INUKAMI!

Omnibus Collection 1

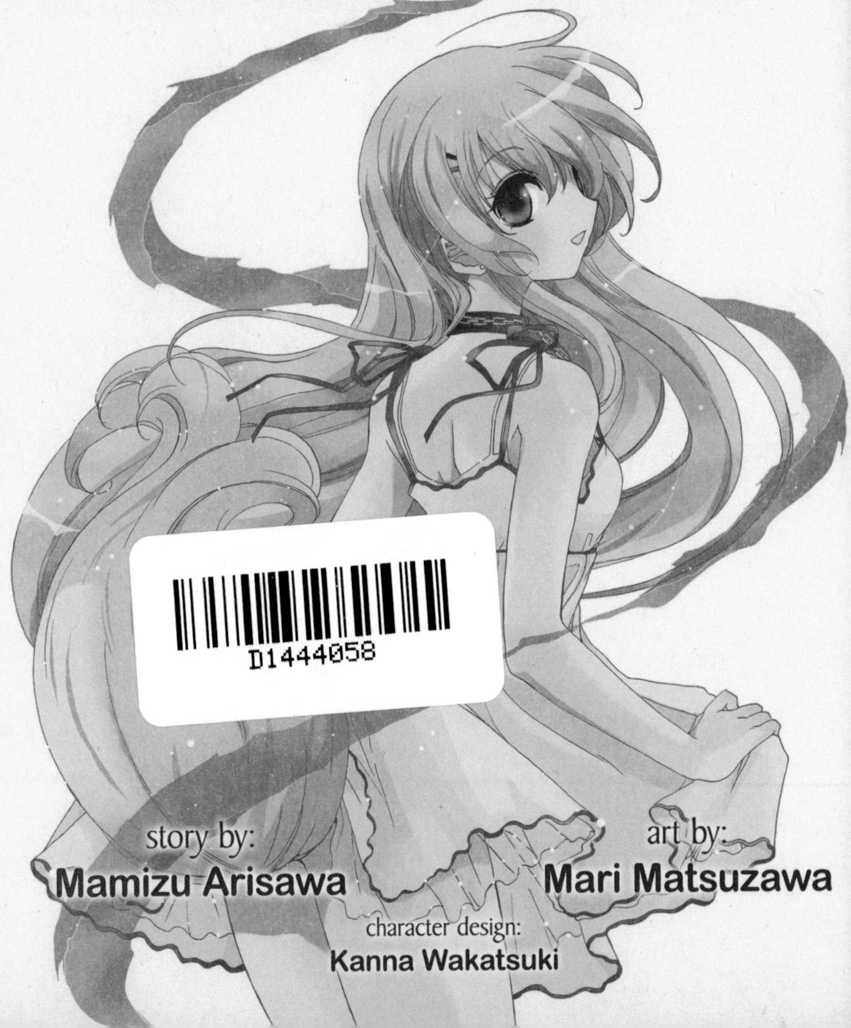

story by:
Mamizu Arisawa

art by:
Mari Matsuzawa

character design:
Kanna Wakatsuki

INUKAMI!

OMNIBUS COLLECTION 1

story by **Mamizu Arisawa**

art by **Mari Matsuzawa**

character design by **Kanna Wakatsuki**

STAFF CREDITS

translation	Rhys Moses, Anastasia Moreno
adaptation	Lorelei Laird
cover design	Nicky Lim
lettering & retouch	Igor Cabbab, Roland Amago, Bambi Eloriaga-Amago
layout	Adam Arnold, Bambi Eloriaga-Amago
copy editor	Erica Friedman
editor	Adam Arnold
publisher	Jason DeAngelis Seven Seas Entertainment

INUKAMI! OMNIBUS COLLECTION 1
Content originally published as Inukami! Vol. 1-3.
Copyright © Mamizu Arisawa / Mari Matsuzawa 2006-2007
First published in 2006-2007 by Media Works Inc., Tokyo, Japan.
English translation rights arranged with ASCII MEDIA WORKS.

ISBN: 978-1-934876-91-6

Printed in Canada

First Printing: November 2010

10 9 8 7 6 5 4 3 2

CONTENTS

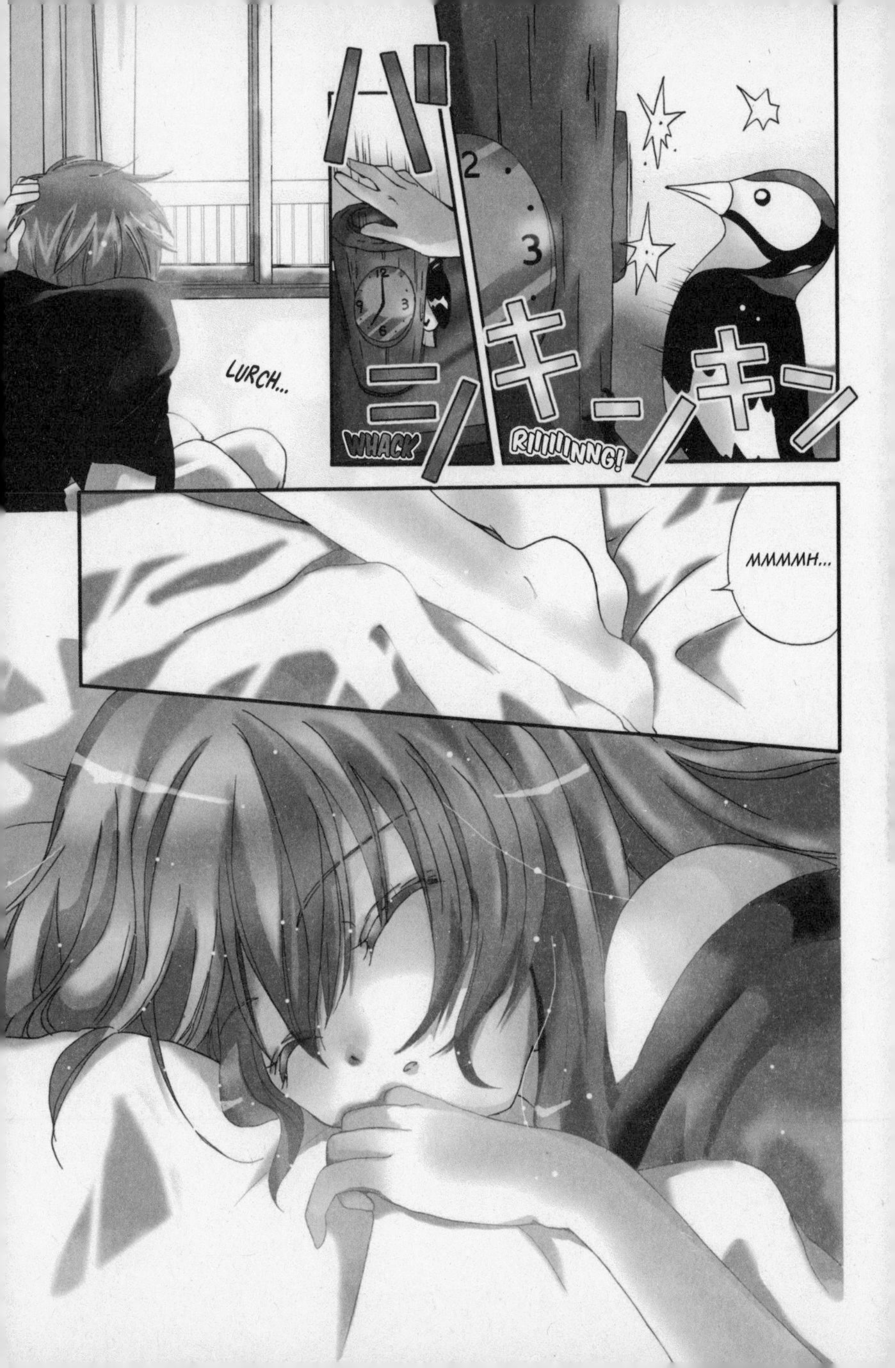
RIIIIIINNG!
WHACK
LURCH...
MMMMH...

Step.1 Boy Meets Dog

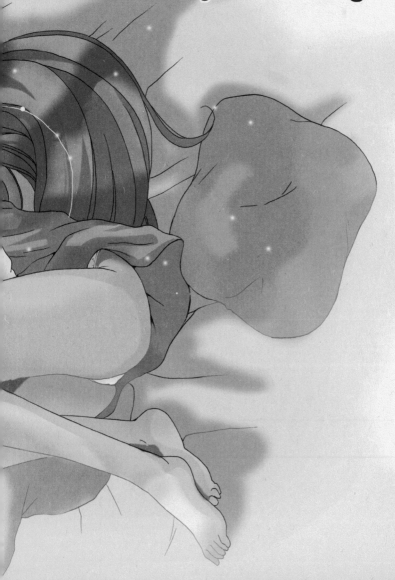

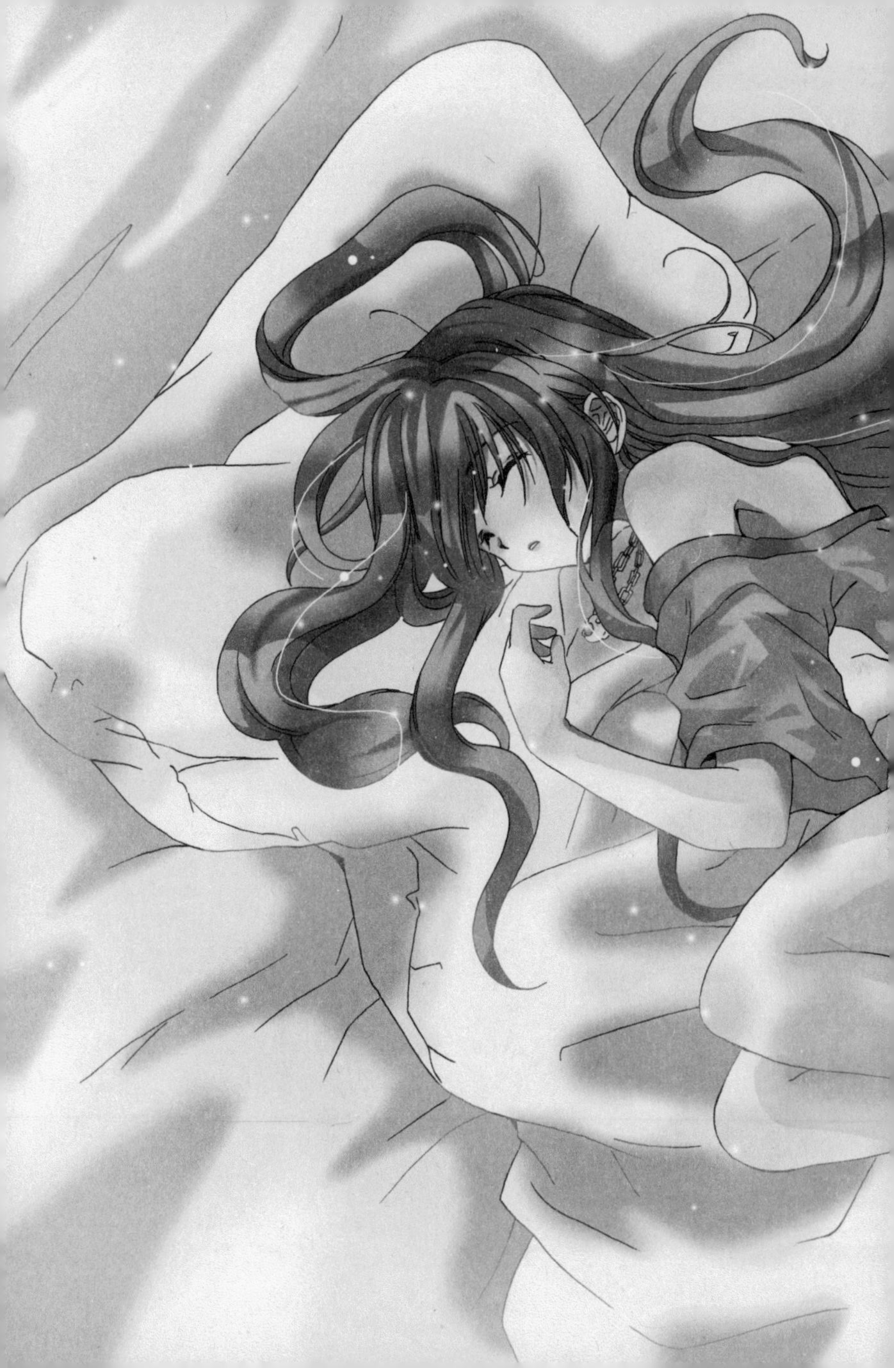

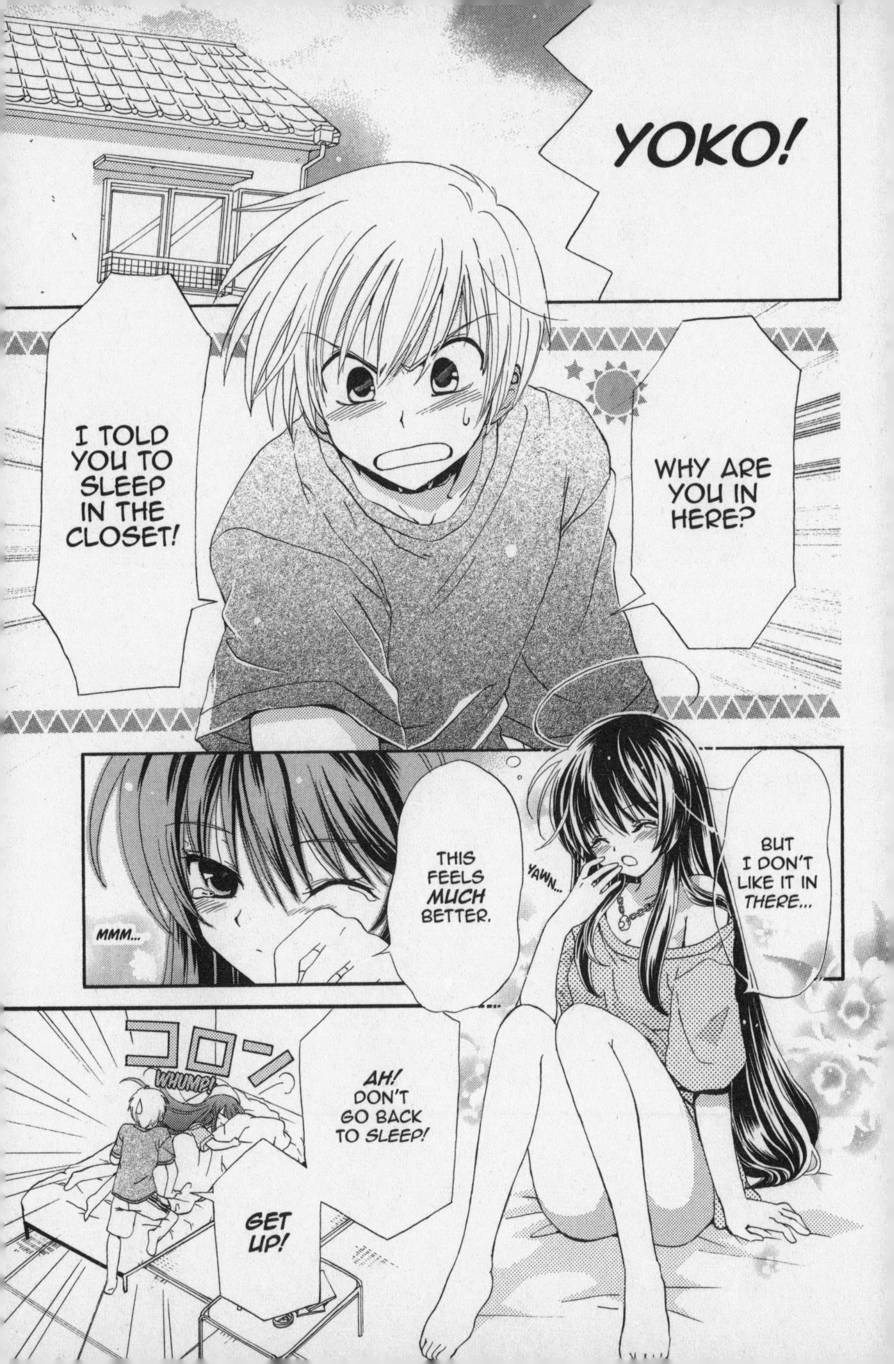

YOKO!
WHY ARE YOU IN HERE?
I TOLD YOU TO SLEEP IN THE CLOSET!
BUT I DON'T LIKE IT IN THERE...
YAWN...
THIS FEELS *MUCH* BETTER.
MMM...
AH! DON'T GO BACK TO SLEEP!
コロン
WHUMP!
GET UP!

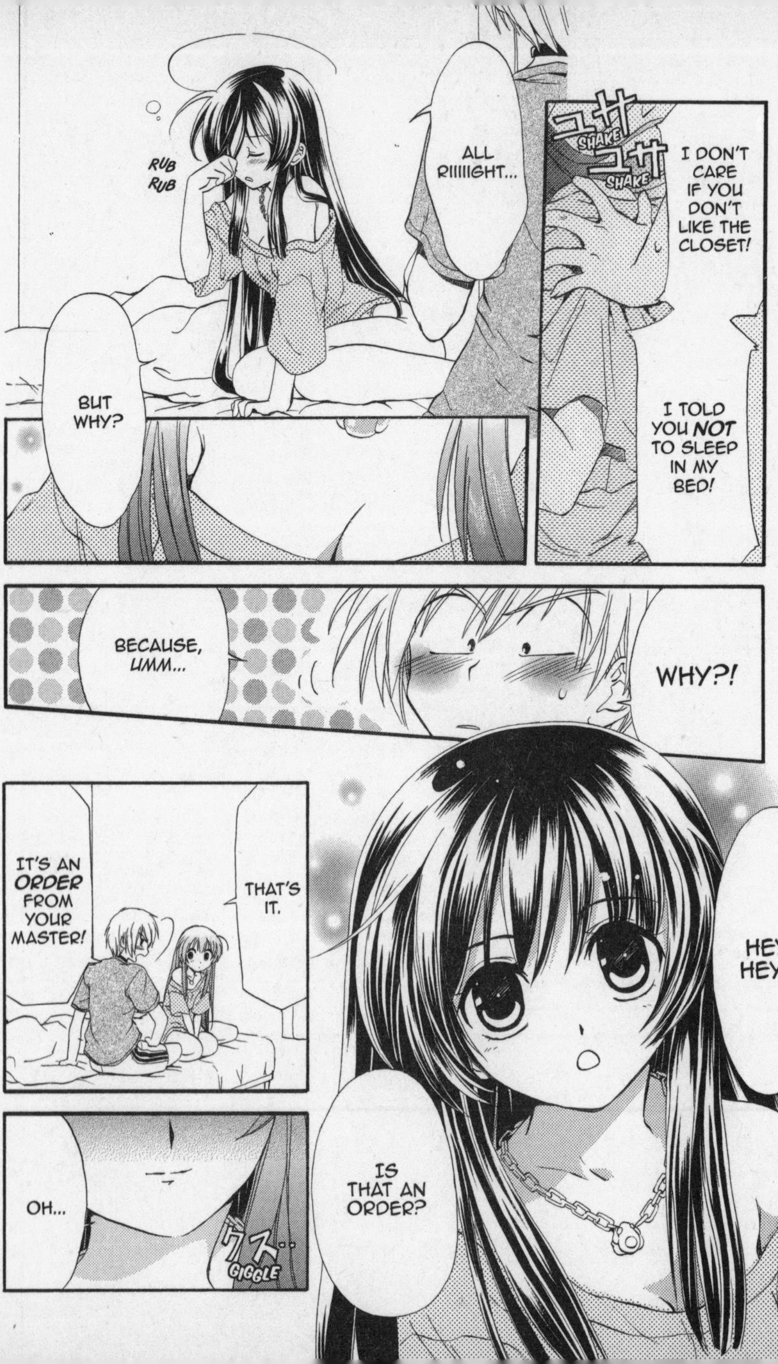

ユサ SHAKE
ユサ SHAKE
I DON'T CARE IF YOU DON'T LIKE THE CLOSET!
I TOLD YOU **NOT** TO SLEEP IN MY BED!
ALL RIIIIGHT...
RUB RUB
BUT WHY?
WHY?!
BECAUSE, UMM...
HEY, HEY...
IS THAT AN ORDER?
THAT'S IT.
IT'S AN ***ORDER*** FROM YOUR MASTER!
OH...
クスー GIGGLE

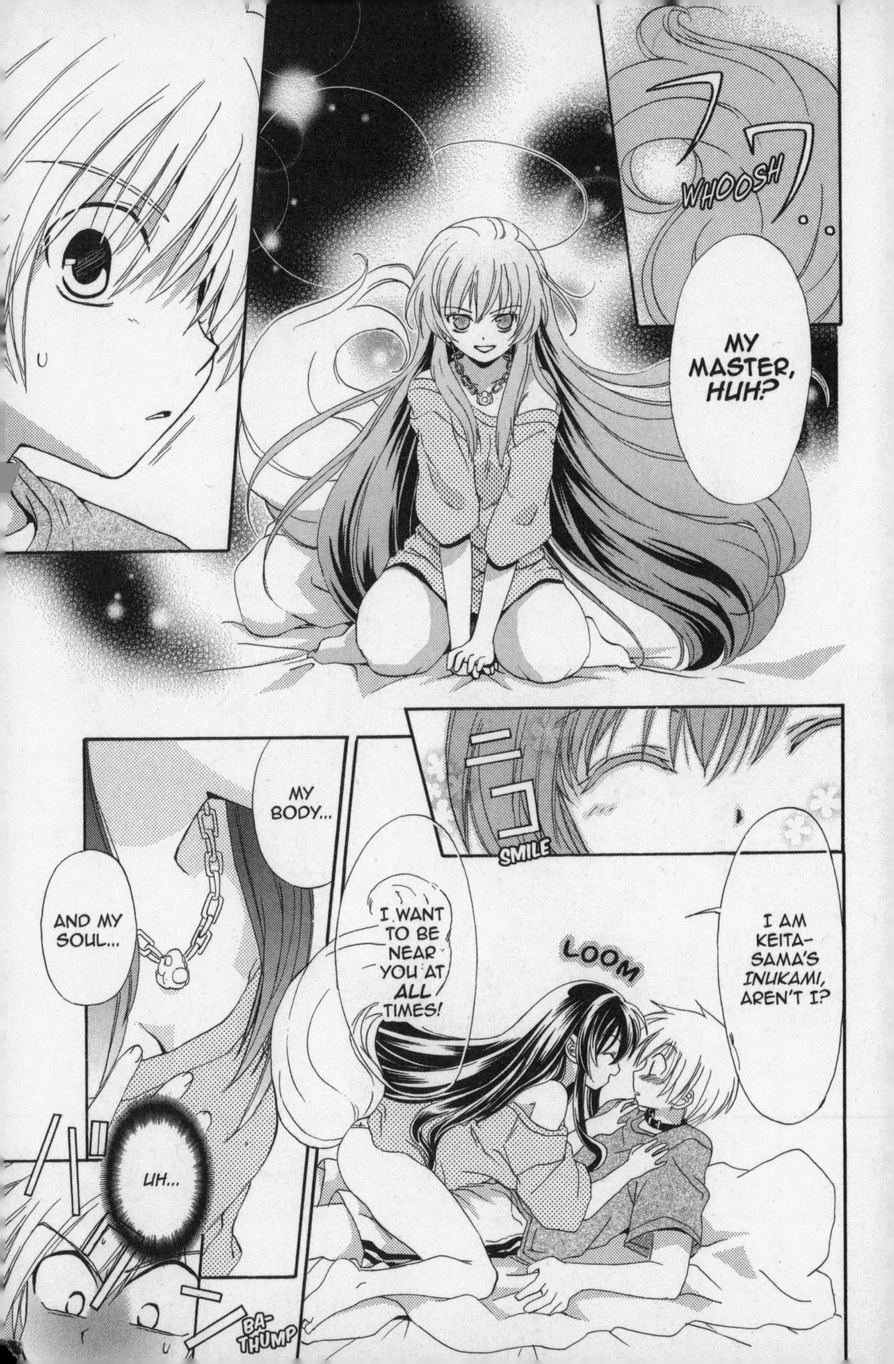
WHOOSH
MY MASTER, HUH?
SMILE
I AM KEITA-SAMA'S INUKAMI, AREN'T I?
LOOM
I WANT TO BE NEAR YOU AT ALL TIMES!
MY BODY...
AND MY SOUL...
UH...
BA-THUMP

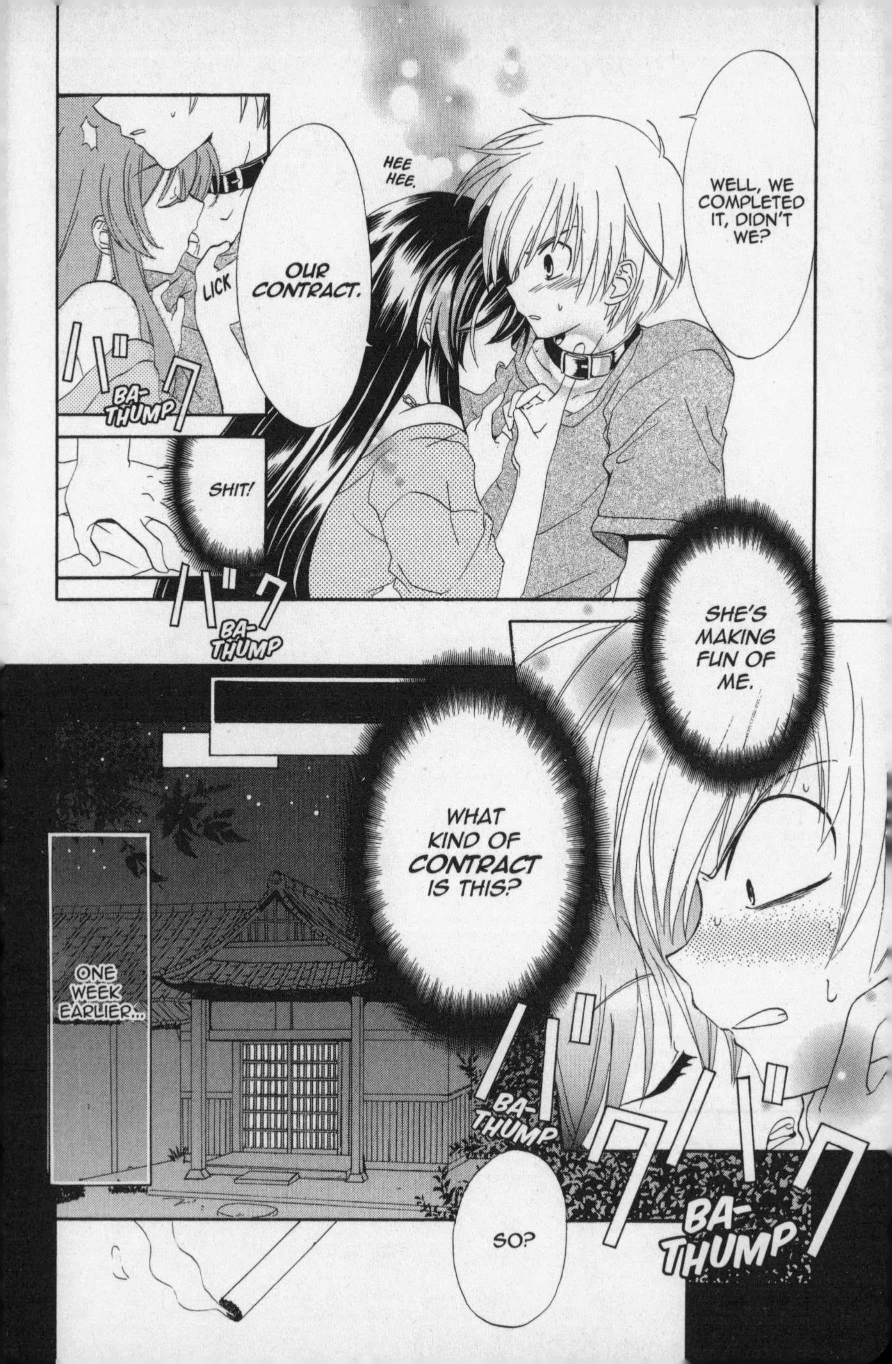
WELL, WE COMPLETED IT, DIDN'T WE?
HEE HEE.
OUR CONTRACT.
LICK
BA-THUMP
SHIT!
BA-THUMP
SHE'S MAKING FUN OF ME.
WHAT KIND OF CONTRACT IS THIS?
BA-THUMP
BA-THUMP
ONE WEEK EARLIER...
SO?

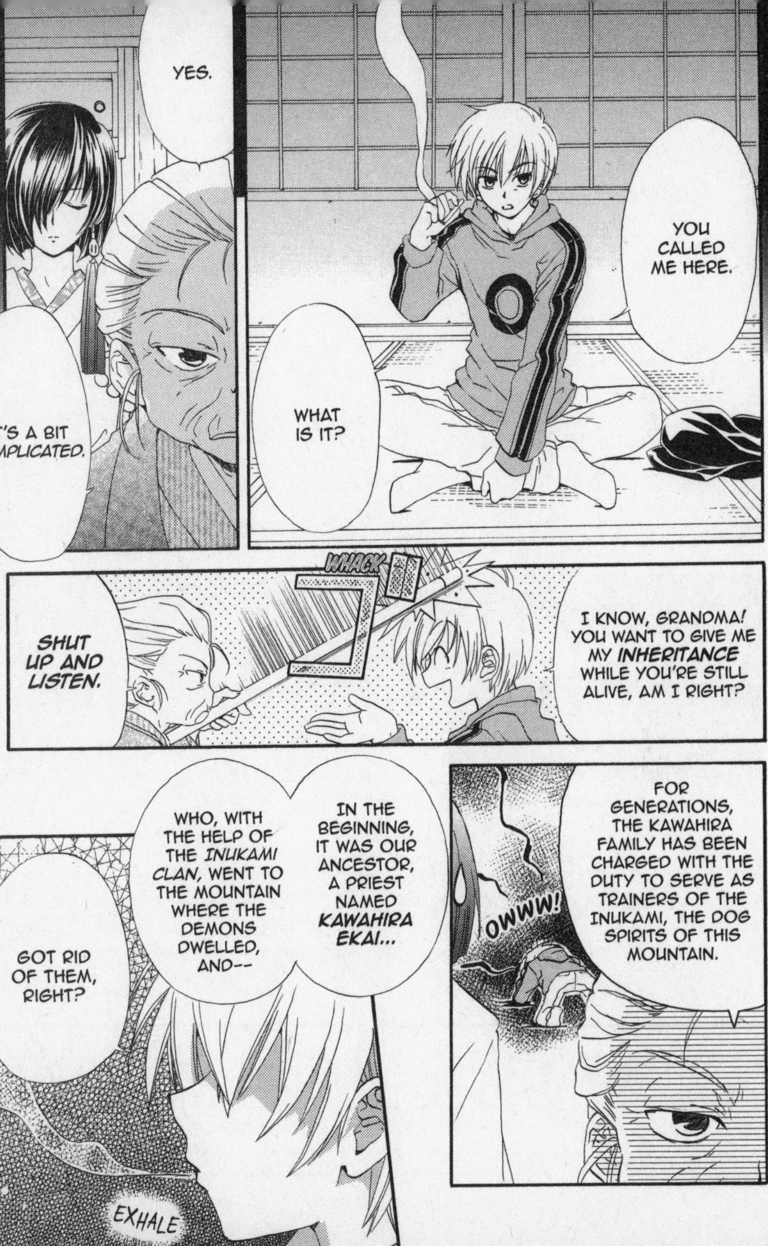
YOU CALLED ME HERE.
WHAT IS IT?
YES.
IT'S A BIT COMPLICATED.
WHACK
I KNOW, GRANDMA! YOU WANT TO GIVE ME MY **INHERITANCE** WHILE YOU'RE STILL ALIVE, AM I RIGHT?
SHUT UP AND LISTEN.
FOR GENERATIONS, THE KAWAHIRA FAMILY HAS BEEN CHARGED WITH THE DUTY TO SERVE AS TRAINERS OF THE INUKAMI, THE DOG SPIRITS OF THIS MOUNTAIN.
OWWW!
IN THE BEGINNING, IT WAS OUR ANCESTOR, A PRIEST NAMED ***KAWAHIRA EKAI...***
WHO, WITH THE HELP OF THE *INUKAMI CLAN*, WENT TO THE MOUNTAIN WHERE THE DEMONS DWELLED, AND--
GOT RID OF THEM, RIGHT?
EXHALE

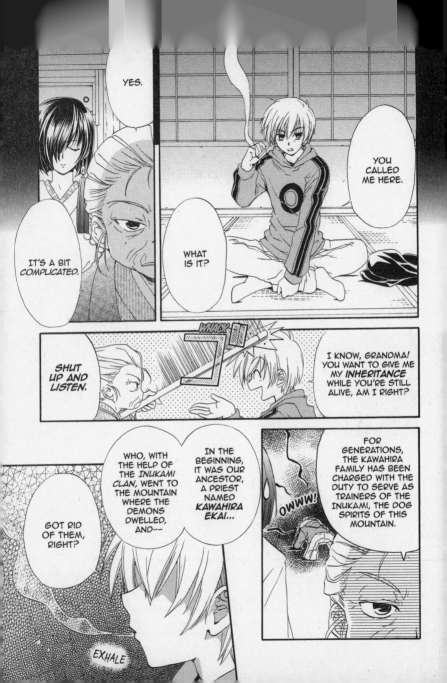

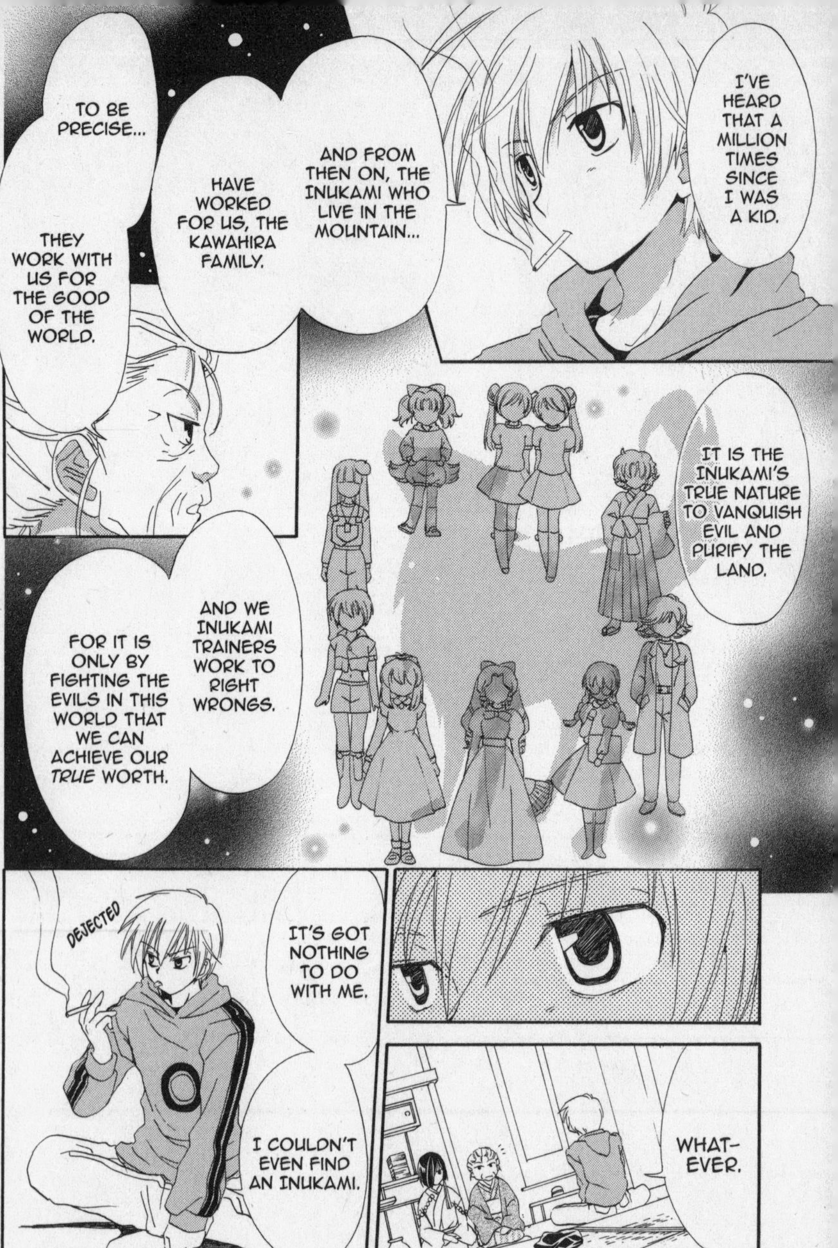
I'VE HEARD THAT A MILLION TIMES SINCE I WAS A KID.
AND FROM THEN ON, THE INUKAMI WHO LIVE IN THE MOUNTAIN...
HAVE WORKED FOR US, THE KAWAHIRA FAMILY.
TO BE PRECISE...
THEY WORK WITH US FOR THE GOOD OF THE WORLD.
IT IS THE INUKAMI'S TRUE NATURE TO VANQUISH EVIL AND PURIFY THE LAND.
AND WE INUKAMI TRAINERS WORK TO RIGHT WRONGS.
FOR IT IS ONLY BY FIGHTING THE EVILS IN THIS WORLD THAT WE CAN ACHIEVE OUR *TRUE* WORTH.
WHAT-EVER.
IT'S GOT NOTHING TO DO WITH ME.
I COULDN'T EVEN FIND AN INUKAMI.
DEJECTED

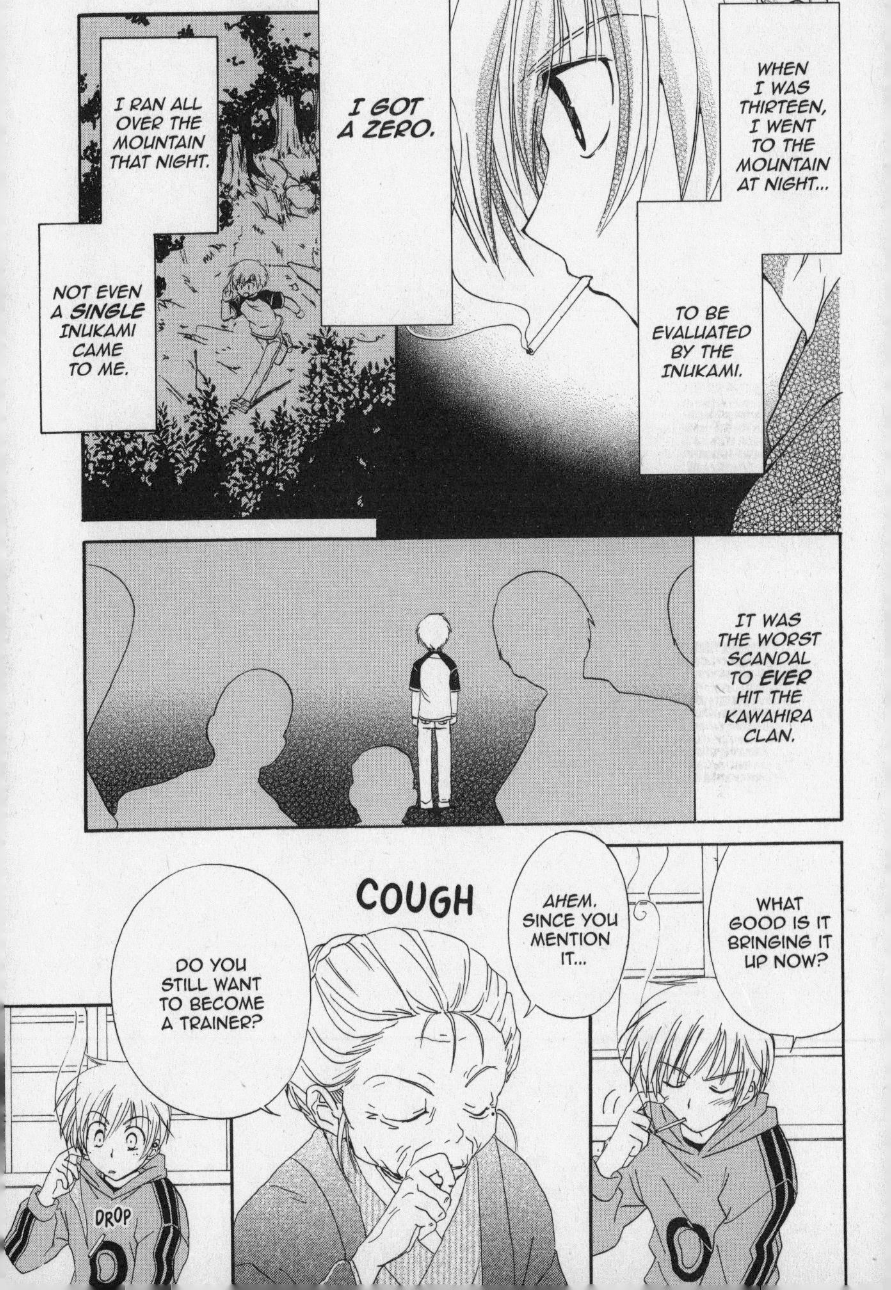

WHEN I WAS THIRTEEN, I WENT TO THE MOUNTAIN AT NIGHT...
TO BE EVALUATED BY THE INUKAMI.
I GOT A ZERO.
I RAN ALL OVER THE MOUNTAIN THAT NIGHT.
NOT EVEN A SINGLE INUKAMI CAME TO ME.
IT WAS THE WORST SCANDAL TO EVER HIT THE KAWAHIRA CLAN.
WHAT GOOD IS IT BRINGING IT UP NOW?
COUGH
AHEM, SINCE YOU MENTION IT...
DO YOU STILL WANT TO BECOME A TRAINER?
DROP

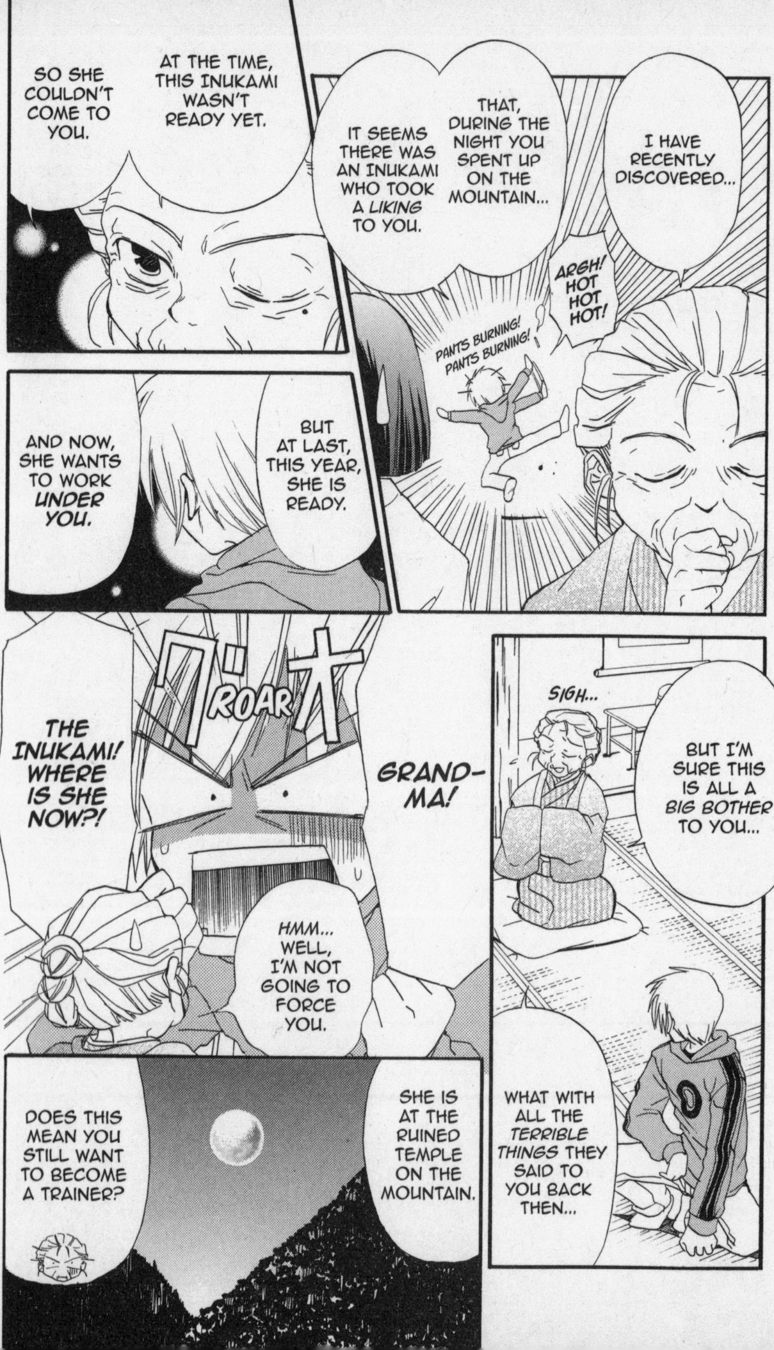

I HAVE RECENTLY DISCOVERED...
THAT, DURING THE NIGHT YOU SPENT UP ON THE MOUNTAIN...
IT SEEMS THERE WAS AN INUKAMI WHO TOOK A *LIKING* TO YOU.
ARGH! HOT HOT HOT!
PANTS BURNING! PANTS BURNING!
AT THE TIME, THIS INUKAMI WASN'T READY YET.
SO SHE COULDN'T COME TO YOU.
BUT AT LAST, THIS YEAR, SHE IS READY.
AND NOW, SHE WANTS TO WORK *UNDER YOU.*
SIGH...
BUT I'M SURE THIS IS ALL A *BIG BOTHER* TO YOU...
WHAT WITH ALL THE *TERRIBLE THINGS* THEY SAID TO YOU BACK THEN...
ROAR
GRAND-MA!
THE INUKAMI! WHERE IS SHE NOW?!
HMM... WELL, I'M NOT GOING TO FORCE YOU.
SHE IS AT THE RUINED TEMPLE ON THE MOUNTAIN.
DOES THIS MEAN YOU STILL WANT TO BECOME A TRAINER?

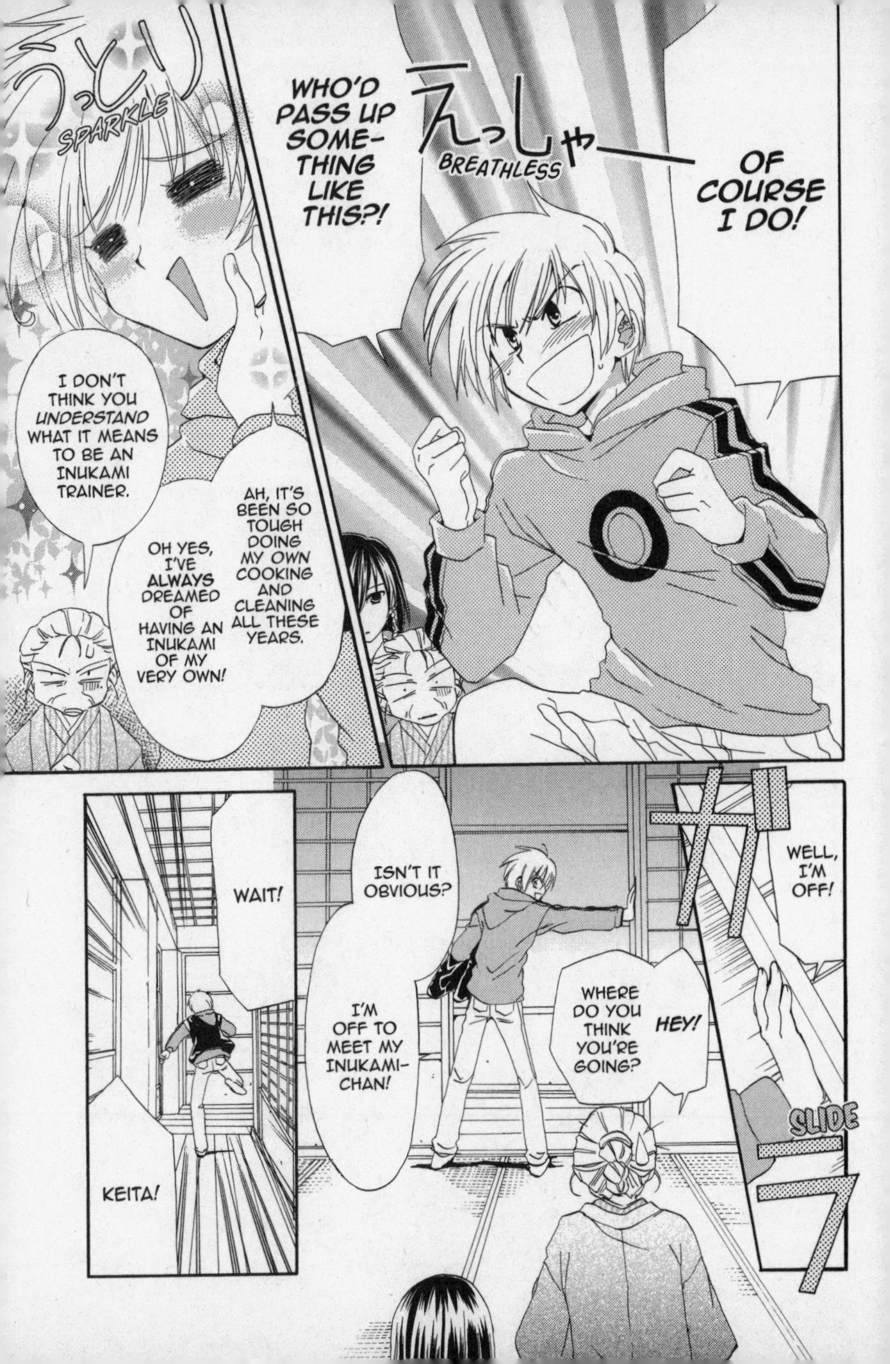
OF COURSE I DO!
WHO'D PASS UP SOME-THING LIKE THIS?!
えっしゃー
BREATHLESS
AH, IT'S BEEN SO TOUGH DOING MY OWN COOKING AND CLEANING ALL THESE YEARS.
OH YES, I'VE ALWAYS DREAMED OF HAVING AN INUKAMI OF MY VERY OWN!
うっとり
SPARKLE
I DON'T THINK YOU UNDERSTAND WHAT IT MEANS TO BE AN INUKAMI TRAINER.
ガ
WELL, I'M OFF!
HEY!
WHERE DO YOU THINK YOU'RE GOING?
SLIDE
ISN'T IT OBVIOUS?
I'M OFF TO MEET MY INUKAMI-CHAN!
WAIT!
KEITA!

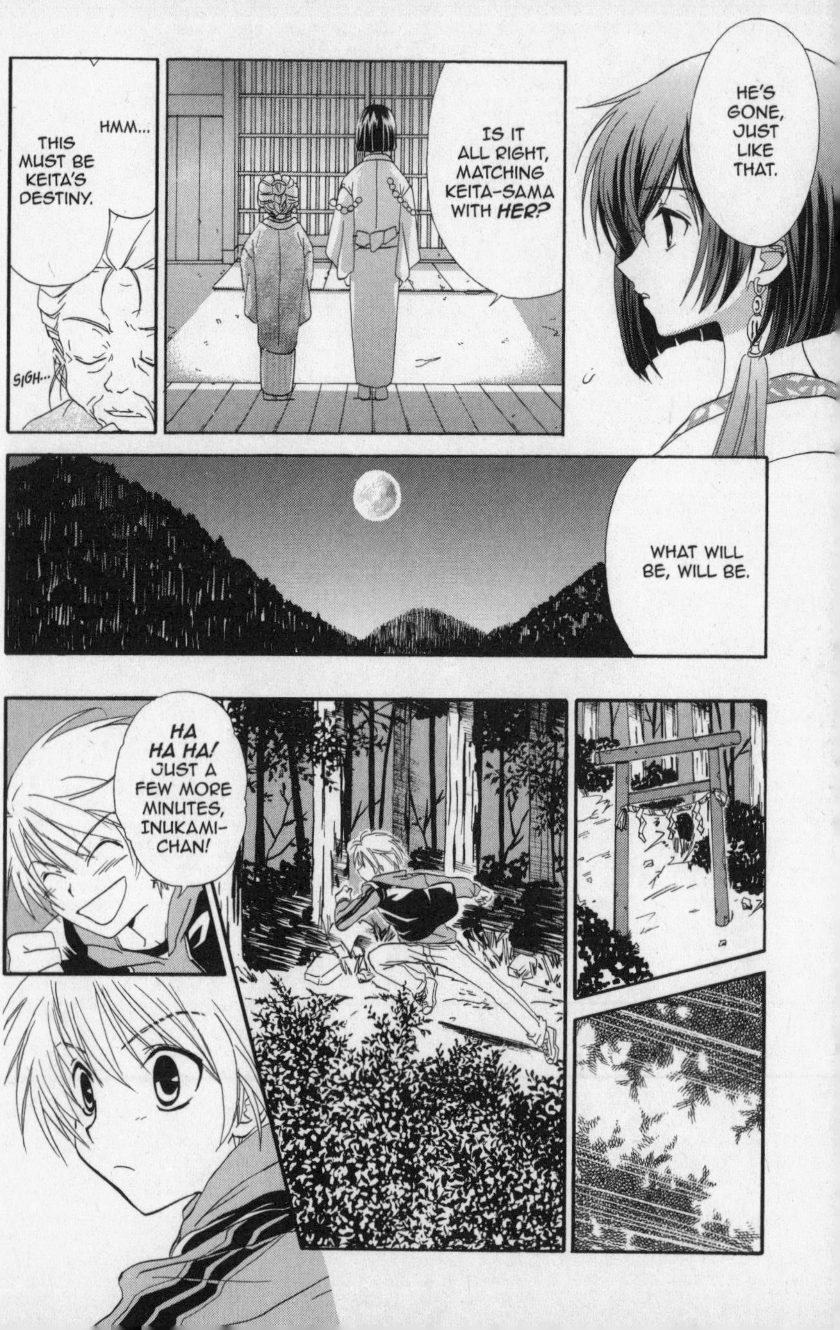
HE'S GONE, JUST LIKE THAT.
IS IT ALL RIGHT, MATCHING KEITA-SAMA WITH **HER?**
HMM...
THIS MUST BE KEITA'S DESTINY.
SIGH...
WHAT WILL BE, WILL BE.
HA HA HA! JUST A FEW MORE MINUTES, INUKAMI-CHAN!

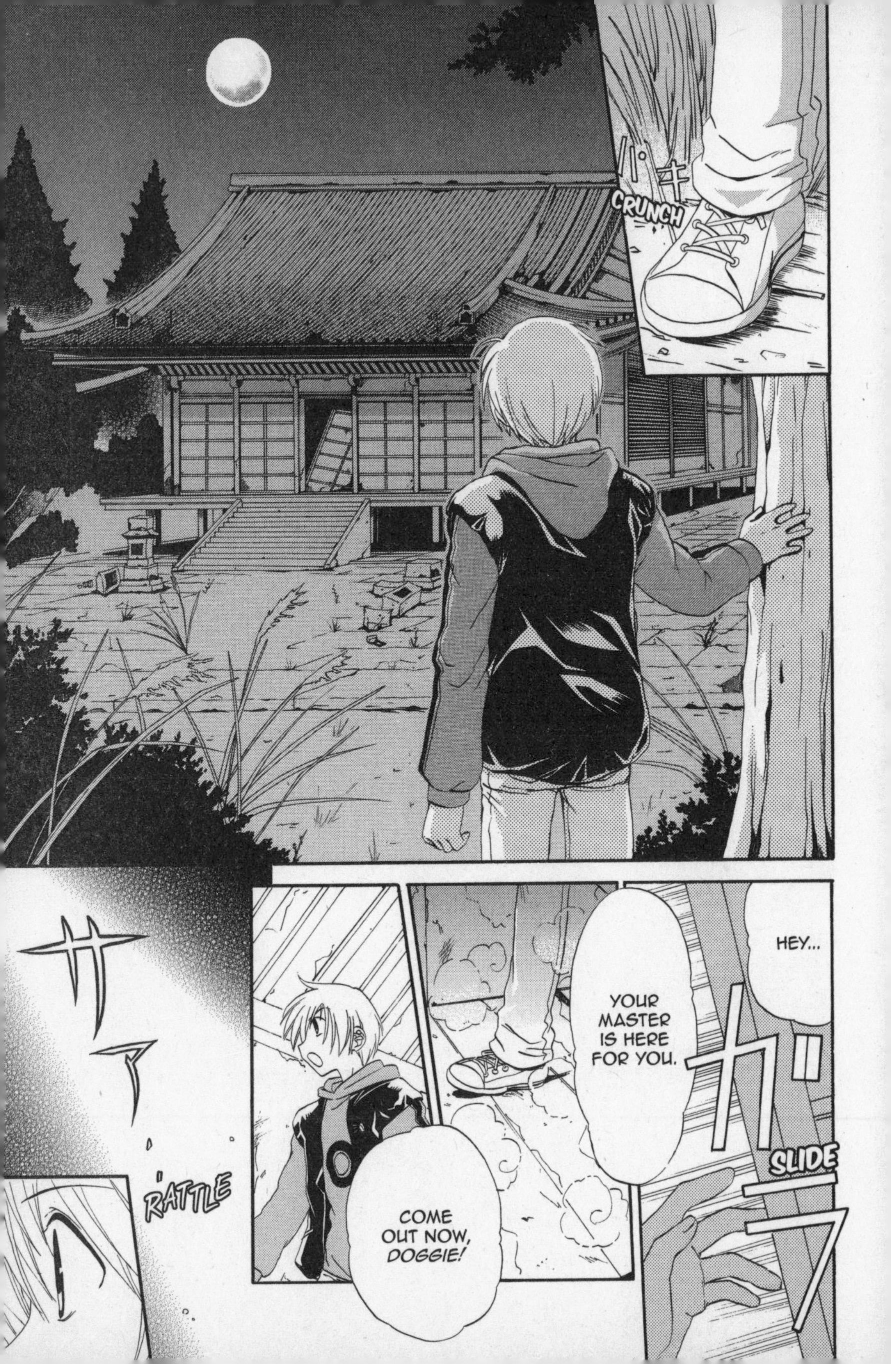
CRUNCH
HEY...
SLIDE
YOUR MASTER IS HERE FOR YOU.
COME OUT NOW, *DOGGIE!*
RATTLE

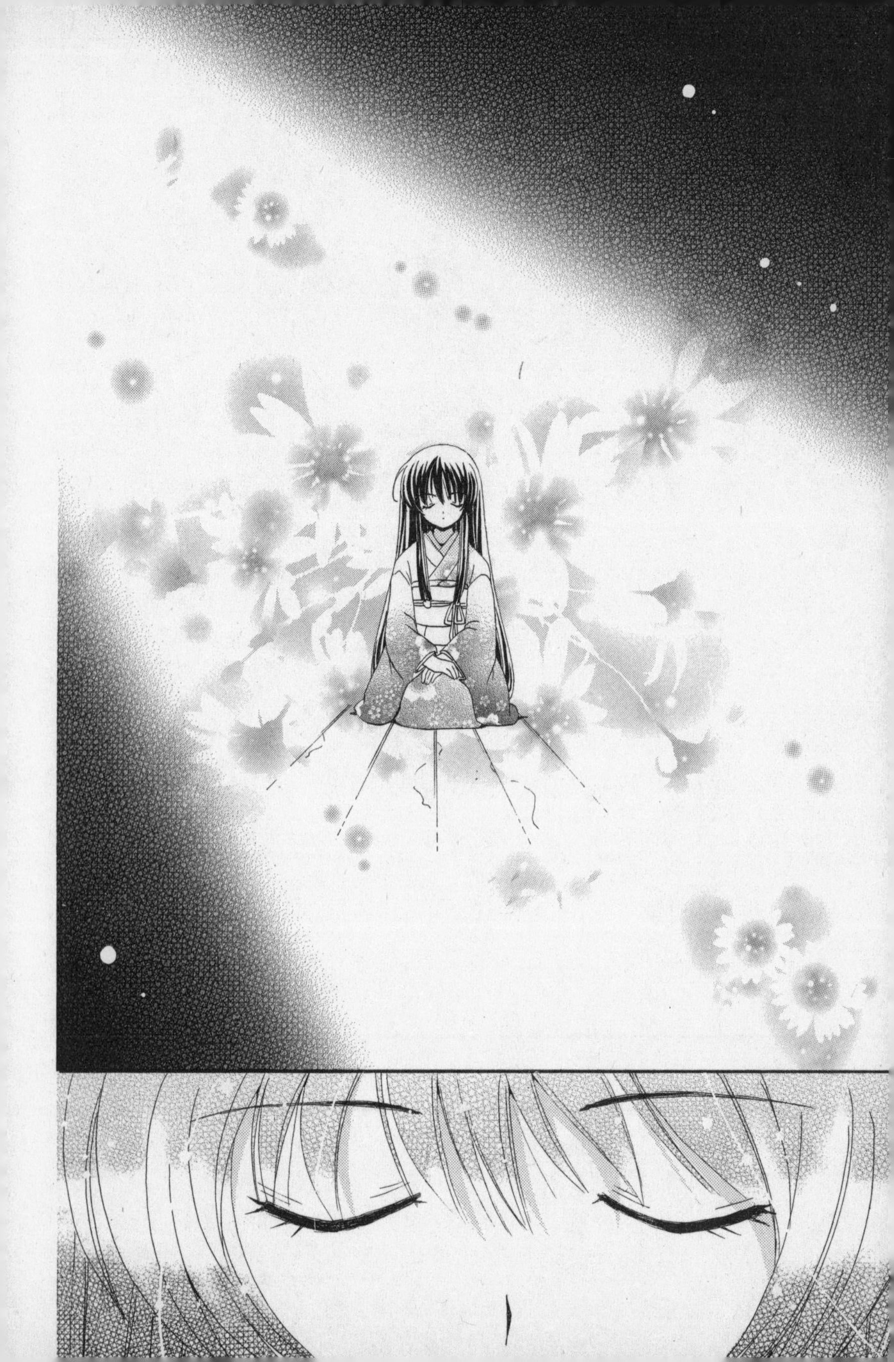

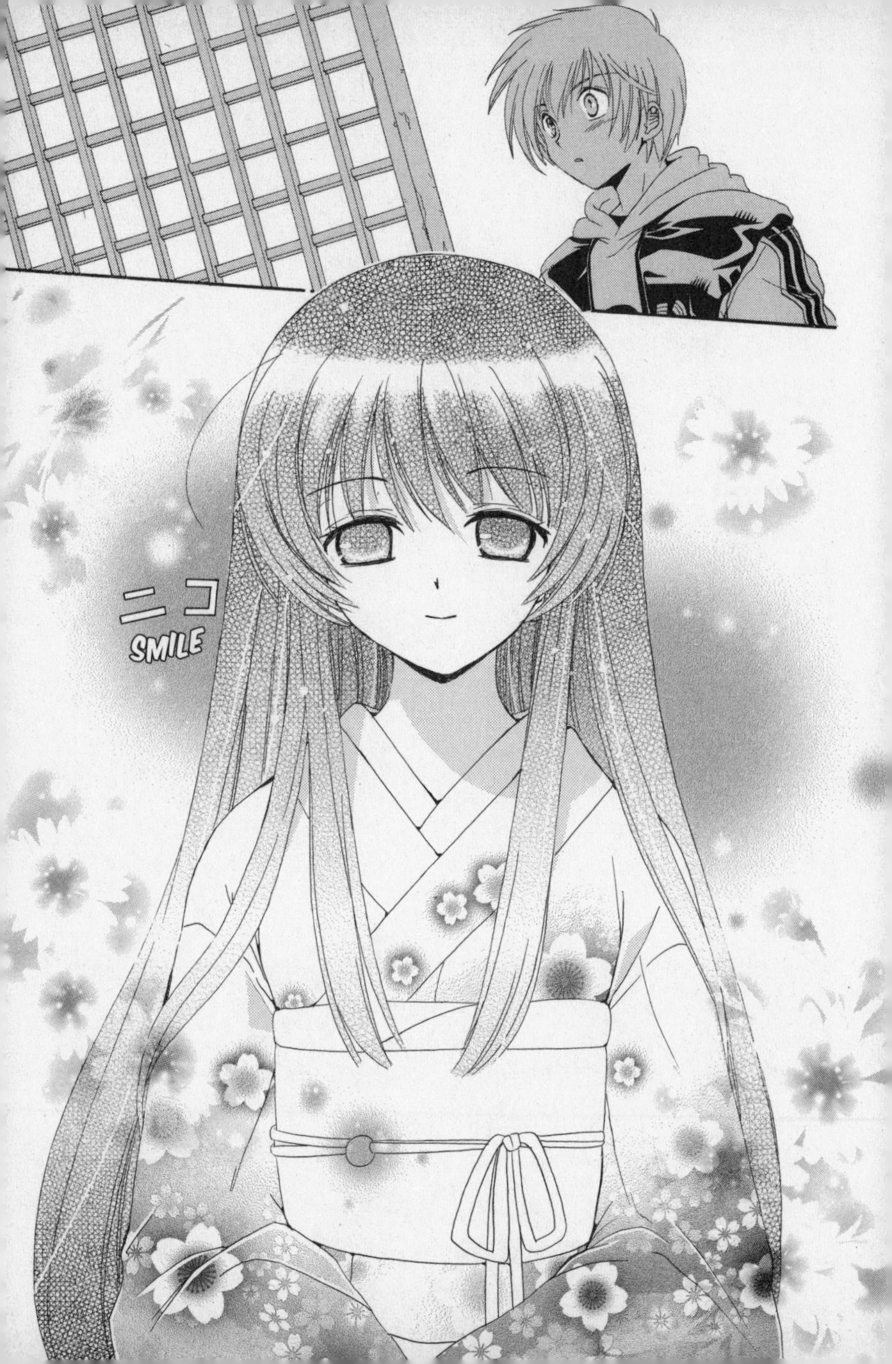
ニコ
SMILE

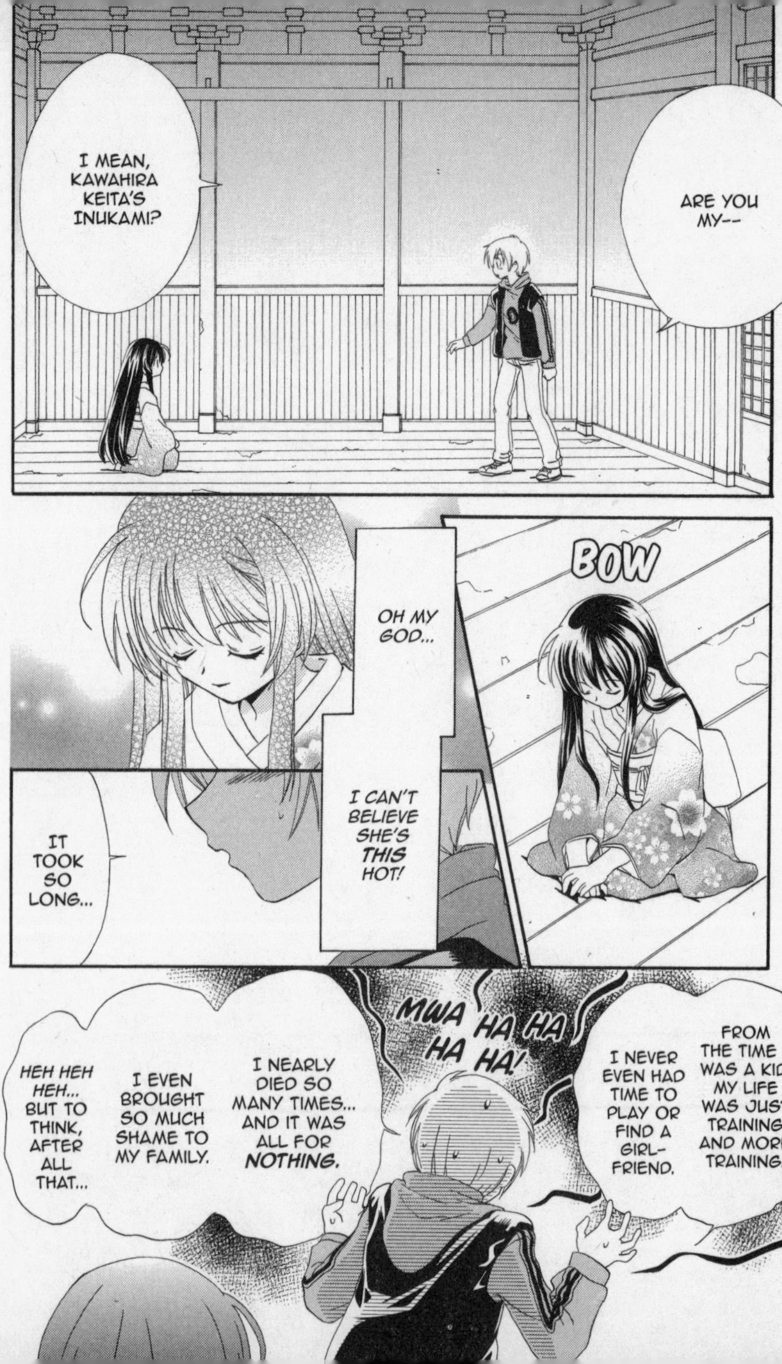
ARE YOU MY--
I MEAN, KAWAHIRA KEITA'S INUKAMI?
BOW
OH MY GOD...
I CAN'T BELIEVE SHE'S THIS HOT!
IT TOOK SO LONG...
FROM THE TIME I WAS A KID, MY LIFE WAS JUST TRAINING AND MORE TRAINING.
I NEVER EVEN HAD TIME TO PLAY OR FIND A GIRL-FRIEND.
MWA HA HA HA HA!
I NEARLY DIED SO MANY TIMES... AND IT WAS ALL FOR NOTHING.
I EVEN BROUGHT SO MUCH SHAME TO MY FAMILY.
HEH HEH HEH... BUT TO THINK, AFTER ALL THAT...

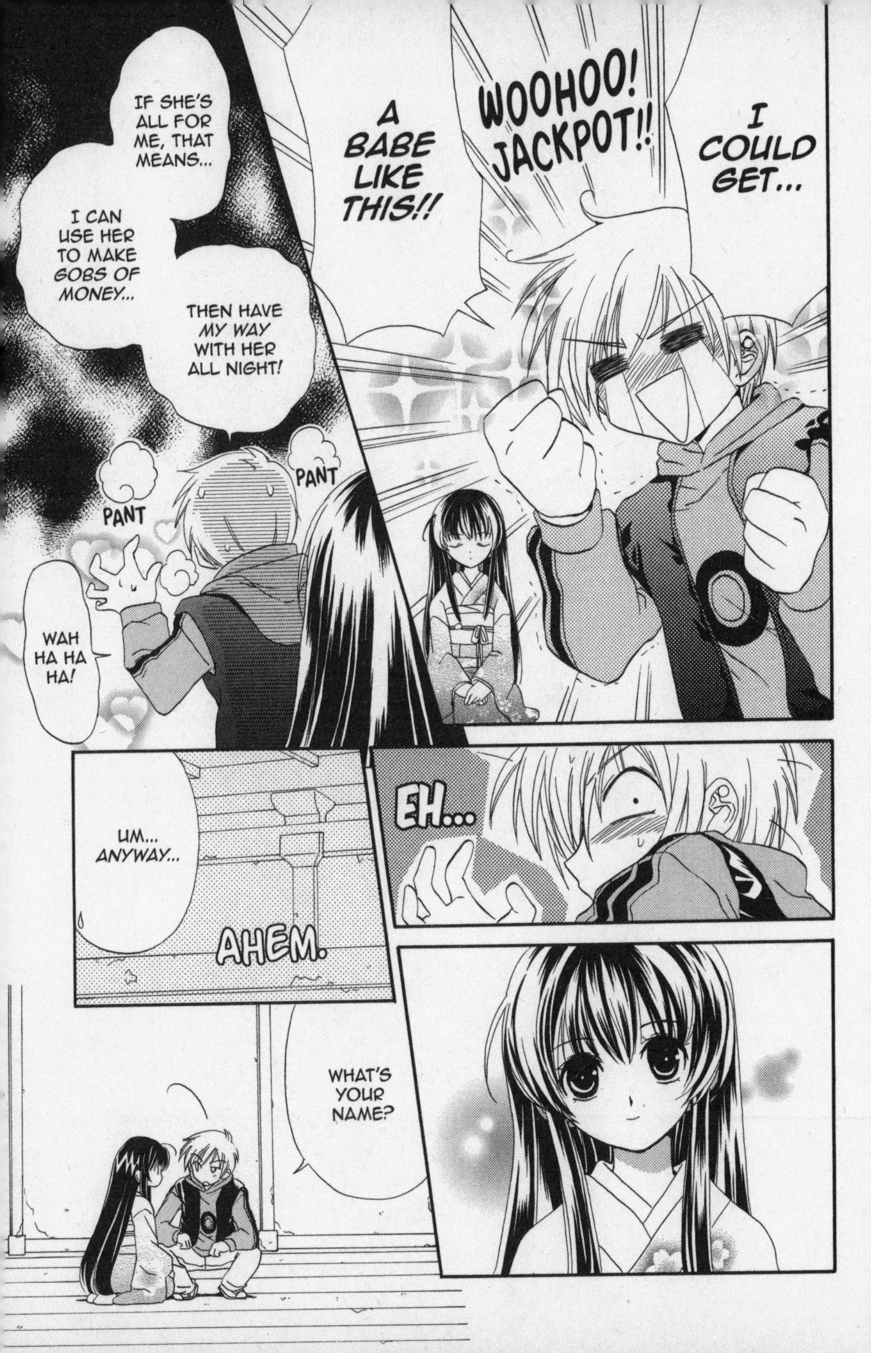

I COULD GET...
WOOHOO! JACKPOT!!
A BABE LIKE THIS!!
IF SHE'S ALL FOR ME, THAT MEANS...
I CAN USE HER TO MAKE GOBS OF MONEY...
THEN HAVE MY WAY WITH HER ALL NIGHT!
PANT
PANT
WAH HA HA HA!
EH...
UM... ANYWAY...
AHEM.
WHAT'S YOUR NAME?

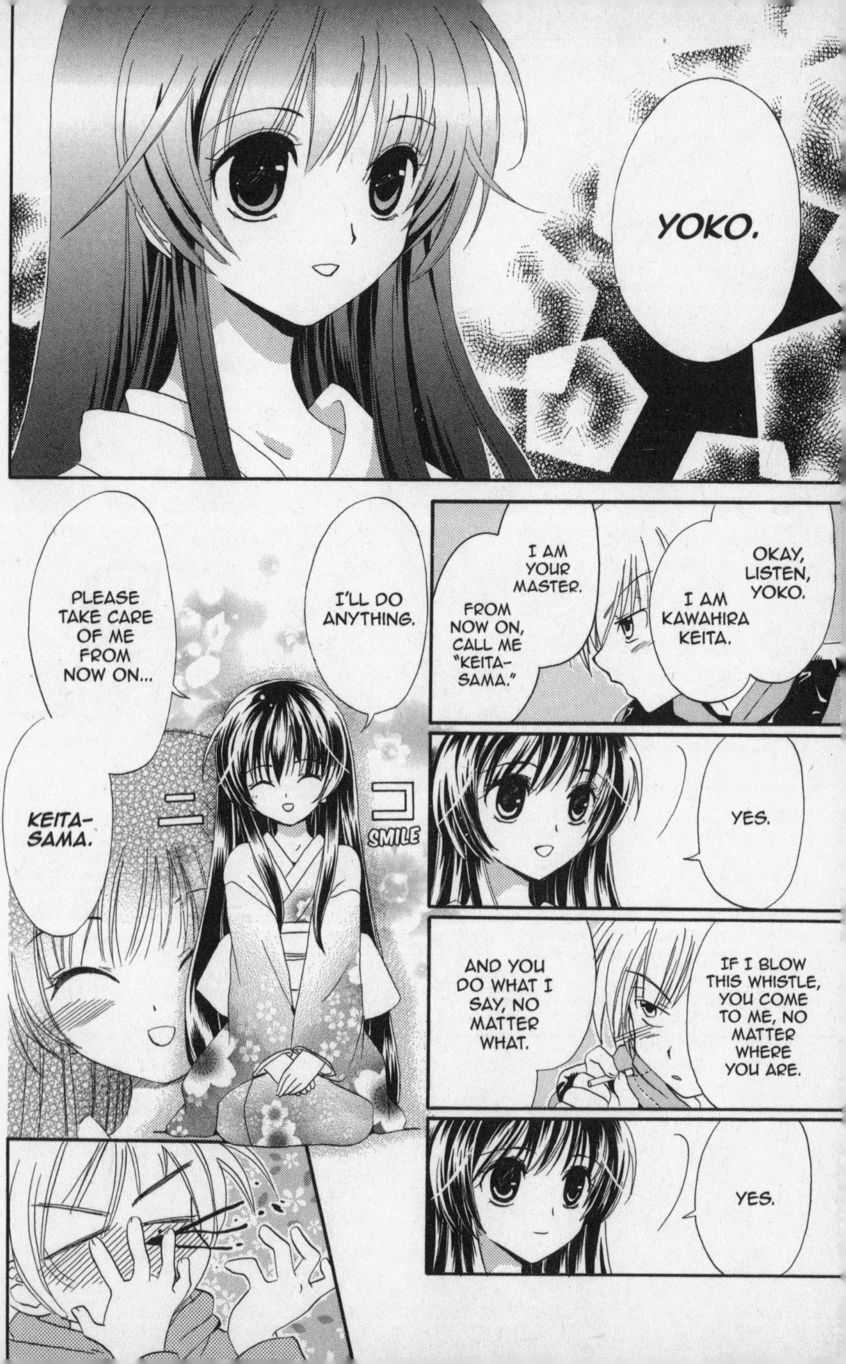
YOKO.
OKAY, LISTEN, YOKO.
I AM KAWAHIRA KEITA.
I AM YOUR MASTER.
FROM NOW ON, CALL ME "KEITA-SAMA."
YES.
IF I BLOW THIS WHISTLE, YOU COME TO ME, NO MATTER WHERE YOU ARE.
AND YOU DO WHAT I SAY, NO MATTER WHAT.
YES.
I'LL DO ANYTHING.
PLEASE TAKE CARE OF ME FROM NOW ON...
KEITA-SAMA.
SMILE

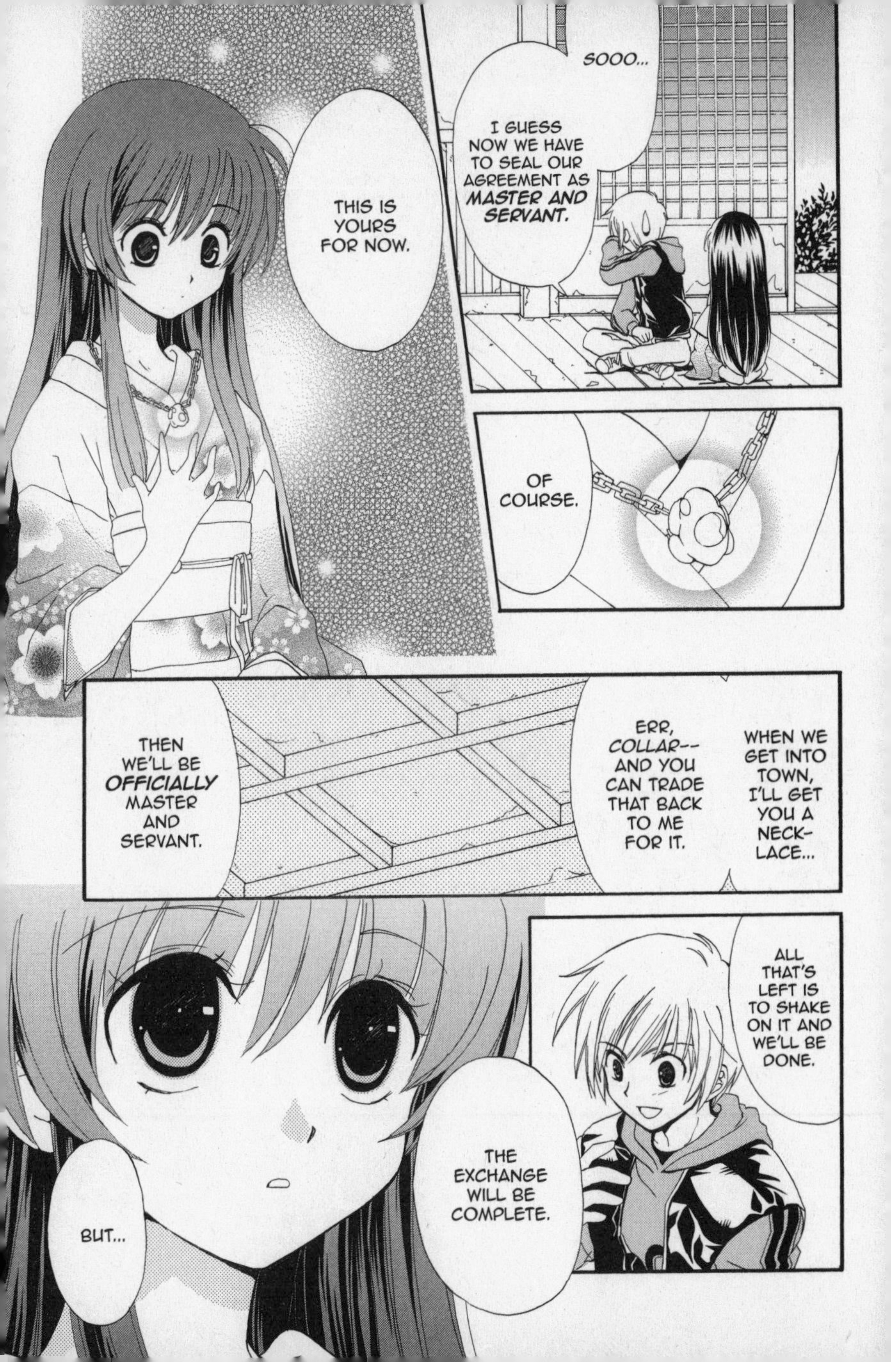
SOOO...
I GUESS NOW WE HAVE TO SEAL OUR AGREEMENT AS MASTER AND SERVANT.
OF COURSE.
THIS IS YOURS FOR NOW.
WHEN WE GET INTO TOWN, I'LL GET YOU A NECK-LACE...
ERR, COLLAR-- AND YOU CAN TRADE THAT BACK TO ME FOR IT.
THEN WE'LL BE OFFICIALLY MASTER AND SERVANT.
ALL THAT'S LEFT IS TO SHAKE ON IT AND WE'LL BE DONE.
THE EXCHANGE WILL BE COMPLETE.
BUT...

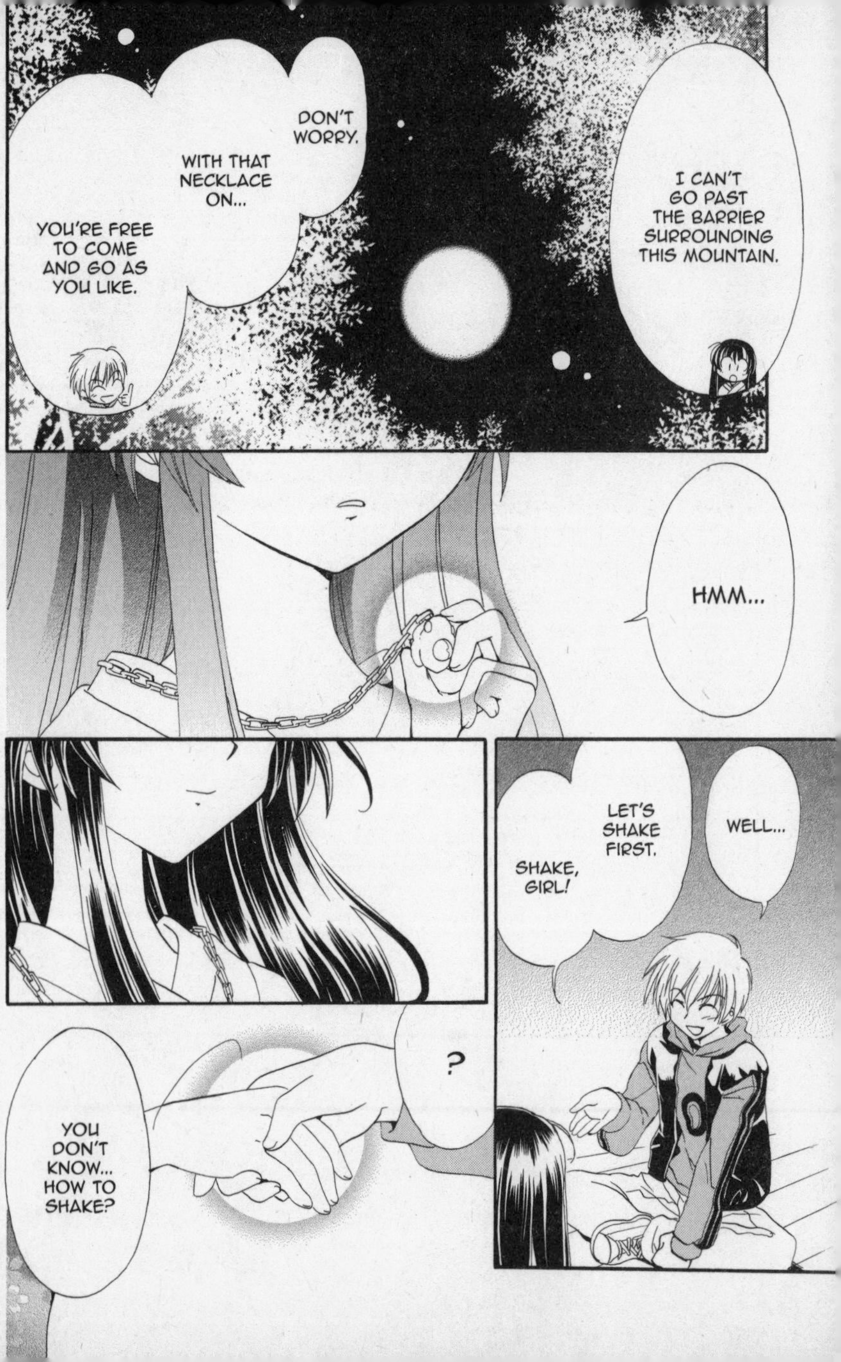
I CAN'T GO PAST THE BARRIER SURROUNDING THIS MOUNTAIN.
DON'T WORRY.
WITH THAT NECKLACE ON...
YOU'RE FREE TO COME AND GO AS YOU LIKE.
HMM...
WELL...
LET'S SHAKE FIRST.
SHAKE, GIRL!
?
YOU DON'T KNOW... HOW TO SHAKE?

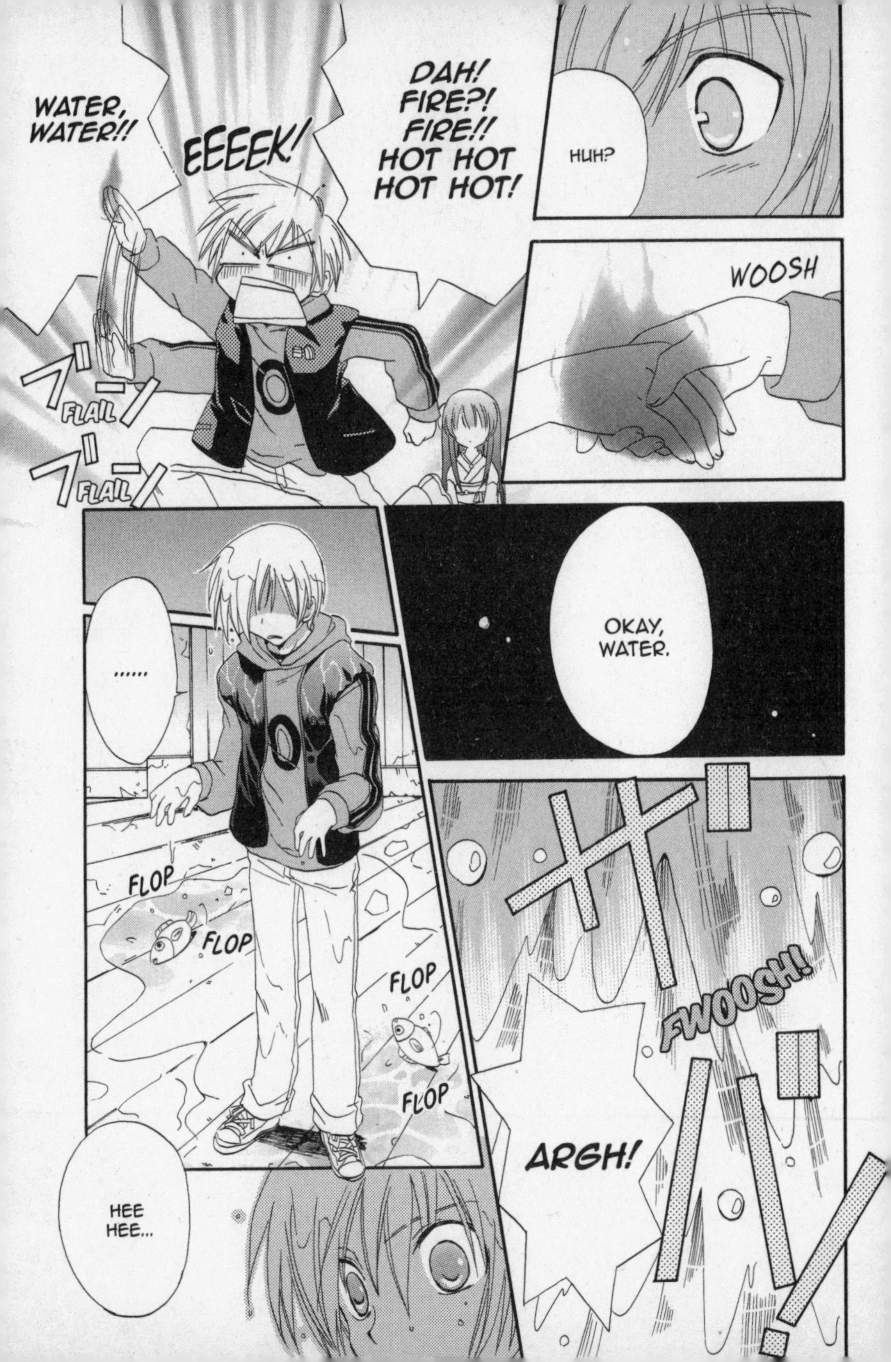

HUH?
WOOSH
DAH! FIRE?! FIRE!! HOT HOT HOT HOT!
EEEEK!
WATER, WATER!!
FLAIL
FLAIL
OKAY, WATER.
FWOOSH!
ARGH!
......
FLOP
FLOP
FLOP
FLOP
HEE HEE...

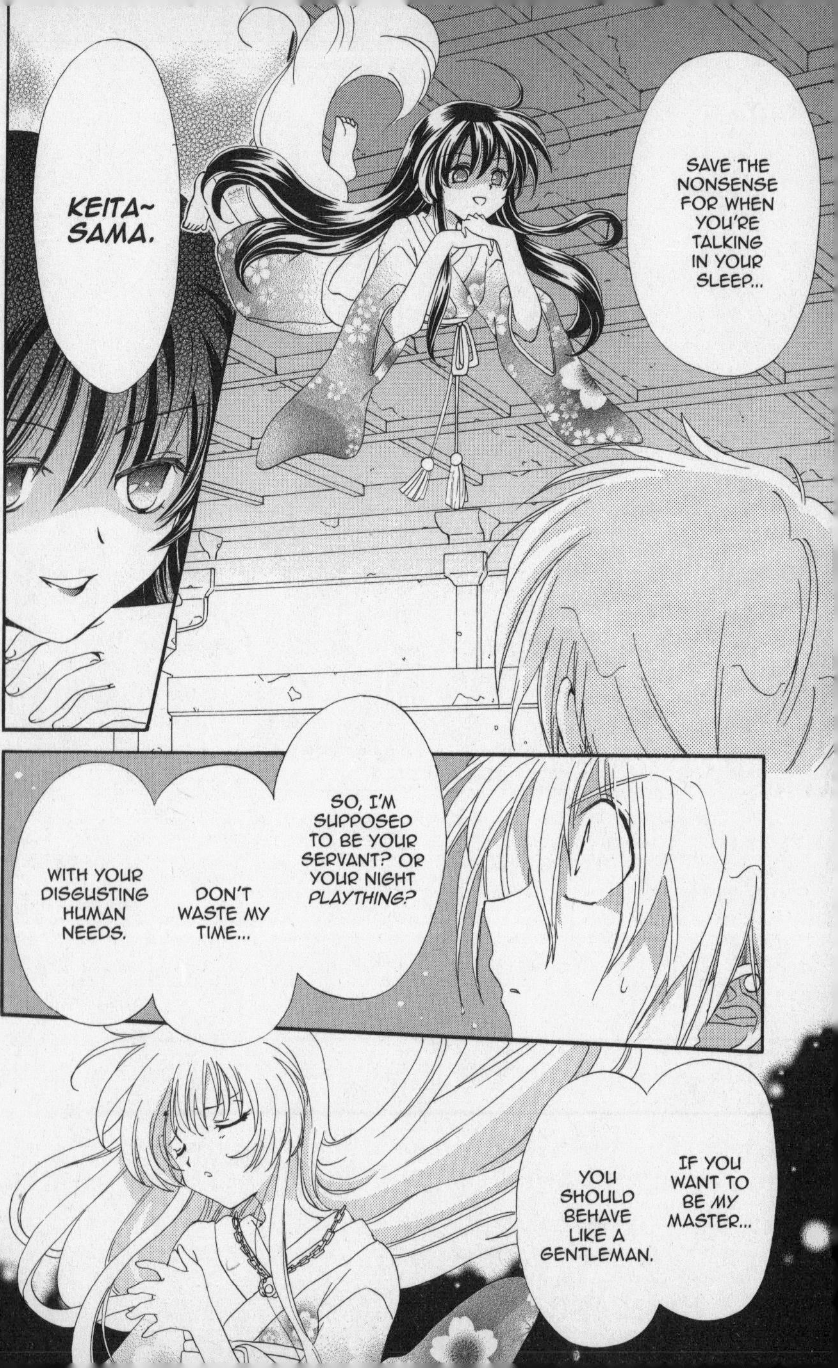
SAVE THE NONSENSE FOR WHEN YOU'RE TALKING IN YOUR SLEEP...
KEITA~ SAMA.
SO, I'M SUPPOSED TO BE YOUR SERVANT? OR YOUR NIGHT *PLAYTHING?*
DON'T WASTE MY TIME...
WITH YOUR DISGUSTING HUMAN NEEDS.
IF YOU WANT TO BE *MY* MASTER...
YOU SHOULD BEHAVE LIKE A GENTLEMAN.

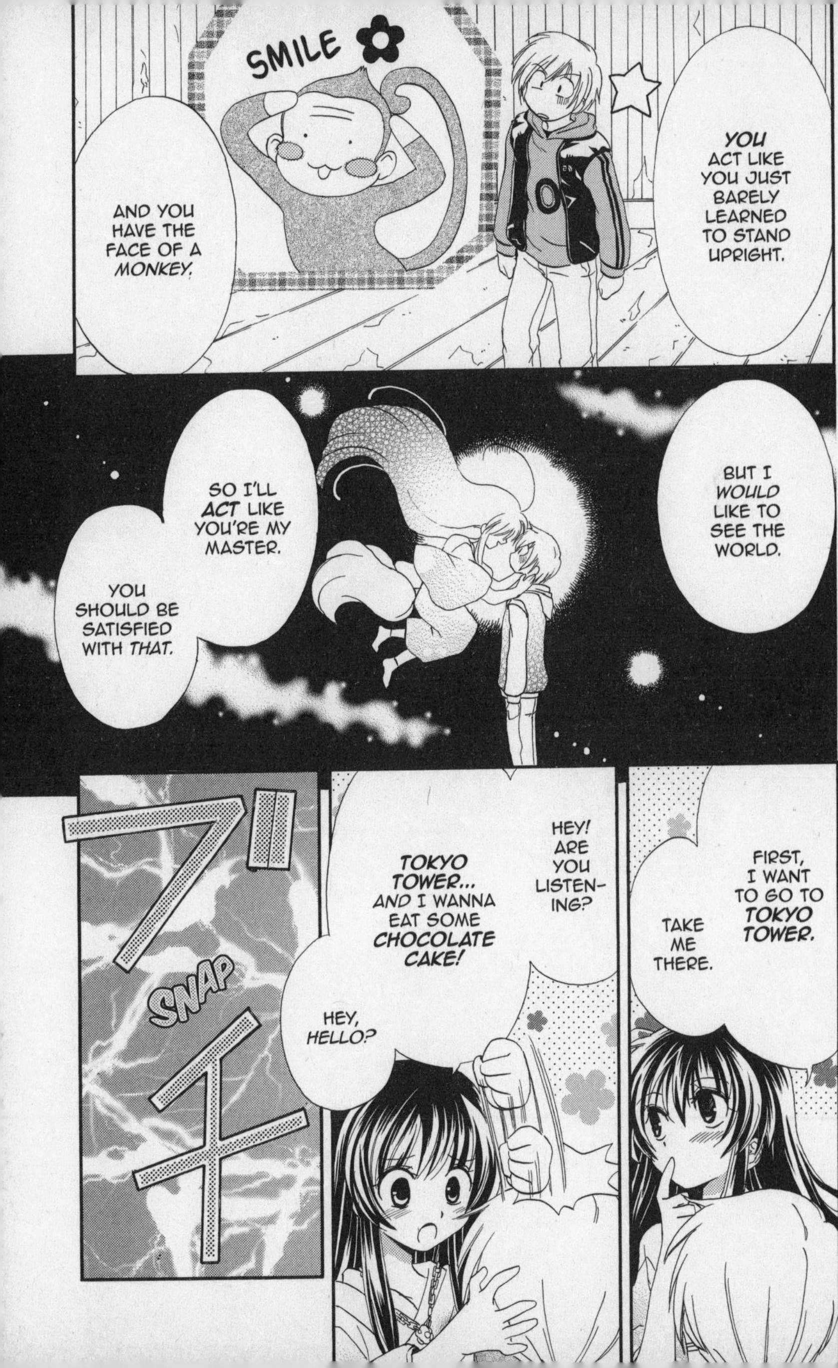
YOU ACT LIKE YOU JUST BARELY LEARNED TO STAND UPRIGHT.
SMILE
AND YOU HAVE THE FACE OF A MONKEY.
BUT I WOULD LIKE TO SEE THE WORLD.
SO I'LL ACT LIKE YOU'RE MY MASTER.
YOU SHOULD BE SATISFIED WITH THAT.
FIRST, I WANT TO GO TO TOKYO TOWER.
TAKE ME THERE.
HEY! ARE YOU LISTENING?
TOKYO TOWER... AND I WANNA EAT SOME CHOCOLATE CAKE!
HEY, HELLO?
ブチ
SNAP

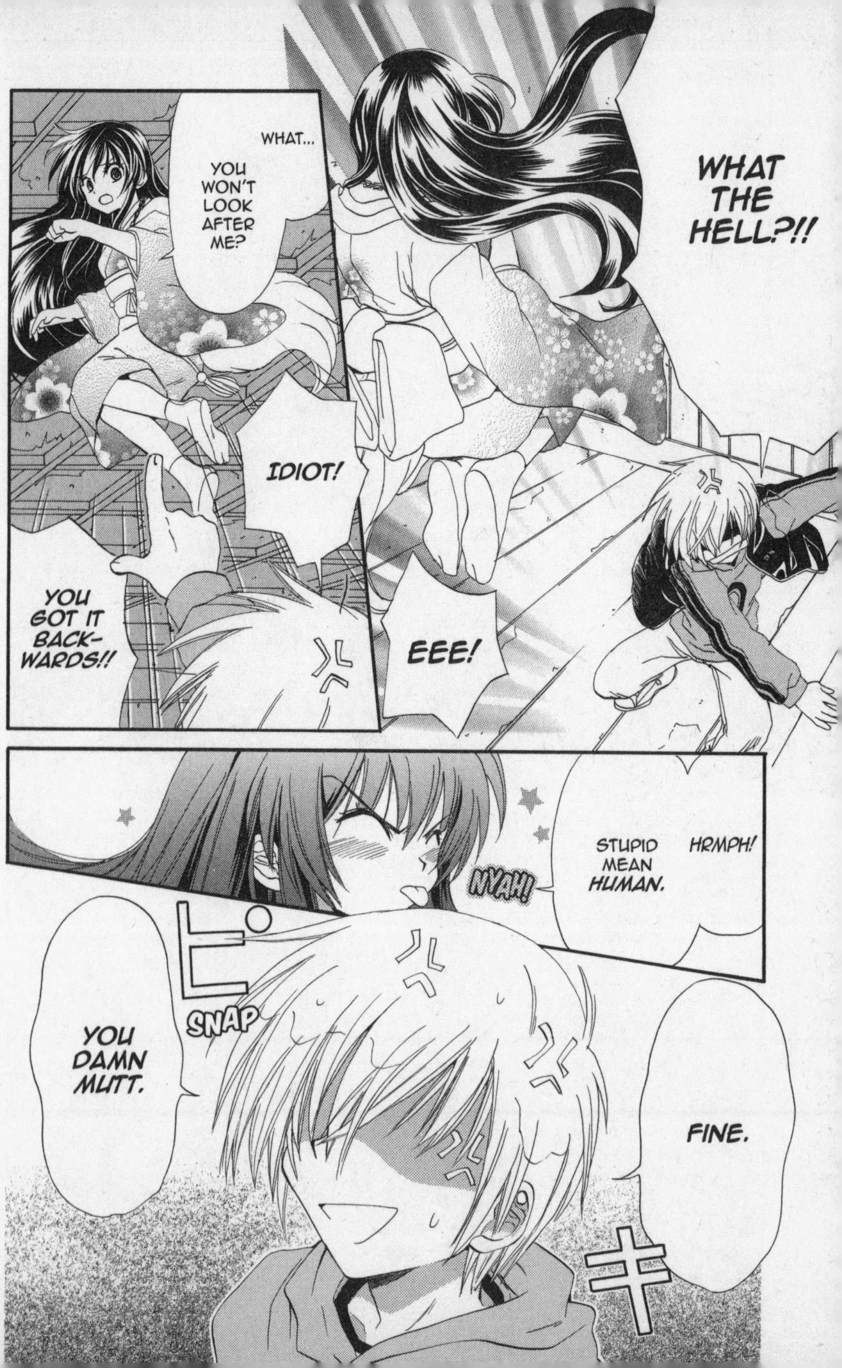
WHAT THE HELL?!!
WHAT...
YOU WON'T LOOK AFTER ME?
IDIOT!
YOU GOT IT BACKWARDS!!
EEE!
HRMPH!
STUPID MEAN HUMAN.
NYAH!
ピ
FINE.
キ
SNAP
YOU DAMN MUTT.

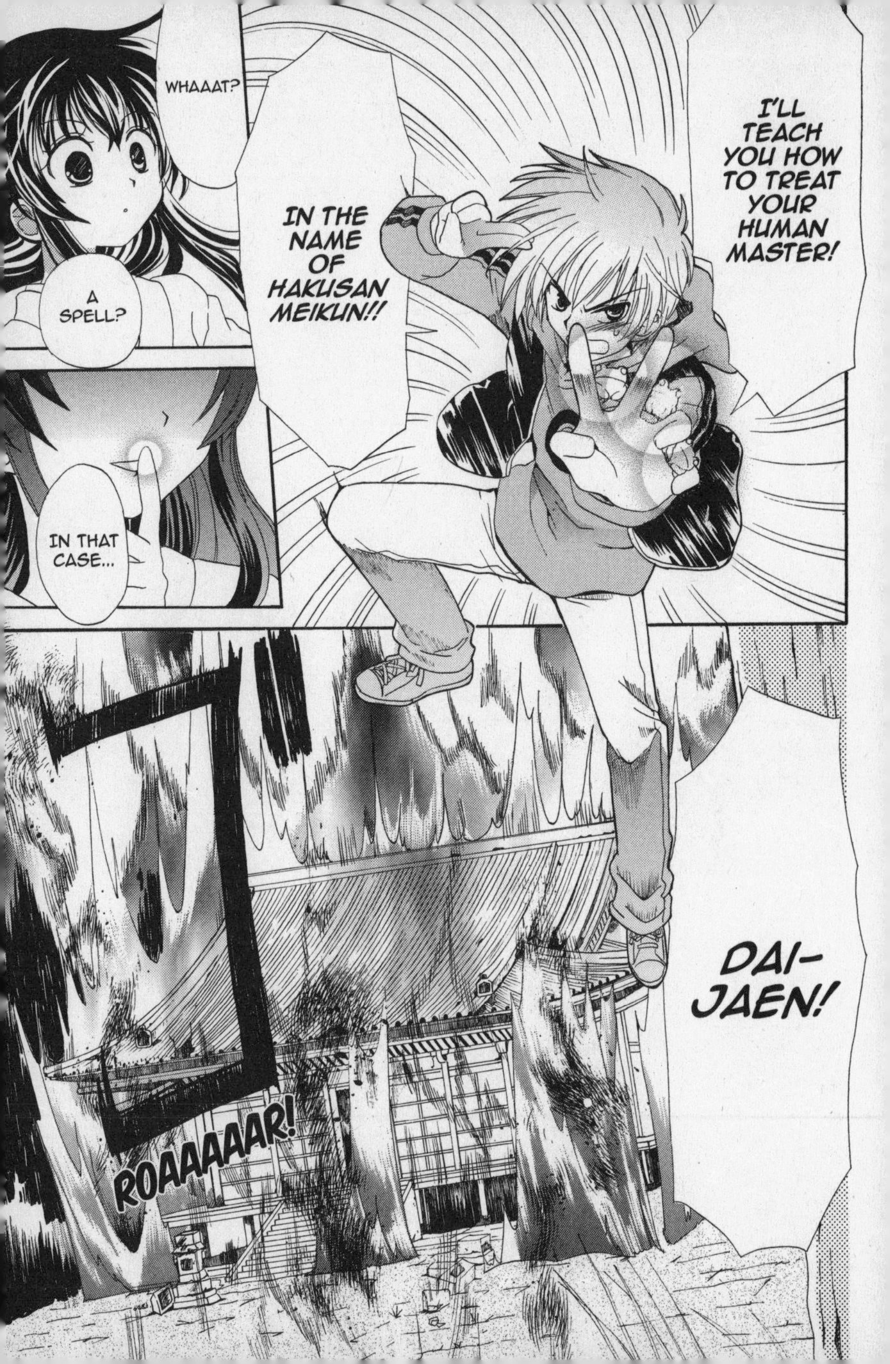
I'LL TEACH YOU HOW TO TREAT YOUR HUMAN MASTER!
IN THE NAME OF HAKUSAN MEIKUN!!
WHAAAT?
A SPELL?
IN THAT CASE...
DAI-JAEN!
ROAAAAAR!

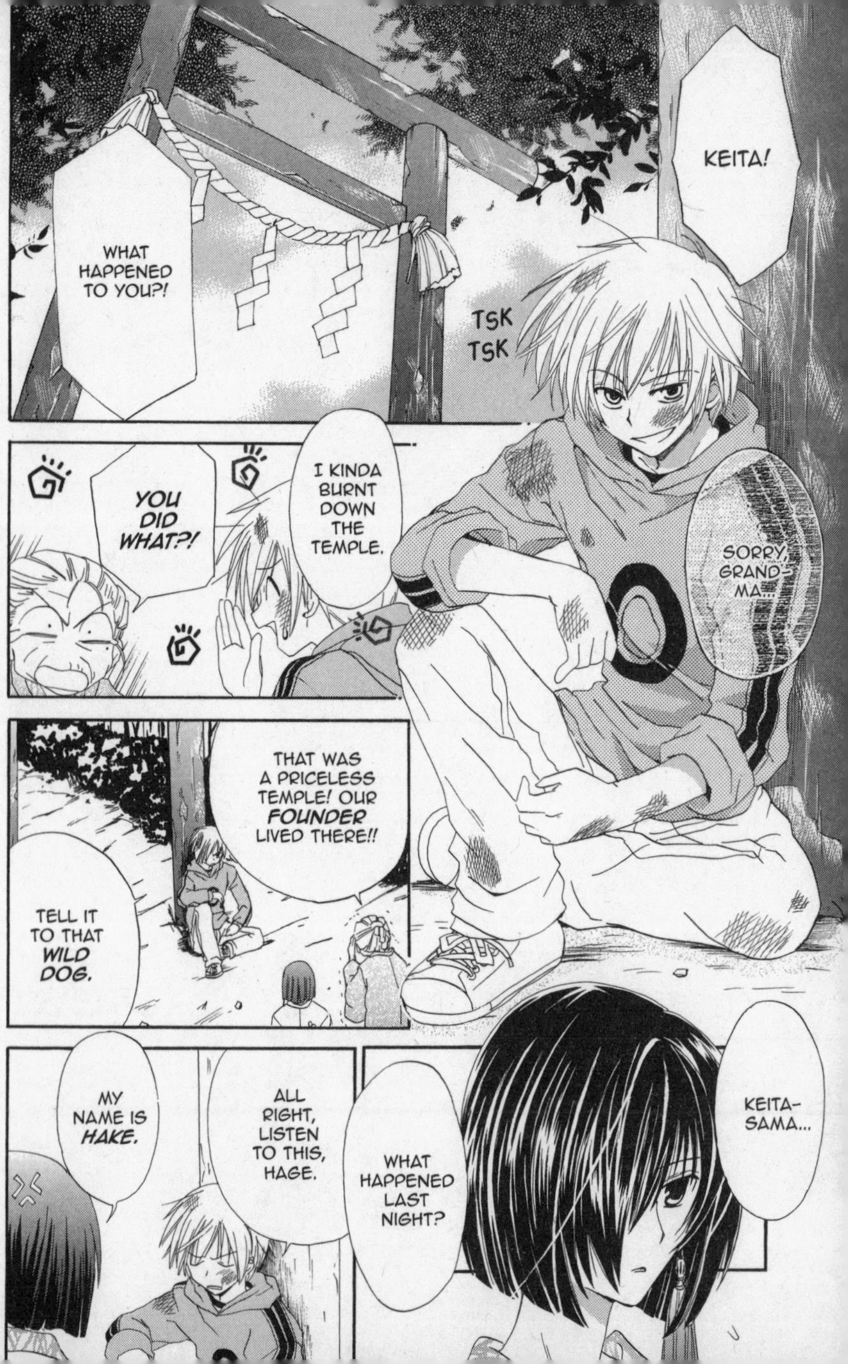
KEITA!
WHAT HAPPENED TO YOU?!
TSK TSK
SORRY, GRAND-MA...
I KINDA BURNT DOWN THE TEMPLE.
YOU DID WHAT?!
THAT WAS A PRICELESS TEMPLE! OUR FOUNDER LIVED THERE!!
TELL IT TO THAT WILD DOG.
KEITA-SAMA...
WHAT HAPPENED LAST NIGHT?
ALL RIGHT, LISTEN TO THIS, HAGE.
MY NAME IS HAKE.

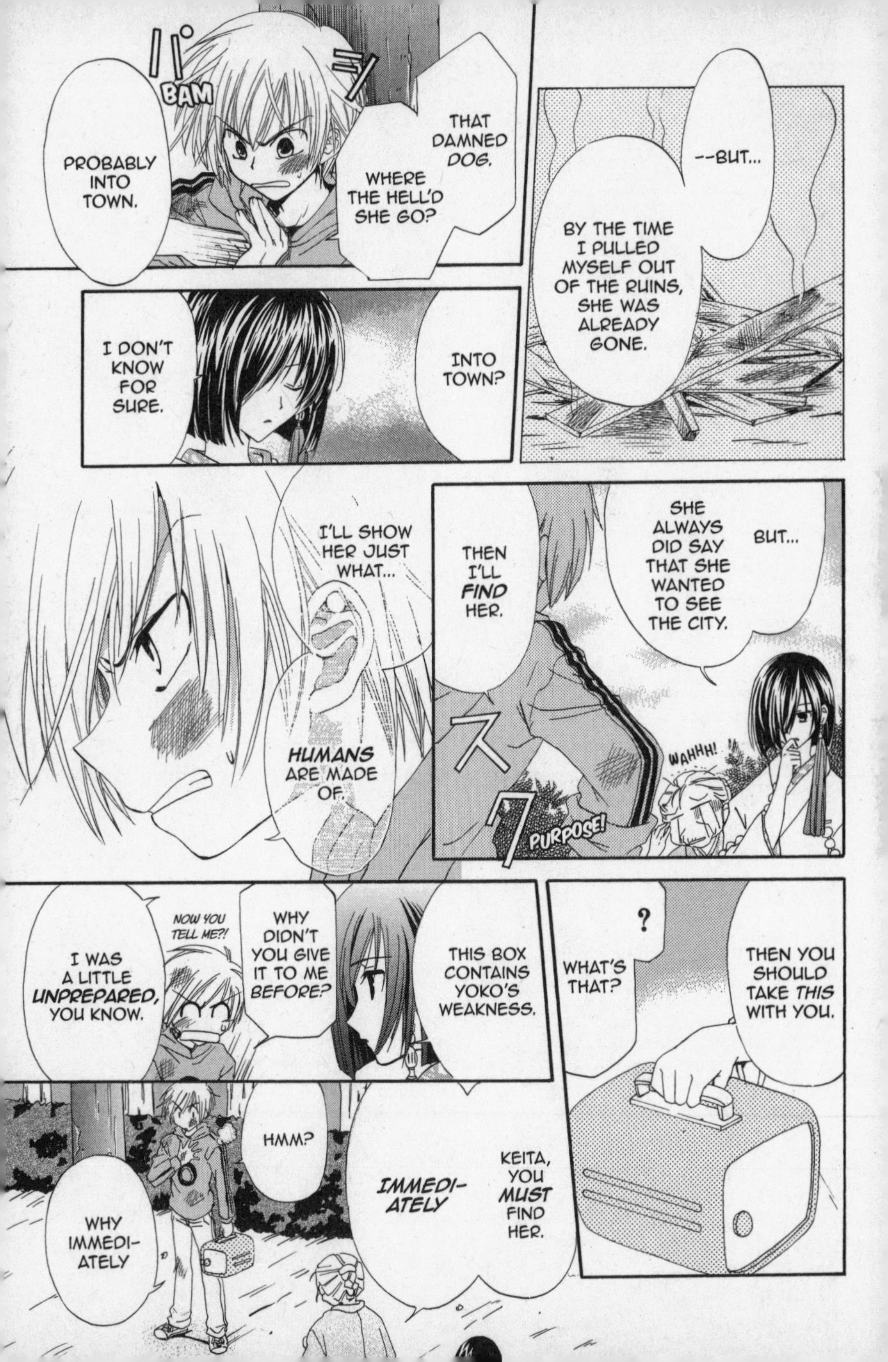

--BUT...
BY THE TIME I PULLED MYSELF OUT OF THE RUINS, SHE WAS ALREADY GONE.
THAT DAMNED DOG.
WHERE THE HELL'D SHE GO?
BAM
PROBABLY INTO TOWN.
INTO TOWN?
I DON'T KNOW FOR SURE.
BUT...
SHE ALWAYS DID SAY THAT SHE WANTED TO SEE THE CITY.
THEN I'LL FIND HER.
WAHHH!
PURPOSE!
I'LL SHOW HER JUST WHAT...
HUMANS ARE MADE OF.
THEN YOU SHOULD TAKE THIS WITH YOU.
?
WHAT'S THAT?
THIS BOX CONTAINS YOKO'S WEAKNESS.
WHY DIDN'T YOU GIVE IT TO ME BEFORE?
NOW YOU TELL ME?!
I WAS A LITTLE UNPREPARED, YOU KNOW.
KEITA, YOU MUST FIND HER.
IMMEDIATELY
HMM?
WHY IMMEDIATELY

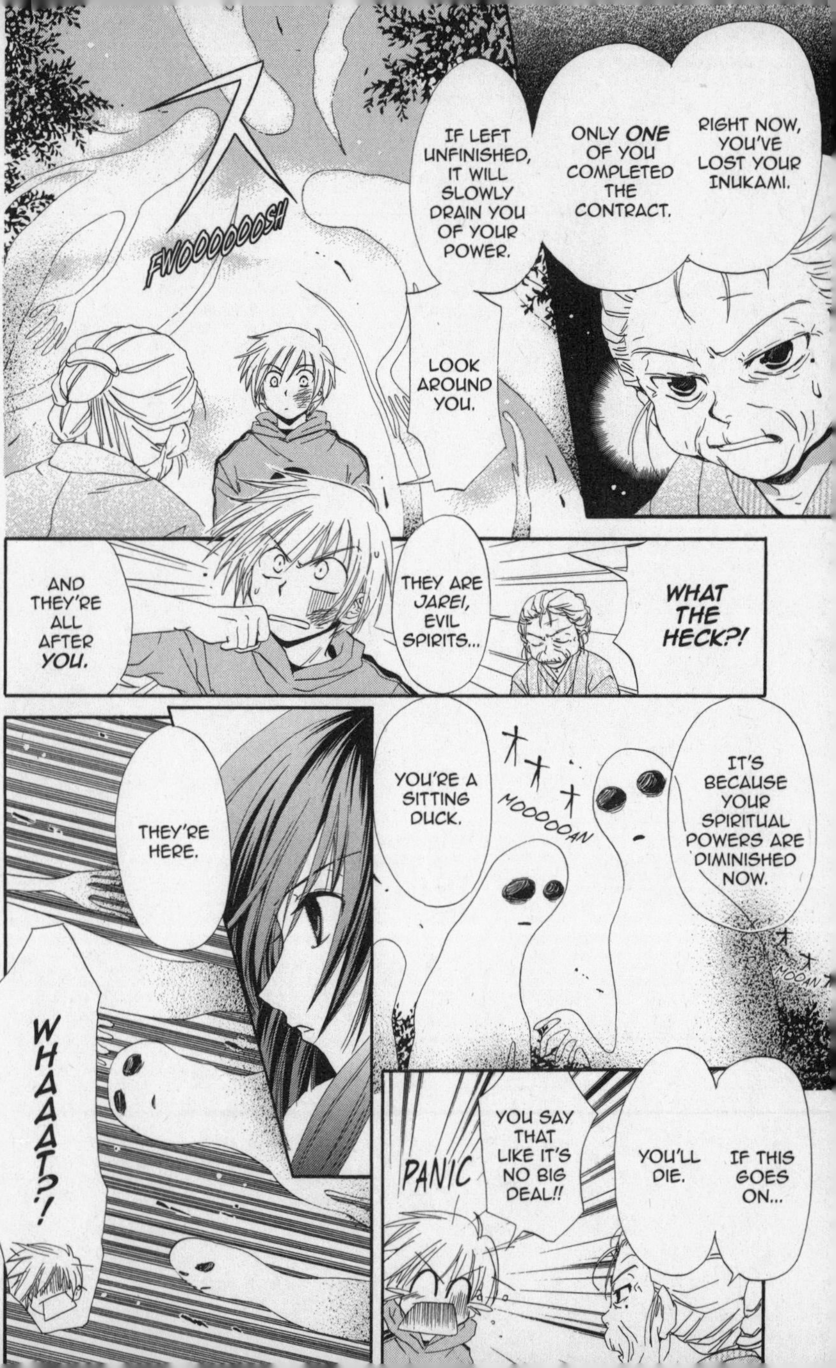
RIGHT NOW, YOU'VE LOST YOUR INUKAMI.
ONLY ONE OF YOU COMPLETED THE CONTRACT.
IF LEFT UNFINISHED, IT WILL SLOWLY DRAIN YOU OF YOUR POWER.
FWOOOOOOOSH
LOOK AROUND YOU.
WHAT THE HECK?!
THEY ARE JAREI, EVIL SPIRITS...
AND THEY'RE ALL AFTER YOU.
IT'S BECAUSE YOUR SPIRITUAL POWERS ARE DIMINISHED NOW.
MOOAN
MOOOOOAN
YOU'RE A SITTING DUCK.
IF THIS GOES ON...
YOU'LL DIE.
YOU SAY THAT LIKE IT'S NO BIG DEAL!!
PANIC
THEY'RE HERE.
WHAAAAT?!

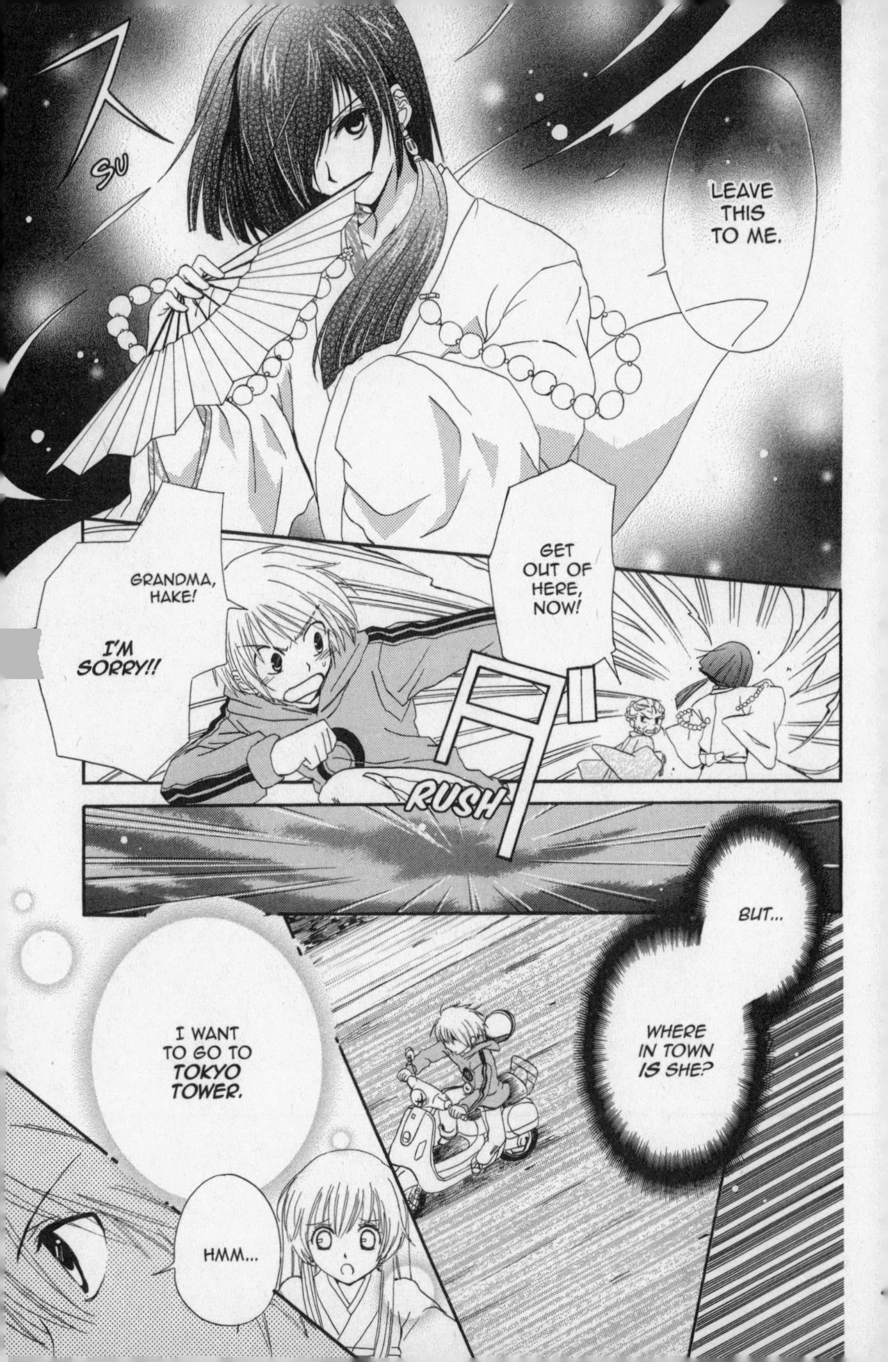
SU
LEAVE THIS TO ME.
GET OUT OF HERE, NOW!
GRANDMA, HAKE!
I'M SORRY!!
RUSH
BUT...
WHERE IN TOWN IS SHE?
I WANT TO GO TO TOKYO TOWER.
HMM...

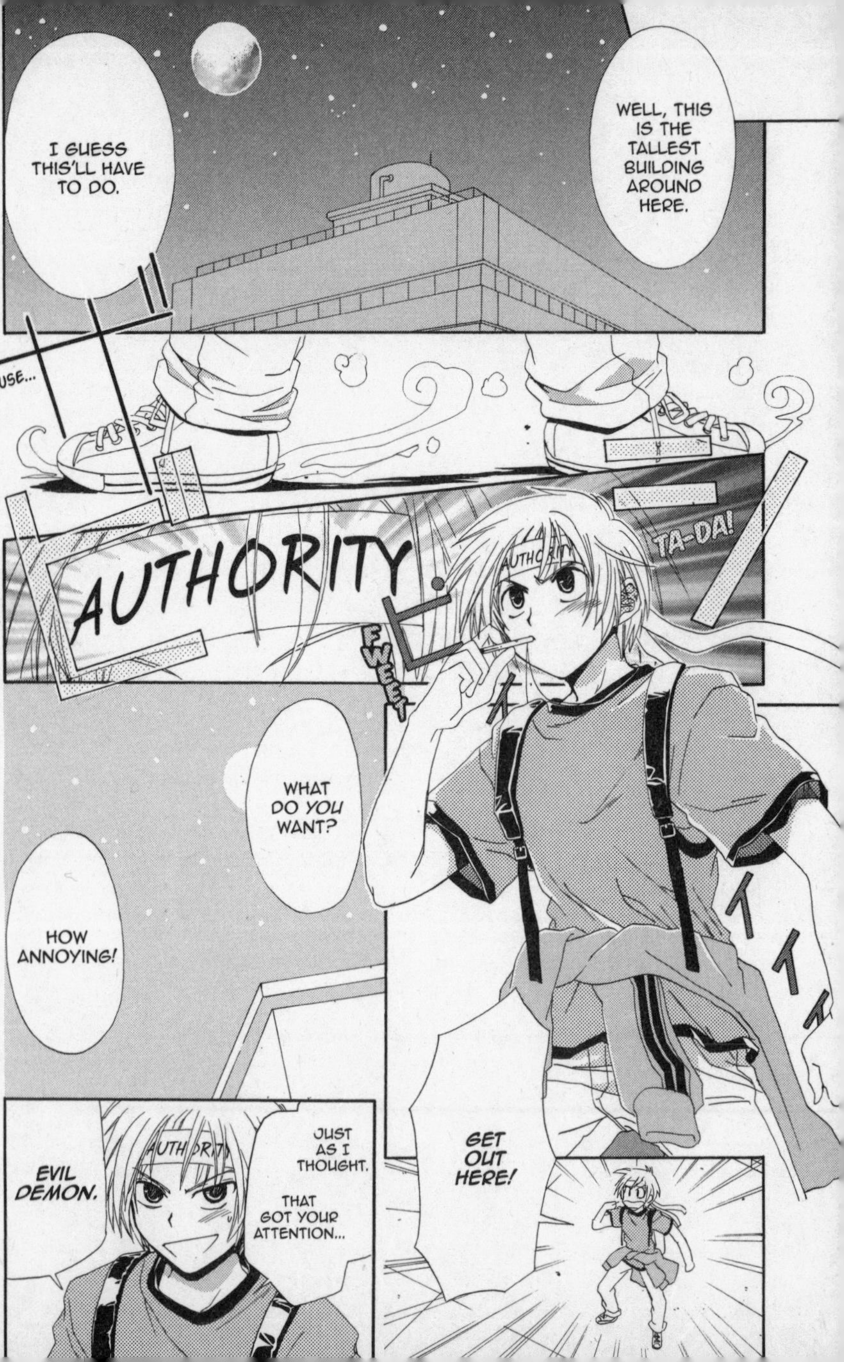
WELL, THIS IS THE TALLEST BUILDING AROUND HERE.
I GUESS THIS'LL HAVE TO DO.
PAUSE...
TA-DA!
AUTHORITY
FWEET
WHAT DO YOU WANT?
HOW ANNOYING!
GET OUT HERE!
JUST AS I THOUGHT.
THAT GOT YOUR ATTENTION...
EVIL DEMON.

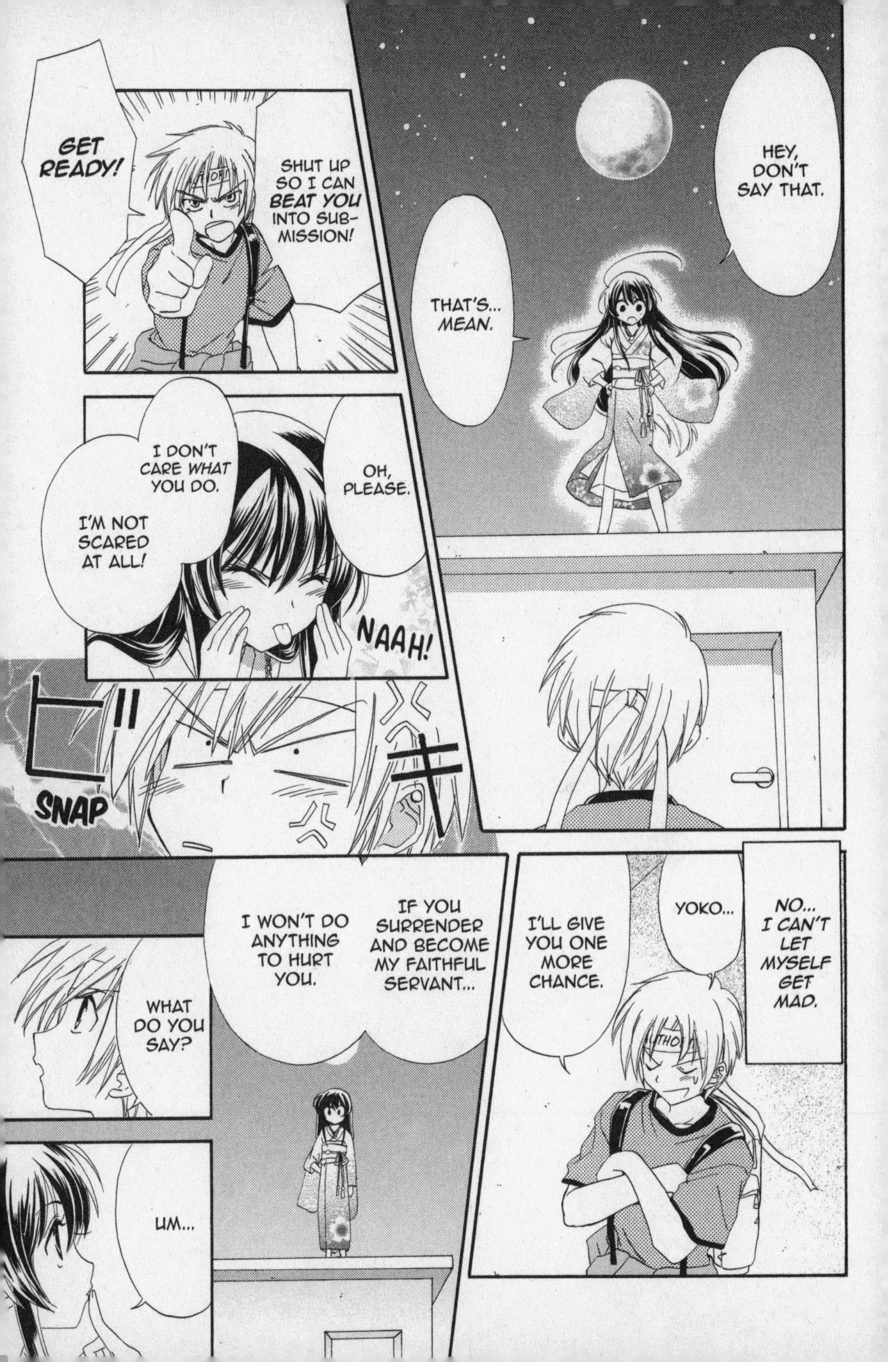
HEY, DON'T SAY THAT.
THAT'S... MEAN.
SHUT UP SO I CAN BEAT YOU INTO SUB-MISSION!
GET READY!
OH, PLEASE.
I DON'T CARE WHAT YOU DO.
I'M NOT SCARED AT ALL!
NAAH!
SNAP
NO... I CAN'T LET MYSELF GET MAD.
YOKO...
I'LL GIVE YOU ONE MORE CHANCE.
IF YOU SURRENDER AND BECOME MY FAITHFUL SERVANT...
I WON'T DO ANYTHING TO HURT YOU.
WHAT DO YOU SAY?
UM...

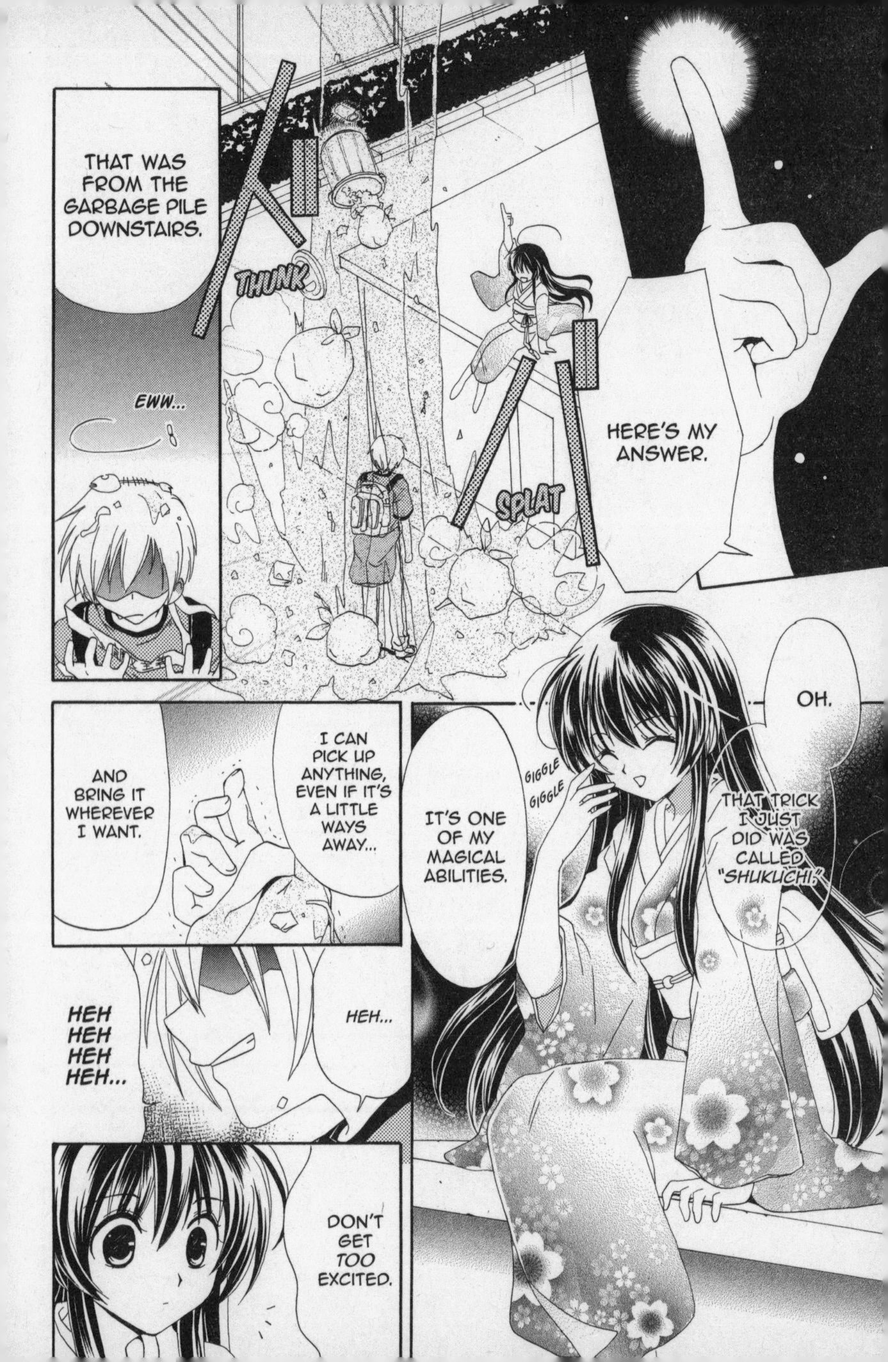
HERE'S MY ANSWER.
SPLAT
THUNK
THAT WAS FROM THE GARBAGE PILE DOWNSTAIRS.
EWW...
OH.
THAT TRICK I JUST DID WAS CALLED "SHUKUCHI."
GIGGLE GIGGLE
IT'S ONE OF MY MAGICAL ABILITIES.
I CAN PICK UP ANYTHING, EVEN IF IT'S A LITTLE WAYS AWAY...
AND BRING IT WHEREVER I WANT.
HEH...
HEH HEH HEH HEH...
DON'T GET *TOO* EXCITED.

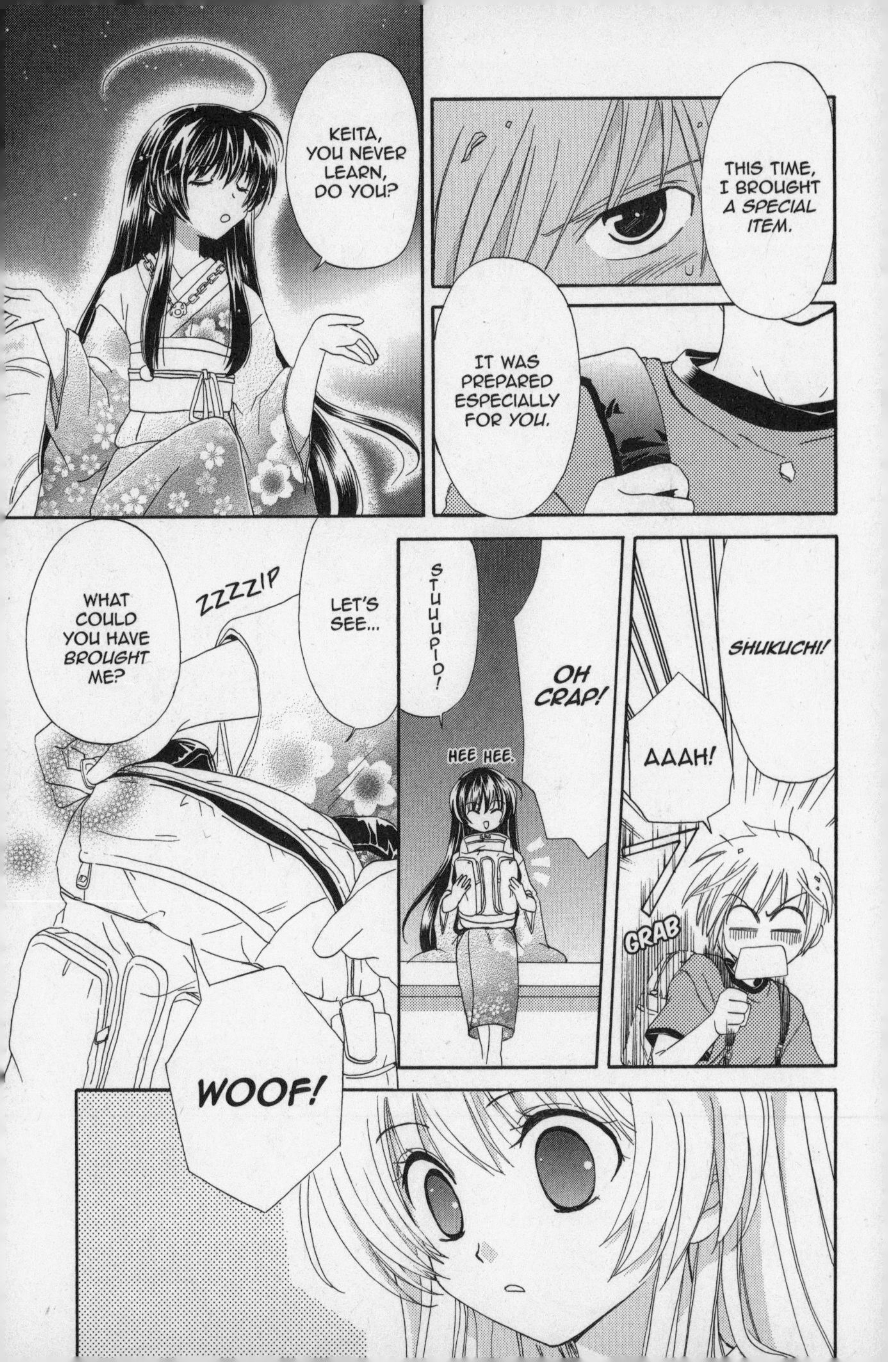
THIS TIME, I BROUGHT A SPECIAL ITEM.
IT WAS PREPARED ESPECIALLY FOR YOU.
KEITA, YOU NEVER LEARN, DO YOU?
SHUKUCHI!
AAAH!
GRAB
STUUUPID!
OH CRAP!
HEE HEE.
LET'S SEE...
ZZZZIP
WHAT COULD YOU HAVE BROUGHT ME?
WOOF!

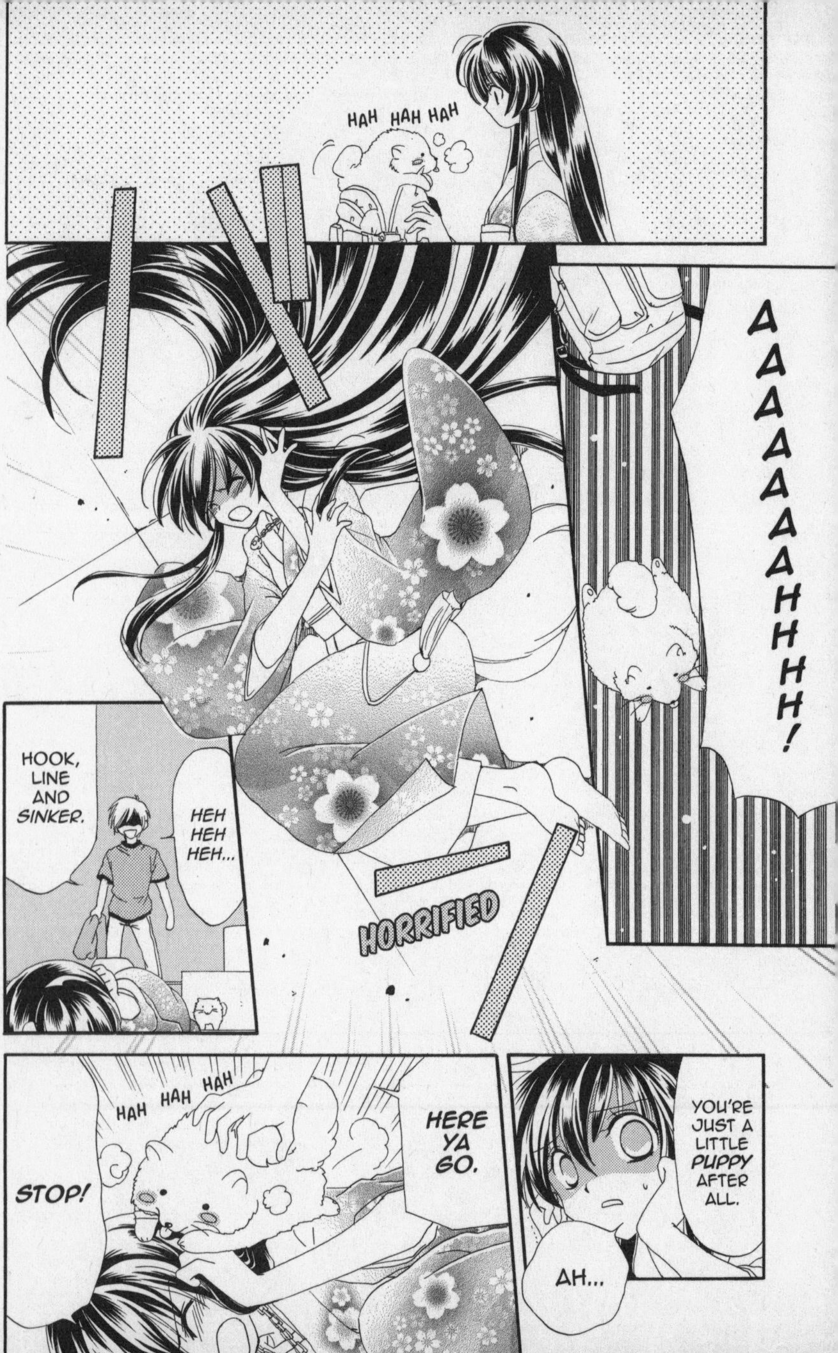
HAH HAH HAH
AAAAAAAHHHH!
HORRIFIED
HEH HEH HEH...
HOOK, LINE AND SINKER.
YOU'RE JUST A LITTLE PUPPY AFTER ALL.
AH...
HERE YA GO.
HAH HAH HAH
STOP!

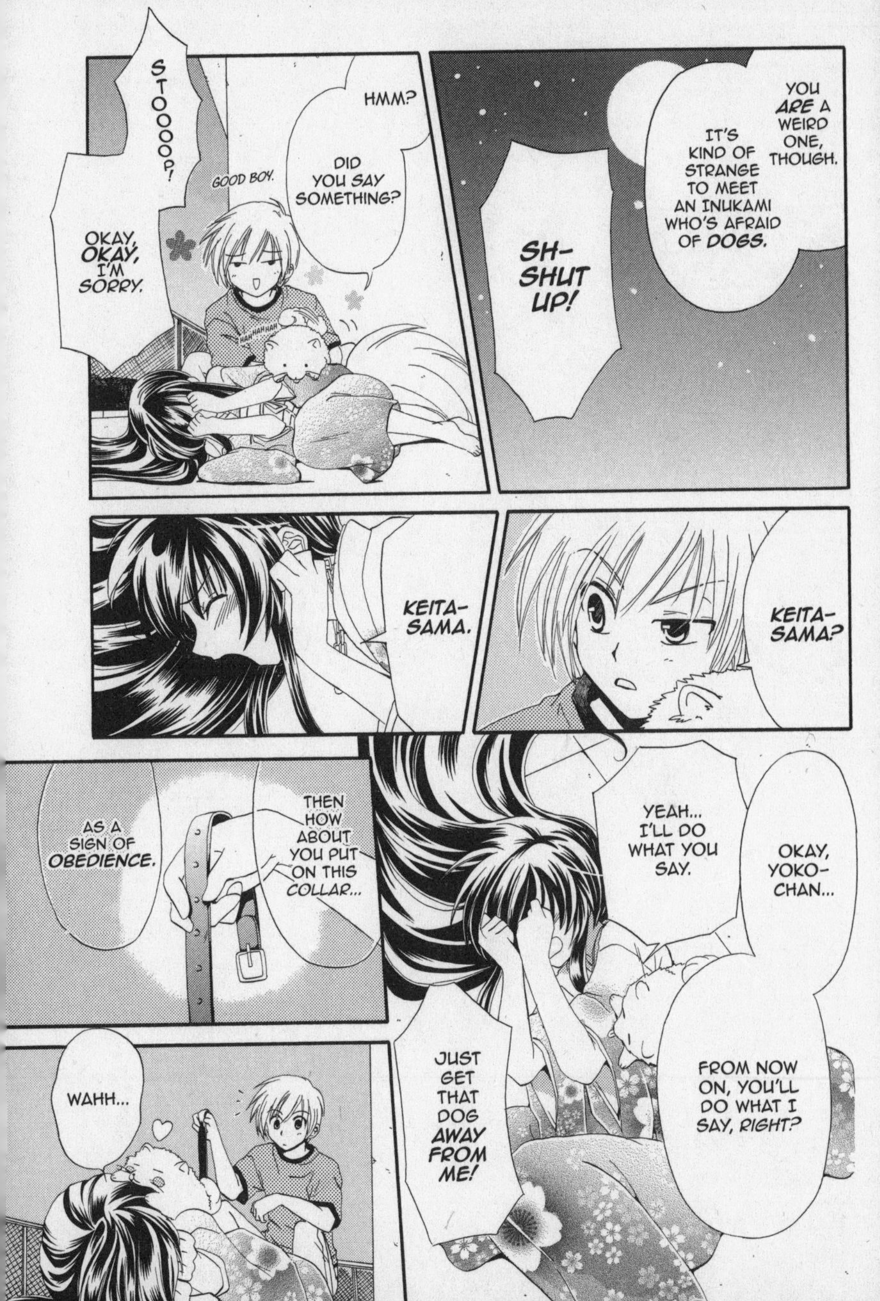
YOU ARE A WEIRD ONE, THOUGH.
IT'S KIND OF STRANGE TO MEET AN INUKAMI WHO'S AFRAID OF DOGS.
SH-SHUT UP!
HMM?
DID YOU SAY SOMETHING?
STOOOOOP!
GOOD BOY.
HAH HAH HAH
OKAY, OKAY, I'M SORRY.
KEITA-SAMA?
KEITA-SAMA.
OKAY, YOKO-CHAN...
YEAH... I'LL DO WHAT YOU SAY.
FROM NOW ON, YOU'LL DO WHAT I SAY, RIGHT?
JUST GET THAT DOG AWAY FROM ME!
THEN HOW ABOUT YOU PUT ON THIS COLLAR...
AS A SIGN OF OBEDIENCE.
WAHH...

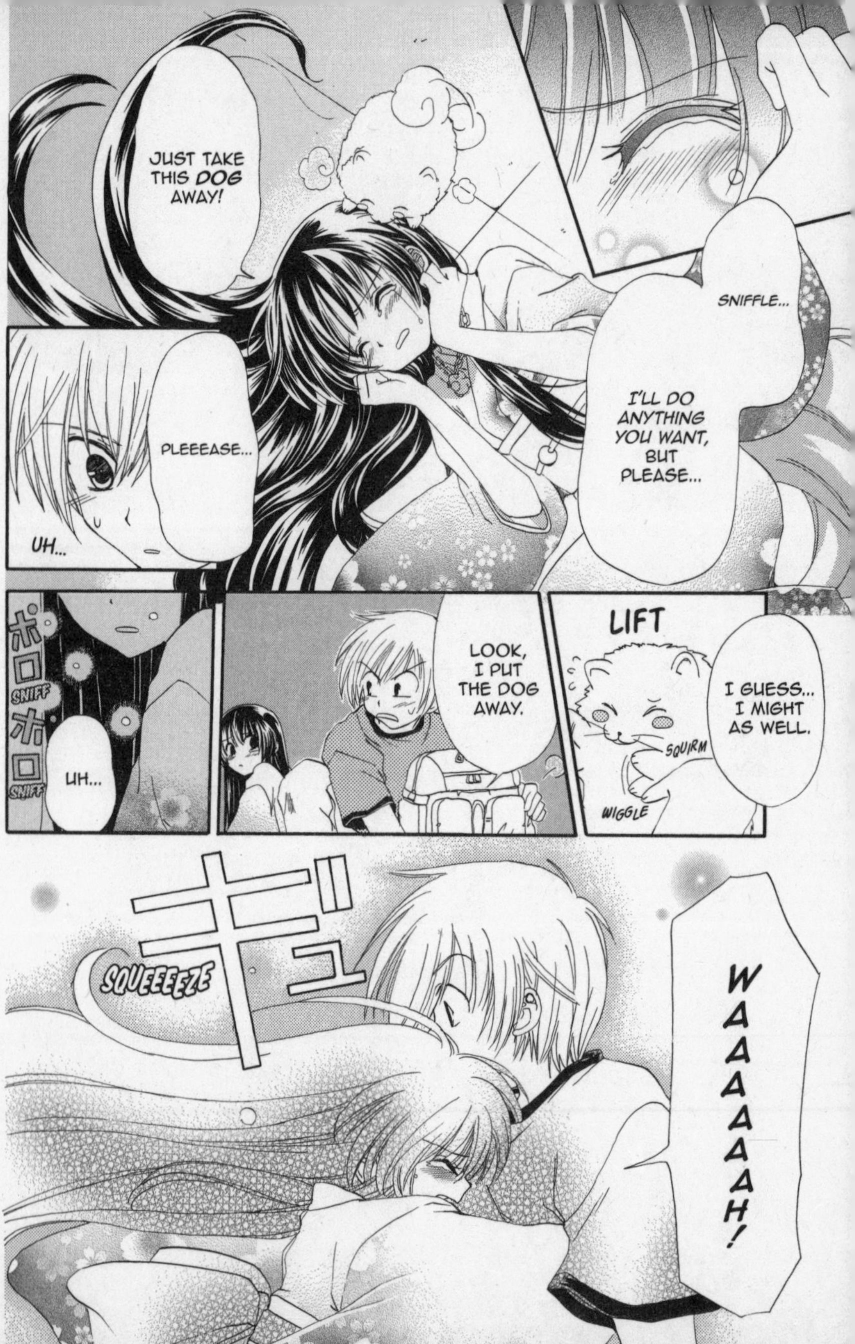
SNIFFLE...
I'LL DO ANYTHING YOU WANT, BUT PLEASE...
JUST TAKE THIS *DOG* AWAY!
PLEEEASE...
UH...
LIFT
I GUESS... I MIGHT AS WELL.
SQUIRM
WIGGLE
LOOK, I PUT THE DOG AWAY.
ポロ
SNIFF
ポロ
SNIFF
UH...
WAAAAAAAH!
ギュ
SQUEEEEEZE

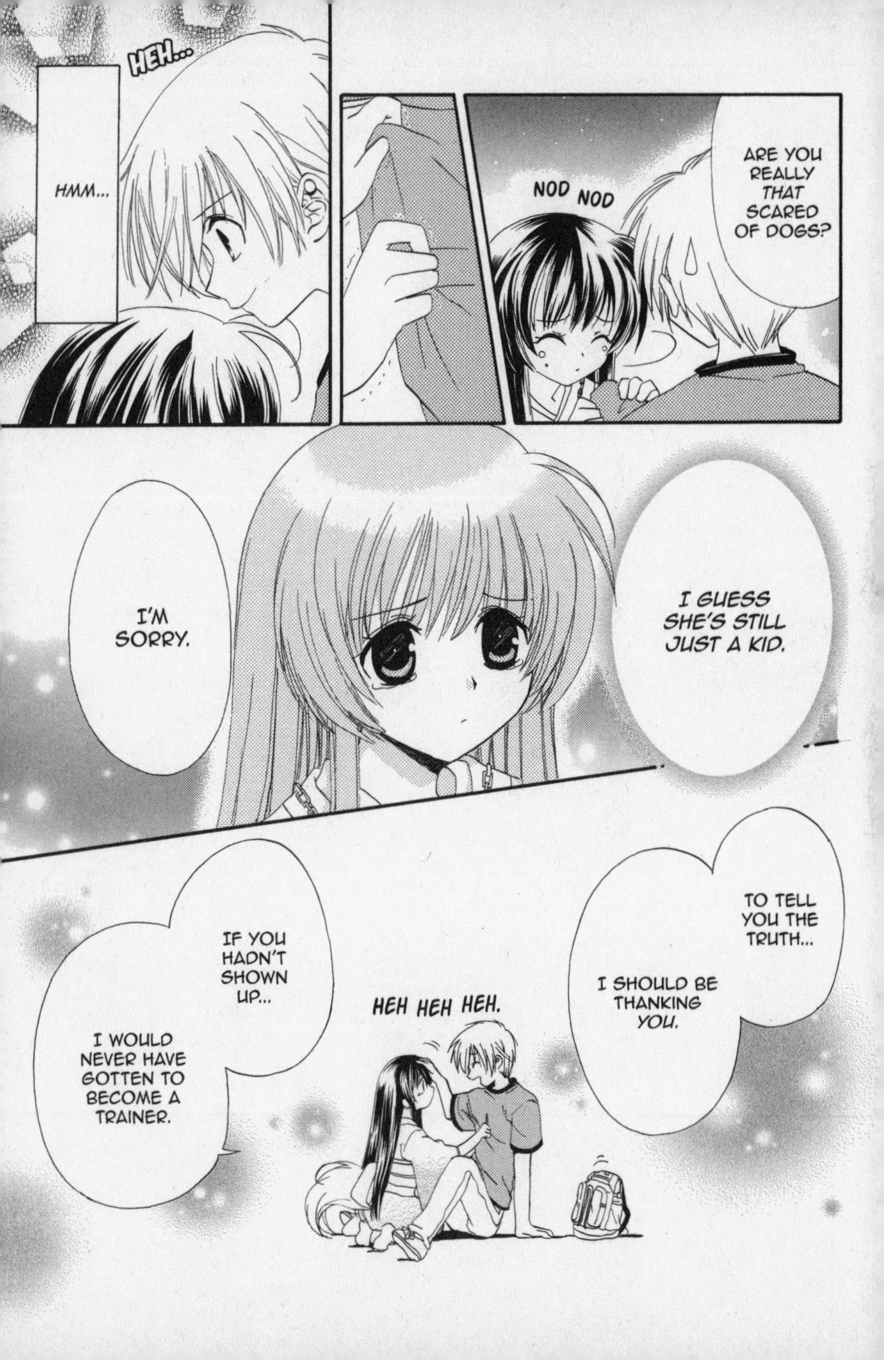
ARE YOU REALLY THAT SCARED OF DOGS?
NOD NOD
HEH...
HMM...
I GUESS SHE'S STILL JUST A KID.
I'M SORRY.
TO TELL YOU THE TRUTH...
I SHOULD BE THANKING YOU.
HEH HEH HEH.
IF YOU HADN'T SHOWN UP...
I WOULD NEVER HAVE GOTTEN TO BECOME A TRAINER.

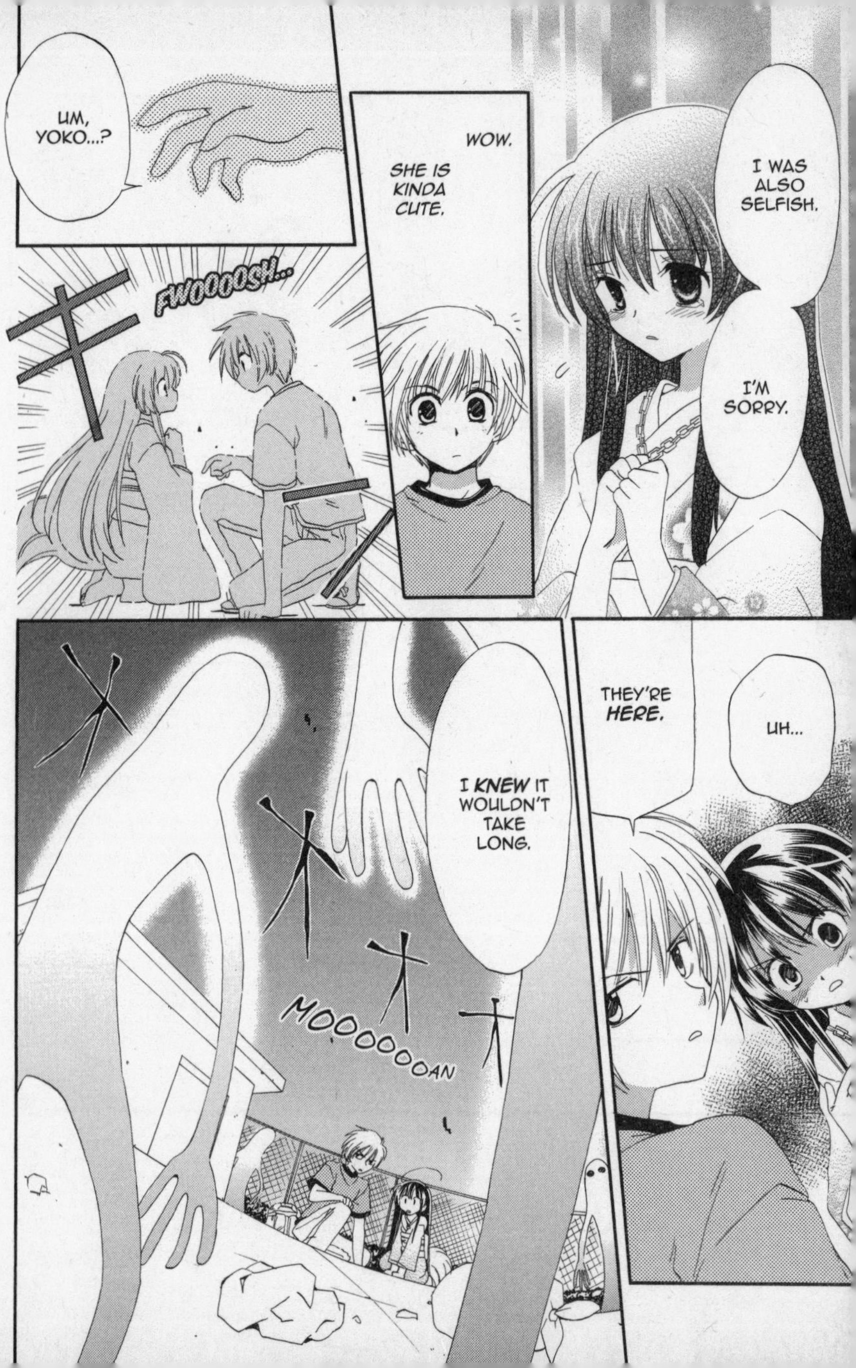
I WAS ALSO SELFISH.
I'M SORRY.
WOW.
SHE IS KINDA CUTE.
UM, YOKO...?
FWOOOOSH...
UH...
THEY'RE *HERE.*
I *KNEW* IT WOULDN'T TAKE LONG.
MOOOOOOOAN

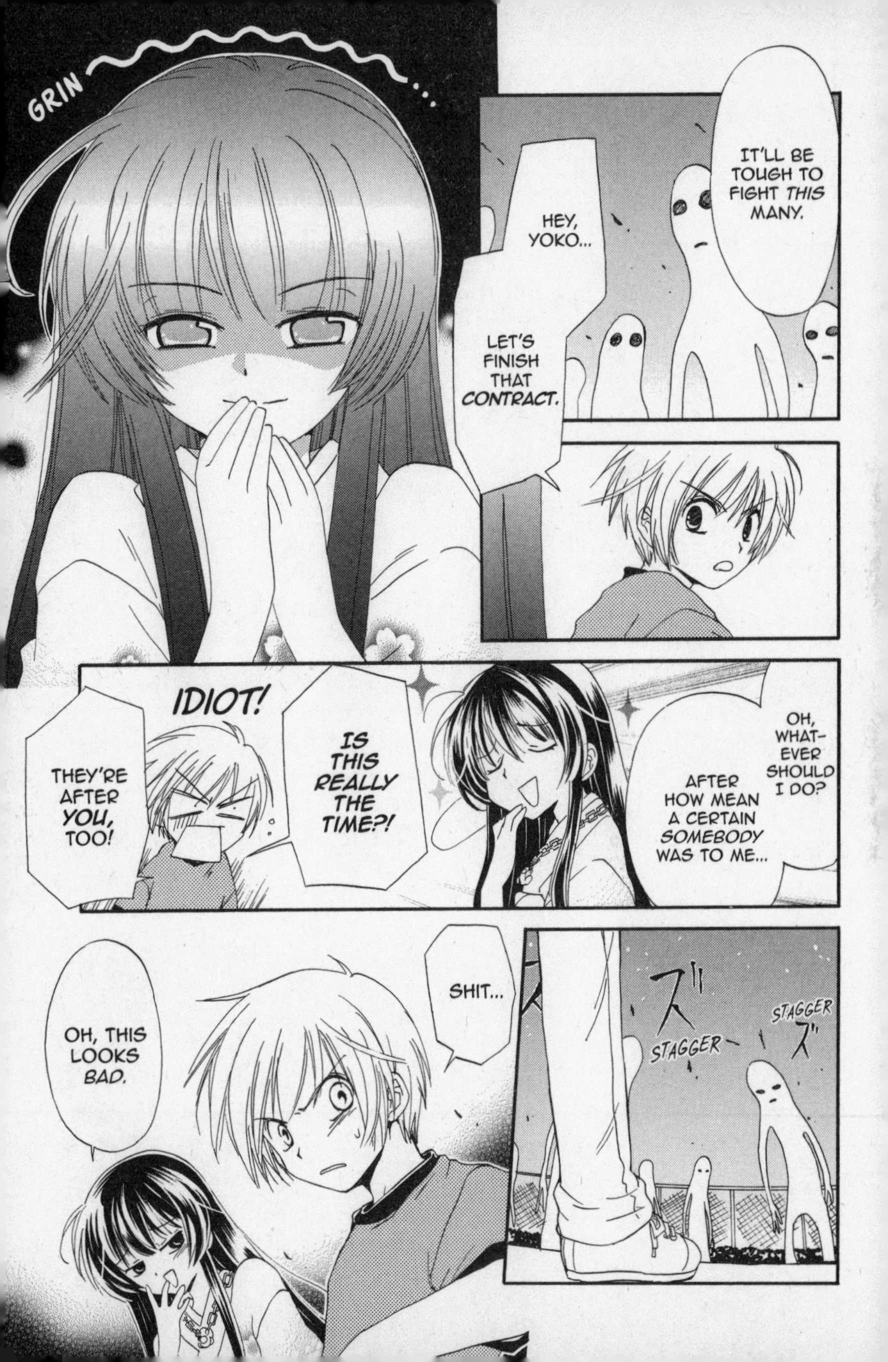
IT'LL BE TOUGH TO FIGHT THIS MANY.
HEY, YOKO...
LET'S FINISH THAT CONTRACT.
GRIN~~~...
OH, WHATEVER SHOULD I DO?
AFTER HOW MEAN A CERTAIN SOMEBODY WAS TO ME...
IS THIS REALLY THE TIME?!
IDIOT!
THEY'RE AFTER YOU, TOO!
ズ
STAGGER
ズ
STAGGER
SHIT...
OH, THIS LOOKS BAD.

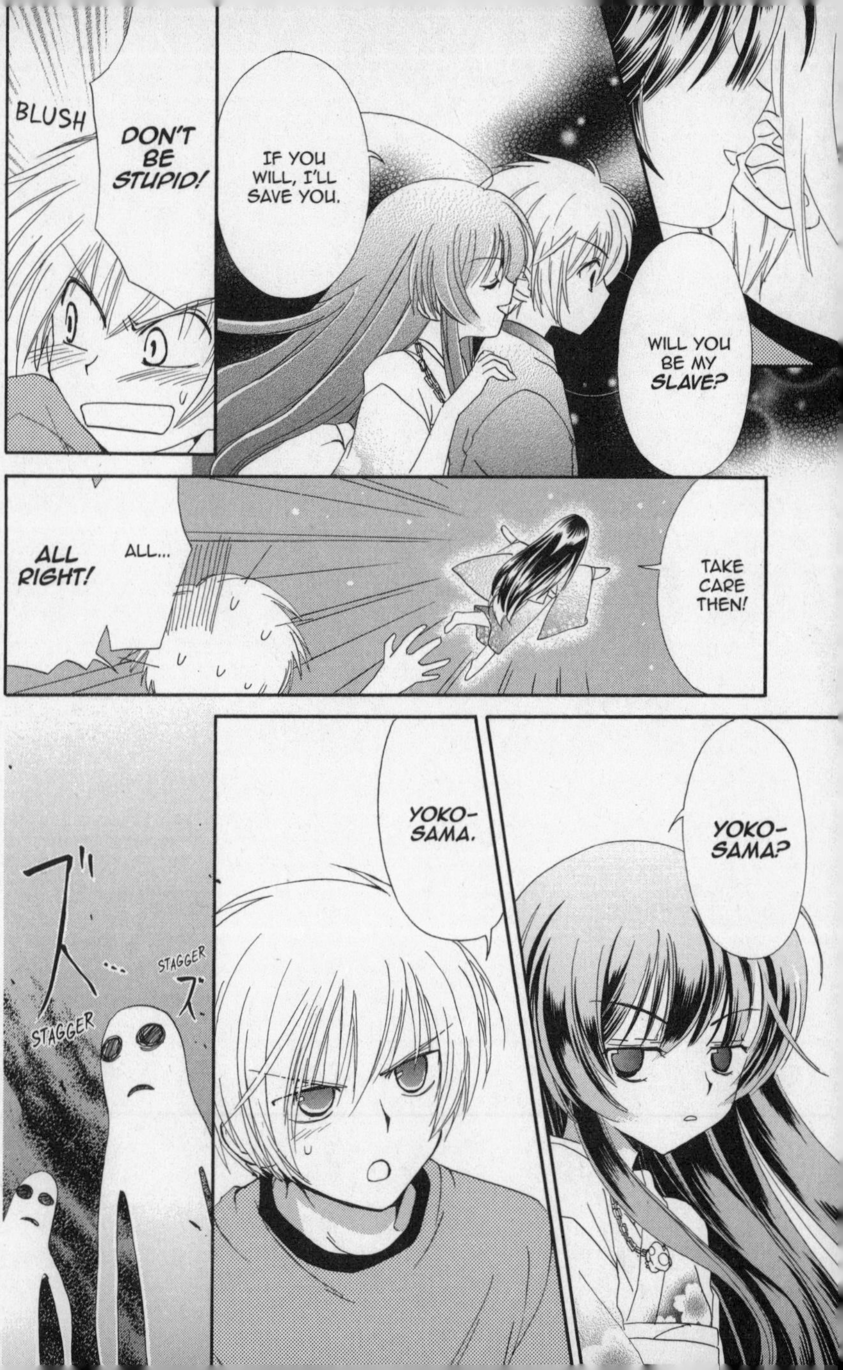
WILL YOU BE MY SLAVE?
IF YOU WILL, I'LL SAVE YOU.
DON'T BE STUPID!
BLUSH
TAKE CARE THEN!
ALL...
ALL RIGHT!
YOKO-SAMA?
YOKO-SAMA.
STAGGER
ズ
ズ...
STAGGER

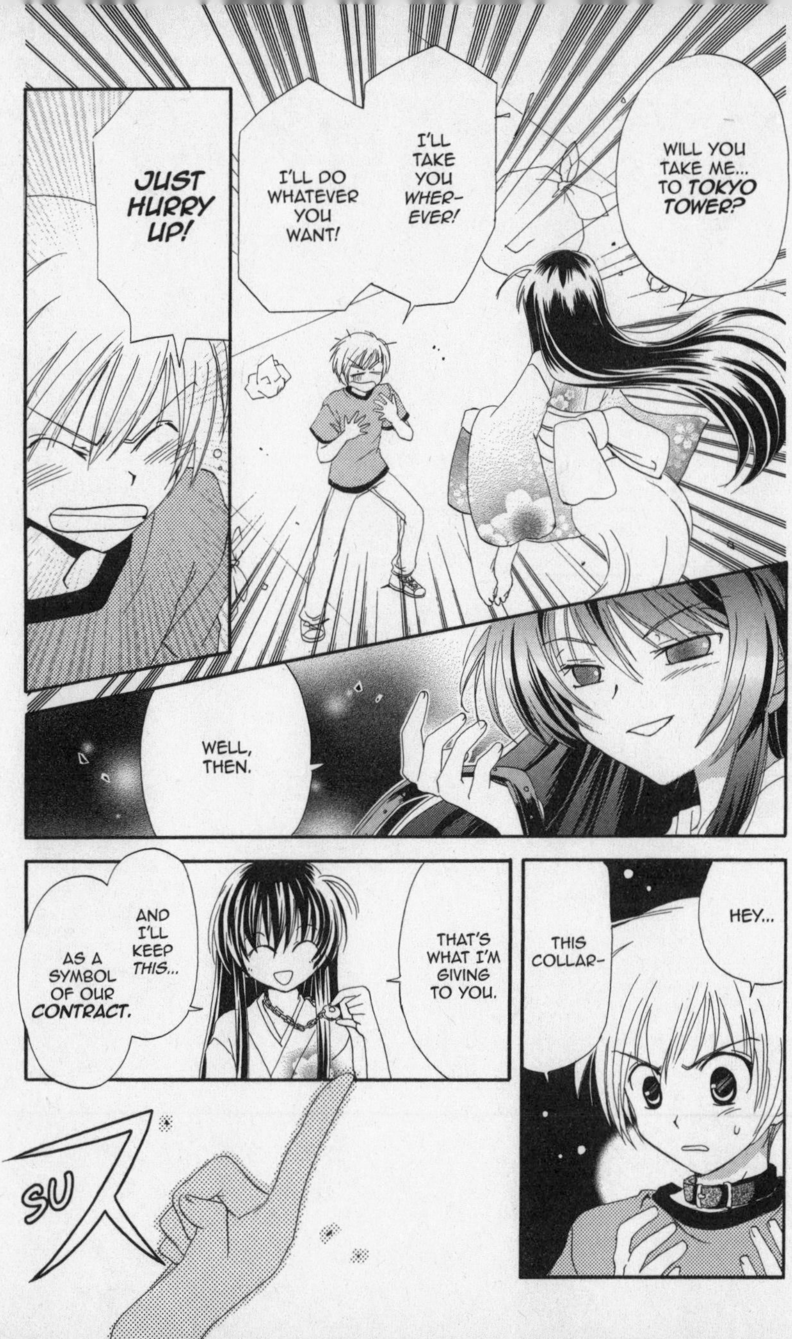
WILL YOU TAKE ME... TO TOKYO TOWER?
I'LL TAKE YOU WHER-EVER!
I'LL DO WHATEVER YOU WANT!
JUST HURRY UP!
WELL, THEN.
HEY...
THIS COLLAR-
THAT'S WHAT I'M GIVING TO YOU.
AND I'LL KEEP THIS...
AS A SYMBOL OF OUR CONTRACT.
SU

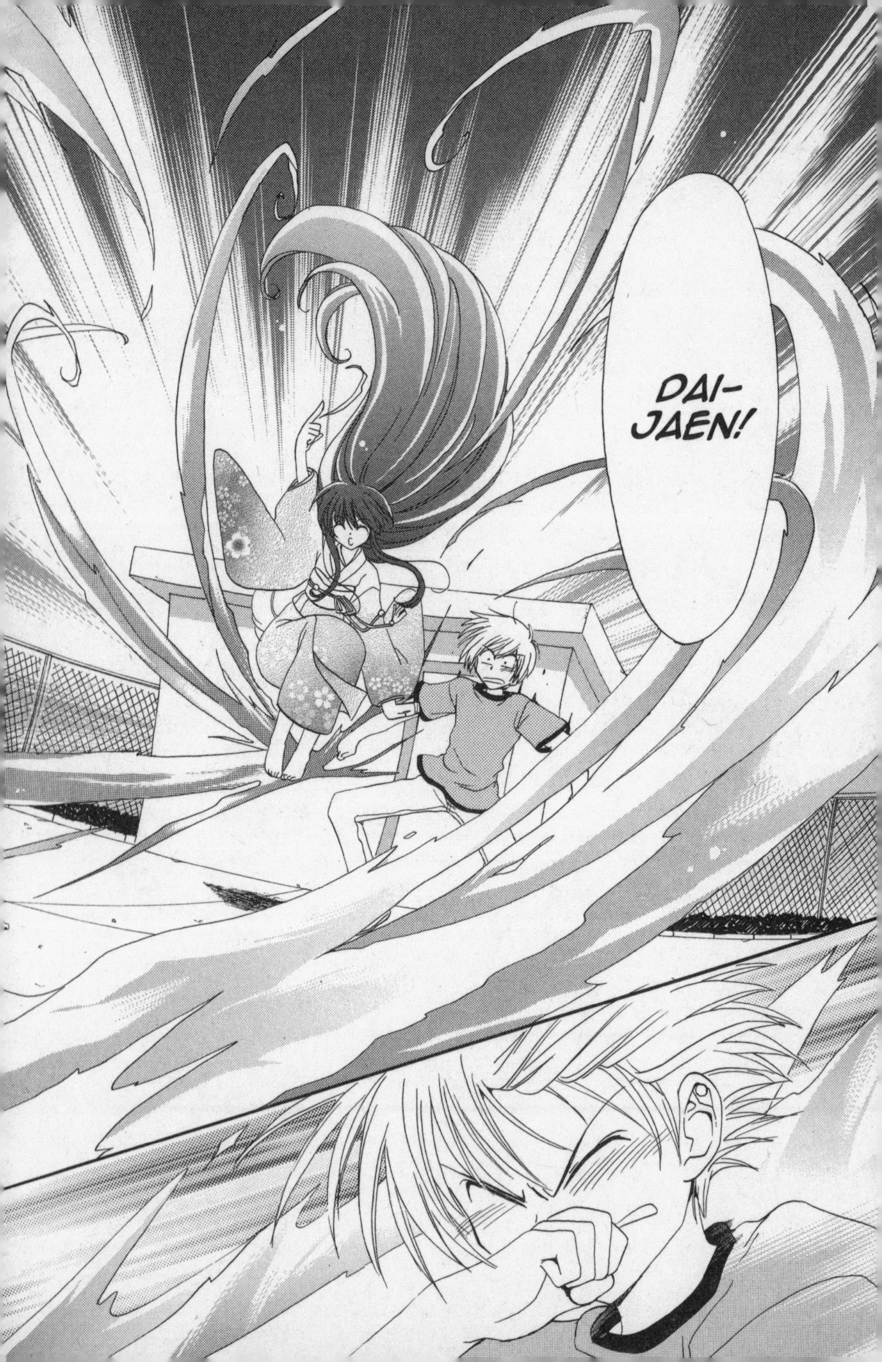
DAI-
JAEN!

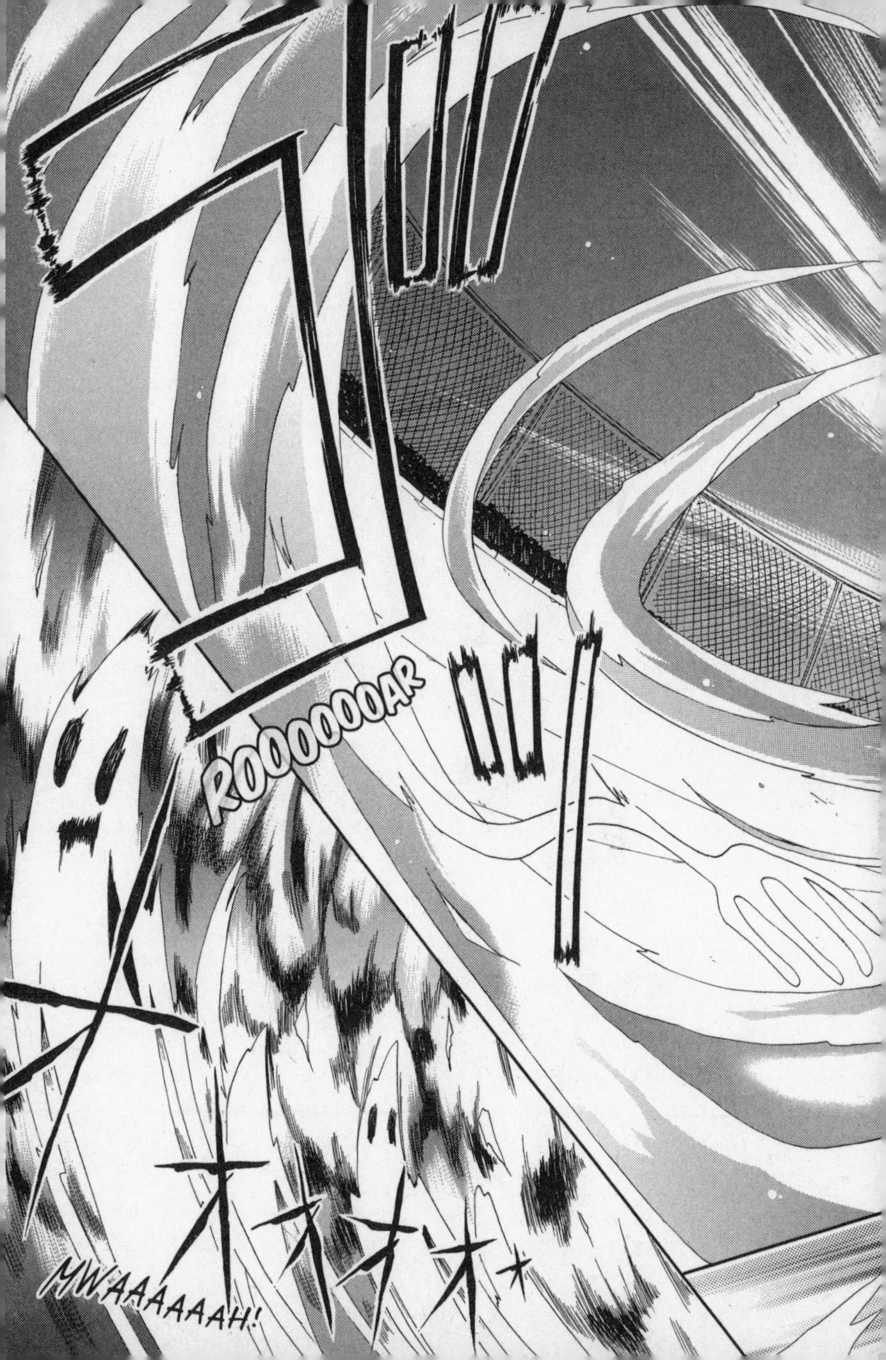
ROOOOOOOAR
MWAAAAAAAH!

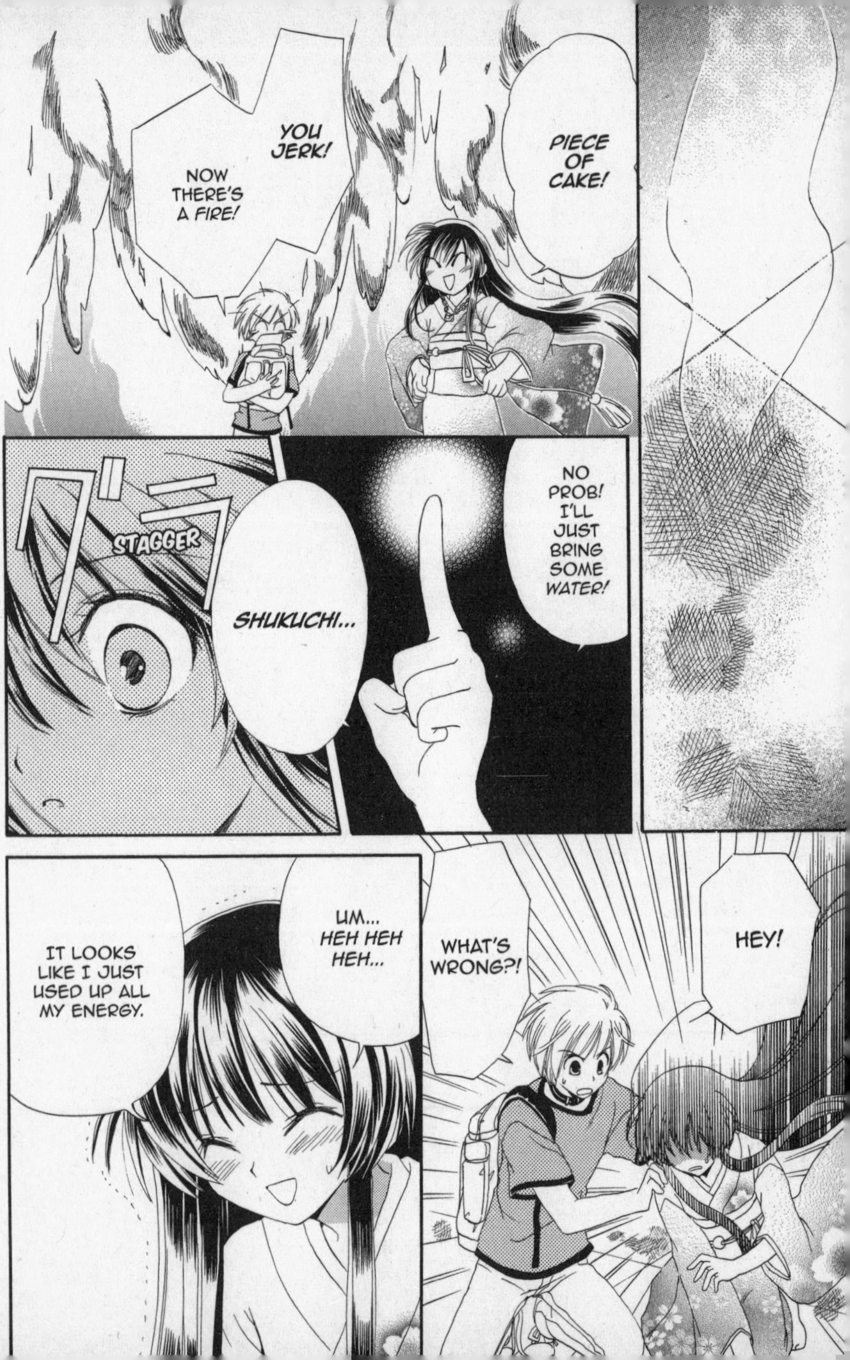
PIECE OF CAKE!
YOU JERK!
NOW THERE'S A FIRE!
NO PROB! I'LL JUST BRING SOME WATER!
SHUKUCHI...
STAGGER
HEY!
WHAT'S WRONG?!
UM... HEH HEH HEH...
IT LOOKS LIKE I JUST USED UP ALL MY ENERGY.

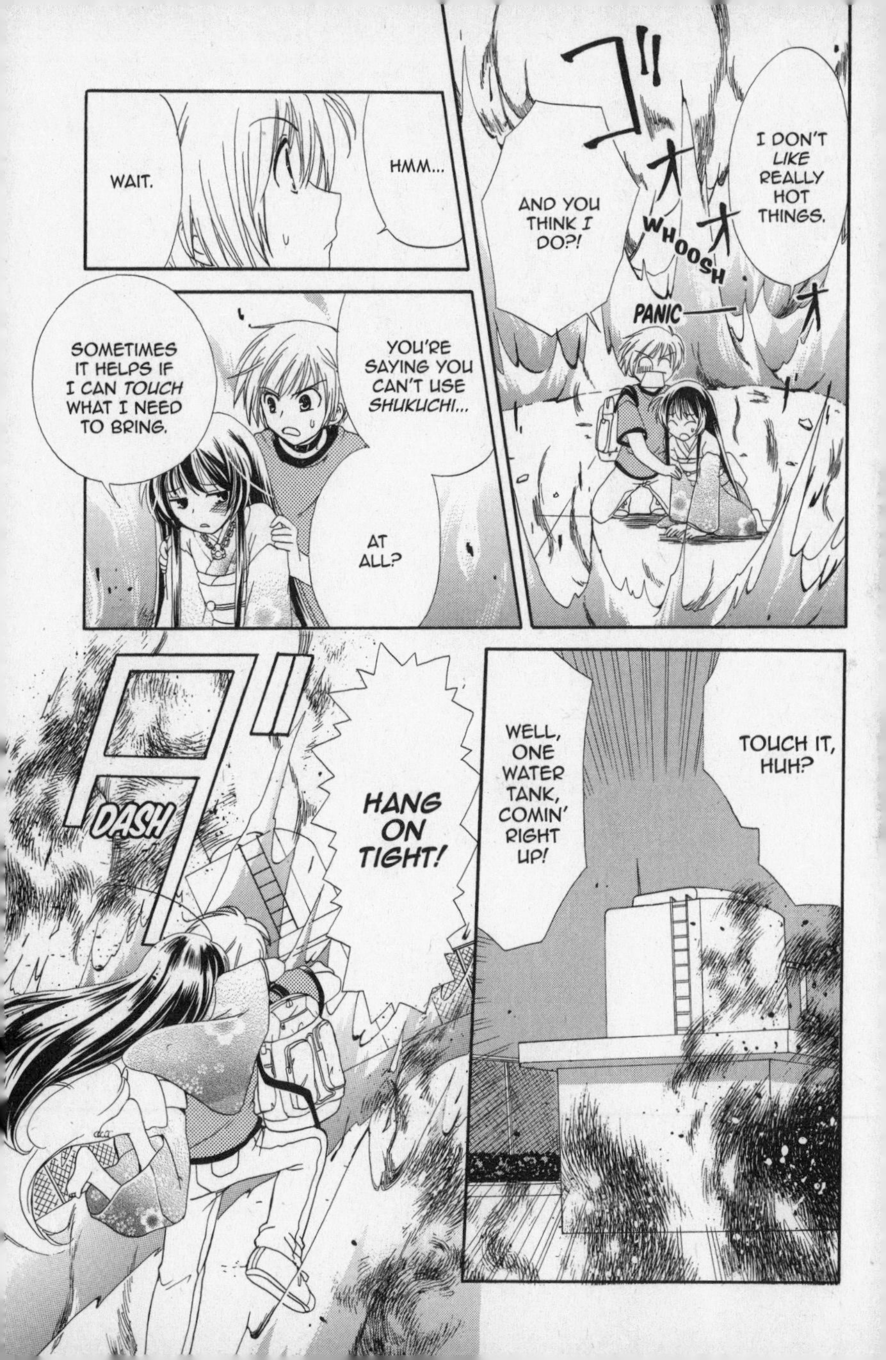

I DON'T *LIKE* REALLY HOT THINGS.
AND YOU THINK I DO?!
WHOOSH
PANIC
HMM...
WAIT.
YOU'RE SAYING YOU CAN'T USE *SHUKUCHI*...
AT ALL?
SOMETIMES IT HELPS IF I CAN *TOUCH* WHAT I NEED TO BRING.
TOUCH IT, HUH?
WELL, ONE WATER TANK, COMIN' RIGHT UP!
HANG ON TIGHT!
DASH

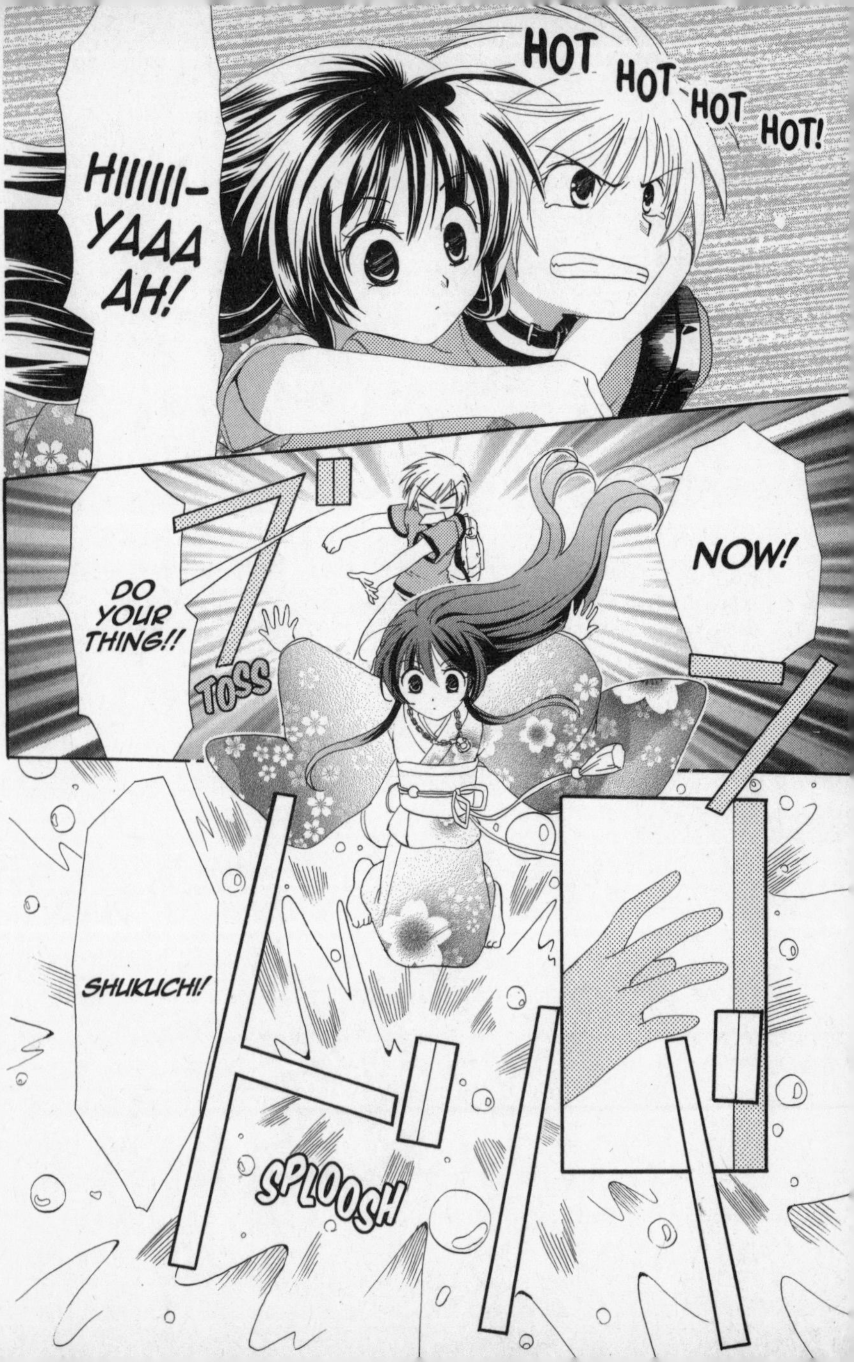
HOT HOT HOT HOT!
HIIIIII-YAAAAH!
NOW!
DO YOUR THING!!
TOSS
SHUKUCHI!
SPLOOSH

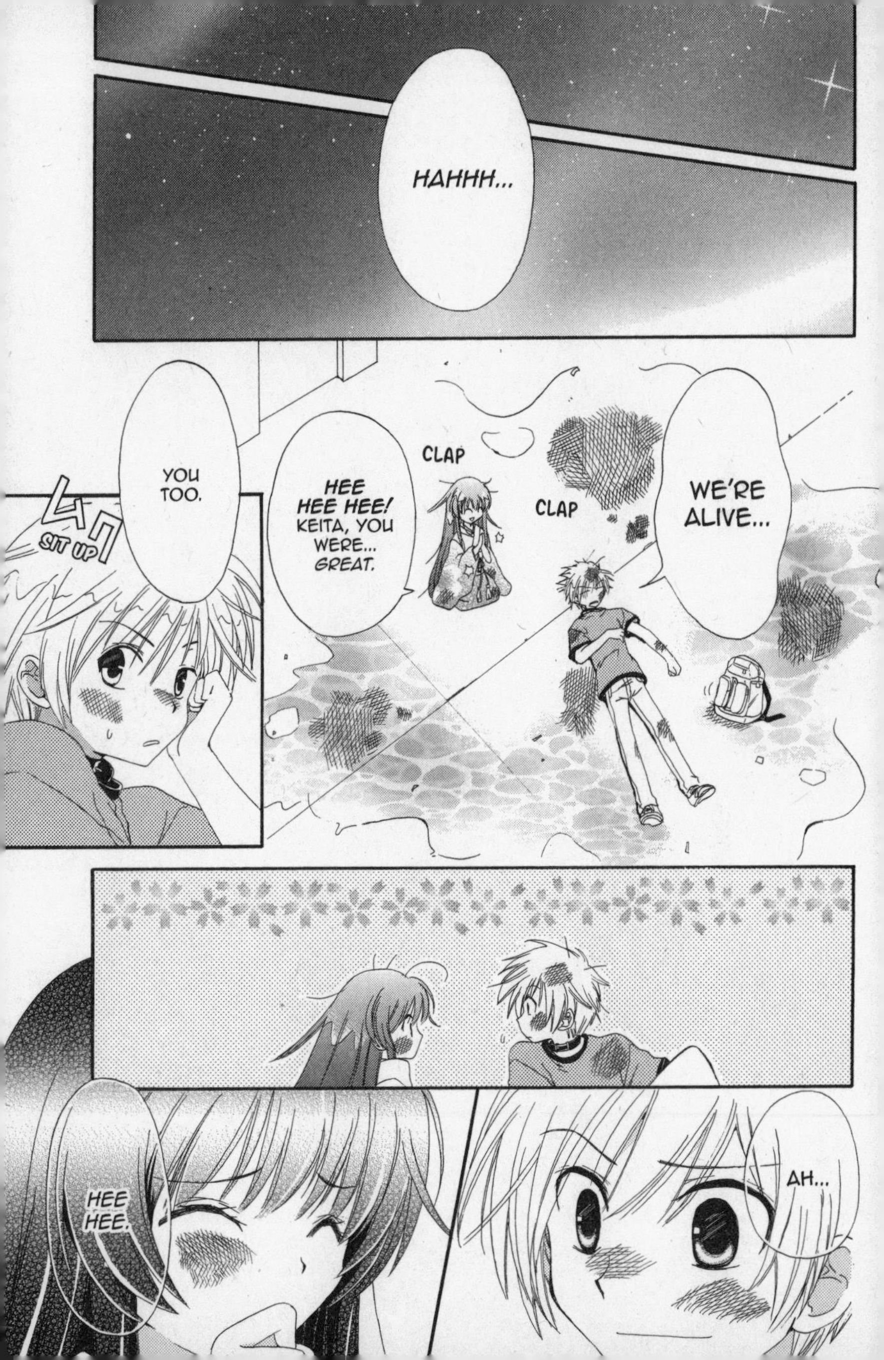
HAHHH...
WE'RE ALIVE...
CLAP
CLAP
HEE HEE HEE! KEITA, YOU WERE... GREAT.
SIT UP
YOU TOO.
AH...
HEE HEE.

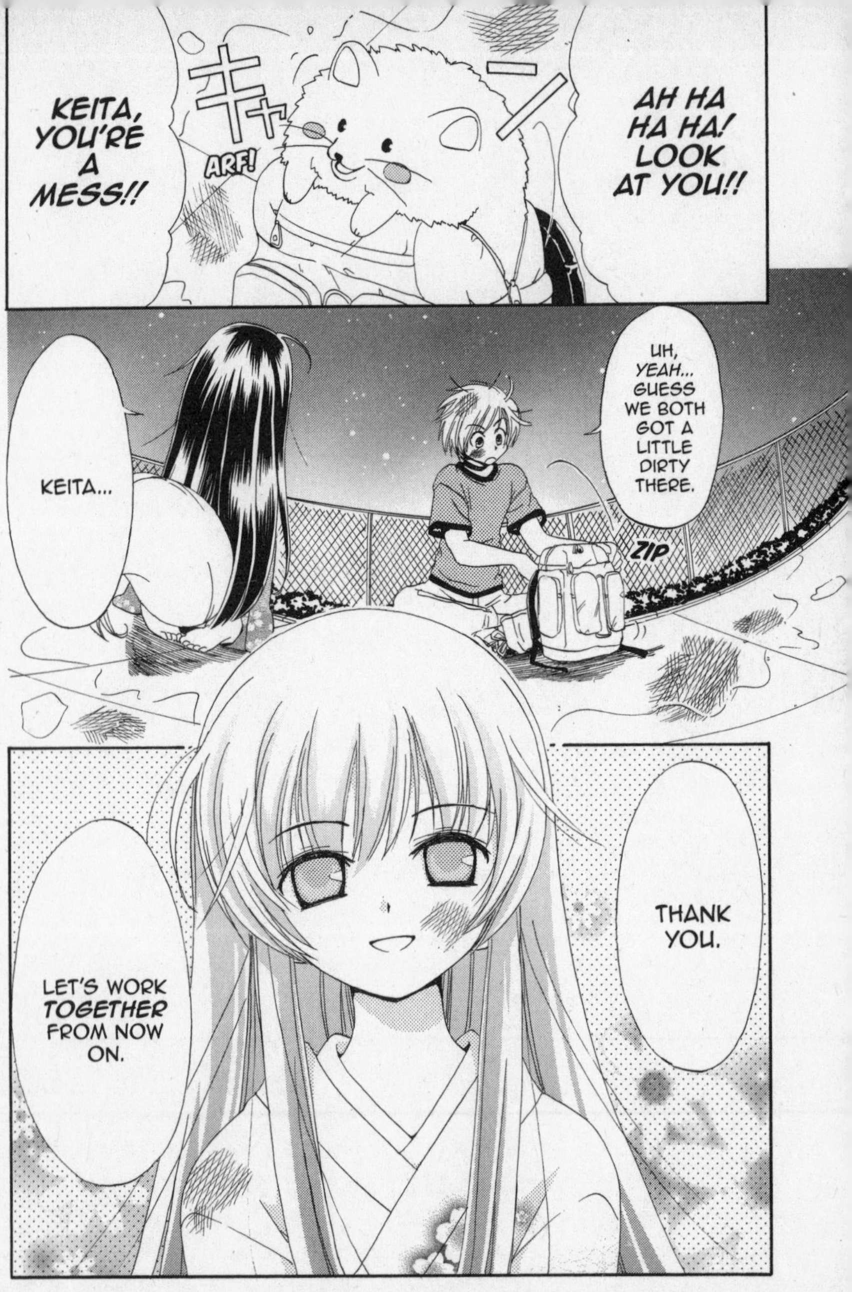
AH HA HA HA! LOOK AT YOU!!
ARF!
KEITA, YOU'RE A MESS!!
UH, YEAH... GUESS WE BOTH GOT A LITTLE DIRTY THERE.
ZIP
KEITA...
THANK YOU.
LET'S WORK *TOGETHER* FROM NOW ON.

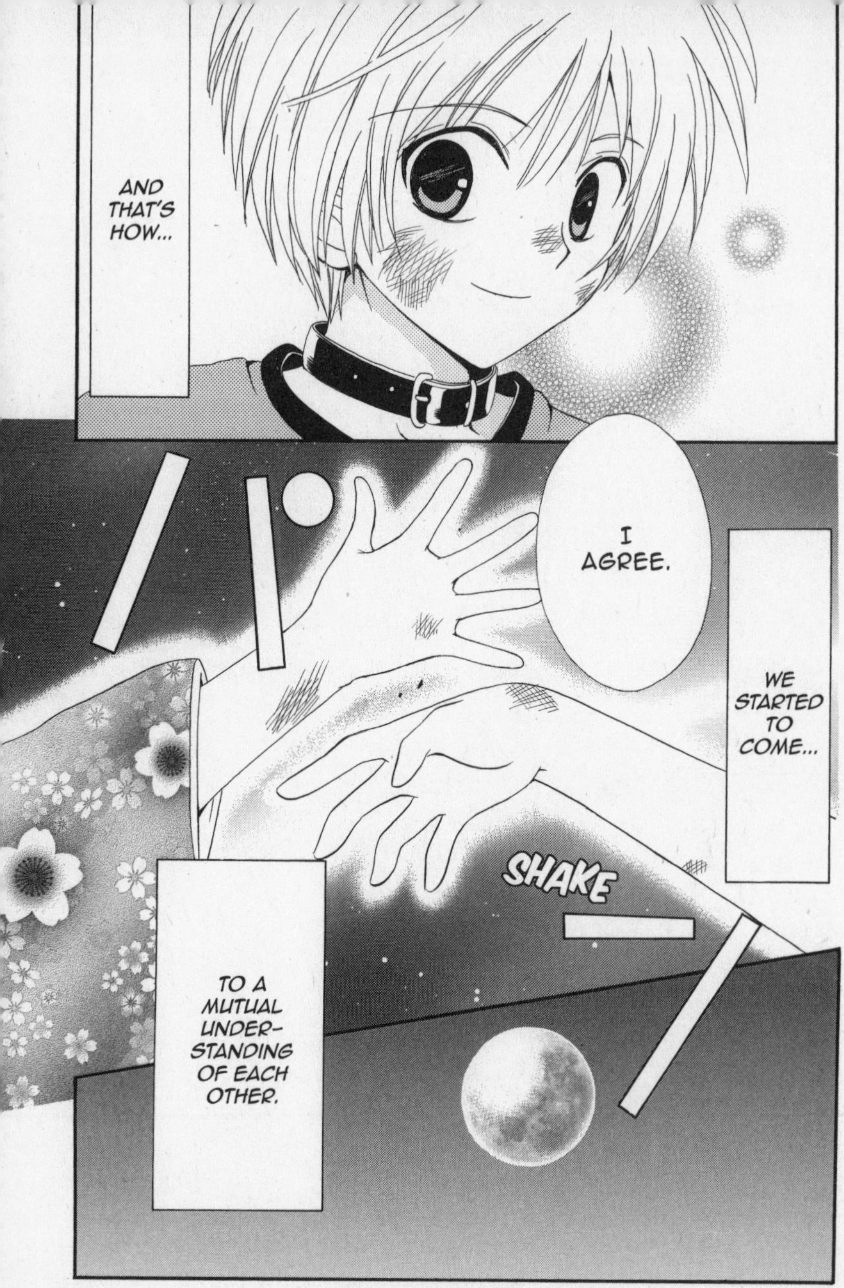
AND THAT'S HOW...
I AGREE.
WE STARTED TO COME...
SHAKE
TO A MUTUAL UNDER-STANDING OF EACH OTHER.

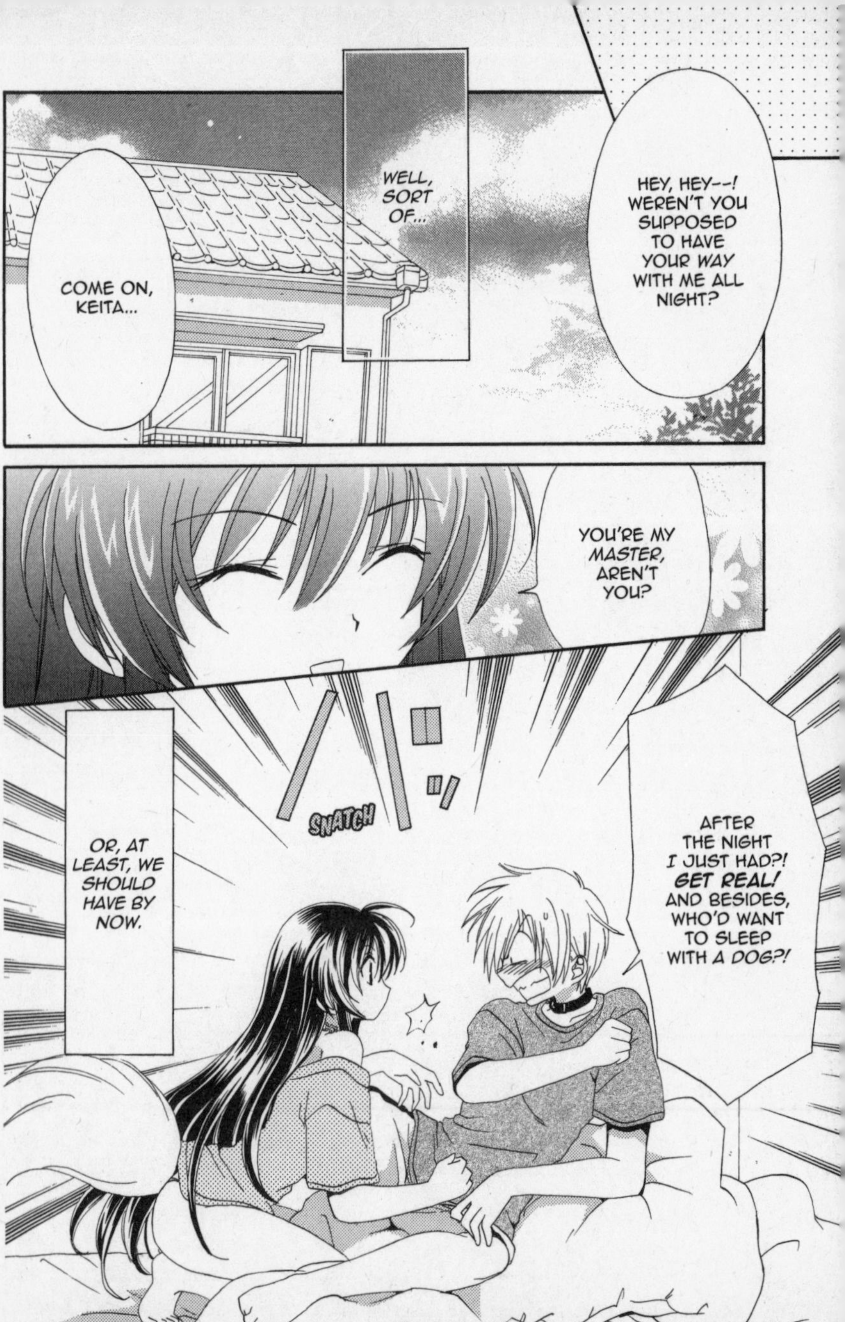
HEY, HEY--! WEREN'T YOU SUPPOSED TO HAVE YOUR WAY WITH ME ALL NIGHT?
WELL, SORT OF...
COME ON, KEITA...
YOU'RE MY *MASTER*, AREN'T YOU?
AFTER THE NIGHT I JUST HAD?! **GET REAL!** AND BESIDES, WHO'D WANT TO SLEEP WITH A *DOG*?!
SNATCH
OR, AT LEAST, WE SHOULD HAVE BY NOW.

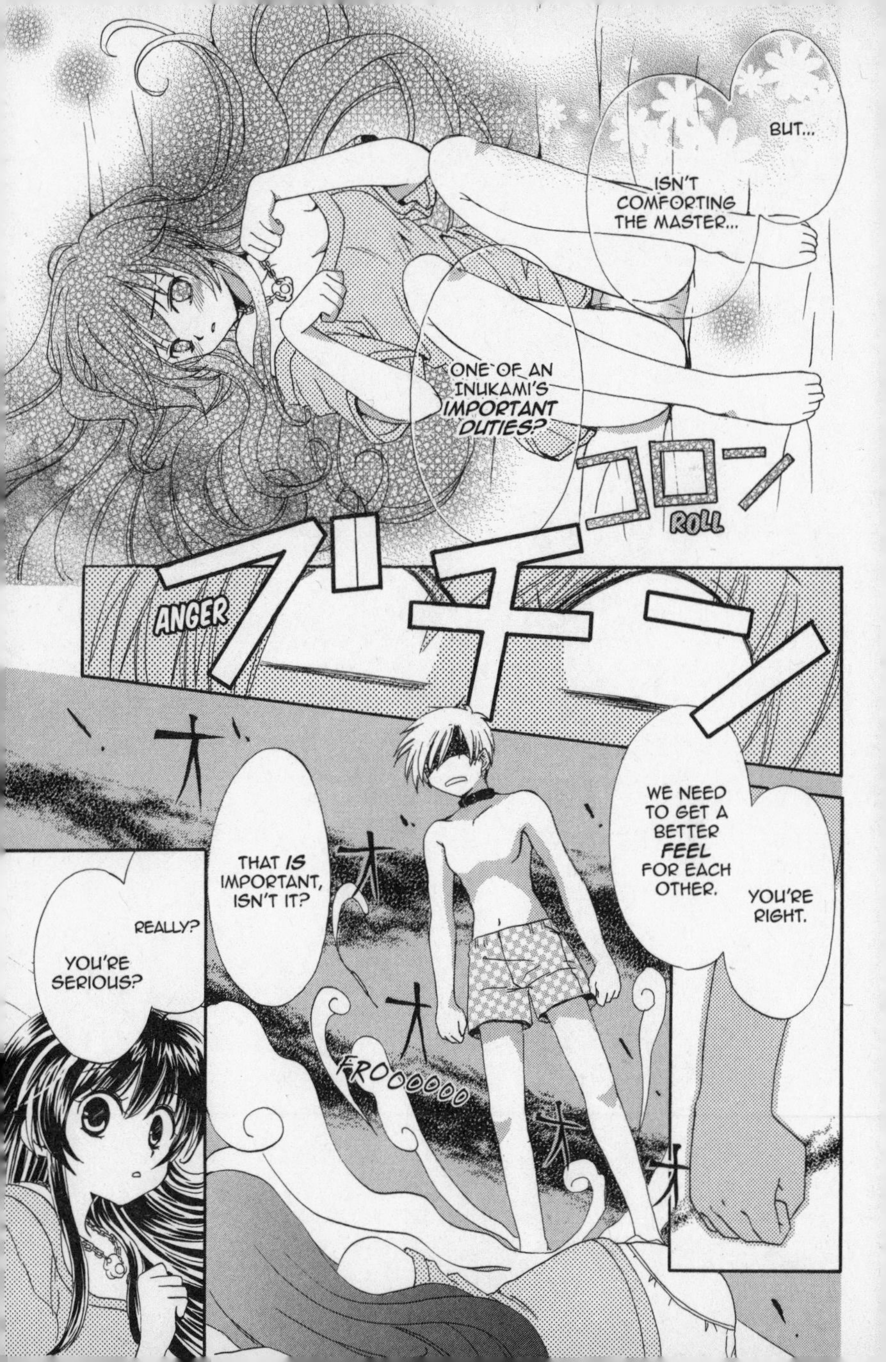
BUT...
ISN'T COMFORTING THE MASTER...
ONE OF AN INUKAMI'S IMPORTANT DUTIES?
コローン
ROLL
ブチーン
ANGER
WE NEED TO GET A BETTER FEEL FOR EACH OTHER.
YOU'RE RIGHT.
THAT IS IMPORTANT, ISN'T IT?
FROOOOOO
REALLY?
YOU'RE SERIOUS?

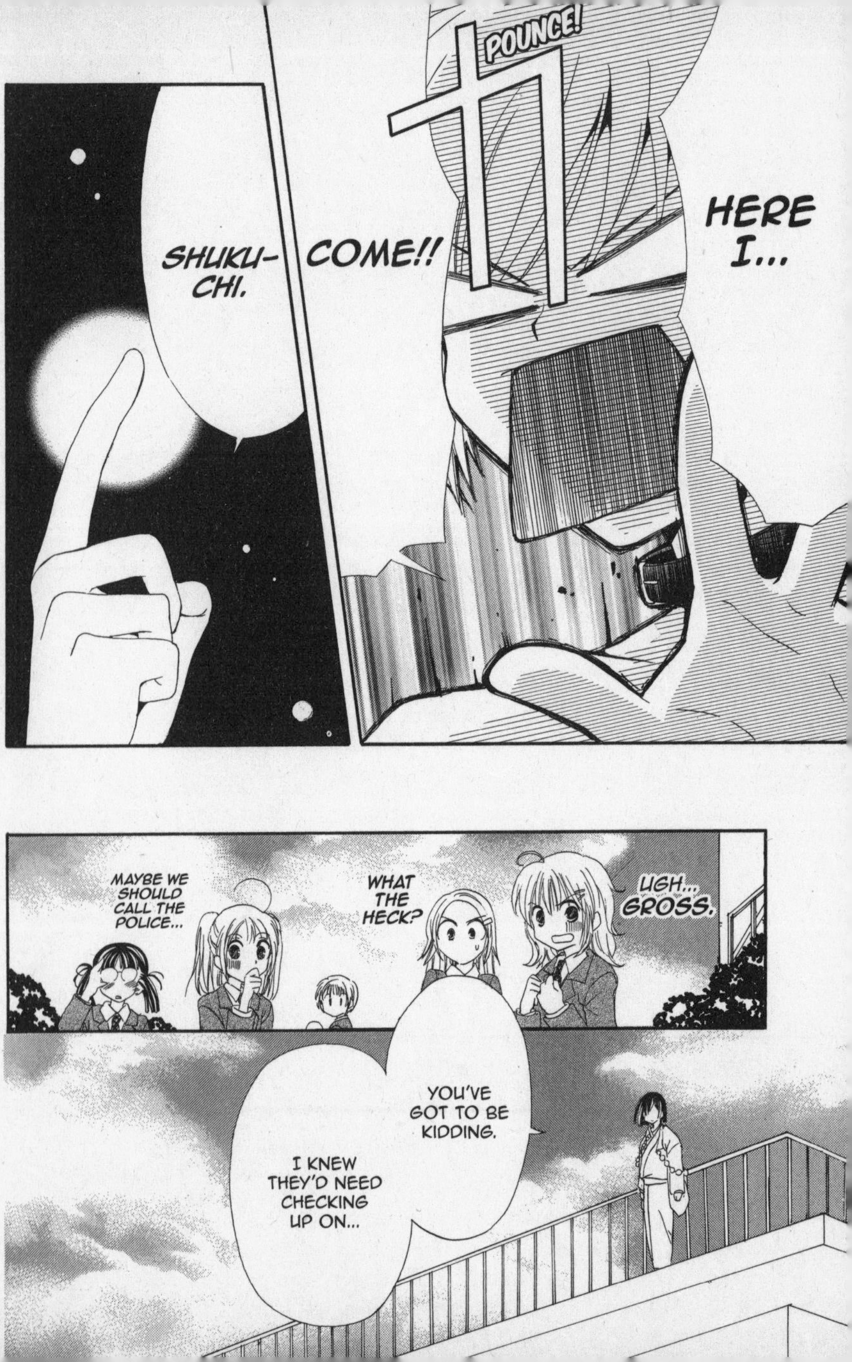
POUNCE!
HERE I...
COME!!
SHUKU-CHI.
UGH... GROSS.
WHAT THE HECK?
MAYBE WE SHOULD CALL THE POLICE...
YOU'VE GOT TO BE KIDDING.
I KNEW THEY'D NEED CHECKING UP ON...

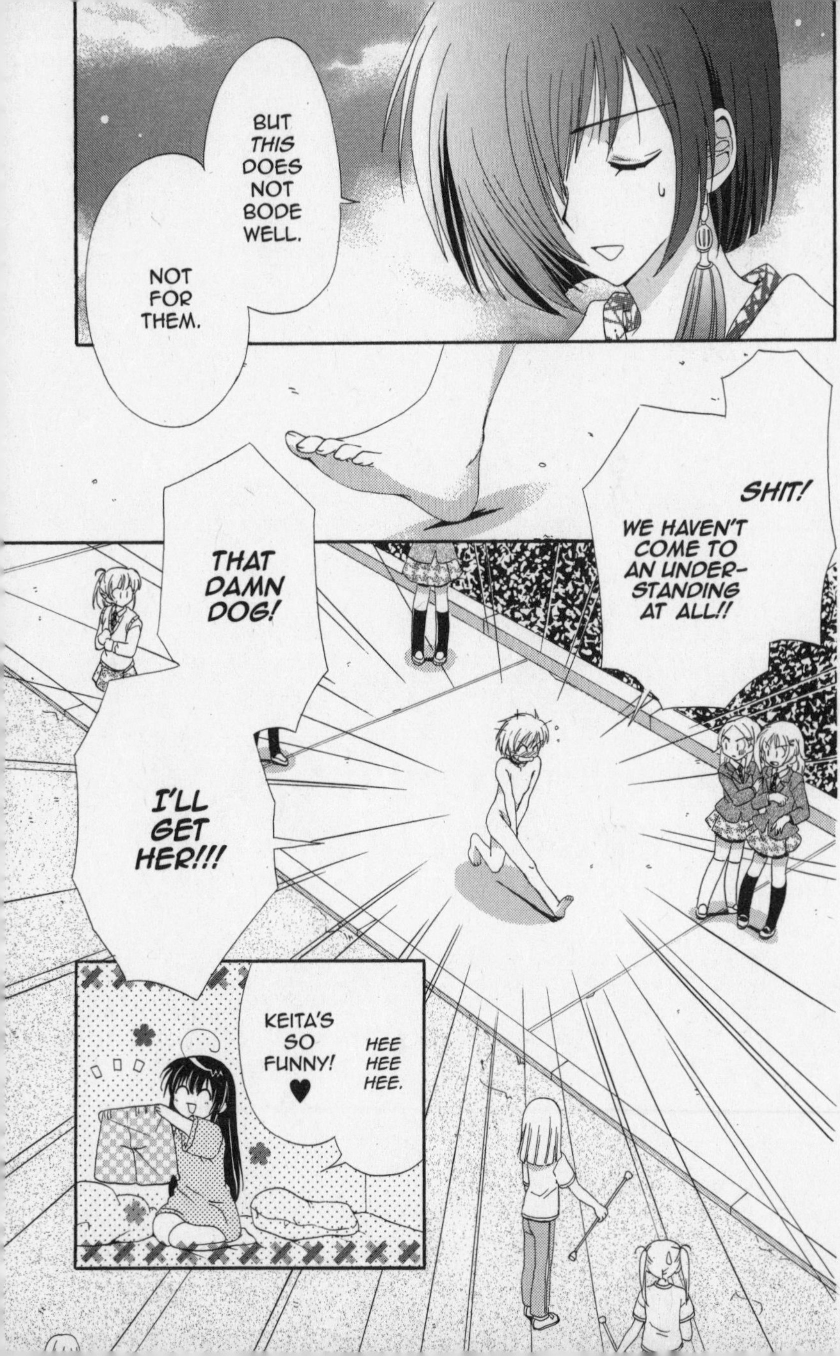
BUT THIS DOES NOT BODE WELL.
NOT FOR THEM.
SHIT!
WE HAVEN'T COME TO AN UNDER-STANDING AT ALL!!
THAT DAMN DOG!
I'LL GET HER!!!
KEITA'S SO FUNNY! ♥
HEE HEE HEE.

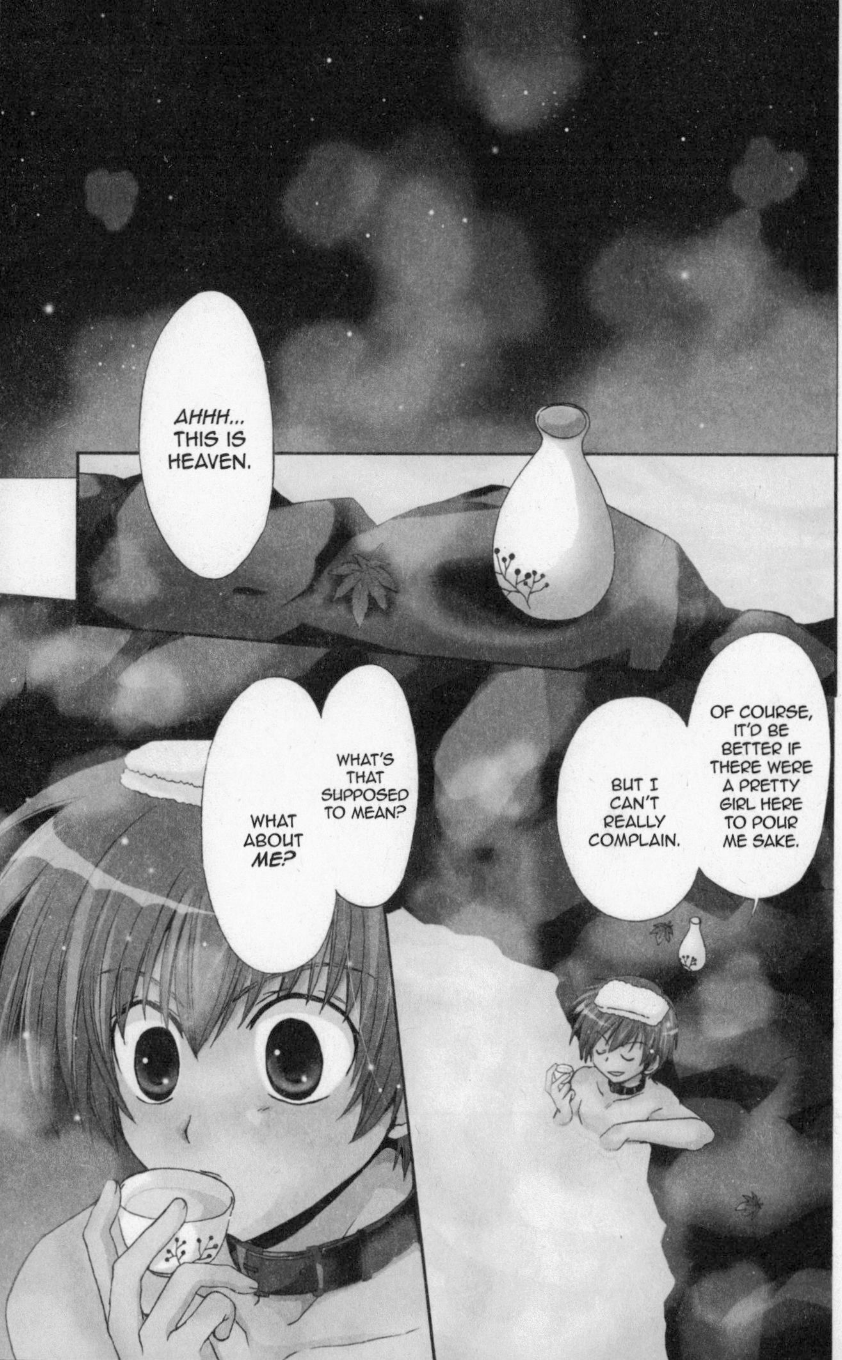
AHHH... THIS IS HEAVEN.
OF COURSE, IT'D BE BETTER IF THERE WERE A PRETTY GIRL HERE TO POUR ME SAKE.
BUT I CAN'T REALLY COMPLAIN.
WHAT'S THAT SUPPOSED TO MEAN?
WHAT ABOUT *ME?*

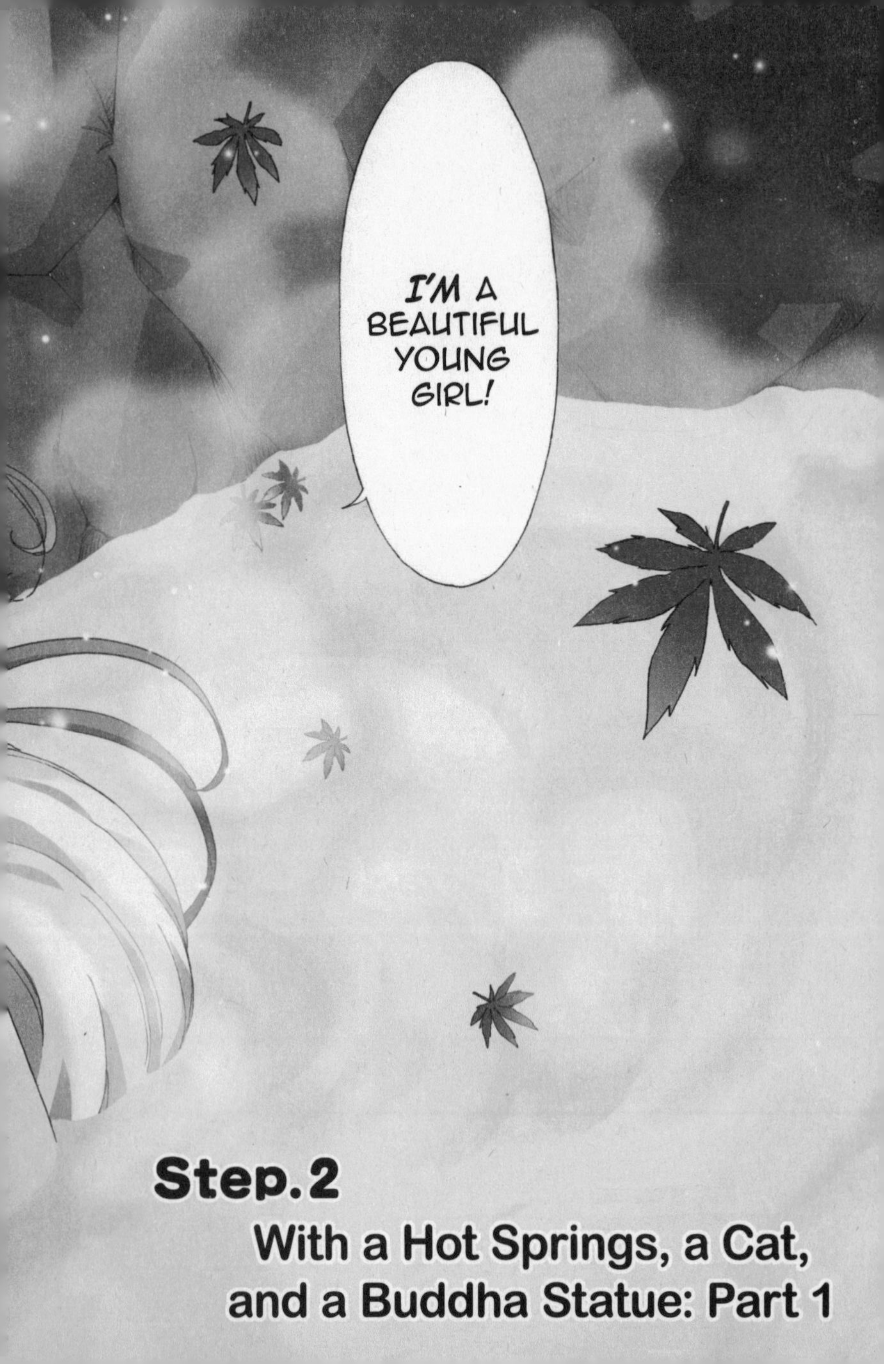
I'M A BEAUTIFUL YOUNG GIRL!

Step. 2
With a Hot Springs, a Cat, and a Buddha Statue: Part 1

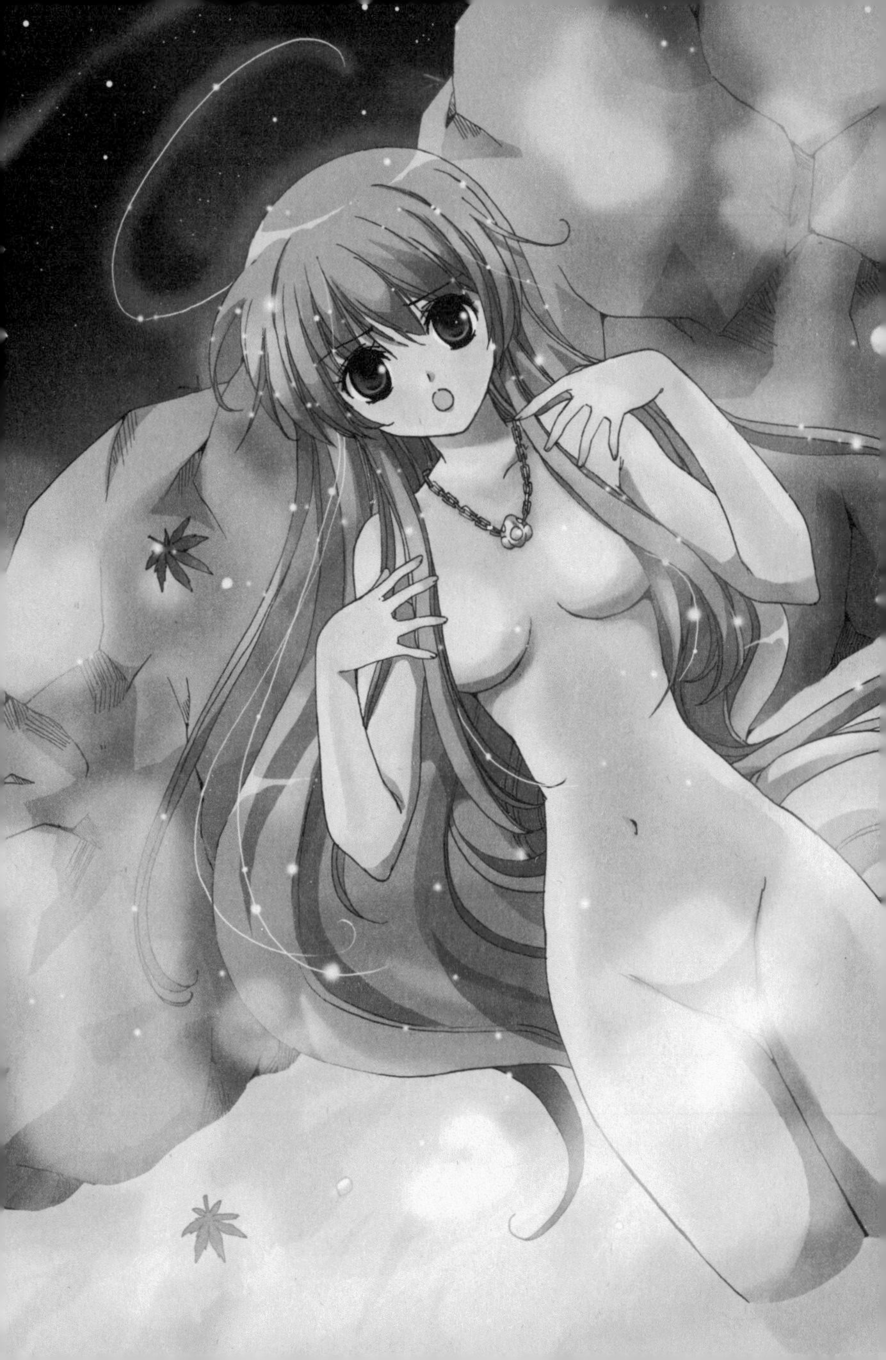

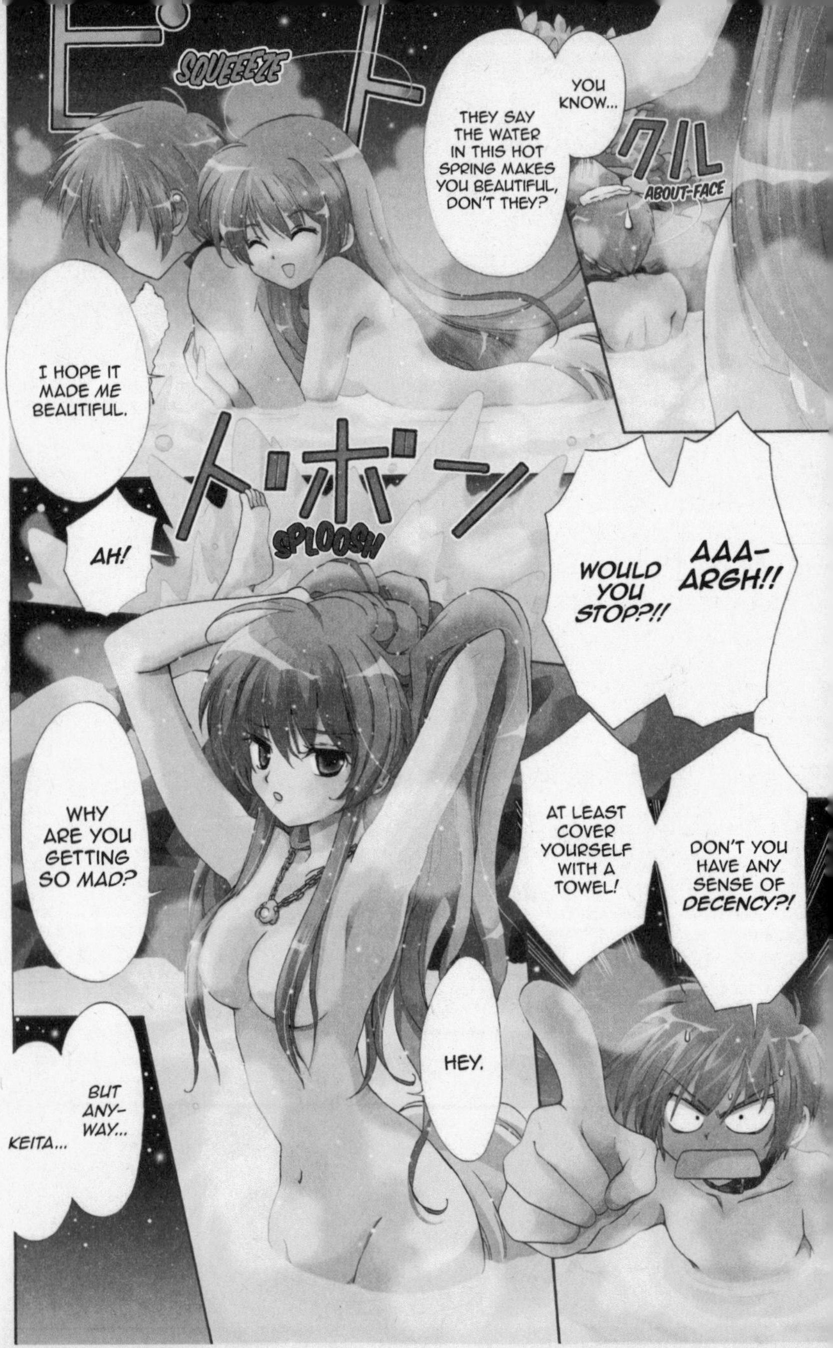

クル
ABOUT-FACE
ピト
SQUEEEZE
YOU KNOW...
THEY SAY THE WATER IN THIS HOT SPRING MAKES YOU BEAUTIFUL, DON'T THEY?
I HOPE IT MADE ME BEAUTIFUL.
AAA-ARGH!!
WOULD YOU STOP?!!
トボーン
SPLOOSH
AH!
DON'T YOU HAVE ANY SENSE OF DECENCY?!
AT LEAST COVER YOURSELF WITH A TOWEL!
WHY ARE YOU GETTING SO MAD?
HEY.
BUT ANY-WAY...
KEITA...

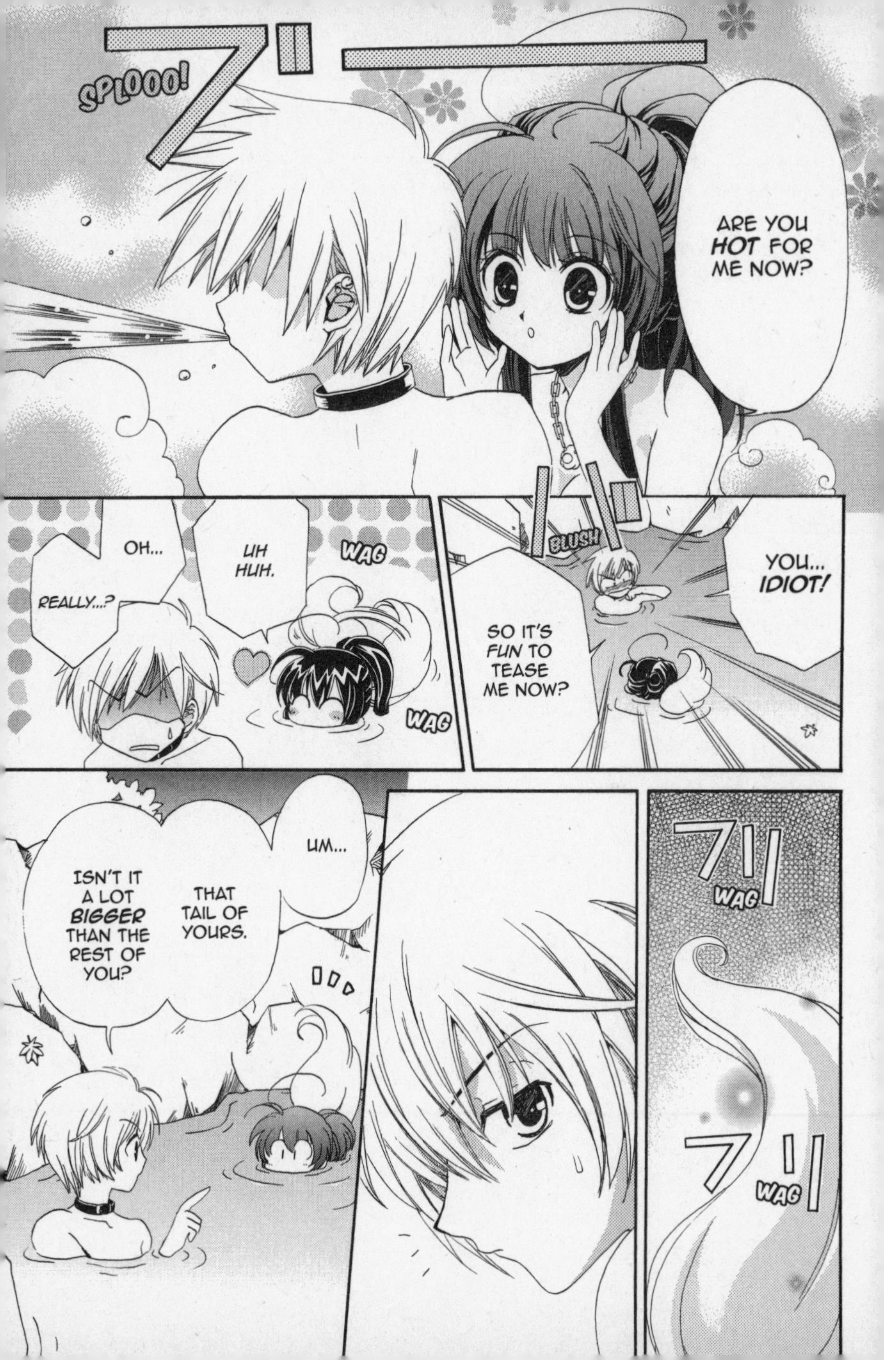
ARE YOU HOT FOR ME NOW?
SPLOOO!
YOU... IDIOT!
BLUSH
SO IT'S FUN TO TEASE ME NOW?
UH HUH.
OH...
REALLY...?
WAG
WAG
WAG
WAG
UM...
THAT TAIL OF YOURS.
ISN'T IT A LOT BIGGER THAN THE REST OF YOU?

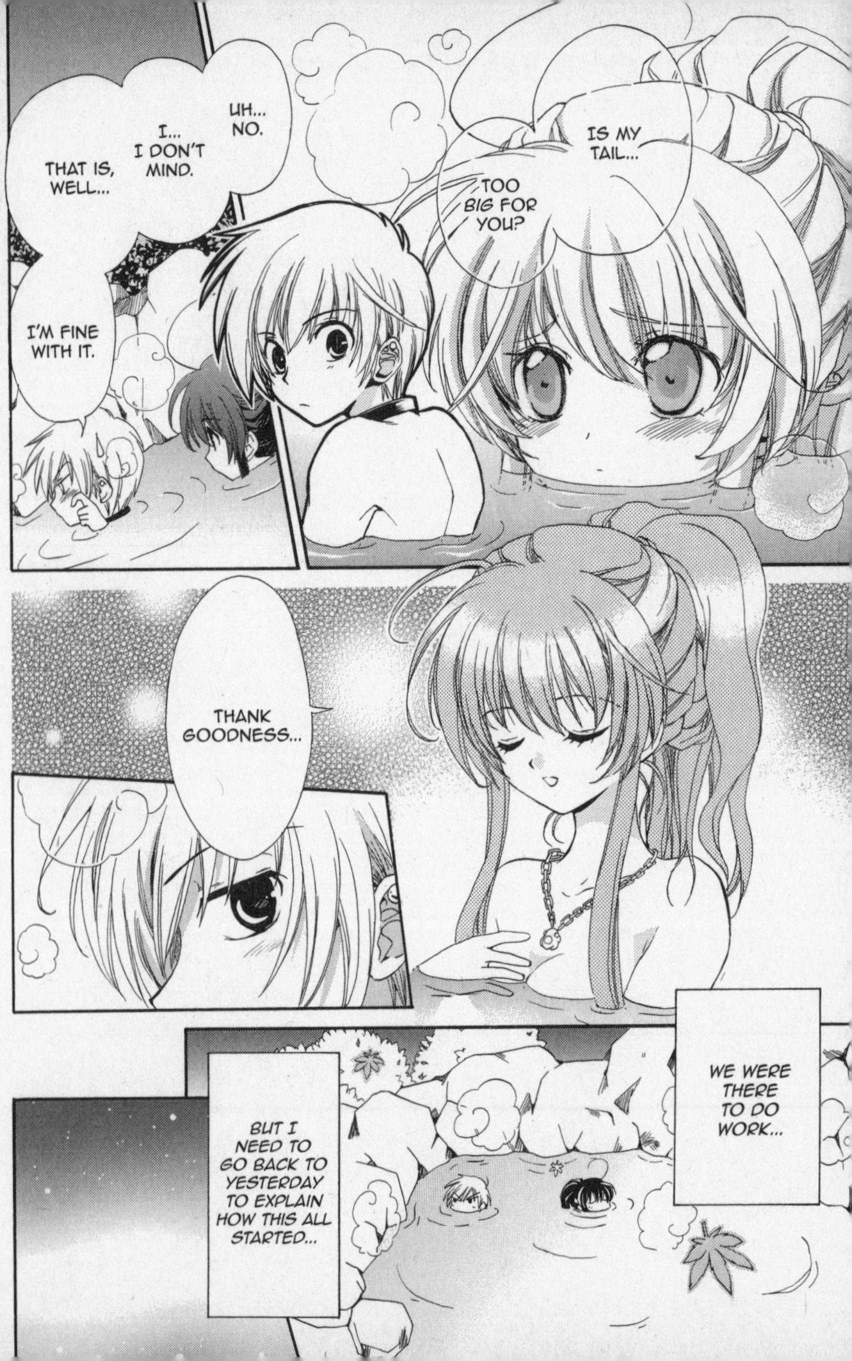
IS MY TAIL...
TOO BIG FOR YOU?
UH... NO.
I... I DON'T MIND.
THAT IS, WELL...
I'M FINE WITH IT.
THANK GOODNESS...
WE WERE THERE TO DO WORK...
BUT I NEED TO GO BACK TO YESTERDAY TO EXPLAIN HOW THIS ALL STARTED...

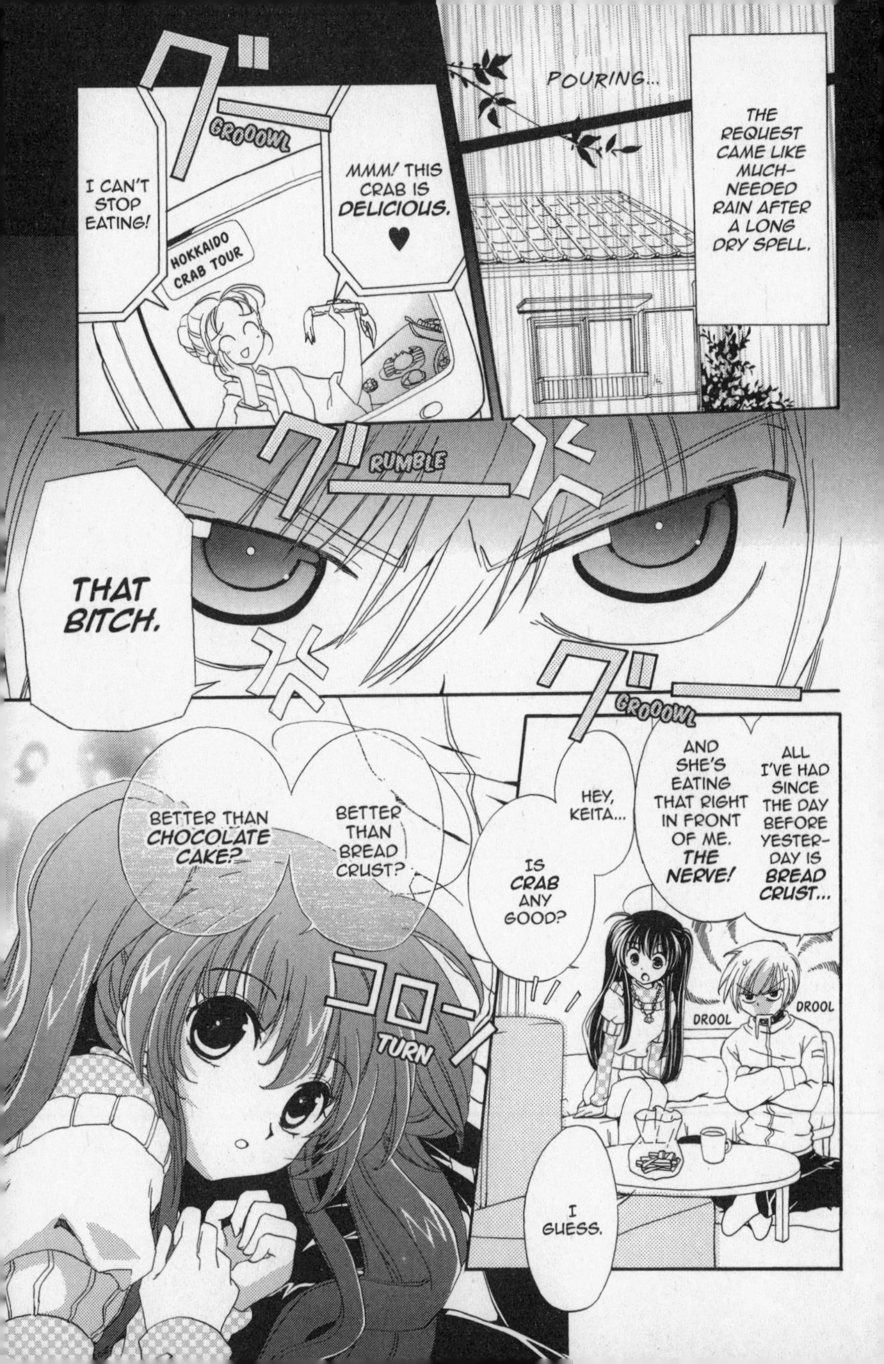

POURING...
THE REQUEST CAME LIKE MUCH-NEEDED RAIN AFTER A LONG DRY SPELL.
MMM! THIS CRAB IS DELICIOUS. ♥
GROOOWL
I CAN'T STOP EATING!
HOKKAIDO CRAB TOUR
RUMBLE
THAT BITCH.
GROOOWL
ALL I'VE HAD SINCE THE DAY BEFORE YESTER-DAY IS BREAD CRUST...
AND SHE'S EATING THAT RIGHT IN FRONT OF ME. THE NERVE!
HEY, KEITA...
IS CRAB ANY GOOD?
DROOL
DROOL
I GUESS.
BETTER THAN BREAD CRUST?
BETTER THAN CHOCOLATE CAKE?
TURN

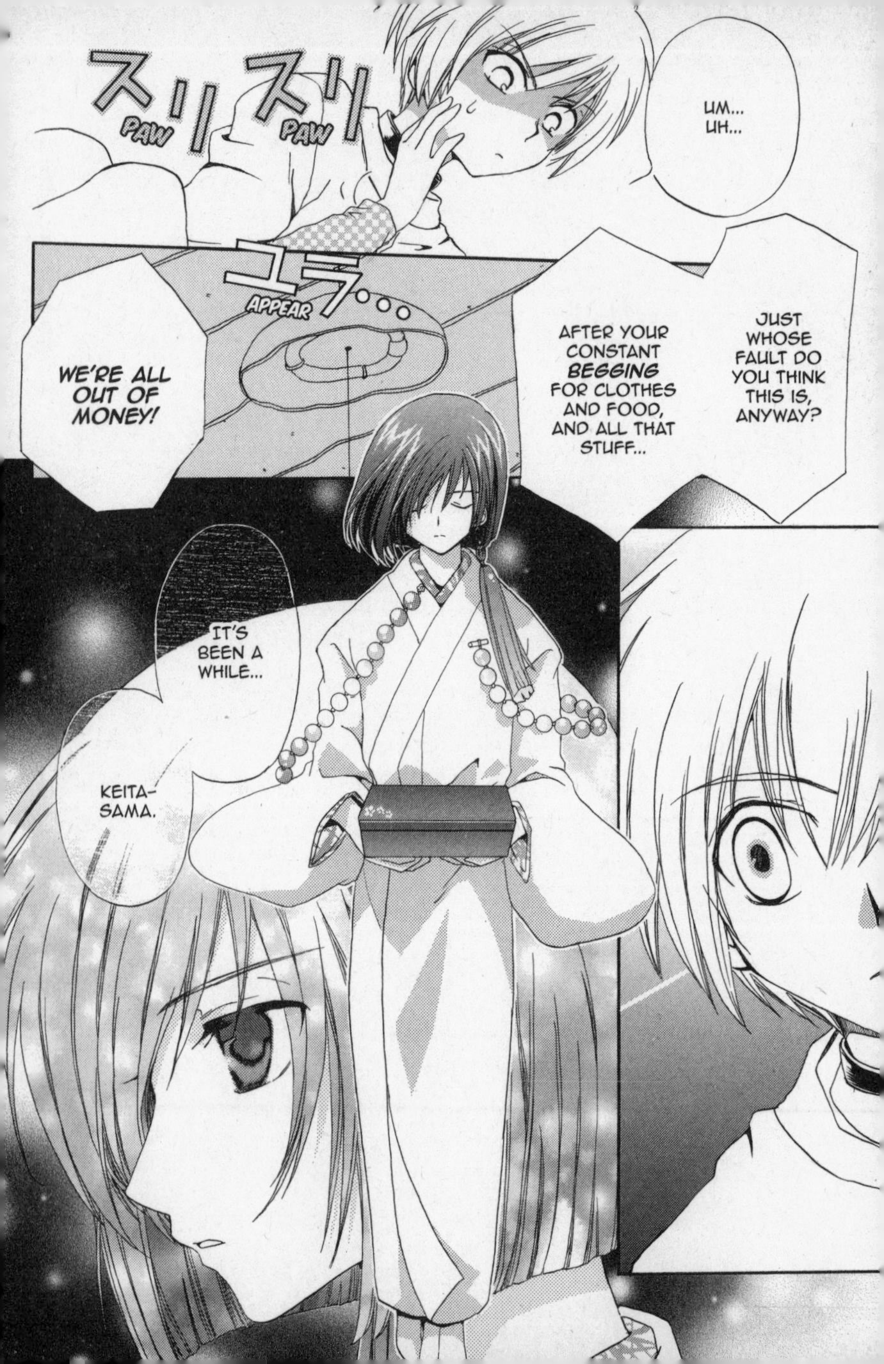
UM... UH...
スリスリ
PAW PAW
JUST WHOSE FAULT DO YOU THINK THIS IS, ANYWAY?
AFTER YOUR CONSTANT *BEGGING* FOR CLOTHES AND FOOD, AND ALL THAT STUFF...
ユラ
APPEAR
WE'RE ALL OUT OF MONEY!
IT'S BEEN A WHILE...
KEITA-SAMA.

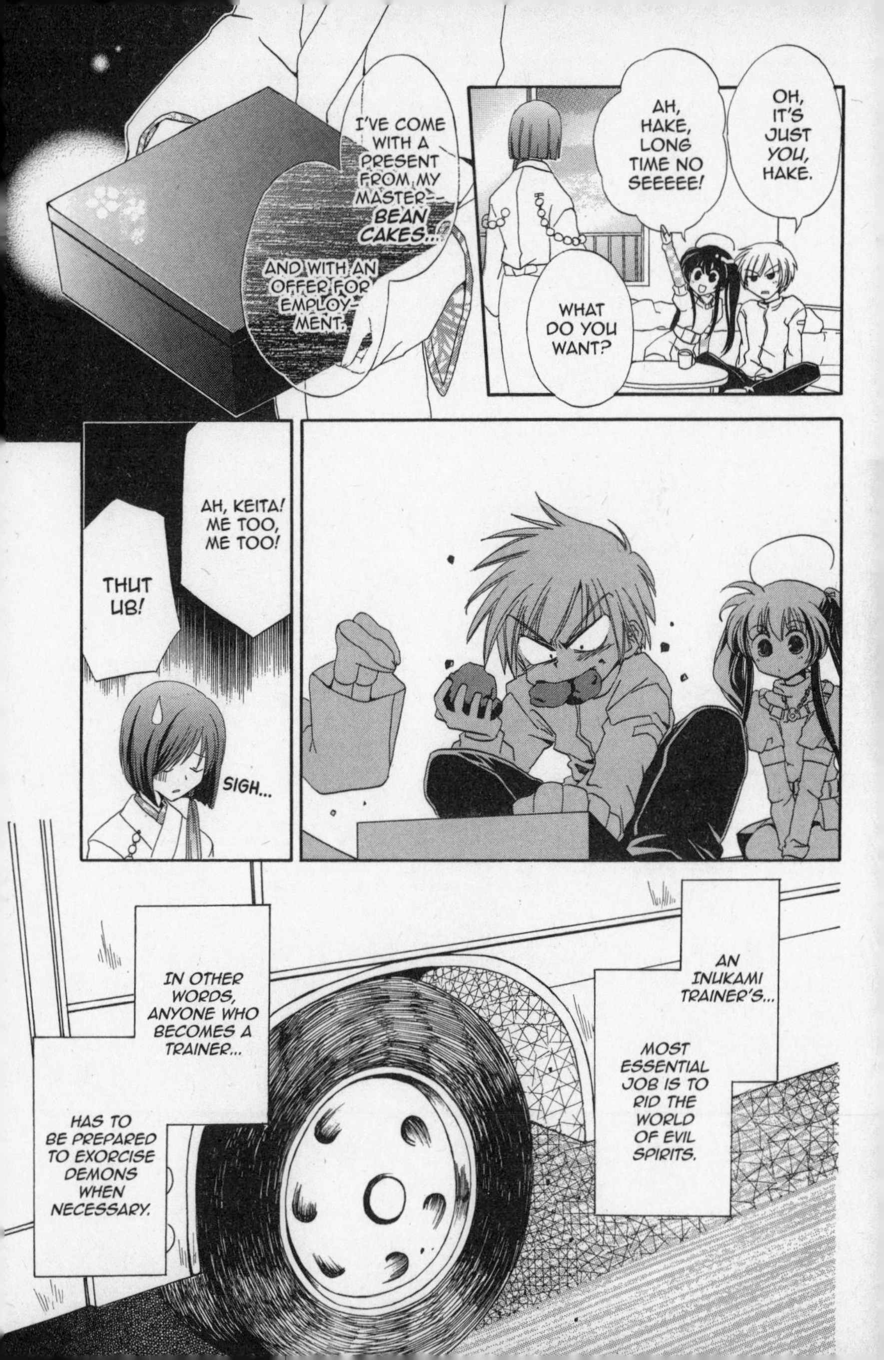
OH, IT'S JUST YOU, HAKE.
AH, HAKE, LONG TIME NO SEEEEE!
WHAT DO YOU WANT?
I'VE COME WITH A PRESENT FROM MY MASTER--BEAN CAKES...
AND WITH AN OFFER FOR EMPLOY-MENT.
AH, KEITA! ME TOO, ME TOO!
THUT UB!
SIGH...
AN INUKAMI TRAINER'S...
MOST ESSENTIAL JOB IS TO RID THE WORLD OF EVIL SPIRITS.
IN OTHER WORDS, ANYONE WHO BECOMES A TRAINER...
HAS TO BE PREPARED TO EXORCISE DEMONS WHEN NECESSARY.

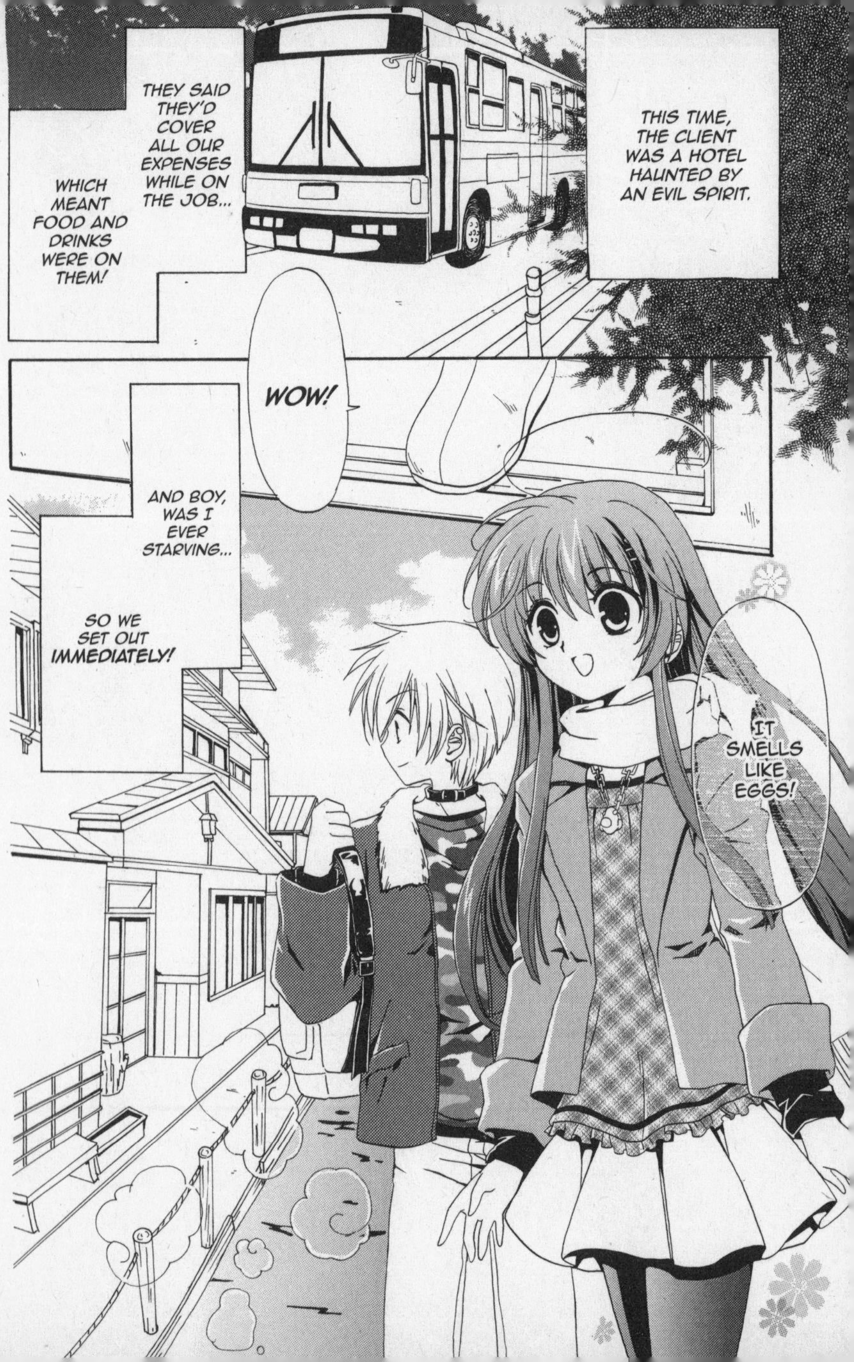
THIS TIME, THE CLIENT WAS A HOTEL HAUNTED BY AN EVIL SPIRIT.
THEY SAID THEY'D COVER ALL OUR EXPENSES WHILE ON THE JOB...
WHICH MEANT FOOD AND DRINKS WERE ON THEM!
WOW!
AND BOY, WAS I EVER STARVING...
SO WE SET OUT IMMEDIATELY!
IT SMELLS LIKE EGGS!

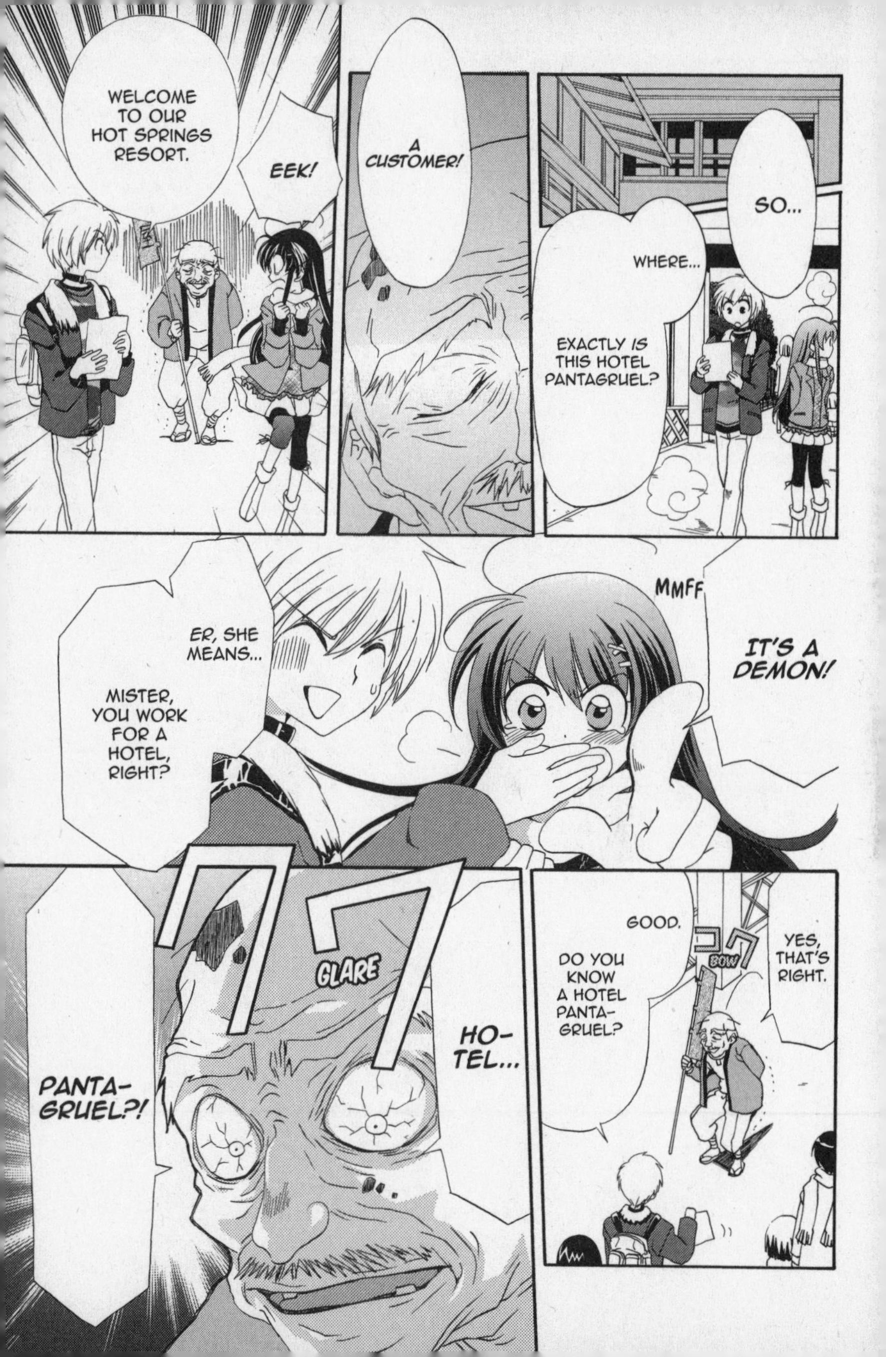
SO...
WHERE...
EXACTLY IS THIS HOTEL PANTAGRUEL?
A CUSTOMER!
WELCOME TO OUR HOT SPRINGS RESORT.
EEK!
MMFF
IT'S A DEMON!
ER, SHE MEANS...
MISTER, YOU WORK FOR A HOTEL, RIGHT?
YES, THAT'S RIGHT.
BOW
GOOD.
DO YOU KNOW A HOTEL PANTA-GRUEL?
GLARE
HO-TEL...
PANTA-GRUEL?!

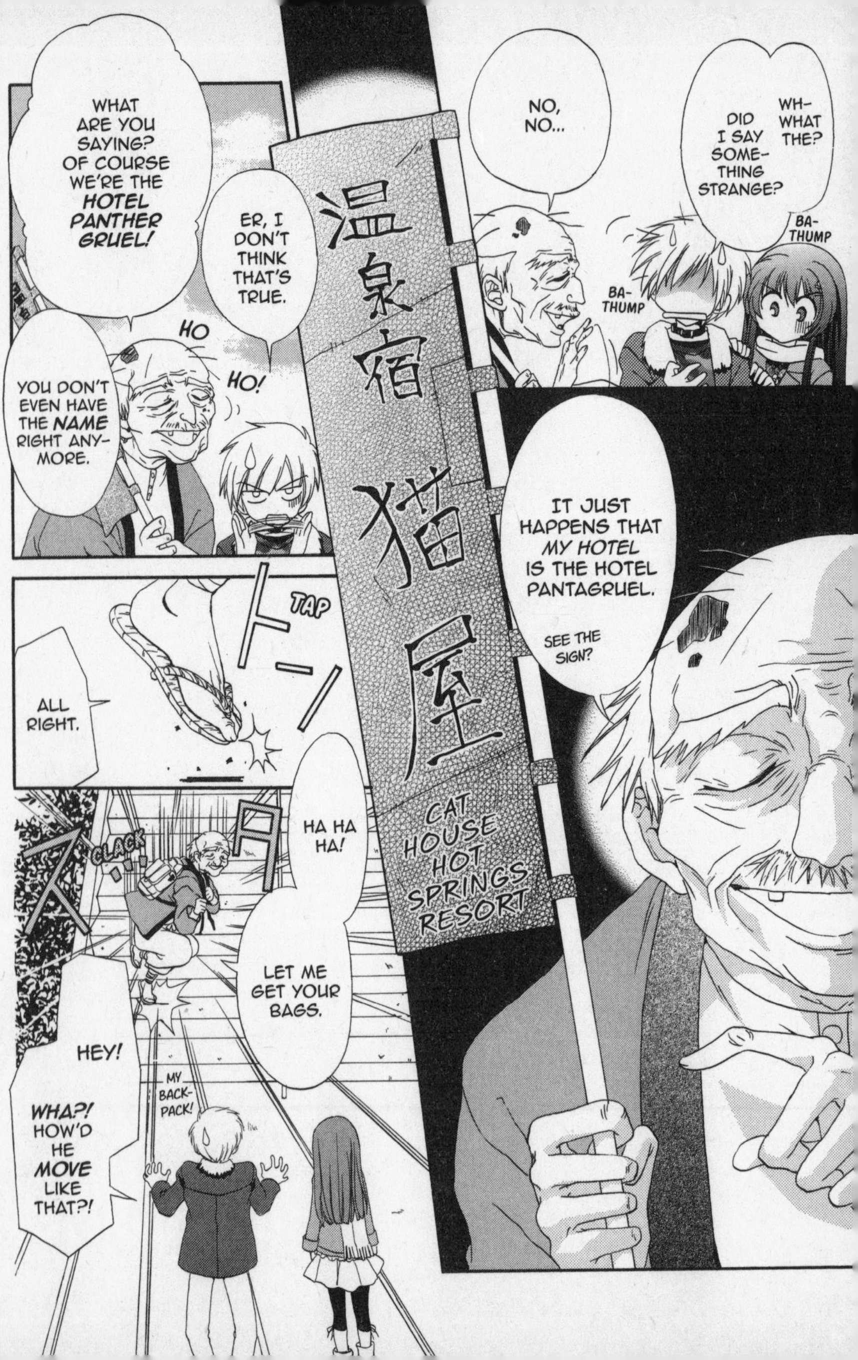
ER, I DON'T THINK THAT'S TRUE.
WHAT ARE YOU SAYING? OF COURSE WE'RE THE ***HOTEL PANTHER GRUEL!***
HO HO!
YOU DON'T EVEN HAVE THE ***NAME*** RIGHT ANY-MORE.
WH-WHAT THE?
DID I SAY SOME-THING STRANGE?
BA-THUMP
BA-THUMP
NO, NO...
IT JUST HAPPENS THAT *MY HOTEL* IS THE HOTEL PANTAGRUEL.
SEE THE SIGN?
温泉宿猫屋
CAT HOUSE HOT SPRINGS RESORT
TAP
ALL RIGHT.
HA HA HA!
LET ME GET YOUR BAGS.
CLACK
HEY!
MY BACK-PACK!
WHA?! HOW'D HE ***MOVE*** LIKE THAT?!

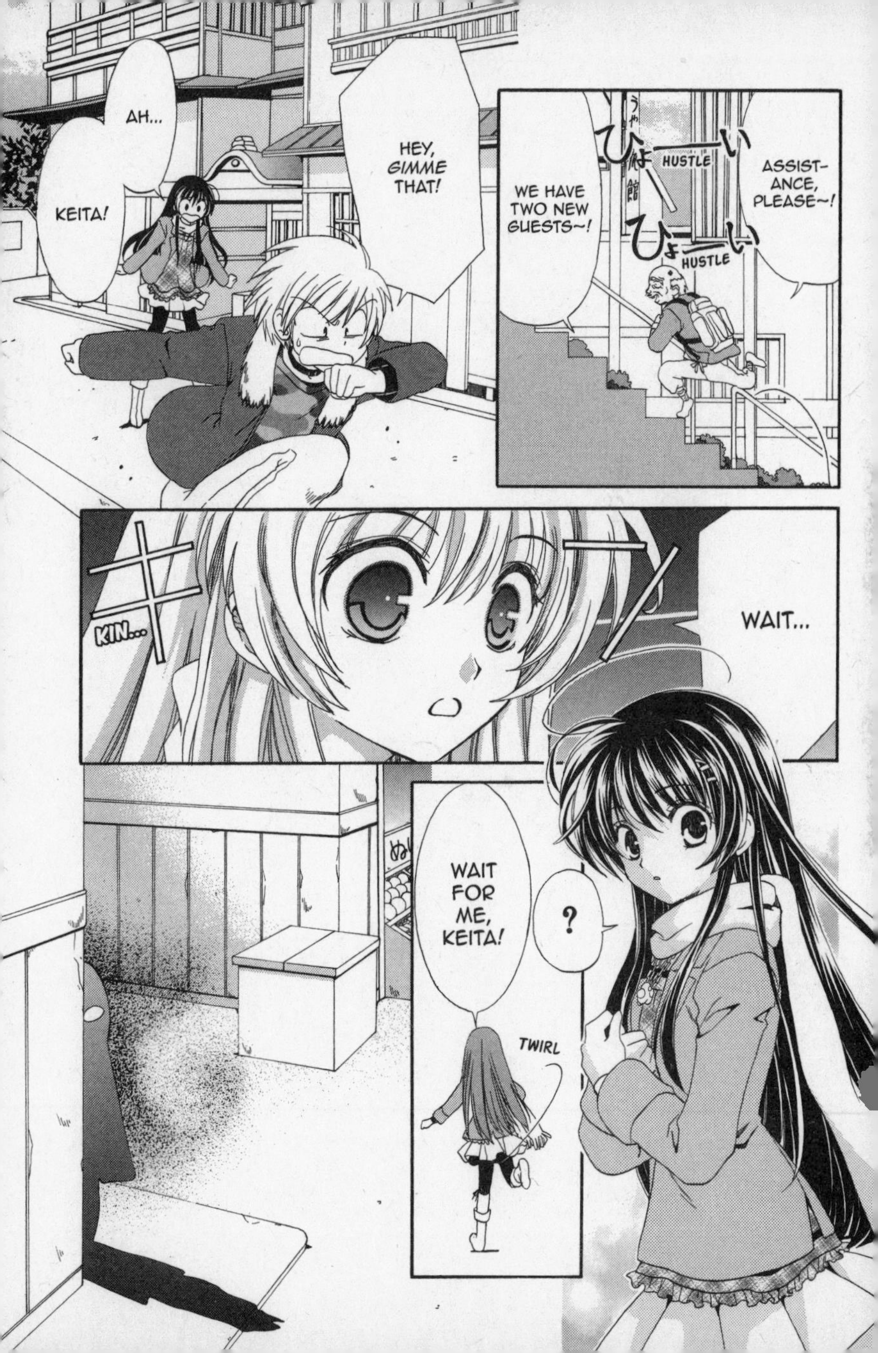
ASSIST-ANCE, PLEASE~!
ひょーい
HUSTLE
ひょーい
HUSTLE
WE HAVE TWO NEW GUESTS~!
HEY, GIMME THAT!
AH...
KEITA!
WAIT...
KIN...
?
WAIT FOR ME, KEITA!
TWIRL

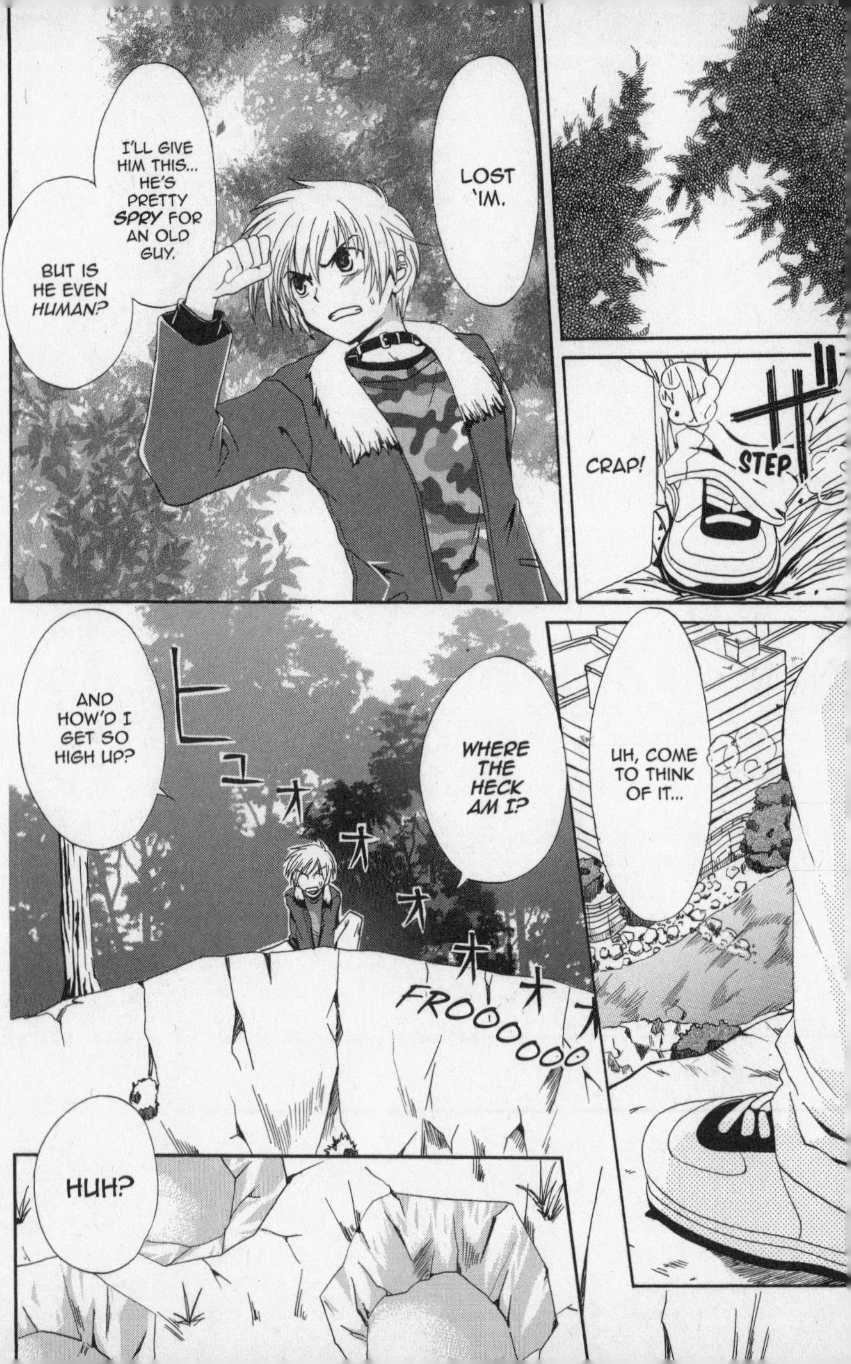
CRAP!
STEP
LOST 'IM.
I'LL GIVE HIM THIS... HE'S PRETTY SPRY FOR AN OLD GUY.
BUT IS HE EVEN HUMAN?
UH, COME TO THINK OF IT...
WHERE THE HECK AM I?
AND HOW'D I GET SO HIGH UP?
ヒュオオオオオオ
FROOOOOOO
HUH?

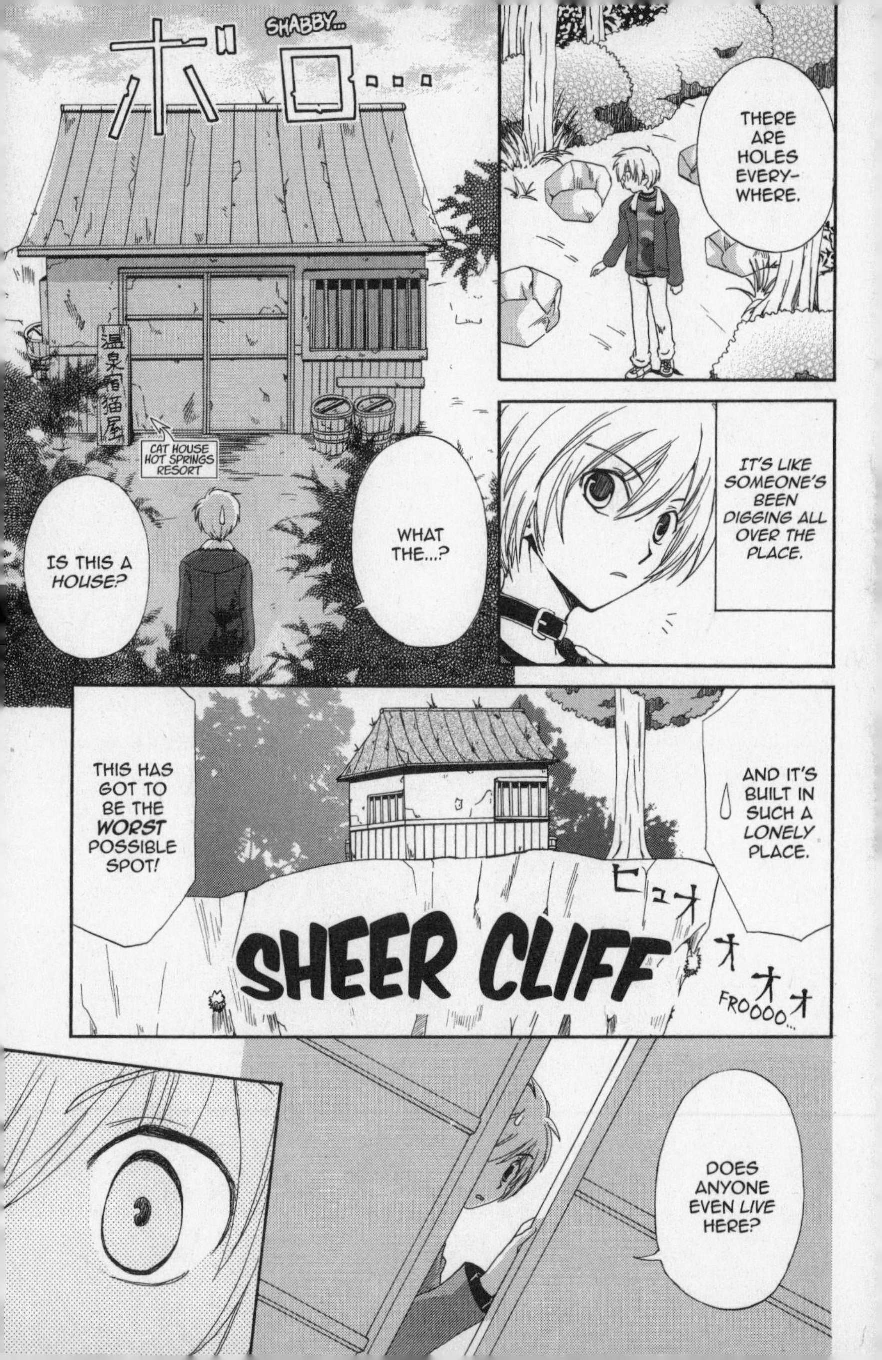
THERE ARE HOLES EVERY-WHERE.
IT'S LIKE SOMEONE'S BEEN DIGGING ALL OVER THE PLACE.
ボロ...
SHABBY...
温泉宿猫屋
CAT HOUSE HOT SPRINGS RESORT
WHAT THE...?
IS THIS A HOUSE?
AND IT'S BUILT IN SUCH A *LONELY* PLACE.
THIS HAS GOT TO BE THE **WORST** POSSIBLE SPOT!
ヒュオォォオ
FROOOO...
SHEER CLIFF
DOES ANYONE EVEN *LIVE* HERE?

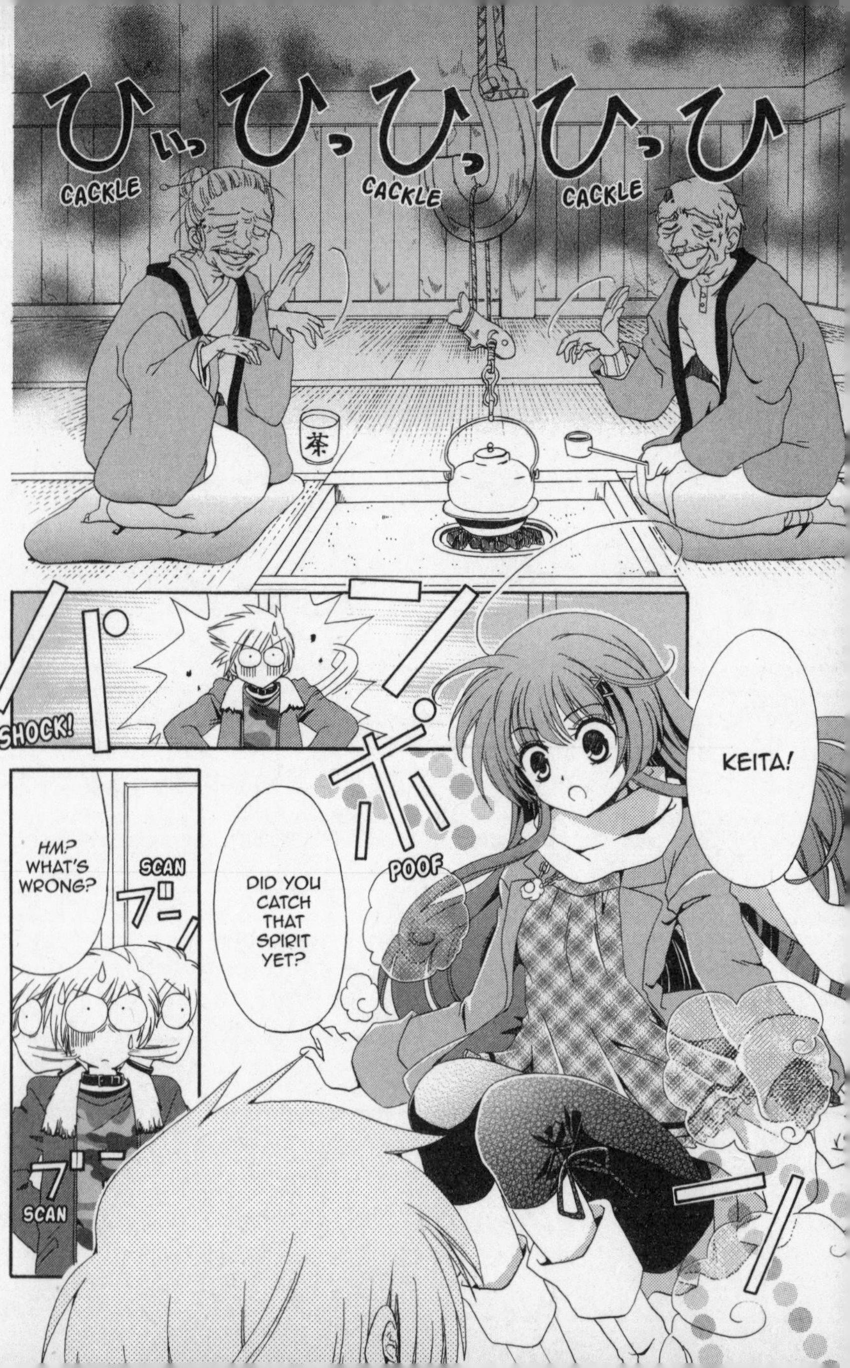
ひぃっひっひっひっひ
CACKLE
CACKLE
CACKLE
KEITA!
DID YOU CATCH THAT SPIRIT YET?
POOF
SHOCK!
HM? WHAT'S WRONG?
SCAN
SCAN

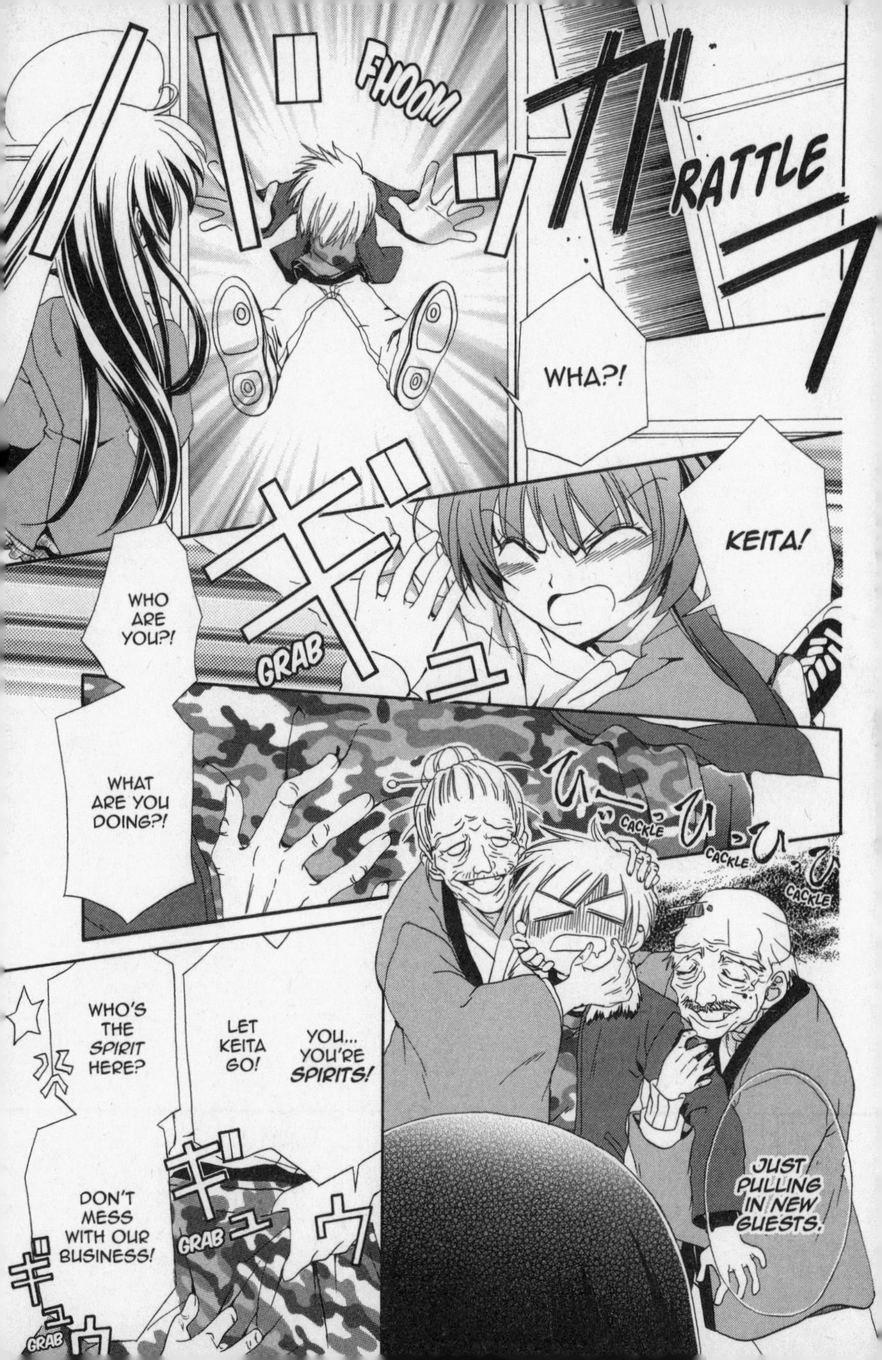
RATTLE
WHA?!
FHOOM
KEITA!
WHO ARE YOU?!
GRAB
CACKLE
CACKLE
CACKLE
WHAT ARE YOU DOING?!
JUST PULLING IN NEW GUESTS.
YOU... YOU'RE SPIRITS!
LET KEITA GO!
WHO'S THE SPIRIT HERE?
DON'T MESS WITH OUR BUSINESS!
GRAB
GRAB

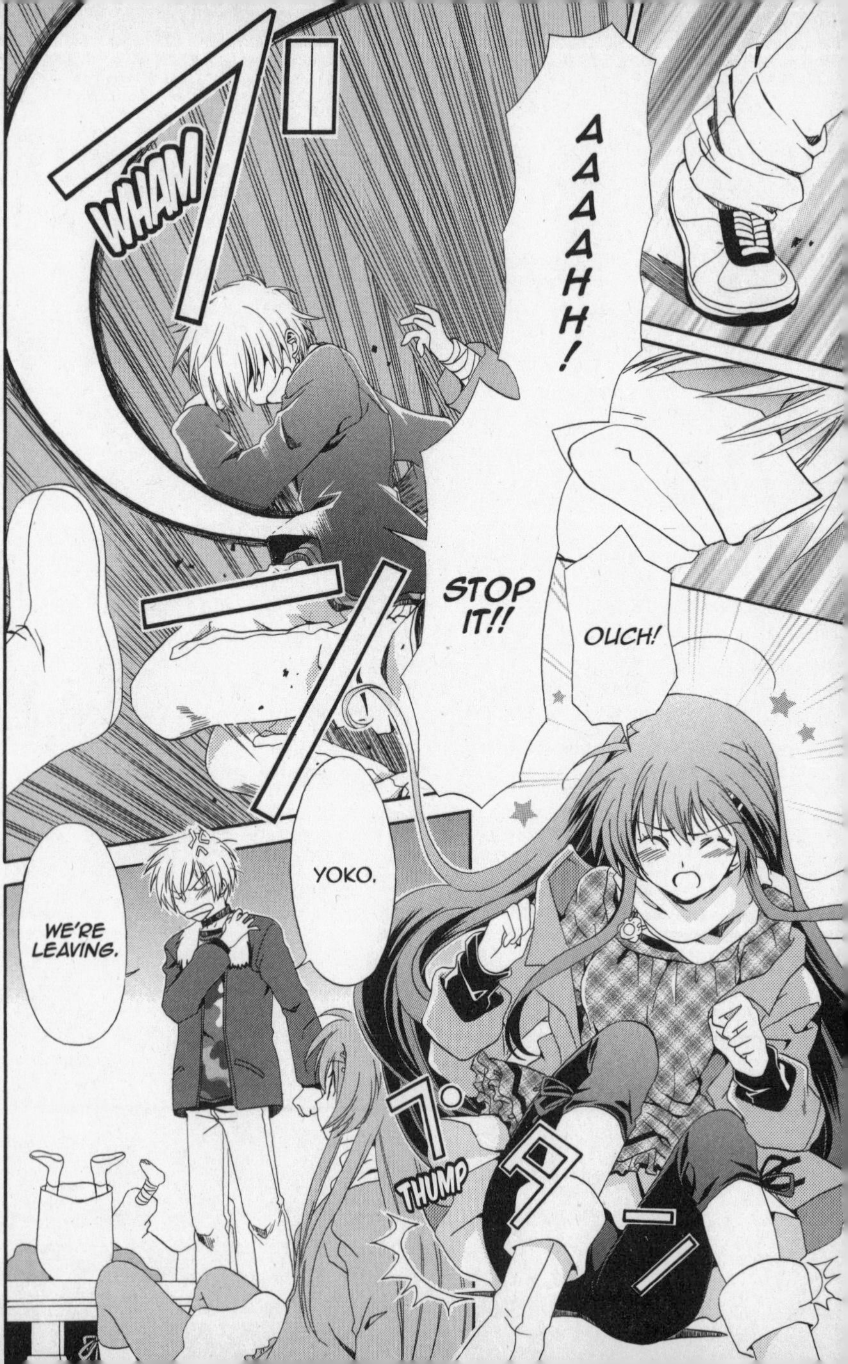
AAAAAHH!
WHAM
OUCH!
STOP IT!!
YOKO.
WE'RE LEAVING.
THUMP

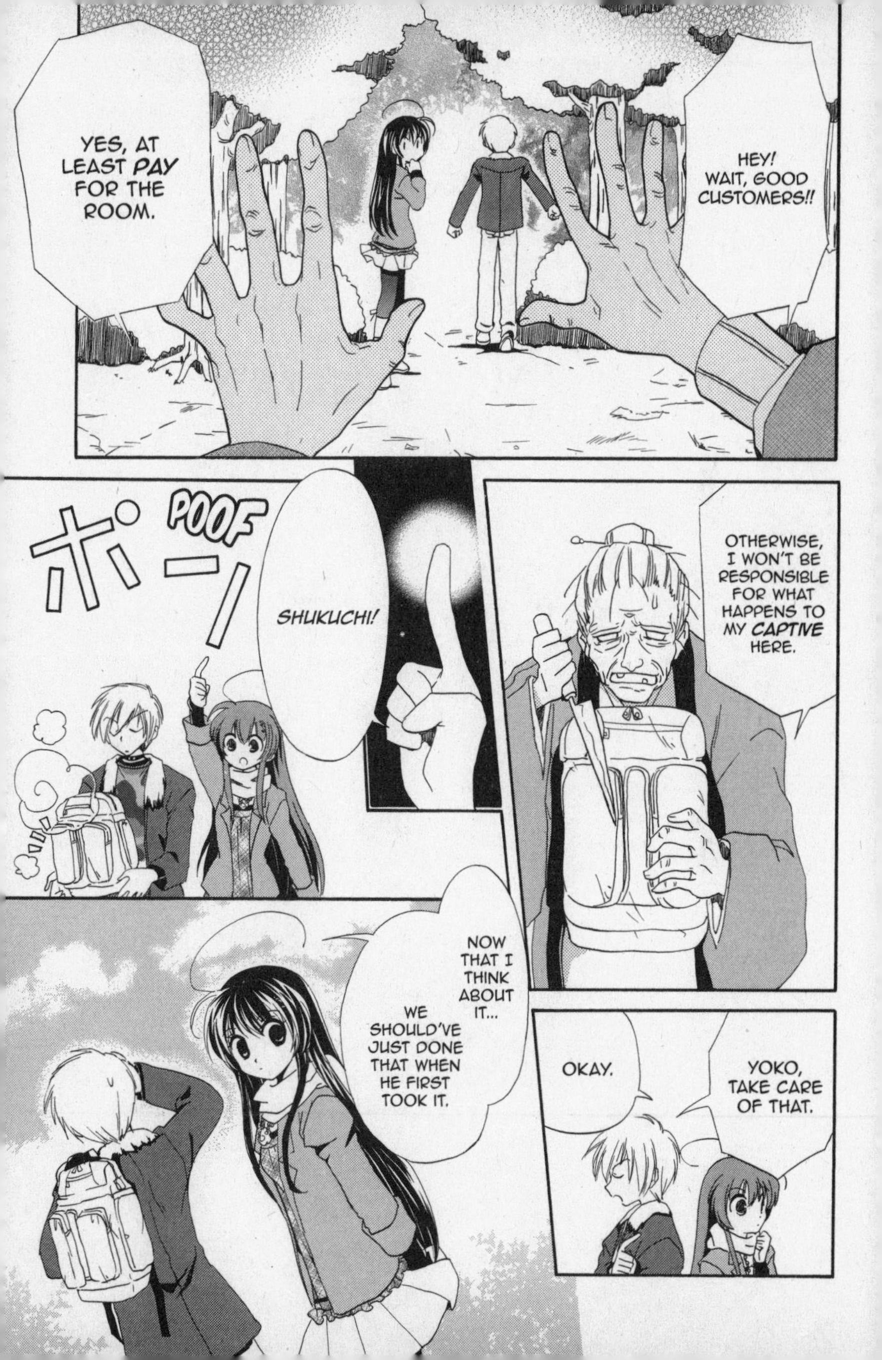
HEY! WAIT, GOOD CUSTOMERS!!
YES, AT LEAST PAY FOR THE ROOM.
OTHERWISE, I WON'T BE RESPONSIBLE FOR WHAT HAPPENS TO MY CAPTIVE HERE.
YOKO, TAKE CARE OF THAT.
OKAY.
SHUKUCHI!
POOF
ポーン
NOW THAT I THINK ABOUT IT...
WE SHOULD'VE JUST DONE THAT WHEN HE FIRST TOOK IT.

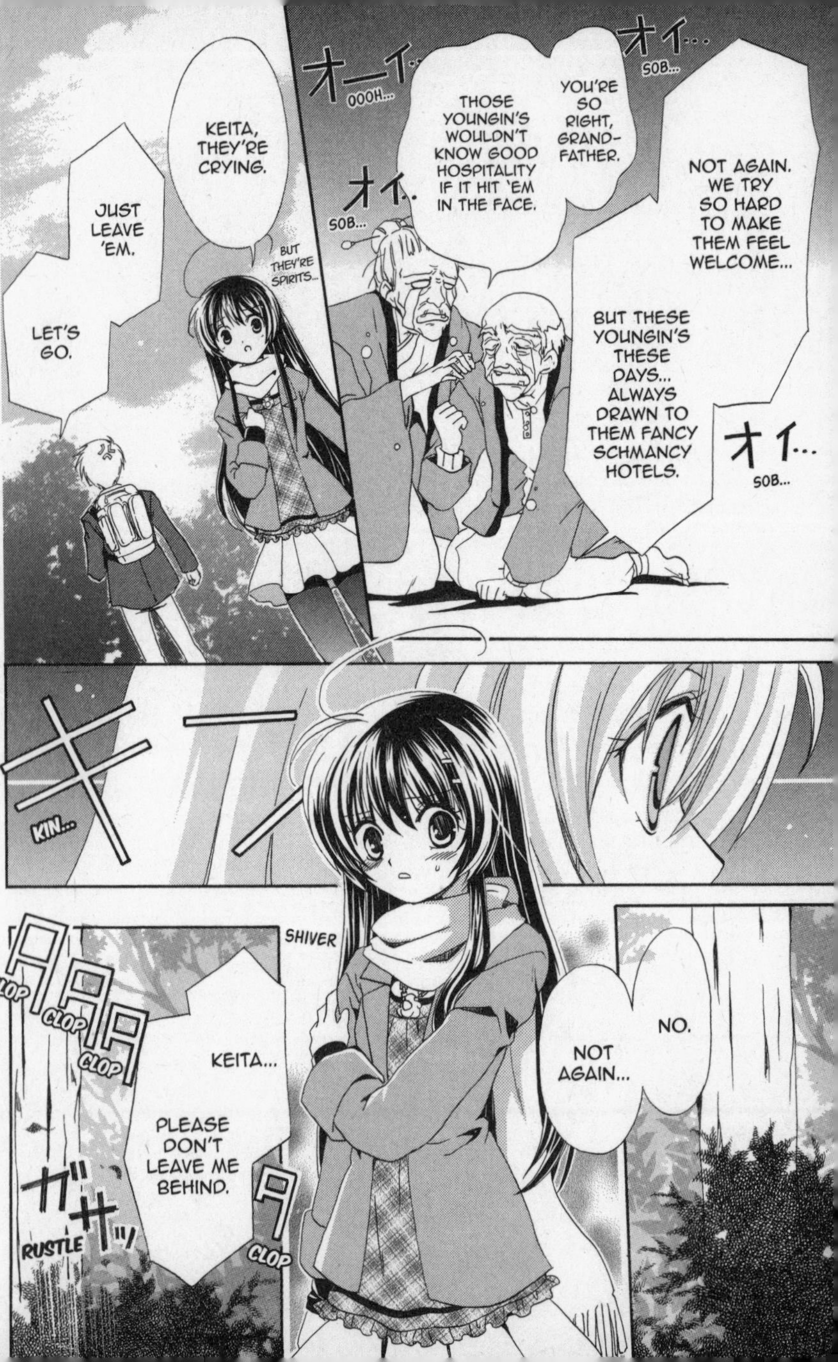

オイ...
SOB...
NOT AGAIN. WE TRY SO HARD TO MAKE THEM FEEL WELCOME...
YOU'RE SO RIGHT, GRAND-FATHER.
THOSE YOUNGIN'S WOULDN'T KNOW GOOD HOSPITALITY IF IT HIT 'EM IN THE FACE.
オーイ...
OOOH...
オイ...
SOB...
BUT THESE YOUNGIN'S THESE DAYS... ALWAYS DRAWN TO THEM FANCY SCHMANCY HOTELS.
オイ...
SOB...
KEITA, THEY'RE CRYING.
BUT THEY'RE SPIRITS...
JUST LEAVE 'EM.
LET'S GO.
キーン
KIN...
NO.
NOT AGAIN...
SHIVER
KEITA...
PLEASE DON'T LEAVE ME BEHIND.
タ
CLOP
タタタ
CLOP
CLOP
CLOP
ガサッ
RUSTLE

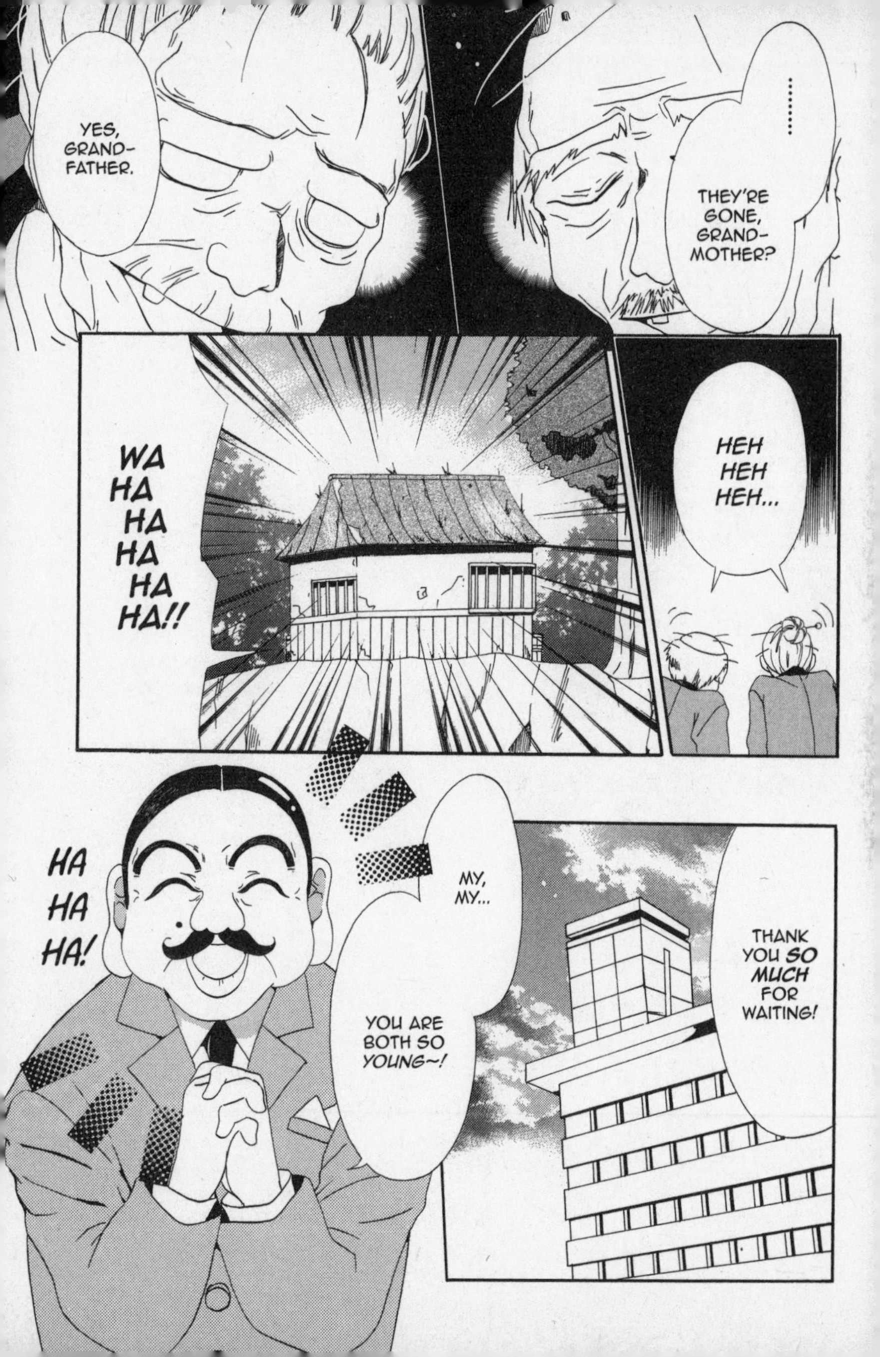
......
THEY'RE GONE, GRANDMOTHER?
YES, GRANDFATHER.
HEH HEH HEH...
WA HA HA HA HA HA!!
THANK YOU *SO MUCH* FOR WAITING!
MY, MY...
YOU ARE BOTH SO *YOUNG*~!
HA HA HA!

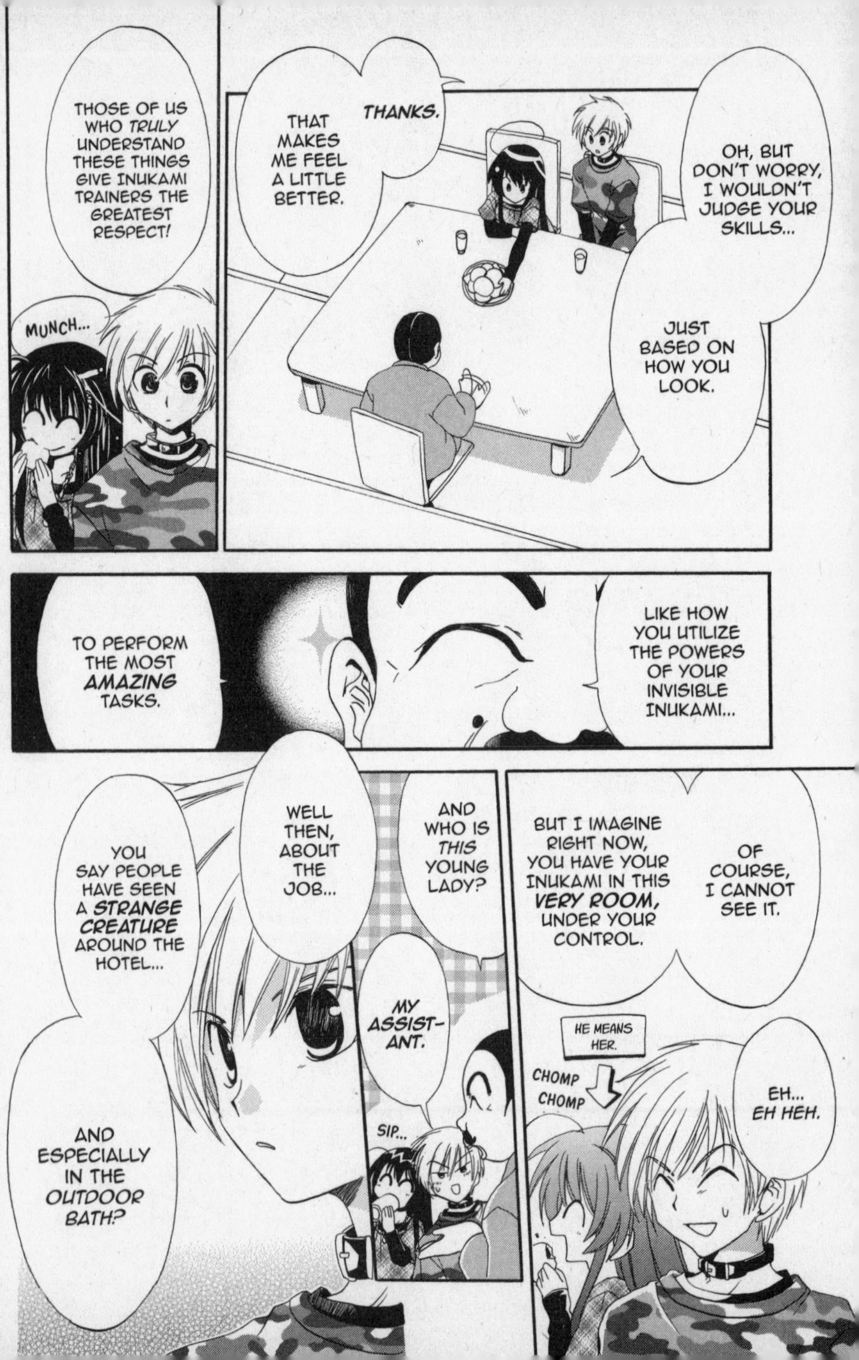
OH, BUT DON'T WORRY, I WOULDN'T JUDGE YOUR SKILLS...
JUST BASED ON HOW YOU LOOK.
THANKS.
THAT MAKES ME FEEL A LITTLE BETTER.
THOSE OF US WHO TRULY UNDERSTAND THESE THINGS GIVE INUKAMI TRAINERS THE GREATEST RESPECT!
MUNCH...
LIKE HOW YOU UTILIZE THE POWERS OF YOUR INVISIBLE INUKAMI...
TO PERFORM THE MOST AMAZING TASKS.
OF COURSE, I CANNOT SEE IT.
BUT I IMAGINE RIGHT NOW, YOU HAVE YOUR INUKAMI IN THIS VERY ROOM, UNDER YOUR CONTROL.
EH... EH HEH.
HE MEANS HER.
CHOMP CHOMP
AND WHO IS THIS YOUNG LADY?
MY ASSIST-ANT.
SIP...
WELL THEN, ABOUT THE JOB...
YOU SAY PEOPLE HAVE SEEN A STRANGE CREATURE AROUND THE HOTEL...
AND ESPECIALLY IN THE OUTDOOR BATH?

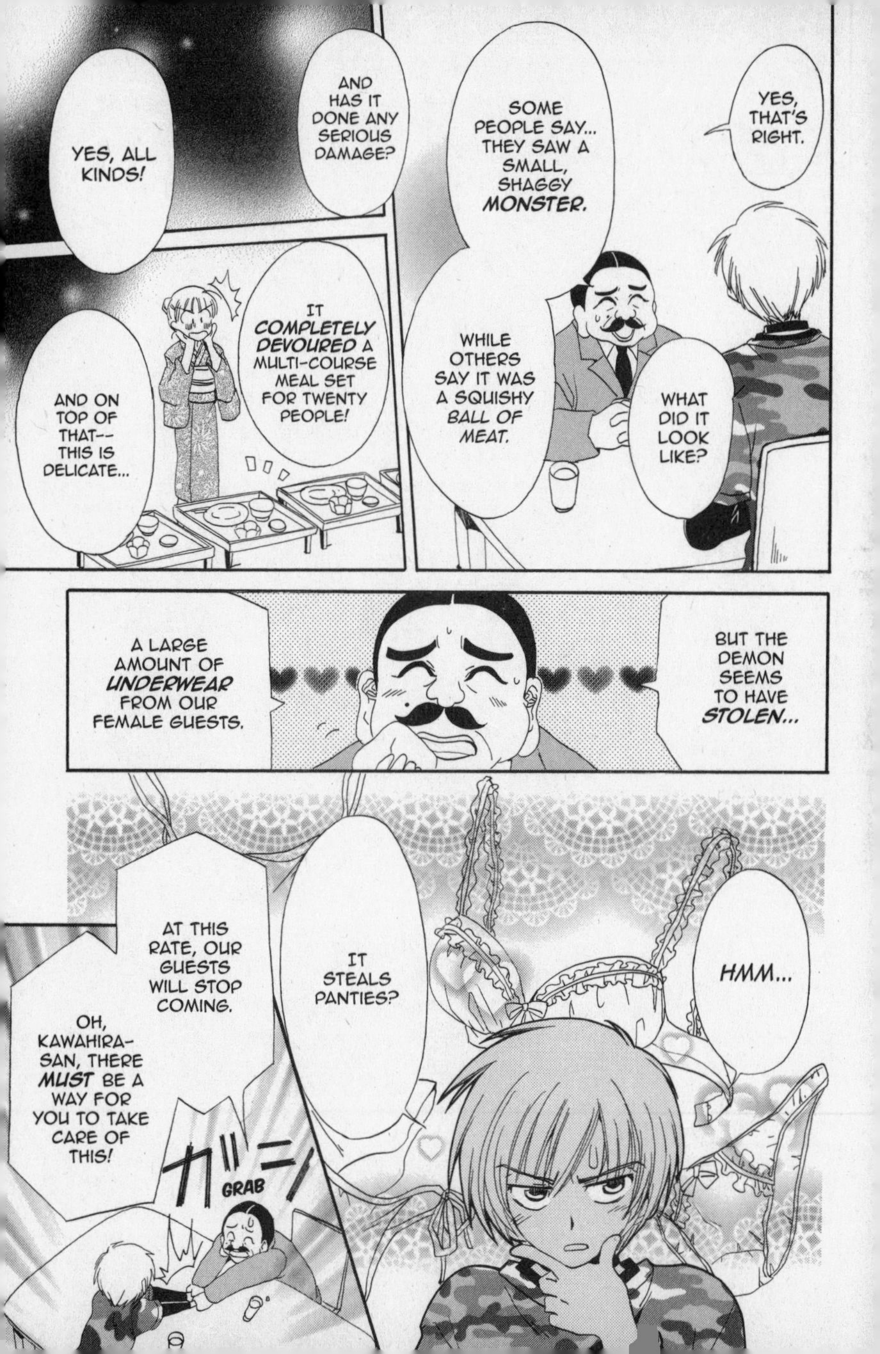

YES, THAT'S RIGHT.
WHAT DID IT LOOK LIKE?
SOME PEOPLE SAY... THEY SAW A SMALL, SHAGGY MONSTER.
WHILE OTHERS SAY IT WAS A SQUISHY BALL OF MEAT.
AND HAS IT DONE ANY SERIOUS DAMAGE?
YES, ALL KINDS!
IT COMPLETELY DEVOURED A MULTI-COURSE MEAL SET FOR TWENTY PEOPLE!
AND ON TOP OF THAT-- THIS IS DELICATE...
BUT THE DEMON SEEMS TO HAVE STOLEN...
A LARGE AMOUNT OF UNDERWEAR FROM OUR FEMALE GUESTS.
HMM...
IT STEALS PANTIES?
AT THIS RATE, OUR GUESTS WILL STOP COMING.
OH, KAWAHIRA-SAN, THERE MUST BE A WAY FOR YOU TO TAKE CARE OF THIS!
GRAB

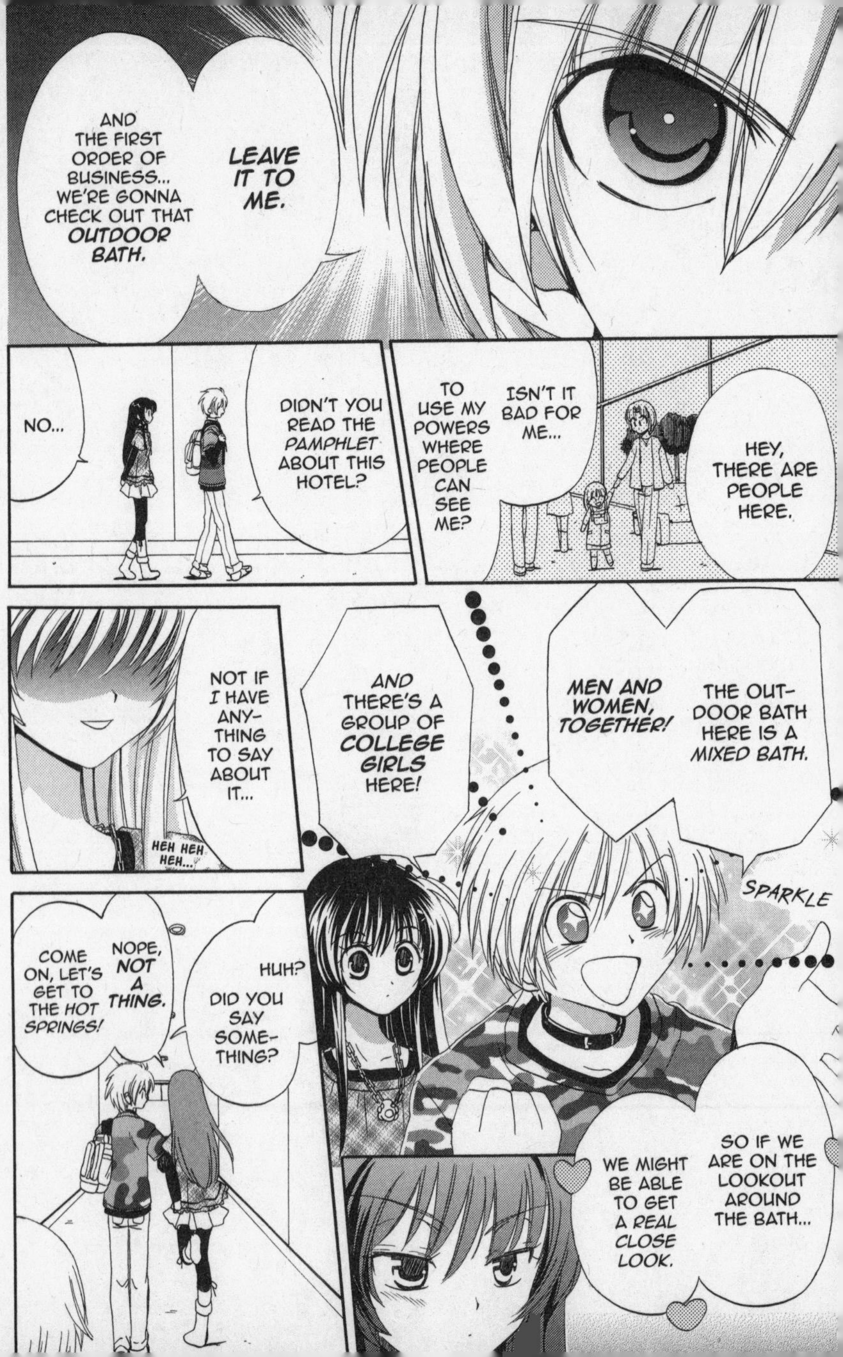
LEAVE IT TO ME.
AND THE FIRST ORDER OF BUSINESS... WE'RE GONNA CHECK OUT THAT OUTDOOR BATH.
HEY, THERE ARE PEOPLE HERE.
ISN'T IT BAD FOR ME...
TO USE MY POWERS WHERE PEOPLE CAN SEE ME?
DIDN'T YOU READ THE PAMPHLET ABOUT THIS HOTEL?
NO...
THE OUT-DOOR BATH HERE IS A MIXED BATH.
MEN AND WOMEN, TOGETHER!
SPARKLE
AND THERE'S A GROUP OF COLLEGE GIRLS HERE!
SO IF WE ARE ON THE LOOKOUT AROUND THE BATH...
WE MIGHT BE ABLE TO GET A REAL CLOSE LOOK.
NOT IF I HAVE ANY-THING TO SAY ABOUT IT...
HEH HEH HEH...
HUH?
DID YOU SAY SOME-THING?
NOPE, NOT A THING.
COME ON, LET'S GET TO THE HOT SPRINGS!

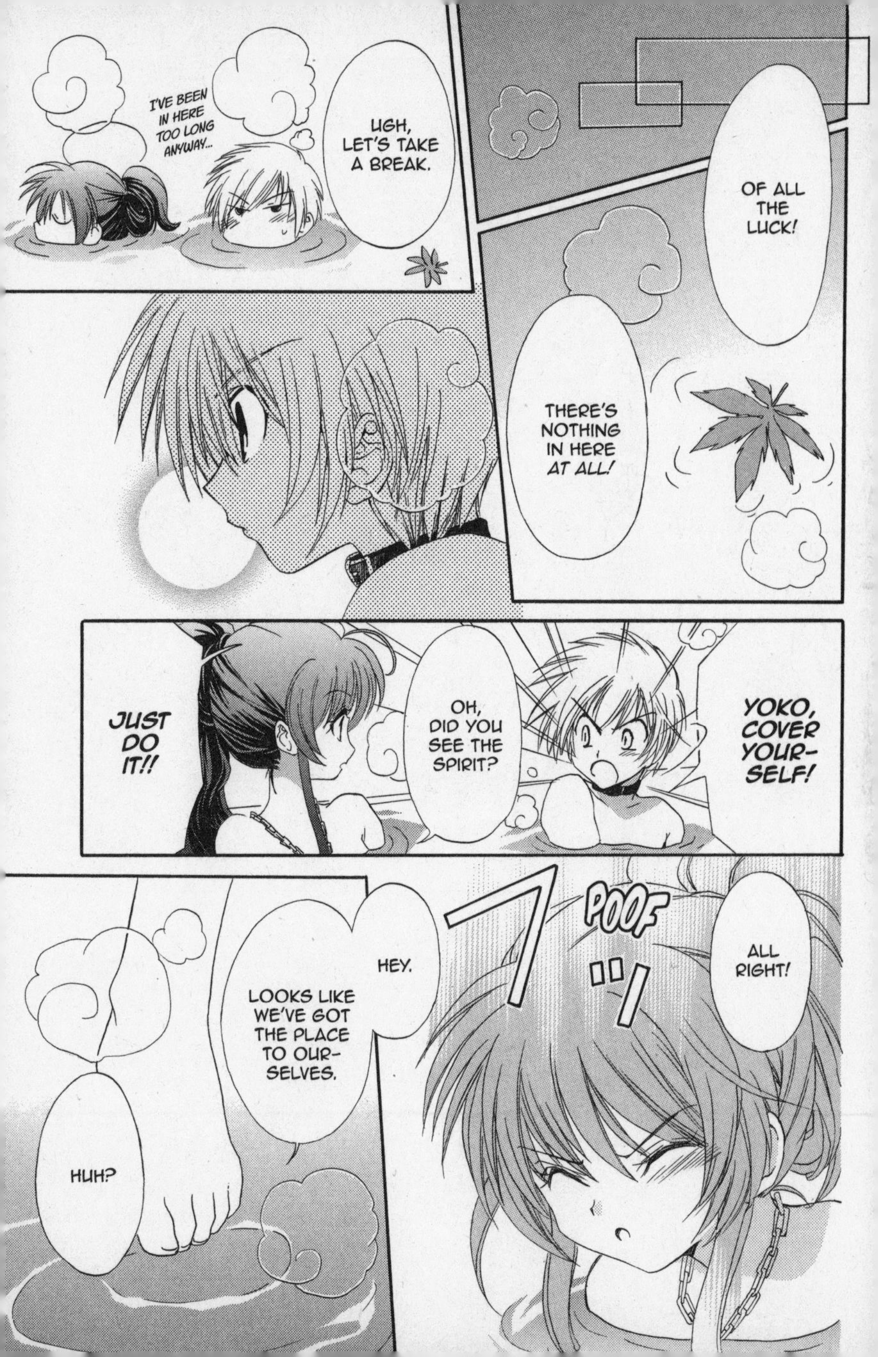
OF ALL THE LUCK!
THERE'S NOTHING IN HERE AT ALL!
UGH, LET'S TAKE A BREAK.
I'VE BEEN IN HERE TOO LONG ANYWAY...
YOKO, COVER YOURSELF!
OH, DID YOU SEE THE SPIRIT?
JUST DO IT!!
POOF
ALL RIGHT!
HEY.
LOOKS LIKE WE'VE GOT THE PLACE TO OURSELVES.
HUH?

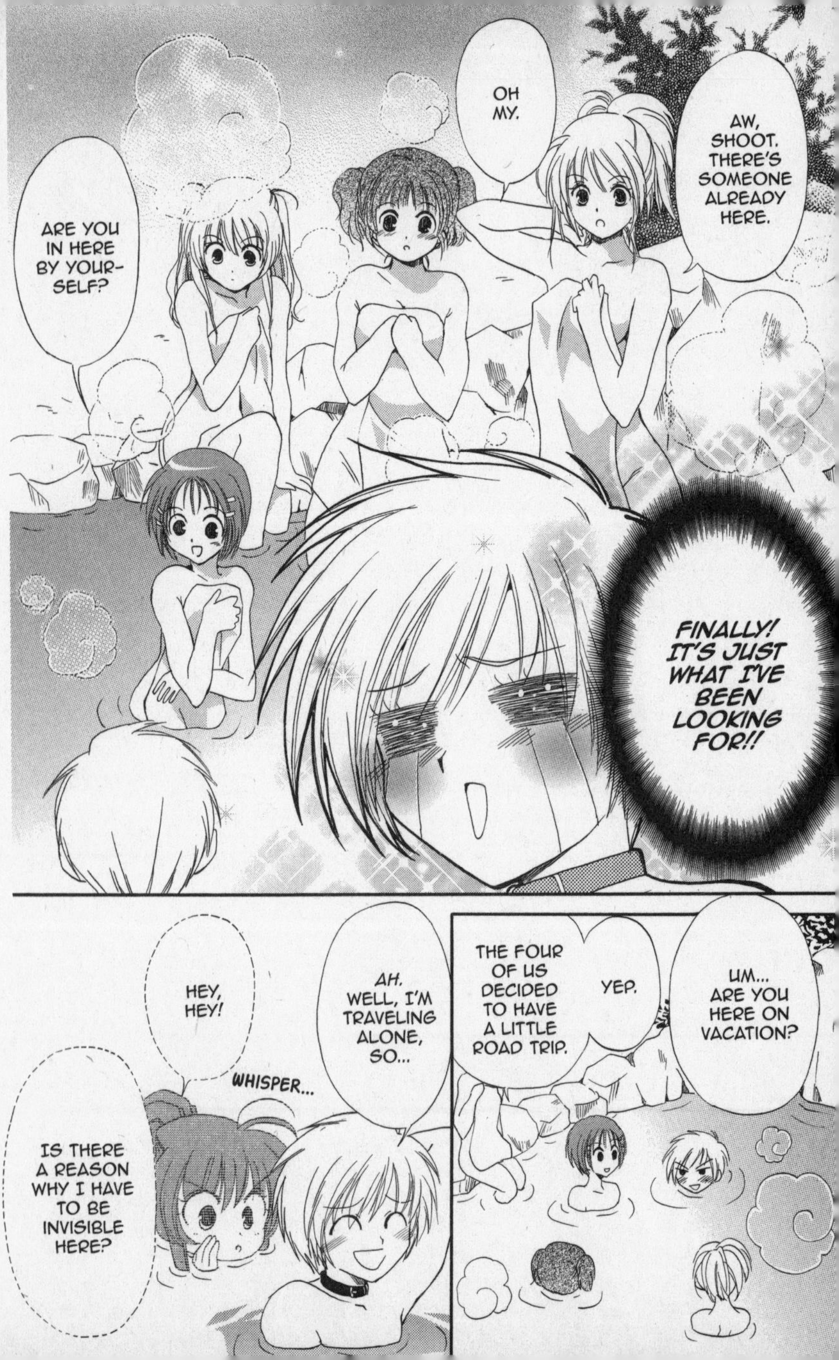
AW, SHOOT. THERE'S SOMEONE ALREADY HERE.
OH MY.
ARE YOU IN HERE BY YOUR-SELF?
FINALLY! IT'S JUST WHAT I'VE BEEN LOOKING FOR!!
UM... ARE YOU HERE ON VACATION?
YEP.
THE FOUR OF US DECIDED TO HAVE A LITTLE ROAD TRIP.
AH. WELL, I'M TRAVELING ALONE, SO...
HEY, HEY!
WHISPER...
IS THERE A REASON WHY I HAVE TO BE INVISIBLE HERE?

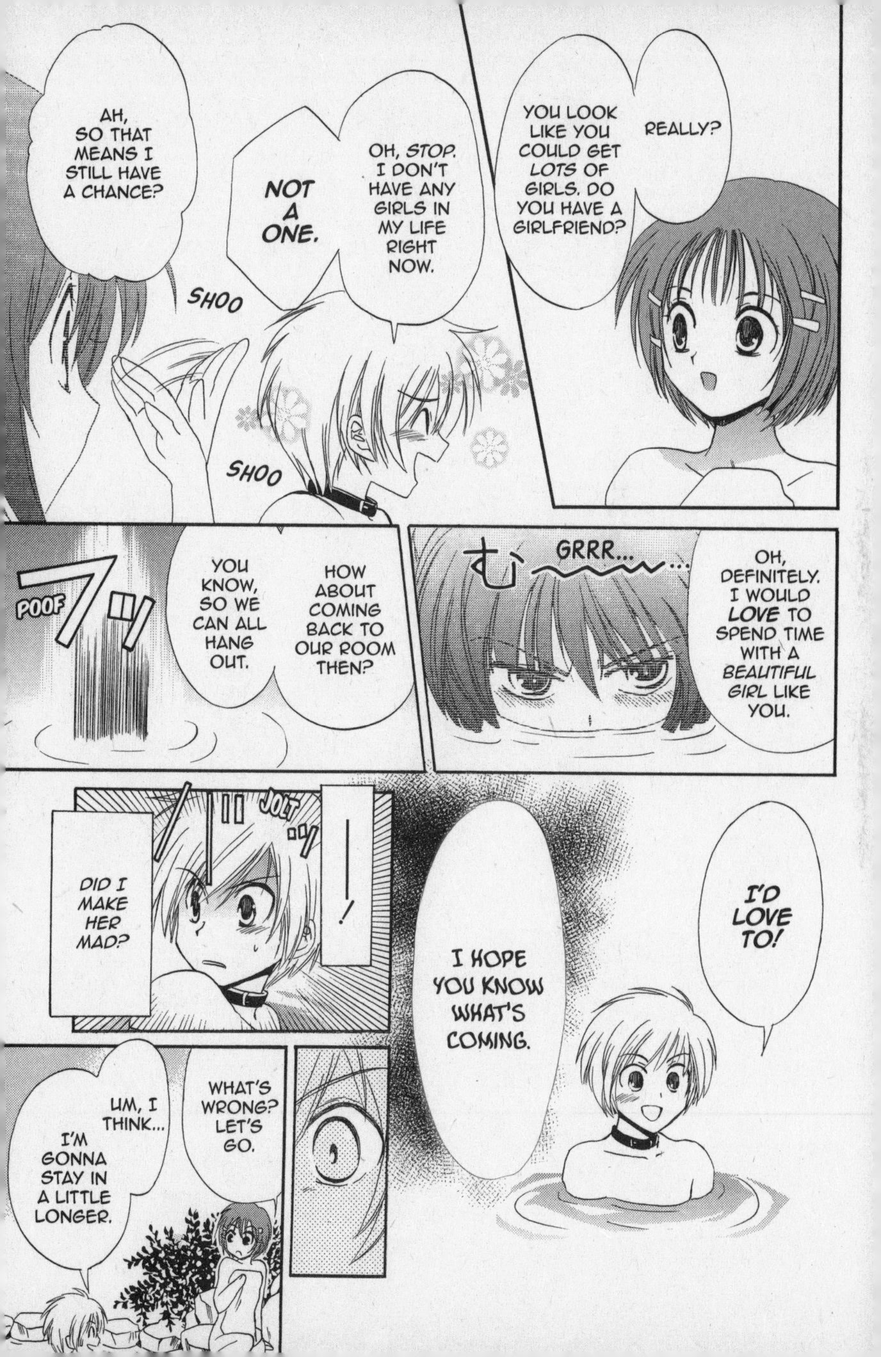
REALLY?
YOU LOOK LIKE YOU COULD GET *LOTS* OF GIRLS. DO YOU HAVE A GIRLFRIEND?
OH, *STOP.* I DON'T HAVE ANY GIRLS IN MY LIFE RIGHT NOW.
NOT A ONE.
SHOO
SHOO
AH, SO THAT MEANS I STILL HAVE A CHANCE?
OH, DEFINITELY. I WOULD **LOVE** TO SPEND TIME WITH A *BEAUTIFUL* GIRL LIKE YOU.
GRRR...
HOW ABOUT COMING BACK TO OUR ROOM THEN?
YOU KNOW, SO WE CAN ALL HANG OUT.
POOF
I'D LOVE TO!
I HOPE YOU KNOW WHAT'S COMING.
JOLT
!
DID I MAKE HER MAD?
WHAT'S WRONG? LET'S GO.
UM, I THINK... I'M GONNA STAY IN A LITTLE LONGER.

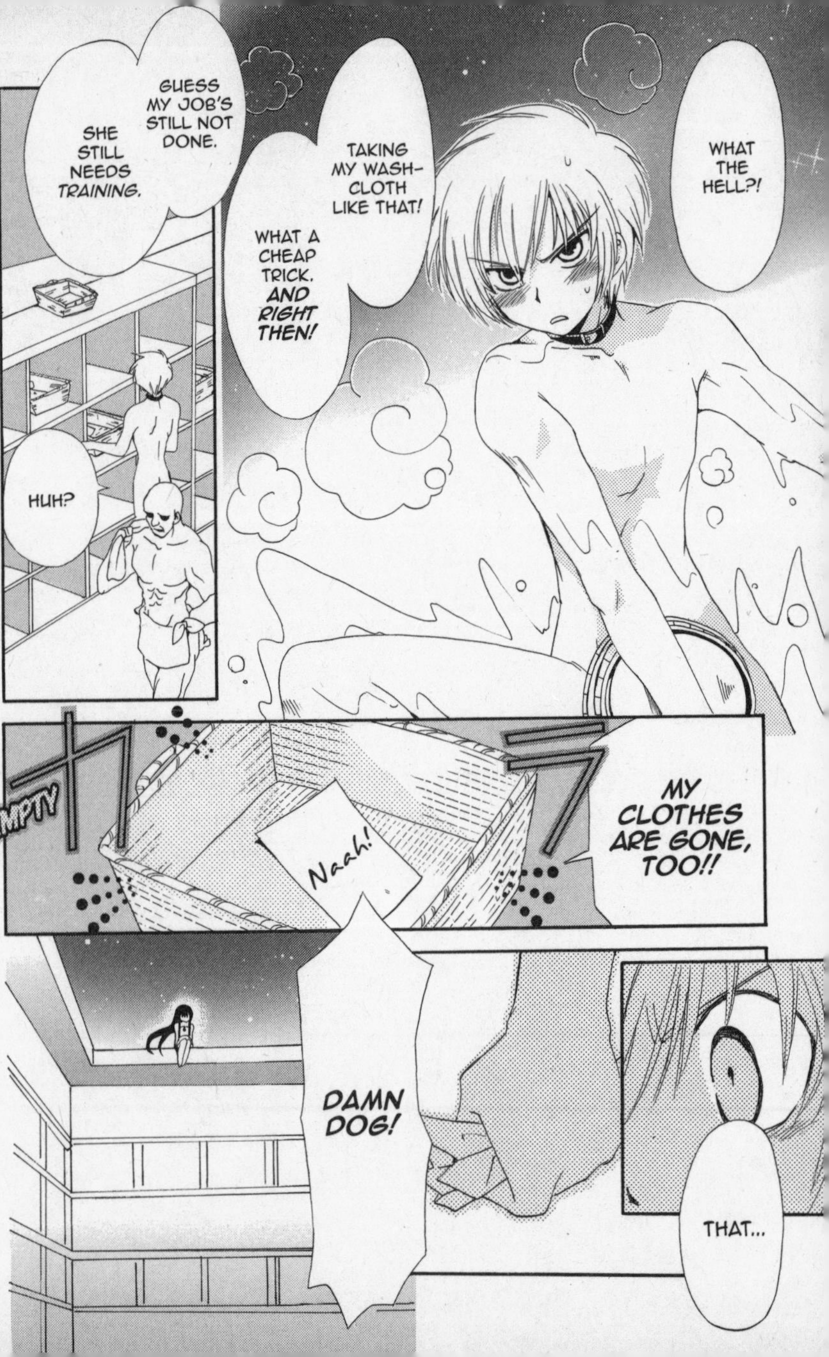
WHAT THE HELL?!
TAKING MY WASH-CLOTH LIKE THAT!
WHAT A CHEAP TRICK. AND RIGHT THEN!
GUESS MY JOB'S STILL NOT DONE.
SHE STILL NEEDS TRAINING.
HUH?
MY CLOTHES ARE GONE, TOO!!
Naah!
EMPTY
THAT...
DAMN DOG!

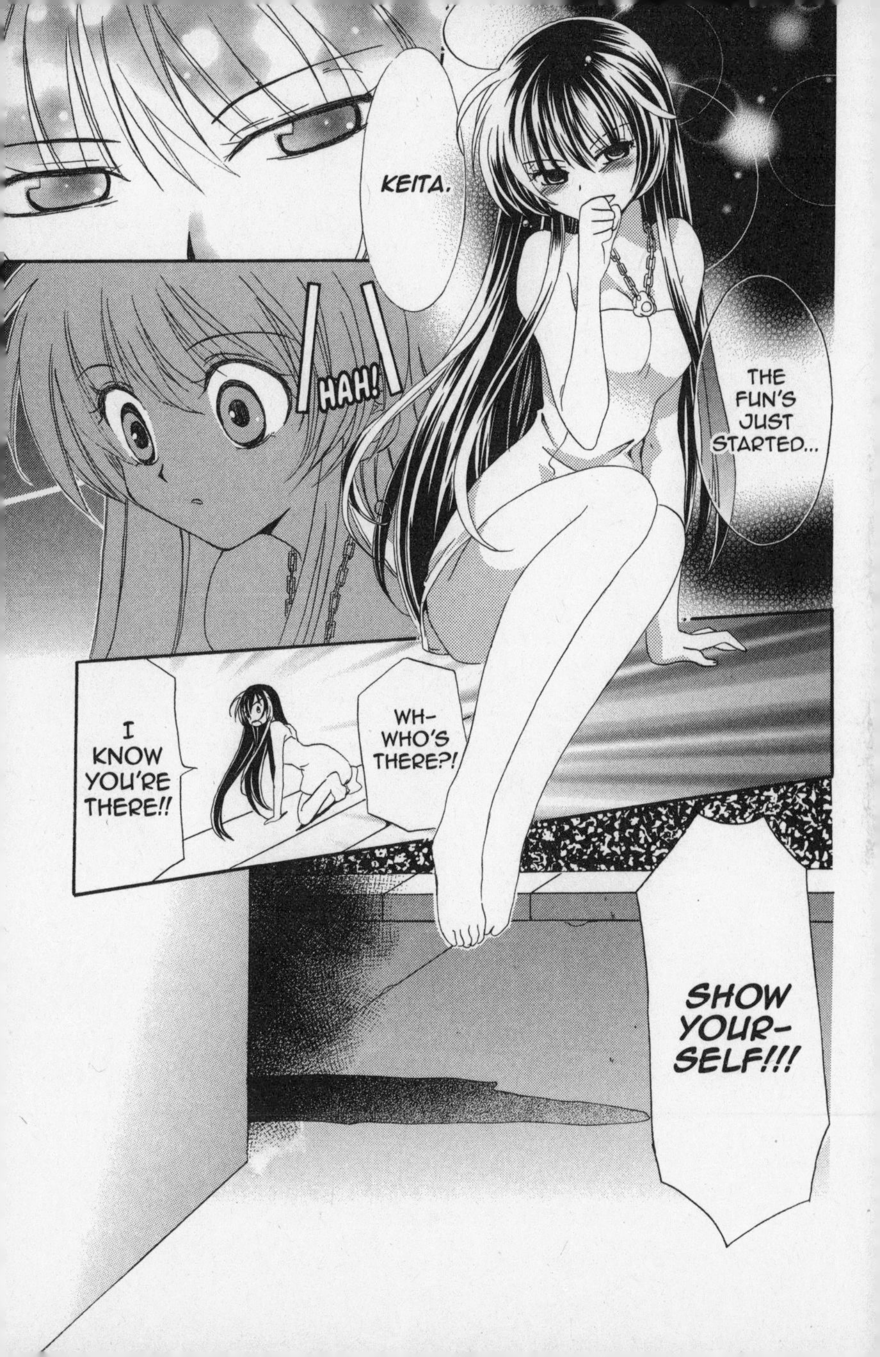
KEITA.
THE FUN'S JUST STARTED...
HAH!
WH- WHO'S THERE?!
I KNOW YOU'RE THERE!!
SHOW YOURSELF!!!

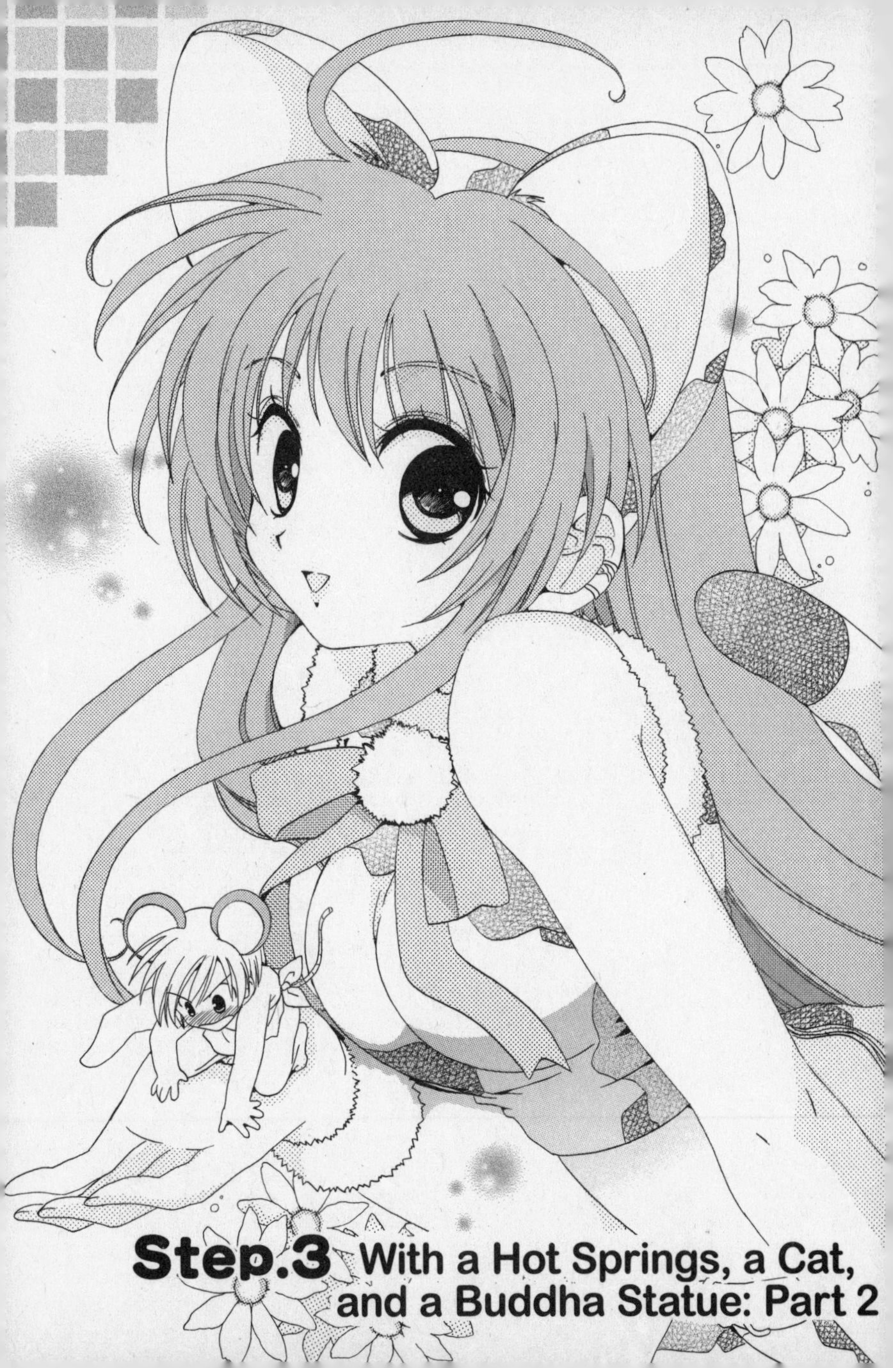

Step.3 With a Hot Springs, a Cat, and a Buddha Statue: Part 2

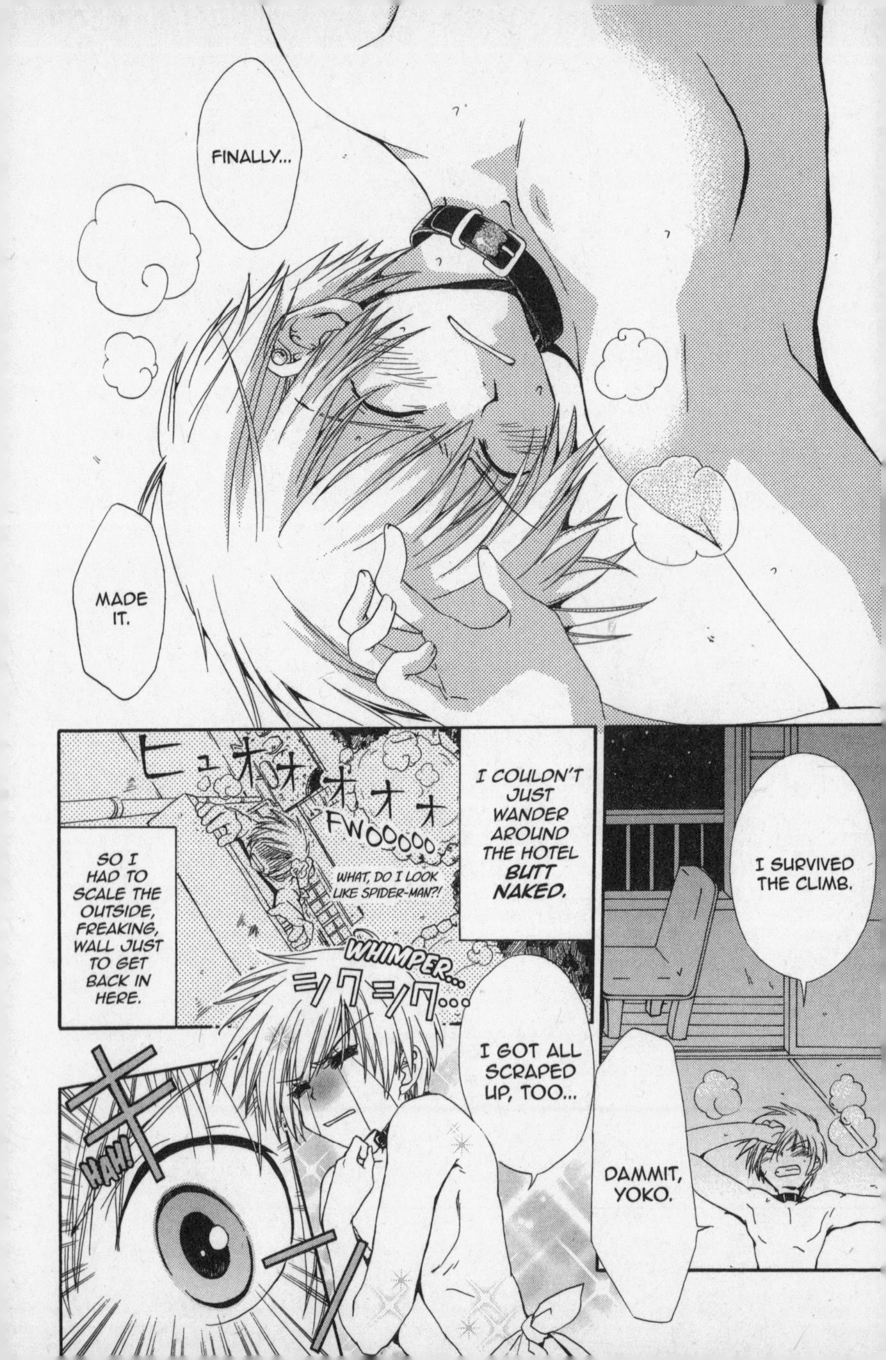
FINALLY...
MADE IT.
I SURVIVED THE CLIMB.
DAMMIT, YOKO.
I COULDN'T JUST WANDER AROUND THE HOTEL BUTT NAKED.
SO I HAD TO SCALE THE OUTSIDE, FREAKING, WALL JUST TO GET BACK IN HERE.
ヒュオオオオオオ
FWOOOOOO
WHAT, DO I LOOK LIKE SPIDER-MAN?!
WHIMPER...
シクシク...
I GOT ALL SCRAPED UP, TOO...
HAH!

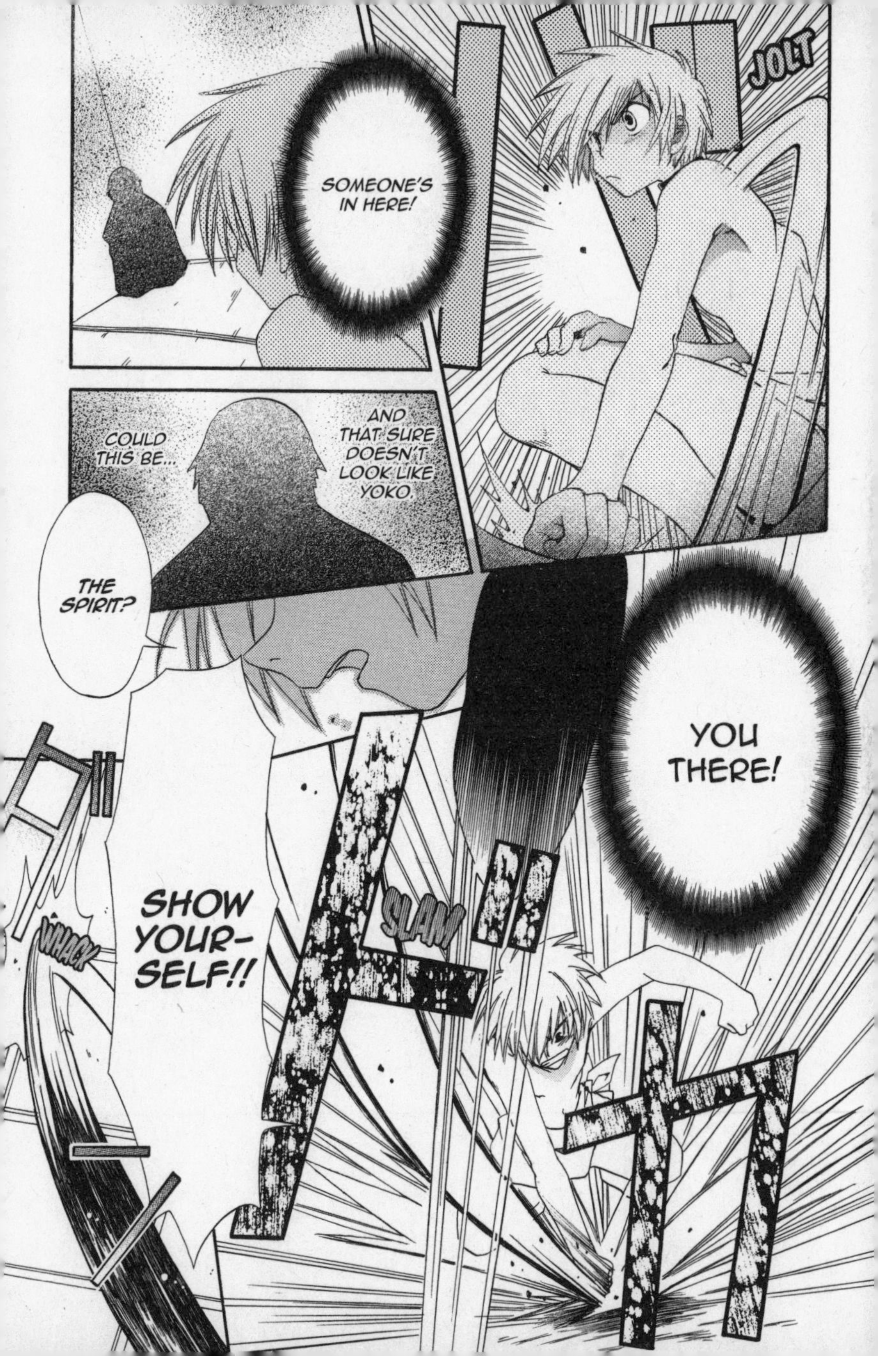
JOLT
SOMEONE'S IN HERE!
AND THAT SURE DOESN'T LOOK LIKE YOKO.
COULD THIS BE...
THE SPIRIT?
YOU THERE!
SLAM
SHOW YOUR-SELF!!
WHACK

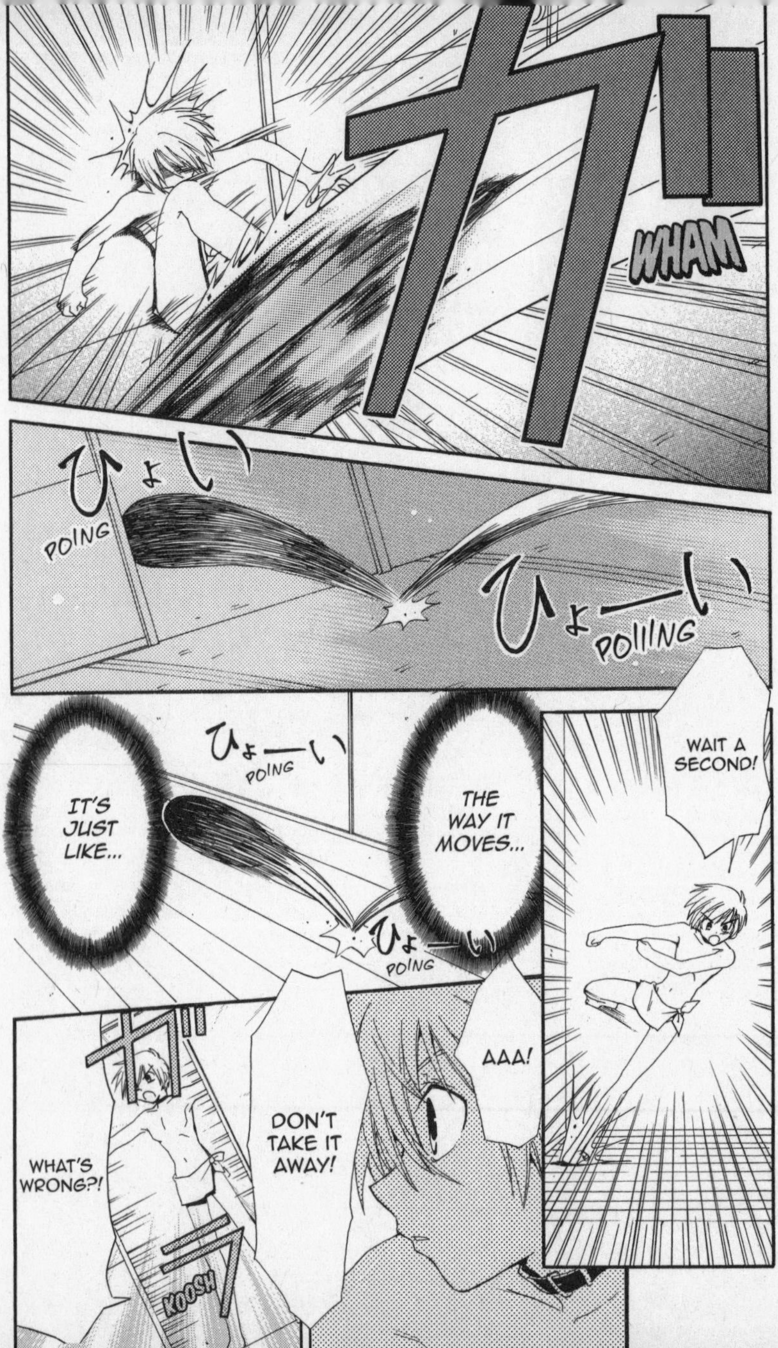

ガッ
WHAM
ひょい
POING
ひょーい
POIIING
WAIT A SECOND!
THE WAY IT MOVES...
ひょーい
POING
IT'S JUST LIKE...
ひょーい
POING
AAA!
DON'T TAKE IT AWAY!
WHAT'S WRONG?!
KOOSH

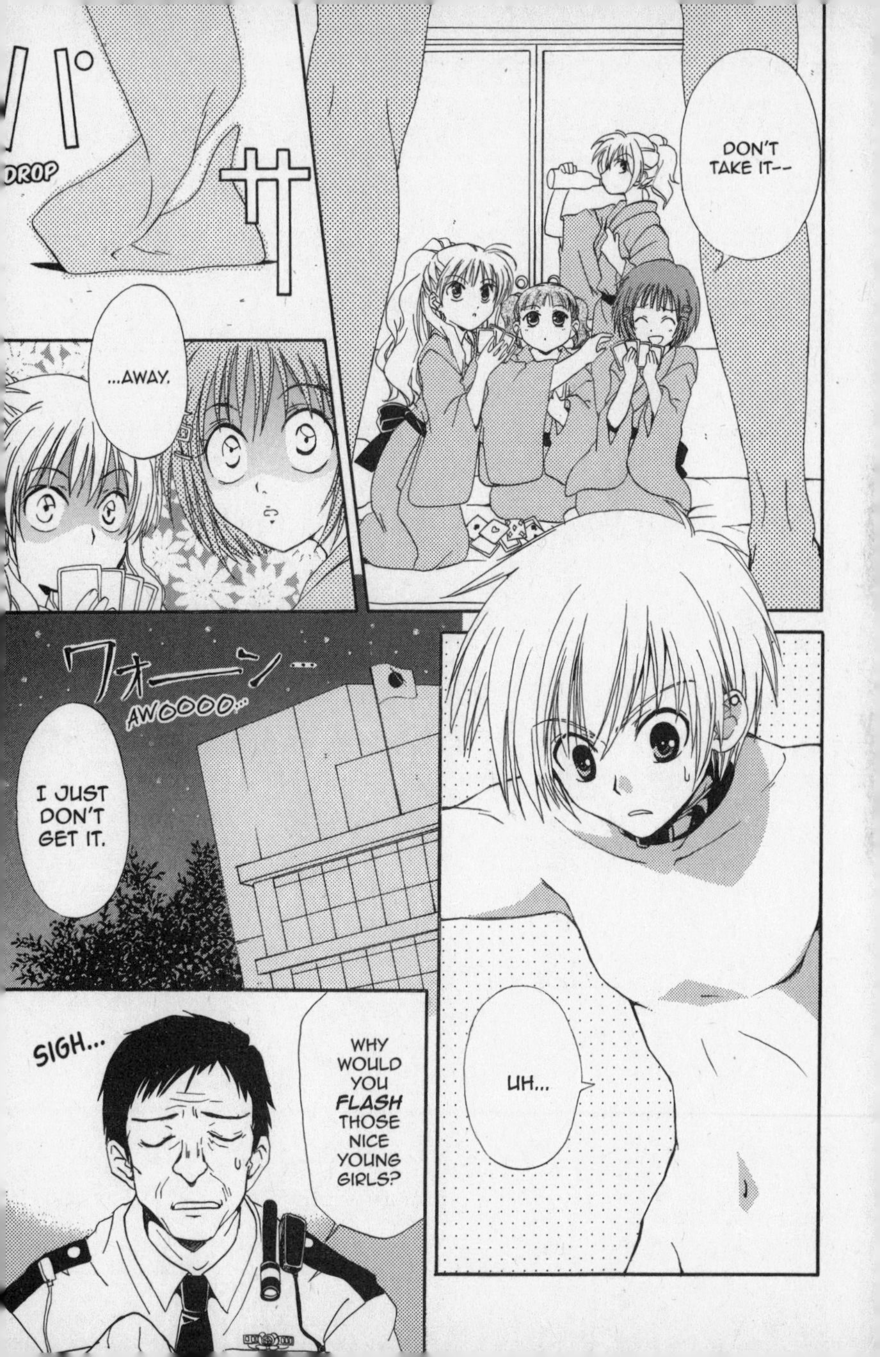
DON'T TAKE IT--
パサ
DROP
...AWAY.
UH...
ワオーン..
AWOOOO..
I JUST DON'T GET IT.
SIGH...
WHY WOULD YOU FLASH THOSE NICE YOUNG GIRLS?

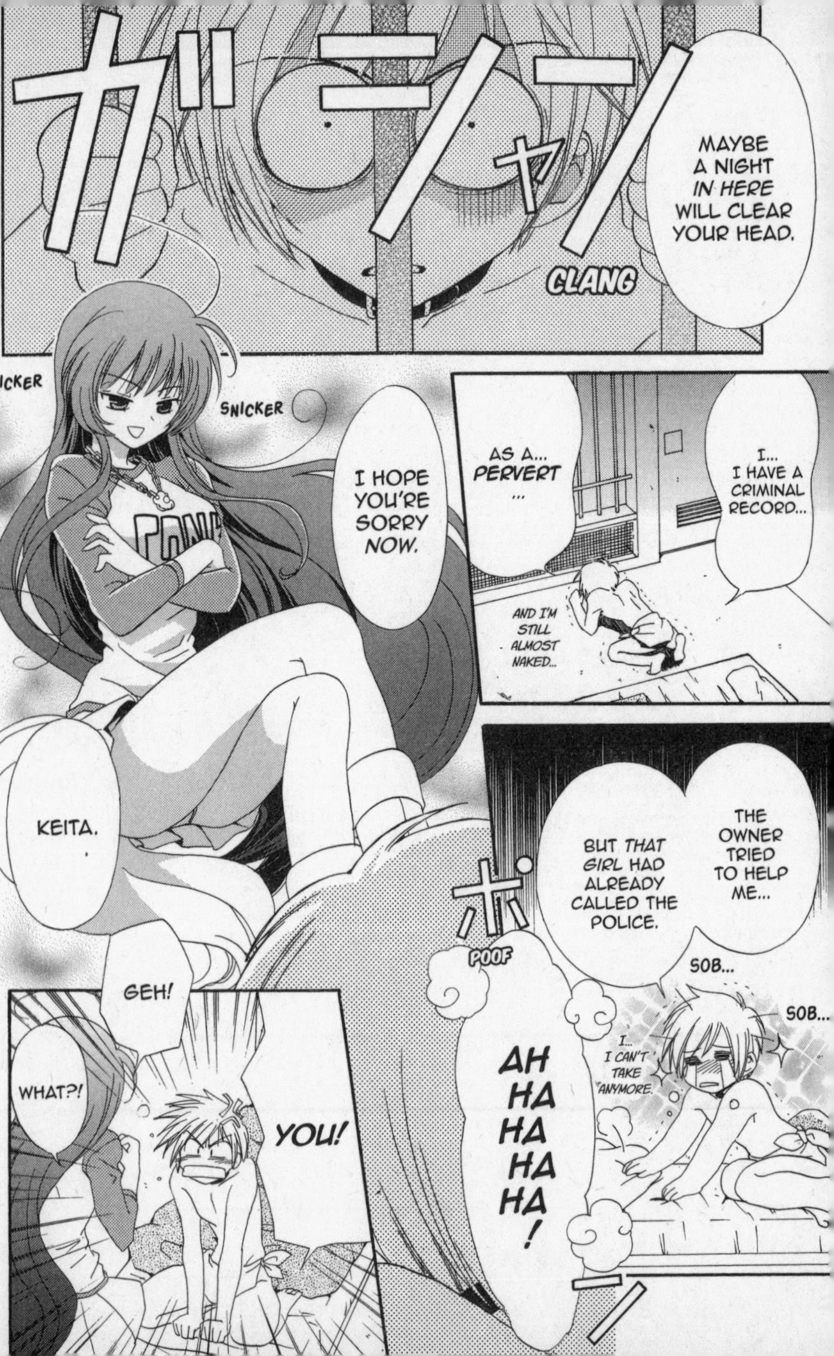
MAYBE A NIGHT *IN HERE* WILL CLEAR YOUR HEAD.
CLANG
ガシャーン
I... I HAVE A CRIMINAL RECORD...
AS A... *PERVERT* ...
AND I'M STILL ALMOST NAKED...
THE OWNER TRIED TO HELP ME...
BUT *THAT* GIRL HAD ALREADY CALLED THE POLICE.
SOB...
SOB...
I... I CAN'T TAKE ANYMORE.
ポ
POOF
I HOPE YOU'RE SORRY *NOW.*
SNICKER
SNICKER
KEITA.
AH HA HA HA HA HA!
GEH!
YOU!
WHAT?!

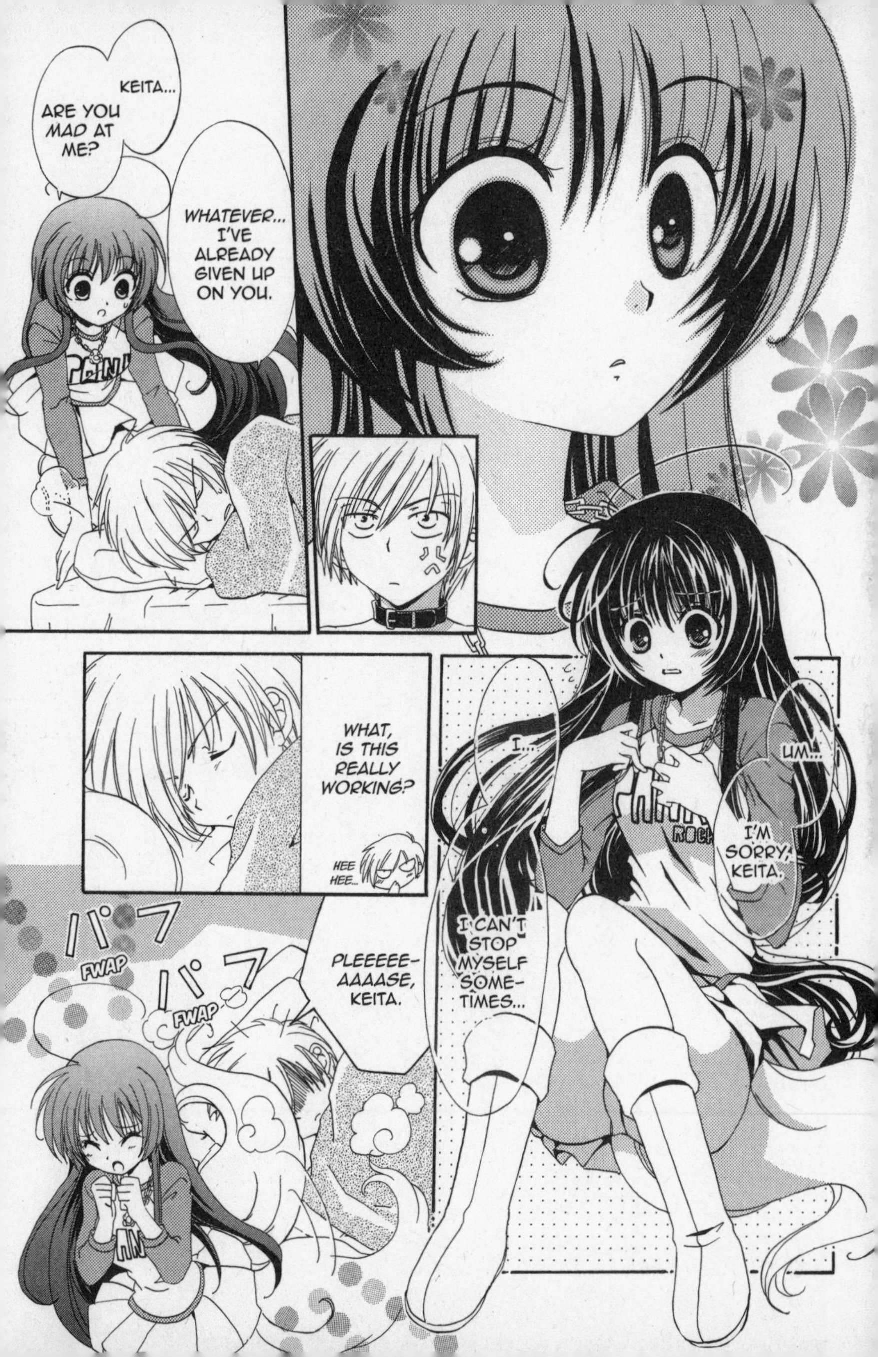

KEITA... ARE YOU MAD AT ME?
WHATEVER... I'VE ALREADY GIVEN UP ON YOU.
UM...
I'M SORRY, KEITA.
I...
I CAN'T STOP MYSELF SOMETIMES...
WHAT, IS THIS REALLY WORKING?
HEE HEE...
PLEEEEE-AAAASE, KEITA.
パフ
FWAP
パフ
FWAP

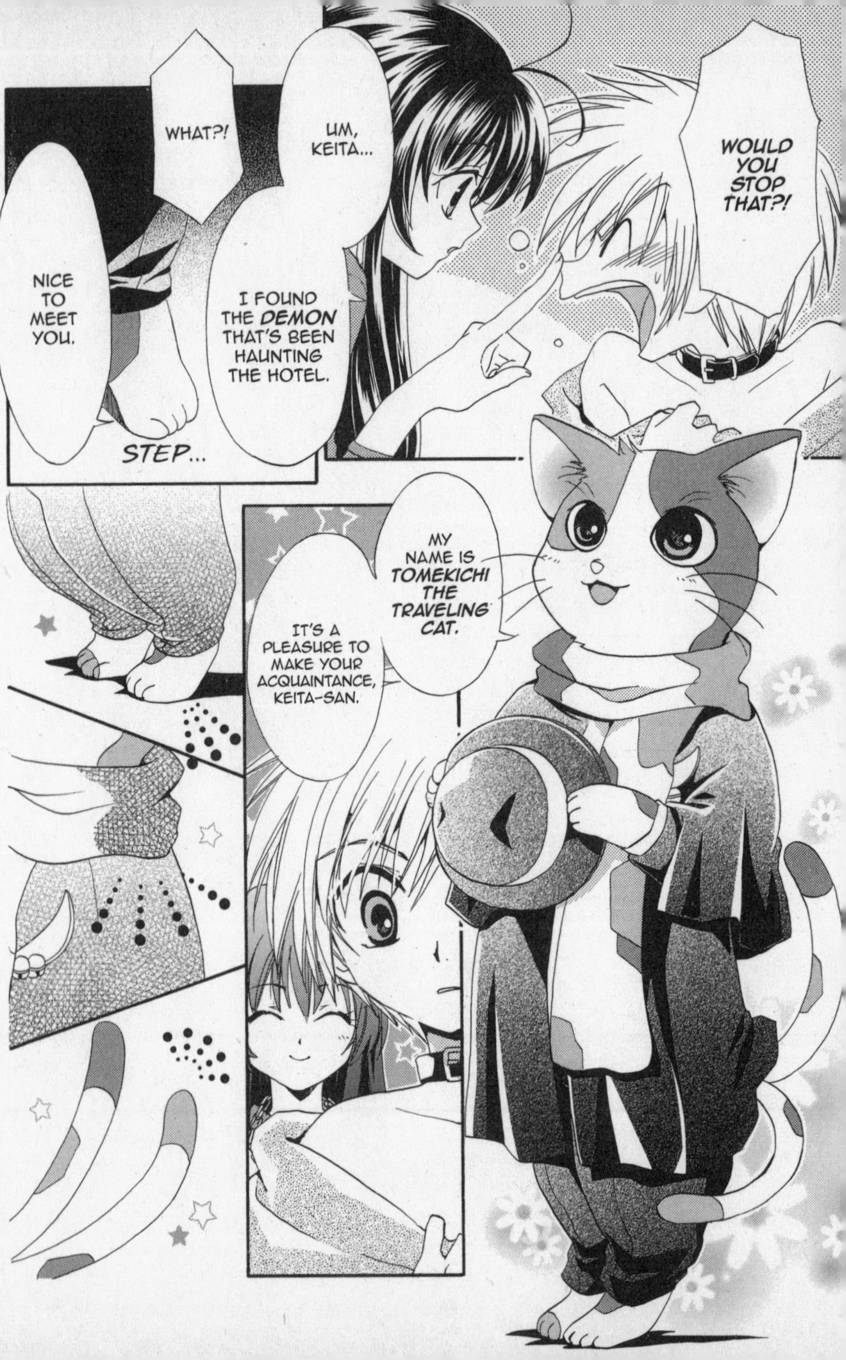
WOULD YOU STOP THAT?!
UM, KEITA...
I FOUND THE *DEMON* THAT'S BEEN HAUNTING THE HOTEL.
WHAT?!
NICE TO MEET YOU.
STEP...
MY NAME IS *TOMEKICHI THE TRAVELING CAT.*
IT'S A PLEASURE TO MAKE YOUR ACQUAINTANCE, KEITA-SAN.

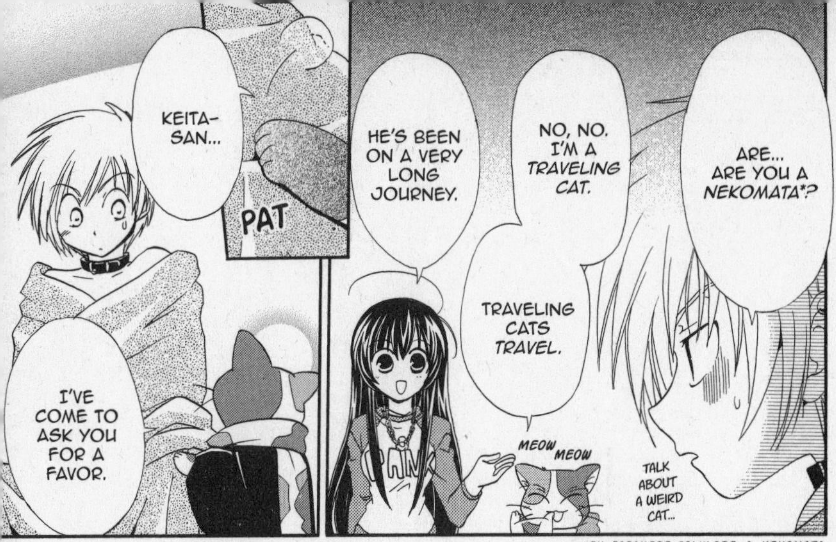
ARE... ARE YOU A *NEKOMATA**?
NO, NO. I'M A *TRAVELING* CAT.
HE'S BEEN ON A VERY LONG JOURNEY.
TRAVELING CATS *TRAVEL*.
MEOW MEOW
TALK ABOUT A WEIRD CAT...
KEITA-SAN...
PAT
I'VE COME TO ASK YOU FOR A FAVOR.

*IN JAPANESE FOLKLORE, A *NEKOMATA* IS A DEMON CAT WITH A FORKED TAIL.

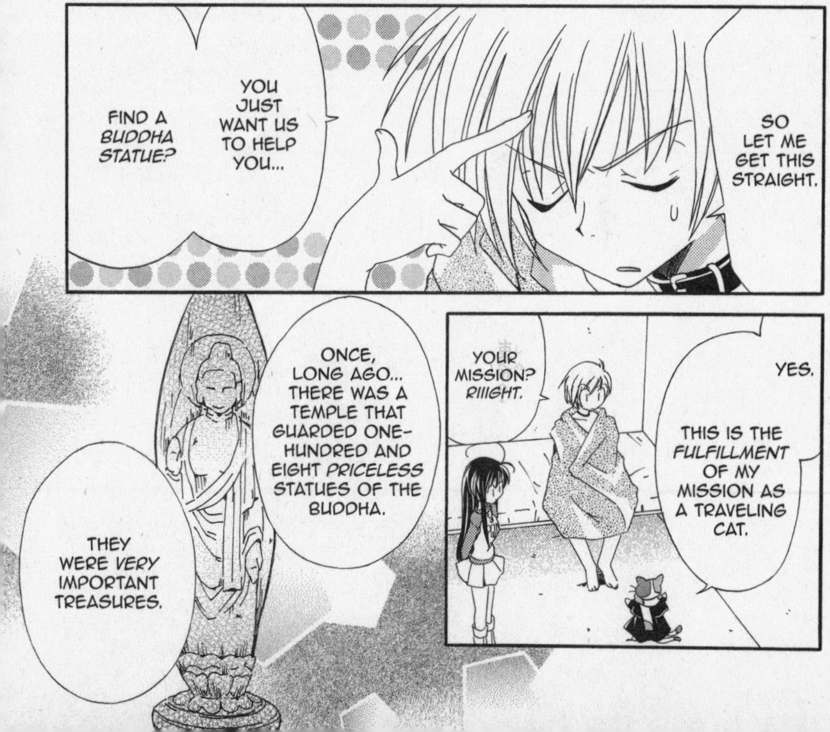
SO LET ME GET THIS STRAIGHT.
YOU JUST WANT US TO HELP YOU...
FIND A *BUDDHA STATUE?*
YES.
THIS IS THE *FULFILLMENT* OF MY MISSION AS A TRAVELING CAT.
YOUR MISSION? *RIIIGHT.*
ONCE, LONG AGO... THERE WAS A TEMPLE THAT GUARDED ONE-HUNDRED AND EIGHT *PRICELESS* STATUES OF THE BUDDHA.
THEY WERE *VERY* IMPORTANT TREASURES.

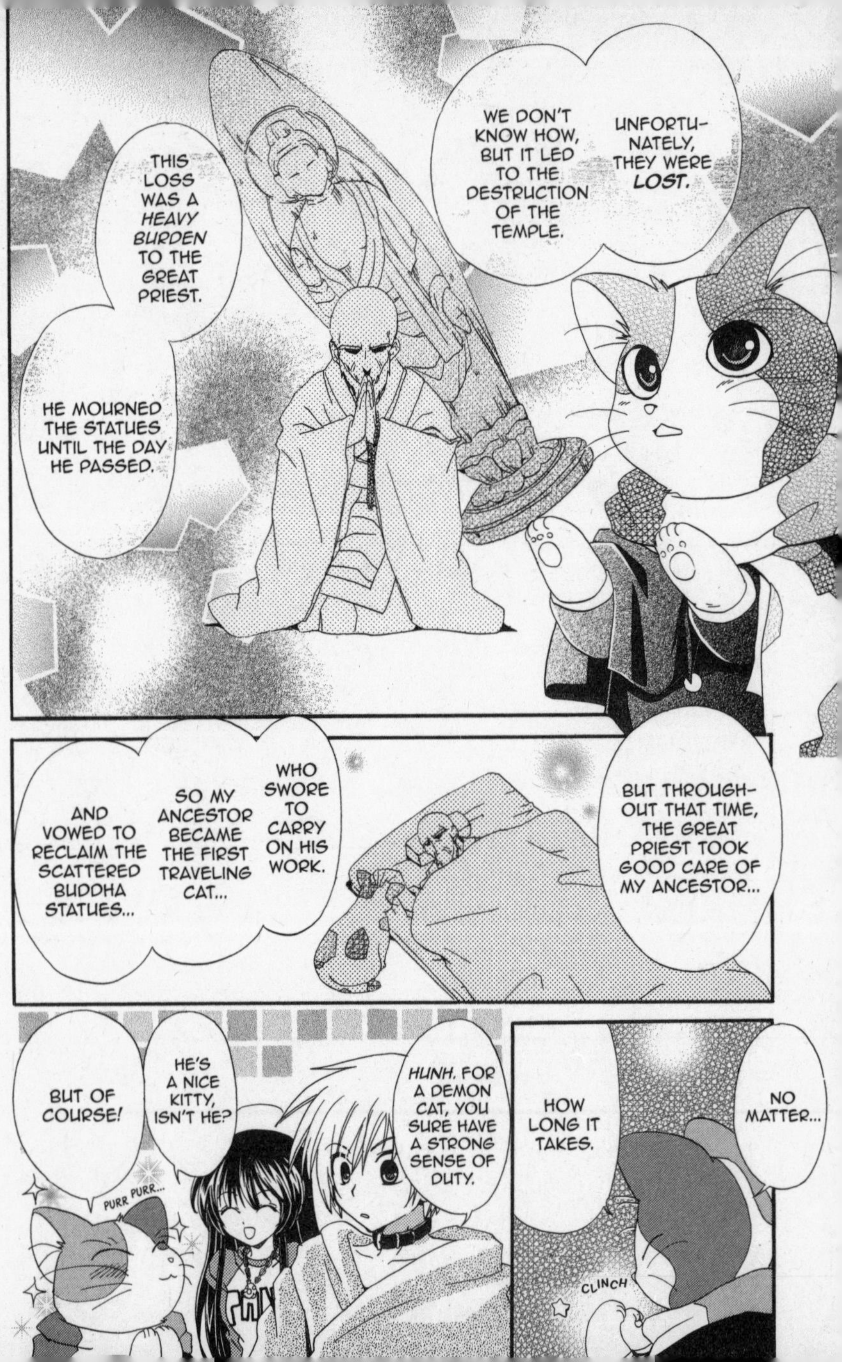
UNFORTUNATELY, THEY WERE *LOST.*
WE DON'T KNOW HOW, BUT IT LED TO THE DESTRUCTION OF THE TEMPLE.
THIS LOSS WAS A *HEAVY BURDEN* TO THE GREAT PRIEST.
HE MOURNED THE STATUES UNTIL THE DAY HE PASSED.
BUT THROUGHOUT THAT TIME, THE GREAT PRIEST TOOK GOOD CARE OF MY ANCESTOR...
WHO SWORE TO CARRY ON HIS WORK.
SO MY ANCESTOR BECAME THE FIRST TRAVELING CAT...
AND VOWED TO RECLAIM THE SCATTERED BUDDHA STATUES...
NO MATTER...
HOW LONG IT TAKES.
CLINCH
HUNH. FOR A DEMON CAT, YOU SURE HAVE A STRONG SENSE OF DUTY.
HE'S A NICE KITTY, ISN'T HE?
BUT OF COURSE!
PURR PURR...

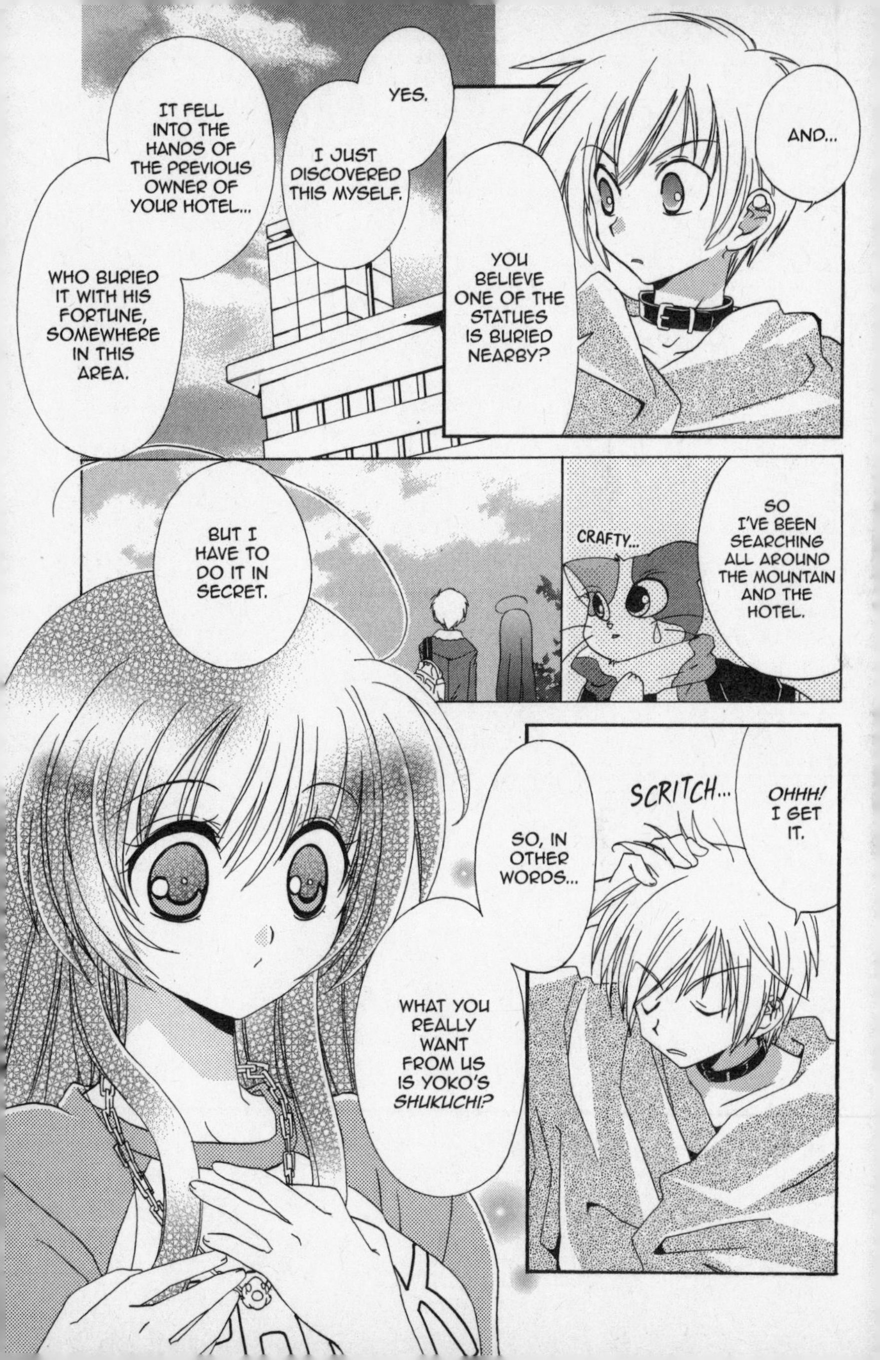
AND...
YOU BELIEVE ONE OF THE STATUES IS BURIED NEARBY?
YES.
I JUST DISCOVERED THIS MYSELF.
IT FELL INTO THE HANDS OF THE PREVIOUS OWNER OF YOUR HOTEL...
WHO BURIED IT WITH HIS FORTUNE, SOMEWHERE IN THIS AREA.
SO I'VE BEEN SEARCHING ALL AROUND THE MOUNTAIN AND THE HOTEL.
CRAFTY...
BUT I HAVE TO DO IT IN SECRET.
OHHH! I GET IT.
SCRITCH...
SO, IN OTHER WORDS...
WHAT YOU REALLY WANT FROM US IS YOKO'S *SHUKUCHI*?

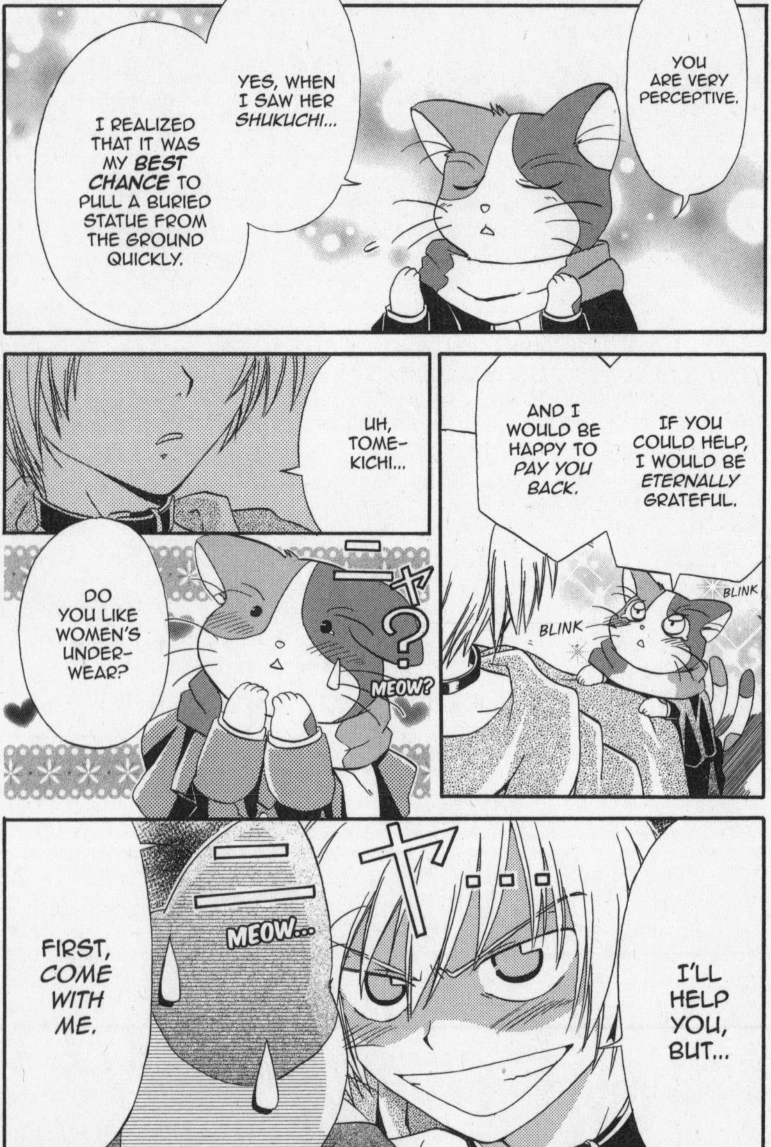
YOU ARE VERY PERCEPTIVE.
YES, WHEN I SAW HER *SHUKUCHI*...
I REALIZED THAT IT WAS MY **BEST CHANCE** TO PULL A BURIED STATUE FROM THE GROUND QUICKLY.
IF YOU COULD HELP, I WOULD BE *ETERNALLY* GRATEFUL.
AND I WOULD BE HAPPY TO *PAY YOU* BACK.
BLINK
BLINK
UH, TOME-KICHI...
MEOW?
DO YOU LIKE WOMEN'S UNDER-WEAR?
I'LL HELP YOU, BUT...
...
MEOW...
FIRST, COME WITH ME.

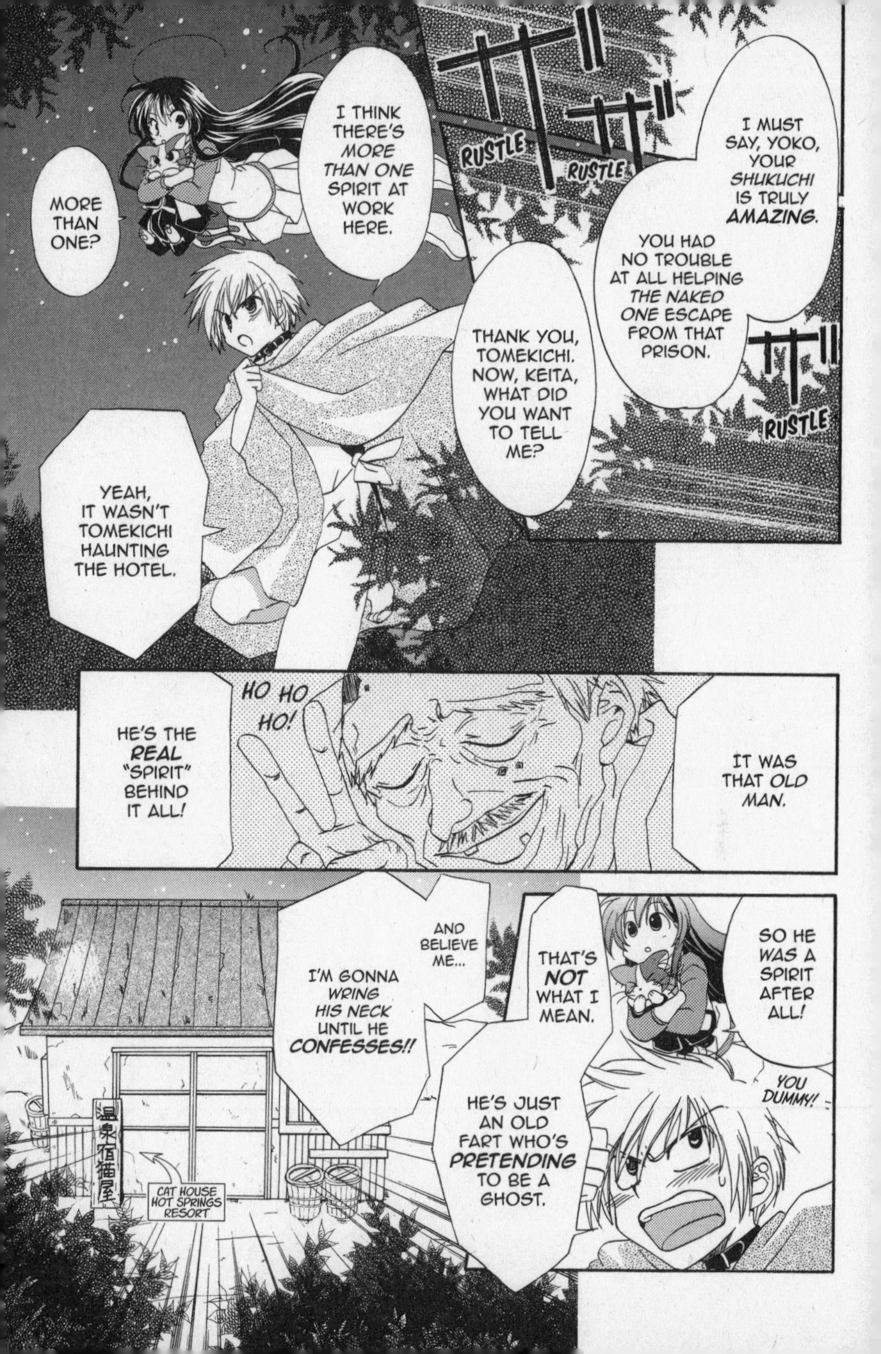
RUSTLE
RUSTLE
RUSTLE
I MUST SAY, YOKO, YOUR SHUKUCHI IS TRULY AMAZING.
YOU HAD NO TROUBLE AT ALL HELPING THE NAKED ONE ESCAPE FROM THAT PRISON.
THANK YOU, TOMEKICHI. NOW, KEITA, WHAT DID YOU WANT TO TELL ME?
I THINK THERE'S MORE THAN ONE SPIRIT AT WORK HERE.
MORE THAN ONE?
YEAH, IT WASN'T TOMEKICHI HAUNTING THE HOTEL.
IT WAS THAT OLD MAN.
HO HO HO!
HE'S THE REAL "SPIRIT" BEHIND IT ALL!
SO HE WAS A SPIRIT AFTER ALL!
THAT'S NOT WHAT I MEAN.
YOU DUMMY!
HE'S JUST AN OLD FART WHO'S PRETENDING TO BE A GHOST.
AND BELIEVE ME...
I'M GONNA WRING HIS NECK UNTIL HE CONFESSES!!
温泉宿猫屋
CAT HOUSE HOT SPRINGS RESORT

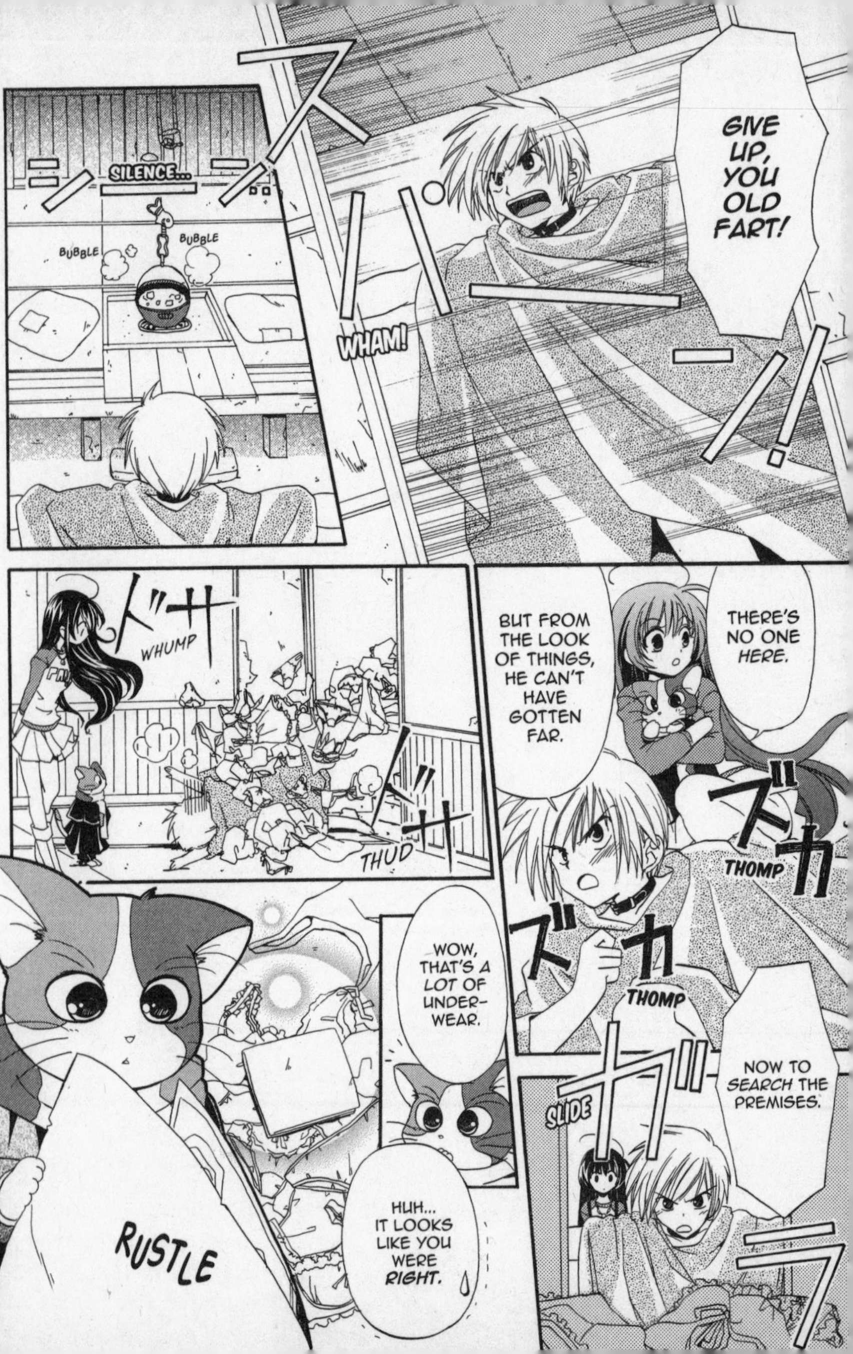

GIVE UP, YOU OLD FART!
WHAM!
SILENCE...
BUBBLE
BUBBLE
THERE'S NO ONE HERE.
BUT FROM THE LOOK OF THINGS, HE CAN'T HAVE GOTTEN FAR.
THOMP
THOMP
WHUMP
THUD
NOW TO SEARCH THE PREMISES.
SLIDE
WOW, THAT'S A LOT OF UNDERWEAR.
HUH... IT LOOKS LIKE YOU WERE RIGHT.
RUSTLE

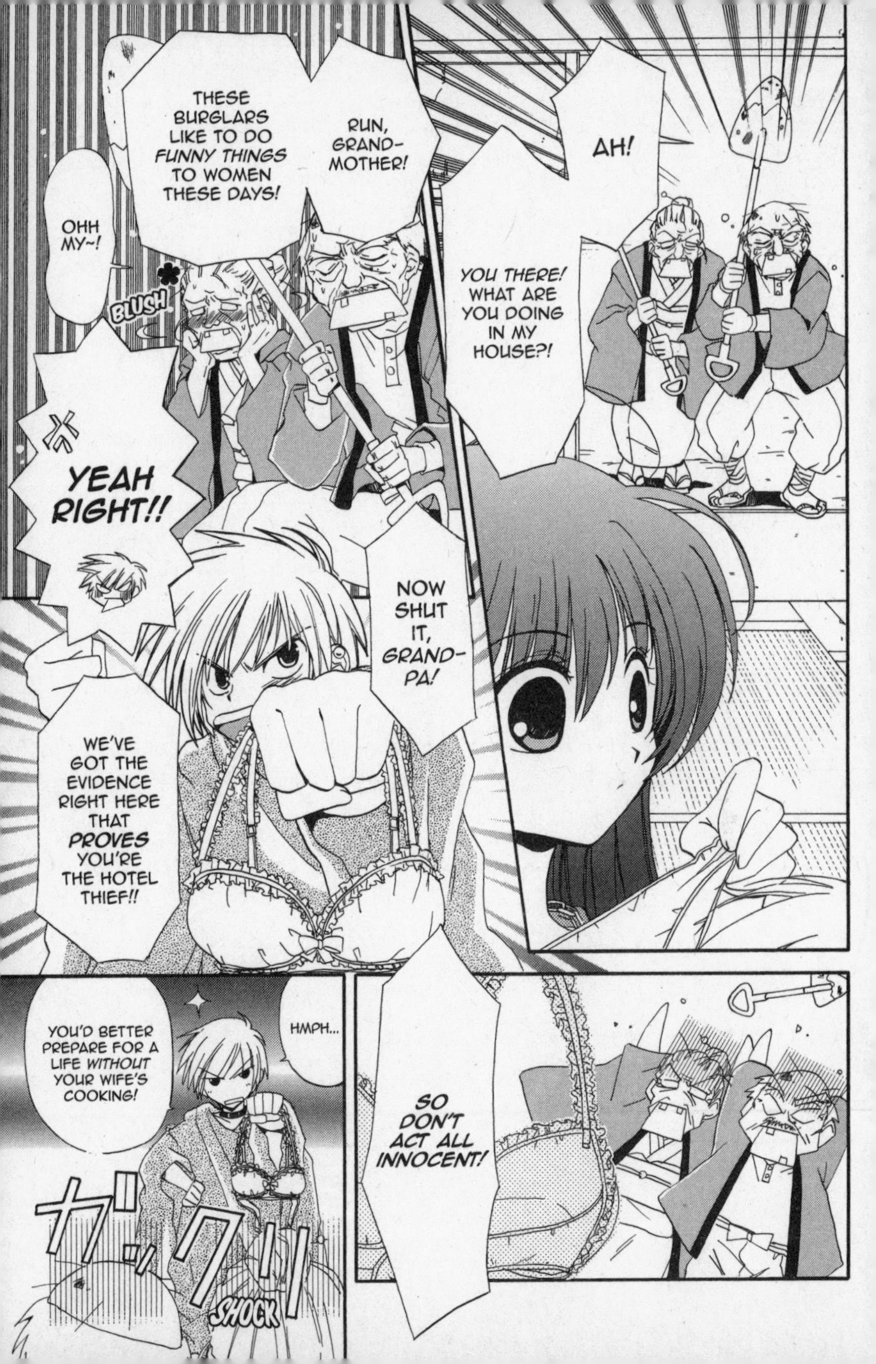
AH!
YOU THERE! WHAT ARE YOU DOING IN MY HOUSE?!
RUN, GRANDMOTHER!
THESE BURGLARS LIKE TO DO FUNNY THINGS TO WOMEN THESE DAYS!
OHH MY~!
BLUSH
YEAH RIGHT!!
NOW SHUT IT, GRANDPA!
WE'VE GOT THE EVIDENCE RIGHT HERE THAT PROVES YOU'RE THE HOTEL THIEF!!
SO DON'T ACT ALL INNOCENT!
HMPH...
YOU'D BETTER PREPARE FOR A LIFE WITHOUT YOUR WIFE'S COOKING!
SHOCK

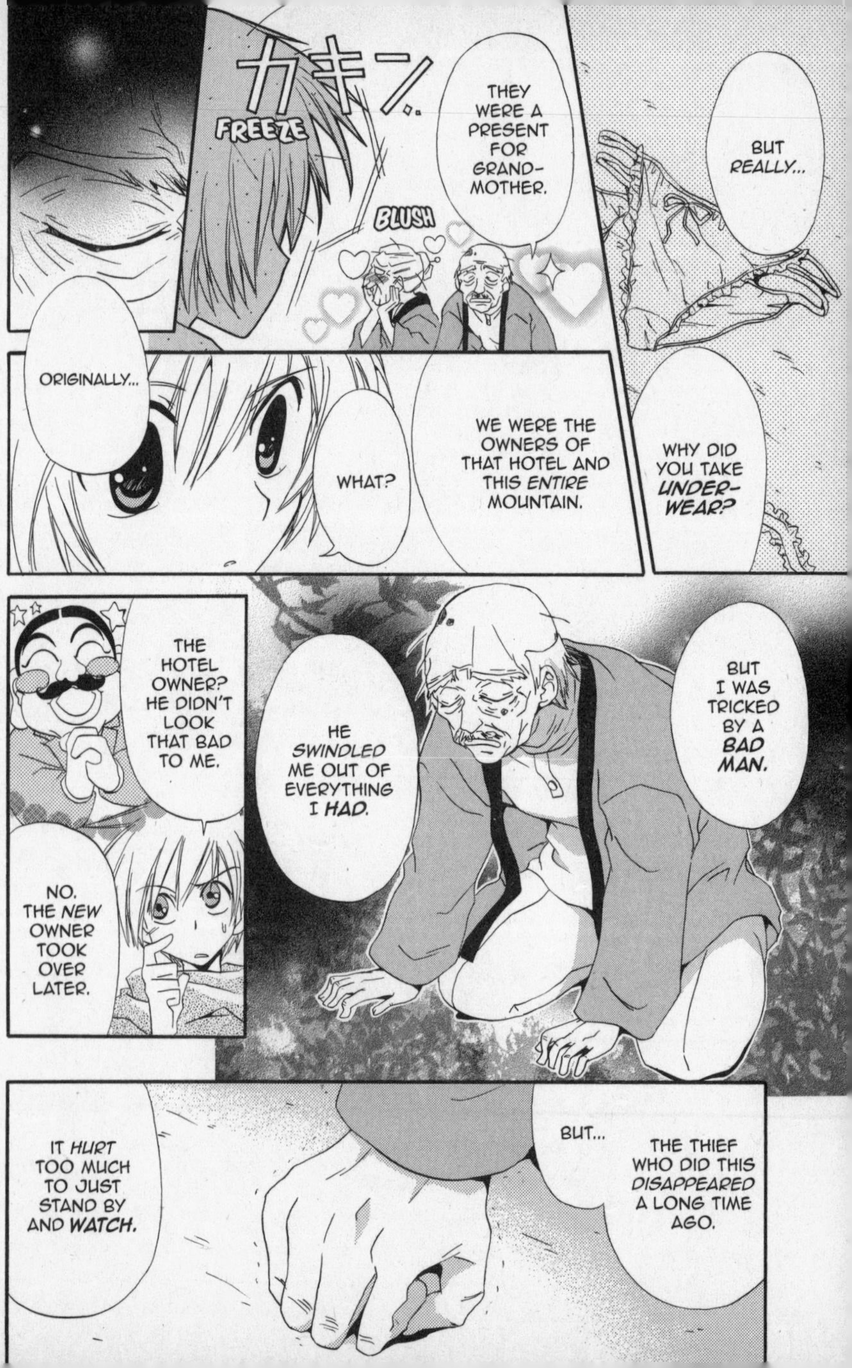

BUT REALLY...
WHY DID YOU TAKE UNDERWEAR?
THEY WERE A PRESENT FOR GRAND-MOTHER.
BLUSH
カキーン。
FREEZE
ORIGINALLY...
WE WERE THE OWNERS OF THAT HOTEL AND THIS ENTIRE MOUNTAIN.
WHAT?
BUT I WAS TRICKED BY A BAD MAN.
HE SWINDLED ME OUT OF EVERYTHING I HAD.
THE HOTEL OWNER? HE DIDN'T LOOK THAT BAD TO ME.
NO. THE NEW OWNER TOOK OVER LATER.
THE THIEF WHO DID THIS DISAPPEARED A LONG TIME AGO.
BUT...
IT HURT TOO MUCH TO JUST STAND BY AND WATCH.

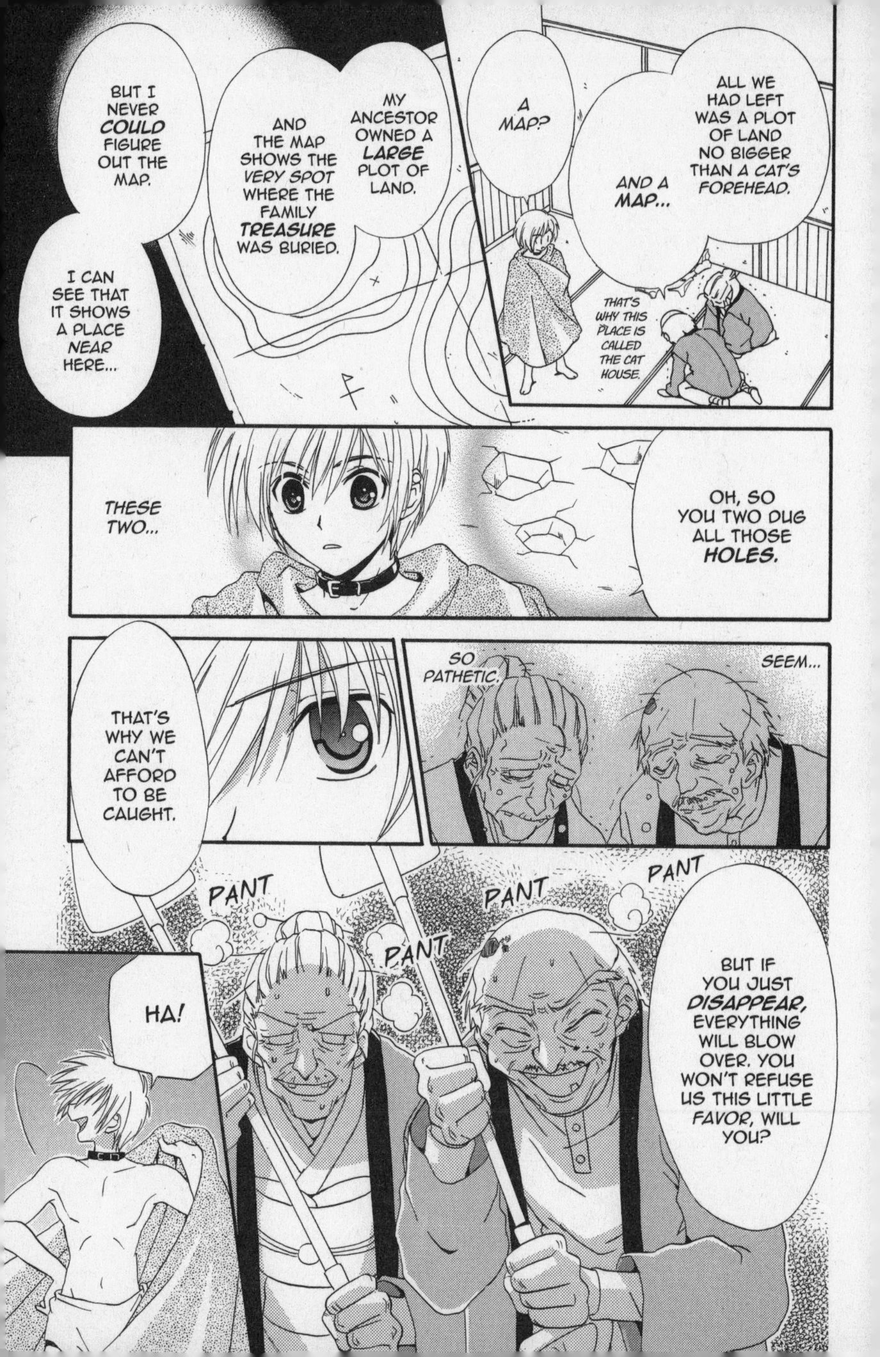
ALL WE HAD LEFT WAS A PLOT OF LAND NO BIGGER THAN A CAT'S FOREHEAD.
AND A MAP...
THAT'S WHY THIS PLACE IS CALLED THE CAT HOUSE.
A MAP?
MY ANCESTOR OWNED A LARGE PLOT OF LAND.
AND THE MAP SHOWS THE VERY SPOT WHERE THE FAMILY TREASURE WAS BURIED.
BUT I NEVER COULD FIGURE OUT THE MAP.
I CAN SEE THAT IT SHOWS A PLACE NEAR HERE...
OH, SO YOU TWO DUG ALL THOSE HOLES.
THESE TWO...
SEEM...
SO PATHETIC.
THAT'S WHY WE CAN'T AFFORD TO BE CAUGHT.
PANT
PANT
PANT
PANT
BUT IF YOU JUST DISAPPEAR, EVERYTHING WILL BLOW OVER. YOU WON'T REFUSE US THIS LITTLE FAVOR, WILL YOU?
HA!

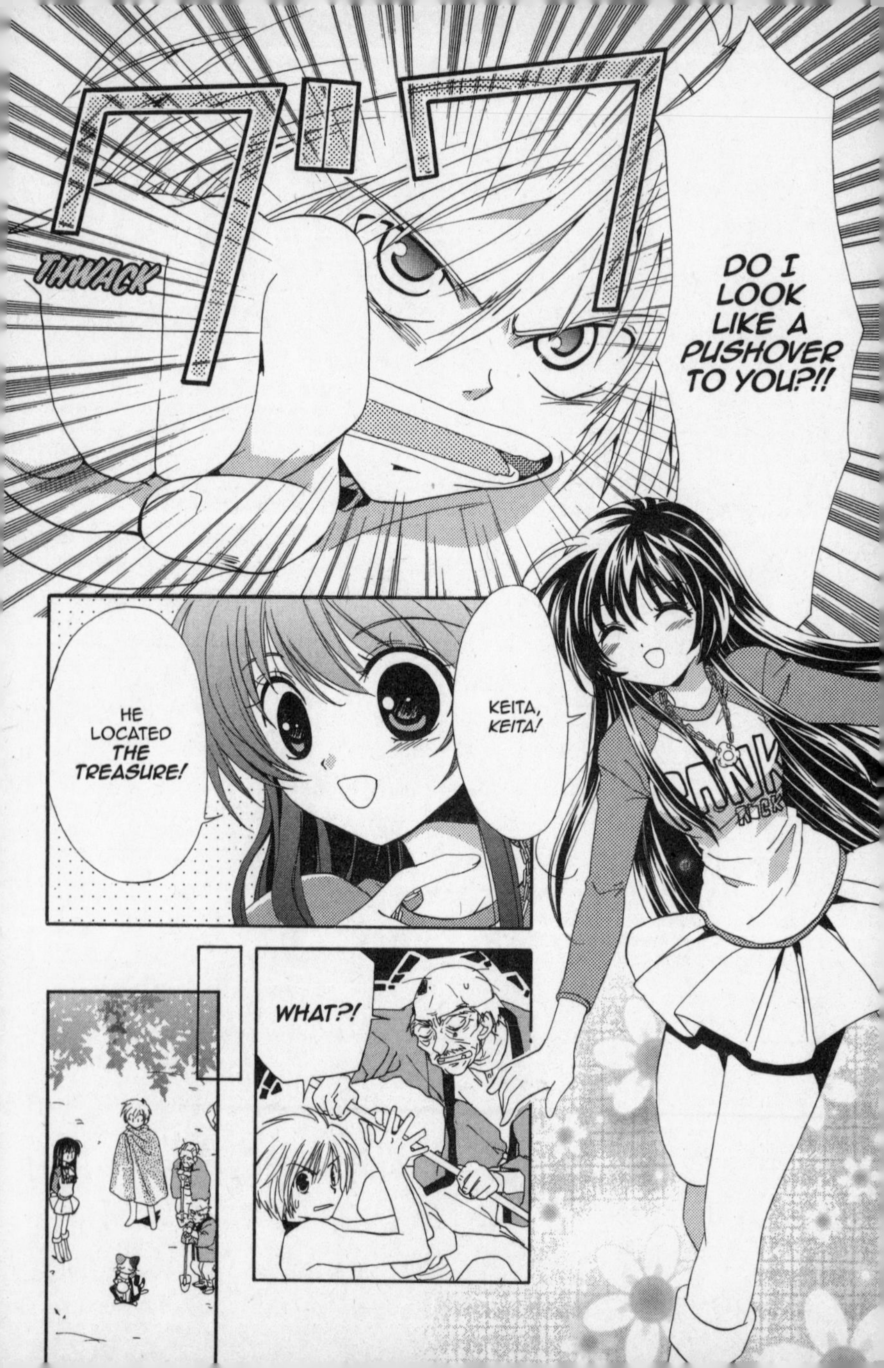
DO I LOOK LIKE A PUSHOVER TO YOU?!!
THWACK
KEITA, KEITA!
HE LOCATED THE TREASURE!
WHAT?!

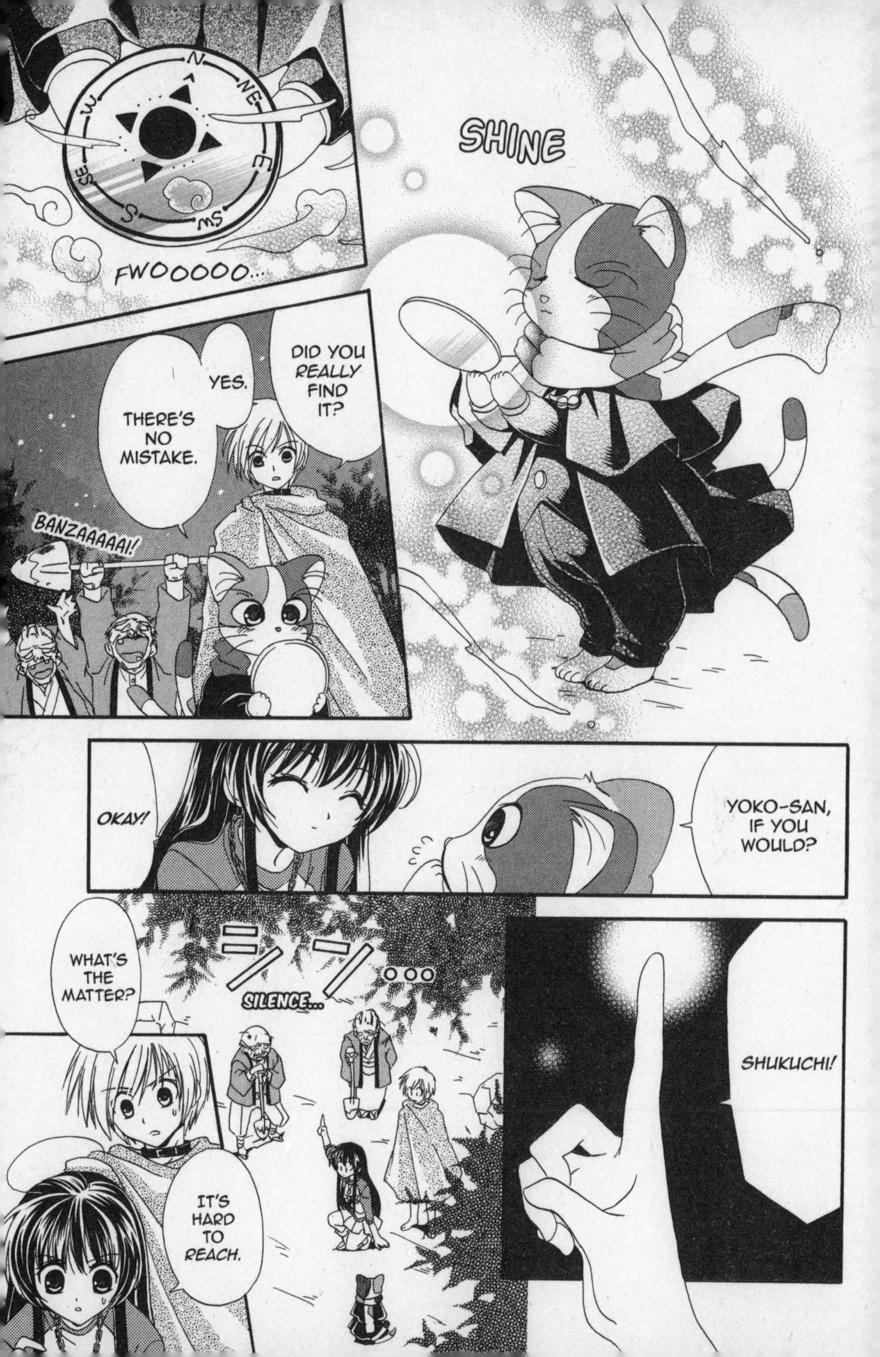
SHINE
FWOOOOO...
N
NE
E
SW
S
SE
W
DID YOU REALLY FIND IT?
YES.
THERE'S NO MISTAKE.
BANZAAAAAI!
YOKO-SAN, IF YOU WOULD?
OKAY!
SHUKUCHI!
...
SILENCE...
WHAT'S THE MATTER?
IT'S HARD TO REACH.

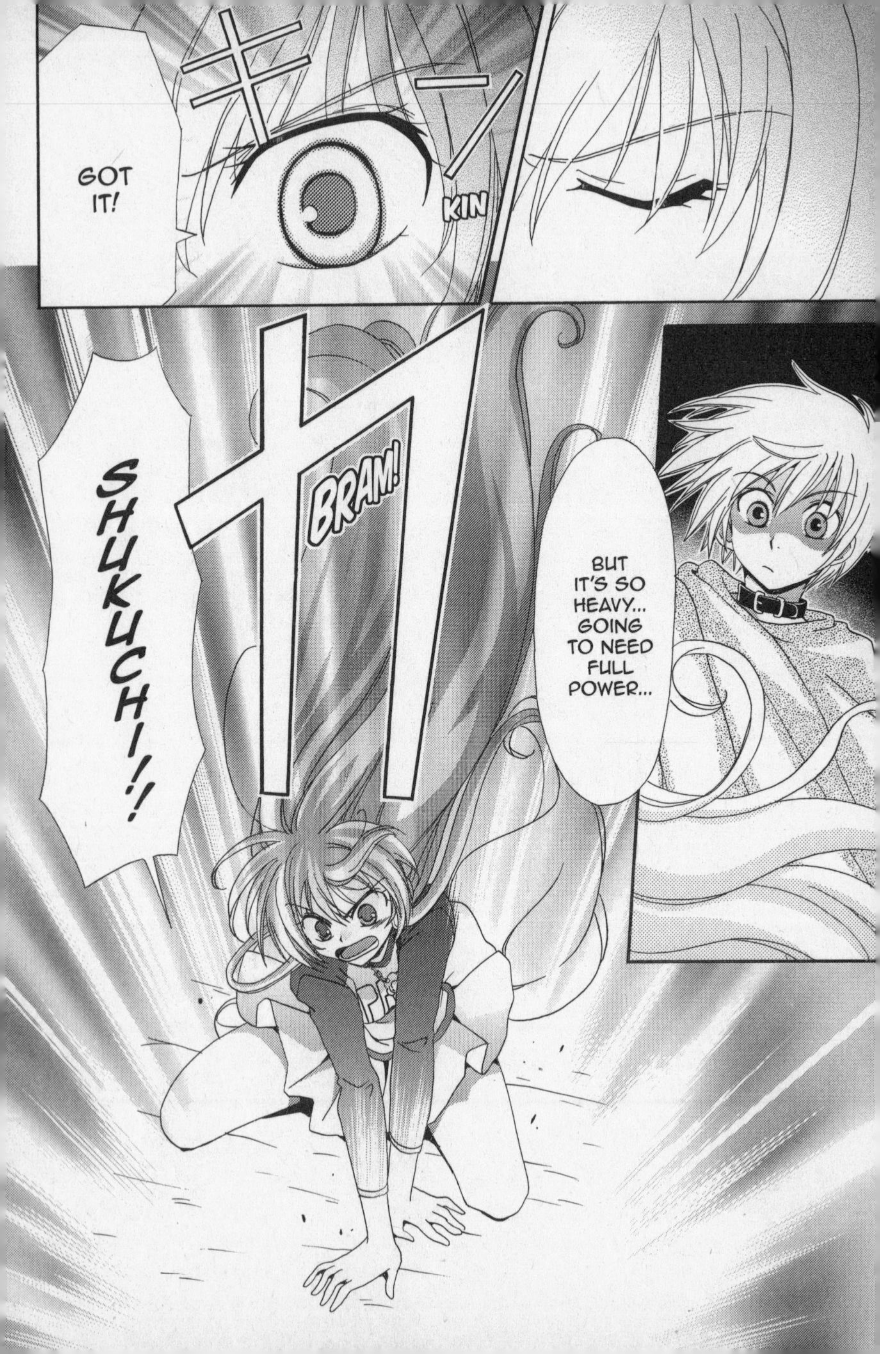

KIN
GOT IT!
BUT IT'S SO HEAVY... GOING TO NEED FULL POWER...
BRAM!
SHUKUCHI!!!

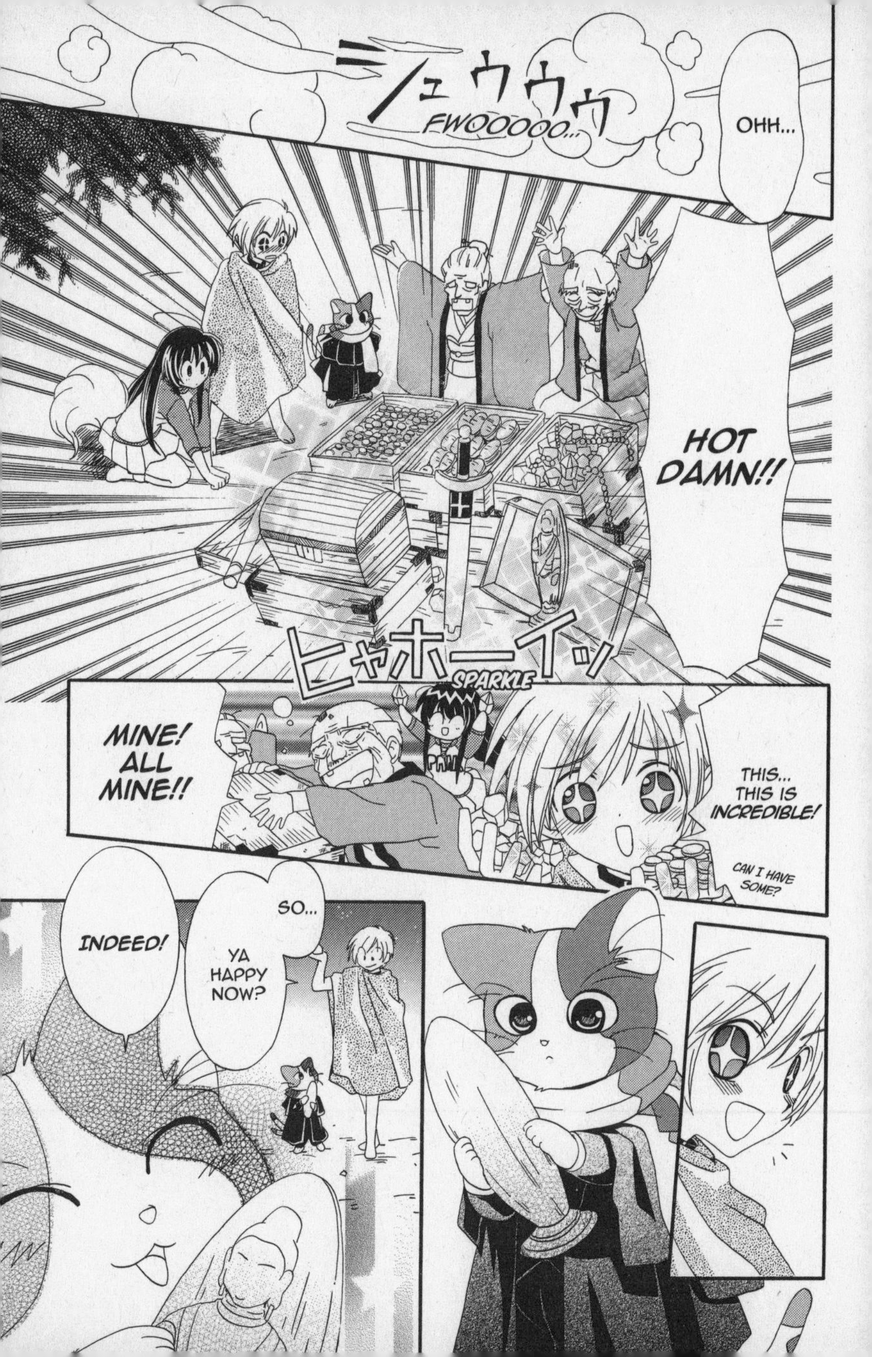

OHH...
シュウウウ
FWOOOOO...
HOT DAMN!!
ヒャホーイッ
THIS... THIS IS INCREDIBLE!
CAN I HAVE SOME?
SPARKLE
MINE! ALL MINE!!
SO...
YA HAPPY NOW?
INDEED!

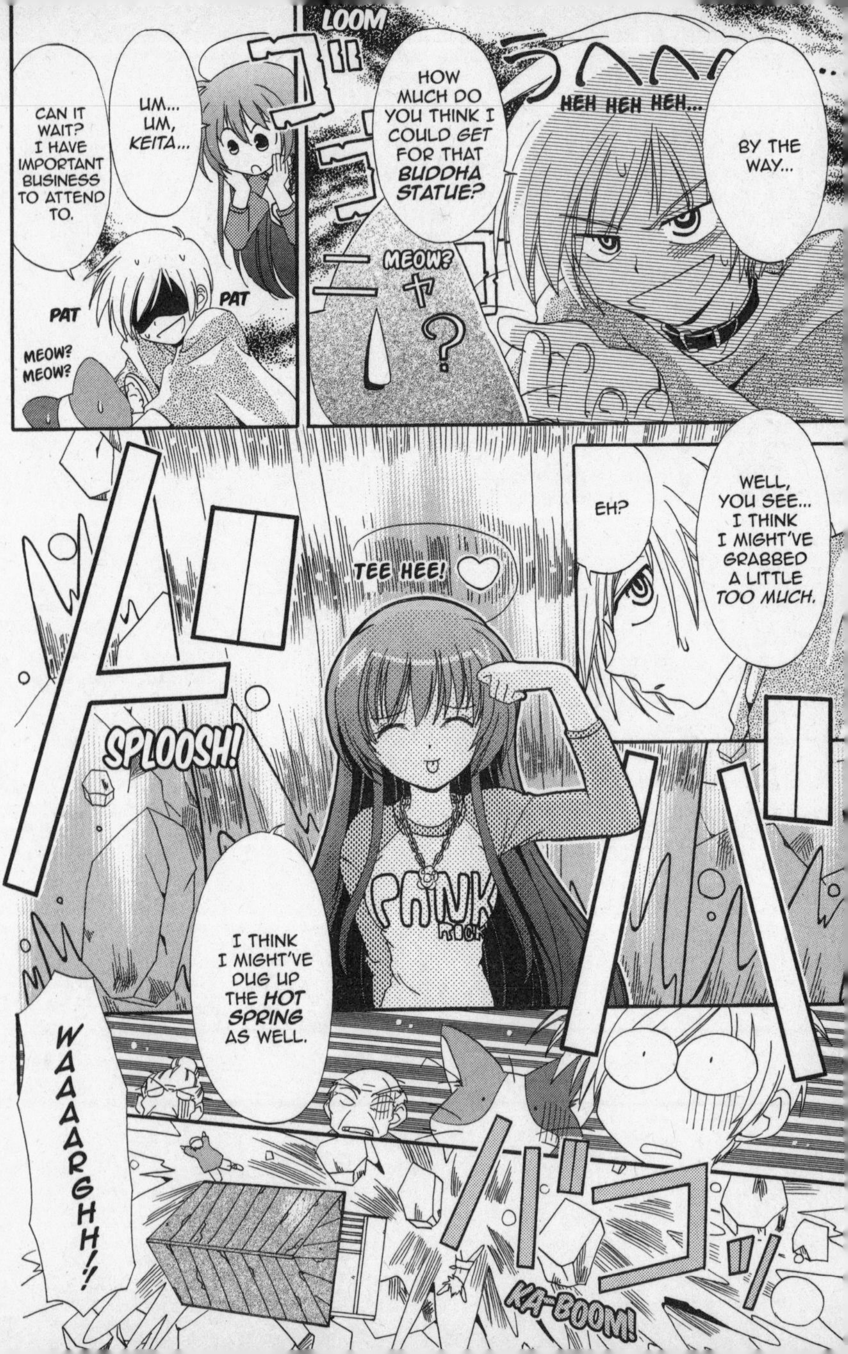
LOOM
BY THE WAY...
HEH HEH HEH...
HOW MUCH DO YOU THINK I COULD GET FOR THAT *BUDDHA STATUE?*
MEOW?
UM... UM, KEITA...
CAN IT WAIT? I HAVE IMPORTANT BUSINESS TO ATTEND TO.
PAT
PAT
MEOW? MEOW?
WELL, YOU SEE... I THINK I MIGHT'VE GRABBED A LITTLE *TOO MUCH.*
EH?
TEE HEE!
SPLOOSH!
I THINK I MIGHT'VE DUG UP THE *HOT SPRING* AS WELL.
WAAAAARGHH!!
KA-BOOM!

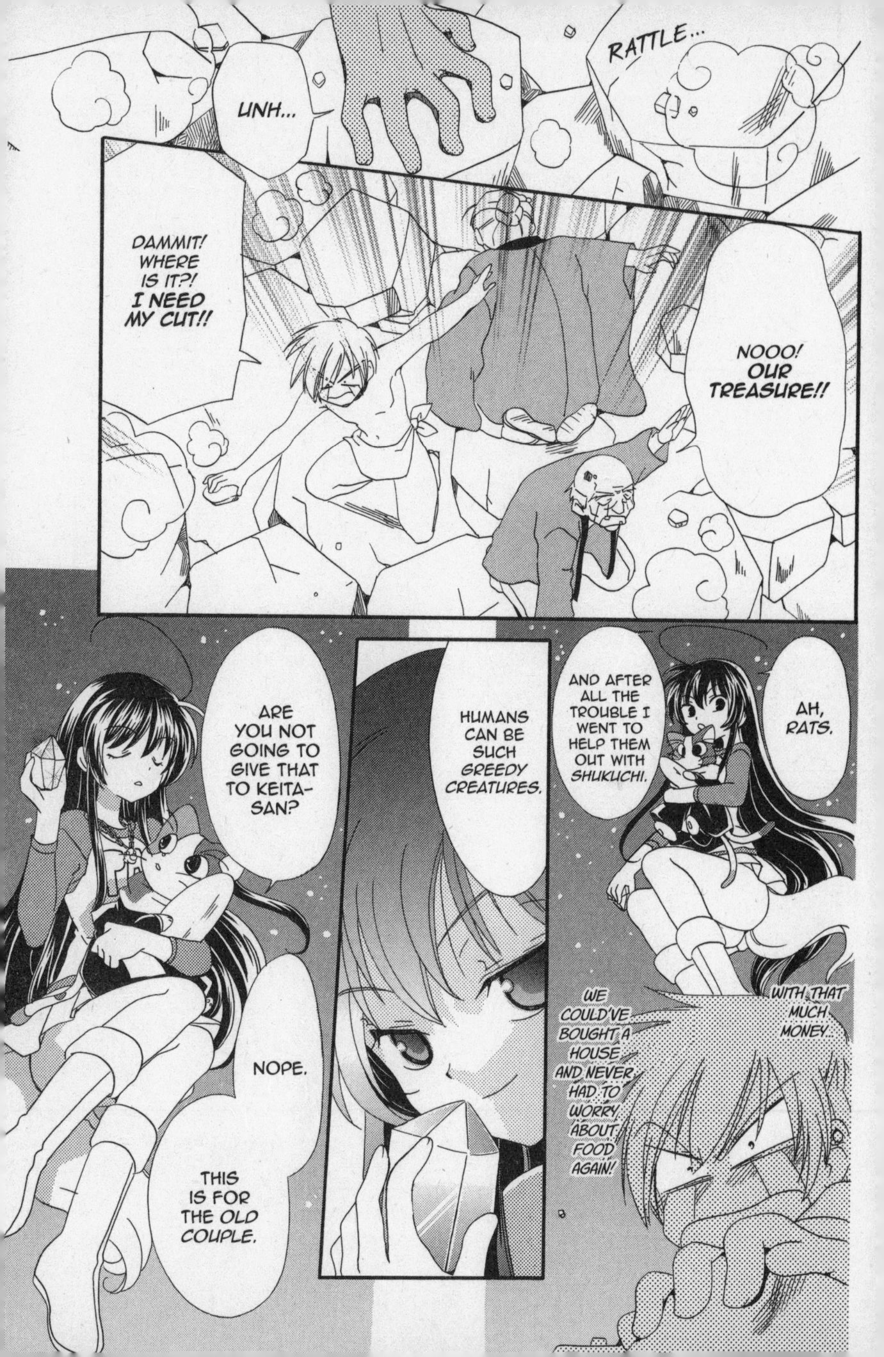
RATTLE...
UNH...
NOOO! OUR TREASURE!!
DAMMIT! WHERE IS IT?! I NEED MY CUT!!
AH, RATS.
AND AFTER ALL THE TROUBLE I WENT TO HELP THEM OUT WITH SHUKUCHI.
WITH THAT MUCH MONEY...
WE COULD'VE BOUGHT A HOUSE AND NEVER HAD TO WORRY ABOUT FOOD AGAIN!
HUMANS CAN BE SUCH GREEDY CREATURES.
ARE YOU NOT GOING TO GIVE THAT TO KEITA-SAN?
NOPE.
THIS IS FOR THE OLD COUPLE.

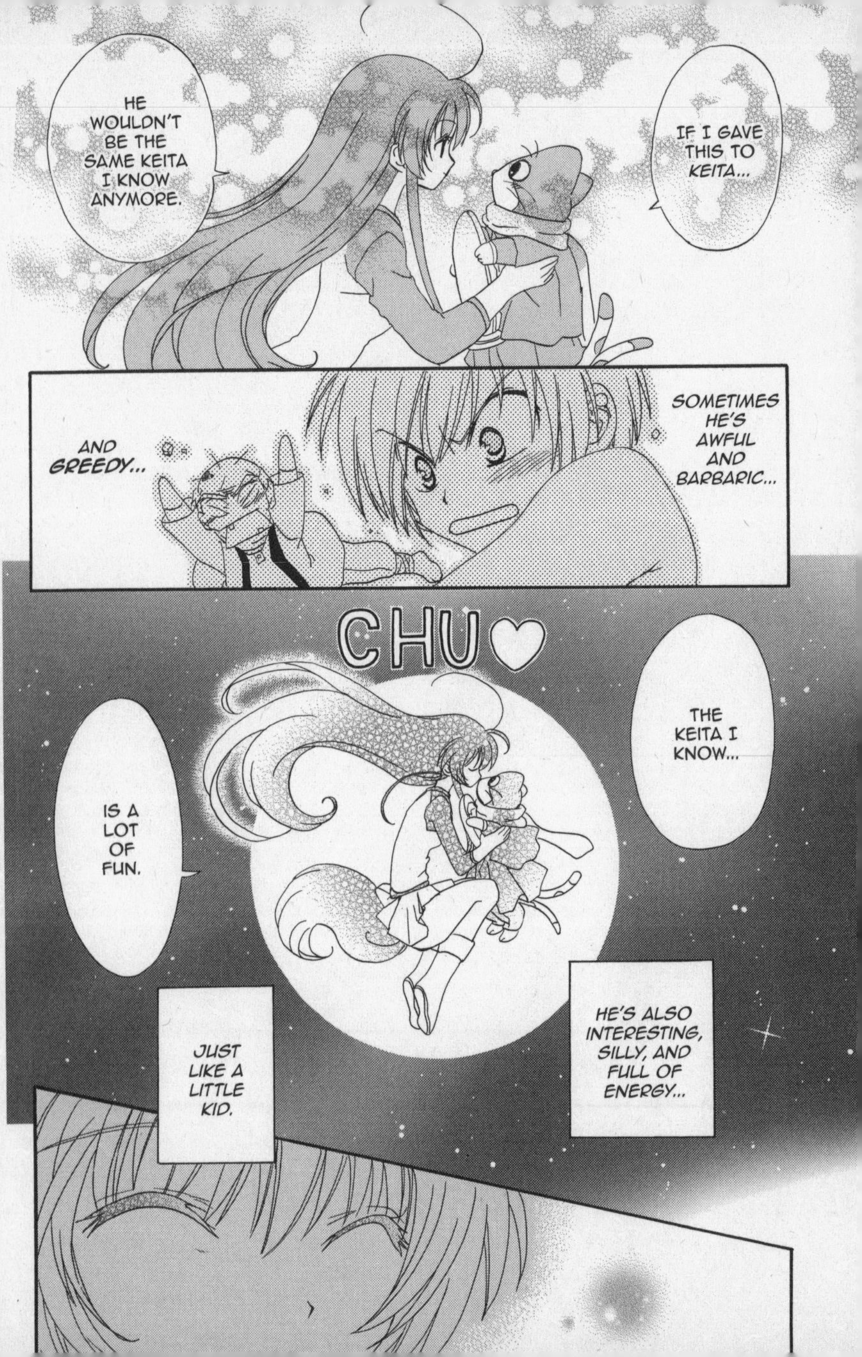
IF I GAVE THIS TO KEITA...
HE WOULDN'T BE THE SAME KEITA I KNOW ANYMORE.
SOMETIMES HE'S AWFUL AND BARBARIC...
AND *GREEDY*...
CHU♥
THE KEITA I KNOW...
IS A LOT OF FUN.
HE'S ALSO INTERESTING, SILLY, AND FULL OF ENERGY...
JUST LIKE A LITTLE KID.

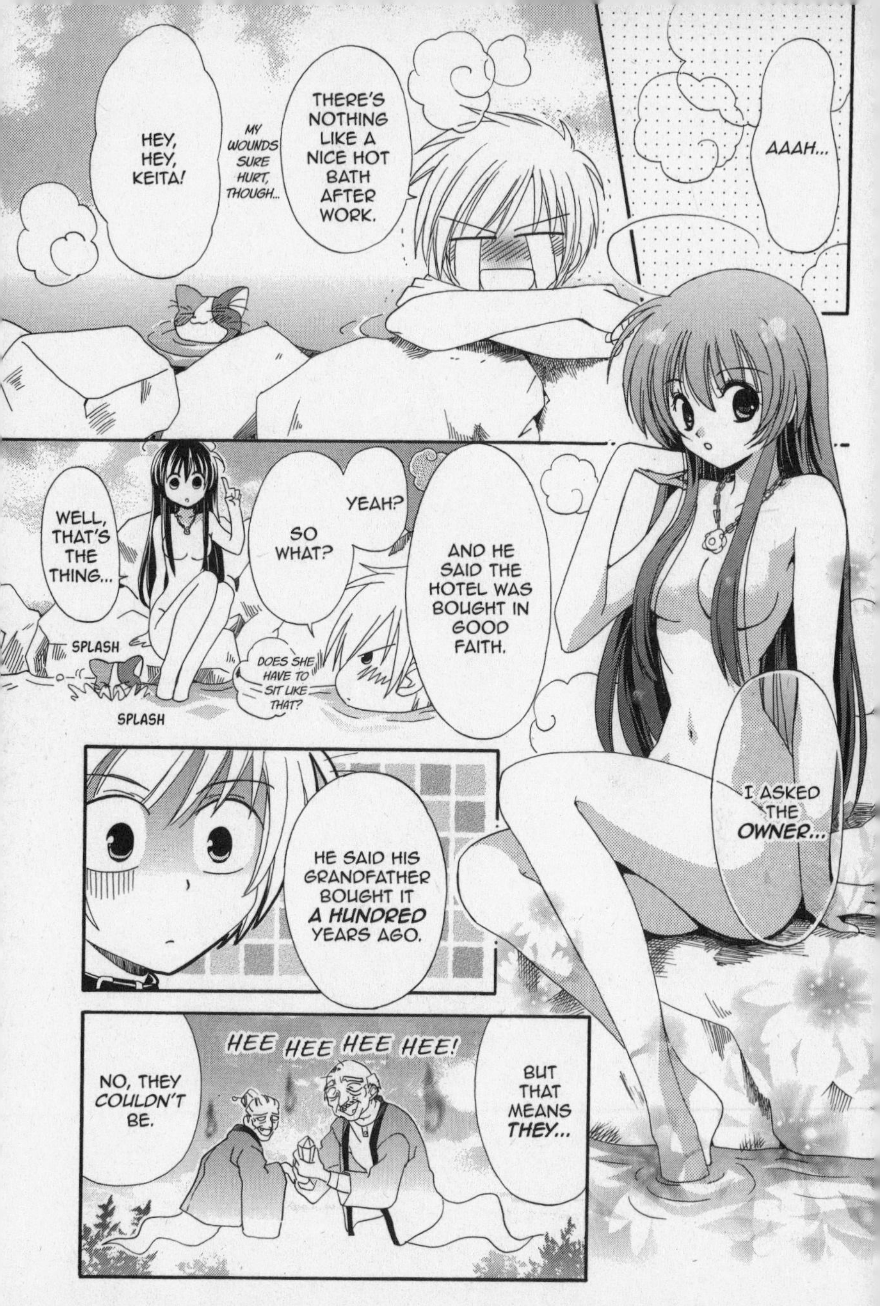
AAAH...
THERE'S NOTHING LIKE A NICE HOT BATH AFTER WORK.
MY WOUNDS SURE HURT, THOUGH...
HEY, HEY, KEITA!
I ASKED THE OWNER...
AND HE SAID THE HOTEL WAS BOUGHT IN GOOD FAITH.
YEAH? SO WHAT?
DOES SHE HAVE TO SIT LIKE THAT?
WELL, THAT'S THE THING...
SPLASH
SPLASH
HE SAID HIS GRANDFATHER BOUGHT IT A HUNDRED YEARS AGO.
BUT THAT MEANS THEY...
HEE HEE HEE HEE!
NO, THEY COULDN'T BE.

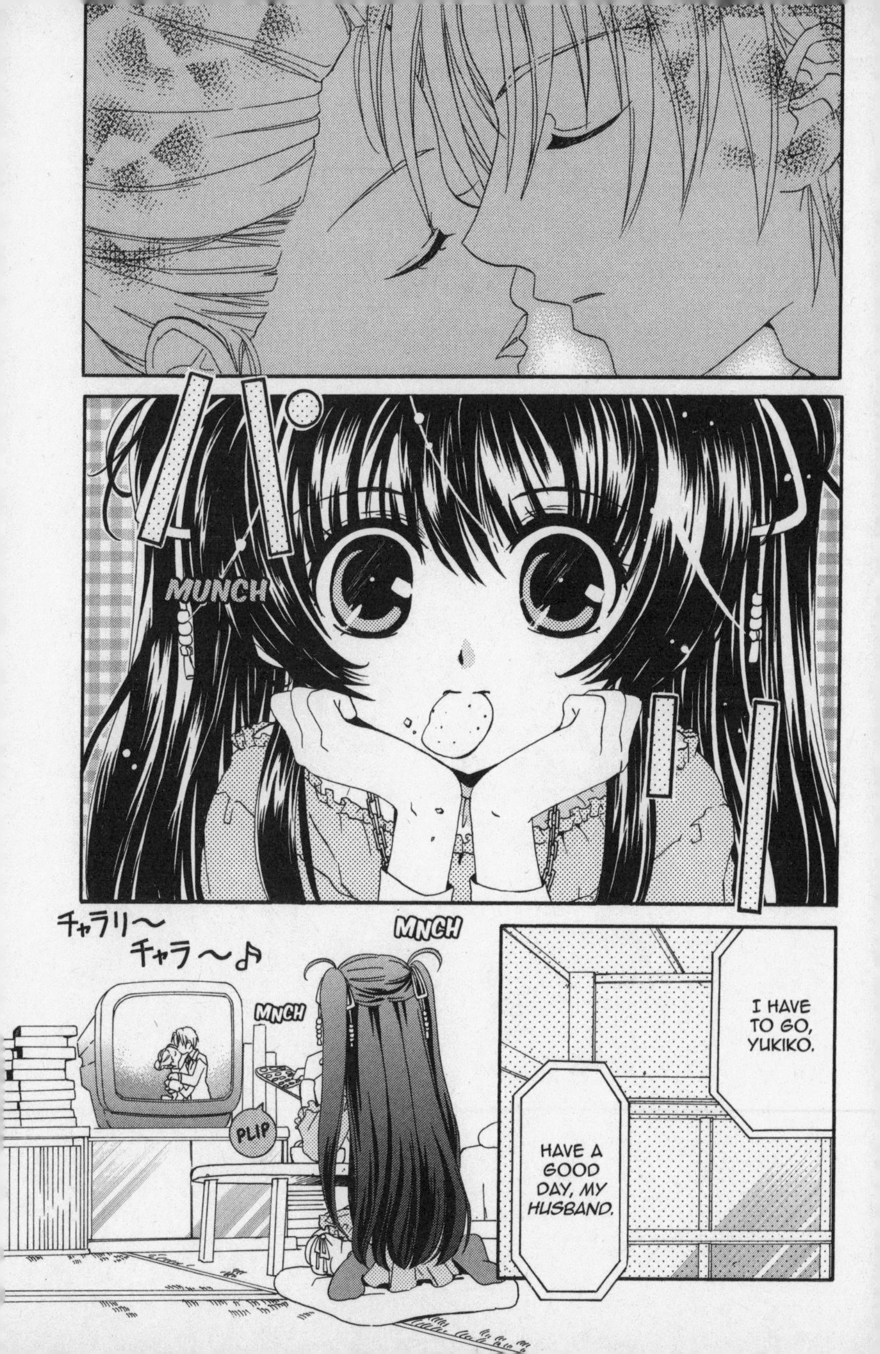
MUNCH
I HAVE TO GO, YUKIKO.
HAVE A GOOD DAY, MY HUSBAND.
チャラリ～
チャラ～♪
MNCH
MNCH
PLIP

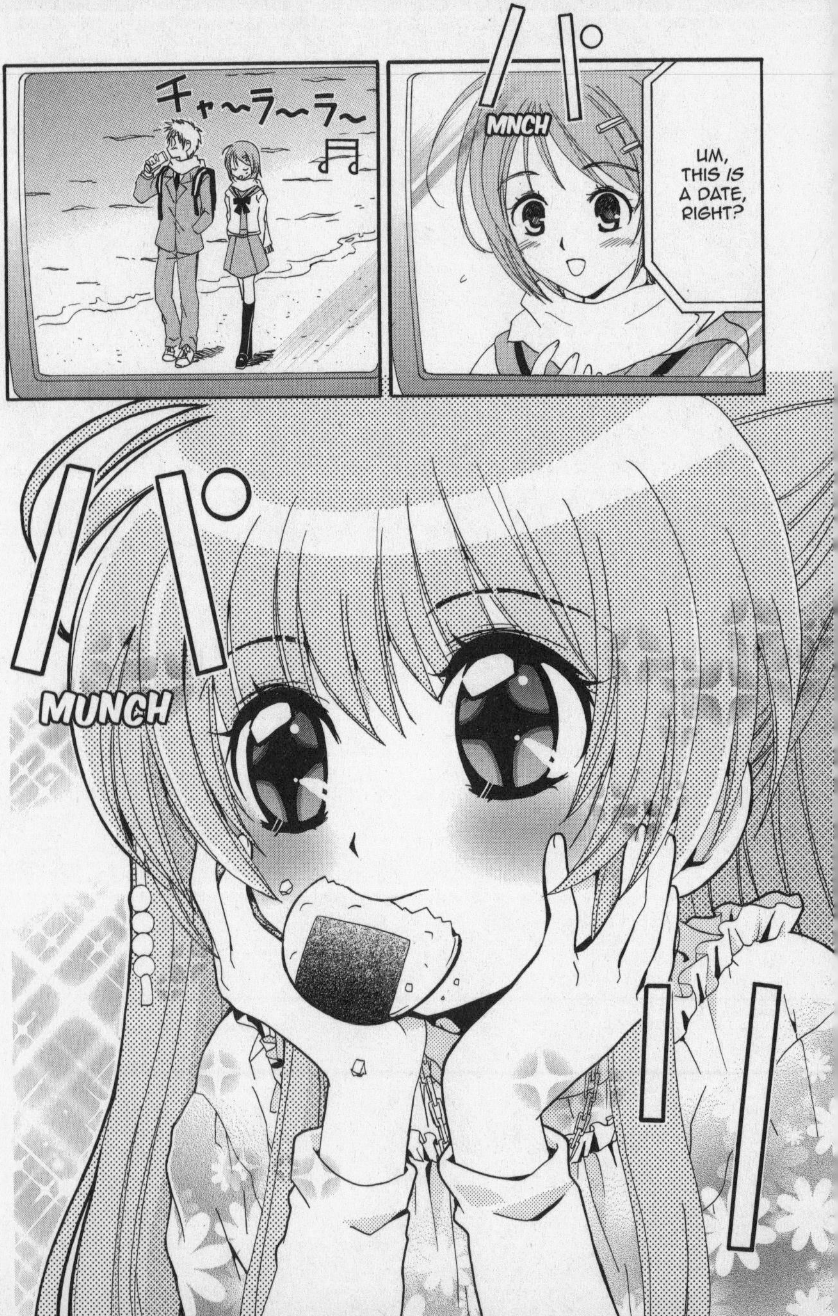
MNCH
UM, THIS IS A DATE, RIGHT?
チャ～ラ～ラ～
MUNCH

Step.4 A Date with Yoko

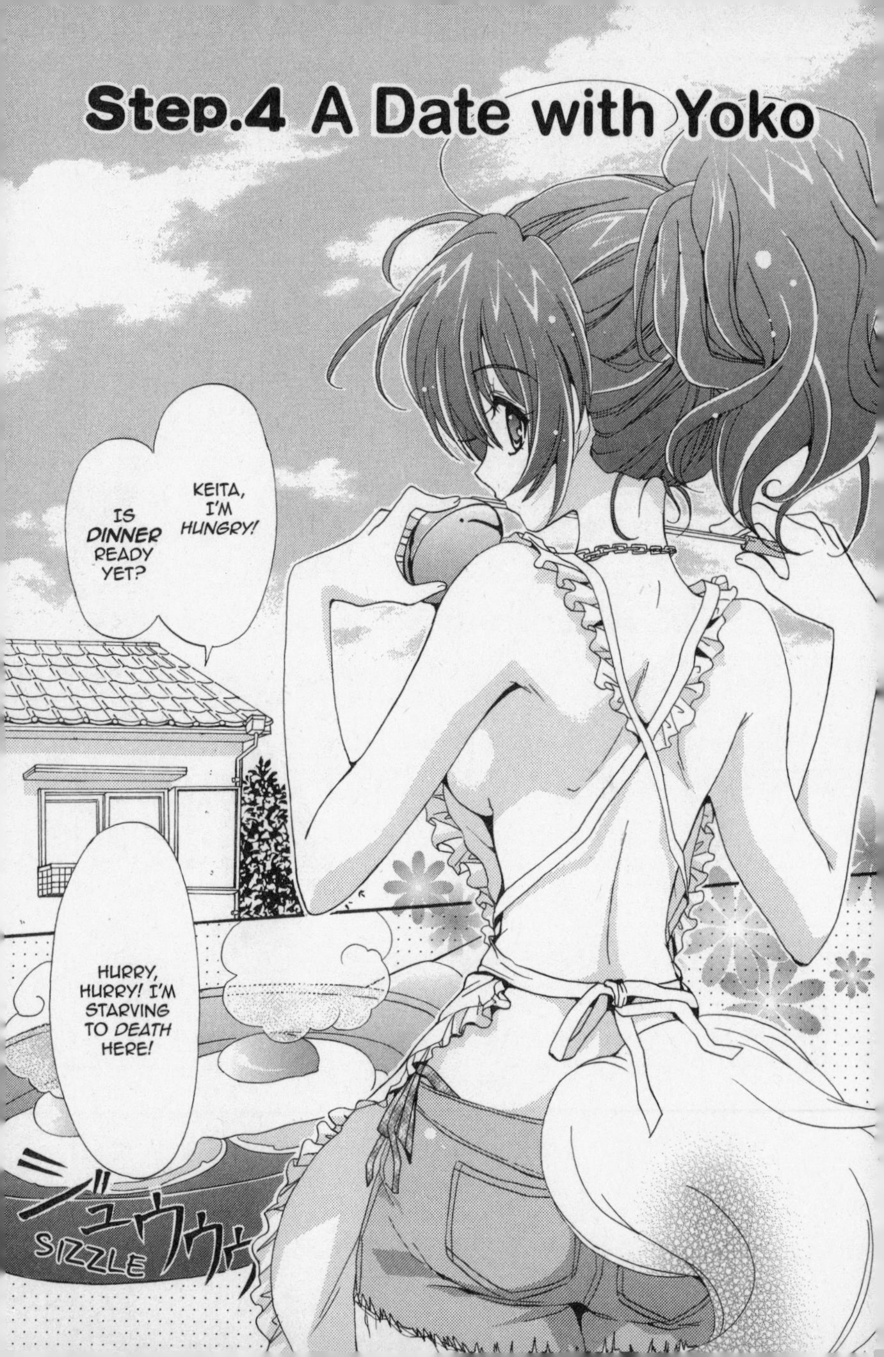
KEITA, I'M HUNGRY!
IS DINNER READY YET?
HURRY, HURRY! I'M STARVING TO DEATH HERE!
ジュウウウ
SIZZLE

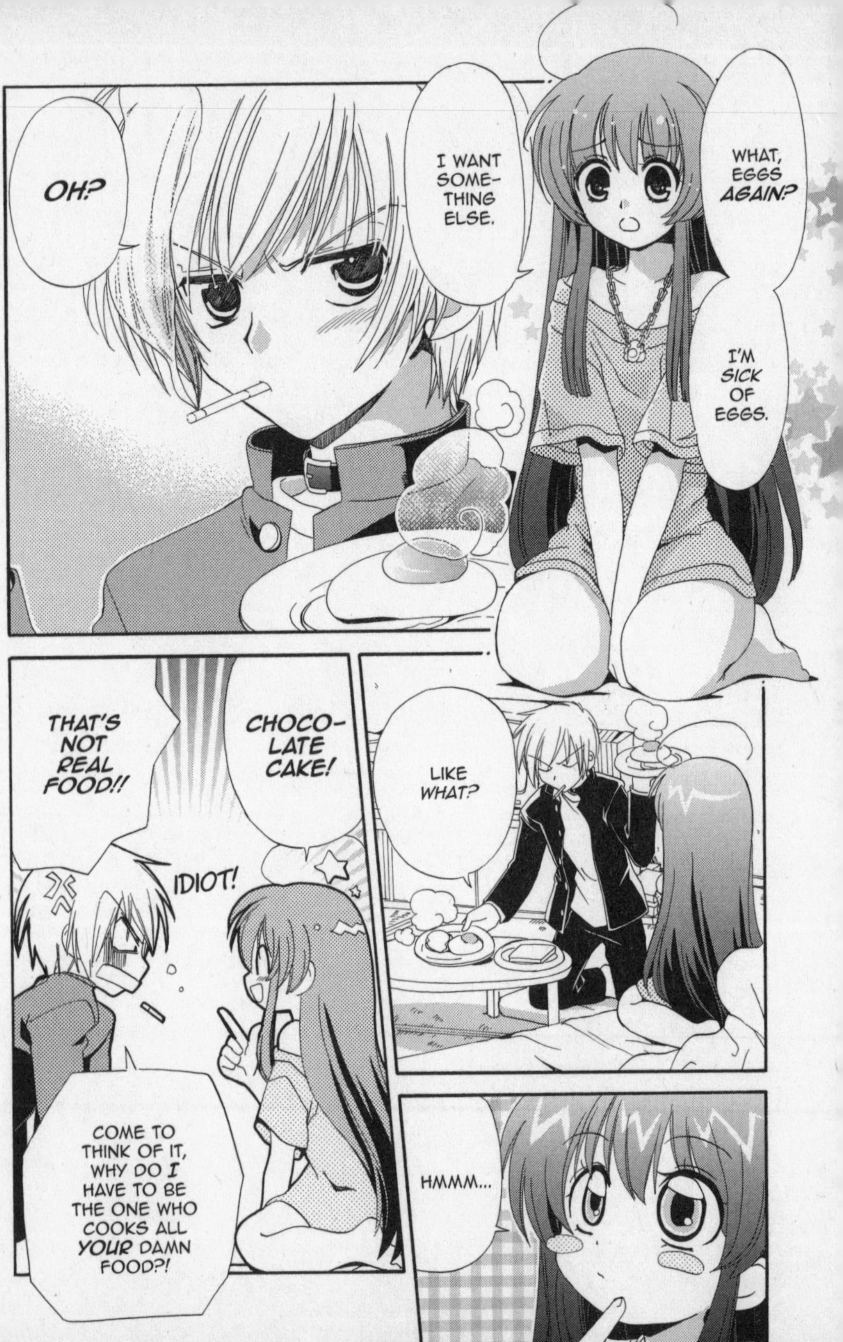
WHAT, EGGS AGAIN?
I'M SICK OF EGGS.
I WANT SOME-THING ELSE.
OH?
LIKE WHAT?
HMMM...
CHOCO-LATE CAKE!
THAT'S NOT REAL FOOD!!
IDIOT!
COME TO THINK OF IT, WHY DO I HAVE TO BE THE ONE WHO COOKS ALL YOUR DAMN FOOD?!

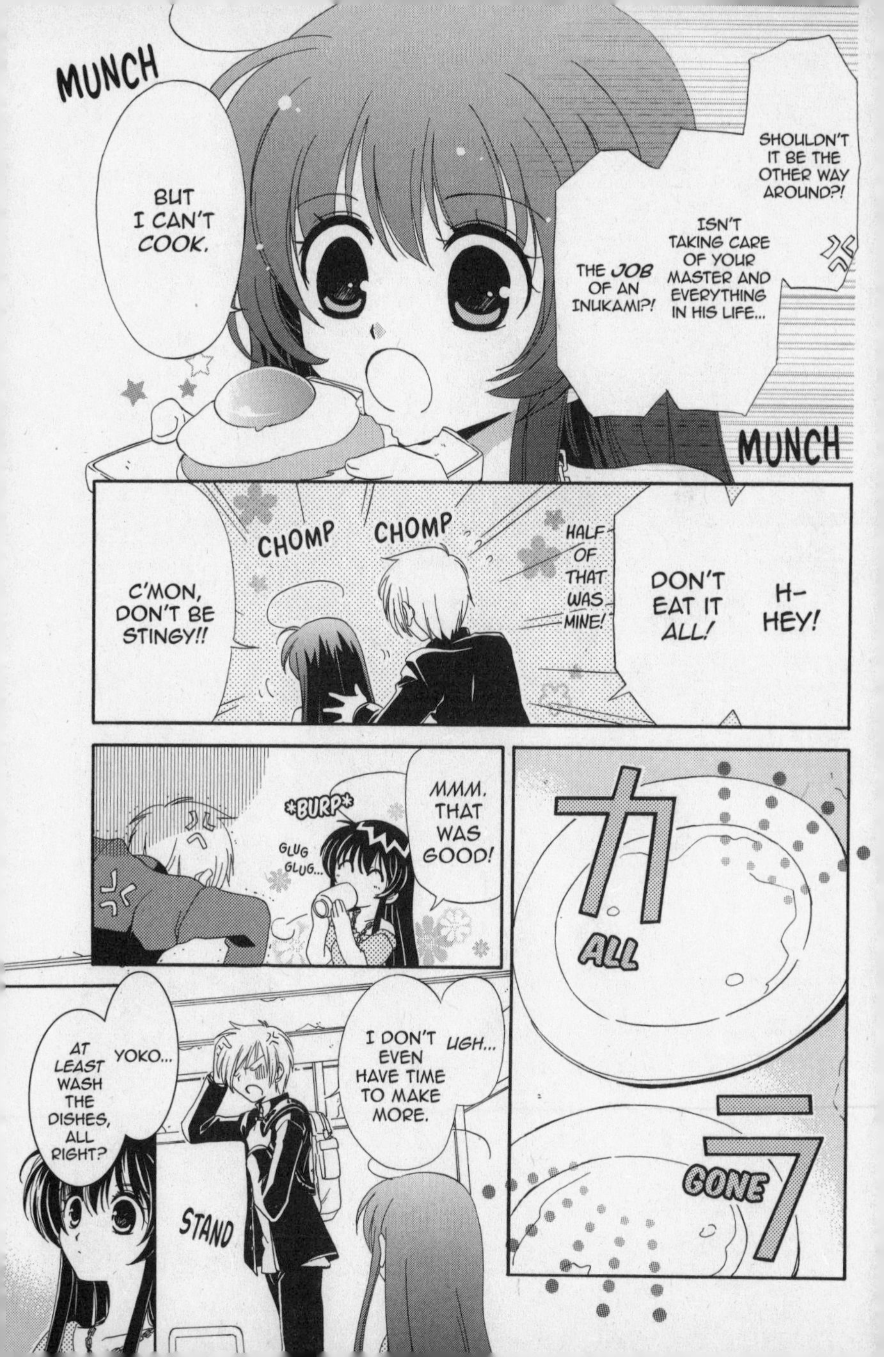
ISN'T TAKING CARE OF YOUR MASTER AND EVERYTHING IN HIS LIFE...
THE *JOB* OF AN INUKAMI?!
SHOULDN'T IT BE THE OTHER WAY AROUND?!
MUNCH
BUT I CAN'T COOK.
MUNCH
H-HEY!
DON'T EAT IT ALL!
HALF OF THAT WAS MINE!
CHOMP
CHOMP
C'MON, DON'T BE STINGY!!
カ
ALL
ラ
GONE
MMM. THAT WAS GOOD!
BURP
GLUG GLUG...
UGH...
I DON'T EVEN HAVE TIME TO MAKE MORE.
STAND
YOKO...
AT LEAST WASH THE DISHES, ALL RIGHT?

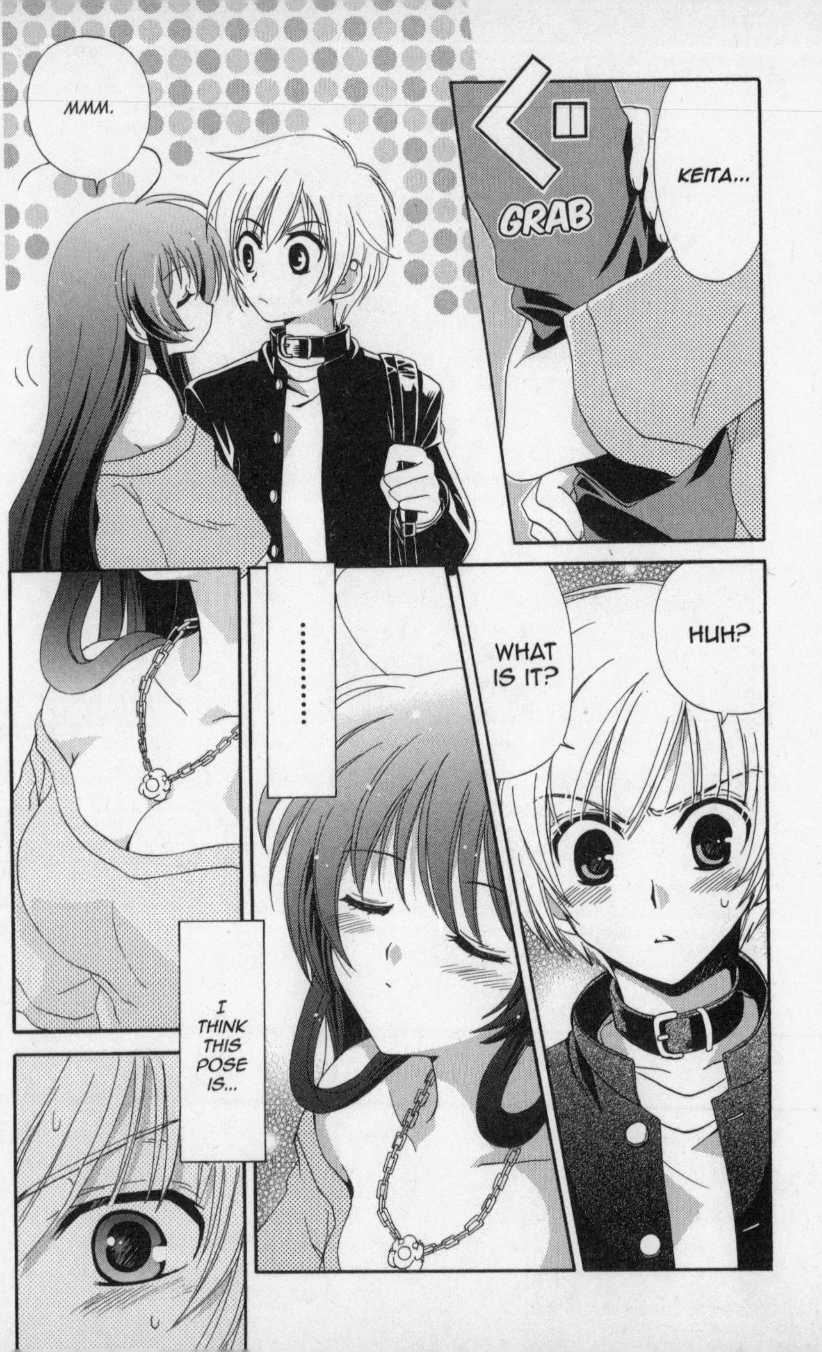
KEITA...
GRAB
MMM.
HUH?
WHAT IS IT?
....
I THINK THIS POSE IS...

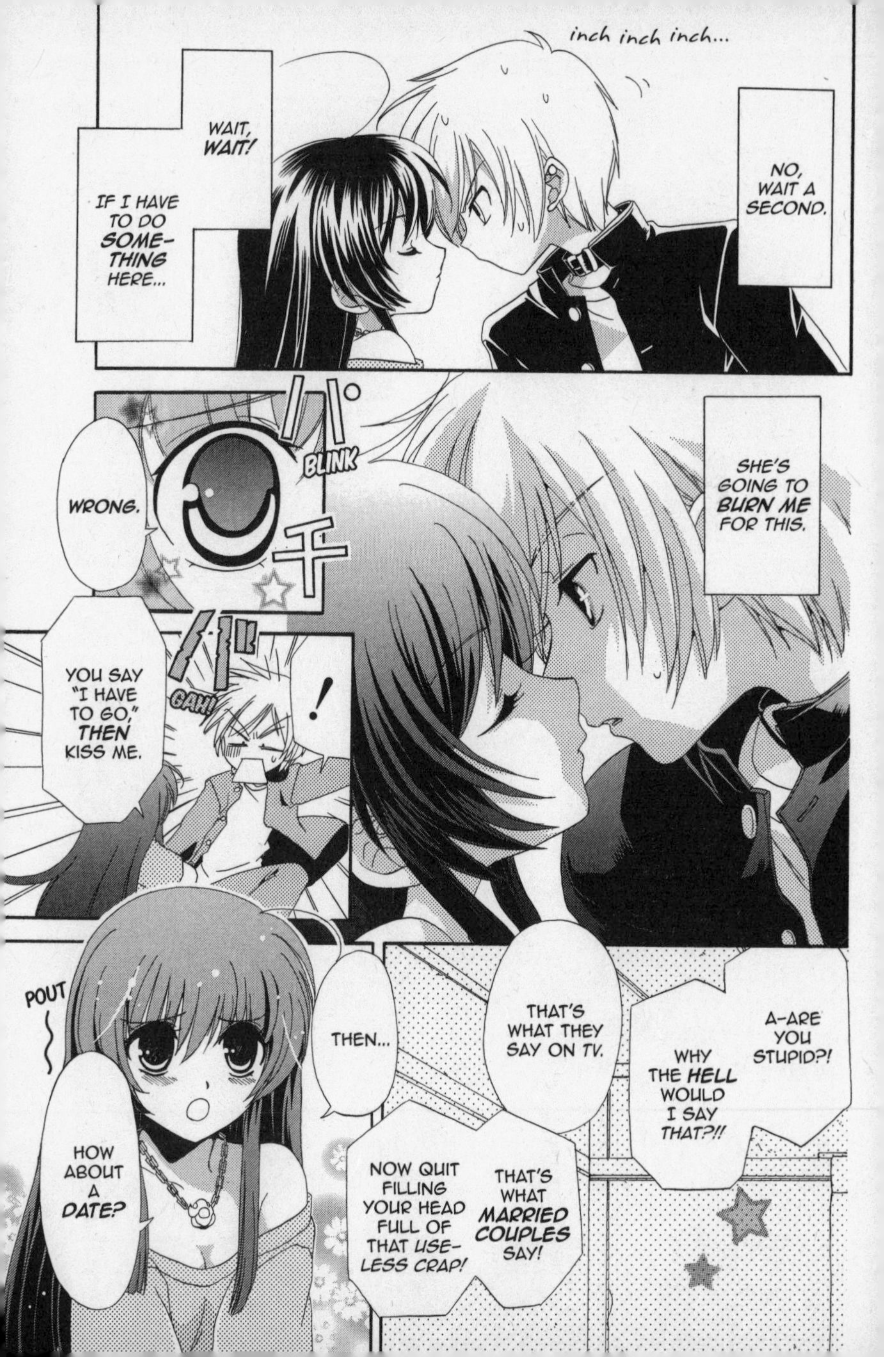
inch inch inch...
NO, WAIT A SECOND.
WAIT, WAIT!
IF I HAVE TO DO SOME-THING HERE...
SHE'S GOING TO BURN ME FOR THIS.
BLINK
WRONG.
GAH!
!
YOU SAY "I HAVE TO GO," THEN KISS ME.
A-ARE YOU STUPID?!
WHY THE HELL WOULD I SAY THAT?!!
THAT'S WHAT THEY SAY ON TV.
THAT'S WHAT MARRIED COUPLES SAY!
NOW QUIT FILLING YOUR HEAD FULL OF THAT USE-LESS CRAP!
THEN...
POUT
HOW ABOUT A DATE?

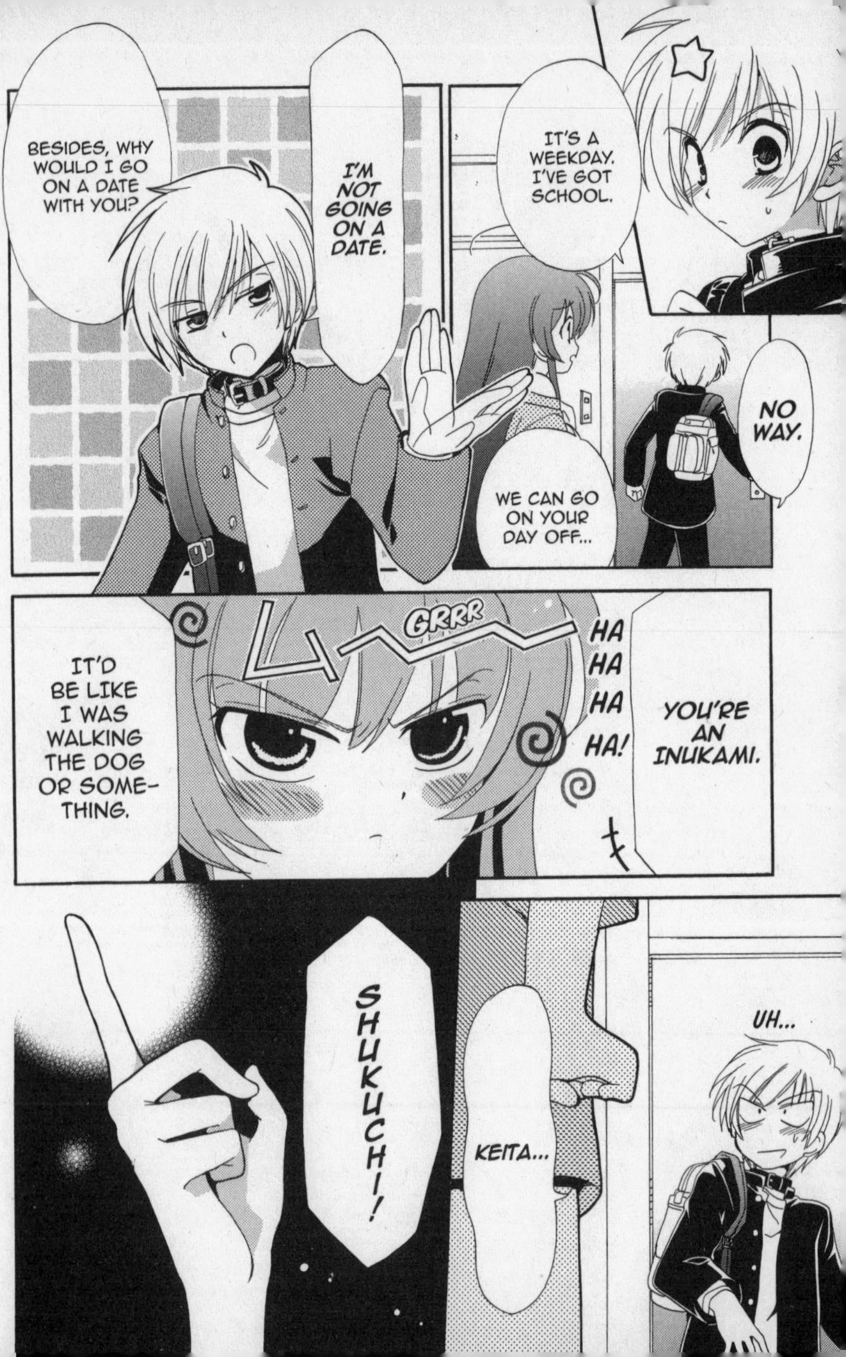
IT'S A WEEKDAY. I'VE GOT SCHOOL.
NO WAY.
WE CAN GO ON YOUR DAY OFF...
I'M NOT GOING ON A DATE.
BESIDES, WHY WOULD I GO ON A DATE WITH YOU?
YOU'RE AN INUKAMI.
HA HA HA HA!
GRRR
IT'D BE LIKE I WAS WALKING THE DOG OR SOME-THING.
UH...
KEITA...
SHUKUCHI!

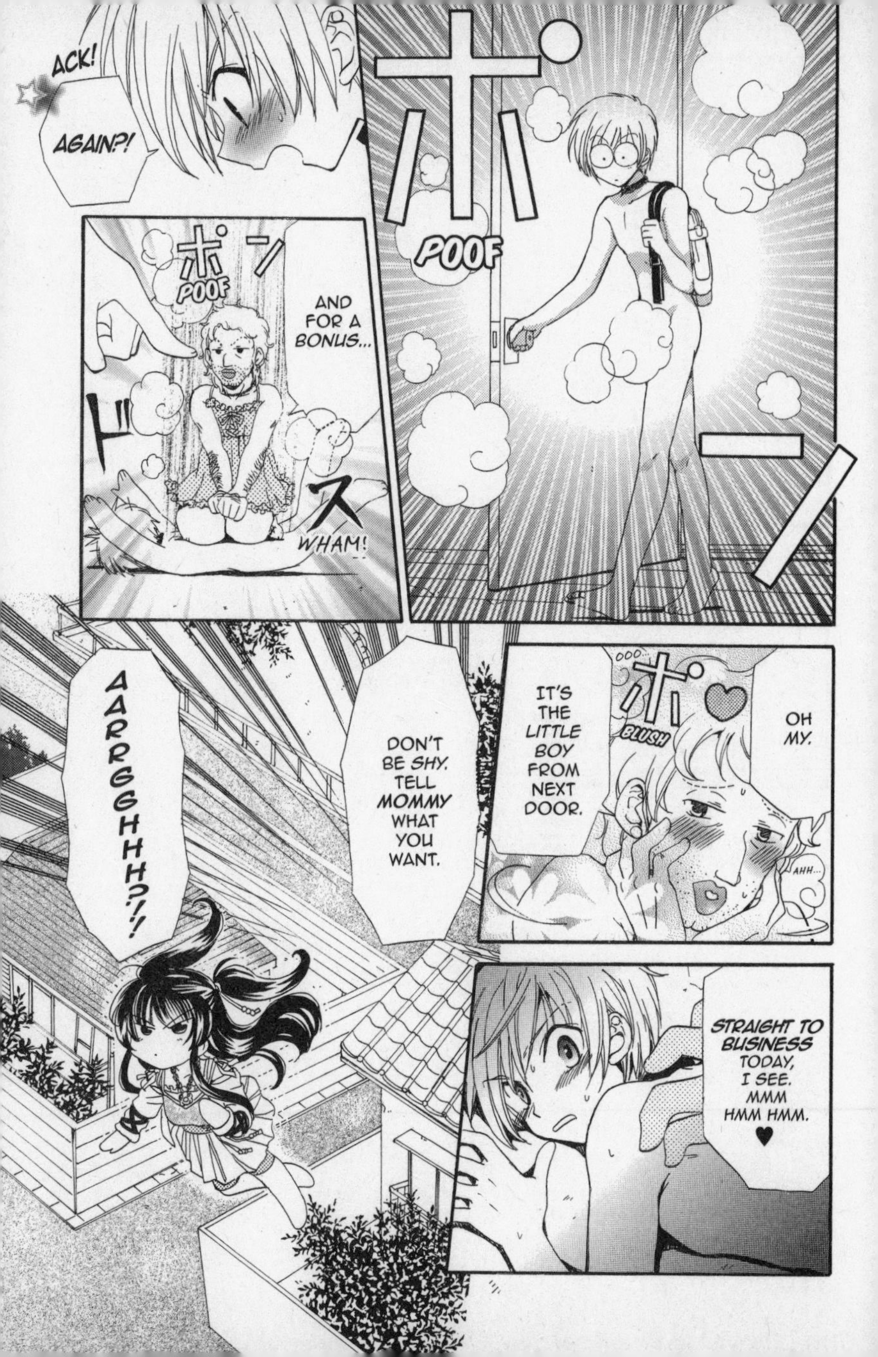
POOF
ACK!
AGAIN?!
POOF
AND FOR A BONUS...
WHAM!
OH MY.
OOO...
BLUSH
IT'S THE *LITTLE* BOY FROM NEXT DOOR.
AHH...
STRAIGHT TO BUSINESS TODAY, I SEE. MMM HMM HMM. ♥
DON'T BE *SHY*. TELL *MOMMY* WHAT YOU WANT.
AARRGGHHH?!!

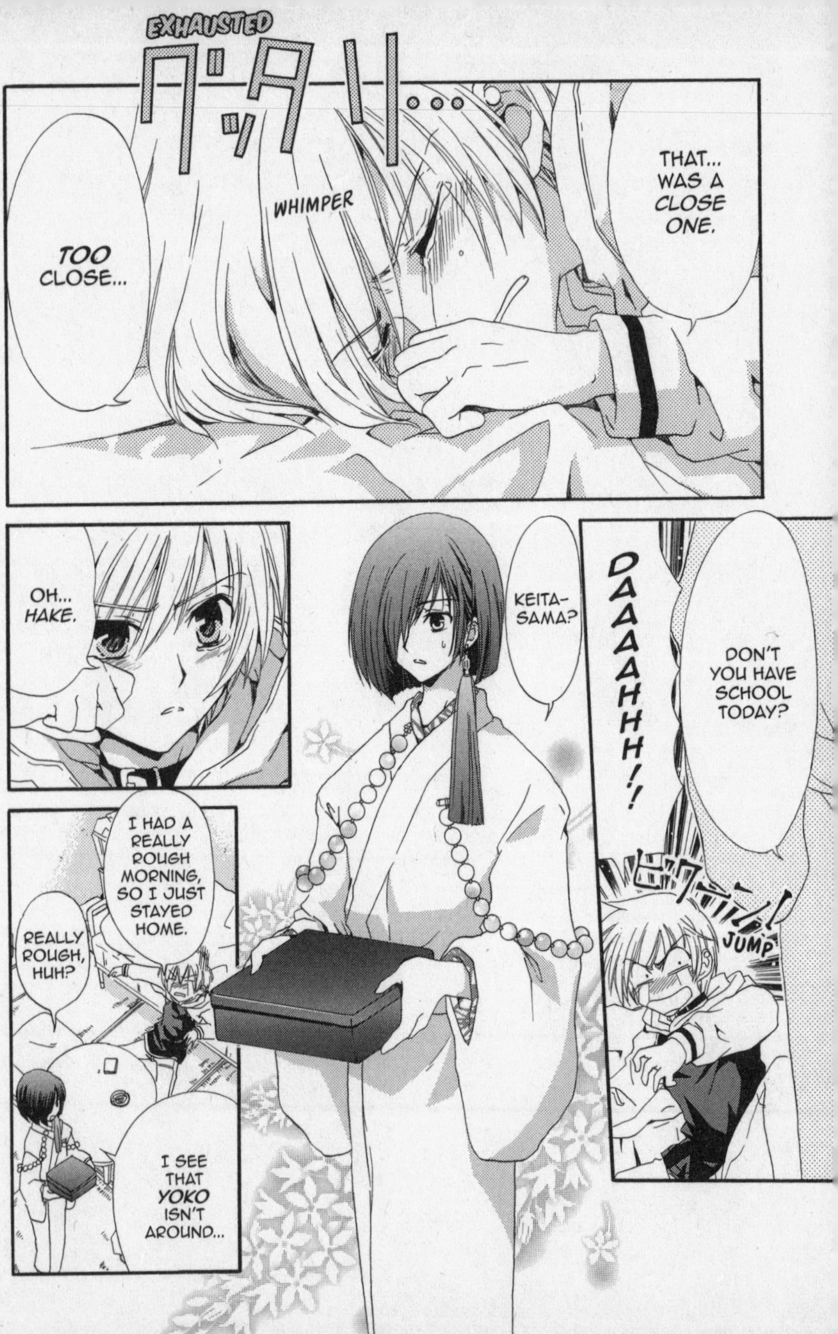
EXHAUSTED
THAT... WAS A CLOSE ONE.
WHIMPER
TOO CLOSE...
DON'T YOU HAVE SCHOOL TODAY?
DAAAAAHHH!!
JUMP
KEITA-SAMA?
OH... HAKE.
I HAD A REALLY ROUGH MORNING, SO I JUST STAYED HOME.
REALLY ROUGH, HUH?
I SEE THAT YOKO ISN'T AROUND...

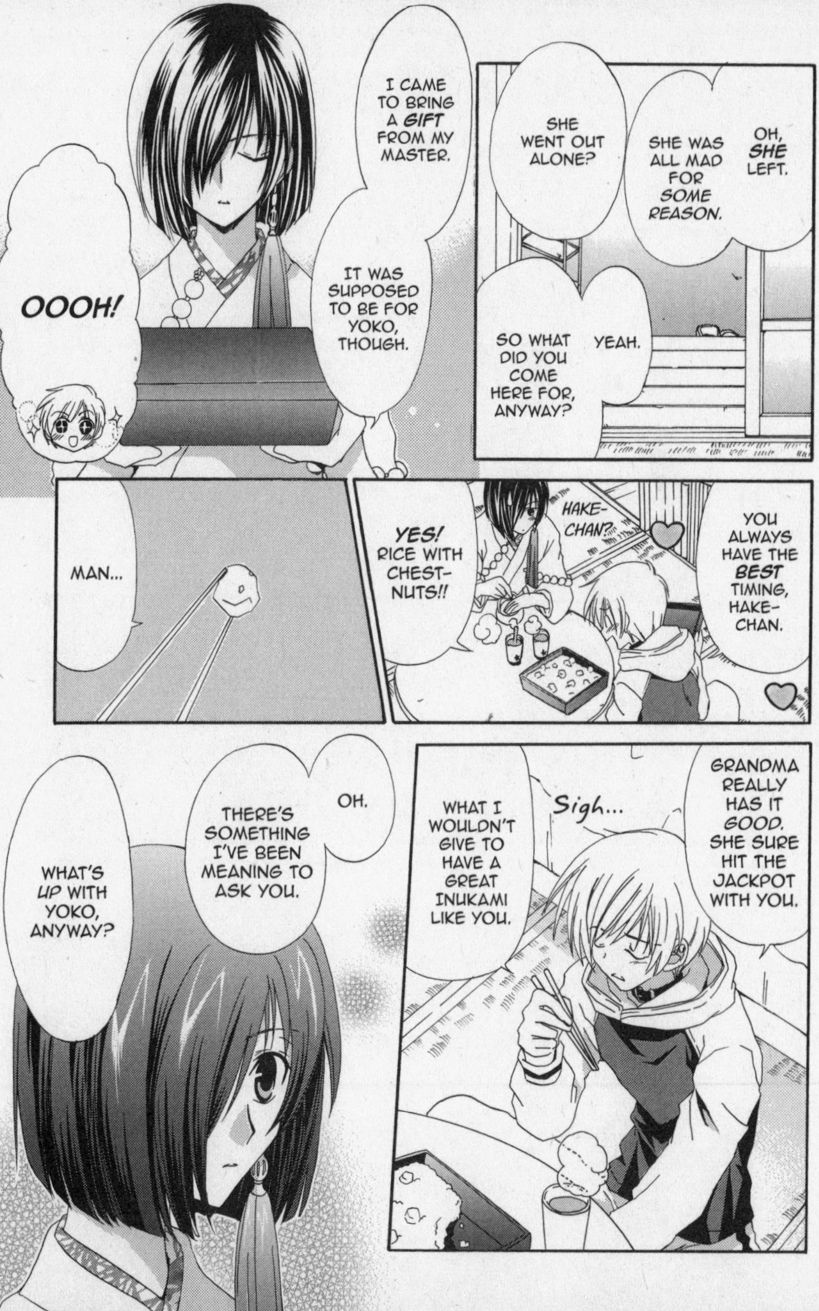
OH, SHE LEFT.
SHE WAS ALL MAD FOR SOME REASON.
SHE WENT OUT ALONE?
YEAH.
SO WHAT DID YOU COME HERE FOR, ANYWAY?
I CAME TO BRING A GIFT FROM MY MASTER.
IT WAS SUPPOSED TO BE FOR YOKO, THOUGH.
OOOH!
YOU ALWAYS HAVE THE BEST TIMING, HAKE-CHAN.
HAKE-CHAN?
YES! RICE WITH CHEST-NUTS!!
MAN...
GRANDMA REALLY HAS IT GOOD. SHE SURE HIT THE JACKPOT WITH YOU.
Sigh...
WHAT I WOULDN'T GIVE TO HAVE A GREAT INUKAMI LIKE YOU.
OH.
THERE'S SOMETHING I'VE BEEN MEANING TO ASK YOU.
WHAT'S UP WITH YOKO, ANYWAY?

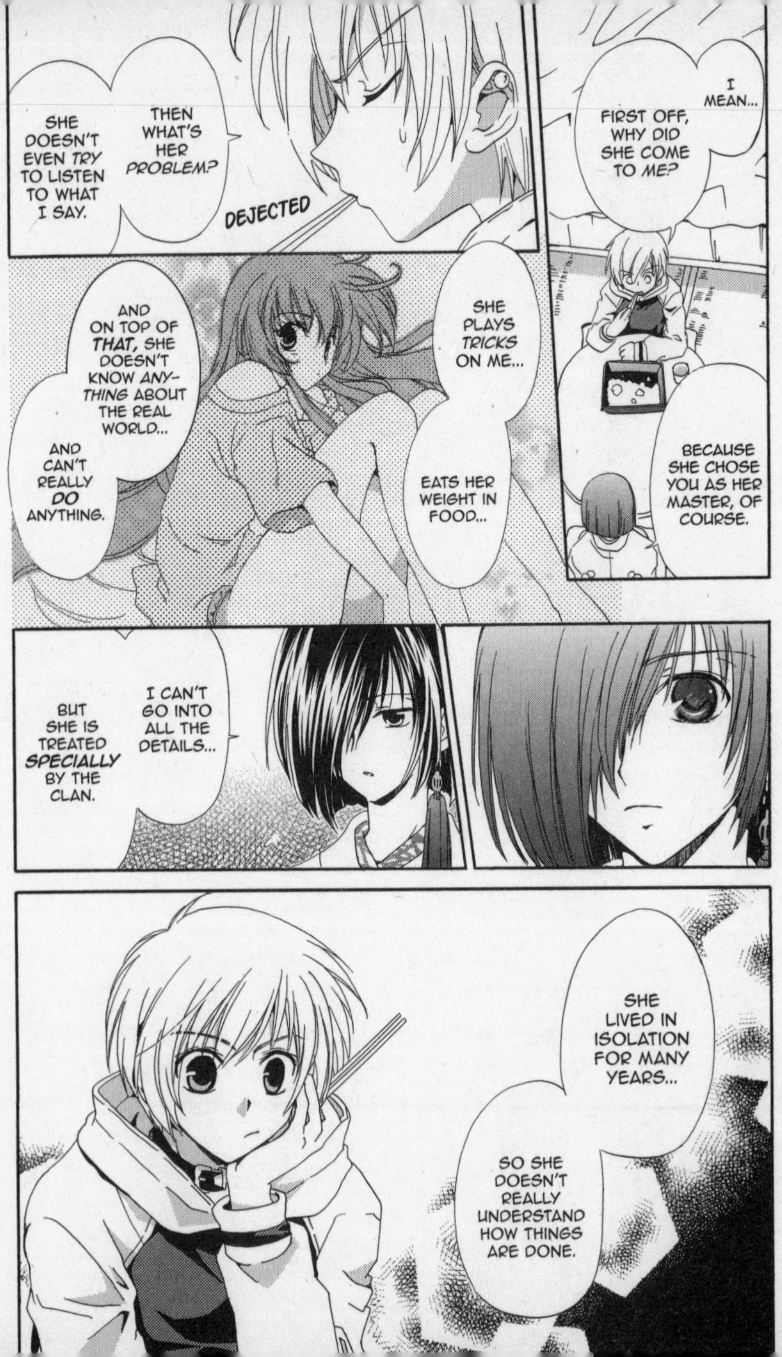
I MEAN...
FIRST OFF, WHY DID SHE COME TO ME?
THEN WHAT'S HER *PROBLEM?*
SHE DOESN'T EVEN *TRY* TO LISTEN TO WHAT I SAY.
DEJECTED
BECAUSE SHE CHOSE YOU AS HER MASTER, OF COURSE.
SHE PLAYS *TRICKS* ON ME...
EATS HER WEIGHT IN FOOD...
AND ON TOP OF **THAT,** SHE DOESN'T KNOW *ANY-THING* ABOUT THE REAL WORLD...
AND CAN'T REALLY *DO* ANYTHING.
I CAN'T GO INTO ALL THE DETAILS...
BUT SHE IS TREATED ***SPECIALLY*** BY THE CLAN.
SHE LIVED IN ISOLATION FOR MANY YEARS...
SO SHE DOESN'T REALLY UNDERSTAND HOW THINGS ARE DONE.

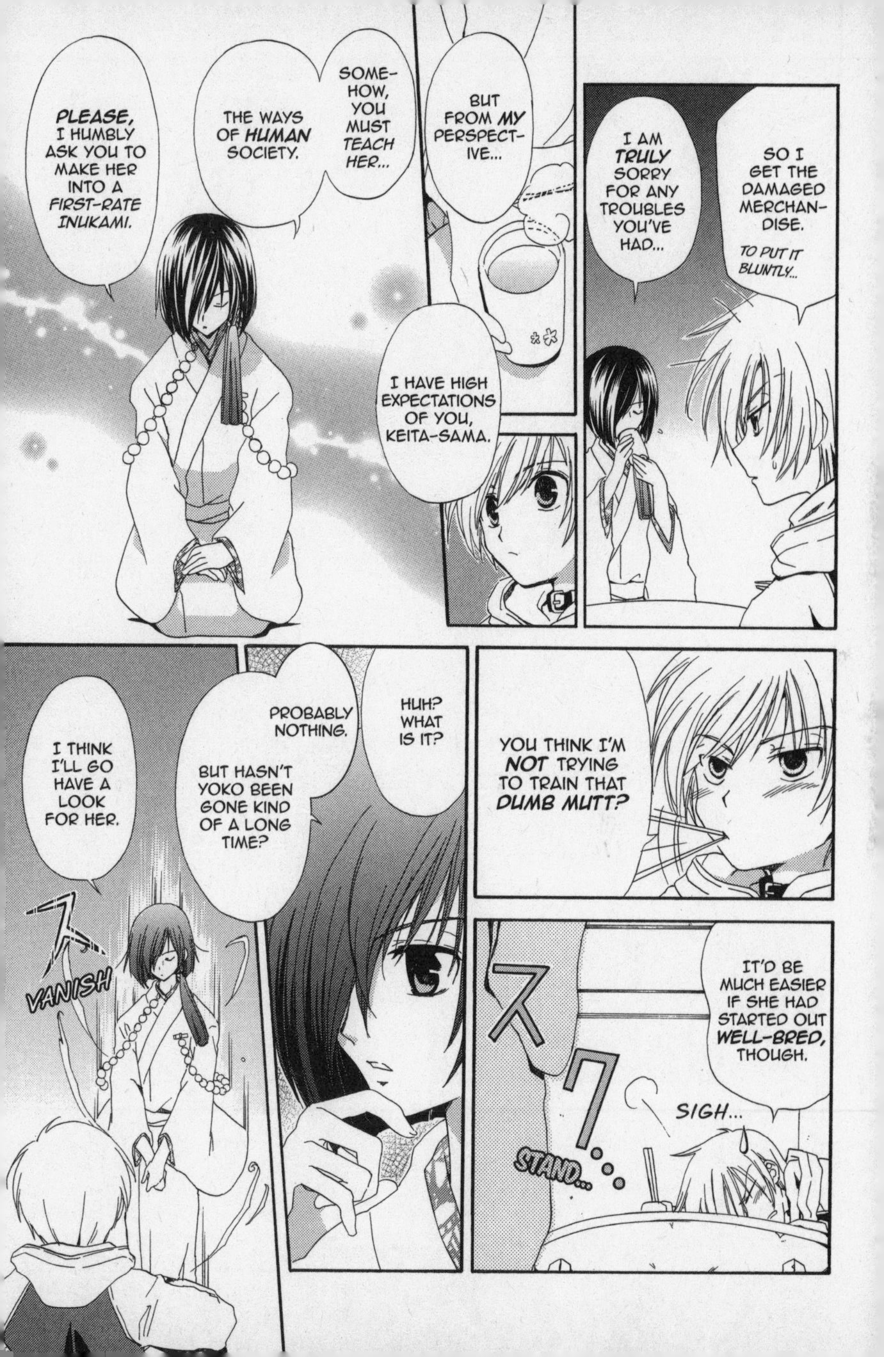
SO I GET THE DAMAGED MERCHANDISE.
TO PUT IT BLUNTLY...
I AM TRULY SORRY FOR ANY TROUBLES YOU'VE HAD...
BUT FROM MY PERSPECTIVE...
I HAVE HIGH EXPECTATIONS OF YOU, KEITA-SAMA.
SOME-HOW, YOU MUST TEACH HER...
THE WAYS OF HUMAN SOCIETY.
PLEASE, I HUMBLY ASK YOU TO MAKE HER INTO A FIRST-RATE INUKAMI.
YOU THINK I'M NOT TRYING TO TRAIN THAT DUMB MUTT?
IT'D BE MUCH EASIER IF SHE HAD STARTED OUT WELL-BRED, THOUGH.
SIGH...
STAND...
HUH? WHAT IS IT?
PROBABLY NOTHING.
BUT HASN'T YOKO BEEN GONE KIND OF A LONG TIME?
I THINK I'LL GO HAVE A LOOK FOR HER.
VANISH

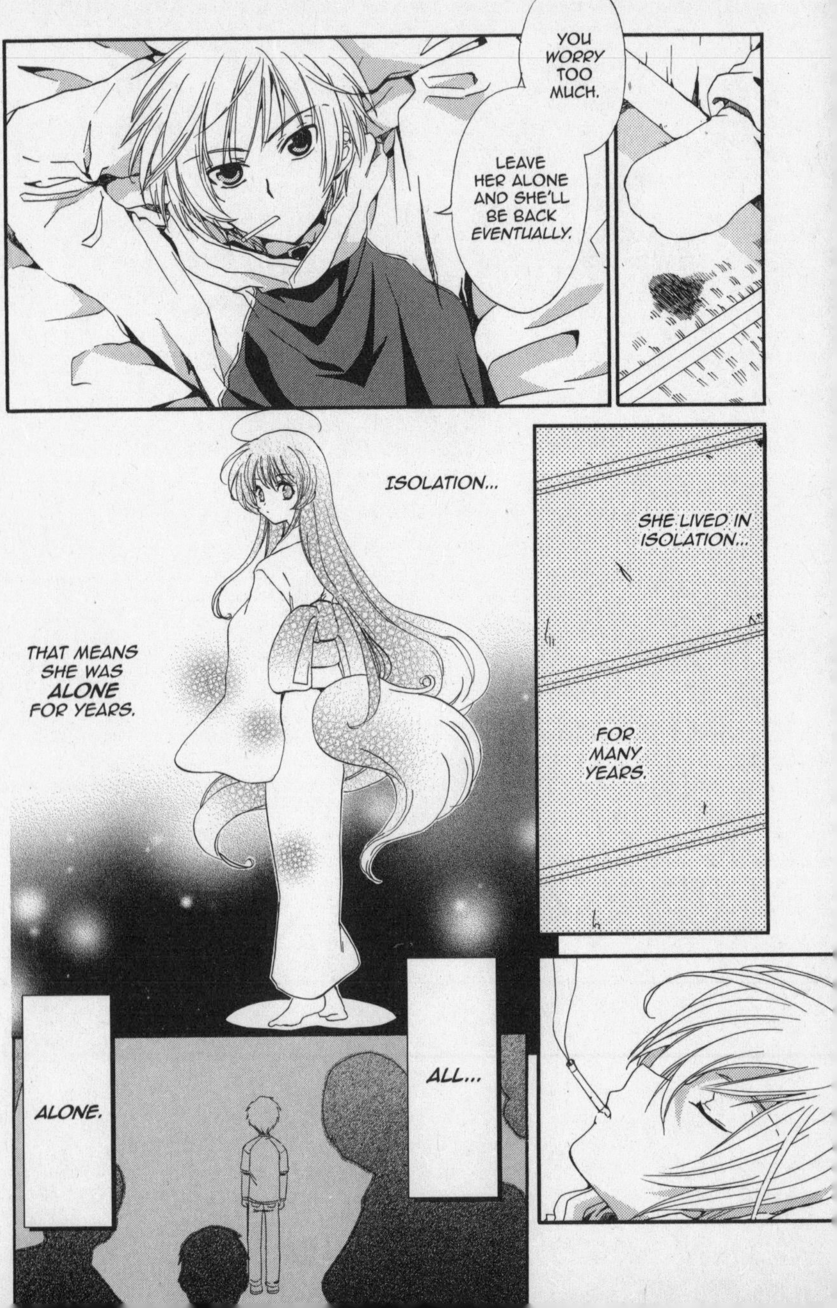
YOU WORRY TOO MUCH.
LEAVE HER ALONE AND SHE'LL BE BACK EVENTUALLY.
SHE LIVED IN ISOLATION...
FOR MANY YEARS.
ISOLATION...
THAT MEANS SHE WAS ALONE FOR YEARS.
ALL...
ALONE.

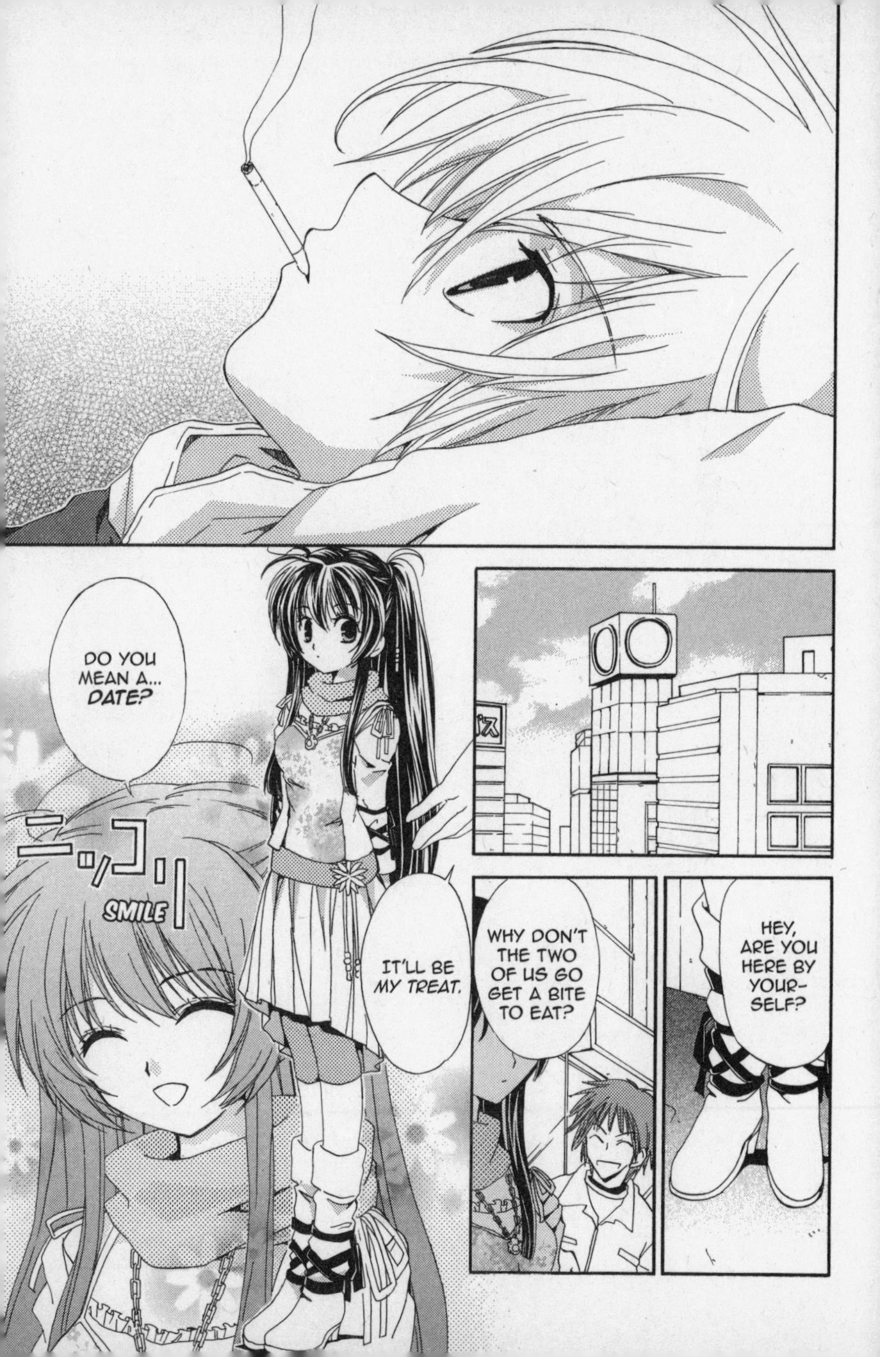
HEY, ARE YOU HERE BY YOURSELF?
WHY DON'T THE TWO OF US GO GET A BITE TO EAT?
IT'LL BE MY TREAT.
DO YOU MEAN A... DATE?
ニッコリ
SMILE

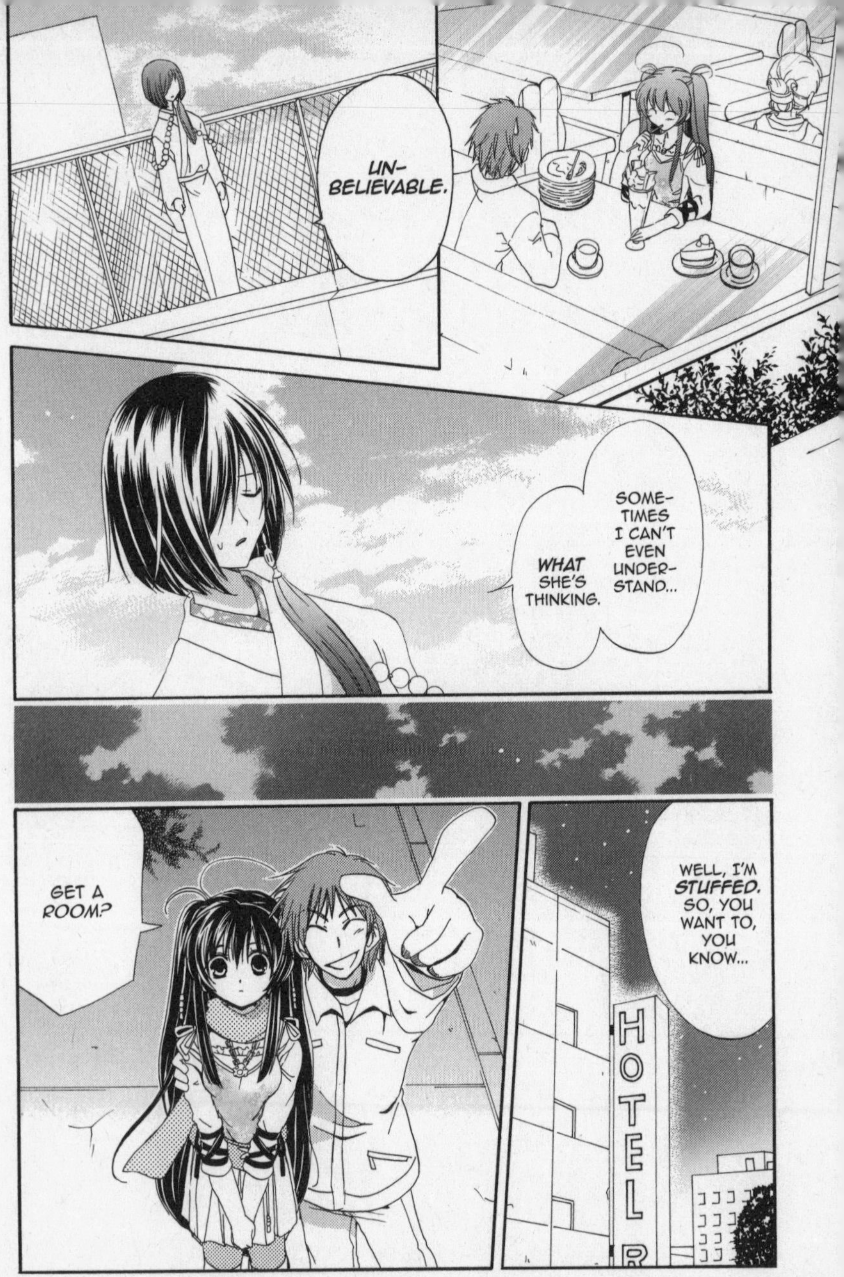
UN-BELIEVABLE.
SOMETIMES I CAN'T EVEN UNDERSTAND... WHAT SHE'S THINKING.
WELL, I'M STUFFED. SO, YOU WANT TO, YOU KNOW...
HOTEL
GET A ROOM?

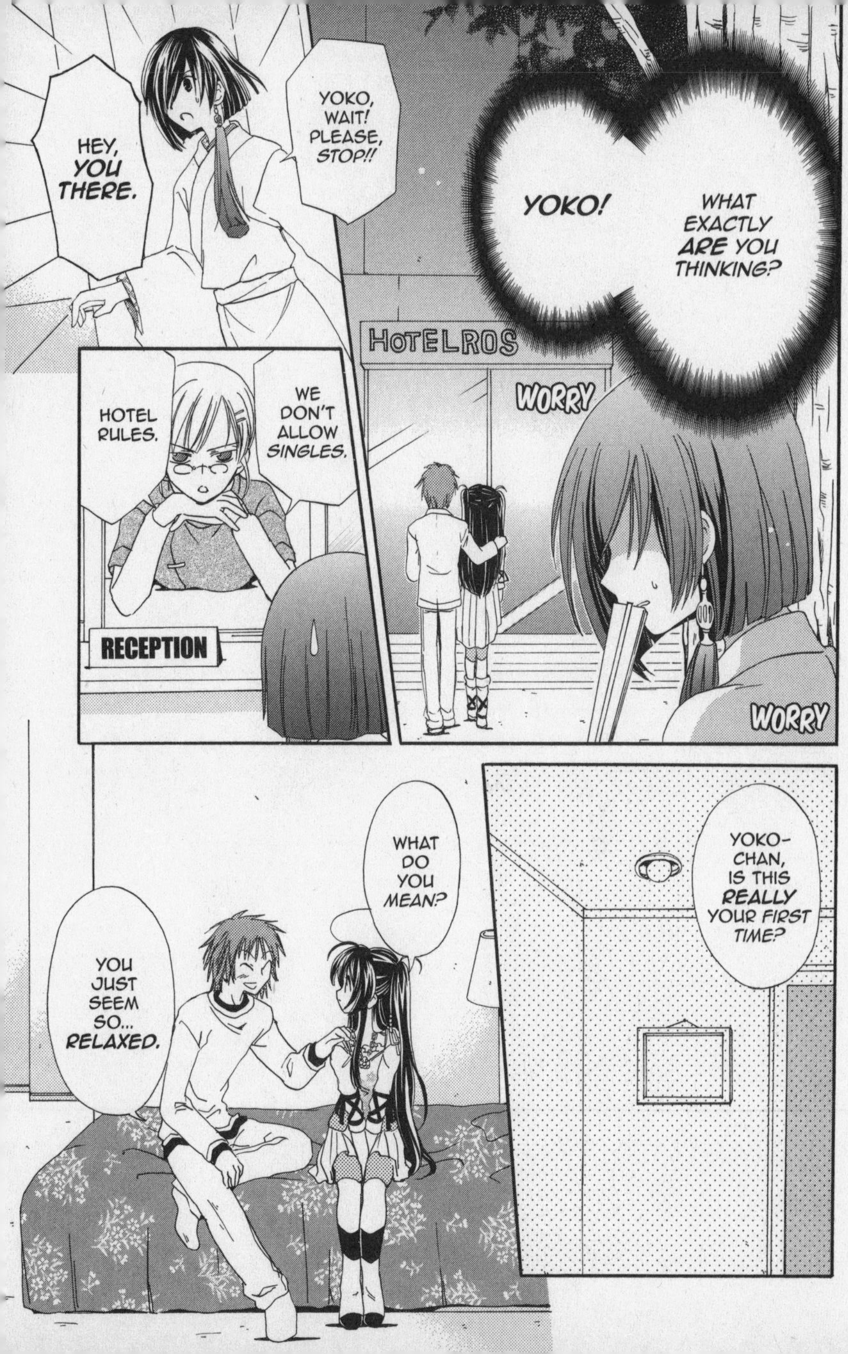
YOKO!
WHAT EXACTLY ARE YOU THINKING?
HOTELROS
WORRY
WORRY
YOKO, WAIT! PLEASE, STOP!!
HEY, YOU THERE.
WE DON'T ALLOW SINGLES.
HOTEL RULES.
RECEPTION
YOKO-CHAN, IS THIS REALLY YOUR FIRST TIME?
WHAT DO YOU MEAN?
YOU JUST SEEM SO... RELAXED.

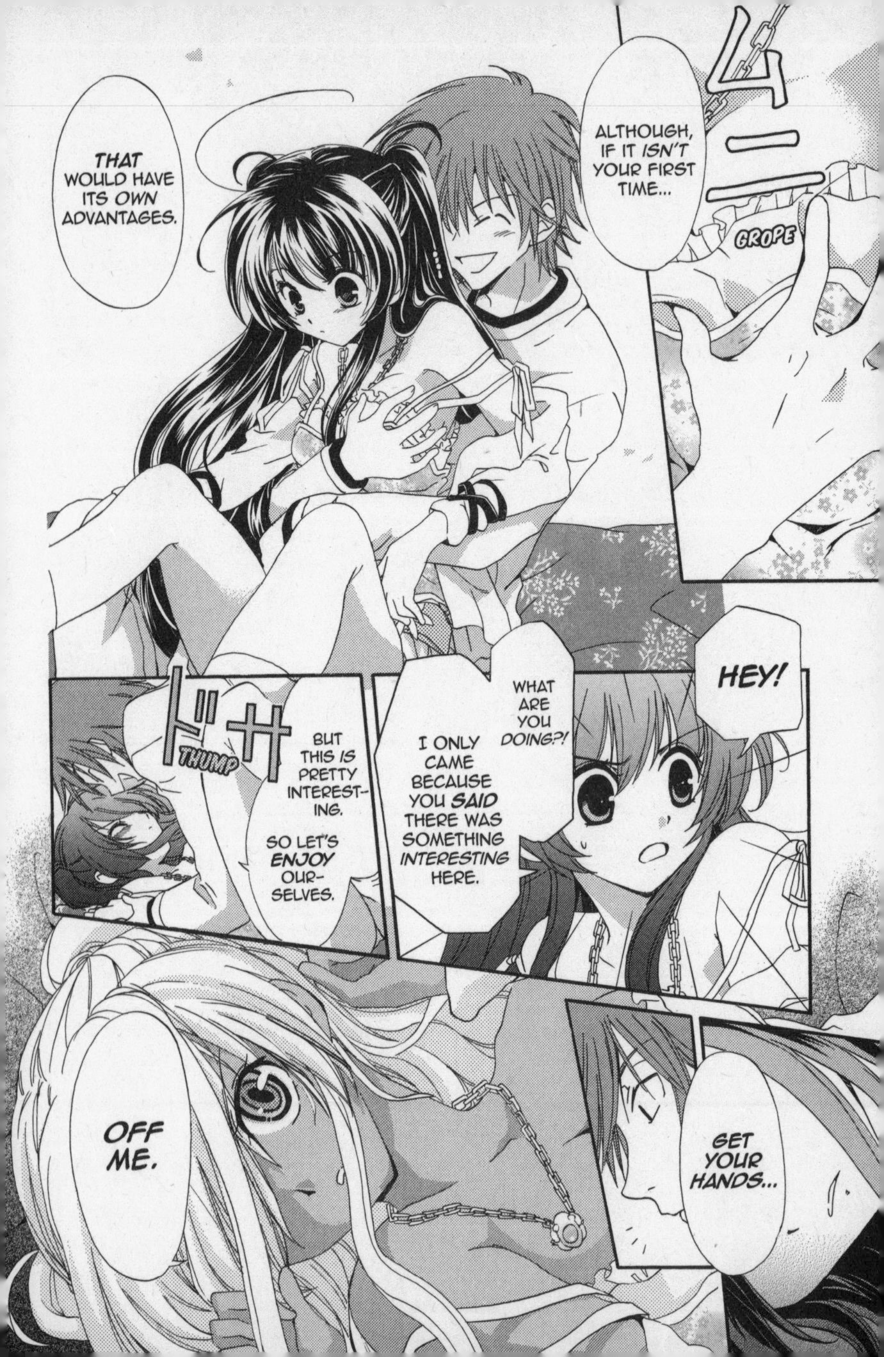

ムーー
GROPE
ALTHOUGH, IF IT *ISN'T* YOUR FIRST TIME...
THAT WOULD HAVE ITS *OWN* ADVANTAGES.
HEY!
WHAT ARE YOU *DOING?!*
I ONLY CAME BECAUSE YOU *SAID* THERE WAS SOMETHING *INTERESTING* HERE.
ドサ
THUMP
BUT THIS *IS* PRETTY INTERESTING.
SO LET'S *ENJOY* OURSELVES.
GET YOUR HANDS...
OFF ME.

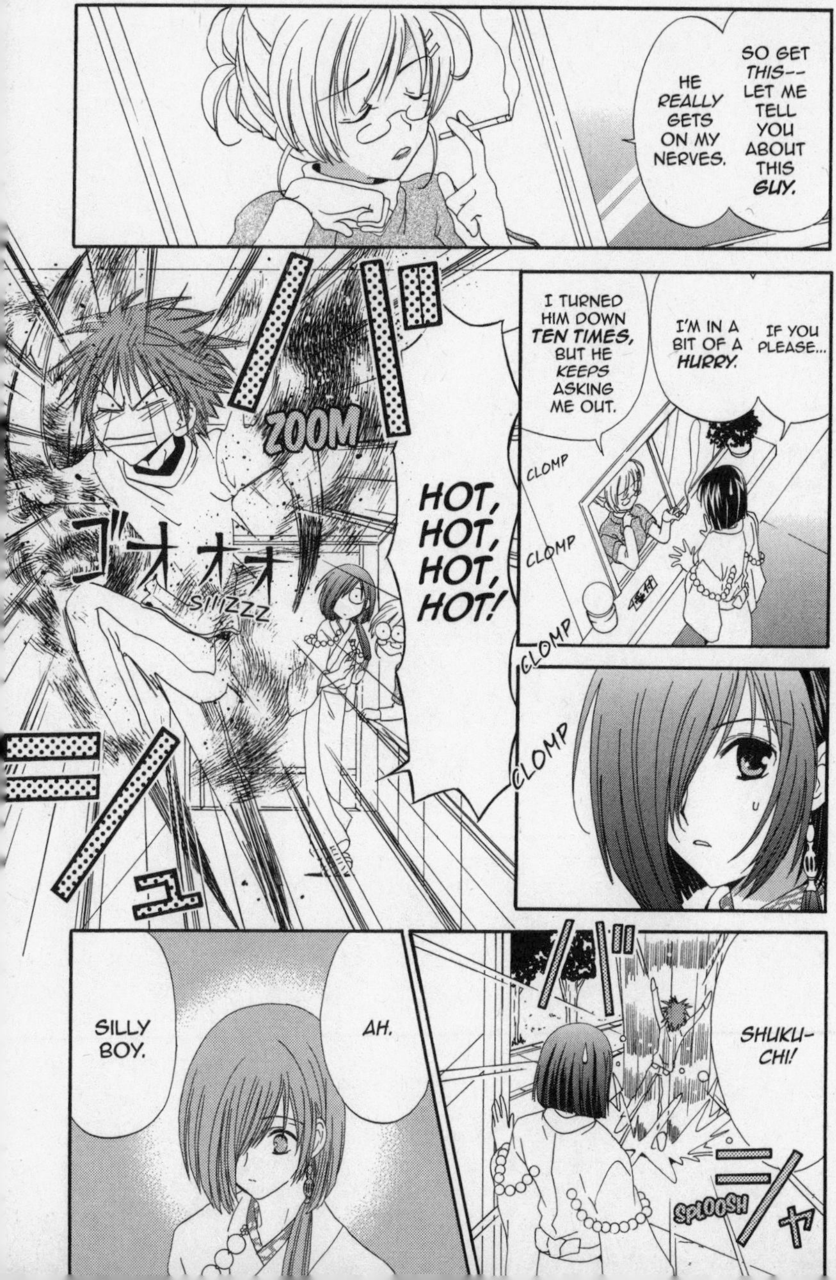
SO GET THIS-- LET ME TELL YOU ABOUT THIS GUY.
HE REALLY GETS ON MY NERVES.
IF YOU PLEASE...
I'M IN A BIT OF A HURRY.
I TURNED HIM DOWN TEN TIMES, BUT HE KEEPS ASKING ME OUT.
CLOMP
CLOMP
CLOMP
CLOMP
HOT, HOT, HOT, HOT!
ZOOM
ゴオオオ
SIIIZZZ
SHUKU-CHI!
SPLOOSH
AH.
SILLY BOY.

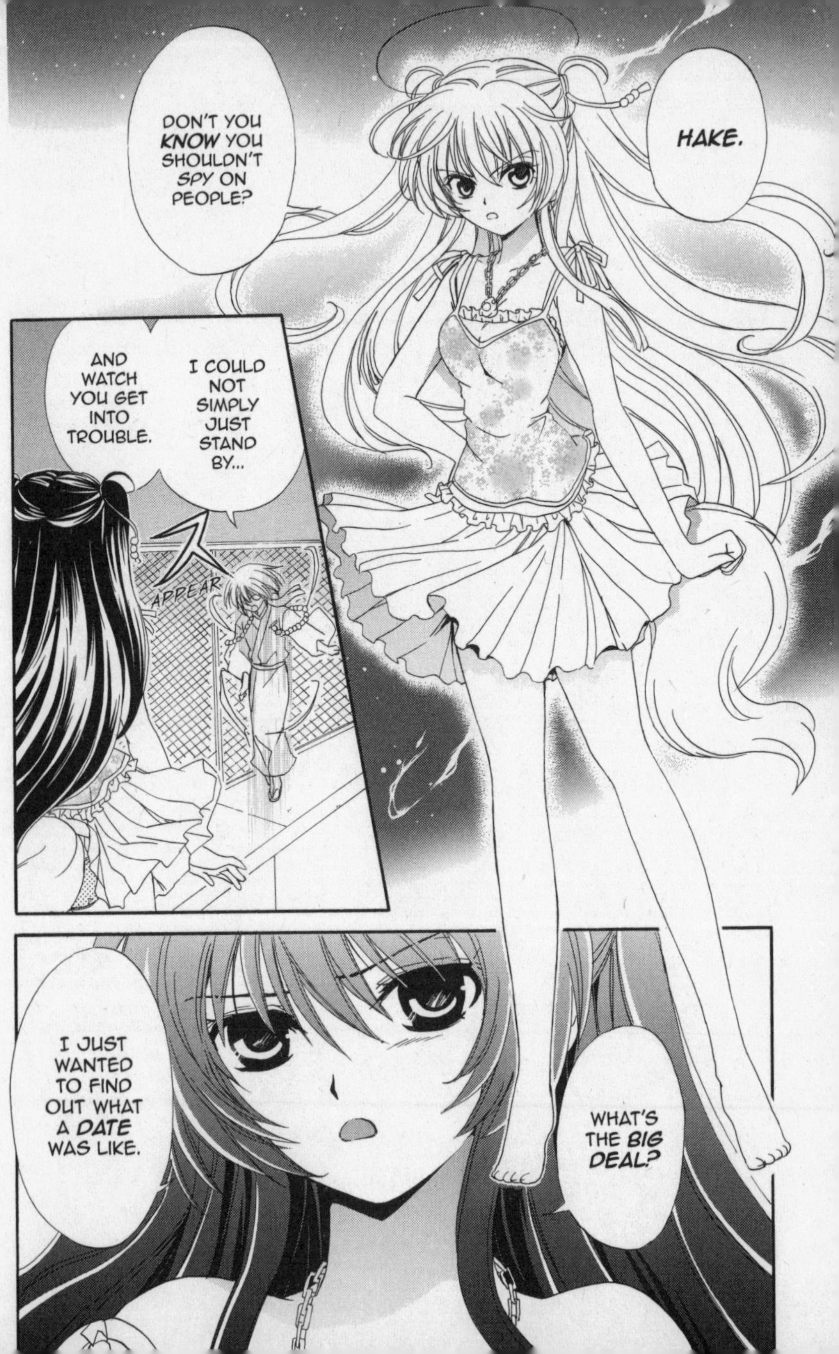
HAKE.
DON'T YOU KNOW YOU SHOULDN'T SPY ON PEOPLE?
I COULD NOT SIMPLY JUST STAND BY...
AND WATCH YOU GET INTO TROUBLE.
APPEAR
WHAT'S THE BIG DEAL?
I JUST WANTED TO FIND OUT WHAT A DATE WAS LIKE.

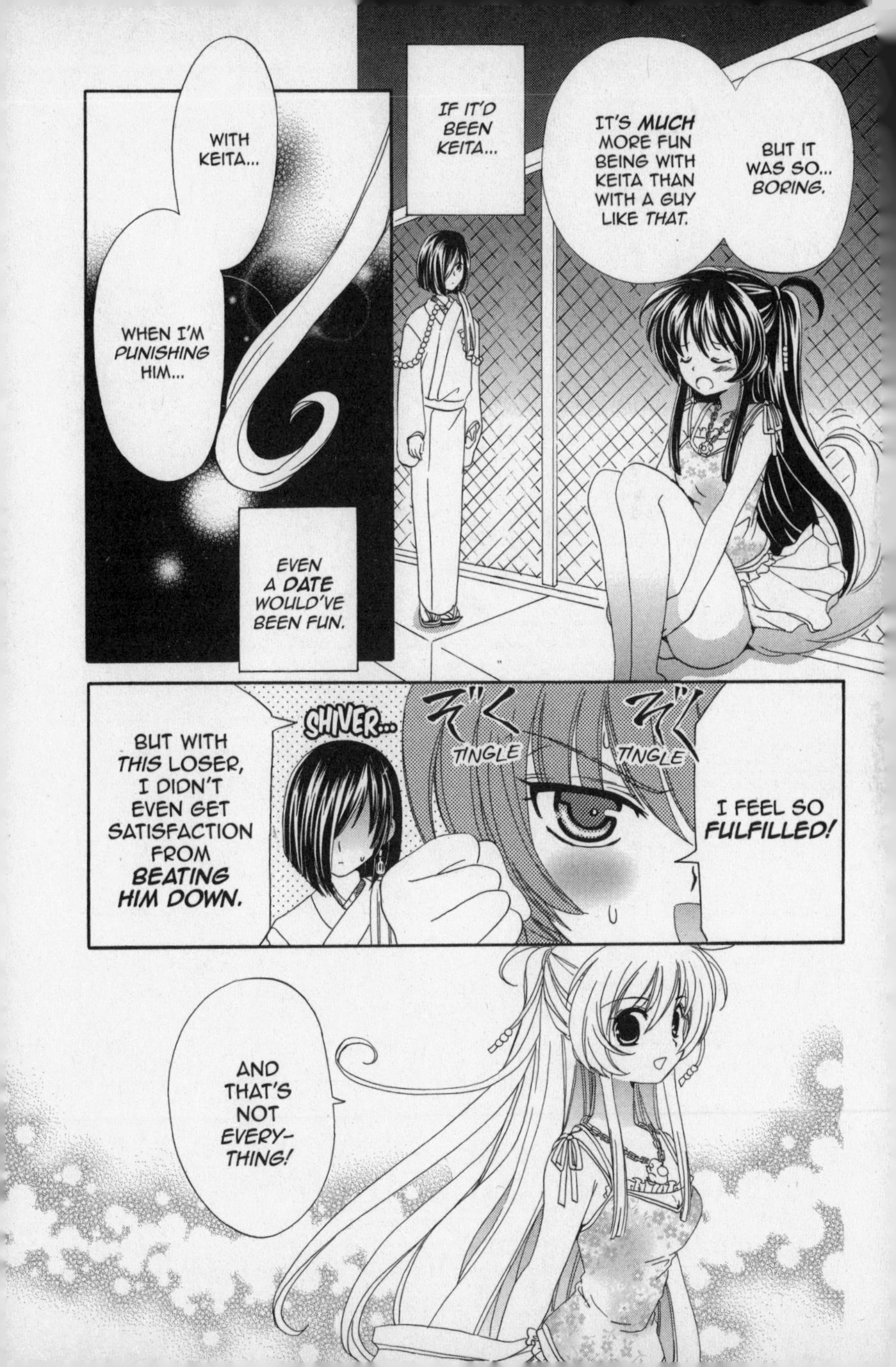
BUT IT WAS SO... BORING.
IT'S MUCH MORE FUN BEING WITH KEITA THAN WITH A GUY LIKE THAT.
IF IT'D BEEN KEITA...
EVEN A DATE WOULD'VE BEEN FUN.
WITH KEITA...
WHEN I'M PUNISHING HIM...
ぞく TINGLE
ぞく TINGLE
I FEEL SO FULFILLED!
SHIVER...
BUT WITH THIS LOSER, I DIDN'T EVEN GET SATISFACTION FROM BEATING HIM DOWN.
AND THAT'S NOT EVERY-THING!

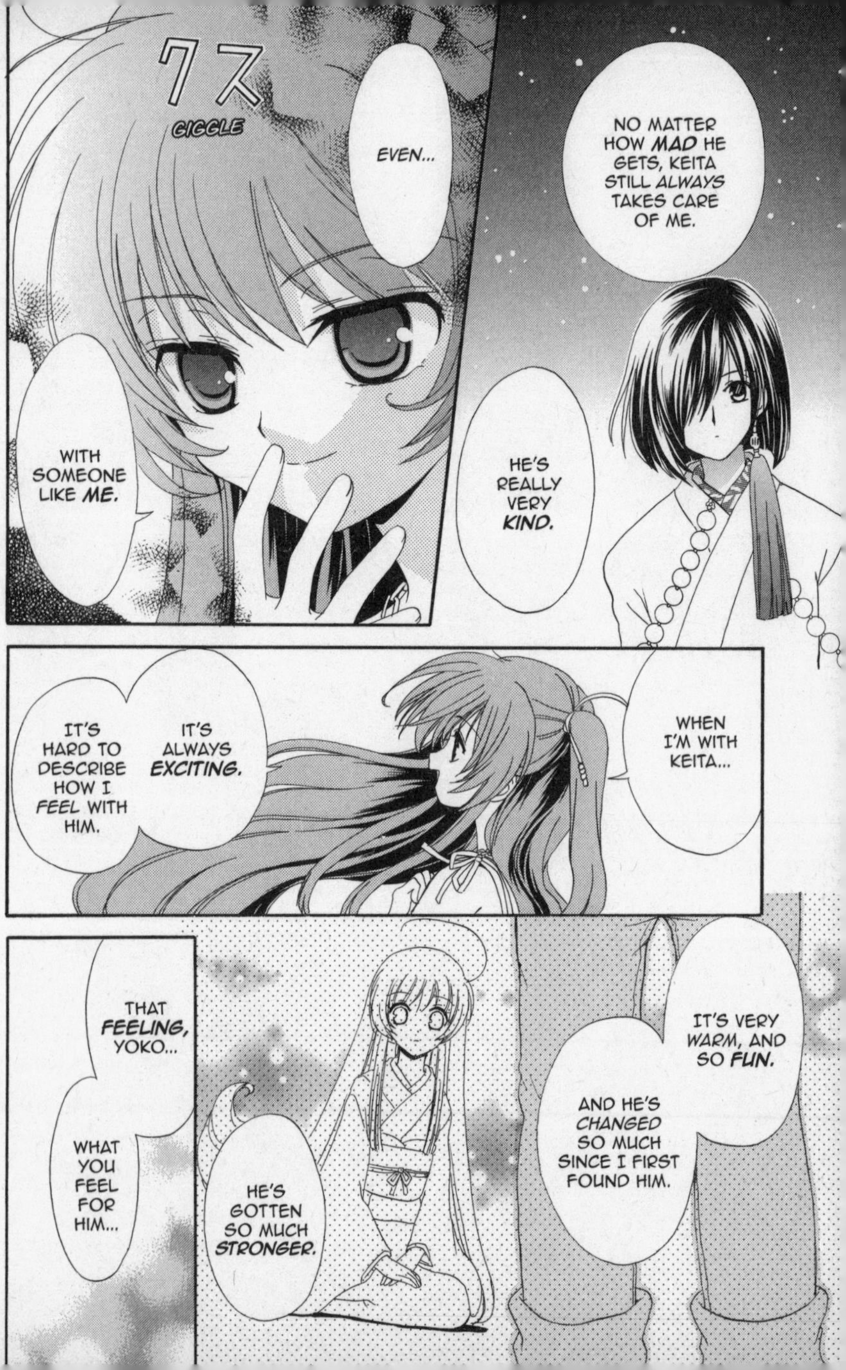

NO MATTER HOW MAD HE GETS, KEITA STILL ALWAYS TAKES CARE OF ME.
HE'S REALLY VERY KIND.
クス
GIGGLE
EVEN...
WITH SOMEONE LIKE ME.
WHEN I'M WITH KEITA...
IT'S ALWAYS EXCITING.
IT'S HARD TO DESCRIBE HOW I FEEL WITH HIM.
IT'S VERY WARM, AND SO FUN.
AND HE'S CHANGED SO MUCH SINCE I FIRST FOUND HIM.
HE'S GOTTEN SO MUCH STRONGER.
THAT FEELING, YOKO...
WHAT YOU FEEL FOR HIM...

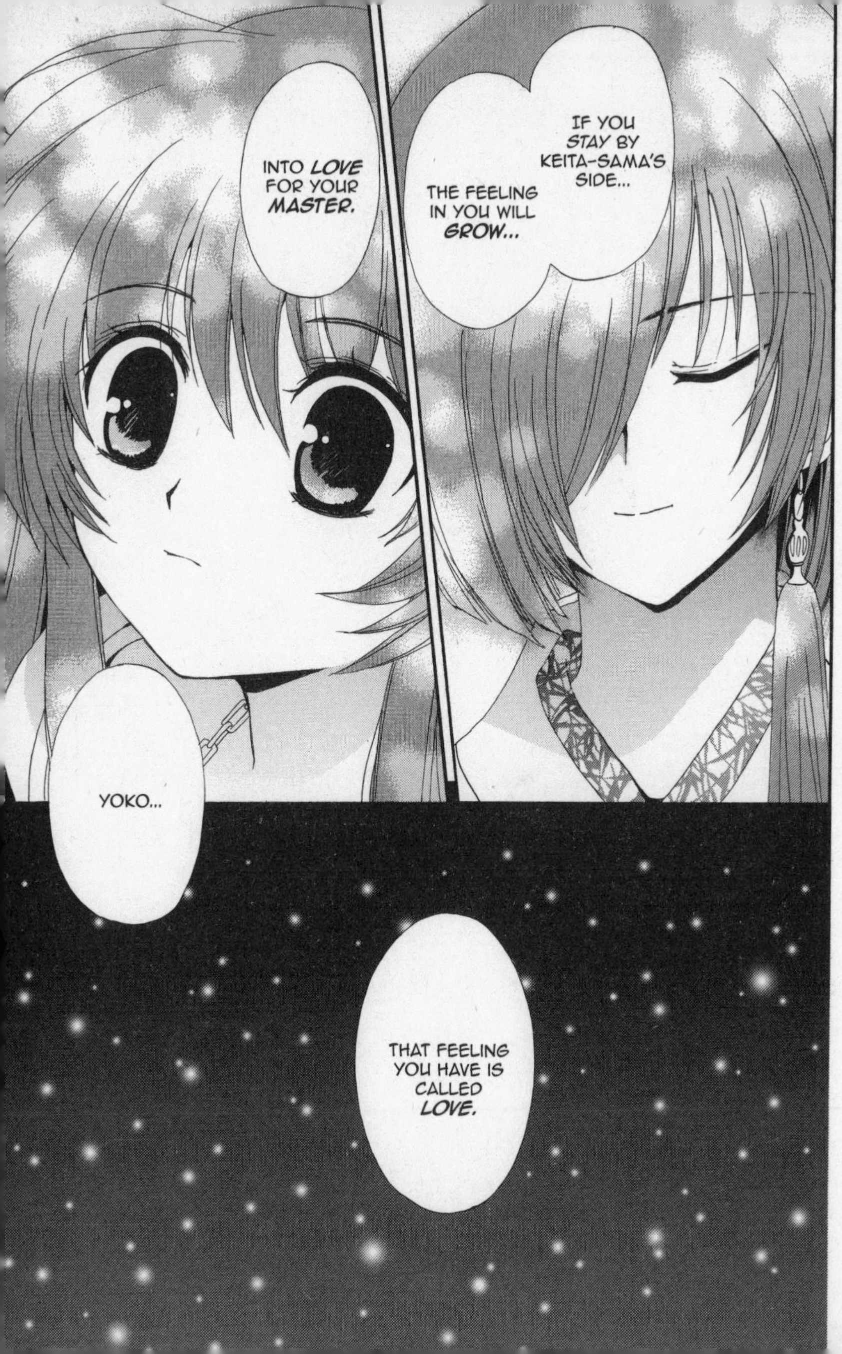
IF YOU STAY BY KEITA-SAMA'S SIDE...
THE FEELING IN YOU WILL GROW...
INTO LOVE FOR YOUR MASTER.
YOKO...
THAT FEELING YOU HAVE IS CALLED LOVE.

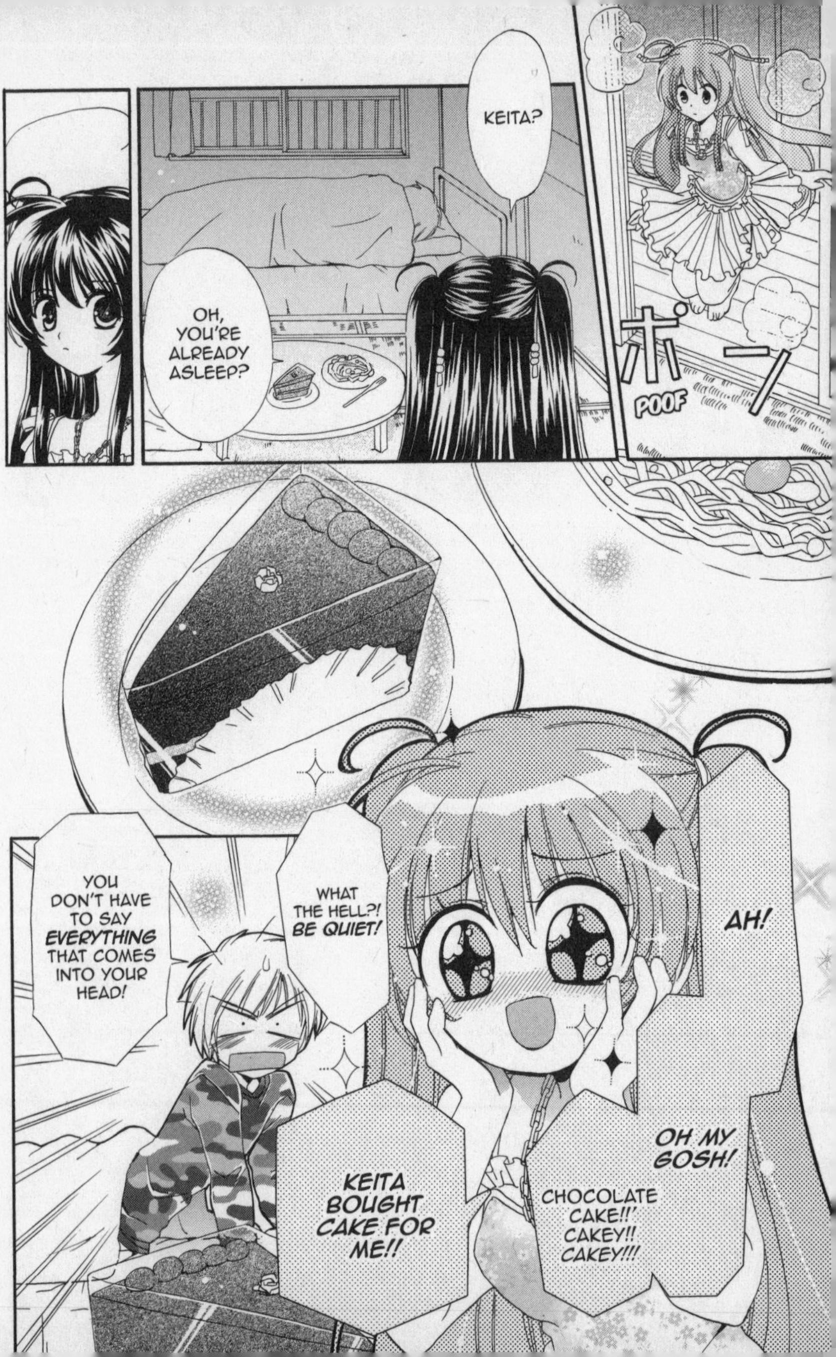
ポーン
POOF
KEITA?
OH, YOU'RE ALREADY ASLEEP?
AH!
OH MY GOSH!
CHOCOLATE CAKE!! CAKEY!! CAKEY!!!
KEITA BOUGHT CAKE FOR ME!!
WHAT THE HELL?! BE QUIET!
YOU DON'T HAVE TO SAY EVERYTHING THAT COMES INTO YOUR HEAD!

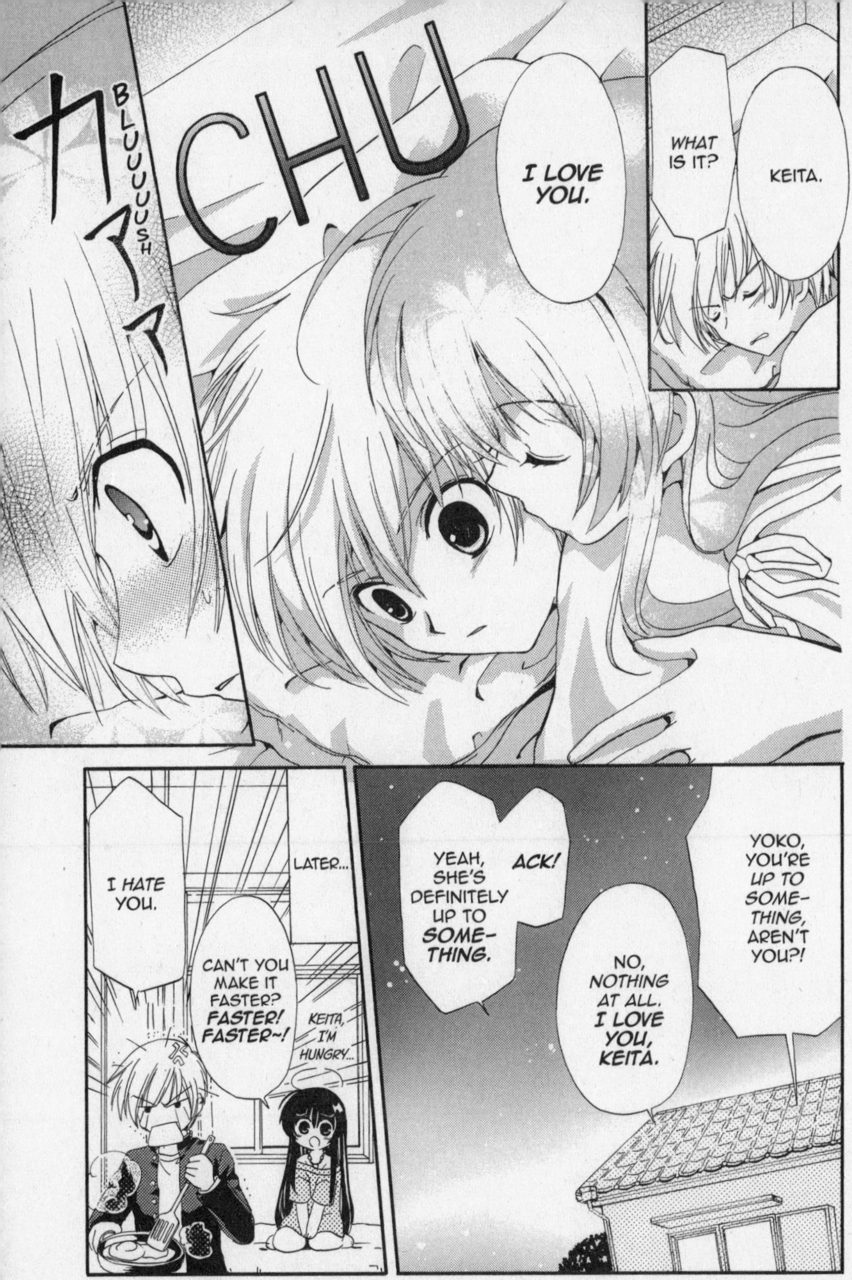
KEITA.
WHAT IS IT?
I LOVE YOU.
CHU
BLUUUUUSH
カァァ
YOKO, YOU'RE UP TO SOME-THING, AREN'T YOU?!
NO, NOTHING AT ALL. I LOVE YOU, KEITA.
ACK!
YEAH, SHE'S DEFINITELY UP TO SOME-THING.
LATER...
I HATE YOU.
CAN'T YOU MAKE IT FASTER? FASTER! FASTER~!
KEITA, I'M HUNGRY...

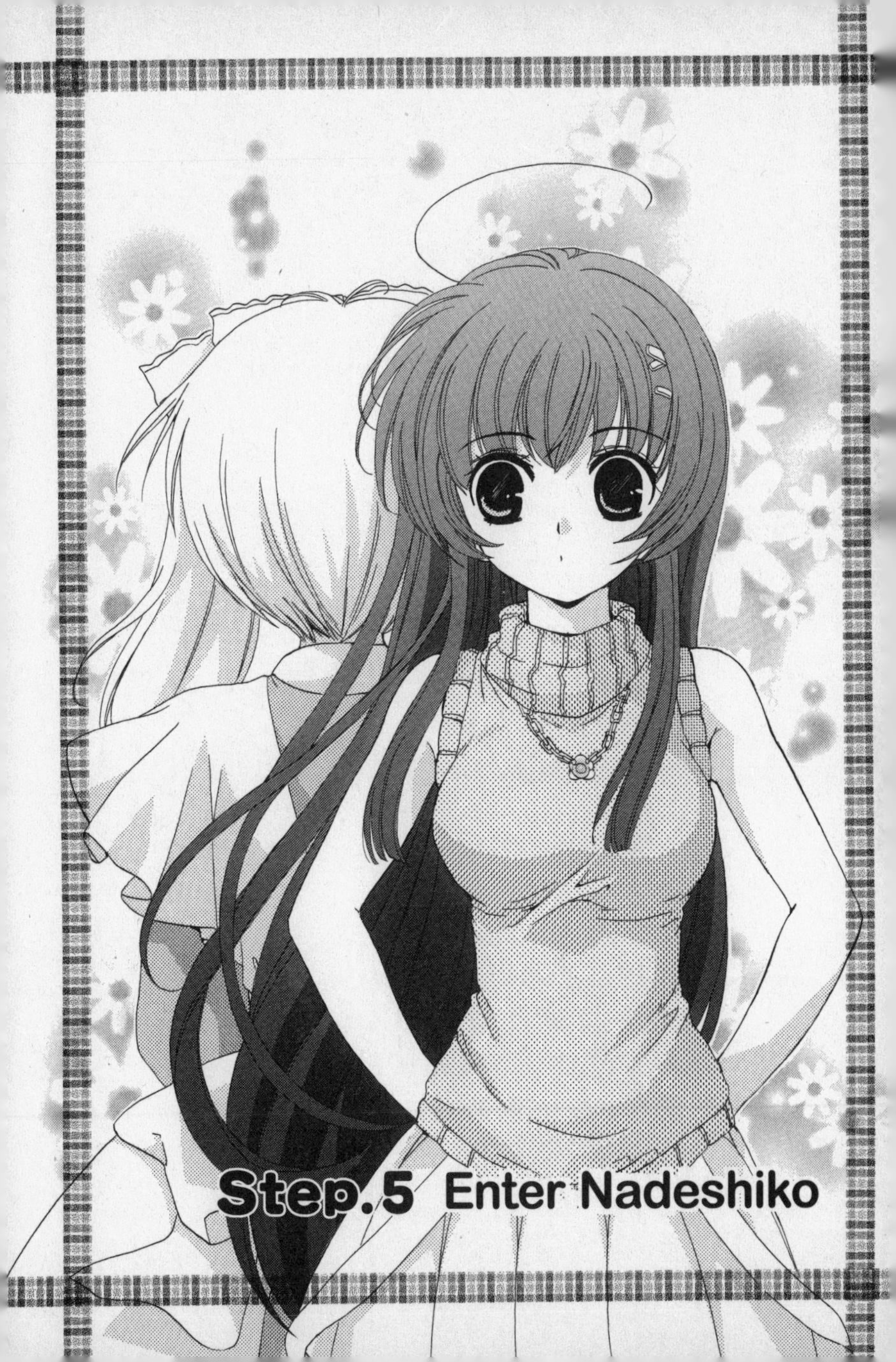
Step.5 Enter Nadeshiko

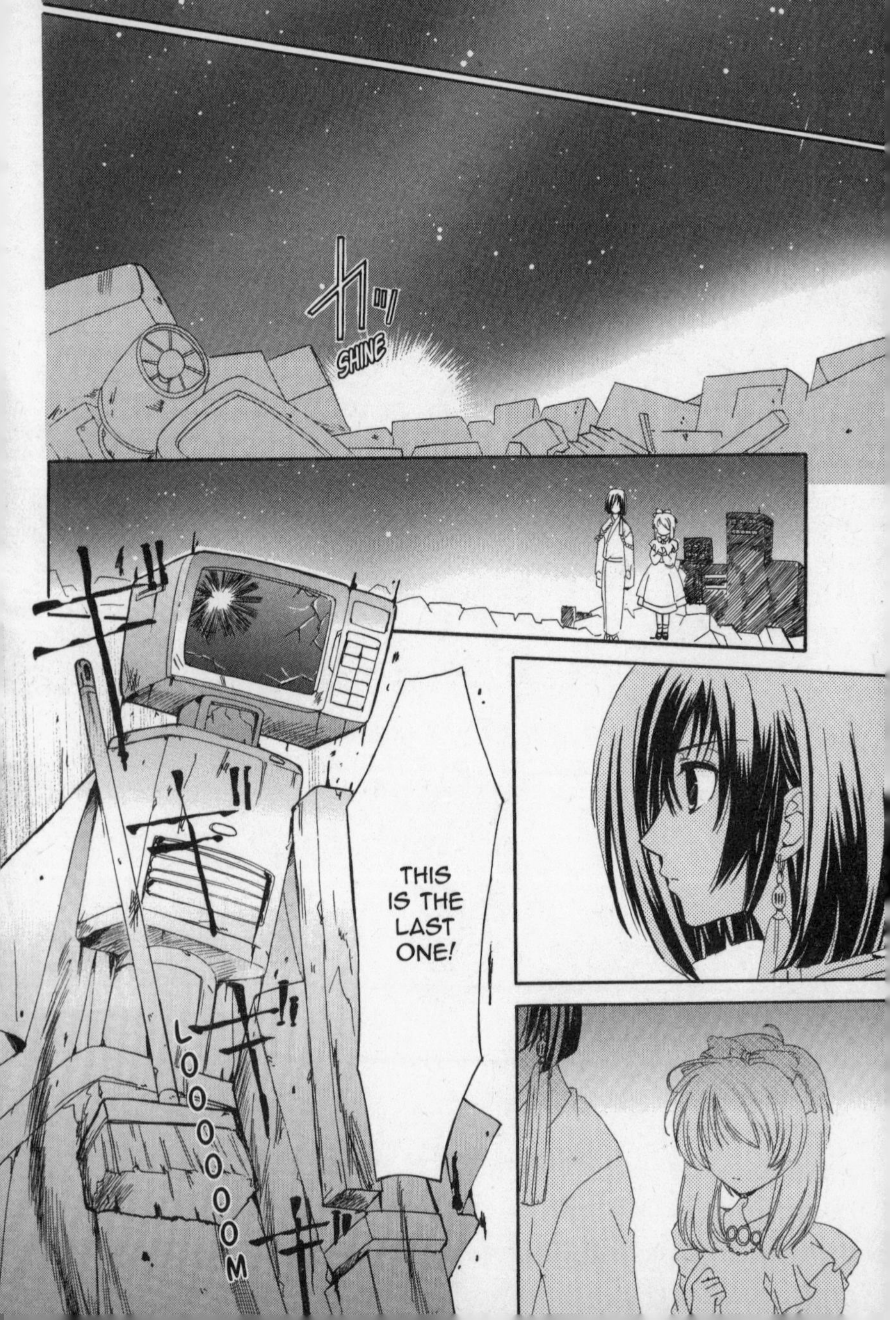
カッ
SHINE
THIS IS THE LAST ONE!
LOOOOOOM

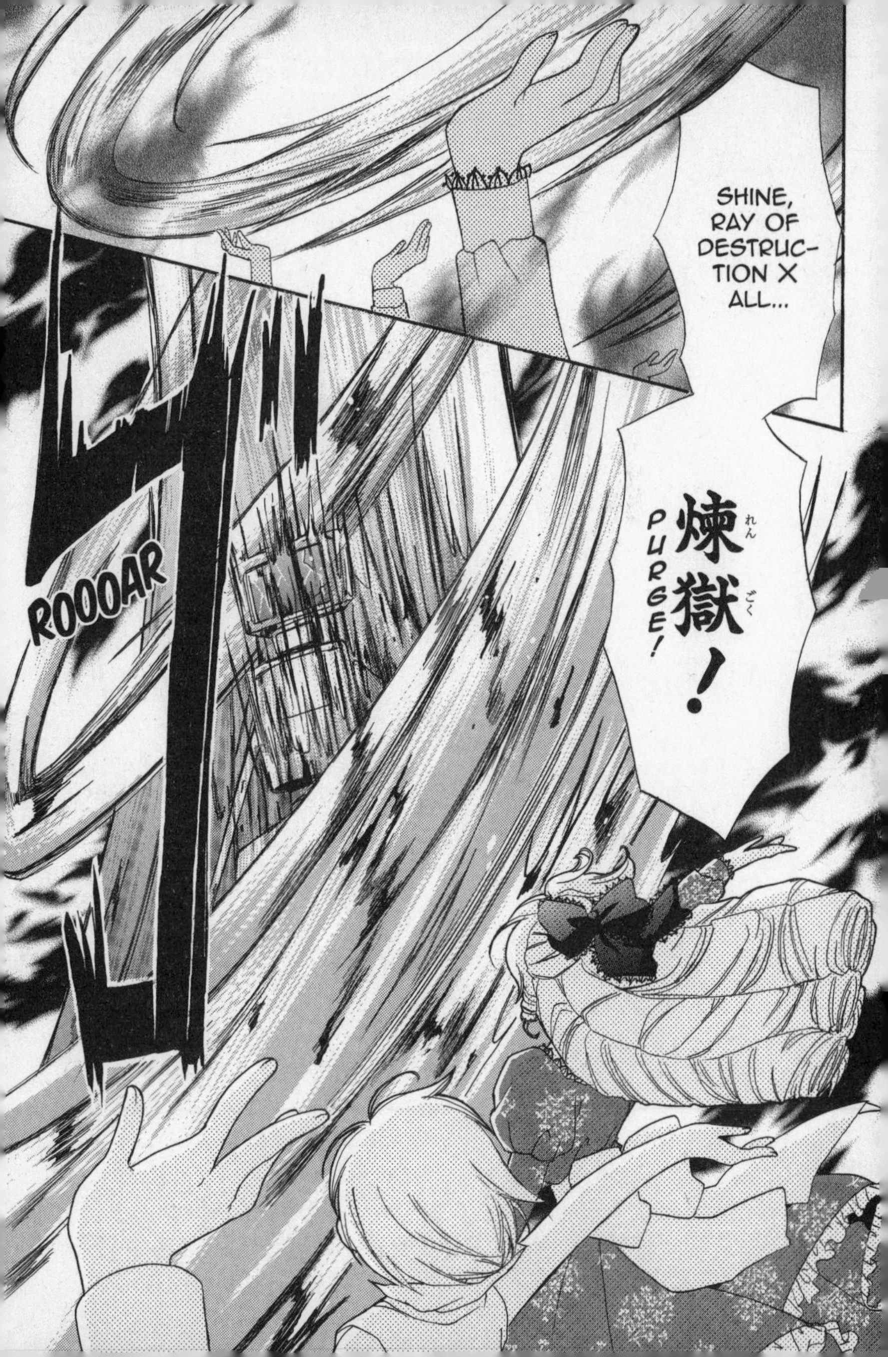
SHINE, RAY OF DESTRUC-TION X ALL...
煉獄！
PURGE!
ROOOAR

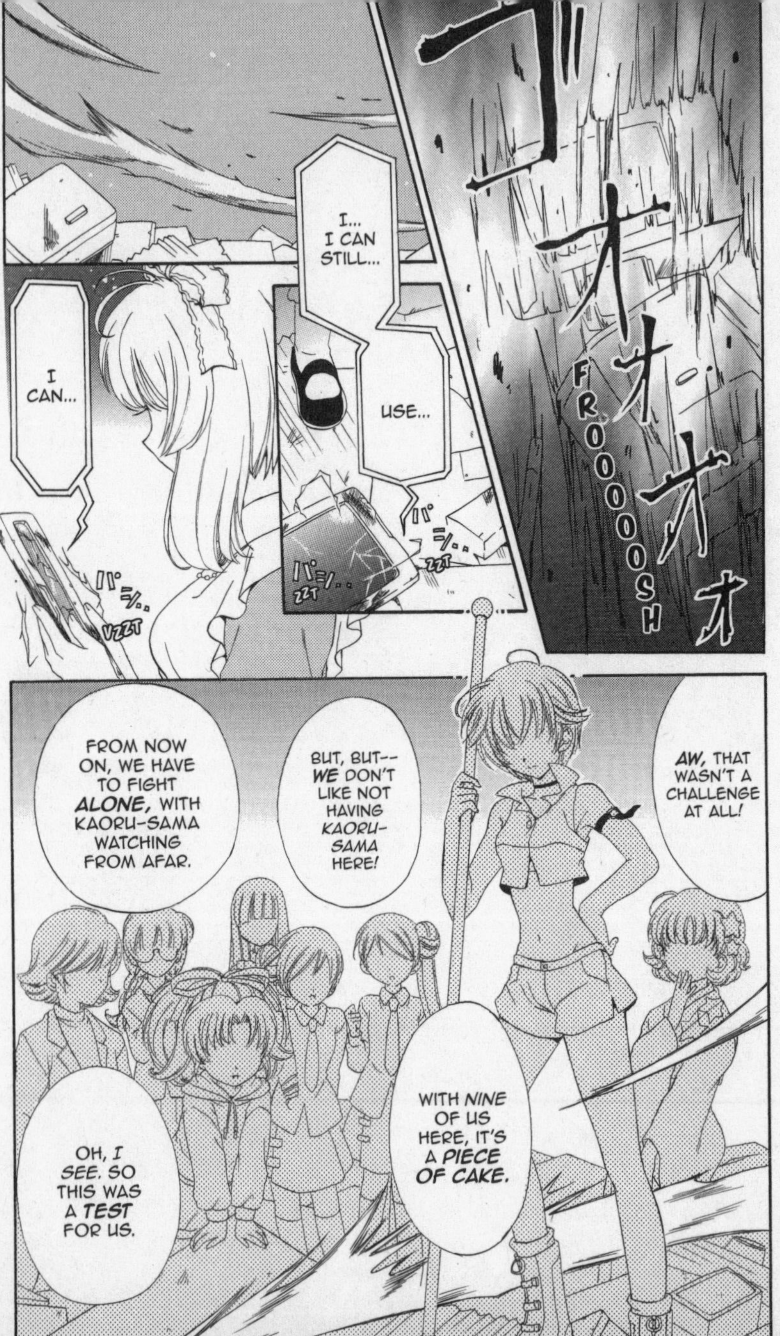
FROOOOOOSH
I... I CAN STILL...
USE...
ZZT
ZZT
I CAN...
VZZT
AW, THAT WASN'T A CHALLENGE AT ALL!
BUT, BUT-- **WE** DON'T LIKE NOT HAVING *KAORU-SAMA* HERE!
FROM NOW ON, WE HAVE TO FIGHT ***ALONE,*** WITH KAORU-SAMA WATCHING FROM AFAR.
WITH *NINE* OF US HERE, IT'S A ***PIECE OF CAKE.***
OH, *I* SEE. SO THIS WAS A ***TEST*** FOR US.

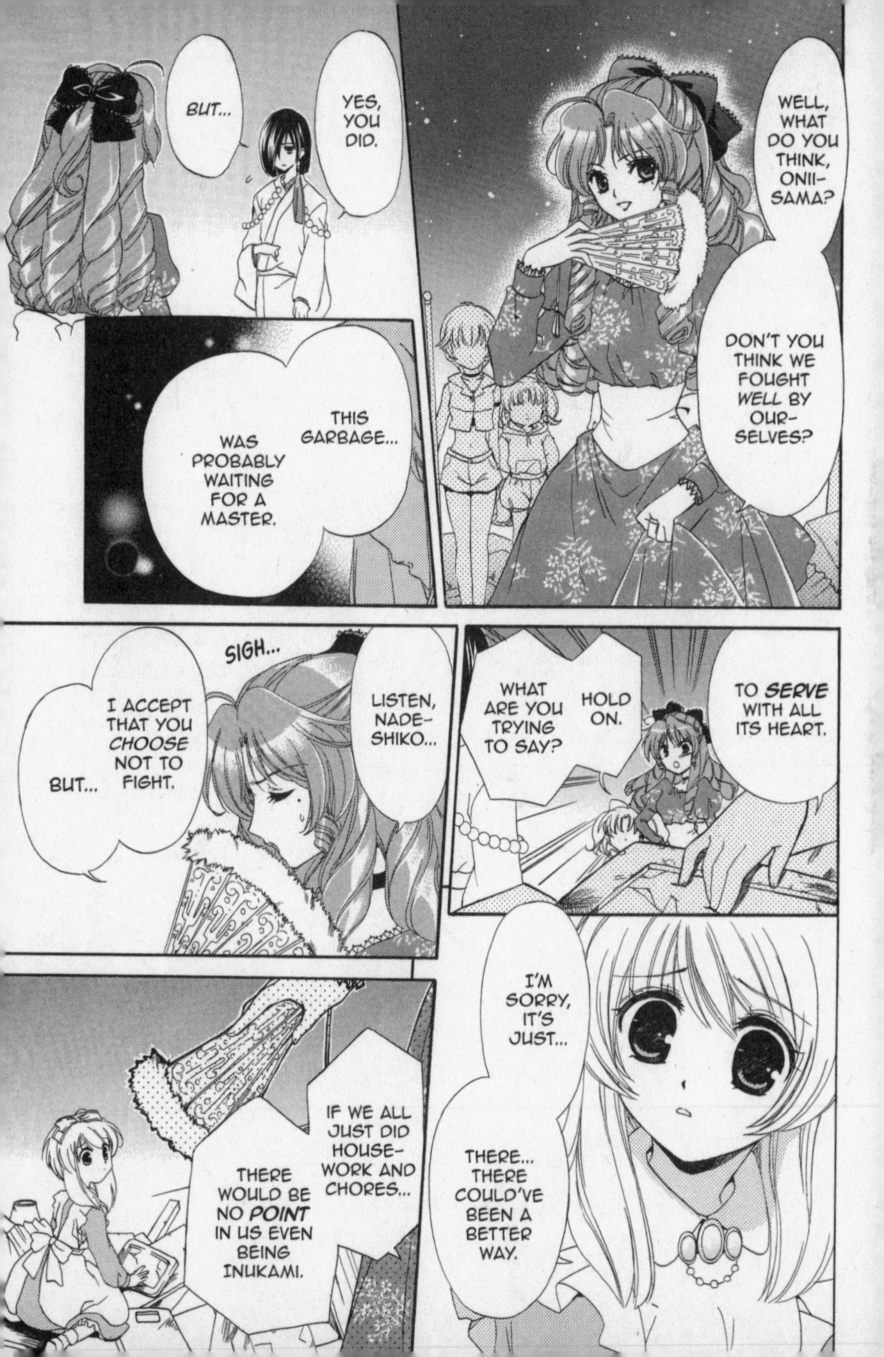
WELL, WHAT DO YOU THINK, ONII-SAMA?
DON'T YOU THINK WE FOUGHT *WELL* BY OURSELVES?
YES, YOU DID.
BUT...
THIS GARBAGE...
WAS PROBABLY WAITING FOR A MASTER.
TO *SERVE* WITH ALL ITS HEART.
HOLD ON.
WHAT ARE YOU TRYING TO SAY?
SIGH...
LISTEN, NADESHIKO...
I ACCEPT THAT YOU *CHOOSE* NOT TO FIGHT.
BUT...
I'M SORRY, IT'S JUST...
THERE... THERE COULD'VE BEEN A BETTER WAY.
IF WE ALL JUST DID HOUSEWORK AND CHORES...
THERE WOULD BE NO *POINT* IN US EVEN BEING INUKAMI.

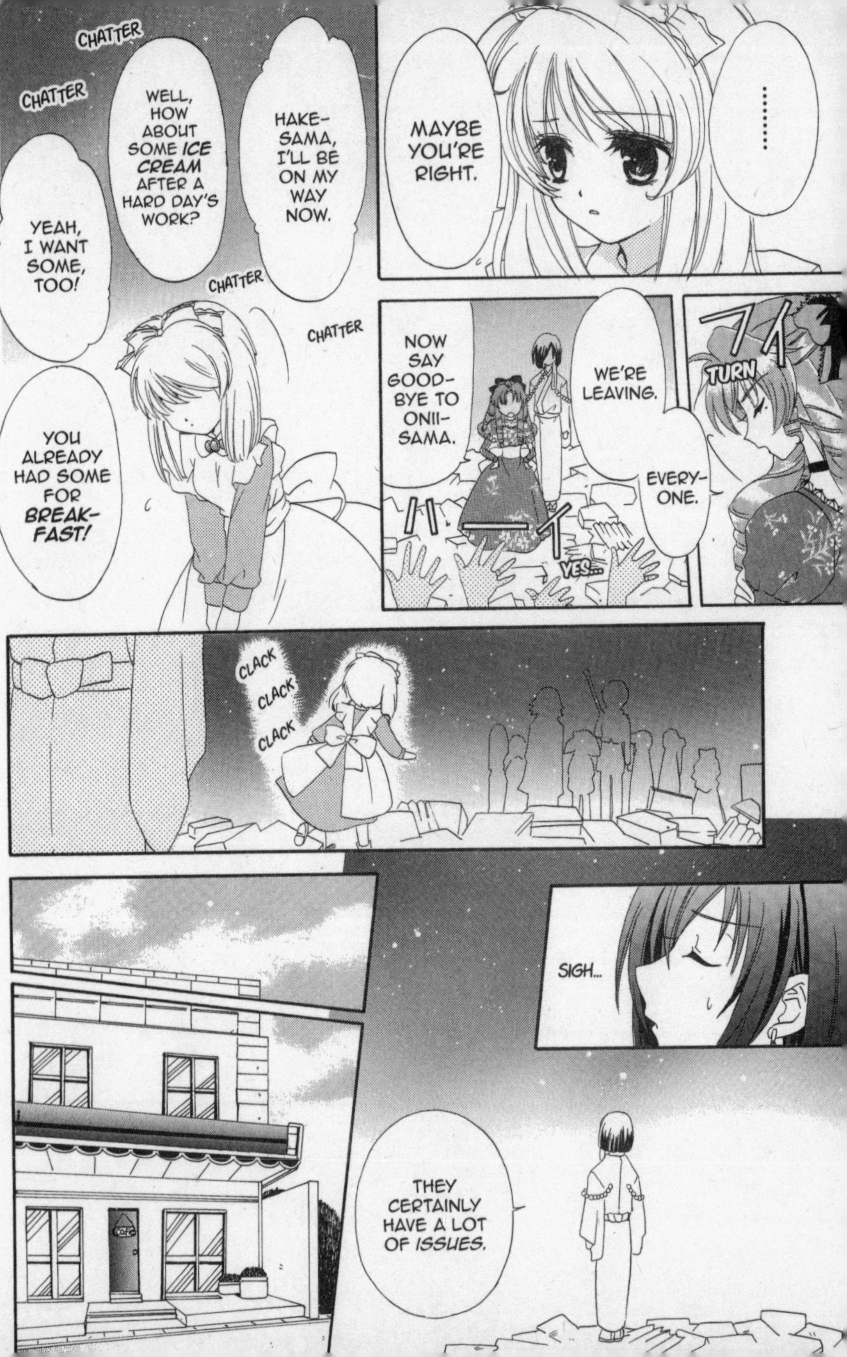
......
MAYBE YOU'RE RIGHT.
フイ
TURN
WE'RE LEAVING.
EVERY-ONE.
NOW SAY GOOD-BYE TO ONII-SAMA.
ハーイ
YES...
HAKE-SAMA, I'LL BE ON MY WAY NOW.
CHATTER
WELL, HOW ABOUT SOME *ICE CREAM* AFTER A HARD DAY'S WORK?
CHATTER
YEAH, I WANT SOME, TOO!
CHATTER
CHATTER
YOU ALREADY HAD SOME FOR ***BREAK-FAST!***
CLACK
CLACK
CLACK
SIGH...
THEY CERTAINLY HAVE A LOT OF *ISSUES*.

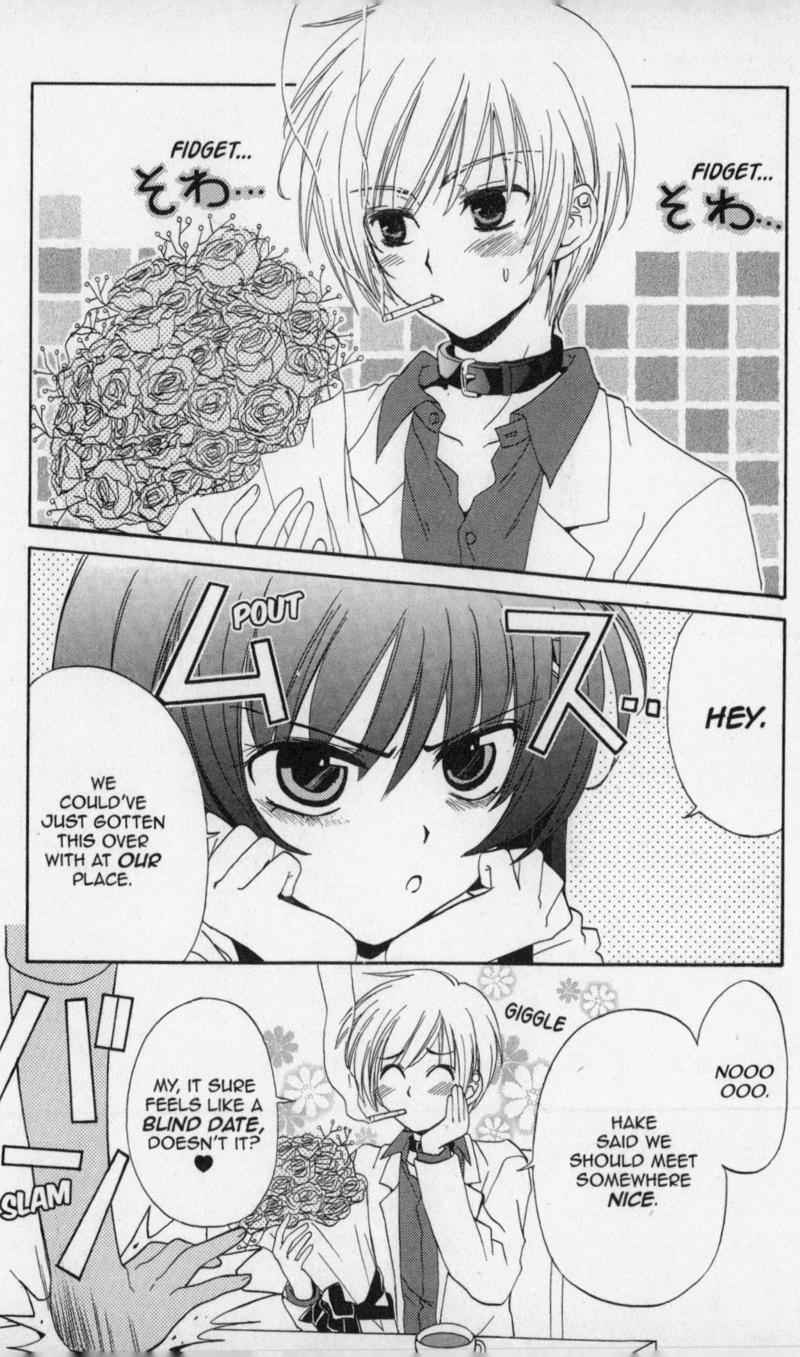

FIDGET...
そわ...
FIDGET...
そわ...
HEY.
POUT
ムス..
WE COULD'VE JUST GOTTEN THIS OVER WITH AT OUR PLACE.
NOOOOOO.
HAKE SAID WE SHOULD MEET SOMEWHERE NICE.
GIGGLE
MY, IT SURE FEELS LIKE A BLIND DATE, DOESN'T IT? ♥
SLAM

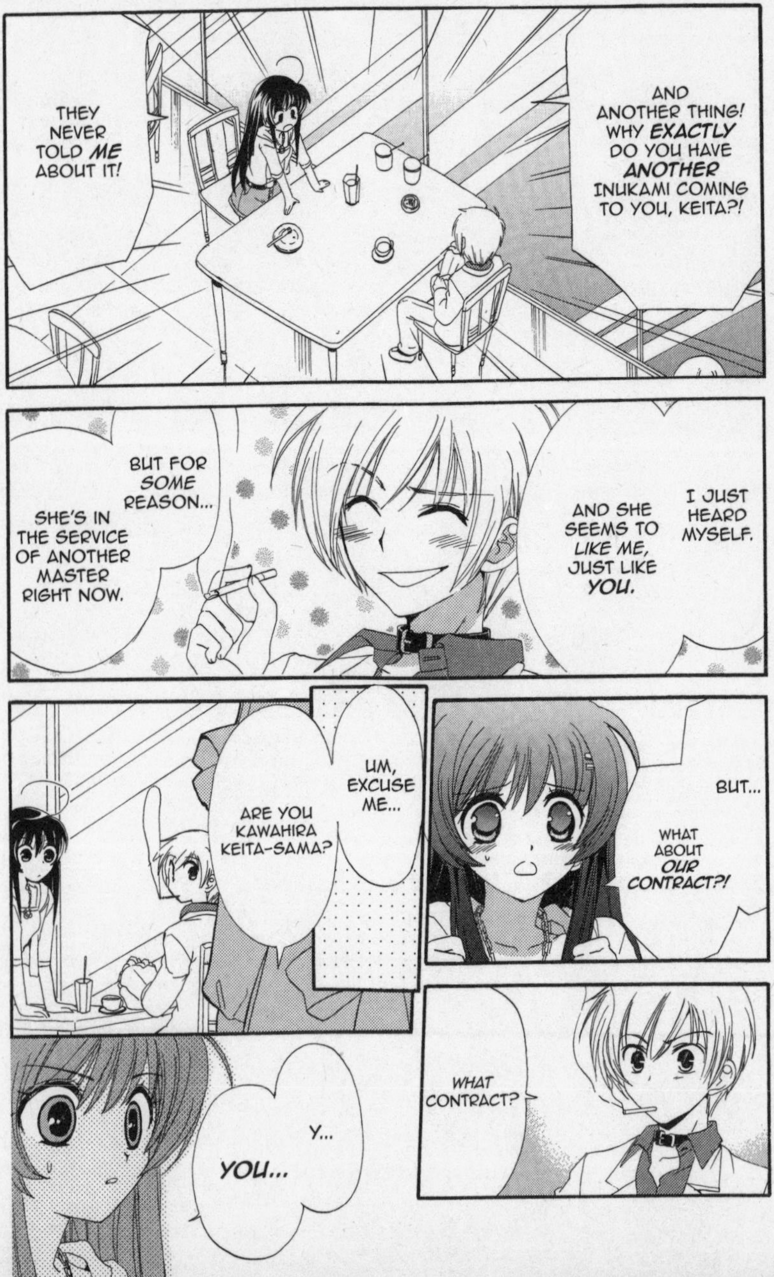
AND ANOTHER THING! WHY *EXACTLY* DO YOU HAVE *ANOTHER* INUKAMI COMING TO YOU, KEITA?!
THEY NEVER TOLD *ME* ABOUT IT!
I JUST HEARD MYSELF.
AND SHE SEEMS TO *LIKE ME,* JUST LIKE *YOU.*
BUT FOR *SOME* REASON...
SHE'S IN THE SERVICE OF ANOTHER MASTER RIGHT NOW.
BUT...
WHAT ABOUT *OUR* CONTRACT?!
UM, EXCUSE ME...
ARE YOU KAWAHIRA KEITA-SAMA?
WHAT CONTRACT?
Y...
YOU...

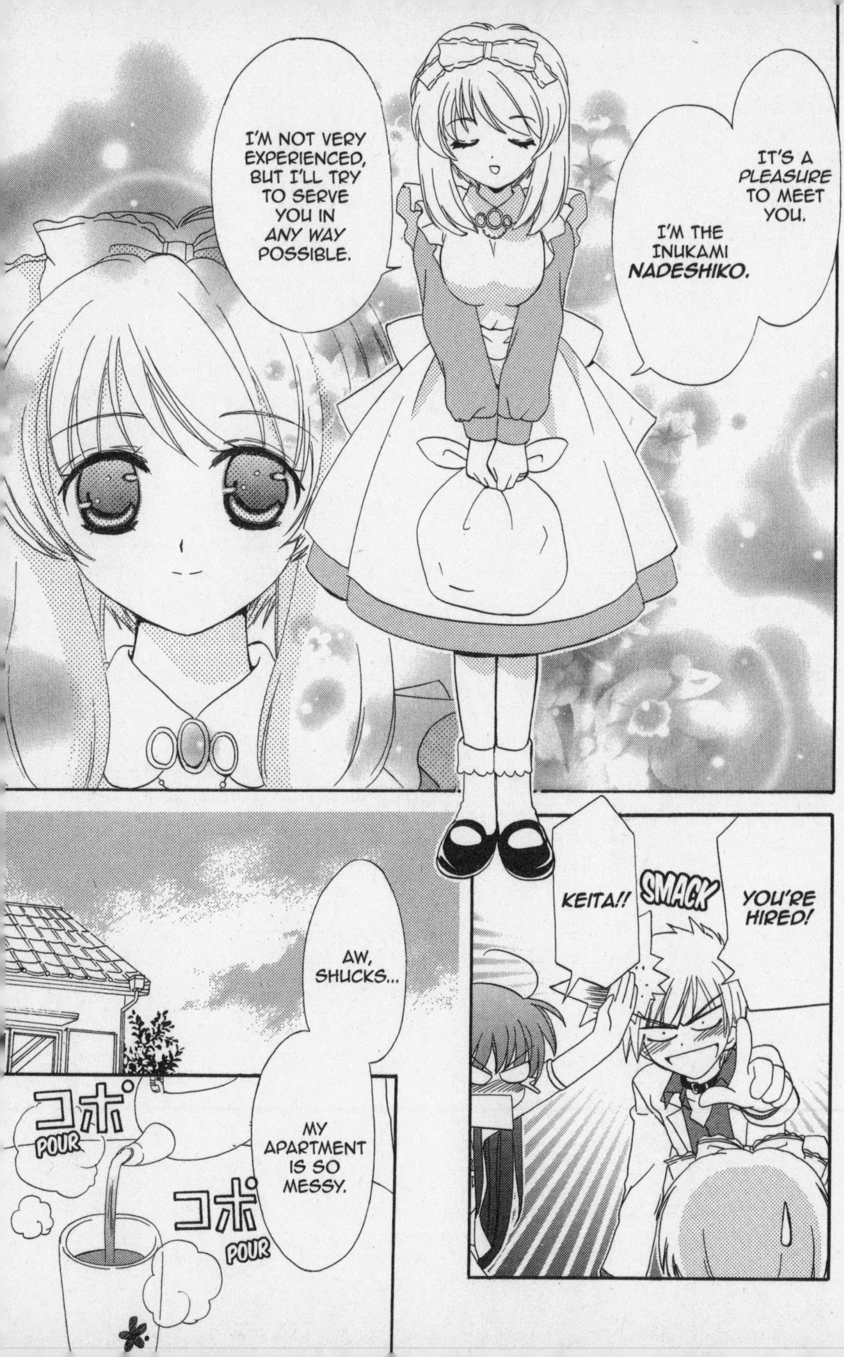
IT'S A PLEASURE TO MEET YOU.
I'M THE INUKAMI NADESHIKO.
I'M NOT VERY EXPERIENCED, BUT I'LL TRY TO SERVE YOU IN ANY WAY POSSIBLE.
YOU'RE HIRED!
SMACK
KEITA!!
AW, SHUCKS...
MY APARTMENT IS SO MESSY.
コポ
POUR
コポ
POUR

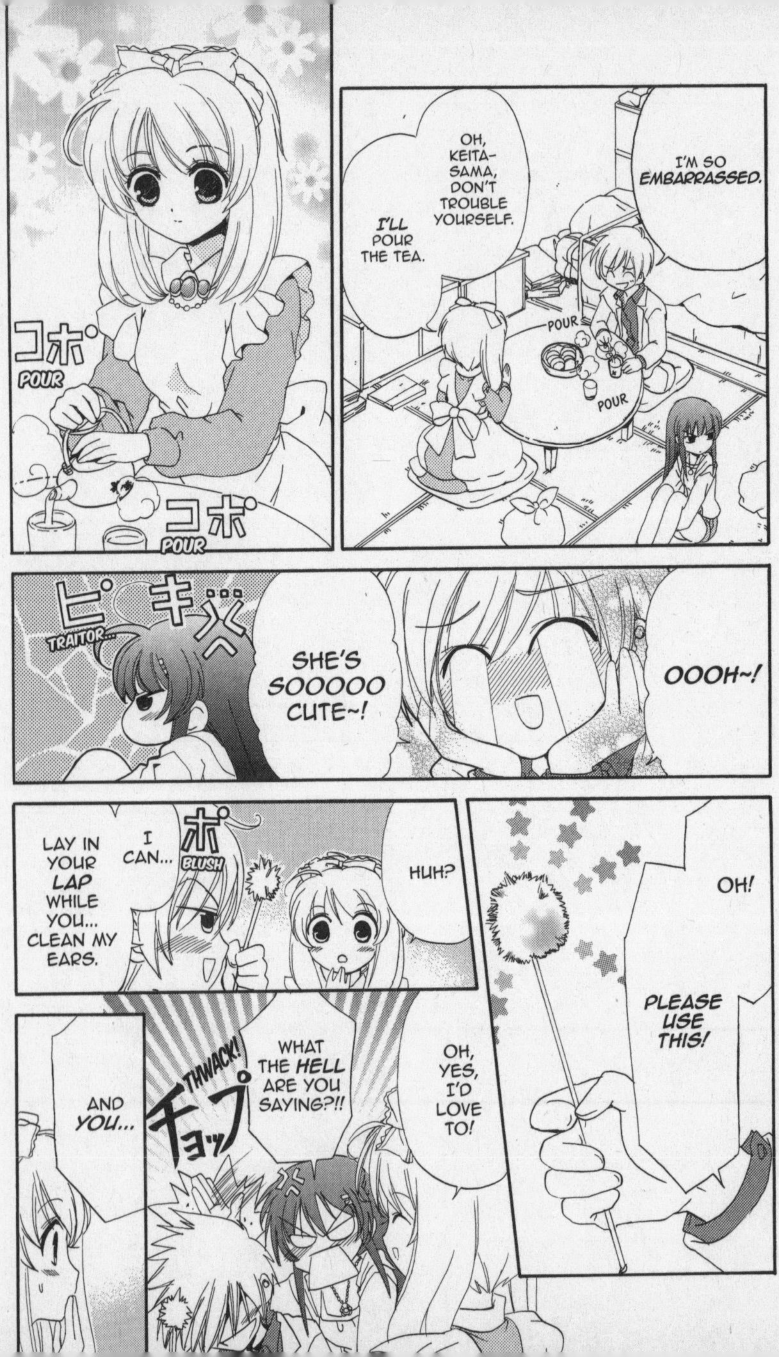
I'M SO EMBARRASSED.
OH, KEITA-SAMA, DON'T TROUBLE YOURSELF.
I'LL POUR THE TEA.
POUR
POUR
コポ
POUR
コポ
POUR
OOOH~!
SHE'S SOOOOO CUTE~!
ピキ
TRAITOR...
OH!
PLEASE USE THIS!
HUH?
I CAN...
ポ
BLUSH
LAY IN YOUR LAP WHILE YOU... CLEAN MY EARS.
OH, YES, I'D LOVE TO!
WHAT THE HELL ARE YOU SAYING?!!
THWACK!
チョップ
AND YOU...

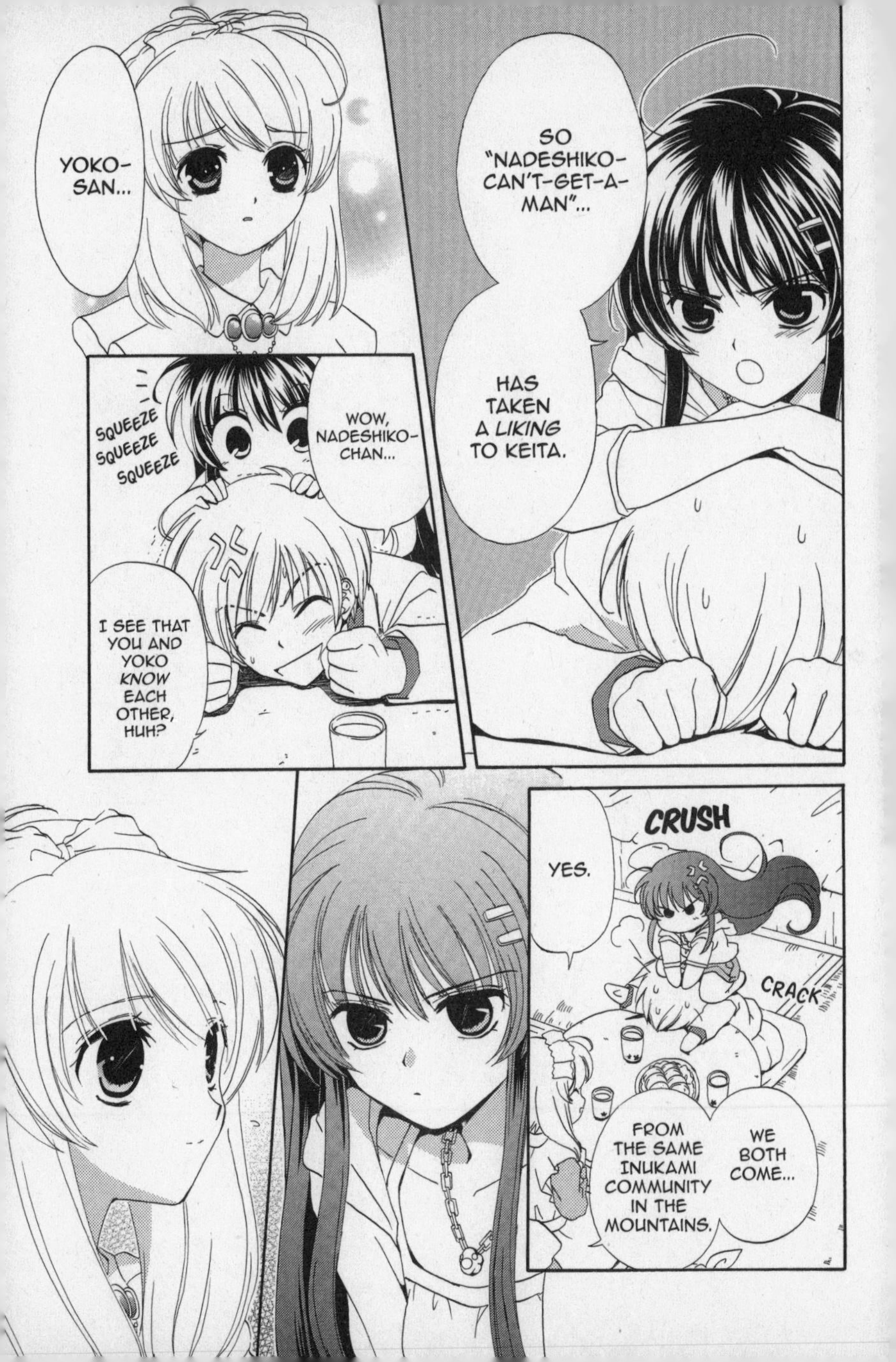
SO "NADESHIKO-CAN'T-GET-A-MAN"...
HAS TAKEN A *LIKING* TO KEITA.
YOKO-SAN...
WOW, NADESHIKO-CHAN...
SQUEEZE SQUEEZE SQUEEZE
I SEE THAT YOU AND YOKO *KNOW* EACH OTHER, HUH?
CRUSH
YES.
CRACK
WE BOTH COME...
FROM THE SAME INUKAMI COMMUNITY IN THE MOUNTAINS.

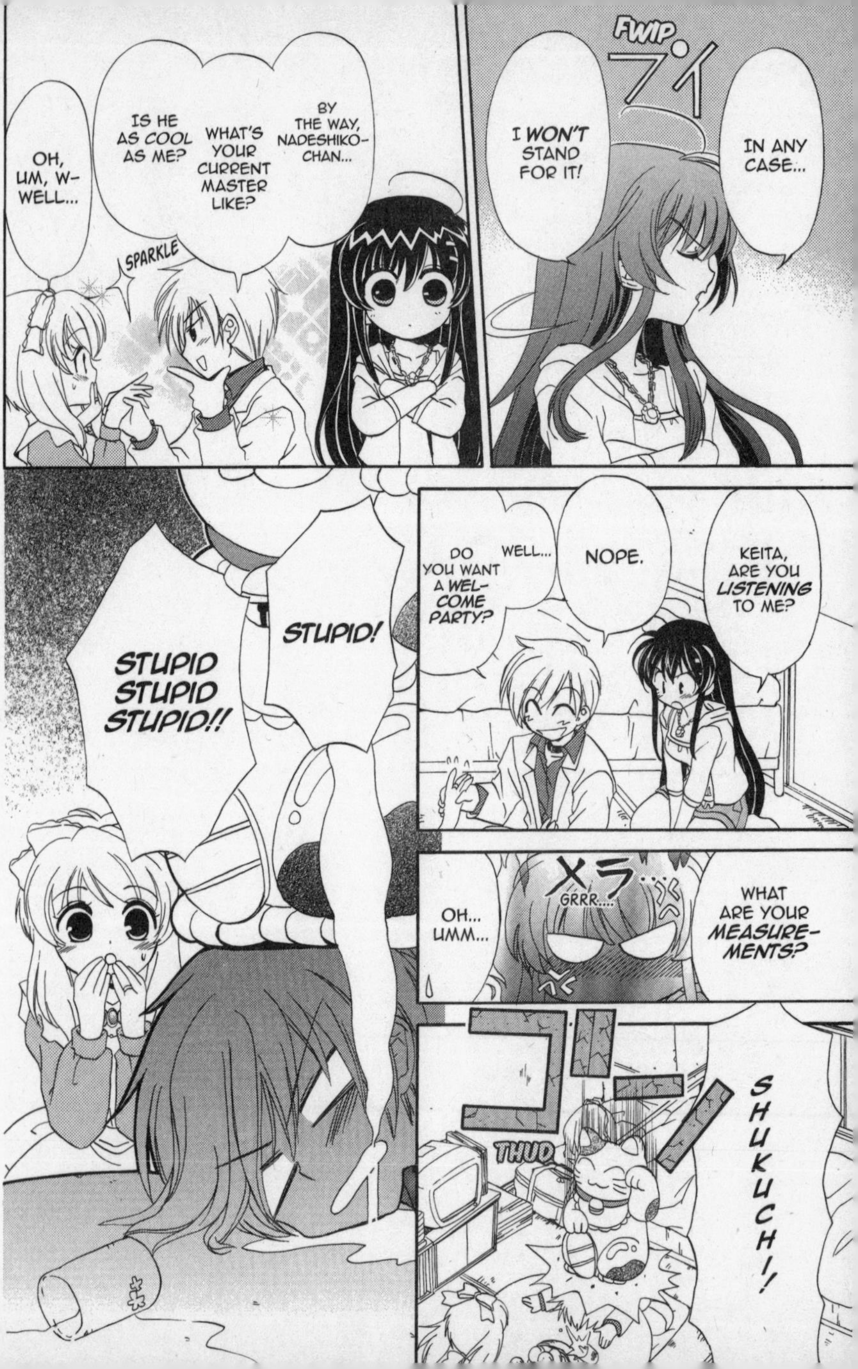
IN ANY CASE...
I WON'T STAND FOR IT!
FWIP
フイ
BY THE WAY, NADESHIKO-CHAN...
WHAT'S YOUR CURRENT MASTER LIKE?
IS HE AS COOL AS ME?
SPARKLE
OH, UM, W-WELL...
KEITA, ARE YOU LISTENING TO ME?
NOPE.
WELL...
DO YOU WANT A WEL-COME PARTY?
WHAT ARE YOUR MEASURE-MENTS?
メラ
GRRR....
OH... UMM...
SHUKUCH!!
THUD
STUPID!
STUPID STUPID STUPID!!

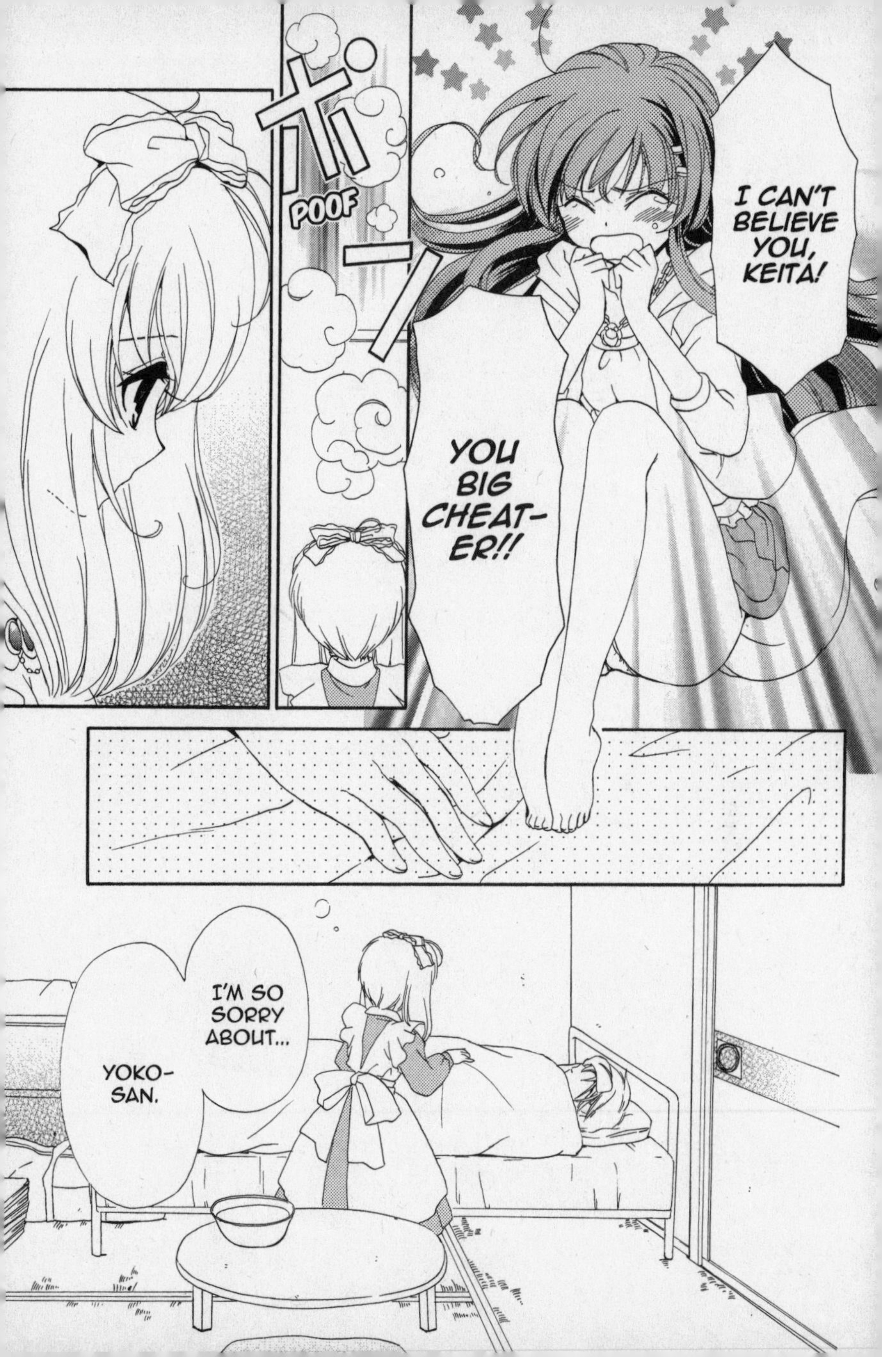

I CAN'T BELIEVE YOU, KEITA!
YOU BIG CHEATER!!
POOF
I'M SO SORRY ABOUT...
YOKO-SAN.

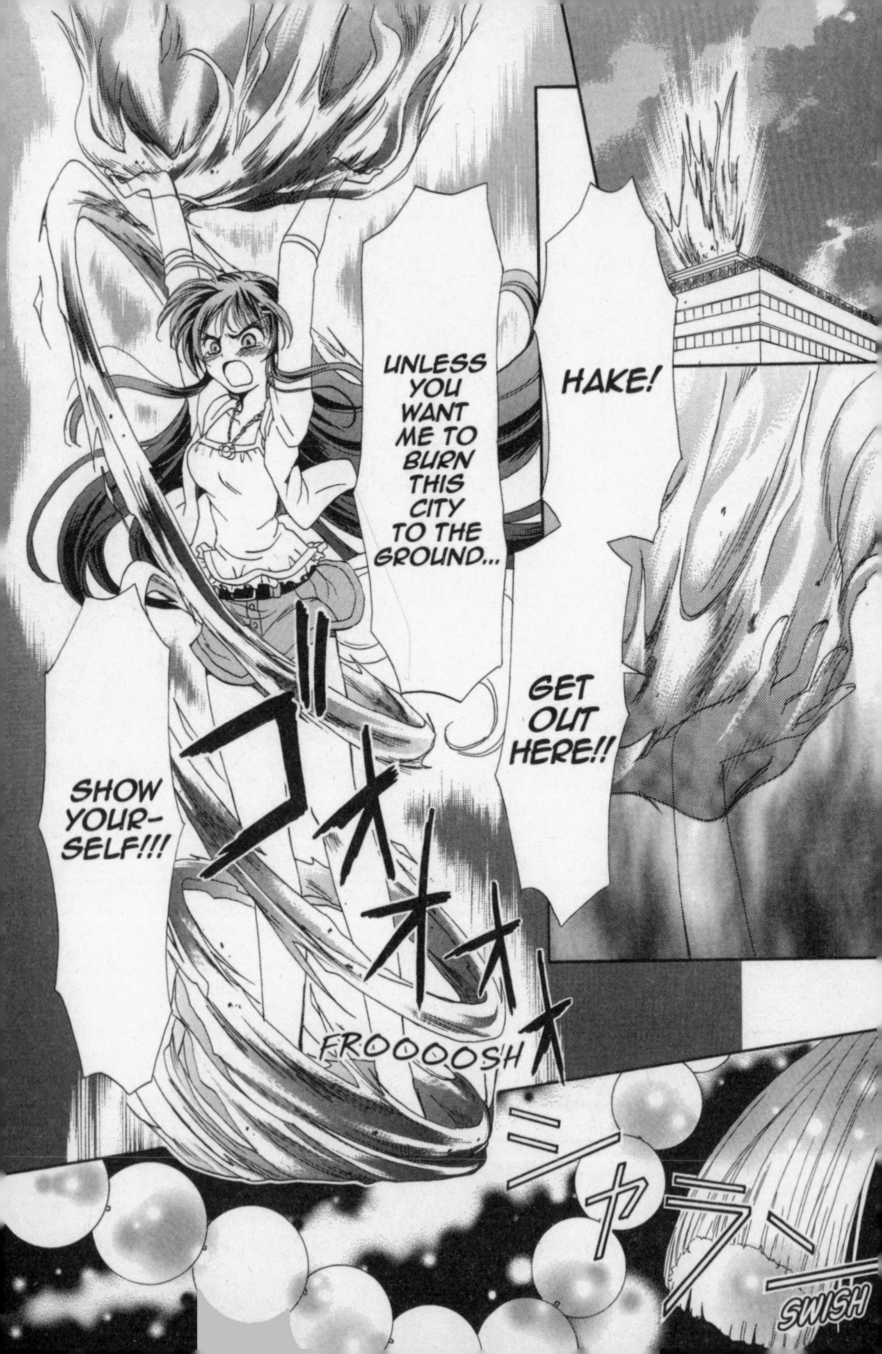
HAKE!
GET OUT HERE!!
UNLESS YOU WANT ME TO BURN THIS CITY TO THE GROUND...
SHOW YOUR-SELF!!!
FROOOOOSH
SWISH

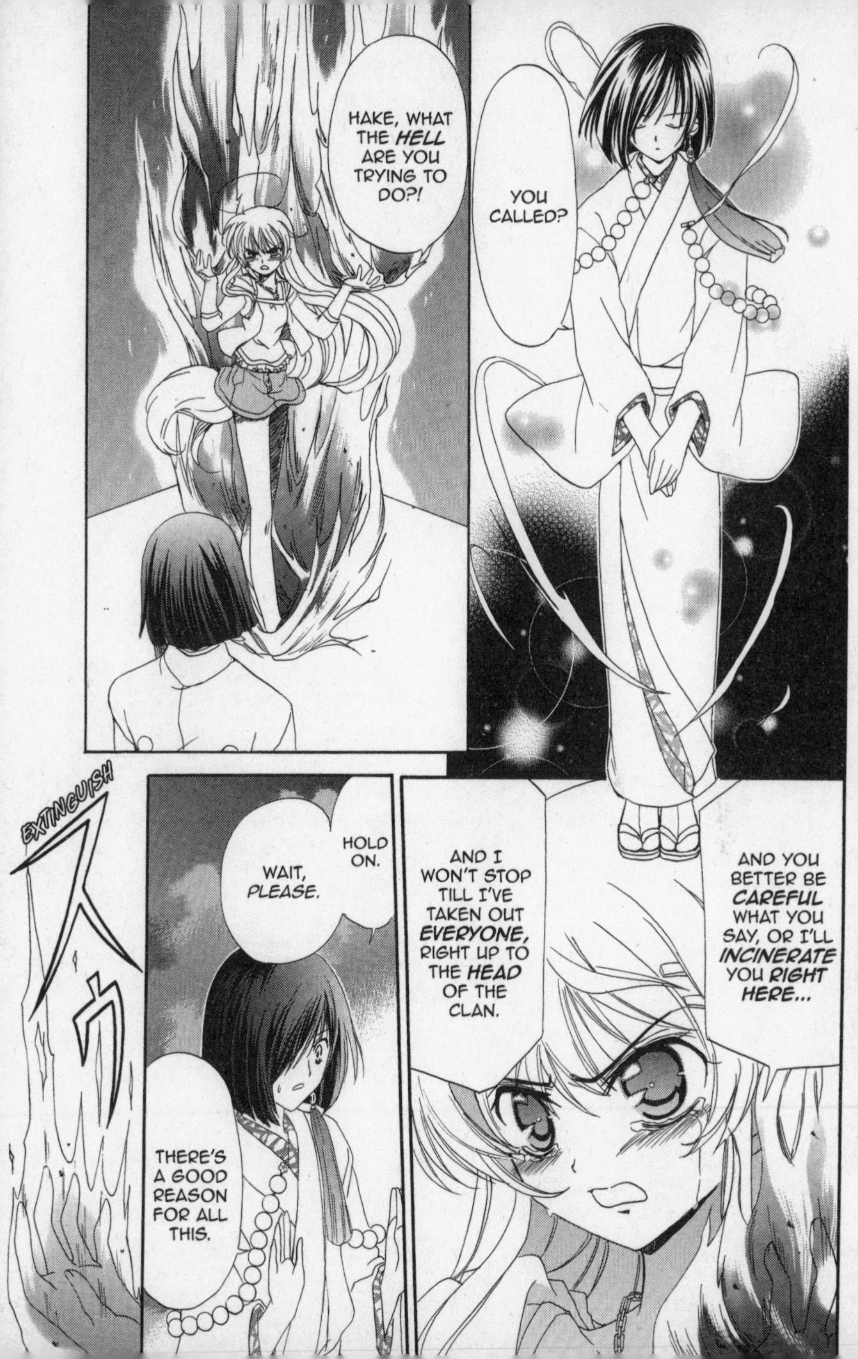
YOU CALLED?
HAKE, WHAT THE HELL ARE YOU TRYING TO DO?!
AND YOU BETTER BE CAREFUL WHAT YOU SAY, OR I'LL INCINERATE YOU RIGHT HERE...
AND I WON'T STOP TILL I'VE TAKEN OUT EVERYONE, RIGHT UP TO THE HEAD OF THE CLAN.
HOLD ON.
WAIT, PLEASE.
THERE'S A GOOD REASON FOR ALL THIS.
EXTINGUISH

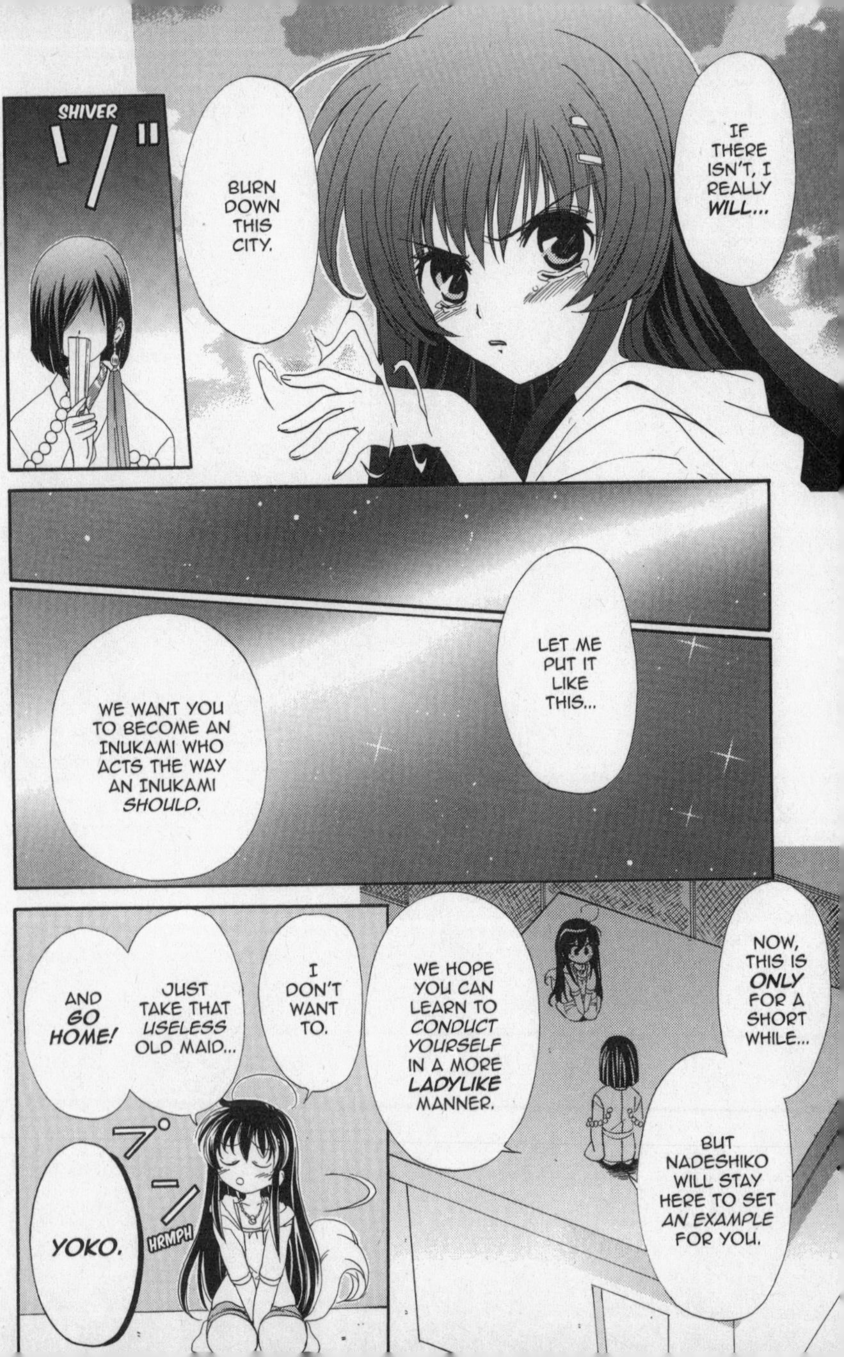
IF THERE ISN'T, I REALLY WILL...
BURN DOWN THIS CITY.
SHIVER
LET ME PUT IT LIKE THIS...
WE WANT YOU TO BECOME AN INUKAMI WHO ACTS THE WAY AN INUKAMI SHOULD.
NOW, THIS IS ONLY FOR A SHORT WHILE...
BUT NADESHIKO WILL STAY HERE TO SET AN EXAMPLE FOR YOU.
WE HOPE YOU CAN LEARN TO CONDUCT YOURSELF IN A MORE LADYLIKE MANNER.
I DON'T WANT TO.
JUST TAKE THAT USELESS OLD MAID...
AND GO HOME!
HRMPH
YOKO.

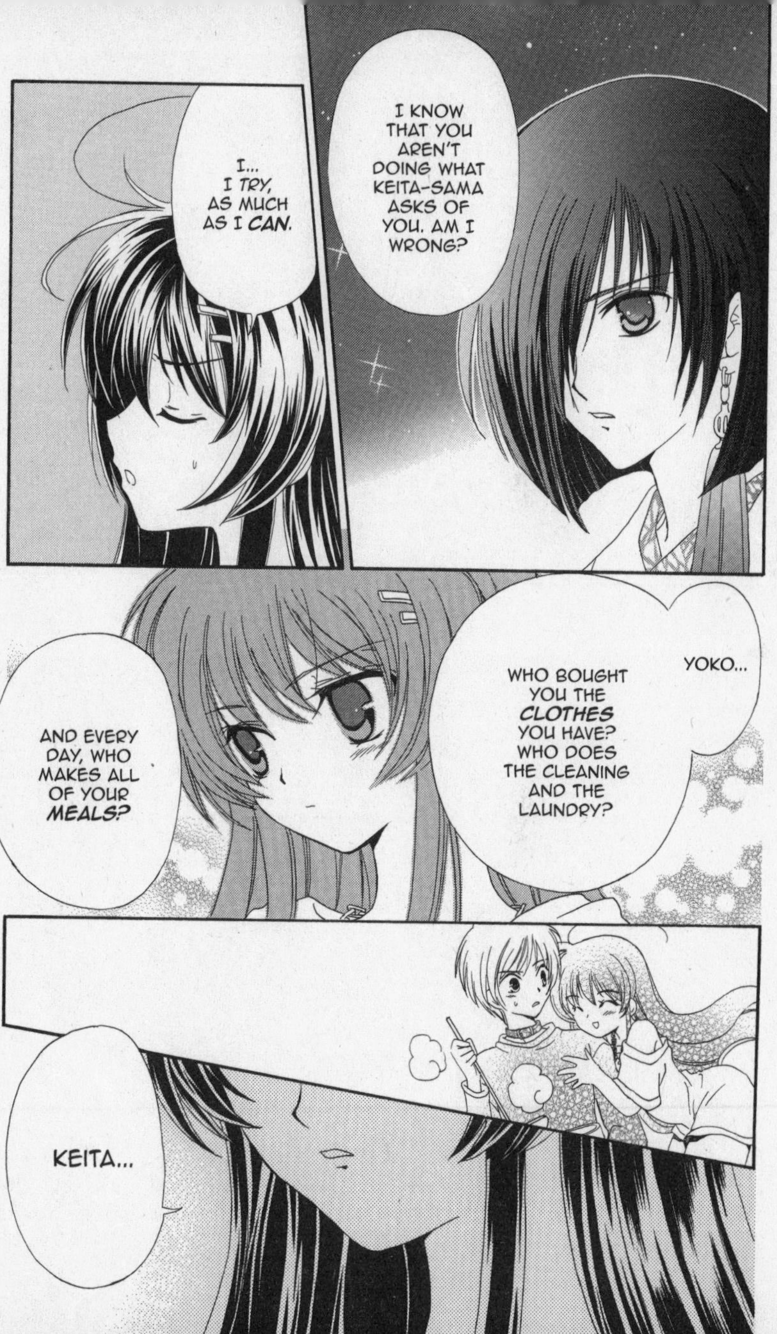
I KNOW THAT YOU AREN'T DOING WHAT KEITA-SAMA ASKS OF YOU. AM I WRONG?
I... I *TRY*, AS MUCH AS I **CAN**.
YOKO...
WHO BOUGHT YOU THE ***CLOTHES*** YOU HAVE? WHO DOES THE CLEANING AND THE LAUNDRY?
AND EVERY DAY, WHO MAKES ALL OF YOUR ***MEALS?***
KEITA...

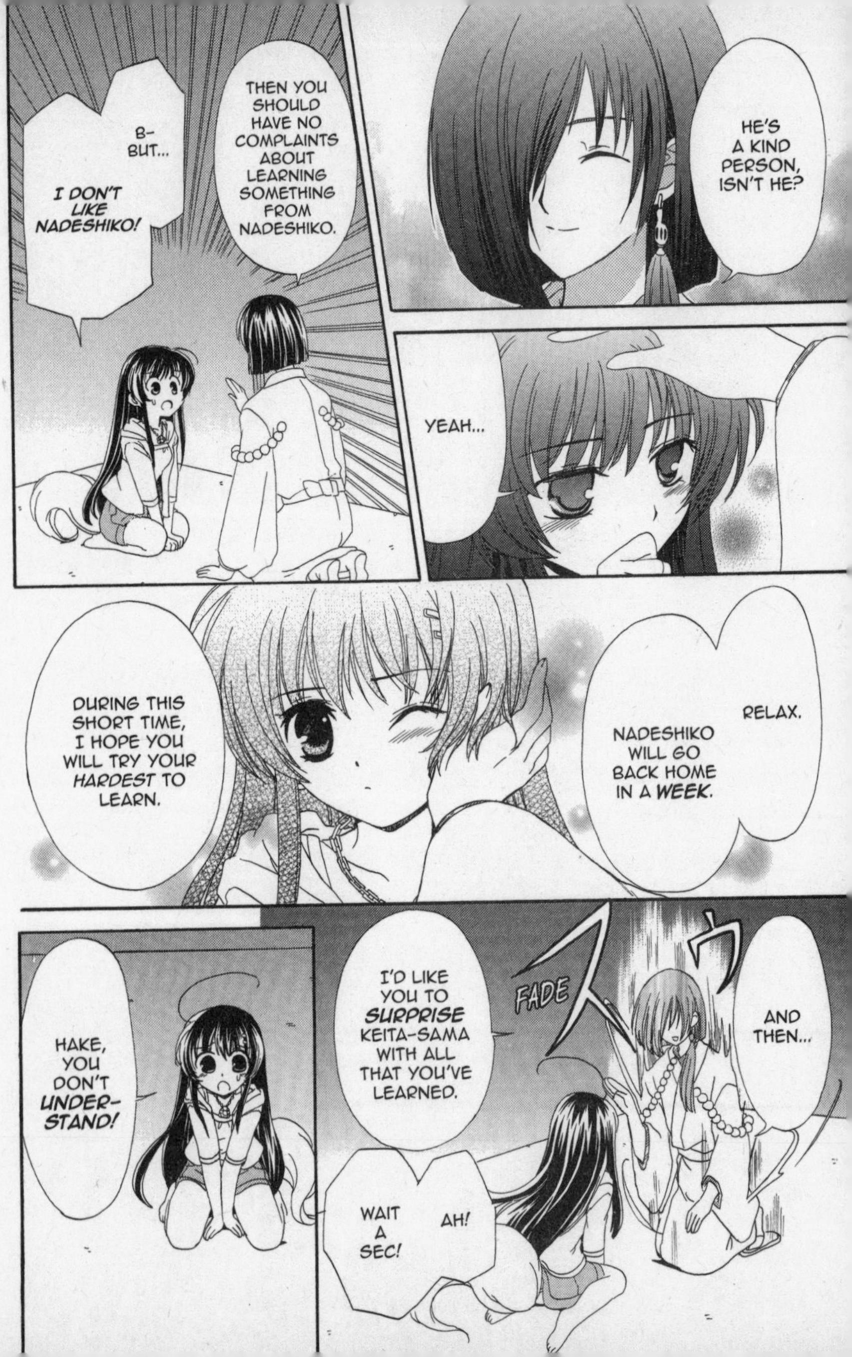
HE'S A KIND PERSON, ISN'T HE?
YEAH...
THEN YOU SHOULD HAVE NO COMPLAINTS ABOUT LEARNING SOMETHING FROM NADESHIKO.
B-BUT... I DON'T LIKE NADESHIKO!
RELAX. NADESHIKO WILL GO BACK HOME IN A WEEK.
DURING THIS SHORT TIME, I HOPE YOU WILL TRY YOUR HARDEST TO LEARN.
AND THEN...
I'D LIKE YOU TO SURPRISE KEITA-SAMA WITH ALL THAT YOU'VE LEARNED.
FADE
AH!
WAIT A SEC!
HAKE, YOU DON'T UNDER-STAND!

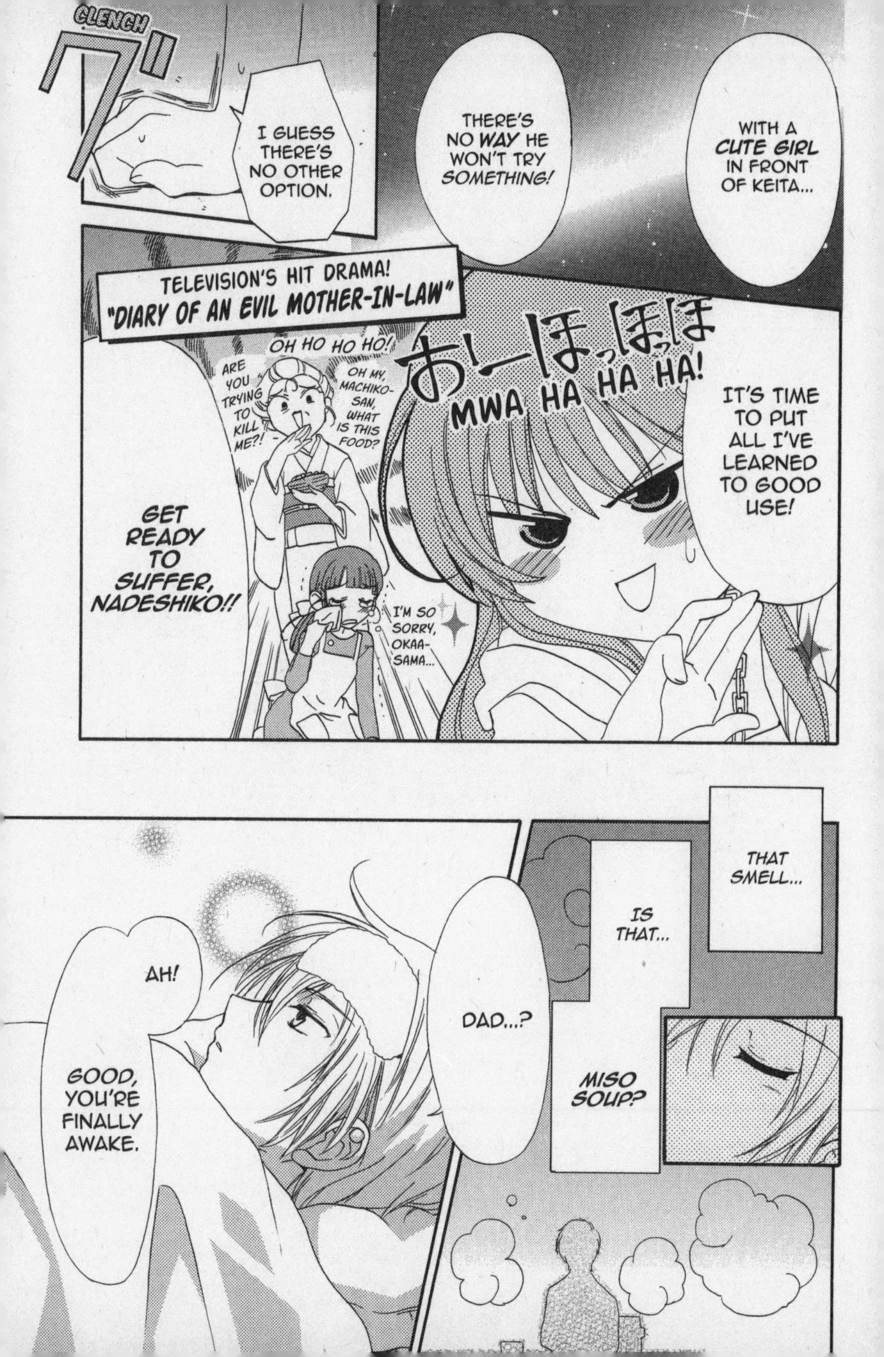
WITH A CUTE GIRL IN FRONT OF KEITA...
THERE'S NO WAY HE WON'T TRY SOMETHING!
CLENCH
I GUESS THERE'S NO OTHER OPTION.
TELEVISION'S HIT DRAMA! "DIARY OF AN EVIL MOTHER-IN-LAW"
IT'S TIME TO PUT ALL I'VE LEARNED TO GOOD USE!
おーほっほほ
MWA HA HA HA!
OH HO HO HO!
OH MY, MACHIKO-SAN, WHAT IS THIS FOOD?
ARE YOU TRYING TO KILL ME?!
I'M SO SORRY, OKAA-SAMA...
GET READY TO SUFFER, NADESHIKO!!
THAT SMELL...
IS THAT...
MISO SOUP?
DAD...?
AH!
GOOD, YOU'RE FINALLY AWAKE.

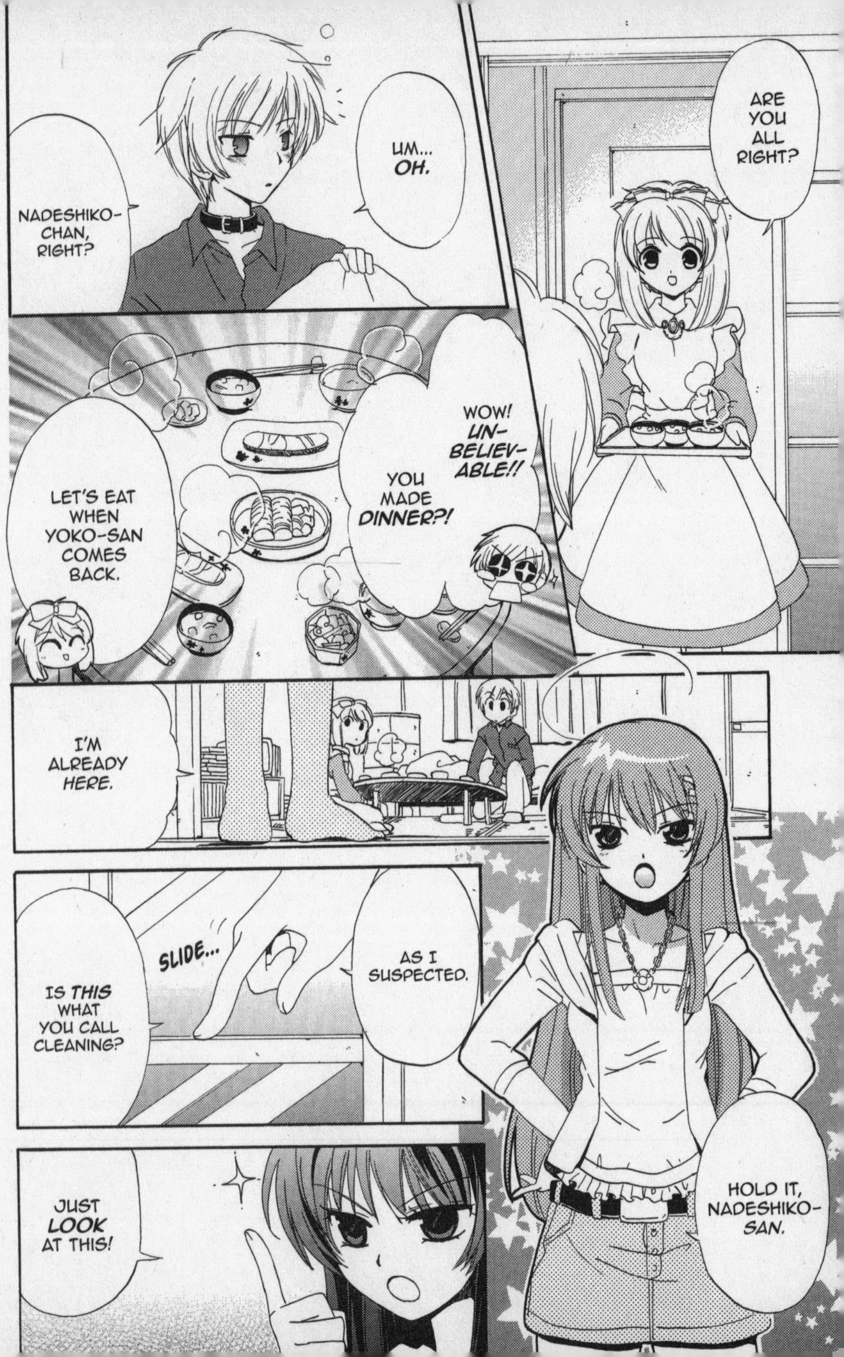
ARE YOU ALL RIGHT?
UM... OH.
NADESHIKO-CHAN, RIGHT?
WOW! UN-BELIEVABLE!!
YOU MADE DINNER?!
LET'S EAT WHEN YOKO-SAN COMES BACK.
I'M ALREADY HERE.
AS I SUSPECTED.
SLIDE...
IS THIS WHAT YOU CALL CLEANING?
HOLD IT, NADESHIKO-SAN.
JUST LOOK AT THIS!

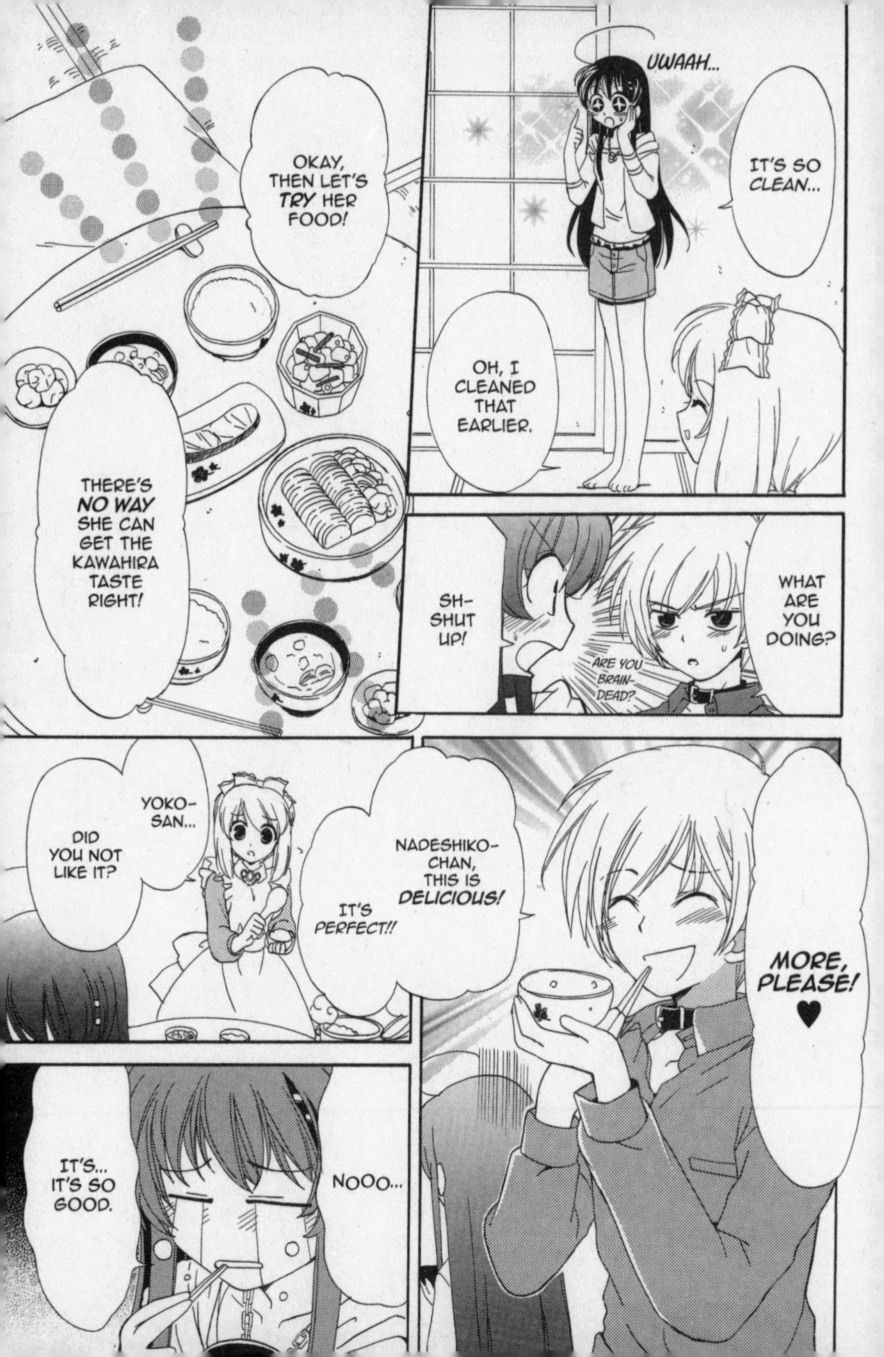
UWAAH...
IT'S SO CLEAN...
OH, I CLEANED THAT EARLIER.
WHAT ARE YOU DOING?
ARE YOU BRAIN-DEAD?
SH-SHUT UP!
OKAY, THEN LET'S TRY HER FOOD!
THERE'S NO WAY SHE CAN GET THE KAWAHIRA TASTE RIGHT!
MORE, PLEASE! ♥
NADESHIKO-CHAN, THIS IS DELICIOUS!
IT'S PERFECT!!
YOKO-SAN...
DID YOU NOT LIKE IT?
NOOO...
IT'S... IT'S SO GOOD.

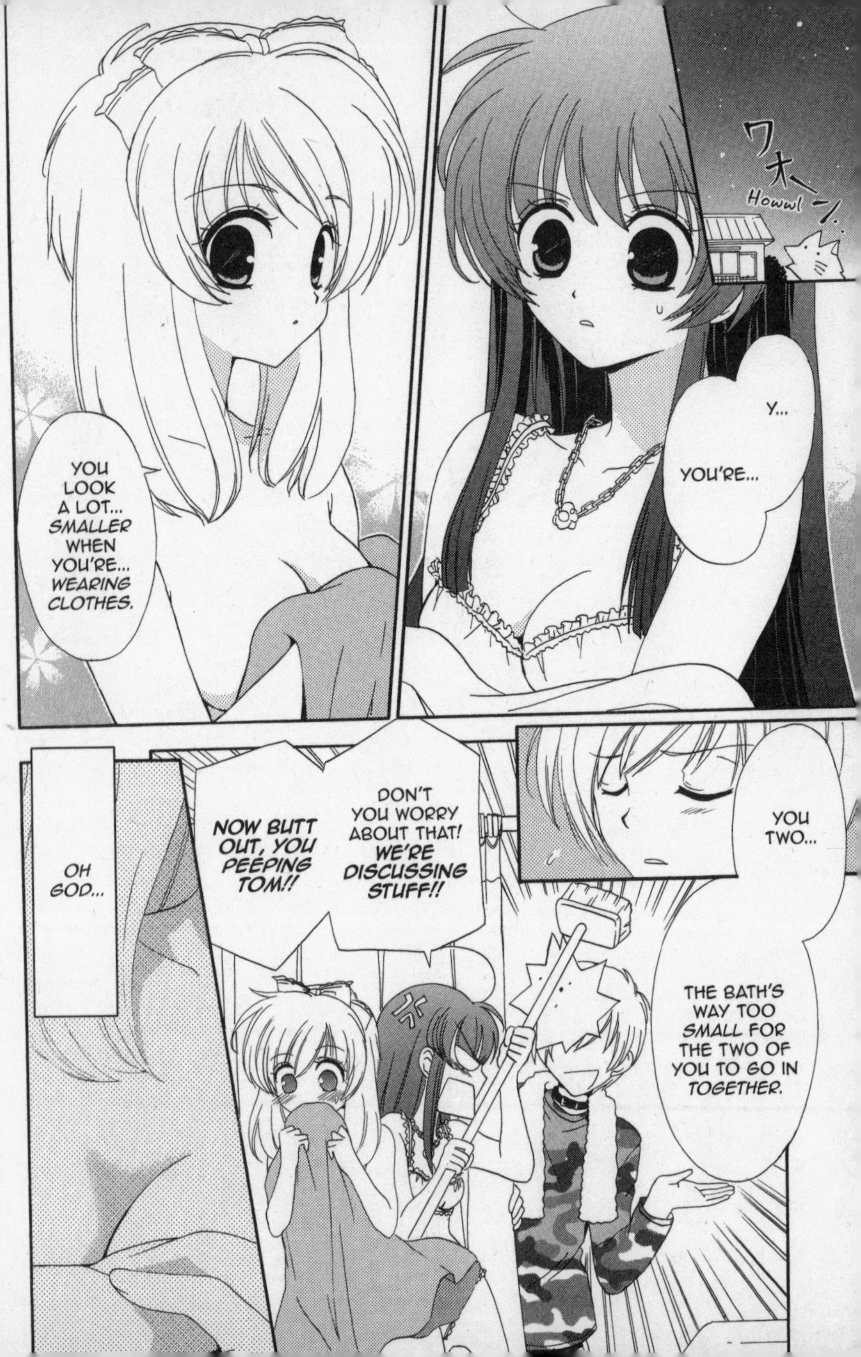
ワオーン
Howwl
Y...
YOU'RE...
YOU LOOK A LOT... *SMALLER* WHEN YOU'RE... *WEARING* CLOTHES.
YOU TWO...
THE BATH'S WAY TOO *SMALL* FOR THE TWO OF YOU TO GO IN *TOGETHER.*
DON'T YOU WORRY ABOUT THAT! *WE'RE DISCUSSING STUFF!!*
NOW BUTT OUT, YOU PEEPING TOM!!
OH GOD...

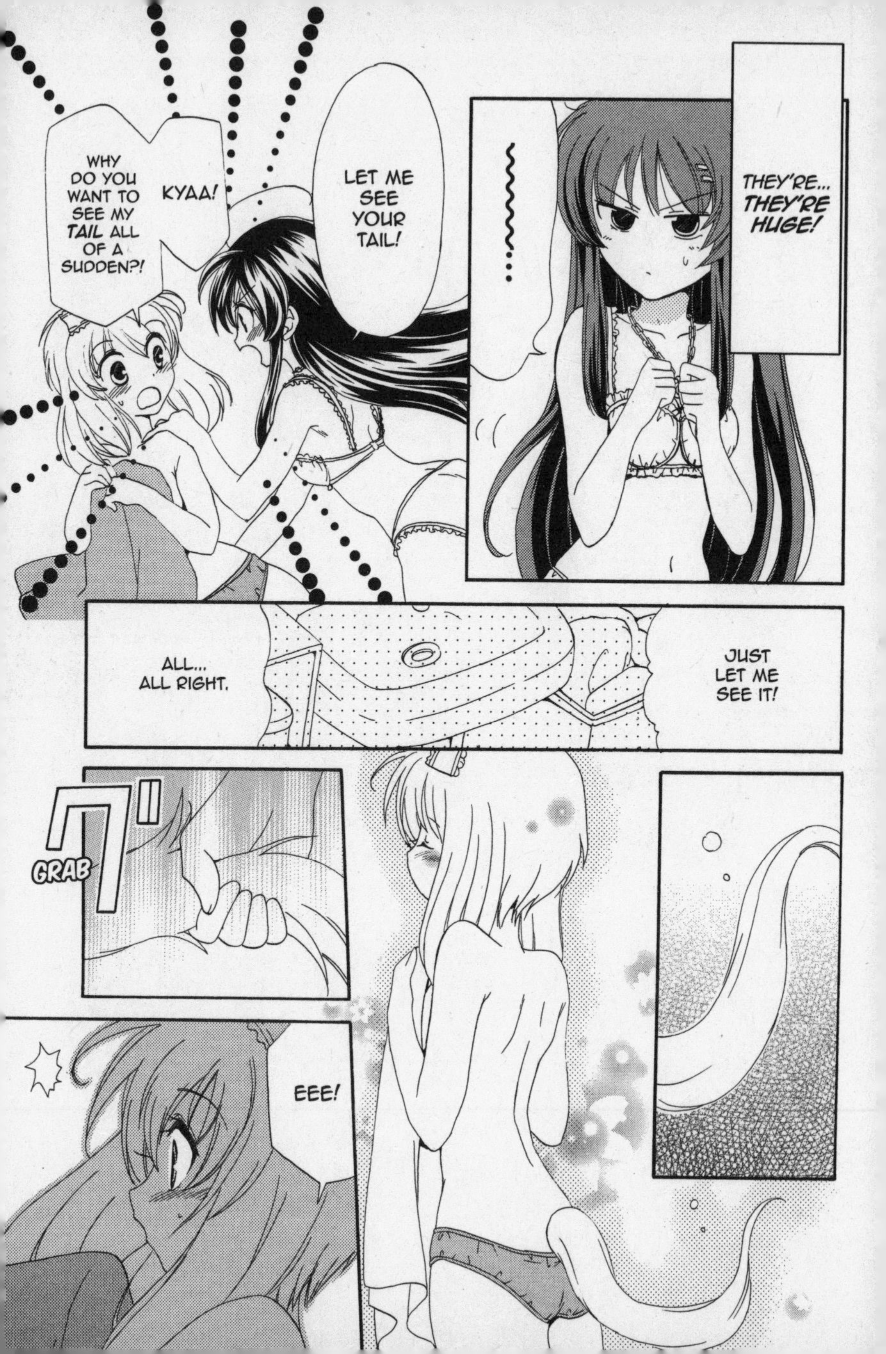
THEY'RE... THEY'RE HUGE!
......
LET ME SEE YOUR TAIL!
KYAA!
WHY DO YOU WANT TO SEE MY TAIL ALL OF A SUDDEN?!
JUST LET ME SEE IT!
ALL... ALL RIGHT.
GRAB
EEE!

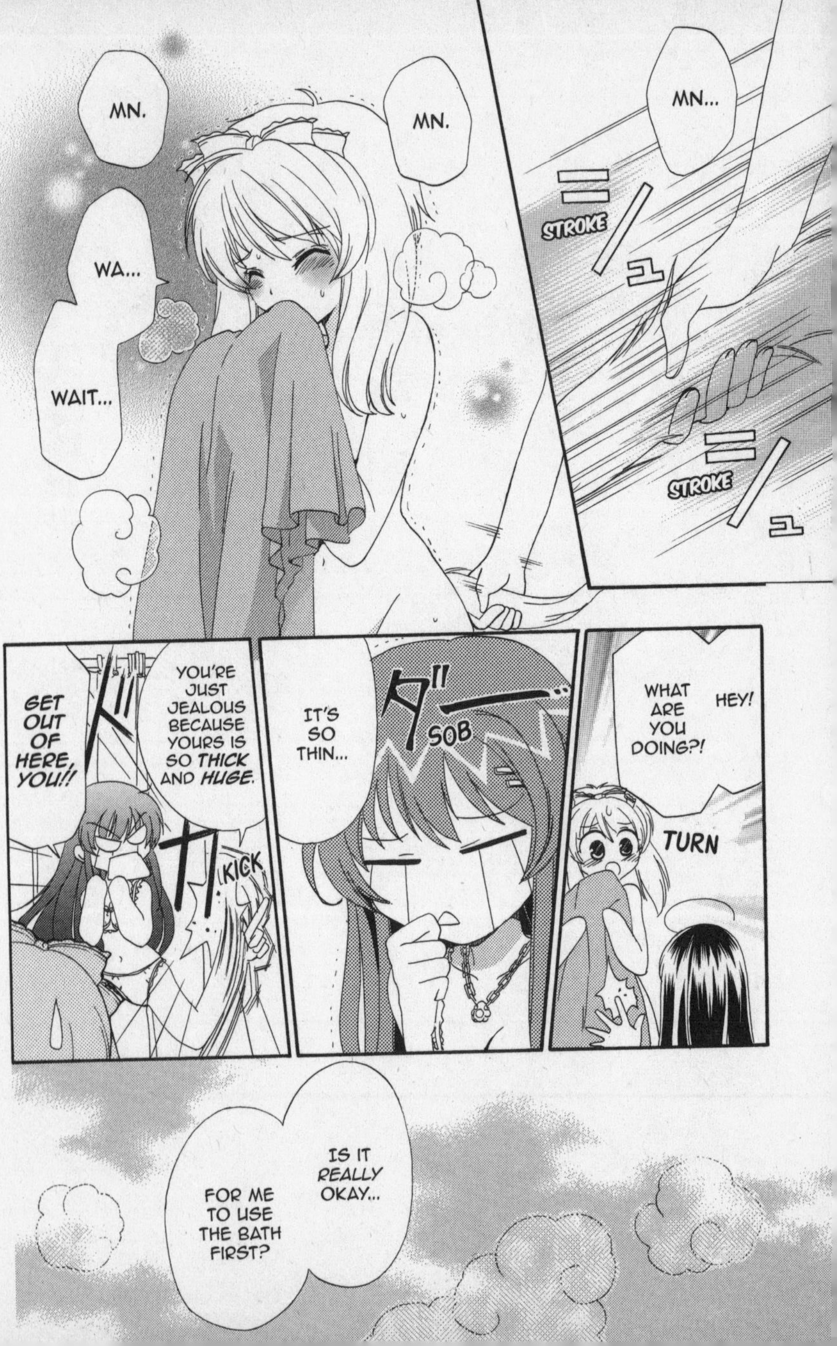
MN...
STROKE
STROKE
MN.
MN.
WA...
WAIT...
HEY!
WHAT ARE YOU DOING?!
TURN
IT'S SO THIN...
SOB
YOU'RE JUST JEALOUS BECAUSE YOURS IS SO THICK AND HUGE.
GET OUT OF HERE, YOU!!
KICK
IS IT REALLY OKAY...
FOR ME TO USE THE BATH FIRST?

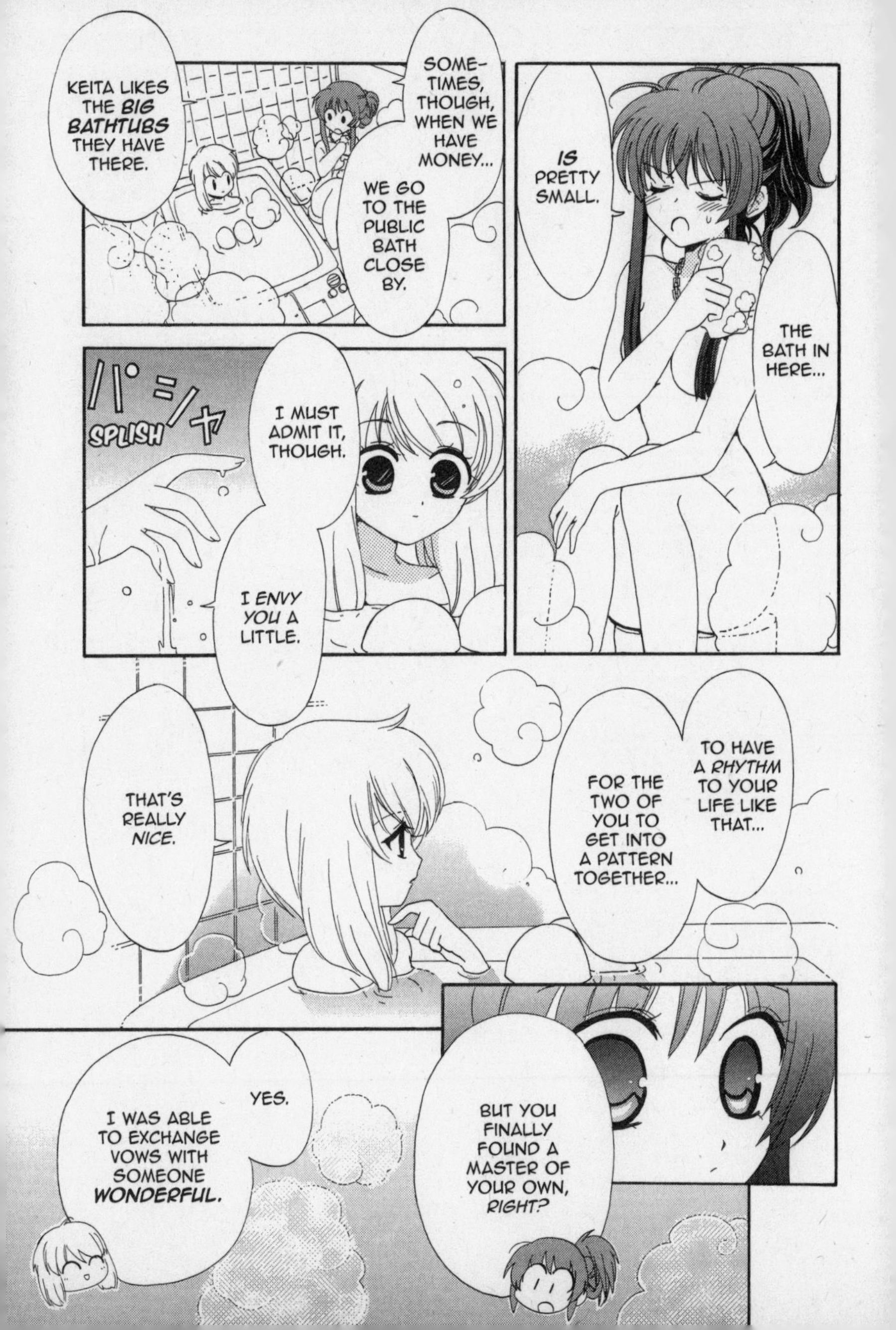
THE BATH IN HERE...
IS PRETTY SMALL.
SOMETIMES, THOUGH, WHEN WE HAVE MONEY...
WE GO TO THE PUBLIC BATH CLOSE BY.
KEITA LIKES THE BIG BATHTUBS THEY HAVE THERE.
パシャ
SPLISH
I MUST ADMIT IT, THOUGH.
I ENVY YOU A LITTLE.
TO HAVE A RHYTHM TO YOUR LIFE LIKE THAT...
FOR THE TWO OF YOU TO GET INTO A PATTERN TOGETHER...
THAT'S REALLY NICE.
BUT YOU FINALLY FOUND A MASTER OF YOUR OWN, RIGHT?
YES.
I WAS ABLE TO EXCHANGE VOWS WITH SOMEONE WONDERFUL.

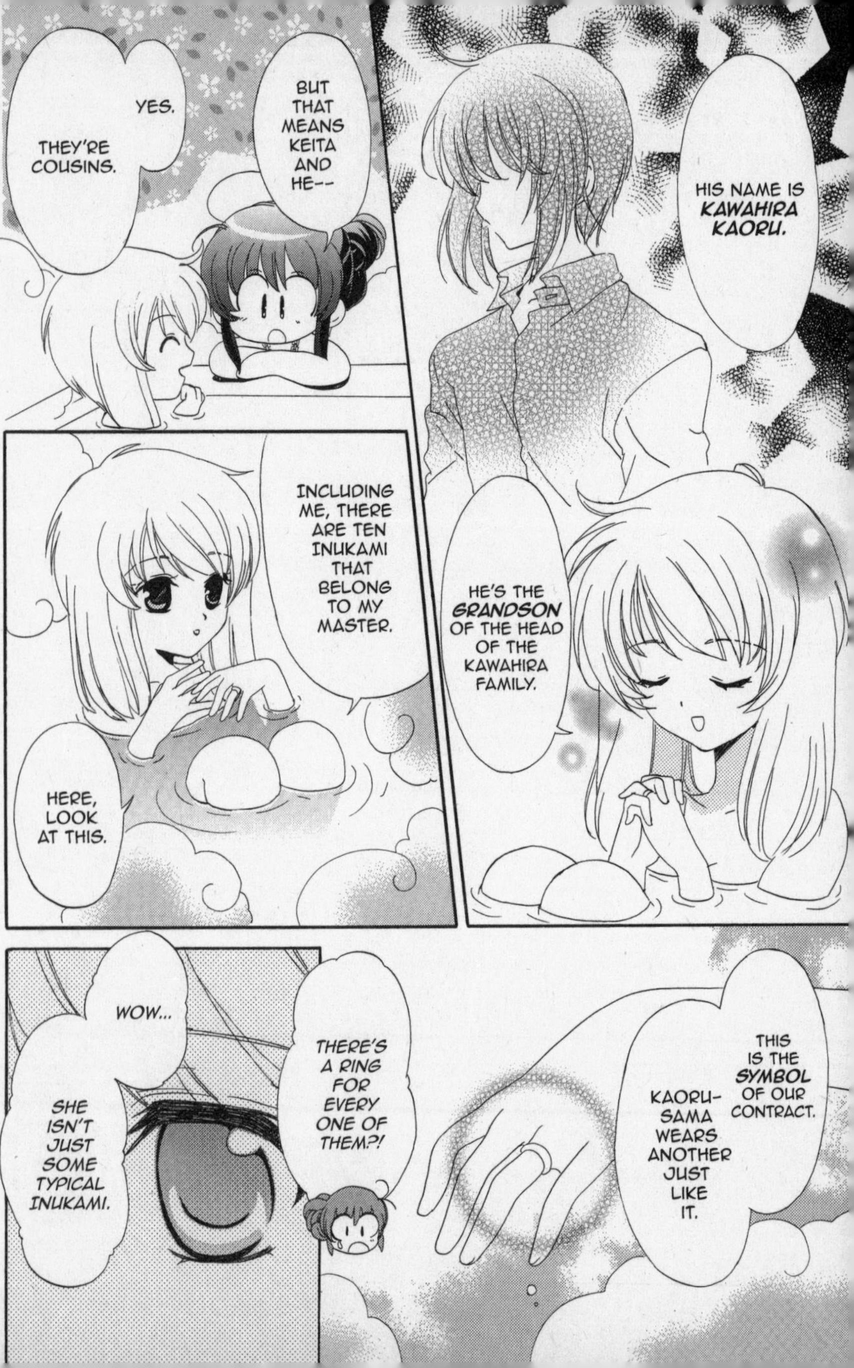
HIS NAME IS KAWAHIRA KAORU.
HE'S THE GRANDSON OF THE HEAD OF THE KAWAHIRA FAMILY.
BUT THAT MEANS KEITA AND HE--
YES.
THEY'RE COUSINS.
INCLUDING ME, THERE ARE TEN INUKAMI THAT BELONG TO MY MASTER.
HERE, LOOK AT THIS.
THIS IS THE SYMBOL OF OUR CONTRACT.
KAORU-SAMA WEARS ANOTHER JUST LIKE IT.
THERE'S A RING FOR EVERY ONE OF THEM?!
WOW...
SHE ISN'T JUST SOME TYPICAL INUKAMI.

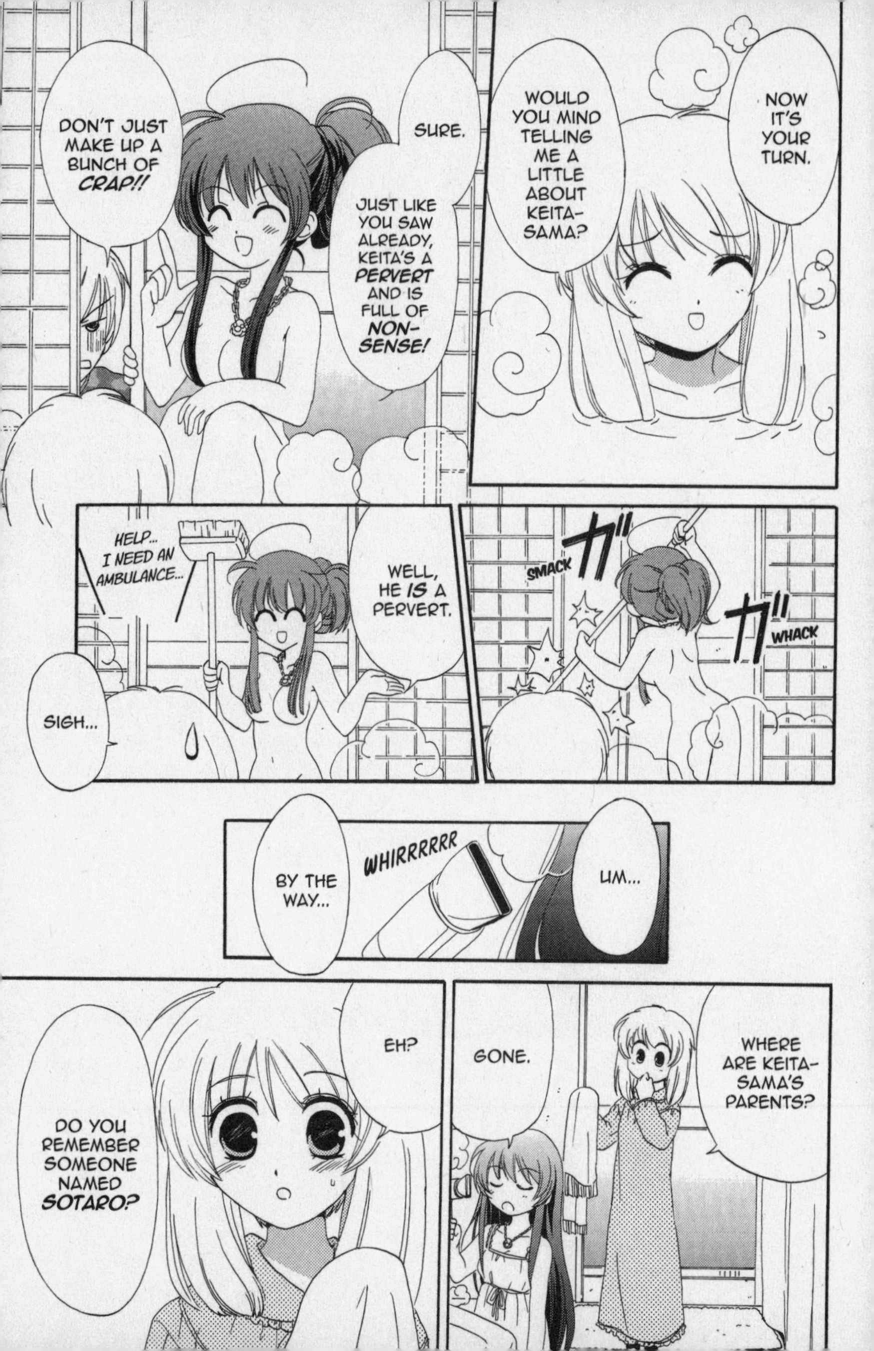
NOW IT'S YOUR TURN.
WOULD YOU MIND TELLING ME A LITTLE ABOUT KEITA-SAMA?
SURE.
JUST LIKE YOU SAW ALREADY, KEITA'S A PERVERT AND IS FULL OF NON-SENSE!
DON'T JUST MAKE UP A BUNCH OF CRAP!!
ガ SMACK
ガ!! WHACK
WELL, HE IS A PERVERT.
HELP... I NEED AN AMBULANCE...
SIGH...
UM...
WHIRRRRR
BY THE WAY...
WHERE ARE KEITA-SAMA'S PARENTS?
GONE.
EH?
DO YOU REMEMBER SOMEONE NAMED SOTARO?

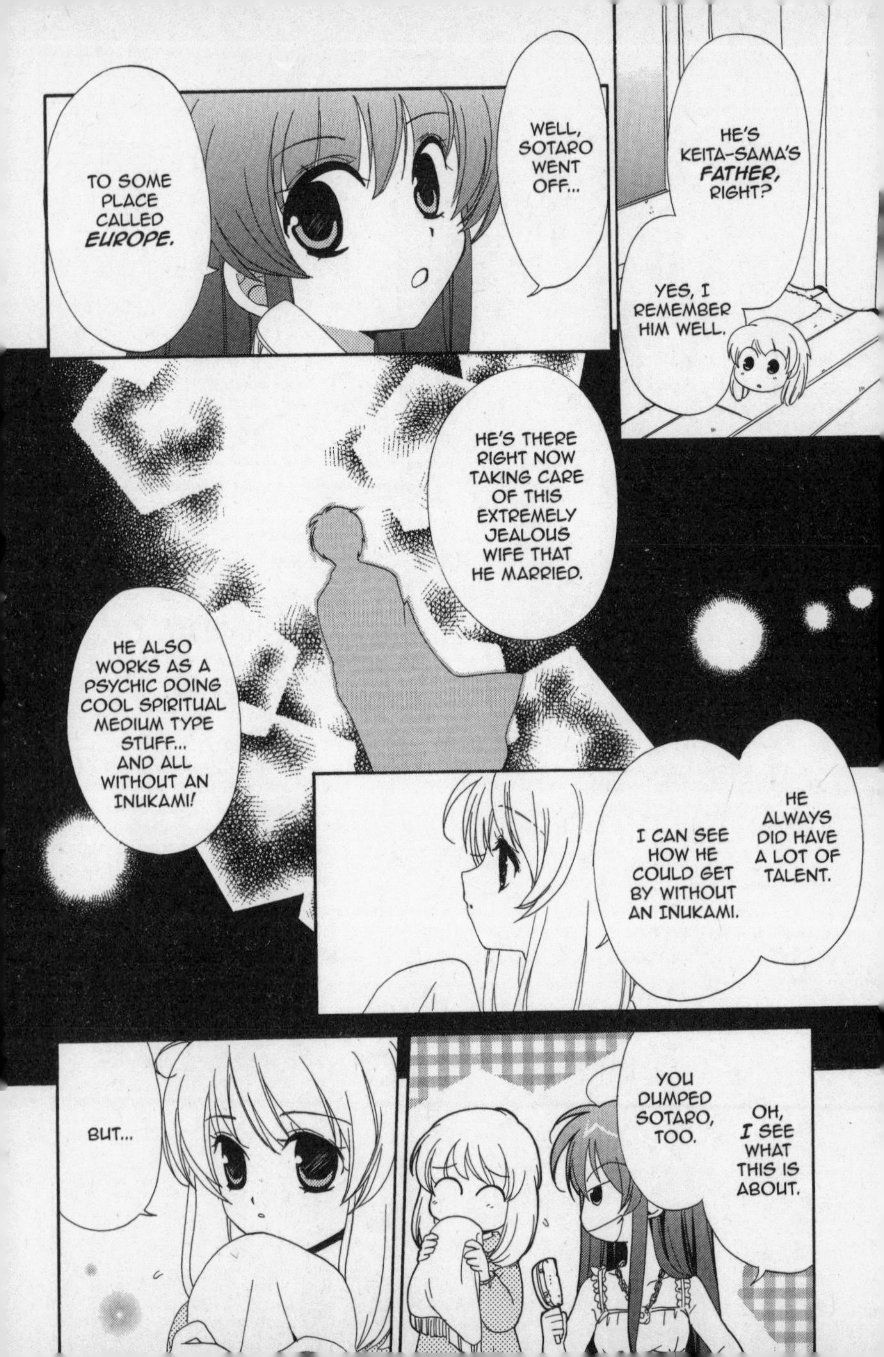
HE'S KEITA-SAMA'S *FATHER,* RIGHT?
YES, I REMEMBER HIM WELL.
WELL, SOTARO WENT OFF...
TO SOME PLACE CALLED *EUROPE.*
HE'S THERE RIGHT NOW TAKING CARE OF THIS EXTREMELY JEALOUS WIFE THAT HE MARRIED.
HE ALSO WORKS AS A PSYCHIC DOING COOL SPIRITUAL MEDIUM TYPE STUFF... AND ALL WITHOUT AN INUKAMI!
HE ALWAYS DID HAVE A LOT OF TALENT.
I CAN SEE HOW HE COULD GET BY WITHOUT AN INUKAMI.
OH, *I* SEE WHAT THIS IS ABOUT.
YOU DUMPED SOTARO, TOO.
BUT...

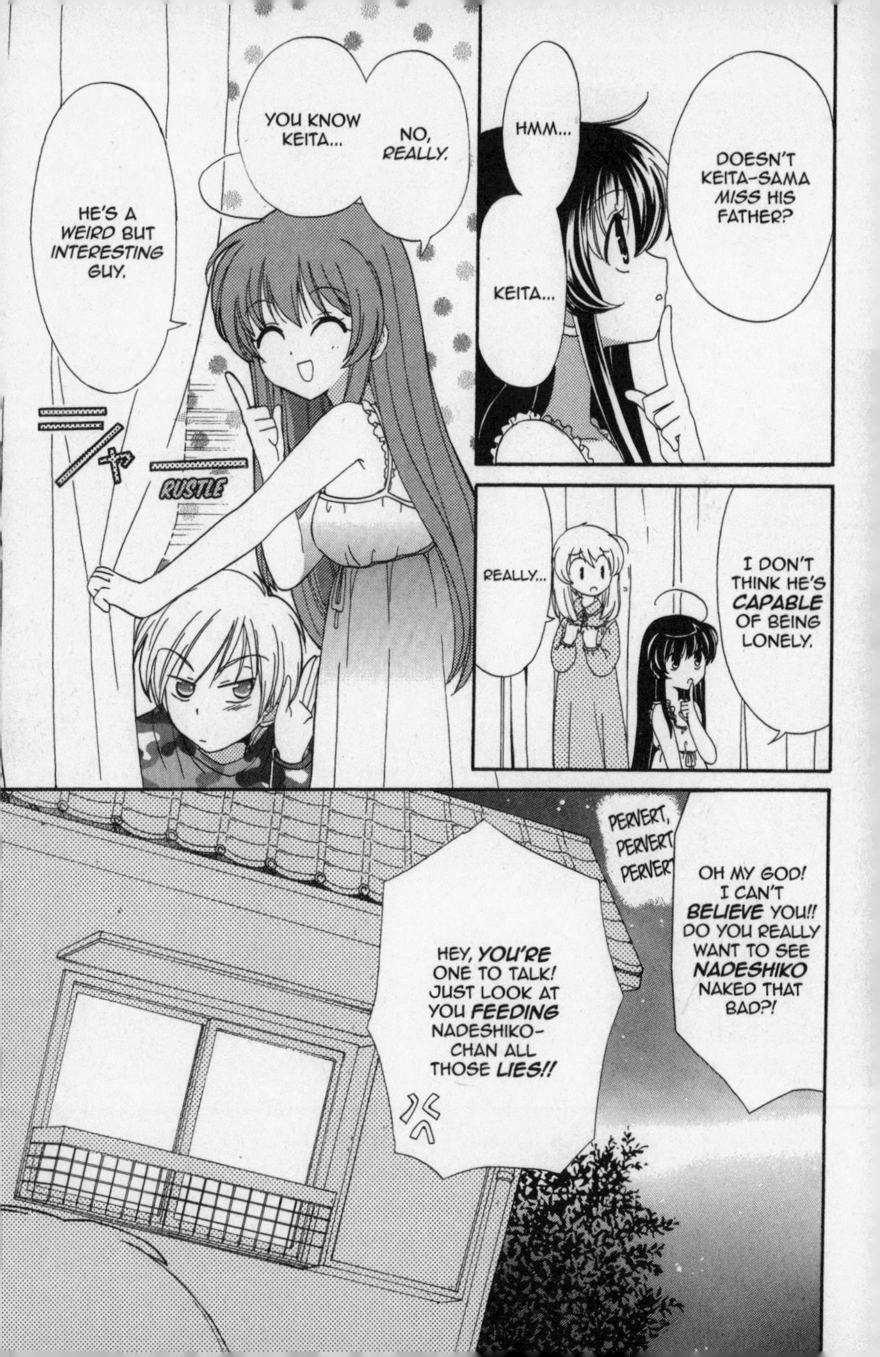
DOESN'T KEITA-SAMA *MISS* HIS FATHER?
HMM...
KEITA...
I DON'T THINK HE'S ***CAPABLE*** OF BEING LONELY.
REALLY...
YOU KNOW KEITA...
NO, *REALLY.*
HE'S A *WEIRD* BUT *INTERESTING* GUY.
RUSTLE
OH MY GOD! I CAN'T ***BELIEVE*** YOU!! DO YOU REALLY WANT TO SEE ***NADESHIKO*** NAKED THAT BAD?!
PERVERT, PERVERT PERVERT
HEY, ***YOU'RE*** ONE TO TALK! JUST LOOK AT YOU ***FEEDING*** NADESHIKO-CHAN ALL THOSE ***LIES!!***

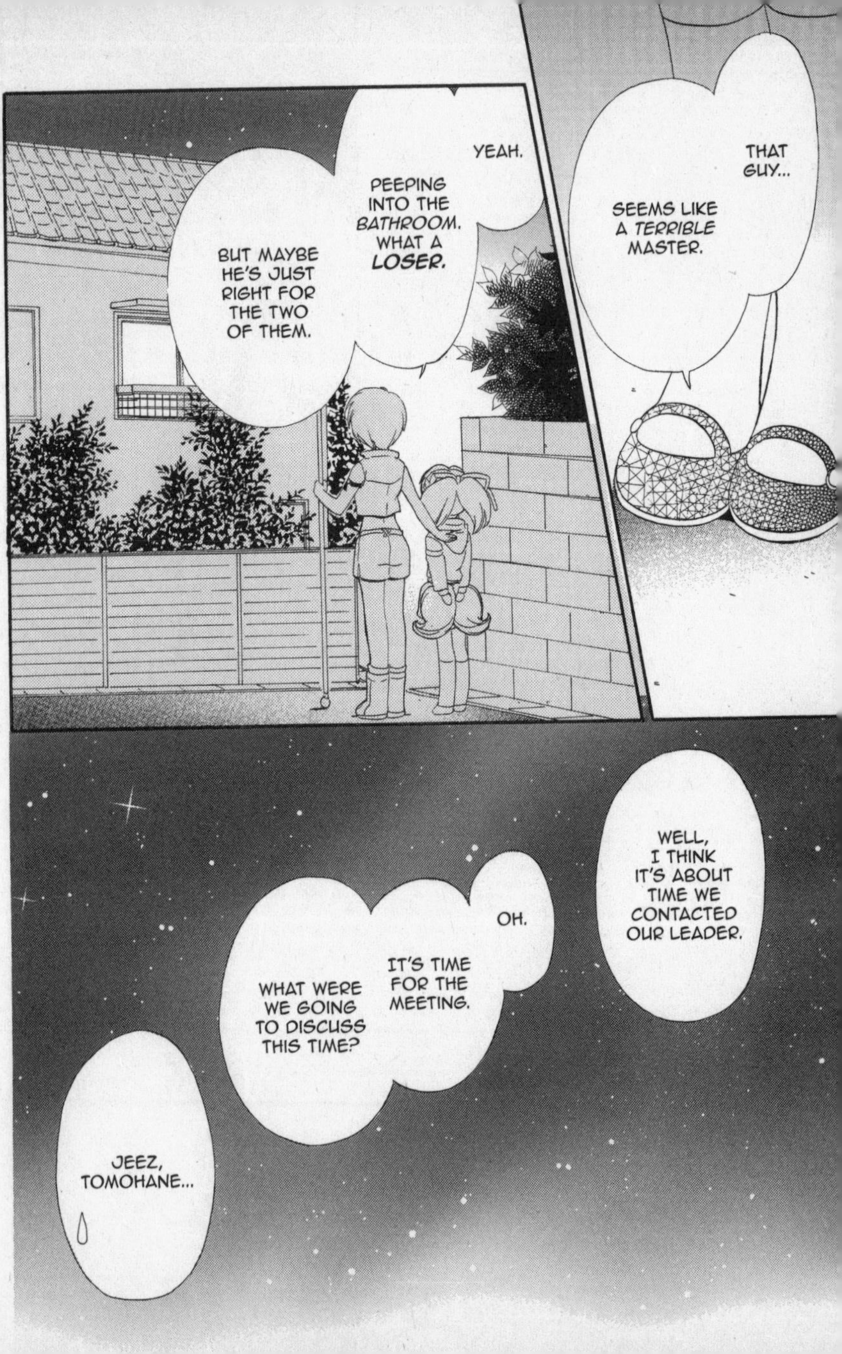
THAT GUY...
SEEMS LIKE A *TERRIBLE* MASTER.
YEAH.
PEEPING INTO THE *BATHROOM*. WHAT A **LOSER.**
BUT MAYBE HE'S JUST RIGHT FOR THE TWO OF THEM.
WELL, I THINK IT'S ABOUT TIME WE CONTACTED OUR LEADER.
OH.
IT'S TIME FOR THE MEETING.
WHAT WERE WE GOING TO DISCUSS THIS TIME?
JEEZ, TOMOHANE...

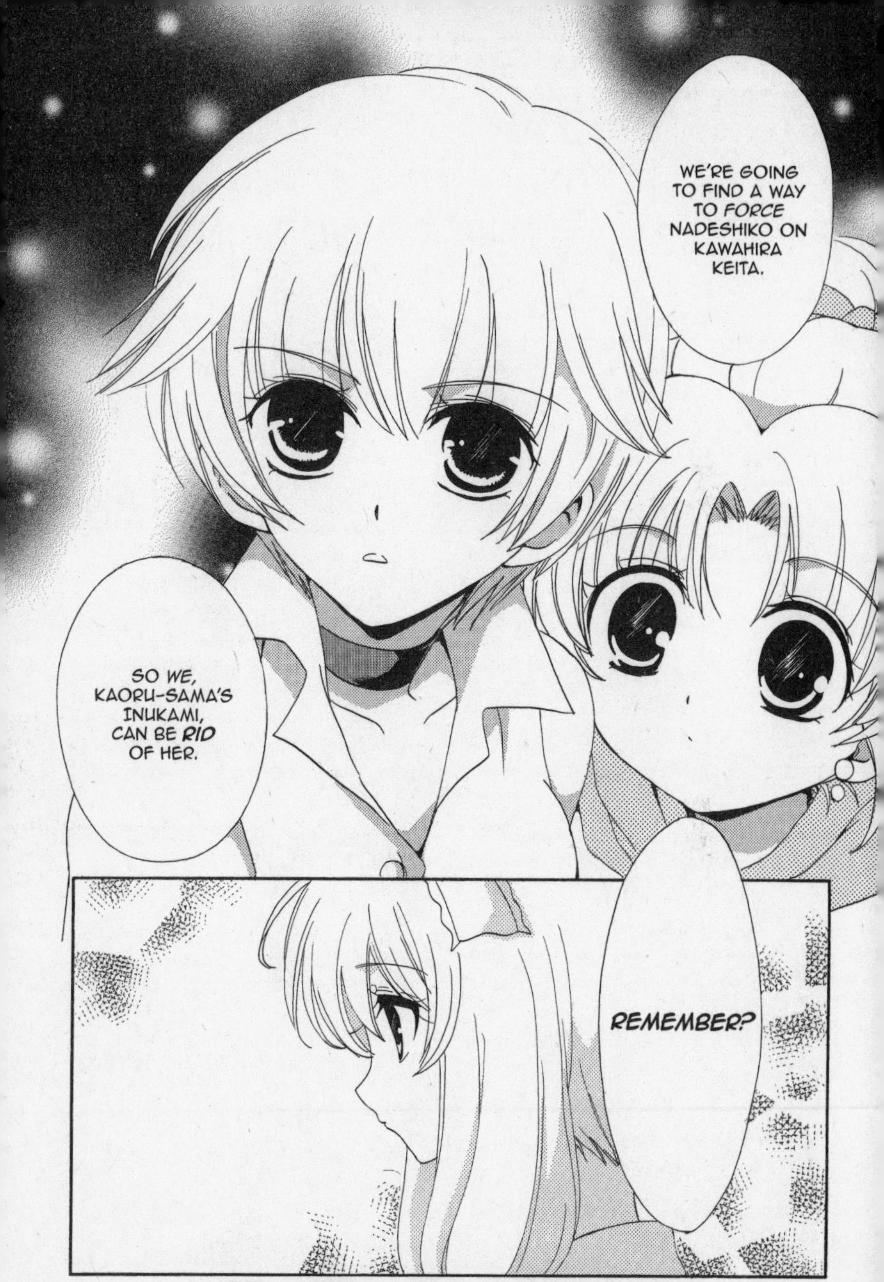
WE'RE GOING TO FIND A WAY TO *FORCE* NADESHIKO ON KAWAHIRA KEITA.
SO WE, KAORU-SAMA'S INUKAMI, CAN BE *RID* OF HER.
REMEMBER?

To Be Continued

Afterword

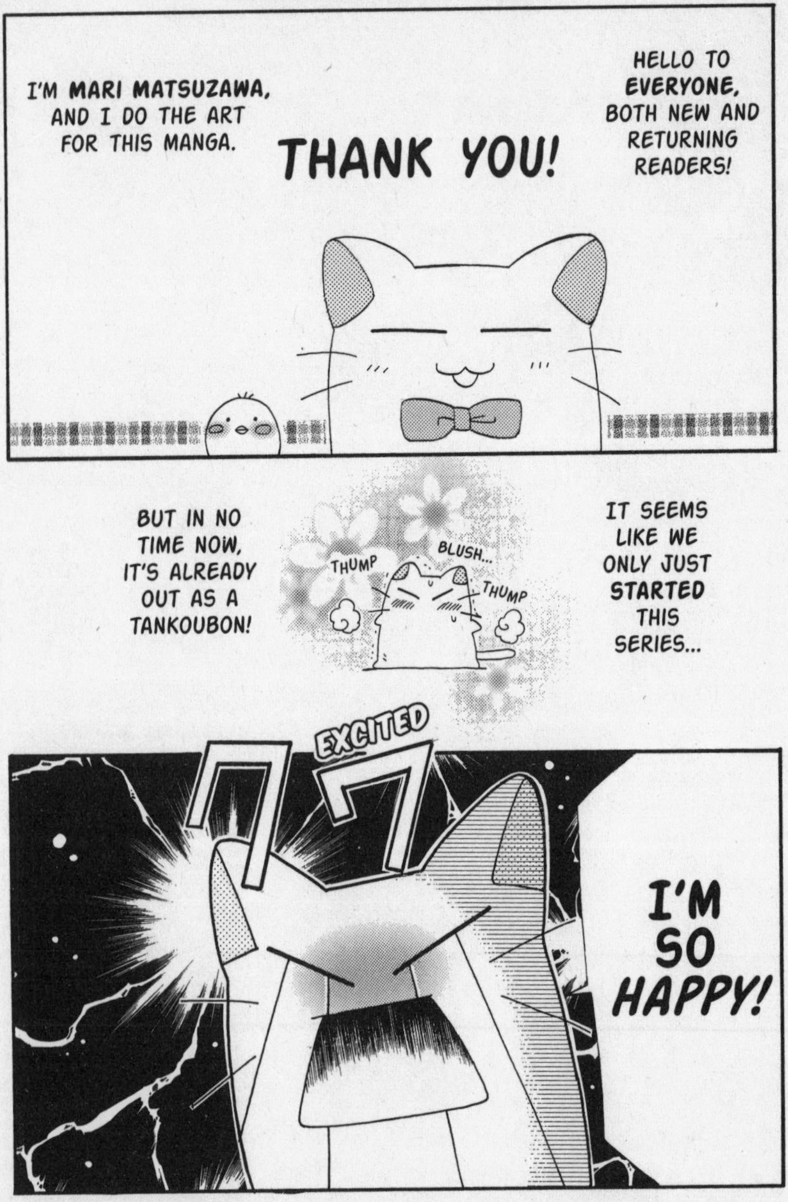
HELLO TO EVERYONE, BOTH NEW AND RETURNING READERS!
THANK YOU!
I'M MARI MATSUZAWA, AND I DO THE ART FOR THIS MANGA.
IT SEEMS LIKE WE ONLY JUST STARTED THIS SERIES...
THUMP
BLUSH...
THUMP
BUT IN NO TIME NOW, IT'S ALREADY OUT AS A TANKOUBON!
I'M SO HAPPY!
EXCITED

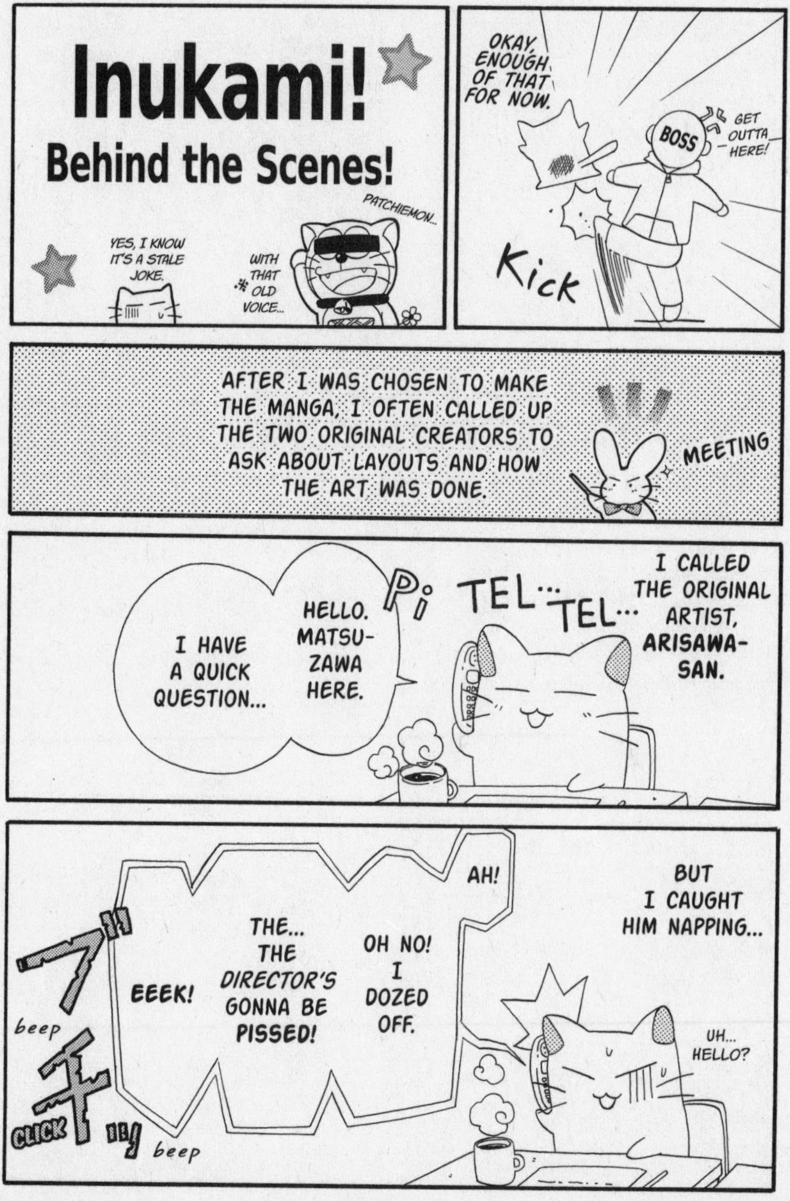
OKAY, ENOUGH OF THAT FOR NOW.
GET OUTTA HERE!
BOSS
Kick
Inukami!
Behind the Scenes!
PATCHIEMON...
WITH THAT * OLD VOICE...
YES, I KNOW IT'S A STALE JOKE.
MEETING
AFTER I WAS CHOSEN TO MAKE THE MANGA, I OFTEN CALLED UP THE TWO ORIGINAL CREATORS TO ASK ABOUT LAYOUTS AND HOW THE ART WAS DONE.
I CALLED THE ORIGINAL ARTIST, ARISAWA-SAN.
TEL... TEL...
Pi
HELLO. MATSUZAWA HERE.
I HAVE A QUICK QUESTION...
BUT I CAUGHT HIM NAPPING...
UH... HELLO?
AH!
OH NO! I DOZED OFF.
THE... THE DIRECTOR'S GONNA BE PISSED!
EEEK!
beep
CLICK
beep

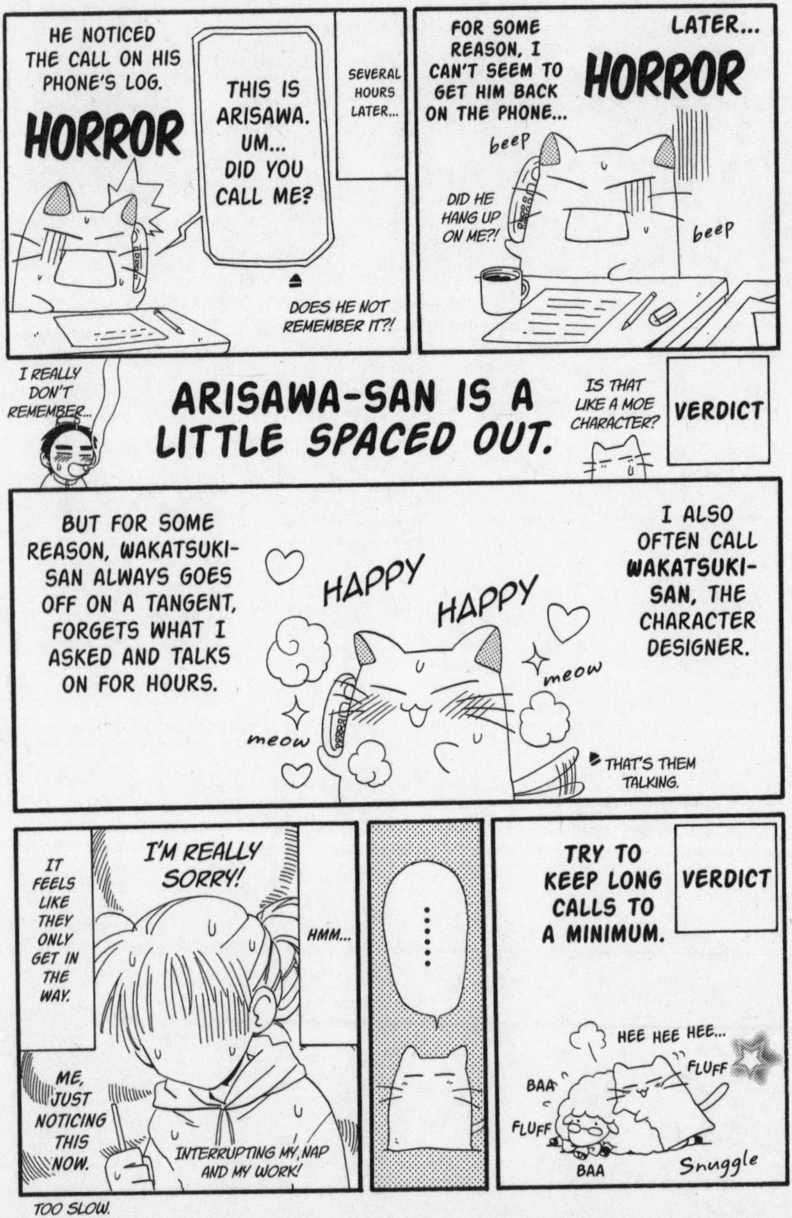

LATER...
HORROR
FOR SOME REASON, I CAN'T SEEM TO GET HIM BACK ON THE PHONE...
beep
DID HE HANG UP ON ME?!
beep
SEVERAL HOURS LATER...
THIS IS ARISAWA. UM... DID YOU CALL ME?
HE NOTICED THE CALL ON HIS PHONE'S LOG.
HORROR
DOES HE NOT REMEMBER IT?!
VERDICT
IS THAT LIKE A MOE CHARACTER?
ARISAWA-SAN IS A LITTLE SPACED OUT.
I REALLY DON'T REMEMBER...
I ALSO OFTEN CALL WAKATSUKI-SAN, THE CHARACTER DESIGNER.
HAPPY
HAPPY
BUT FOR SOME REASON, WAKATSUKI-SAN ALWAYS GOES OFF ON A TANGENT, FORGETS WHAT I ASKED AND TALKS ON FOR HOURS.
meow
meow
THAT'S THEM TALKING.
VERDICT
TRY TO KEEP LONG CALLS TO A MINIMUM.
HEE HEE HEE...
FLUFF
BAA
FLUFF
BAA
Snuggle
......
HMM...
I'M REALLY SORRY!
IT FEELS LIKE THEY ONLY GET IN THE WAY.
INTERRUPTING MY NAP AND MY WORK!
ME, JUST NOTICING THIS NOW.
TOO SLOW.

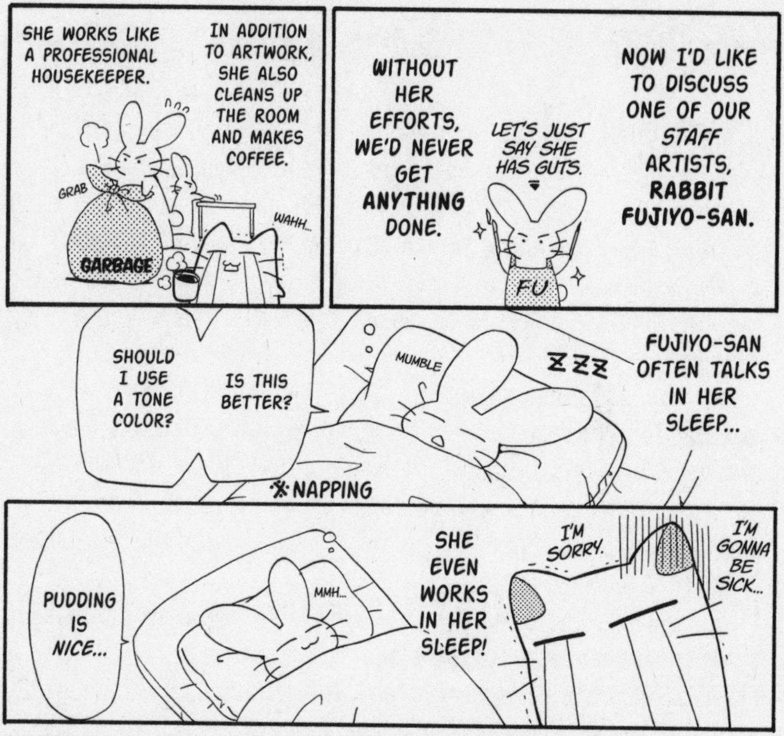
NOW I'D LIKE TO DISCUSS ONE OF OUR STAFF ARTISTS, RABBIT FUJIYO-SAN.
WITHOUT HER EFFORTS, WE'D NEVER GET ANYTHING DONE.
LET'S JUST SAY SHE HAS GUTS.
FU
IN ADDITION TO ARTWORK, SHE ALSO CLEANS UP THE ROOM AND MAKES COFFEE.
SHE WORKS LIKE A PROFESSIONAL HOUSEKEEPER.
WAHH...
GRAB
GARBAGE
FUJIYO-SAN OFTEN TALKS IN HER SLEEP...
ZZZ
MUMBLE
IS THIS BETTER?
SHOULD I USE A TONE COLOR?
※NAPPING
I'M GONNA BE SICK...
I'M SORRY.
SHE EVEN WORKS IN HER SLEEP!
MMH...
PUDDING IS NICE...

INUKAMI'S MANGA WOULDN'T EXIST WITHOUT THE HELP OF SO MANY PEOPLE. I'D LIKE TO GIVE MY **SINCEREST THANKS** TO EVERY ONE OF THEM.

AND TO ALL MY READERS: I'D BE SO HAPPY TO LEARN THAT YOU GOT EVEN A LITTLE ENJOYMENT OUT OF THIS MANGA.

I KNOW I'VE STILL GOT A LOT TO LEARN, BUT I'LL KEEP TRYING.

SEE YOU IN THE NEXT ISSUE!

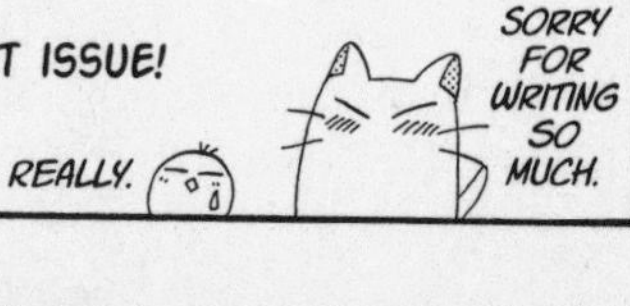
SORRY FOR WRITING SO MUCH.
REALLY.

Special Thanks

MAMIZU ARISAWA-SAMA

KANNA WAKATSUKI-SAMA

KISHO FUJIYO-SAMA

ALL THE DIVISION CHIEFS.

MY FAMILY.

AND EVERYONE!

From the Creator and Character Designers

CONGRATULATIONS ON THE FIRST VOLUME OF THE MANGA! ORIGINAL CREATOR ARISAWA HERE. THANK YOU FOR YOUR CONTINUING SUPPORT, EVERYONE.

WHEN I FIRST HEARD A WOMAN WOULD BE IN CHARGE OF MAKING THE *INUKAMI!* MANGA, I WAS A LITTLE WORRIED. "WOULD A WOMAN BE OKAY WITH WRITING A MANGA FULL OF RISQUÉ JOKES LIKE THIS?" WAS MY FIRST THOUGHT.

MY SECOND THOUGHT WAS, "I HAVE TO APOLOGIZE TO HER." BUT WHEN IT WAS FINISHED AND I OPENED IT UP, WHAT SHE'D PREPARED FOR ME COMPLETELY EXCEEDED MY EXPECTATIONS. I CAN SAY THAT WITHOUT EXAGGERATION OR FLATTERY. THIS MANGA IS MORE INTERESTING THAN THE ORIGINAL LIGHT NOVELS.

OOPS, I SAID IT...

I KNOW IT'S NOT SOMETHING A WRITER IS SUPPOSED TO SAY, BUT THAT'S HOW GREAT MATSUZAWA-SENSEI'S *INUKAMI!* MANGA IS. YOKO IS A PERVERT! KEITA'S A REAL DUMMY! FROM THE ACTION TO THE CUTE STUFF, WITH A LITTLE GUTTER HUMOR THROWN IN, THERE ISN'T A PART THAT DOESN'T FIT. I HOPE YOU'LL ENJOY IT.

AND, IF YOU CAN, PLEASE TAKE A LOOK AT THE ORIGINAL *INUKAMI!* LIGHT NOVELS. THE *INUKAMI!* ANIME IS ALSO STARTING IN APRIL IN JAPAN, SO IF YOU LIKE THE MANGA, PLEASE GIVE THE ANIME A TRY. I HOPE THAT YOU WILL PICK UP THE NEXT VOLUME OF THE MANGA, TOO!

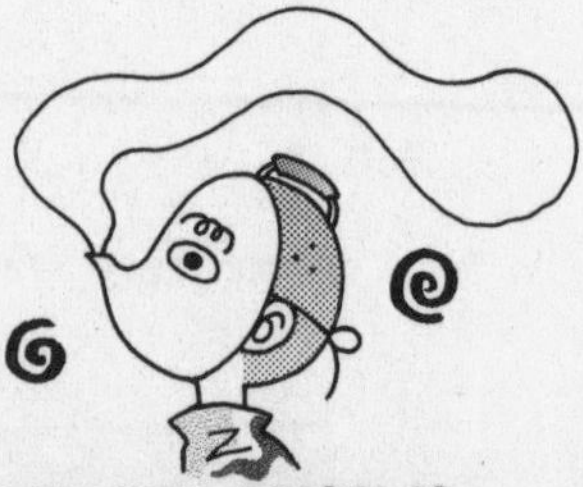

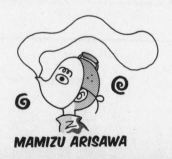

MAMIZU ARISAWA

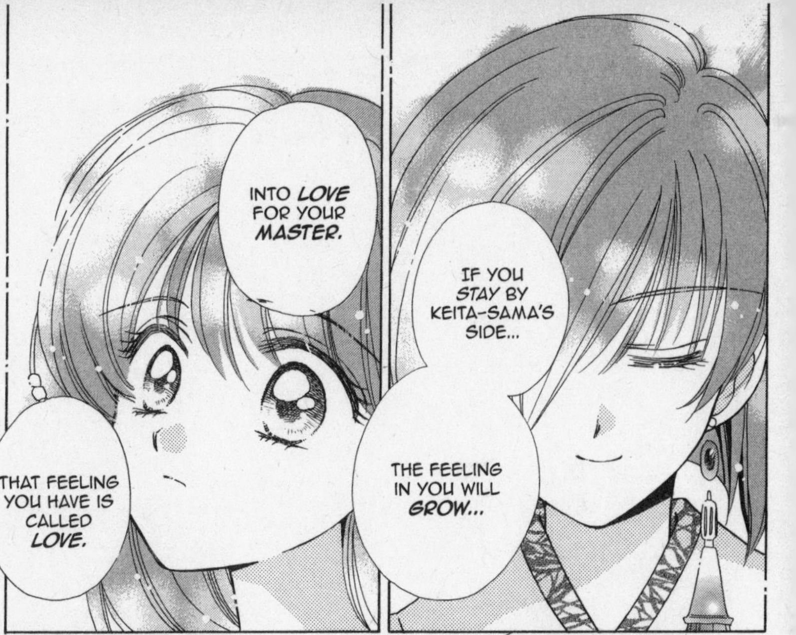
IF YOU STAY BY KEITA-SAMA'S SIDE...
THE FEELING IN YOU WILL GROW...
INTO LOVE FOR YOUR MASTER.
THAT FEELING YOU HAVE IS CALLED LOVE.

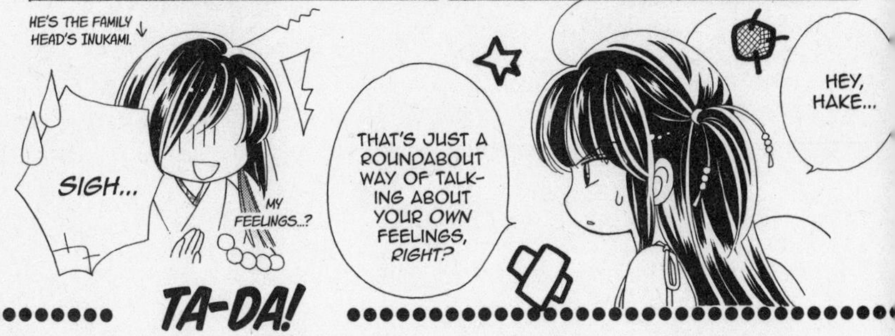
HEY, HAKE...
THAT'S JUST A ROUNDABOUT WAY OF TALK-ING ABOUT YOUR OWN FEELINGS, RIGHT?
MY FEELINGS...?
SIGH...
HE'S THE FAMILY HEAD'S INUKAMI.
TA-DA!

AM I THE ONLY ONE WHO THOUGHT THAT? HI THERE, THIS IS **KANNA WAKATSUKI.** CONGRATULATIONS ON THE FIRST VOLUME OF THE *INUKAMI!* MANGA! I WISH I COULD'VE BEEN IN BETTER SHAPE, MENTALLY AND PHYSICALLY, WHEN SHE CALLED ME. **SORRY!** I'M REALLY WORN OUT. I HAVE TO THANK MATSUZAWA-SAN FOR ALWAYS BEING THERE TO CHEER ME UP, EVEN WHEN SHE WAS UNDER DEADLINE PRESSURE. I HOPE SHE CAN GIVE ME PIGGYBACK RIDES AGAIN. (HEE HEE!) AND, AND...! WHEN WE OPEN THE MANUSCRIPT, LET'S GO TO A HOT SPRING. I'LL TRY TO BE FREE TO GO ALONG.

P.S. I'M SO *HAPPY* THAT HAKE HAS A LOT OF SCENES. **HAKE!**

(IN THE MANGA.)

06.3

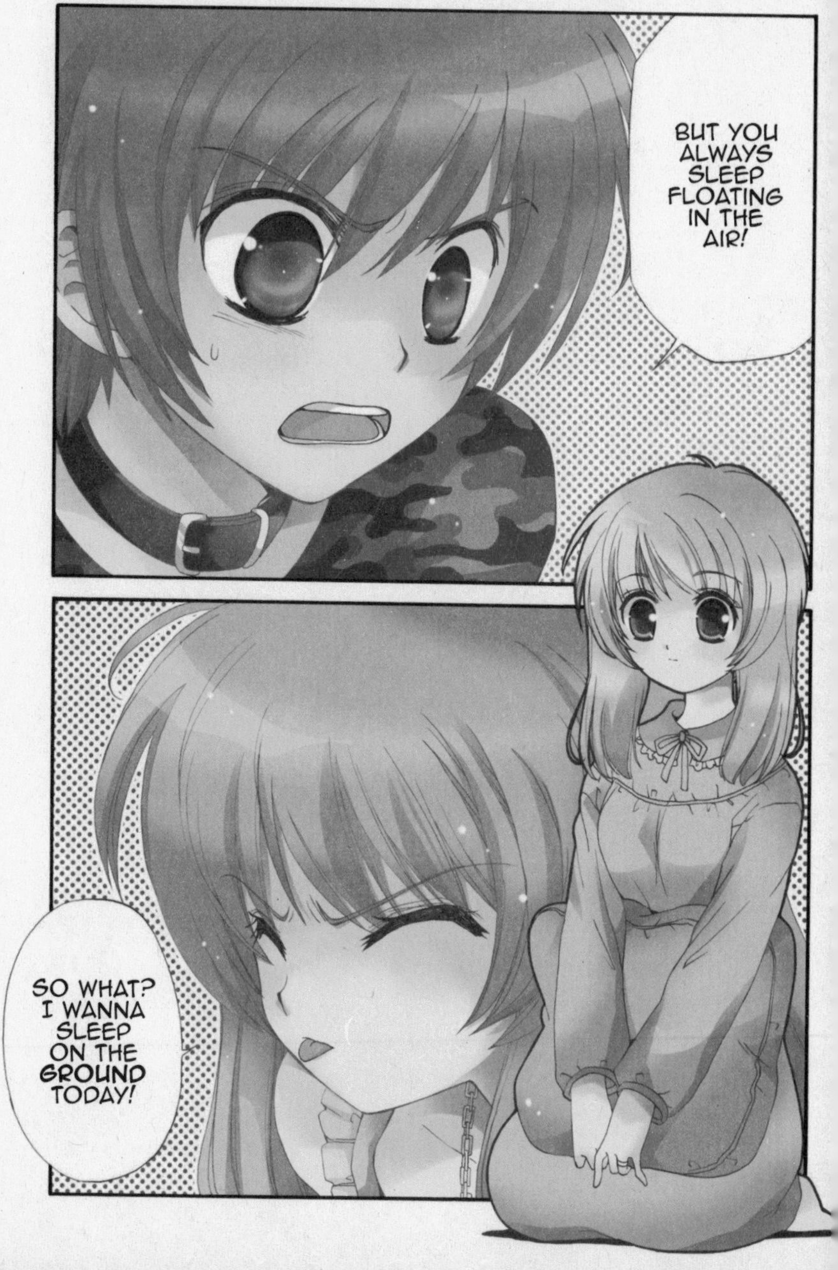
BUT YOU ALWAYS SLEEP FLOATING IN THE AIR!
SO WHAT? I WANNA SLEEP ON THE GROUND TODAY!

Step.6 Enter Nadeshiko: Part 2

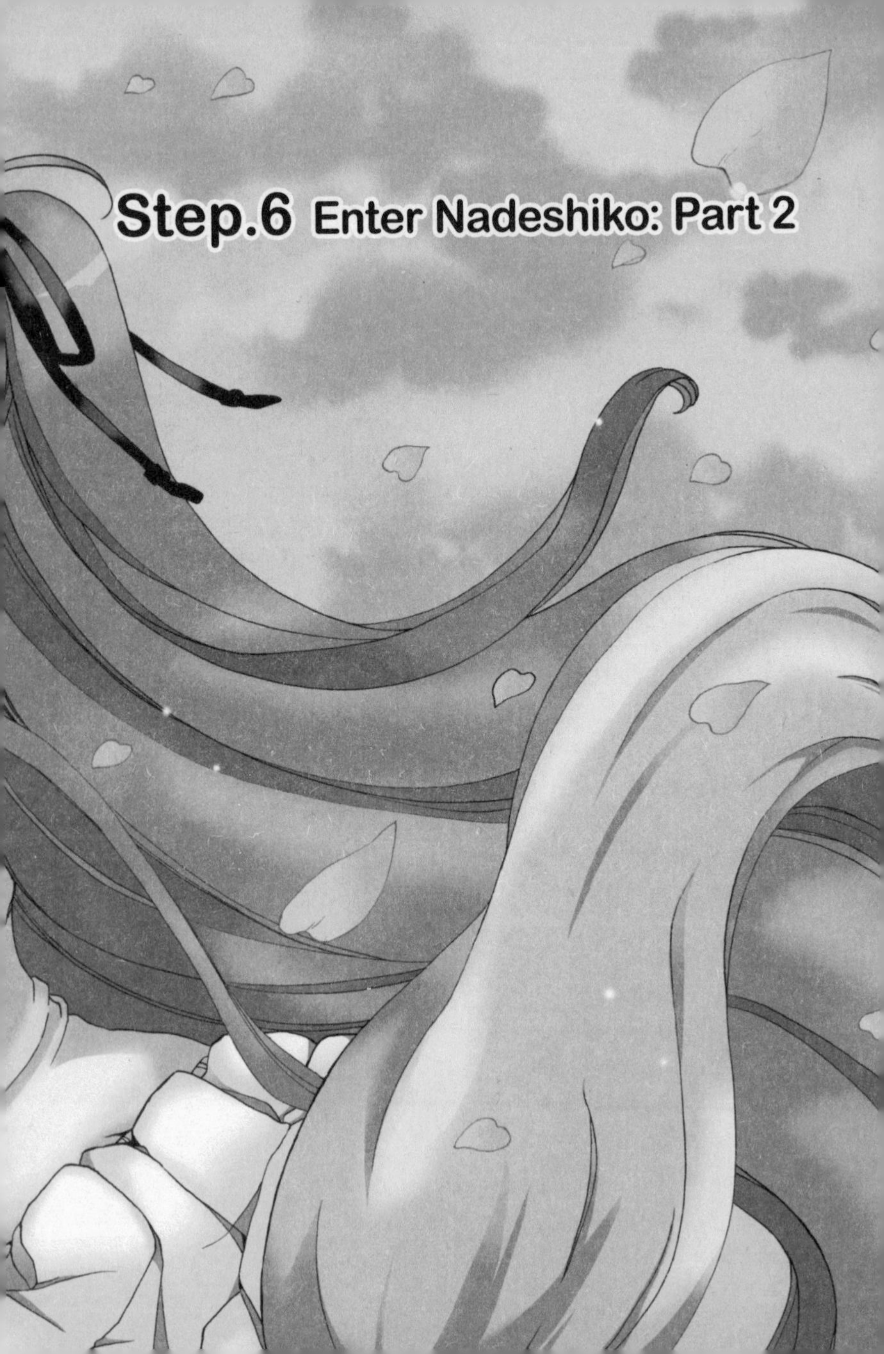

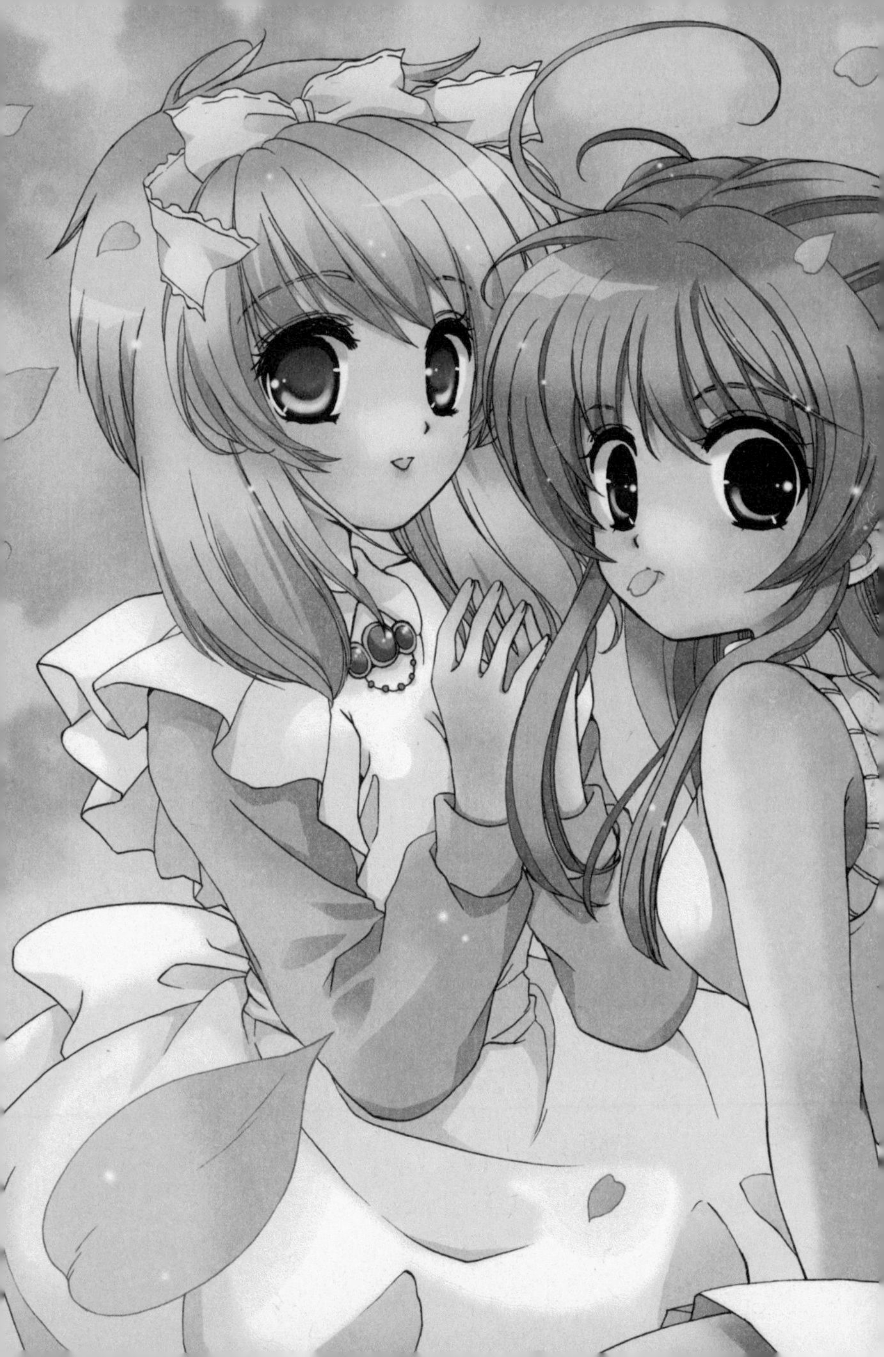

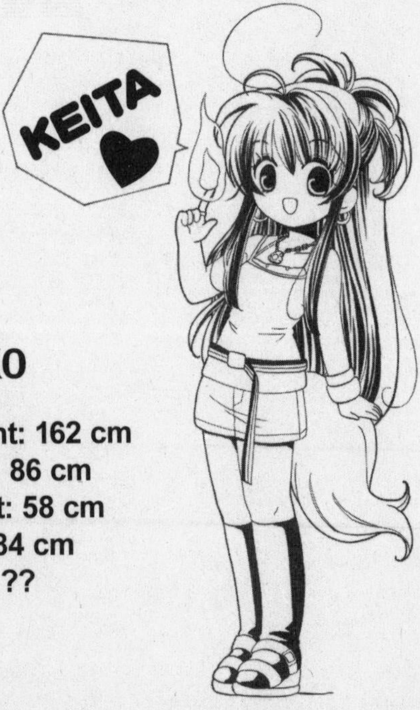
KEITA ♥

YOKO

Height: 162 cm
Bust: 86 cm
Waist: 58 cm
Hip: 84 cm
Age: ??

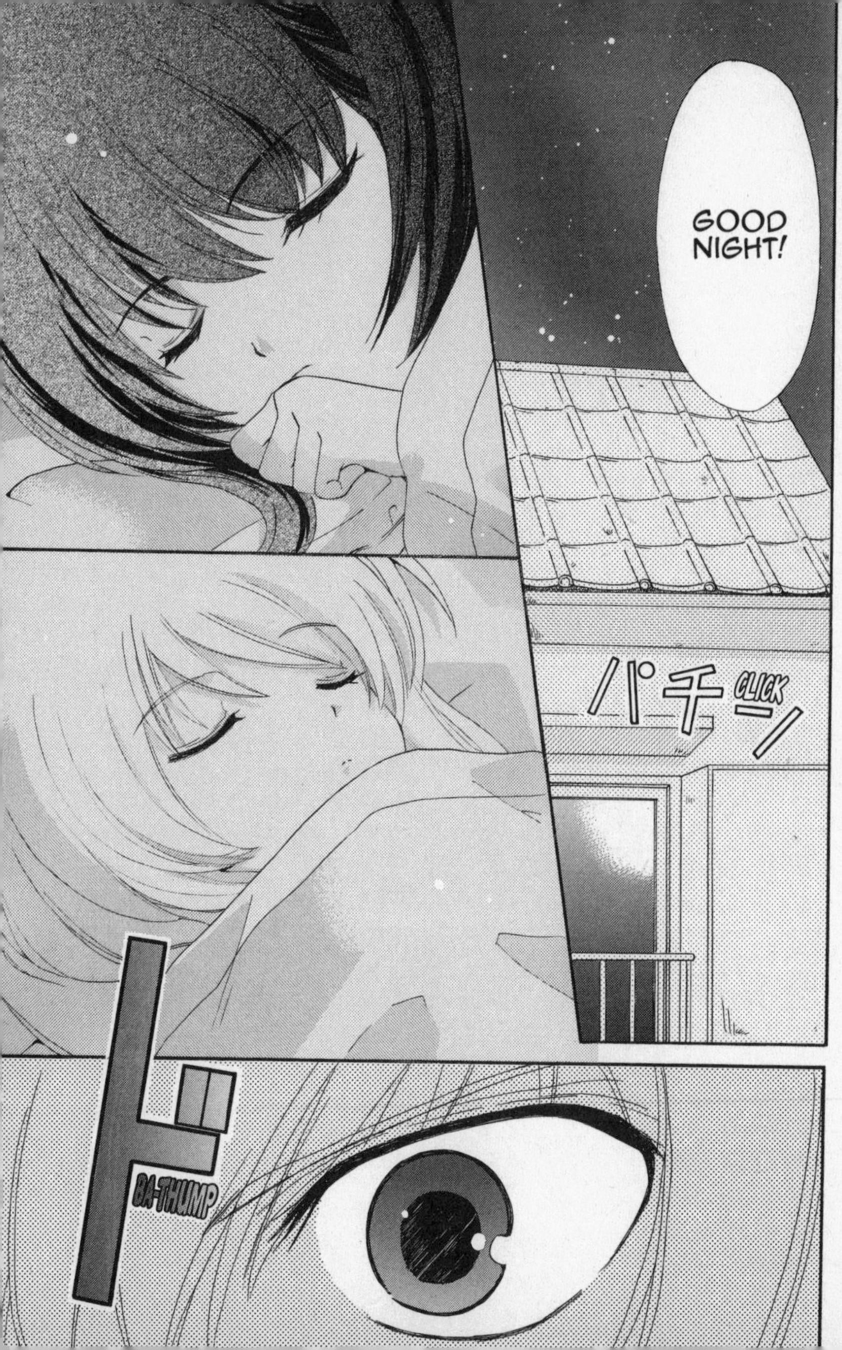
GOOD NIGHT!
パチーン
CLICK
ド
BA-THUMP

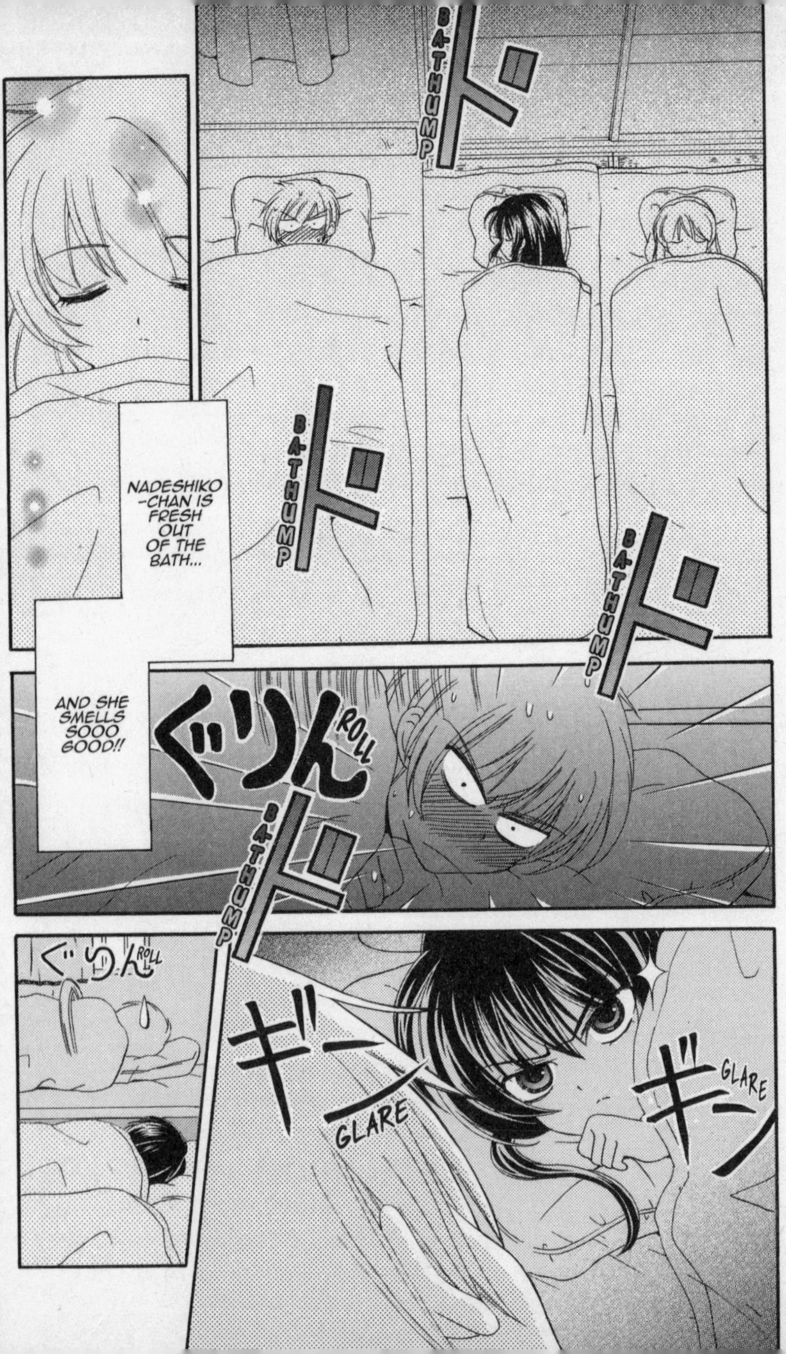
ド BATHUMP
ド BATHUMP
ド BATHUMP
NADESHIKO-CHAN IS FRESH OUT OF THE BATH...
AND SHE SMELLS SOOO GOOD!!
ぐりん ROLL
ド BATHUMP
ギン GLARE
ギン GLARE
ぐりん ROLL

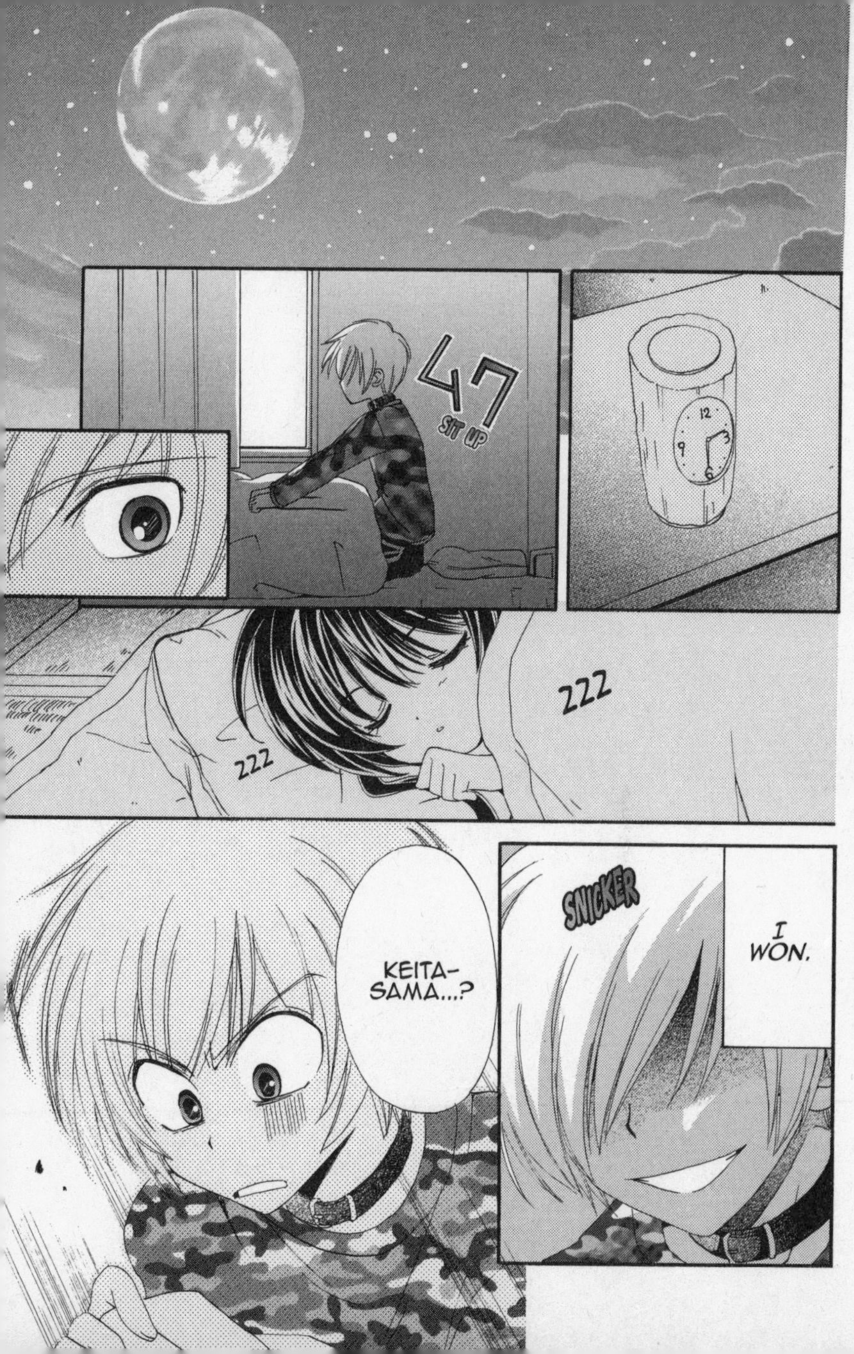
SIT UP
ZZZ
ZZZ
SNICKER
I WON.
KEITA-SAMA...?

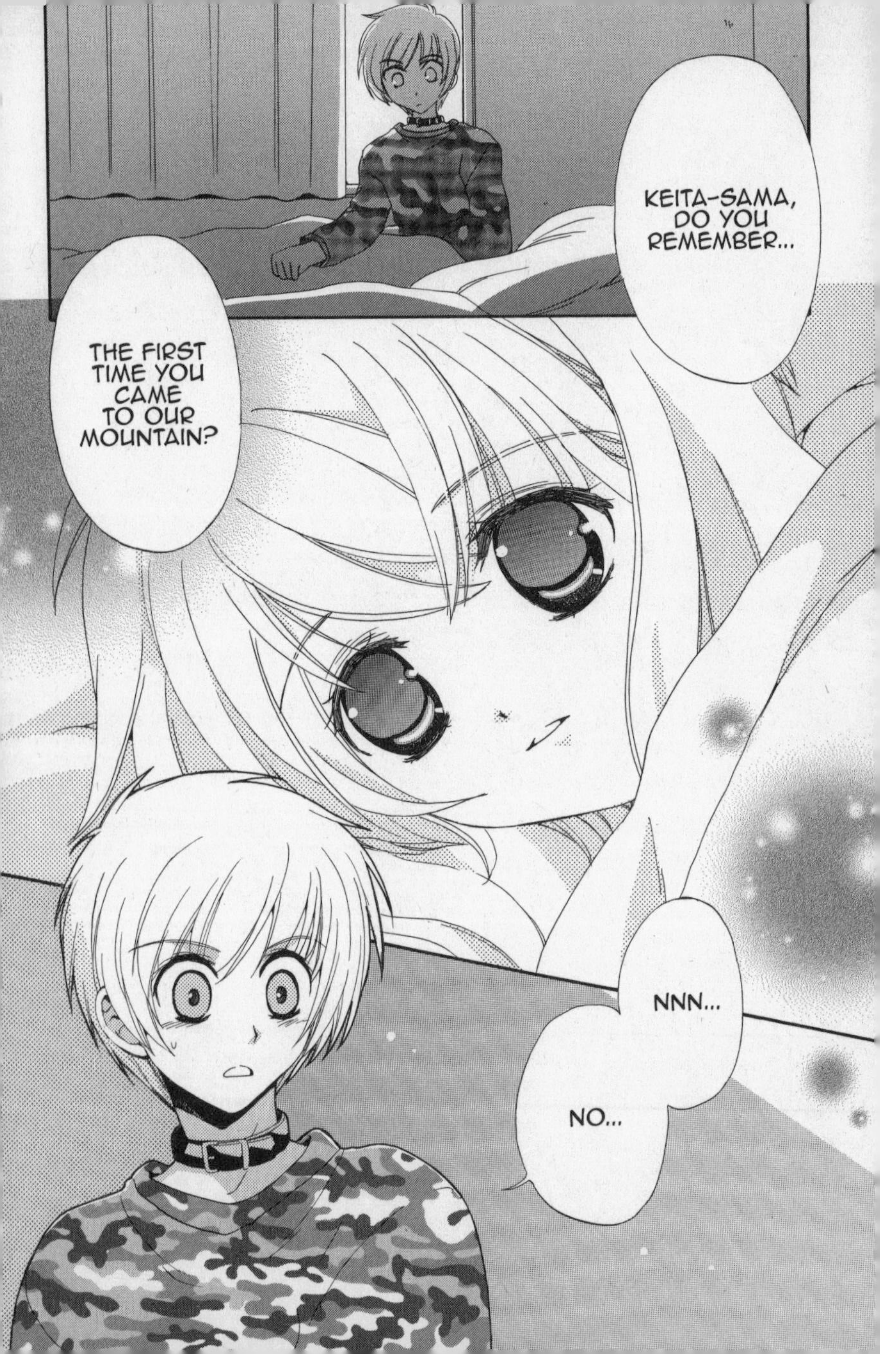
KEITA-SAMA, DO YOU REMEMBER...
THE FIRST TIME YOU CAME TO OUR MOUNTAIN?
NNN...
NO...

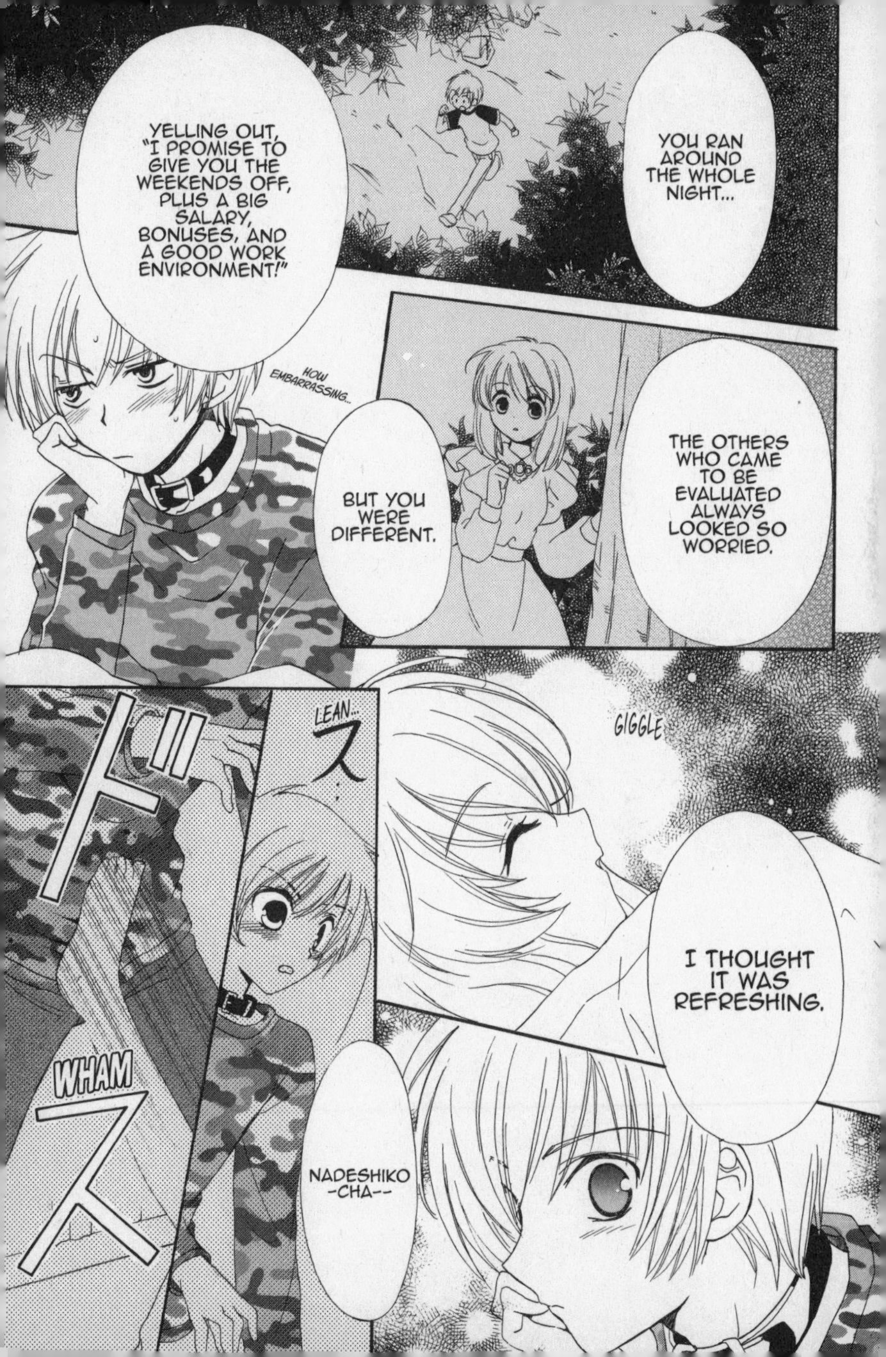
YOU RAN AROUND THE WHOLE NIGHT...
YELLING OUT, "I PROMISE TO GIVE YOU THE WEEKENDS OFF, PLUS A BIG SALARY, BONUSES, AND A GOOD WORK ENVIRONMENT!"
THE OTHERS WHO CAME TO BE EVALUATED ALWAYS LOOKED SO WORRIED.
BUT YOU WERE DIFFERENT.
HOW EMBARRASSING...
GIGGLE
I THOUGHT IT WAS REFRESHING.
NADESHIKO-CHA--
LEAN...
WHAM

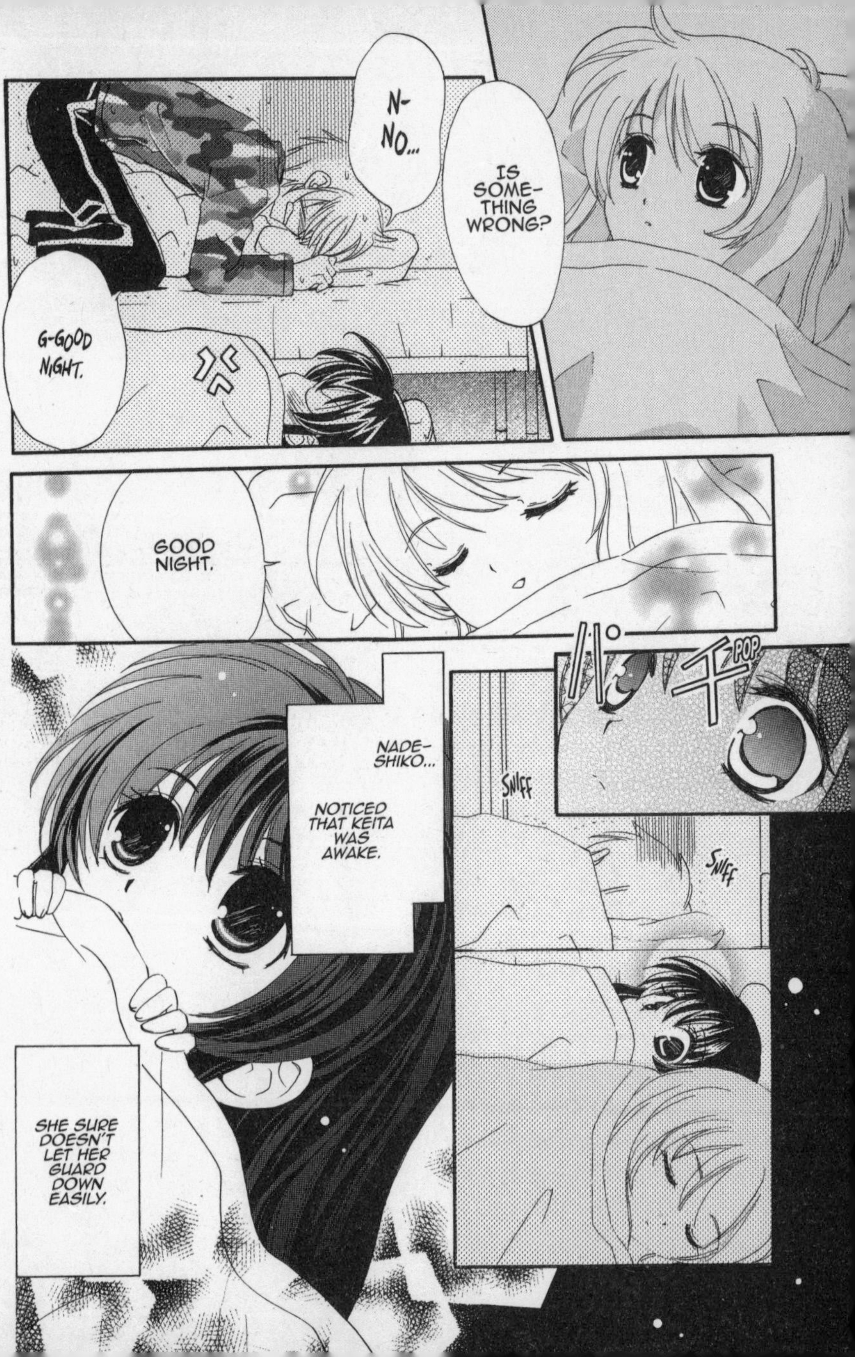
IS SOMETHING WRONG?
N-NO...
G-GOOD NIGHT.
GOOD NIGHT.
パチ
POP
SNIFF
SNIFF
NADESHIKO...
NOTICED THAT KEITA WAS AWAKE.
SHE SURE DOESN'T LET HER GUARD DOWN EASILY.

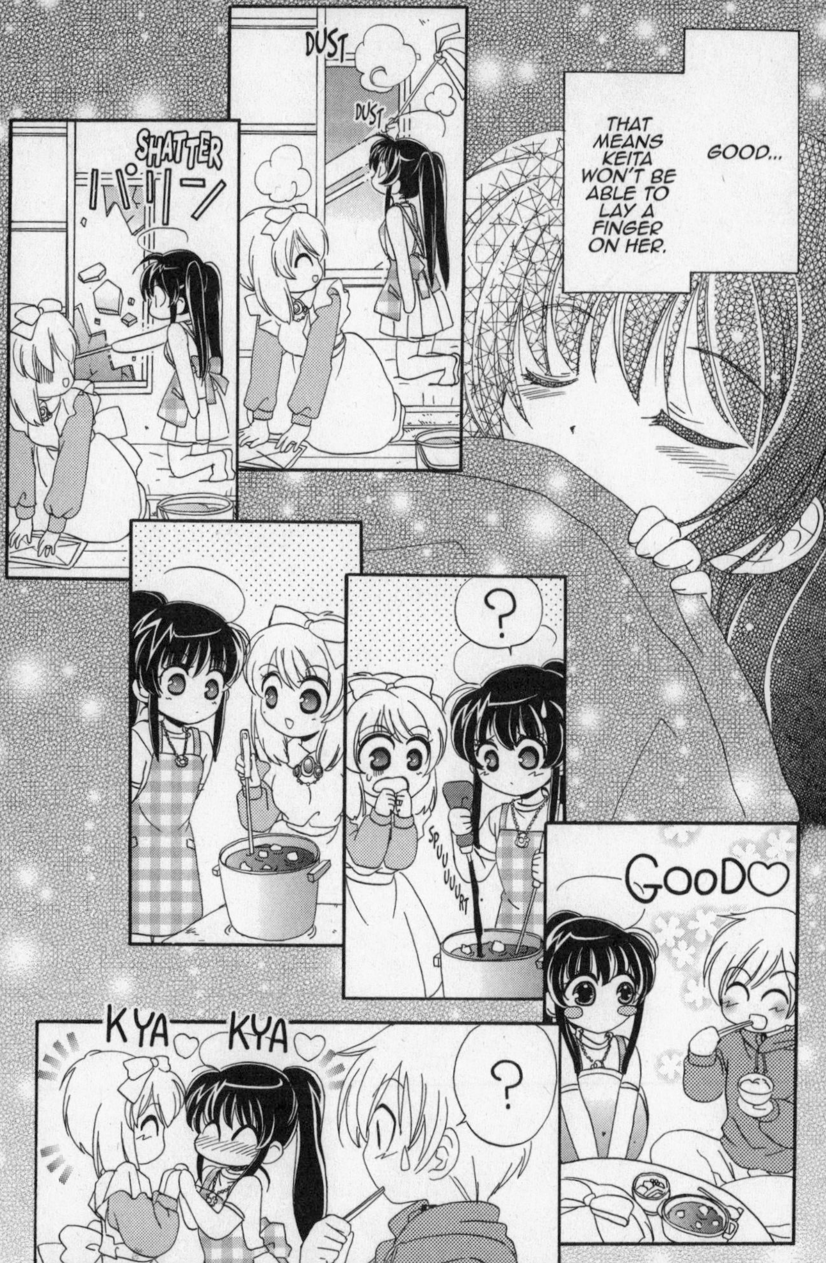
GOOD...
THAT MEANS KEITA WON'T BE ABLE TO LAY A FINGER ON HER.
DUST
DUST
SHATTER
パリーン
?
SPRUUUUURT
GOOD♡
KYA♡ KYA♡
?

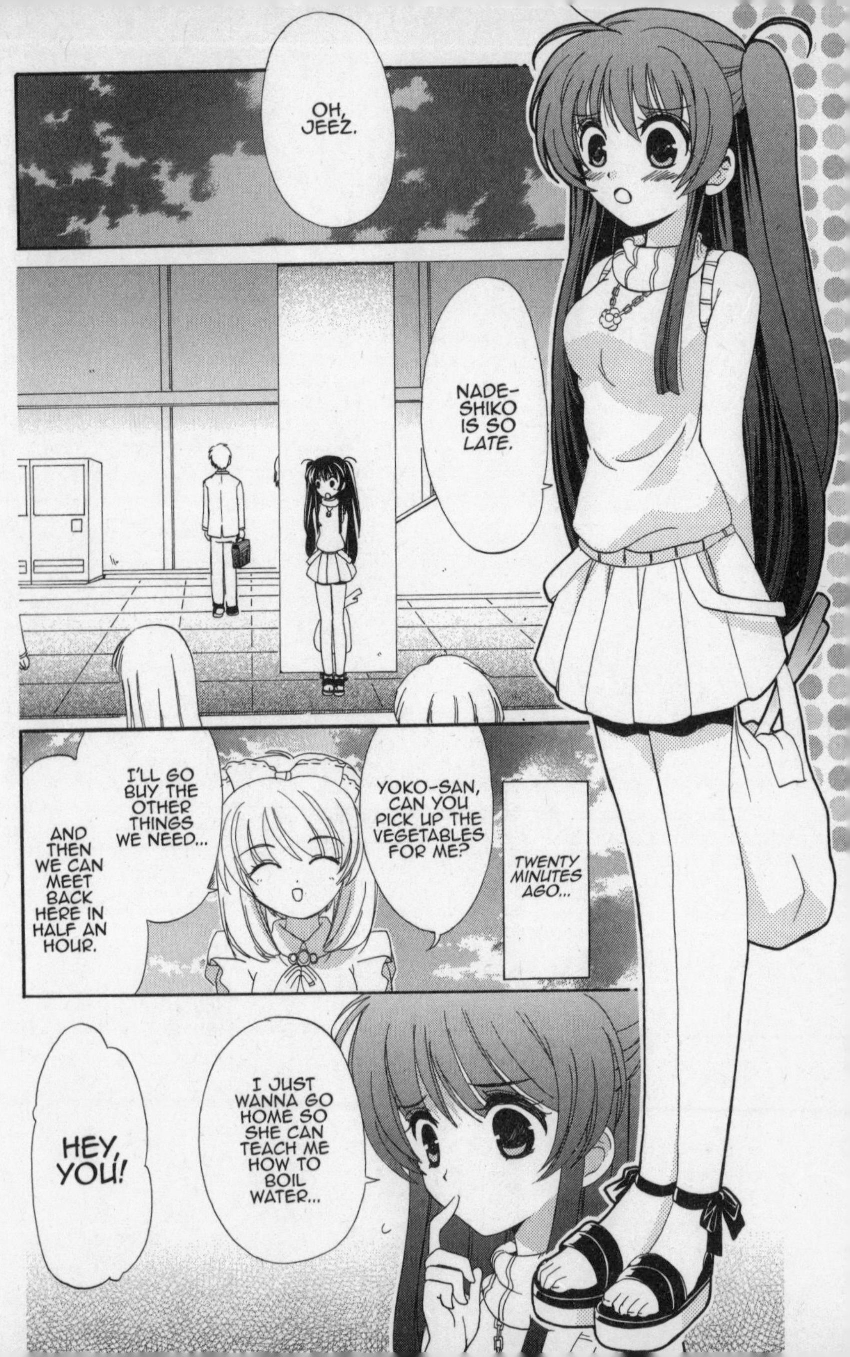
OH, JEEZ.
NADE-SHIKO IS SO LATE.
TWENTY MINUTES AGO...
YOKO-SAN, CAN YOU PICK UP THE VEGETABLES FOR ME?
I'LL GO BUY THE OTHER THINGS WE NEED...
AND THEN WE CAN MEET BACK HERE IN HALF AN HOUR.
I JUST WANNA GO HOME SO SHE CAN TEACH ME HOW TO BOIL WATER...
HEY, YOU!

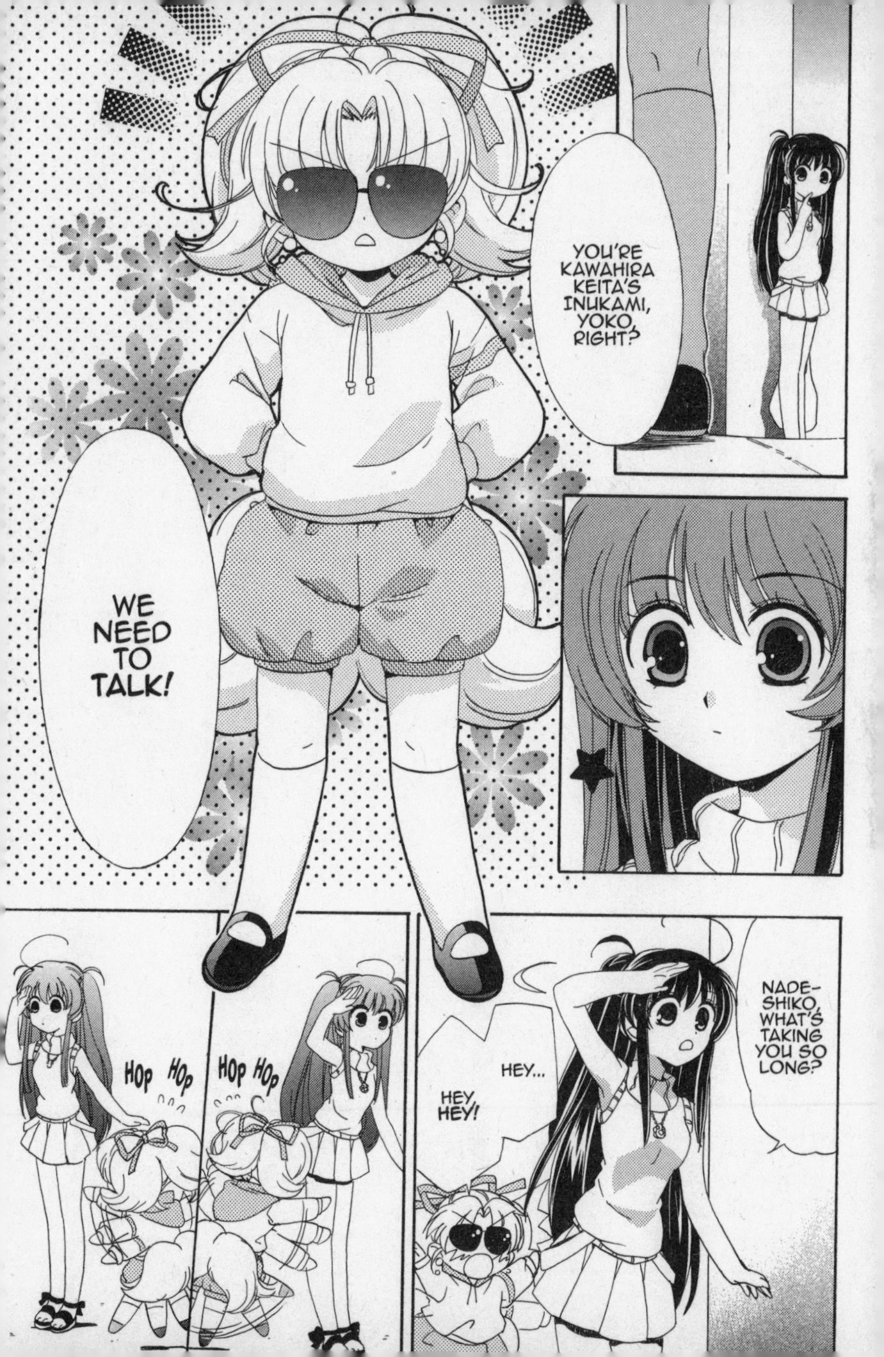
YOU'RE KAWAHIRA KEITA'S INUKAMI, YOKO, RIGHT?
WE NEED TO TALK!
NADE-SHIKO, WHAT'S TAKING YOU SO LONG?
HEY...
HEY, HEY!
HOP HOP
HOP HOP

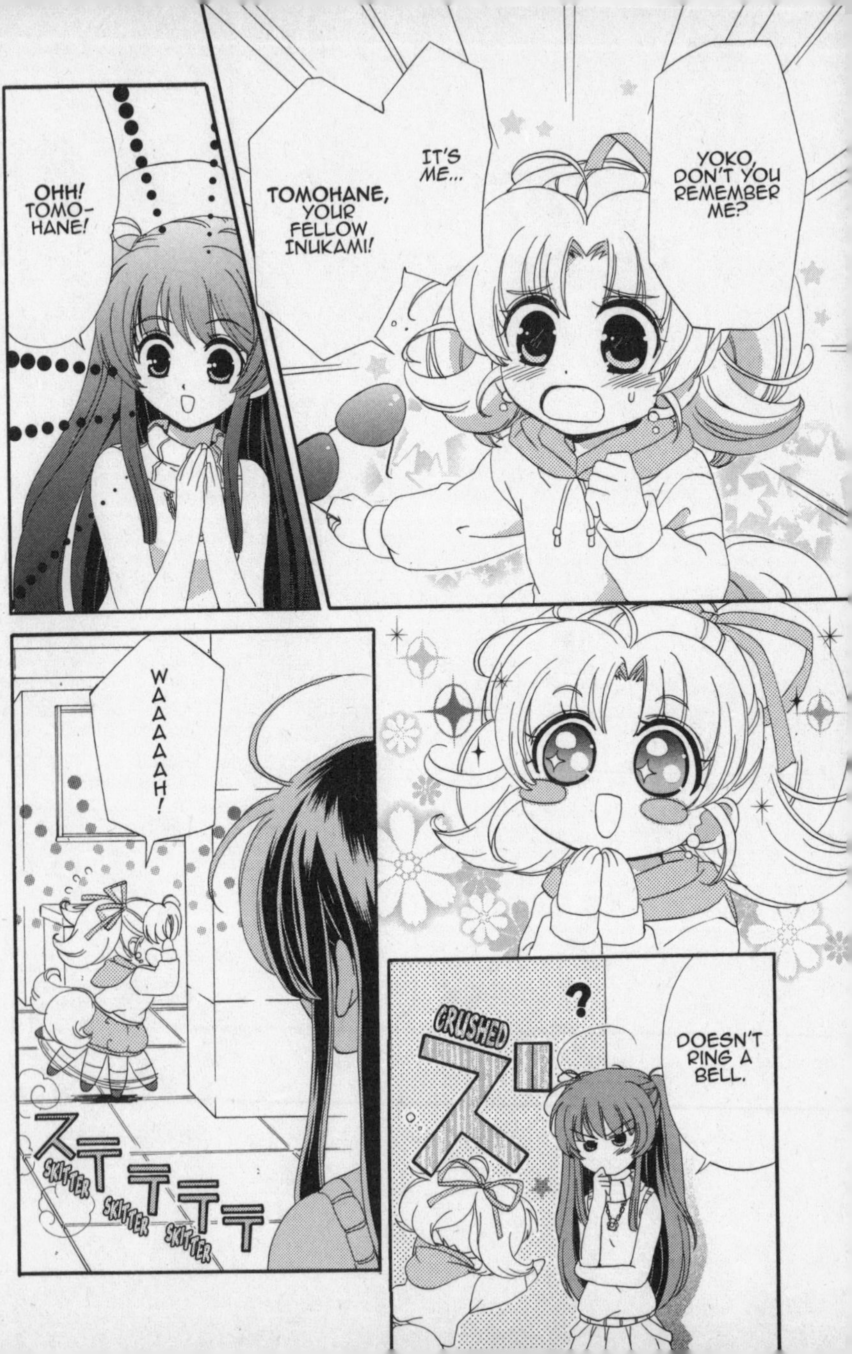
YOKO, DON'T YOU REMEMBER ME?
IT'S ME...
TOMOHANE, YOUR FELLOW INUKAMI!
OHH! TOMO-HANE!
?
DOESN'T RING A BELL.
ズ
CRUSHED
WAAAAAAH!
ステテテテテ
SKITTER
SKITTER
SKITTER

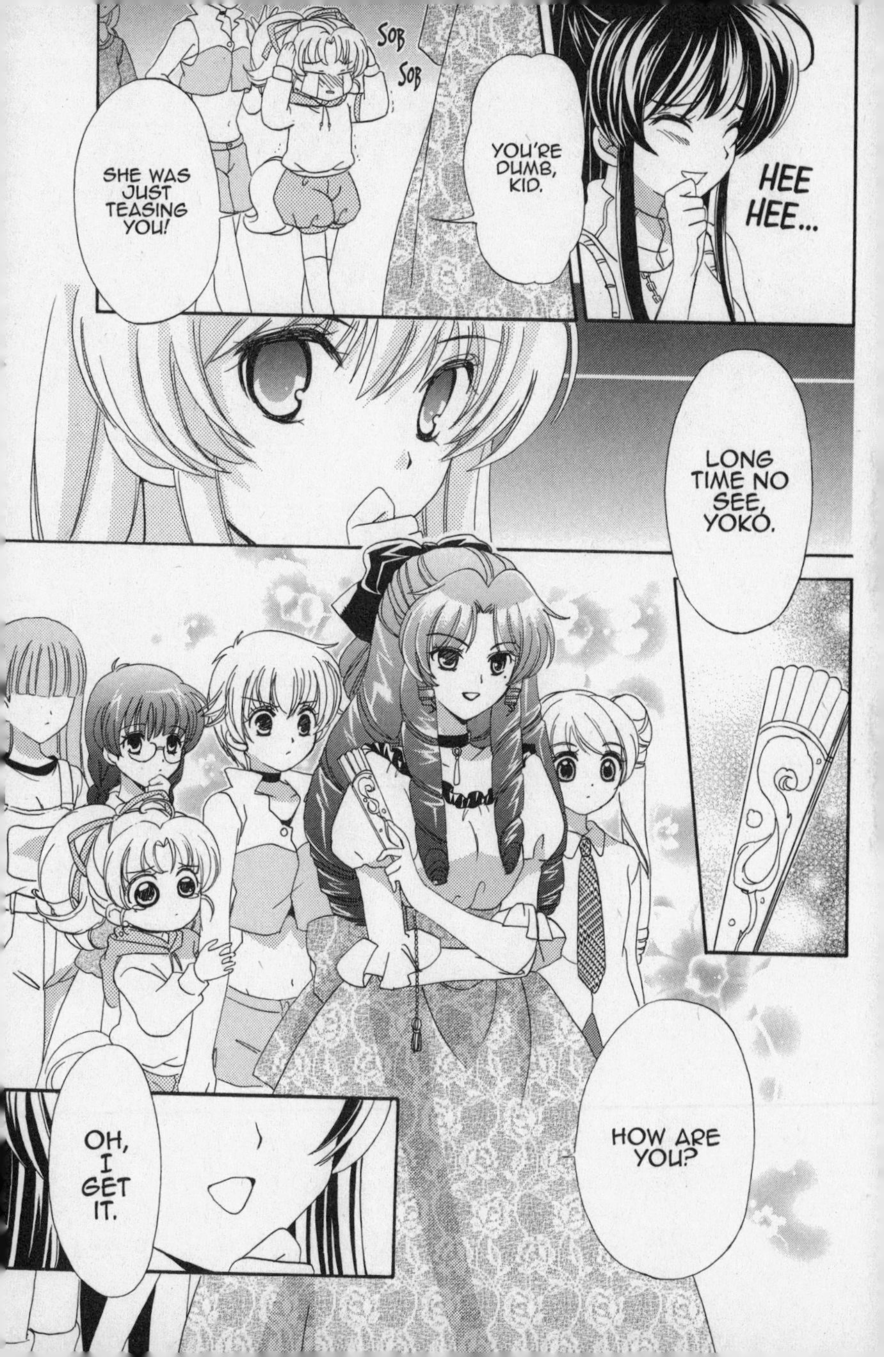
HEE HEE...
YOU'RE DUMB, KID.
SOB SOB
SHE WAS JUST TEASING YOU!
LONG TIME NO SEE, YOKO.
HOW ARE YOU?
OH, I GET IT.

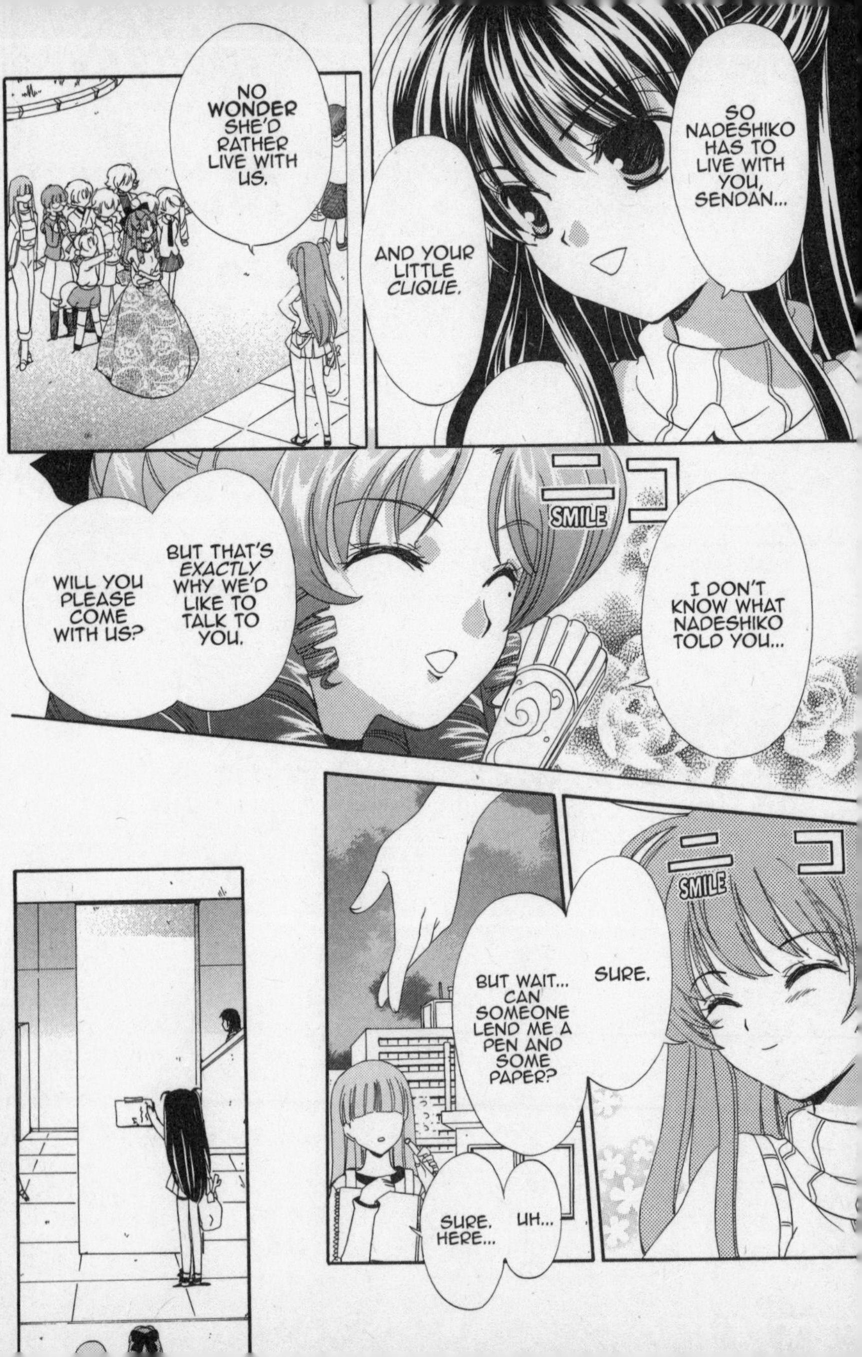
SO NADESHIKO HAS TO LIVE WITH YOU, SENDAN...
AND YOUR LITTLE *CLIQUE*.
NO WONDER SHE'D RATHER LIVE WITH US.
I DON'T KNOW WHAT NADESHIKO TOLD YOU...
SMILE
BUT THAT'S *EXACTLY* WHY WE'D LIKE TO TALK TO YOU.
WILL YOU PLEASE COME WITH US?
SMILE
SURE.
BUT WAIT... CAN SOMEONE LEND ME A PEN AND SOME PAPER?
UH...
SURE. HERE...

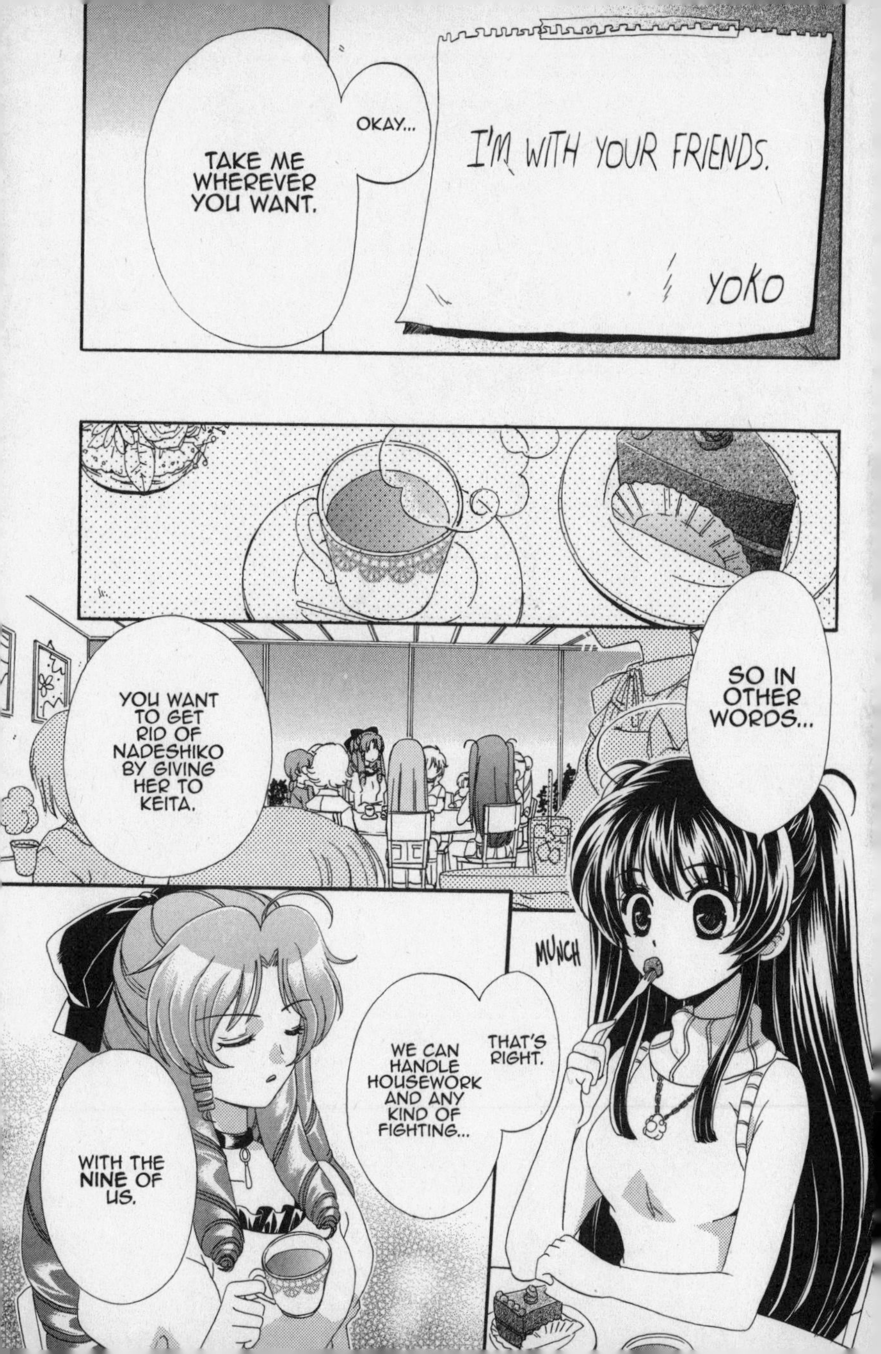
I'M WITH YOUR FRIENDS.
YOKO
OKAY...
TAKE ME WHEREVER YOU WANT.
SO IN OTHER WORDS...
YOU WANT TO GET RID OF NADESHIKO BY GIVING HER TO KEITA.
MUNCH
THAT'S RIGHT.
WE CAN HANDLE HOUSEWORK AND ANY KIND OF FIGHTING...
WITH THE NINE OF US.

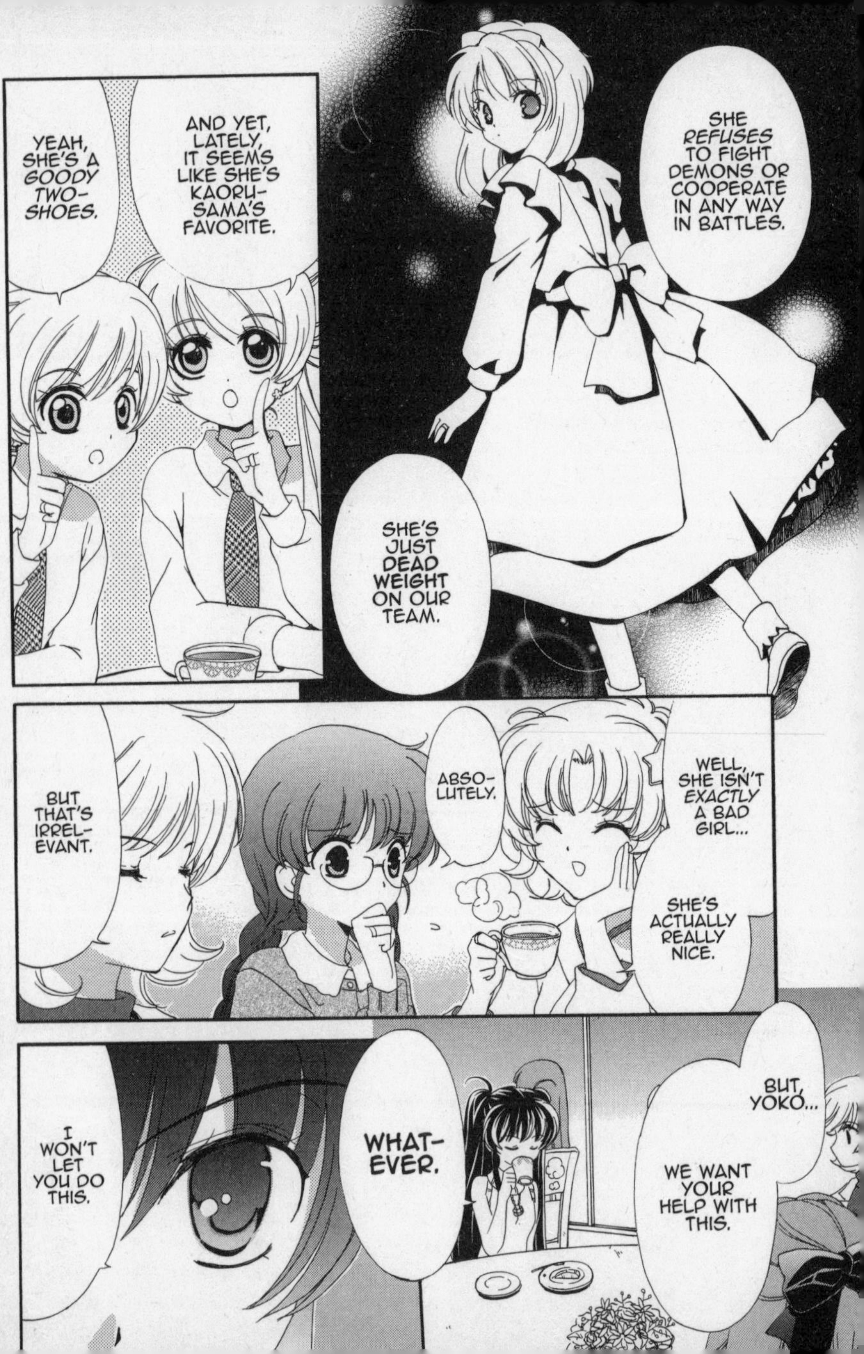
SHE REFUSES TO FIGHT DEMONS OR COOPERATE IN ANY WAY IN BATTLES.
SHE'S JUST DEAD WEIGHT ON OUR TEAM.
AND YET, LATELY, IT SEEMS LIKE SHE'S KAORU-SAMA'S FAVORITE.
YEAH, SHE'S A GOODY TWO-SHOES.
WELL, SHE ISN'T EXACTLY A BAD GIRL...
SHE'S ACTUALLY REALLY NICE.
ABSO-LUTELY.
BUT THAT'S IRREL-EVANT.
BUT, YOKO...
WE WANT YOUR HELP WITH THIS.
WHAT-EVER.
I WON'T LET YOU DO THIS.

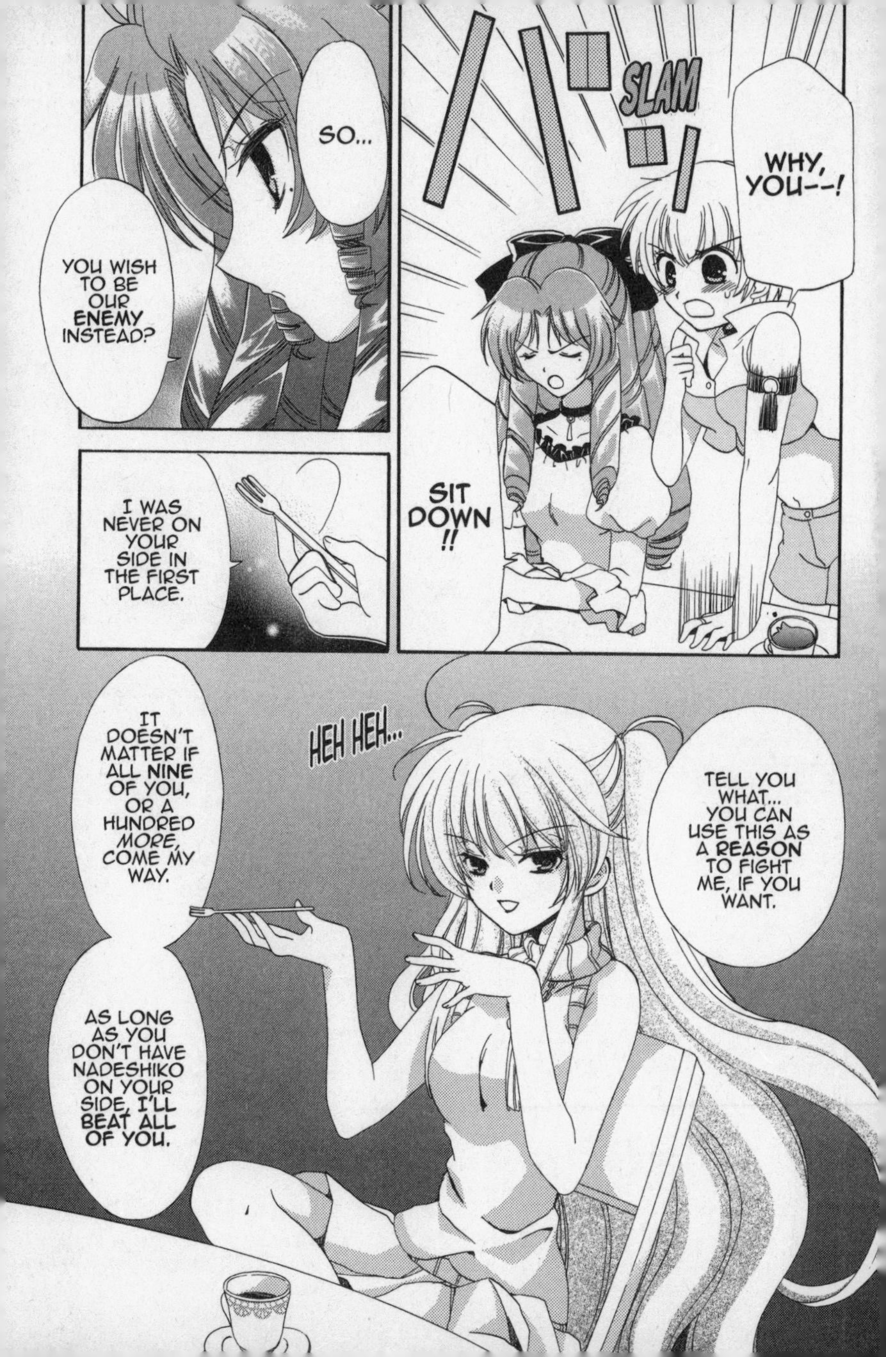
SLAM
WHY, YOU--!
SIT DOWN !!
SO...
YOU WISH TO BE OUR ENEMY INSTEAD?
I WAS NEVER ON YOUR SIDE IN THE FIRST PLACE.
TELL YOU WHAT... YOU CAN USE THIS AS A REASON TO FIGHT ME, IF YOU WANT.
HEH HEH...
IT DOESN'T MATTER IF ALL NINE OF YOU, OR A HUNDRED MORE, COME MY WAY.
AS LONG AS YOU DON'T HAVE NADESHIKO ON YOUR SIDE, I'LL BEAT ALL OF YOU.

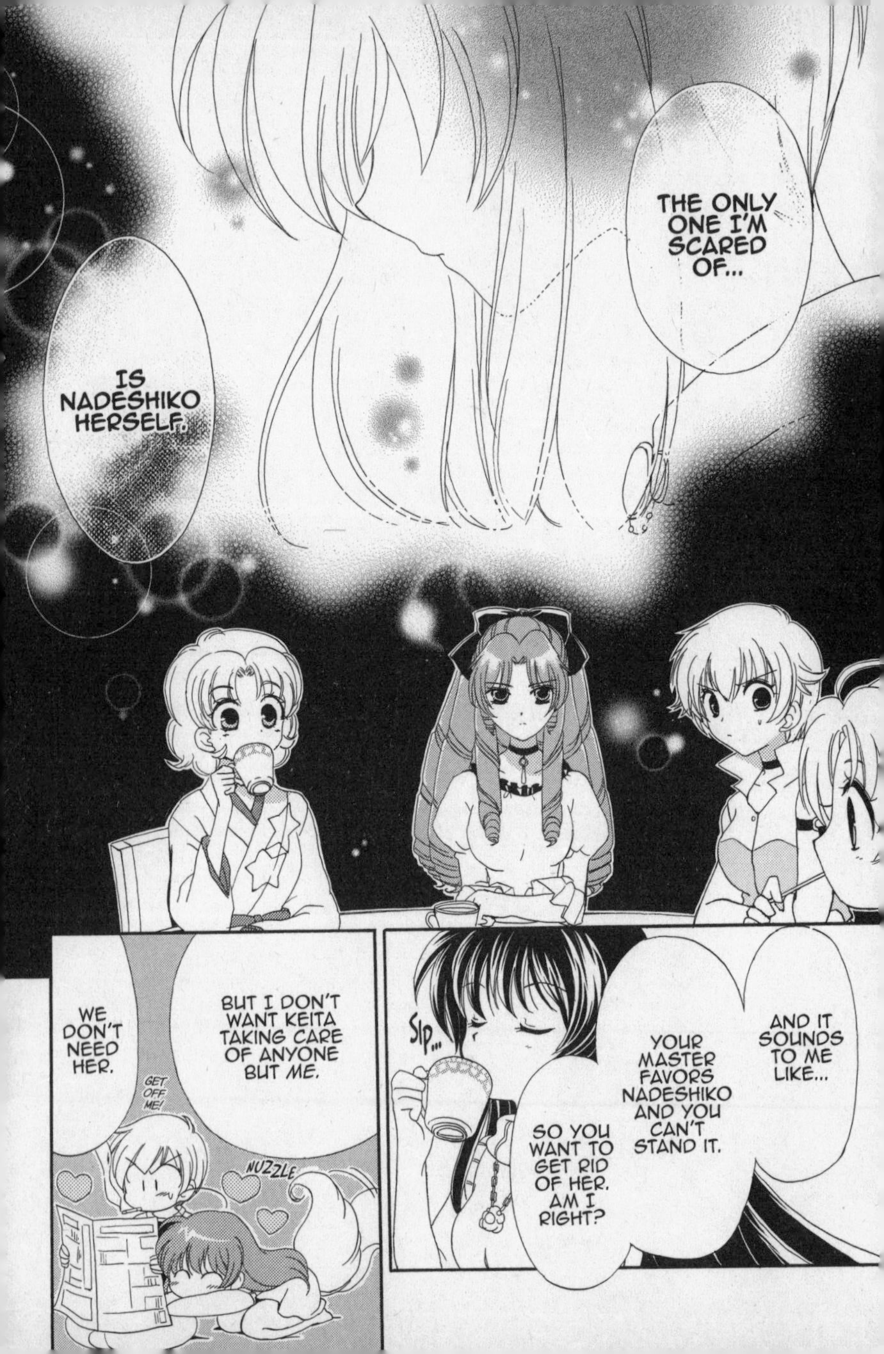
THE ONLY ONE I'M SCARED OF...
IS NADESHIKO HERSELF.
AND IT SOUNDS TO ME LIKE...
YOUR MASTER FAVORS NADESHIKO AND YOU CAN'T STAND IT.
SO YOU WANT TO GET RID OF HER. AM I RIGHT?
Sip...
BUT I DON'T WANT KEITA TAKING CARE OF ANYONE BUT ME.
WE DON'T NEED HER.
GET OFF ME!
NUZZLE

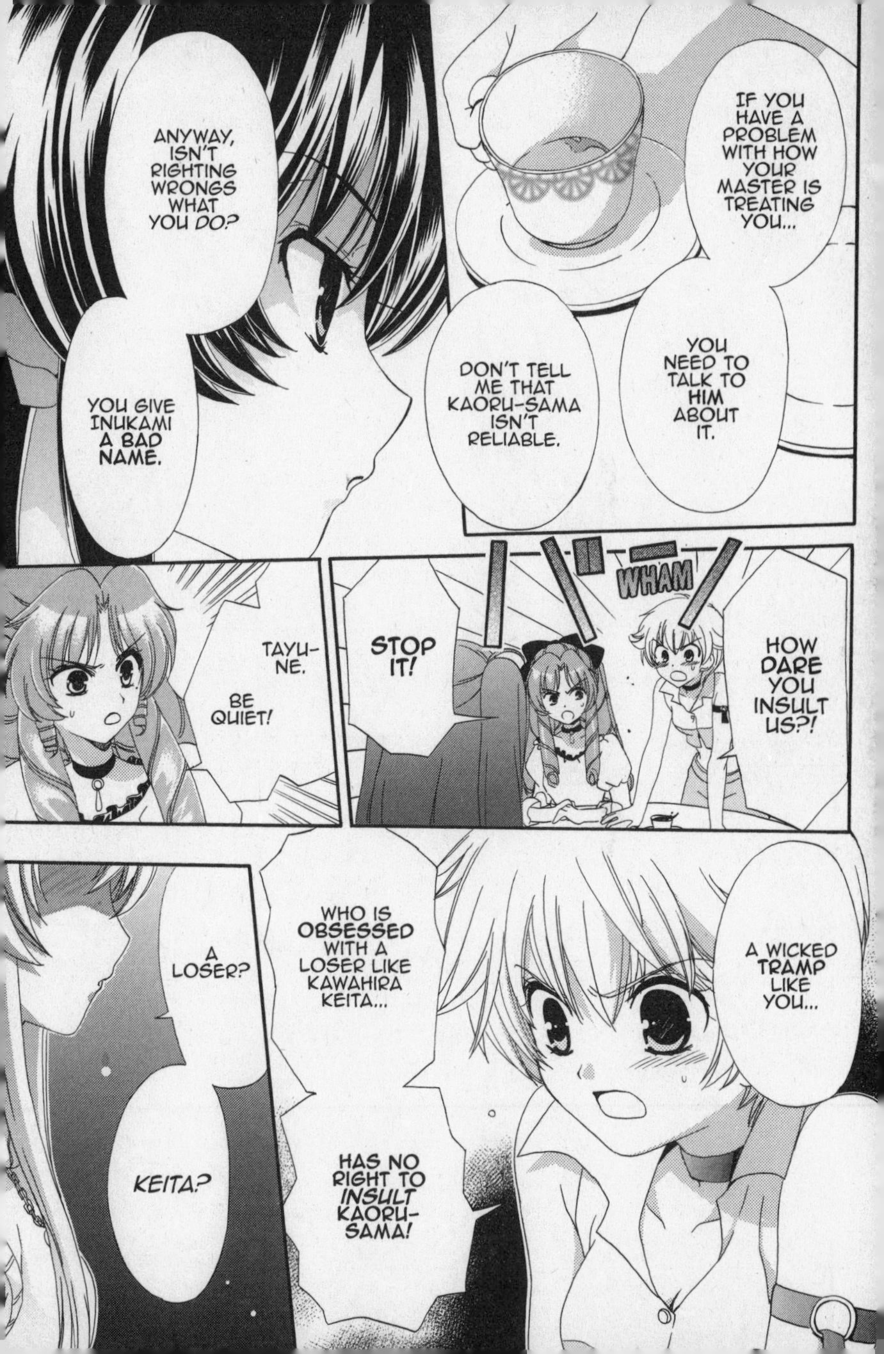
IF YOU HAVE A PROBLEM WITH HOW YOUR MASTER IS TREATING YOU...
YOU NEED TO TALK TO HIM ABOUT IT.
DON'T TELL ME THAT KAORU-SAMA ISN'T RELIABLE.
ANYWAY, ISN'T RIGHTING WRONGS WHAT YOU *DO*?
YOU GIVE INUKAMI A BAD NAME.
WHAM
HOW DARE YOU INSULT US?!
STOP IT!
TAYU-NE.
BE QUIET!
A WICKED TRAMP LIKE YOU...
WHO IS OBSESSED WITH A LOSER LIKE KAWAHIRA KEITA...
HAS NO RIGHT TO *INSULT* KAORU-SAMA!
A LOSER?
KEITA?

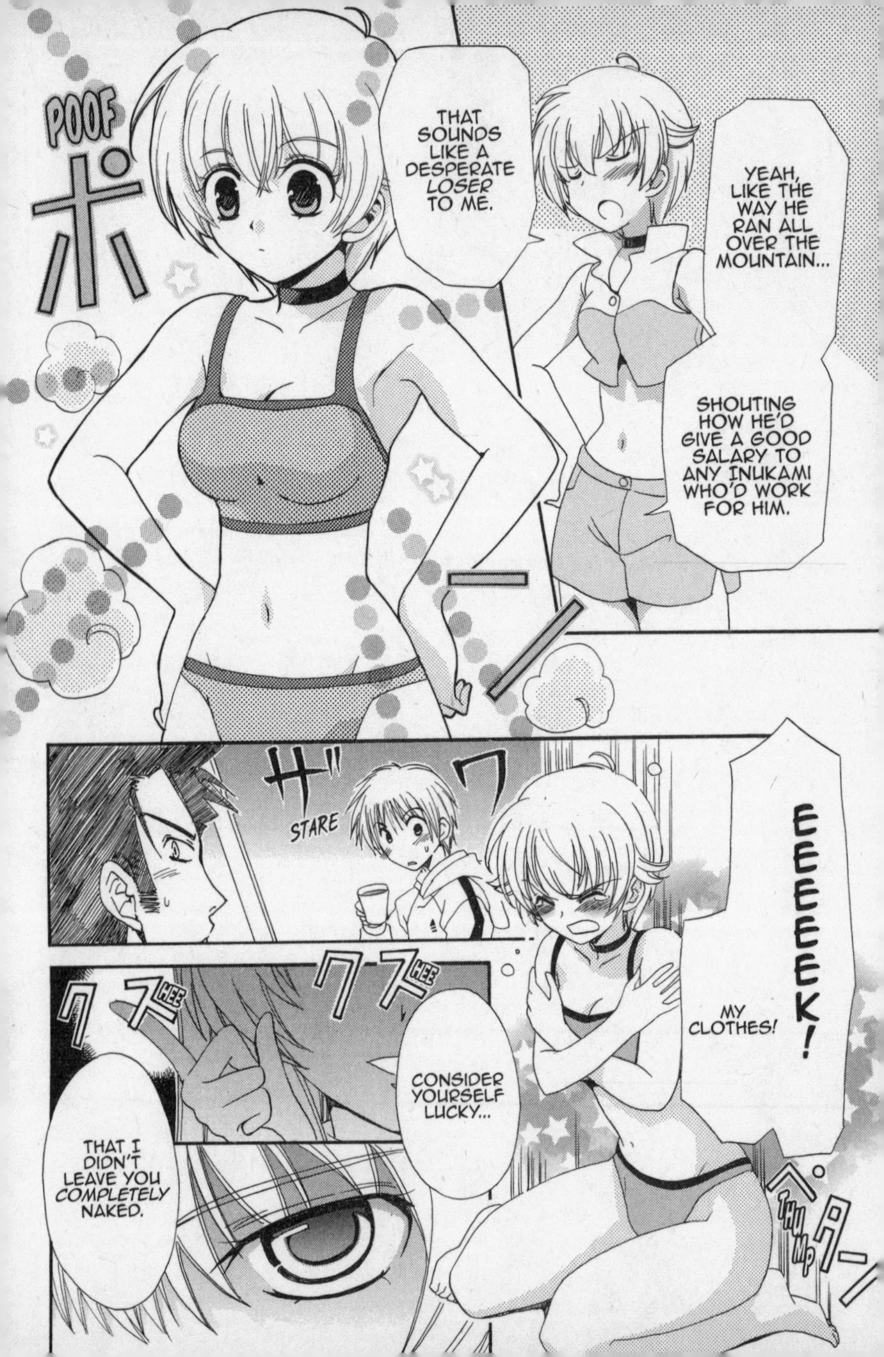
THAT SOUNDS LIKE A DESPERATE *LOSER* TO ME.
YEAH, LIKE THE WAY HE RAN ALL OVER THE MOUNTAIN...
SHOUTING HOW HE'D GIVE A GOOD SALARY TO ANY INUKAMI WHO'D WORK FOR HIM.
POOF
ポ
ーー
EEEEEEEK!
MY CLOTHES!
ザワ
STARE
クス HEE
クス HEE
CONSIDER YOURSELF LUCKY...
THAT I DIDN'T LEAVE YOU COMPLETELY NAKED.
ペターー
THUMP

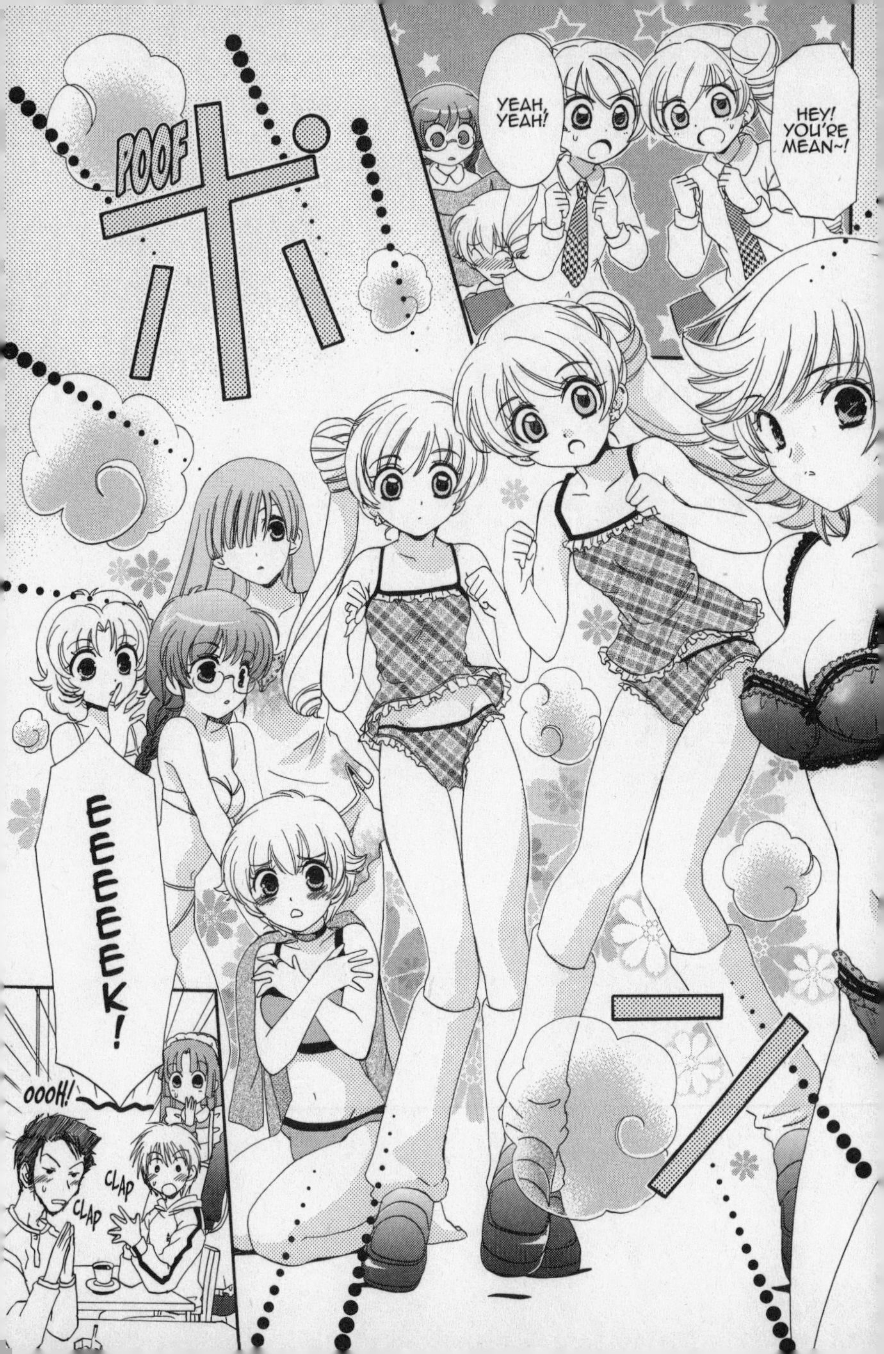
HEY! YOU'RE MEAN~!
YEAH, YEAH!
POOF
EEEEEEK!
OOOH!
CLAP
CLAP

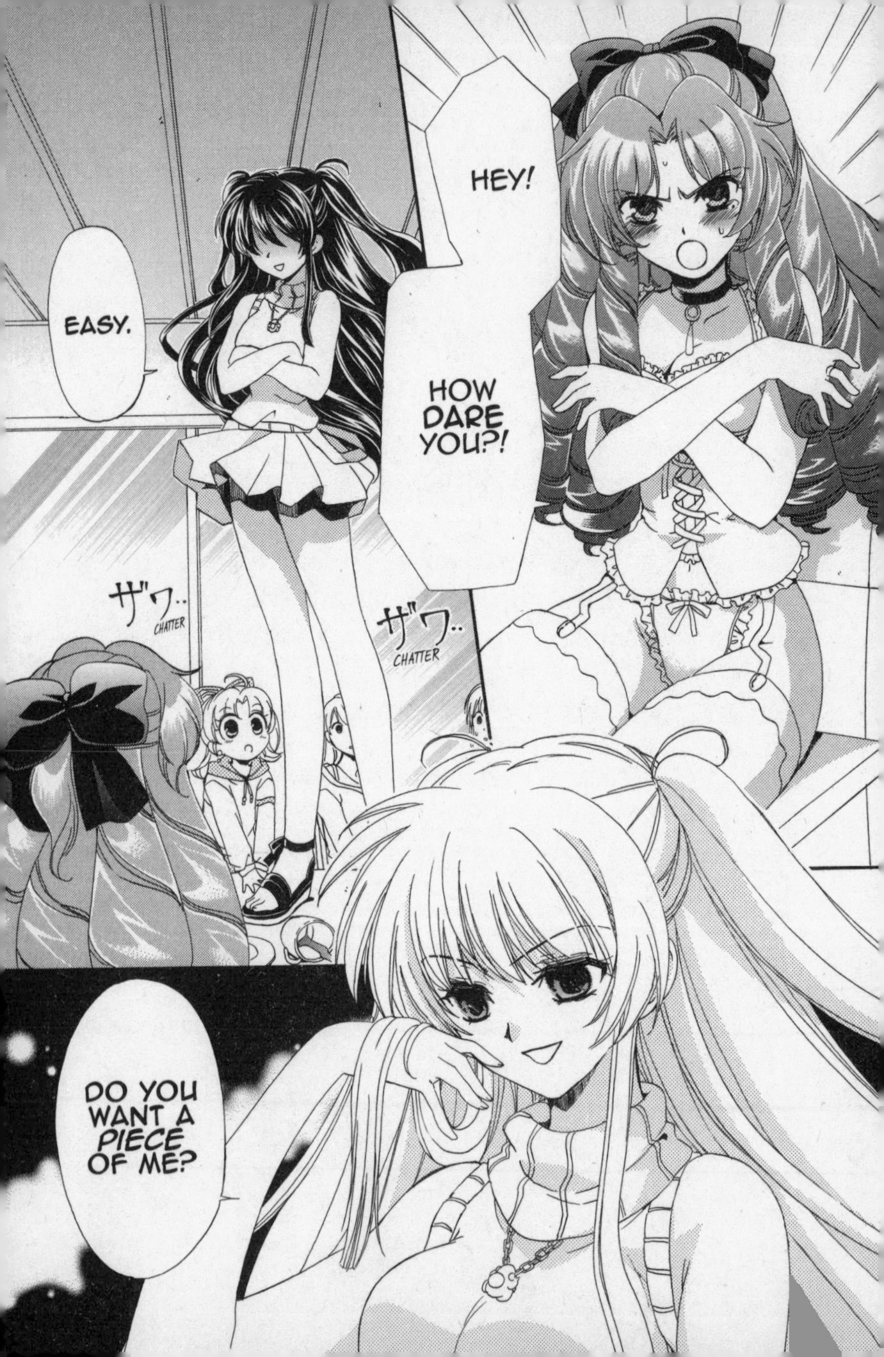
HEY!
HOW DARE YOU?!
EASY.
ザワ..
CHATTER
ザワ..
CHATTER
DO YOU WANT A PIECE OF ME?

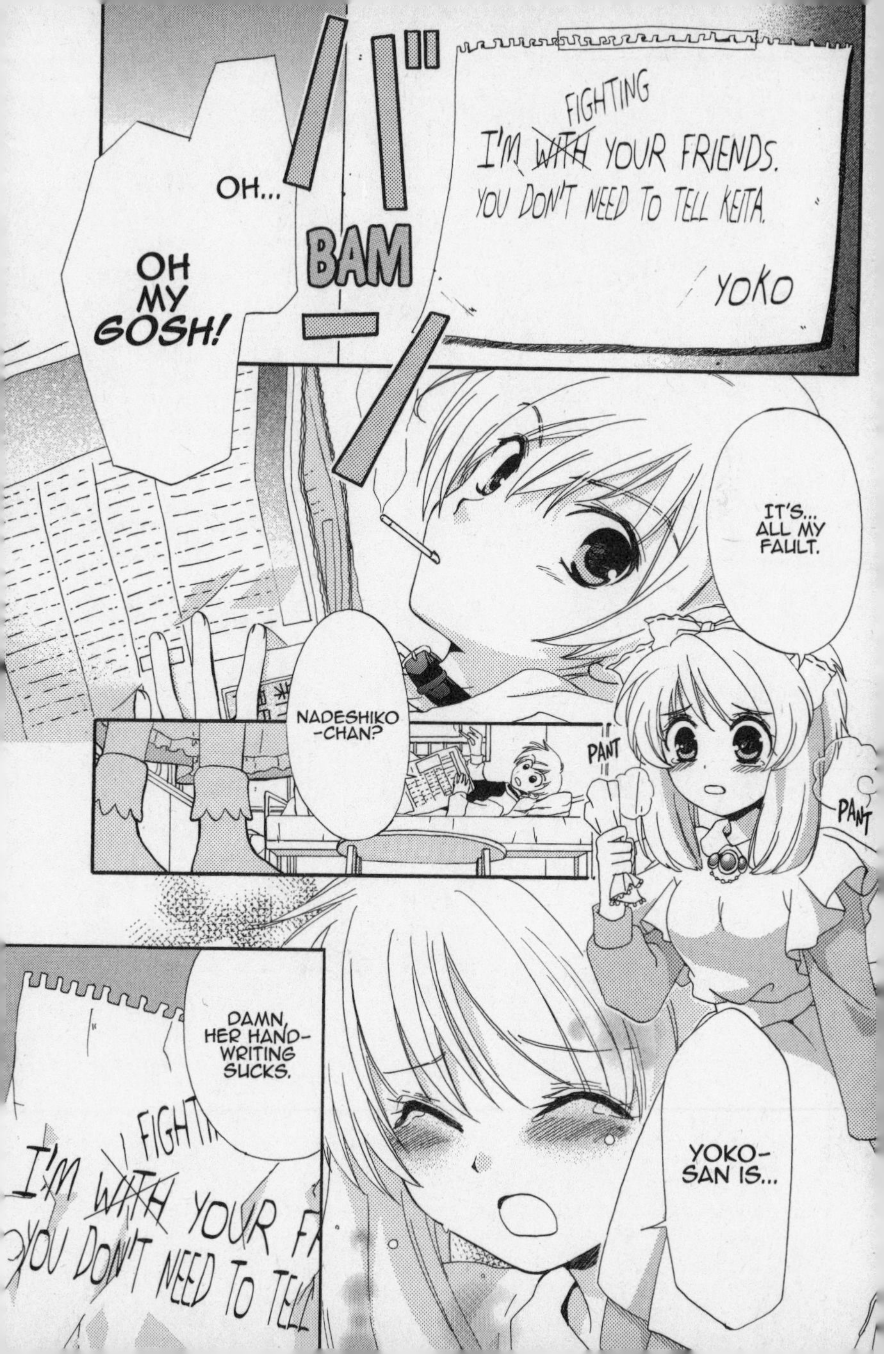

FIGHTING
I'M WITH YOUR FRIENDS.
YOU DON'T NEED TO TELL KEITA.
YOKO
BAM
OH...
OH MY GOSH!
IT'S... ALL MY FAULT.
PANT
PANT
NADESHIKO-CHAN?
YOKO-SAN IS...
DAMN, HER HAND-WRITING SUCKS.
FIGHTI
I'M WITH YOUR F
YOU DON'T NEED TO TEL

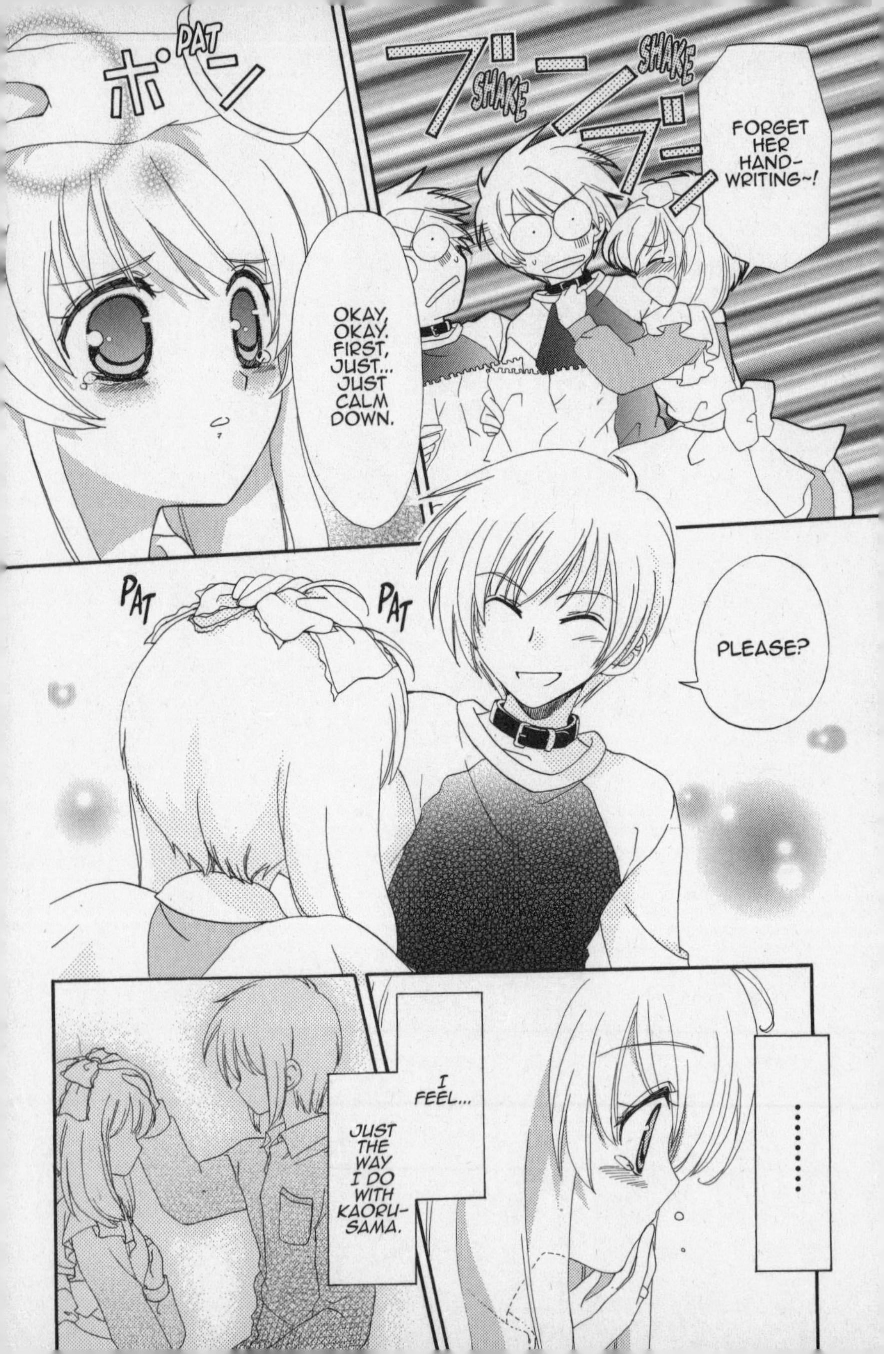
SHAKE
SHAKE
FORGET HER HAND-WRITING~!
OKAY, OKAY. FIRST, JUST... JUST CALM DOWN.
PAT
PAT
PAT
PLEASE?
....
I FEEL...
JUST THE WAY I DO WITH KAORU-SAMA.

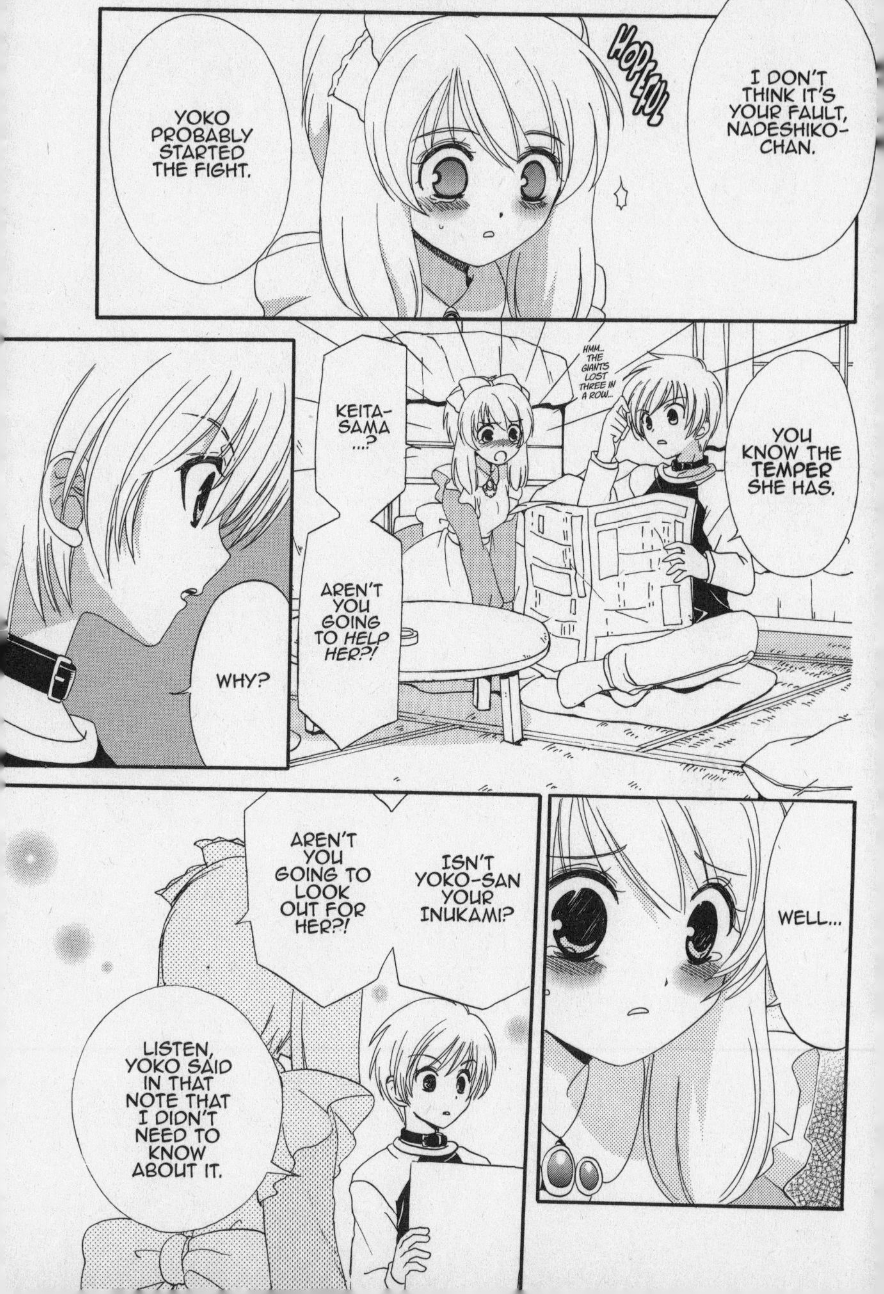
I DON'T THINK IT'S YOUR FAULT, NADESHIKO-CHAN.
HOPEFUL
YOKO PROBABLY STARTED THE FIGHT.
YOU KNOW THE TEMPER SHE HAS.
HMM... THE GIANTS LOST THREE IN A ROW...
KEITA-SAMA ...?
AREN'T YOU GOING TO HELP HER?!
WHY?
WELL...
ISN'T YOKO-SAN YOUR INUKAMI?
AREN'T YOU GOING TO LOOK OUT FOR HER?!
LISTEN, YOKO SAID IN THAT NOTE THAT I DIDN'T NEED TO KNOW ABOUT IT.

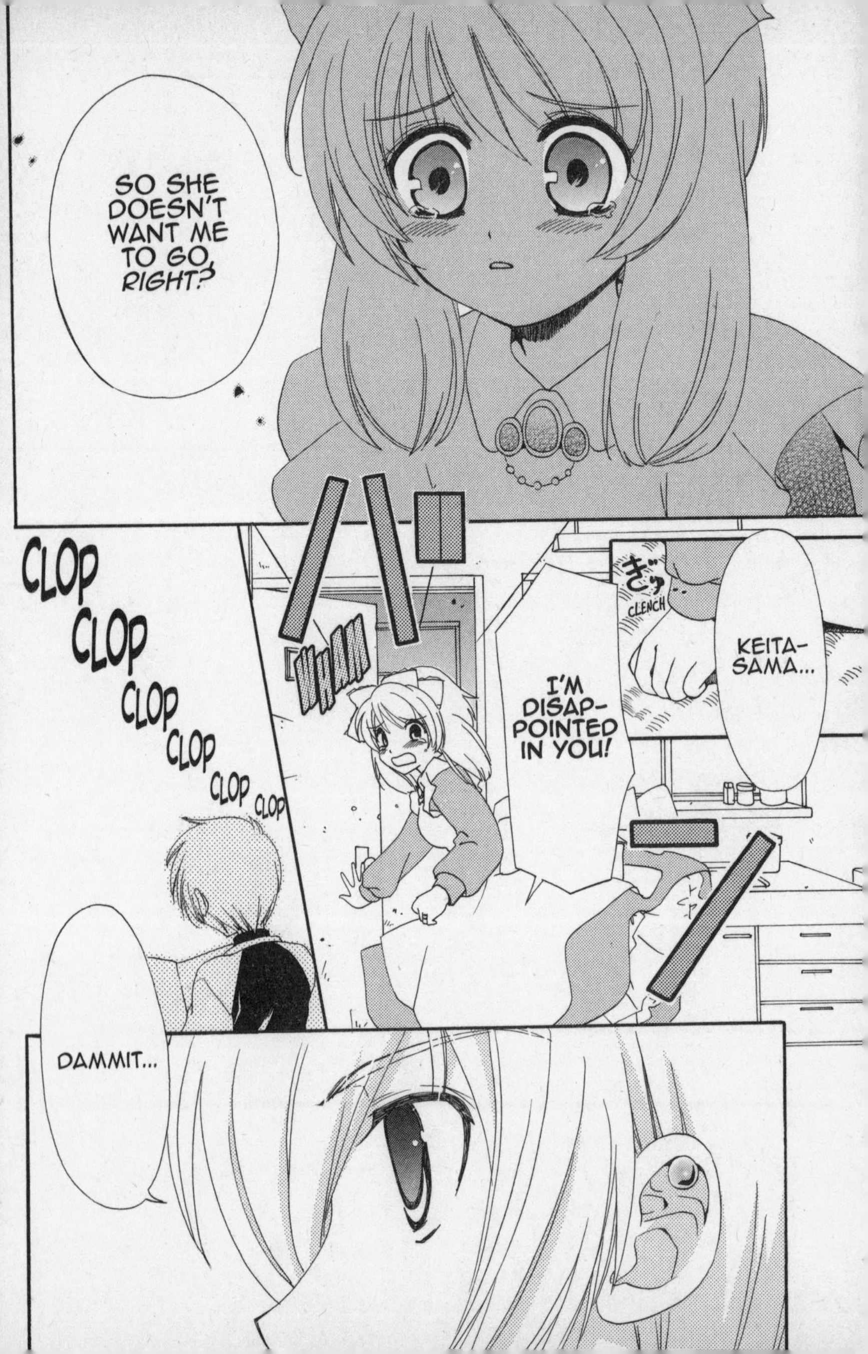
SO SHE DOESN'T WANT ME TO GO, RIGHT?
KEITA-SAMA...
ぎゅ CLENCH
I'M DISAP-POINTED IN YOU!
CLOP CLOP CLOP CLOP CLOP CLOP
DAMMIT...

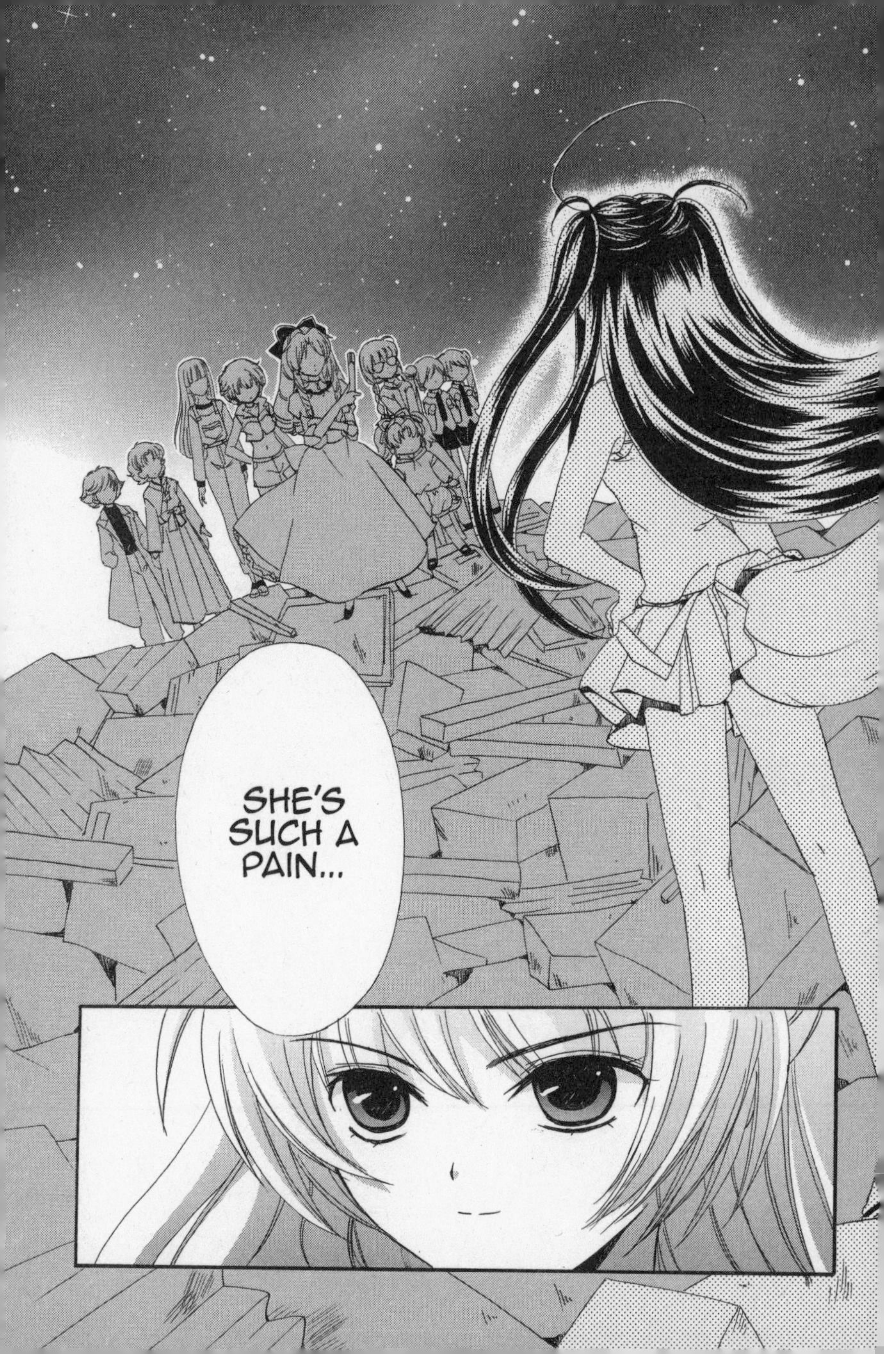
SHE'S SUCH A PAIN...

WHAT?

**KEITA
KAWAHIRA**

Height: 174 cm
Weight: 64 kg
Age: 17

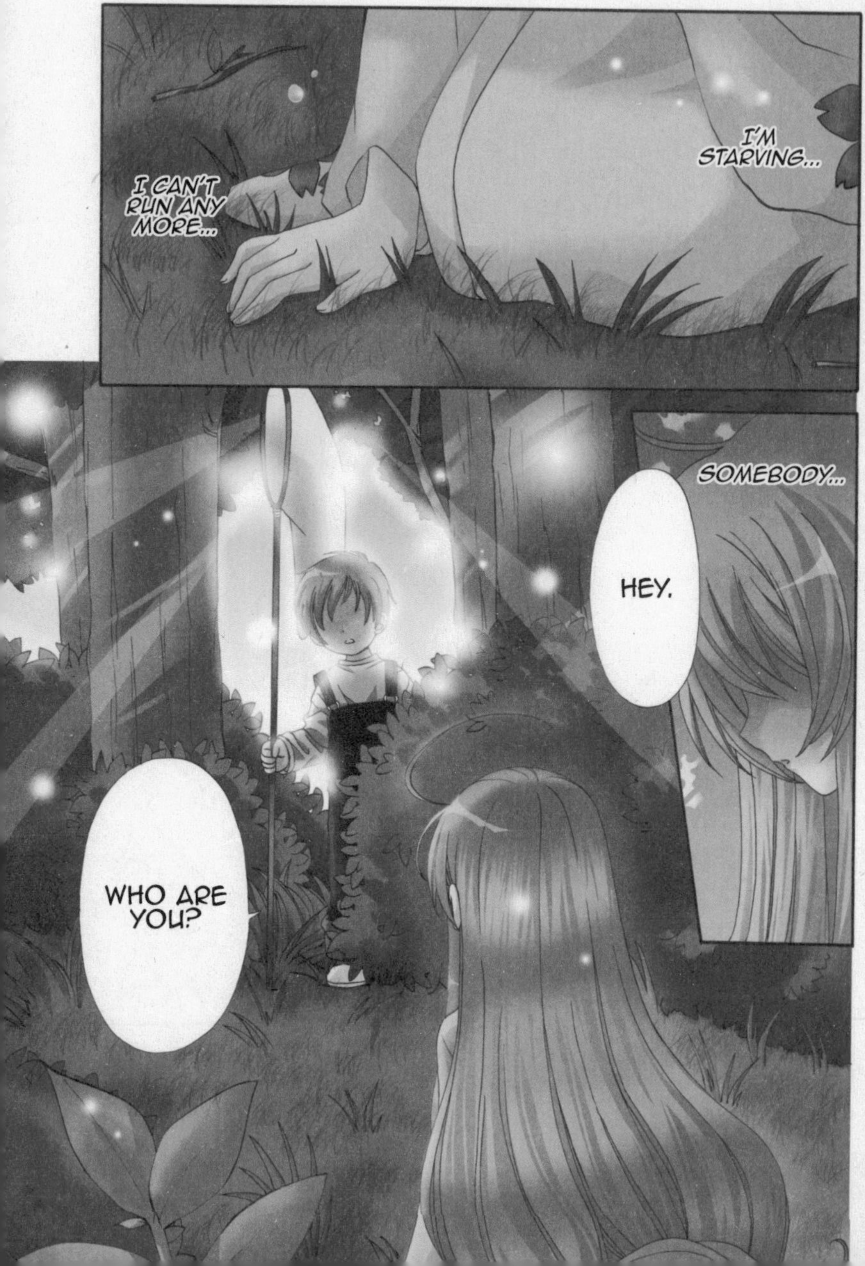
I'M STARVING...
I CAN'T RUN ANY MORE...
SOMEBODY...
HEY.
WHO ARE YOU?

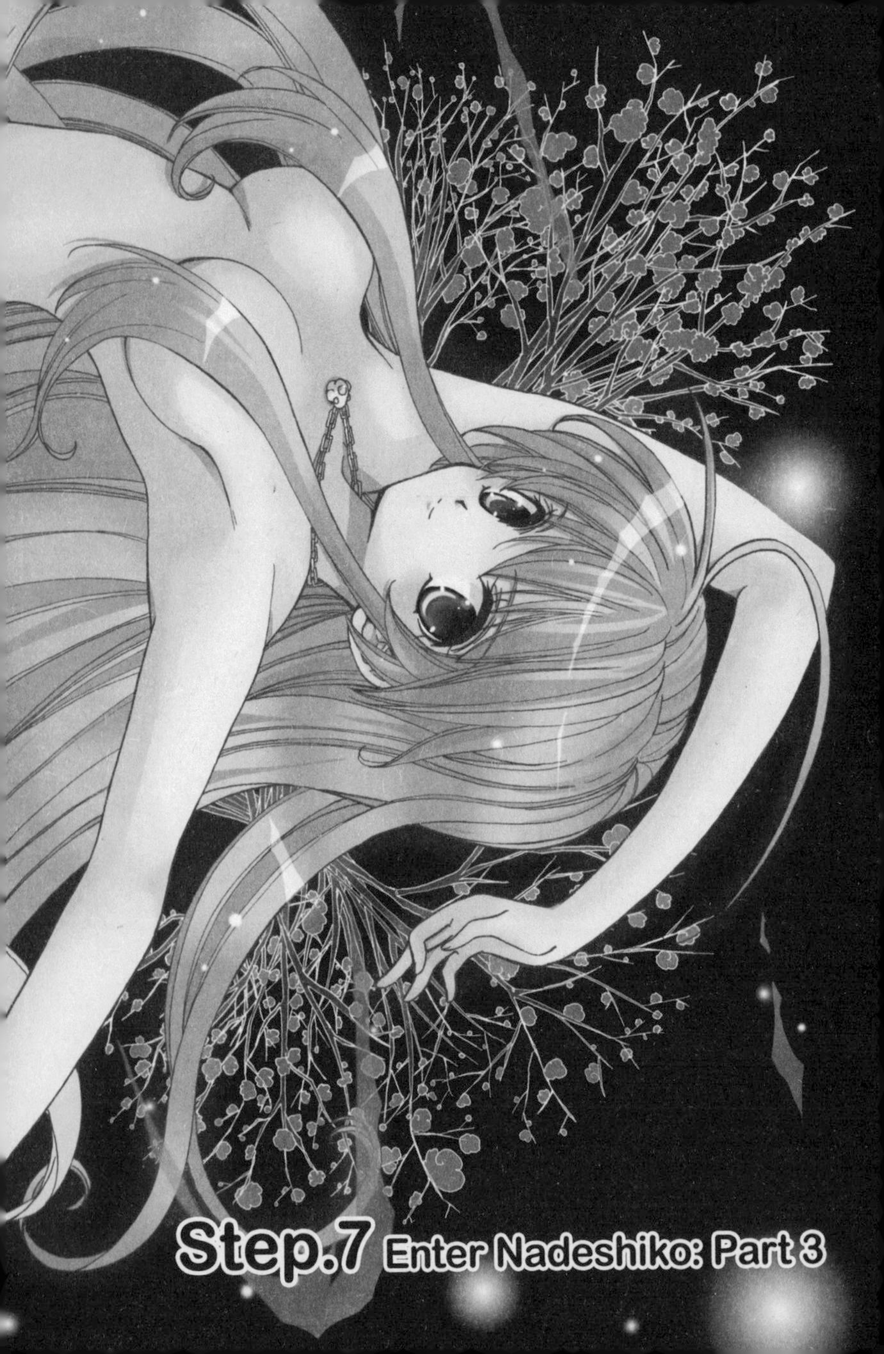
Step.7 Enter Nadeshiko: Part 3

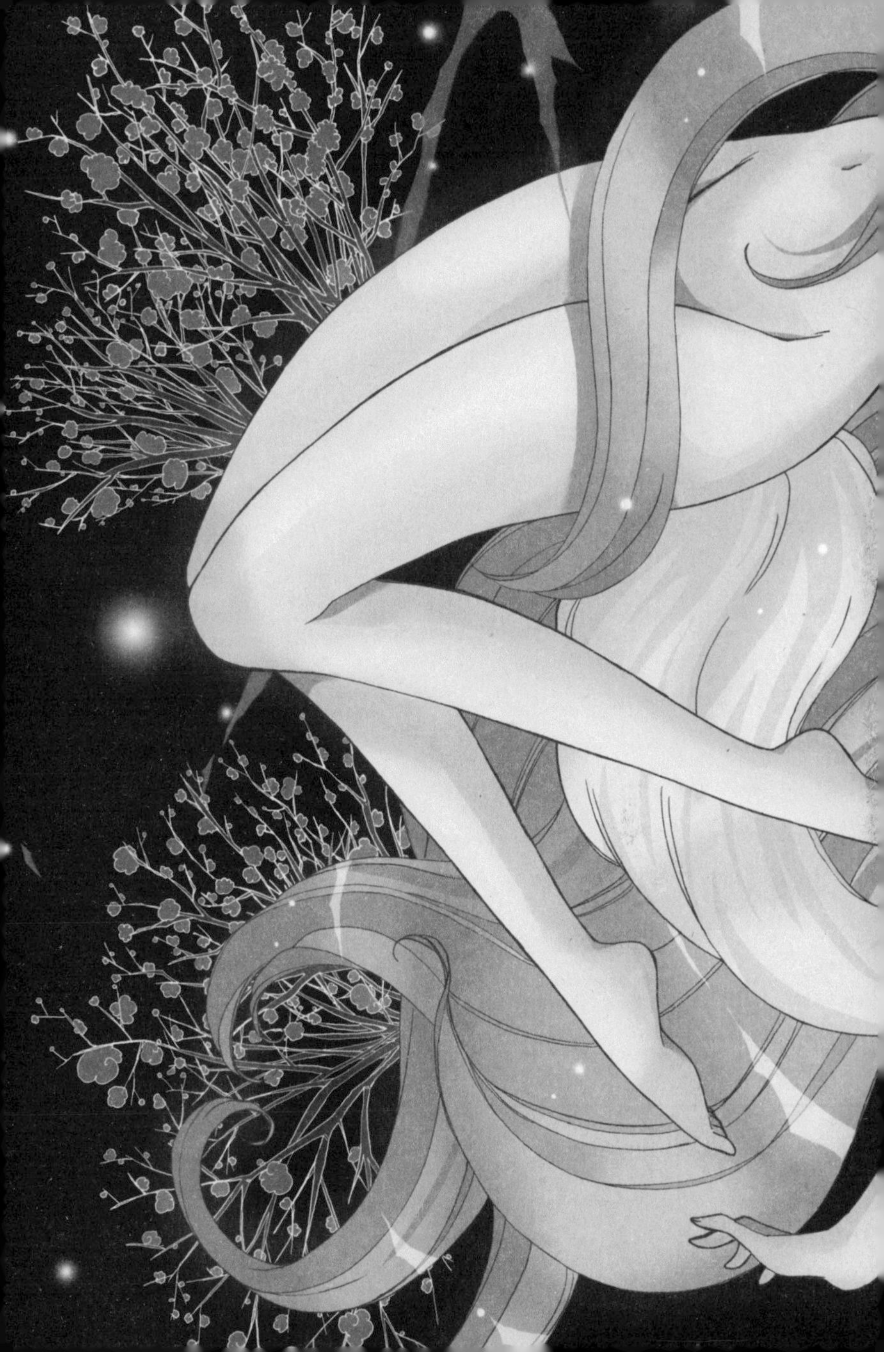

PLEASE.

NADESHIKO

Height: 160 cm
Bust: 92 cm
Waist: 61 cm
Hip: 88 cm
Age: ??

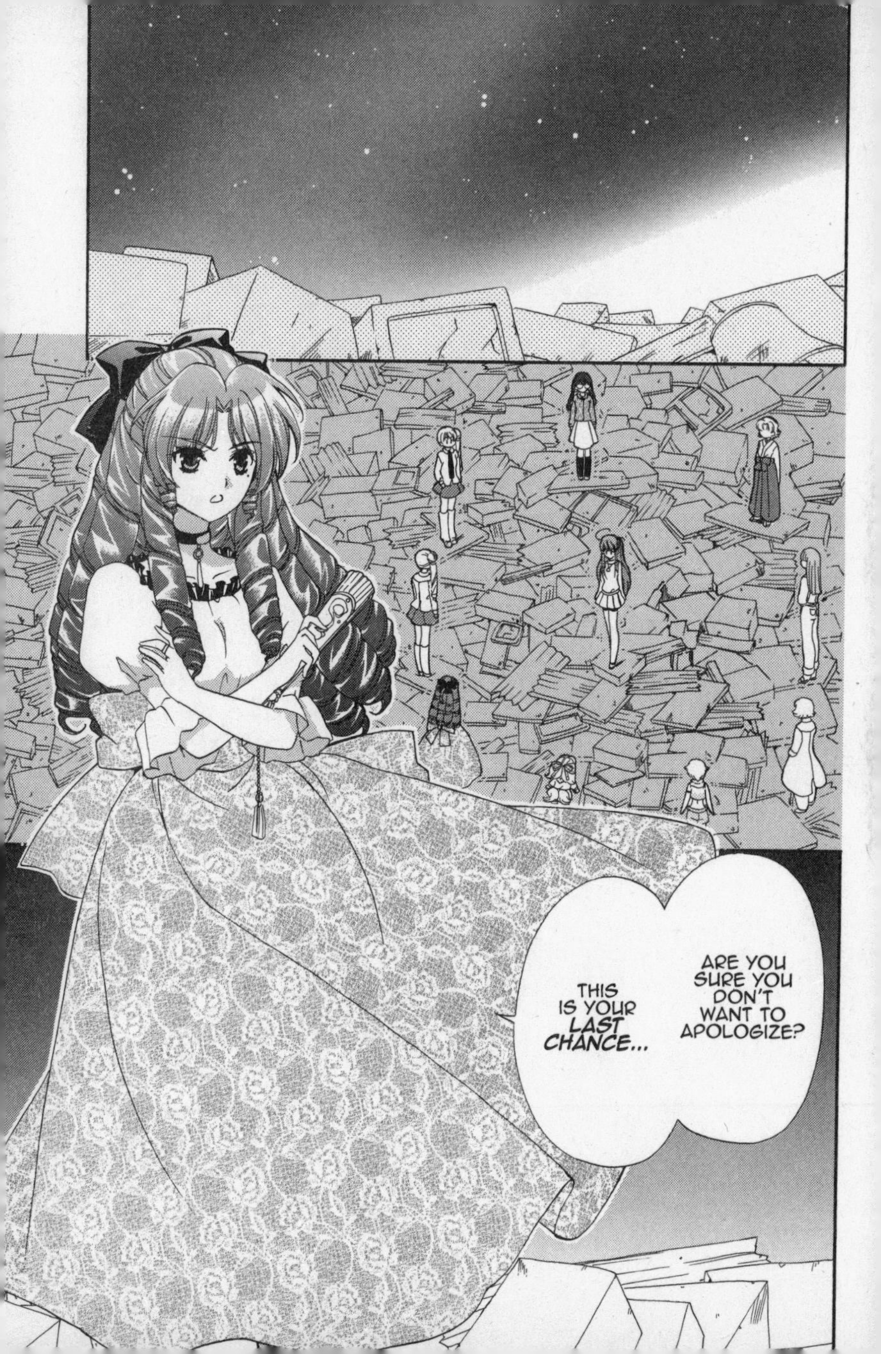
ARE YOU SURE YOU DON'T WANT TO APOLOGIZE?
THIS IS YOUR *LAST CHANCE...*

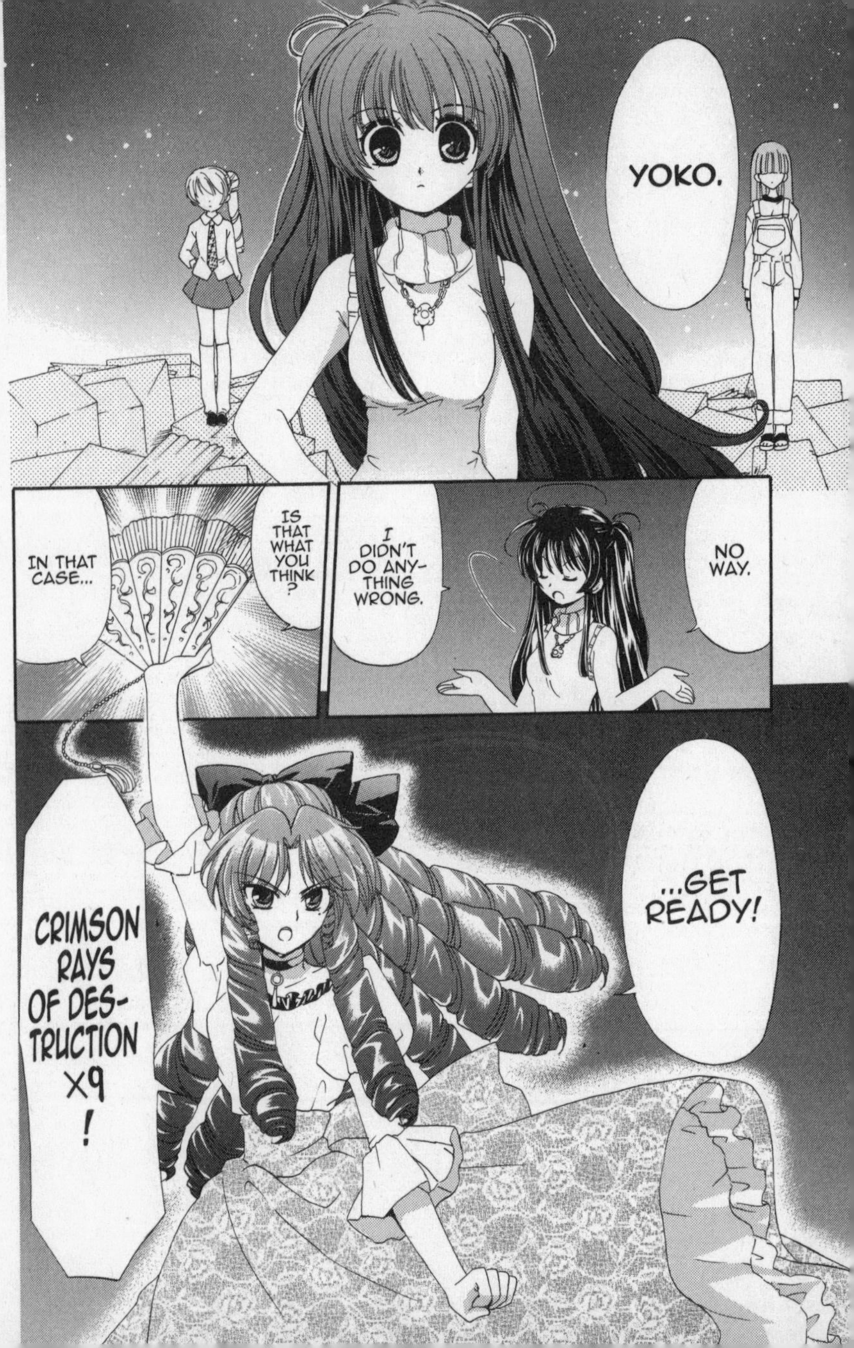
YOKO.
NO WAY.
I DIDN'T DO ANY-THING WRONG.
IS THAT WHAT YOU THINK?
IN THAT CASE...
...GET READY!
CRIMSON RAYS OF DES-TRUCTION x9!

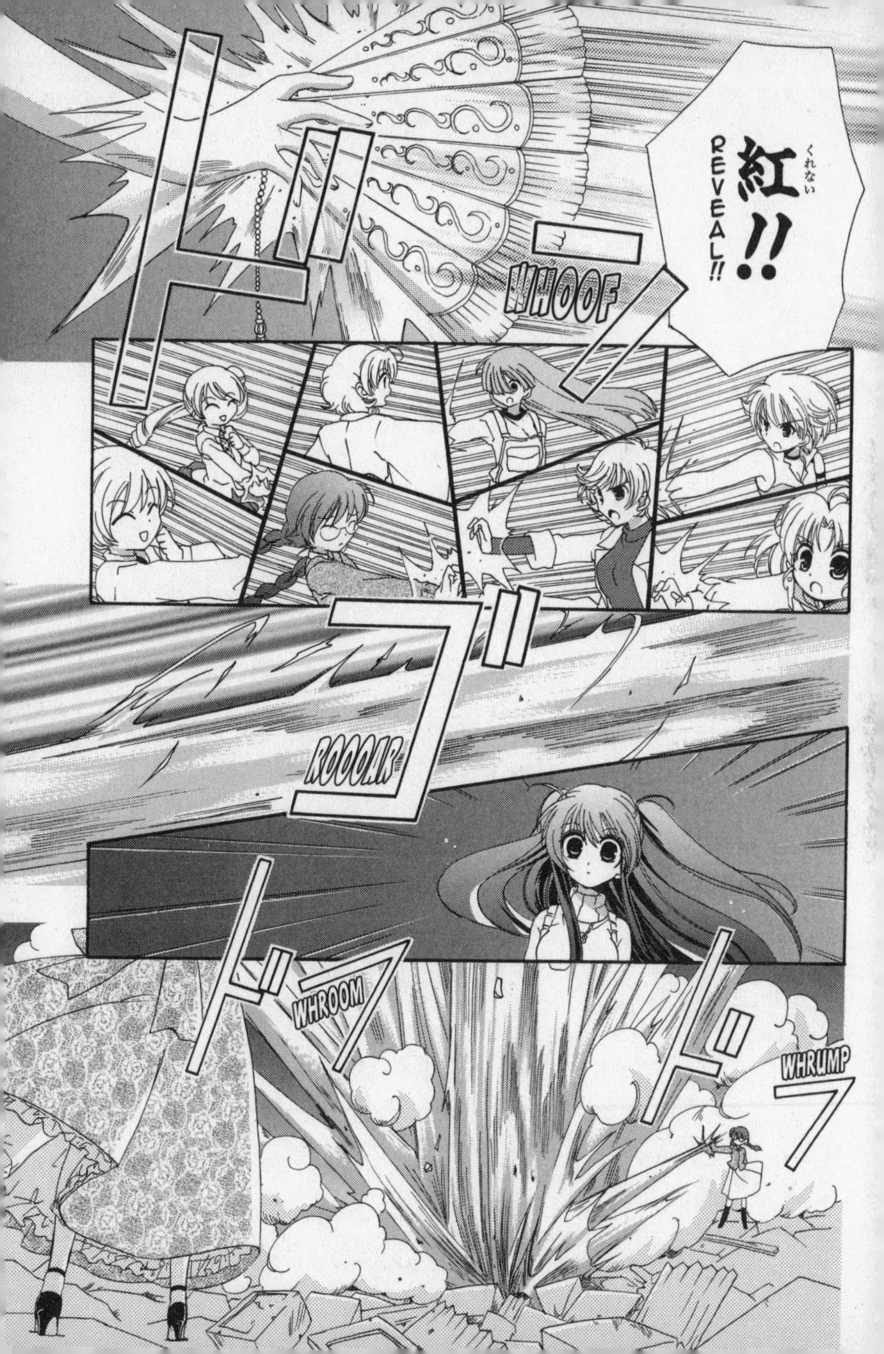
くれない
紅!!
REVEAL!!
WHOOF
ROOOAR
WHRUMP
WHROOM

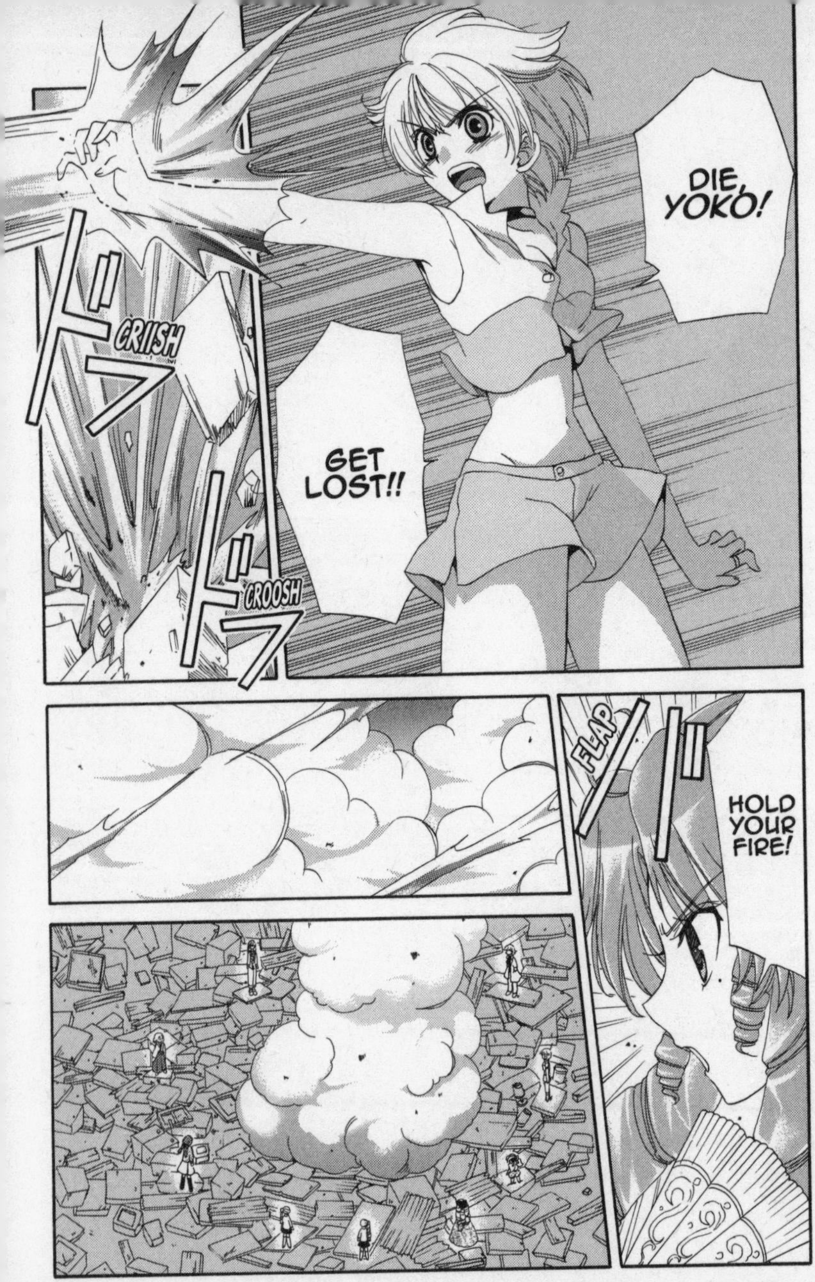
DIE, YOKO!
GET LOST!!
CRIISH
CROOSH
FLAP
HOLD YOUR FIRE!

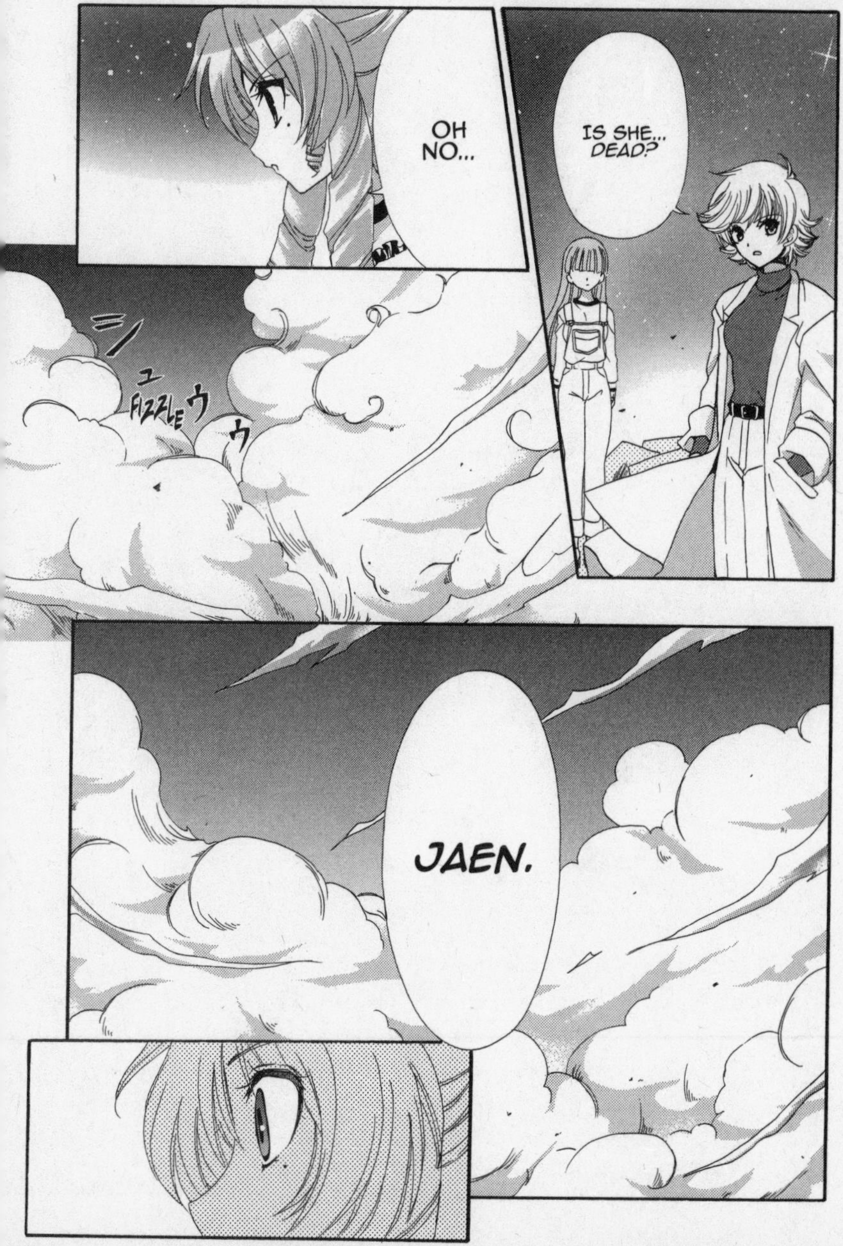
IS SHE... DEAD?
OH NO...
シュウウ
FIZZLE
JAEN.

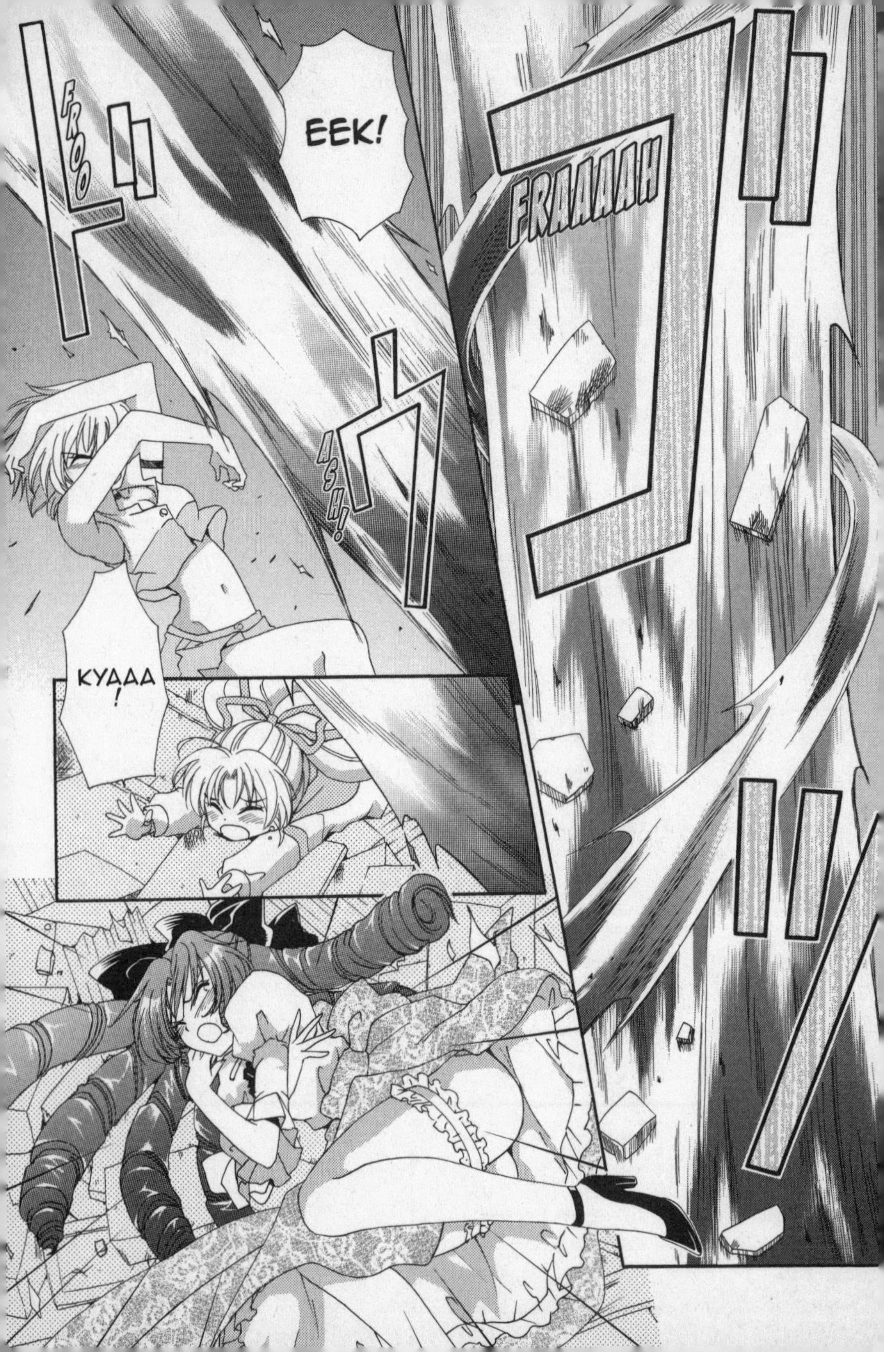
FRAAAAH
EEK!
FROO
ASH!
KYAAA!

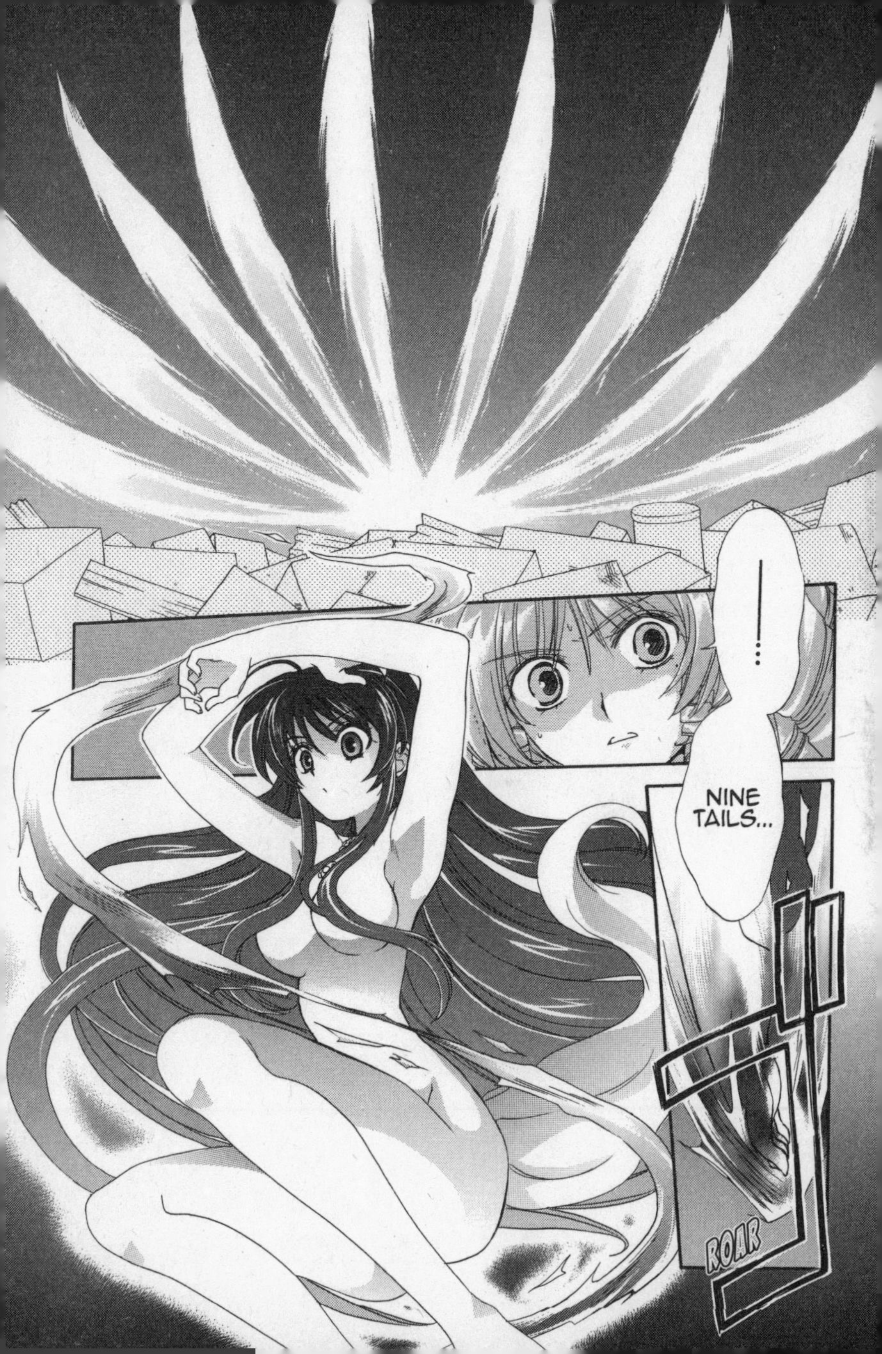
...!
NINE TAILS...
ROAR

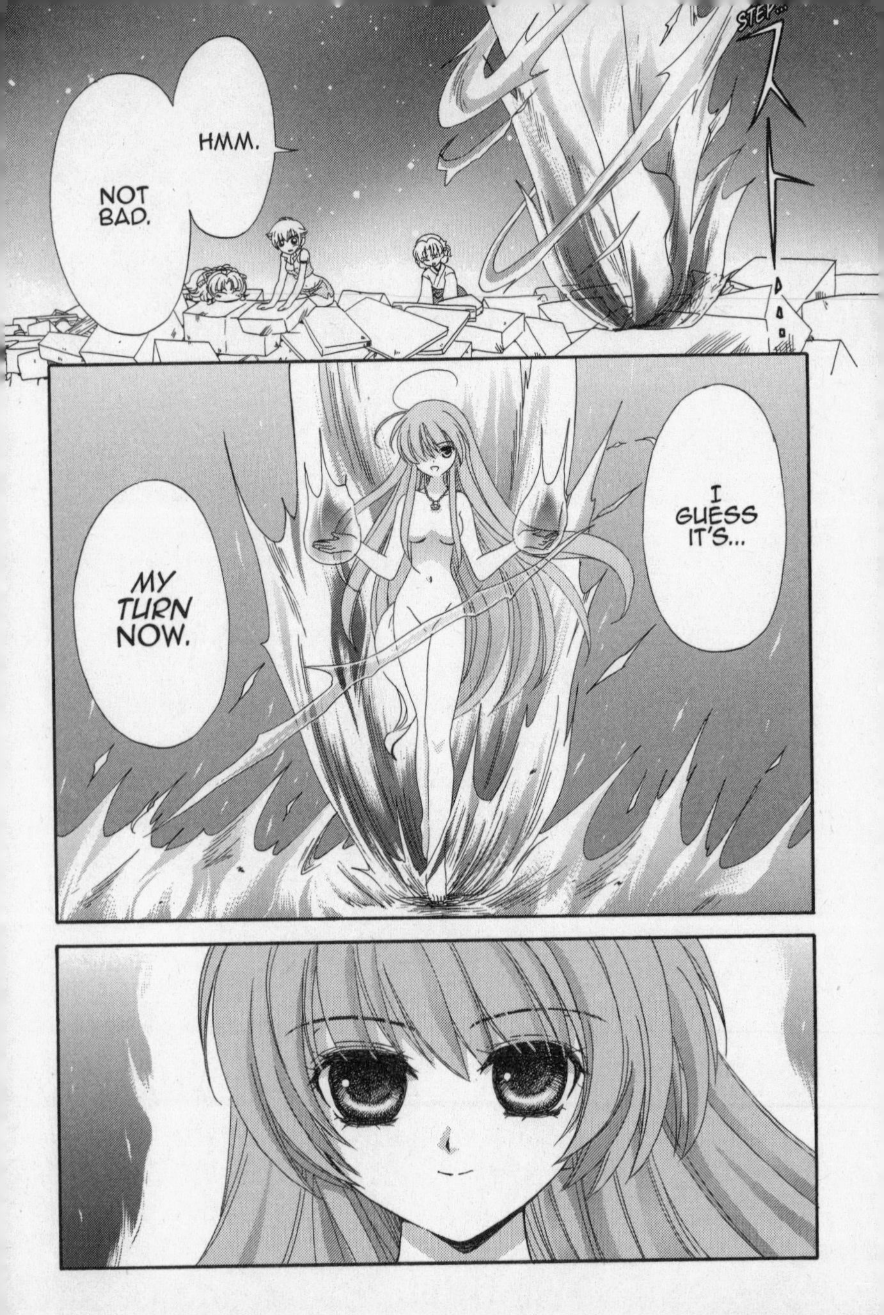
STEP...
HMM.
NOT BAD.
I GUESS IT'S...
MY TURN NOW.

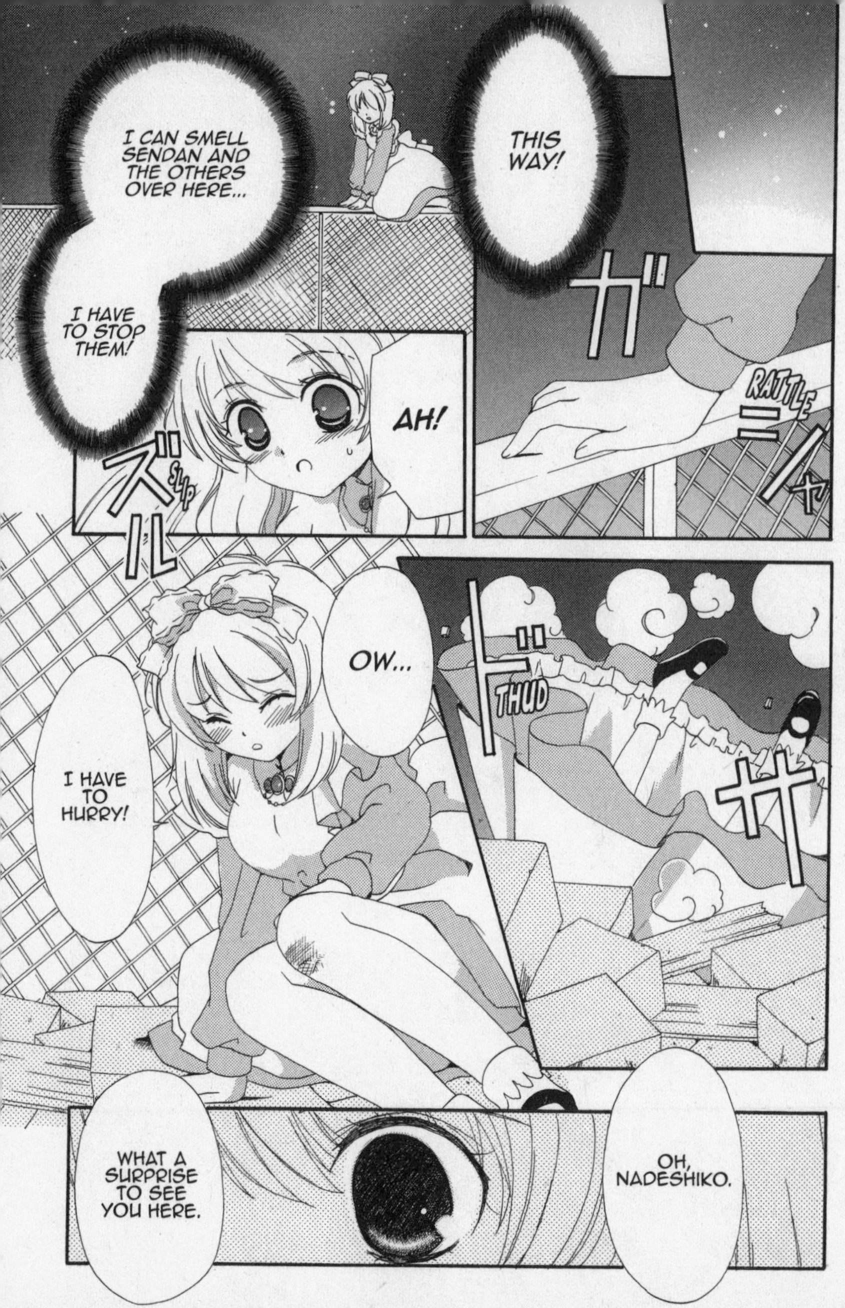
THIS WAY!
I CAN SMELL SENDAN AND THE OTHERS OVER HERE...
I HAVE TO STOP THEM!
RATTLE
AH!
SLIP
THUD
OW...
I HAVE TO HURRY!
OH, NADESHIKO.
WHAT A SURPRISE TO SEE YOU HERE.

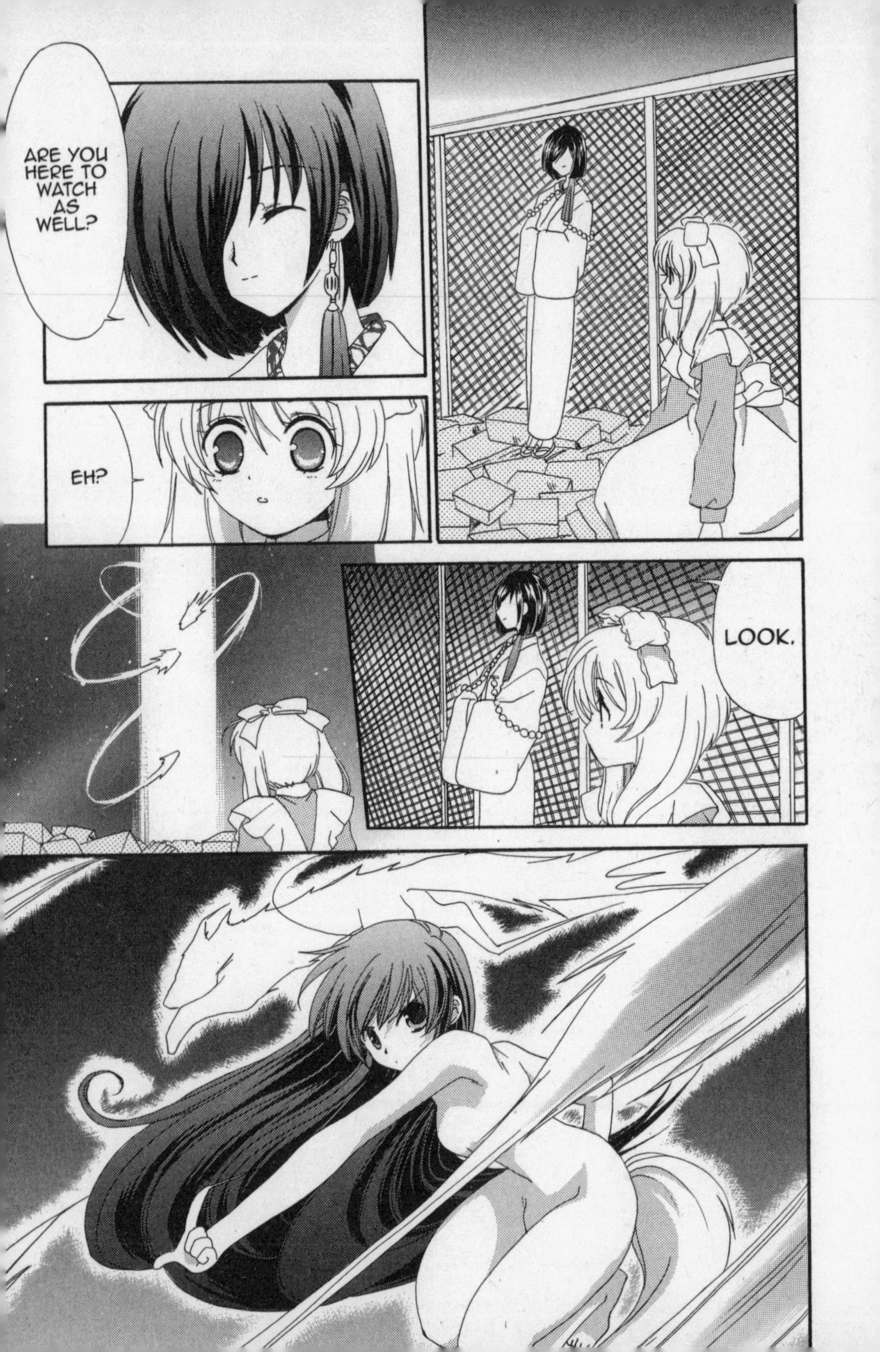
ARE YOU HERE TO WATCH AS WELL?
EH?
LOOK.

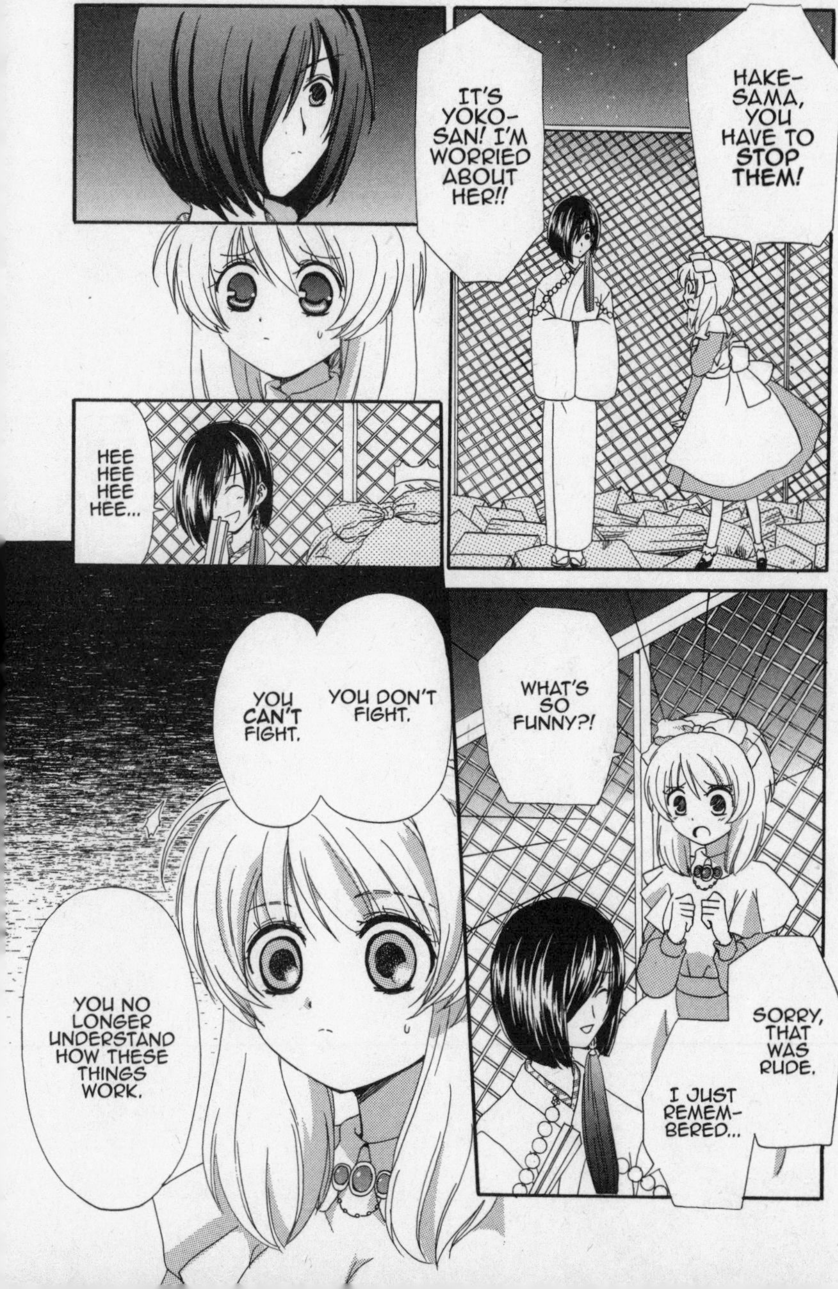
HAKE-SAMA, YOU HAVE TO STOP THEM!
IT'S YOKO-SAN! I'M WORRIED ABOUT HER!!
HEE HEE HEE HEE...
WHAT'S SO FUNNY?!
SORRY, THAT WAS RUDE.
I JUST REMEMBERED...
YOU DON'T FIGHT.
YOU CAN'T FIGHT.
YOU NO LONGER UNDERSTAND HOW THESE THINGS WORK.

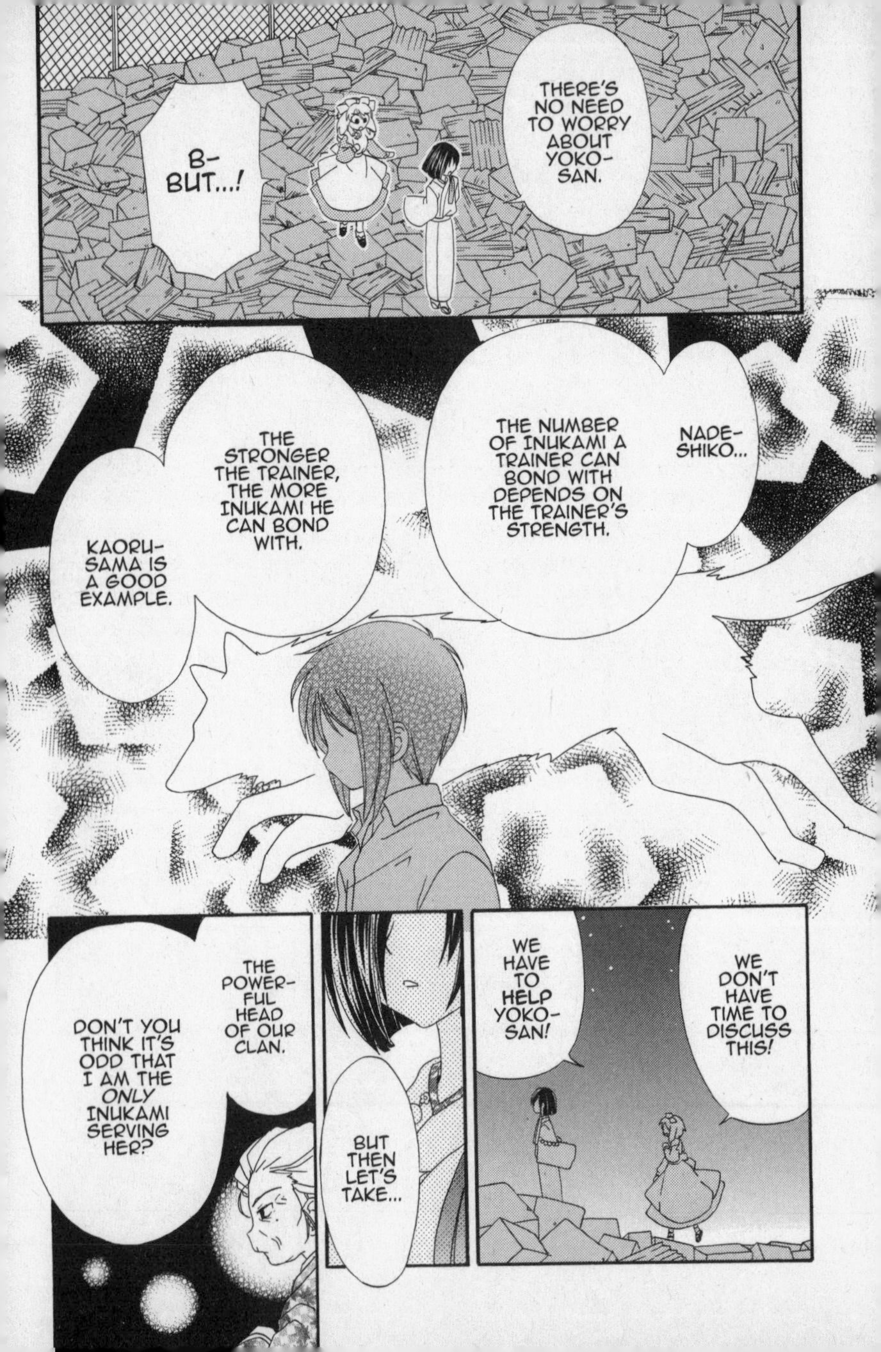
THERE'S NO NEED TO WORRY ABOUT YOKO-SAN.
B-BUT...!
NADE-SHIKO...
THE NUMBER OF INUKAMI A TRAINER CAN BOND WITH DEPENDS ON THE TRAINER'S STRENGTH.
THE STRONGER THE TRAINER, THE MORE INUKAMI HE CAN BOND WITH.
KAORU-SAMA IS A GOOD EXAMPLE.
WE DON'T HAVE TIME TO DISCUSS THIS!
WE HAVE TO HELP YOKO-SAN!
BUT THEN LET'S TAKE...
THE POWER-FUL HEAD OF OUR CLAN.
DON'T YOU THINK IT'S ODD THAT I AM THE *ONLY* INUKAMI SERVING HER?

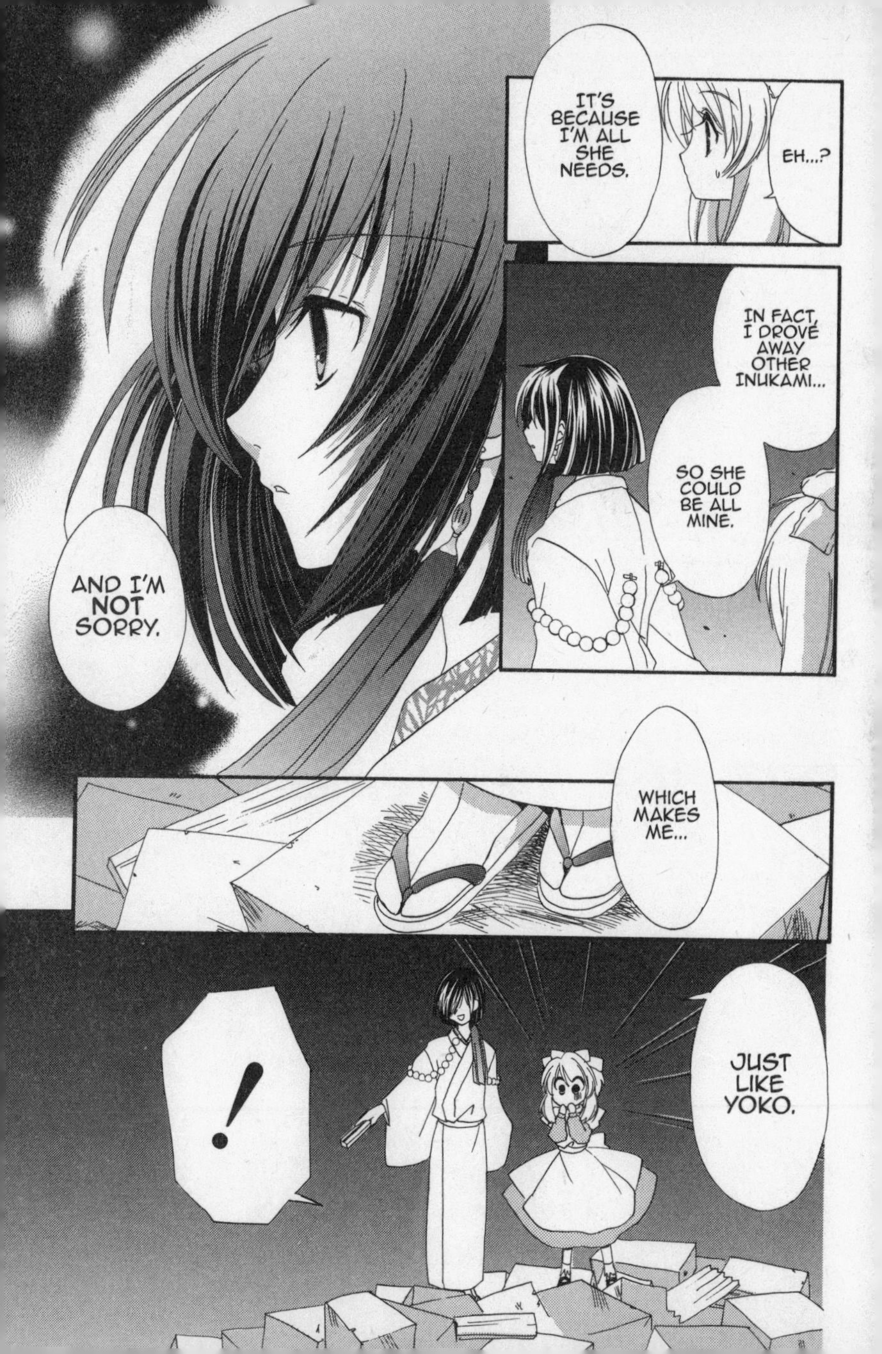
EH...?
IT'S BECAUSE I'M ALL SHE NEEDS.
IN FACT, I DROVE AWAY OTHER INUKAMI...
SO SHE COULD BE ALL MINE.
AND I'M NOT SORRY.
WHICH MAKES ME...
JUST LIKE YOKO.
!

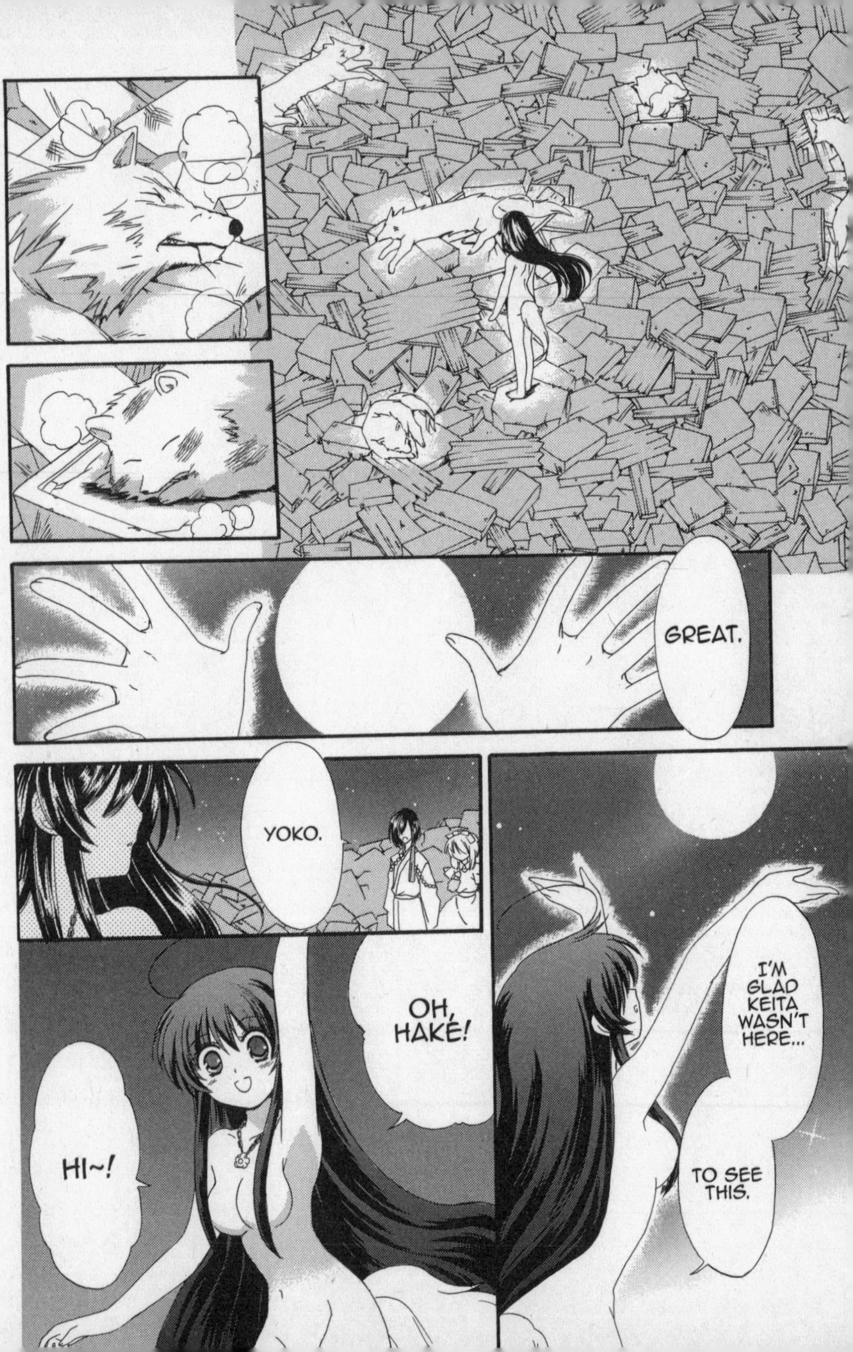
GREAT.
I'M GLAD KEITA WASN'T HERE...
TO SEE THIS.
YOKO.
OH, HAKÉ!
HI~!

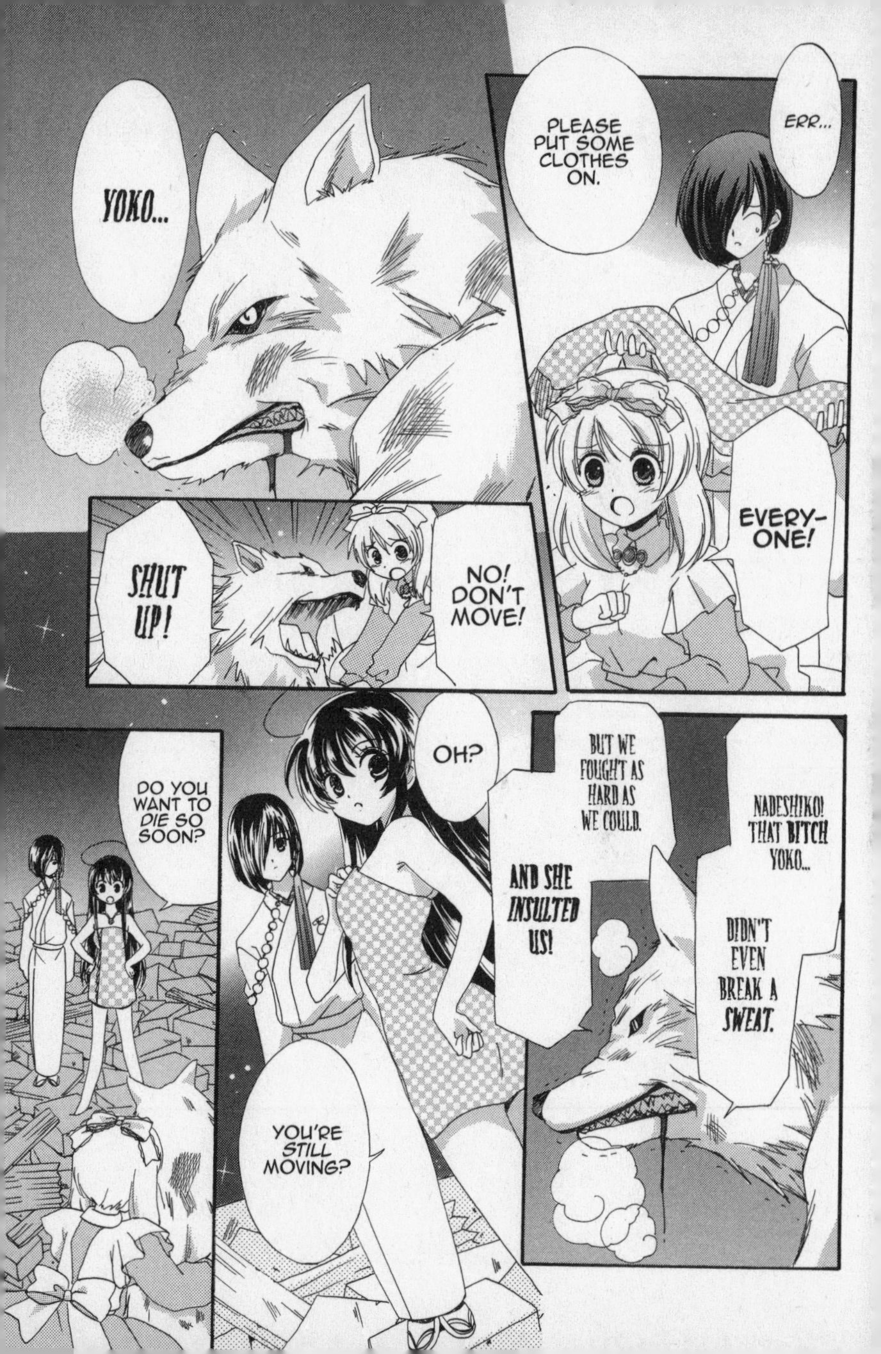
ERR...
PLEASE PUT SOME CLOTHES ON.
EVERY-ONE!
YOKO...
NO! DON'T MOVE!
SHUT UP!
NADESHIKO! THAT BITCH YOKO...
BUT WE FOUGHT AS HARD AS WE COULD.
DIDN'T EVEN BREAK A SWEAT.
AND SHE INSULTED US!
OH?
YOU'RE STILL MOVING?
DO YOU WANT TO DIE SO SOON?

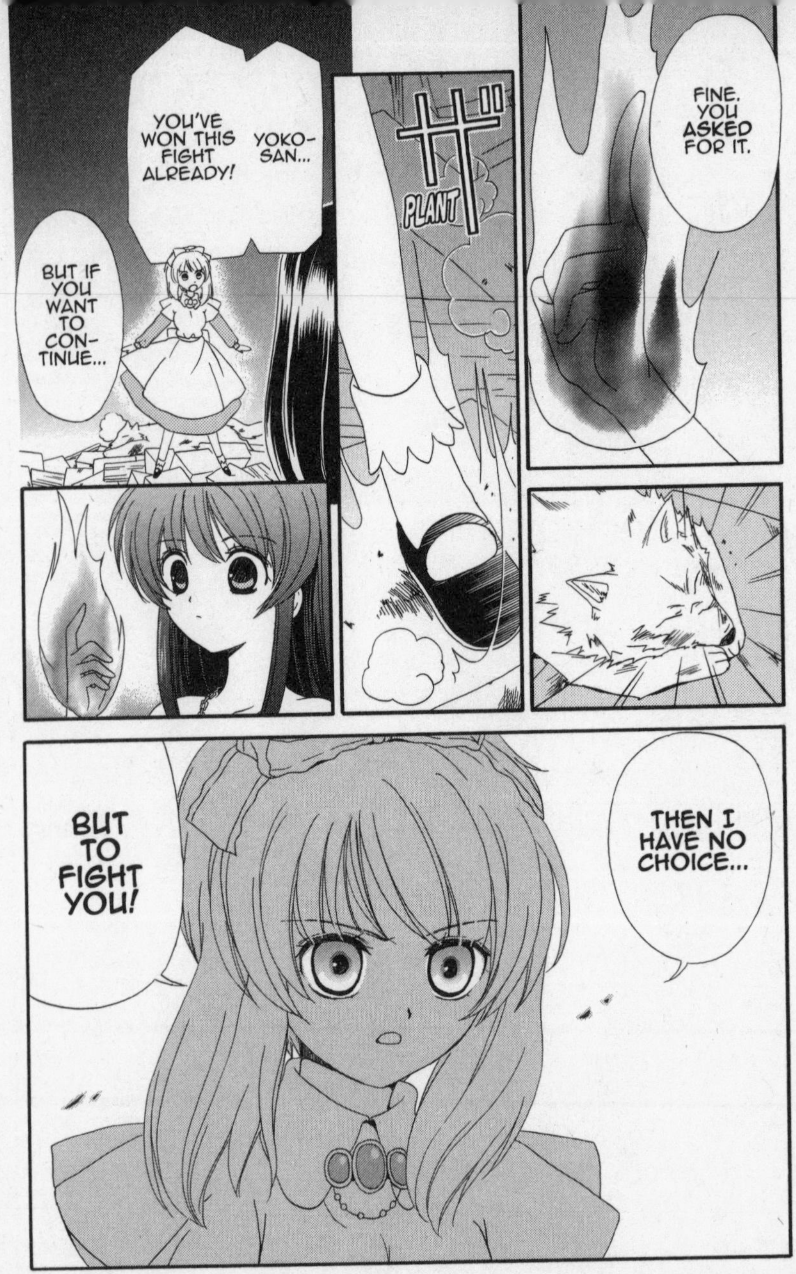
FINE. YOU ASKED FOR IT.
PLANT
YOKO-SAN...
YOU'VE WON THIS FIGHT ALREADY!
BUT IF YOU WANT TO CON-TINUE...
THEN I HAVE NO CHOICE...
BUT TO FIGHT YOU!

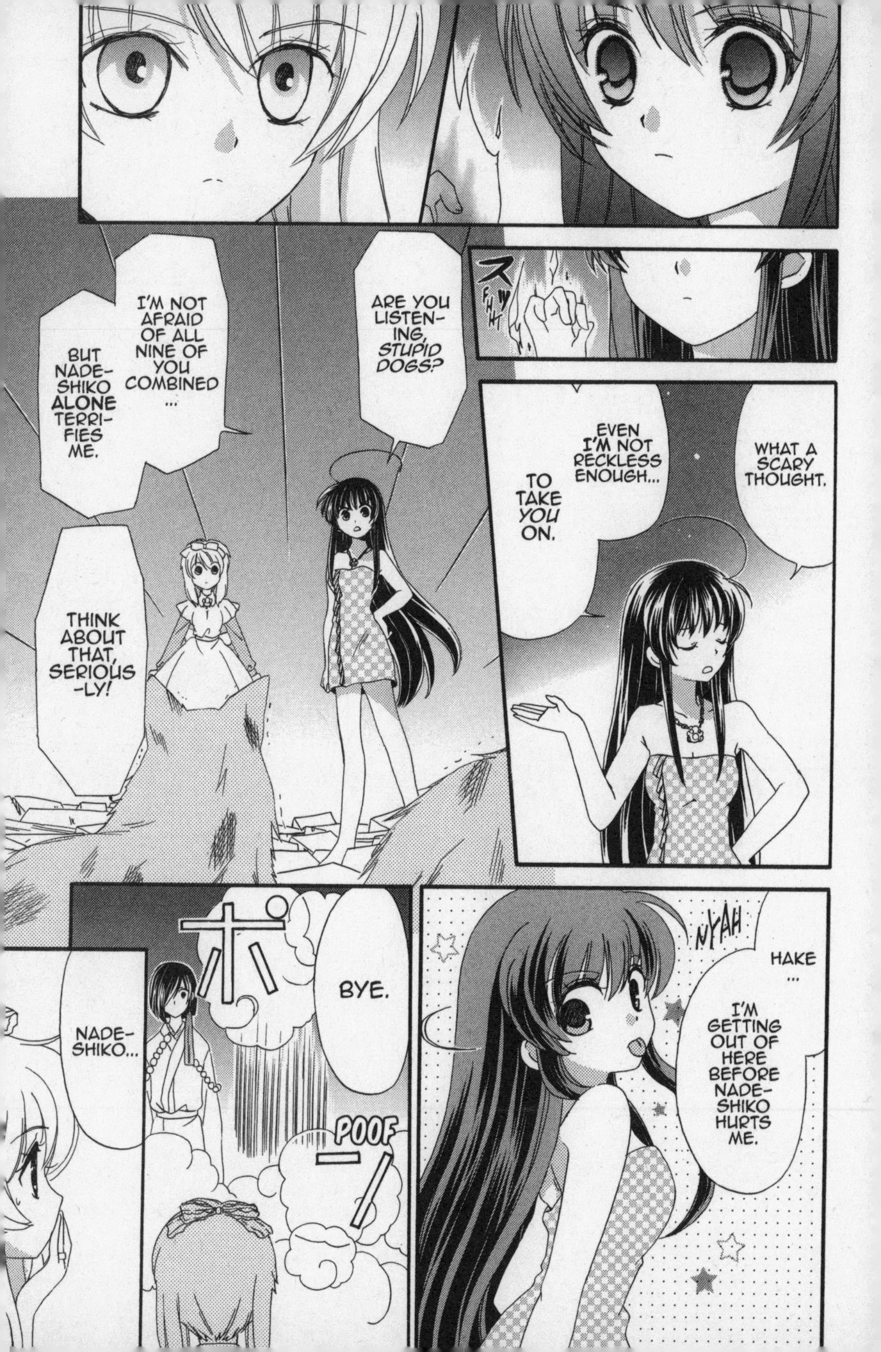

ス
WHAT A SCARY THOUGHT.
EVEN I'M NOT RECKLESS ENOUGH...
TO TAKE *YOU* ON.
ARE YOU LISTENING, *STUPID DOGS?*
I'M NOT AFRAID OF ALL NINE OF YOU COMBINED...
BUT NADESHIKO **ALONE** TERRIFIES ME.
THINK ABOUT THAT, SERIOUSLY!
NYAH
HAKE...
I'M GETTING OUT OF HERE BEFORE NADESHIKO HURTS ME.
BYE.
ポ
POOF
NADESHIKO...

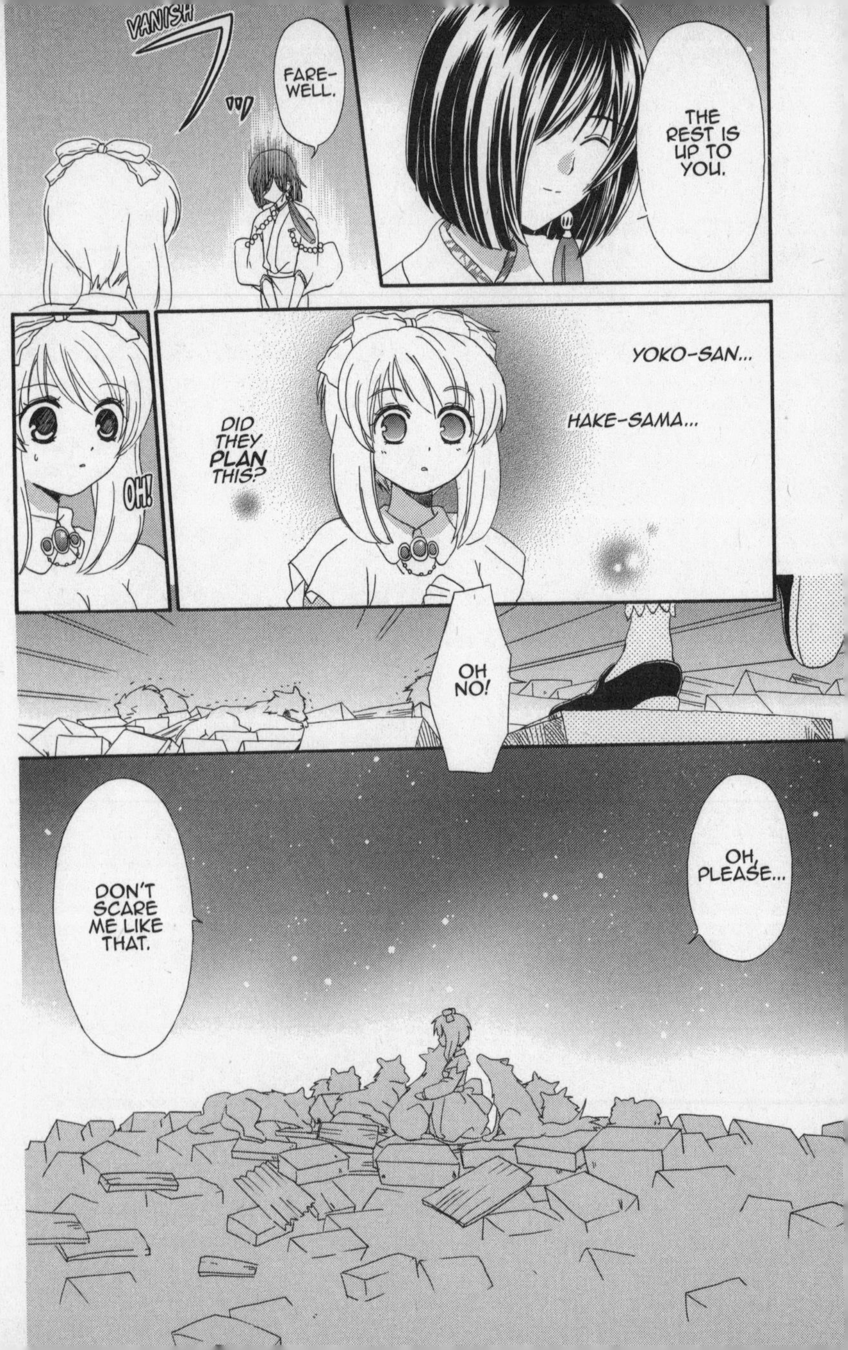
THE REST IS UP TO YOU.
FARE-WELL.
VANISH
YOKO-SAN...
HAKE-SAMA...
DID THEY PLAN THIS?
OH!
OH NO!
OH, PLEASE...
DON'T SCARE ME LIKE THAT.

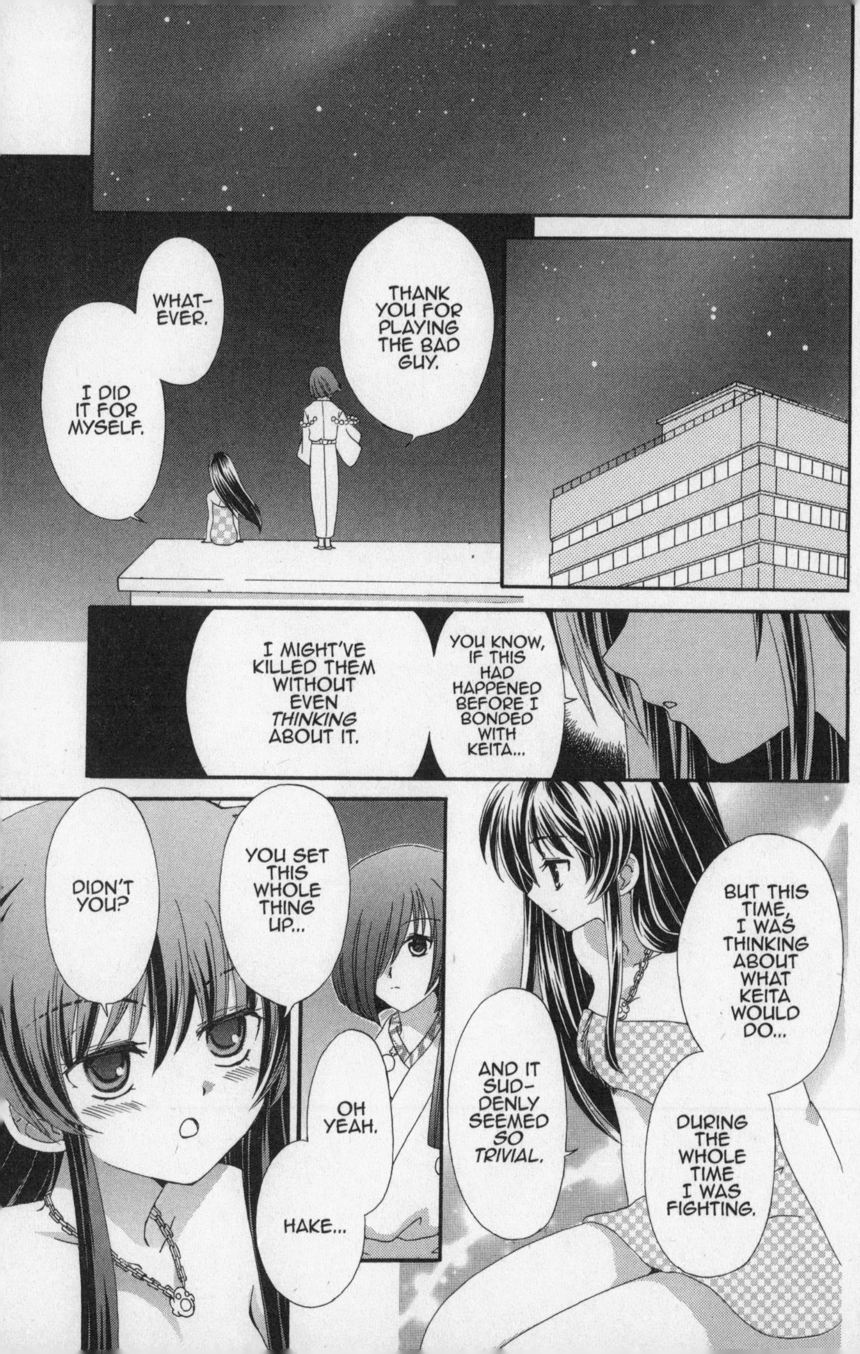
THANK YOU FOR PLAYING THE BAD GUY.
WHAT-EVER.
I DID IT FOR MYSELF.
YOU KNOW, IF THIS HAD HAPPENED BEFORE I BONDED WITH KEITA...
I MIGHT'VE KILLED THEM WITHOUT EVEN *THINKING* ABOUT IT.
BUT THIS TIME, I WAS THINKING ABOUT WHAT KEITA WOULD DO...
DURING THE WHOLE TIME I WAS FIGHTING.
AND IT SUD-DENLY SEEMED *SO TRIVIAL.*
YOU SET THIS WHOLE THING UP...
DIDN'T YOU?
OH YEAH.
HAKE...

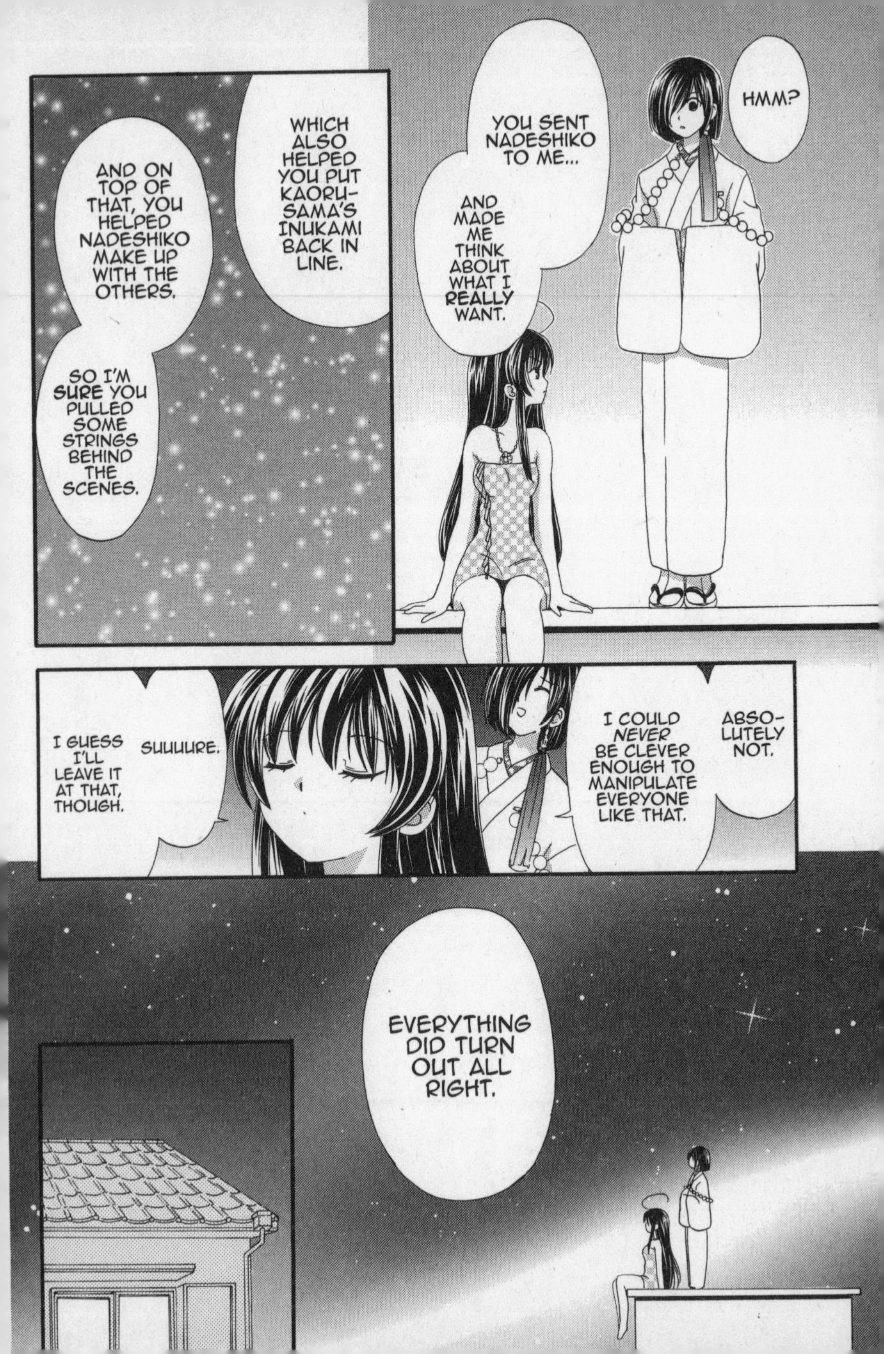
HMM?
YOU SENT NADESHIKO TO ME...
AND MADE ME THINK ABOUT WHAT I *REALLY* WANT.
WHICH ALSO HELPED YOU PUT KAORU-SAMA'S INUKAMI BACK IN LINE.
AND ON TOP OF THAT, YOU HELPED NADESHIKO MAKE UP WITH THE OTHERS.
SO I'M **SURE** YOU PULLED SOME STRINGS BEHIND THE SCENES.
ABSOLUTELY NOT.
I COULD *NEVER* BE CLEVER ENOUGH TO MANIPULATE EVERYONE LIKE THAT.
SUUUURE.
I GUESS I'LL LEAVE IT AT THAT, THOUGH.
EVERYTHING DID TURN OUT ALL RIGHT.

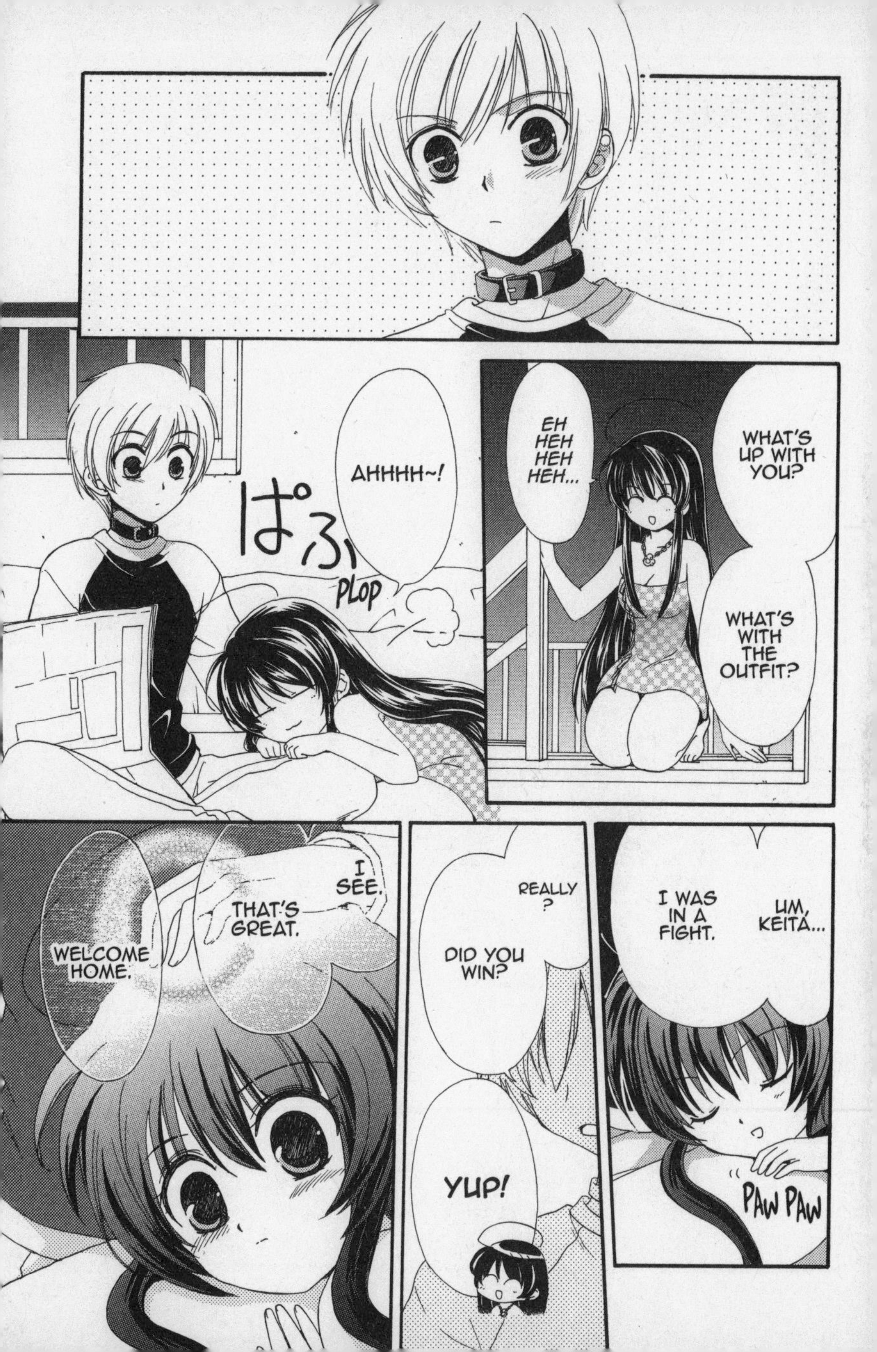
WHAT'S UP WITH YOU?
EH HEH HEH HEH...
WHAT'S WITH THE OUTFIT?
AHHHH~!
ぱふ
PLOP
UM, KEITA...
I WAS IN A FIGHT.
PAW PAW
REALLY?
DID YOU WIN?
YUP!
I SEE.
THAT'S GREAT.
WELCOME HOME.

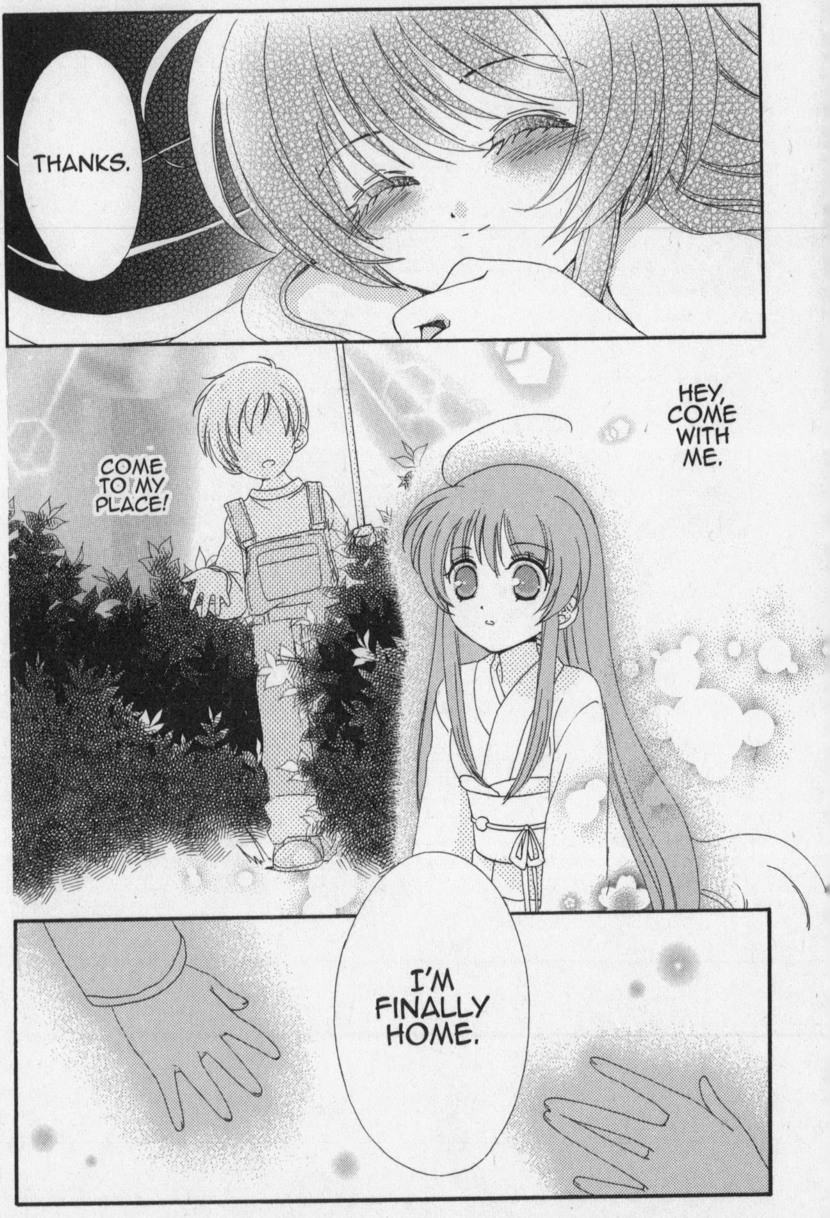
THANKS.
HEY, COME WITH ME.
COME TO MY PLACE!
I'M FINALLY HOME.

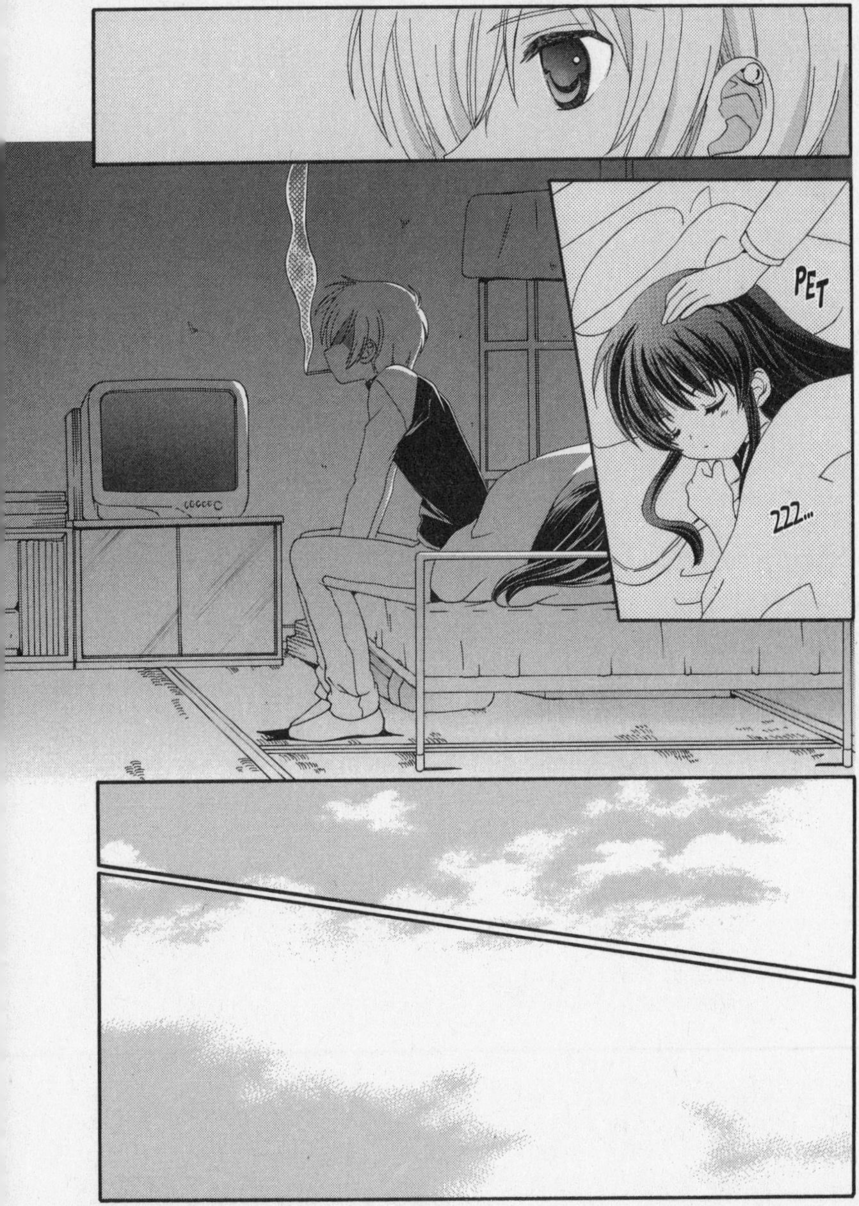
PET
ZZZ...

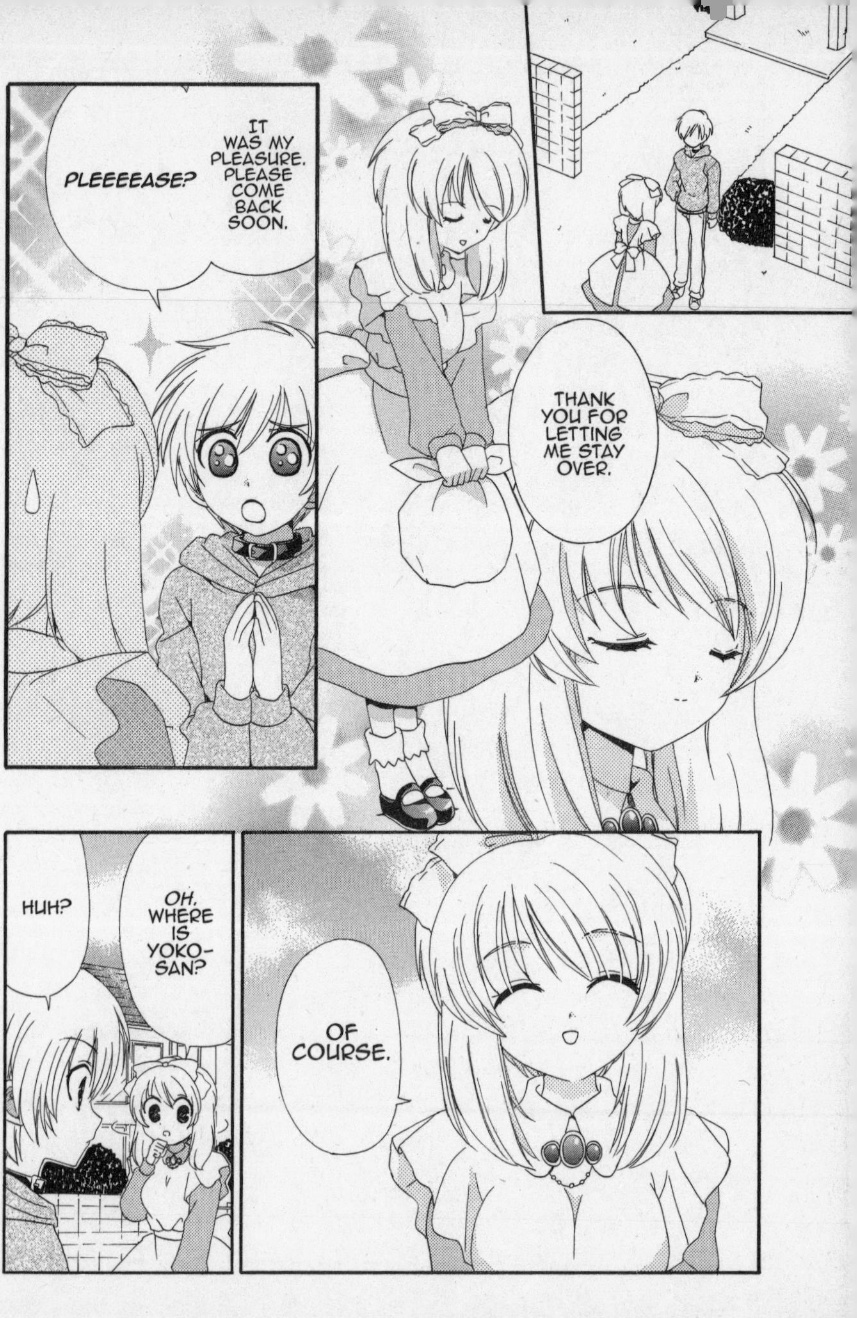
THANK YOU FOR LETTING ME STAY OVER.
IT WAS MY PLEASURE. PLEASE COME BACK SOON.
PLEEEEASE?
OF COURSE.
OH. WHERE IS YOKO-SAN?
HUH?

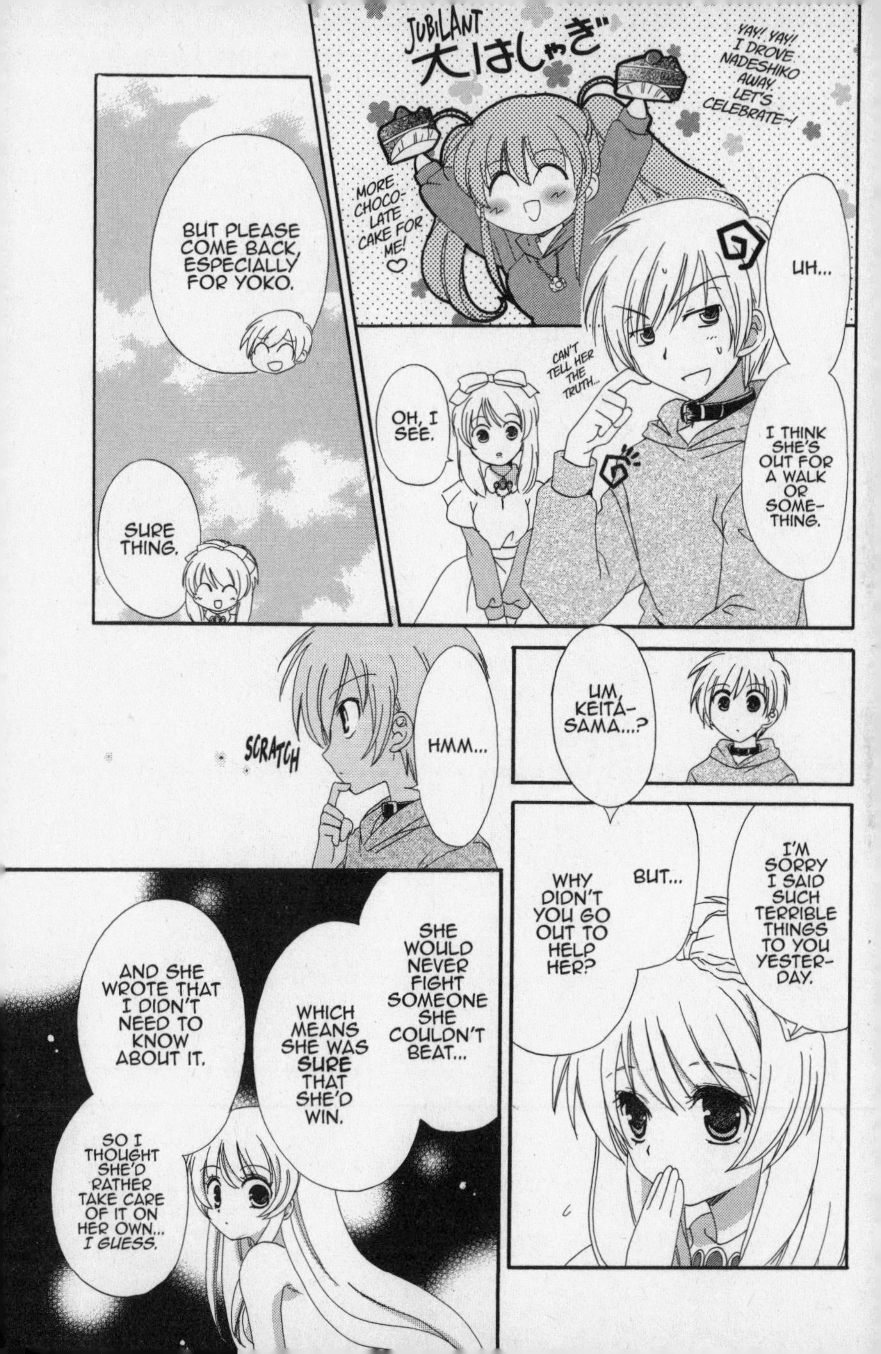
UH...
JUBILANT 大はしゃぎ
YAY! YAY! I DROVE NADESHIKO AWAY. LET'S CELEBRATE~!
MORE CHOCO-LATE CAKE FOR ME! ♡
I THINK SHE'S OUT FOR A WALK OR SOME-THING.
CAN'T TELL HER THE TRUTH...
OH, I SEE.
BUT PLEASE COME BACK, ESPECIALLY FOR YOKO.
SURE THING.
UM, KEITA-SAMA...?
HMM...
SCRATCH
I'M SORRY I SAID SUCH TERRIBLE THINGS TO YOU YESTER-DAY.
BUT...
WHY DIDN'T YOU GO OUT TO HELP HER?
SHE WOULD NEVER FIGHT SOMEONE SHE COULDN'T BEAT...
WHICH MEANS SHE WAS SURE THAT SHE'D WIN.
AND SHE WROTE THAT I DIDN'T NEED TO KNOW ABOUT IT.
SO I THOUGHT SHE'D RATHER TAKE CARE OF IT ON HER OWN... I GUESS.

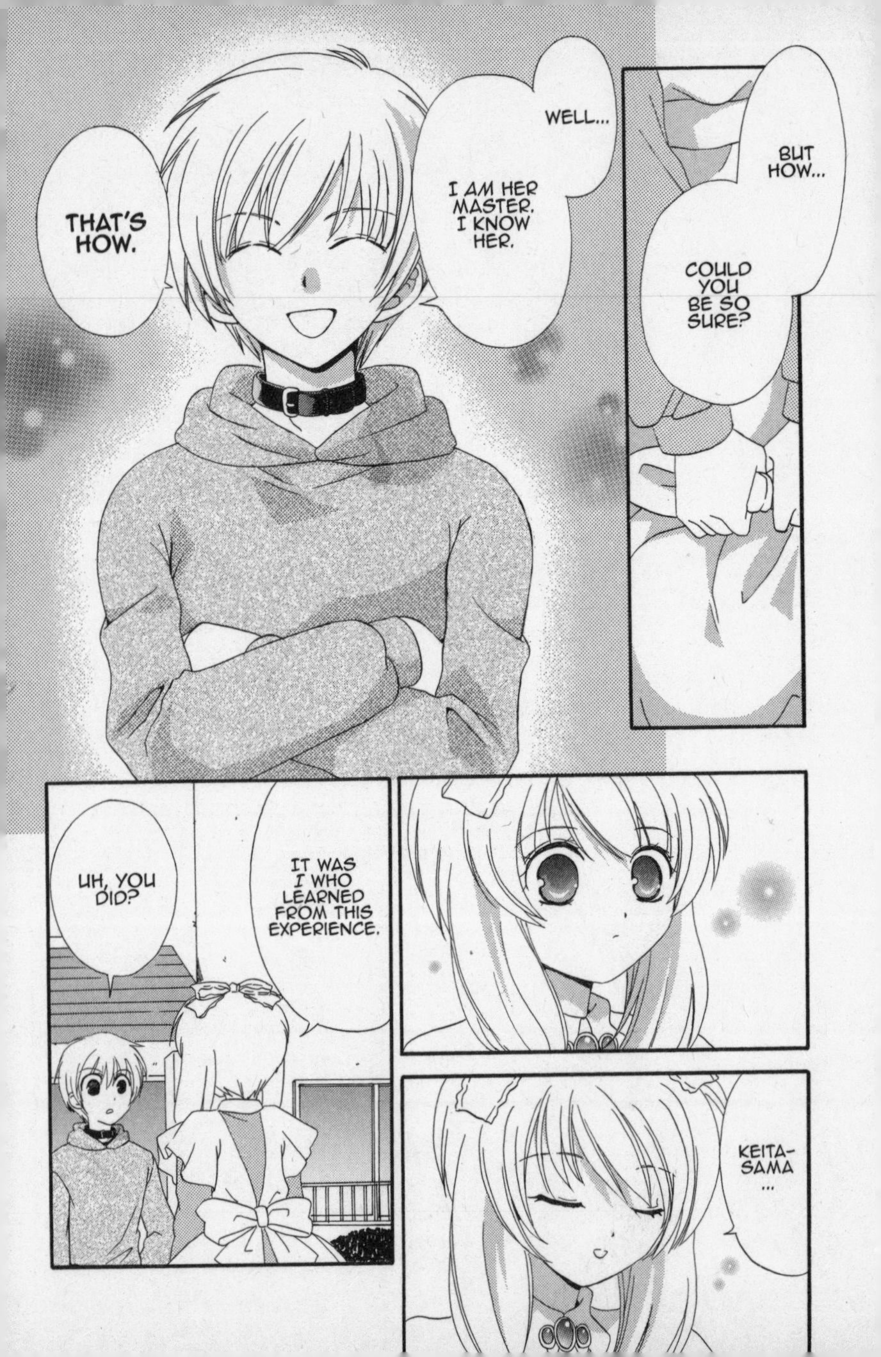
BUT HOW...
COULD YOU BE SO SURE?
WELL...
I AM HER MASTER. I KNOW HER.
THAT'S HOW.
KEITA-SAMA ...
IT WAS I WHO LEARNED FROM THIS EXPERIENCE.
UH, YOU DID?

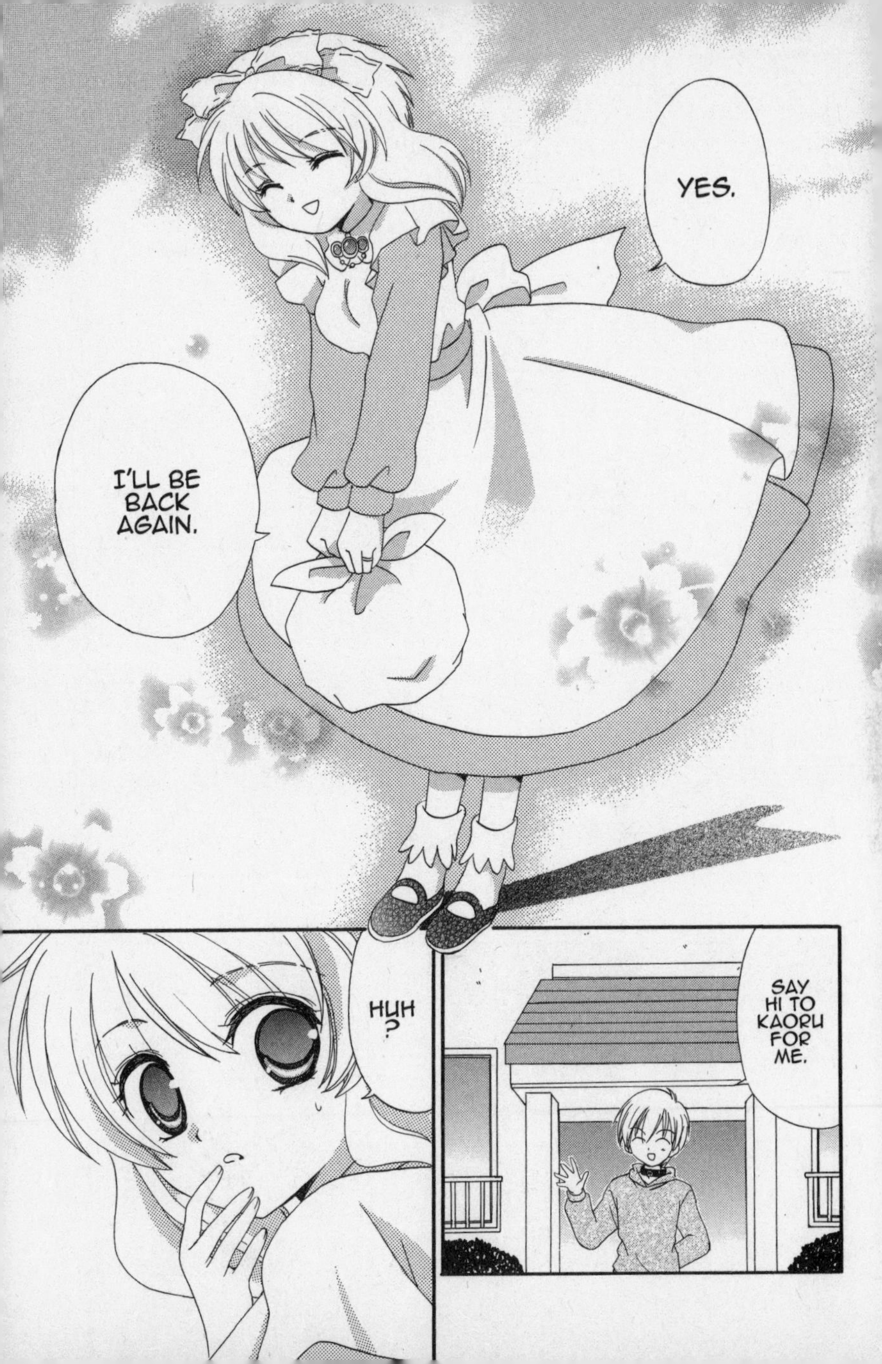
YES.
I'LL BE BACK AGAIN.
SAY HI TO KAORU FOR ME.
HUH?

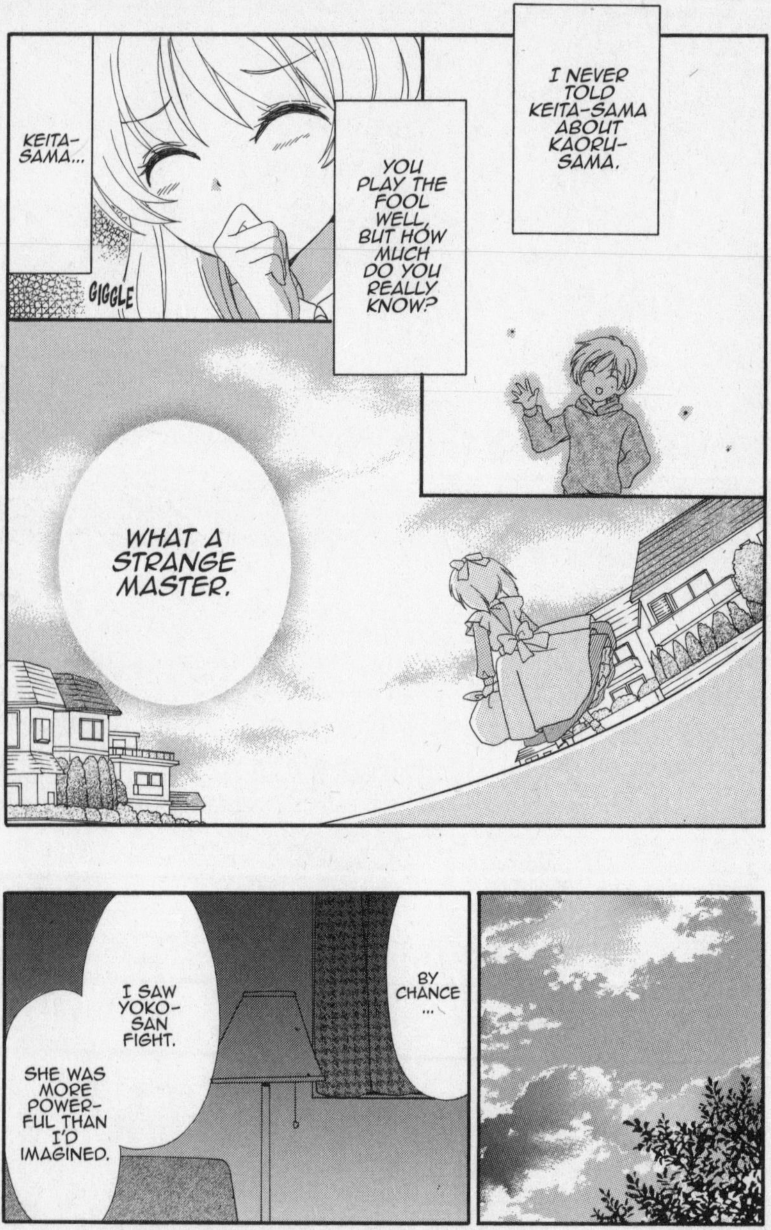
I NEVER TOLD KEITA-SAMA ABOUT KAORU-SAMA.
YOU PLAY THE FOOL WELL, BUT HOW MUCH DO YOU REALLY KNOW?
KEITA-SAMA...
GIGGLE
WHAT A STRANGE MASTER.
BY CHANCE...
I SAW YOKO-SAN FIGHT.
SHE WAS MORE POWERFUL THAN I'D IMAGINED.

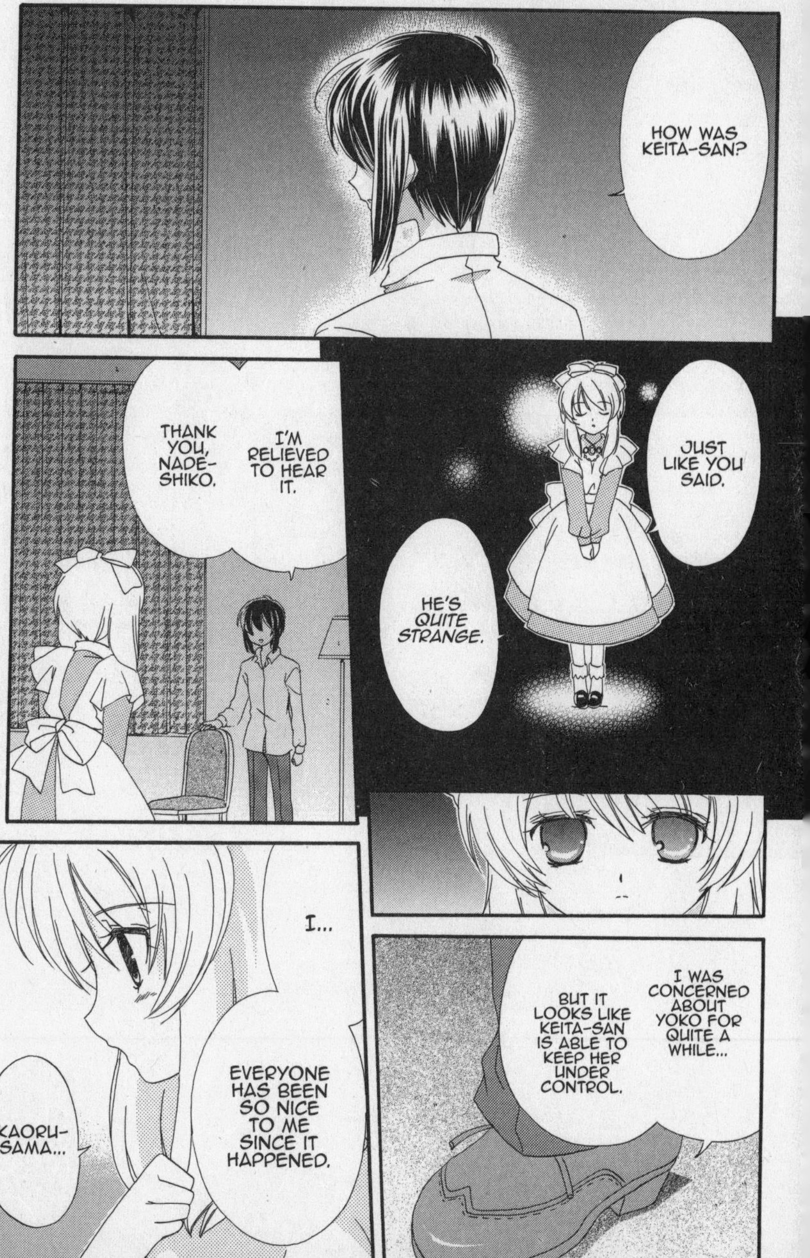
HOW WAS KEITA-SAN?
JUST LIKE YOU SAID.
HE'S QUITE STRANGE.
I'M RELIEVED TO HEAR IT.
THANK YOU, NADE-SHIKO.
I WAS CONCERNED ABOUT YOKO FOR QUITE A WHILE...
BUT IT LOOKS LIKE KEITA-SAN IS ABLE TO KEEP HER UNDER CONTROL.
I...
EVERYONE HAS BEEN SO NICE TO ME SINCE IT HAPPENED.
KAORU-SAMA...

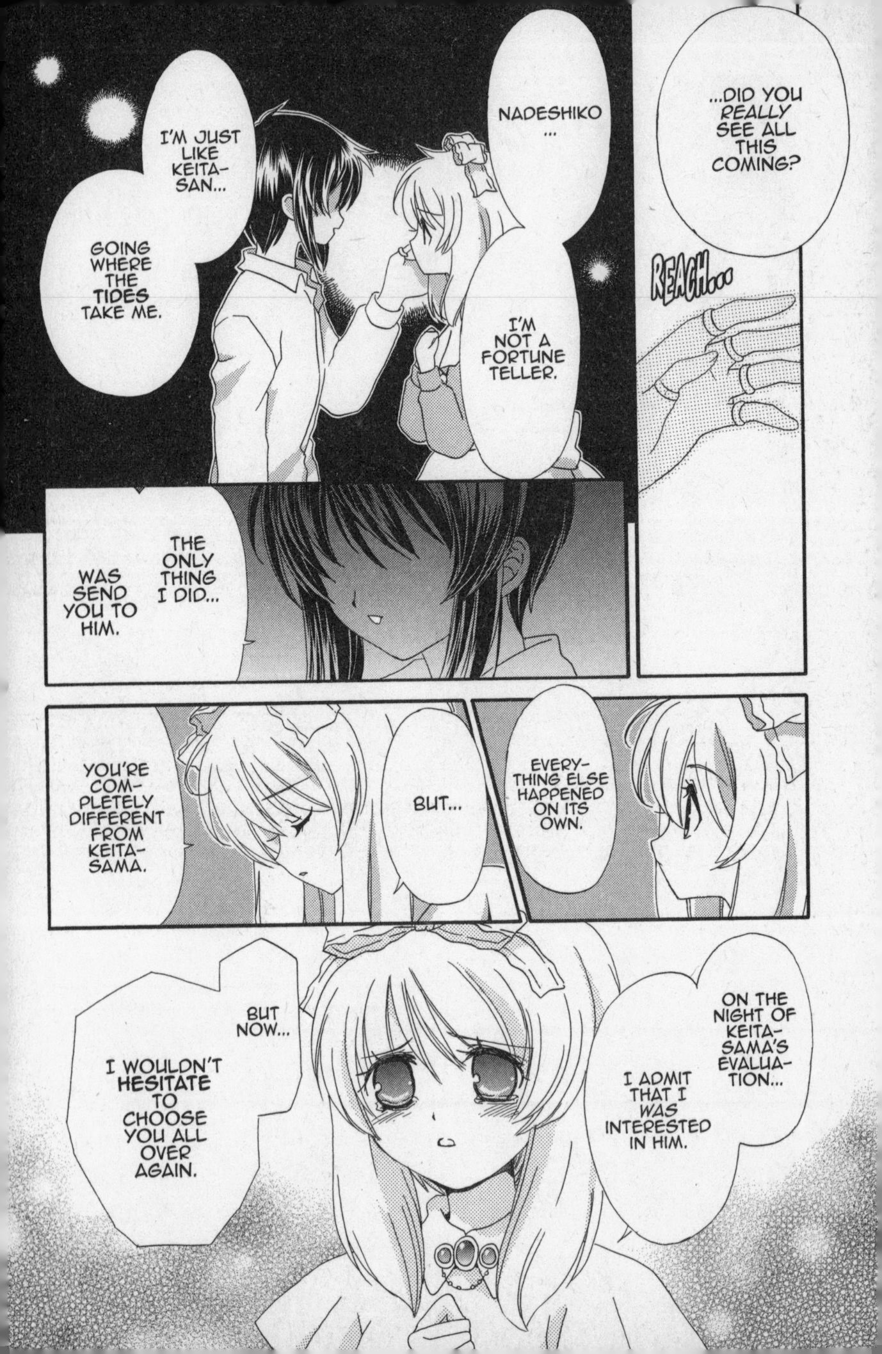
...DID YOU REALLY SEE ALL THIS COMING?
REACH...
NADESHIKO...
I'M NOT A FORTUNE TELLER.
I'M JUST LIKE KEITA-SAN...
GOING WHERE THE TIDES TAKE ME.
THE ONLY THING I DID...
WAS SEND YOU TO HIM.
EVERY-THING ELSE HAPPENED ON ITS OWN.
BUT...
YOU'RE COM-PLETELY DIFFERENT FROM KEITA-SAMA.
ON THE NIGHT OF KEITA-SAMA'S EVALUA-TION...
I ADMIT THAT I WAS INTERESTED IN HIM.
BUT NOW...
I WOULDN'T HESITATE TO CHOOSE YOU ALL OVER AGAIN.

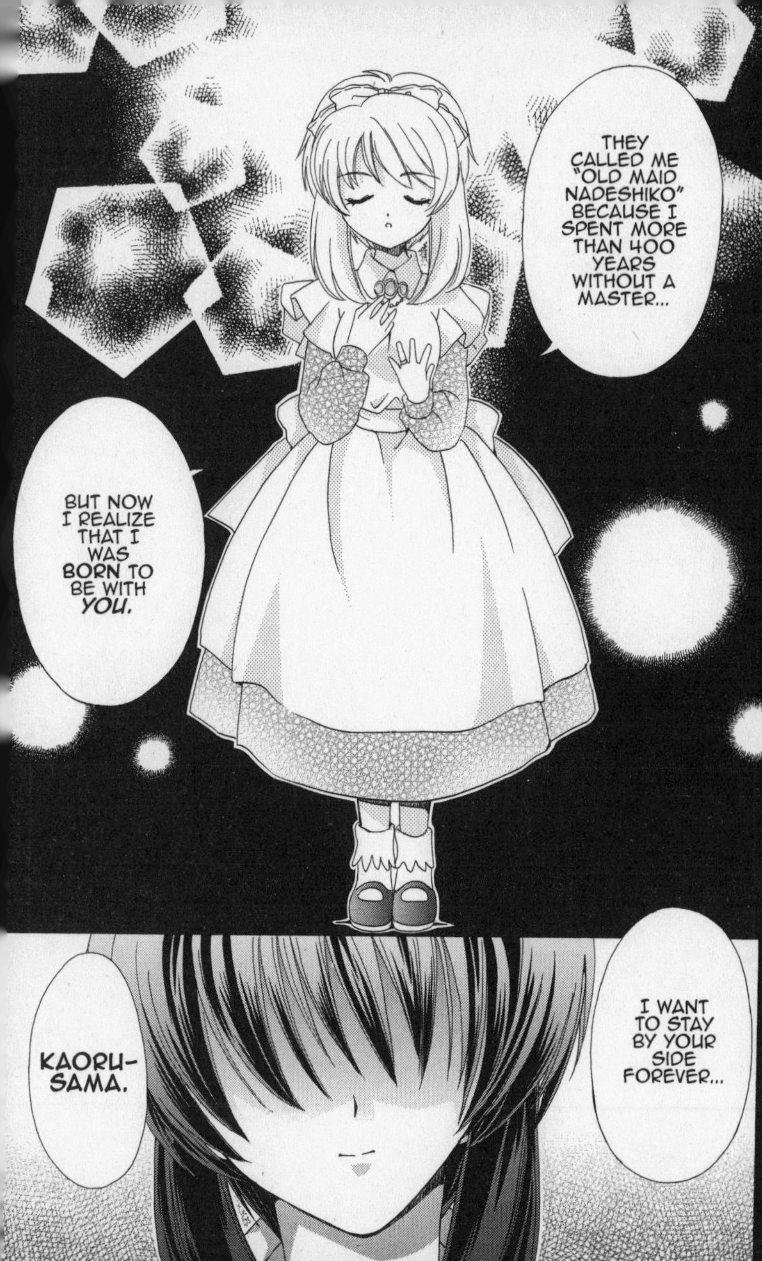
THEY CALLED ME "OLD MAID NADESHIKO" BECAUSE I SPENT MORE THAN 400 YEARS WITHOUT A MASTER...
BUT NOW I REALIZE THAT I WAS BORN TO BE WITH *YOU*.
I WANT TO STAY BY YOUR SIDE FOREVER...
KAORU-SAMA.

PLAY WITH ME! ☆

TOMOHANE

Height: 144 cm
Bust: ??
Waist: ??
Hip: ??
Age: 11

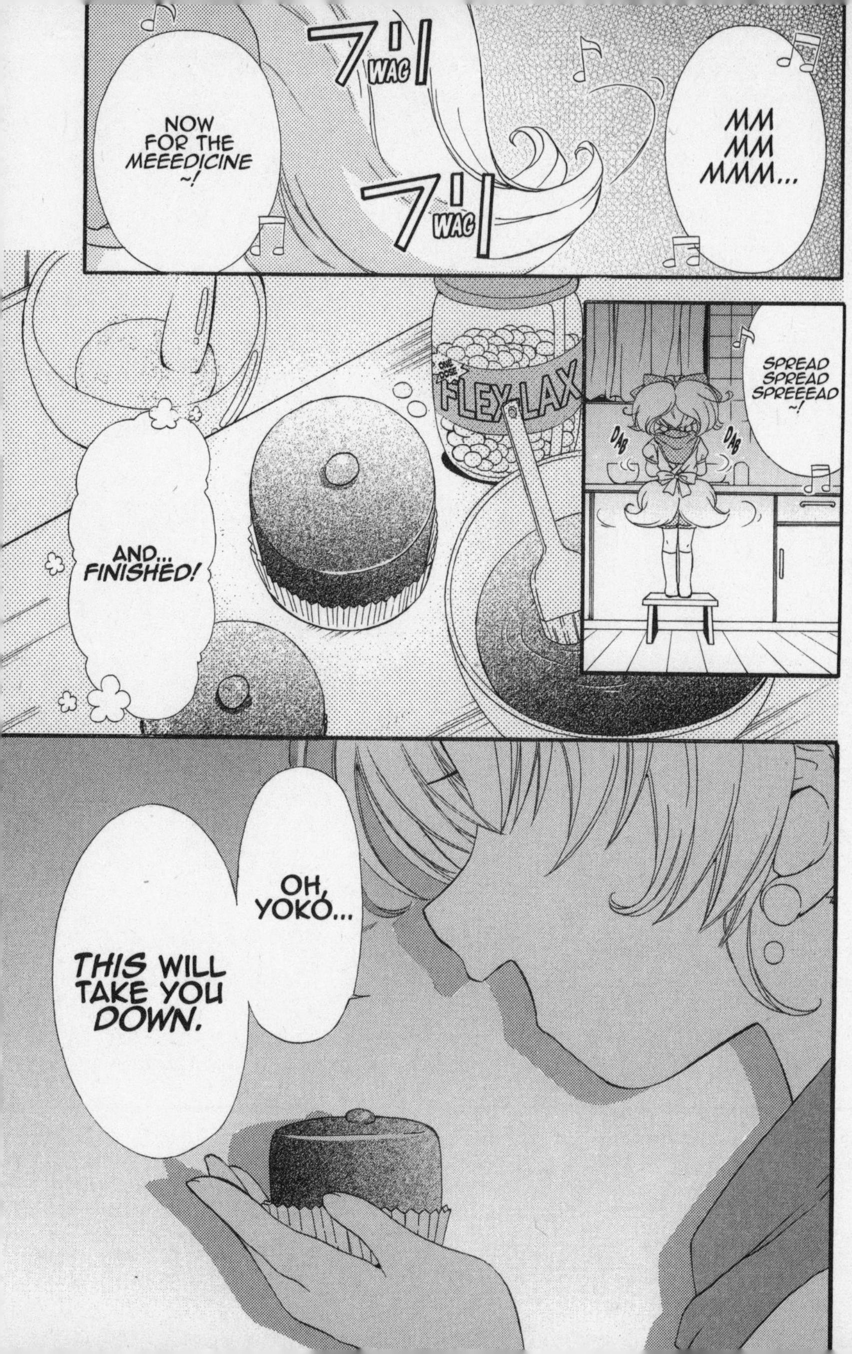
MM MM MMM...
WAG
WAG
NOW FOR THE MEEEDICINE ~!
SPREAD SPREAD SPREEEAD ~!
DAB
DAB
ONE DOSE
FLEX-LAX
AND... FINISHED!
OH, YOKO...
THIS WILL TAKE YOU DOWN.

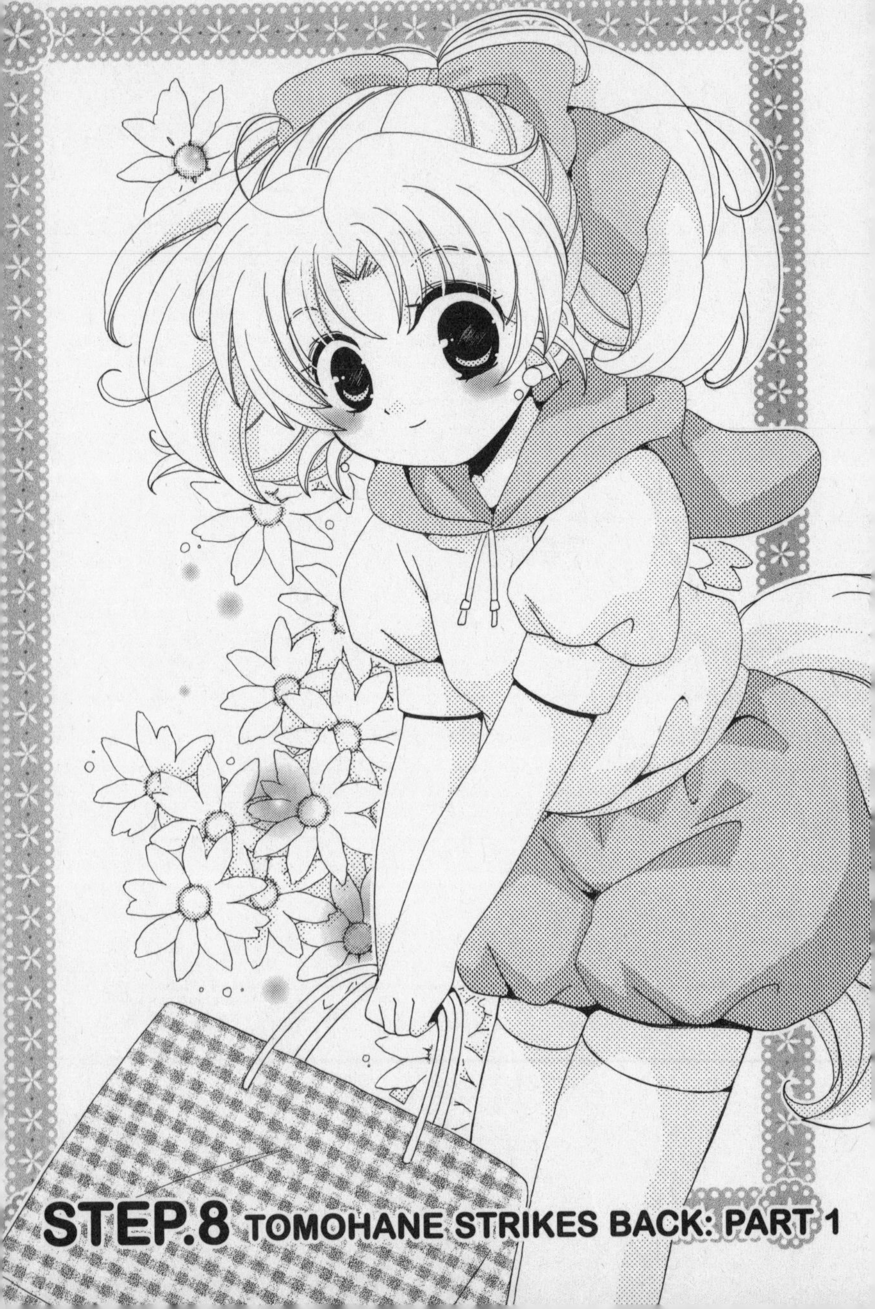

STEP.8 TOMOHANE STRIKES BACK: PART 1

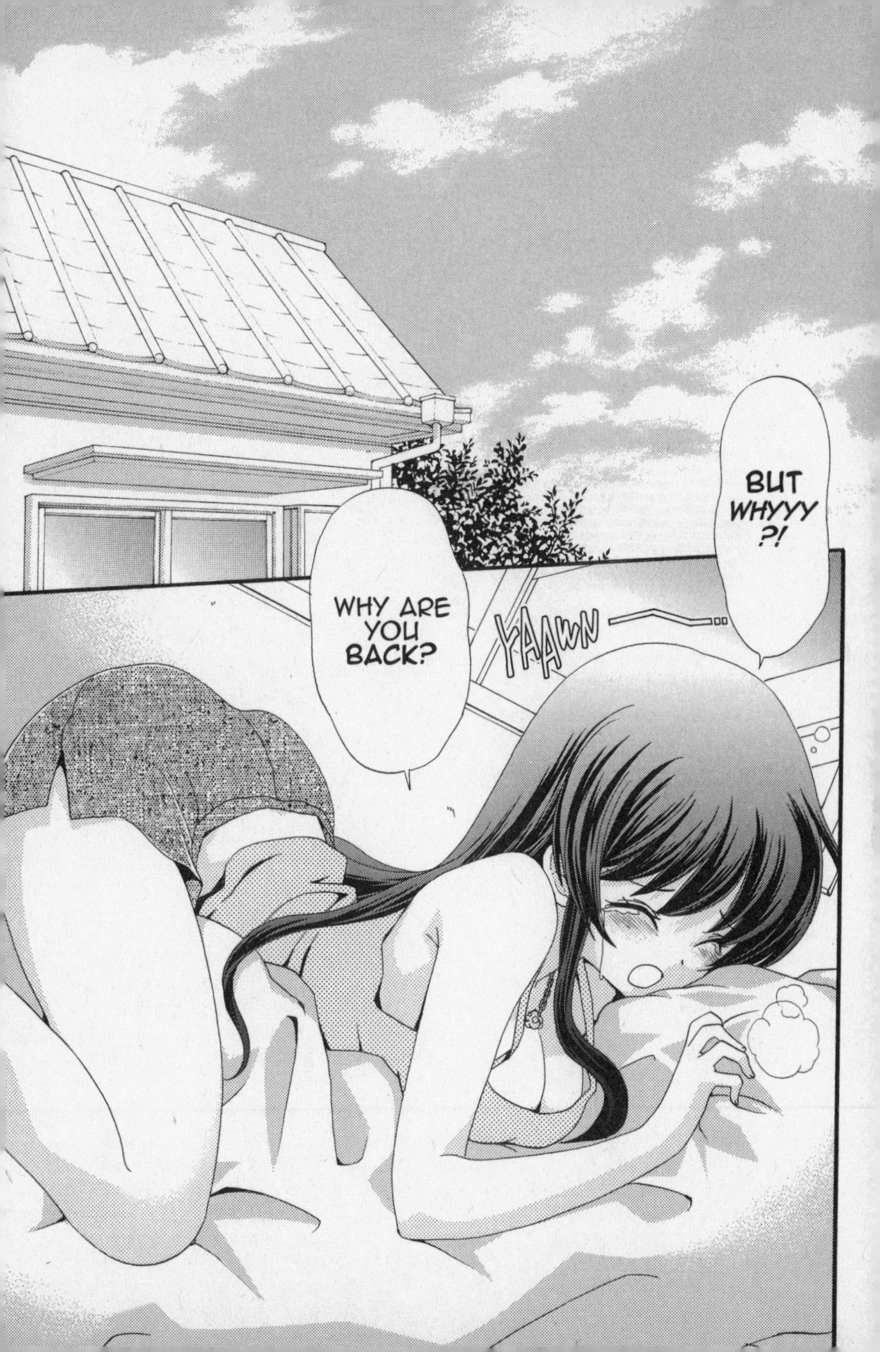
BUT WHYYY ?!
YAAWN
WHY ARE YOU BACK?

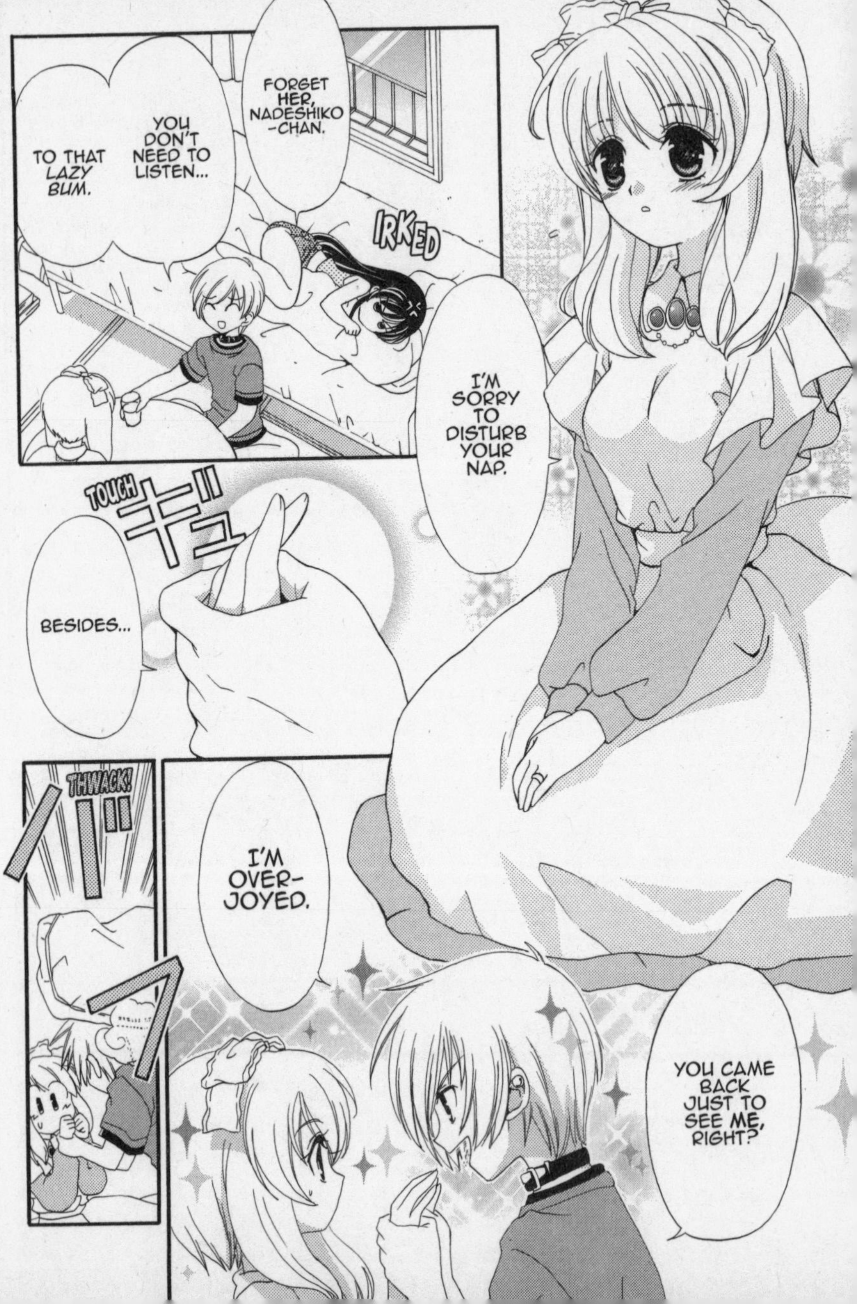

I'M SORRY TO DISTURB YOUR NAP.
FORGET HER, NADESHIKO-CHAN.
YOU DON'T NEED TO LISTEN...
TO THAT LAZY BUM.
IRKED
TOUCH
BESIDES...
YOU CAME BACK JUST TO SEE ME, RIGHT?
I'M OVER-JOYED.
THWACK!

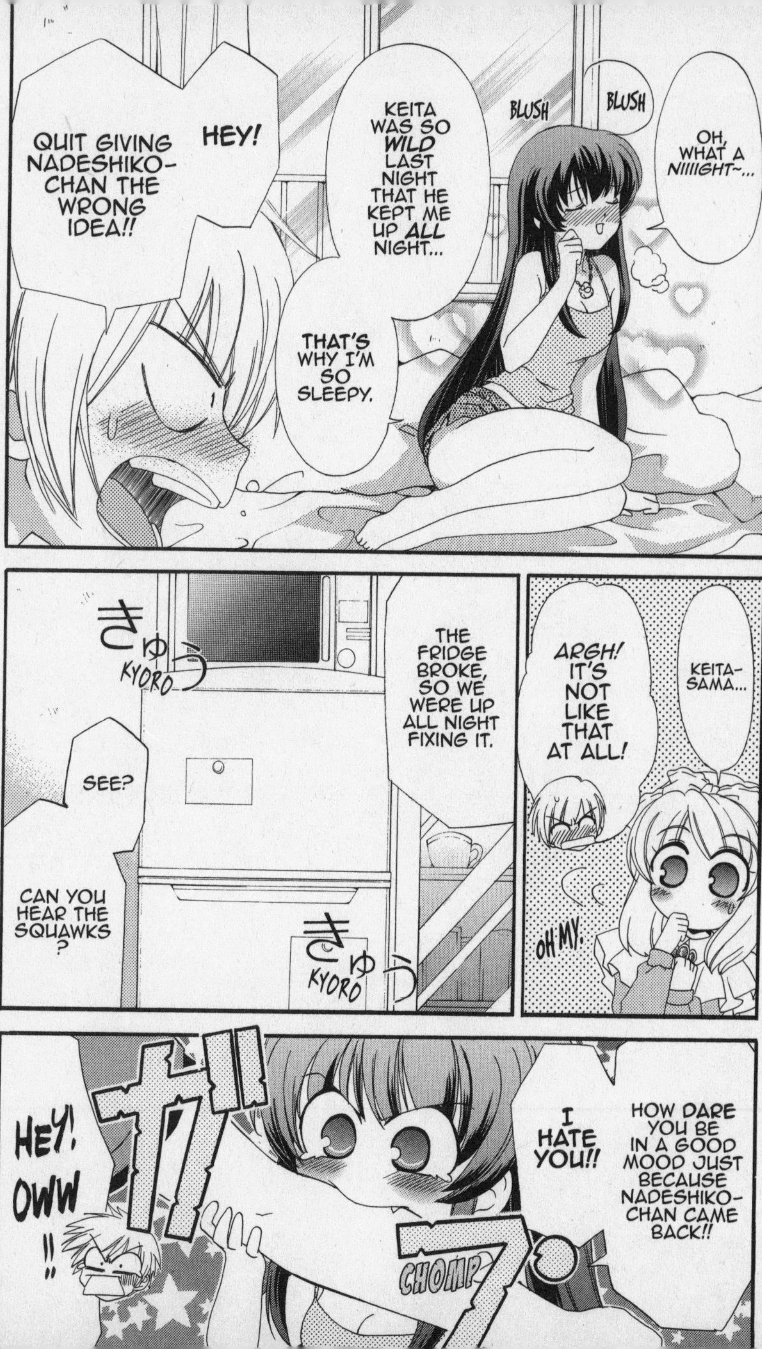
OH, WHAT A NIIIIGHT~...
BLUSH
BLUSH
KEITA WAS SO WILD LAST NIGHT THAT HE KEPT ME UP ALL NIGHT...
THAT'S WHY I'M SO SLEEPY.
HEY!
QUIT GIVING NADESHIKO-CHAN THE WRONG IDEA!!
KEITA-SAMA...
ARGH! IT'S NOT LIKE THAT AT ALL!
OH MY.
THE FRIDGE BROKE, SO WE WERE UP ALL NIGHT FIXING IT.
きゅう
KYORO
SEE?
CAN YOU HEAR THE SQUAWKS?
きゅう
KYORO
HOW DARE YOU BE IN A GOOD MOOD JUST BECAUSE NADESHIKO-CHAN CAME BACK!!
I HATE YOU!!
CHOMP
HEY! OWW!!

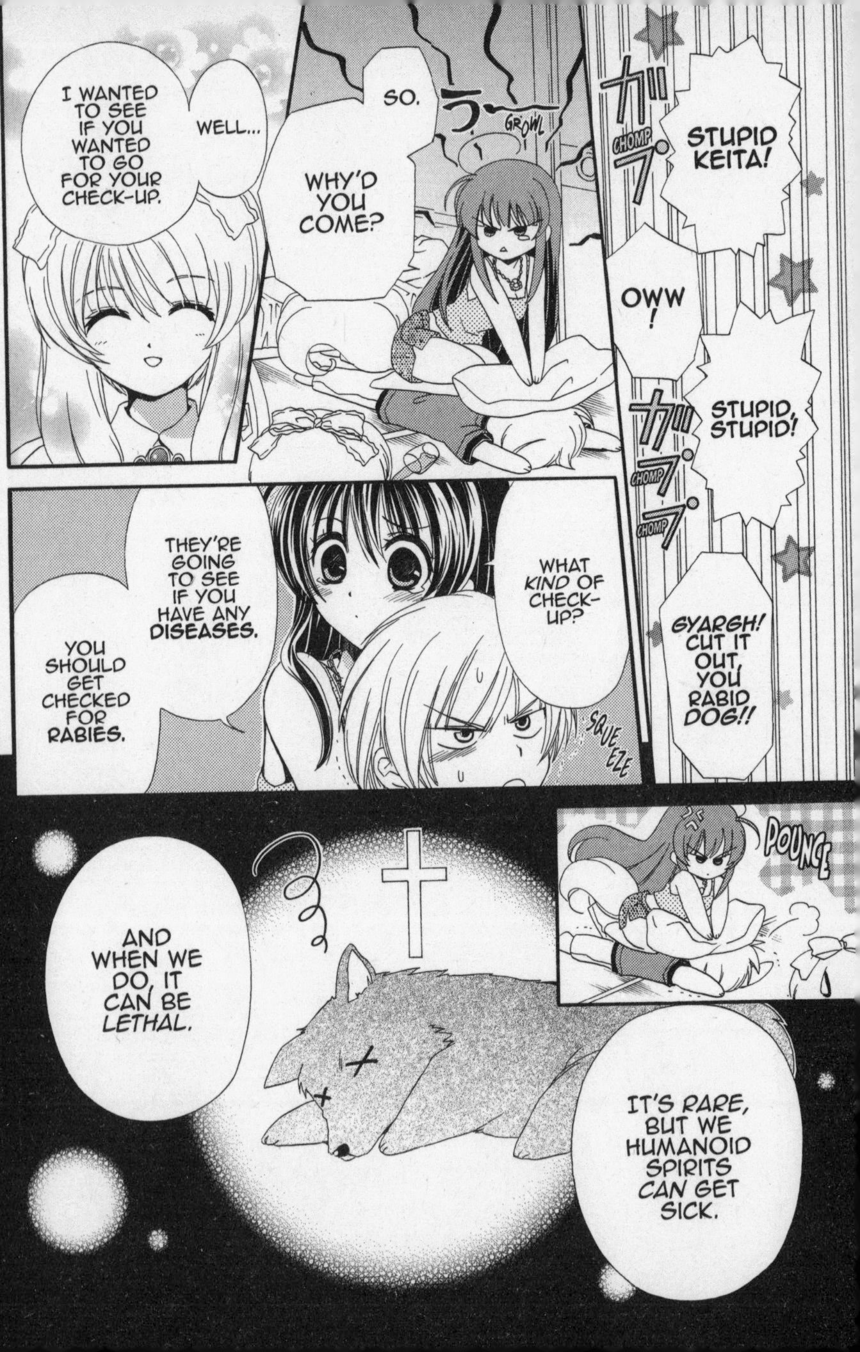

ガブ
CHOMP
STUPID KEITA!
OWW!
STUPID, STUPID!
CHOMP
CHOMP
GYARGH! CUT IT OUT, YOU RABID DOG!!
GROWL
SO.
WHY'D YOU COME?
WELL...
I WANTED TO SEE IF YOU WANTED TO GO FOR YOUR CHECK-UP.
WHAT KIND OF CHECK-UP?
THEY'RE GOING TO SEE IF YOU HAVE ANY DISEASES.
YOU SHOULD GET CHECKED FOR RABIES.
SQUEEZE
POUNCE
IT'S RARE, BUT WE HUMANOID SPIRITS CAN GET SICK.
AND WHEN WE DO, IT CAN BE LETHAL.

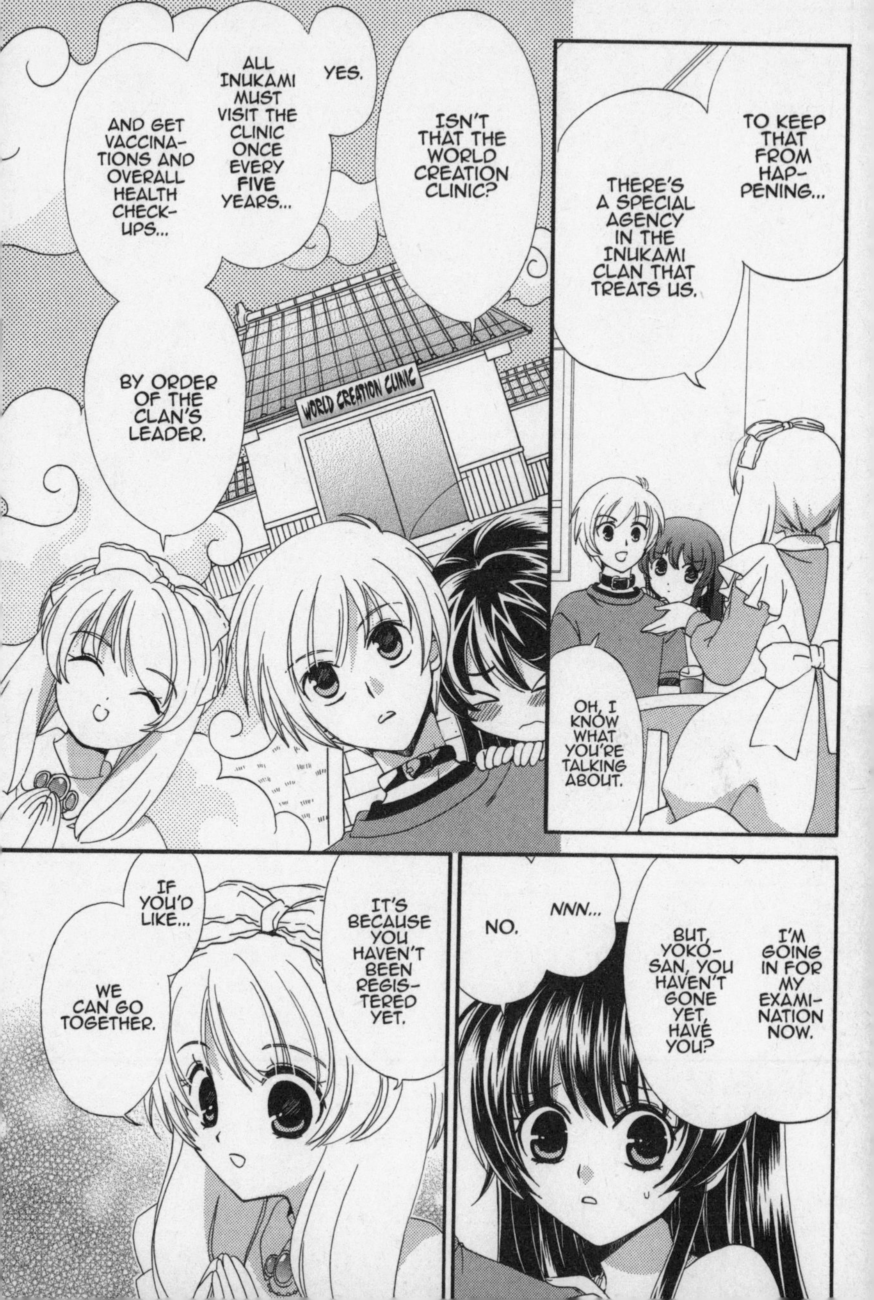
TO KEEP THAT FROM HAPPENING...
THERE'S A SPECIAL AGENCY IN THE INUKAMI CLAN THAT TREATS US.
OH, I KNOW WHAT YOU'RE TALKING ABOUT.
ISN'T THAT THE WORLD CREATION CLINIC?
YES.
ALL INUKAMI MUST VISIT THE CLINIC ONCE EVERY FIVE YEARS...
AND GET VACCINATIONS AND OVERALL HEALTH CHECK-UPS...
WORLD CREATION CLINIC
BY ORDER OF THE CLAN'S LEADER.
I'M GOING IN FOR MY EXAMINATION NOW.
BUT, YOKO-SAN, YOU HAVEN'T GONE YET, HAVE YOU?
NNN...
NO.
IT'S BECAUSE YOU HAVEN'T BEEN REGISTERED YET.
IF YOU'D LIKE...
WE CAN GO TOGETHER.

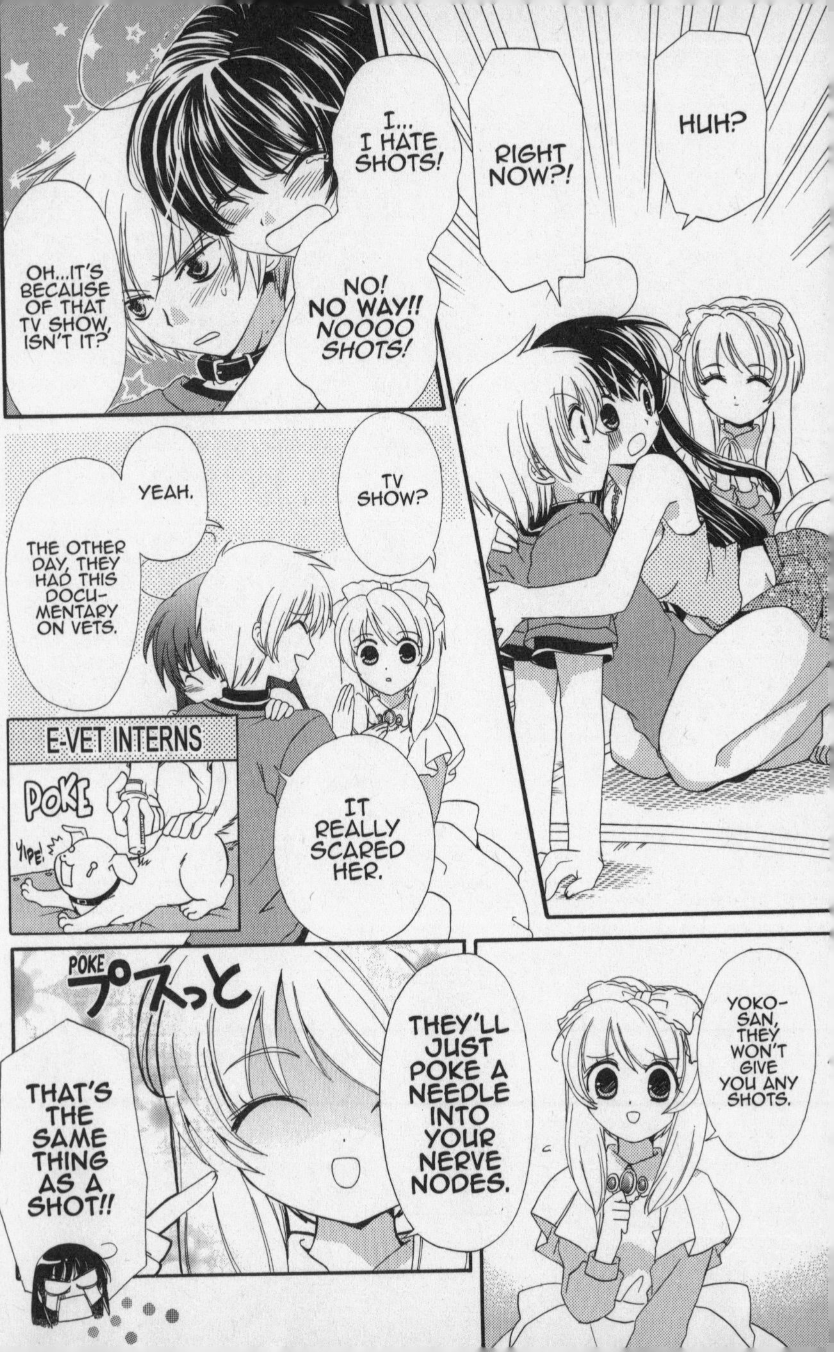
HUH?
RIGHT NOW?!
I... I HATE SHOTS!
NO! NO WAY!! NOOOO SHOTS!
OH...IT'S BECAUSE OF THAT TV SHOW, ISN'T IT?
TV SHOW?
YEAH.
THE OTHER DAY, THEY HAD THIS DOCU-MENTARY ON VETS.
IT REALLY SCARED HER.
E-VET INTERNS
POKE
YIPE!
YOKO-SAN, THEY WON'T GIVE YOU ANY SHOTS.
POKE
プスっと
THEY'LL JUST POKE A NEEDLE INTO YOUR NERVE NODES.
THAT'S THE SAME THING AS A SHOT!!

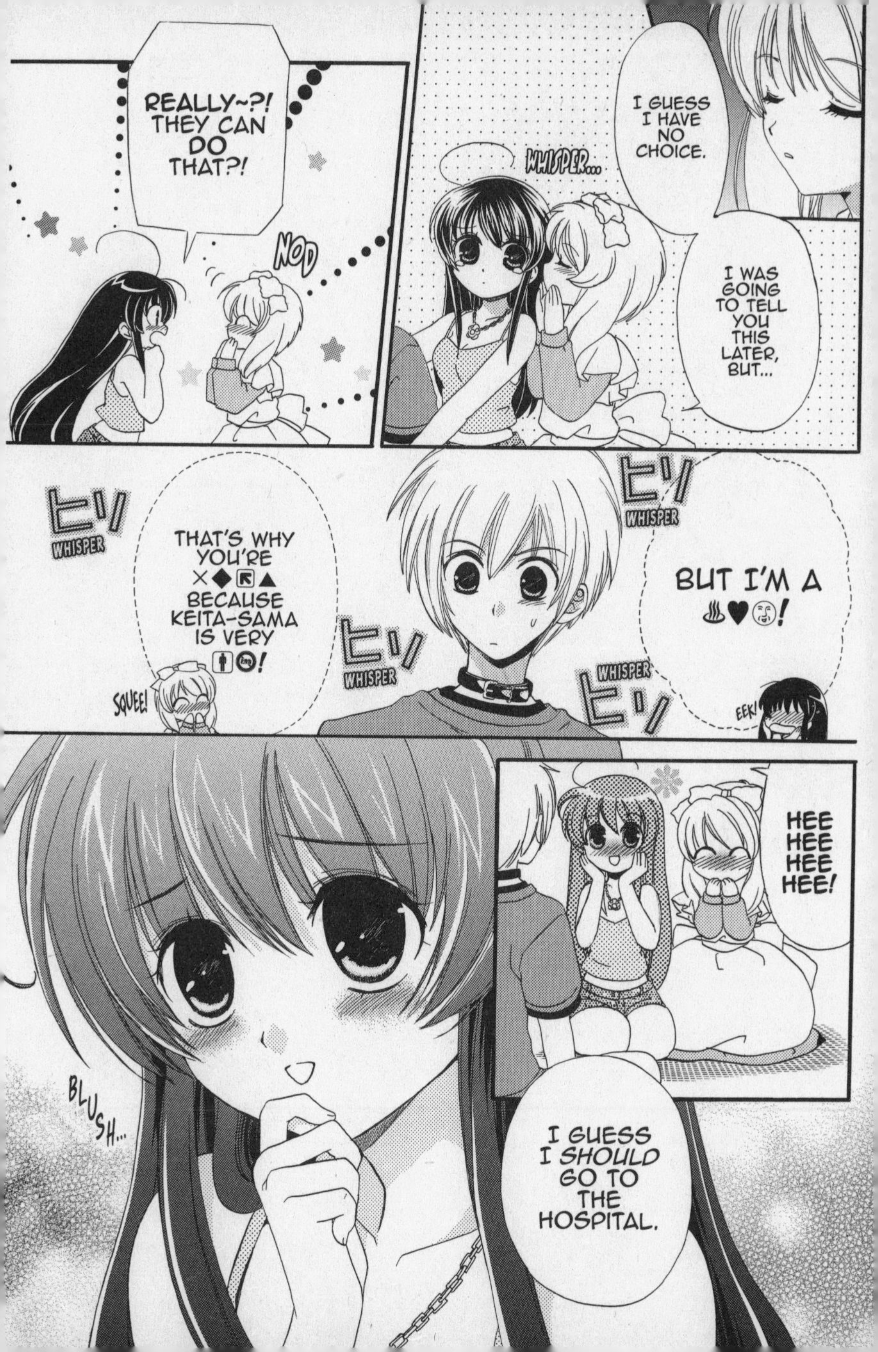
I GUESS I HAVE NO CHOICE.
WHISPER...
I WAS GOING TO TELL YOU THIS LATER, BUT...
REALLY~?! THEY CAN DO THAT?!
NOD
ヒソ WHISPER
BUT I'M A ♨♥!
WHISPER ヒソ
EEK!
ヒソ WHISPER
ヒソ WHISPER
THAT'S WHY YOU'RE ×◆▲ BECAUSE KEITA-SAMA IS VERY !
SQUEE!
HEE HEE HEE HEE!
I GUESS I SHOULD GO TO THE HOSPITAL.
BLUSH...

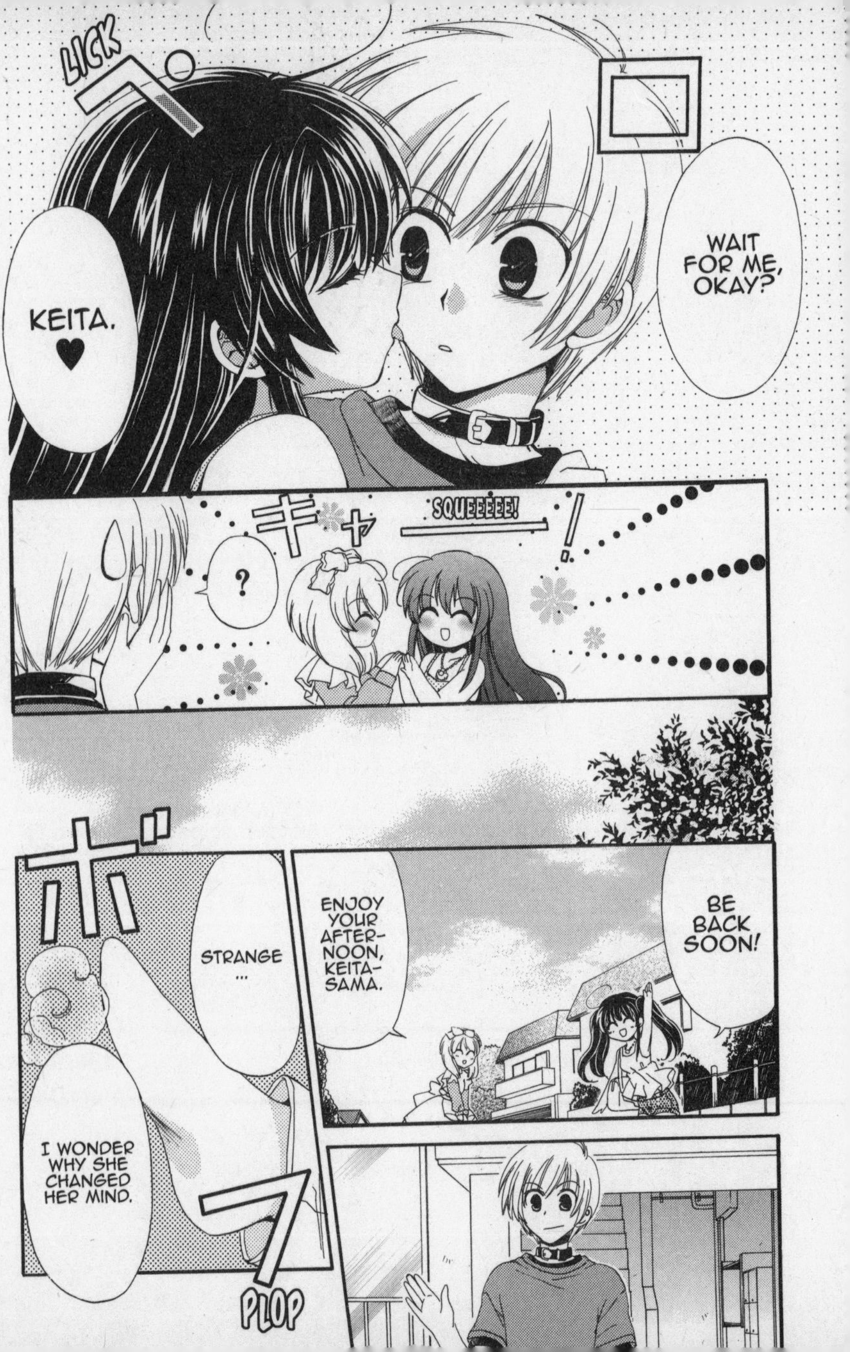
LICK
WAIT FOR ME, OKAY?
KEITA. ♥
キャ
SQUEEEEEE!
?
BE BACK SOON!
ENJOY YOUR AFTERNOON, KEITA-SAMA.
ボ
STRANGE ...
I WONDER WHY SHE CHANGED HER MIND.
フ
PLOP

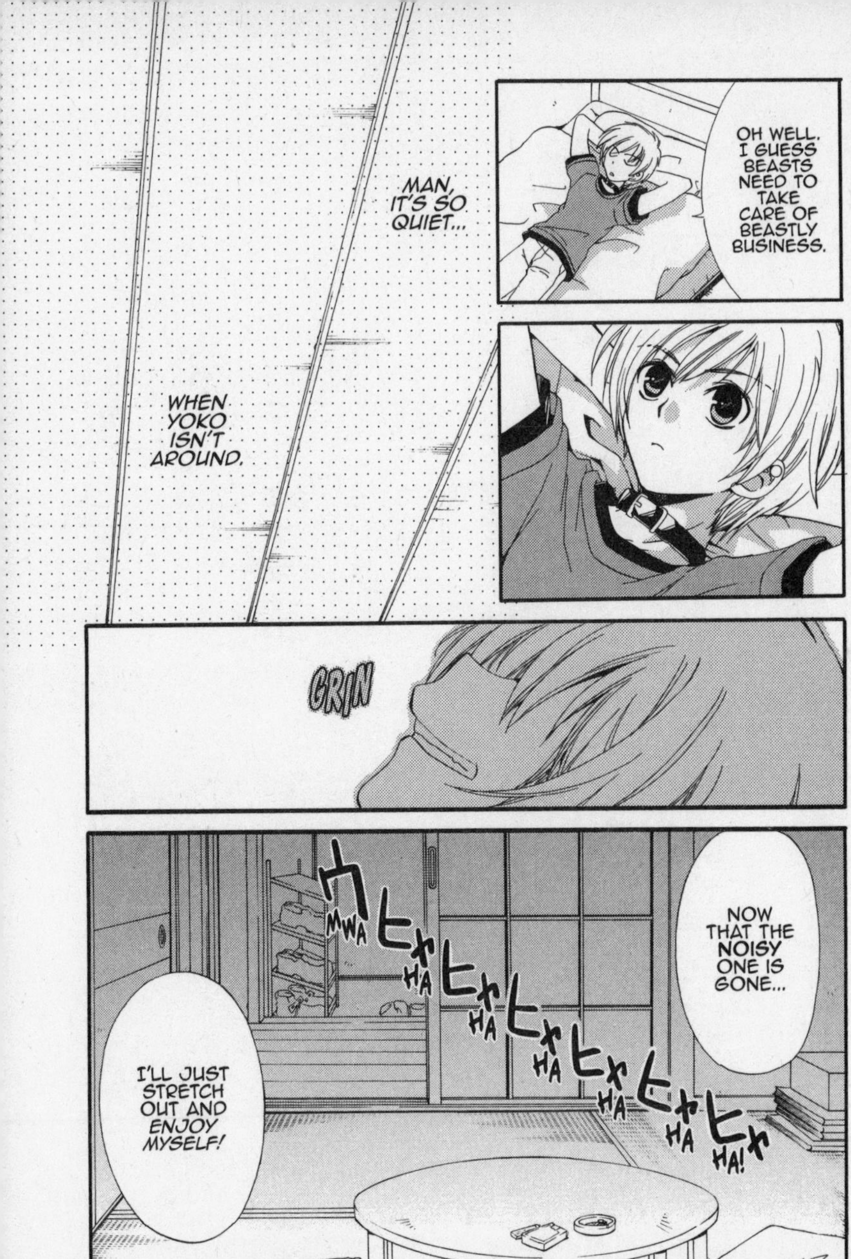
OH WELL. I GUESS BEASTS NEED TO TAKE CARE OF BEASTLY BUSINESS.
MAN, IT'S SO QUIET...
WHEN YOKO ISN'T AROUND.
GRIN
NOW THAT THE NOISY ONE IS GONE...
MWA HA HA HA HA HA HA!
I'LL JUST STRETCH OUT AND ENJOY MYSELF!

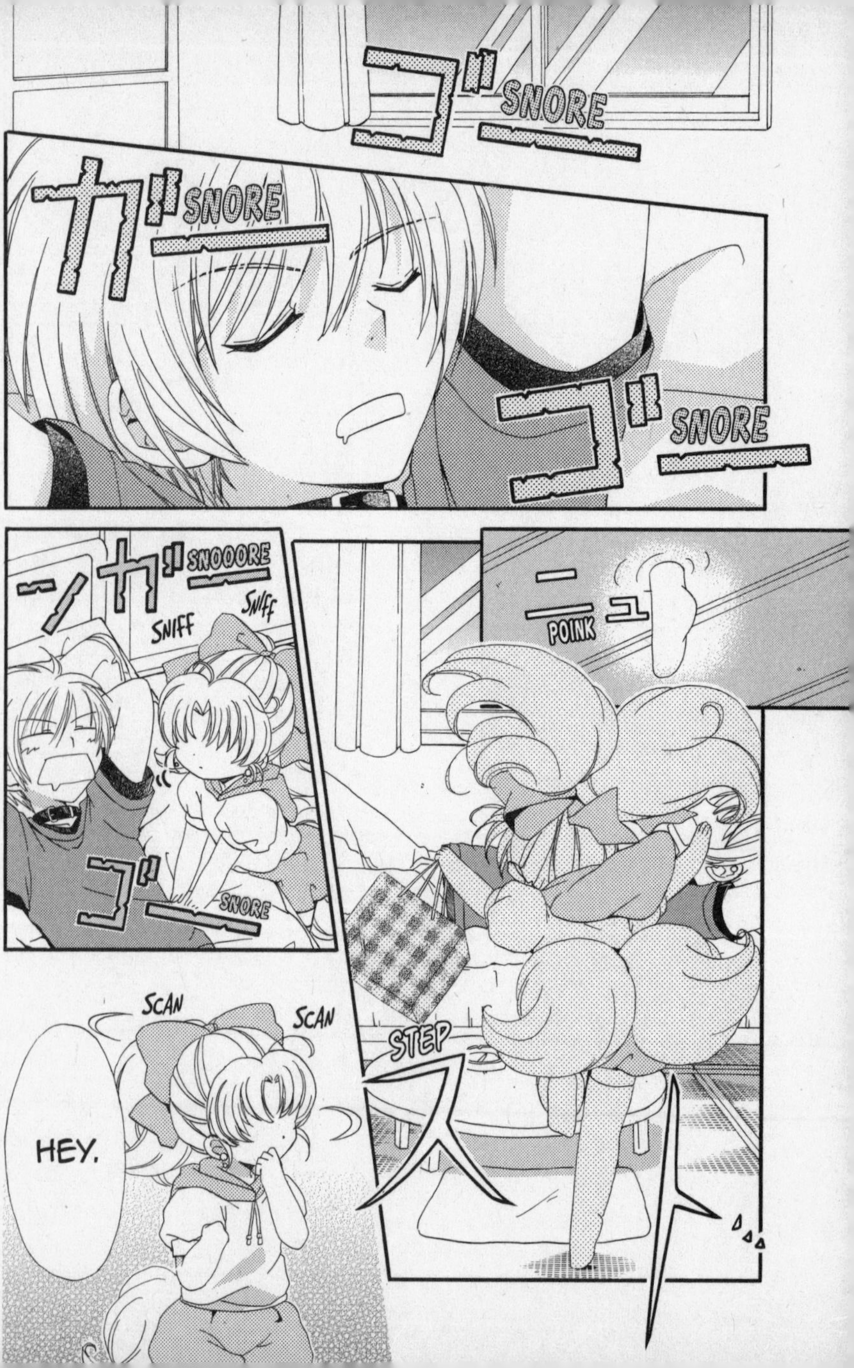

SNORE
SNORE
SNORE
POINK
SNOOORE
SNIFF
SNIFF
SNORE
STEP
SCAN
SCAN
HEY.

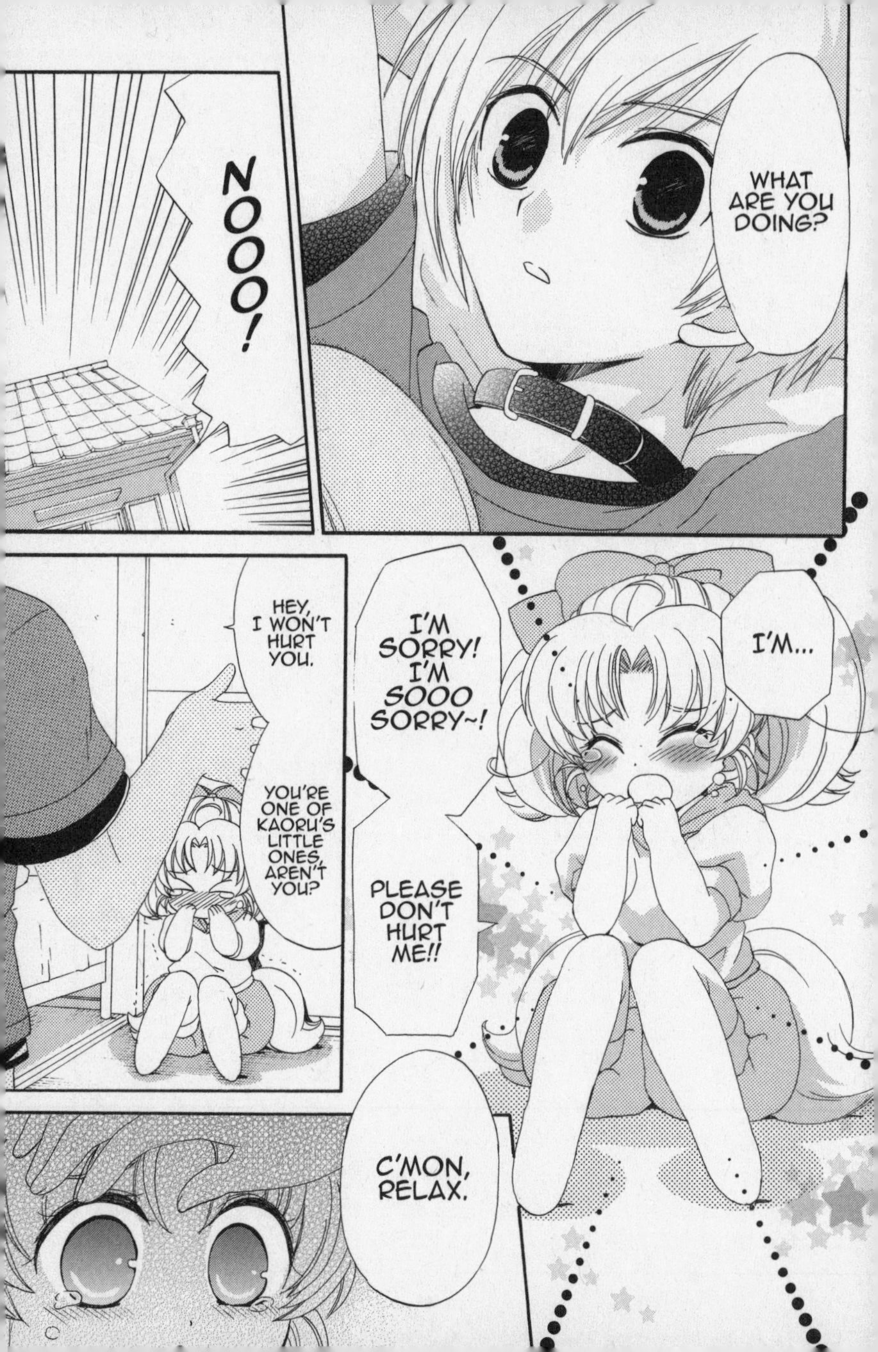
WHAT ARE YOU DOING?
NOOOO!
I'M...
I'M SORRY! I'M SOOO SORRY~!
PLEASE DON'T HURT ME!!
HEY, I WON'T HURT YOU.
YOU'RE ONE OF KAORU'S LITTLE ONES, AREN'T YOU?
C'MON, RELAX.

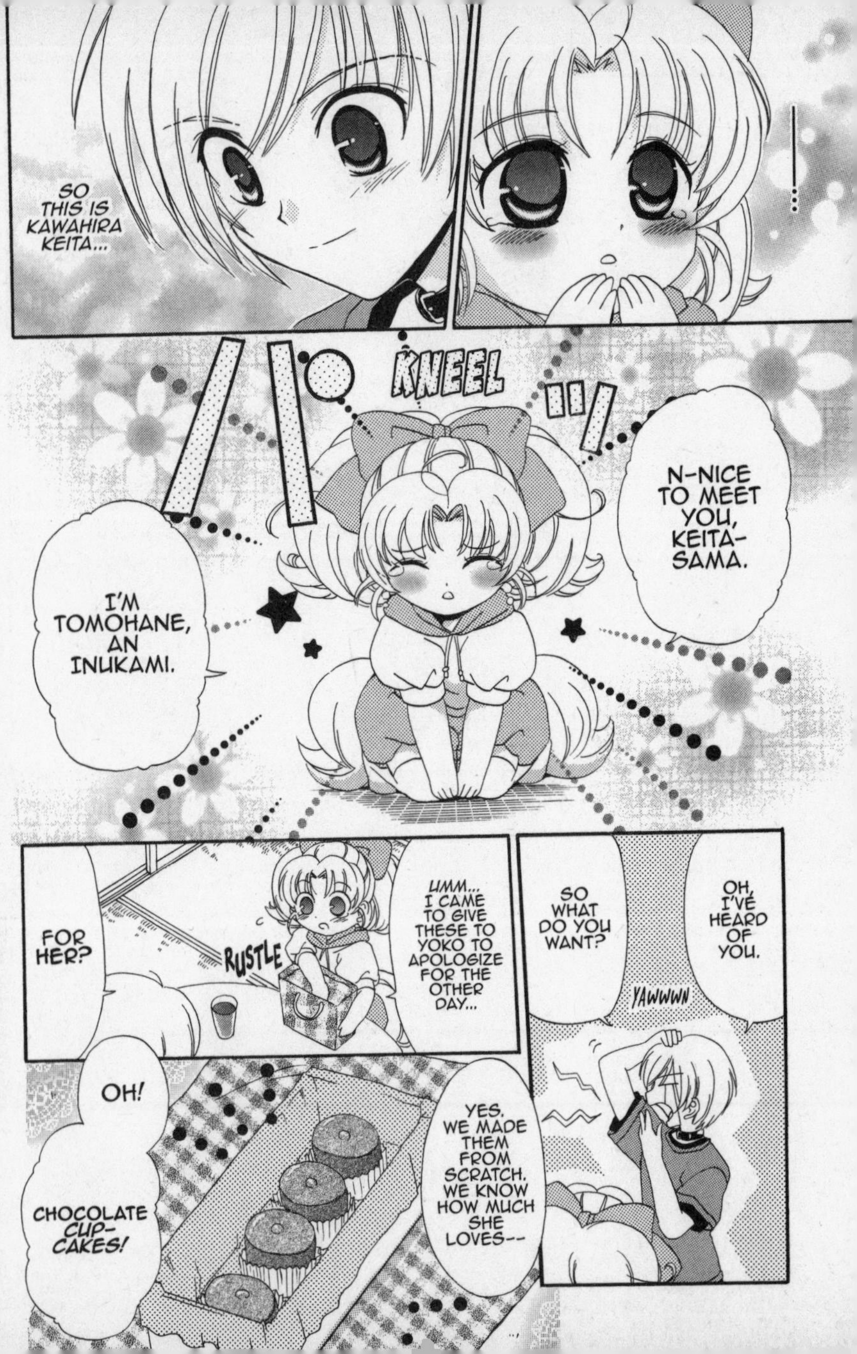
...!
SO THIS IS KAWAHIRA KEITA...
KNEEL
N-NICE TO MEET YOU, KEITA-SAMA.
I'M TOMOHANE, AN INUKAMI.
OH, I'VE HEARD OF YOU.
YAWWWN
SO WHAT DO YOU WANT?
UMM... I CAME TO GIVE THESE TO YOKO TO APOLOGIZE FOR THE OTHER DAY...
RUSTLE
FOR HER?
YES. WE MADE THEM FROM SCRATCH. WE KNOW HOW MUCH SHE LOVES--
OH!
CHOCOLATE CUP-CAKES!

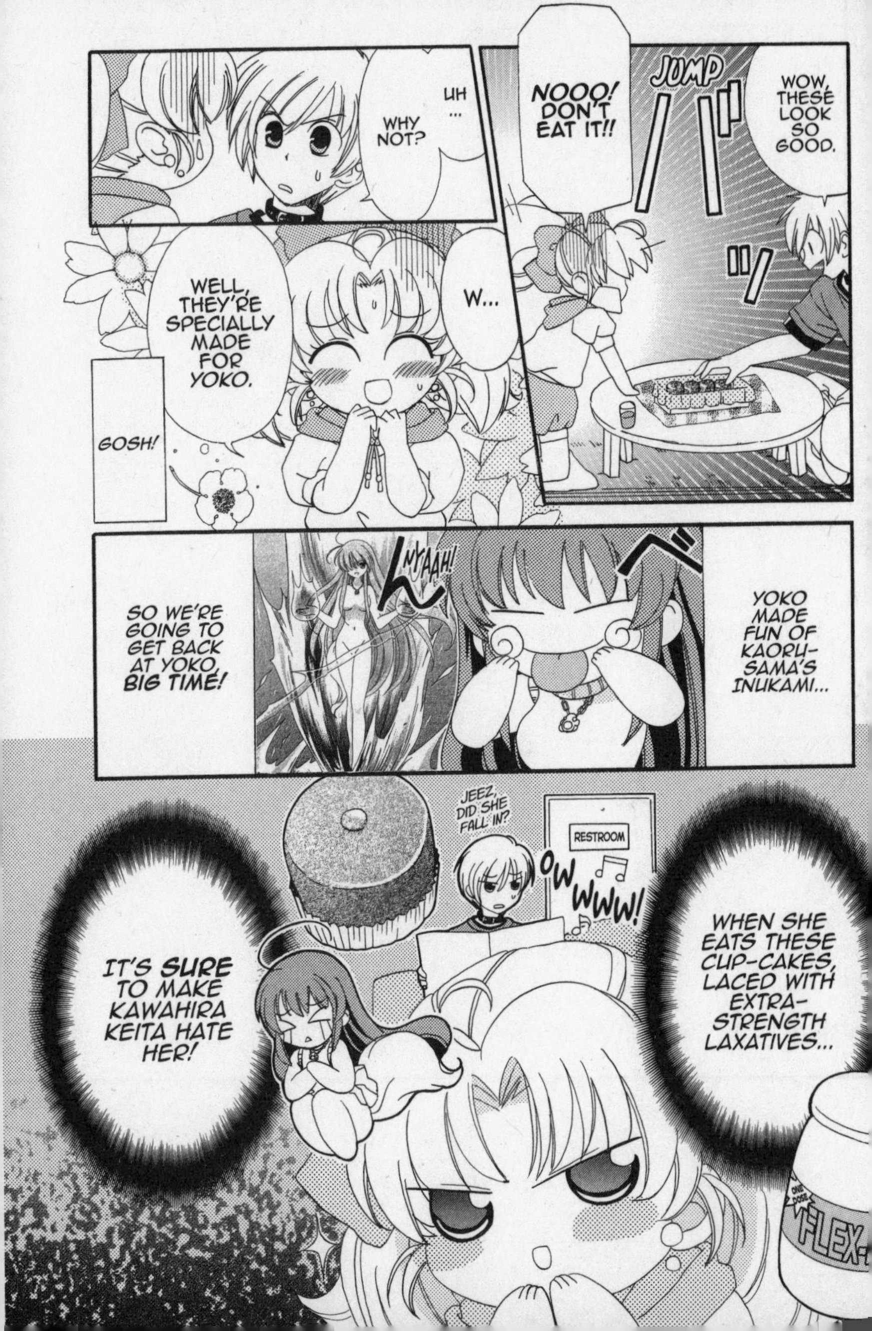
WOW, THESE LOOK SO GOOD.
JUMP
NOOO! DON'T EAT IT!!
UH ...
WHY NOT?
W...
WELL, THEY'RE SPECIALLY MADE FOR YOKO.
GOSH!
YOKO MADE FUN OF KAORU-SAMA'S INUKAMI...
NYAAH!
SO WE'RE GOING TO GET BACK AT YOKO, BIG TIME!
WHEN SHE EATS THESE CUP-CAKES, LACED WITH EXTRA-STRENGTH LAXATIVES...
RESTROOM
OWWWW!
JEEZ, DID SHE FALL IN?
IT'S SURE TO MAKE KAWAHIRA KEITA HATE HER!
ONE DOSE

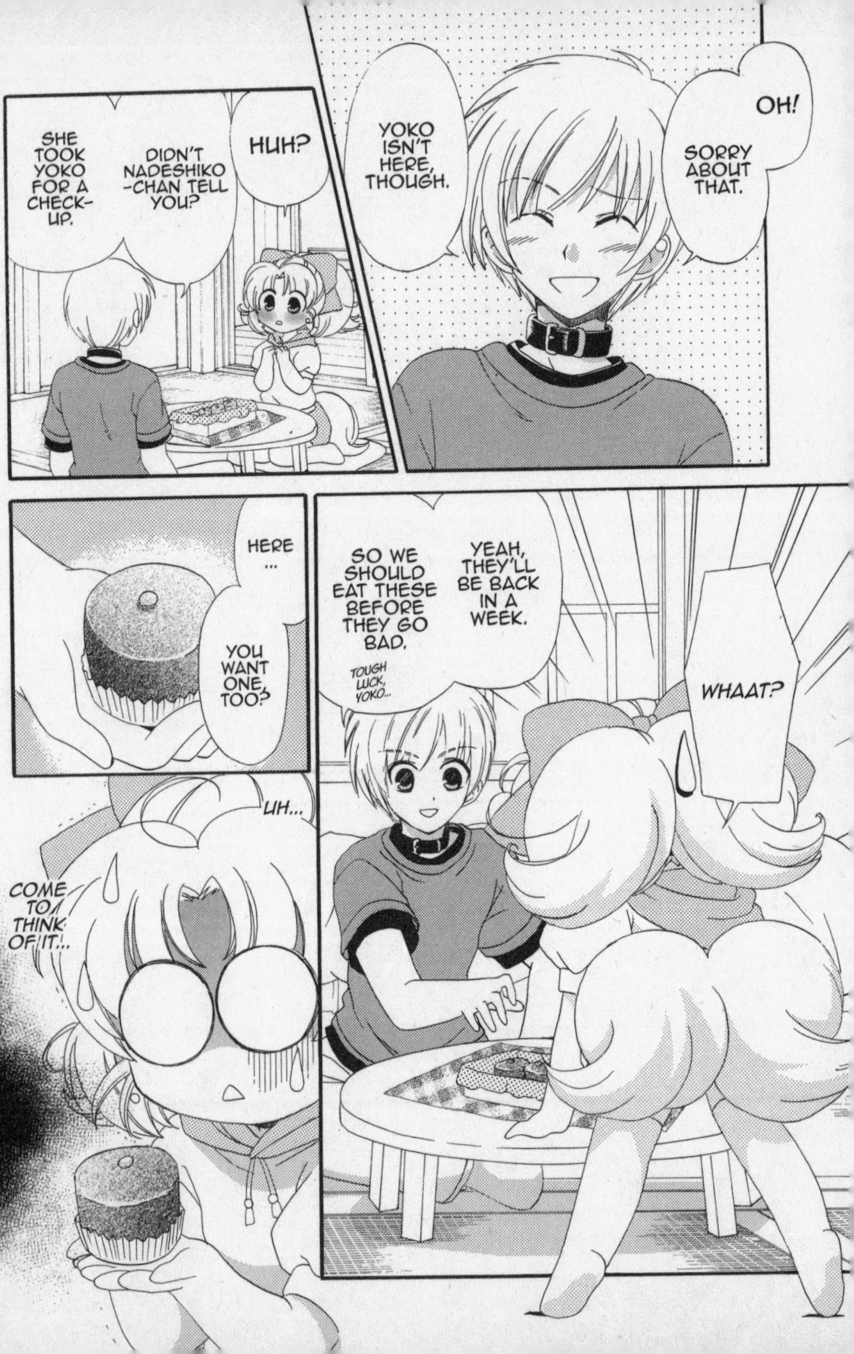
OH!
SORRY ABOUT THAT.
YOKO ISN'T HERE, THOUGH.
HUH?
DIDN'T NADESHIKO-CHAN TELL YOU?
SHE TOOK YOKO FOR A CHECK-UP.
WHAAT?
YEAH, THEY'LL BE BACK IN A WEEK.
SO WE SHOULD EAT THESE BEFORE THEY GO BAD.
TOUGH LUCK, YOKO...
HERE...
YOU WANT ONE, TOO?
UH...
COME TO THINK OF IT...

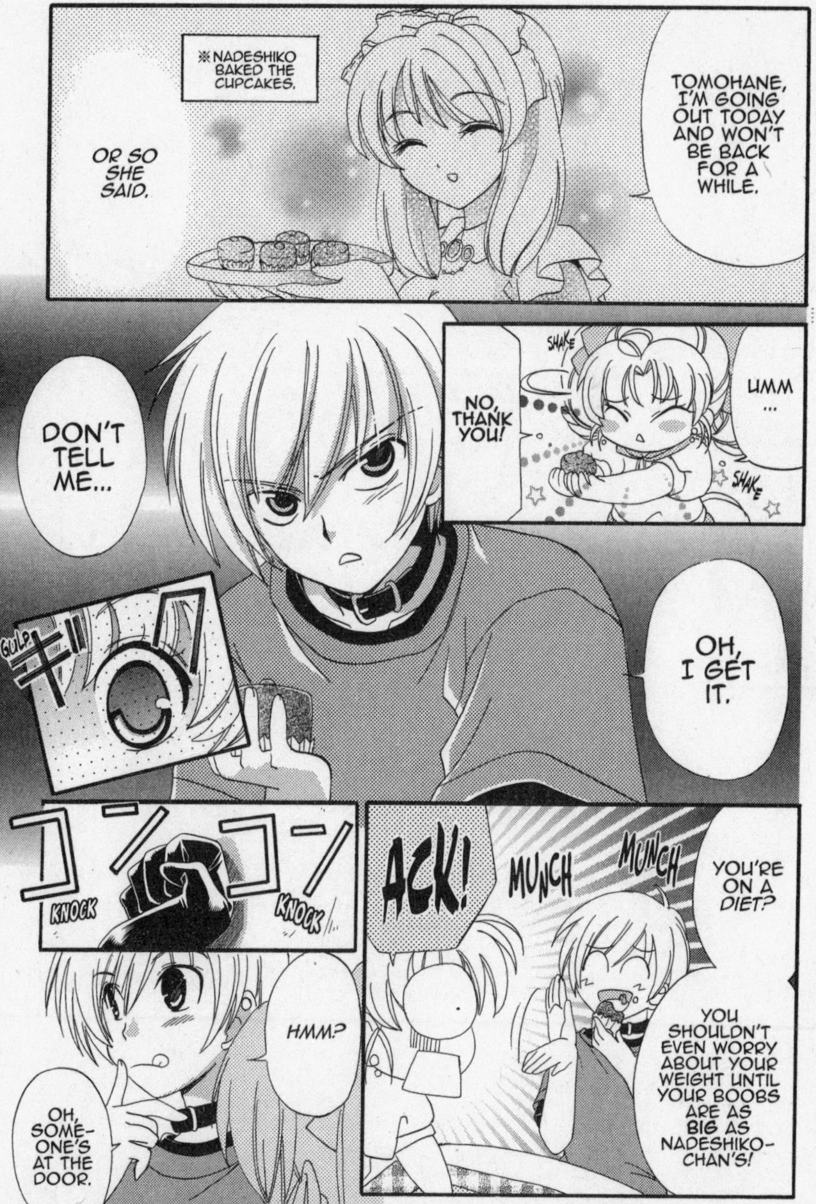
TOMOHANE, I'M GOING OUT TODAY AND WON'T BE BACK FOR A WHILE.
※NADESHIKO BAKED THE CUPCAKES.
OR SO SHE SAID.
UMM ...
SHAKE
NO, THANK YOU!
SHAKE
OH, I GET IT.
DON'T TELL ME...
GULP
YOU'RE ON A DIET?
MUNCH
MUNCH
YOU SHOULDN'T EVEN WORRY ABOUT YOUR WEIGHT UNTIL YOUR BOOBS ARE AS BIG AS NADESHIKO-CHAN'S!
ACK!
KNOCK
KNOCK
HMM?
OH, SOME-ONE'S AT THE DOOR.

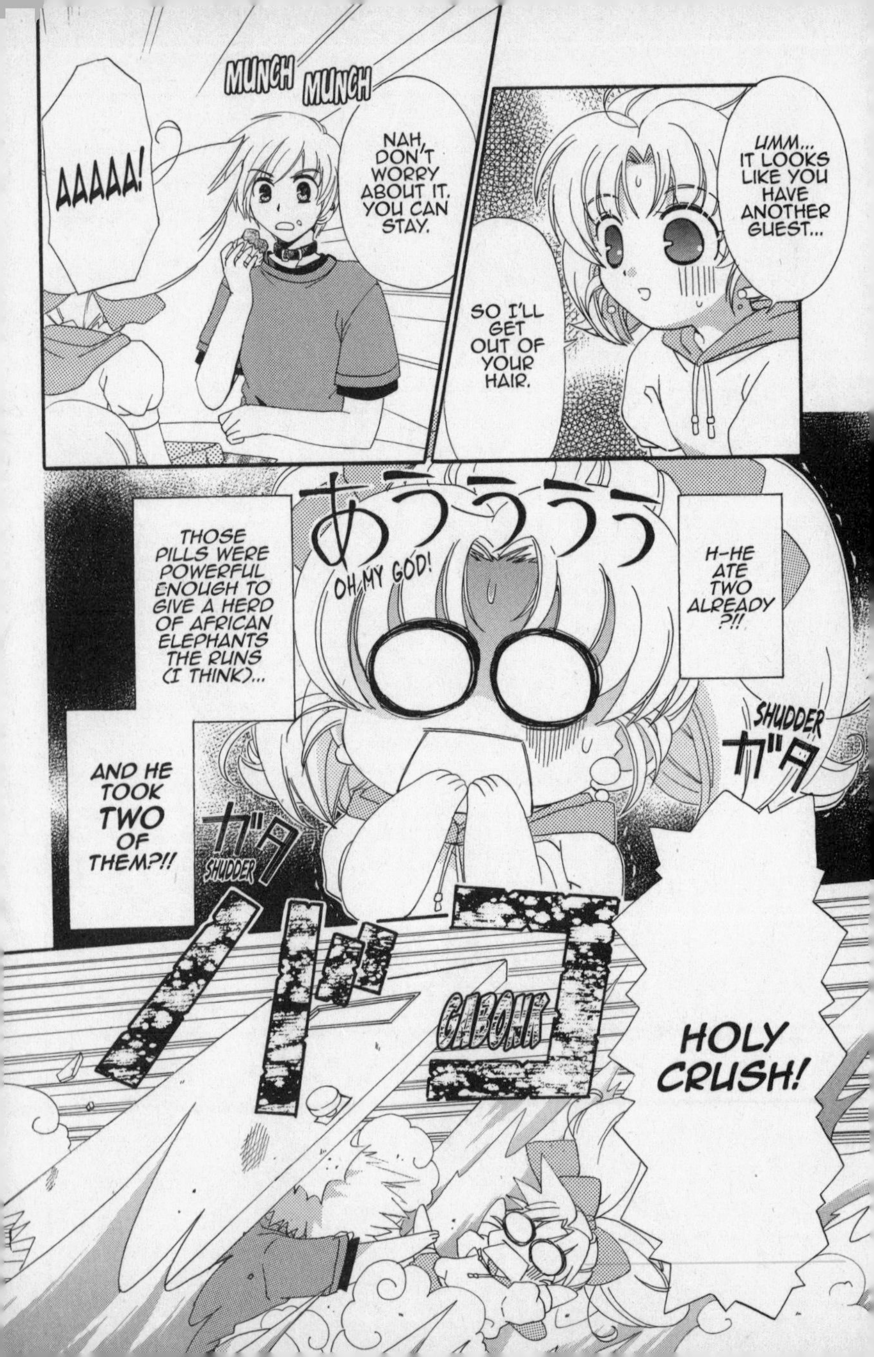
UMM... IT LOOKS LIKE YOU HAVE ANOTHER GUEST...
SO I'LL GET OUT OF YOUR HAIR.
MUNCH MUNCH
NAH, DON'T WORRY ABOUT IT. YOU CAN STAY.
AAAAA!
H-HE ATE TWO ALREADY?!!
あうううう
OH MY GOD!
THOSE PILLS WERE POWERFUL ENOUGH TO GIVE A HERD OF AFRICAN ELEPHANTS THE RUNS (I THINK)...
SHUDDER ガタ
AND HE TOOK TWO OF THEM?!!
ガタ SHUDDER
GABONK
HOLY CRUSH!

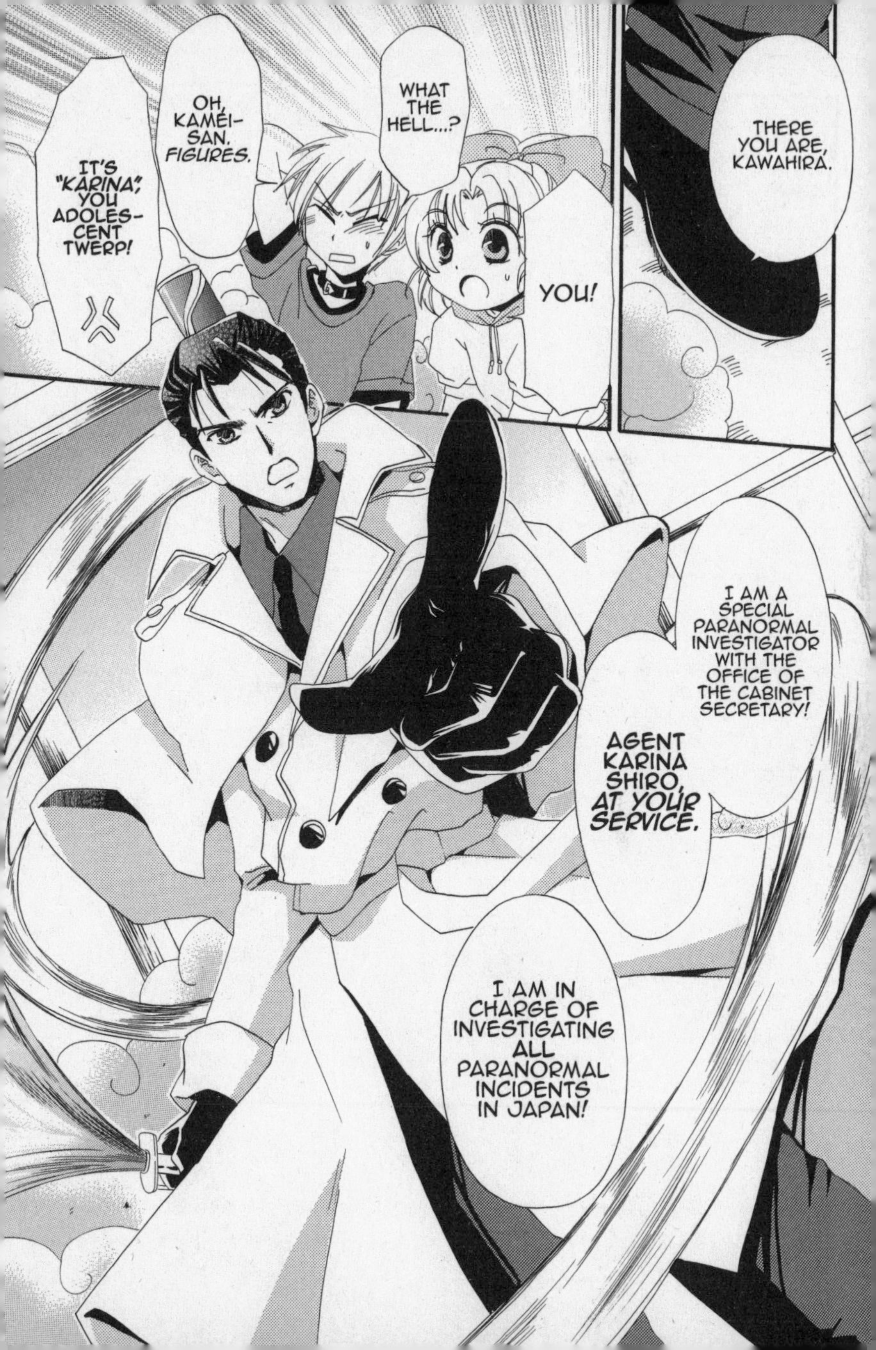
THERE YOU ARE, KAWAHIRA.
YOU!
WHAT THE HELL...?
OH, KAMEI-SAN. FIGURES.
IT'S "KARINA," YOU ADOLESCENT TWERP!
I AM A SPECIAL PARANORMAL INVESTIGATOR WITH THE OFFICE OF THE CABINET SECRETARY!
AGENT KARINA SHIRO, AT YOUR SERVICE.
I AM IN CHARGE OF INVESTIGATING ALL PARANORMAL INCIDENTS IN JAPAN!

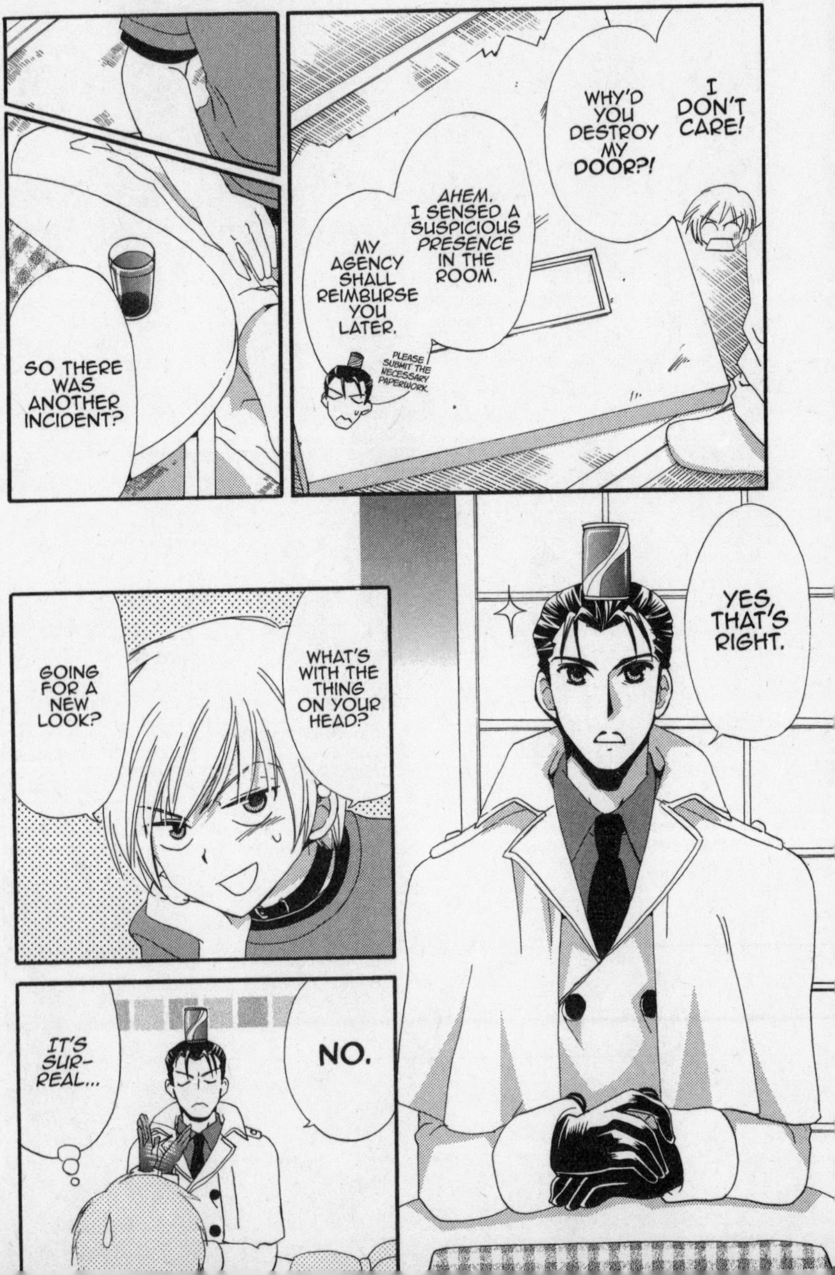
I DON'T CARE!
WHY'D YOU DESTROY MY DOOR?!
AHEM. I SENSED A SUSPICIOUS PRESENCE IN THE ROOM.
MY AGENCY SHALL REIMBURSE YOU LATER.
PLEASE SUBMIT THE NECESSARY PAPERWORK.
SO THERE WAS ANOTHER INCIDENT?
YES, THAT'S RIGHT.
WHAT'S WITH THE THING ON YOUR HEAD?
GOING FOR A NEW LOOK?
NO.
IT'S SUR-REAL...

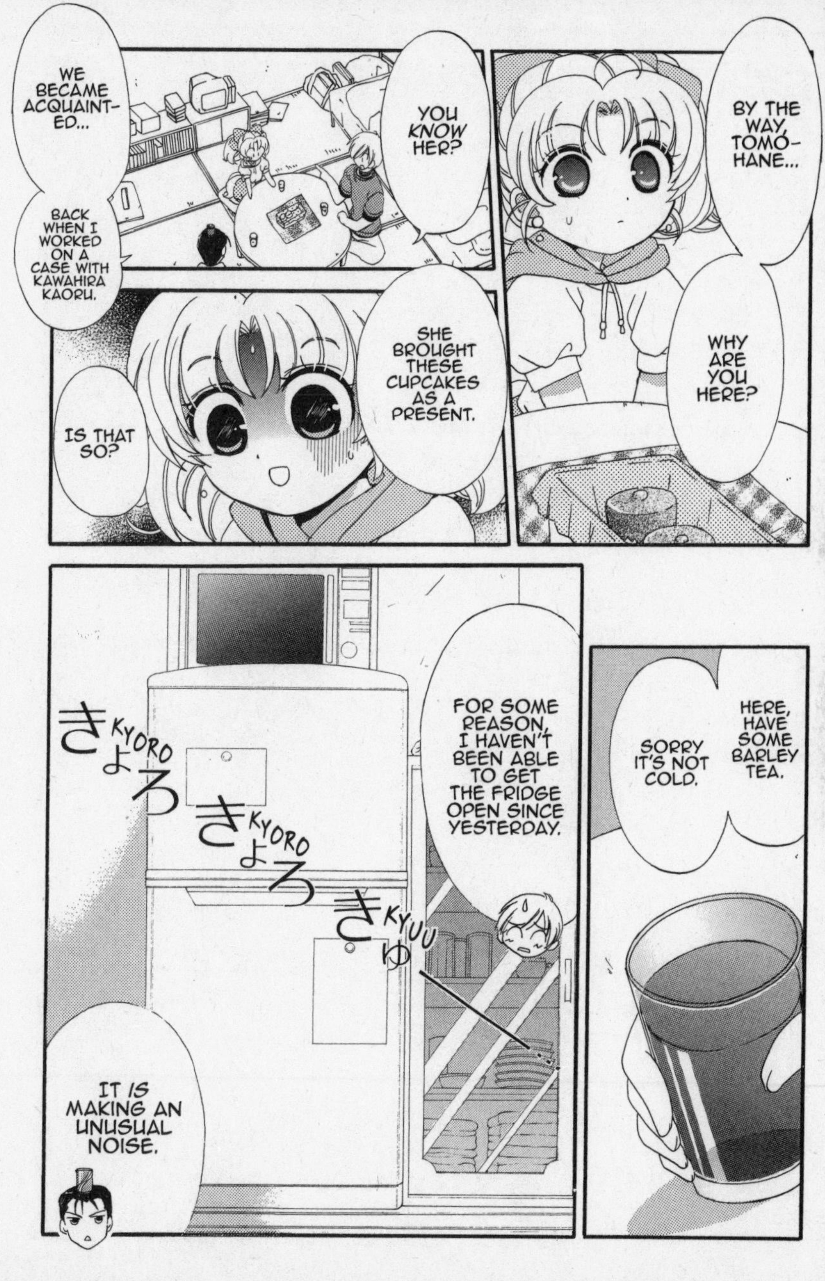
BY THE WAY, TOMO-HANE...
WHY ARE YOU HERE?
YOU KNOW HER?
WE BECAME ACQUAINT-ED...
BACK WHEN I WORKED ON A CASE WITH KAWAHIRA KAORU.
SHE BROUGHT THESE CUPCAKES AS A PRESENT.
IS THAT SO?
HERE, HAVE SOME BARLEY TEA.
SORRY IT'S NOT COLD.
FOR SOME REASON, I HAVEN'T BEEN ABLE TO GET THE FRIDGE OPEN SINCE YESTERDAY.
きょろ KYORO
きょろ KYORO
きゅ KYUU
IT IS MAKING AN UNUSUAL NOISE.

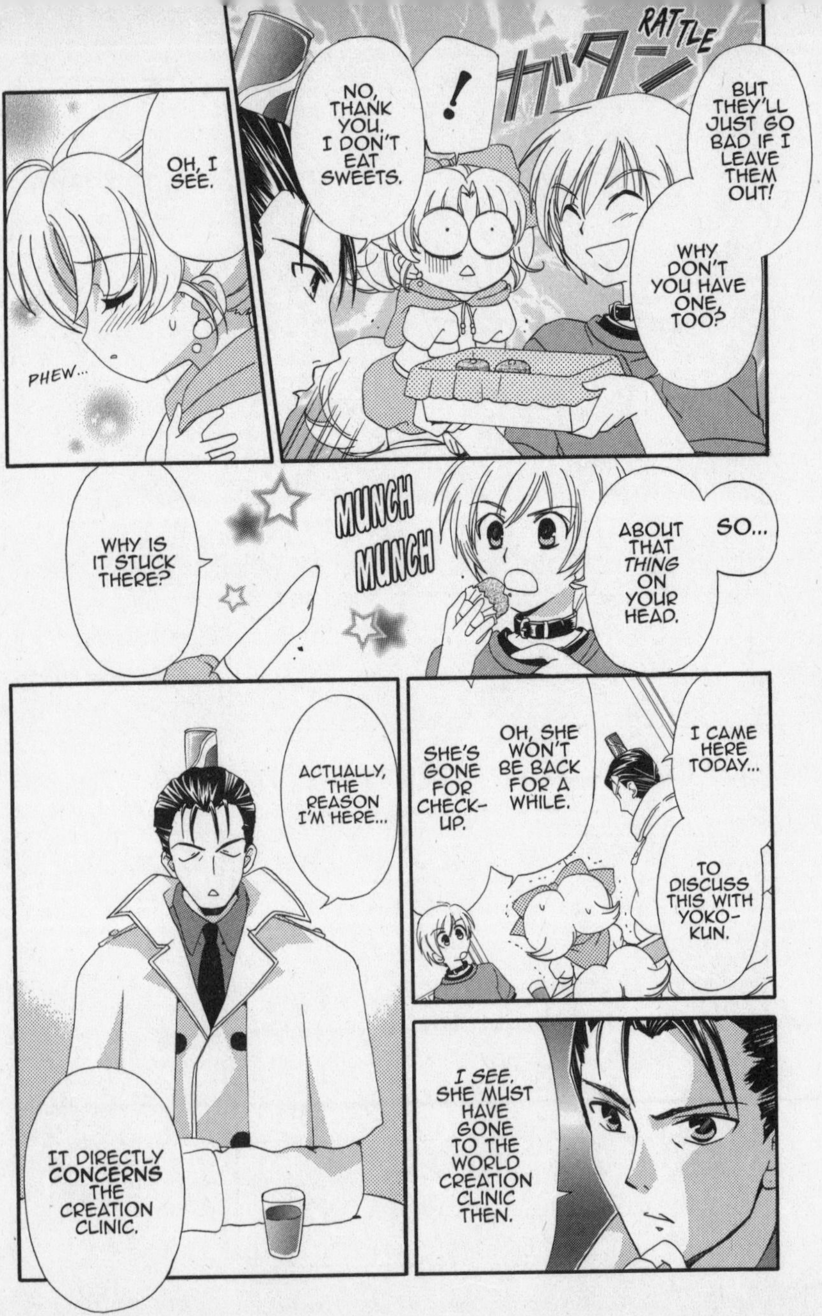
RATTLE
BUT THEY'LL JUST GO BAD IF I LEAVE THEM OUT!
WHY DON'T YOU HAVE ONE, TOO?
!
NO, THANK YOU. I DON'T EAT SWEETS.
OH, I SEE.
PHEW...
SO...
ABOUT THAT *THING* ON YOUR HEAD.
MUNCH MUNCH
WHY IS IT STUCK THERE?
I CAME HERE TODAY...
TO DISCUSS THIS WITH YOKO-KUN.
OH, SHE WON'T BE BACK FOR A WHILE.
SHE'S GONE FOR CHECK-UP.
I SEE. SHE MUST HAVE GONE TO THE WORLD CREATION CLINIC THEN.
ACTUALLY, THE REASON I'M HERE...
IT DIRECTLY **CONCERNS** THE CREATION CLINIC.

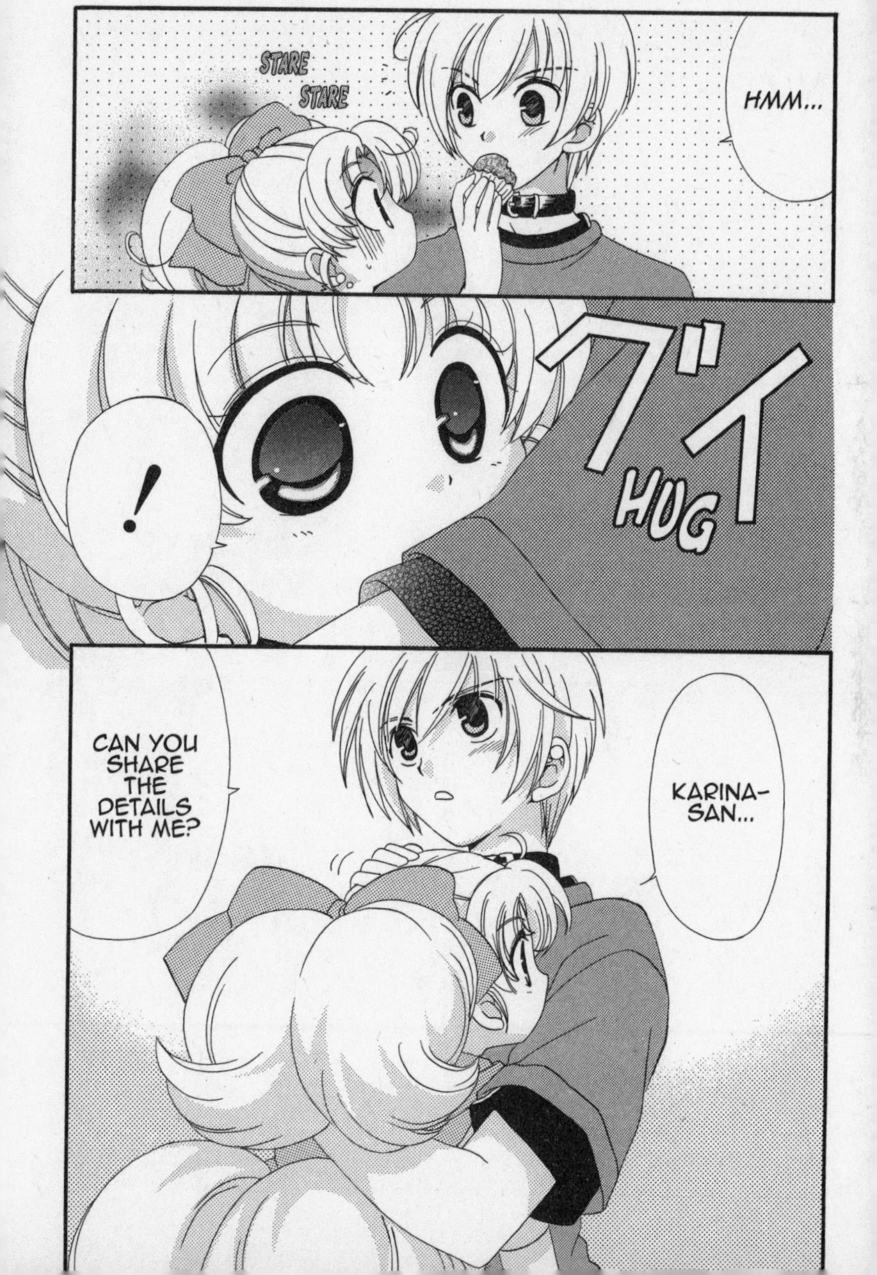
HMM...
STARE
STARE
グイ
HUG
!
KARINA-SAN...
CAN YOU SHARE THE DETAILS WITH ME?

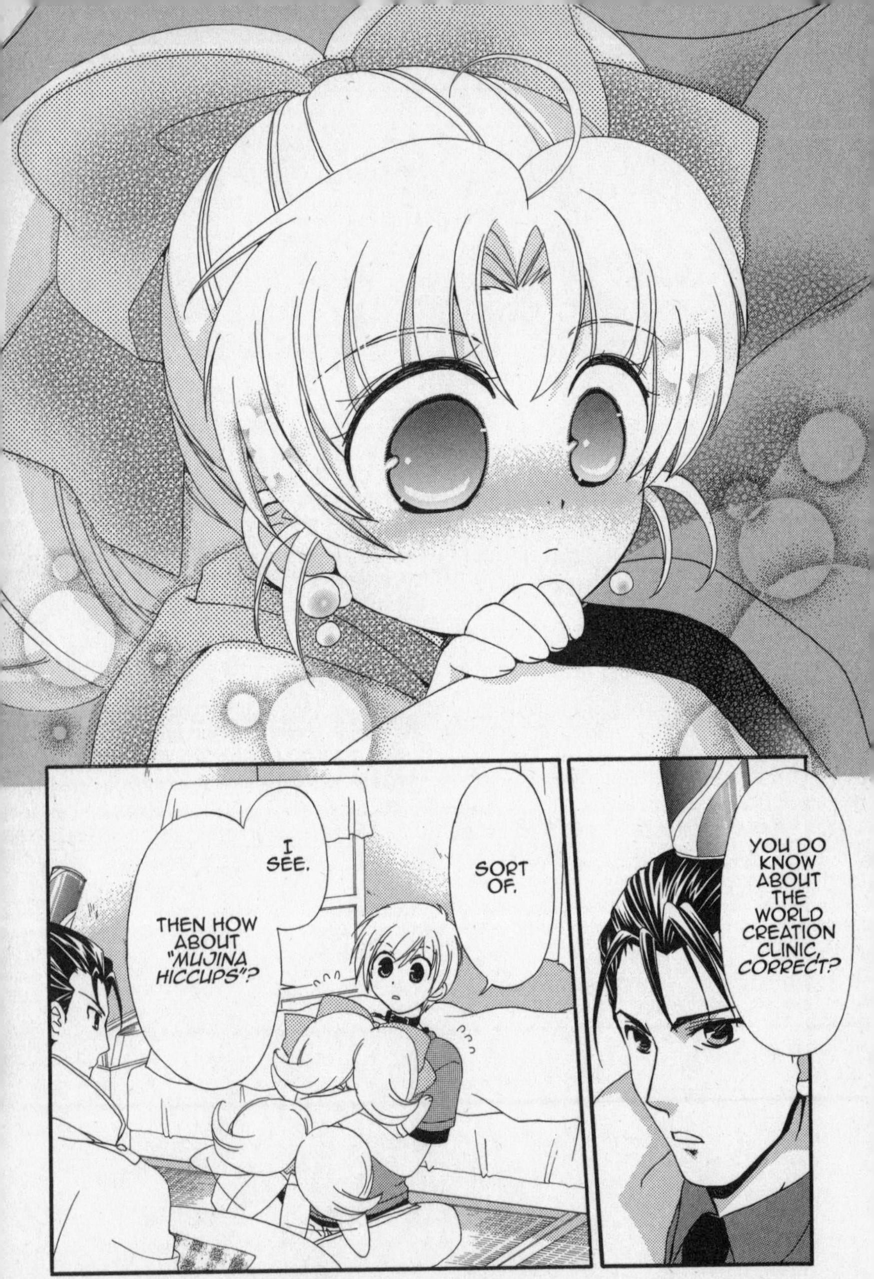
YOU DO KNOW ABOUT THE WORLD CREATION CLINIC, CORRECT?
SORT OF.
I SEE.
THEN HOW ABOUT "MUJINA HICCUPS"?

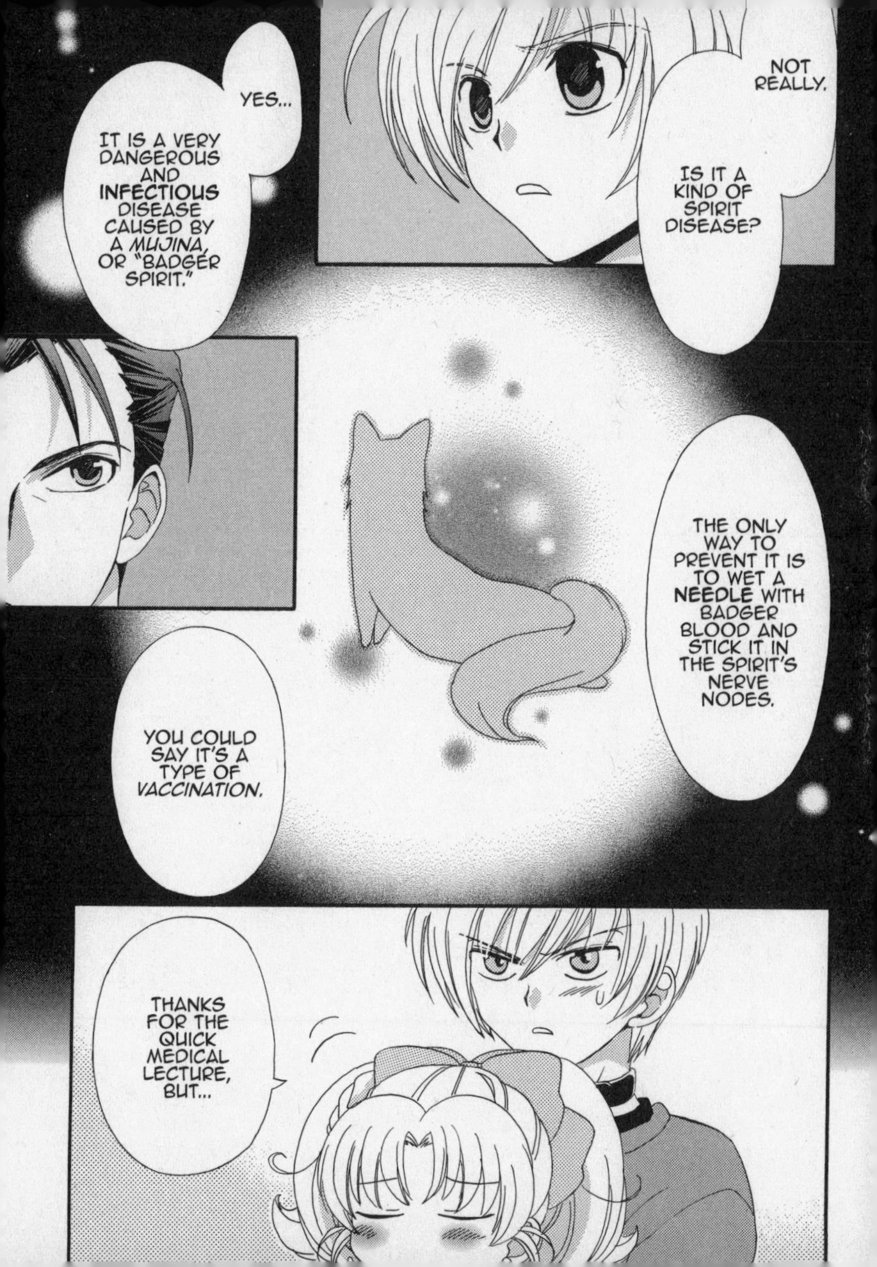
NOT REALLY.
IS IT A KIND OF SPIRIT DISEASE?
YES...
IT IS A VERY DANGEROUS AND **INFECTIOUS** DISEASE CAUSED BY A *MUJINA*, OR "BADGER SPIRIT."
THE ONLY WAY TO PREVENT IT IS TO WET A **NEEDLE** WITH BADGER BLOOD AND STICK IT IN THE SPIRIT'S NERVE NODES.
YOU COULD SAY IT'S A TYPE OF *VACCINATION*.
THANKS FOR THE QUICK MEDICAL LECTURE, BUT...

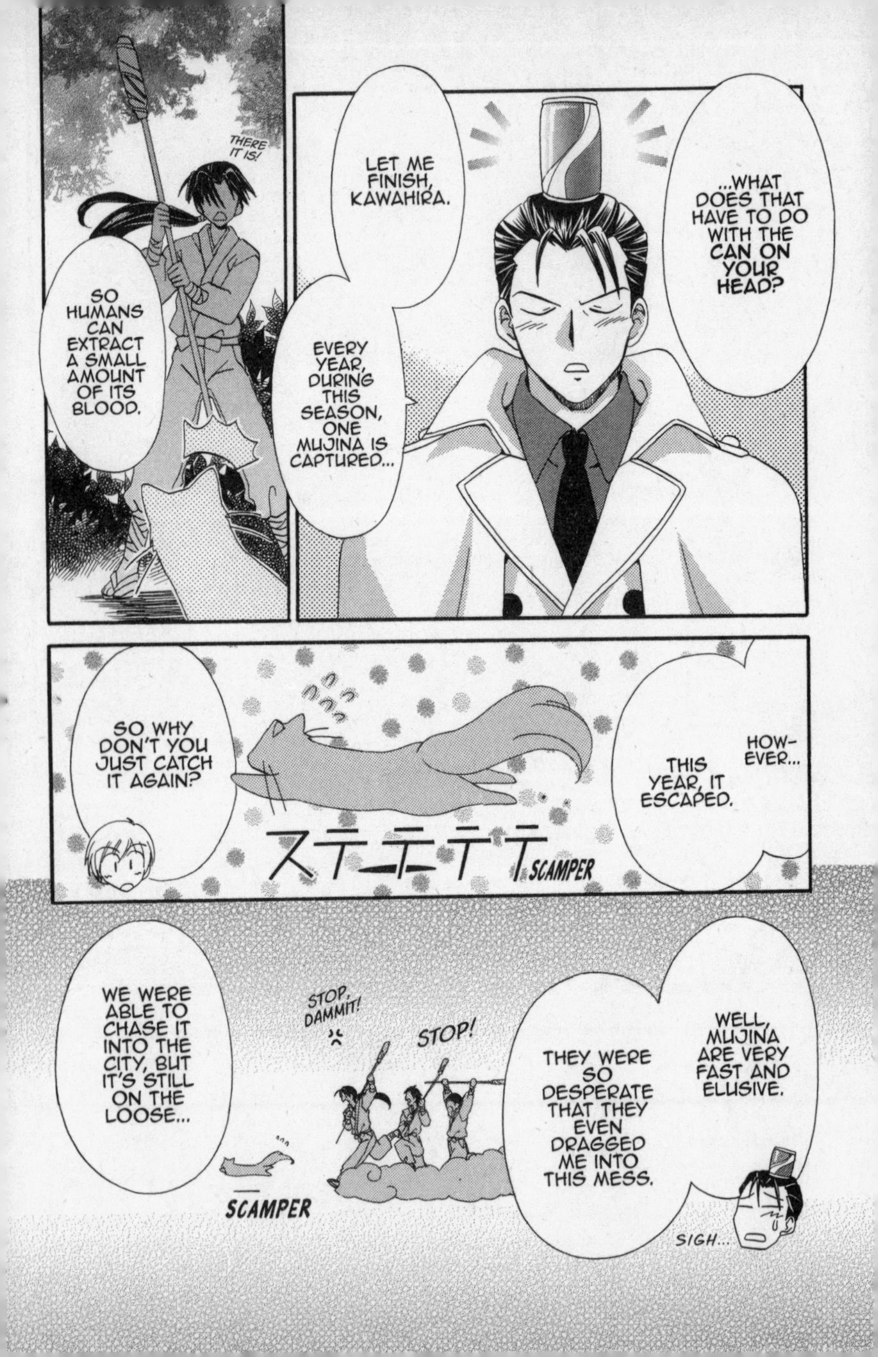

...WHAT DOES THAT HAVE TO DO WITH THE CAN ON YOUR HEAD?
LET ME FINISH, KAWAHIRA.
EVERY YEAR, DURING THIS SEASON, ONE MUJINA IS CAPTURED...
THERE IT IS!
SO HUMANS CAN EXTRACT A SMALL AMOUNT OF ITS BLOOD.
HOW-EVER...
THIS YEAR, IT ESCAPED.
SCAMPER
SO WHY DON'T YOU JUST CATCH IT AGAIN?
WELL, MUJINA ARE VERY FAST AND ELUSIVE.
THEY WERE SO DESPERATE THAT THEY EVEN DRAGGED ME INTO THIS MESS.
SIGH...
STOP!
STOP, DAMMIT!
WE WERE ABLE TO CHASE IT INTO THE CITY, BUT IT'S STILL ON THE LOOSE...
SCAMPER

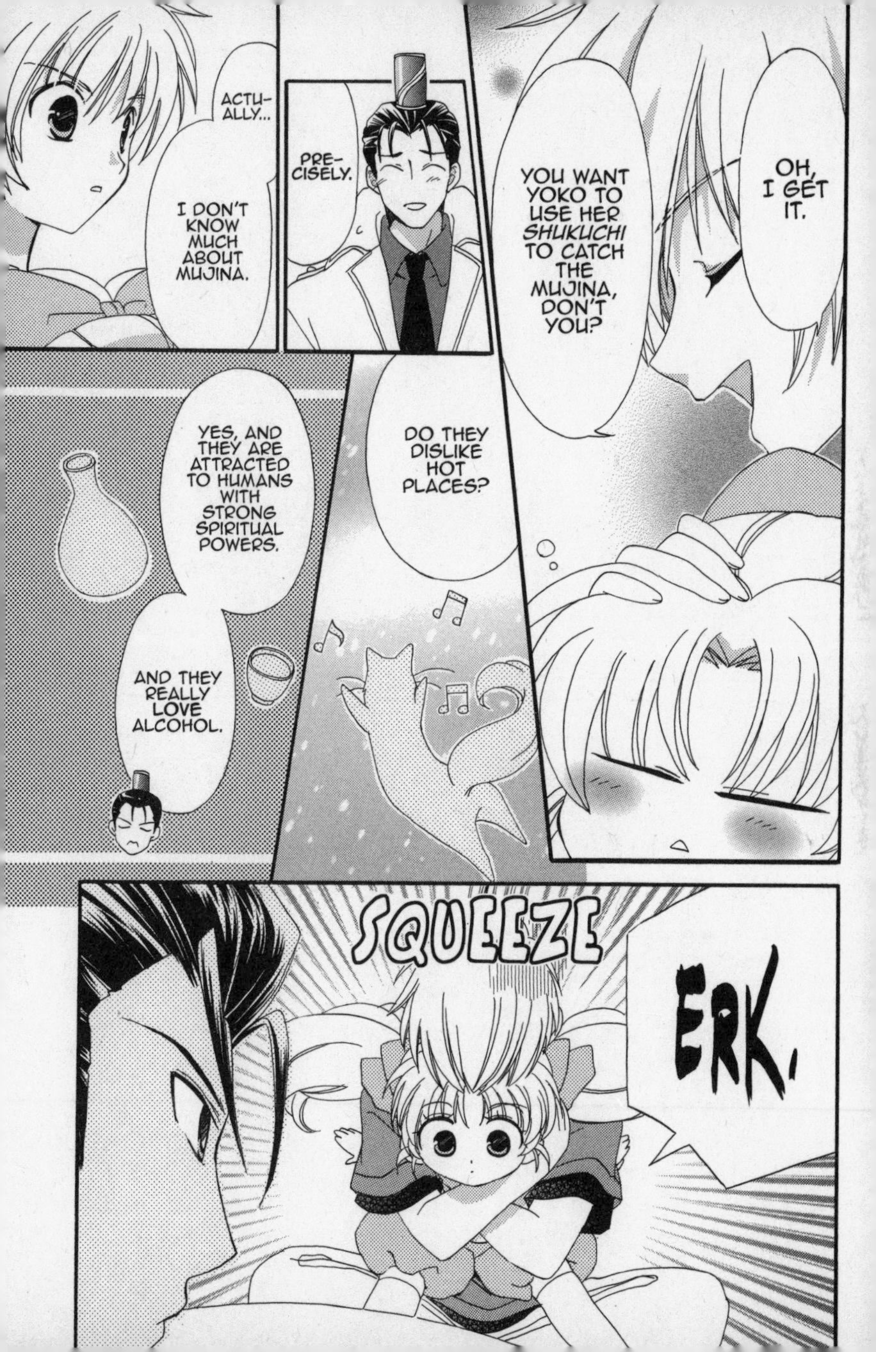
OH, I GET IT.
YOU WANT YOKO TO USE HER *SHUKUCHI* TO CATCH THE MUJINA, DON'T YOU?
PRE-CISELY.
ACTU-ALLY...
I DON'T KNOW MUCH ABOUT MUJINA.
DO THEY DISLIKE HOT PLACES?
YES, AND THEY ARE ATTRACTED TO HUMANS WITH STRONG SPIRITUAL POWERS.
AND THEY REALLY LOVE ALCOHOL.
ERK.
SQUEEZE

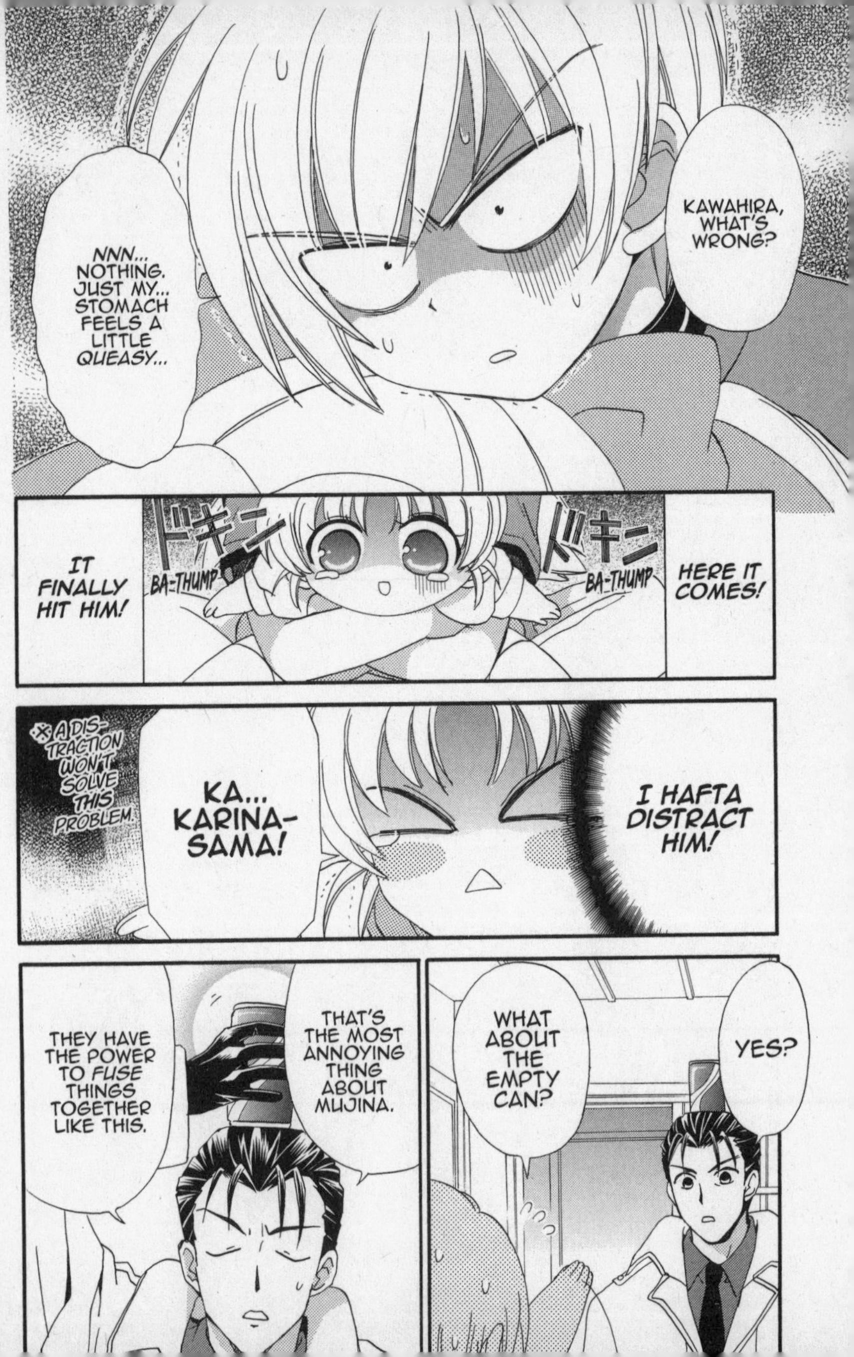

KAWAHIRA, WHAT'S WRONG?
NNN... NOTHING. JUST MY... STOMACH FEELS A LITTLE QUEASY...
HERE IT COMES!
ドキン
BA-THUMP
ドキーン
BA-THUMP
IT FINALLY HIT HIM!
I HAFTA DISTRACT HIM!
KA... KARINA-SAMA!
※A DISTRACTION WON'T SOLVE THIS PROBLEM.
YES?
WHAT ABOUT THE EMPTY CAN?
THAT'S THE MOST ANNOYING THING ABOUT MUJINA.
THEY HAVE THE POWER TO *FUSE* THINGS TOGETHER LIKE THIS.

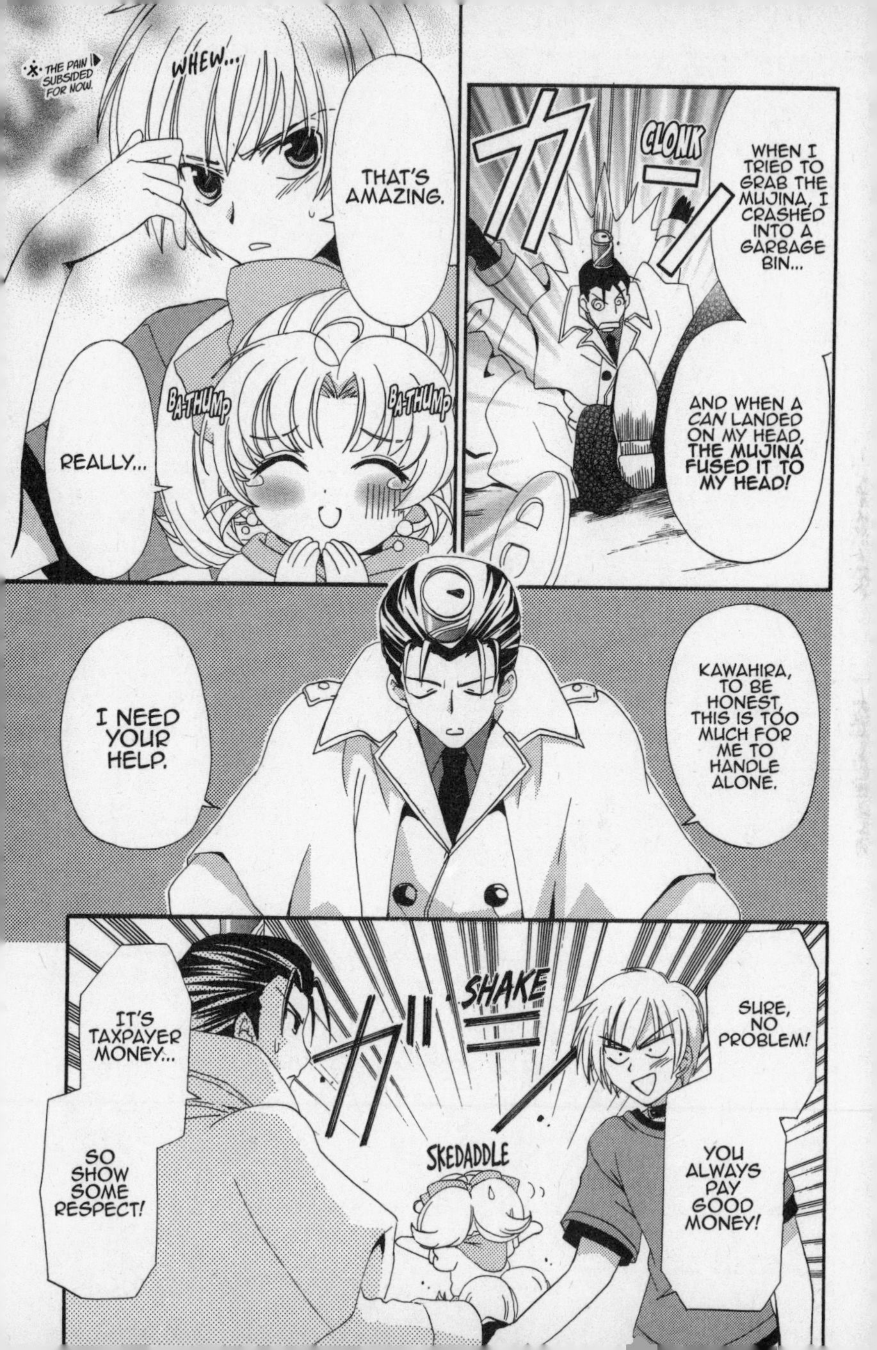

CLONK
WHEN I TRIED TO GRAB THE MUJINA, I CRASHED INTO A GARBAGE BIN...
AND WHEN A CAN LANDED ON MY HEAD, THE MUJINA FUSED IT TO MY HEAD!
THE PAIN SUBSIDED FOR NOW.
WHEW...
THAT'S AMAZING.
BA-THUMP BA-THUMP
REALLY...
KAWAHIRA, TO BE HONEST, THIS IS TOO MUCH FOR ME TO HANDLE ALONE.
I NEED YOUR HELP.
SURE, NO PROBLEM!
YOU ALWAYS PAY GOOD MONEY!
SHAKE
SKEDADDLE
IT'S TAXPAYER MONEY...
SO SHOW SOME RESPECT!

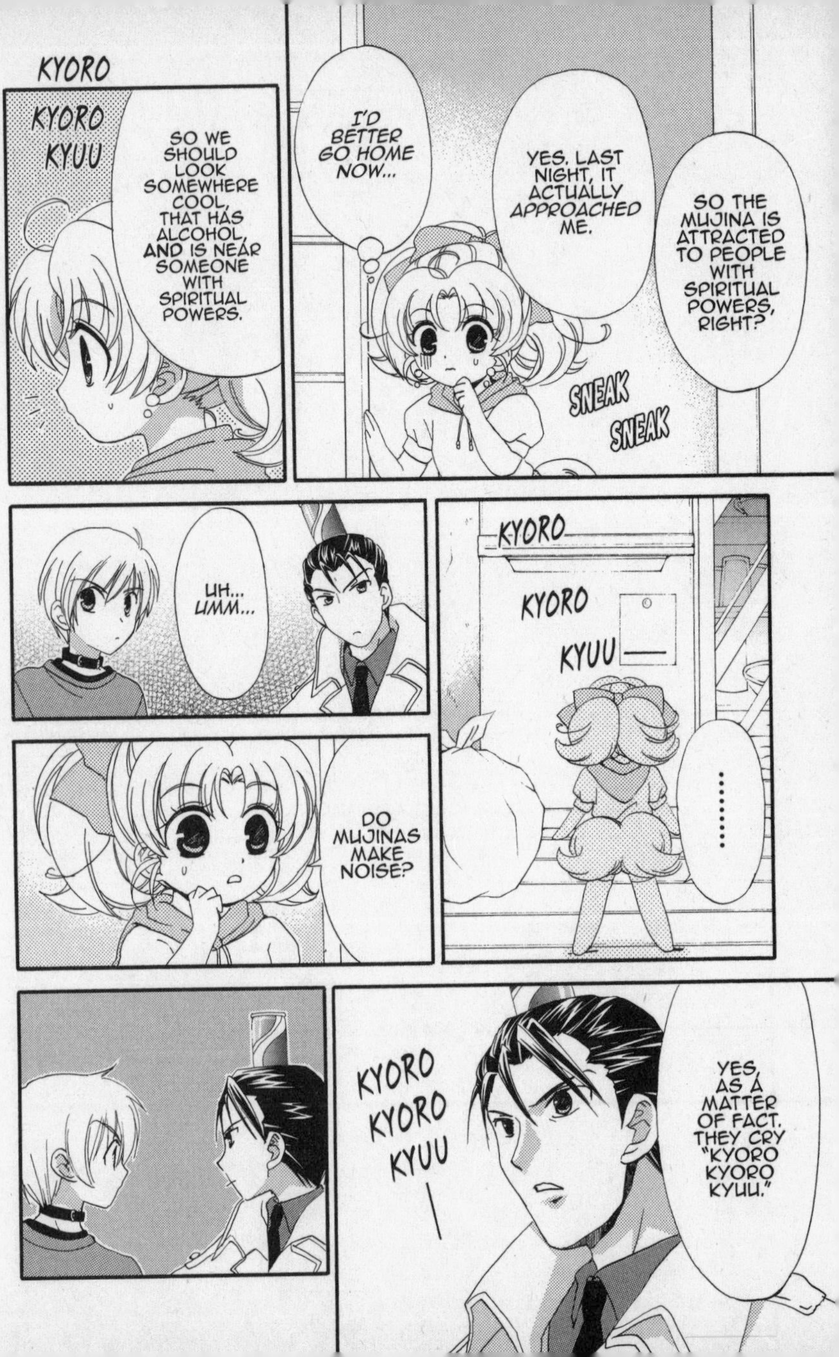

SO THE MUJINA IS ATTRACTED TO PEOPLE WITH SPIRITUAL POWERS, RIGHT?
YES. LAST NIGHT, IT ACTUALLY APPROACHED ME.
I'D BETTER GO HOME NOW...
SNEAK SNEAK
KYORO
KYORO KYUU
SO WE SHOULD LOOK SOMEWHERE COOL, THAT HAS ALCOHOL, AND IS NEAR SOMEONE WITH SPIRITUAL POWERS.
KYORO
KYORO
KYUU—
......
UH... UMM...
DO MUJINAS MAKE NOISE?
YES, AS A MATTER OF FACT. THEY CRY "KYORO KYORO KYUU."
KYORO KYORO KYUU

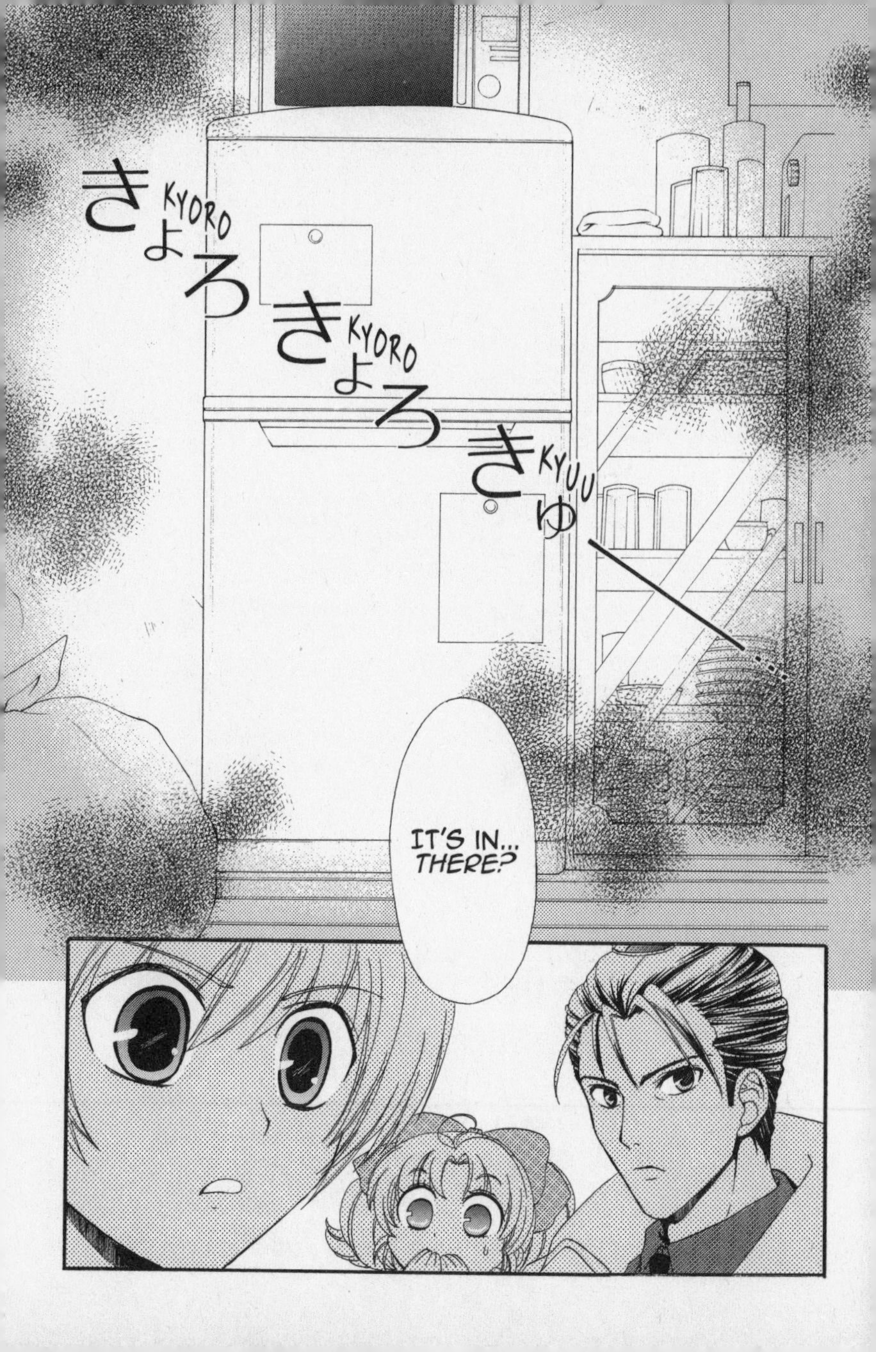

きょろ KYORO
きょろ KYORO
きゅー... KYUU
IT'S IN... THERE?

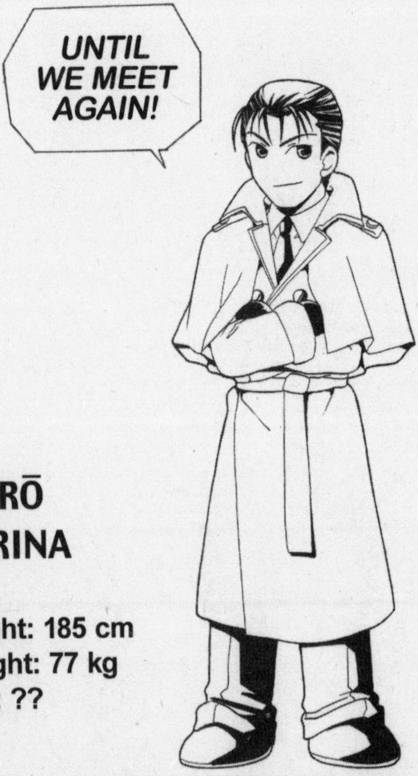
UNTIL WE MEET AGAIN!

SHIRŌ KARINA

Height: 185 cm
Weight: 77 kg
Age: ??

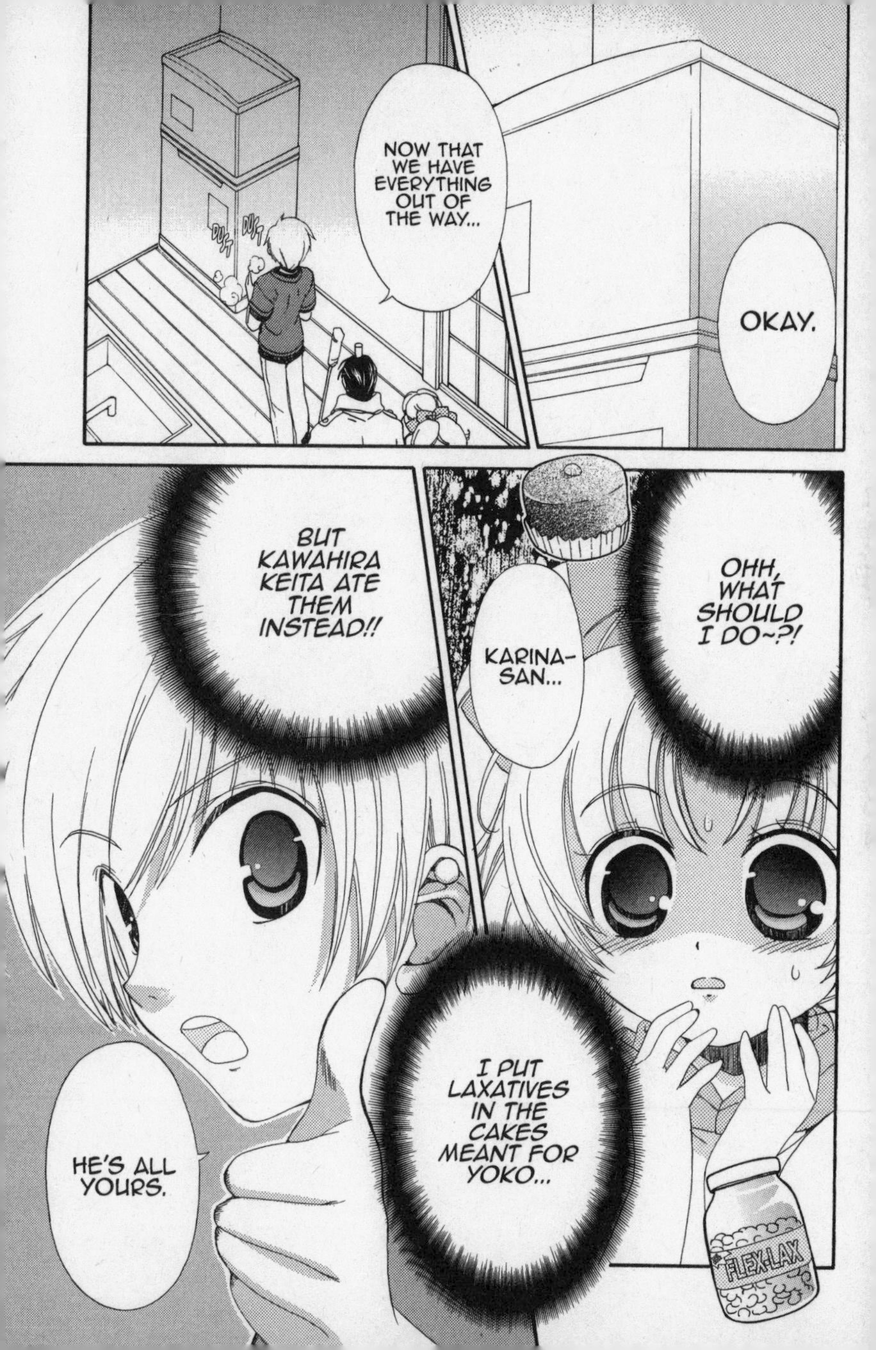
OKAY.
NOW THAT WE HAVE EVERYTHING OUT OF THE WAY...
DUST
DUST
OHH, WHAT SHOULD I DO~?!
KARINA-SAN...
I PUT LAXATIVES IN THE CAKES MEANT FOR YOKO...
FLEX-LAX
BUT KAWAHIRA KEITA ATE THEM INSTEAD!!
HE'S ALL YOURS.

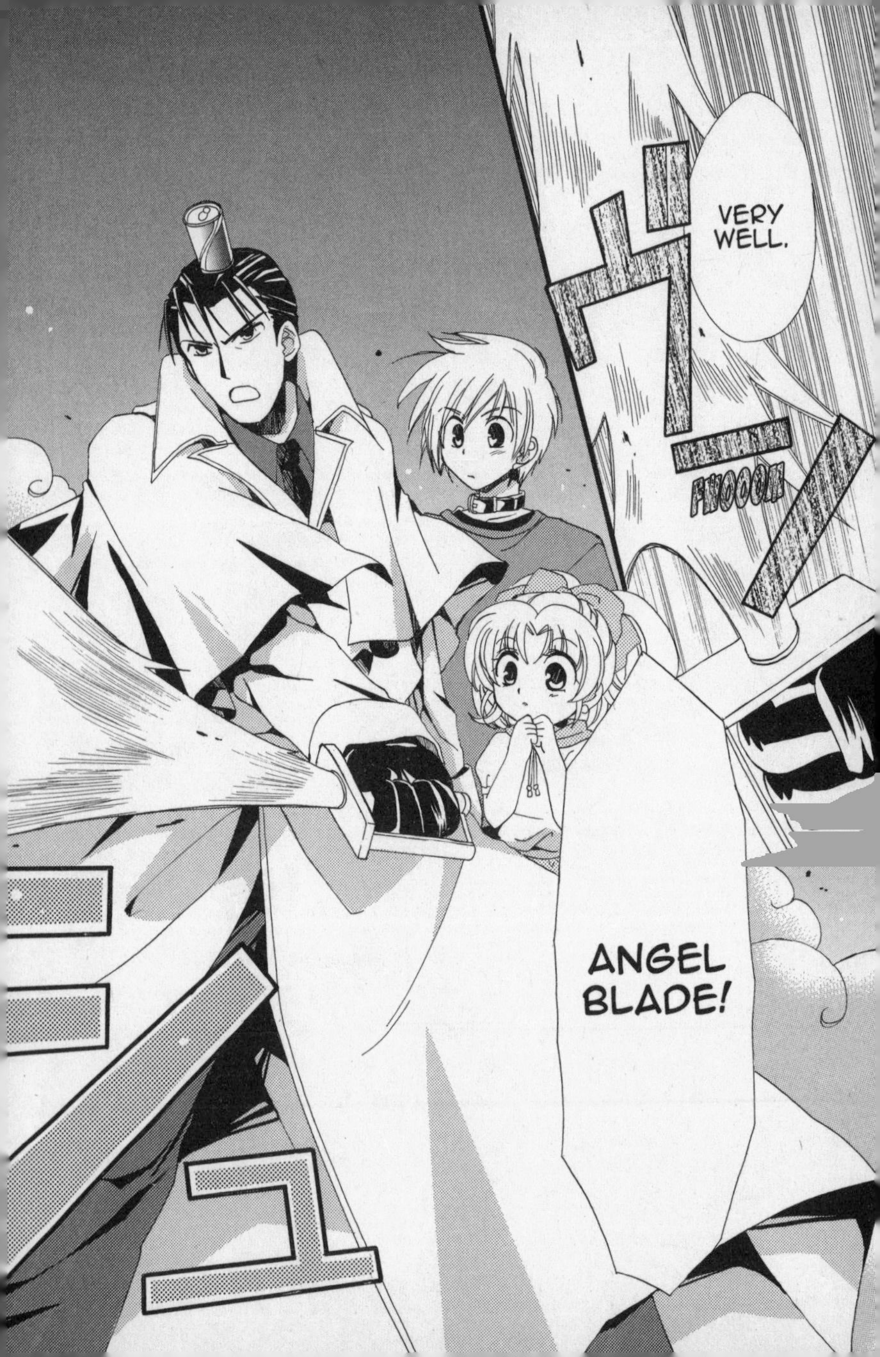
VERY WELL.
FWOOOM
ANGEL BLADE!

Step.9 Tomohane Strikes Back: Part 2

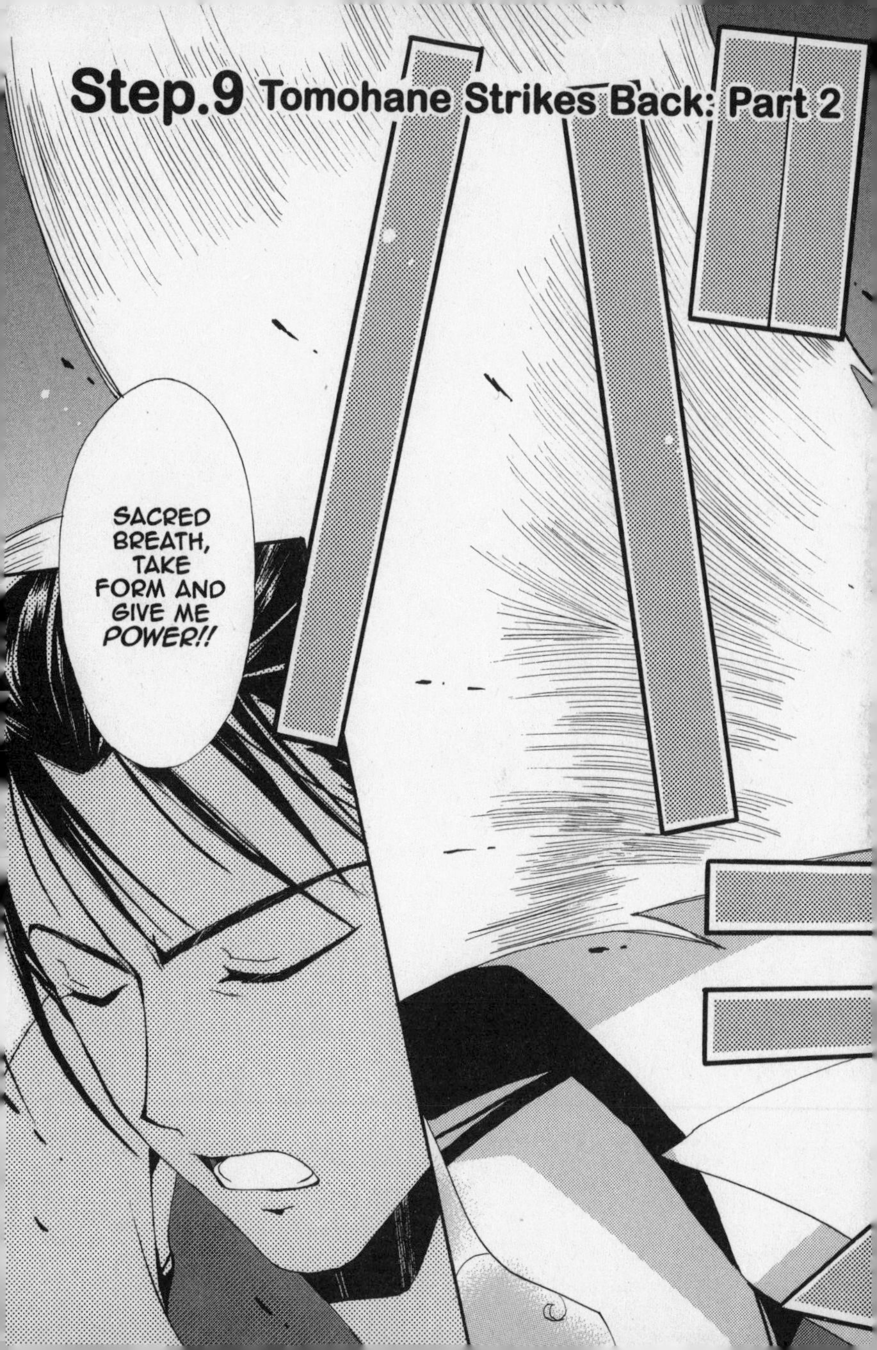
SACRED BREATH, TAKE FORM AND GIVE ME POWER!!

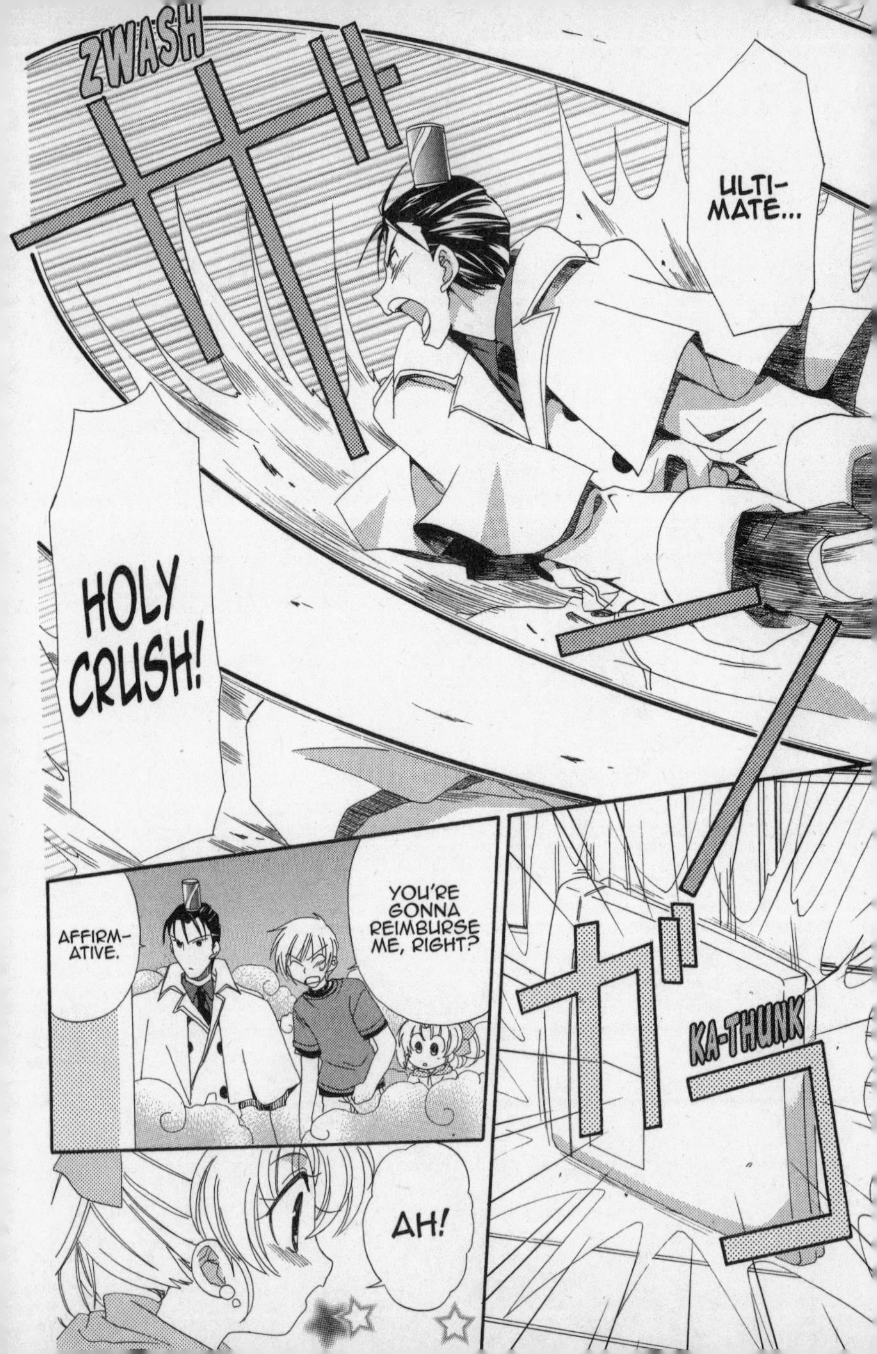
ULTI-
MATE...
ZWASH
HOLY CRUSH!
KA-THUNK
YOU'RE GONNA REIMBURSE ME, RIGHT?
AFFIRM-
ATIVE.
AH!

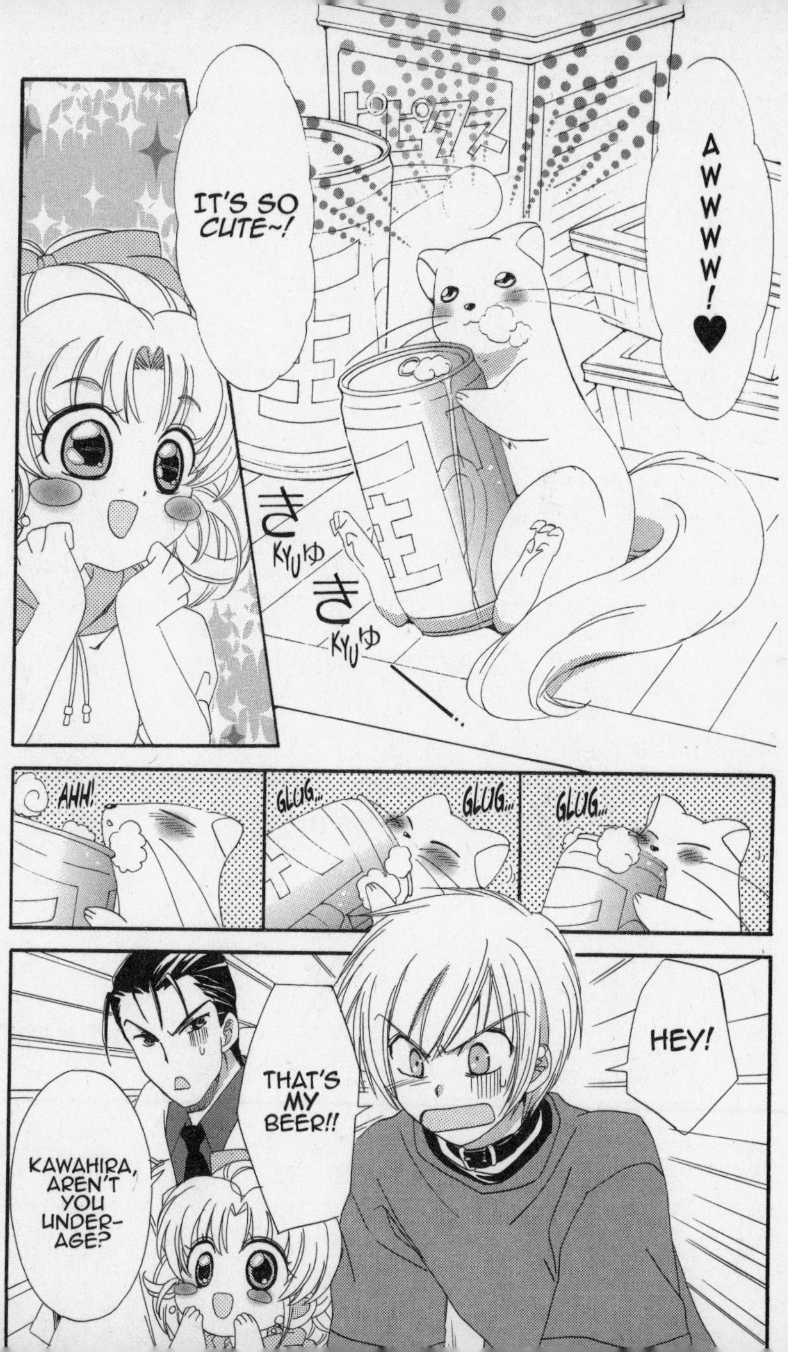
AWWWWW! ♥
IT'S SO CUTE~!
きゅ KYU
きゅ KYU
GLUG...
GLUG...
GLUG...
AHH!
HEY!
THAT'S MY BEER!!
KAWAHIRA, AREN'T YOU UNDER-AGE?

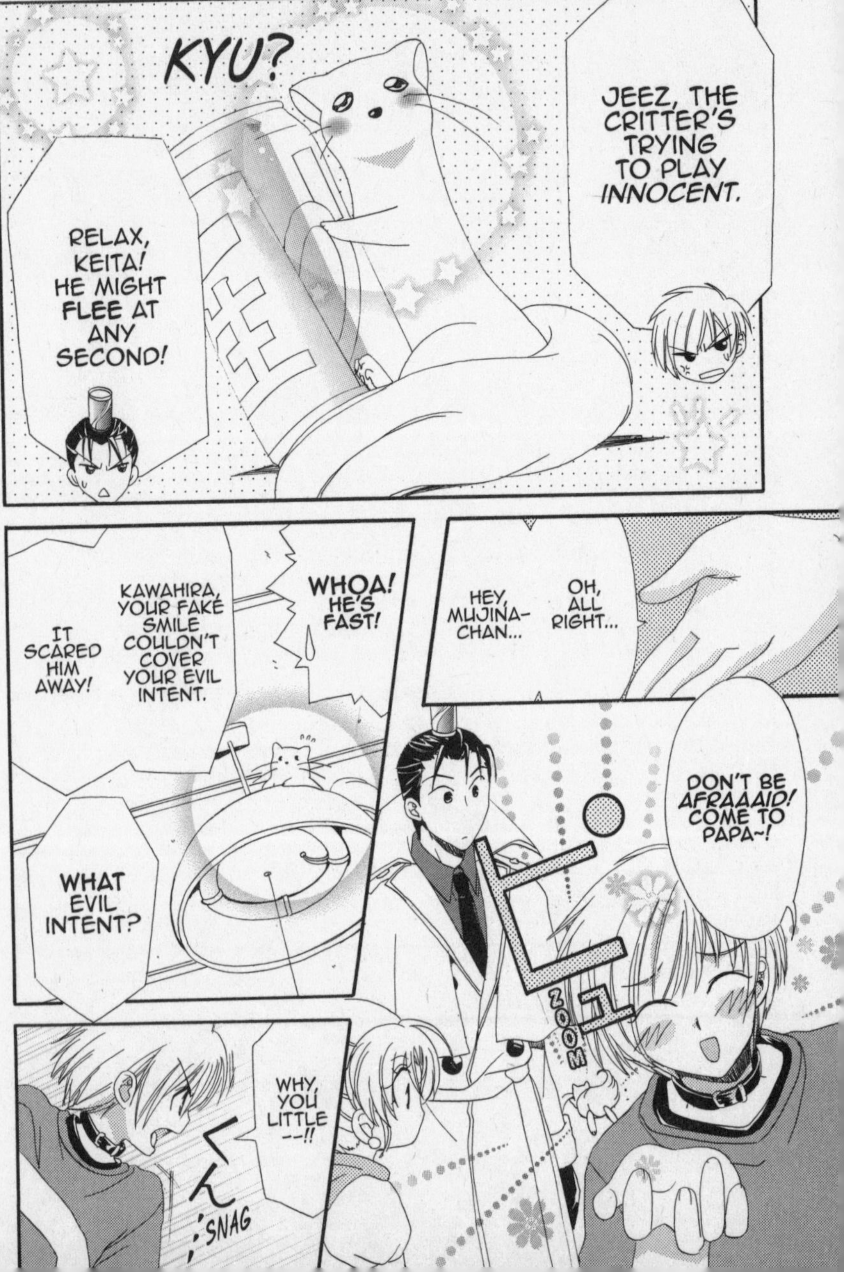
JEEZ, THE CRITTER'S TRYING TO PLAY INNOCENT.
KYU?
RELAX, KEITA! HE MIGHT FLEE AT ANY SECOND!
OH, ALL RIGHT...
HEY, MUJINA-CHAN...
DON'T BE AFRAAAID! COME TO PAPA~!
ZOOM
WHOA! HE'S FAST!
KAWAHIRA, YOUR FAKE SMILE COULDN'T COVER YOUR EVIL INTENT.
IT SCARED HIM AWAY!
WHAT EVIL INTENT?
WHY, YOU LITTLE --!!
SNAG

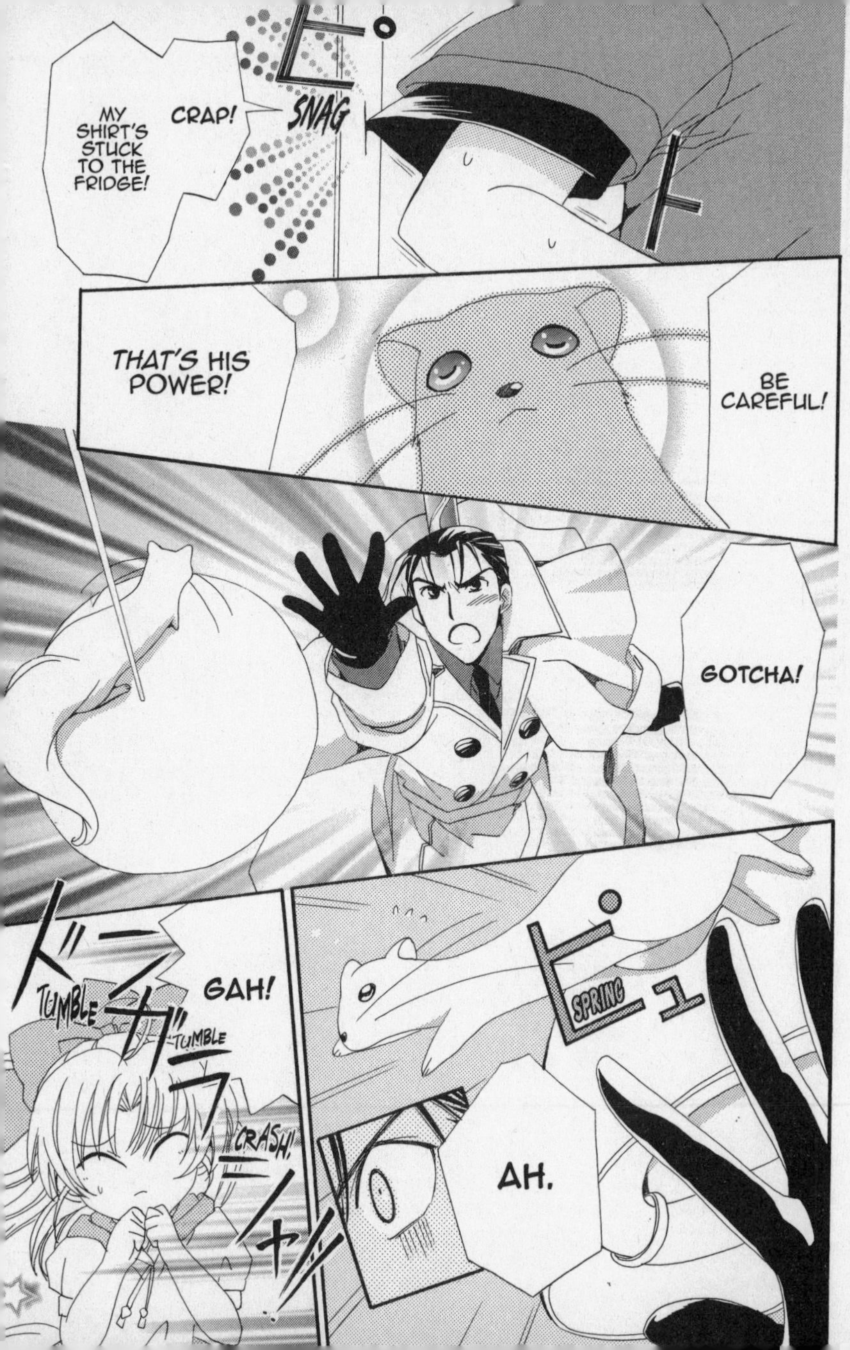
SNAG
CRAP!
MY SHIRT'S STUCK TO THE FRIDGE!
BE CAREFUL!
THAT'S HIS POWER!
GOTCHA!
SPRING
AH.
GAH!
TUMBLE
TUMBLE
CRASH!

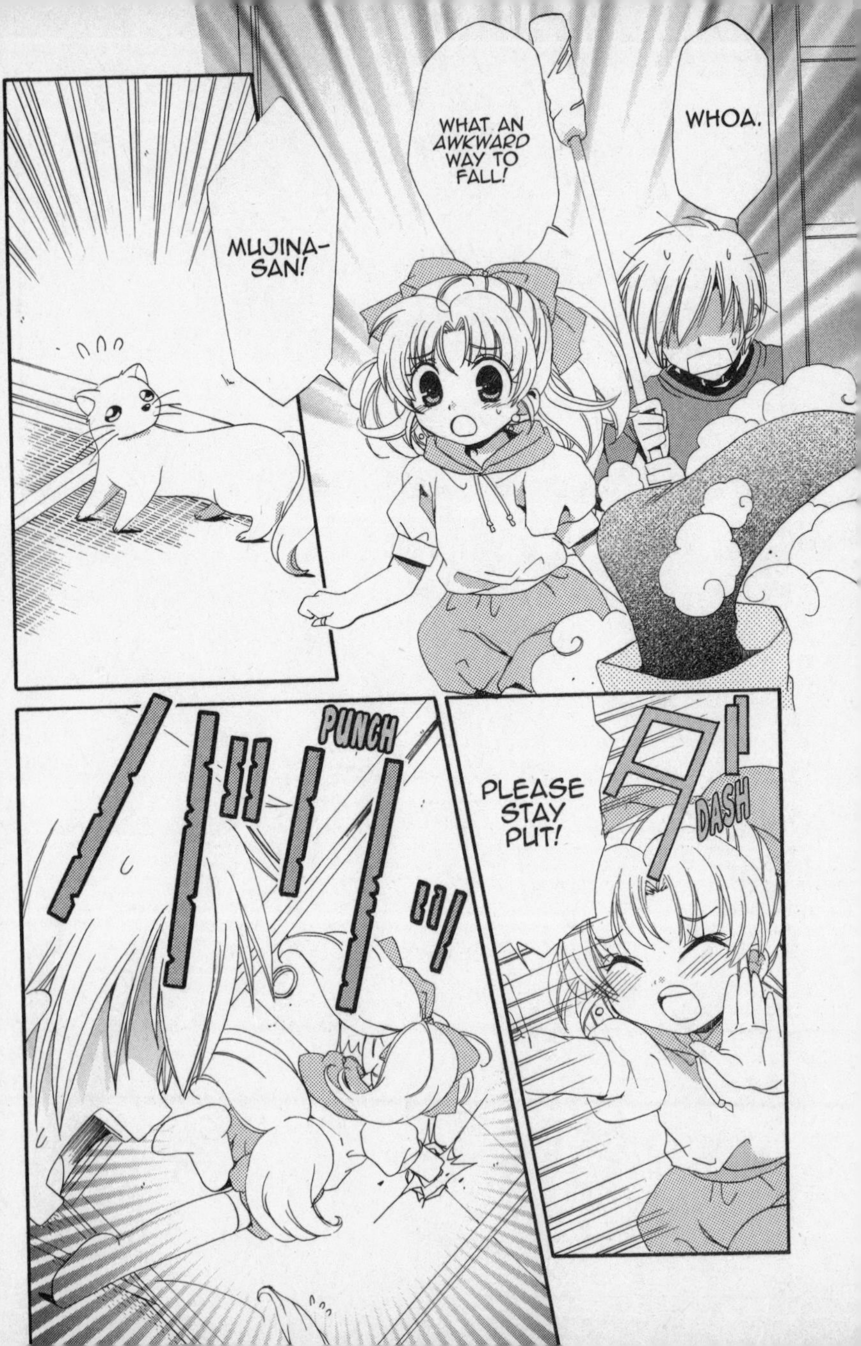
WHOA.
WHAT AN AWKWARD WAY TO FALL!
MUJINA-SAN!
PLEASE STAY PUT!
DASH
PUNCH

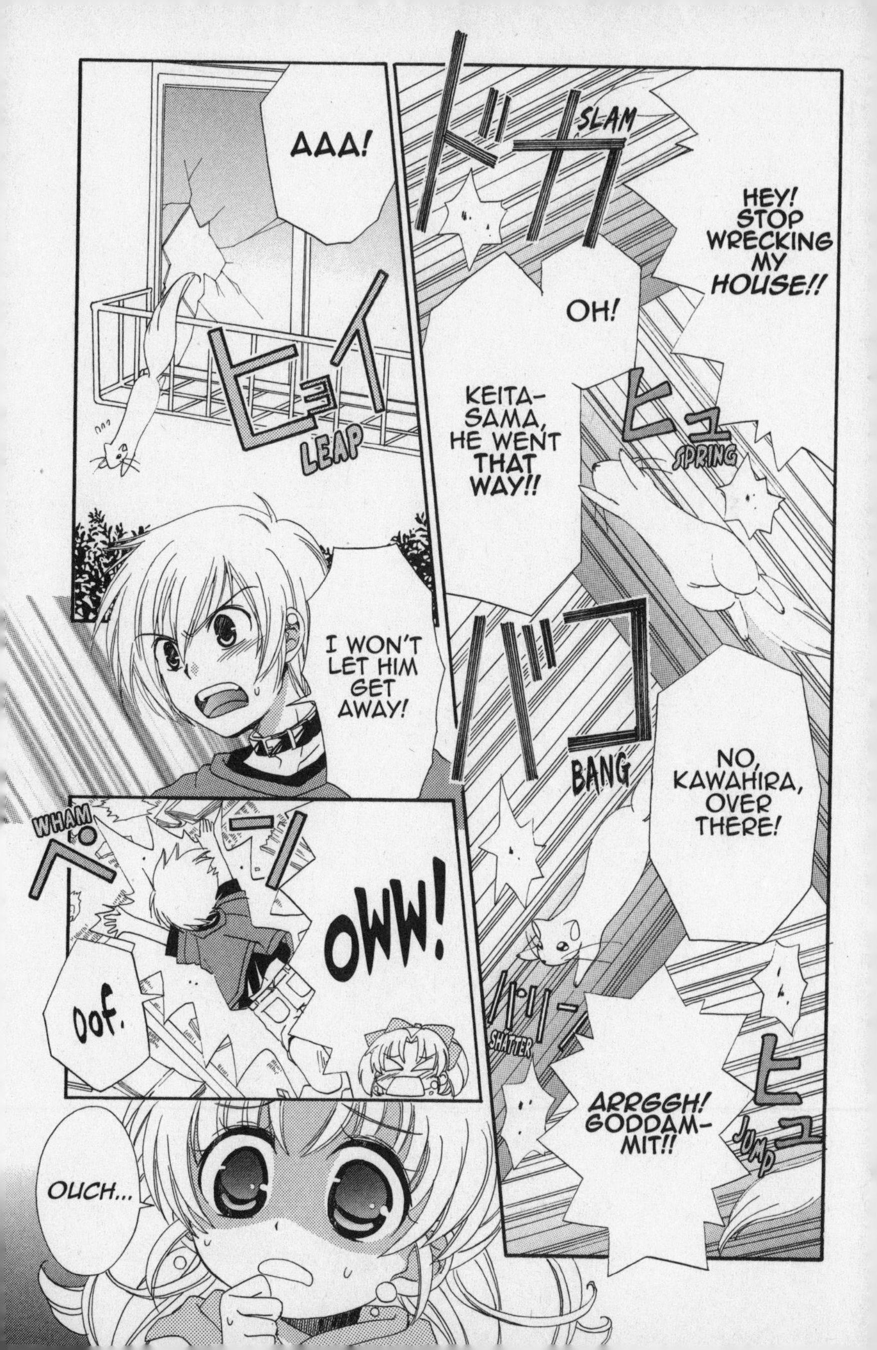
SLAM
HEY! STOP WRECKING MY HOUSE!!
OH!
KEITA-SAMA, HE WENT THAT WAY!!
SPRING
BANG
NO, KAWAHIRA, OVER THERE!
SHATTER
ARRGGH! GODDAM-MIT!!
JUMP
AAA!
LEAP
I WON'T LET HIM GET AWAY!
WHAM
OWW!
Oof.
OUCH...

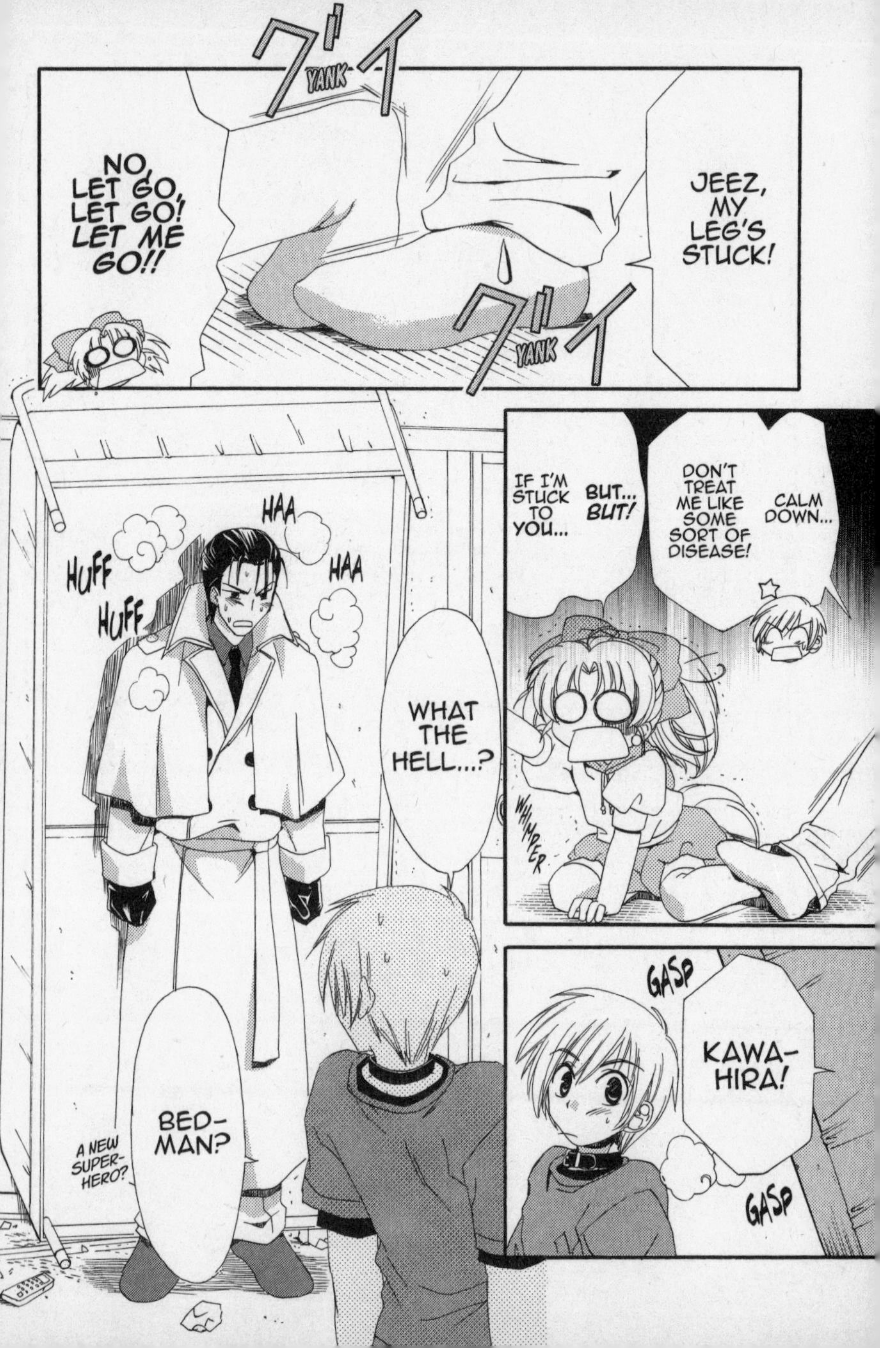
YANK
JEEZ, MY LEG'S STUCK!
NO, LET GO, LET GO! LET ME GO!!
YANK
CALM DOWN...
DON'T TREAT ME LIKE SOME SORT OF DISEASE!
BUT... BUT!
IF I'M STUCK TO YOU...
WHIMPER
GASP
KAWA-HIRA!
GASP
HAA
HAA
HUFF
HUFF
WHAT THE HELL...?
BED-MAN?
A NEW SUPER-HERO?

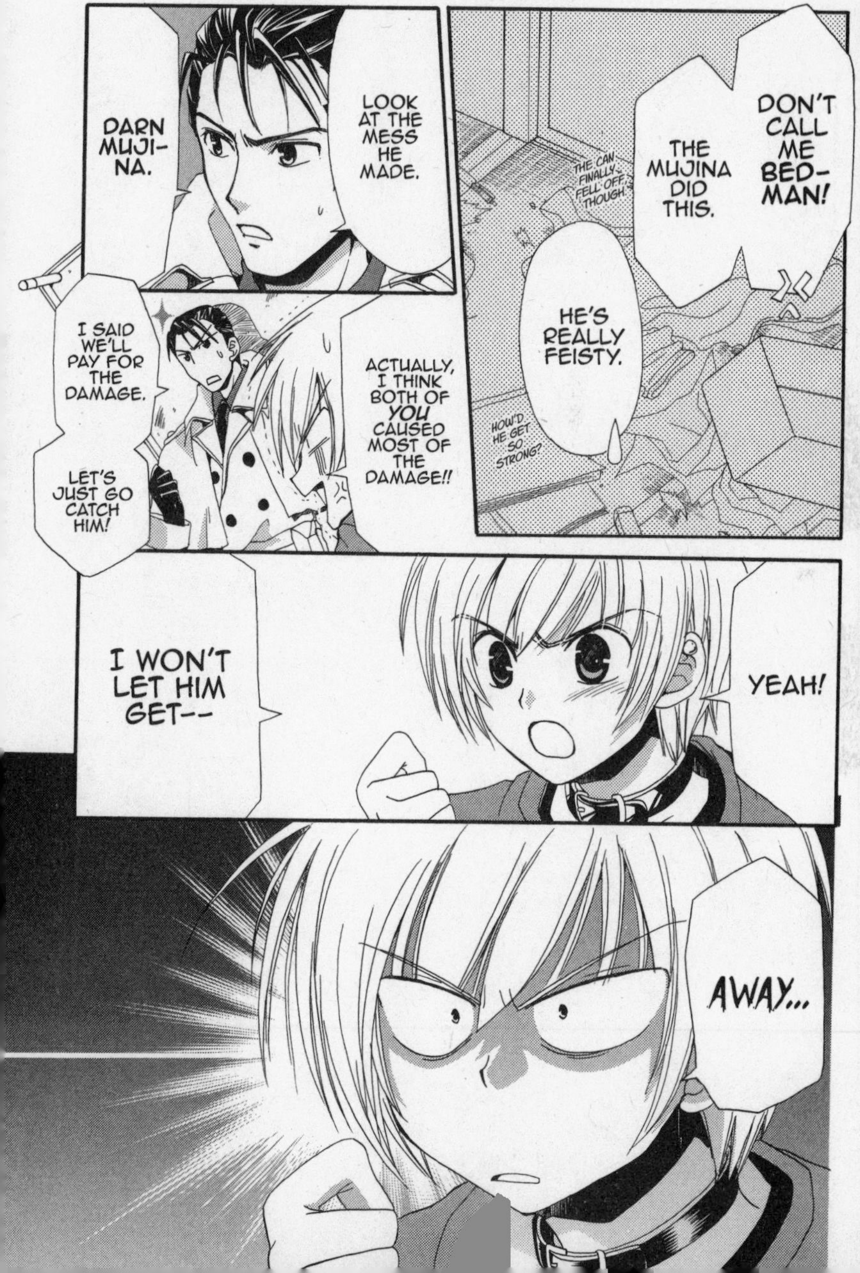
DON'T CALL ME BED-MAN!
THE MUJINA DID THIS.
THE CAN FINALLY FELL OFF, THOUGH.
HE'S REALLY FEISTY.
HOW'D HE GET SO STRONG?
LOOK AT THE MESS HE MADE.
DARN MUJINA.
ACTUALLY, I THINK BOTH OF YOU CAUSED MOST OF THE DAMAGE!!
I SAID WE'LL PAY FOR THE DAMAGE.
LET'S JUST GO CATCH HIM!
YEAH!
I WON'T LET HIM GET--
AWAY...

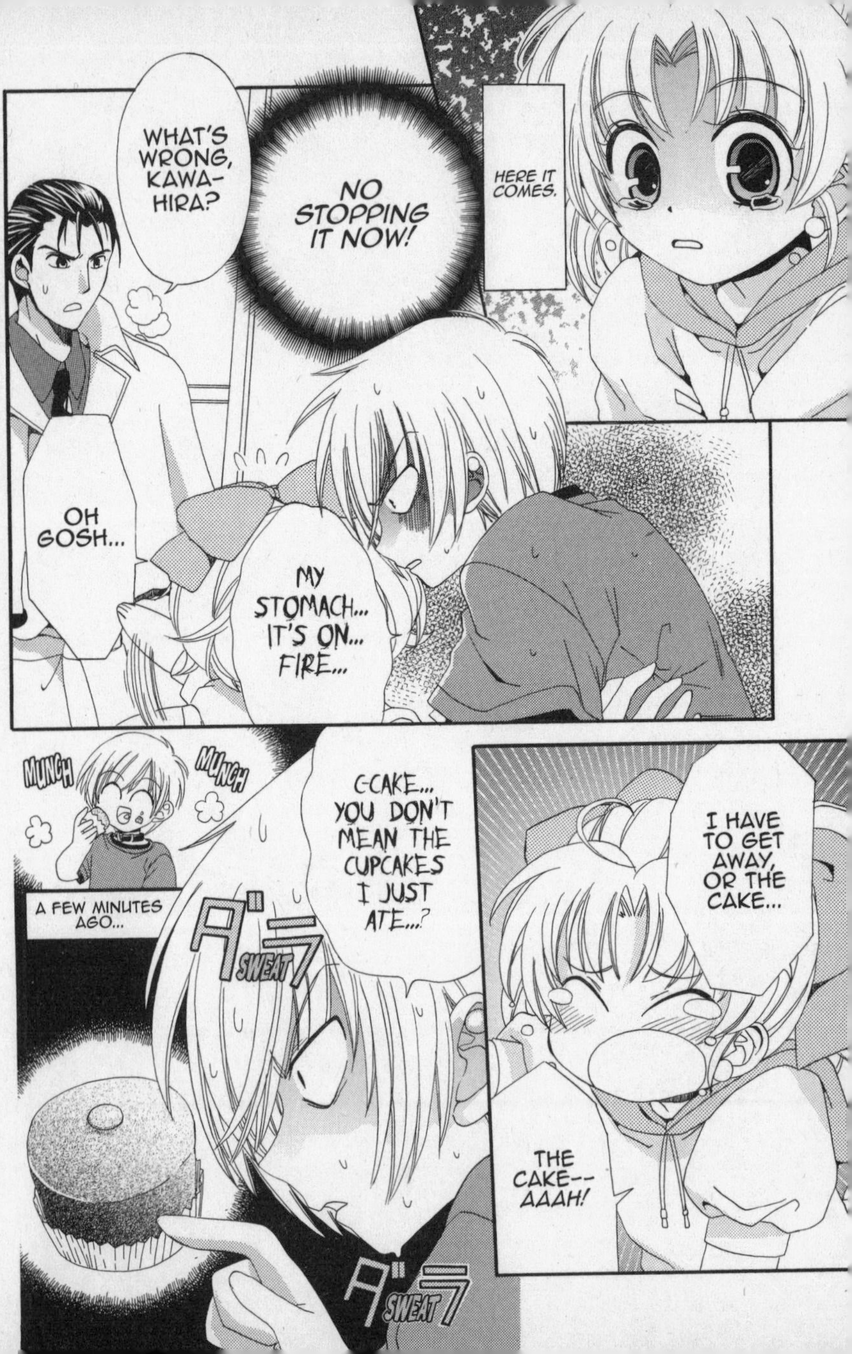
HERE IT COMES.
NO STOPPING IT NOW!
WHAT'S WRONG, KAWA-HIRA?
MY STOMACH... IT'S ON... FIRE...
OH GOSH...
I HAVE TO GET AWAY, OR THE CAKE...
THE CAKE--AAAH!
C-CAKE... YOU DON'T MEAN THE CUPCAKES I JUST ATE...?
MUNCH
MUNCH
A FEW MINUTES AGO...
SWEAT
SWEAT

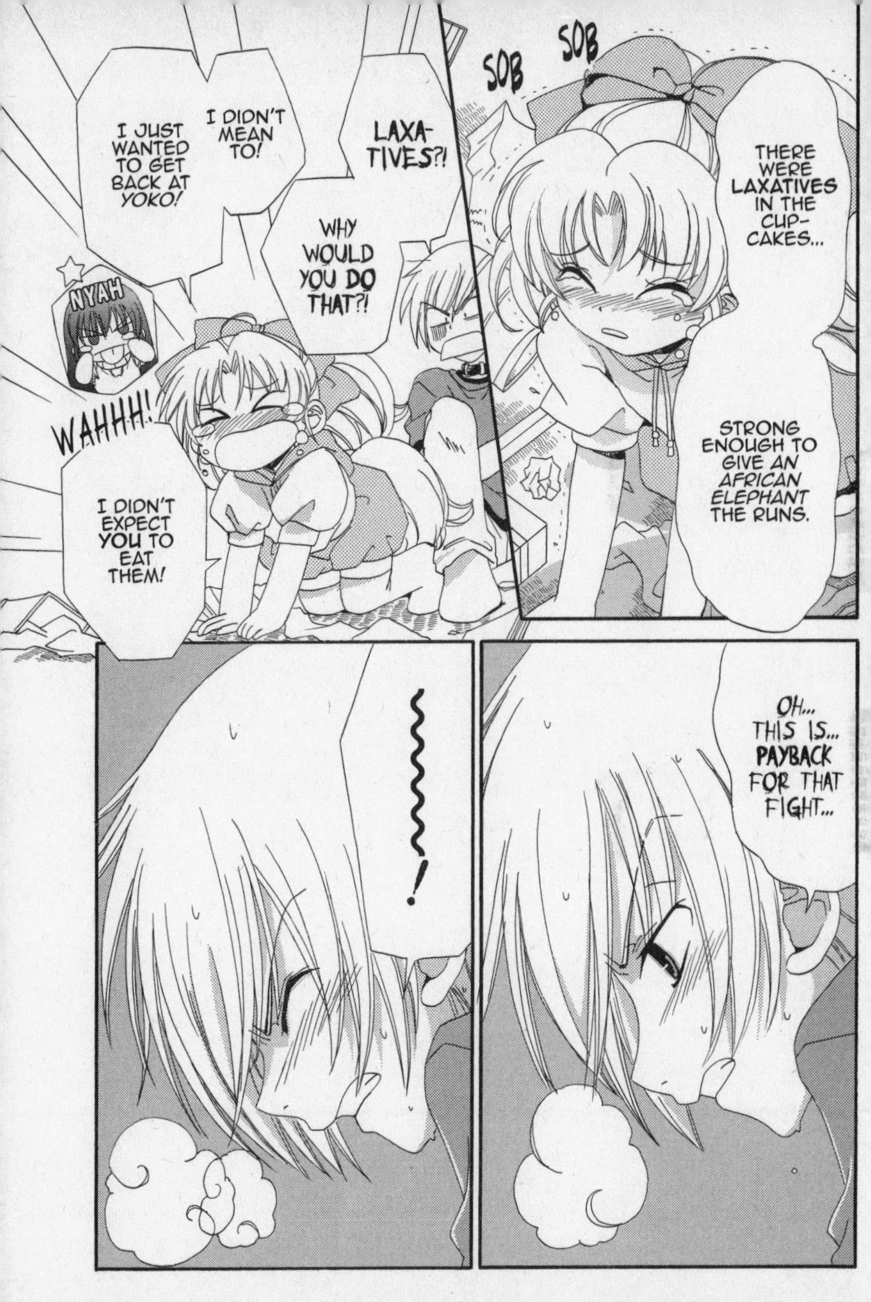
SOB
SOB
THERE WERE LAXATIVES IN THE CUP-CAKES...
STRONG ENOUGH TO GIVE AN AFRICAN ELEPHANT THE RUNS.
LAXA-TIVES?!
WHY WOULD YOU DO THAT?!
I DIDN'T MEAN TO!
I JUST WANTED TO GET BACK AT YOKO!
NYAH
WAHHH!
I DIDN'T EXPECT YOU TO EAT THEM!
OH... THIS IS... PAYBACK FOR THAT FIGHT...
~~~~!
~~~~

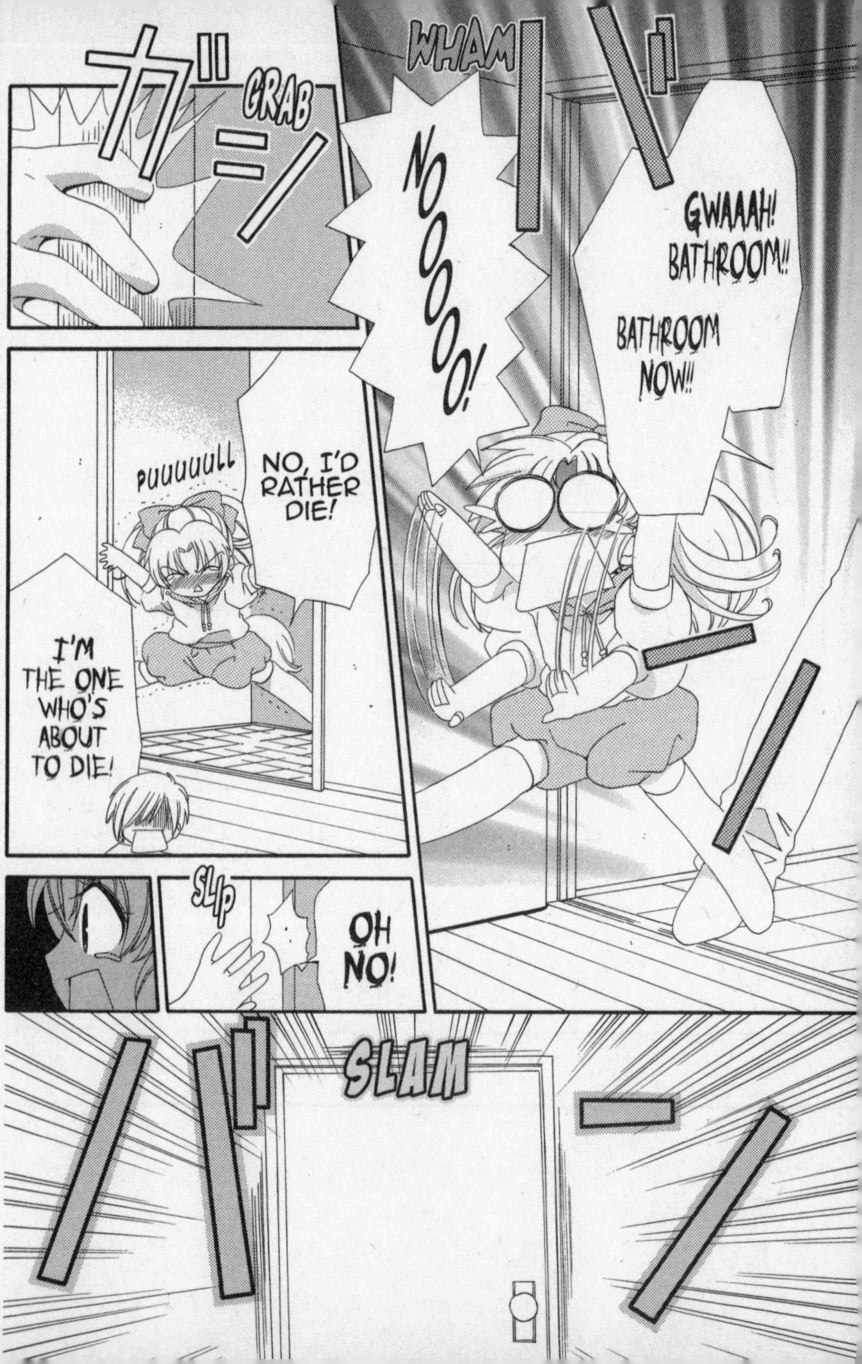
WHAM
GWAAAH! BATHROOM!!
BATHROOM NOW!!
NOOOOOO!
GRAB
NO, I'D RATHER DIE!
PUUUUULL
I'M THE ONE WHO'S ABOUT TO DIE!
OH NO!
SLIP
SLAM

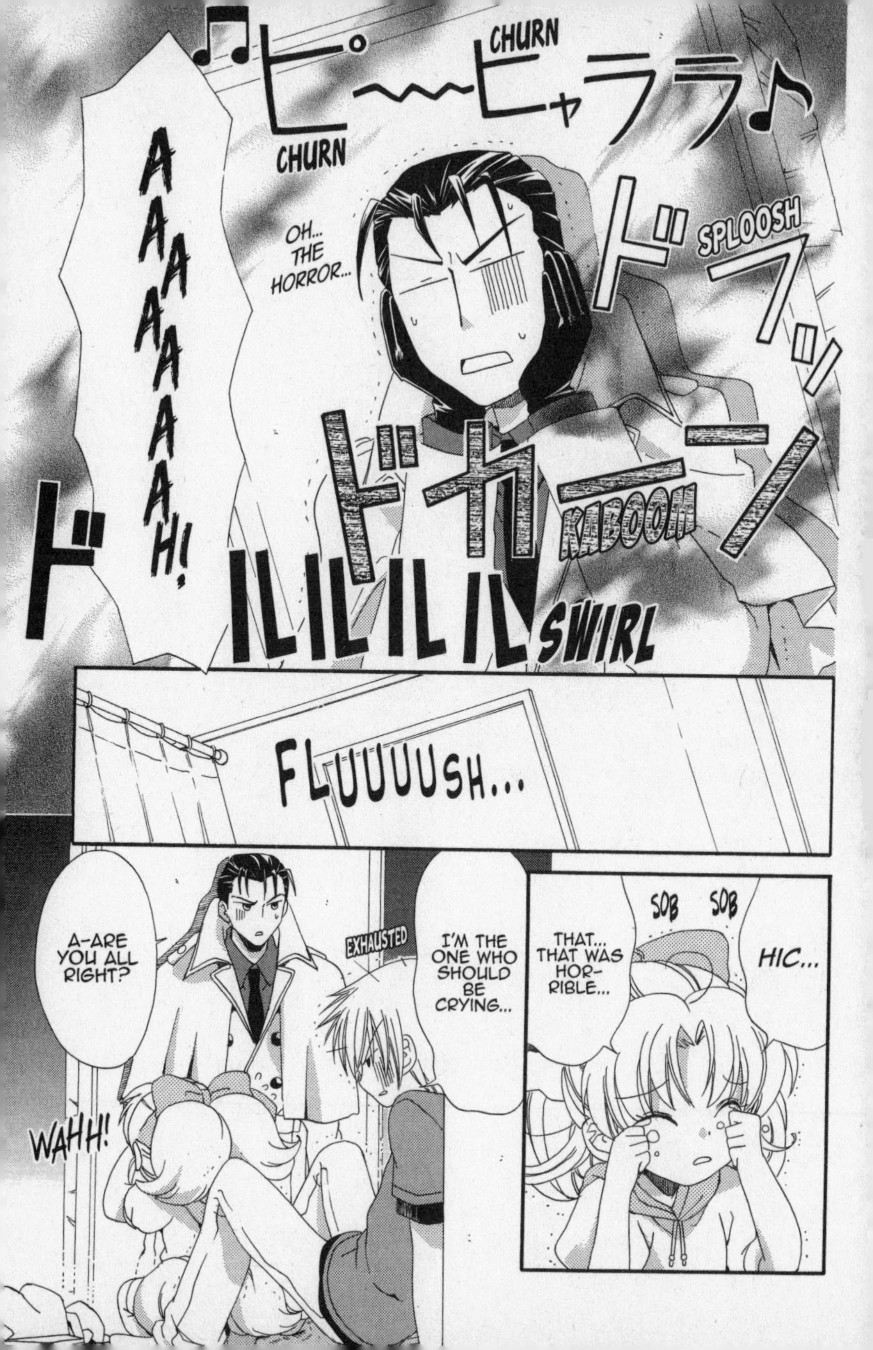

♫ピ〜〜ヒャララ♪
CHURN
CHURN
SPLOOSH
ドフッ
OH... THE HORROR...
ドガーン
KABOOM
AAAAAAAH!
ド
ルルルル
SWIRL
FLUUUUSH...
SOB SOB
HIC...
THAT... THAT WAS HOR-RIBLE...
I'M THE ONE WHO SHOULD BE CRYING...
EXHAUSTED
A-ARE YOU ALL RIGHT?
WAHH!

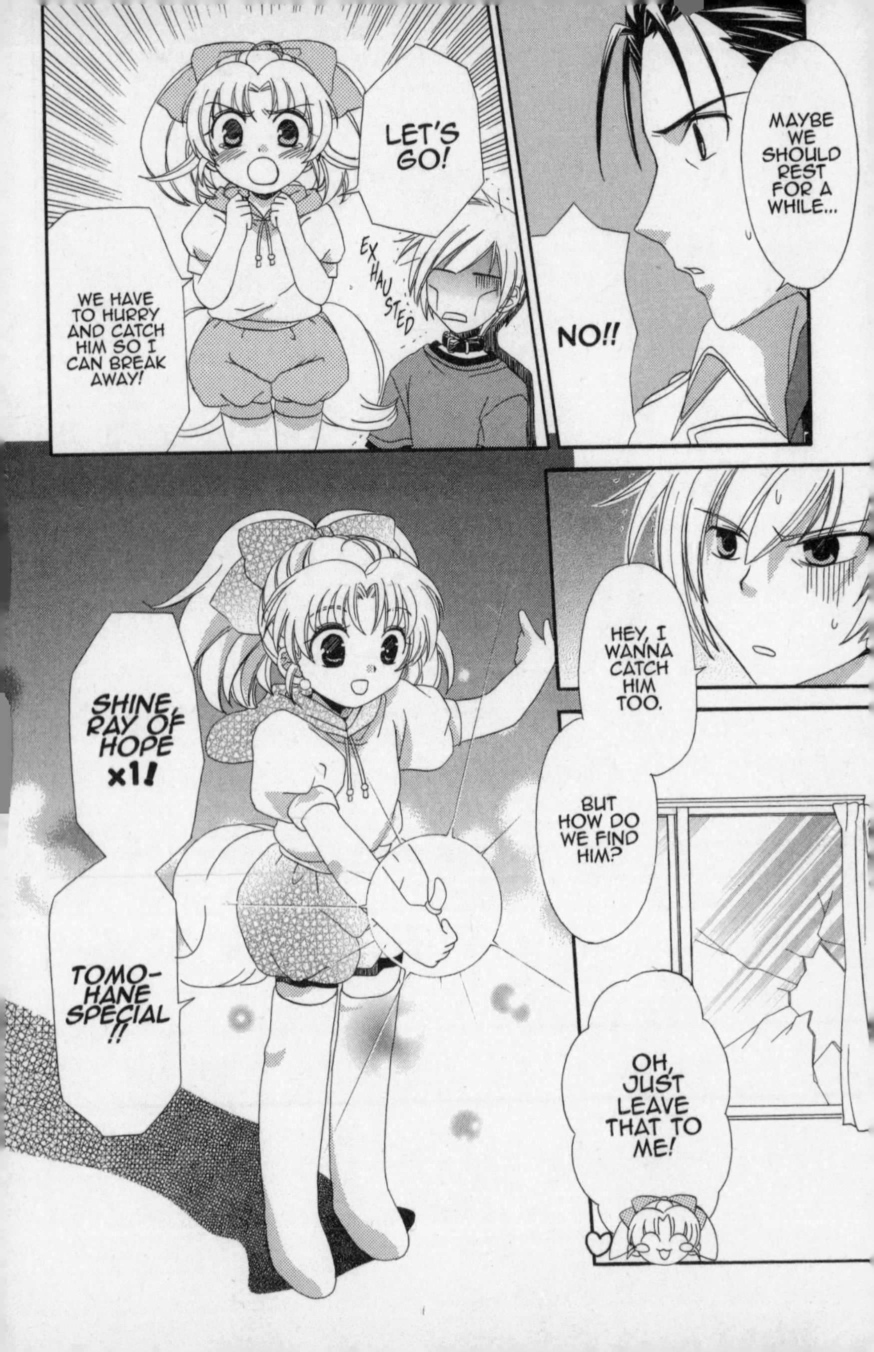
MAYBE WE SHOULD REST FOR A WHILE...
NO!!
LET'S GO!
EXHAUSTED
WE HAVE TO HURRY AND CATCH HIM SO I CAN BREAK AWAY!
HEY, I WANNA CATCH HIM TOO.
BUT HOW DO WE FIND HIM?
OH, JUST LEAVE THAT TO ME!
SHINE, RAY OF HOPE x1!
TOMO-HANE SPECIAL!!

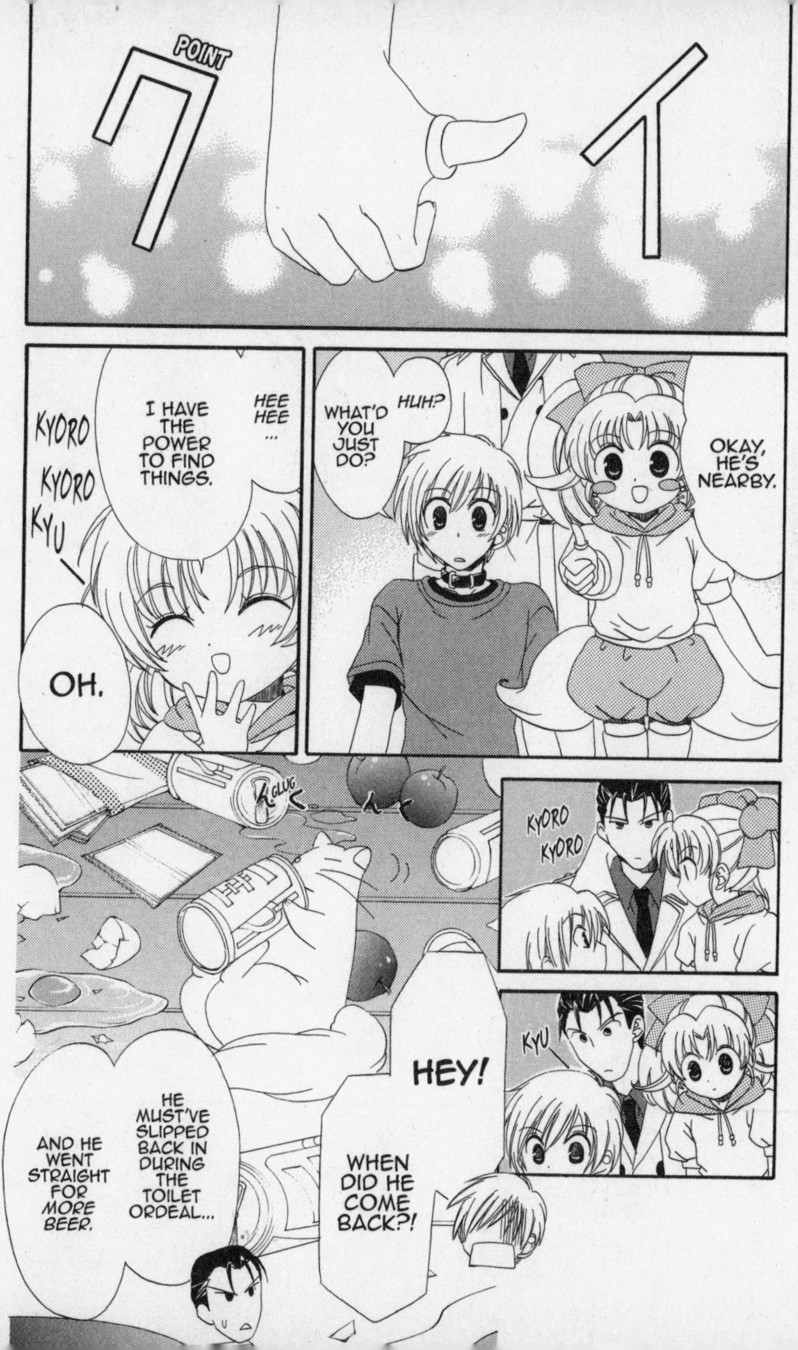
POINT
OKAY, HE'S NEARBY.
HUH?
WHAT'D YOU JUST DO?
HEE HEE ...
I HAVE THE POWER TO FIND THINGS.
KYORO KYORO KYU
OH.
KYORO KYORO
KYU
HEY!
GLUG
WHEN DID HE COME BACK?!
HE MUST'VE SLIPPED BACK IN DURING THE TOILET ORDEAL...
AND HE WENT STRAIGHT FOR MORE BEER.

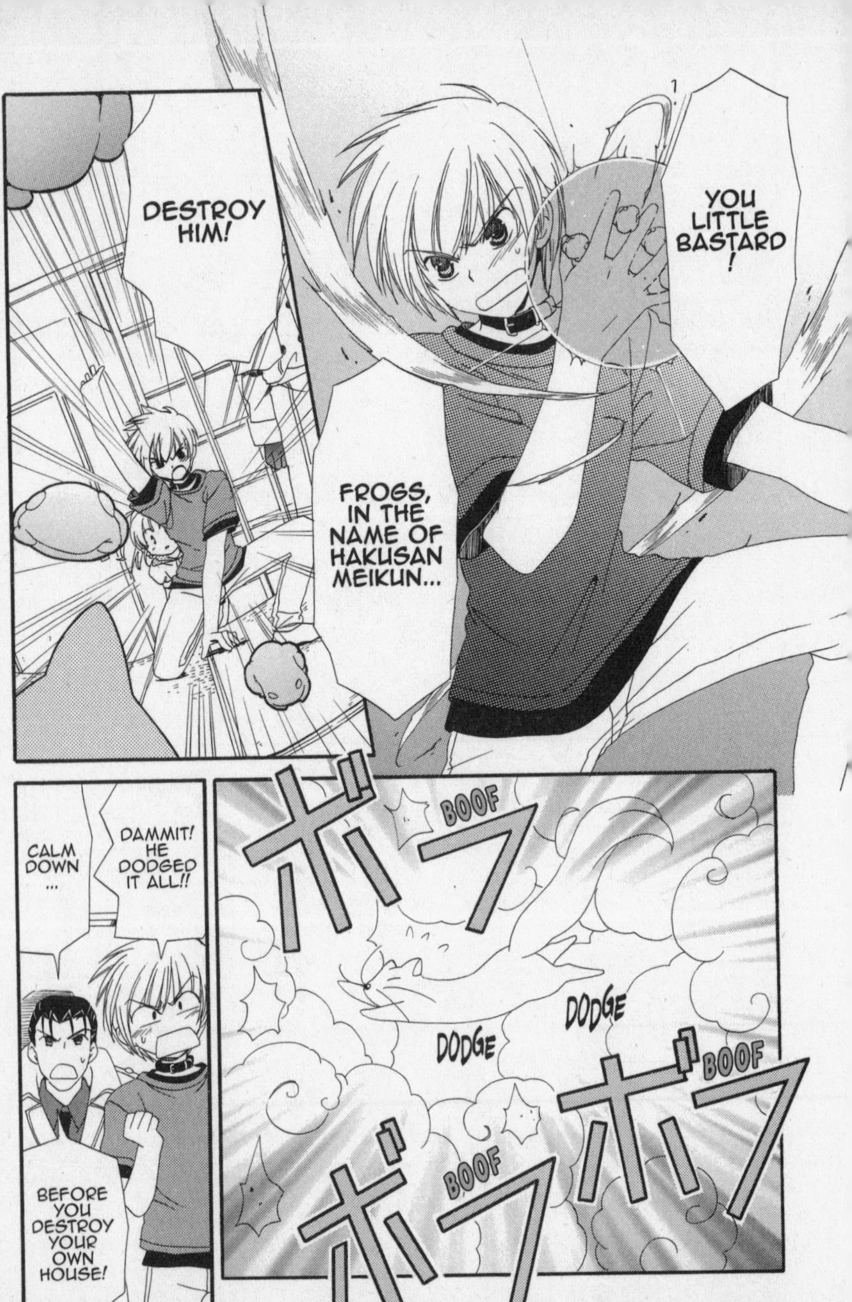
YOU LITTLE BASTARD!
FROGS, IN THE NAME OF HAKUSAN MEIKUN...
DESTROY HIM!
BOOF
DODGE
DODGE
BOOF
BOOF
DAMMIT! HE DODGED IT ALL!!
CALM DOWN...
BEFORE YOU DESTROY YOUR OWN HOUSE!

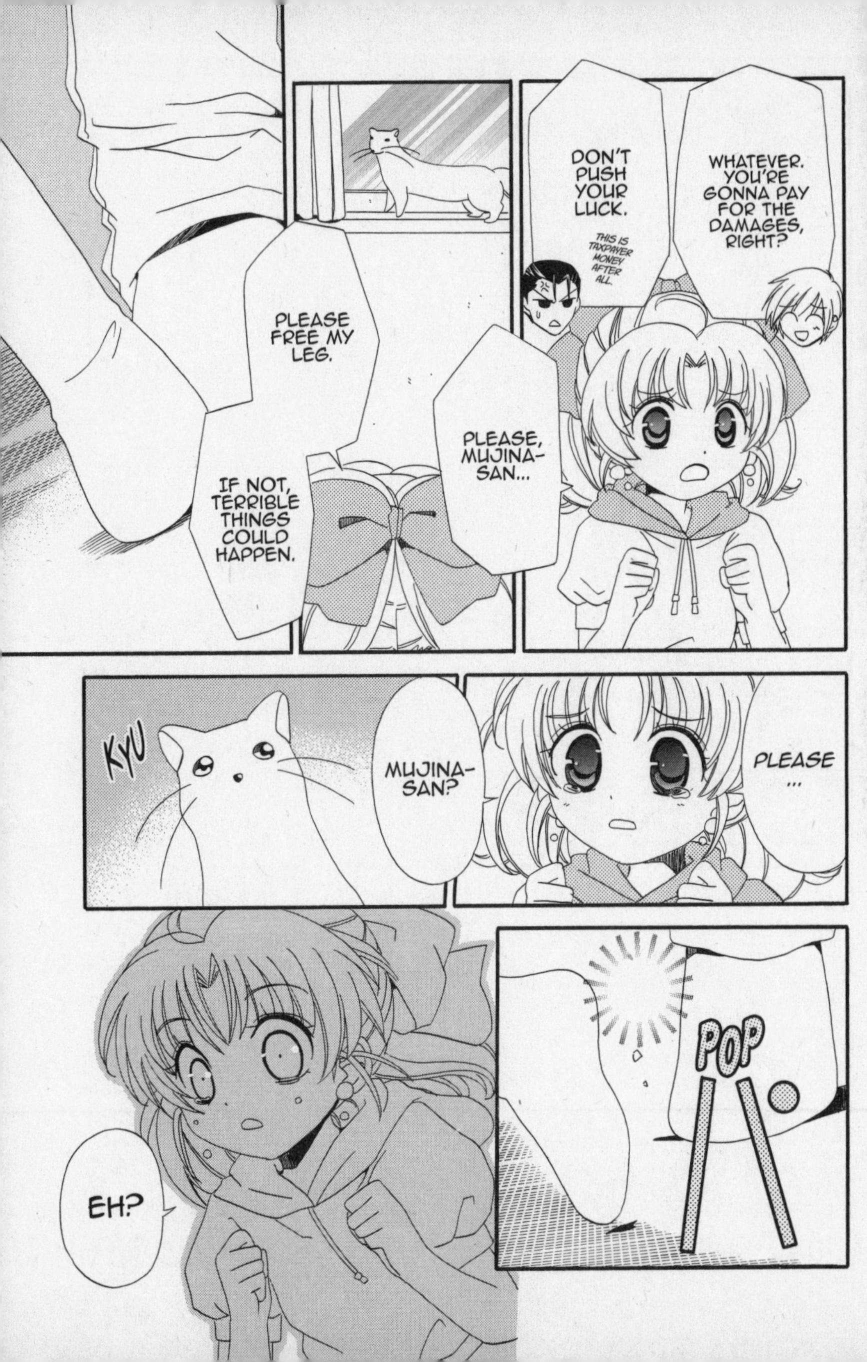
WHATEVER. YOU'RE GONNA PAY FOR THE DAMAGES, RIGHT?
DON'T PUSH YOUR LUCK.
THIS IS TAXPAYER MONEY AFTER ALL.
PLEASE, MUJINA-SAN...
PLEASE FREE MY LEG.
IF NOT, TERRIBLE THINGS COULD HAPPEN.
PLEASE ...
MUJINA-SAN?
KYU
POP
EH?

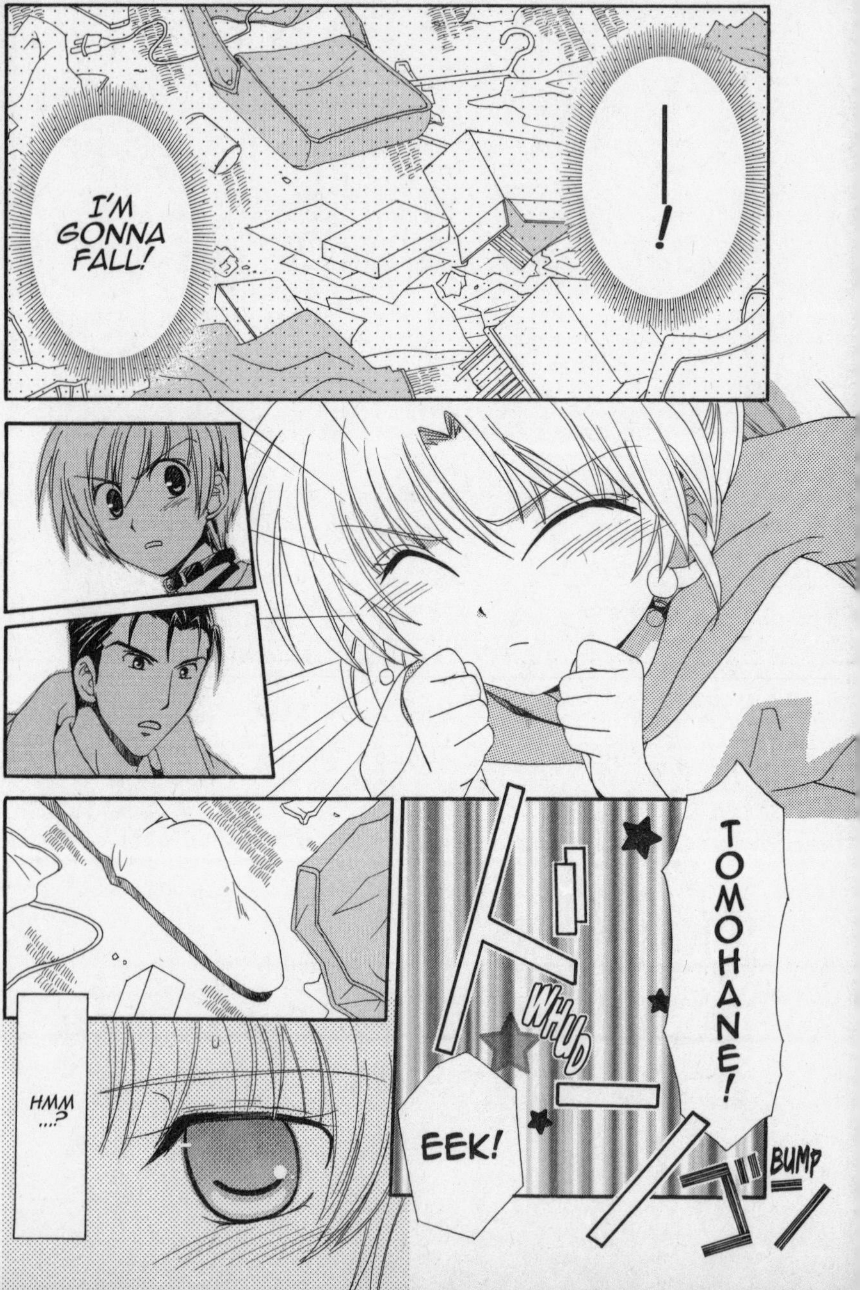
—!
I'M GONNA FALL!
TOMOHANE!
WHUD
EEK!
BUMP
HMM ...?

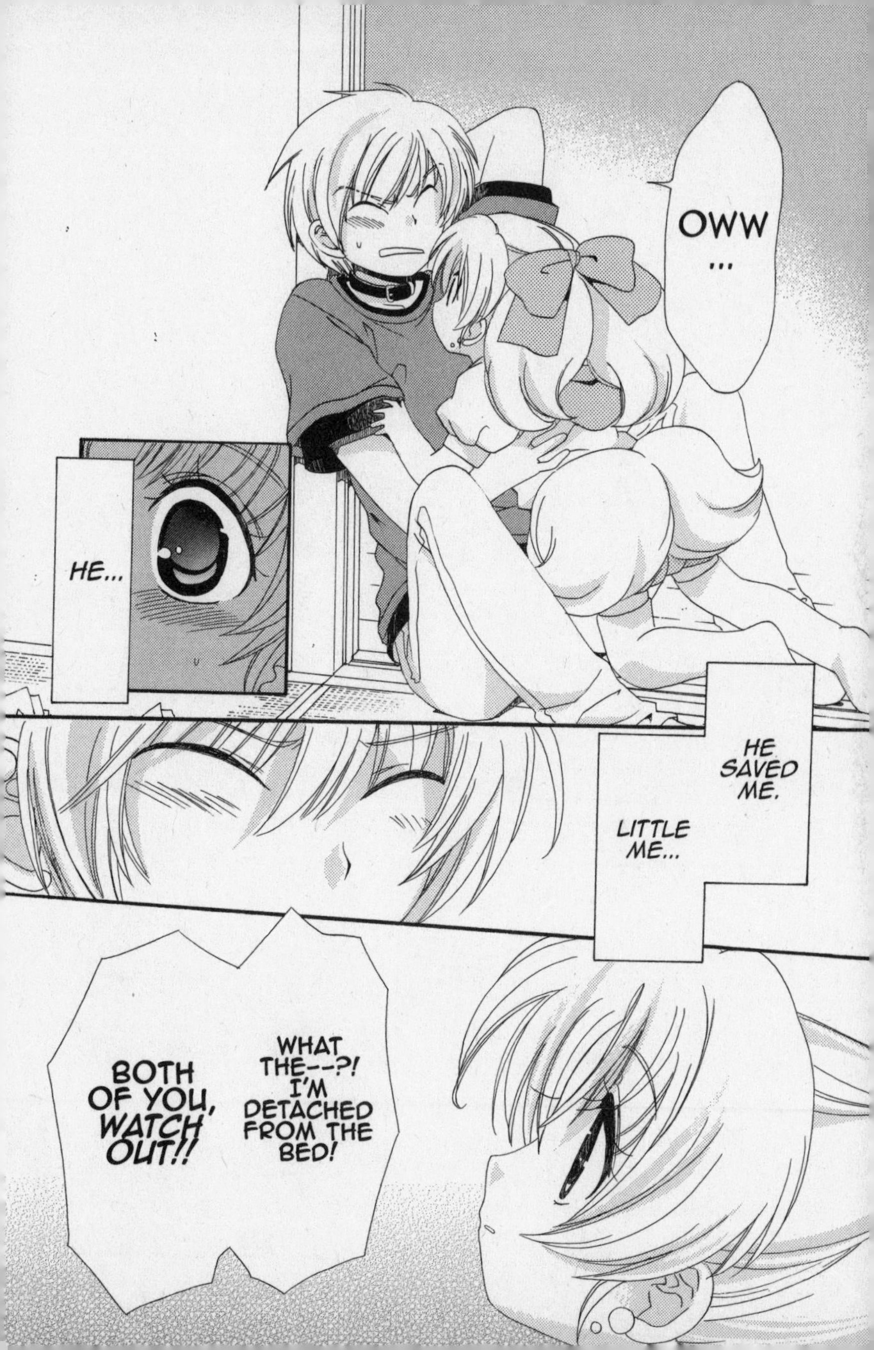
OWW ...
HE...
HE SAVED ME.
LITTLE ME...
WHAT THE--?! I'M DETACHED FROM THE BED!
BOTH OF YOU, WATCH OUT!!

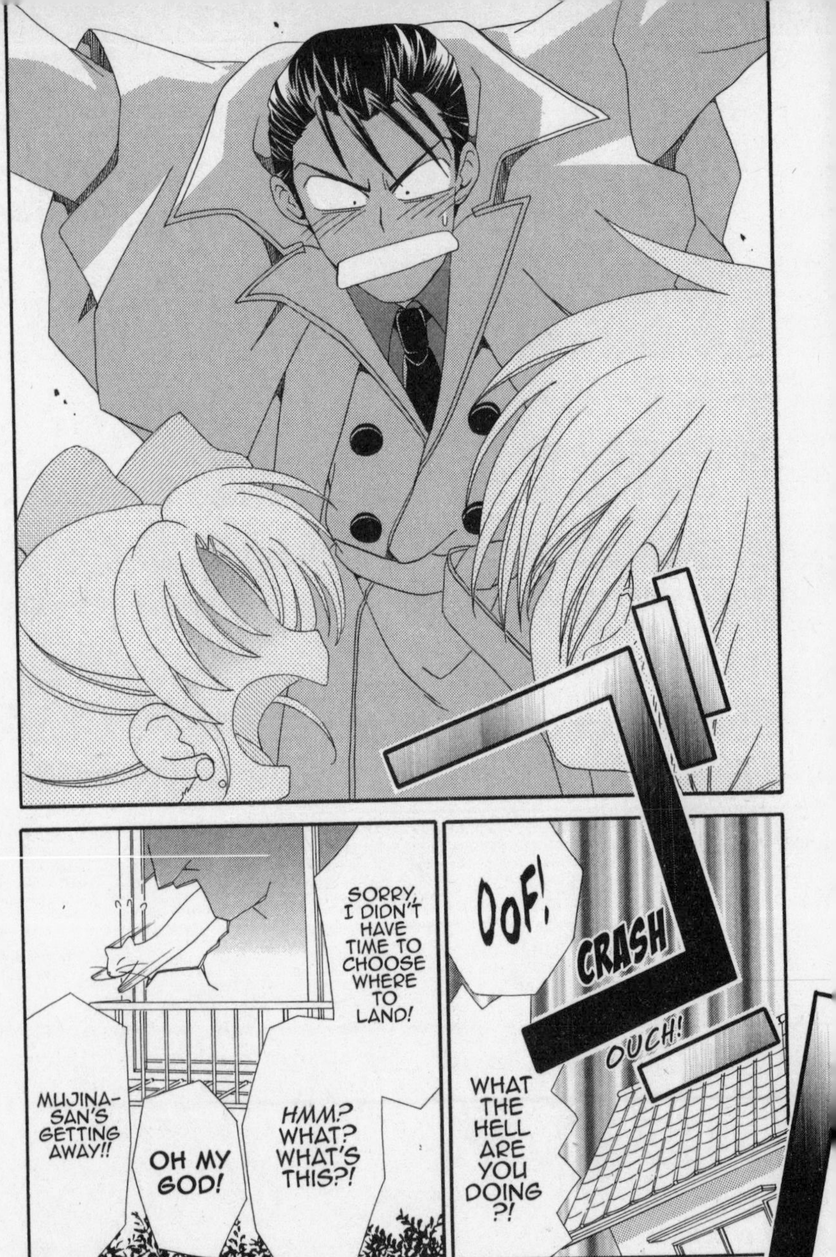
CRASH
OOF!
OUCH!
WHAT THE HELL ARE YOU DOING?!
SORRY, I DIDN'T HAVE TIME TO CHOOSE WHERE TO LAND!
HMM? WHAT? WHAT'S THIS?!
OH MY GOD!
MUJINA-SAN'S GETTING AWAY!!

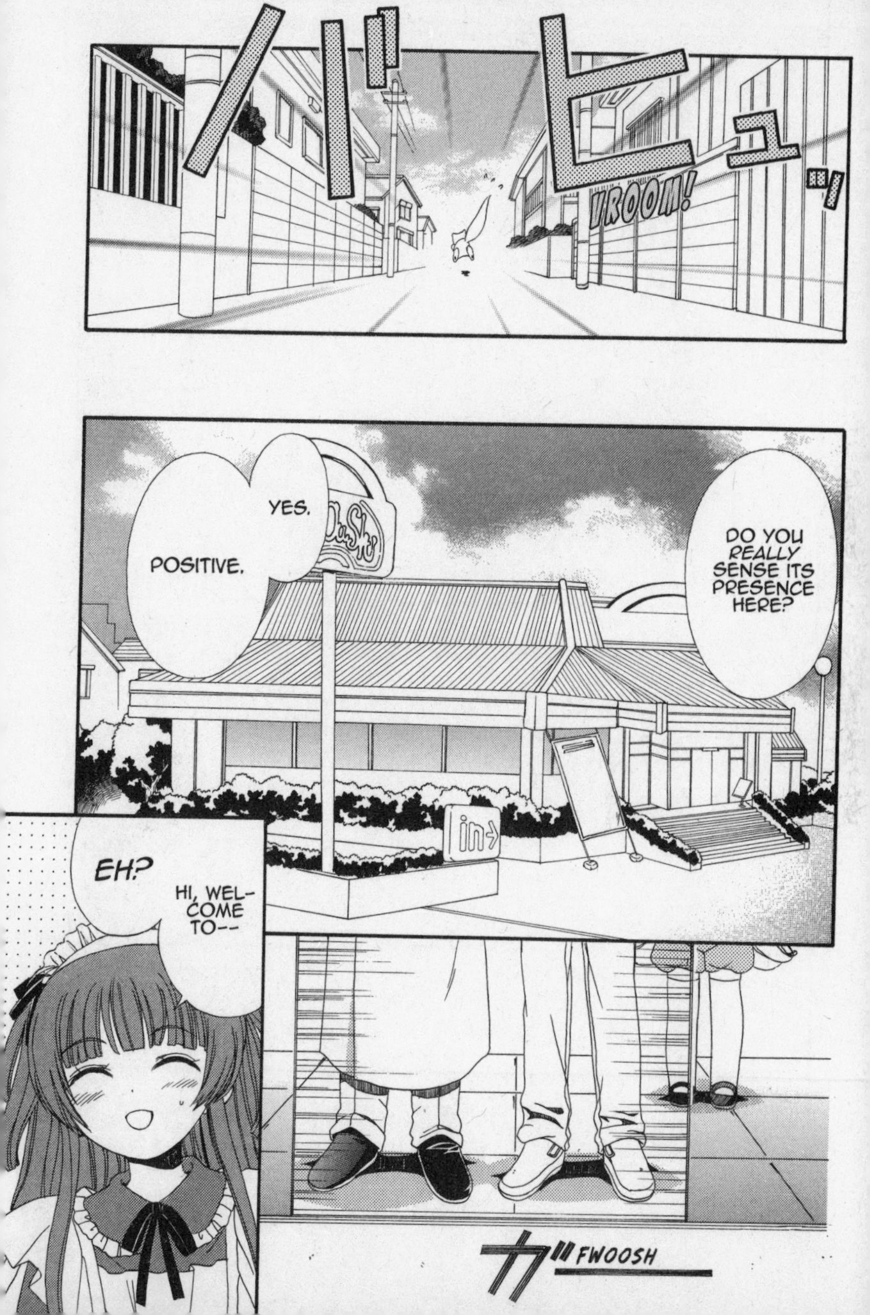
VROOM!
DO YOU REALLY SENSE ITS PRESENCE HERE?
YES.
POSITIVE.
FWOOSH
HI, WELCOME TO--
EH?

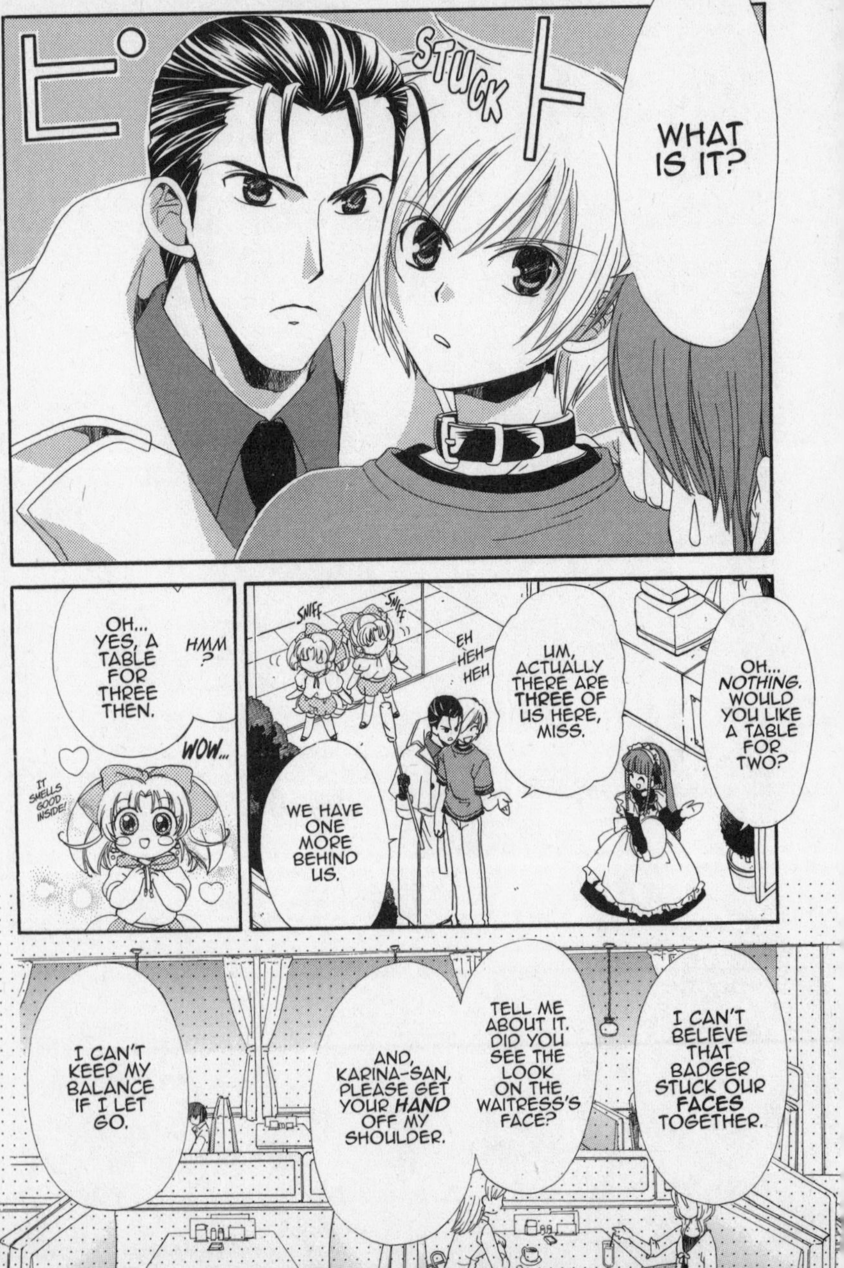

WHAT IS IT?
STUCK
ピト
OH... *NOTHING.* WOULD YOU LIKE A TABLE FOR TWO?
UM, ACTUALLY THERE ARE THREE OF US HERE, MISS.
EH HEH HEH
SNIFF
SNIFF
WE HAVE ONE MORE BEHIND US.
HMM?
OH... YES, A TABLE FOR THREE THEN.
WOW...
IT SMELLS GOOD INSIDE!
I CAN'T BELIEVE THAT BADGER STUCK OUR FACES TOGETHER.
TELL ME ABOUT IT. DID YOU SEE THE LOOK ON THE WAITRESS'S FACE?
AND, KARINA-SAN, PLEASE GET YOUR *HAND* OFF MY SHOULDER.
I CAN'T KEEP MY BALANCE IF I LET GO.

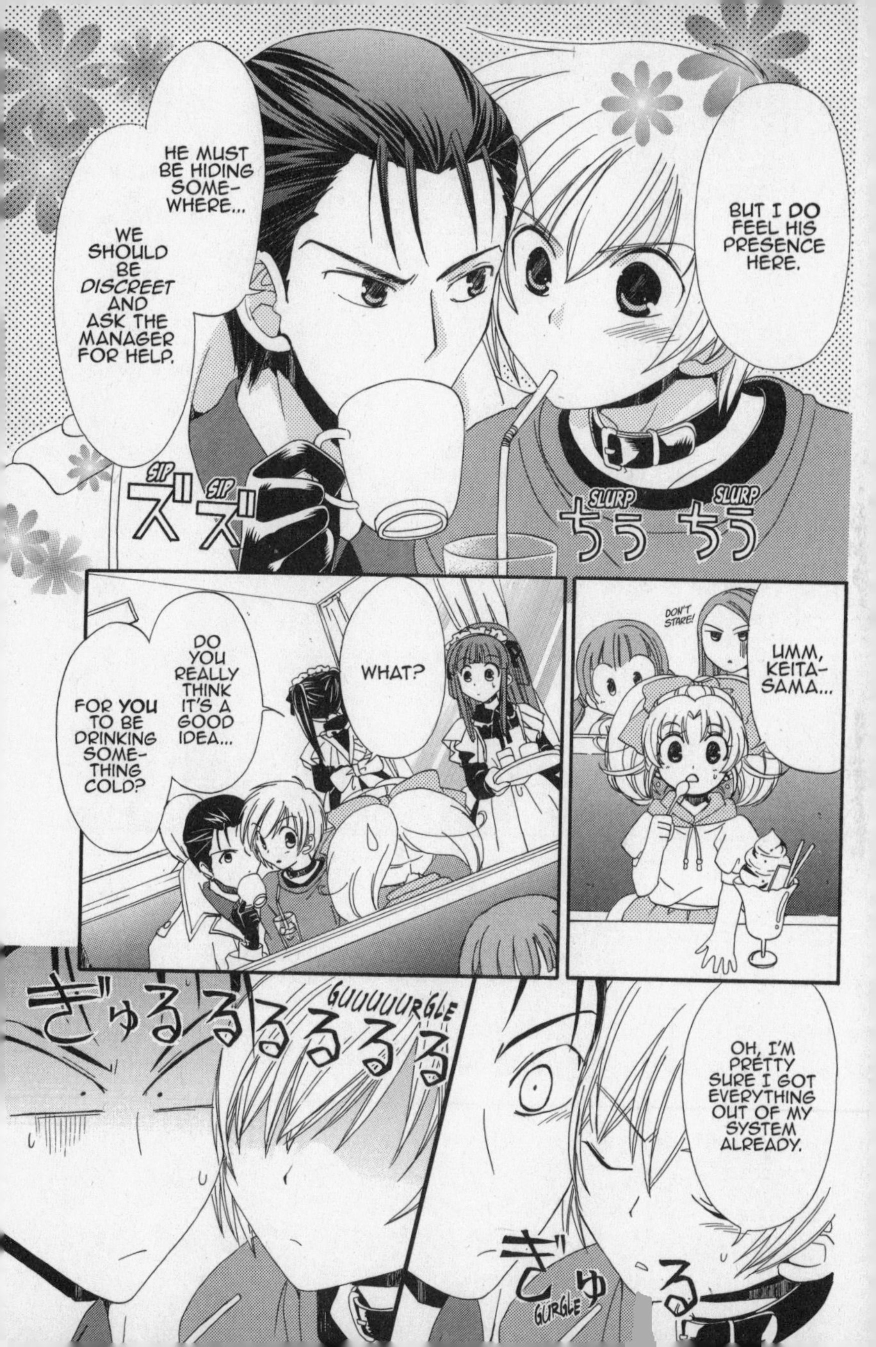
BUT I DO FEEL HIS PRESENCE HERE.
HE MUST BE HIDING SOME-WHERE...
WE SHOULD BE DISCREET AND ASK THE MANAGER FOR HELP.
SLURP SLURP
ちう ちう
SIP SIP
ズズ
UMM, KEITA-SAMA...
DON'T STARE!
WHAT?
DO YOU REALLY THINK IT'S A GOOD IDEA...
FOR YOU TO BE DRINKING SOME-THING COLD?
OH, I'M PRETTY SURE I GOT EVERYTHING OUT OF MY SYSTEM ALREADY.
ぎゅる
GURGLE
ぎゅるるるるるる
GUUUUURGLE

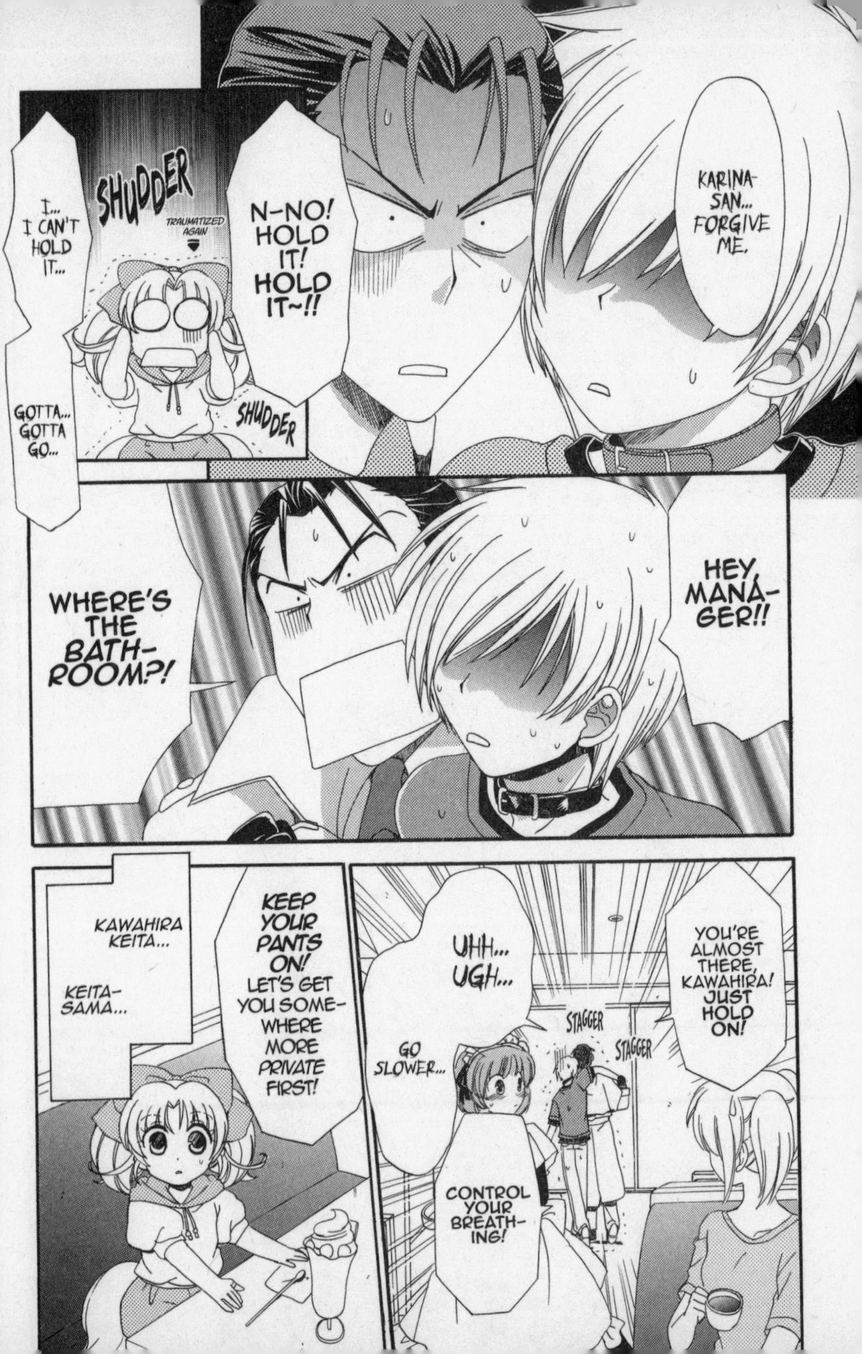
KARINA-SAN... FORGIVE ME.
N-NO! HOLD IT! HOLD IT~!!
SHUDDER
I... I CAN'T HOLD IT...
TRAUMATIZED AGAIN
SHUDDER
GOTTA... GOTTA GO...
HEY MANAGER!!
WHERE'S THE BATHROOM?!
YOU'RE ALMOST THERE, KAWAHIRA! JUST HOLD ON!
STAGGER
STAGGER
UHH... UGH...
GO SLOWER...
CONTROL YOUR BREATHING!
KEEP YOUR PANTS ON! LET'S GET YOU SOMEWHERE MORE PRIVATE FIRST!
KAWAHIRA KEITA...
KEITA-SAMA...

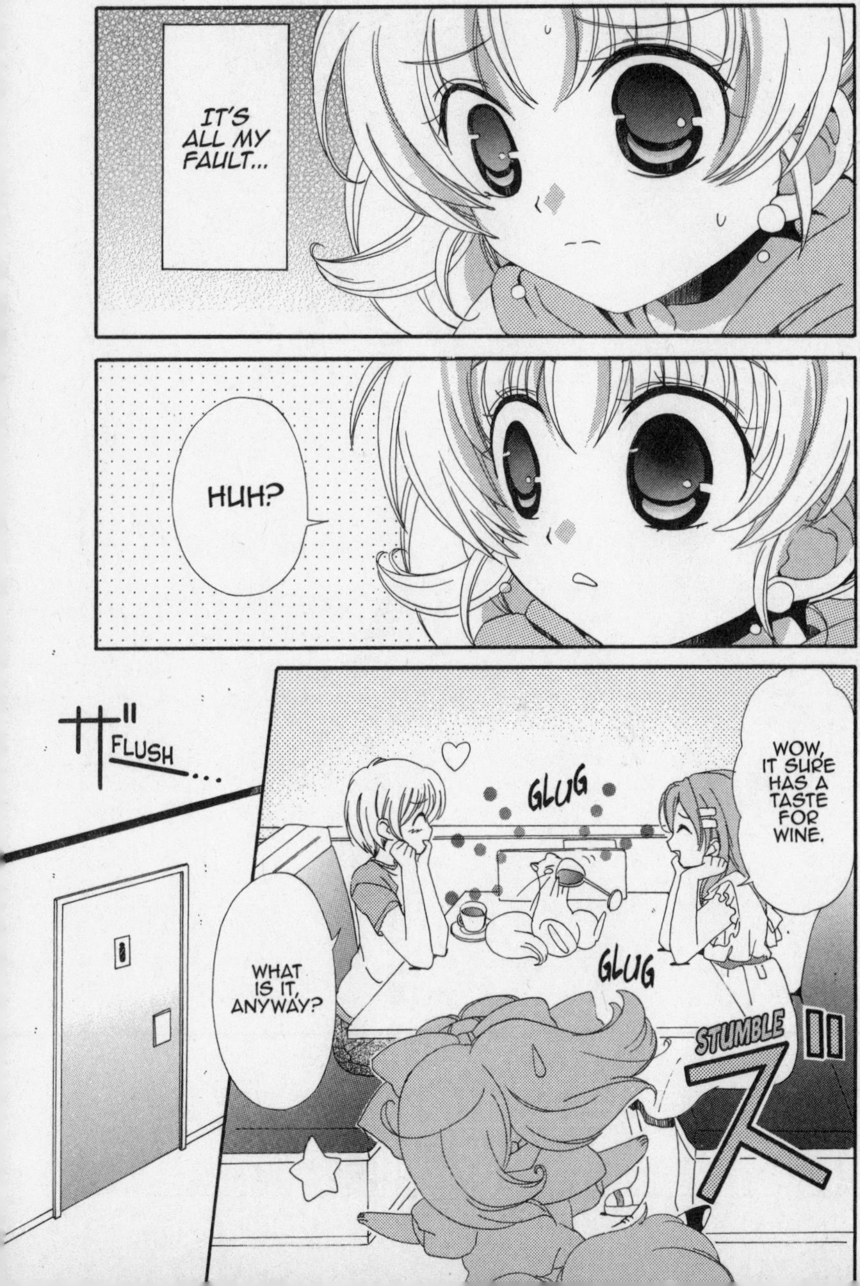
IT'S ALL MY FAULT...
HUH?
WOW, IT SURE HAS A TASTE FOR WINE.
GLUG
FLUSH...
GLUG
WHAT IS IT, ANYWAY?
STUMBLE

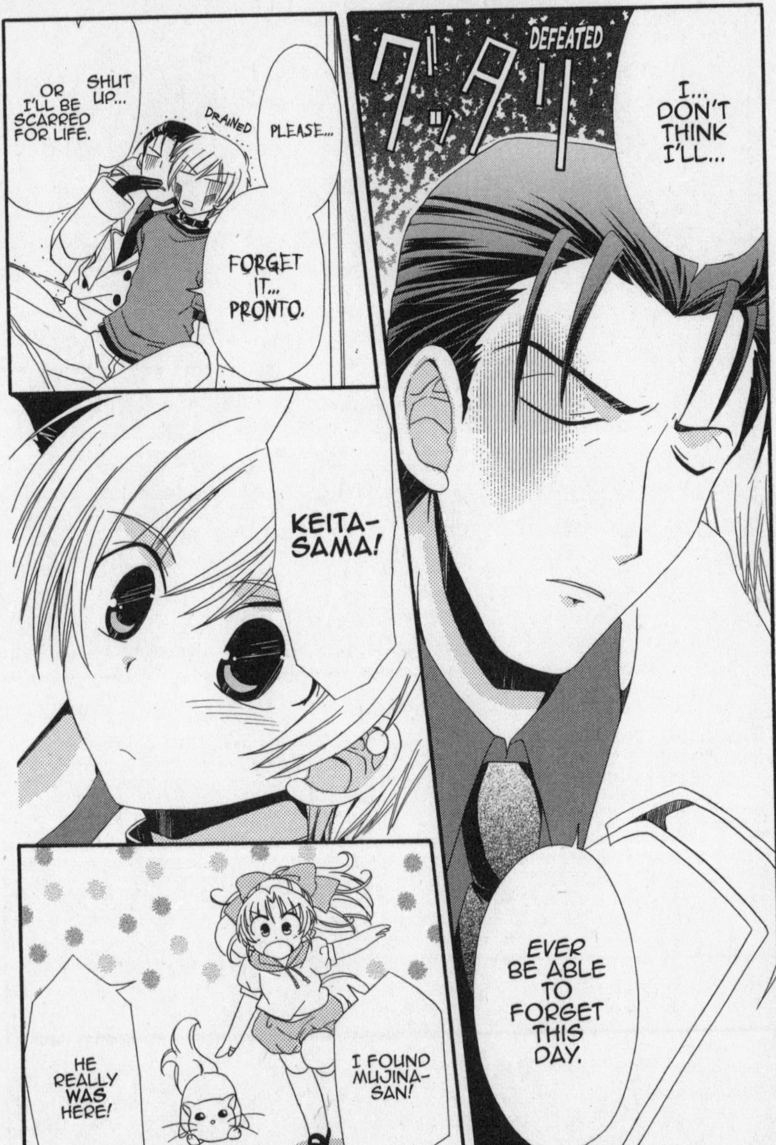
DEFEATED
I... DON'T THINK I'LL...
EVER BE ABLE TO FORGET THIS DAY.
PLEASE...
DRAINED
FORGET IT... PRONTO.
SHUT UP...
OR I'LL BE SCARRED FOR LIFE.
KEITA-SAMA!
I FOUND MUJINA-SAN!
HE REALLY WAS HERE!

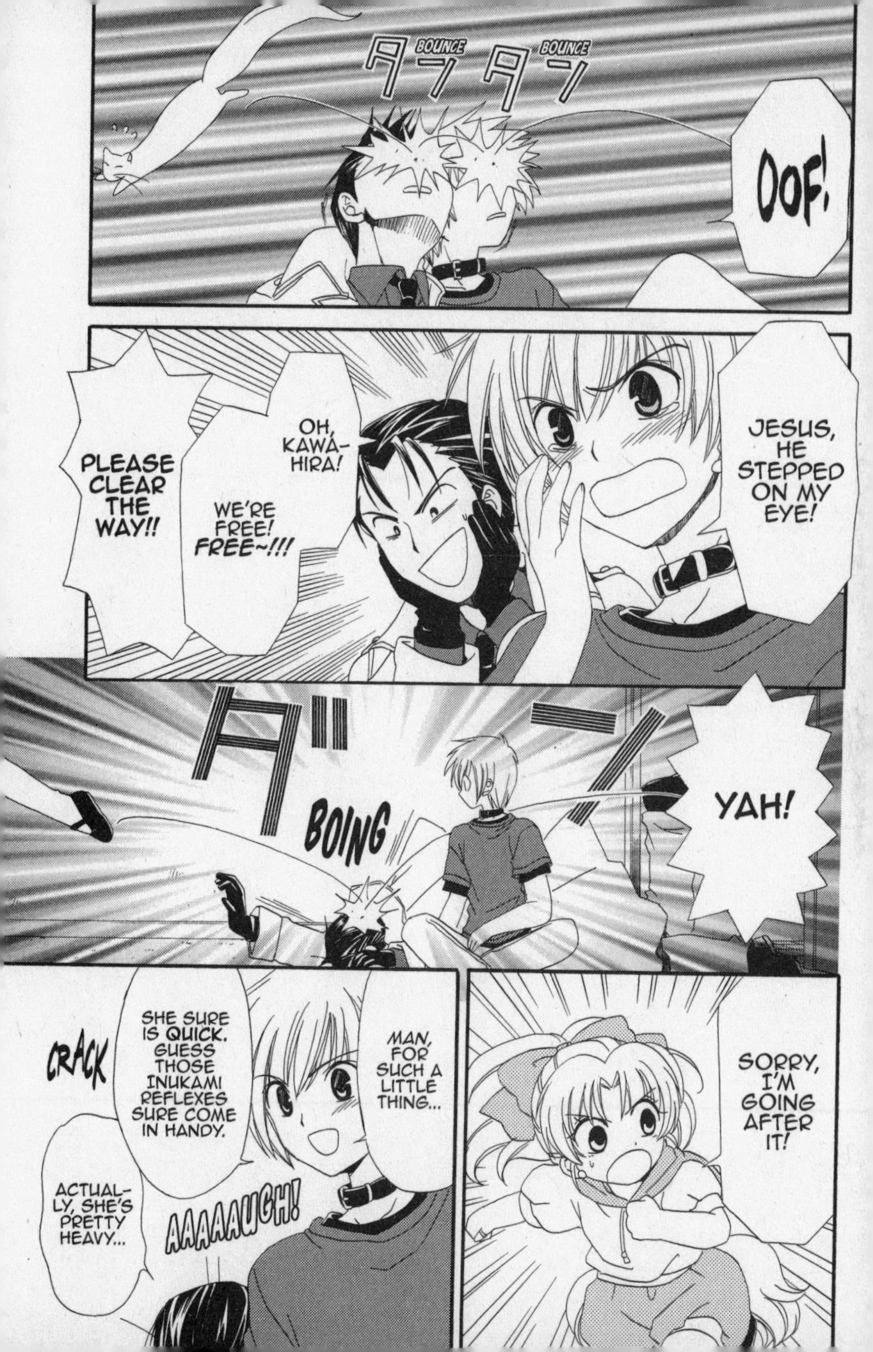
OOF!
BOUNCE
BOUNCE
JESUS, HE STEPPED ON MY EYE!
OH, KAWA-HIRA!
WE'RE FREE! FREE~!!!
PLEASE CLEAR THE WAY!!
YAH!
BOING
SORRY, I'M GOING AFTER IT!
MAN, FOR SUCH A LITTLE THING...
SHE SURE IS QUICK. GUESS THOSE INUKAMI REFLEXES SURE COME IN HANDY.
CRACK
ACTUAL-LY, SHE'S PRETTY HEAVY...
AAAAAUGH!

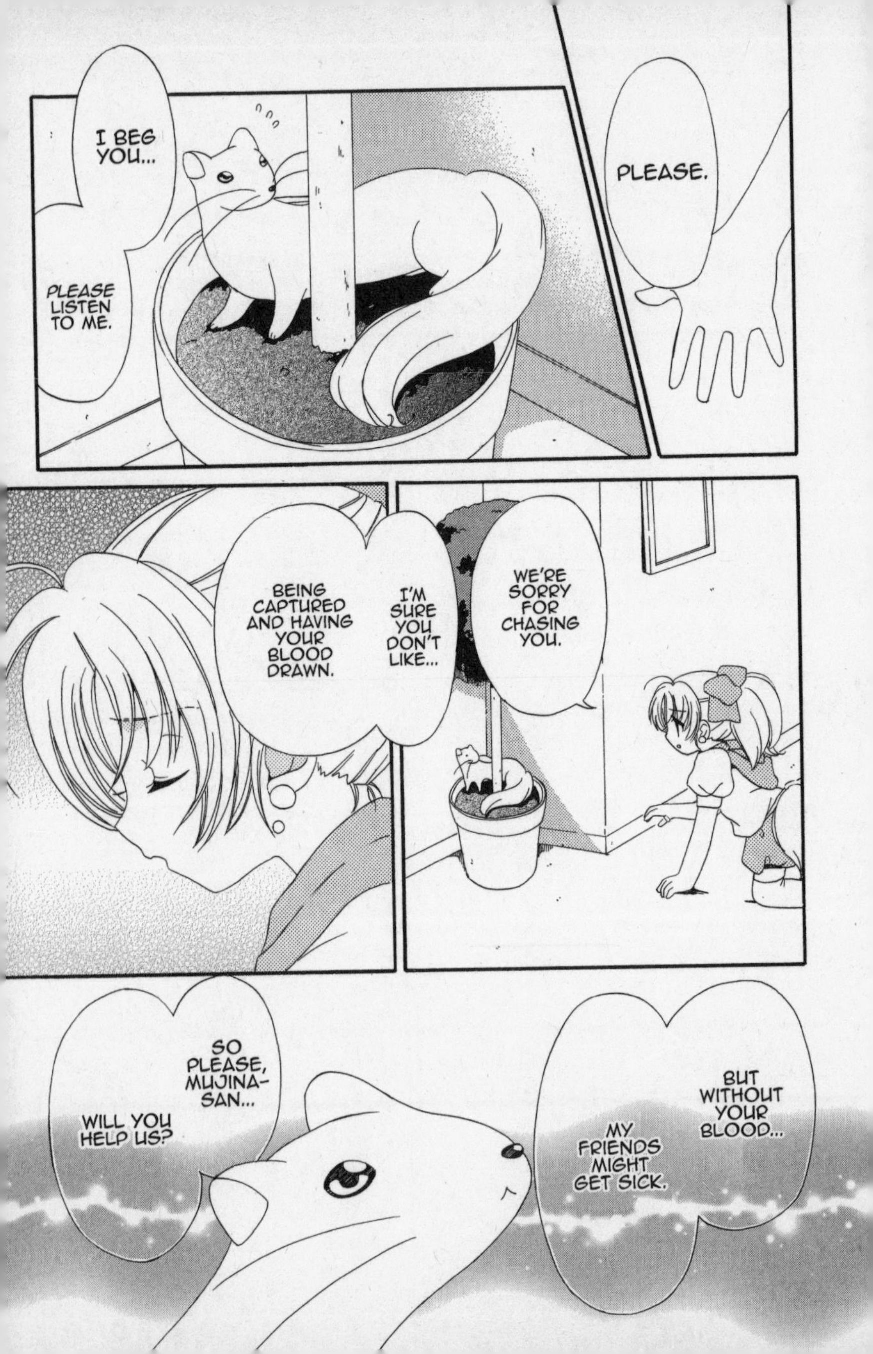
PLEASE.
I BEG YOU...
PLEASE LISTEN TO ME.
WE'RE SORRY FOR CHASING YOU.
I'M SURE YOU DON'T LIKE...
BEING CAPTURED AND HAVING YOUR BLOOD DRAWN.
BUT WITHOUT YOUR BLOOD...
MY FRIENDS MIGHT GET SICK.
SO PLEASE, MUJINA-SAN...
WILL YOU HELP US?

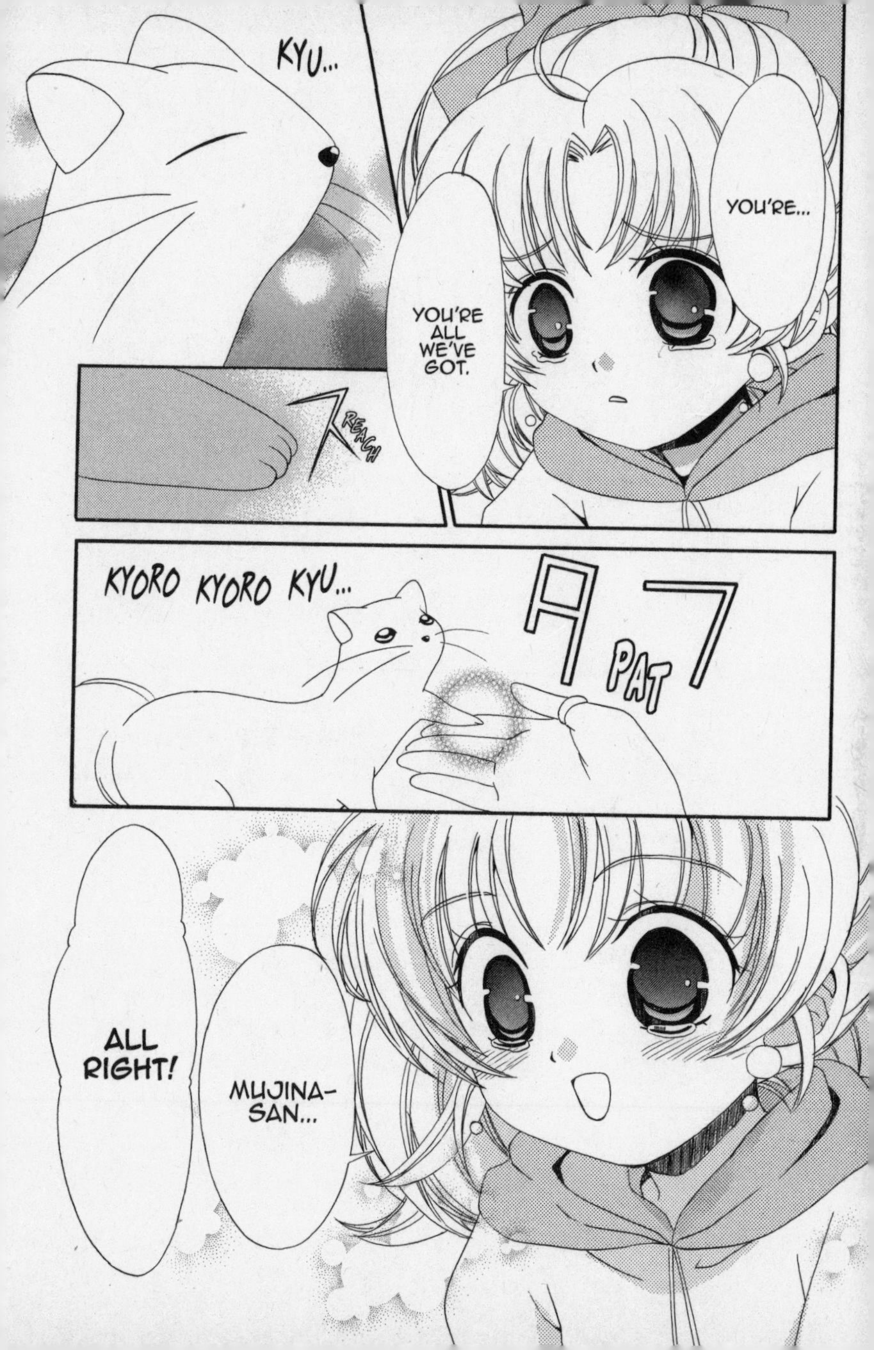
YOU'RE...
YOU'RE ALL WE'VE GOT.
KYU...
REACH
PAT
KYORO KYORO KYU...
MUJINA-SAN...
ALL RIGHT!

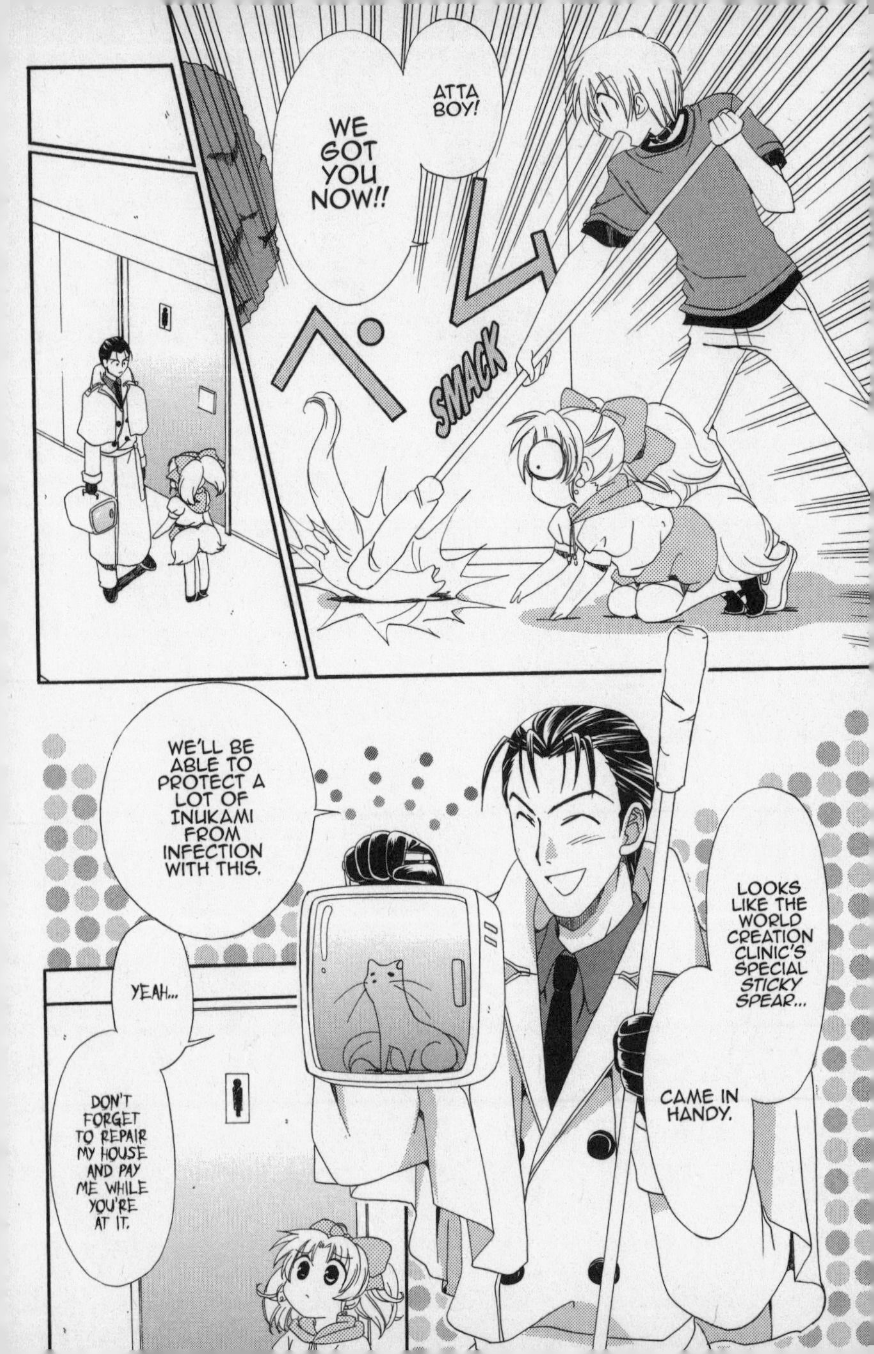
ATTA BOY!
WE GOT YOU NOW!!
SMACK
LOOKS LIKE THE WORLD CREATION CLINIC'S SPECIAL STICKY SPEAR...
CAME IN HANDY.
WE'LL BE ABLE TO PROTECT A LOT OF INUKAMI FROM INFECTION WITH THIS.
YEAH...
DON'T FORGET TO REPAIR MY HOUSE AND PAY ME WHILE YOU'RE AT IT.

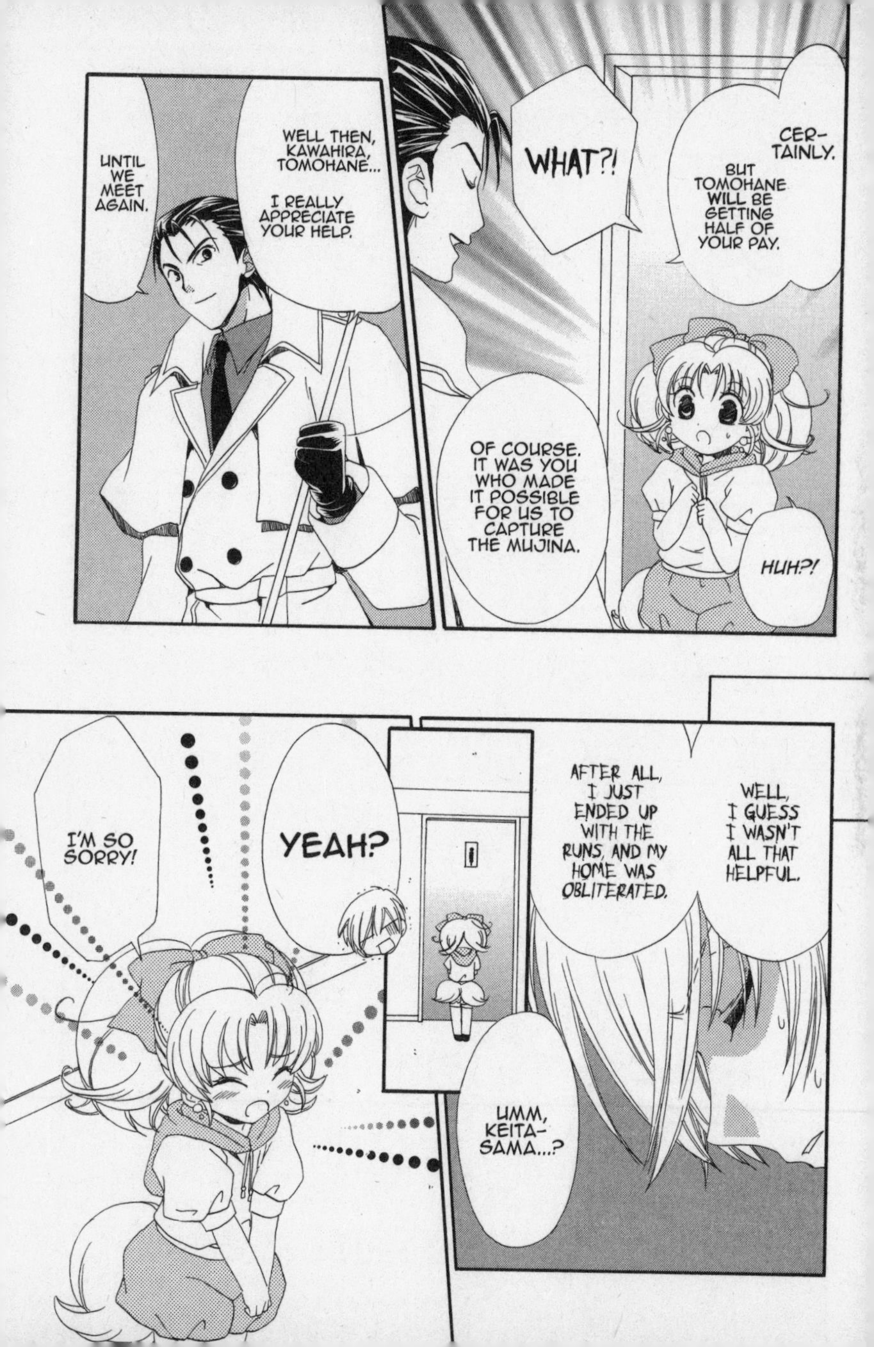
CER-TAINLY.
BUT TOMOHANE WILL BE GETTING HALF OF YOUR PAY.
WHAT?!
OF COURSE. IT WAS YOU WHO MADE IT POSSIBLE FOR US TO CAPTURE THE MUJINA.
HUH?!
WELL THEN, KAWAHIRA, TOMOHANE...
I REALLY APPRECIATE YOUR HELP.
UNTIL WE MEET AGAIN.
WELL, I GUESS I WASN'T ALL THAT HELPFUL.
AFTER ALL, I JUST ENDED UP WITH THE RUNS, AND MY HOME WAS OBLITERATED.
UMM, KEITA-SAMA...?
YEAH?
I'M SO SORRY!

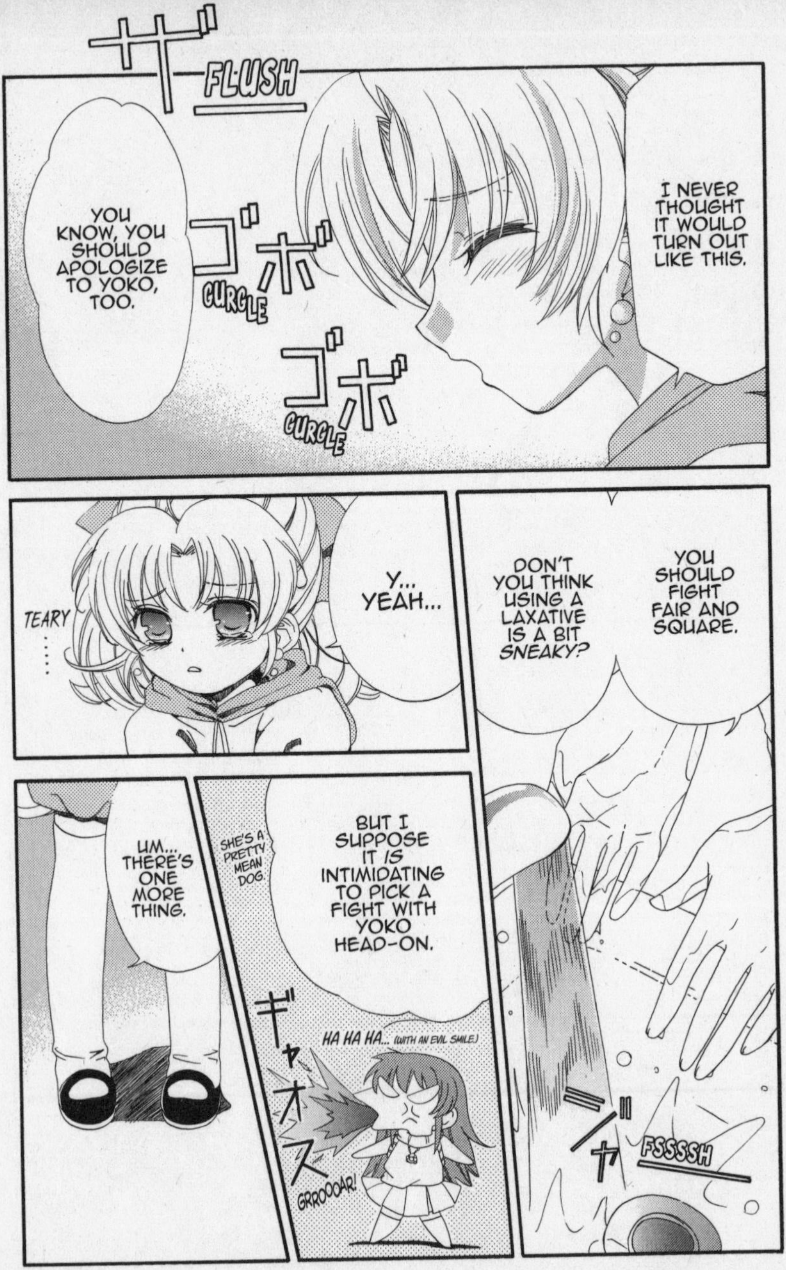
FLUSH
I NEVER THOUGHT IT WOULD TURN OUT LIKE THIS.
YOU KNOW, YOU SHOULD APOLOGIZE TO YOKO, TOO.
ゴボ
GURGLE
ゴボ
GURGLE
YOU SHOULD FIGHT FAIR AND SQUARE.
DON'T YOU THINK USING A LAXATIVE IS A BIT *SNEAKY*?
FSSSSH
Y... YEAH...
TEARY
.....
BUT I SUPPOSE IT *IS* INTIMIDATING TO PICK A FIGHT WITH YOKO HEAD-ON.
SHE'S A PRETTY MEAN DOG.
HA HA HA... (WITH AN EVIL SMILE)
GRROOOAR!
UM... THERE'S ONE MORE THING.

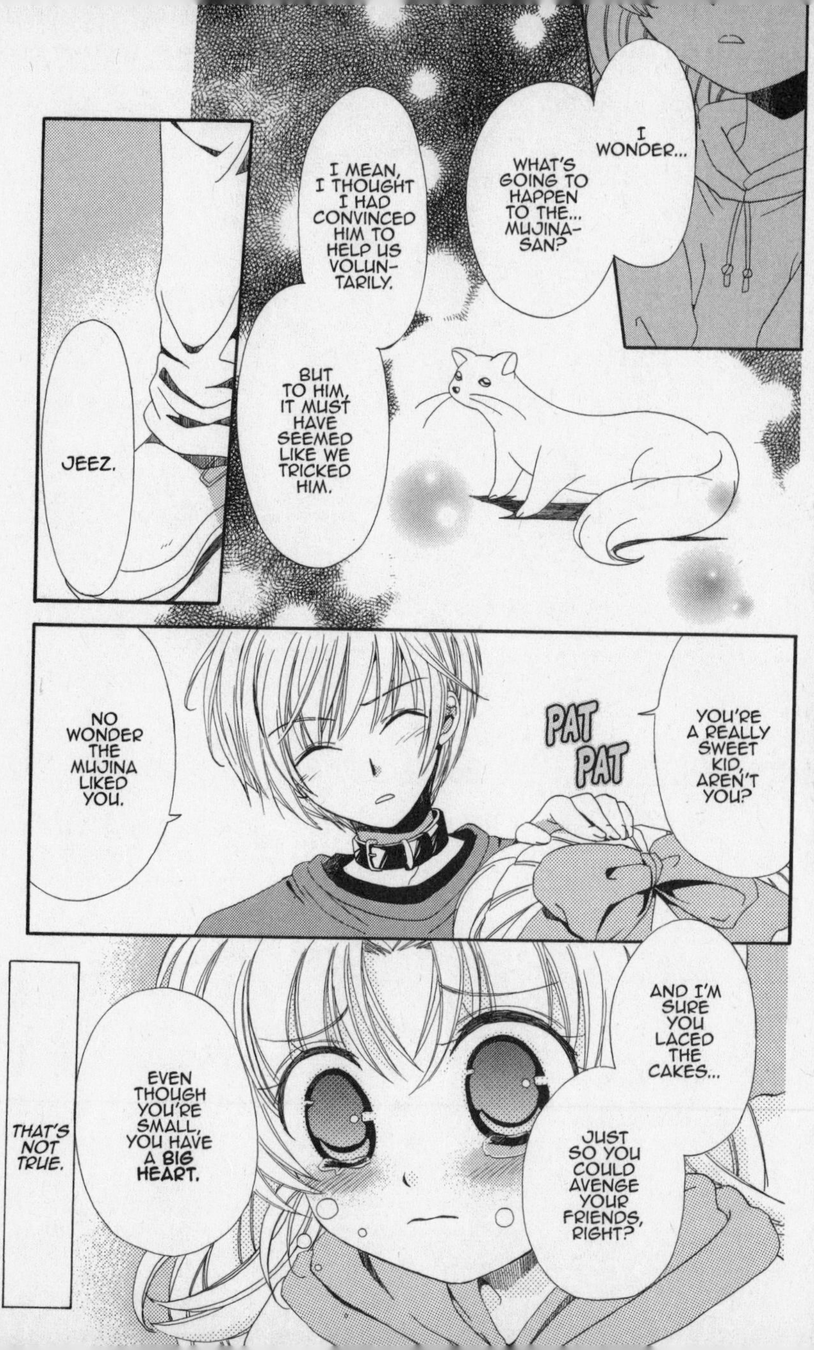
I WONDER... WHAT'S GOING TO HAPPEN TO THE... MUJINA-SAN?
I MEAN, I THOUGHT I HAD CONVINCED HIM TO HELP US VOLUNTARILY.
BUT TO HIM, IT MUST HAVE SEEMED LIKE WE TRICKED HIM.
JEEZ.
YOU'RE A REALLY SWEET KID, AREN'T YOU?
PAT PAT
NO WONDER THE MUJINA LIKED YOU.
AND I'M SURE YOU LACED THE CAKES...
JUST SO YOU COULD AVENGE YOUR FRIENDS, RIGHT?
EVEN THOUGH YOU'RE SMALL, YOU HAVE A BIG HEART.
THAT'S NOT TRUE.

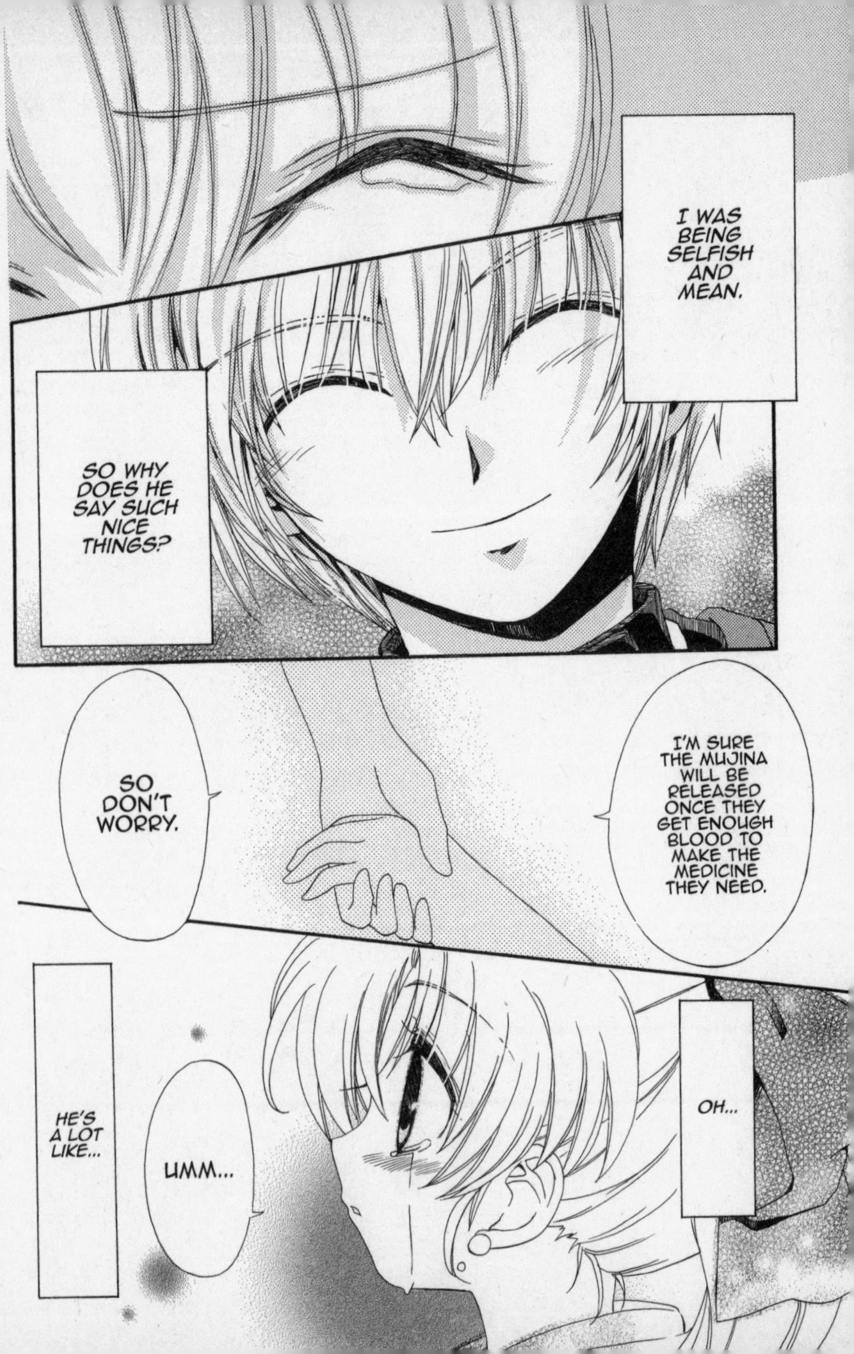
I WAS BEING SELFISH AND MEAN.
SO WHY DOES HE SAY SUCH NICE THINGS?
I'M SURE THE MUJINA WILL BE RELEASED ONCE THEY GET ENOUGH BLOOD TO MAKE THE MEDICINE THEY NEED.
SO DON'T WORRY.
OH...
UMM...
HE'S A LOT LIKE...

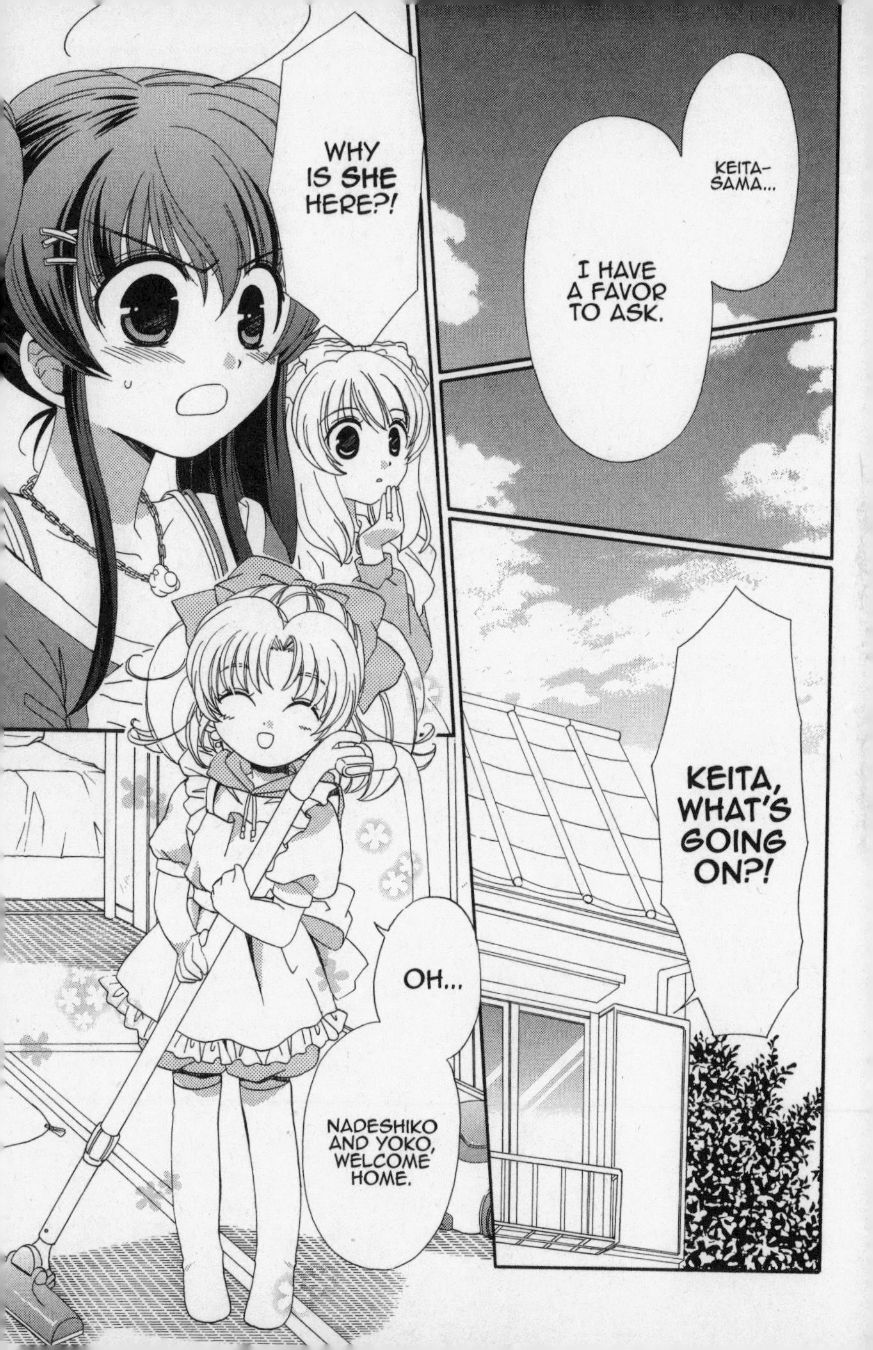
KEITA-SAMA...
I HAVE A FAVOR TO ASK.
KEITA, WHAT'S GOING ON?!
WHY IS SHE HERE?!
OH...
NADESHIKO AND YOKO, WELCOME HOME.

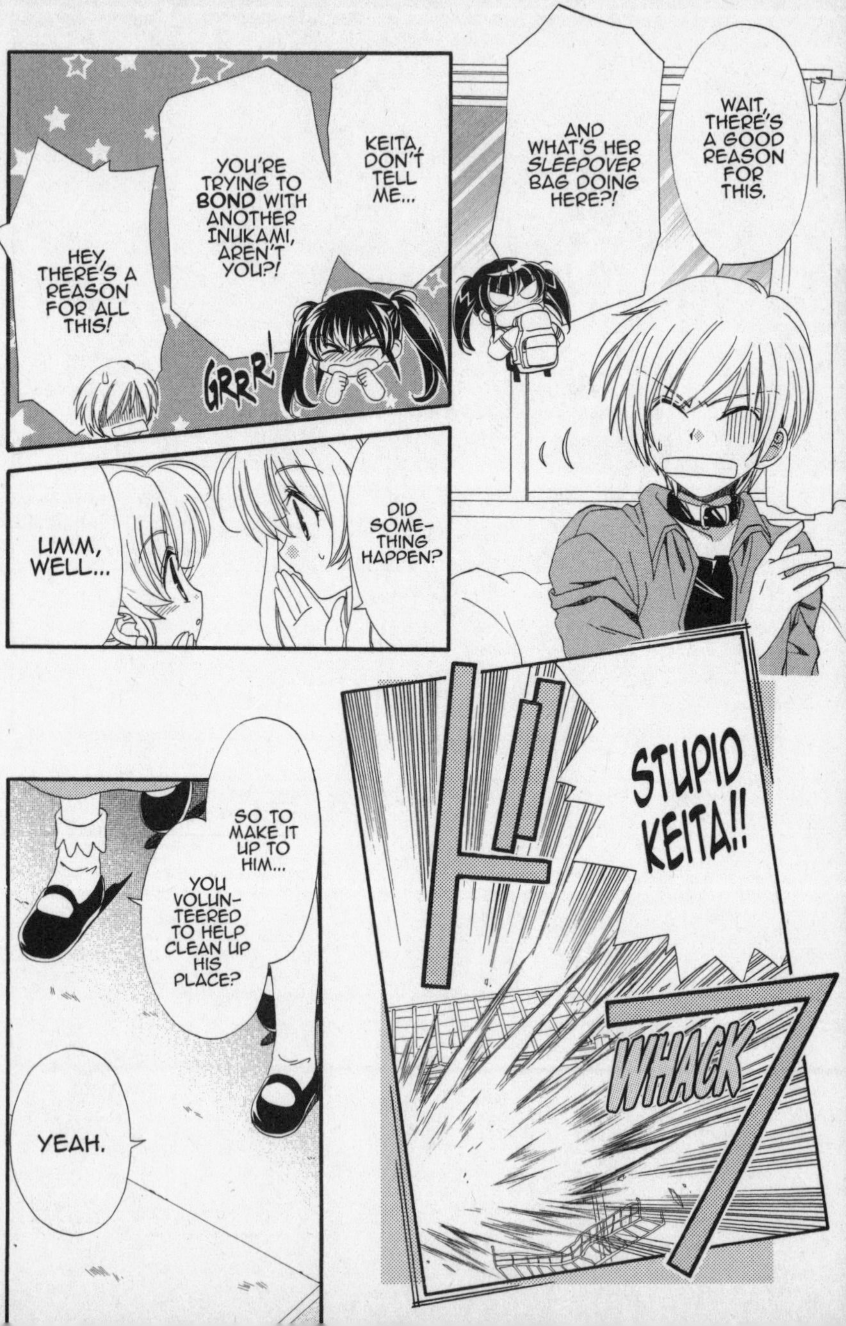
WAIT, THERE'S A GOOD REASON FOR THIS.
AND WHAT'S HER *SLEEPOVER* BAG DOING HERE?!
KEITA, DON'T TELL ME...
YOU'RE TRYING TO **BOND** WITH ANOTHER INUKAMI, AREN'T YOU?!
GRRR!
HEY, THERE'S A REASON FOR ALL THIS!
DID SOME-THING HAPPEN?
UMM, WELL...
STUPID KEITA!!
WHACK
SO TO MAKE IT UP TO HIM...
YOU VOLUN-TEERED TO HELP CLEAN UP HIS PLACE?
YEAH.

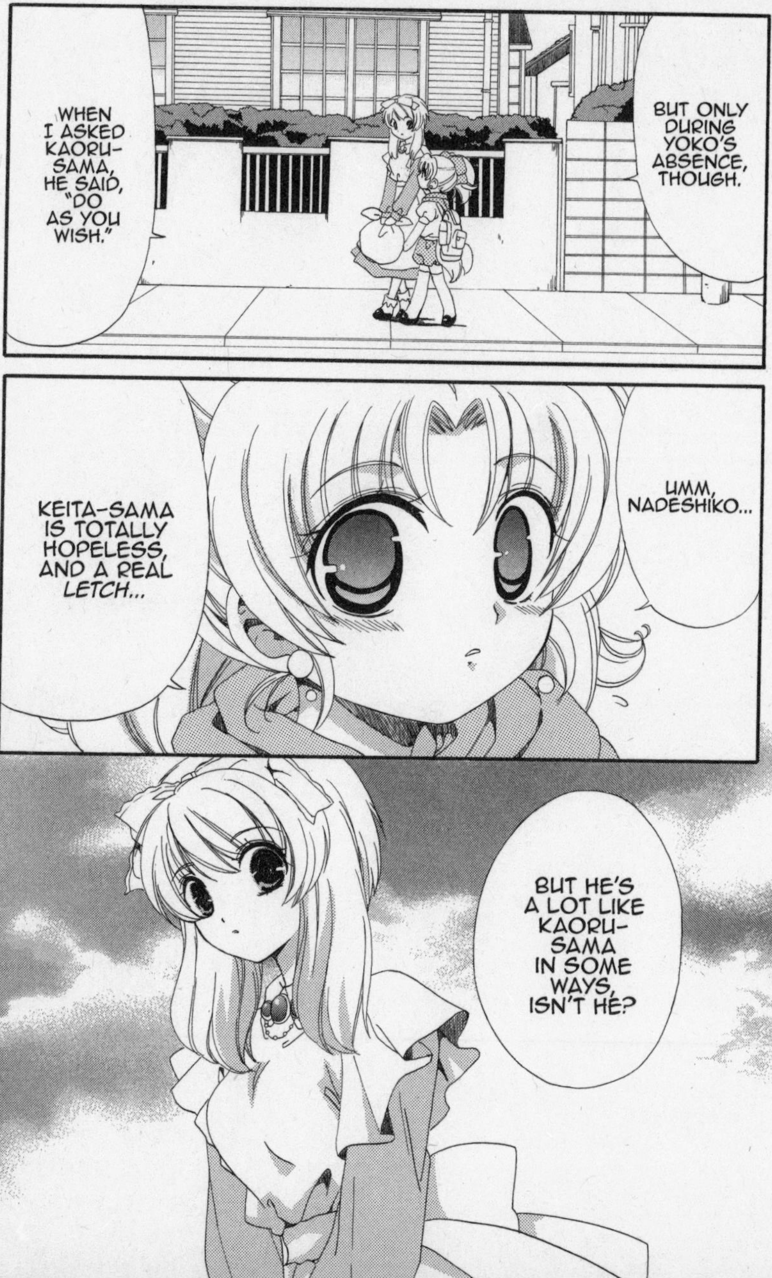
BUT ONLY DURING YOKO'S ABSENCE, THOUGH.
WHEN I ASKED KAORU-SAMA, HE SAID, "DO AS YOU WISH."
UMM, NADESHIKO...
KEITA-SAMA IS TOTALLY HOPELESS, AND A REAL *LETCH*...
BUT HE'S A LOT LIKE KAORU-SAMA IN SOME WAYS, ISN'T HE?

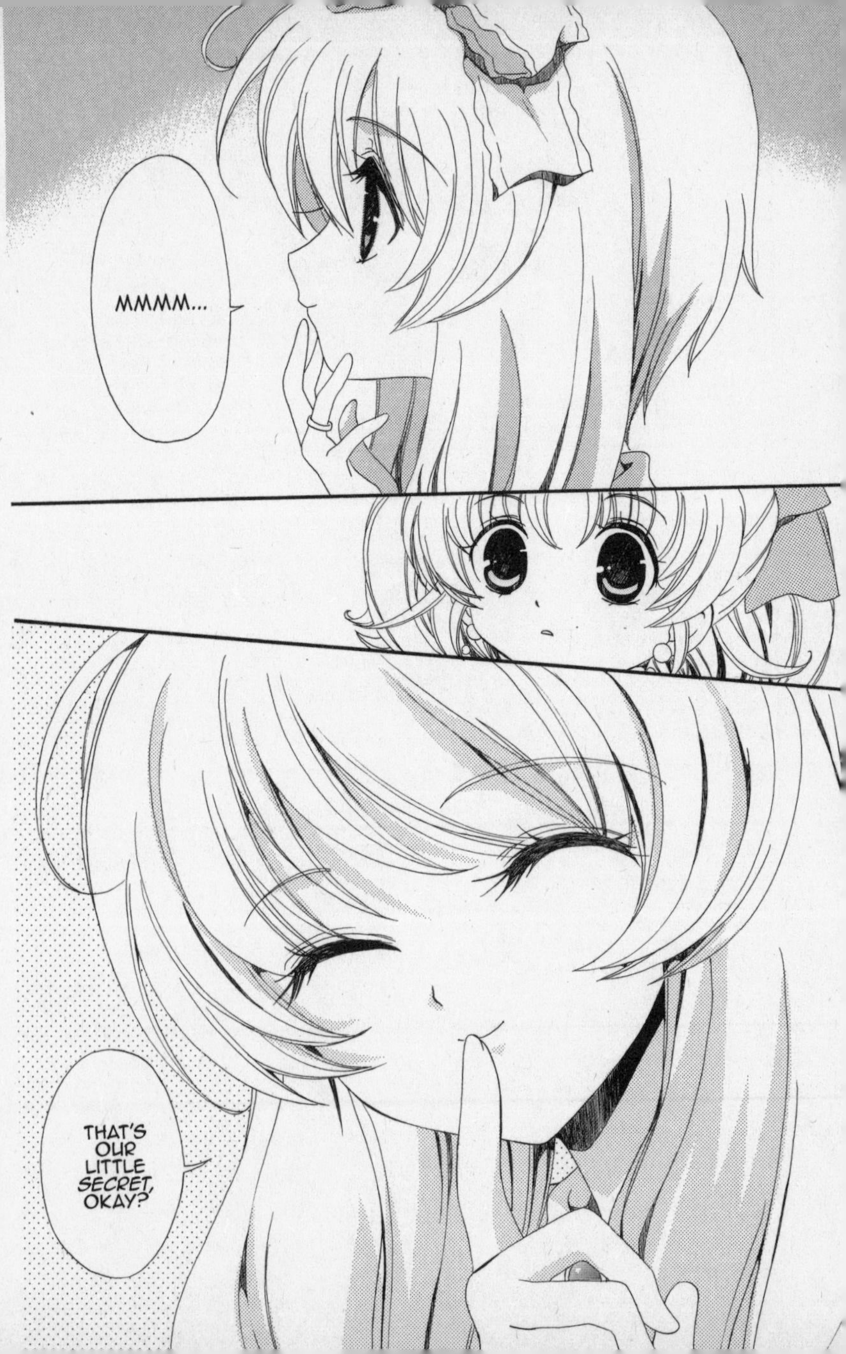
MMMM...
THAT'S OUR LITTLE SECRET, OKAY?

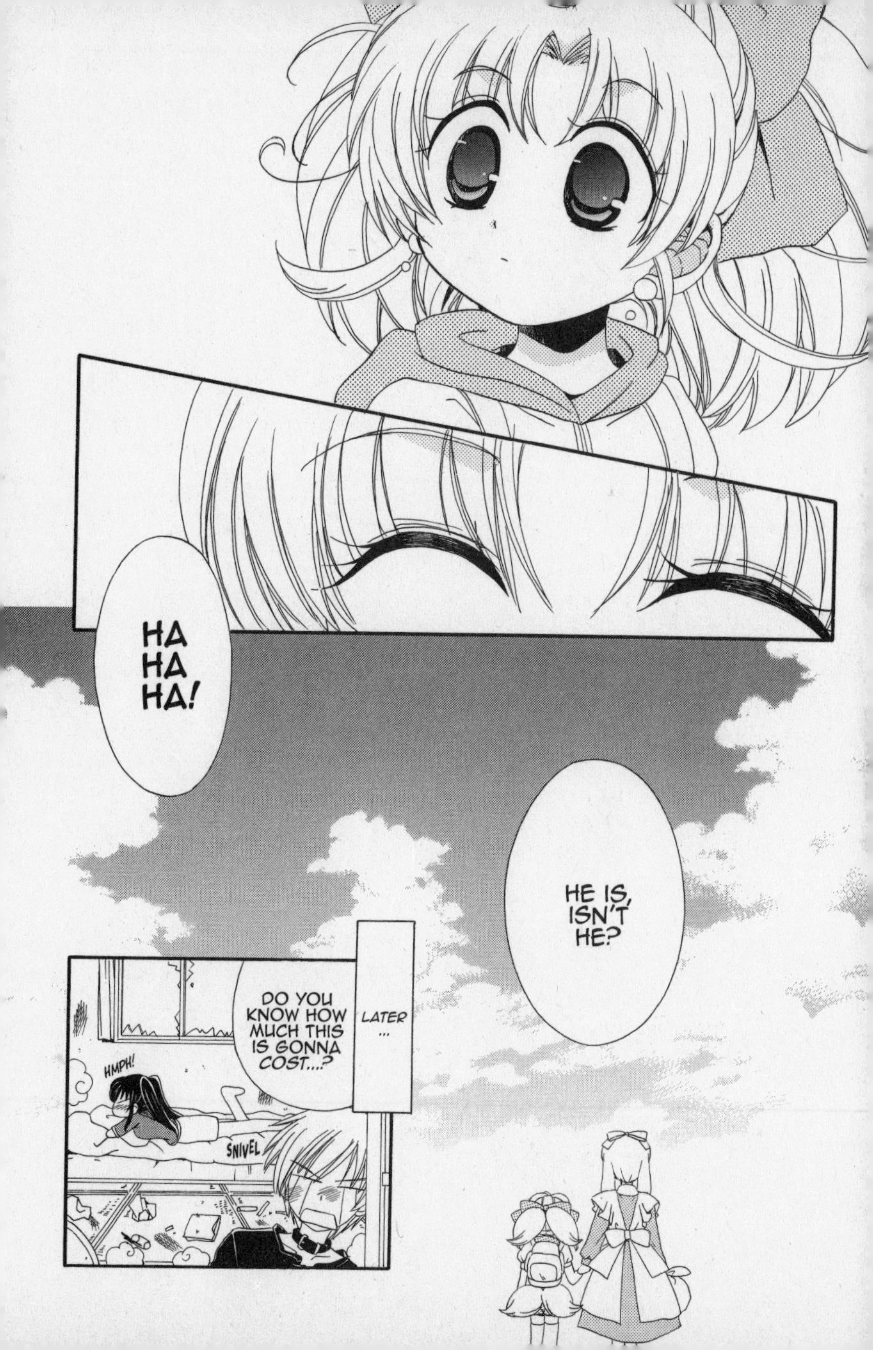
HA HA HA!
HE IS, ISN'T HE?
LATER ...
DO YOU KNOW HOW MUCH THIS IS GONNA COST...?
HMPH!
SNIVEL

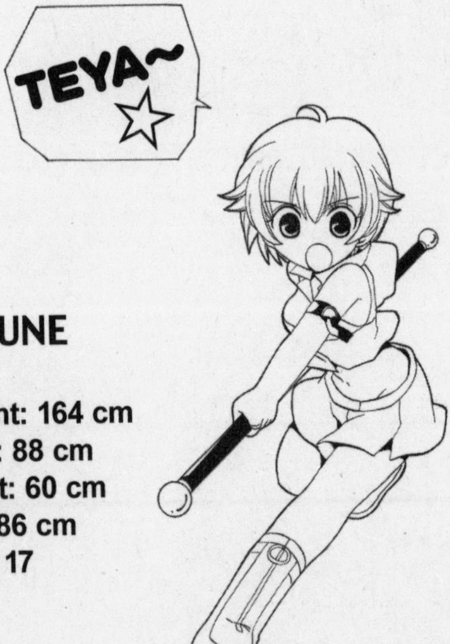
TEYA~ ☆

TAYUNE

Height: 164 cm
Bust: 88 cm
Waist: 60 cm
Hip: 86 cm
Age: 17

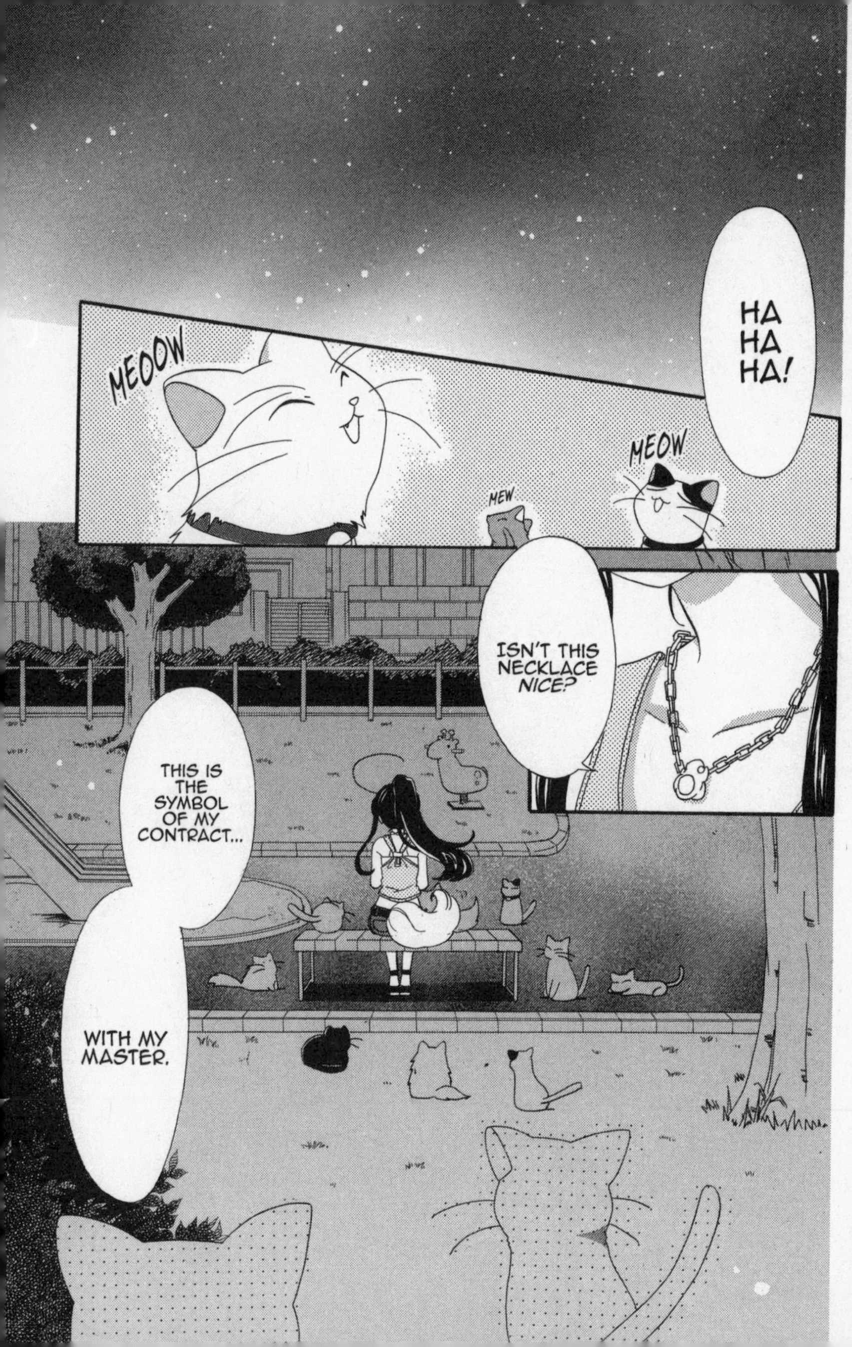
HA HA HA!
MEOW
MEW
MEOOW
ISN'T THIS NECKLACE NICE?
THIS IS THE SYMBOL OF MY CONTRACT...
WITH MY MASTER.

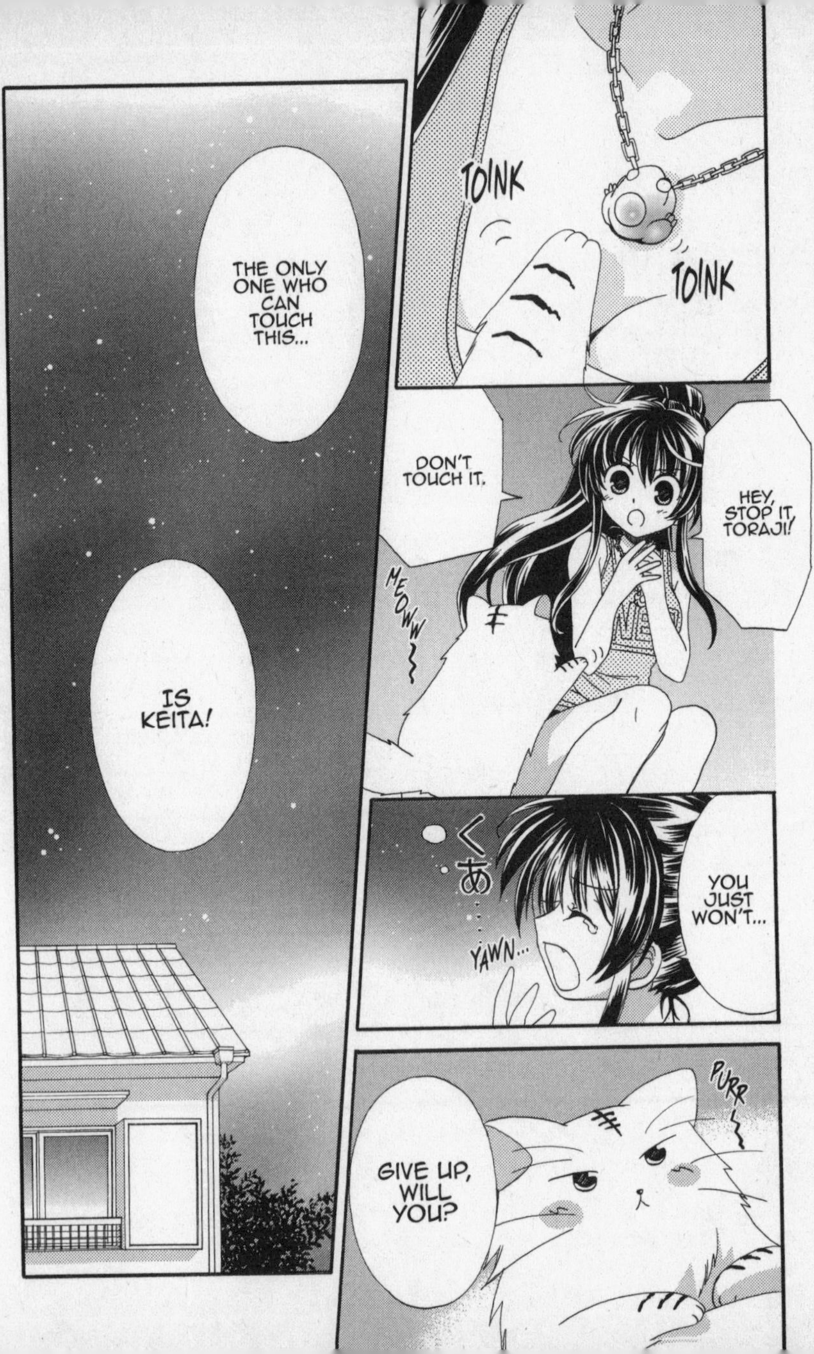
TOINK
TOINK
HEY, STOP IT, TORAJI!
DON'T TOUCH IT.
MEOWW~
YOU JUST WON'T...
くあ…
YAWN...
PURR~
GIVE UP, WILL YOU?
THE ONLY ONE WHO CAN TOUCH THIS...
IS KEITA!

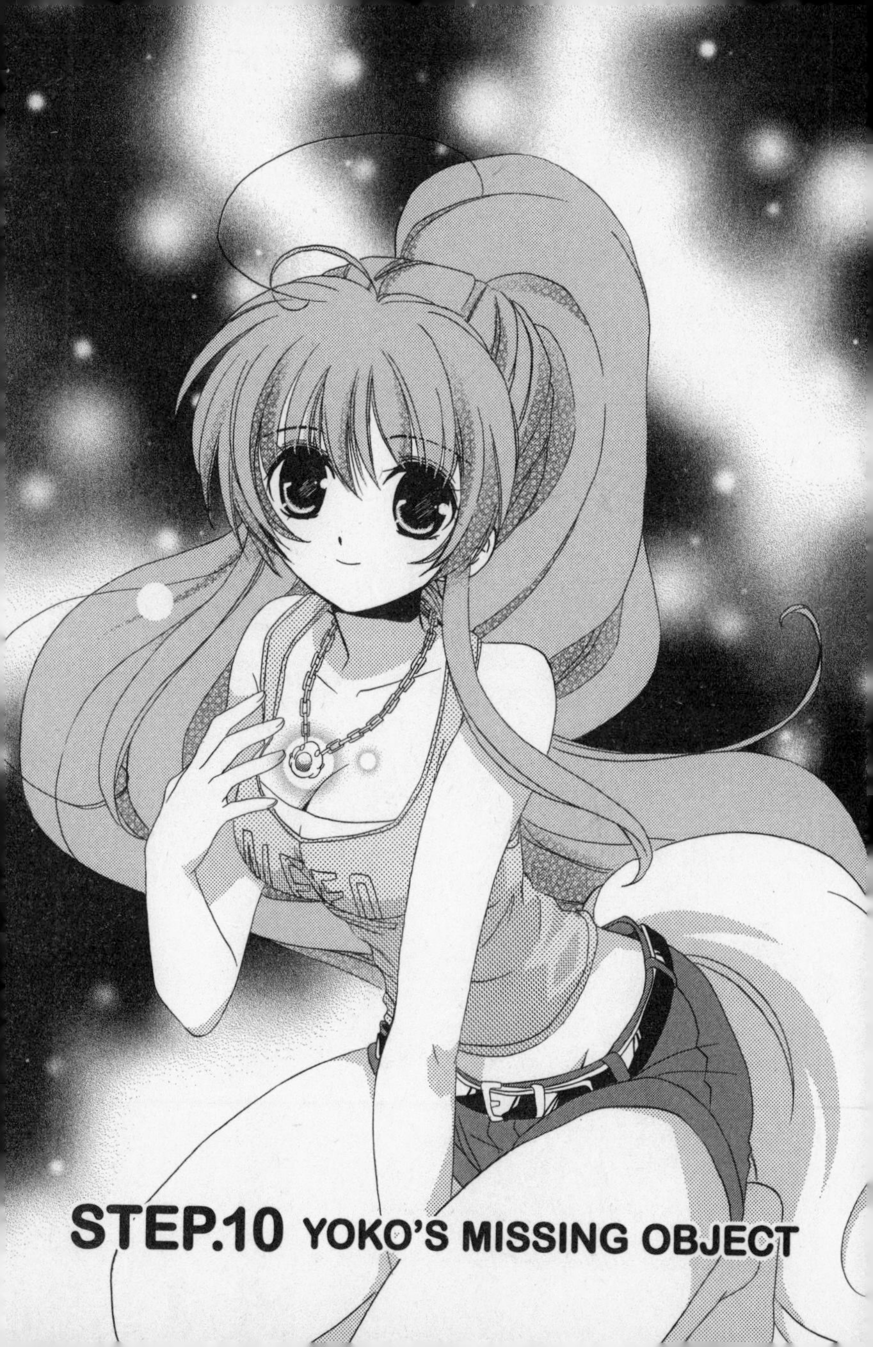

STEP.10 YOKO'S MISSING OBJECT

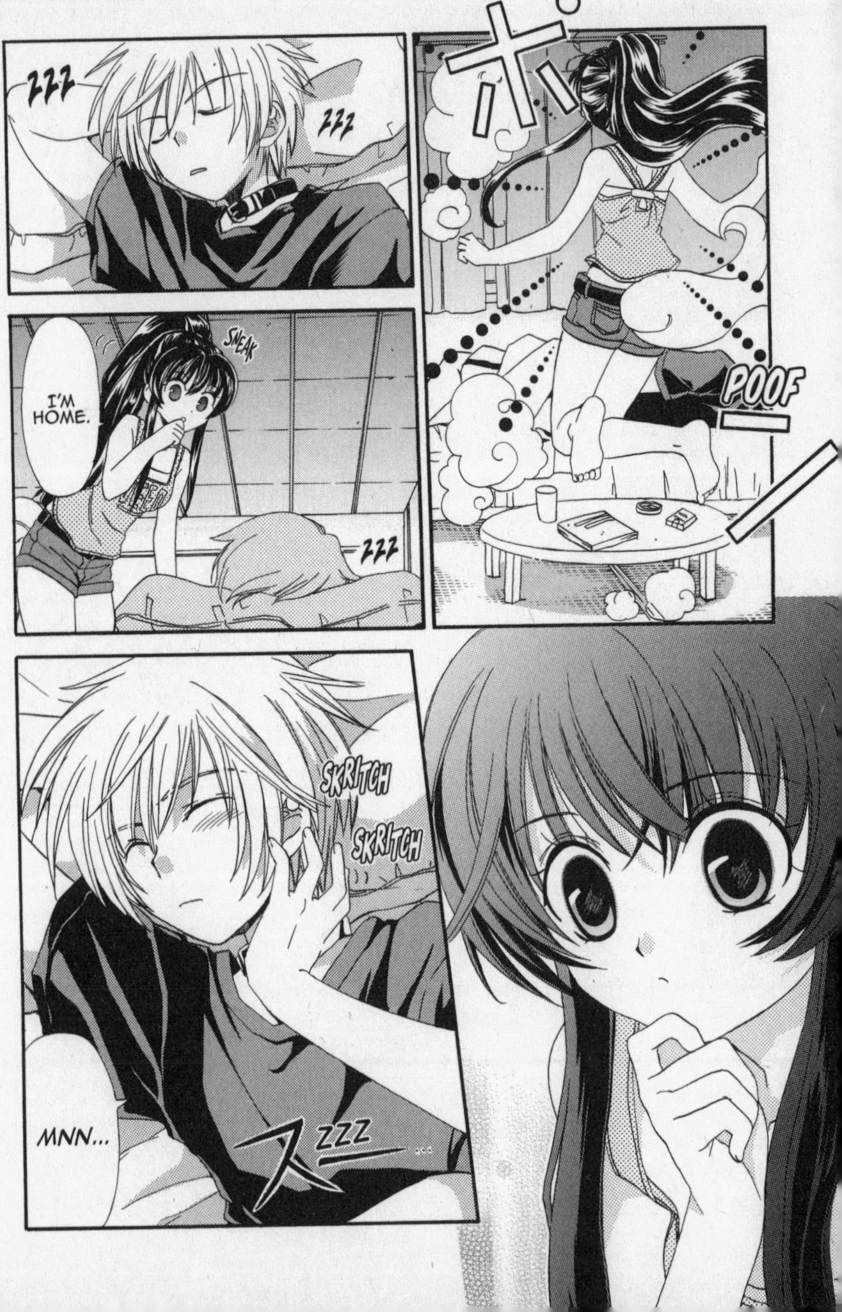

ZZZ
ZZZ
POOF
SNEAK
I'M HOME.
ZZZ
SKRITCH
SKRITCH
MNN...
ZZZ

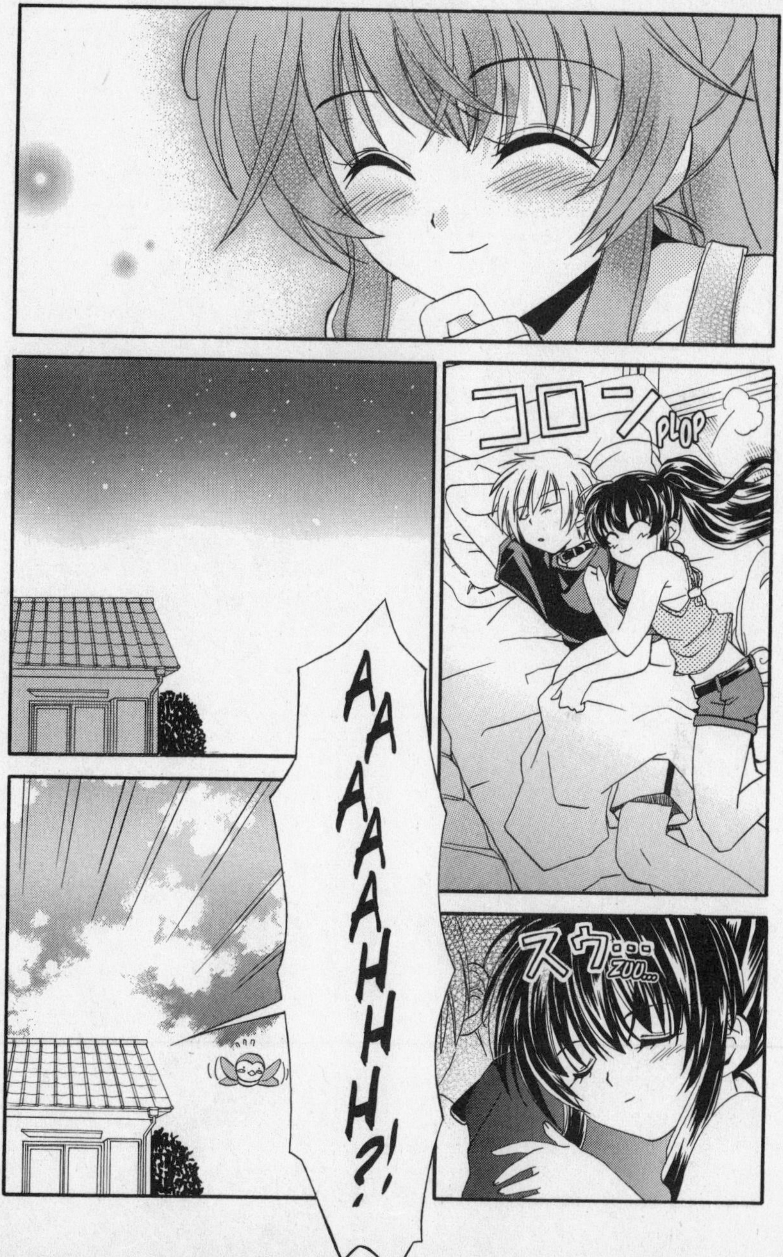

コロン
PLOP
スウ...
ZUU...
AAAAAHHH?!

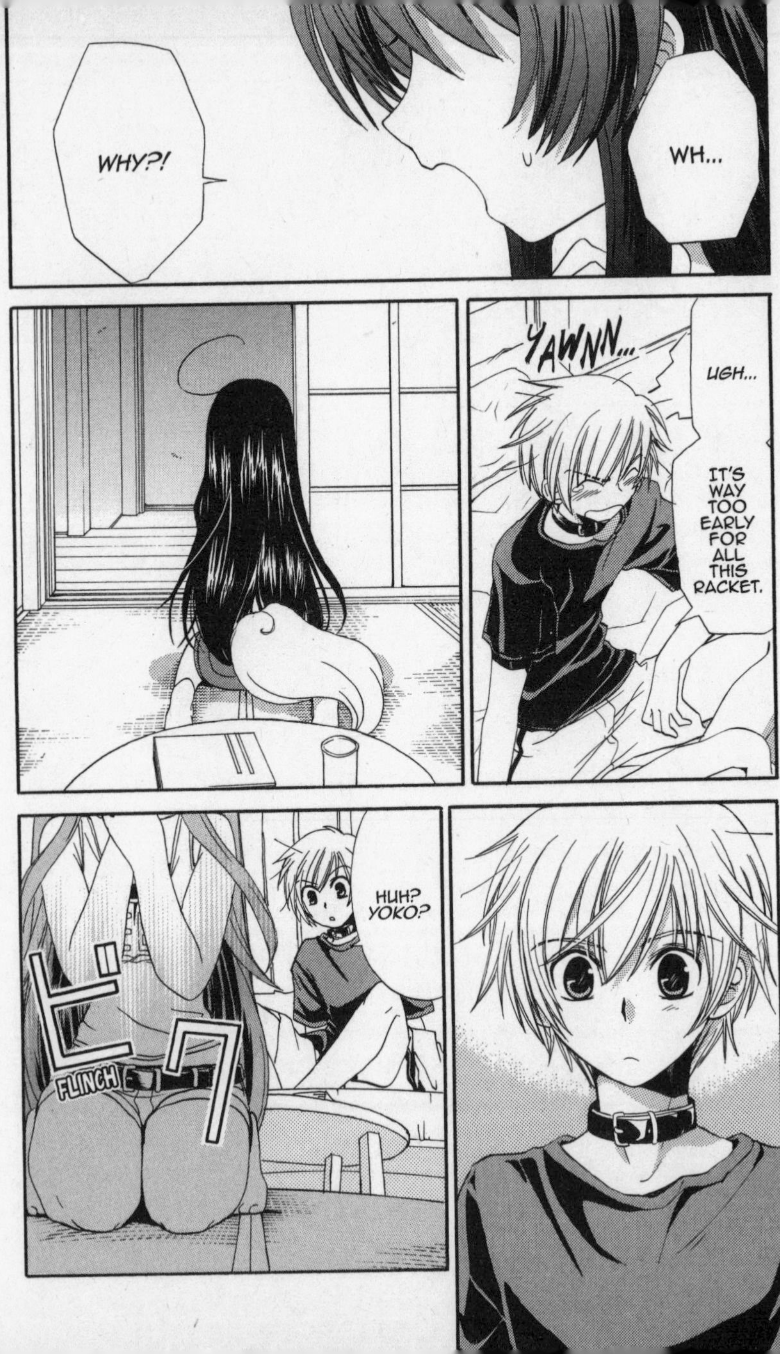
WH...
WHY?!
YAWNN...
UGH...
IT'S WAY TOO EARLY FOR ALL THIS RACKET.
HUH? YOKO?
ビク
FLINCH

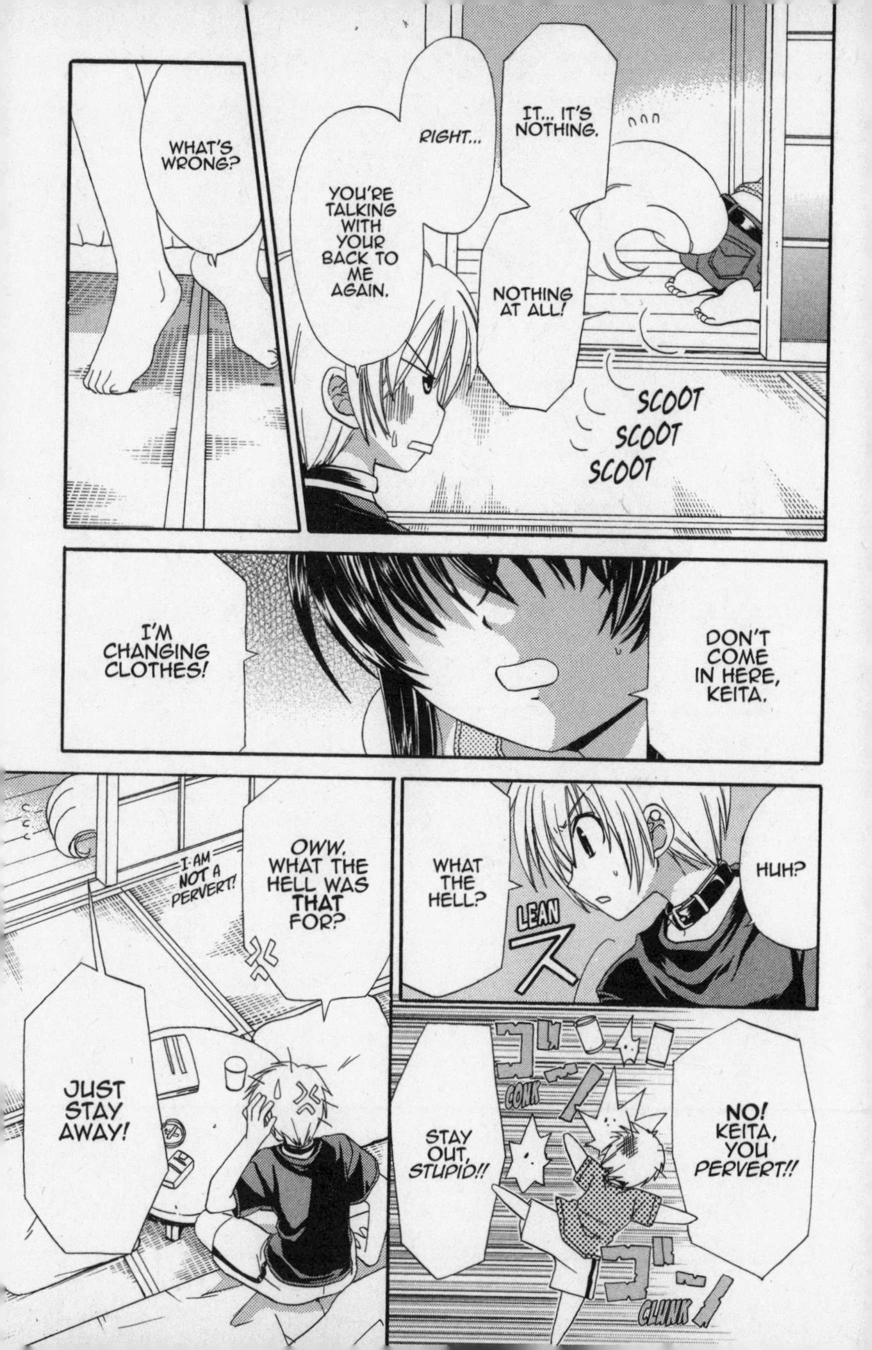
IT... IT'S NOTHING.
RIGHT...
YOU'RE TALKING WITH YOUR BACK TO ME AGAIN.
NOTHING AT ALL!
SCOOT SCOOT SCOOT
WHAT'S WRONG?
DON'T COME IN HERE, KEITA.
I'M CHANGING CLOTHES!
HUH?
WHAT THE HELL?
LEAN
NO! KEITA, YOU PERVERT!!
STAY OUT, STUPID!!
CONK
CLUNK
OWW. WHAT THE HELL WAS THAT FOR?
I-AM NOT A PERVERT!
JUST STAY AWAY!

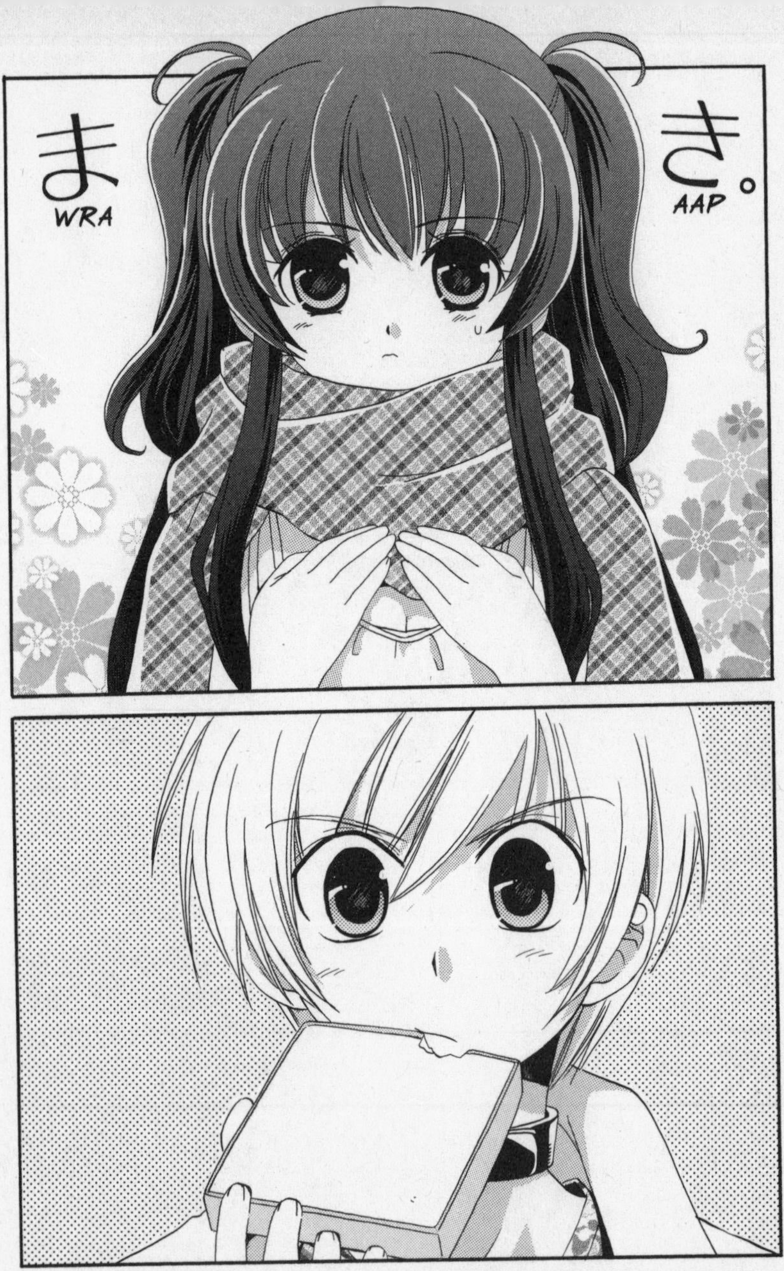
ま
WRA
き。
AAP

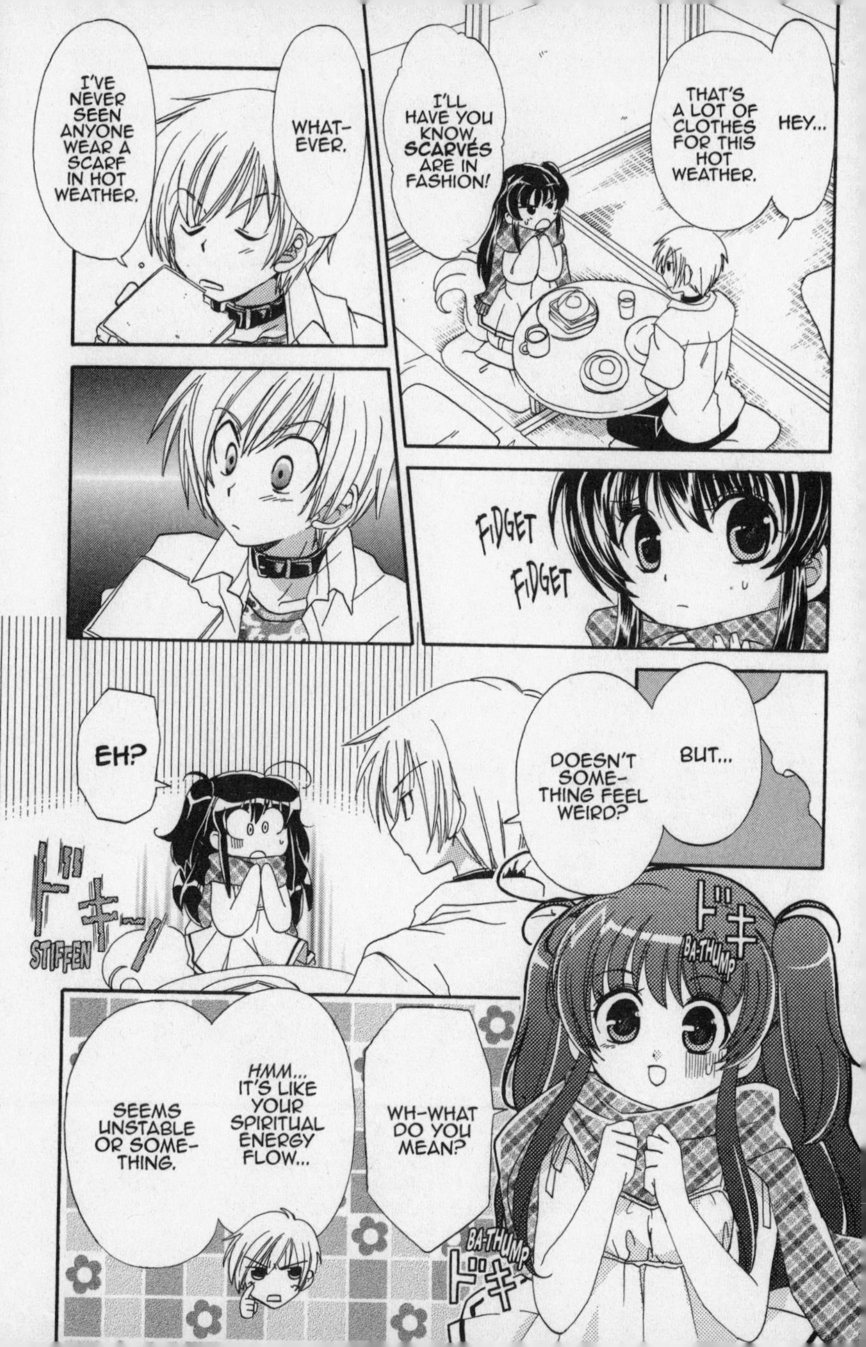
HEY...
THAT'S A LOT OF CLOTHES FOR THIS HOT WEATHER.
I'LL HAVE YOU KNOW, SCARVES ARE IN FASHION!
WHAT-EVER.
I'VE NEVER SEEN ANYONE WEAR A SCARF IN HOT WEATHER.
FIDGET
FIDGET
BUT...
DOESN'T SOME-THING FEEL WEIRD?
ドキー
STIFFEN
EH?
ドキ
BA-THUMP
WH-WHAT DO YOU MEAN?
HMM... IT'S LIKE YOUR SPIRITUAL ENERGY FLOW...
SEEMS UNSTABLE OR SOME-THING.
BA-THUMP
ドキ

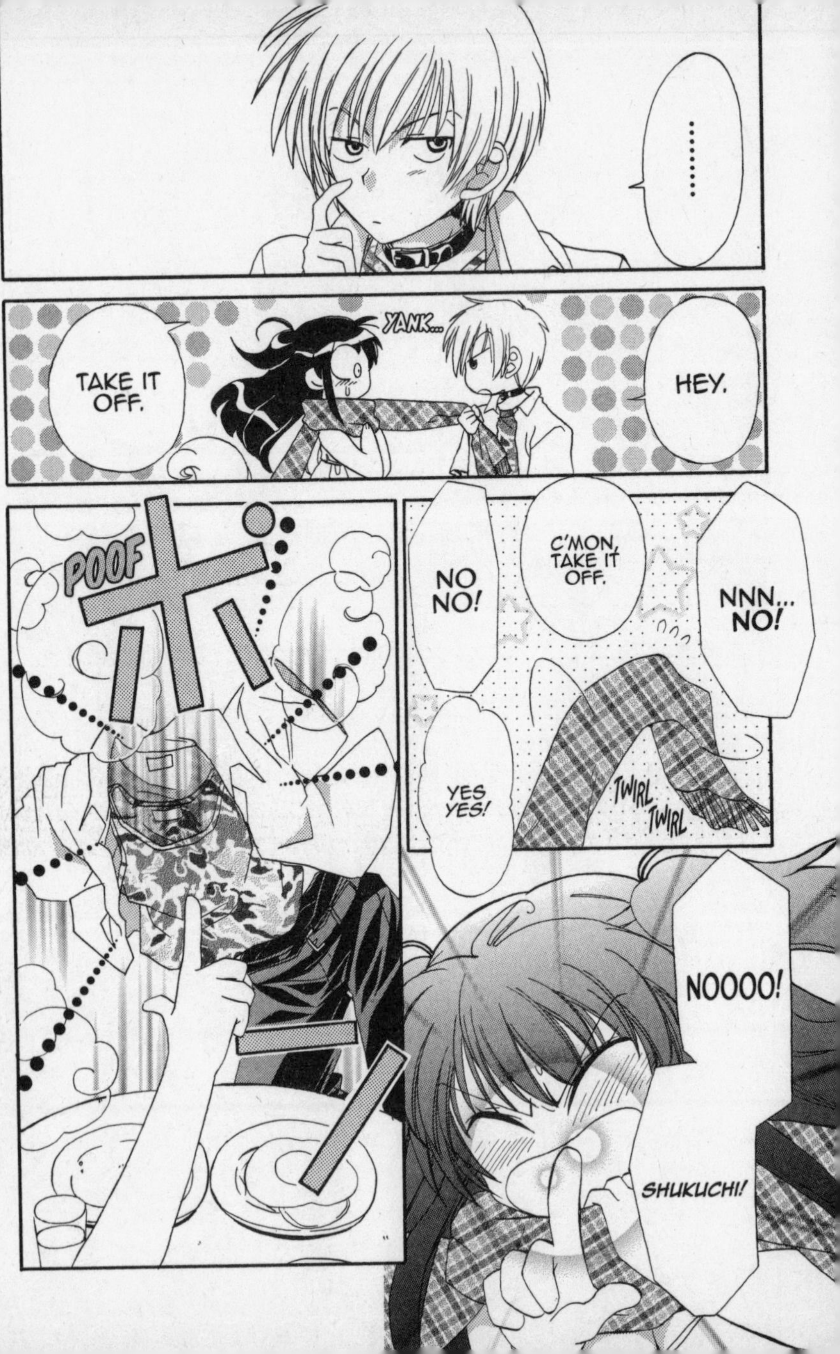
......
HEY.
YANK...
TAKE IT OFF.
NNN... NO!
C'MON, TAKE IT OFF.
NO NO!
YES YES!
TWIRL TWIRL
NOOOO!
SHUKUCHI!
POOF

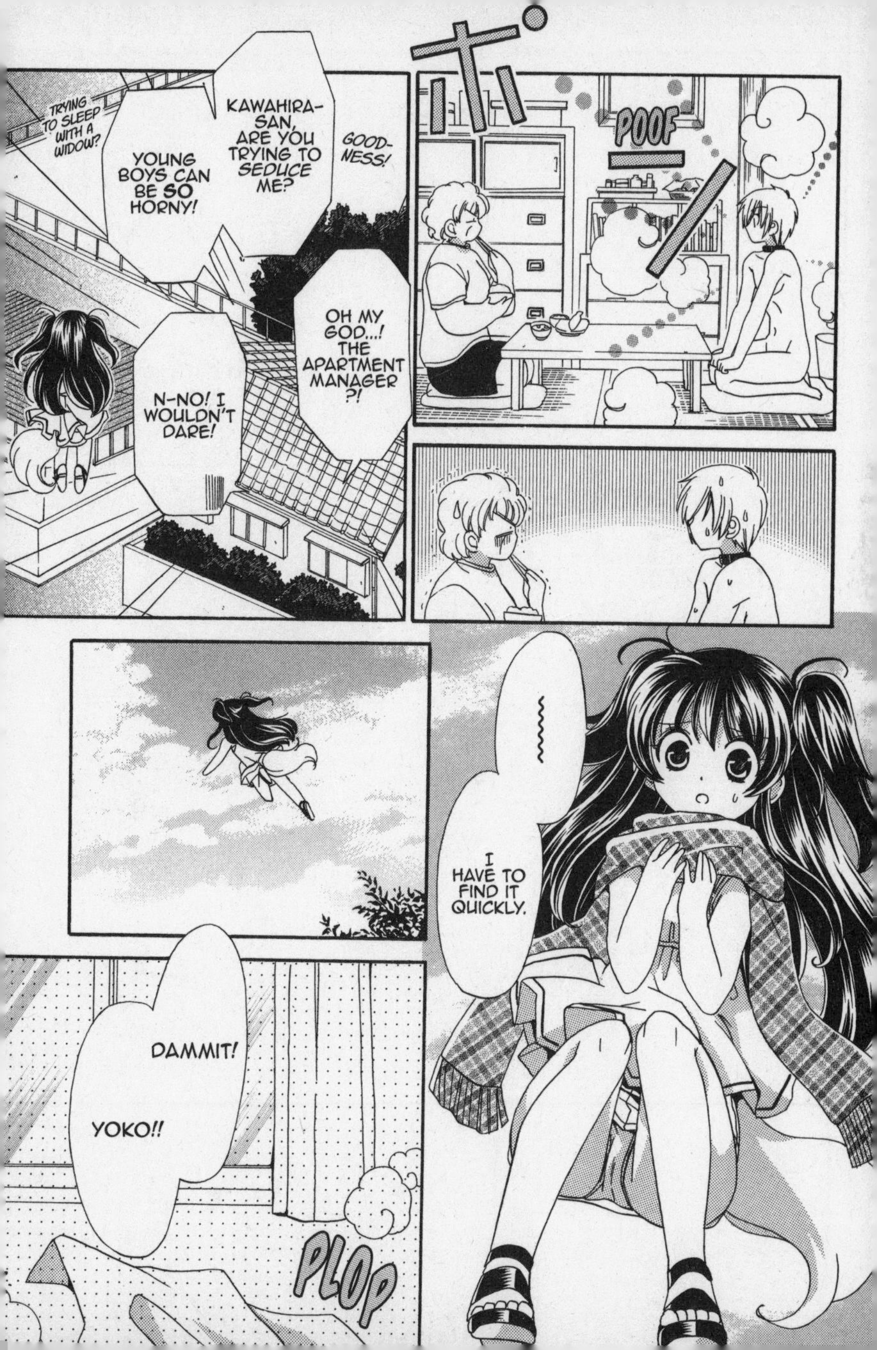
POOF
GOOD-NESS!
KAWAHIRA-SAN, ARE YOU TRYING TO SEDUCE ME?
YOUNG BOYS CAN BE SO HORNY!
TRYING TO SLEEP WITH A WIDOW?
OH MY GOD...! THE APARTMENT MANAGER?!
N-NO! I WOULDN'T DARE!
...
I HAVE TO FIND IT QUICKLY.
DAMMIT!
YOKO!!
PLOP

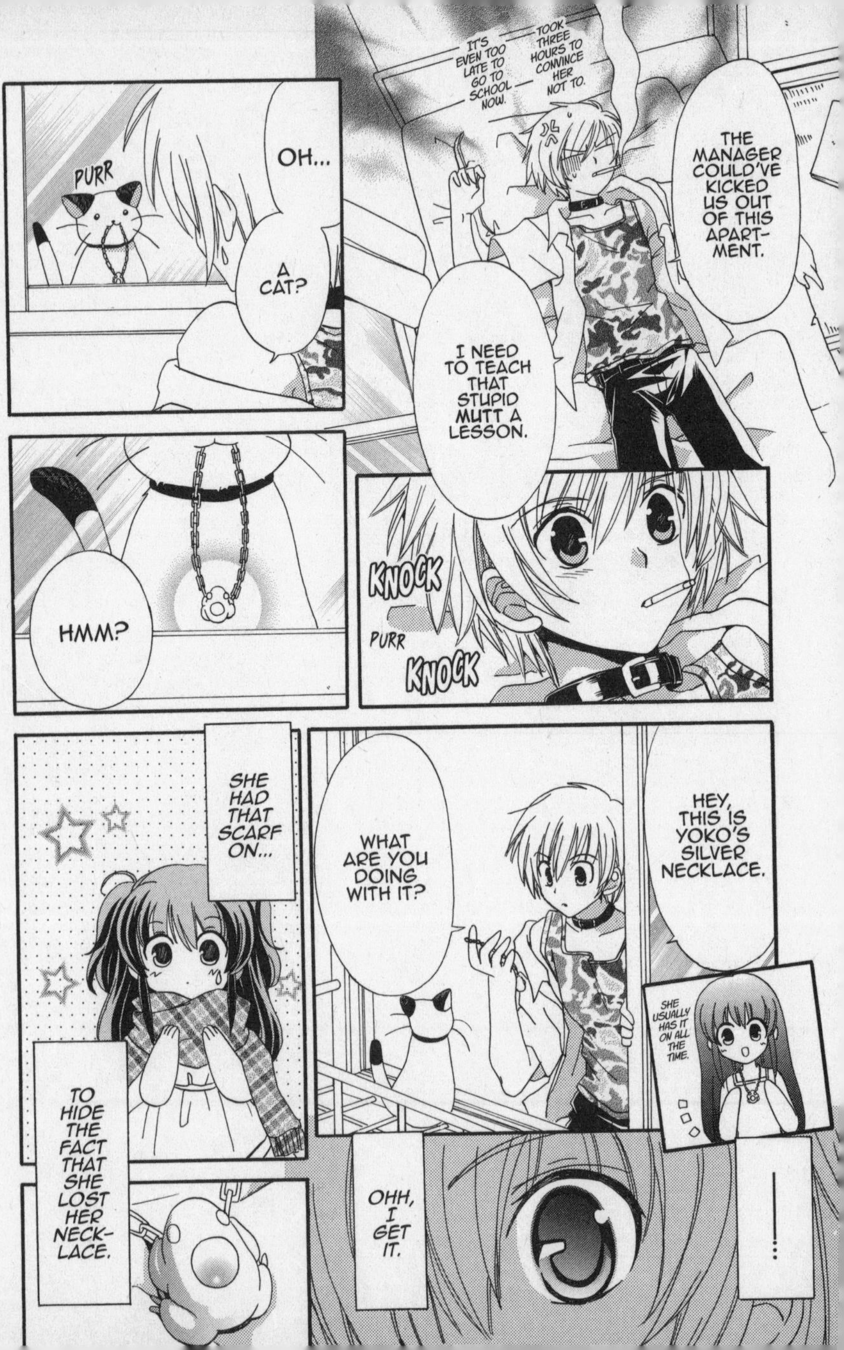
TOOK THREE HOURS TO CONVINCE HER NOT TO.
IT'S EVEN TOO LATE TO GO TO SCHOOL NOW.
THE MANAGER COULD'VE KICKED US OUT OF THIS APARTMENT.
I NEED TO TEACH THAT STUPID MUTT A LESSON.
PURR
OH...
A CAT?
KNOCK
PURR
KNOCK
HMM?
HEY, THIS IS YOKO'S SILVER NECKLACE.
WHAT ARE YOU DOING WITH IT?
SHE USUALLY HAS IT ON ALL THE TIME.
......
OHH, I GET IT.
SHE HAD THAT SCARF ON...
TO HIDE THE FACT THAT SHE LOST HER NECKLACE.

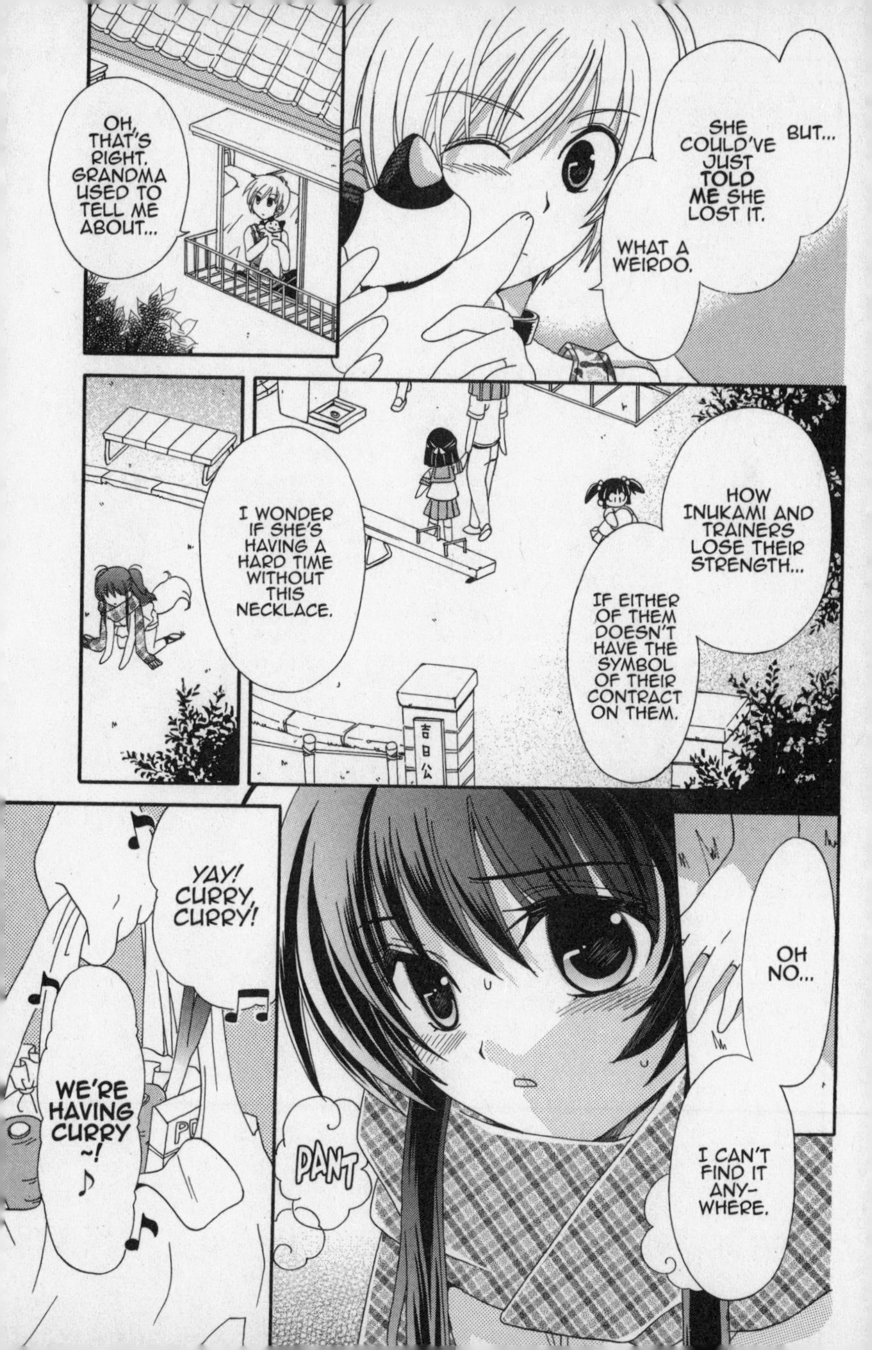
BUT...
SHE COULD'VE JUST TOLD ME SHE LOST IT.
WHAT A WEIRDO.
OH, THAT'S RIGHT. GRANDMA USED TO TELL ME ABOUT...
HOW INUKAMI AND TRAINERS LOSE THEIR STRENGTH...
IF EITHER OF THEM DOESN'T HAVE THE SYMBOL OF THEIR CONTRACT ON THEM.
吉日公
I WONDER IF SHE'S HAVING A HARD TIME WITHOUT THIS NECKLACE.
OH NO...
I CAN'T FIND IT ANY-WHERE.
PANT
YAY! CURRY, CURRY!
WE'RE HAVING CURRY ~! ♪

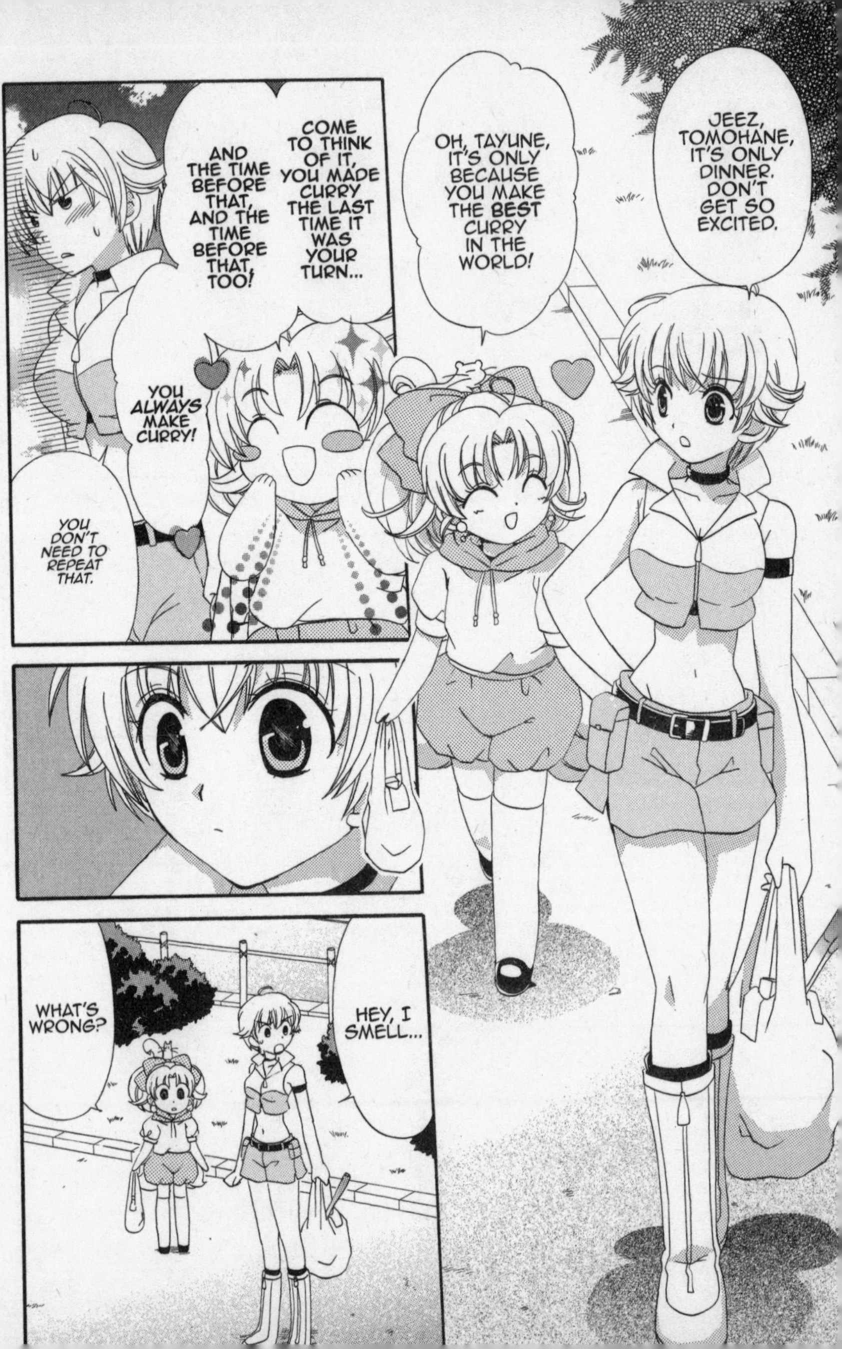
JEEZ, TOMOHANE, IT'S ONLY DINNER. DON'T GET SO EXCITED.
OH, TAYUNE, IT'S ONLY BECAUSE YOU MAKE THE BEST CURRY IN THE WORLD!
COME TO THINK OF IT, YOU MADE CURRY THE LAST TIME IT WAS YOUR TURN...
AND THE TIME BEFORE THAT, AND THE TIME BEFORE THAT, TOO!
YOU ALWAYS MAKE CURRY!
YOU DON'T NEED TO REPEAT THAT.
HEY, I SMELL...
WHAT'S WRONG?

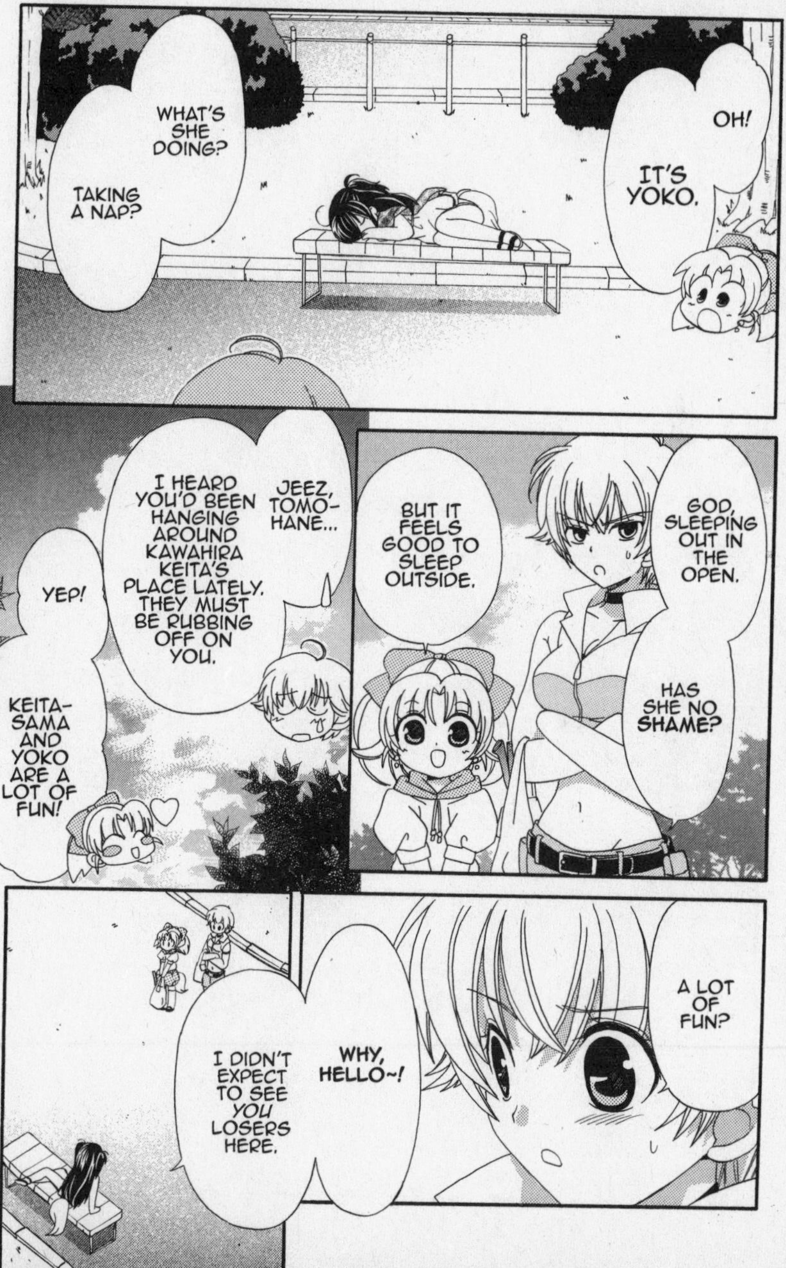
OH!
IT'S YOKO.
WHAT'S SHE DOING?
TAKING A NAP?
GOD, SLEEPING OUT IN THE OPEN.
HAS SHE NO SHAME?
BUT IT FEELS GOOD TO SLEEP OUTSIDE.
JEEZ, TOMO-HANE...
I HEARD YOU'D BEEN HANGING AROUND KAWAHIRA KEITA'S PLACE LATELY. THEY MUST BE RUBBING OFF ON YOU.
YEP!
KEITA-SAMA AND YOKO ARE A LOT OF FUN!
A LOT OF FUN?
WHY, HELLO~!
I DIDN'T EXPECT TO SEE *YOU* LOSERS HERE.

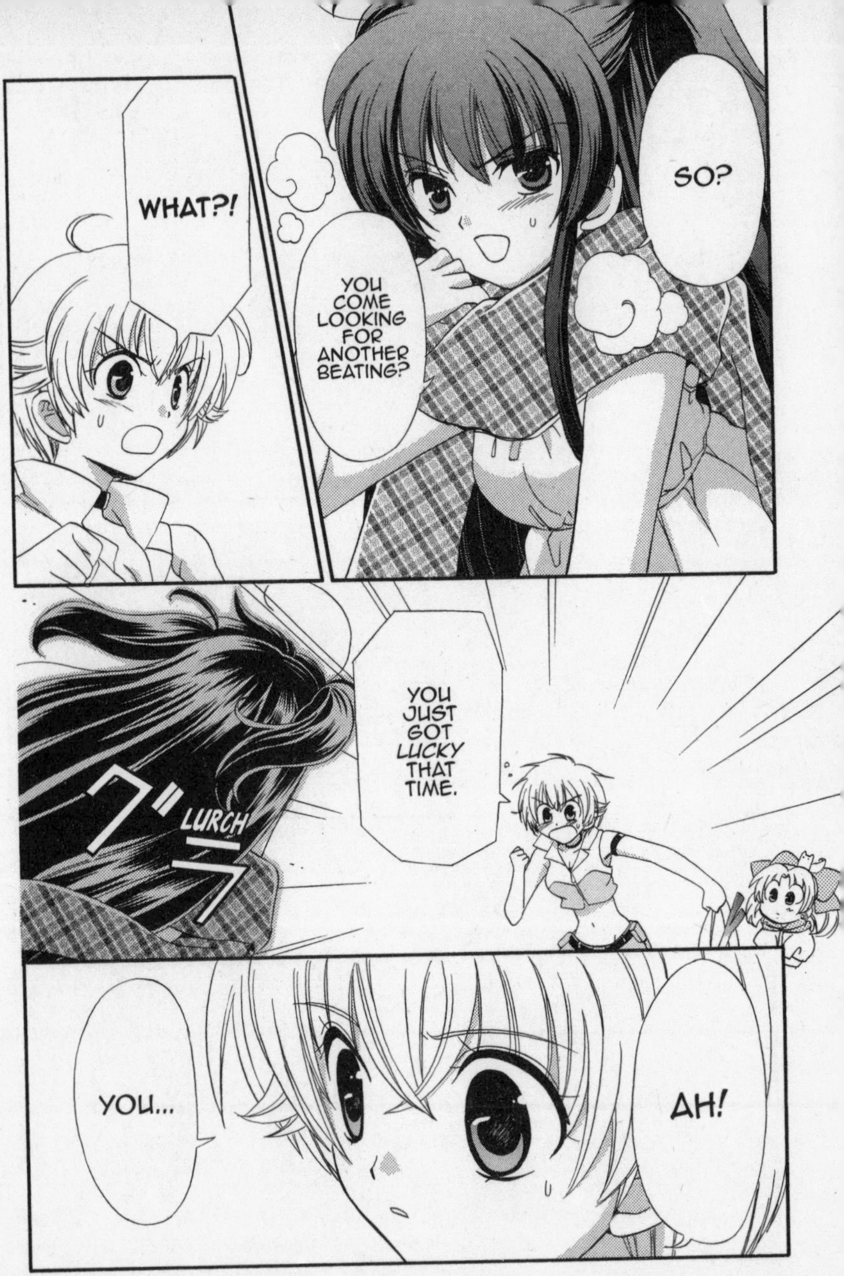
SO?
YOU COME LOOKING FOR ANOTHER BEATING?
WHAT?!
YOU JUST GOT LUCKY THAT TIME.
LURCH
AH!
YOU...

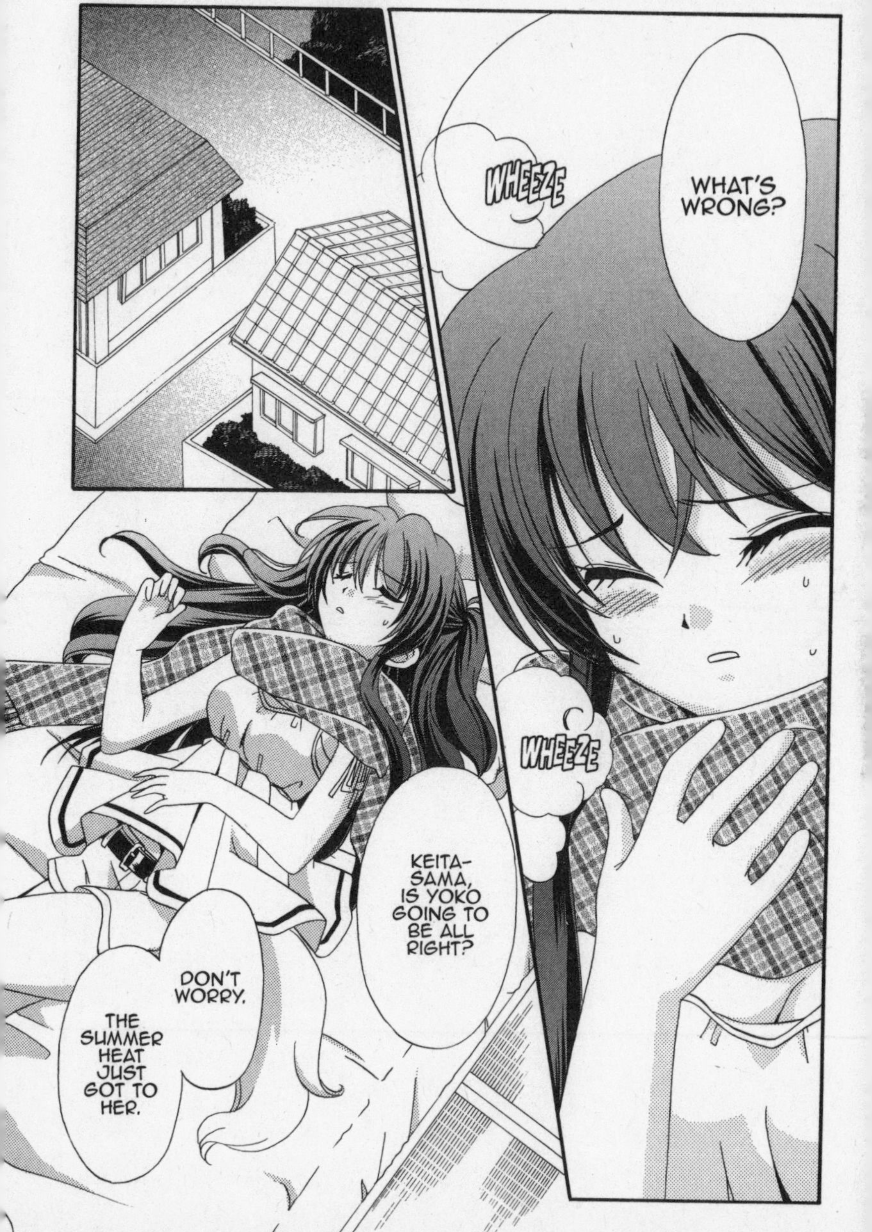
WHAT'S WRONG?
WHEEZE
WHEEZE
KEITA-SAMA, IS YOKO GOING TO BE ALL RIGHT?
DON'T WORRY.
THE SUMMER HEAT JUST GOT TO HER.

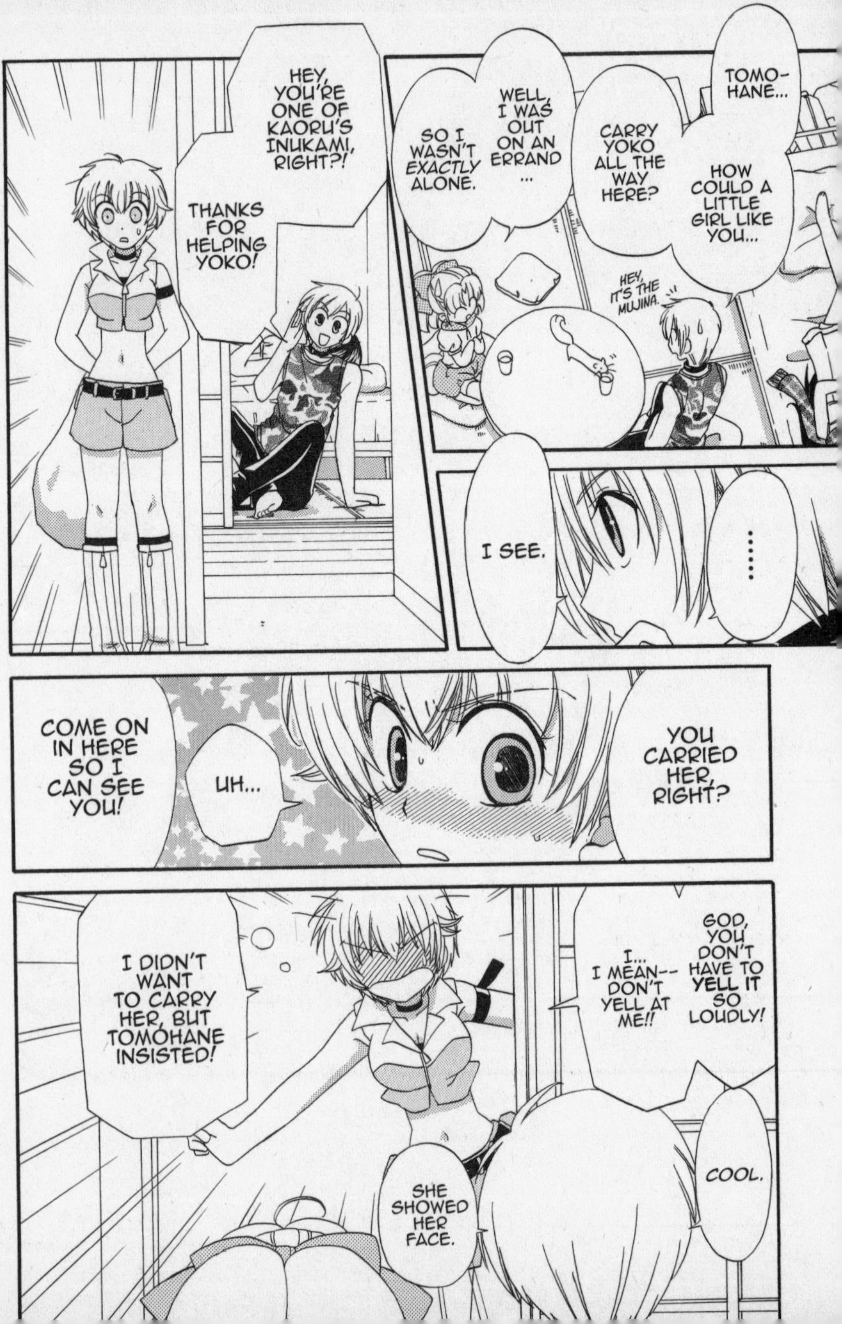
TOMO-HANE...
HOW COULD A LITTLE GIRL LIKE YOU...
CARRY YOKO ALL THE WAY HERE?
WELL, I WAS OUT ON AN ERRAND ...
SO I WASN'T *EXACTLY* ALONE.
HEY, IT'S THE MUJINA.
......
I SEE.
HEY, YOU'RE ONE OF KAORU'S INUKAMI, RIGHT?!
THANKS FOR HELPING YOKO!
YOU CARRIED HER, RIGHT?
UH...
COME ON IN HERE SO I CAN SEE YOU!
GOD, YOU DON'T HAVE TO **YELL IT** SO LOUDLY!
I... I MEAN-- DON'T YELL AT ME!!
I DIDN'T WANT TO CARRY HER, BUT TOMOHANE INSISTED!
COOL.
SHE SHOWED HER FACE.

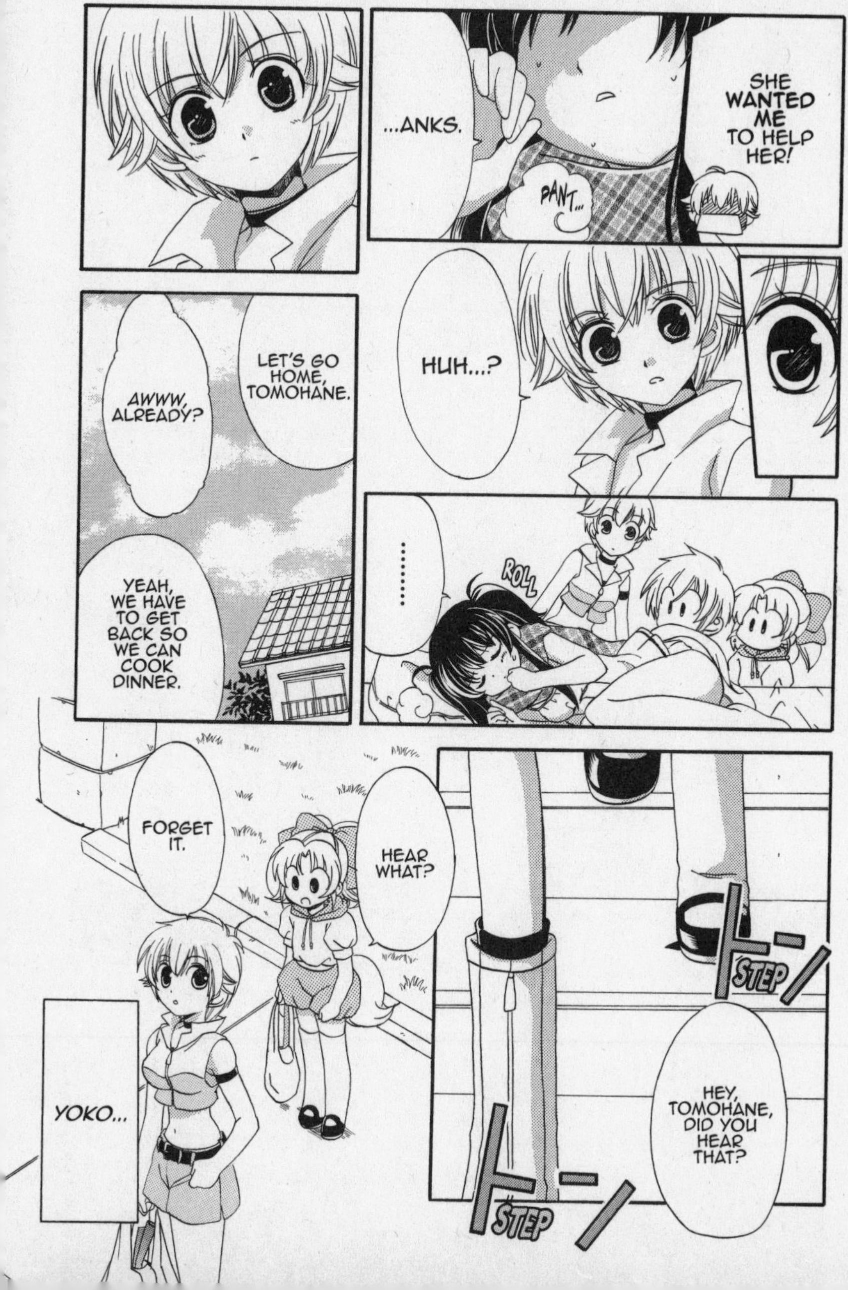
SHE WANTED ME TO HELP HER!
...ANKS.
PANT...
HUH...?
......
ROLL
LET'S GO HOME, TOMOHANE.
AWWW, ALREADY?
YEAH, WE HAVE TO GET BACK SO WE CAN COOK DINNER.
STEP
STEP
HEY, TOMOHANE, DID YOU HEAR THAT?
HEAR WHAT?
FORGET IT.
YOKO...

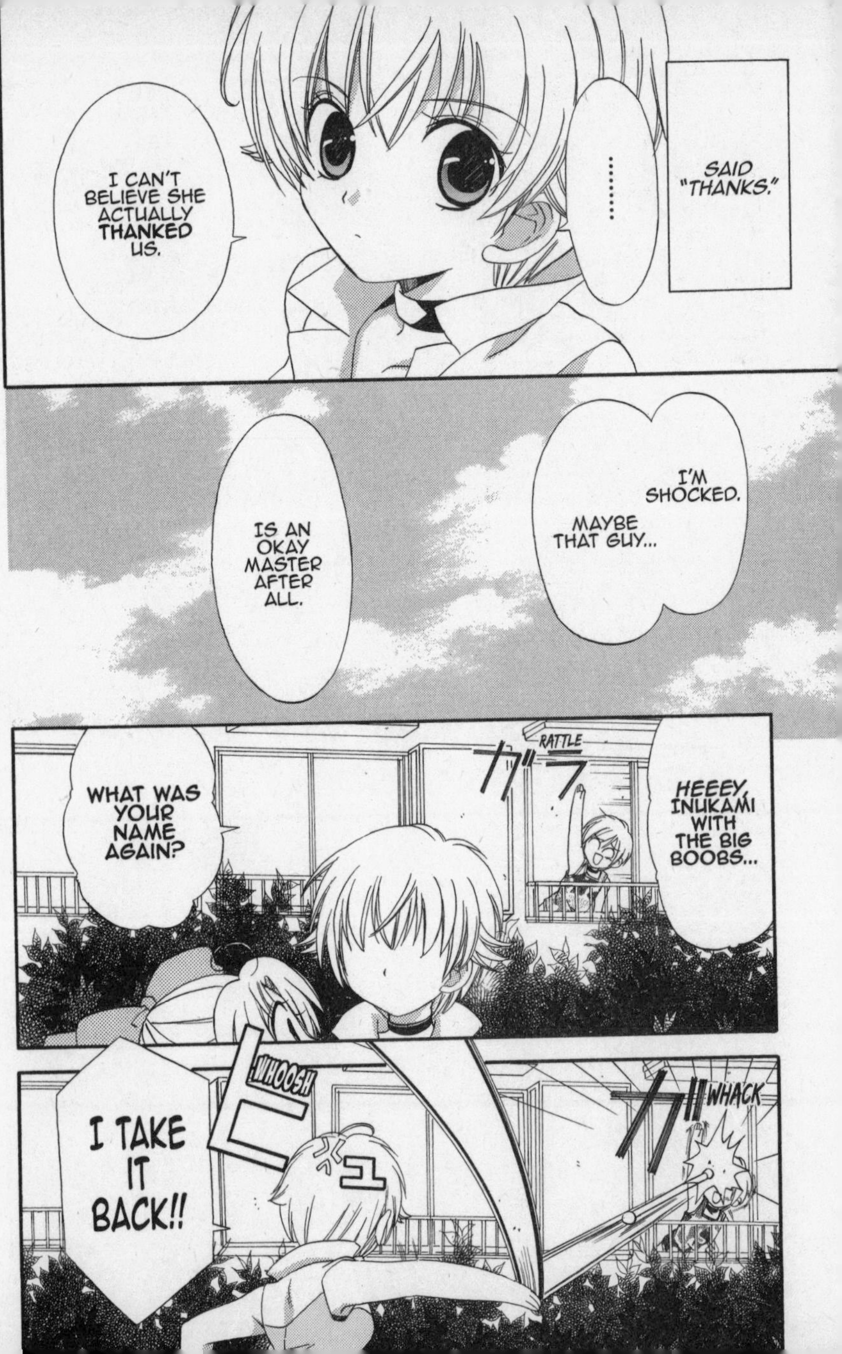
SAID "THANKS."
......
I CAN'T BELIEVE SHE ACTUALLY THANKED US.
I'M SHOCKED.
MAYBE THAT GUY...
IS AN OKAY MASTER AFTER ALL.
RATTLE
HEEEY, INUKAMI WITH THE BIG BOOBS...
WHAT WAS YOUR NAME AGAIN?
WHACK
WHOOSH
I TAKE IT BACK!!

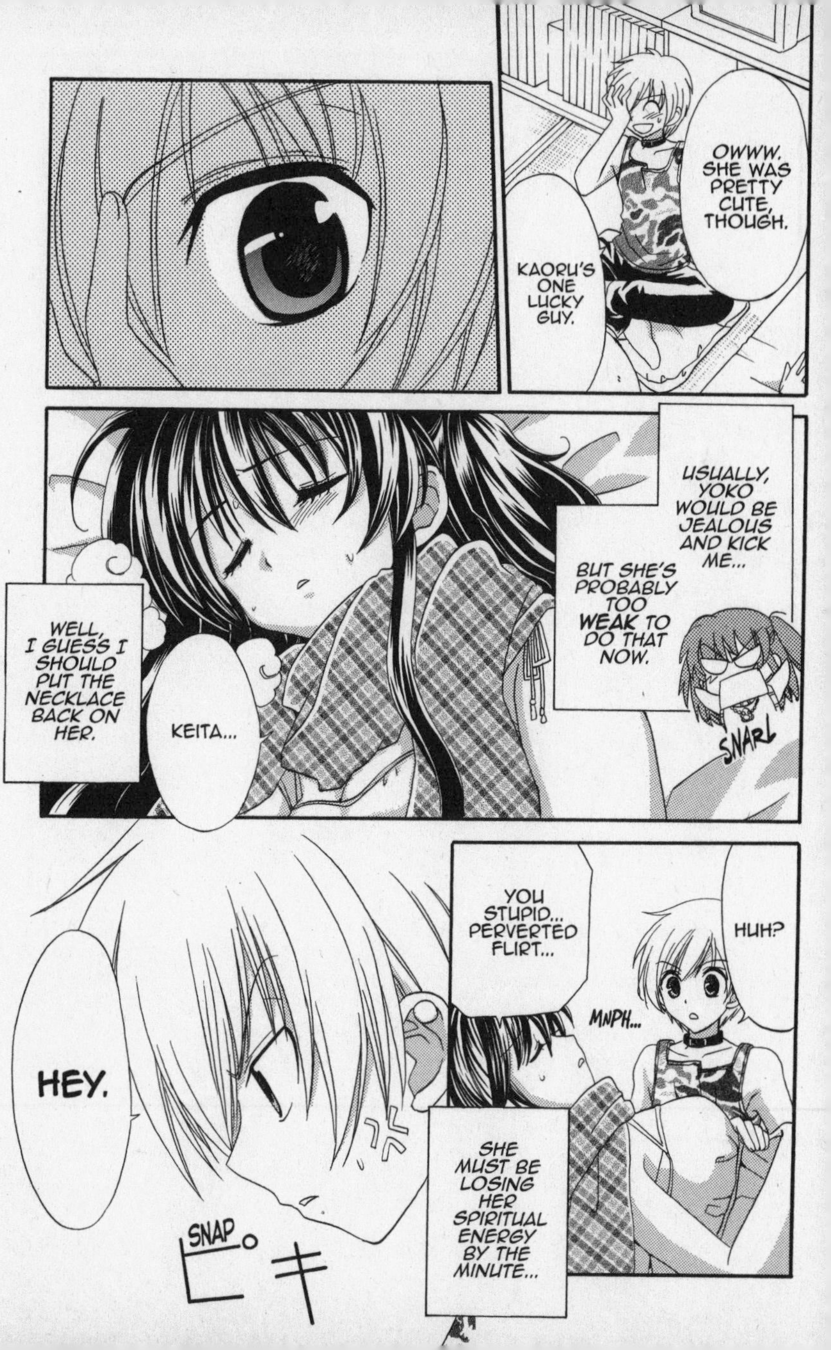
OWWW. SHE WAS PRETTY CUTE, THOUGH.
KAORU'S ONE LUCKY GUY.
USUALLY, YOKO WOULD BE JEALOUS AND KICK ME...
BUT SHE'S PROBABLY TOO WEAK TO DO THAT NOW.
SNARL
KEITA...
WELL, I GUESS I SHOULD PUT THE NECKLACE BACK ON HER.
HUH?
YOU STUPID... PERVERTED FLIRT...
MNPH...
SHE MUST BE LOSING HER SPIRITUAL ENERGY BY THE MINUTE...
HEY.
SNAP

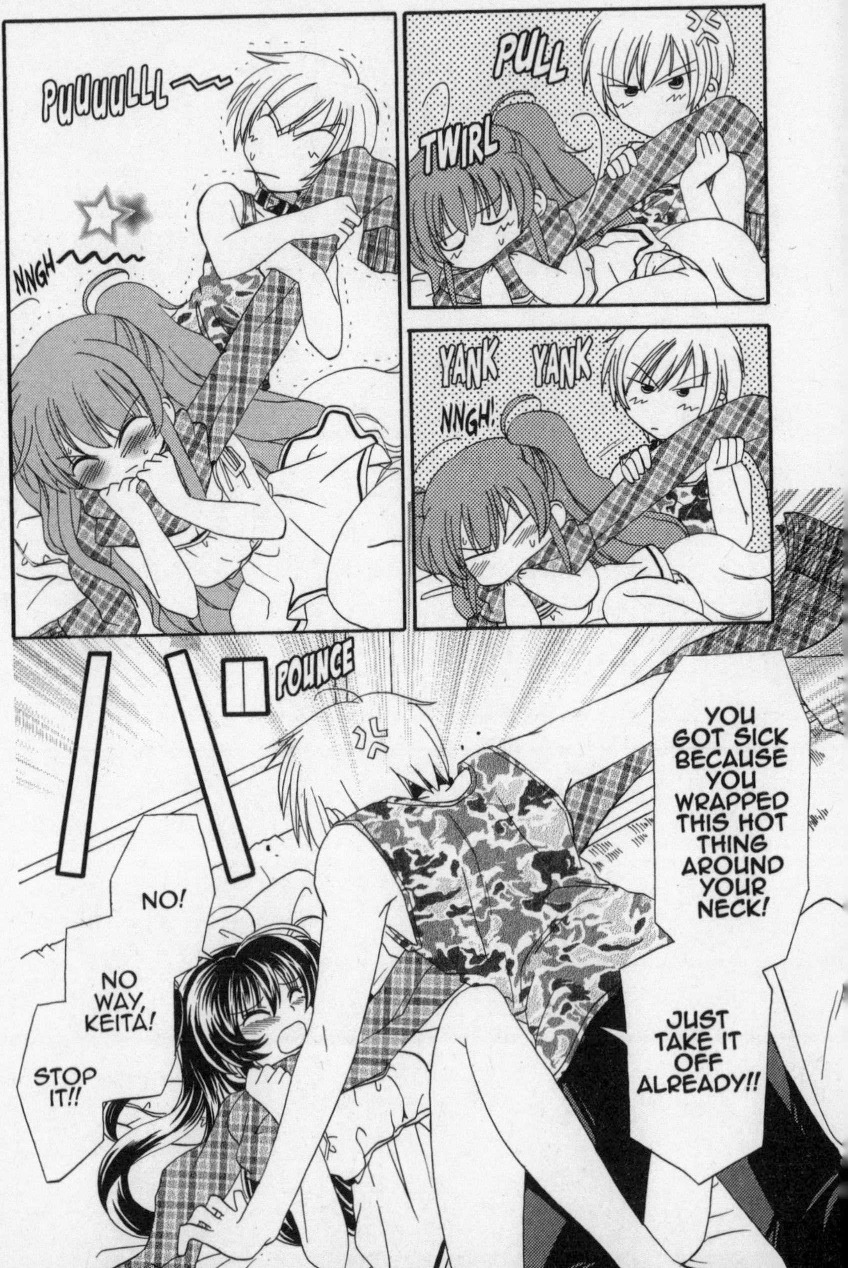
PULL
TWIRL
YANK YANK
NNGH!
PUUUULLL
NNGH
POUNCE
YOU GOT SICK BECAUSE YOU WRAPPED THIS HOT THING AROUND YOUR NECK!
JUST TAKE IT OFF ALREADY!!
NO!
NO WAY, KEITA!
STOP IT!!

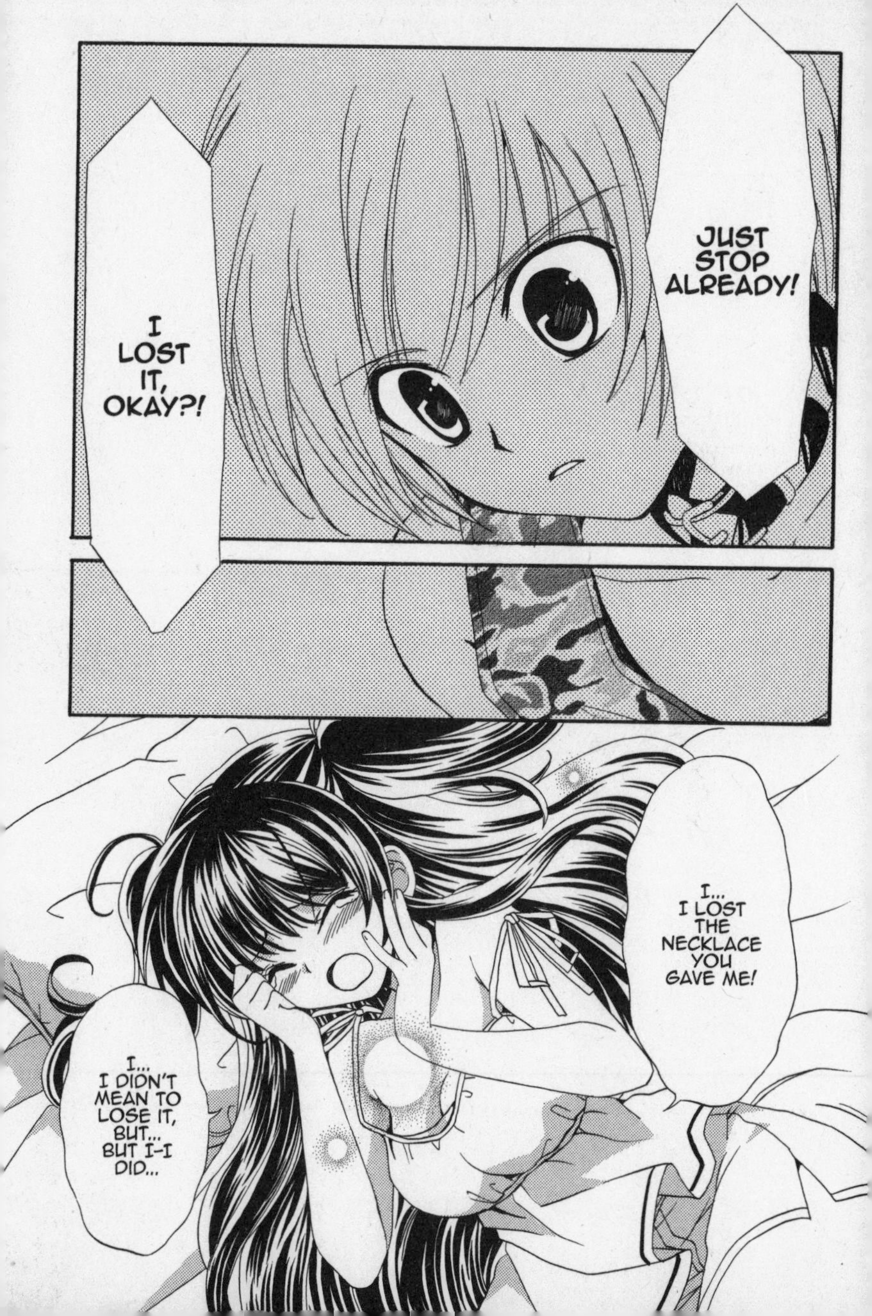
JUST STOP ALREADY!
I LOST IT, OKAY?!
I... I LOST THE NECKLACE YOU GAVE ME!
I... I DIDN'T MEAN TO LOSE IT, BUT... BUT I-I DID...

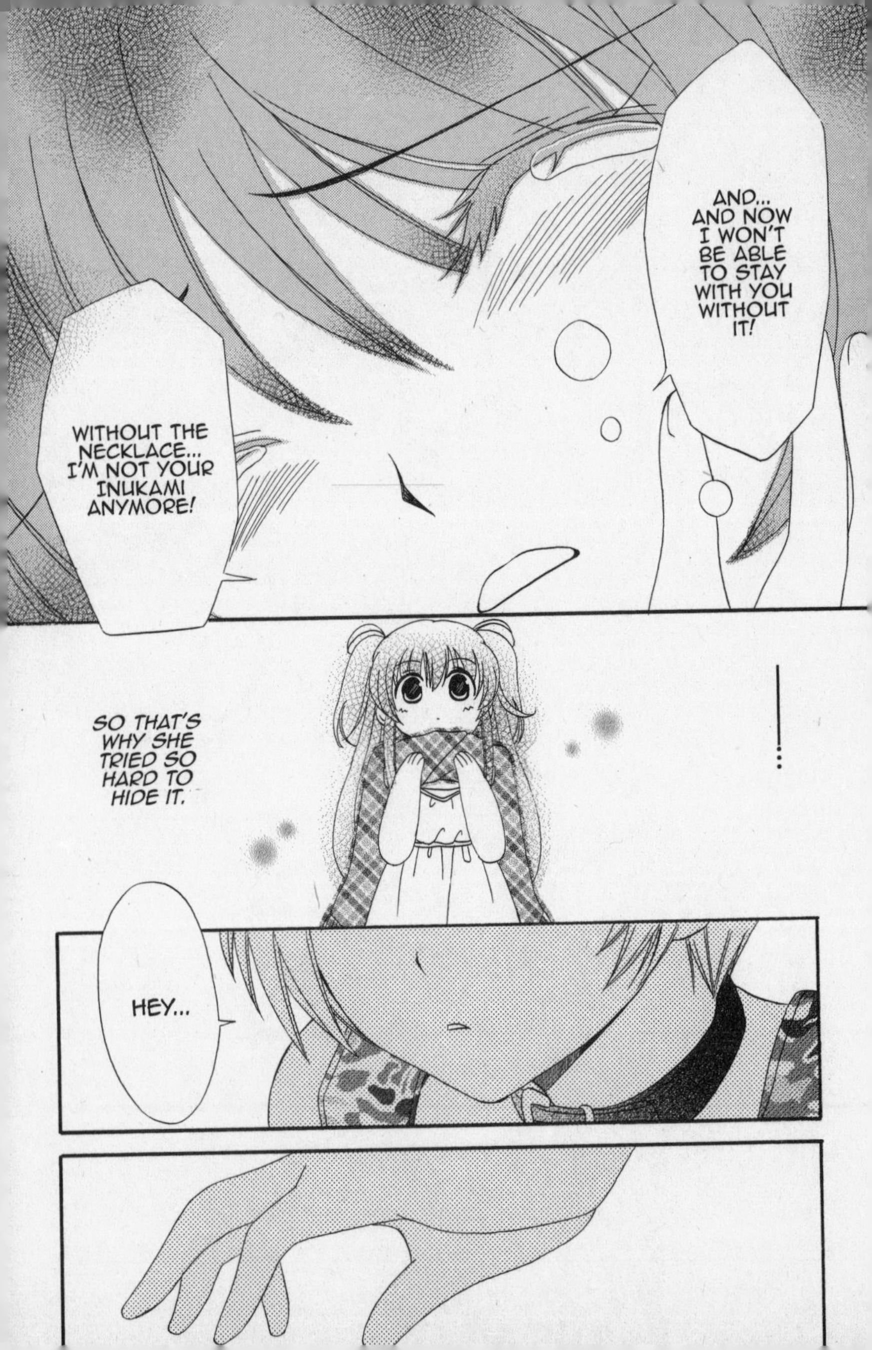
AND... AND NOW I WON'T BE ABLE TO STAY WITH YOU WITHOUT IT!
WITHOUT THE NECKLACE... I'M NOT YOUR INUKAMI ANYMORE!
SO THAT'S WHY SHE TRIED SO HARD TO HIDE IT.
HEY...

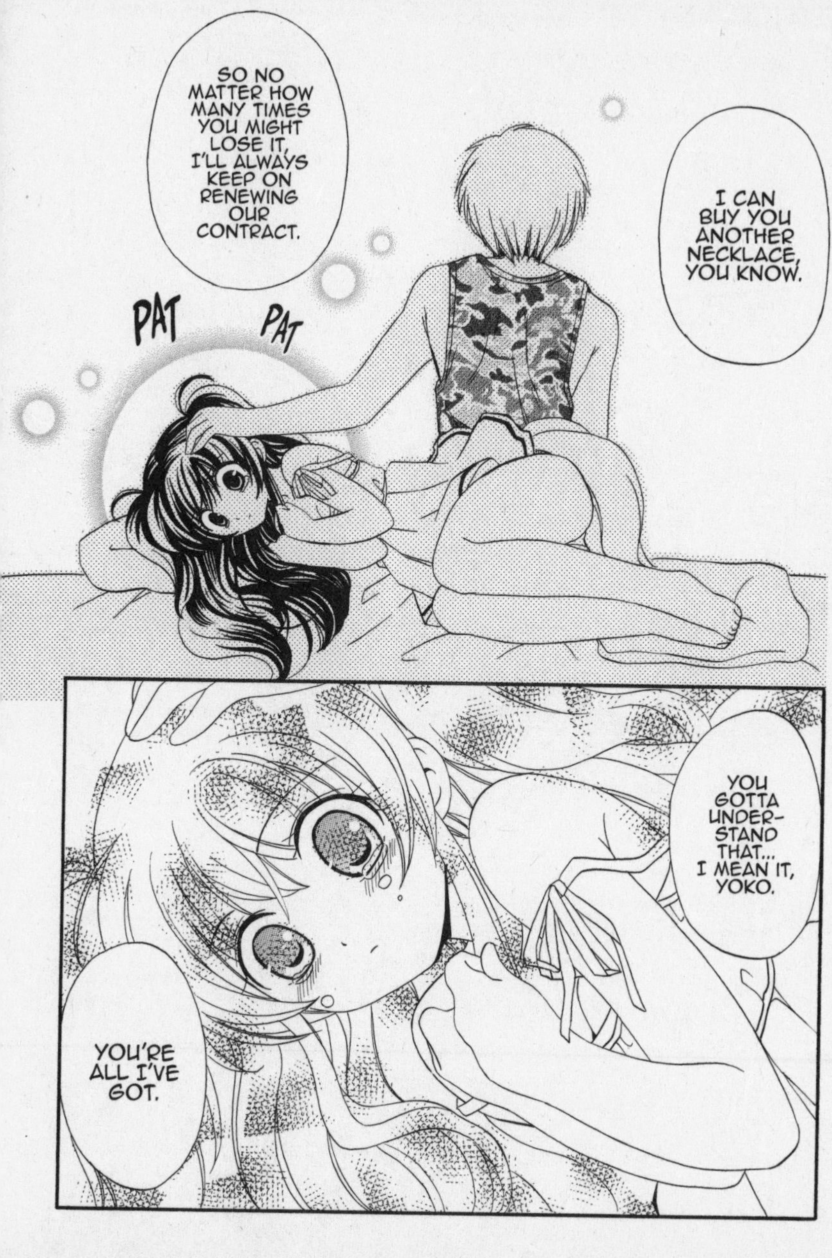
I CAN BUY YOU ANOTHER NECKLACE, YOU KNOW.
SO NO MATTER HOW MANY TIMES YOU MIGHT LOSE IT, I'LL ALWAYS KEEP ON RENEWING OUR CONTRACT.
PAT PAT
YOU GOTTA UNDER-STAND THAT... I MEAN IT, YOKO.
YOU'RE ALL I'VE GOT.

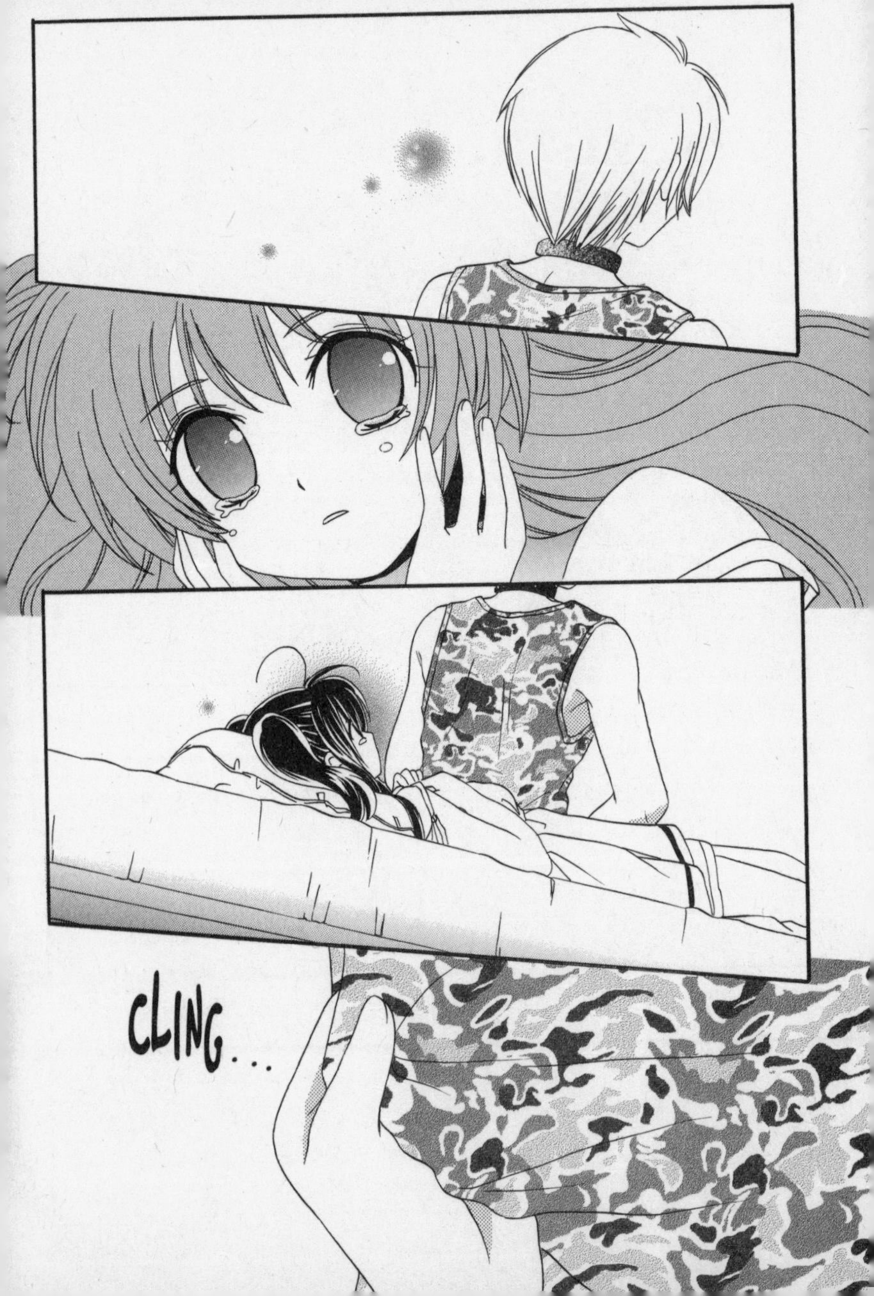
CLING...

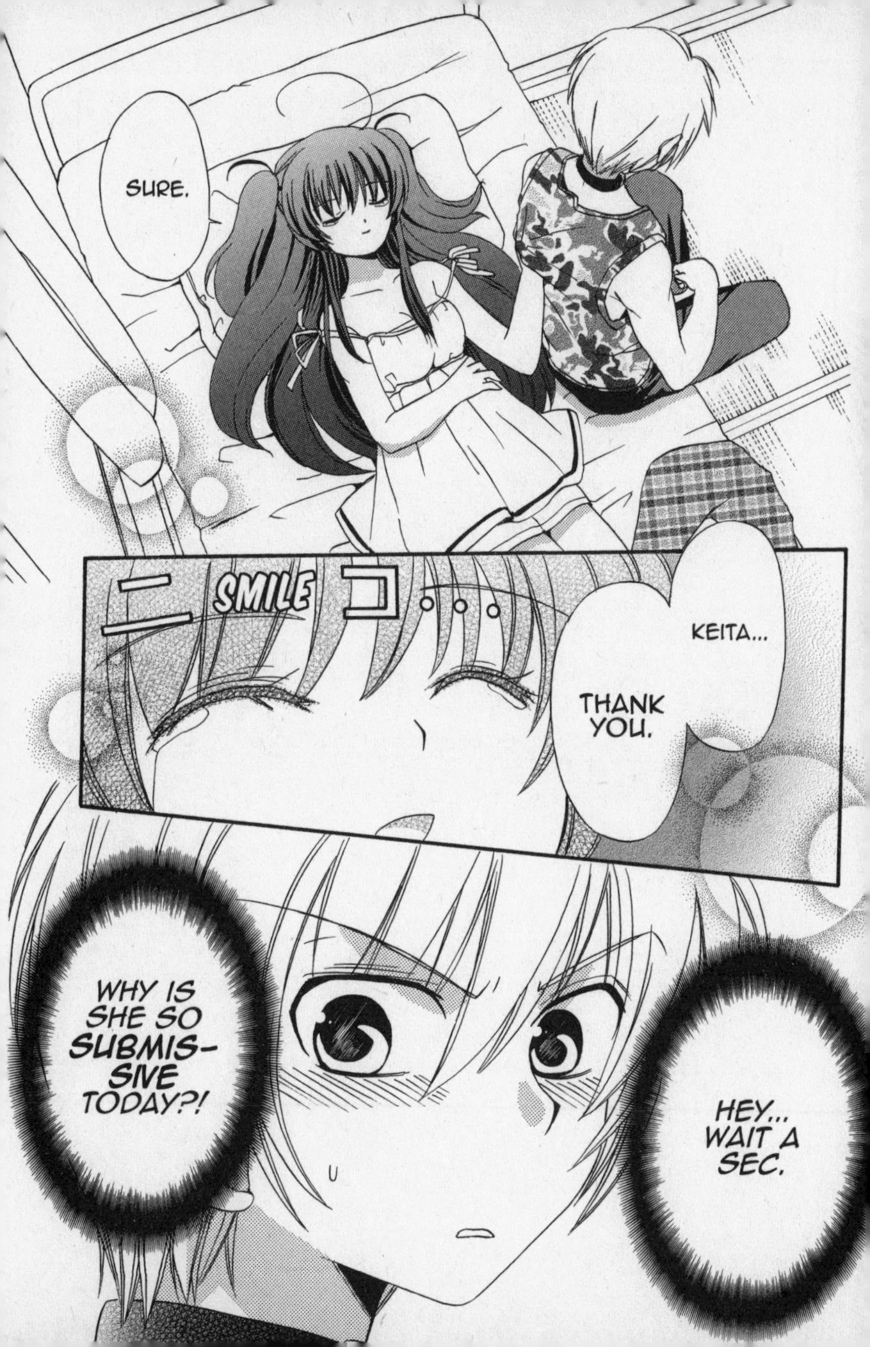
SURE.
KEITA... THANK YOU.
SMILE
HEY... WAIT A SEC.
WHY IS SHE SO SUBMIS-SIVE TODAY?!

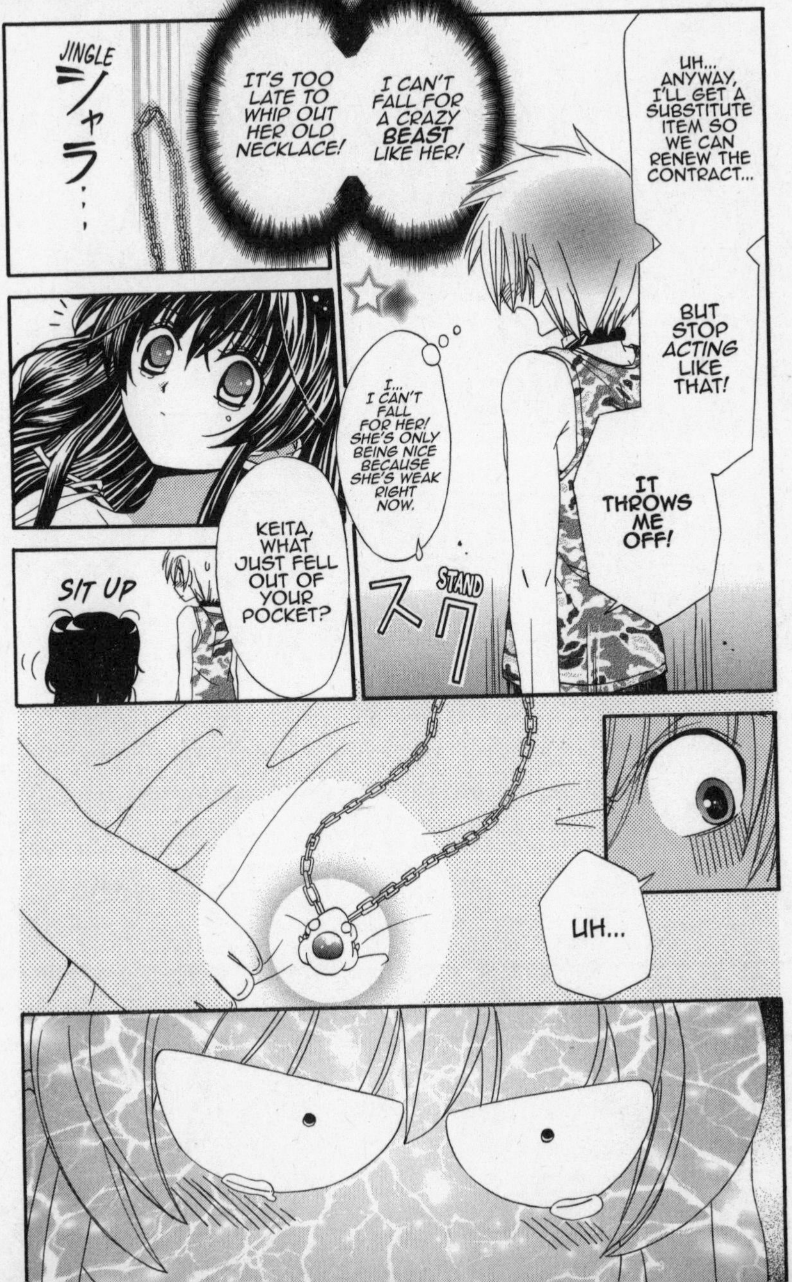
UH... ANYWAY, I'LL GET A SUBSTITUTE ITEM SO WE CAN RENEW THE CONTRACT...
BUT STOP ACTING LIKE THAT!
IT THROWS ME OFF!
I CAN'T FALL FOR A CRAZY BEAST LIKE HER!
IT'S TOO LATE TO WHIP OUT HER OLD NECKLACE!
I... I CAN'T FALL FOR HER! SHE'S ONLY BEING NICE BECAUSE SHE'S WEAK RIGHT NOW.
STAND
スク
JINGLE
シャラ・・・
SIT UP
KEITA, WHAT JUST FELL OUT OF YOUR POCKET?
UH...

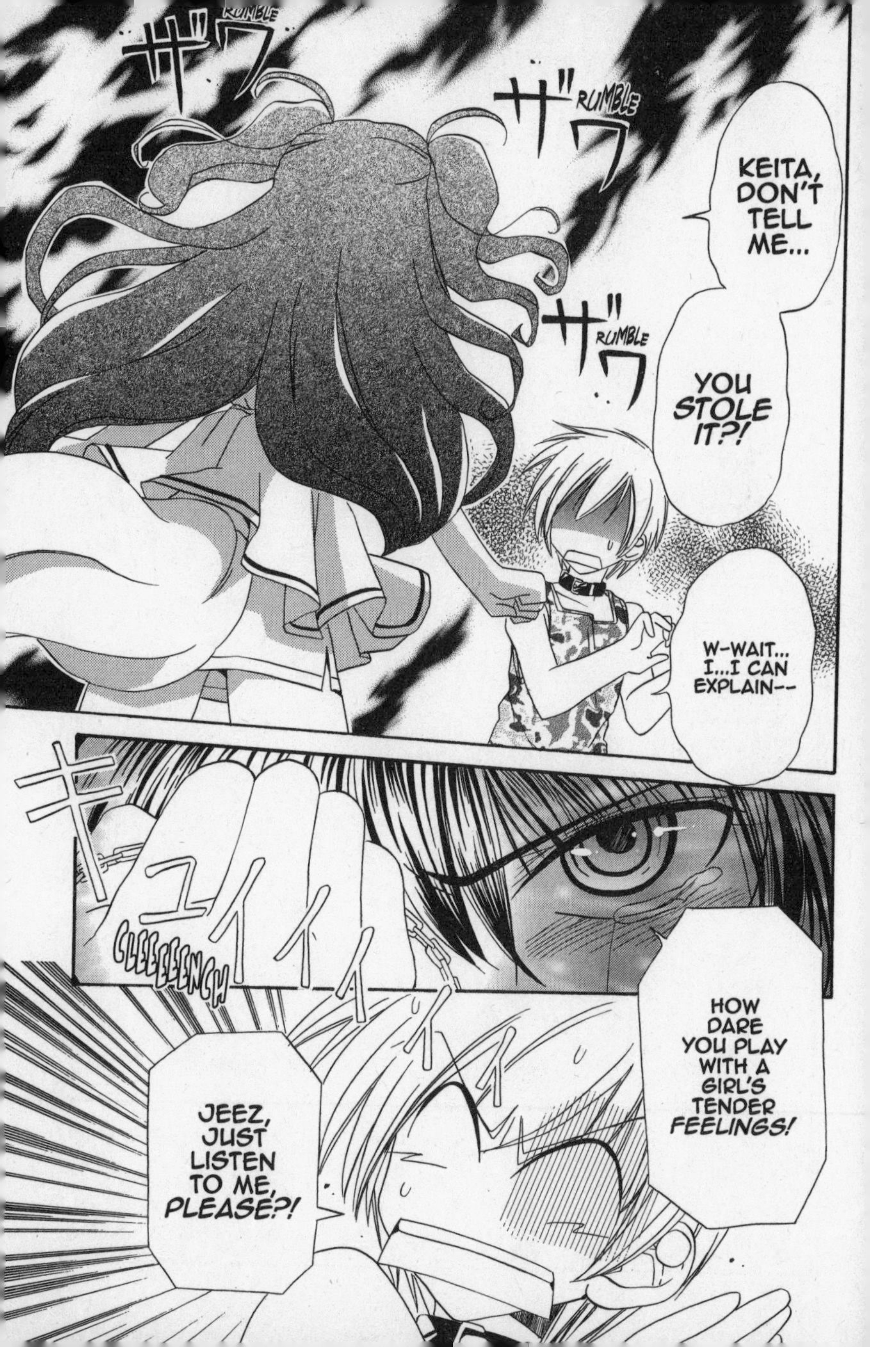
ザワ RUMBLE
KEITA, DON'T TELL ME...
ザワ RUMBLE
ザワ RUMBLE
YOU STOLE IT?!
W-WAIT... I...I CAN EXPLAIN--
キュイイイイ CLEEEEENCH
HOW DARE YOU PLAY WITH A GIRL'S TENDER FEELINGS!
JEEZ, JUST LISTEN TO ME, PLEASE?!

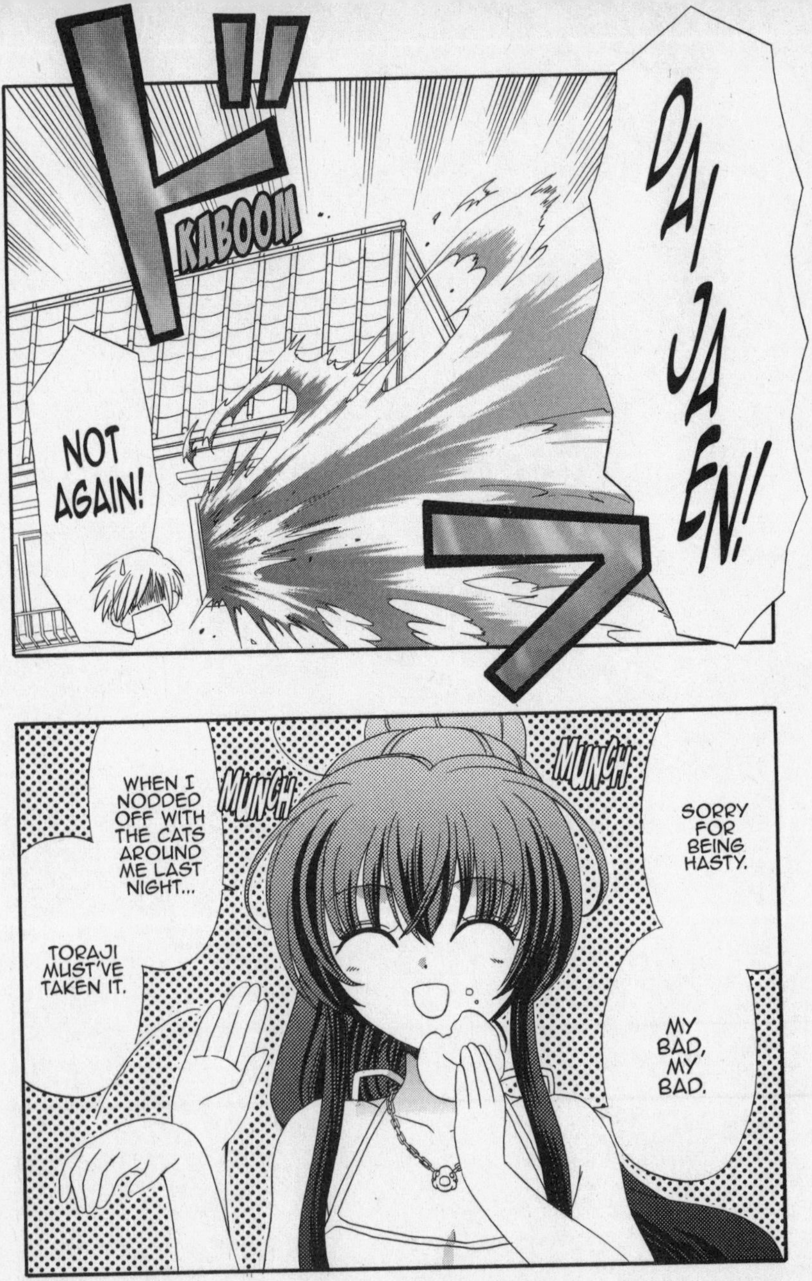
DAI JA EN!!
KABOOM
NOT AGAIN!
SORRY FOR BEING HASTY.
MY BAD, MY BAD.
MUNCH
MUNCH
WHEN I NODDED OFF WITH THE CATS AROUND ME LAST NIGHT...
TORAJI MUST'VE TAKEN IT.

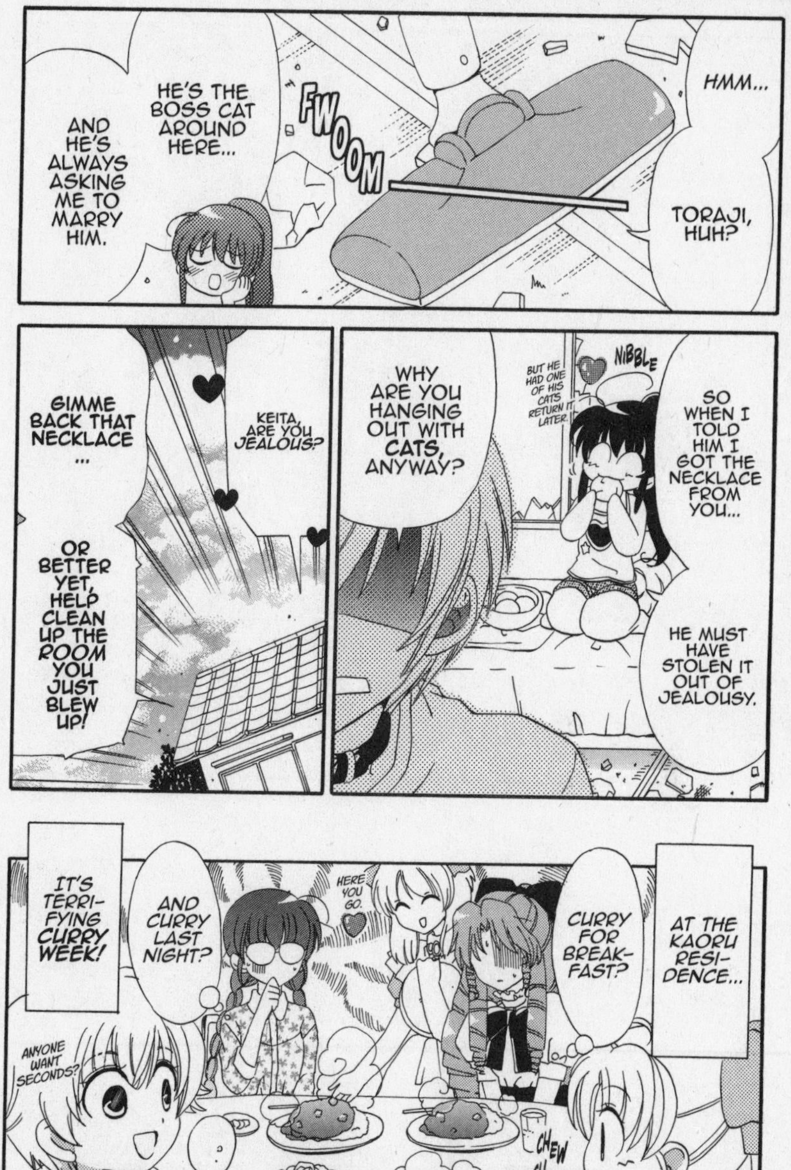
HMM...
TORAJI, HUH?
FWOOM
HE'S THE BOSS CAT AROUND HERE...
AND HE'S ALWAYS ASKING ME TO MARRY HIM.
SO WHEN I TOLD HIM I GOT THE NECKLACE FROM YOU...
NIBBLE
BUT HE HAD ONE OF HIS CATS RETURN IT LATER.
HE MUST HAVE STOLEN IT OUT OF JEALOUSY.
WHY ARE YOU HANGING OUT WITH CATS, ANYWAY?
KEITA, ARE YOU JEALOUS?
GIMME BACK THAT NECKLACE ...
OR BETTER YET, HELP CLEAN UP THE ROOM YOU JUST BLEW UP!
AT THE KAORU RESIDENCE...
CURRY FOR BREAKFAST?
HERE YOU GO.
AND CURRY LAST NIGHT?
IT'S TERRIFYING CURRY WEEK!
ANYONE WANT SECONDS?
CHEW CHEW

To Be Continued

Afterword!

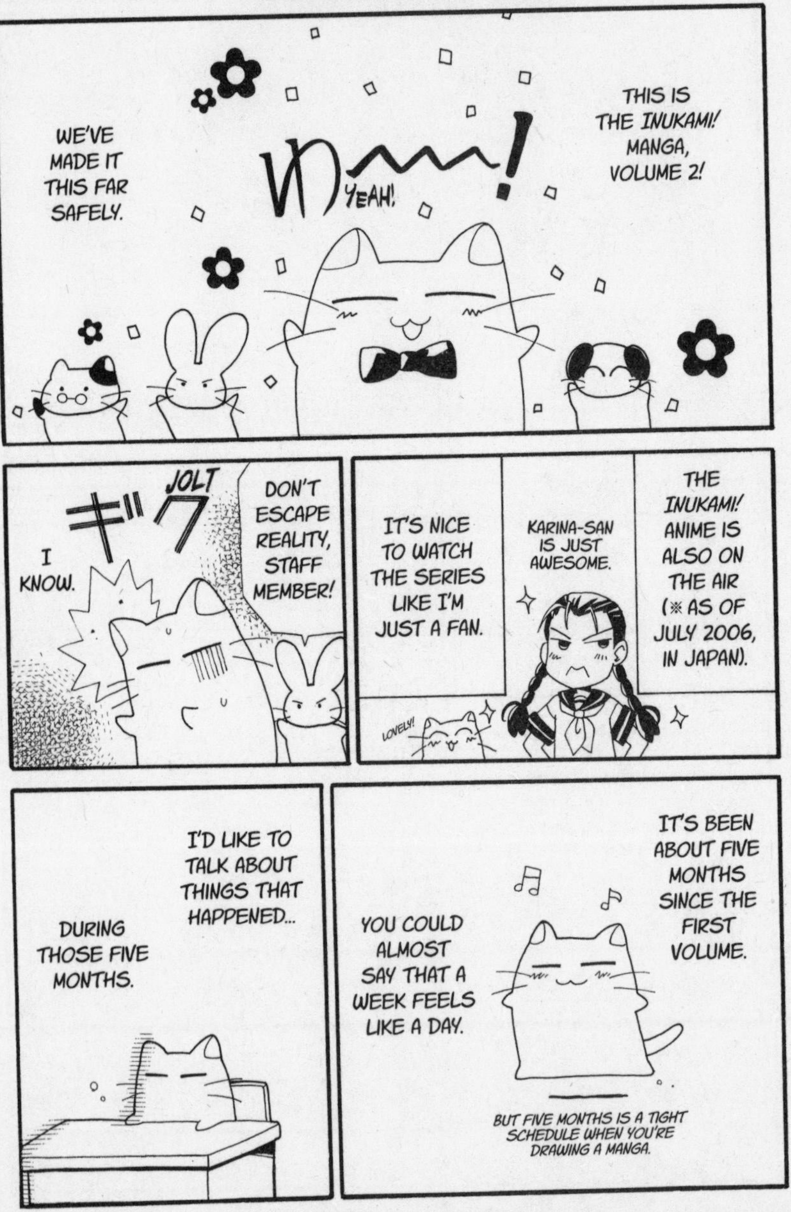
THIS IS THE INUKAMI! MANGA, VOLUME 2!
YEAH!
WE'VE MADE IT THIS FAR SAFELY.
THE INUKAMI! ANIME IS ALSO ON THE AIR (※ AS OF JULY 2006, IN JAPAN).
KARINA-SAN IS JUST AWESOME.
IT'S NICE TO WATCH THE SERIES LIKE I'M JUST A FAN.
LOVELY!
DON'T ESCAPE REALITY, STAFF MEMBER!
ギク
JOLT
I KNOW.
IT'S BEEN ABOUT FIVE MONTHS SINCE THE FIRST VOLUME.
YOU COULD ALMOST SAY THAT A WEEK FEELS LIKE A DAY.
BUT FIVE MONTHS IS A TIGHT SCHEDULE WHEN YOU'RE DRAWING A MANGA.
I'D LIKE TO TALK ABOUT THINGS THAT HAPPENED...
DURING THOSE FIVE MONTHS.

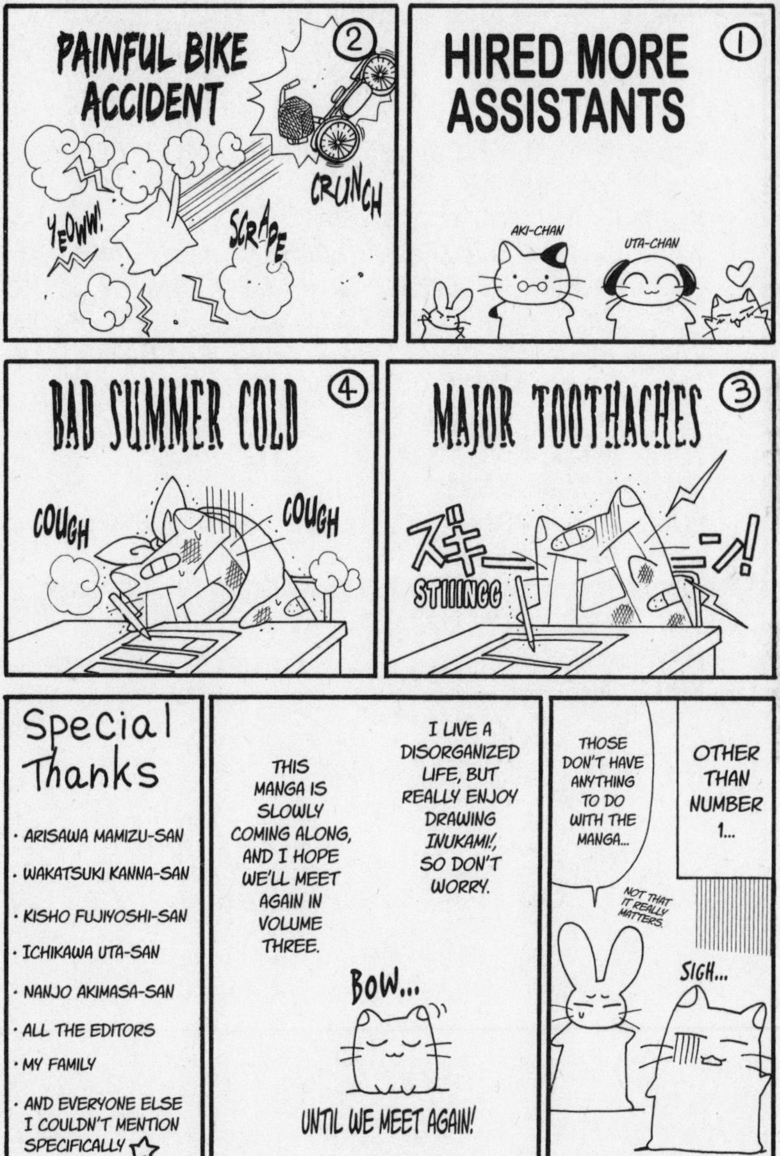
HIRED MORE ASSISTANTS
①
UTA-CHAN
AKI-CHAN
PAINFUL BIKE ACCIDENT
②
CRUNCH
SCRAPE
YEOWW!
MAJOR TOOTHACHES
③
ズキーーン!
STIIINGG
BAD SUMMER COLD
④
COUGH
COUGH
OTHER THAN NUMBER 1...
THOSE DON'T HAVE ANYTHING TO DO WITH THE MANGA...
NOT THAT IT REALLY MATTERS.
SIGH...
I LIVE A DISORGANIZED LIFE, BUT REALLY ENJOY DRAWING INUKAMI!, SO DON'T WORRY.
THIS MANGA IS SLOWLY COMING ALONG, AND I HOPE WE'LL MEET AGAIN IN VOLUME THREE.
BOW...
UNTIL WE MEET AGAIN!
Special Thanks
· ARISAWA MAMIZU-SAN
· WAKATSUKI KANNA-SAN
· KISHO FUJIYOSHI-SAN
· ICHIKAWA UTA-SAN
· NANJO AKIMASA-SAN
· ALL THE EDITORS
· MY FAMILY
· AND EVERYONE ELSE I COULDN'T MENTION SPECIFICALLY ☆

From the Creator and Character Designers

YOKO: KEITA, I WANT TO KNOW SOMETHING. WHY DO YOU LIKE FROGS?

KEITA: HUH? WHAT DO YOU MEAN?

YOKO: KEITA, YOU USE FROG ERASERS, RIGHT? AND YOU GAVE ME A NECKLACE WITH A FROG TRINKET. SO I JUST THOUGHT, YOU KNOW, YOU MUST LIKE FROGS.

KEITA: OH, THAT... (WITH A FARAWAY LOOK) IT'S KIND OF A LONG STORY. IT GOES BACK TO WHEN I WAS STILL IN TRAINING.

YOKO: YAWN~♪

KEITA: HEY, WAKE UP!

YOKO: JUST KIDDING.♪ SO, TELL ME ABOUT IT. GIMME ALL THE DETAILS.

KEITA: LIKE I SAID, I WAS IN TRAINING THEN. SUDDENLY, THIS SILLY FROG...

YOKO: SNOOZE~

KEITA: HEEEEY!!

WHY DOES KEITA USE FROG ERASERS?
I'LL PUT THAT QUESTION ASIDE FOR NOW.
CONGRATULATIONS ON THE RELEASE OF INUKAMI! VOLUME TWO.
I'M GLAD THAT THE SERIES IS PROGRESSING AT A STEADY PACE.
I LOOK FORWARD TO HAVING THE OPPORTUNITY TO ANSWER THAT QUESTION IN A FUTURE VOLUME OF THE MANGA.

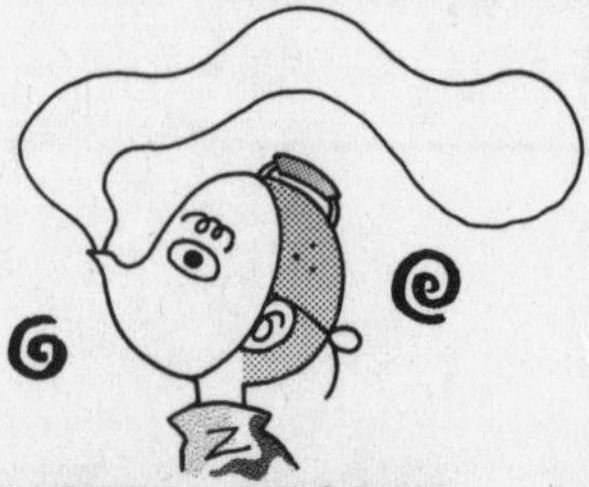

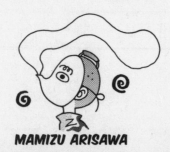

MAMIZU ARISAWA

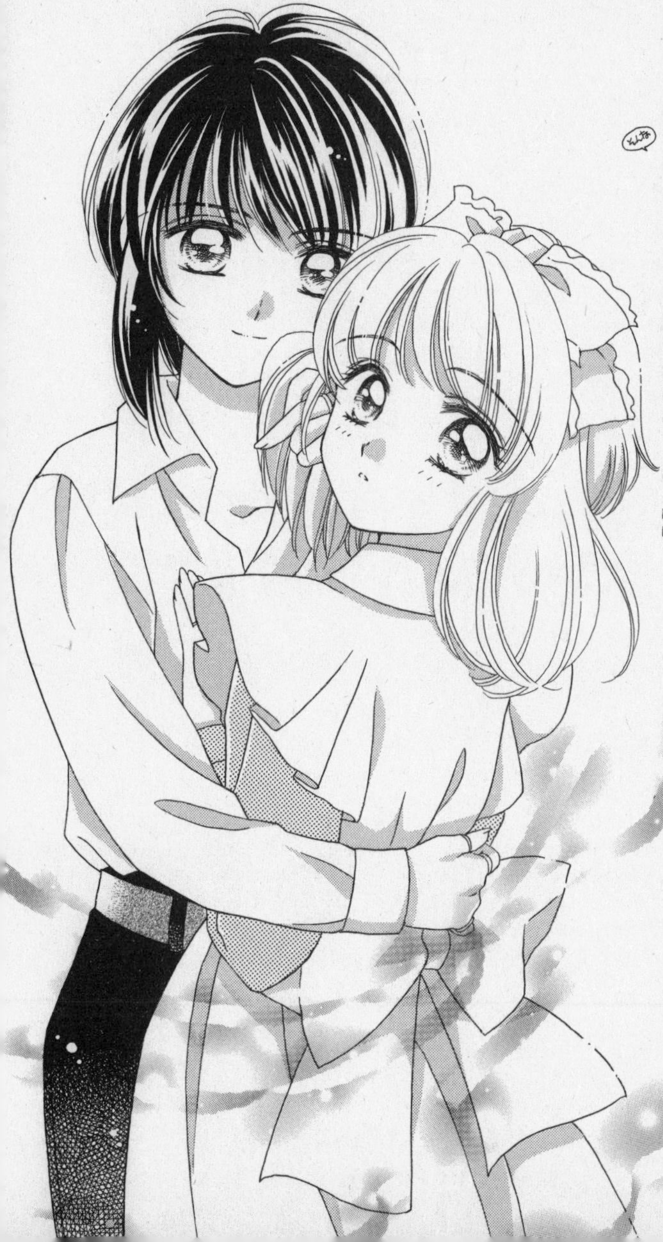

CONGRATULATIONS ON THE RELEASE OF VOLUME TWO. CLAP CLAP! MATSUZAWA-SAN, THANK YOU FOR LISTENING TO MY WHINY COMMENTS SO PATIENTLY OVER THE PHONE... SORRY FOR TROUBLING YOU. I HOPE I CAN MAKE IT UP TO YOU WITH THIS PICTURE OF KAORU AND NADESHIKO THAT YOU REQUESTED. I LOOK FORWARD TO WORKING WITH YOU AGAIN!

FROM KANNA WAKATSUKI.

P.S. MATSUZAWA-SAN DRAWS NADESHIKO SO ADORABLY.

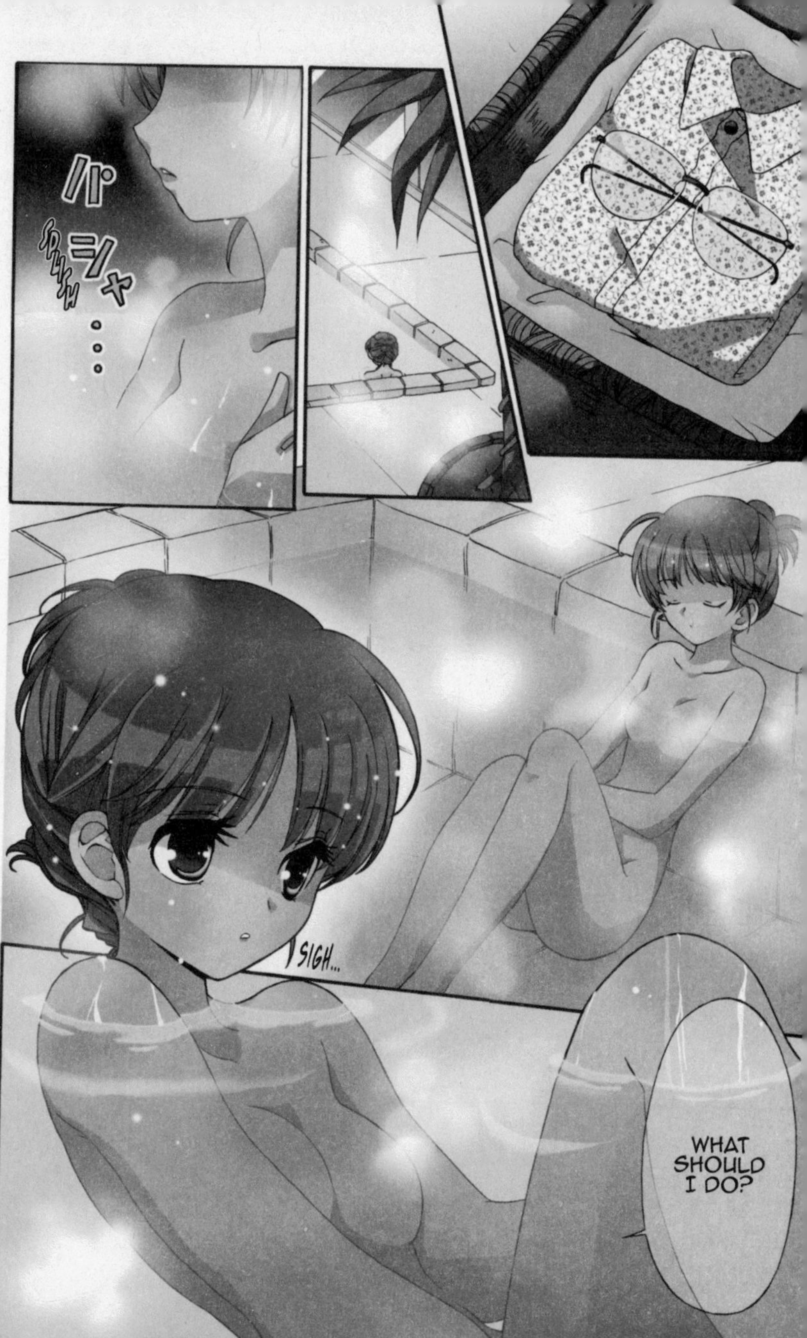
パシャ
SPLASH
...
SIGH...
WHAT SHOULD I DO?

Step.11 Little Red Riding Hoods, Beware! Part 1

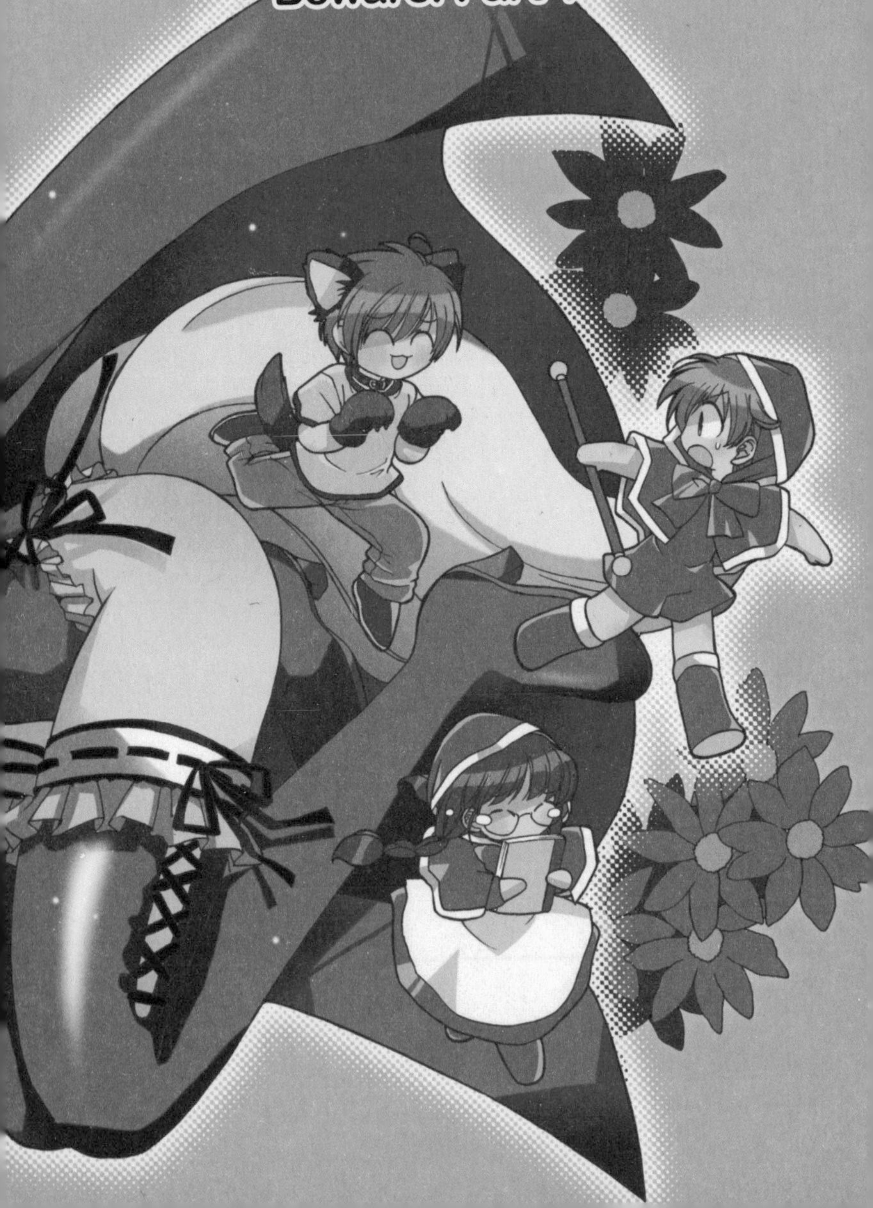

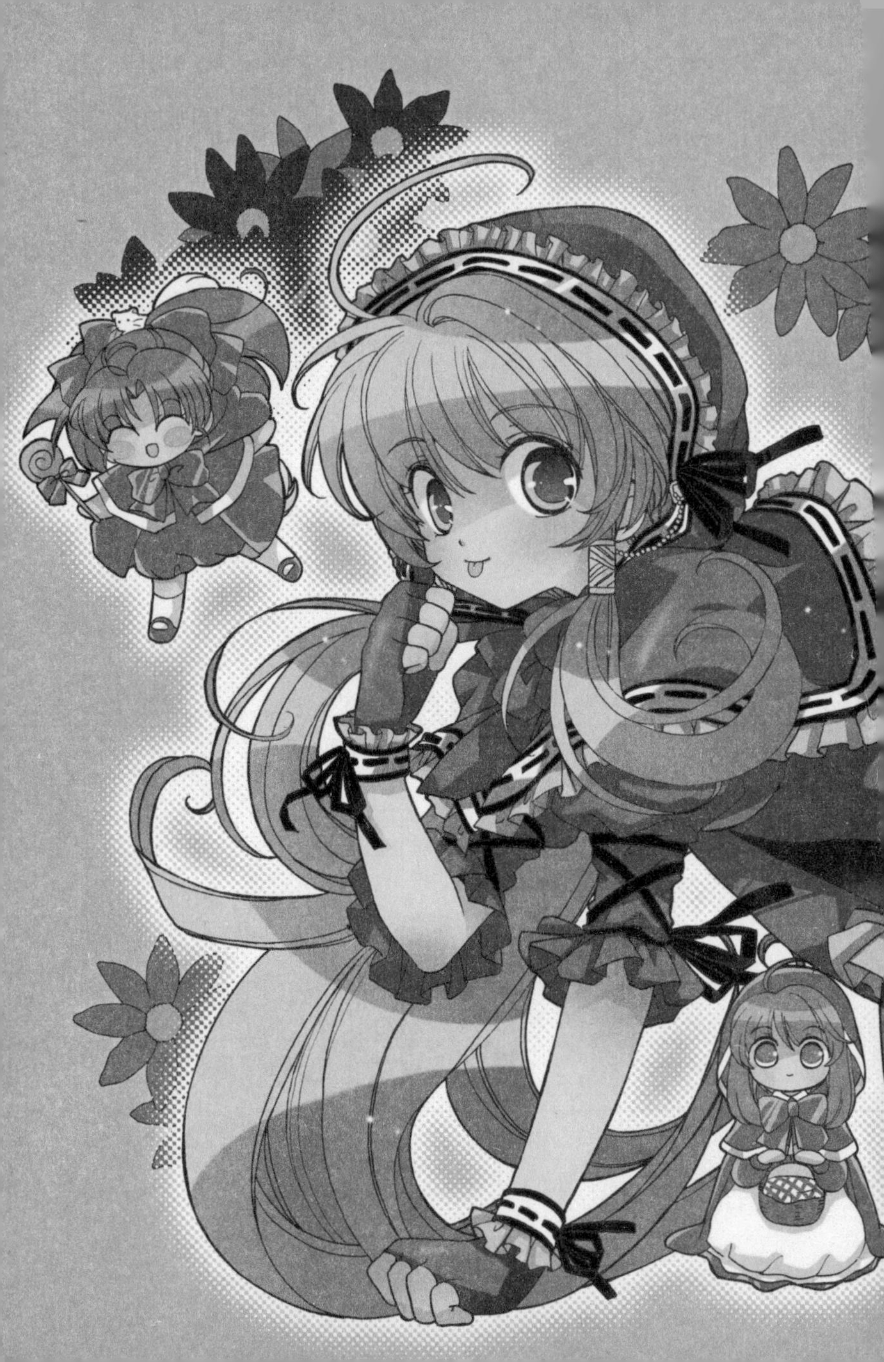

NICE TO MEET YOU.

SENDAN

Height: 162 cm
Bust: 82 cm
Waist: 58 cm
Hip: 83 cm
Age: 124

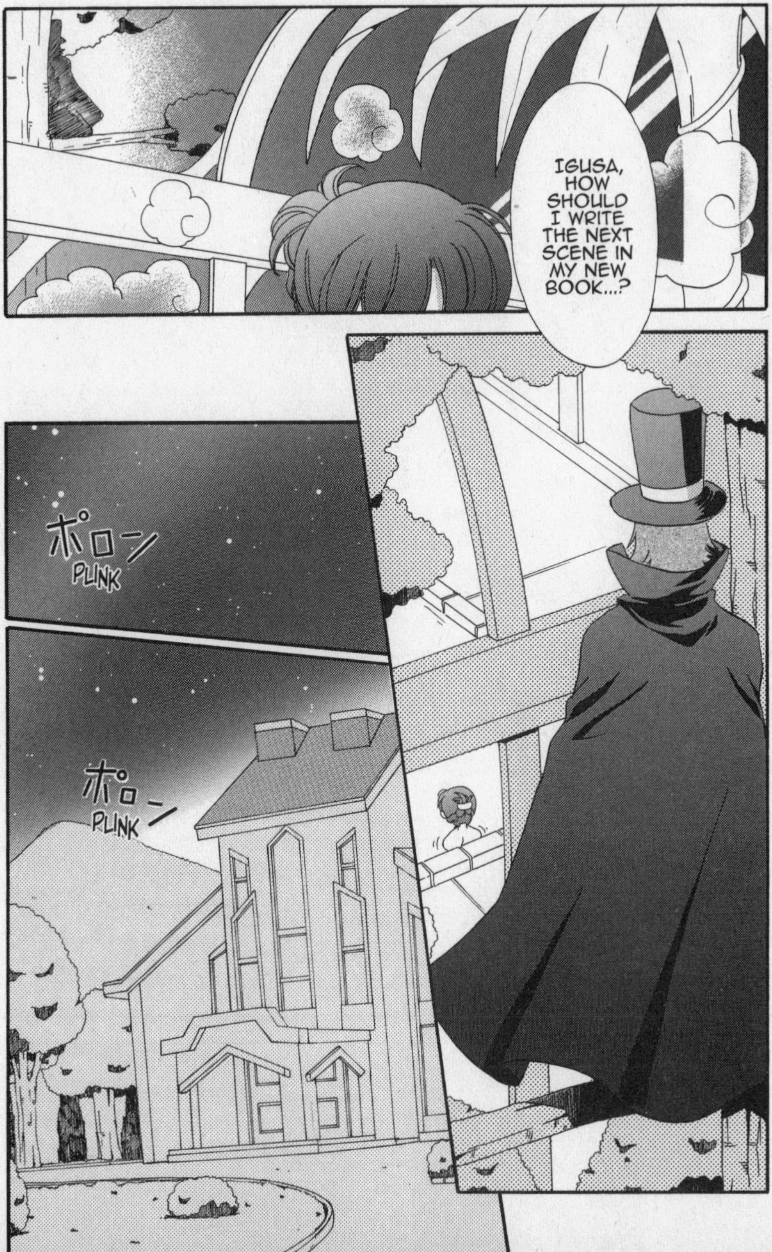
IGUSA, HOW SHOULD I WRITE THE NEXT SCENE IN MY NEW BOOK...?
ポロン
PLINK
ポロ—
PLINK

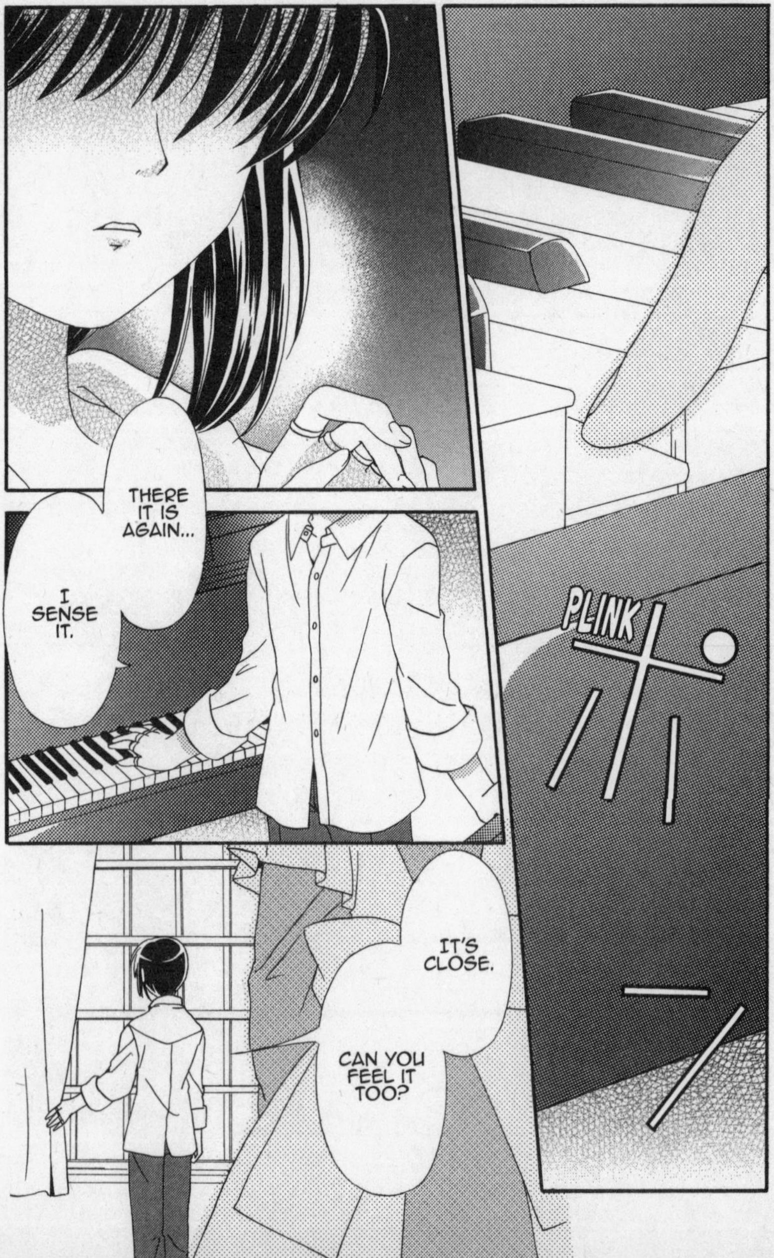
PLINK
THERE IT IS AGAIN...
I SENSE IT.
IT'S CLOSE.
CAN YOU FEEL IT TOO?

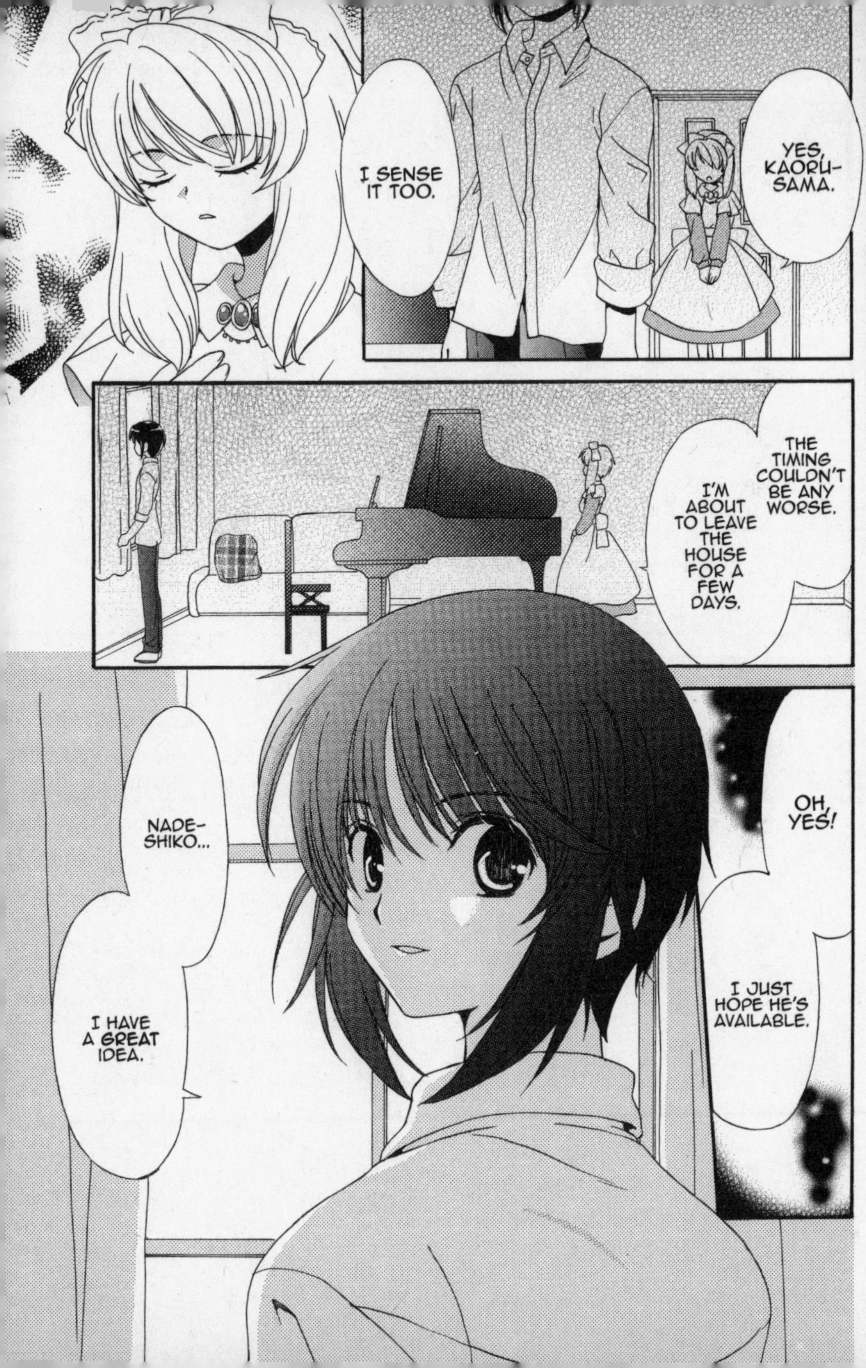
YES, KAORU-SAMA.
I SENSE IT TOO.
THE TIMING COULDN'T BE ANY WORSE.
I'M ABOUT TO LEAVE THE HOUSE FOR A FEW DAYS.
OH, YES!
I JUST HOPE HE'S AVAILABLE.
NADESHIKO...
I HAVE A GREAT IDEA.

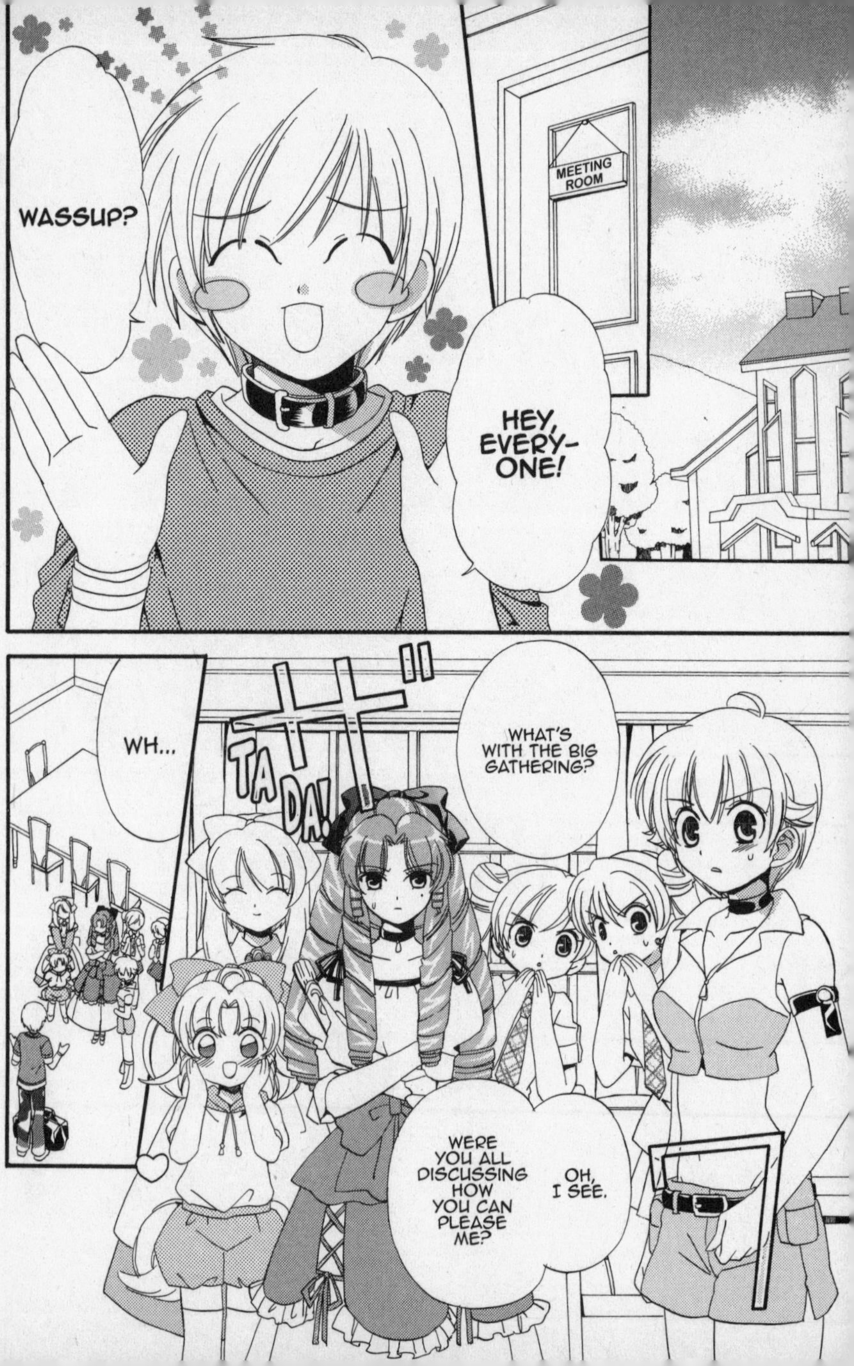
MEETING ROOM
HEY, EVERY-ONE!
WASSUP?
WHAT'S WITH THE BIG GATHERING?
TA DA!
WH...
OH, I SEE.
WERE YOU ALL DISCUSSING HOW YOU CAN PLEASE ME?

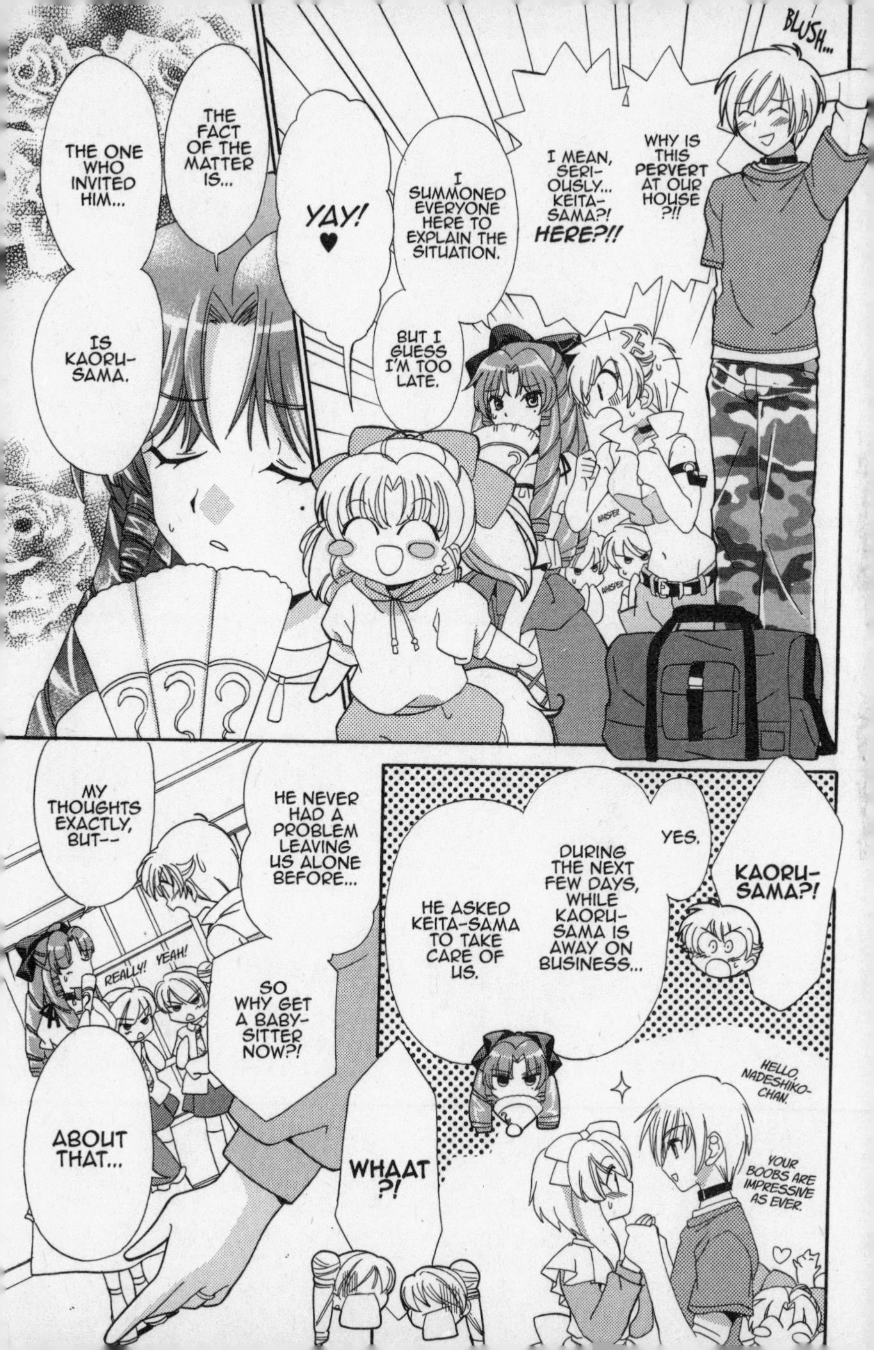
BLUSH...
WHY IS THIS PERVERT AT OUR HOUSE?!!
I MEAN, SERIOUSLY... KEITA-SAMA?! HERE?!!
I SUMMONED EVERYONE HERE TO EXPLAIN THE SITUATION.
YAY! ♥
BUT I GUESS I'M TOO LATE.
WHISPER
WHISPER
THE FACT OF THE MATTER IS...
THE ONE WHO INVITED HIM...
IS KAORU-SAMA.
KAORU-SAMA?!
YES.
DURING THE NEXT FEW DAYS, WHILE KAORU-SAMA IS AWAY ON BUSINESS...
HE ASKED KEITA-SAMA TO TAKE CARE OF US.
HELLO, NADESHIKO-CHAN.
YOUR BOOBS ARE IMPRESSIVE AS EVER.
WHAAT?!
HE NEVER HAD A PROBLEM LEAVING US ALONE BEFORE...
MY THOUGHTS EXACTLY, BUT--
REALLY!
YEAH!
SO WHY GET A BABY-SITTER NOW?!
ABOUT THAT...

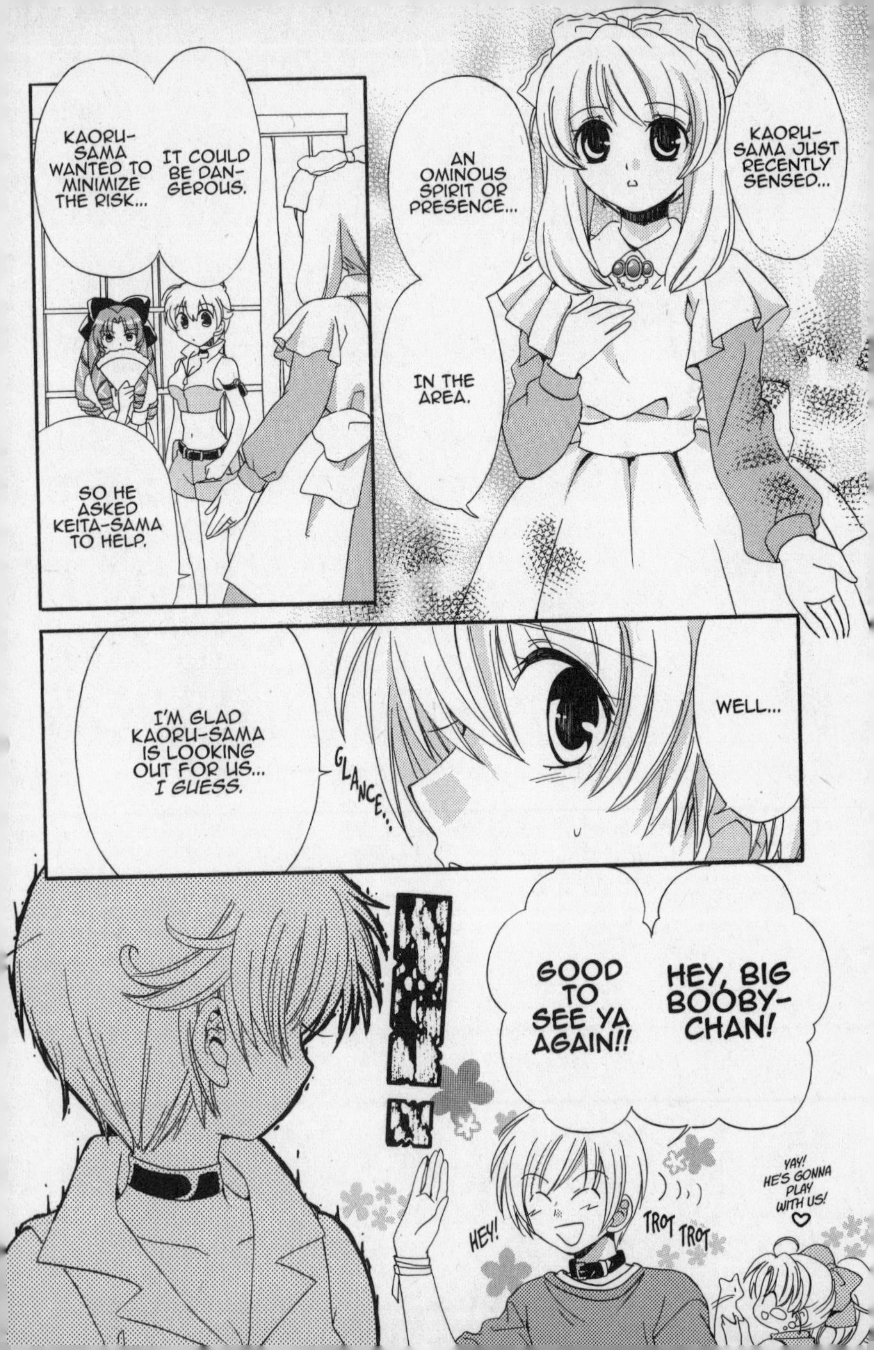
KAORU-SAMA JUST RECENTLY SENSED...
AN OMINOUS SPIRIT OR PRESENCE...
IN THE AREA.
IT COULD BE DAN-GEROUS.
KAORU-SAMA WANTED TO MINIMIZE THE RISK...
SO HE ASKED KEITA-SAMA TO HELP.
WELL...
GLANCE...
I'M GLAD KAORU-SAMA IS LOOKING OUT FOR US... I GUESS.
HEY, BIG BOOBY-CHAN!
GOOD TO SEE YA AGAIN!!
YAY! HE'S GONNA PLAY WITH US! ♡
TROT TROT
HEY!

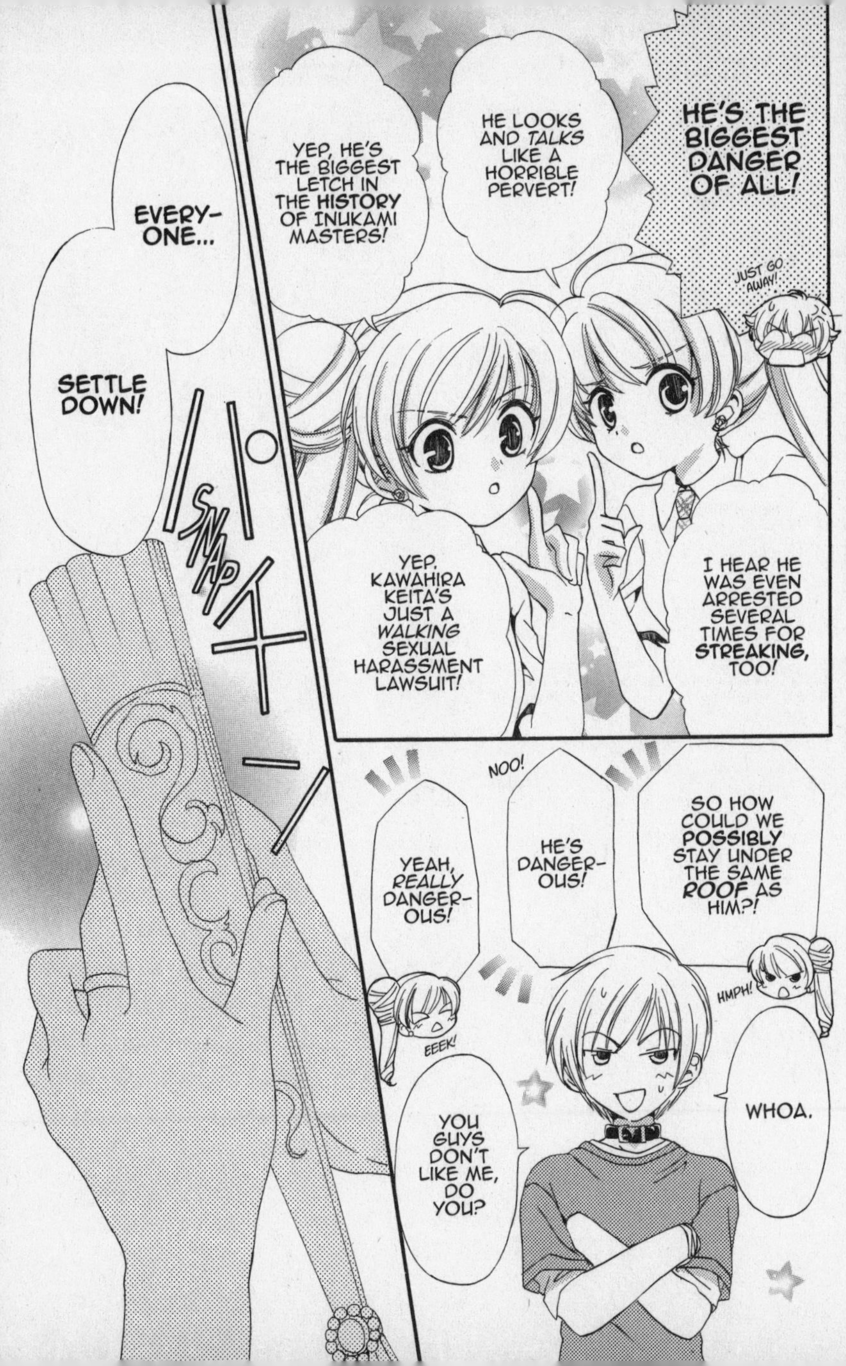
HE'S THE BIGGEST DANGER OF ALL!
JUST GO AWAY!
HE LOOKS AND TALKS LIKE A HORRIBLE PERVERT!
YEP, HE'S THE BIGGEST LETCH IN THE HISTORY OF INUKAMI MASTERS!
I HEAR HE WAS EVEN ARRESTED SEVERAL TIMES FOR STREAKING, TOO!
YEP. KAWAHIRA KEITA'S JUST A WALKING SEXUAL HARASSMENT LAWSUIT!
SO HOW COULD WE POSSIBLY STAY UNDER THE SAME ROOF AS HIM?!
NOO!
HE'S DANGER-OUS!
YEAH, REALLY DANGER-OUS!
HMPH!
WHOA.
EEEK!
YOU GUYS DON'T LIKE ME, DO YOU?
EVERY-ONE...
SETTLE DOWN!
SNAP

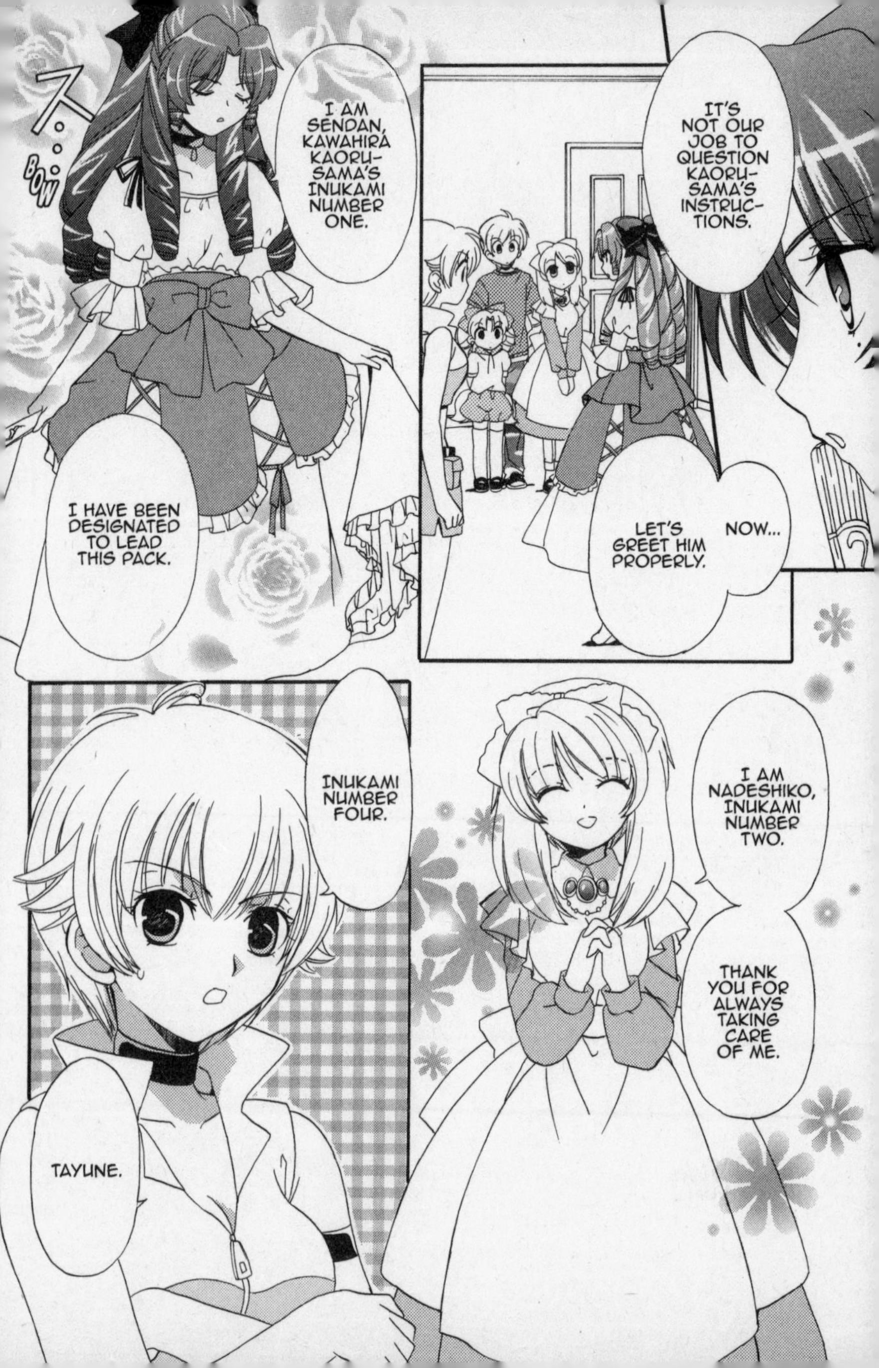
IT'S NOT OUR JOB TO QUESTION KAORU-SAMA'S INSTRUCTIONS.
NOW...
LET'S GREET HIM PROPERLY.
ス...
BOW
I AM SENDAN, KAWAHIRA KAORU-SAMA'S INUKAMI NUMBER ONE.
I HAVE BEEN DESIGNATED TO LEAD THIS PACK.
I AM NADESHIKO, INUKAMI NUMBER TWO.
THANK YOU FOR ALWAYS TAKING CARE OF ME.
INUKAMI NUMBER FOUR.
TAYUNE.

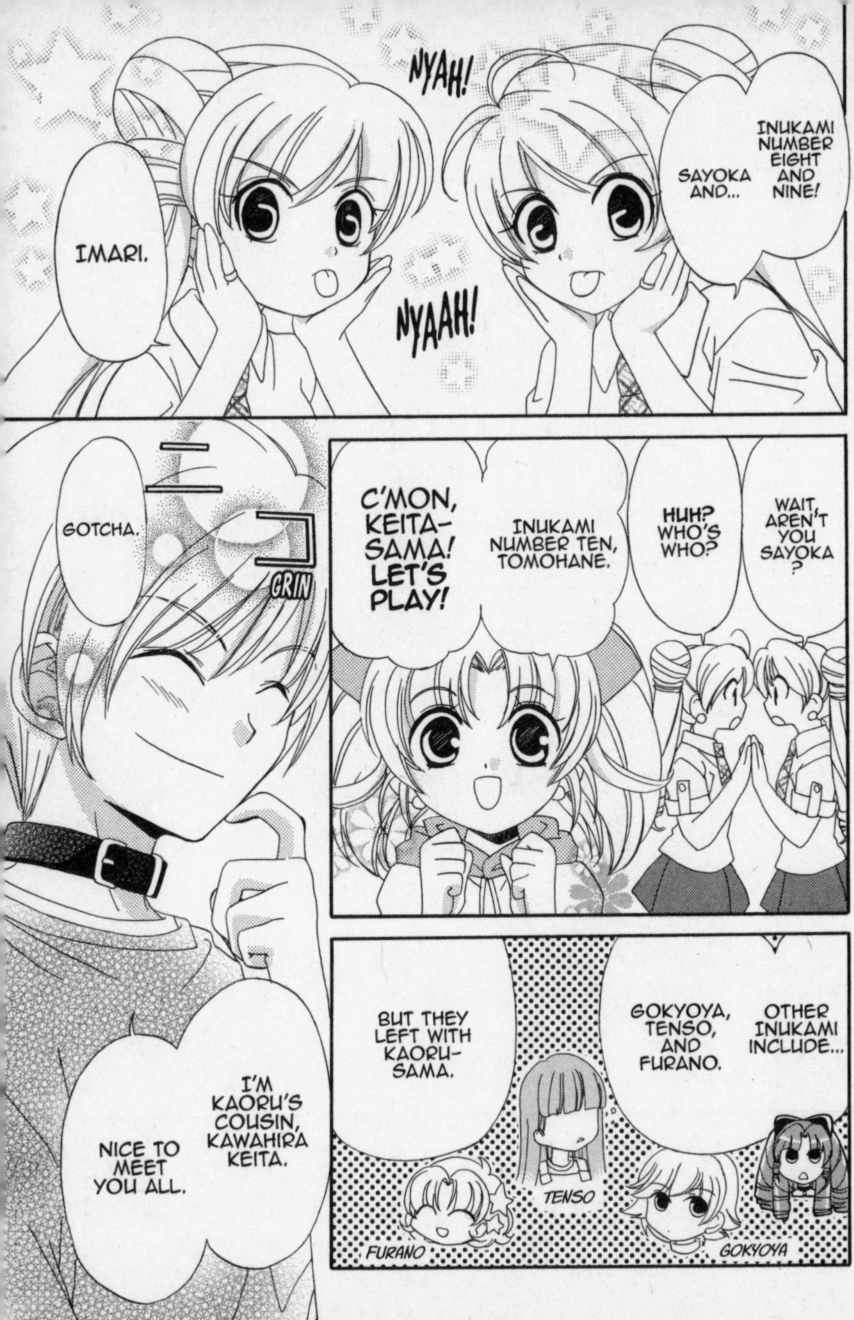
INUKAMI NUMBER EIGHT AND NINE!
SAYOKA AND...
NYAH!
NYAAH!
IMARI.
WAIT, AREN'T YOU SAYOKA?
HUH? WHO'S WHO?
INUKAMI NUMBER TEN, TOMOHANE.
C'MON, KEITA-SAMA! LET'S PLAY!
OTHER INUKAMI INCLUDE...
GOKYOYA, TENSO, AND FURANO.
BUT THEY LEFT WITH KAORU-SAMA.
TENSO
GOKYOYA
FURANO
GOTCHA.
GRIN
I'M KAORU'S COUSIN, KAWAHIRA KEITA.
NICE TO MEET YOU ALL.

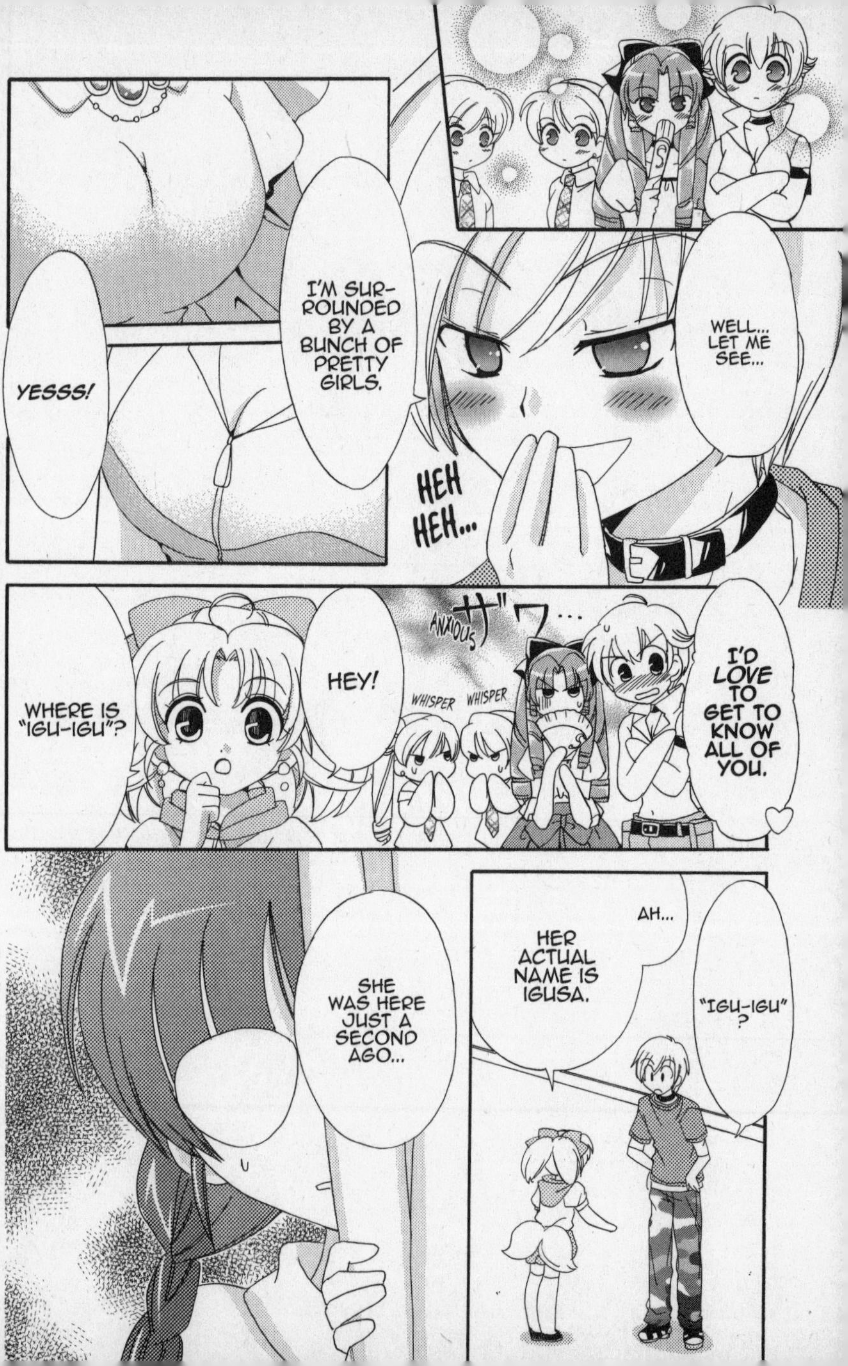
WELL... LET ME SEE...
HEH HEH...
I'M SUR-ROUNDED BY A BUNCH OF PRETTY GIRLS.
YESSS!
I'D LOVE TO GET TO KNOW ALL OF YOU.
ザワ...
ANXIOUS
WHISPER WHISPER
HEY!
WHERE IS "IGU-IGU"?
"IGU-IGU"?
AH...
HER ACTUAL NAME IS IGUSA.
SHE WAS HERE JUST A SECOND AGO...

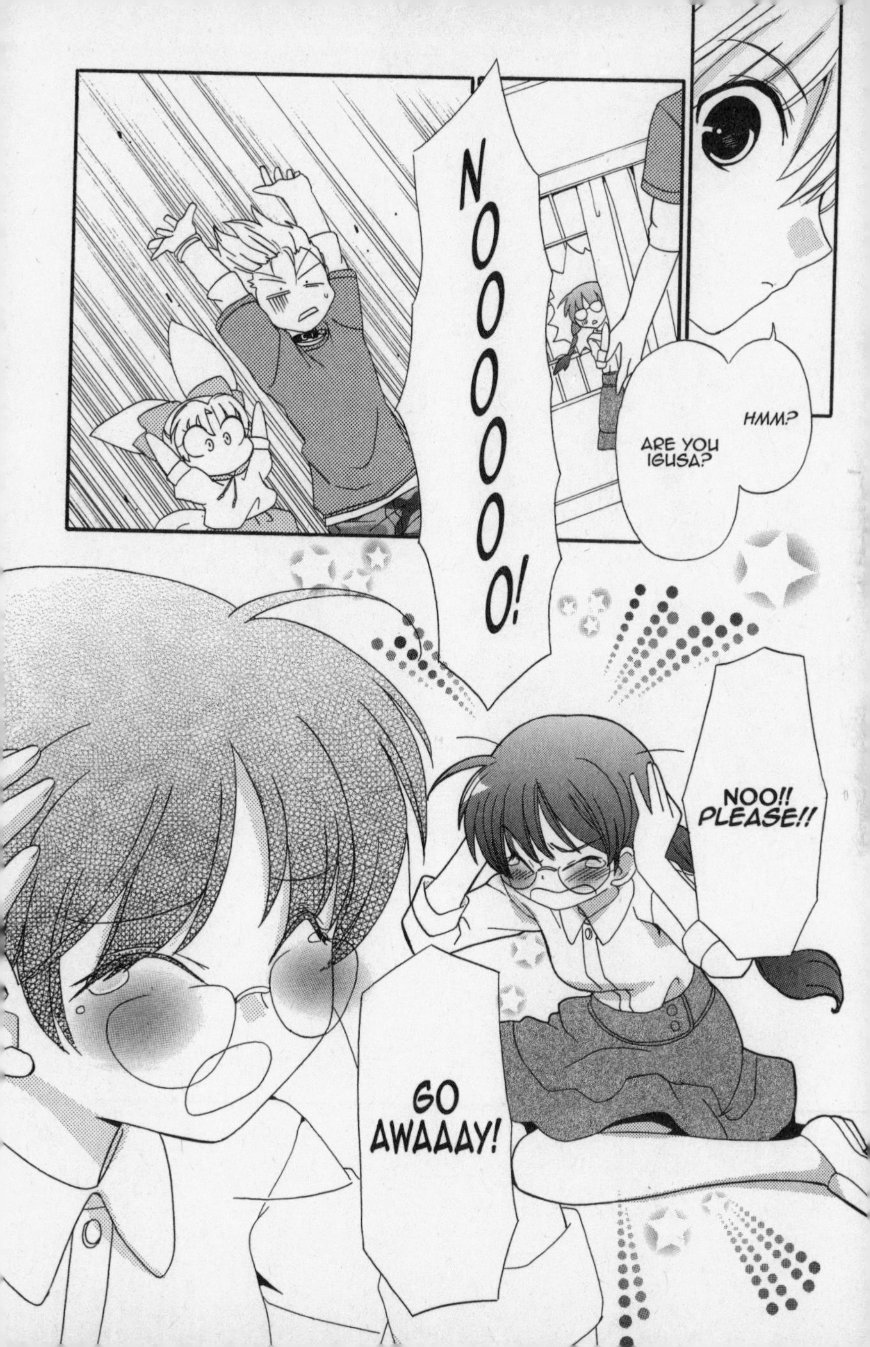
HMM?
ARE YOU IGUSA?
NOOOOOOO!
NOO!! PLEASE!!
GO AWAAAY!

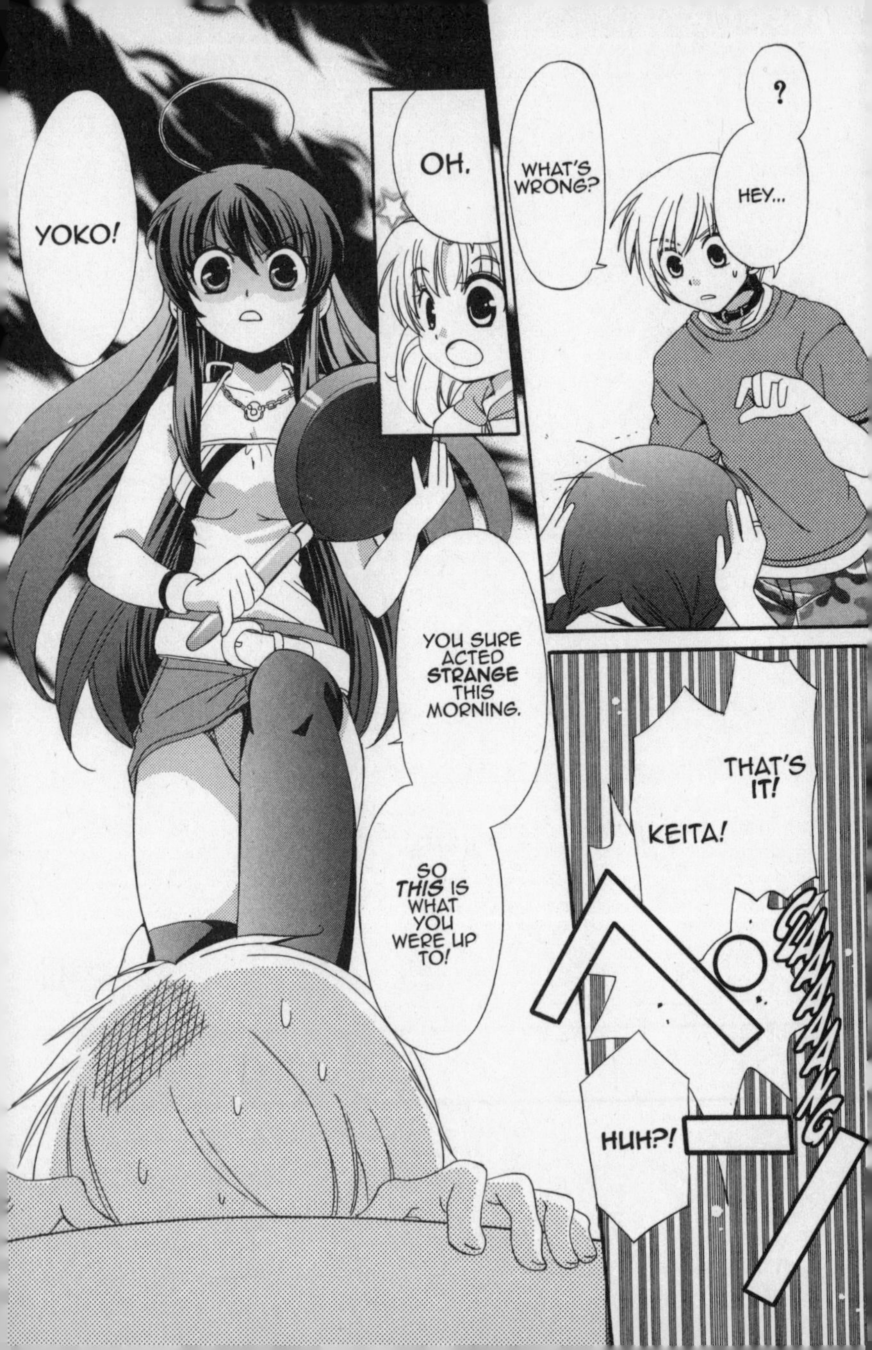
?
HEY...
WHAT'S WRONG?
OH.
THAT'S IT!
KEITA!
HUH?!
CLAAAANG
YOKO!
YOU SURE ACTED STRANGE THIS MORNING.
SO THIS IS WHAT YOU WERE UP TO!

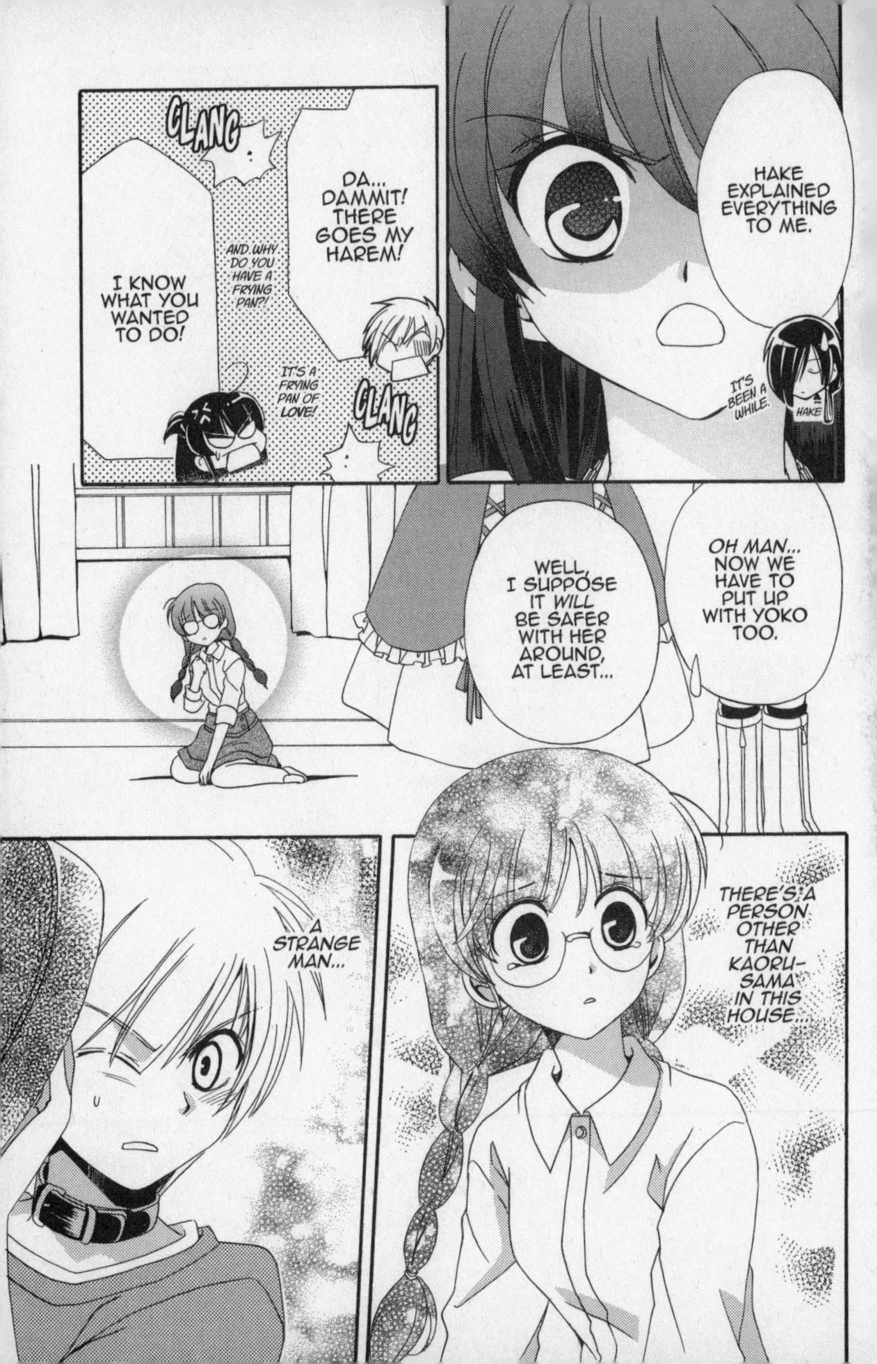
HAKE EXPLAINED EVERYTHING TO ME.
IT'S BEEN A WHILE.
HAKE
DA... DAMMIT! THERE GOES MY HAREM!
AND WHY DO YOU HAVE A FRYING PAN?!
CLANG
I KNOW WHAT YOU WANTED TO DO!
IT'S A FRYING PAN OF LOVE!
CLANG
OH MAN... NOW WE HAVE TO PUT UP WITH YOKO TOO.
WELL, I SUPPOSE IT WILL BE SAFER WITH HER AROUND, AT LEAST...
THERE'S A PERSON OTHER THAN KAORU-SAMA IN THIS HOUSE...
A STRANGE MAN...

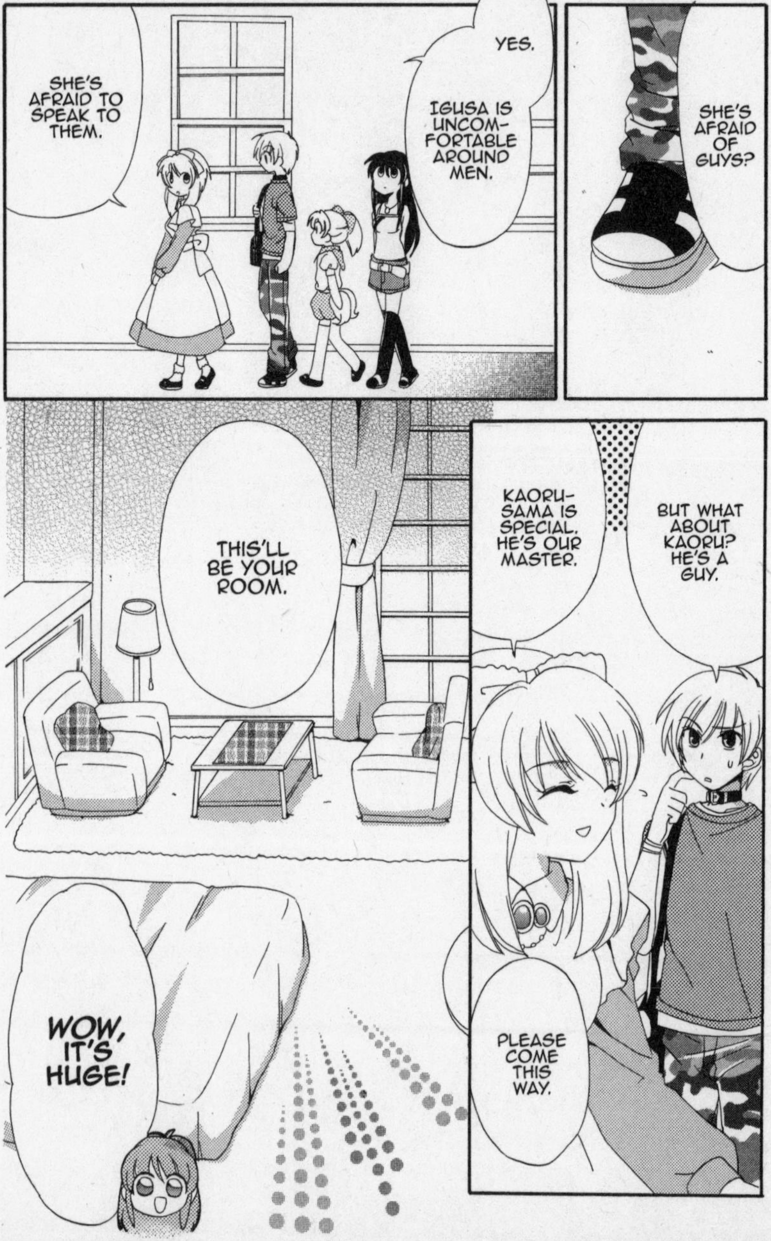
SHE'S AFRAID OF GUYS?
YES.
IGUSA IS UNCOM- FORTABLE AROUND MEN.
SHE'S AFRAID TO SPEAK TO THEM.
BUT WHAT ABOUT KAORU? HE'S A GUY.
KAORU- SAMA IS SPECIAL. HE'S OUR MASTER.
PLEASE COME THIS WAY.
THIS'LL BE YOUR ROOM.
WOW, IT'S HUGE!

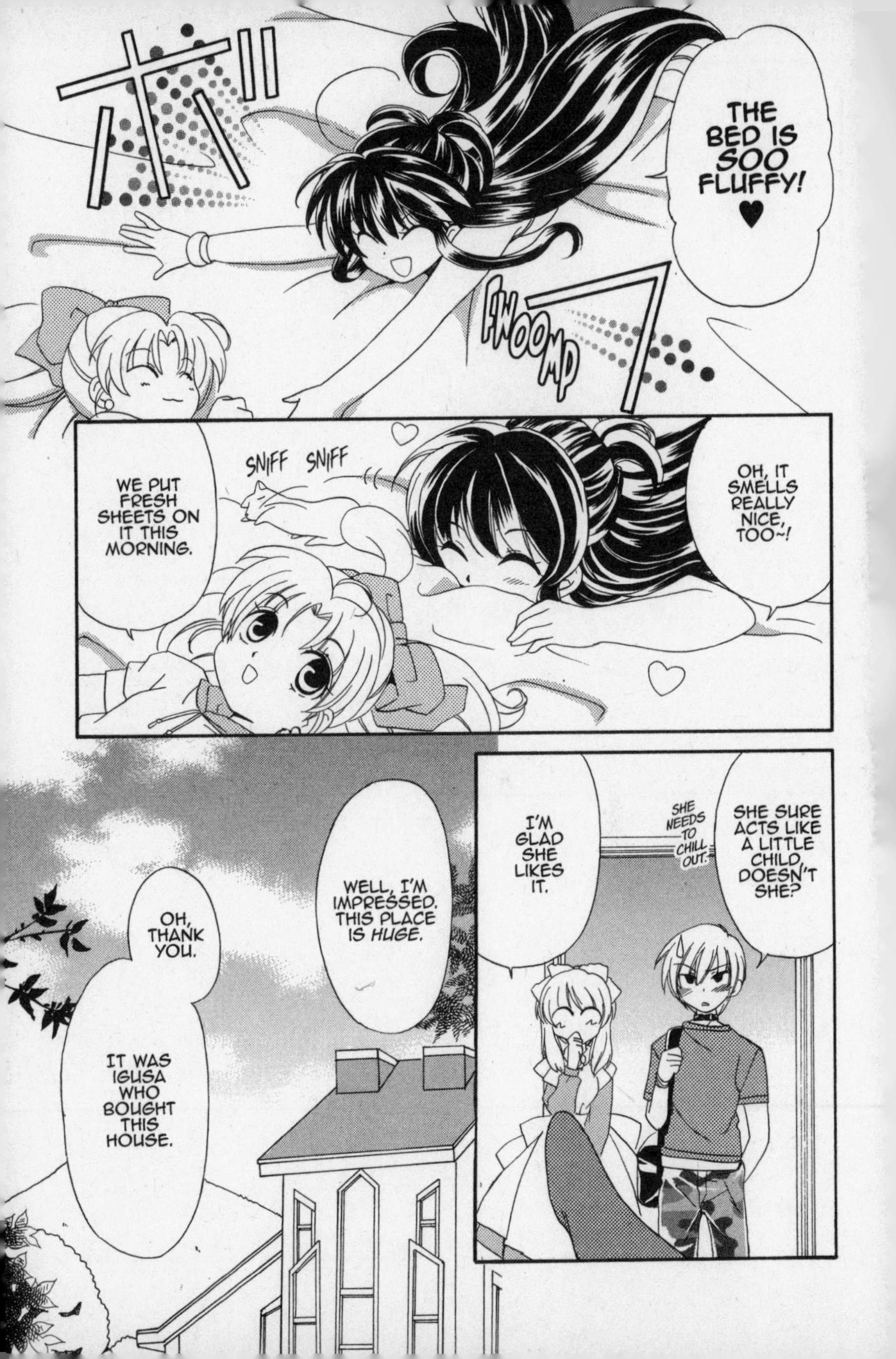
THE BED IS SOO FLUFFY! ♥
FWOOMP
OH, IT SMELLS REALLY NICE, TOO~!
SNIFF SNIFF
WE PUT FRESH SHEETS ON IT THIS MORNING.
SHE SURE ACTS LIKE A LITTLE CHILD, DOESN'T SHE?
SHE NEEDS TO CHILL OUT.
I'M GLAD SHE LIKES IT.
WELL, I'M IMPRESSED. THIS PLACE IS *HUGE*.
OH, THANK YOU.
IT WAS IGUSA WHO BOUGHT THIS HOUSE.

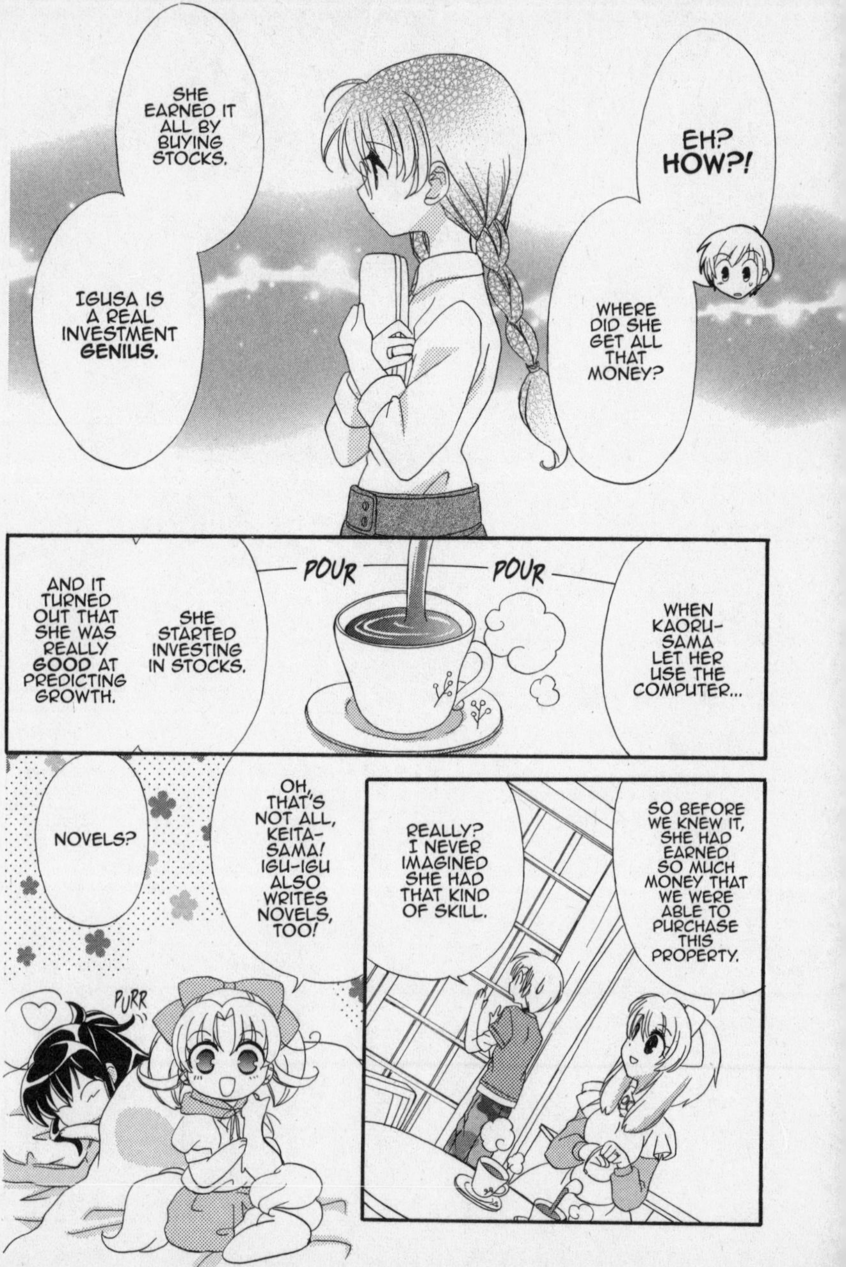
EH? HOW?!
WHERE DID SHE GET ALL THAT MONEY?
SHE EARNED IT ALL BY BUYING STOCKS.
IGUSA IS A REAL INVESTMENT GENIUS.
WHEN KAORU-SAMA LET HER USE THE COMPUTER...
POUR
POUR
SHE STARTED INVESTING IN STOCKS.
AND IT TURNED OUT THAT SHE WAS REALLY GOOD AT PREDICTING GROWTH.
SO BEFORE WE KNEW IT, SHE HAD EARNED SO MUCH MONEY THAT WE WERE ABLE TO PURCHASE THIS PROPERTY.
REALLY? I NEVER IMAGINED SHE HAD THAT KIND OF SKILL.
OH, THAT'S NOT ALL, KEITA-SAMA! IGU-IGU ALSO WRITES NOVELS, TOO!
NOVELS?
PURR

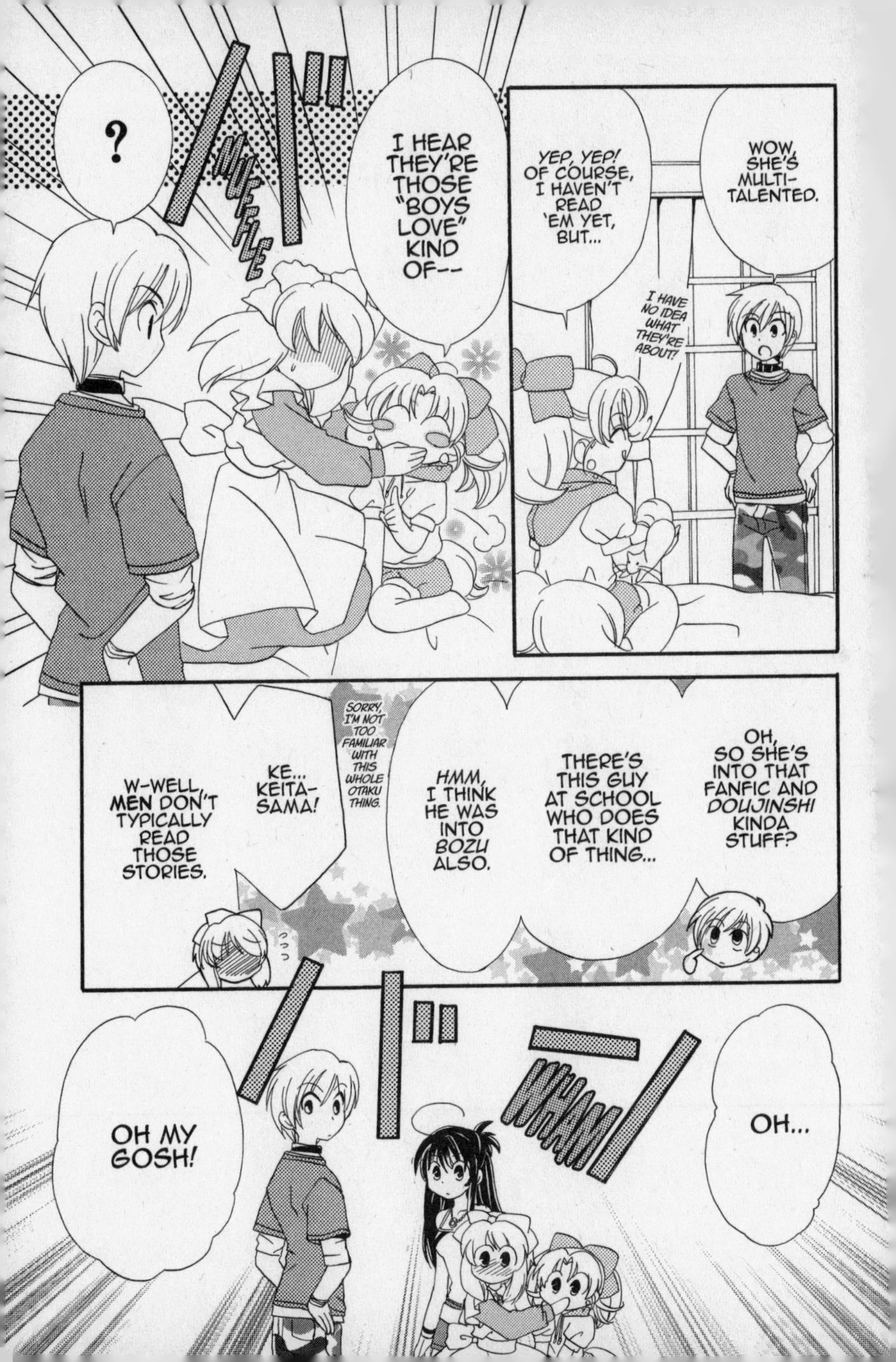
WOW, SHE'S MULTI-TALENTED.
YEP, YEP! OF COURSE, I HAVEN'T READ 'EM YET, BUT...
I HAVE NO IDEA WHAT THEY'RE ABOUT!
I HEAR THEY'RE THOSE "BOYS LOVE" KIND OF--
MUFFLE
?
OH, SO SHE'S INTO THAT FANFIC AND *DOUJINSHI* KINDA STUFF?
THERE'S THIS GUY AT SCHOOL WHO DOES THAT KIND OF THING...
HMM, I THINK HE WAS INTO *BOZU* ALSO.
SORRY, I'M NOT TOO FAMILIAR WITH THIS WHOLE OTAKU THING.
KE... KEITA-SAMA!
W-WELL, MEN DON'T TYPICALLY READ THOSE STORIES.
OH...
WHAM!
OH MY GOSH!

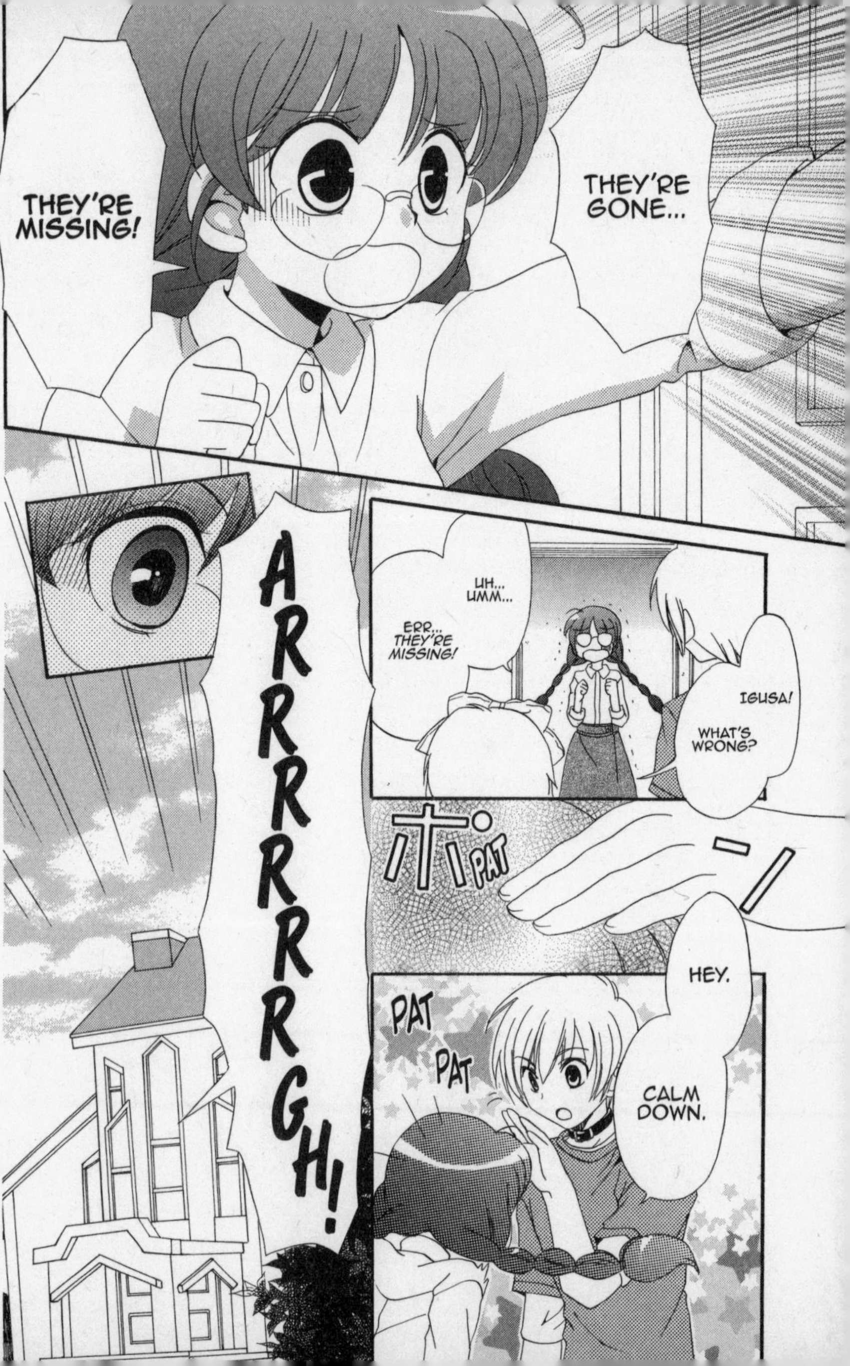
THEY'RE GONE...
THEY'RE MISSING!
IGUSA!
WHAT'S WRONG?
UH... UMM...
ERR... THEY'RE MISSING!
PAT
HEY.
CALM DOWN.
PAT PAT
ARRRRRRGH!

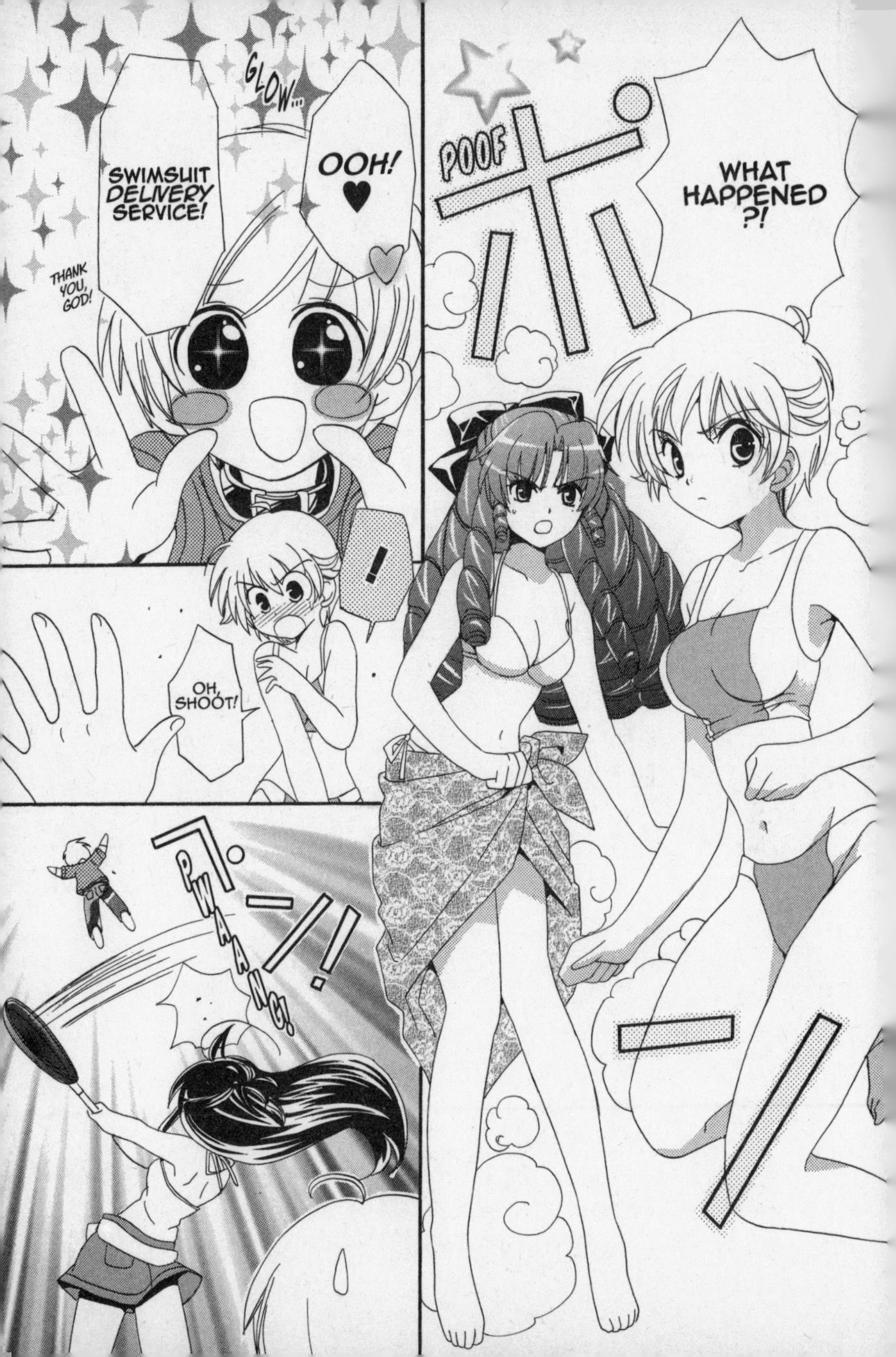
POOF
WHAT HAPPENED ?!
OOH! ♥
GLOW...
SWIMSUIT DELIVERY SERVICE!
THANK YOU, GOD!
!
OH, SHOOT!
PWAAANG!

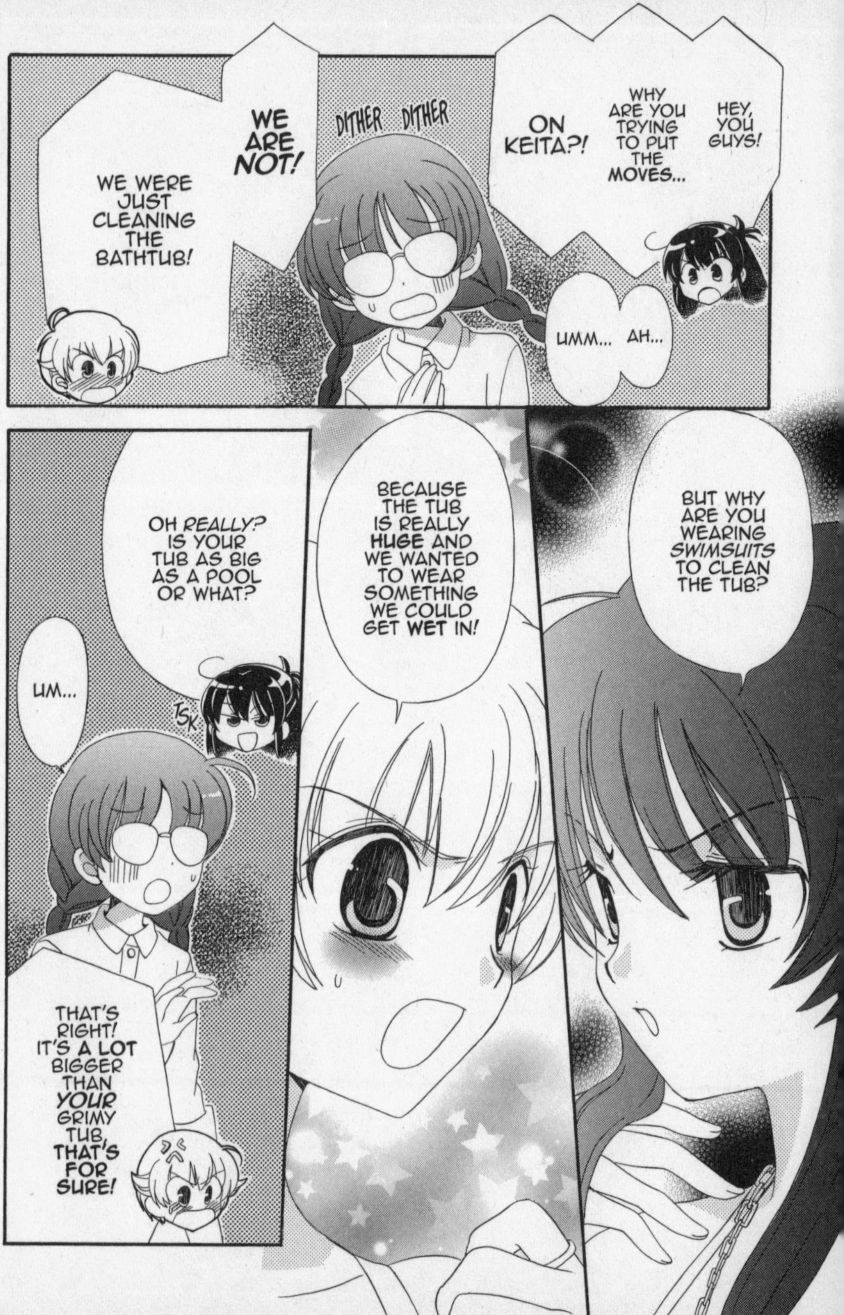
HEY, YOU GUYS!
WHY ARE YOU TRYING TO PUT THE MOVES...
ON KEITA?!
UMM... AH...
DITHER DITHER
WE ARE NOT!
WE WERE JUST CLEANING THE BATHTUB!
BUT WHY ARE YOU WEARING SWIMSUITS TO CLEAN THE TUB?
BECAUSE THE TUB IS REALLY HUGE AND WE WANTED TO WEAR SOMETHING WE COULD GET WET IN!
OH REALLY? IS YOUR TUB AS BIG AS A POOL OR WHAT?
UM...
TSK
THAT'S RIGHT! IT'S A LOT BIGGER THAN YOUR GRIMY TUB, THAT'S FOR SURE!

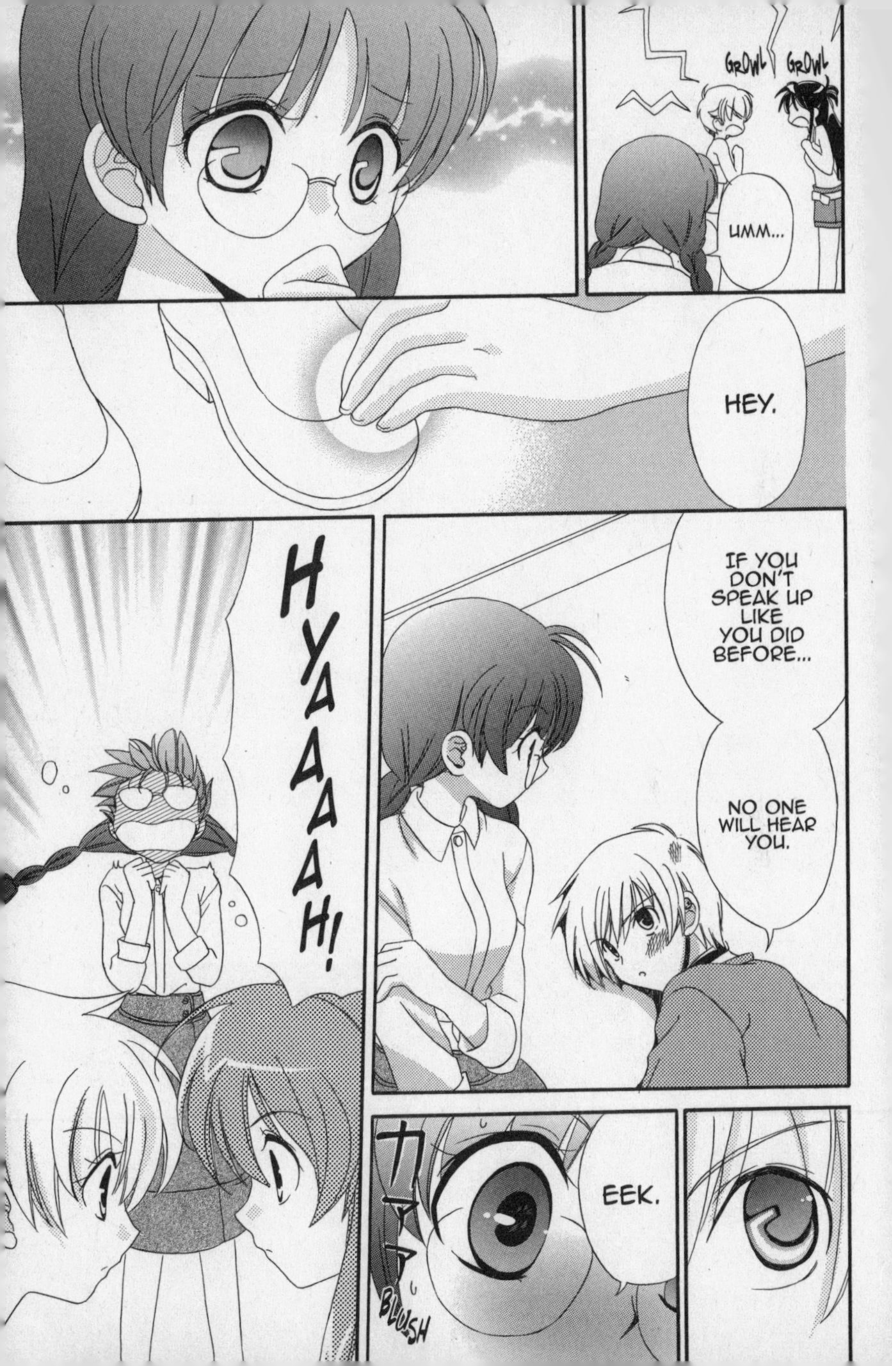
GROWL GROWL
UMM...
HEY.
IF YOU DON'T SPEAK UP LIKE YOU DID BEFORE...
NO ONE WILL HEAR YOU.
EEK.
カァァ
BLUSH
HYAAAAH!

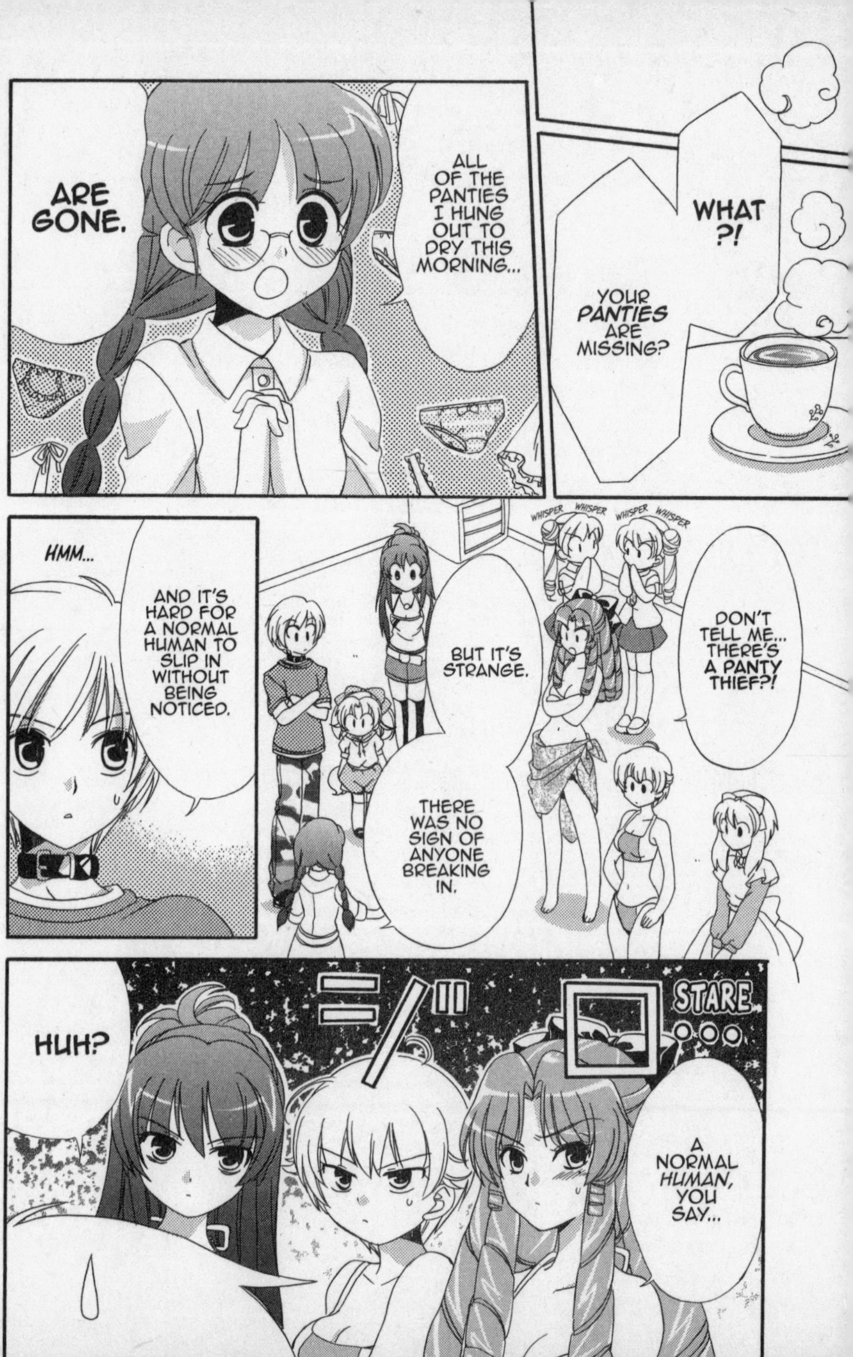
WHAT ?!
YOUR PANTIES ARE MISSING?
ALL OF THE PANTIES I HUNG OUT TO DRY THIS MORNING...
ARE GONE.
WHISPER WHISPER WHISPER WHISPER
DON'T TELL ME... THERE'S A PANTY THIEF?!
BUT IT'S STRANGE.
THERE WAS NO SIGN OF ANYONE BREAKING IN.
HMM...
AND IT'S HARD FOR A NORMAL HUMAN TO SLIP IN WITHOUT BEING NOTICED.
STARE
A NORMAL HUMAN, YOU SAY...
HUH?

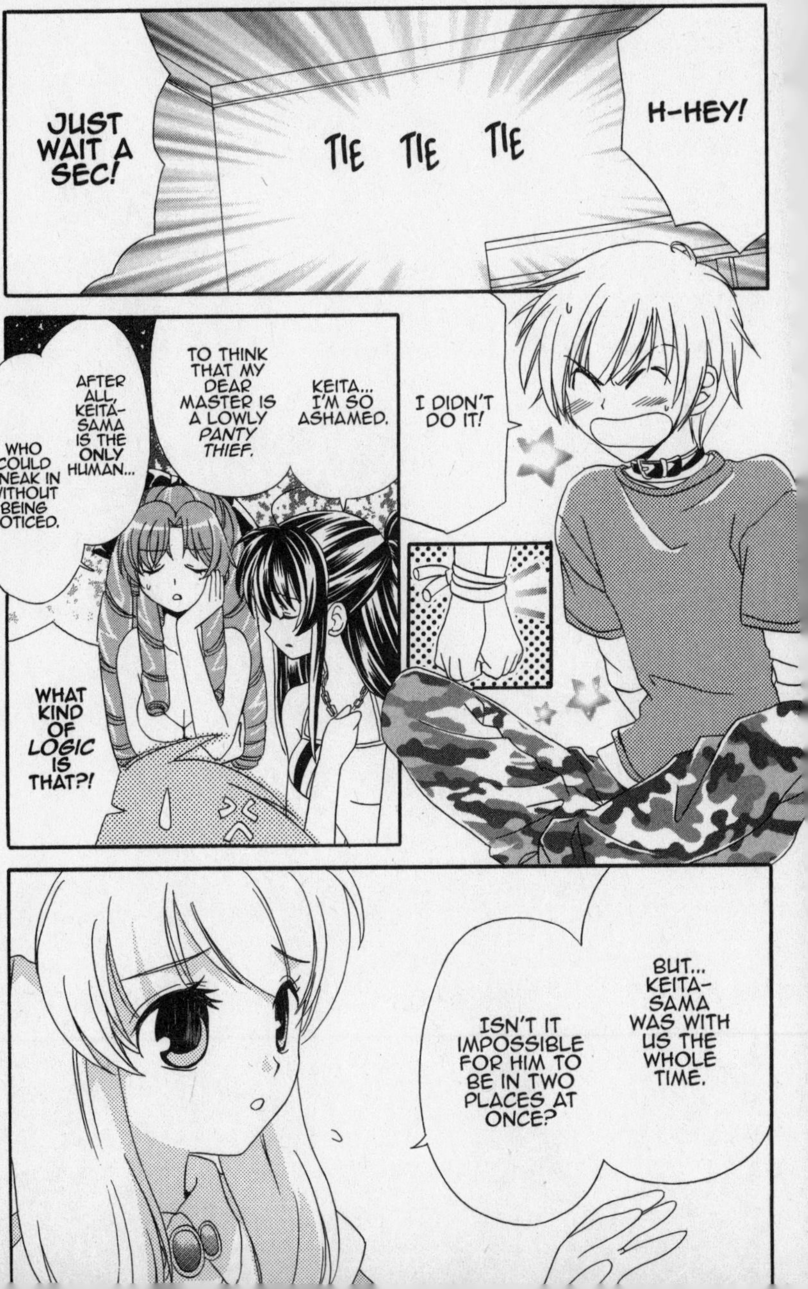
H-HEY!
TIE TIE TIE
JUST WAIT A SEC!
I DIDN'T DO IT!
KEITA... I'M SO ASHAMED.
TO THINK THAT MY DEAR MASTER IS A LOWLY *PANTY THIEF.*
AFTER ALL, KEITA-SAMA IS THE ONLY HUMAN...
WHO COULD SNEAK IN WITHOUT BEING NOTICED.
WHAT KIND OF *LOGIC* IS THAT?!
BUT... KEITA-SAMA WAS WITH US THE WHOLE TIME.
ISN'T IT IMPOSSIBLE FOR HIM TO BE IN TWO PLACES AT ONCE?

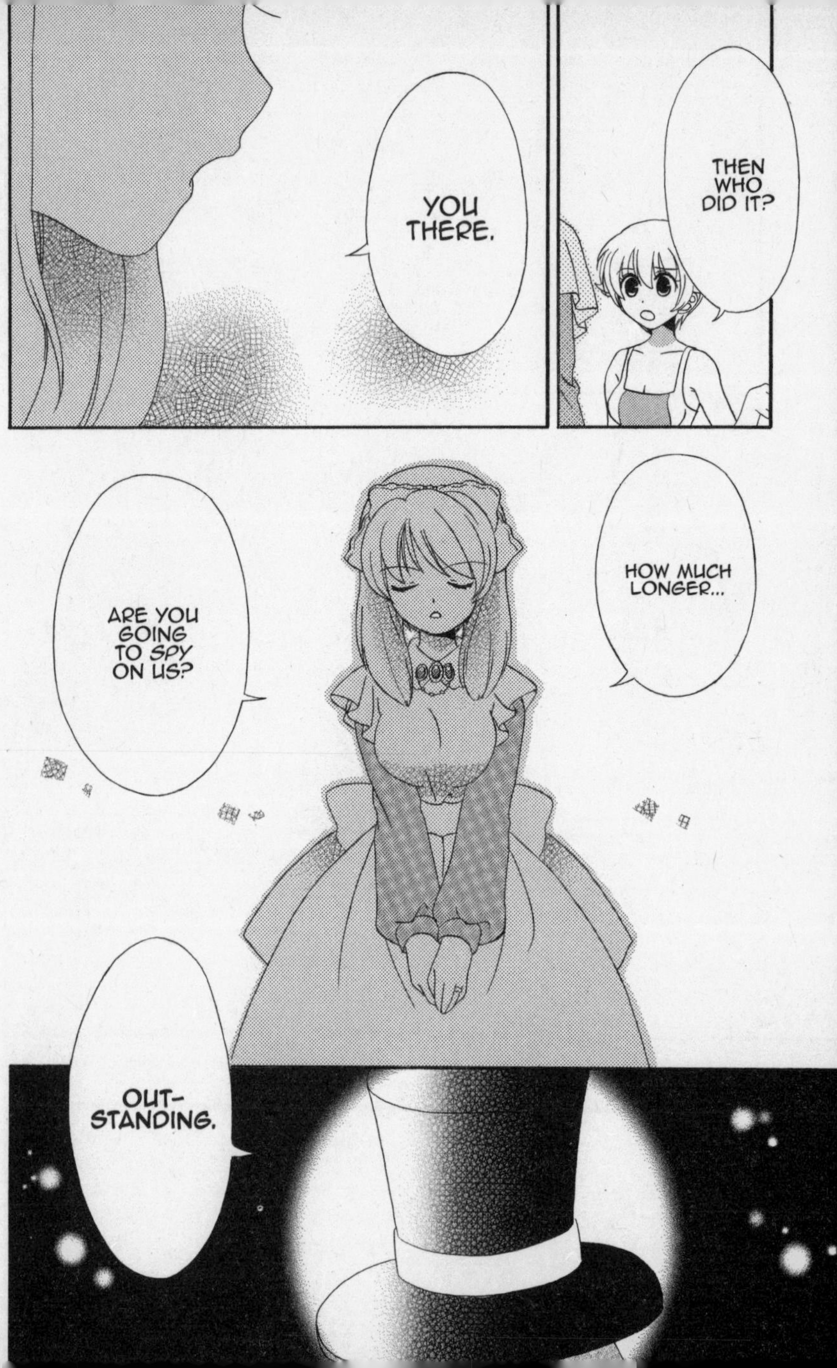
THEN WHO DID IT?
YOU THERE.
HOW MUCH LONGER...
ARE YOU GOING TO SPY ON US?
OUT-STANDING.

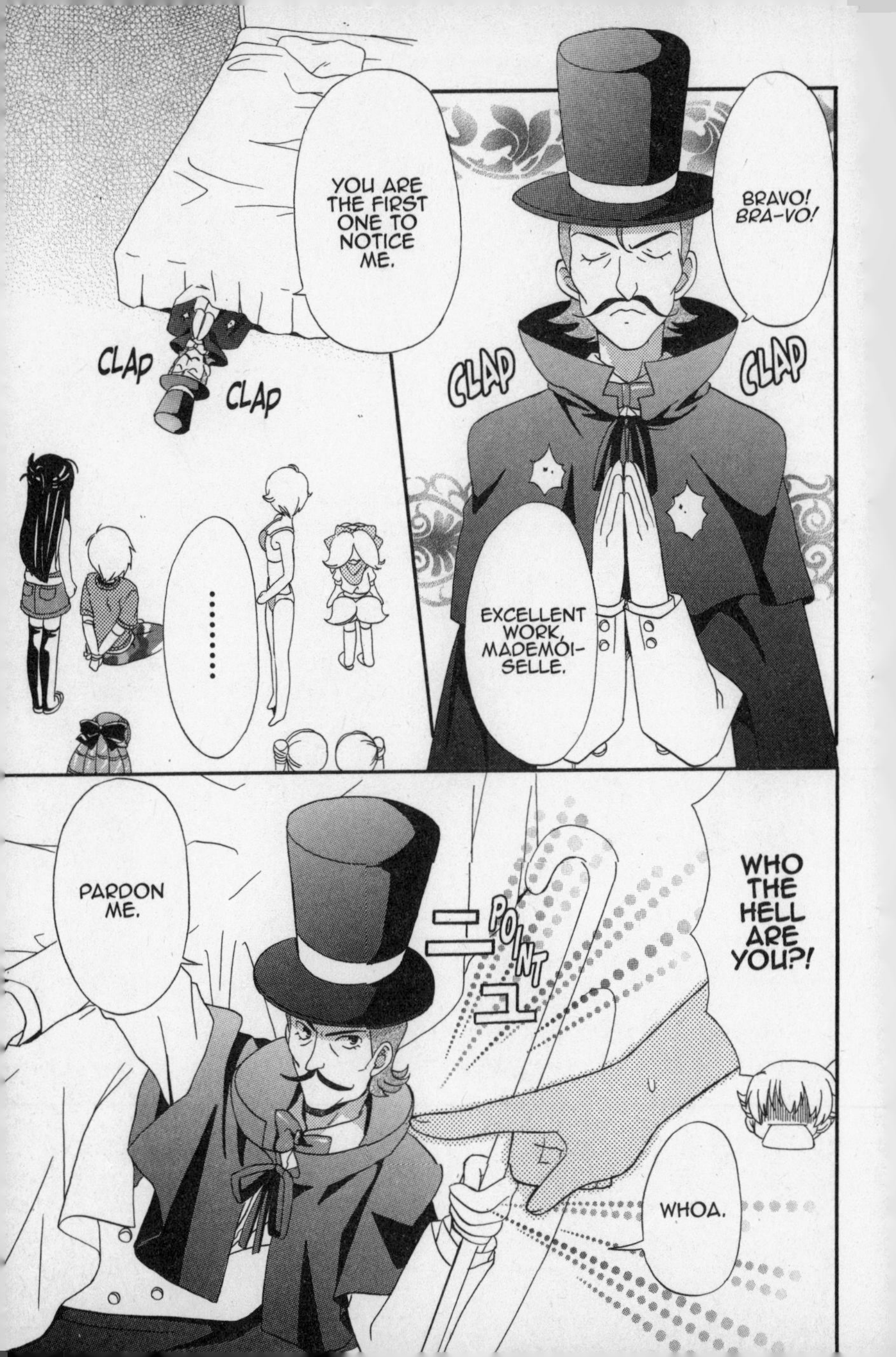
BRAVO! BRA-VO!
CLAP
CLAP
EXCELLENT WORK, MADEMOISELLE.
YOU ARE THE FIRST ONE TO NOTICE ME.
CLAP
CLAP
....
WHO THE HELL ARE YOU?!
POINT
PARDON ME.
WHOA.

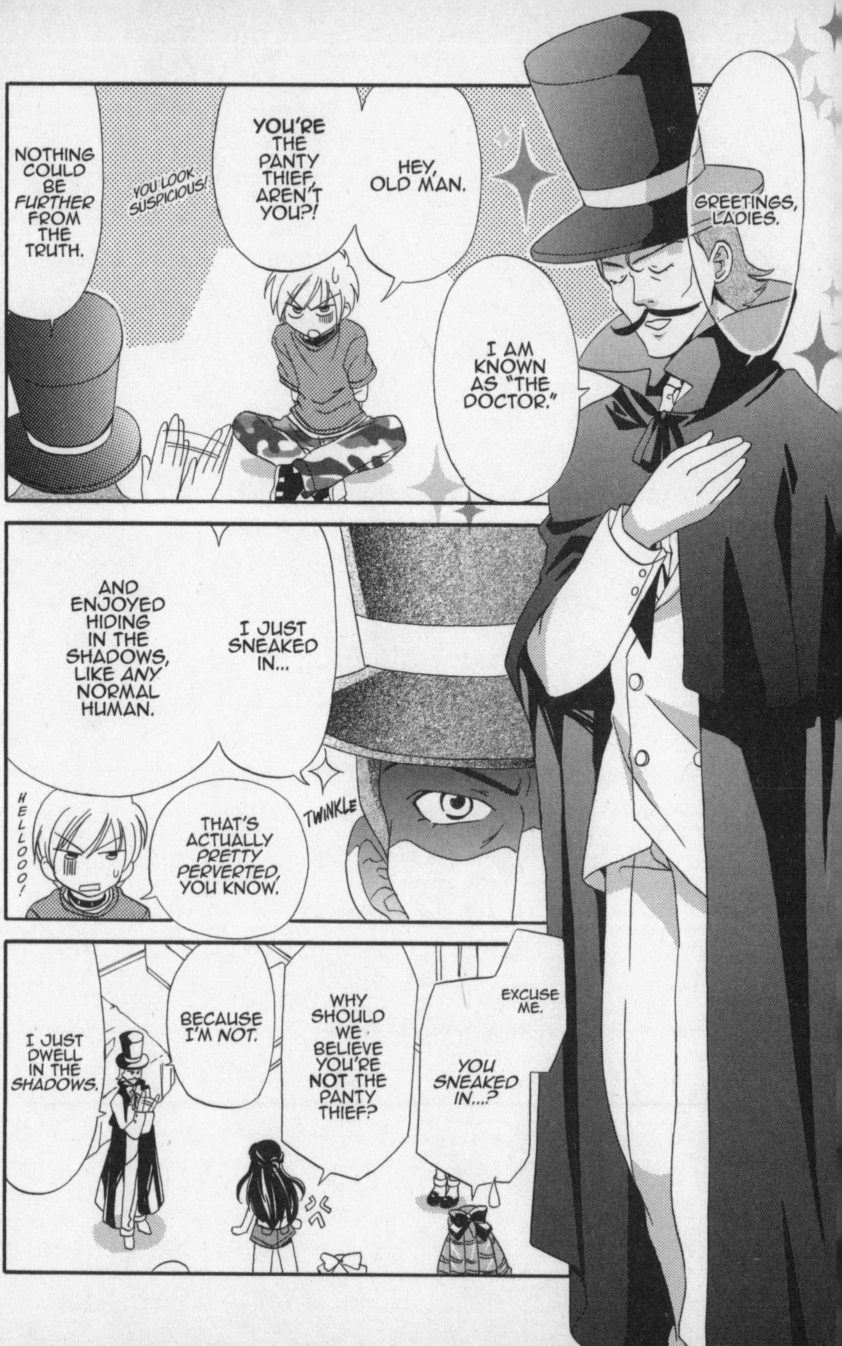
GREETINGS, LADIES.
I AM KNOWN AS "THE DOCTOR."
HEY, OLD MAN.
YOU'RE THE PANTY THIEF, AREN'T YOU?!
YOU LOOK SUSPICIOUS!
NOTHING COULD BE *FURTHER* FROM THE TRUTH.
I JUST SNEAKED IN...
AND ENJOYED HIDING IN THE SHADOWS, LIKE *ANY* NORMAL HUMAN.
TWINKLE
THAT'S ACTUALLY *PRETTY* PERVERTED, YOU KNOW.
HELLOOOO!
EXCUSE ME.
YOU SNEAKED IN...?
WHY SHOULD WE BELIEVE YOU'RE NOT THE PANTY THIEF?
BECAUSE I'M *NOT.*
I JUST DWELL IN THE *SHADOWS.*

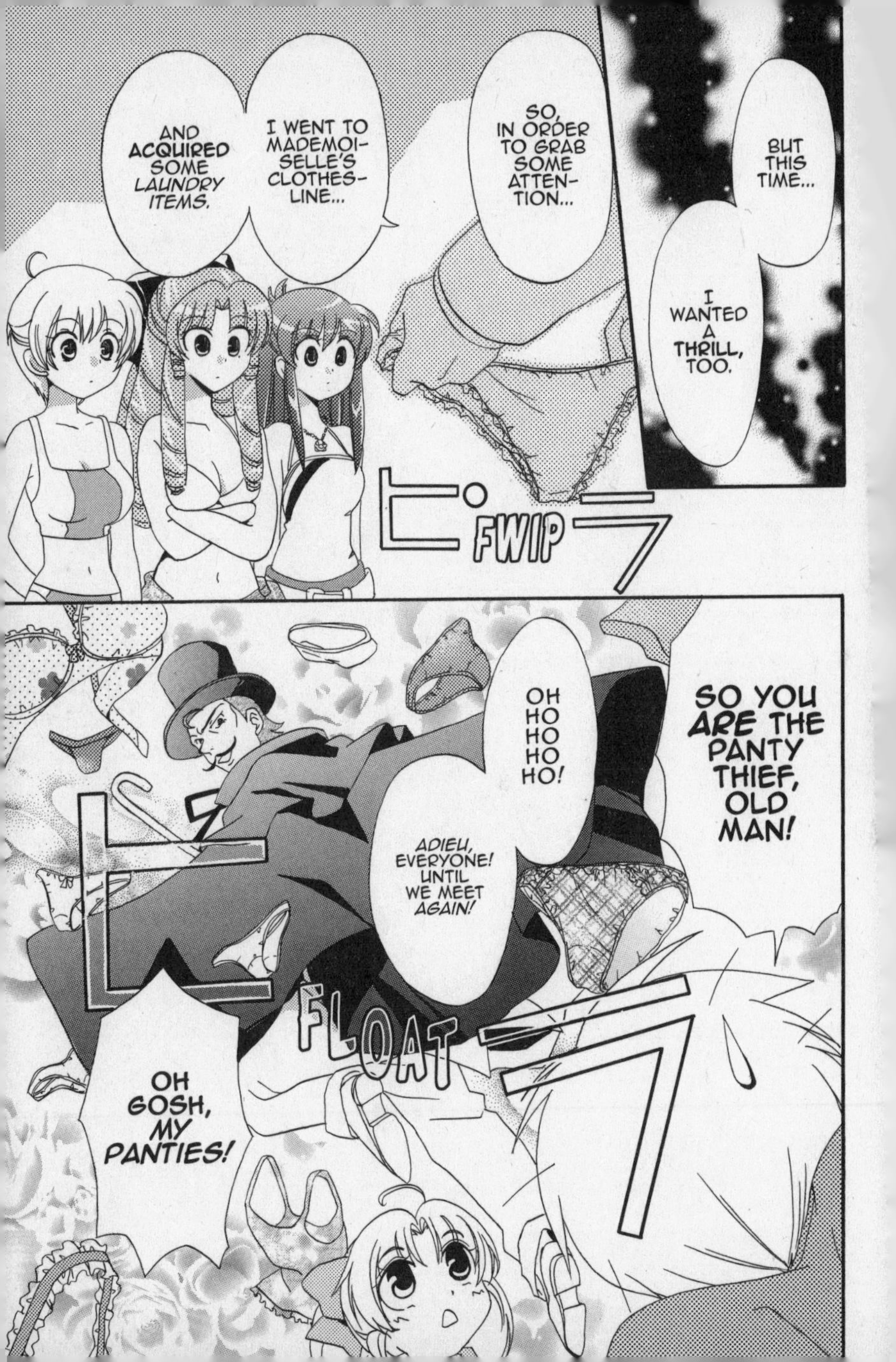

BUT THIS TIME...
I WANTED A THRILL, TOO.
SO, IN ORDER TO GRAB SOME ATTEN-TION...
I WENT TO MADEMOI-SELLE'S CLOTHES-LINE...
AND ACQUIRED SOME LAUNDRY ITEMS.
FWIP
SO YOU ARE THE PANTY THIEF, OLD MAN!
OH HO HO HO HO HO!
ADIEU, EVERYONE! UNTIL WE MEET AGAIN!
FLOAT
OH GOSH, MY PANTIES!

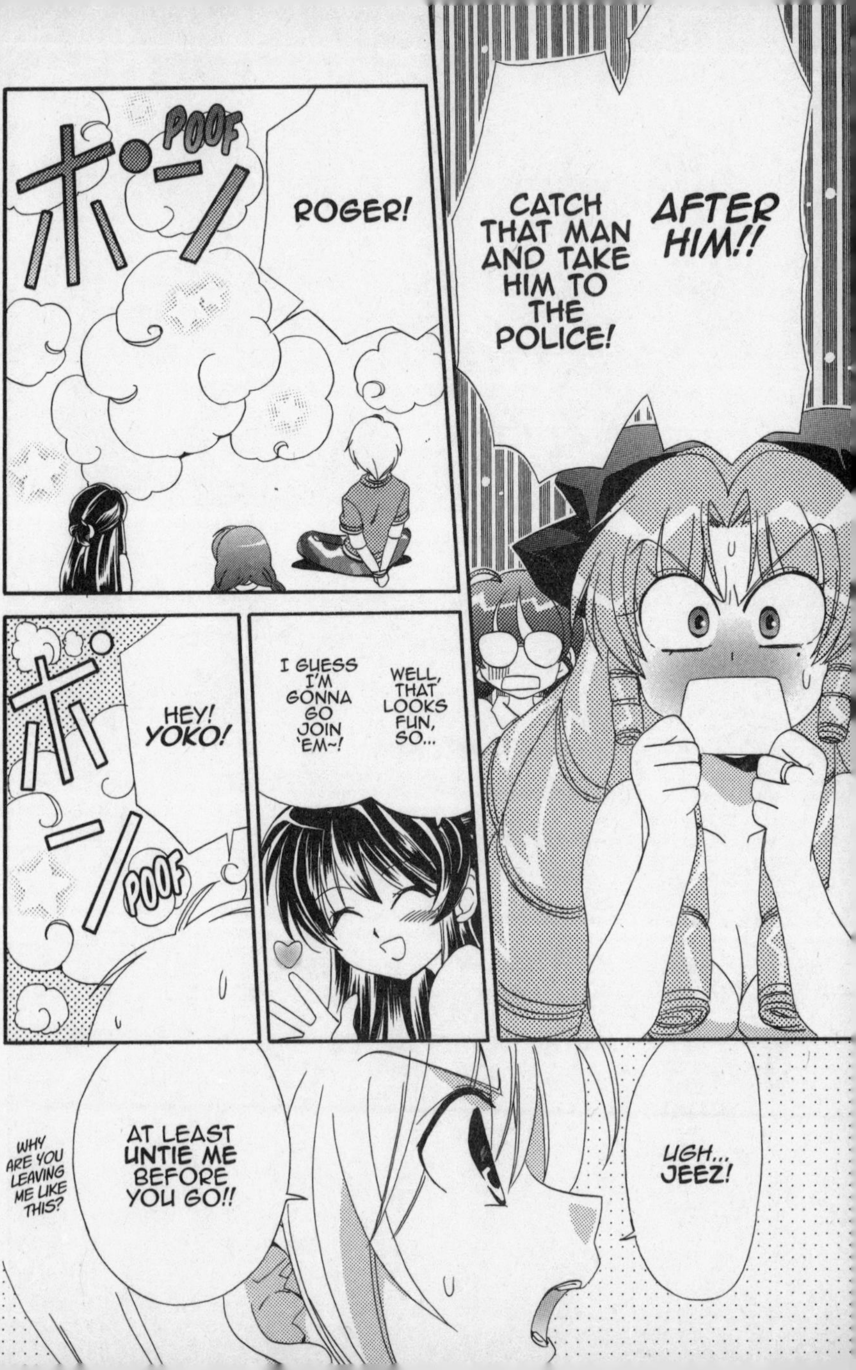
AFTER HIM!!
CATCH THAT MAN AND TAKE HIM TO THE POLICE!
ポーン
POOF
ROGER!
WELL, THAT LOOKS FUN, SO...
I GUESS I'M GONNA GO JOIN 'EM~!
HEY! YOKO!
ポーン
POOF
UGH... JEEZ!
AT LEAST UNTIE ME BEFORE YOU GO!!
WHY ARE YOU LEAVING ME LIKE THIS?

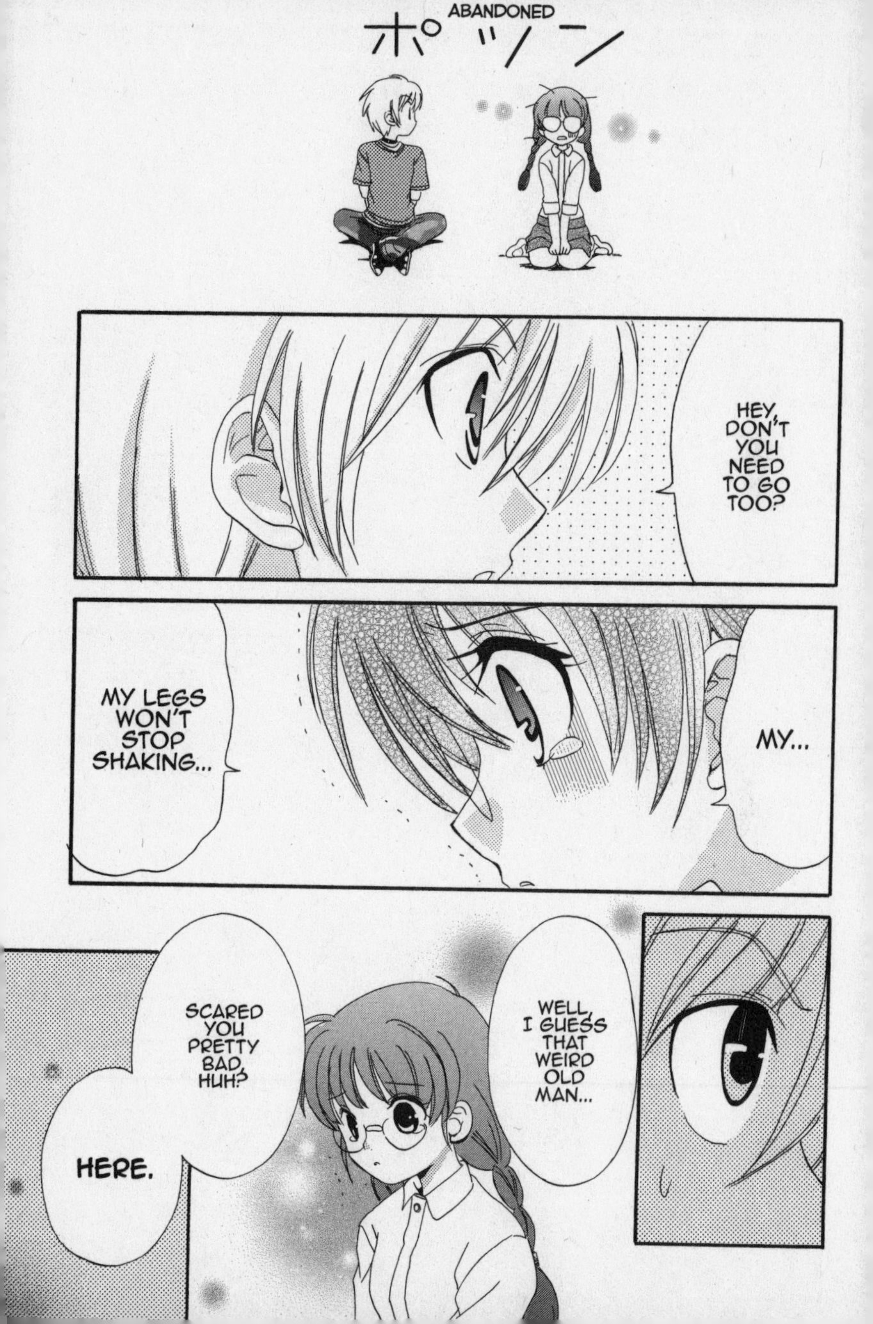

ABANDONED
ポツーン
HEY, DON'T YOU NEED TO GO TOO?
MY...
MY LEGS WON'T STOP SHAKING...
WELL, I GUESS THAT WEIRD OLD MAN...
SCARED YOU PRETTY BAD, HUH?
HERE.

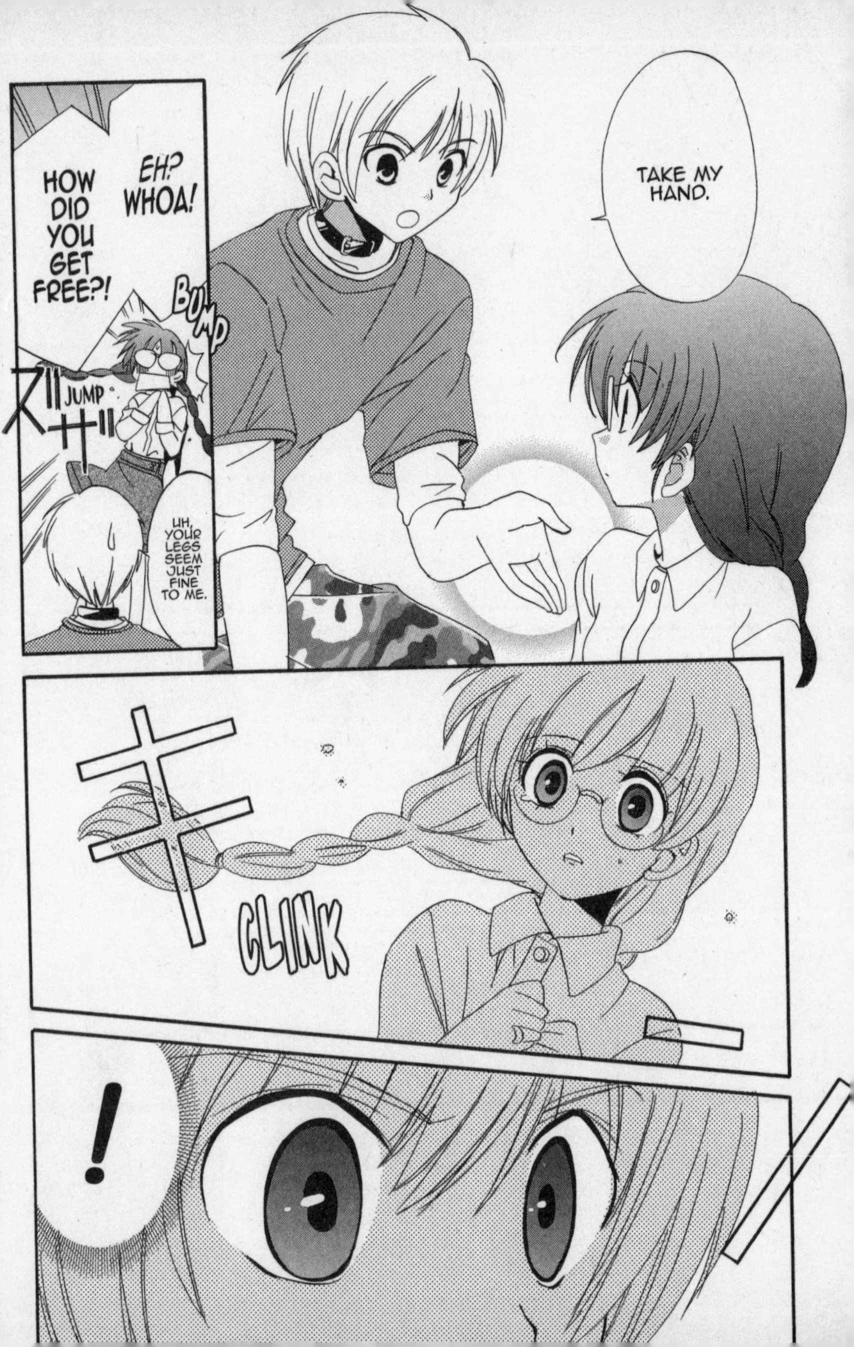
TAKE MY HAND.
EH? WHOA!
HOW DID YOU GET FREE?!
BUMP
JUMP
UH, YOUR LEGS SEEM JUST FINE TO ME.
CLINK
!

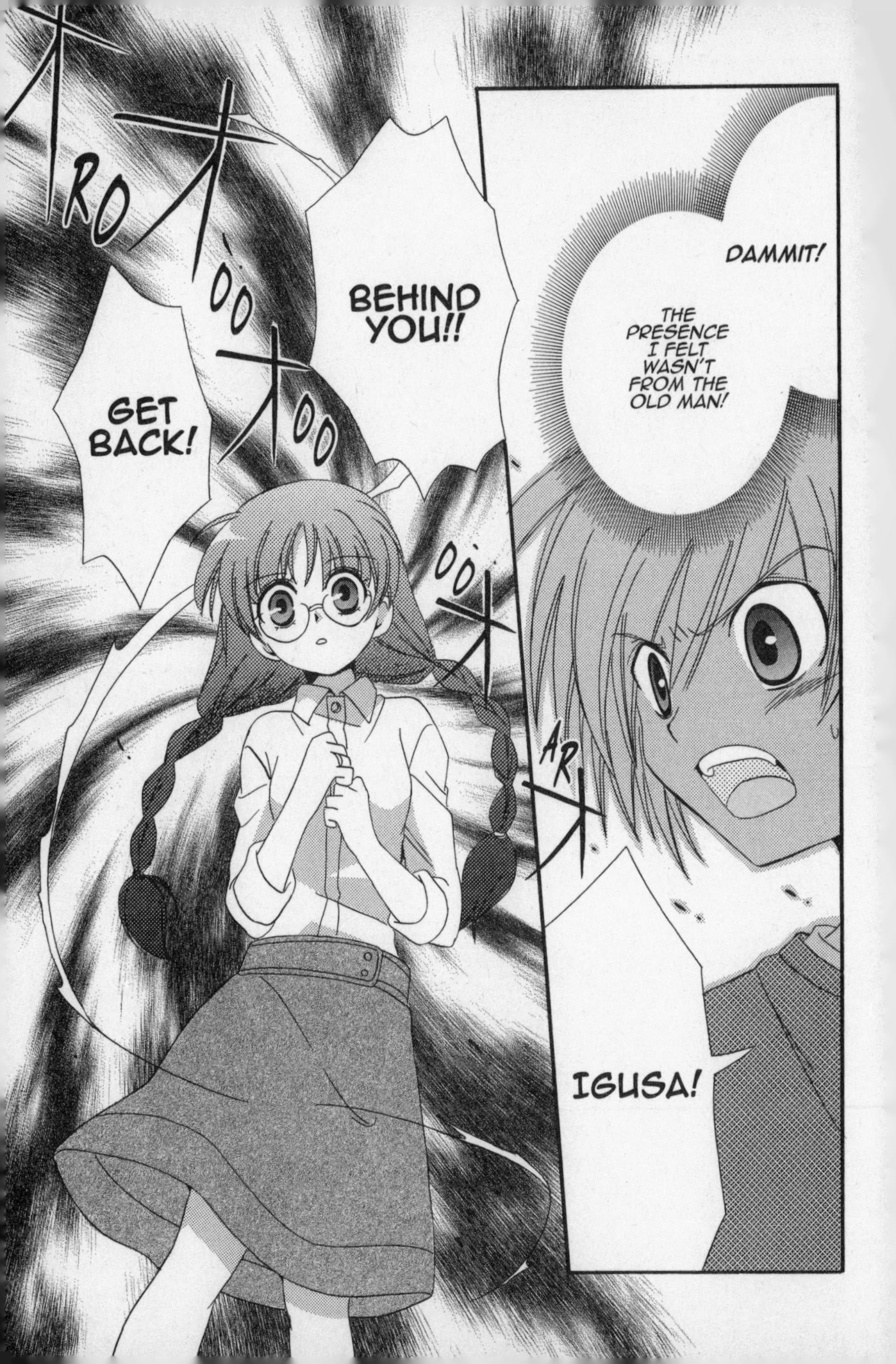
DAMMIT!
THE PRESENCE I FELT WASN'T FROM THE OLD MAN!
IGUSA!
AR
BEHIND YOU!!
GET BACK!
RO
OO
OO
OO

UH...
UMM...

IGUSA

Height: 164 cm
Bust: 78 cm
Waist: 56 cm
Hip: 80 cm
Age: 124

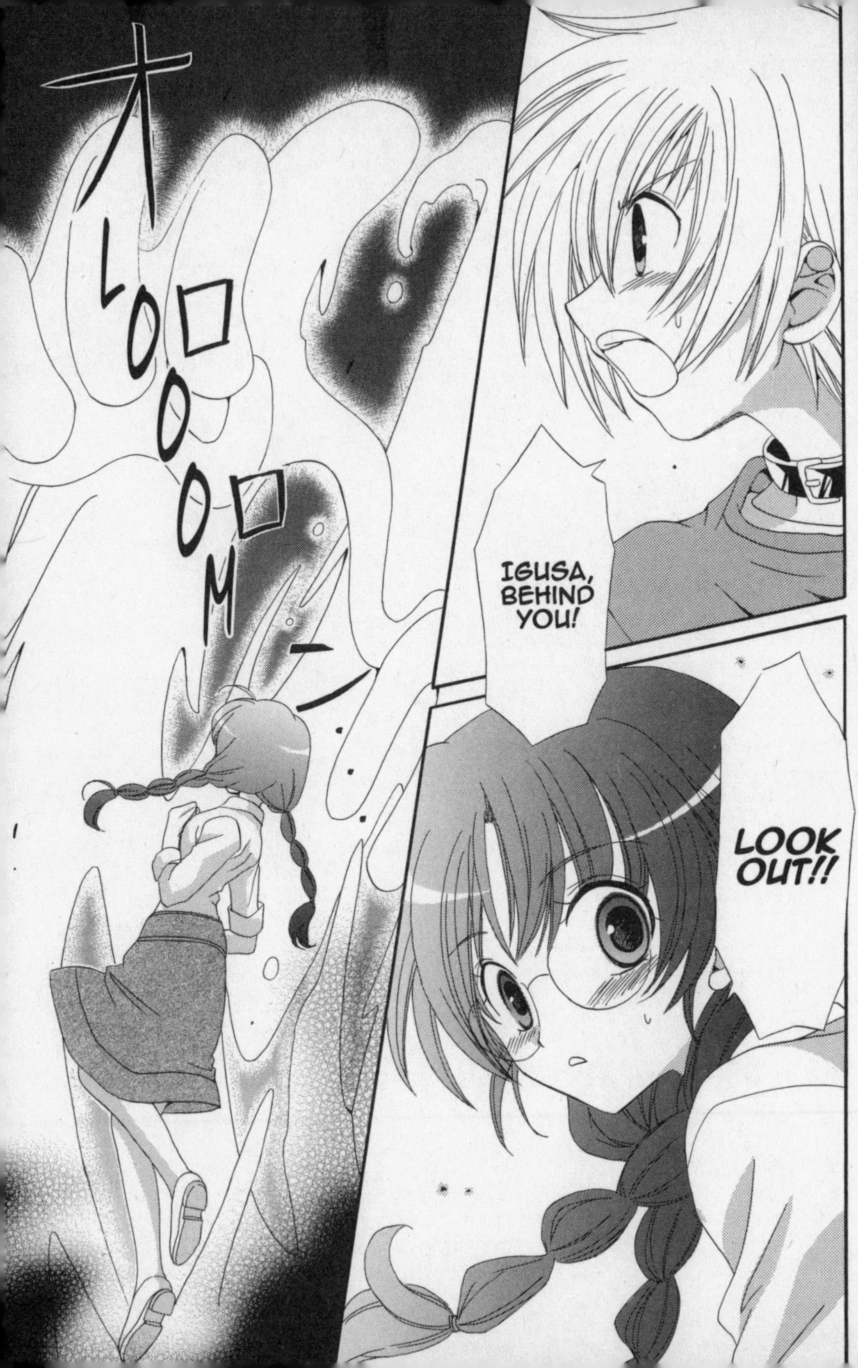
IGUSA, BEHIND YOU!
LOOK OUT!!
LOOOOM

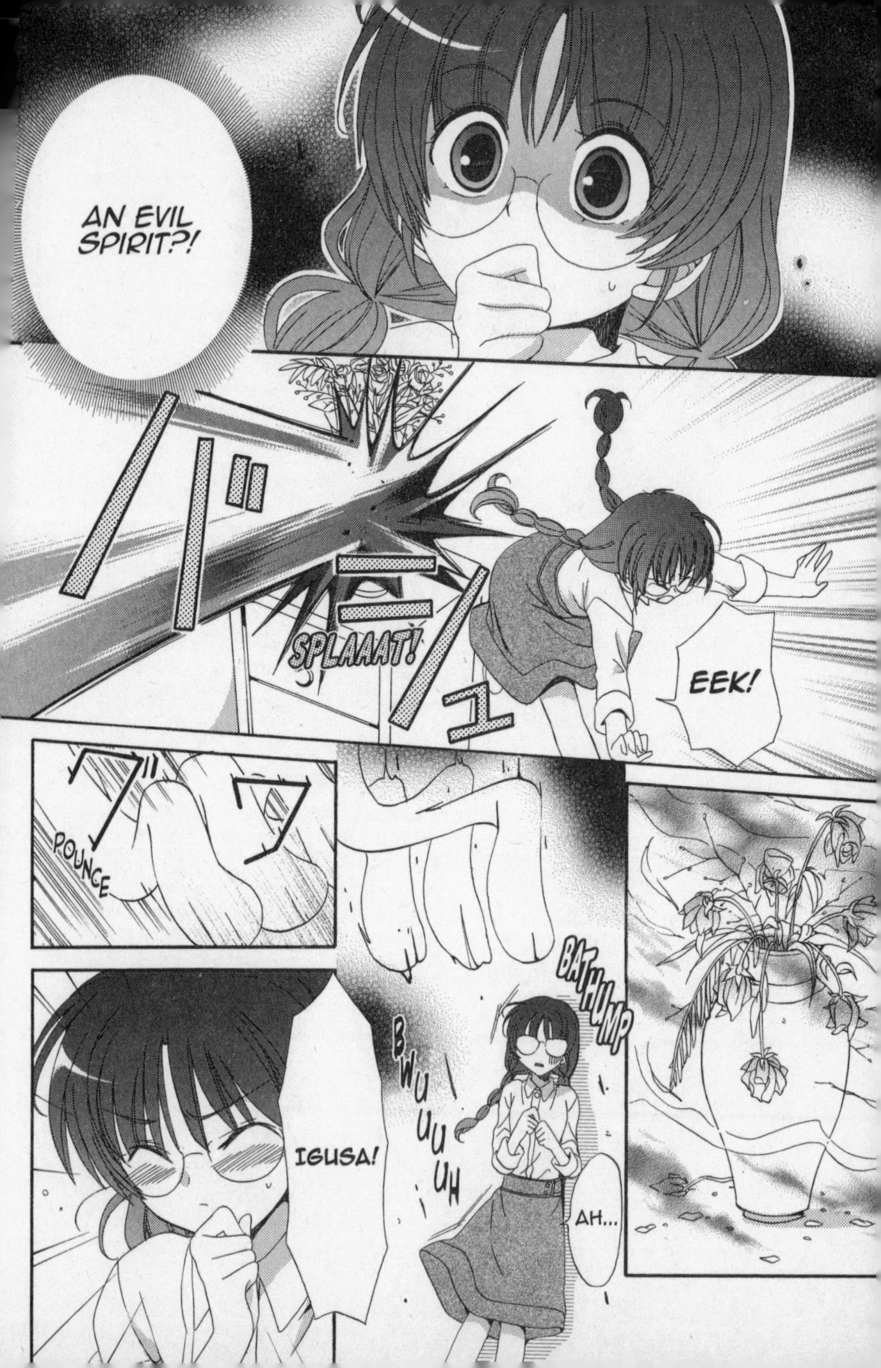
AN EVIL SPIRIT?!
EEK!
SPLAAAT!
POUNCE
BATHUMP
BWUUUUUH
AH...
IGUSA!

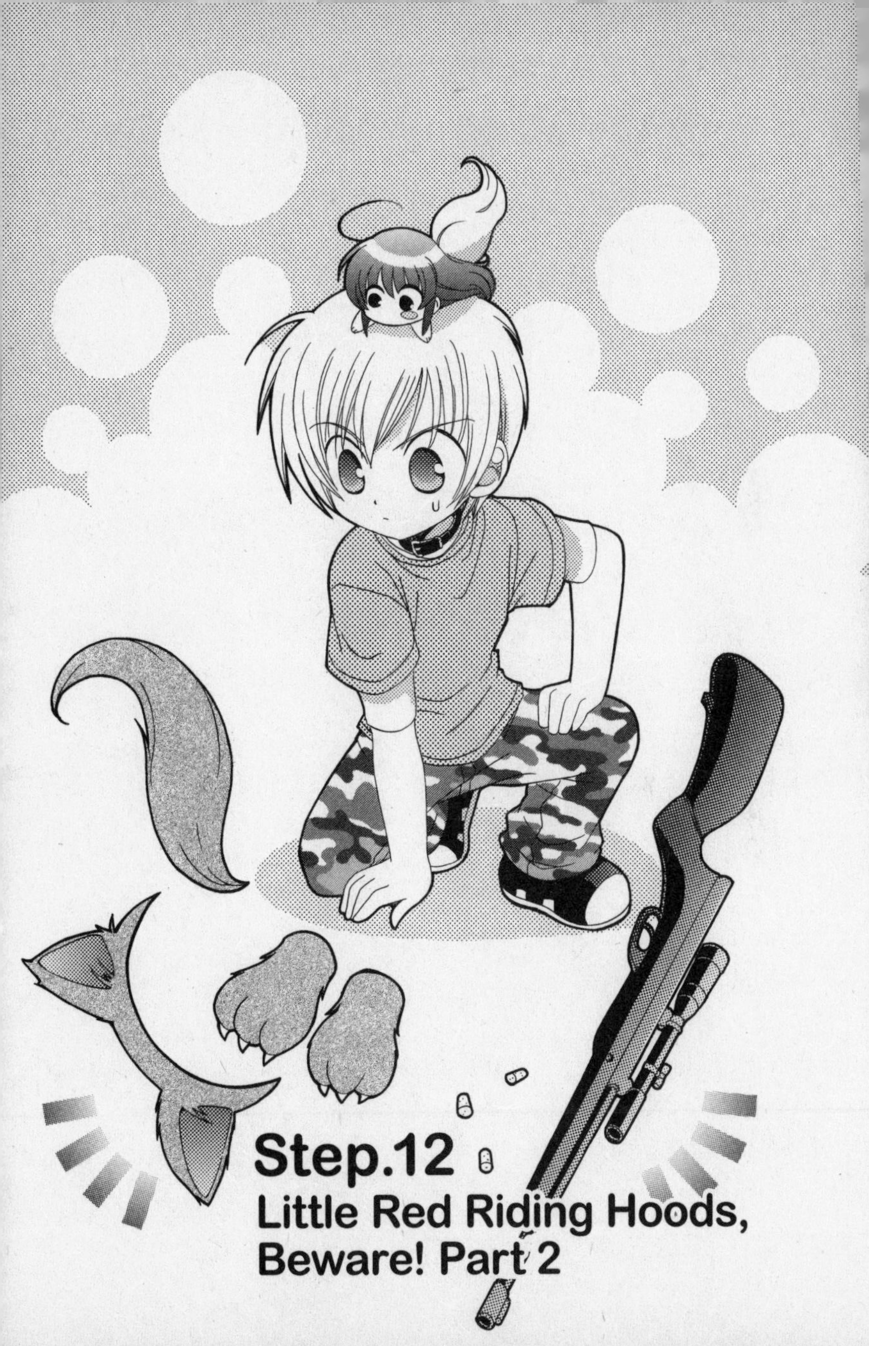

Step.12
Little Red Riding Hoods, Beware! Part 2

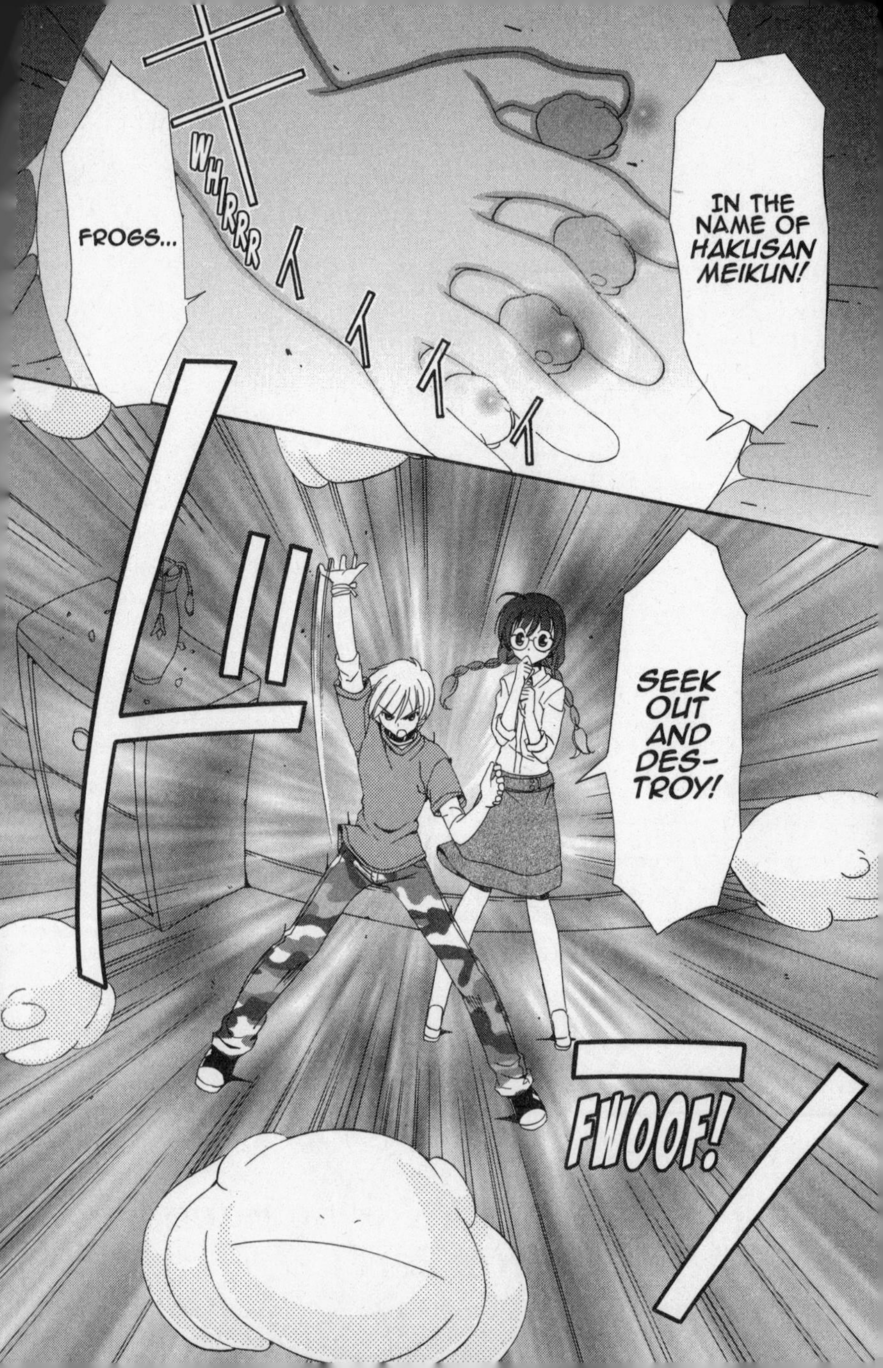
IN THE NAME OF HAKUSAN MEIKUN!
WHIRRR
FROGS...
SEEK OUT AND DES-TROY!
FWOOF!

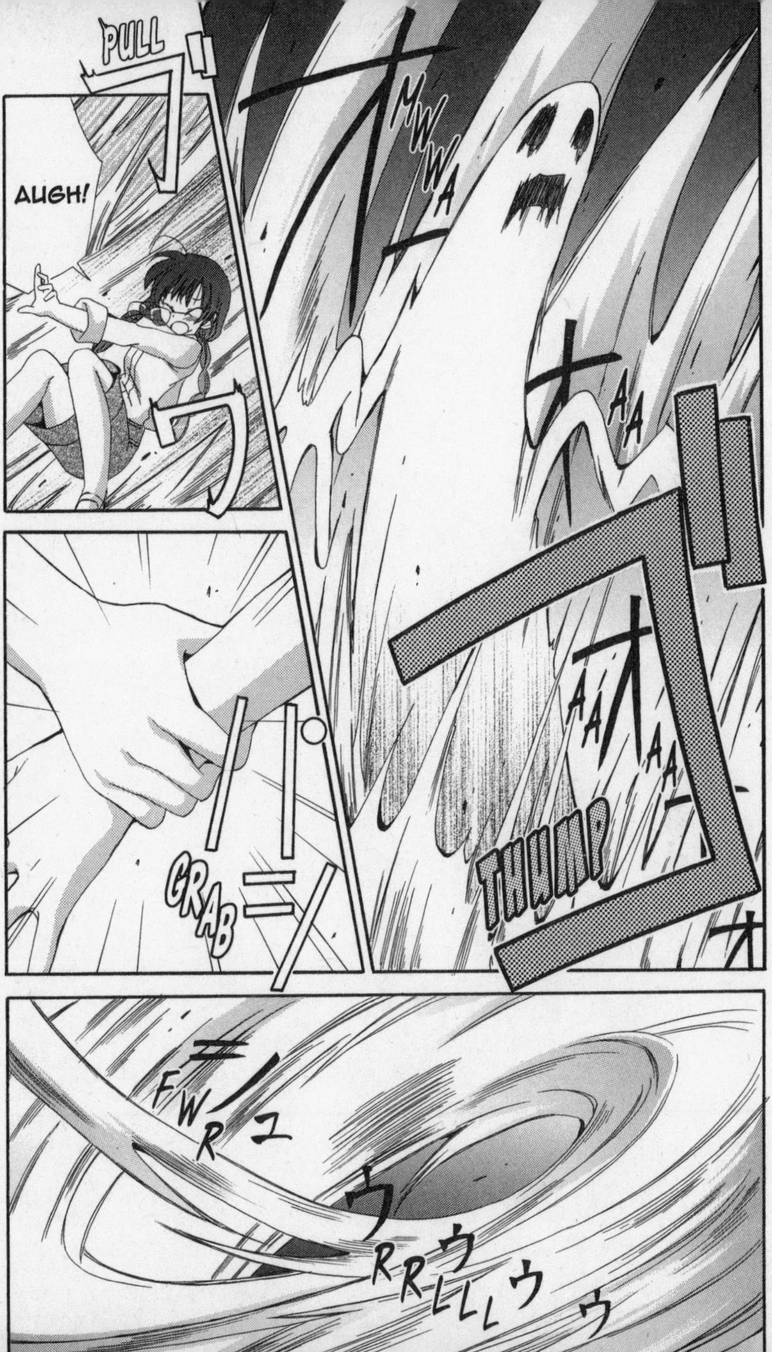

MWWA
AA
AAAA
THUMP
PULL
AUGH!
GRAB
FWR
RRLLL

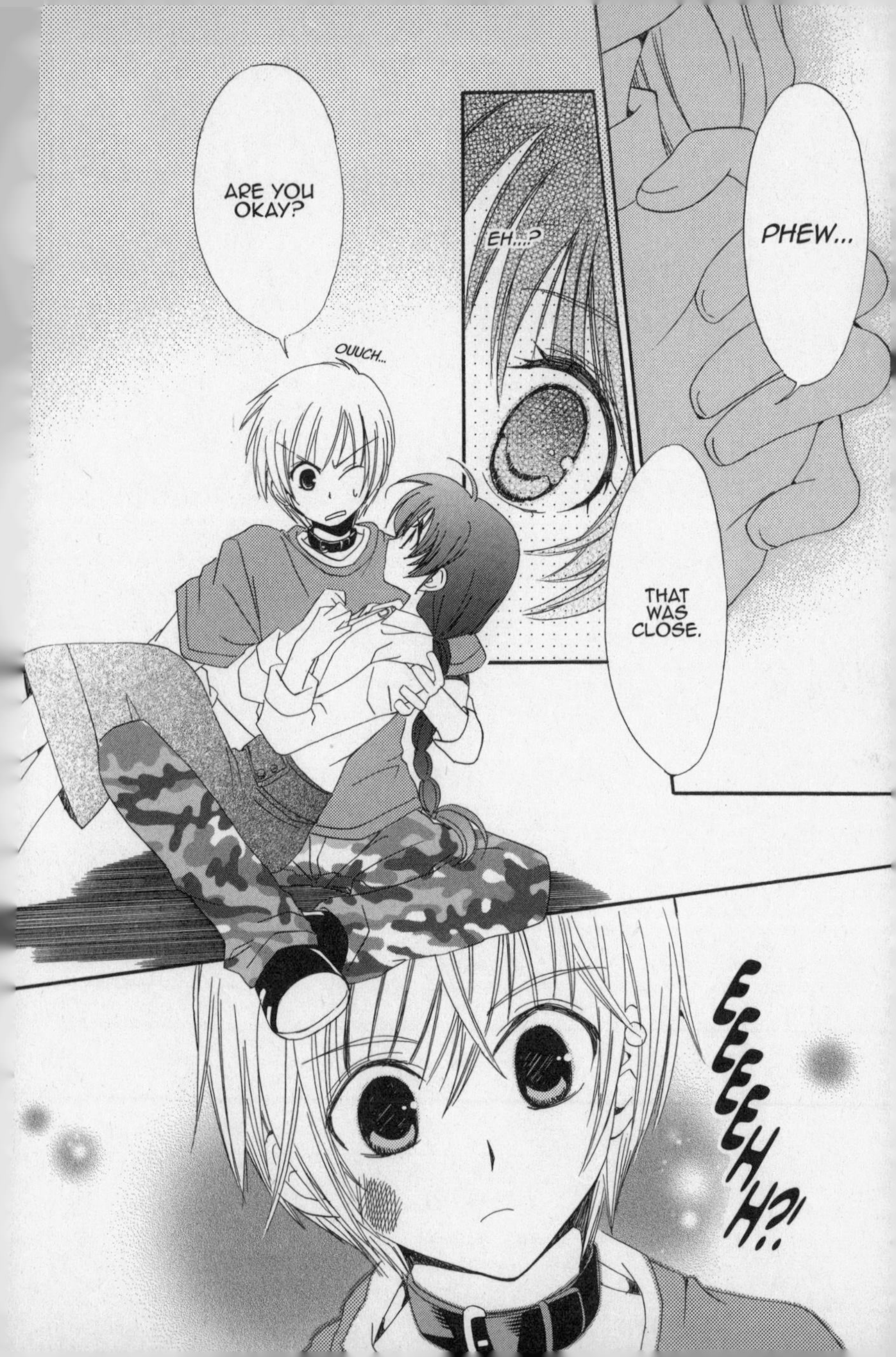
PHEW...
THAT WAS CLOSE.
EH...?
ARE YOU OKAY?
OUUCH...
EEEEEHH?!

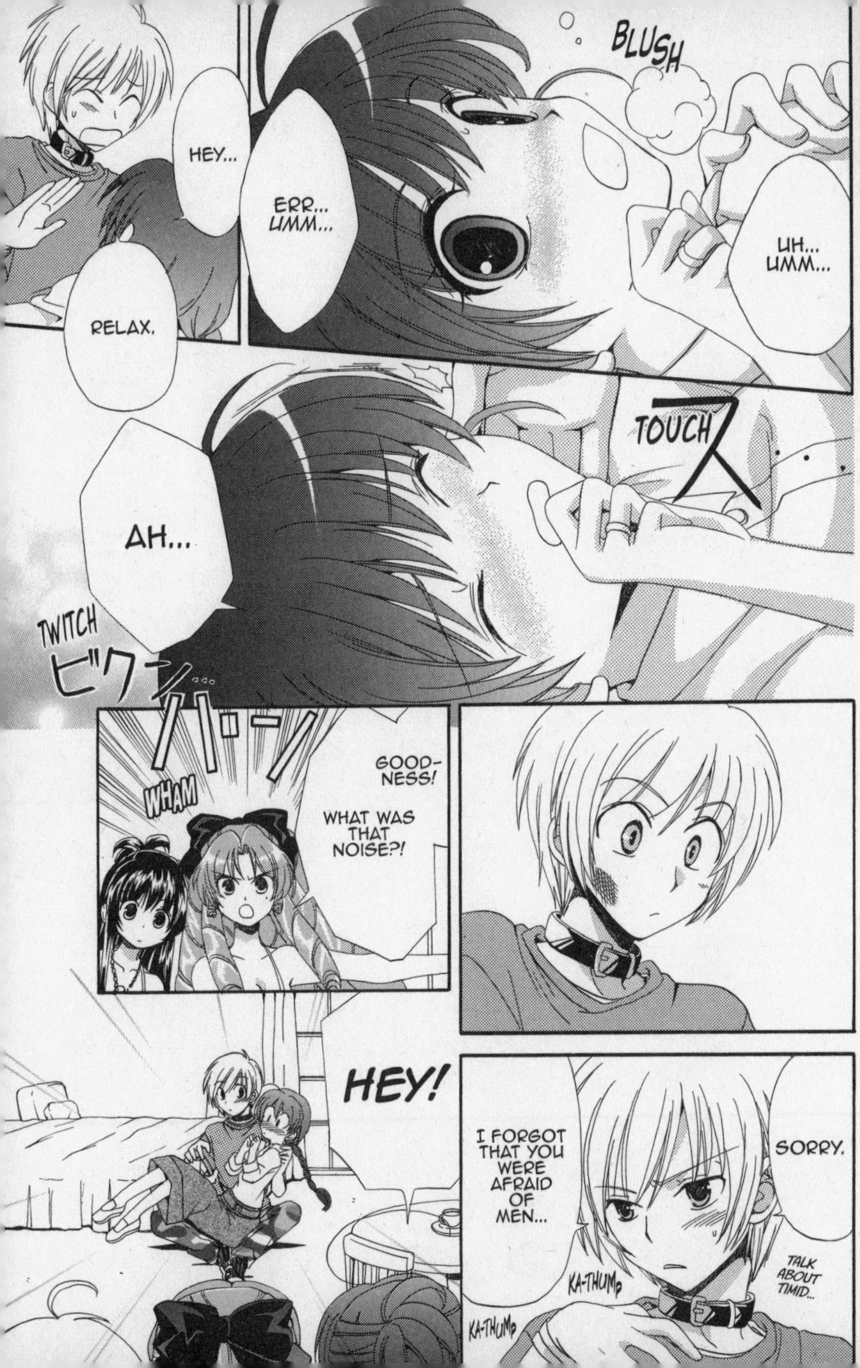
BLUSH
UH... UMM...
ERR... UMM...
HEY...
RELAX.
TOUCH
AH...
TWITCH
WHAM
GOOD-NESS!
WHAT WAS THAT NOISE?!
SORRY.
I FORGOT THAT YOU WERE AFRAID OF MEN...
TALK ABOUT TIMID...
KA-THUMP
KA-THUMP
HEY!

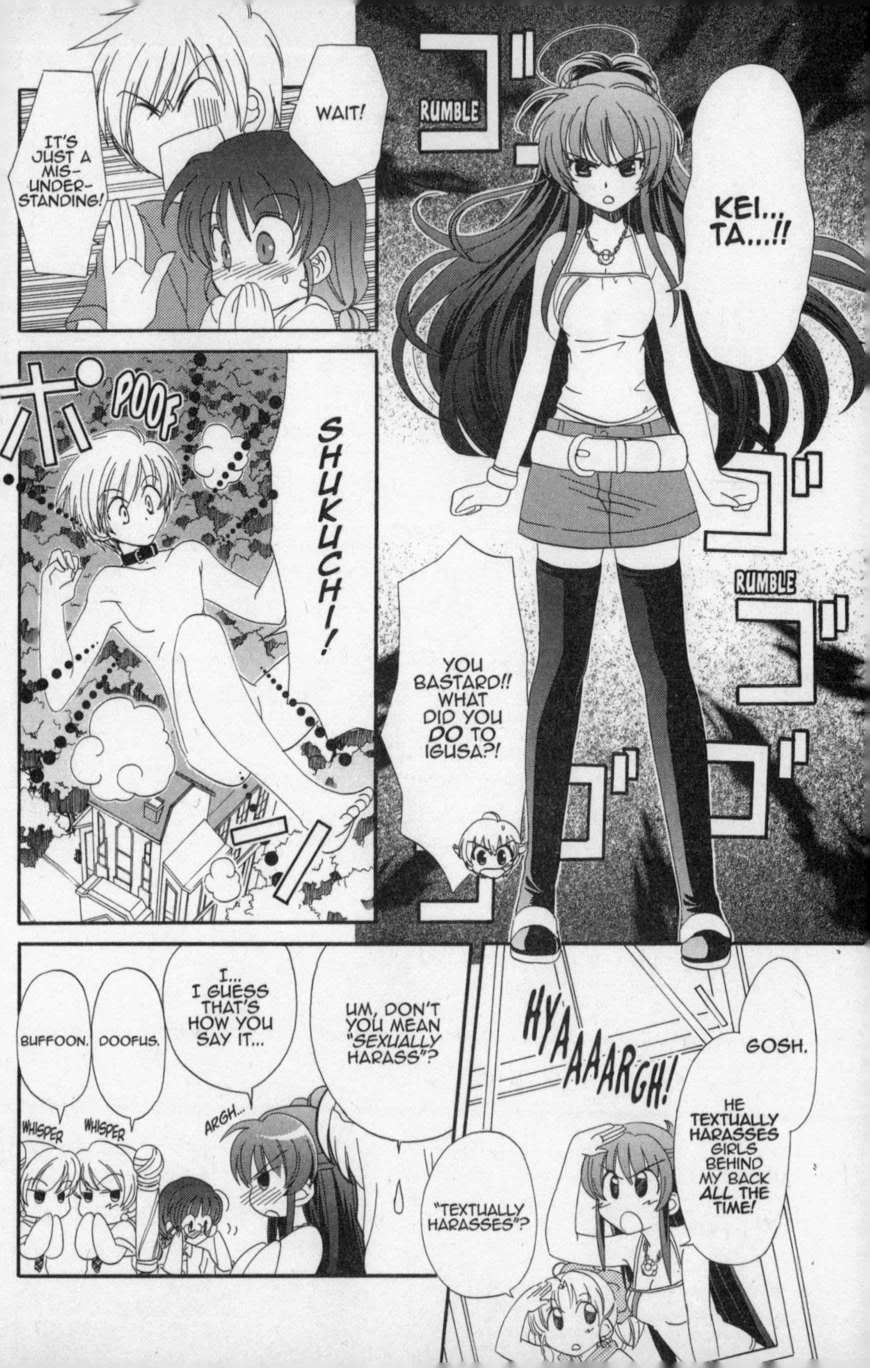
RUMBLE
KEI... TA...!!
RUMBLE
YOU BASTARD!! WHAT DID YOU *DO* TO IGUSA?!
WAIT!
IT'S JUST A MIS-UNDER-STANDING!
POOF
SHUKUCHI!
HYAAAARGH!
GOSH.
HE TEXTUALLY HARASSES GIRLS BEHIND MY BACK **ALL** THE TIME!
"TEXTUALLY HARASSES"?
UM, DON'T YOU MEAN "*SEXUALLY* HARASS"?
I... I GUESS THAT'S HOW YOU SAY IT...
ARGH...
DOOFUS.
WHISPER
BUFFOON.
WHISPER

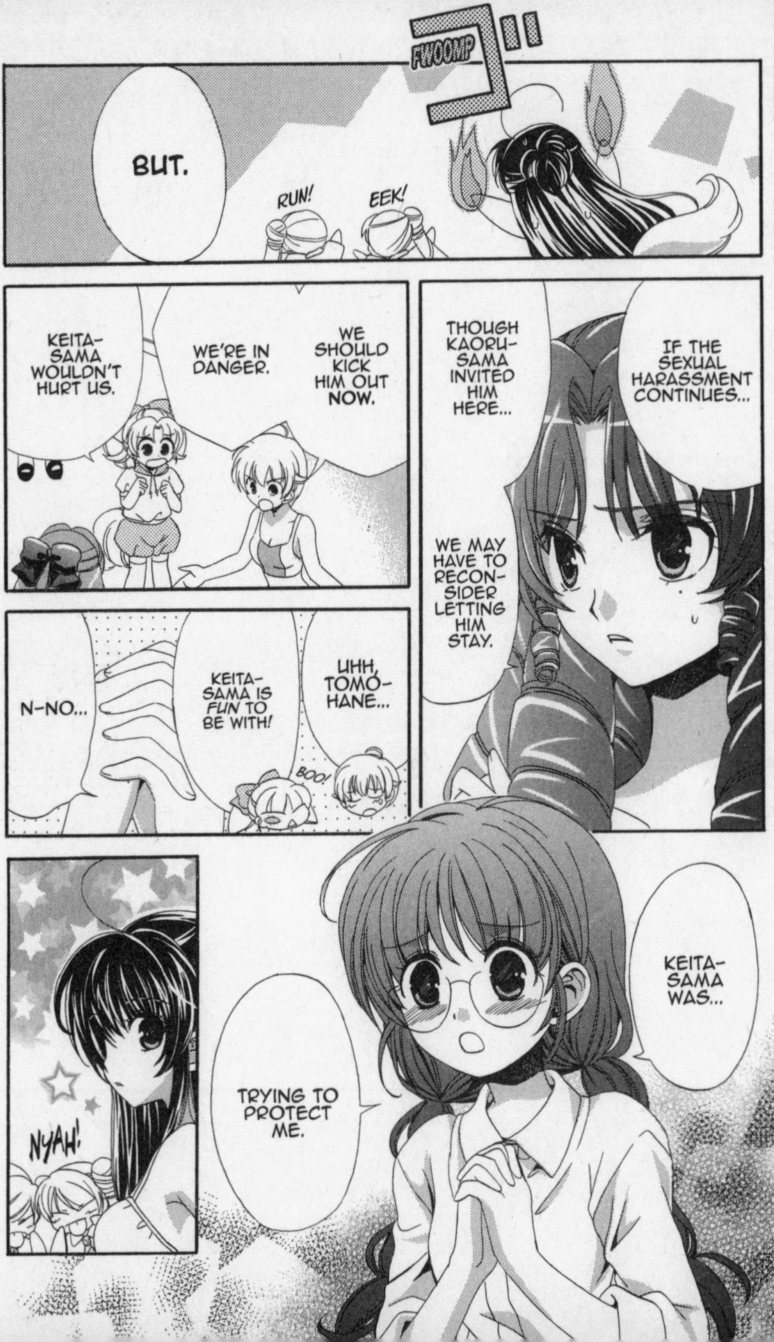
FWOOMP
BUT.
EEK!
RUN!
IF THE SEXUAL HARASSMENT CONTINUES...
THOUGH KAORU-SAMA INVITED HIM HERE...
WE MAY HAVE TO RECONSIDER LETTING HIM STAY.
WE SHOULD KICK HIM OUT NOW.
WE'RE IN DANGER.
KEITA-SAMA WOULDN'T HURT US.
UHH, TOMOHANE...
KEITA-SAMA IS *FUN* TO BE WITH!
BOO!
N-NO...
KEITA-SAMA WAS...
TRYING TO PROTECT ME.
NYAH!

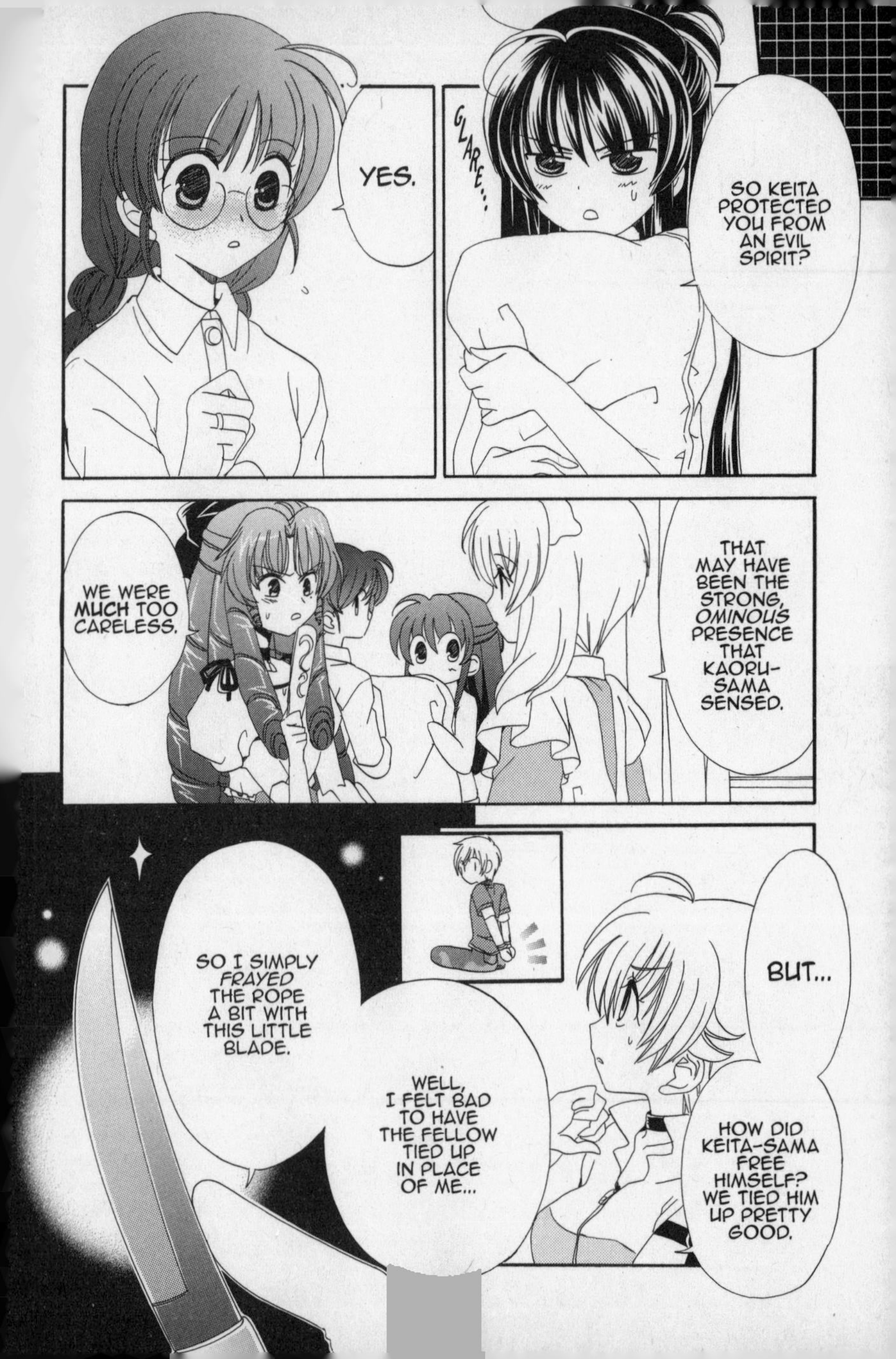
GLARE...
SO KEITA PROTECTED YOU FROM AN EVIL SPIRIT?
YES.
THAT MAY HAVE BEEN THE STRONG, *OMINOUS* PRESENCE THAT KAORU-SAMA SENSED.
WE WERE **MUCH** TOO CARELESS.
BUT...
HOW DID KEITA-SAMA FREE HIMSELF? WE TIED HIM UP PRETTY GOOD.
WELL, I FELT BAD TO HAVE THE FELLOW TIED UP IN PLACE OF ME...
SO I SIMPLY *FRAYED* THE ROPE A BIT WITH THIS LITTLE BLADE.

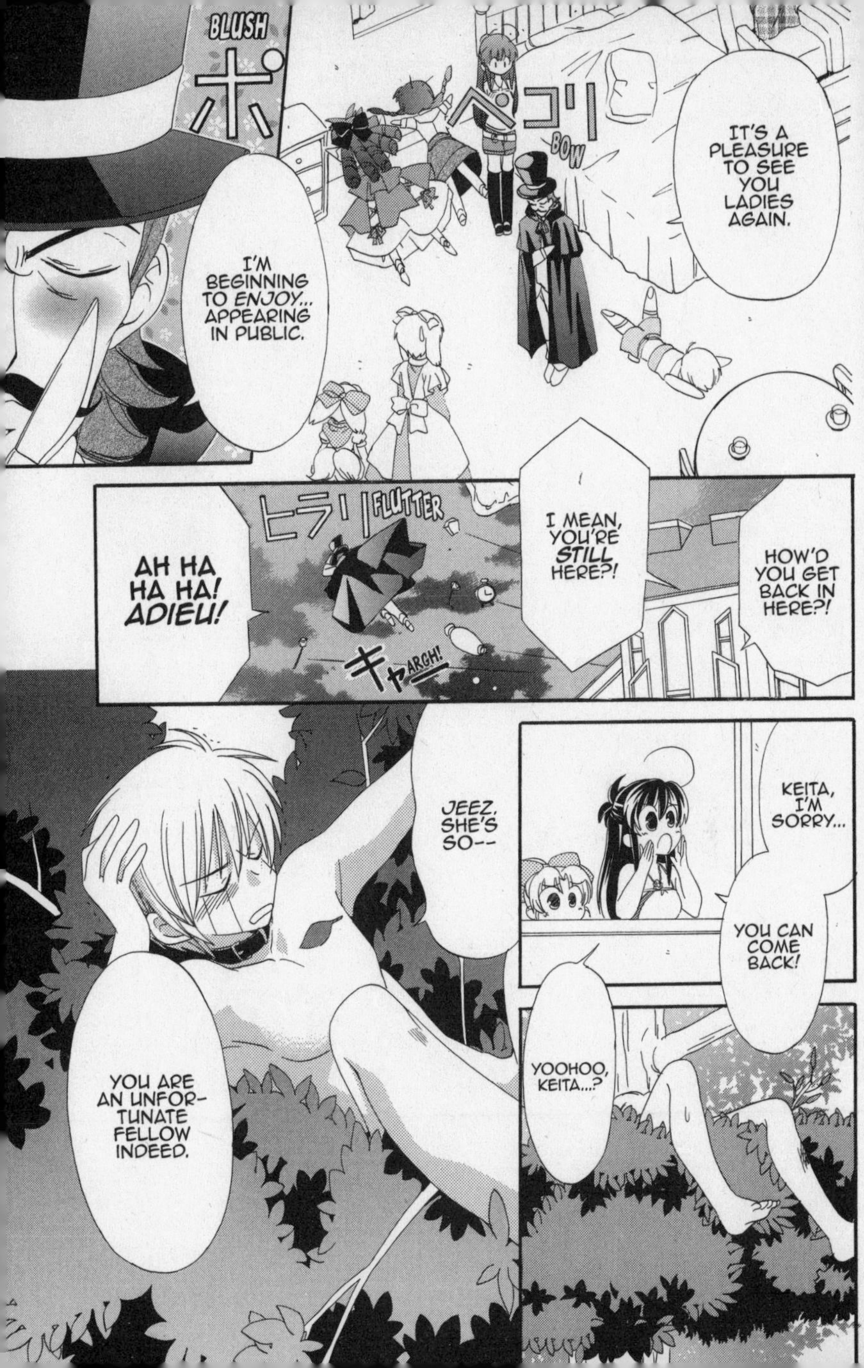
ペコリ
BOW
IT'S A PLEASURE TO SEE YOU LADIES AGAIN.
ポ
BLUSH
I'M BEGINNING TO ENJOY... APPEARING IN PUBLIC.
HOW'D YOU GET BACK IN HERE?!
I MEAN, YOU'RE STILL HERE?!
ヒラー
FLUTTER
AH HA HA HA! ADIEU!
キャ
ARGH!
KEITA, I'M SORRY...
YOU CAN COME BACK!
JEEZ. SHE'S SO--
YOOHOO, KEITA...?
YOU ARE AN UNFORTUNATE FELLOW INDEED.

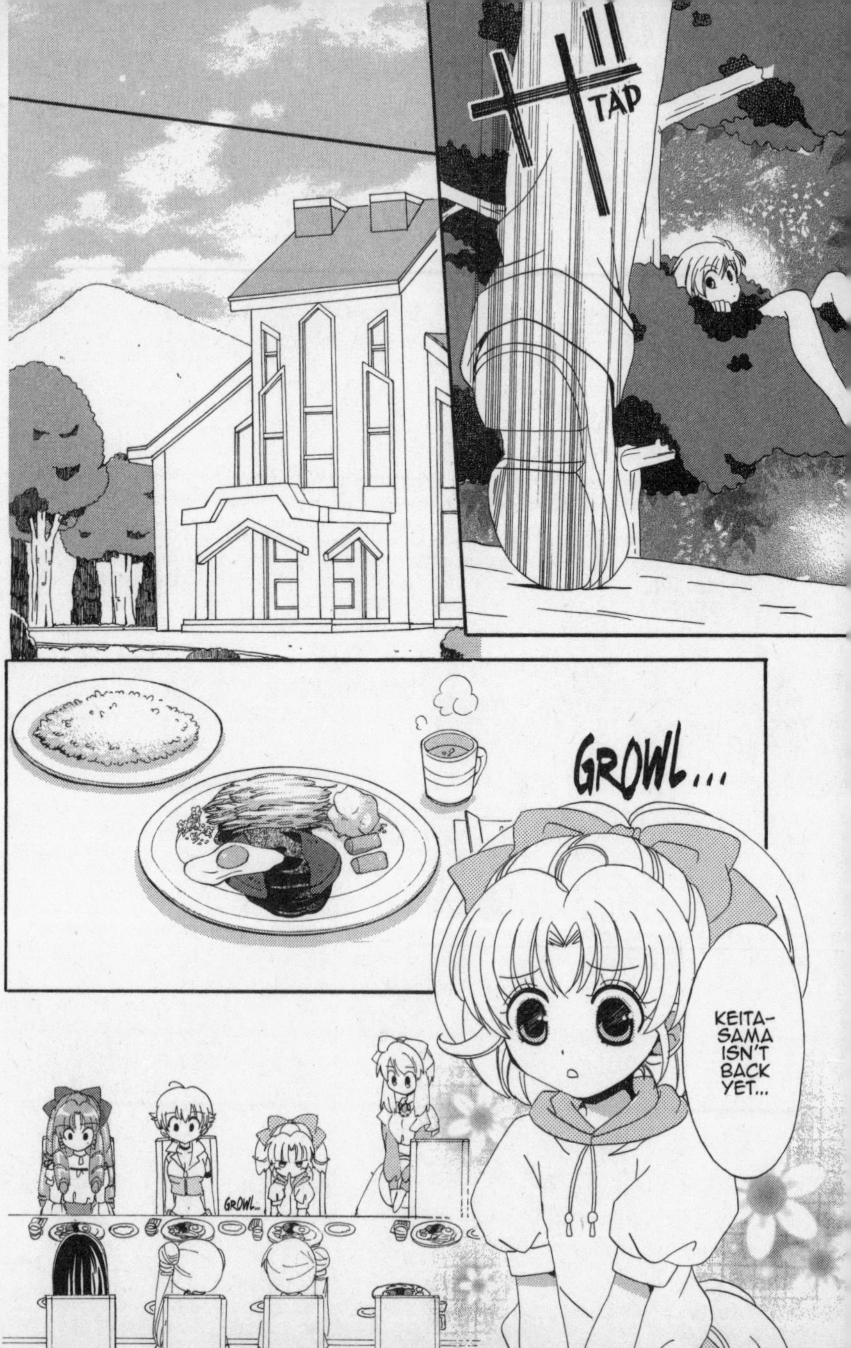
TAP
GROWL...
KEITA-SAMA ISN'T BACK YET...
GROWL...

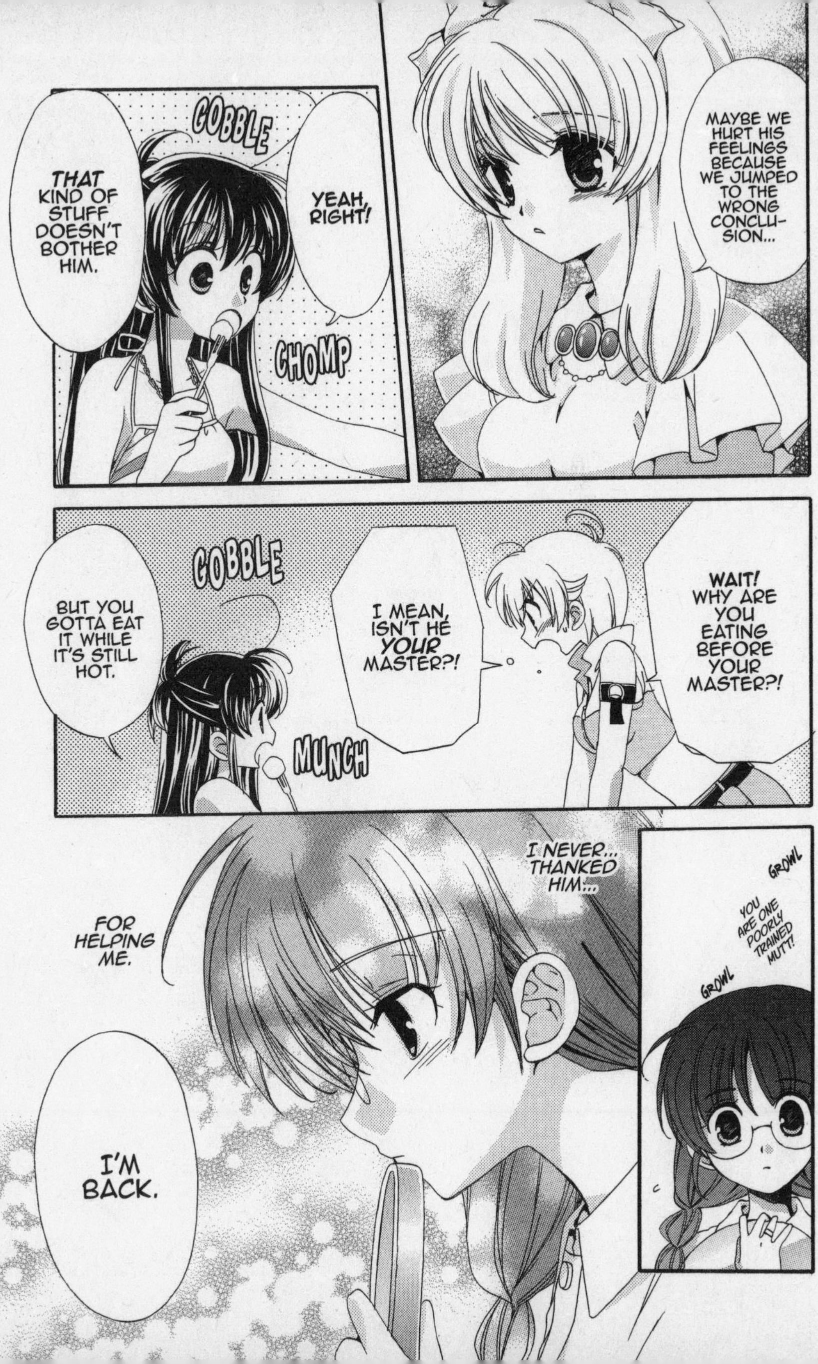
MAYBE WE HURT HIS FEELINGS BECAUSE WE JUMPED TO THE WRONG CONCLUSION...
GOBBLE
YEAH, RIGHT!
THAT KIND OF STUFF DOESN'T BOTHER HIM.
CHOMP
WAIT! WHY ARE YOU EATING BEFORE YOUR MASTER?!
I MEAN, ISN'T HE YOUR MASTER?!
GOBBLE
BUT YOU GOTTA EAT IT WHILE IT'S STILL HOT.
MUNCH
GROWL
YOU ARE ONE POORLY TRAINED MUTT!
GROWL
I NEVER... THANKED HIM...
FOR HELPING ME.
I'M BACK.

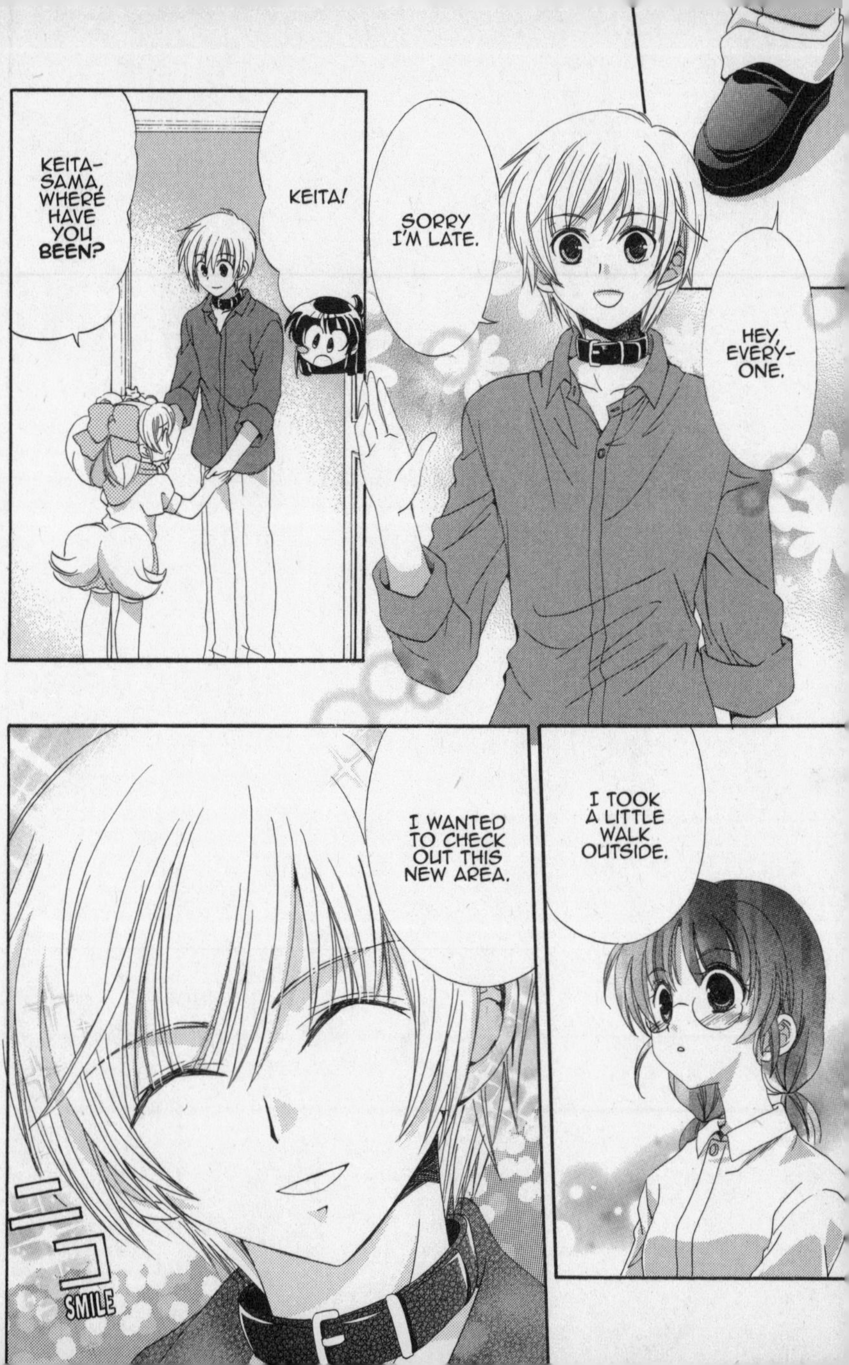
HEY, EVERY-ONE.
SORRY I'M LATE.
KEITA!
KEITA-SAMA, WHERE HAVE YOU BEEN?
I TOOK A LITTLE WALK OUTSIDE.
I WANTED TO CHECK OUT THIS NEW AREA.
SMILE

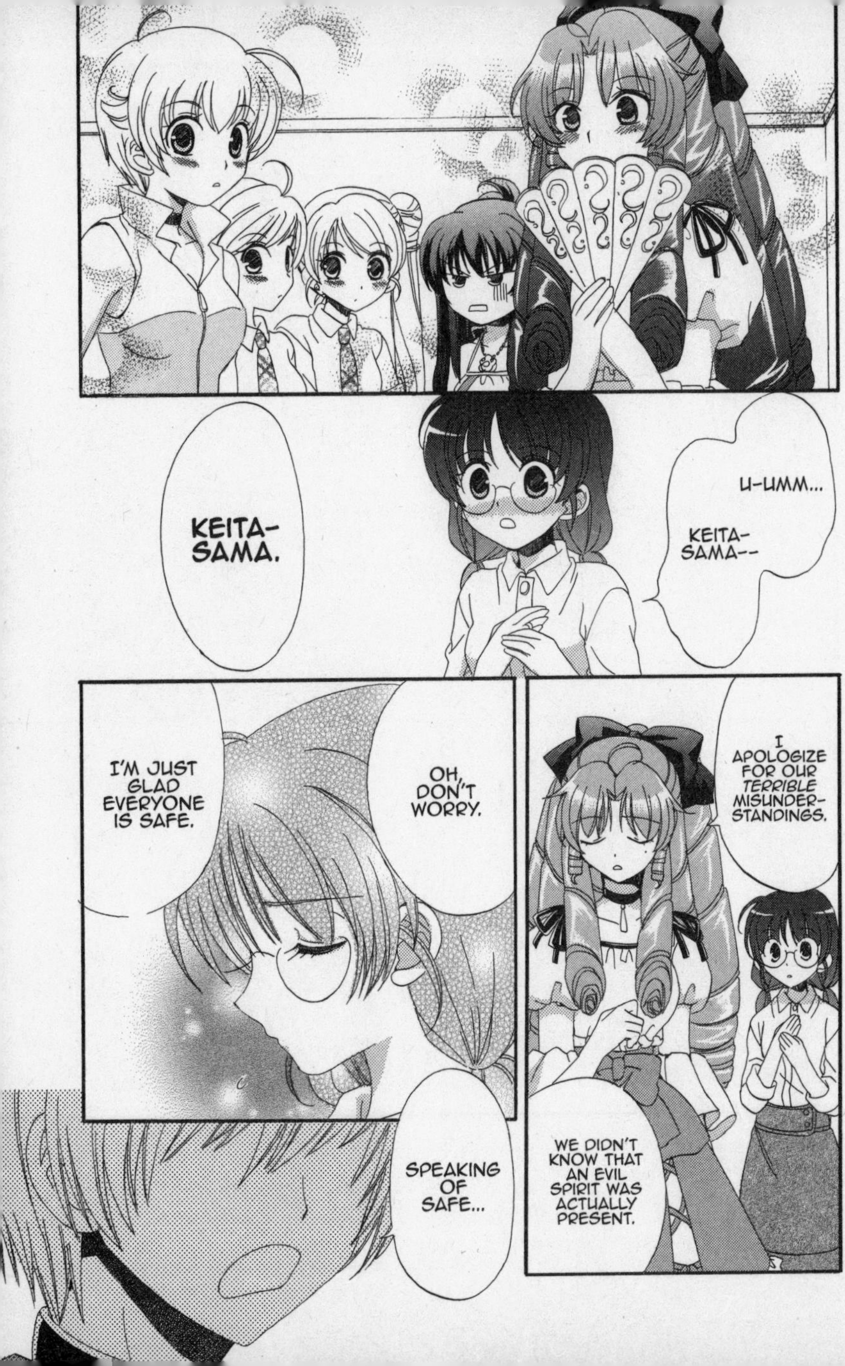
U-UMM...
KEITA-SAMA--
KEITA-SAMA.
I APOLOGIZE FOR OUR *TERRIBLE* MISUNDERSTANDINGS.
WE DIDN'T KNOW THAT AN EVIL SPIRIT WAS ACTUALLY PRESENT.
OH, DON'T WORRY.
I'M JUST GLAD EVERYONE IS SAFE.
SPEAKING OF SAFE...

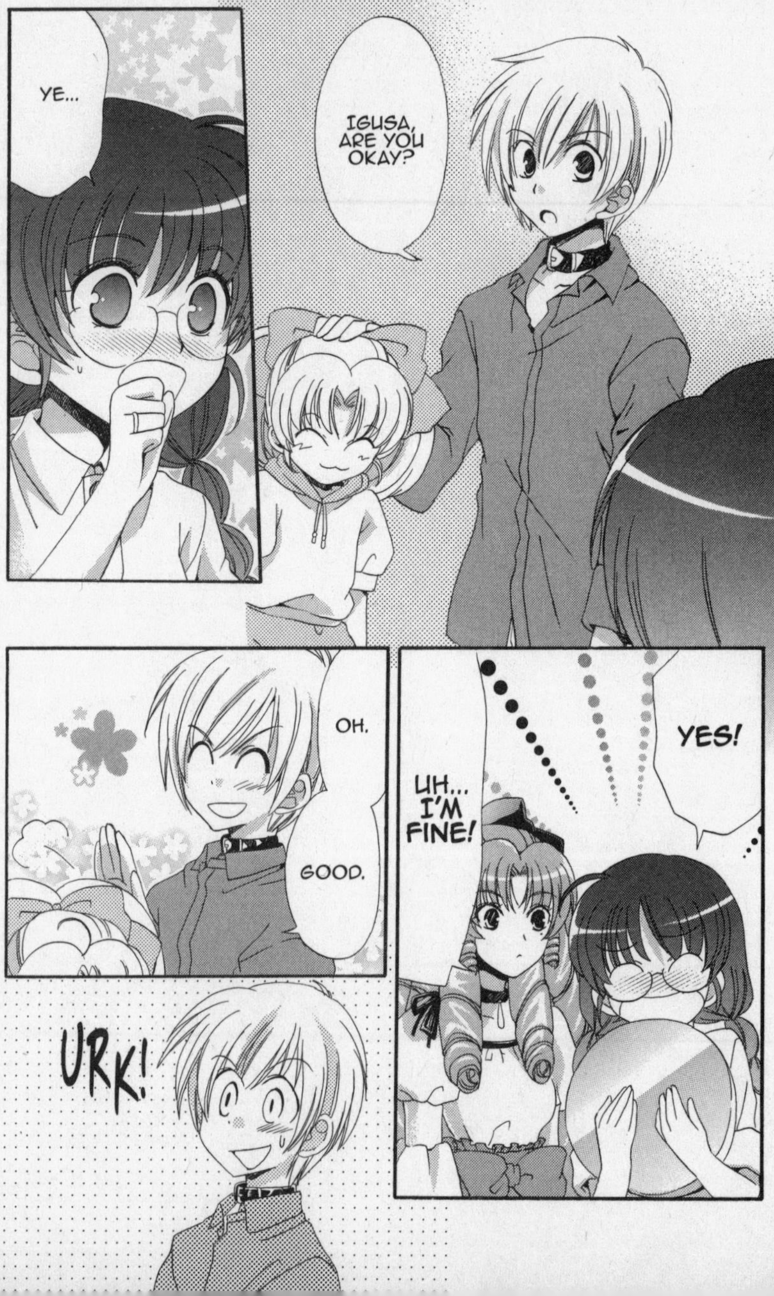
IGUSA, ARE YOU OKAY?
YE...
YES!
UH... I'M FINE!
OH.
GOOD.
URK!

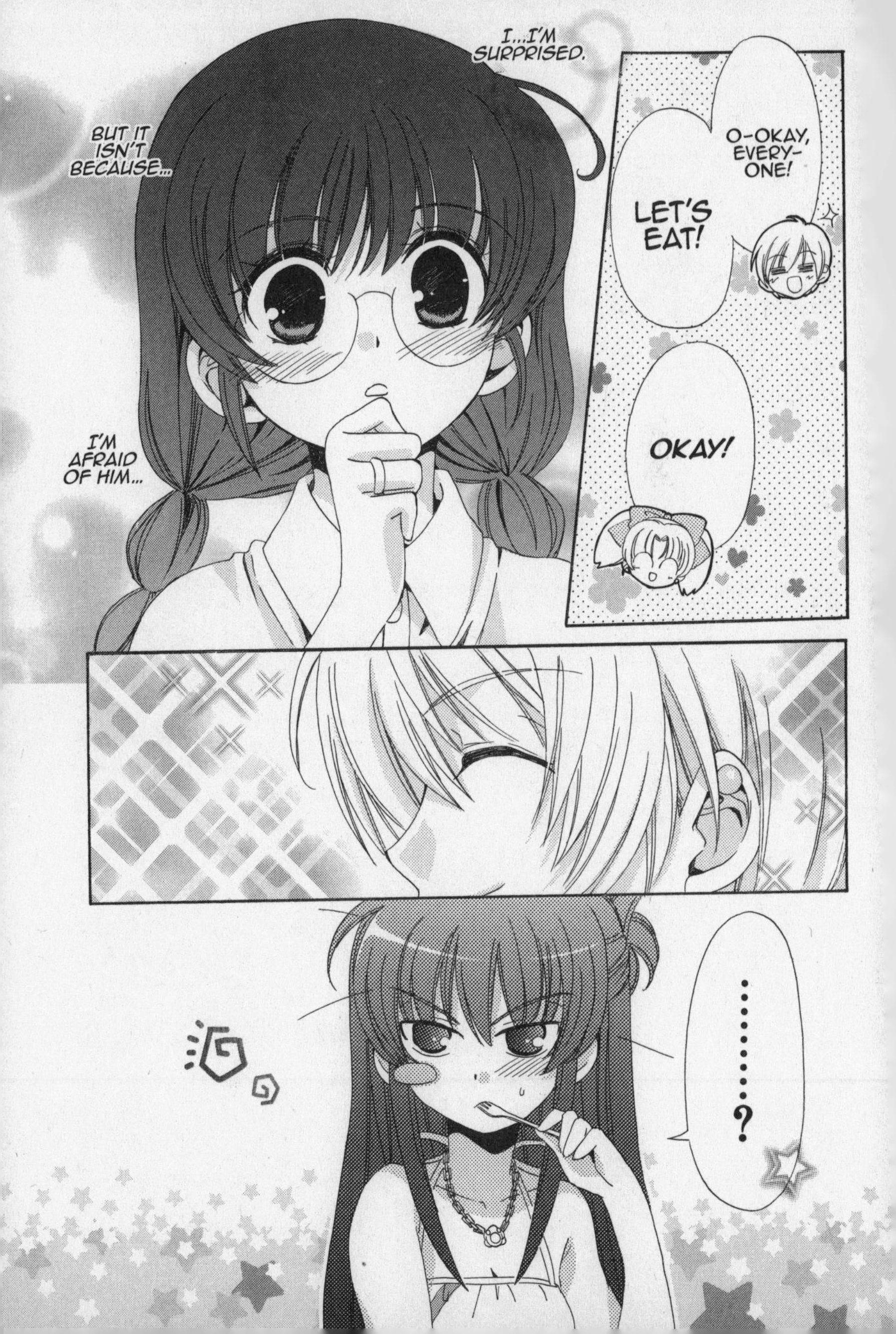
O-OKAY, EVERY-ONE!
LET'S EAT!
OKAY!
I...I'M SURPRISED.
BUT IT ISN'T BECAUSE...
I'M AFRAID OF HIM...
......?

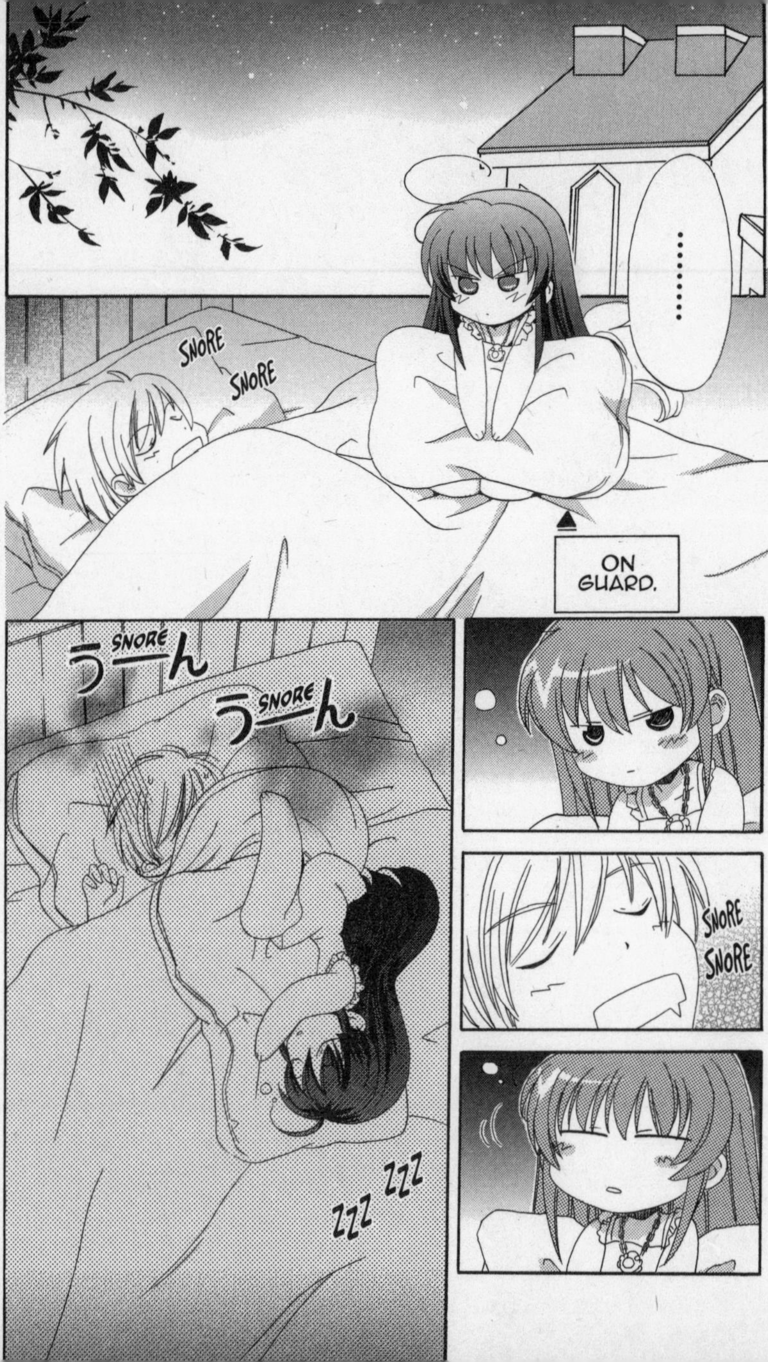
......
SNORE SNORE
ON GUARD.
SNORE SNORE
うーん SNORE
うーん SNORE
ZZZ ZZZ

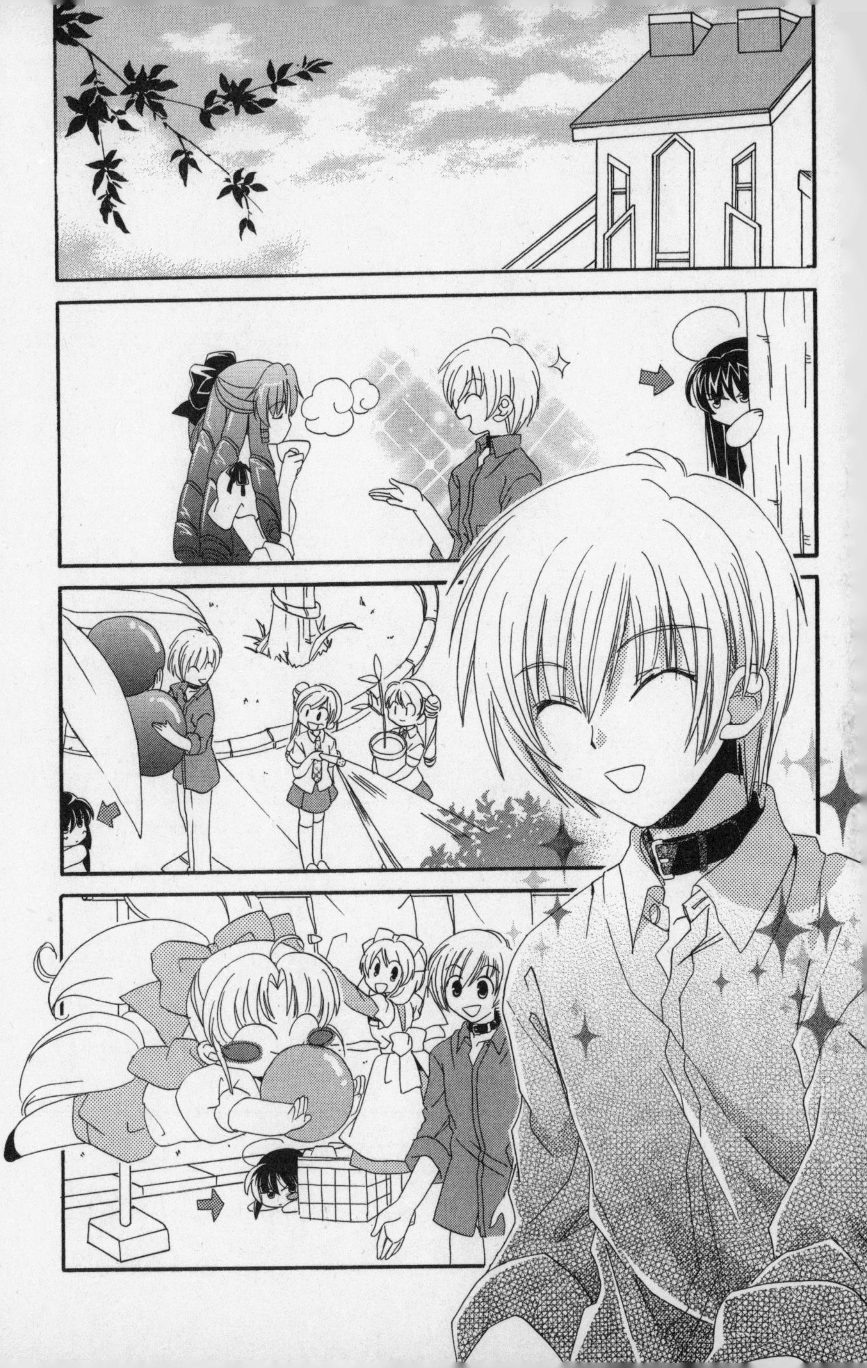

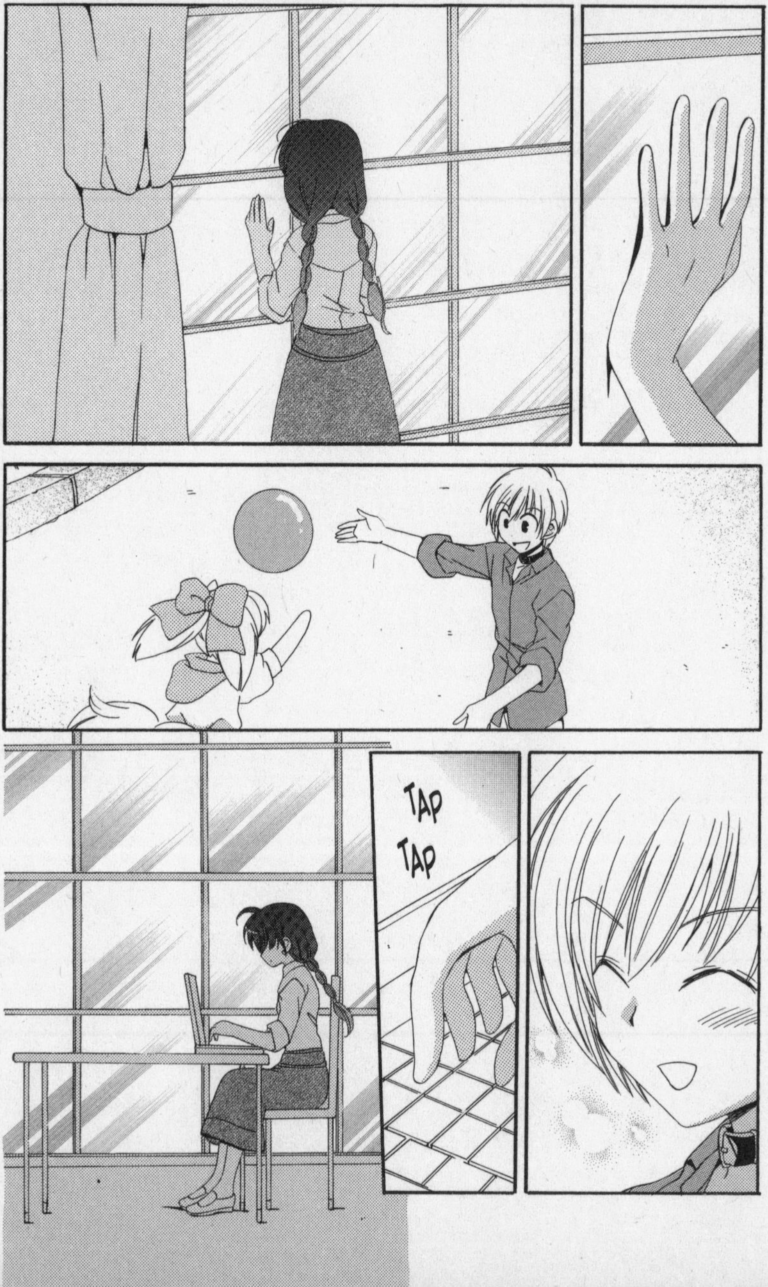
TAP
TAP

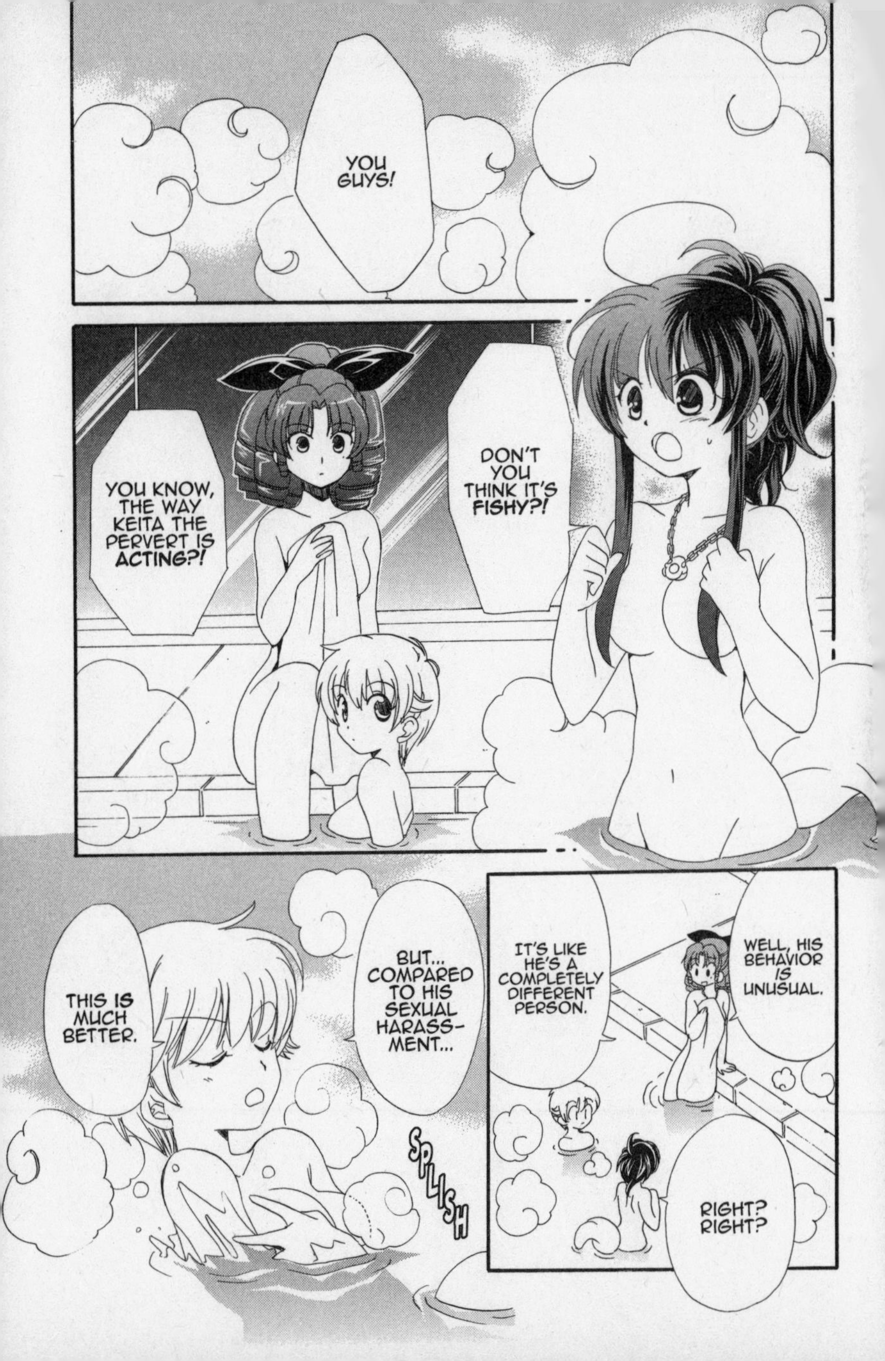
YOU GUYS!
DON'T YOU THINK IT'S FISHY?!
YOU KNOW, THE WAY KEITA THE PERVERT IS ACTING?!
WELL, HIS BEHAVIOR IS UNUSUAL.
IT'S LIKE HE'S A COMPLETELY DIFFERENT PERSON.
RIGHT? RIGHT?
BUT... COMPARED TO HIS SEXUAL HARASS- MENT...
THIS IS MUCH BETTER.
SPLISH

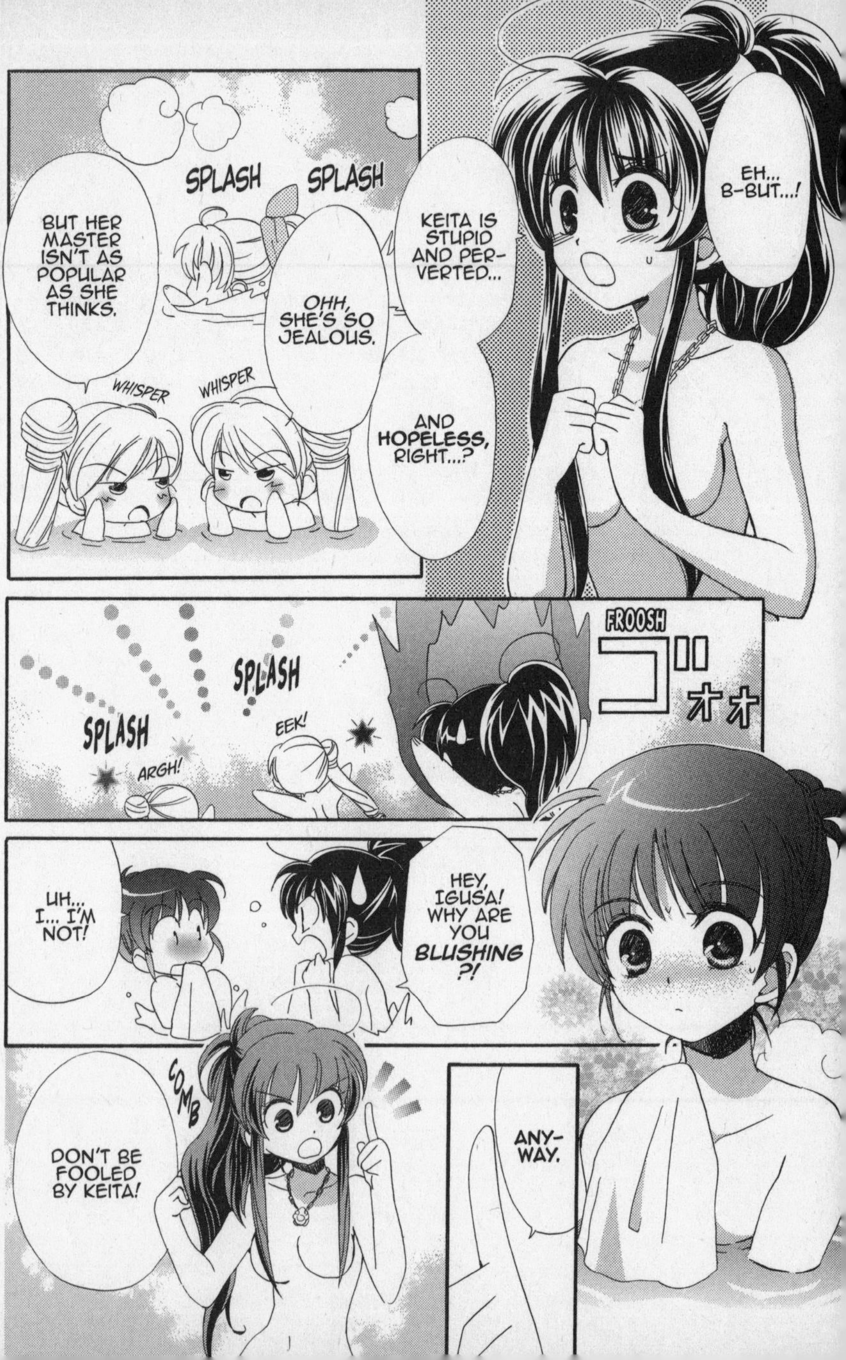

EH... B-BUT...!
KEITA IS STUPID AND PER-VERTED...
AND HOPELESS, RIGHT...?
SPLASH
SPLASH
OHH, SHE'S SO JEALOUS.
BUT HER MASTER ISN'T AS POPULAR AS SHE THINKS.
WHISPER
WHISPER
FROOSH
ゴォォ
SPLASH
EEK!
SPLASH
ARGH!
HEY, IGUSA! WHY ARE YOU BLUSHING?!
UH... I... I'M NOT!
ANY-WAY.
COMB
DON'T BE FOOLED BY KEITA!

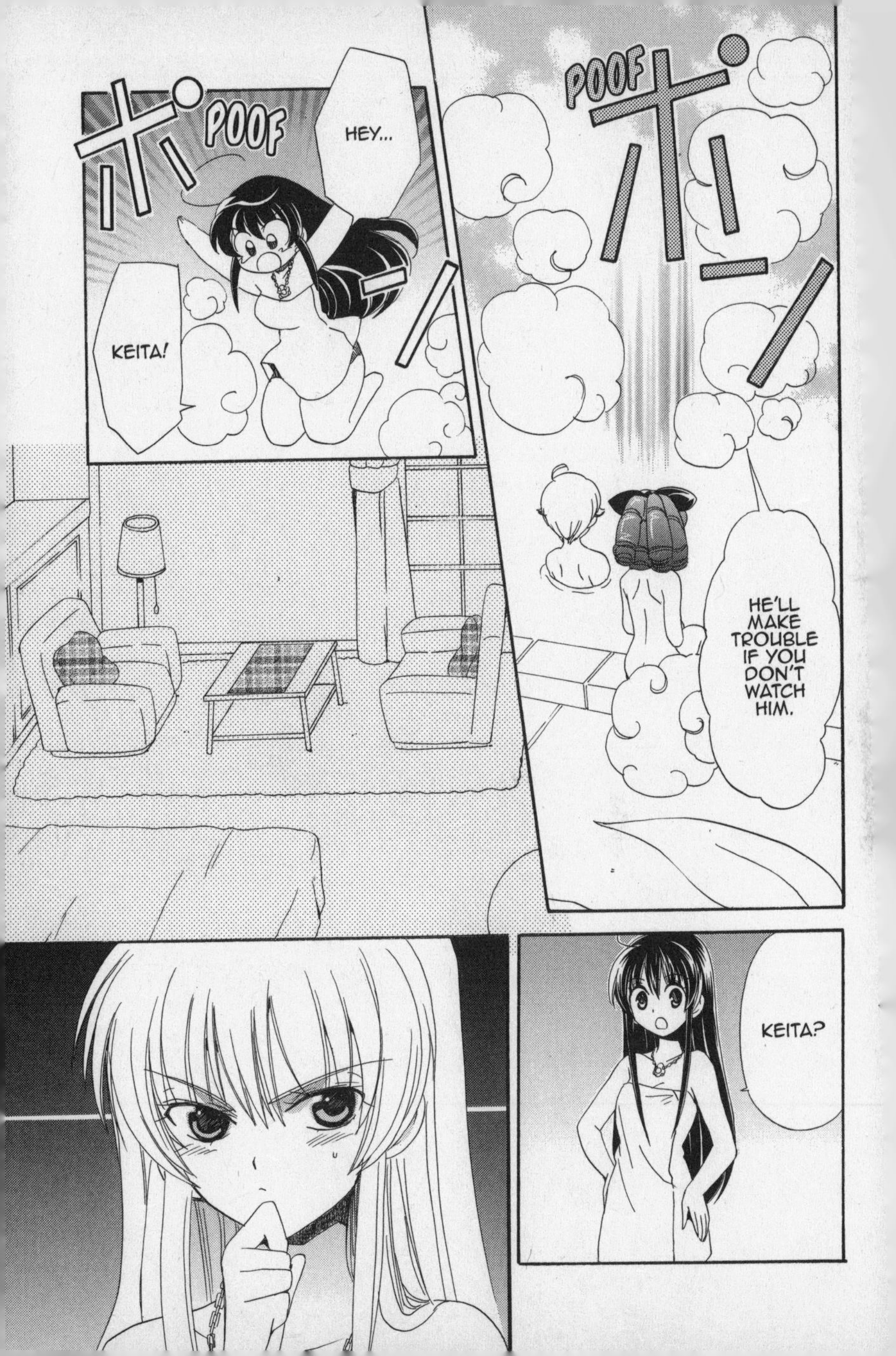
POOF
HE'LL MAKE TROUBLE IF YOU DON'T WATCH HIM.
POOF
HEY...
KEITA!
KEITA?

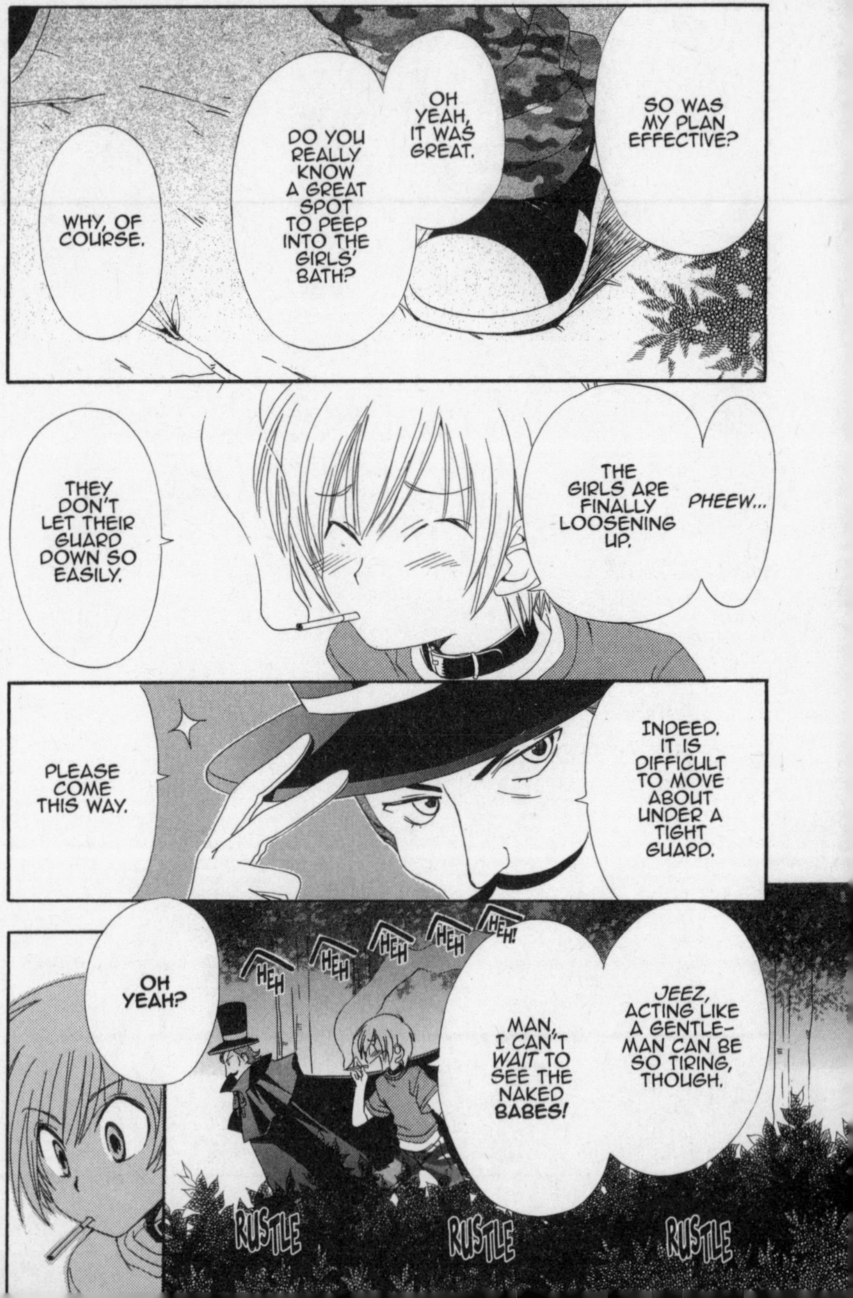
SO WAS MY PLAN EFFECTIVE?
OH YEAH, IT WAS GREAT.
DO YOU REALLY KNOW A GREAT SPOT TO PEEP INTO THE GIRLS' BATH?
WHY, OF COURSE.
PHEEW...
THE GIRLS ARE FINALLY LOOSENING UP.
THEY DON'T LET THEIR GUARD DOWN SO EASILY.
INDEED. IT IS DIFFICULT TO MOVE ABOUT UNDER A TIGHT GUARD.
PLEASE COME THIS WAY.
HEH HEH HEH HEH HEH HEH!
JEEZ, ACTING LIKE A GENTLEMAN CAN BE SO TIRING, THOUGH.
MAN, I CAN'T *WAIT* TO SEE THE NAKED BABES!
RUSTLE
RUSTLE
RUSTLE
OH YEAH?

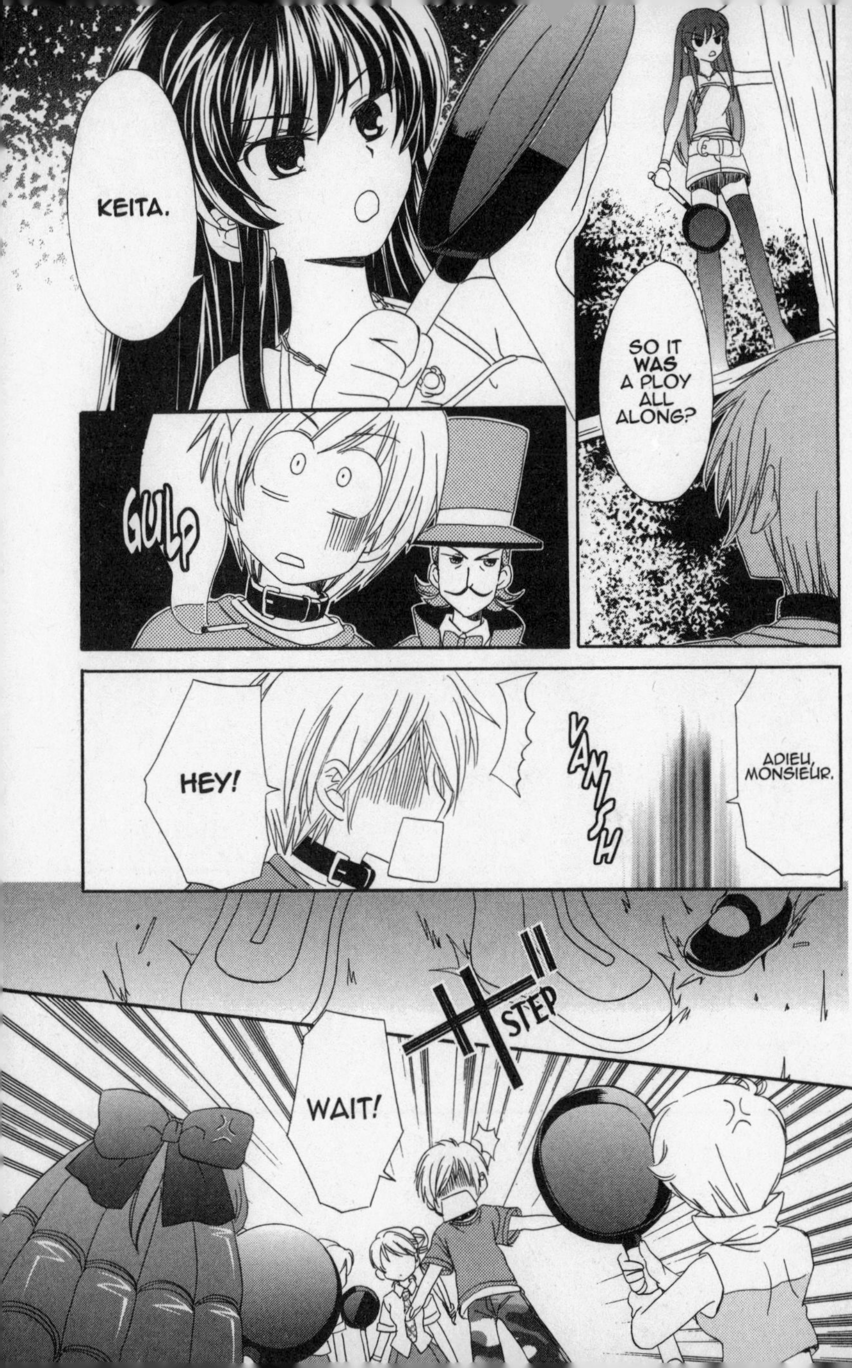
SO IT WAS A PLOY ALL ALONG?
KEITA.
GULP
ADIEU, MONSIEUR.
VANISH
HEY!
STEP
WAIT!

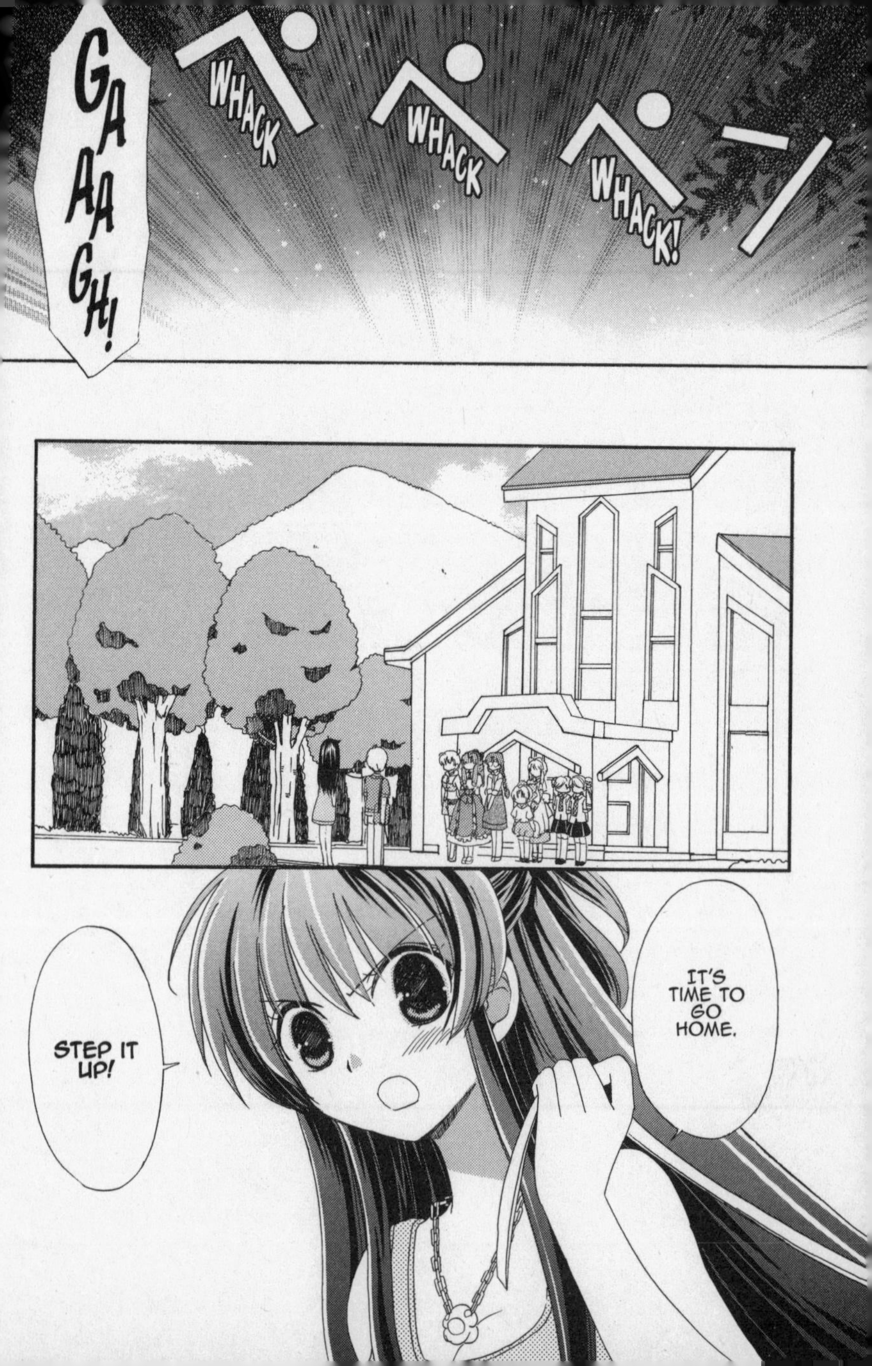
WHACK
WHACK
WHACK!
GAAAGH!
IT'S TIME TO GO HOME.
STEP IT UP!

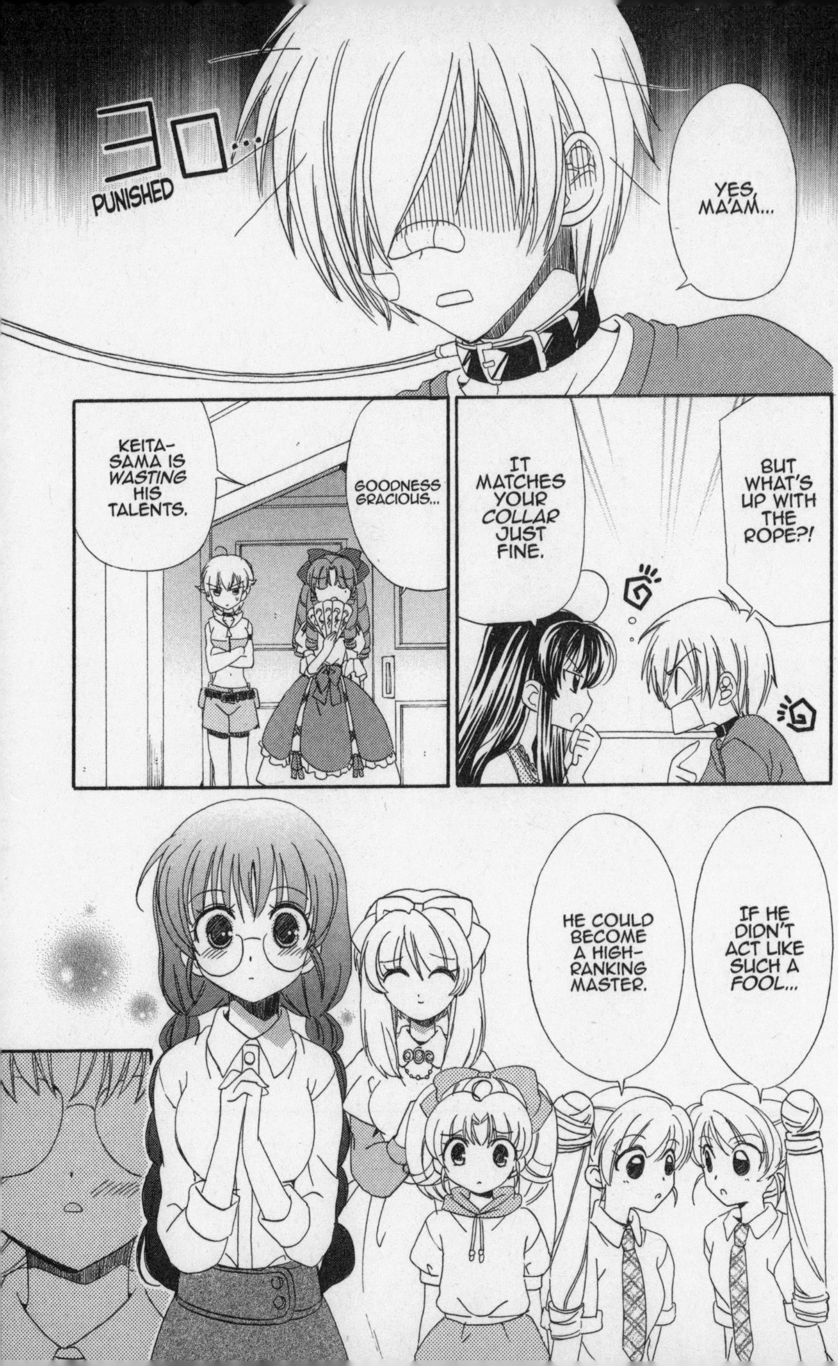
YES, MA'AM...
ヨロ...
PUNISHED
BUT WHAT'S UP WITH THE ROPE?!
IT MATCHES YOUR COLLAR JUST FINE.
GOODNESS GRACIOUS...
KEITA-SAMA IS WASTING HIS TALENTS.
IF HE DIDN'T ACT LIKE SUCH A FOOL...
HE COULD BECOME A HIGH-RANKING MASTER.

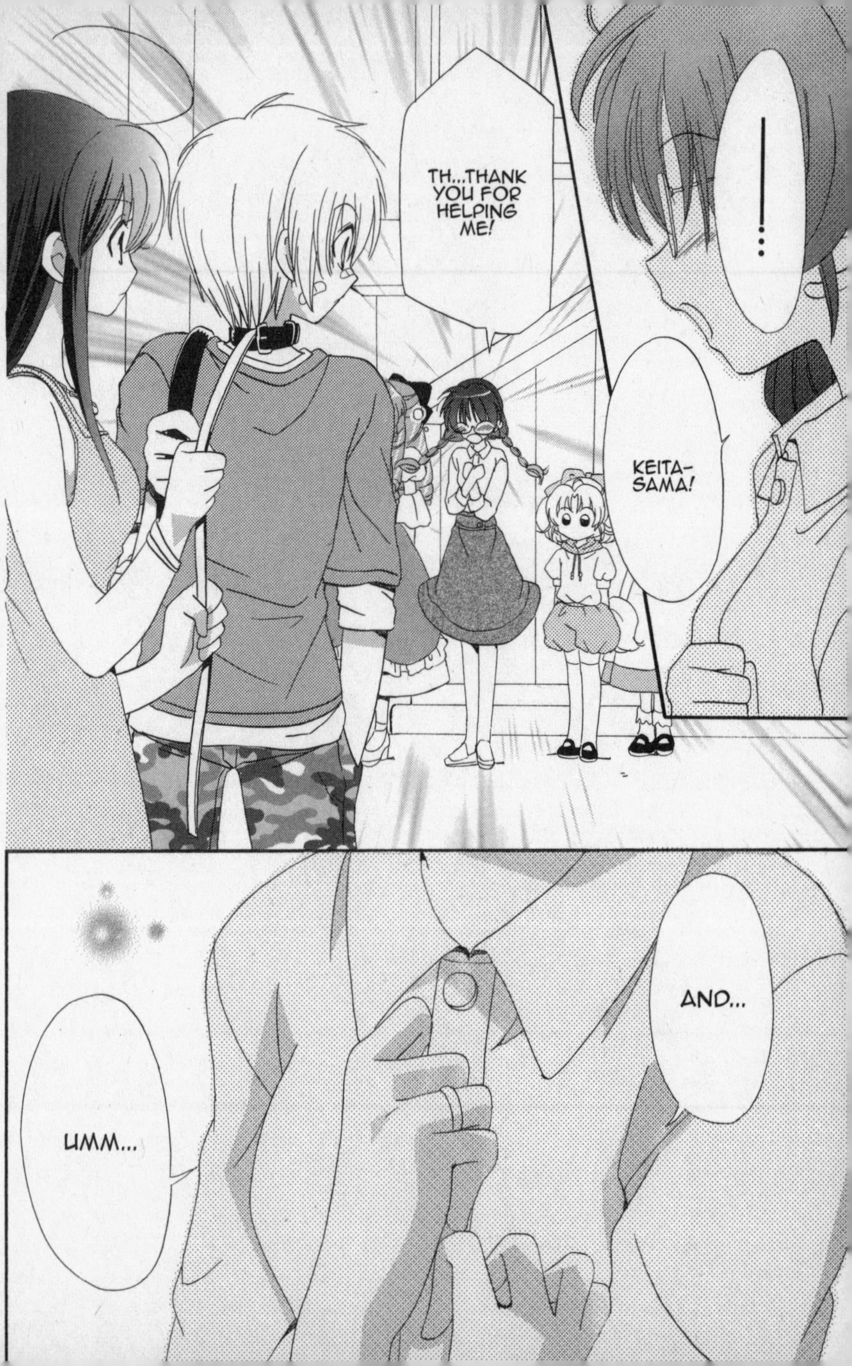
......
KEITA-SAMA!
TH...THANK YOU FOR HELPING ME!
AND...
UMM...

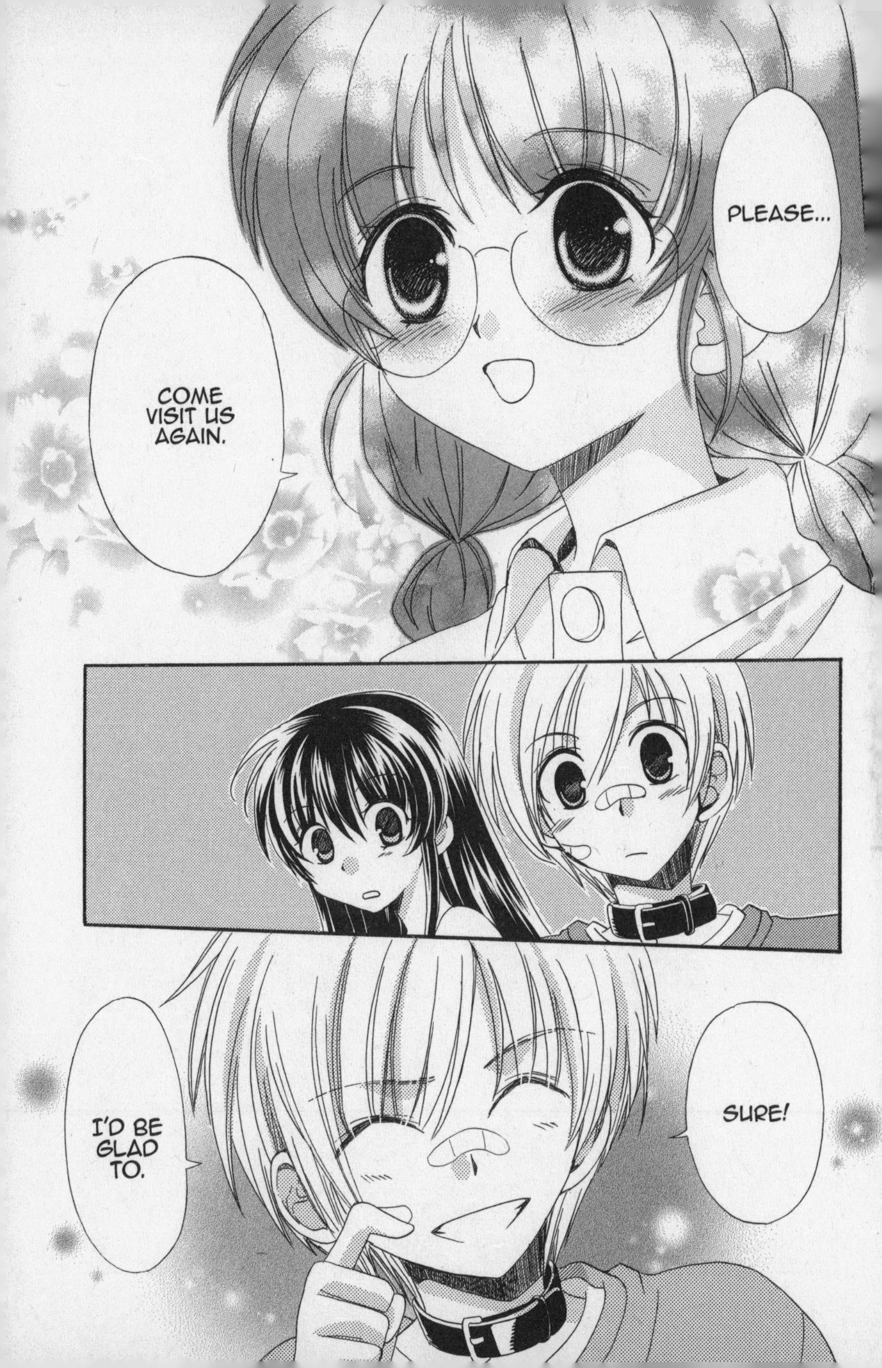
PLEASE...
COME VISIT US AGAIN.
SURE!
I'D BE GLAD TO.

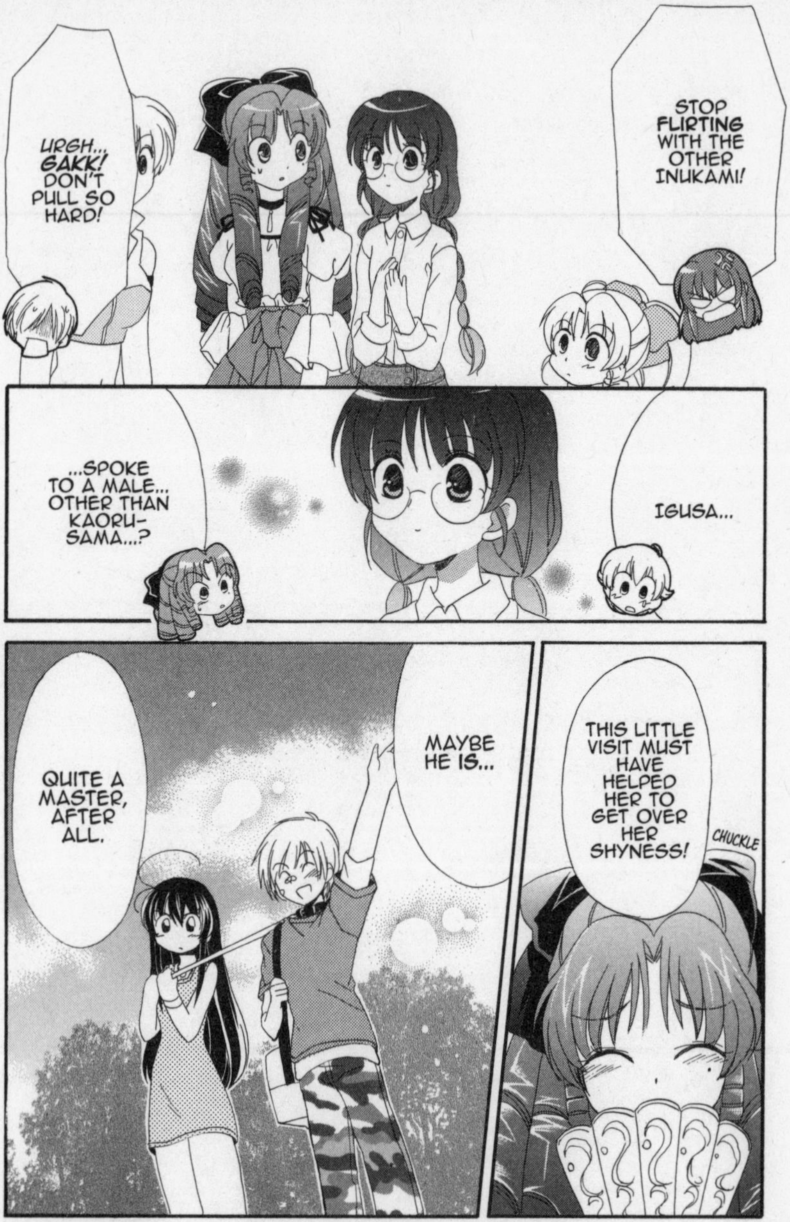
STOP FLIRTING WITH THE OTHER INUKAMI!
URGH... GAKK! DON'T PULL SO HARD!
IGUSA...
...SPOKE TO A MALE... OTHER THAN KAORU-SAMA...?
THIS LITTLE VISIT MUST HAVE HELPED HER TO GET OVER HER SHYNESS!
CHUCKLE
MAYBE HE IS...
QUITE A MASTER, AFTER ALL.

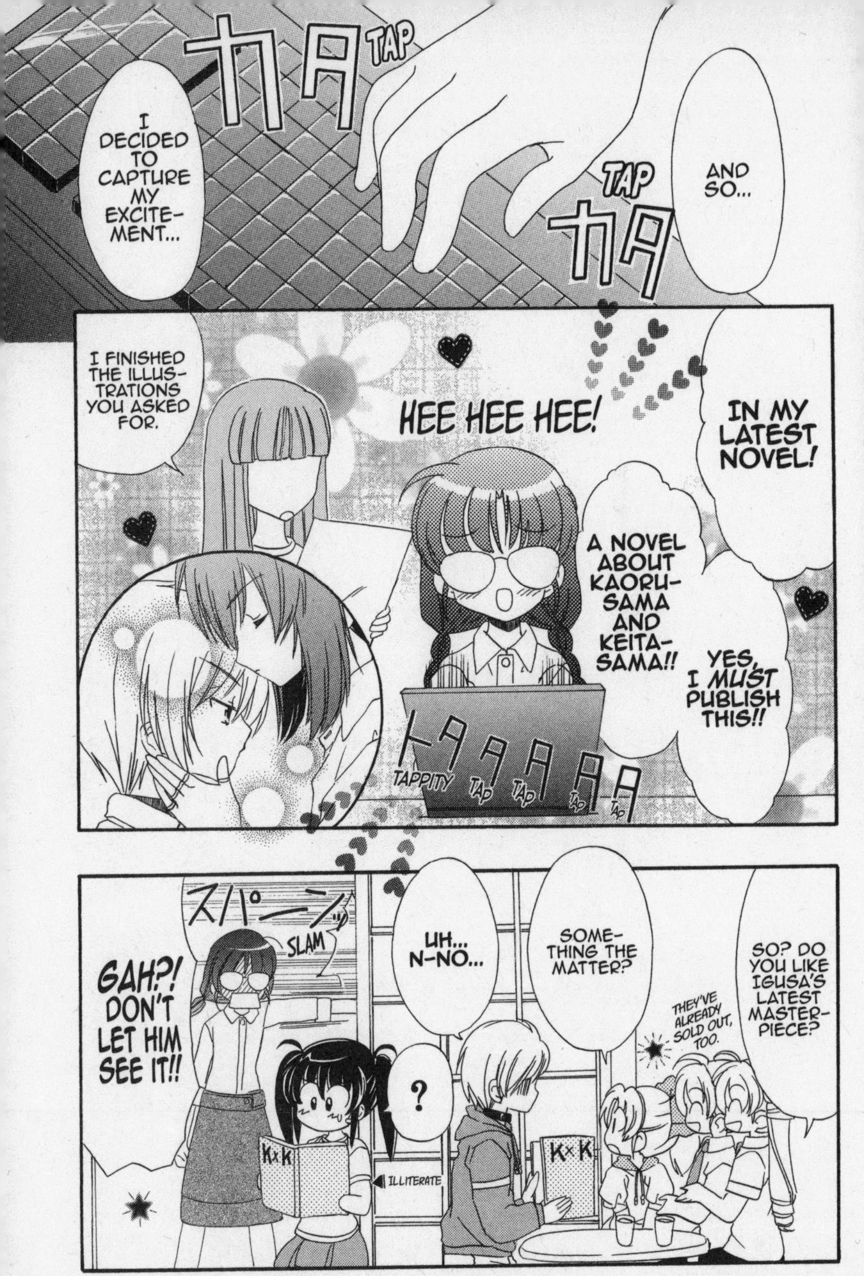
TAP
AND SO...
TAP
I DECIDED TO CAPTURE MY EXCITEMENT...
IN MY LATEST NOVEL!
HEE HEE HEE!
YES, I MUST PUBLISH THIS!!
A NOVEL ABOUT KAORU-SAMA AND KEITA-SAMA!!
I FINISHED THE ILLUSTRATIONS YOU ASKED FOR.
TAPPITY TAP TAP TAP TAP
SO? DO YOU LIKE IGUSA'S LATEST MASTERPIECE?
THEY'VE ALREADY SOLD OUT, TOO.
K×K
SOMETHING THE MATTER?
UH... N-NO...
?
ILLITERATE
K×K
SLAM
GAH?! DON'T LET HIM SEE IT!!

HEE HEE
HEE...

IMARI
& SAYOKA

Height: 156 cm
Bust: 79 cm
Waist: 57 cm
Hip: 83 cm
Age: 100...?

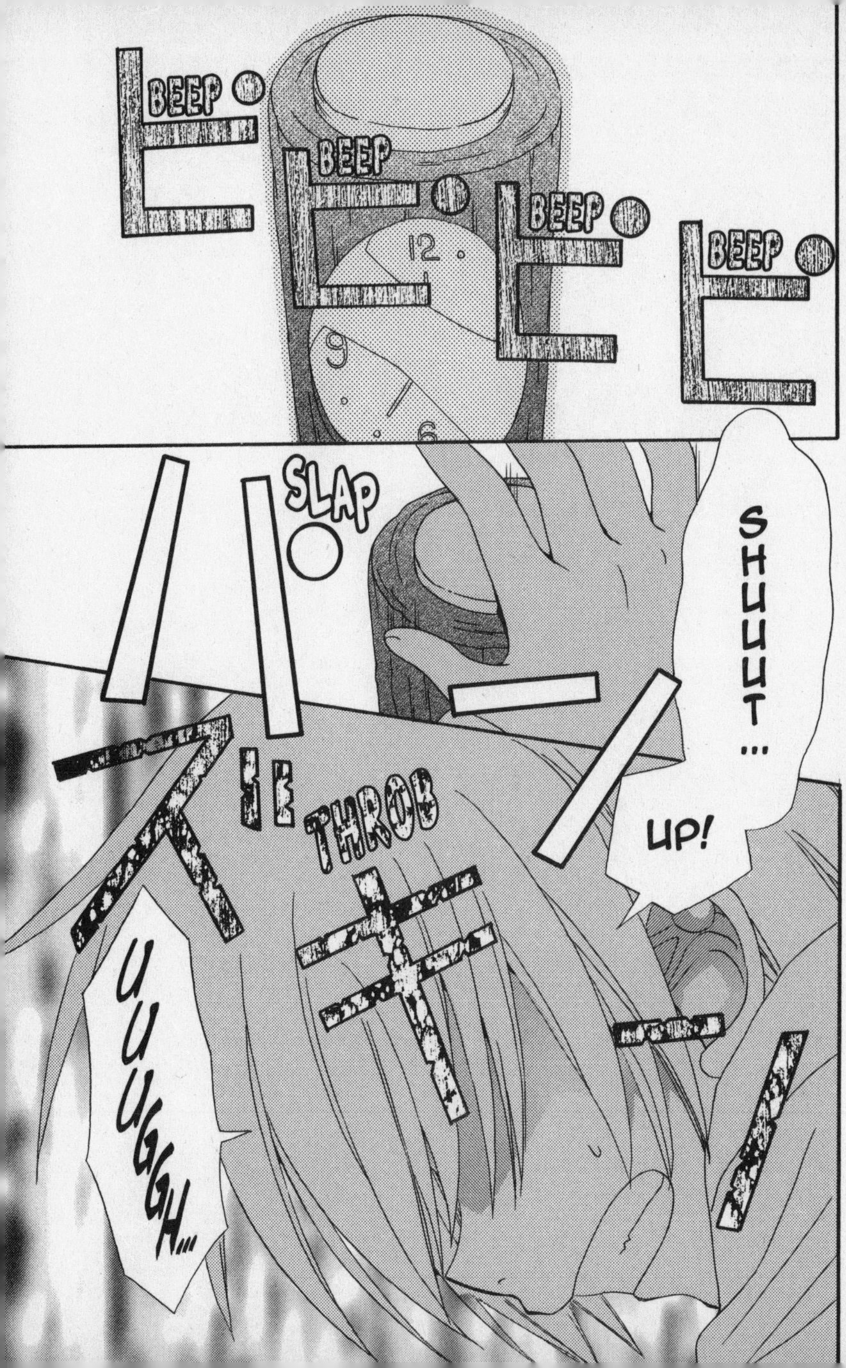
BEEP
BEEP
BEEP
BEEP
SHUUUT... UP!
SLAP
THROB
UUUUGGGH...

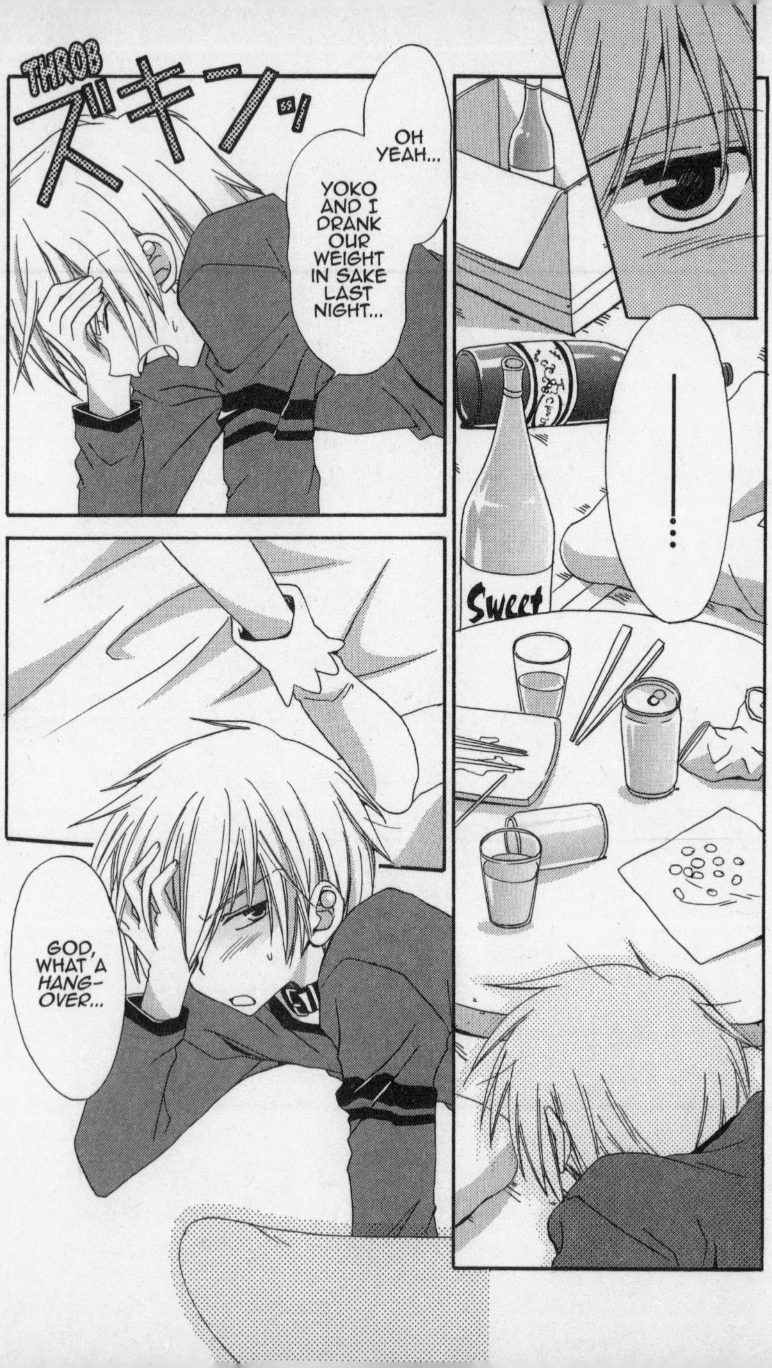

—…
THROB
ズキンッ
OH YEAH...
YOKO AND I DRANK OUR WEIGHT IN SAKE LAST NIGHT...
Sweet
GOD, WHAT A HANG-OVER...

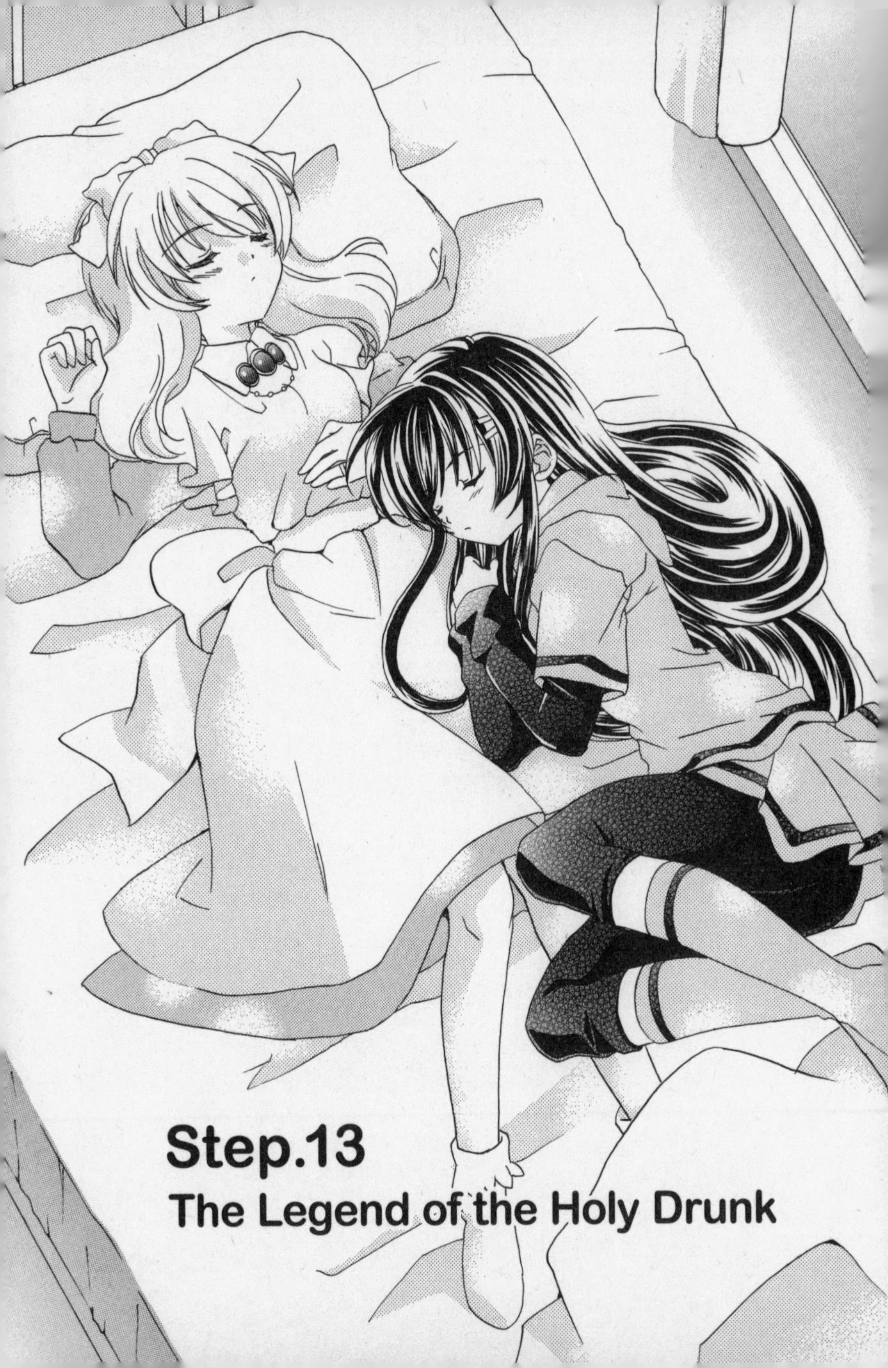

Step.13
The Legend of the Holy Drunk

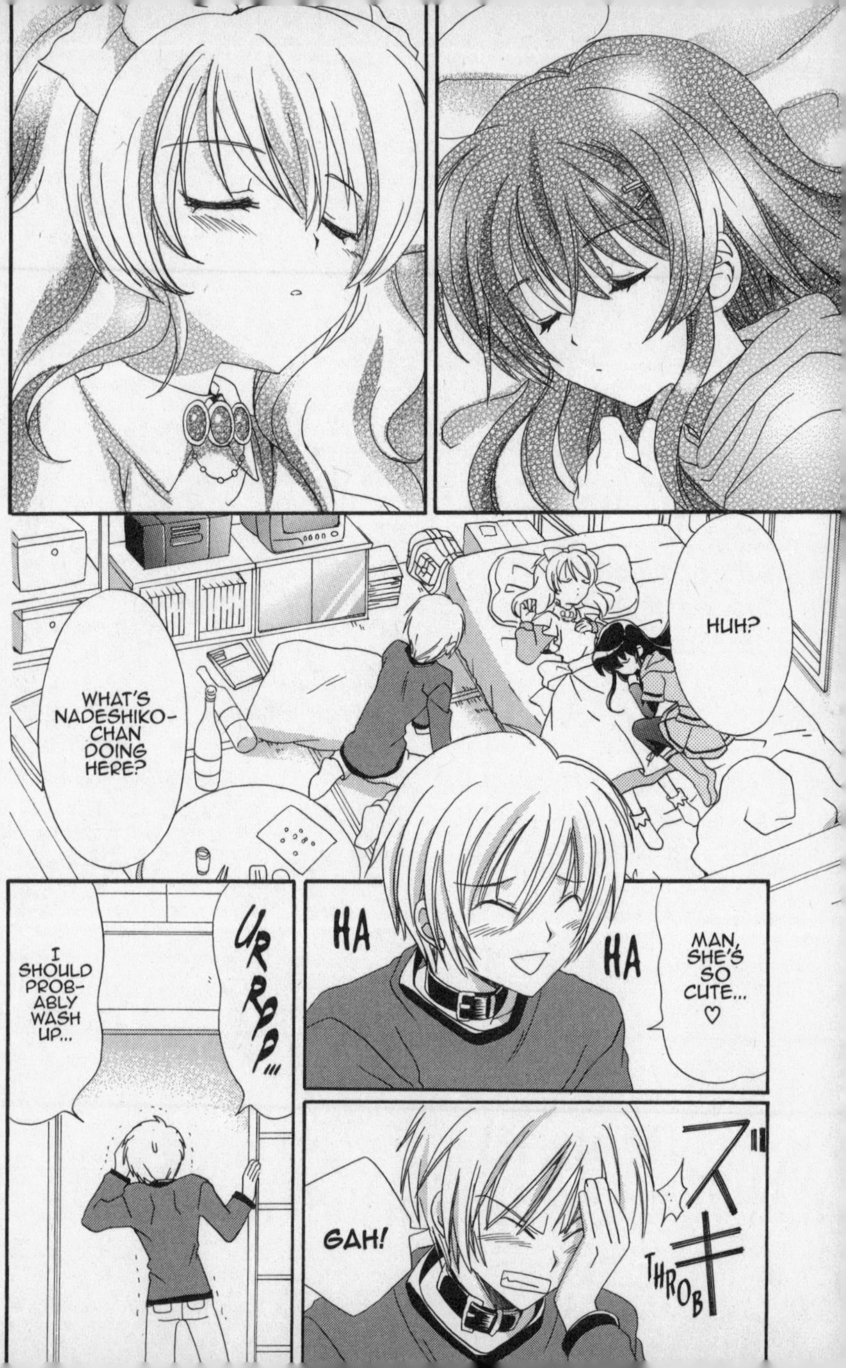
HUH?
WHAT'S NADESHIKO-CHAN DOING HERE?
MAN, SHE'S SO CUTE... ♡
HA
HA
THROB
GAH!
URPPP...
I SHOULD PROB-ABLY WASH UP...

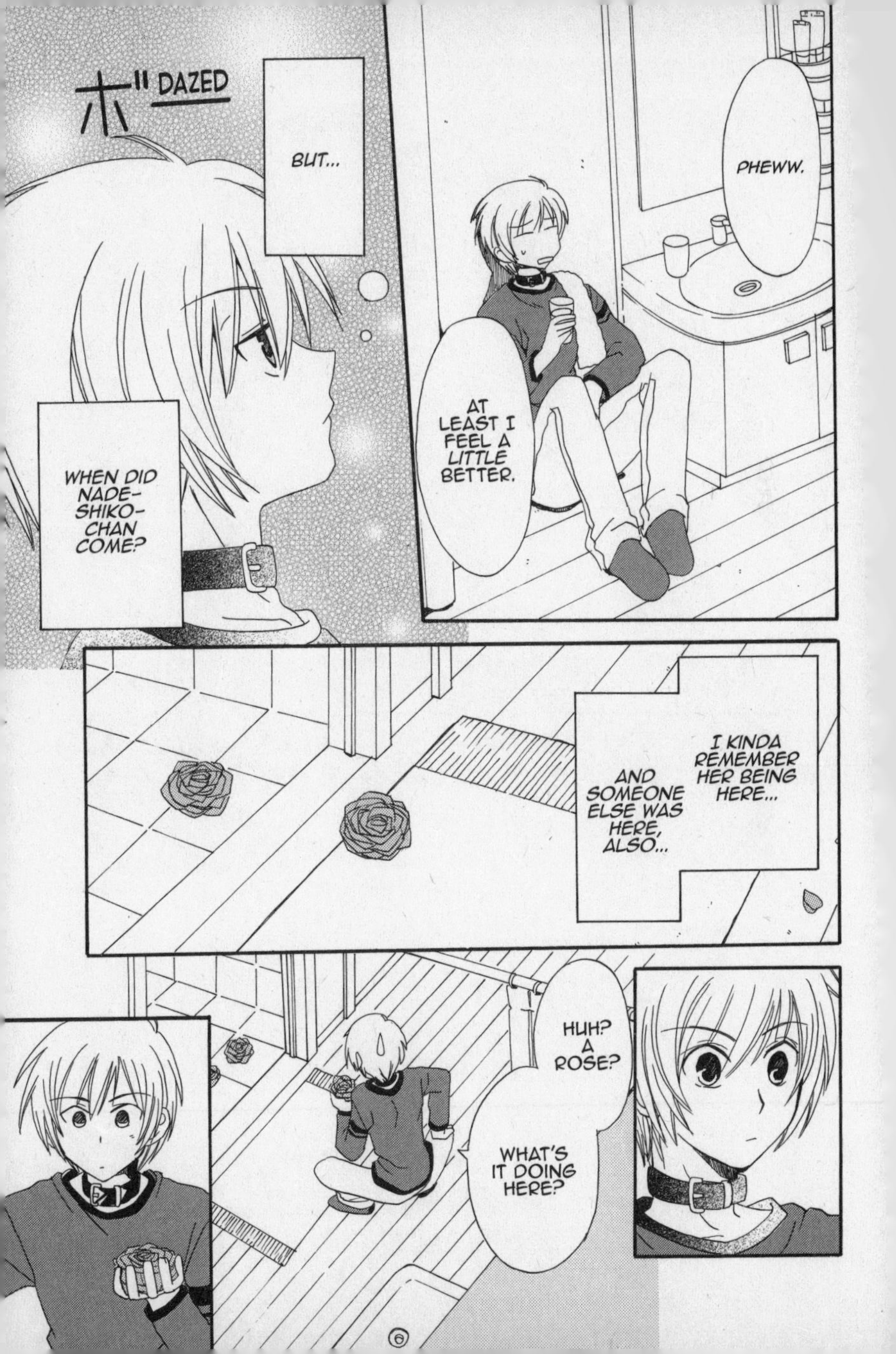
PHEWW.
AT LEAST I FEEL A LITTLE BETTER.
ホ" DAZED
BUT...
WHEN DID NADE-SHIKO-CHAN COME?
I KINDA REMEMBER HER BEING HERE...
AND SOMEONE ELSE WAS HERE, ALSO...
HUH? A ROSE?
WHAT'S IT DOING HERE?

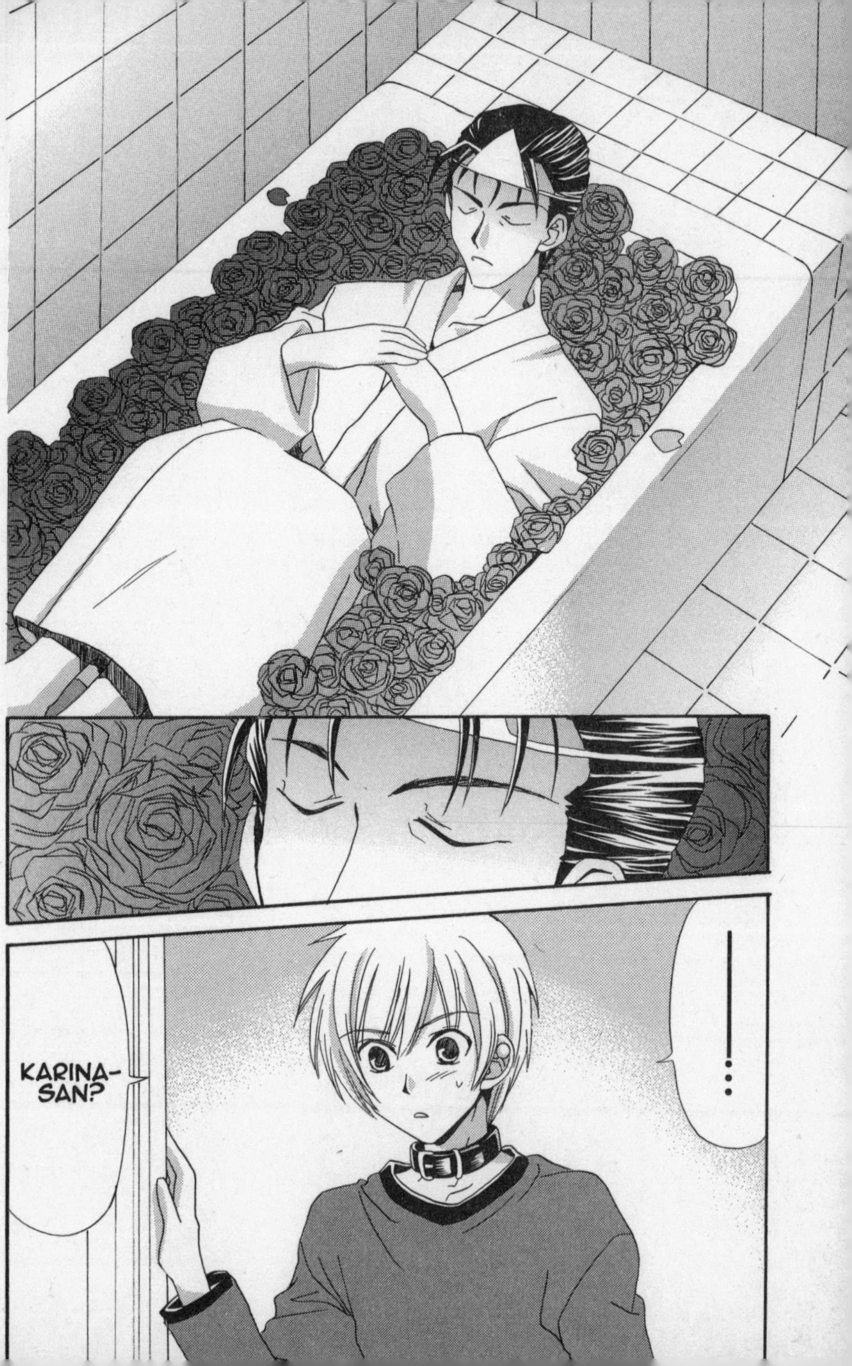
—...
KARINA-SAN?

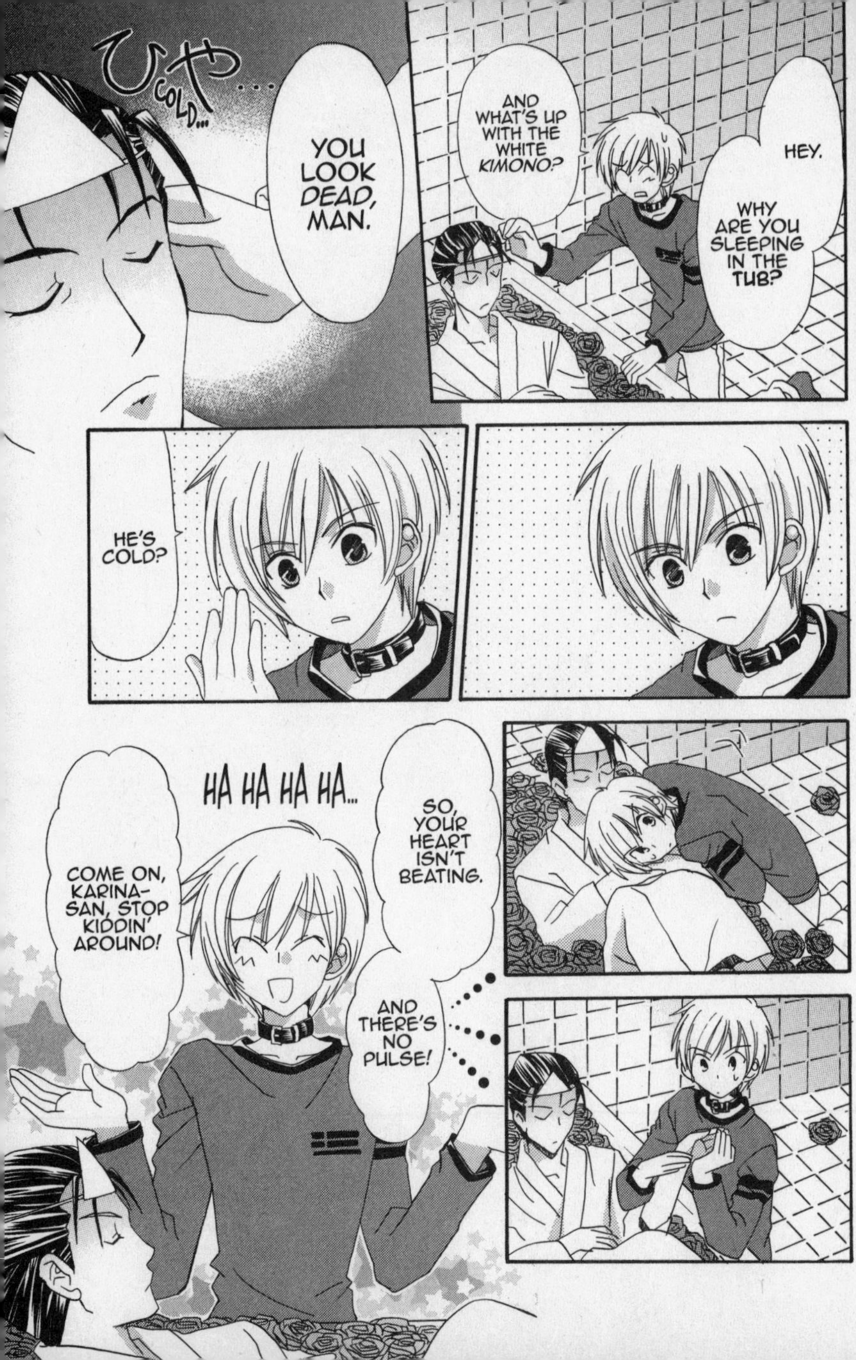
HEY.
WHY ARE YOU SLEEPING IN THE TUB?
AND WHAT'S UP WITH THE WHITE KIMONO?
ひや... COLD...
YOU LOOK DEAD, MAN.
HE'S COLD?
SO, YOUR HEART ISN'T BEATING.
AND THERE'S NO PULSE!
HA HA HA HA...
COME ON, KARINA-SAN, STOP KIDDIN' AROUND!

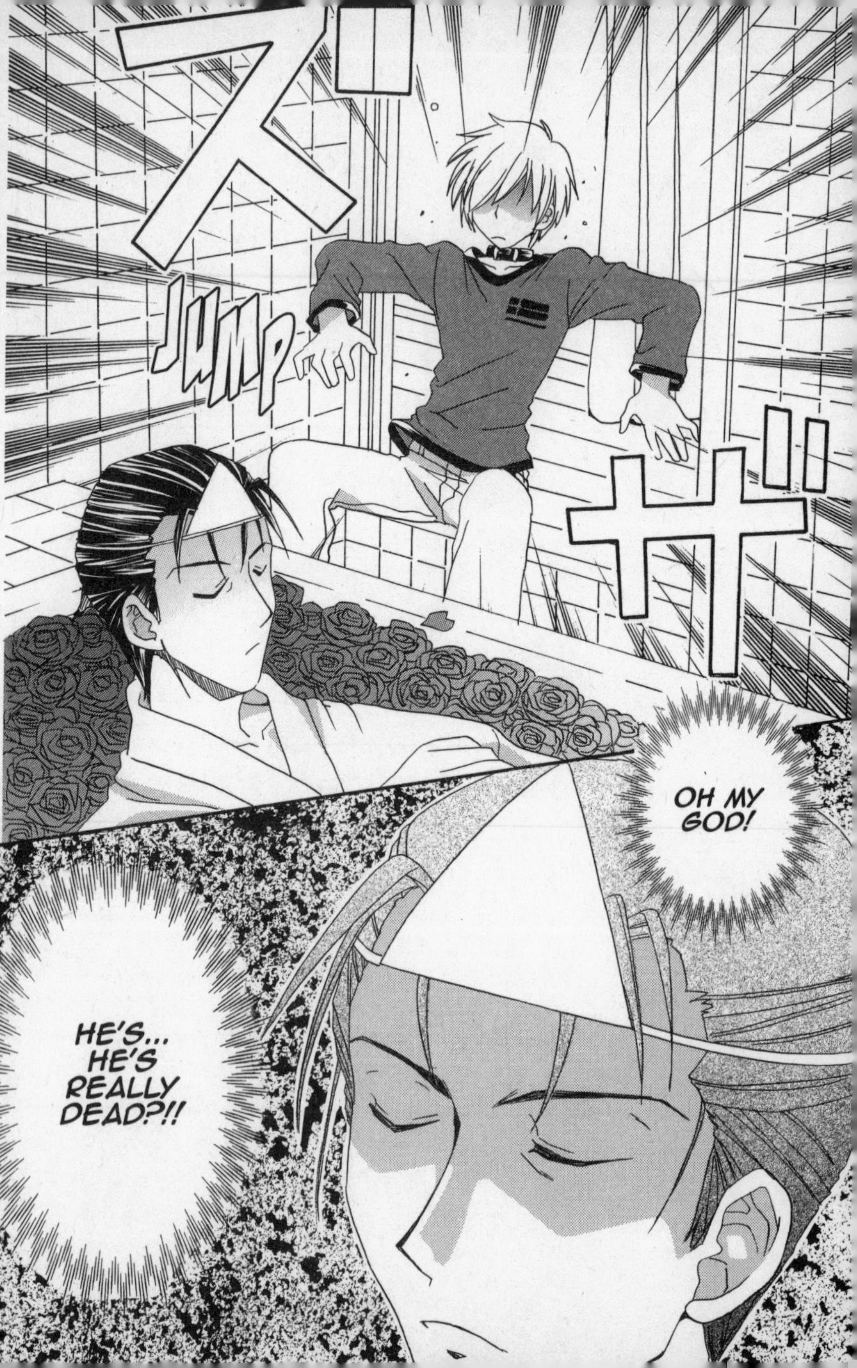
ズ
JUMP
ザ
OH MY GOD!
HE'S... HE'S REALLY DEAD?!!

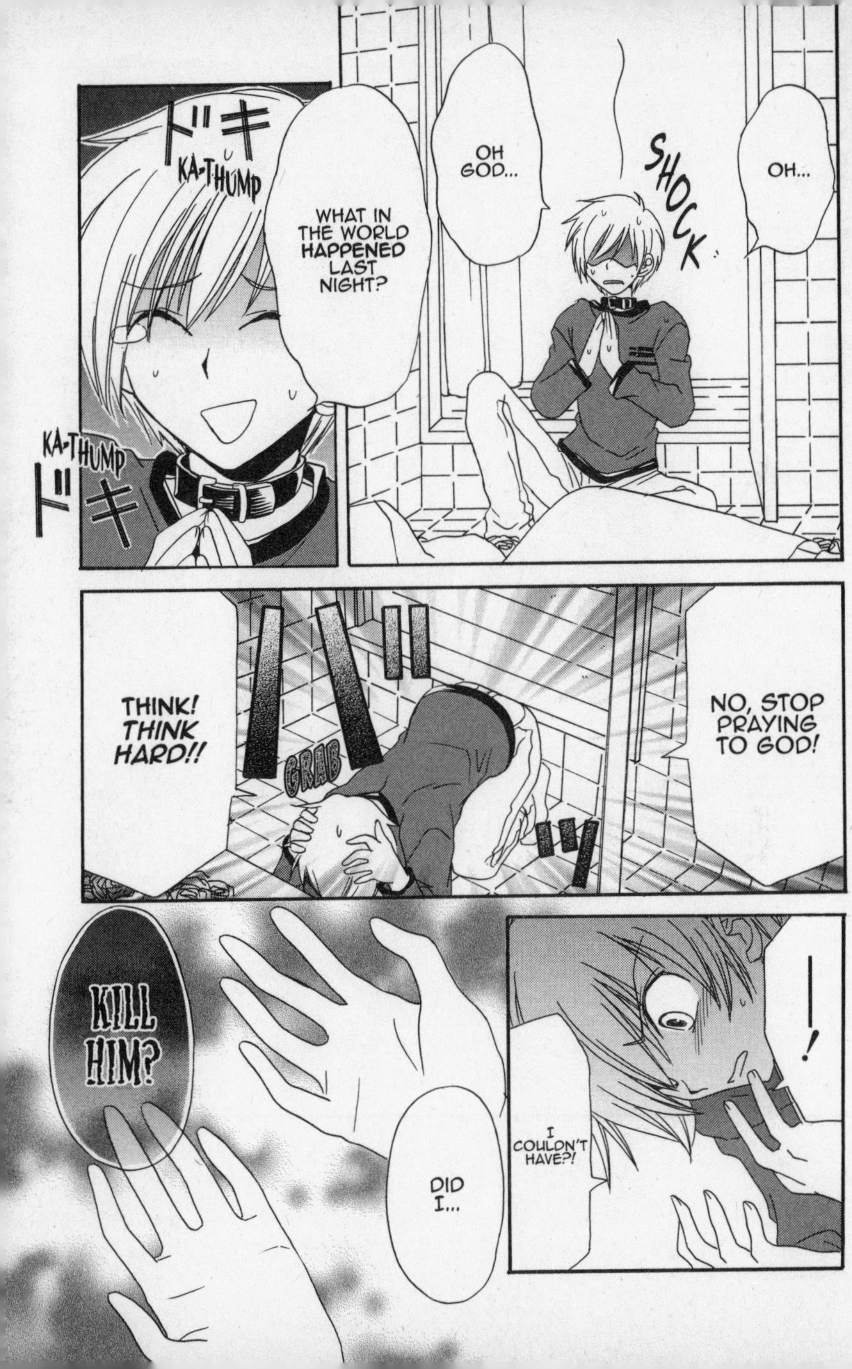
OH...
SHOCK
OH GOD...
ドキ
KA-THUMP
WHAT IN THE WORLD HAPPENED LAST NIGHT?
KA-THUMP
ドキ
NO, STOP PRAYING TO GOD!
THINK! THINK HARD!!
GRAB
!
I COULDN'T HAVE?!
DID I...
KILL HIM?

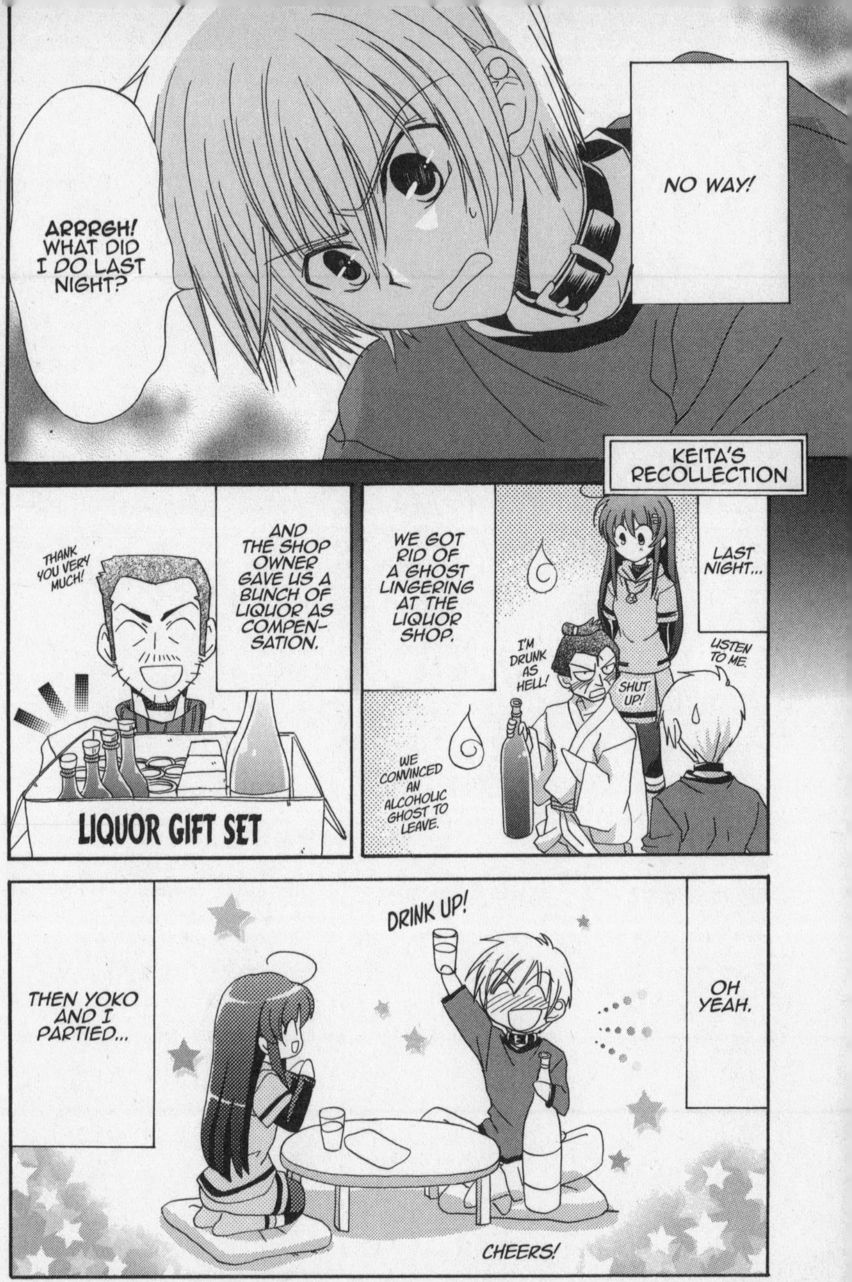
NO WAY!
ARRRGH! WHAT DID I DO LAST NIGHT?
KEITA'S RECOLLECTION
LAST NIGHT...
LISTEN TO ME.
SHUT UP!
I'M DRUNK AS HELL!
WE GOT RID OF A GHOST LINGERING AT THE LIQUOR SHOP.
WE CONVINCED AN ALCOHOLIC GHOST TO LEAVE.
AND THE SHOP OWNER GAVE US A BUNCH OF LIQUOR AS COMPENSATION.
THANK YOU VERY MUCH!
LIQUOR GIFT SET
OH YEAH.
DRINK UP!
THEN YOKO AND I PARTIED...
CHEERS!

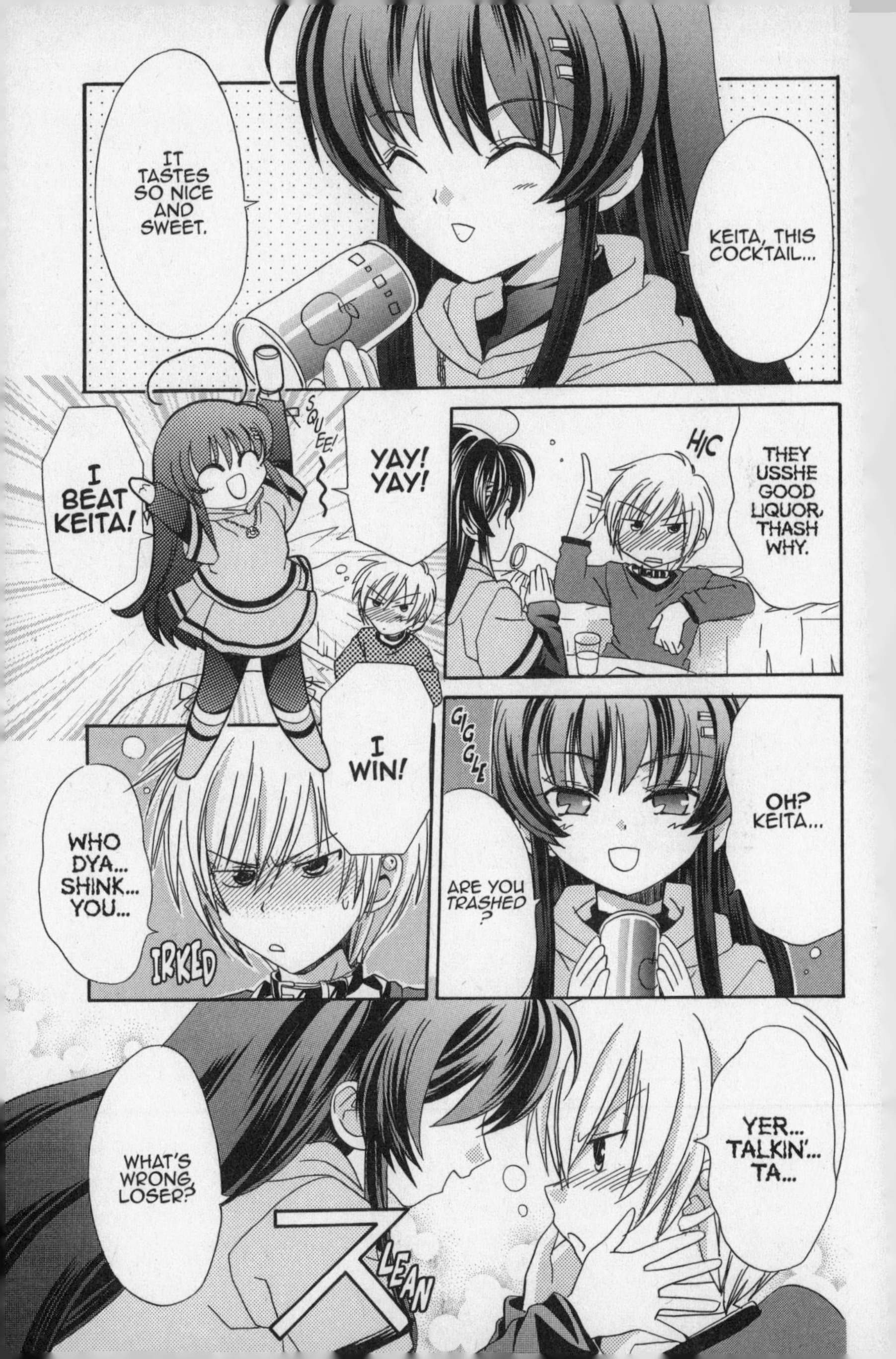
KEITA, THIS COCKTAIL...
IT TASTES SO NICE AND SWEET.
HIC
THEY USSHE GOOD LIQUOR, THASH WHY.
YAY! YAY!
SQUEEE!
I BEAT KEITA!
OH? KEITA...
GIGGLE
ARE YOU TRASHED?
I WIN!
WHO DYA... SHINK... YOU...
IRKED
YER... TALKIN'... TA...
LEAN
WHAT'S WRONG, LOSER?

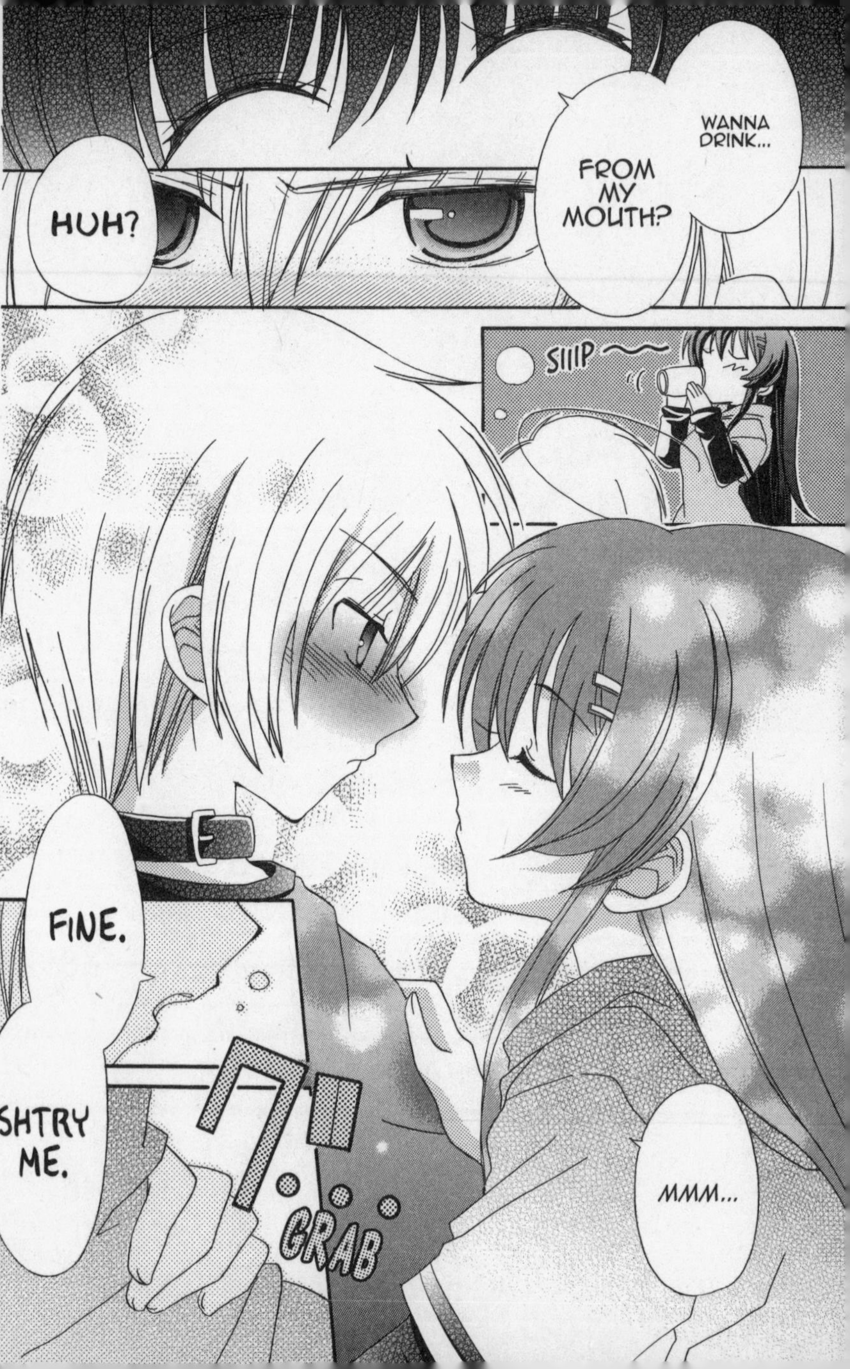
WANNA DRINK...
FROM MY MOUTH?
HUH?
SIIIP
FINE.
MMM...
SHTRY ME.
GRAB

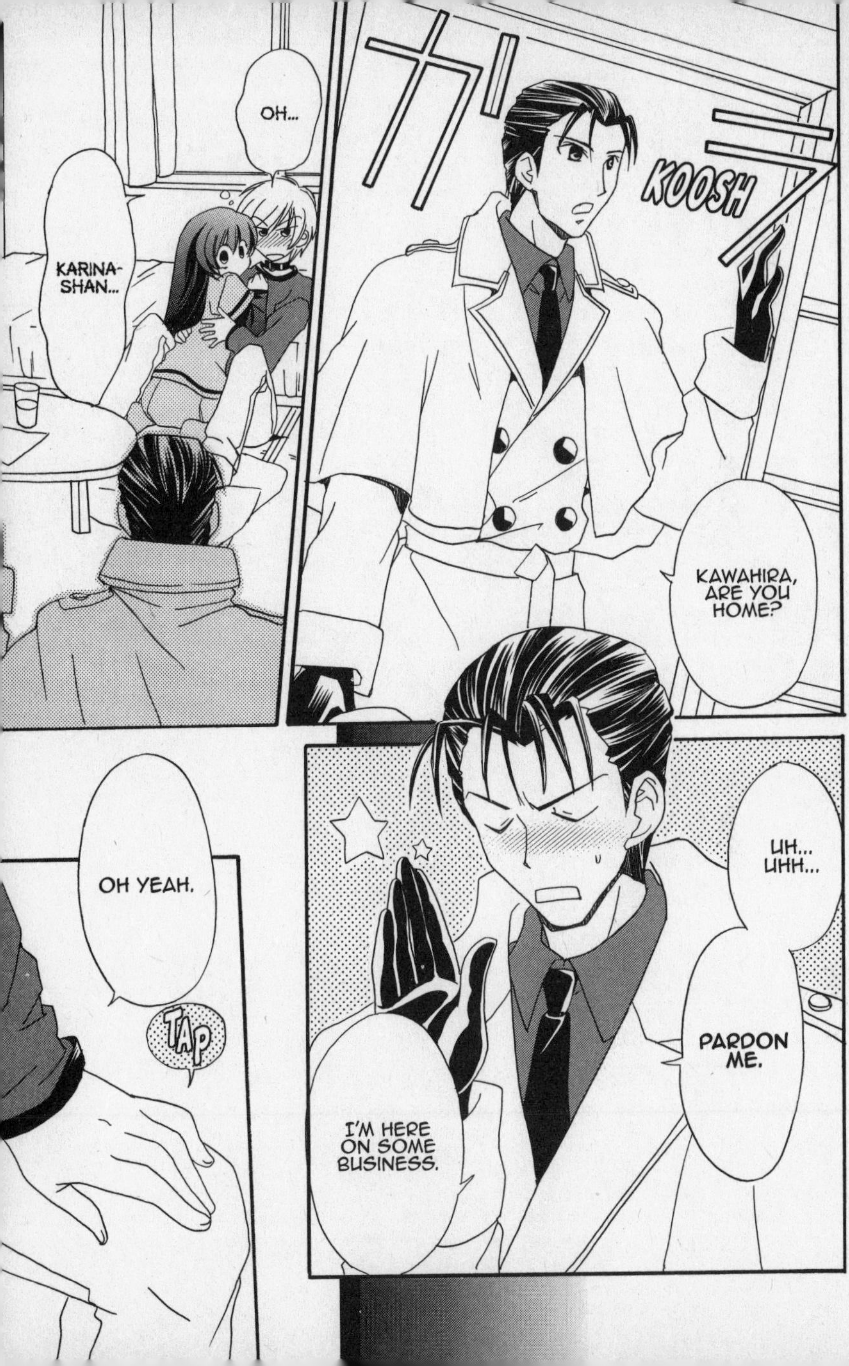
KOOSH
KAWAHIRA, ARE YOU HOME?
OH...
KARINA-SHAN...
UH... UHH...
PARDON ME.
I'M HERE ON SOME BUSINESS.
OH YEAH.
TAP

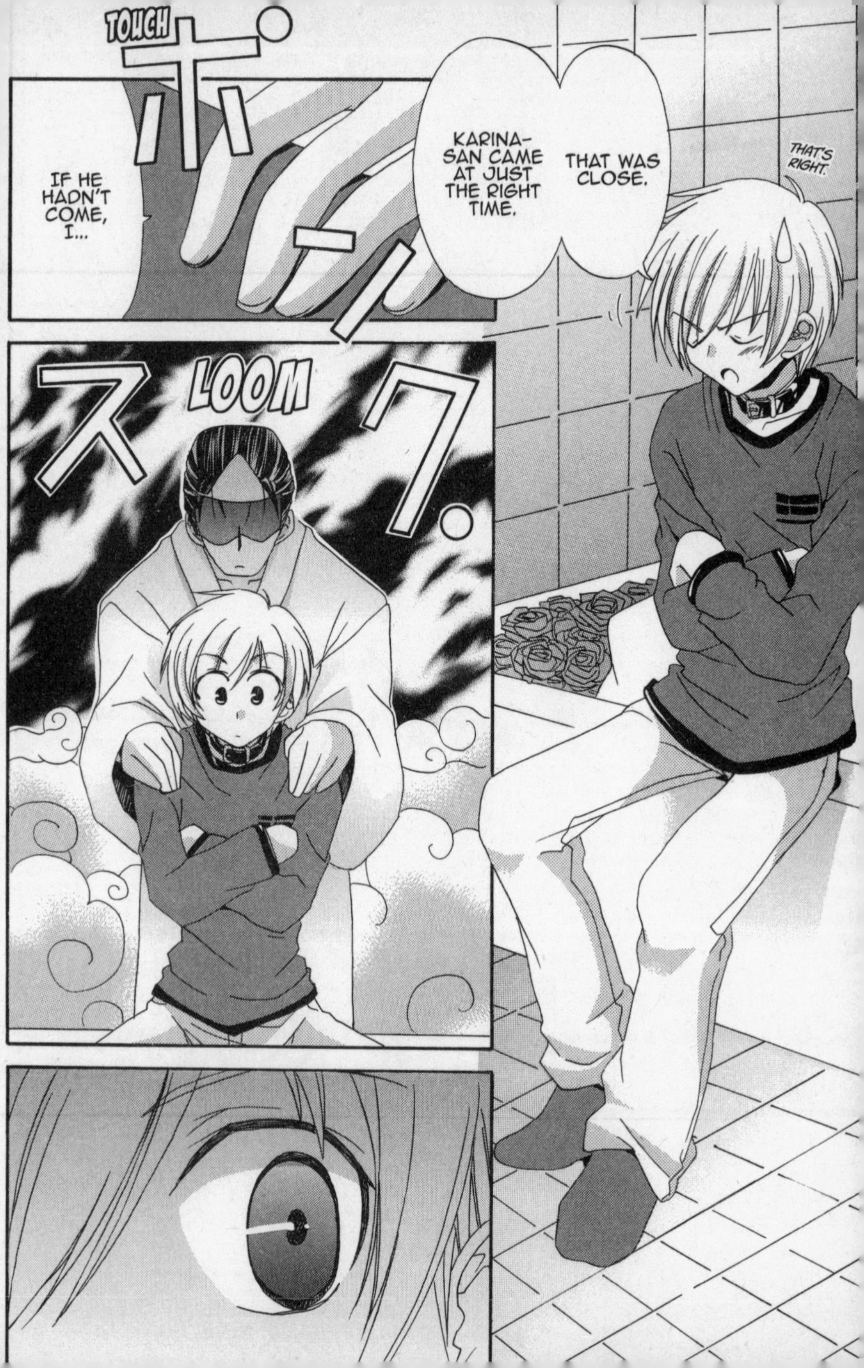
THAT WAS CLOSE.
KARINA-SAN CAME AT JUST THE RIGHT TIME.
THAT'S RIGHT.
TOUCH
IF HE HADN'T COME, I...
LOOM

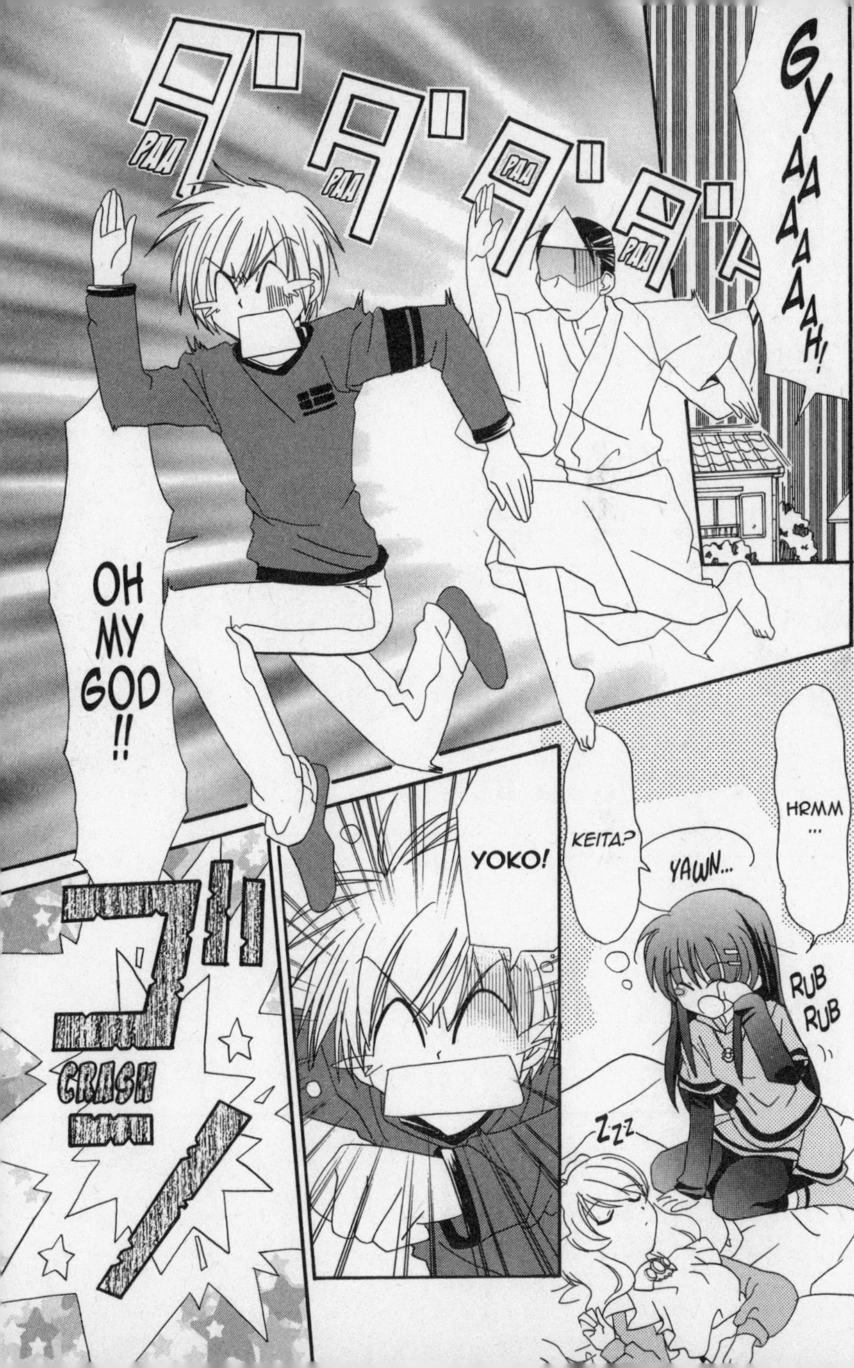

GYAAAAAAAH!
PAA
PAA
PAA
PAA
OH MY GOD !!
HRMM ...
YAWN...
KEITA?
RUB RUB
Z-z-z
YOKO!
CRASH

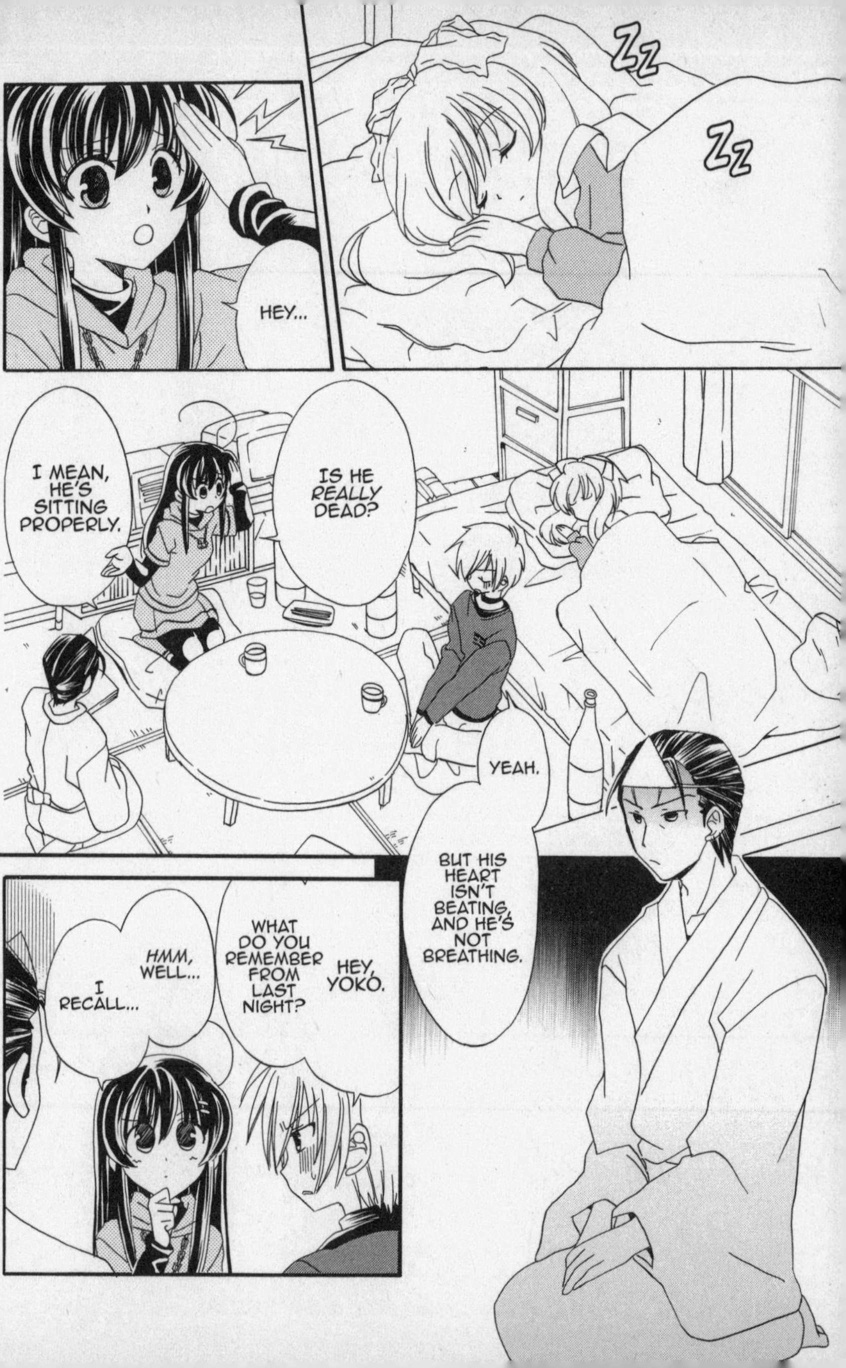

ZZ
ZZ
HEY...
IS HE REALLY DEAD?
I MEAN, HE'S SITTING PROPERLY.
YEAH.
BUT HIS HEART ISN'T BEATING, AND HE'S NOT BREATHING.
HEY, YOKO.
WHAT DO YOU REMEMBER FROM LAST NIGHT?
HMM, WELL...
I RECALL...

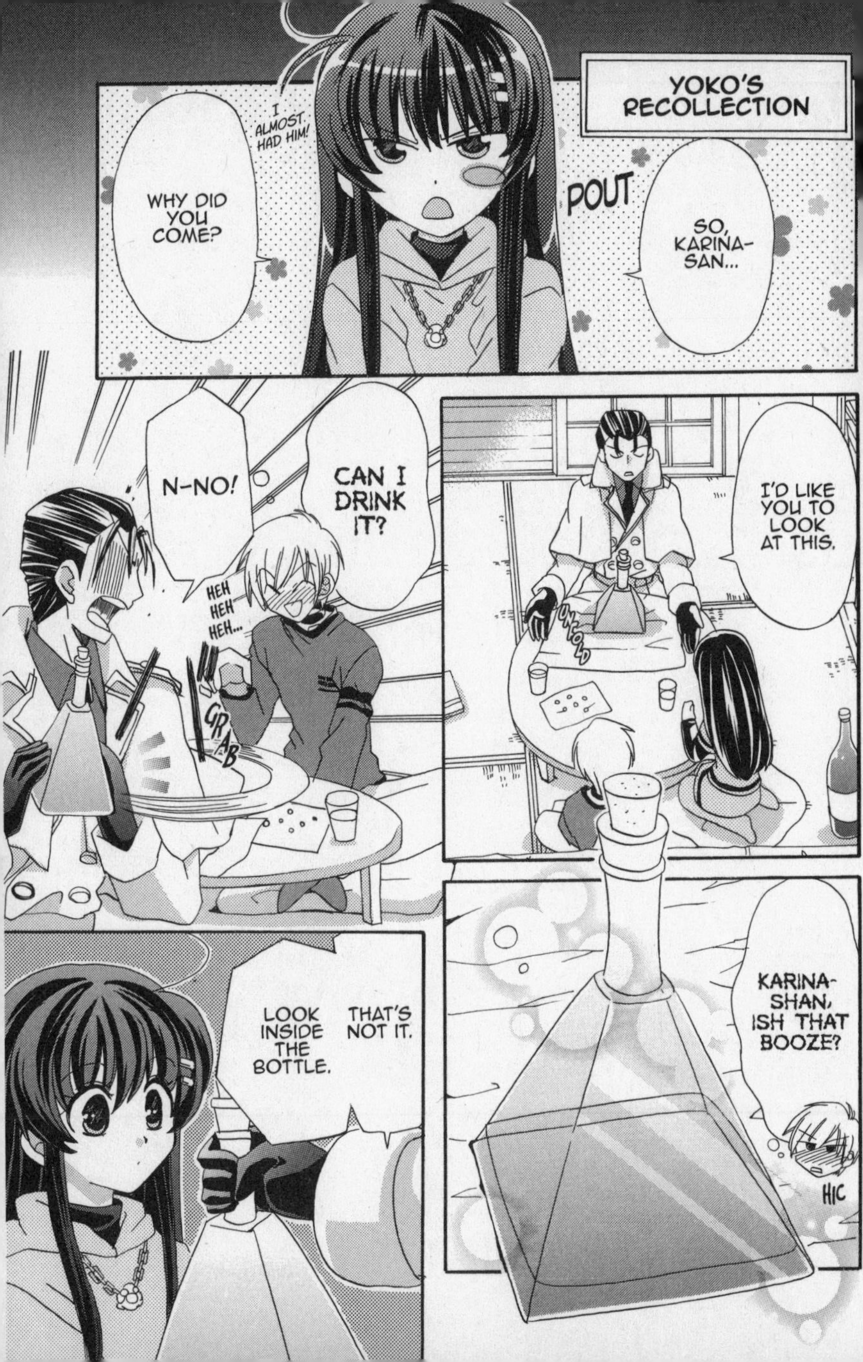
YOKO'S RECOLLECTION
SO, KARINA-SAN...
POUT
I ALMOST HAD HIM!
WHY DID YOU COME?
I'D LIKE YOU TO LOOK AT THIS.
UNFOLD
CAN I DRINK IT?
N-NO!
HEH HEH HEH...
GRAB
KARINA-SHAN, ISH THAT BOOZE?
HIC
THAT'S NOT IT.
LOOK INSIDE THE BOTTLE.

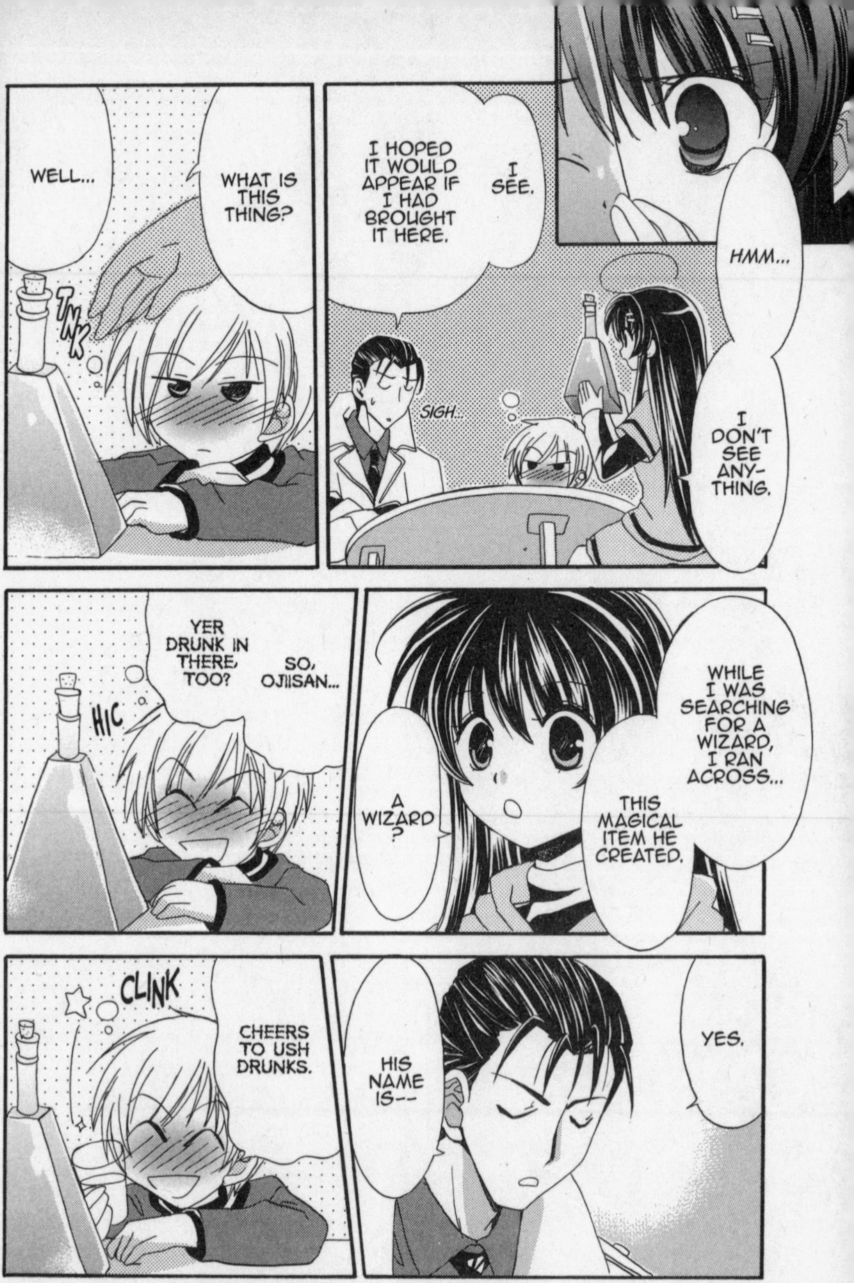

HMM...
I DON'T SEE ANY-THING.
I SEE.
I HOPED IT WOULD APPEAR IF I HAD BROUGHT IT HERE.
SIGH...
WHAT IS THIS THING?
WELL...
TNK
WHILE I WAS SEARCHING FOR A WIZARD, I RAN ACROSS...
THIS MAGICAL ITEM HE CREATED.
A WIZARD?
SO, OJIISAN...
YER DRUNK IN THERE, TOO?
HIC
YES.
HIS NAME IS--
CHEERS TO USH DRUNKS.
CLINK

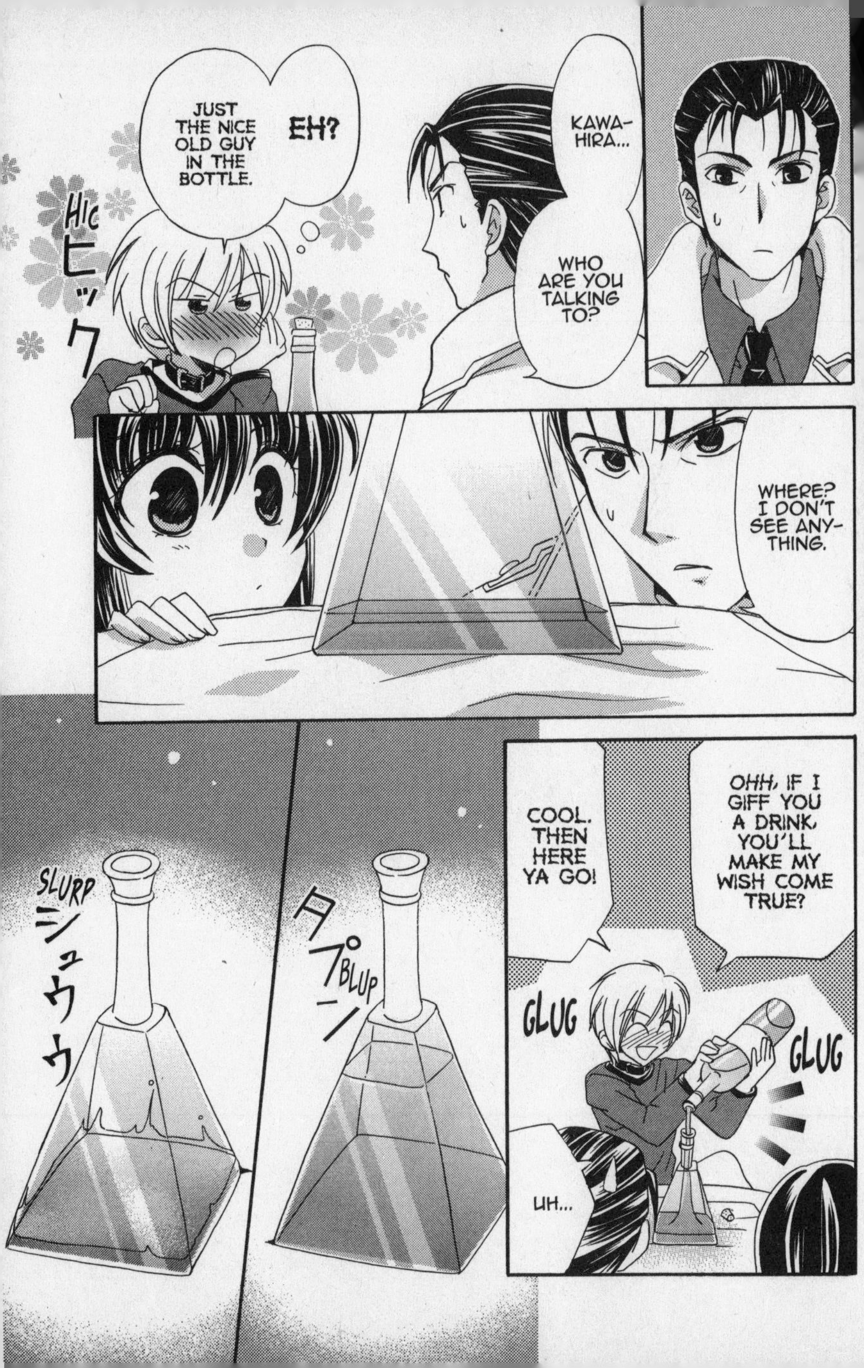
KAWA-HIRA...
WHO ARE YOU TALKING TO?
EH?
JUST THE NICE OLD GUY IN THE BOTTLE.
HIC ヒック
WHERE? I DON'T SEE ANY-THING.
OHH, IF I GIFF YOU A DRINK, YOU'LL MAKE MY WISH COME TRUE?
COOL. THEN HERE YA GO!
GLUG
GLUG
UH...
タプン BLUP
SLURP シュウウウ

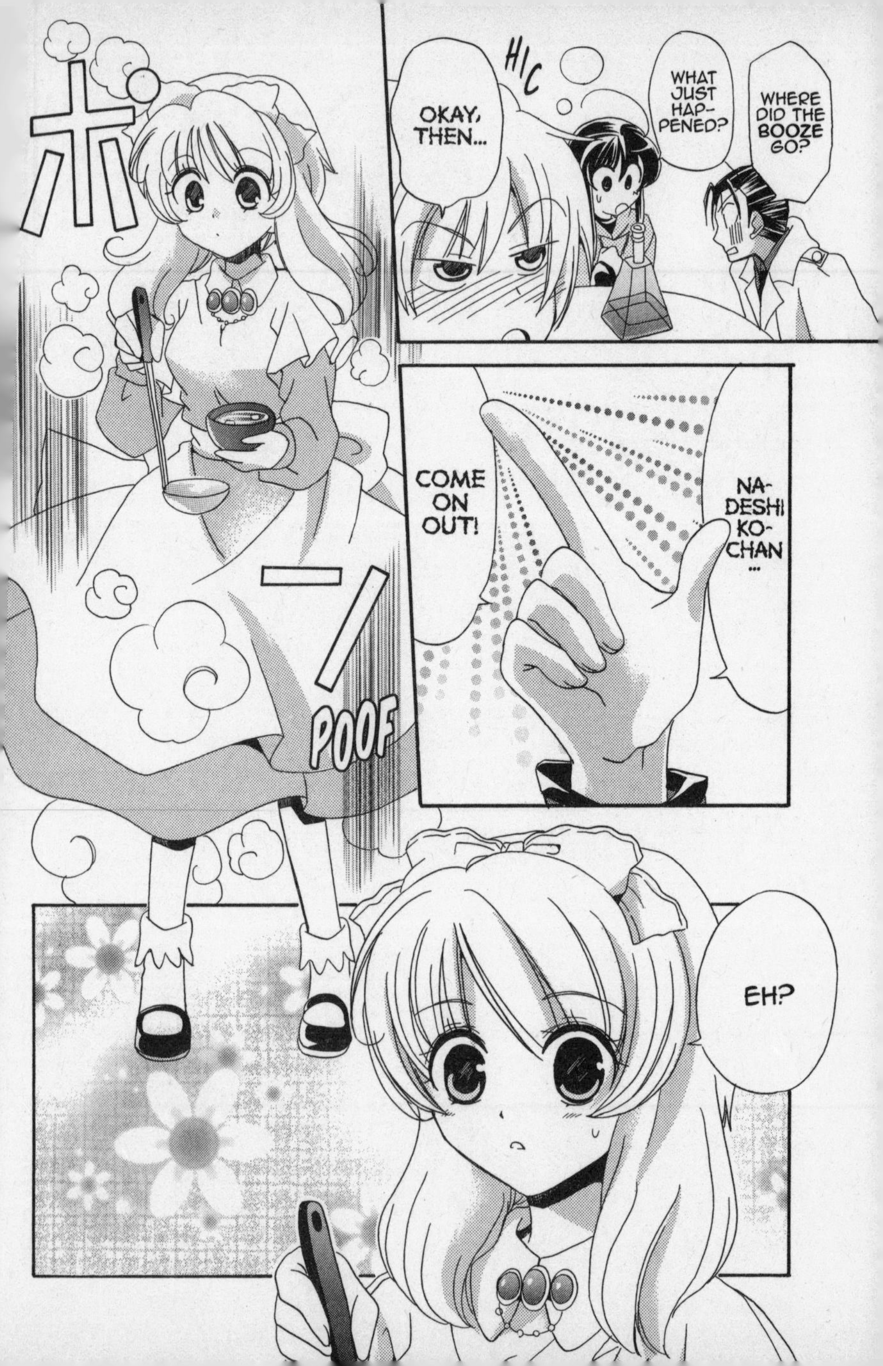
WHERE DID THE BOOZE GO?
WHAT JUST HAP-PENED?
HIC
OKAY, THEN...
NA-DESHI KO-CHAN...
COME ON OUT!
ポ
POOF
EH?

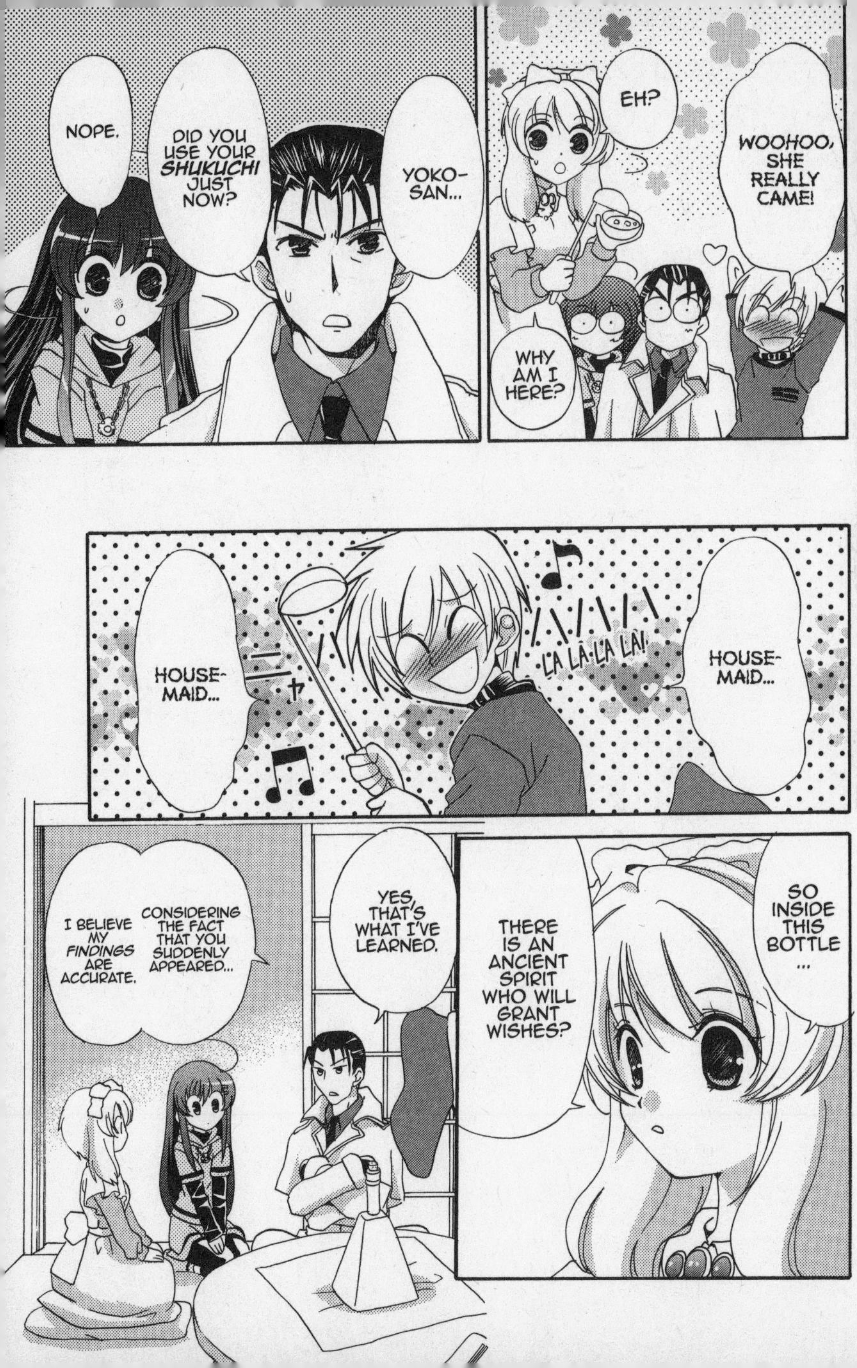
WOOHOO, SHE REALLY CAME!
EH?
WHY AM I HERE?
YOKO-SAN...
DID YOU USE YOUR SHUKUCHI JUST NOW?
NOPE.
HOUSE-MAID...
LA LA LA LA!
HOUSE-MAID...
SO INSIDE THIS BOTTLE ...
THERE IS AN ANCIENT SPIRIT WHO WILL GRANT WISHES?
YES, THAT'S WHAT I'VE LEARNED.
CONSIDERING THE FACT THAT YOU SUDDENLY APPEARED...
I BELIEVE MY FINDINGS ARE ACCURATE.

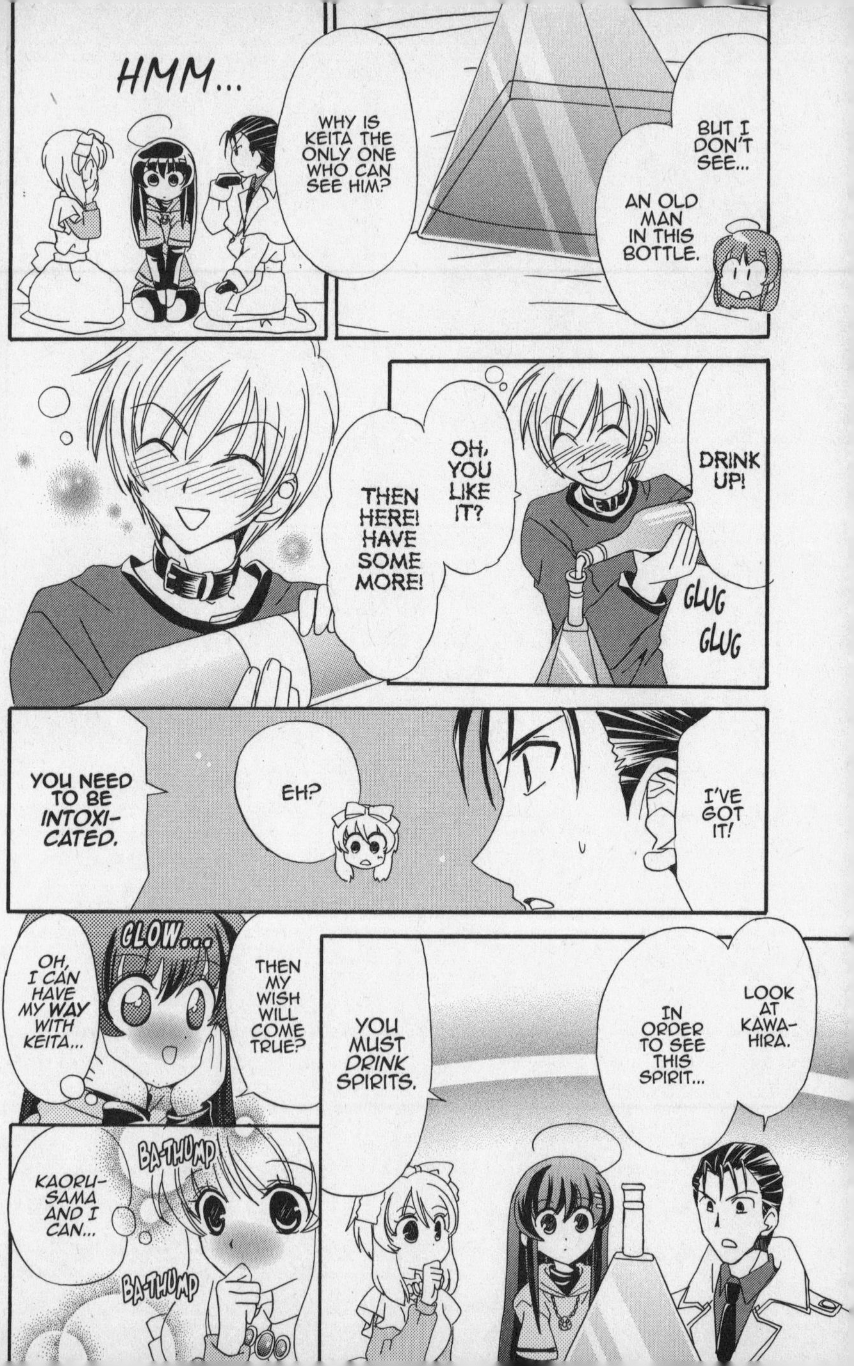
BUT I DON'T SEE...
AN OLD MAN IN THIS BOTTLE.
WHY IS KEITA THE ONLY ONE WHO CAN SEE HIM?
HMM...
DRINK UP!
GLUG GLUG
OH, YOU LIKE IT?
THEN HERE! HAVE SOME MORE!
I'VE GOT IT!
EH?
YOU NEED TO BE INTOXICATED.
LOOK AT KAWAHIRA.
IN ORDER TO SEE THIS SPIRIT...
YOU MUST DRINK SPIRITS.
THEN MY WISH WILL COME TRUE?
GLOW...
OH, I CAN HAVE MY WAY WITH KEITA...
BA-THUMP
KAORU-SAMA AND I CAN...
BA-THUMP

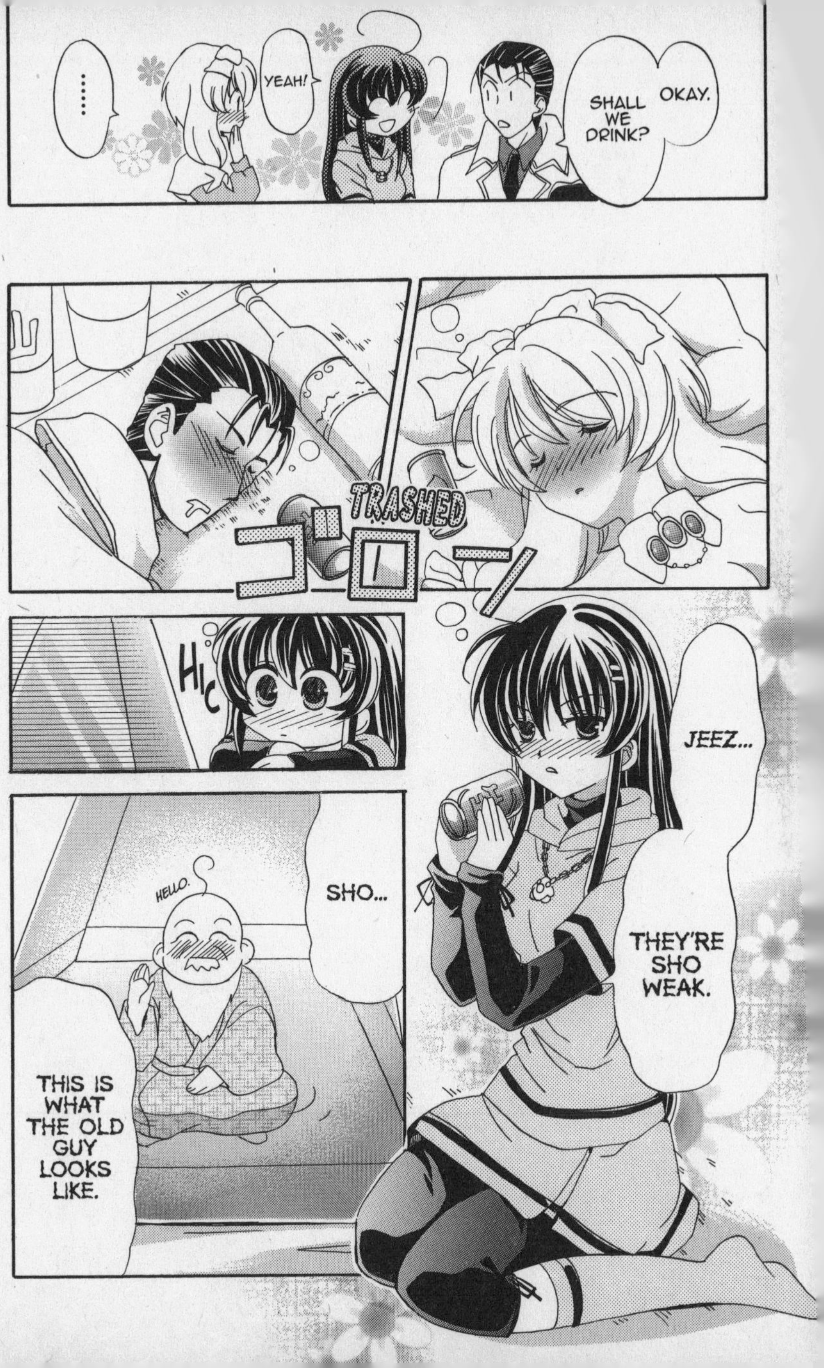
OKAY.
SHALL WE DRINK?
YEAH!
......
TRASHED
ゴローン
JEEZ...
THEY'RE SHO WEAK.
HIC
SHO...
HELLO.
THIS IS WHAT THE OLD GUY LOOKS LIKE.

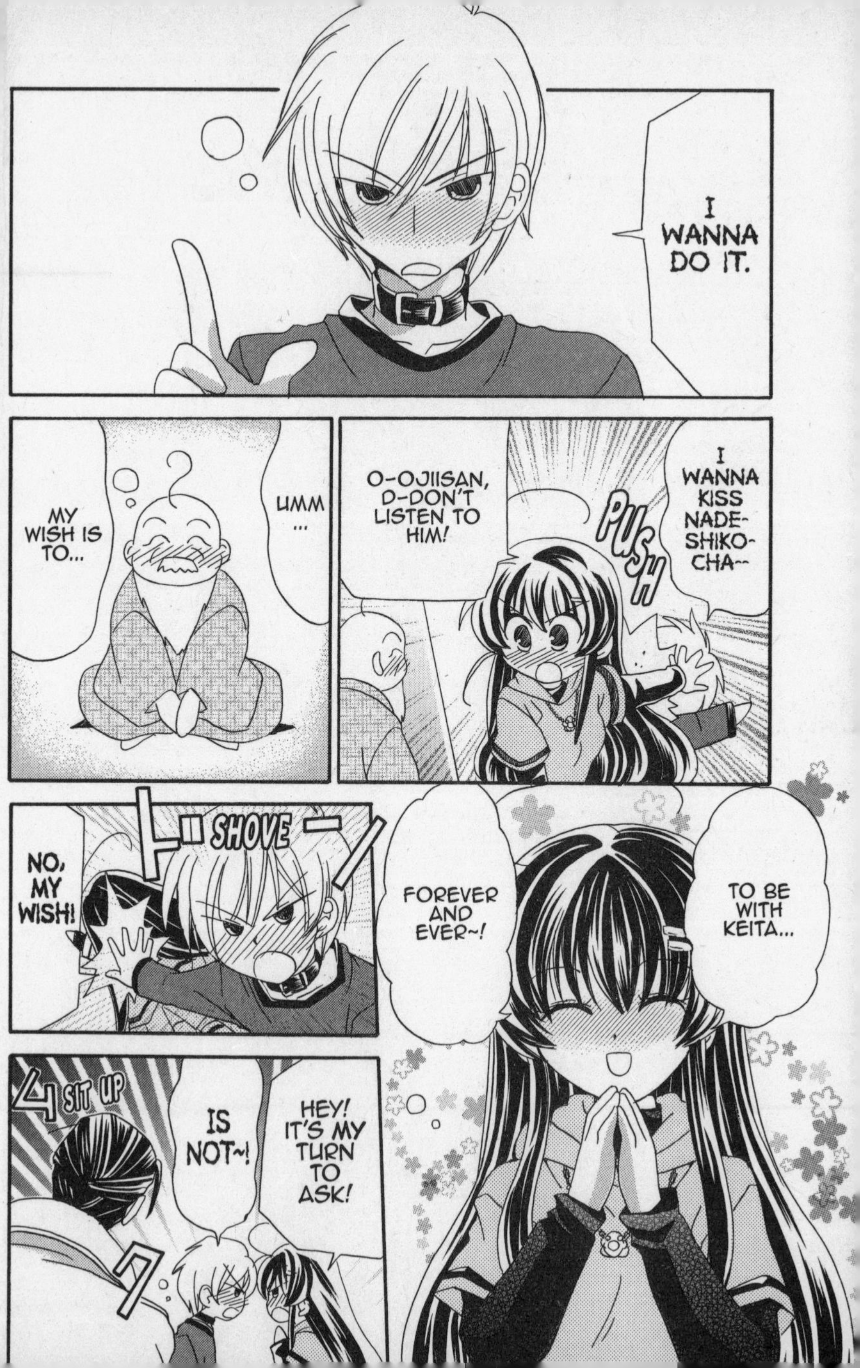
I WANNA DO IT.
I WANNA KISS NADE-SHIKO-CHA--
PUSH
O-OJIISAN, D-DON'T LISTEN TO HIM!
UMM ...
MY WISH IS TO...
TO BE WITH KEITA...
FOREVER AND EVER~!
SHOVE
NO, MY WISH!
HEY! IT'S MY TURN TO ASK!
IS NOT~!
SIT UP

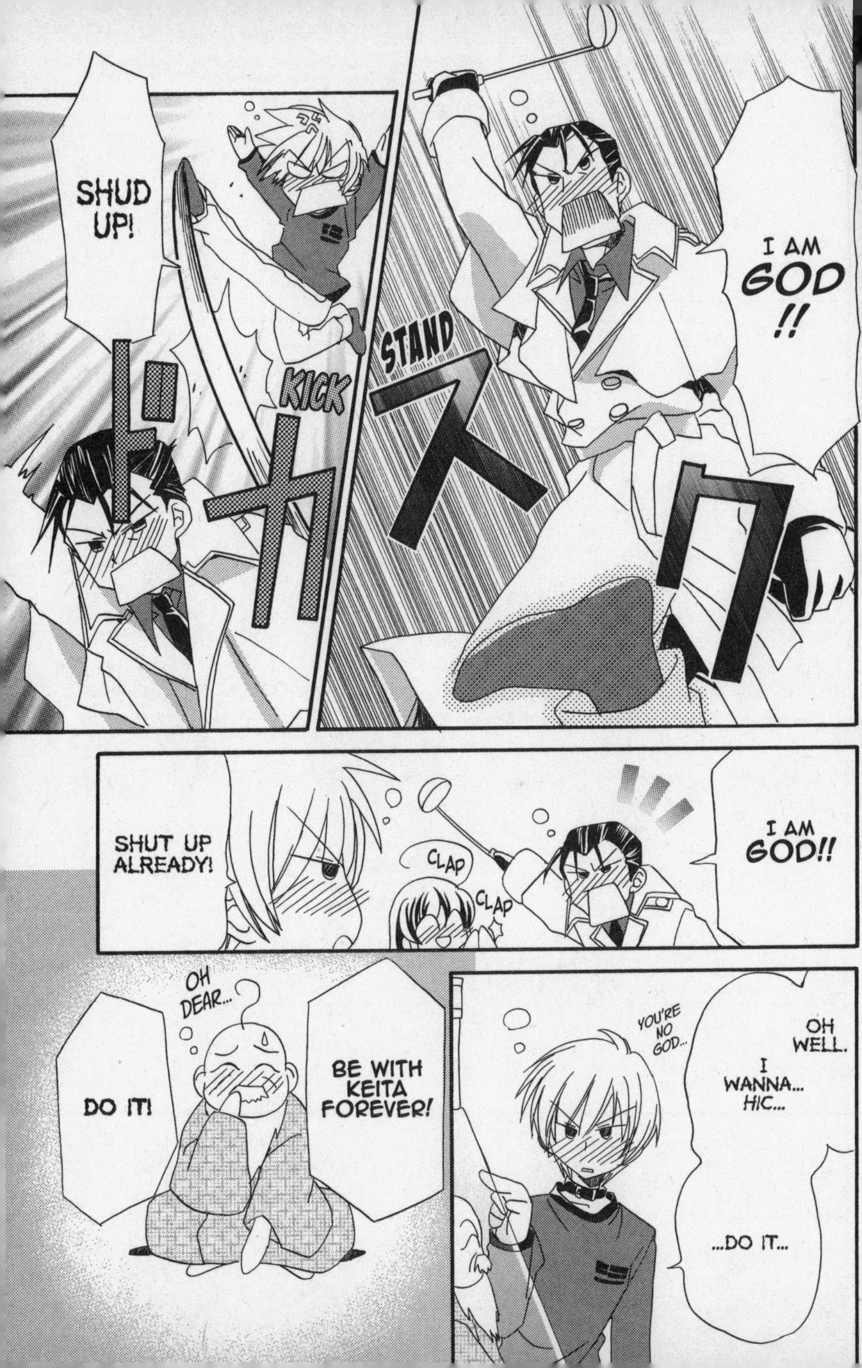
I AM GOD!!
STAND
スク
SHUD UP!
KICK
ドカ
I AM GOD!!
CLAP
CLAP
SHUT UP ALREADY!
OH WELL.
I WANNA... HIC...
...DO IT...
YOU'RE NO GOD...
BE WITH KEITA FOREVER!
OH DEAR...
DO IT!

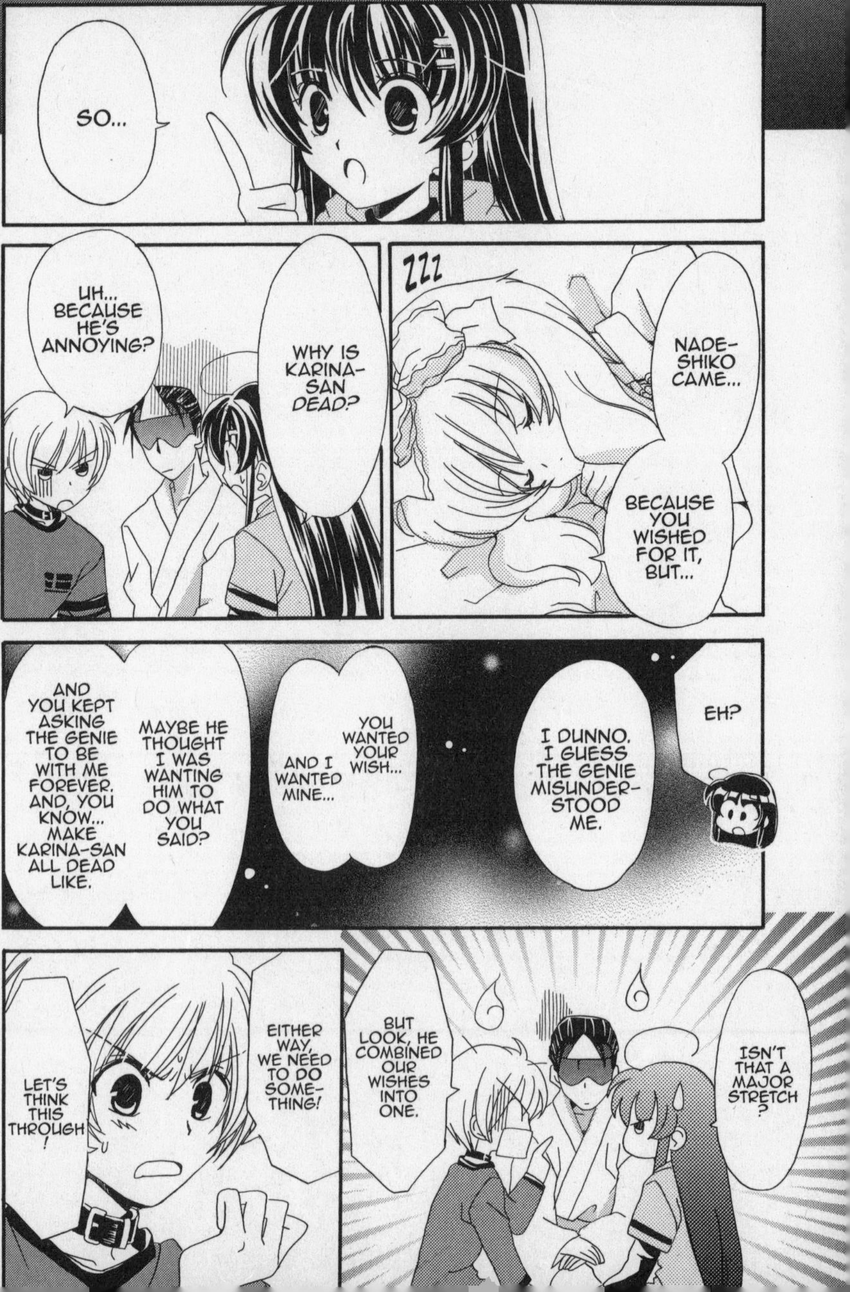
SO...
NADE-SHIKO CAME...
BECAUSE YOU WISHED FOR IT, BUT...
WHY IS KARINA-SAN DEAD?
UH... BECAUSE HE'S ANNOYING?
ZZZ
EH?
I DUNNO. I GUESS THE GENIE MISUNDERSTOOD ME.
YOU WANTED YOUR WISH...
AND I WANTED MINE...
MAYBE HE THOUGHT I WAS WANTING HIM TO DO WHAT YOU SAID?
AND YOU KEPT ASKING THE GENIE TO BE WITH ME FOREVER. AND, YOU KNOW... MAKE KARINA-SAN ALL DEAD LIKE.
ISN'T THAT A MAJOR STRETCH?
BUT LOOK, HE COMBINED OUR WISHES INTO ONE.
EITHER WAY, WE NEED TO DO SOMETHING!
LET'S THINK THIS THROUGH!

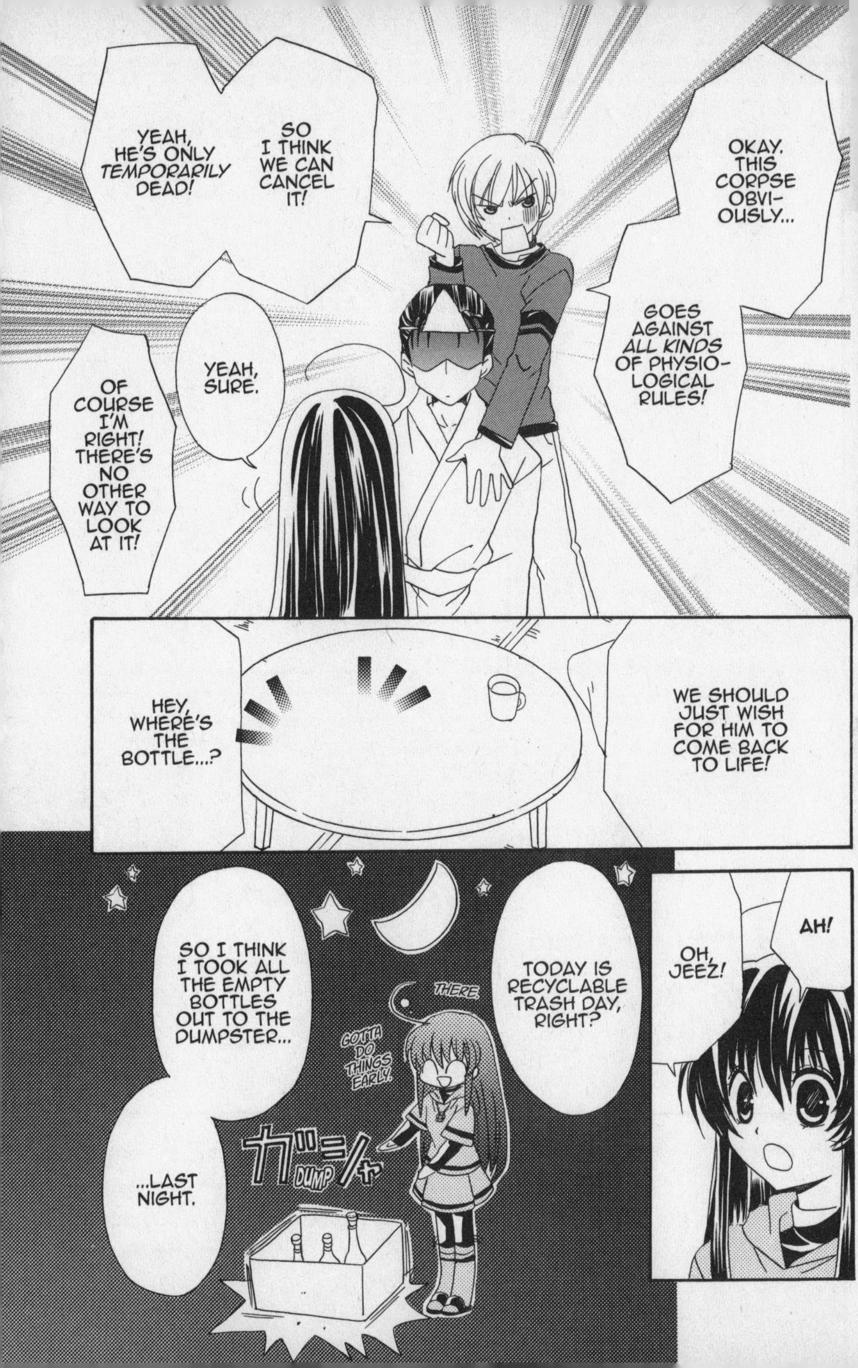

OKAY. THIS CORPSE OBVIOUSLY...
GOES AGAINST ALL KINDS OF PHYSIOLOGICAL RULES!
YEAH, HE'S ONLY TEMPORARILY DEAD! SO I THINK WE CAN CANCEL IT!
YEAH, SURE.
OF COURSE I'M RIGHT! THERE'S NO OTHER WAY TO LOOK AT IT!
WE SHOULD JUST WISH FOR HIM TO COME BACK TO LIFE!
HEY, WHERE'S THE BOTTLE...?
AH!
OH, JEEZ!
TODAY IS RECYCLABLE TRASH DAY, RIGHT?
THERE.
GOTTA DO THINGS EARLY.
SO I THINK I TOOK ALL THE EMPTY BOTTLES OUT TO THE DUMPSTER...
DUMP
...LAST NIGHT.

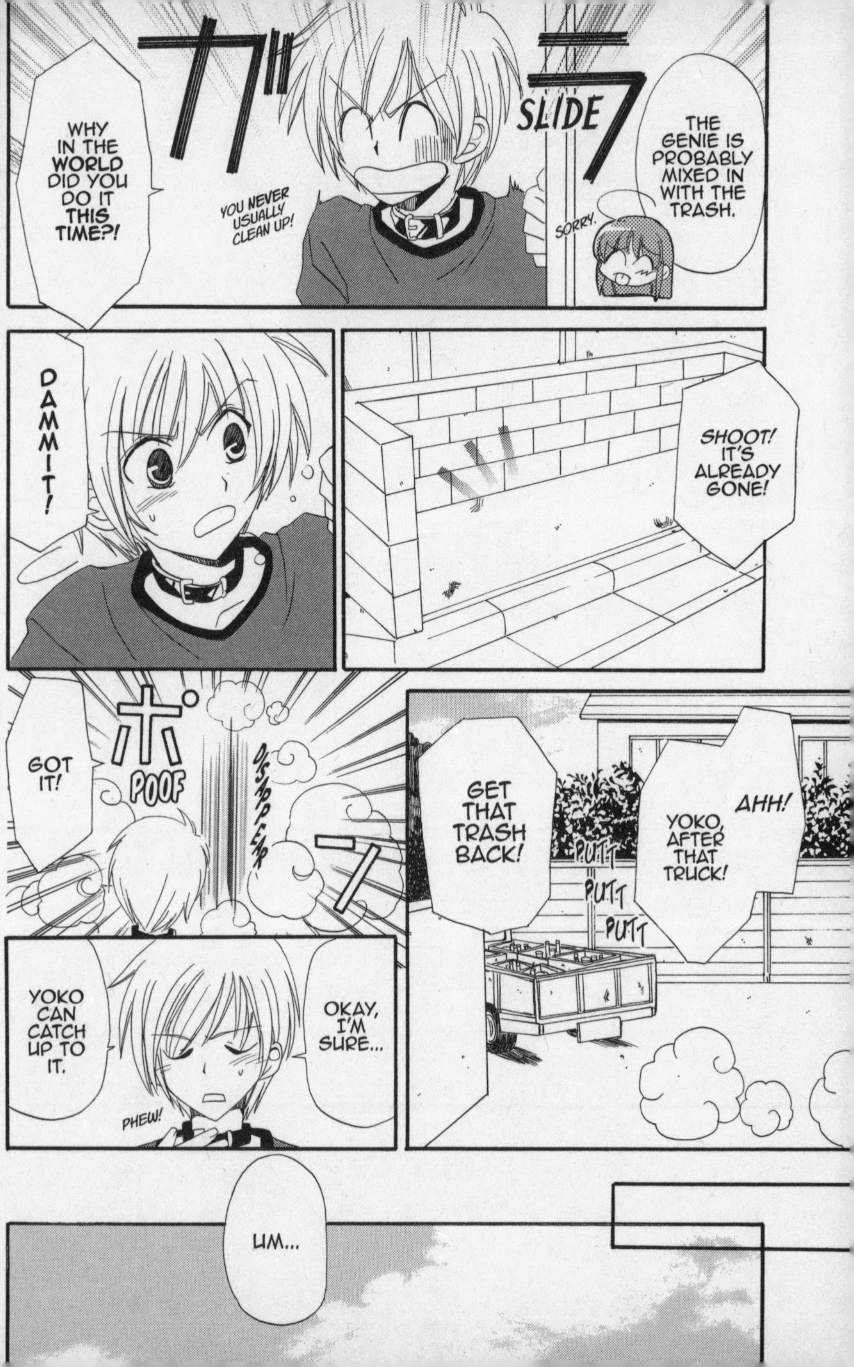
ガラ
SLIDE
THE GENIE IS PROBABLY MIXED IN WITH THE TRASH.
SORRY.
YOU NEVER USUALLY CLEAN UP!
WHY IN THE WORLD DID YOU DO IT THIS TIME?!
SHOOT! IT'S ALREADY GONE!
DAMMIT!
AHH! YOKO, AFTER THAT TRUCK!
GET THAT TRASH BACK!
PUTT
PUTT
PUTT
ポ
POOF
DISAPPEAR
GOT IT!
OKAY, I'M SURE...
YOKO CAN CATCH UP TO IT.
PHEW!
UM...

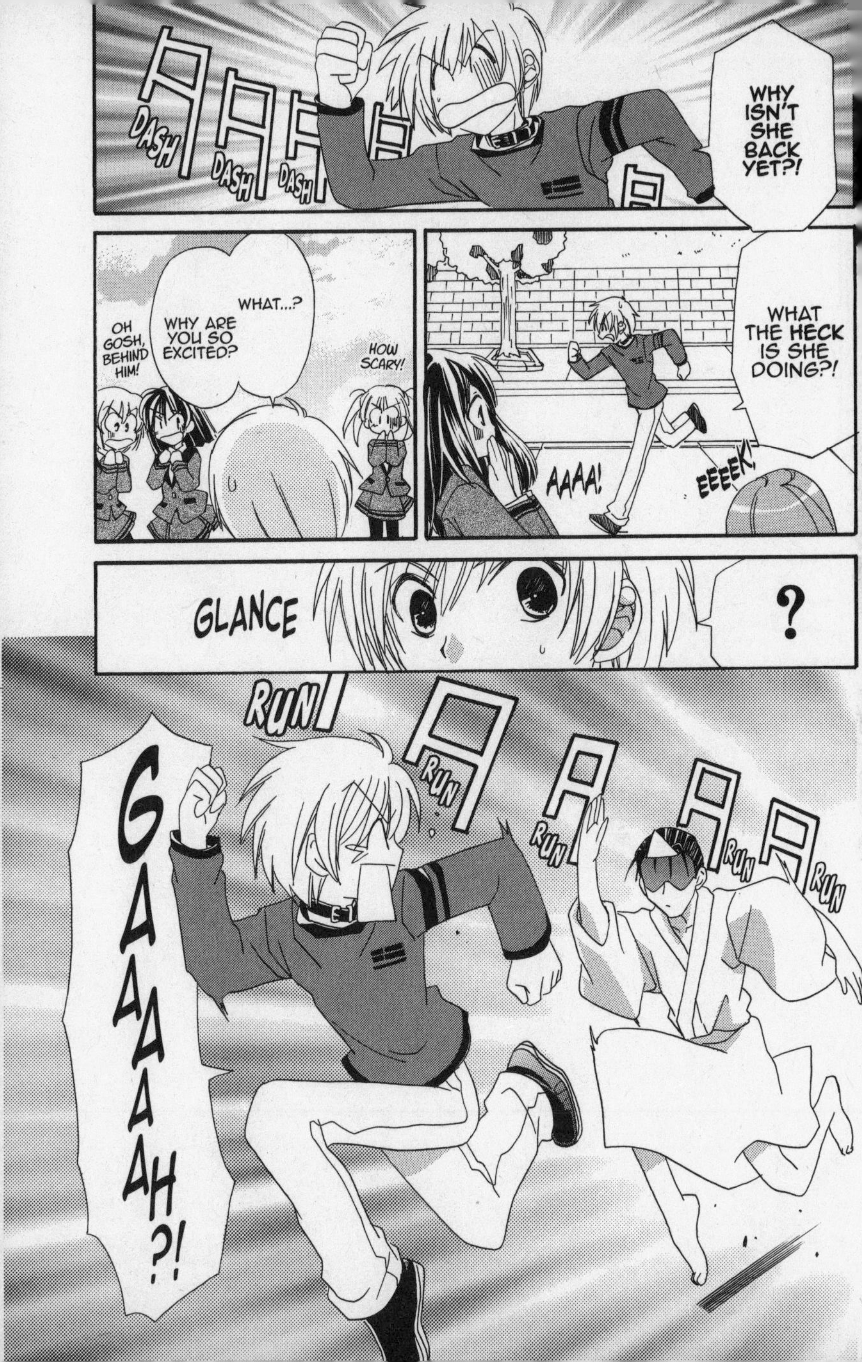
WHY ISN'T SHE BACK YET?!
DASH DASH DASH
WHAT THE HECK IS SHE DOING?!
EEEEK!
AAAA!
WHAT...?
WHY ARE YOU SO EXCITED?
HOW SCARY!
OH GOSH, BEHIND HIM!
?
GLANCE
RUN RUN RUN RUN RUN RUN
GAAAAAH?!

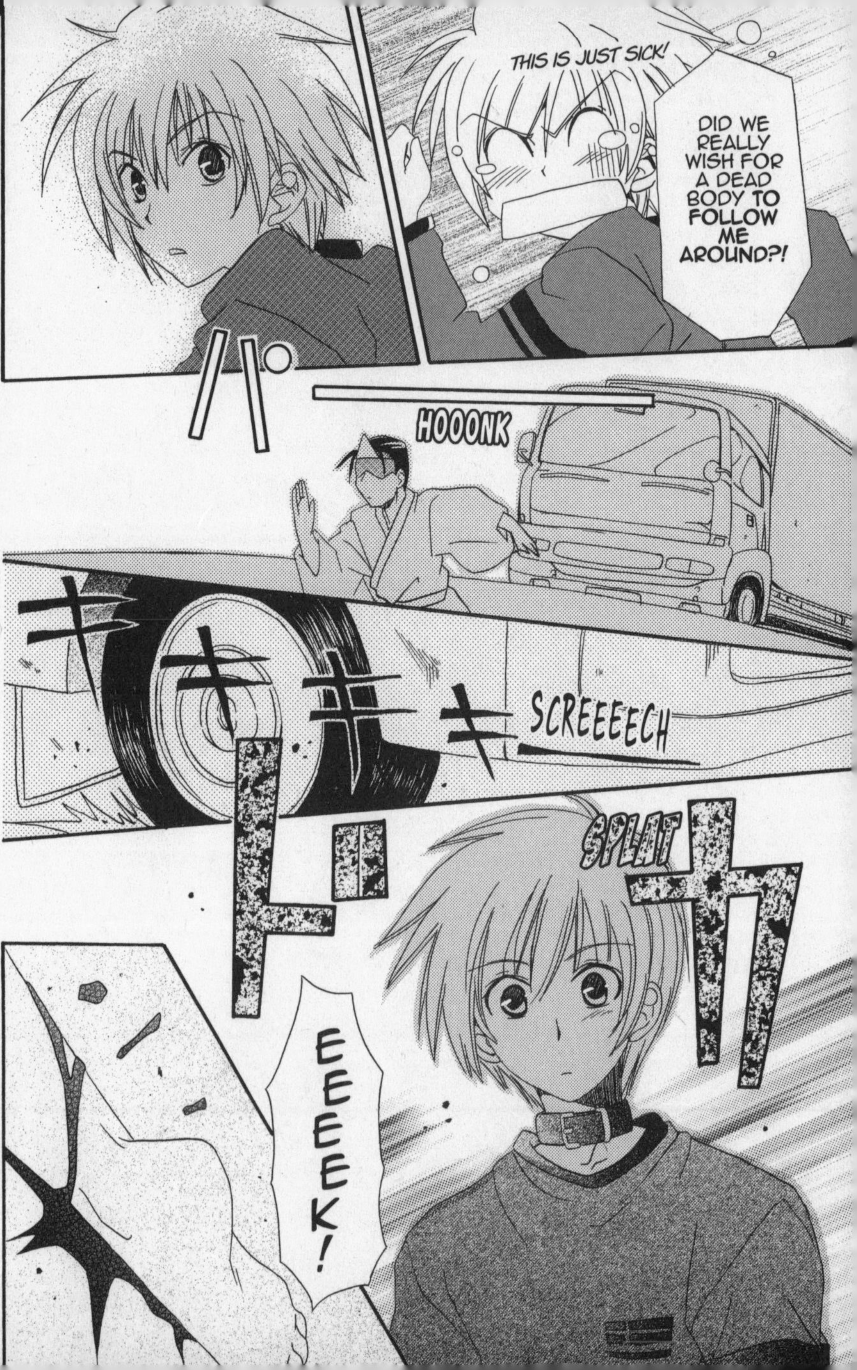
THIS IS JUST SICK!
DID WE REALLY WISH FOR A DEAD BODY TO FOLLOW ME AROUND?!
HOOONK
SCREEEECH
SPLAT
EEEEEK!

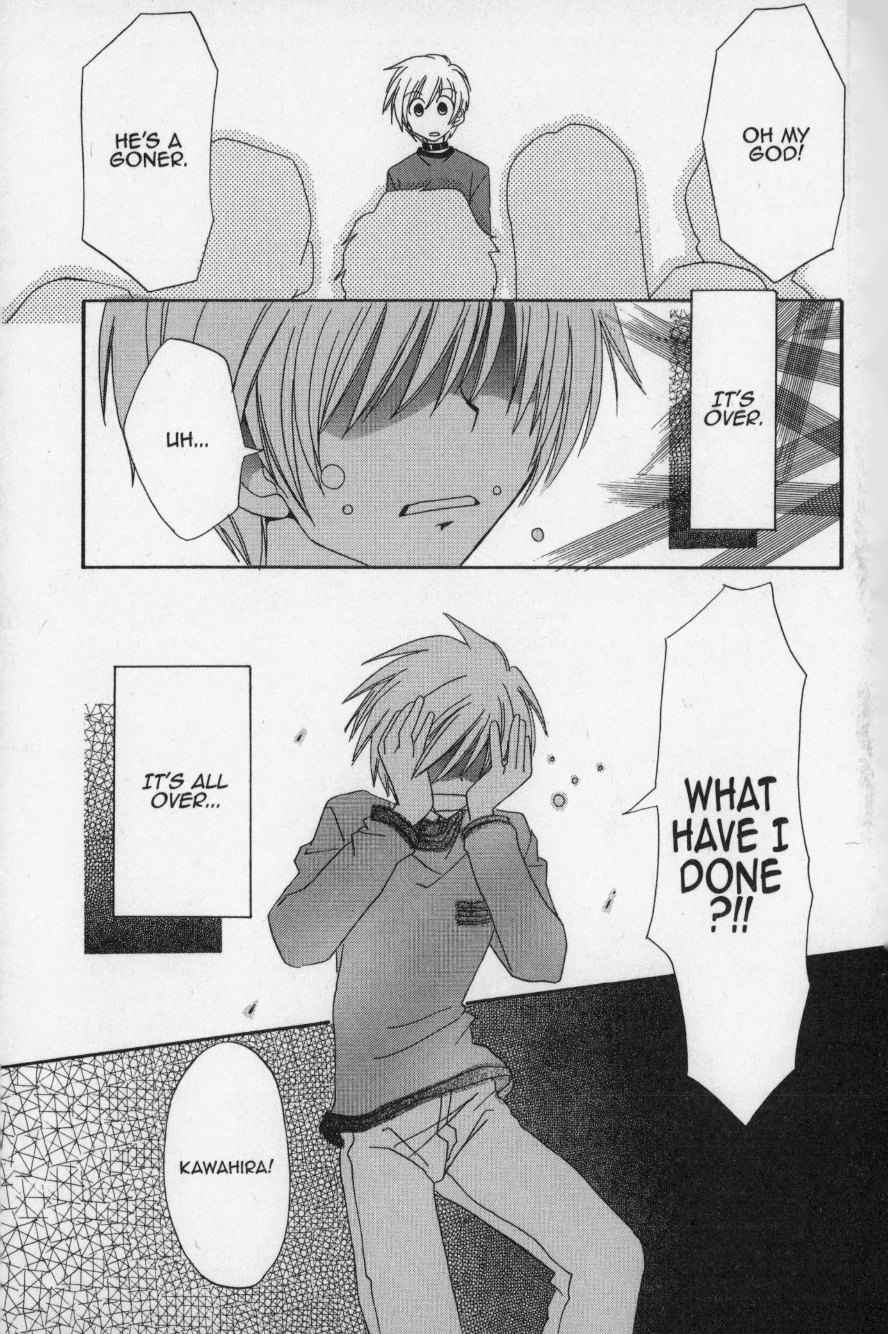
OH MY GOD!
HE'S A GONER.
IT'S OVER.
UH...
WHAT HAVE I DONE ?!!
IT'S ALL OVER...
KAWAHIRA!

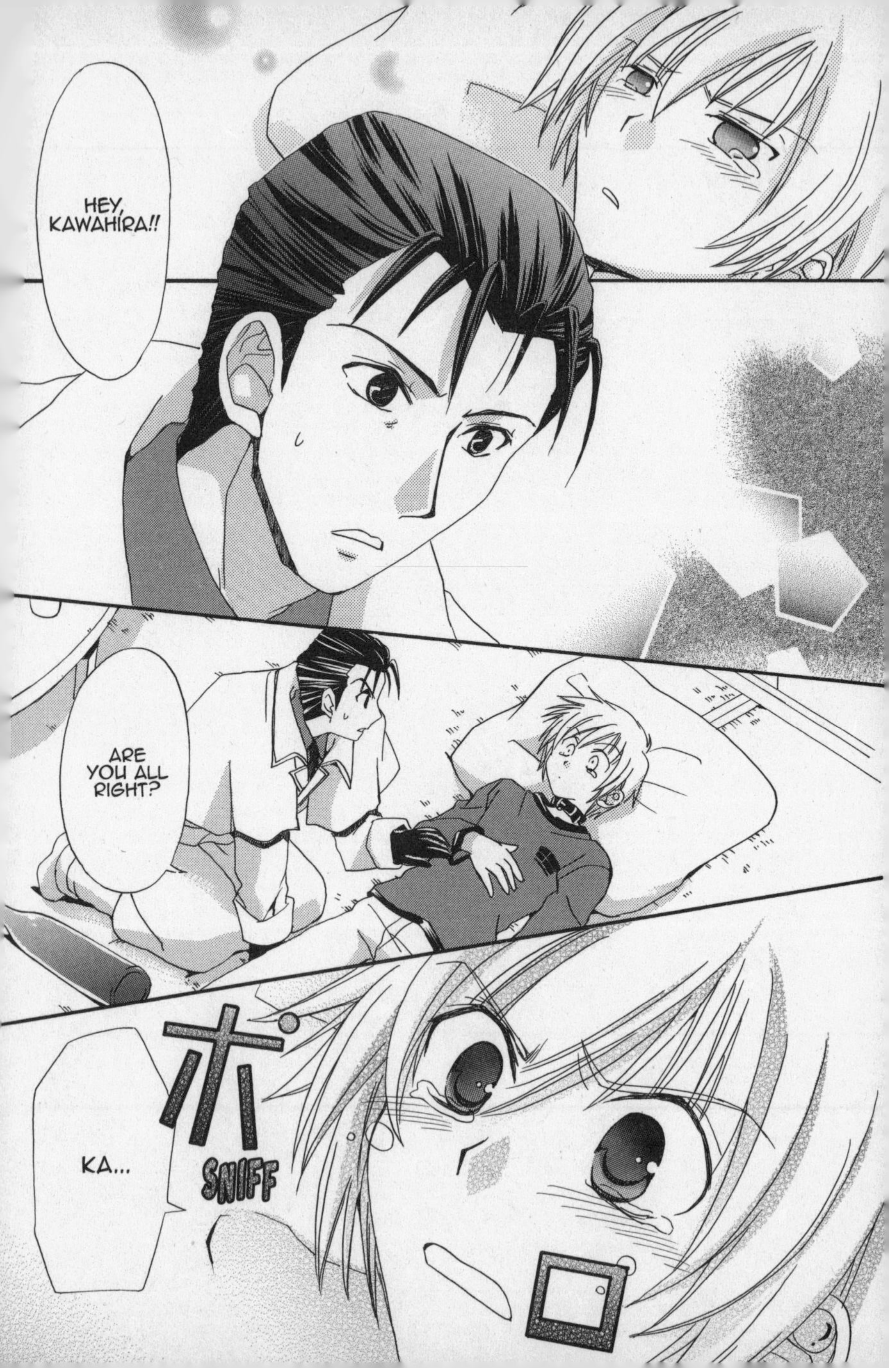
HEY, KAWAHIRA!!
ARE YOU ALL RIGHT?
ポ
SNIFF
KA...

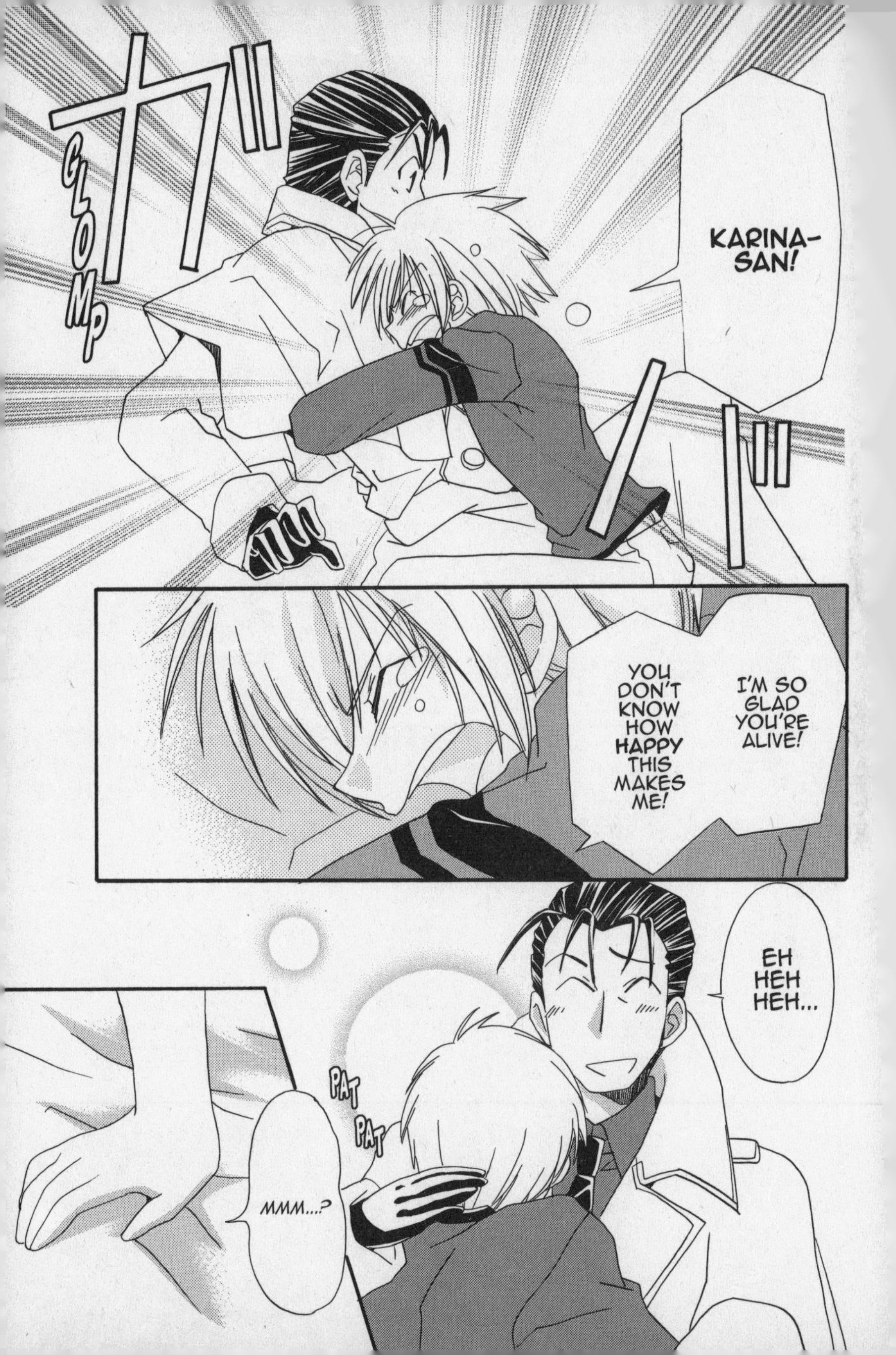
KARINA-SAN!
GLOMP
I'M SO GLAD YOU'RE ALIVE!
YOU DON'T KNOW HOW HAPPY THIS MAKES ME!
EH HEH HEH...
PAT PAT
MMM...?

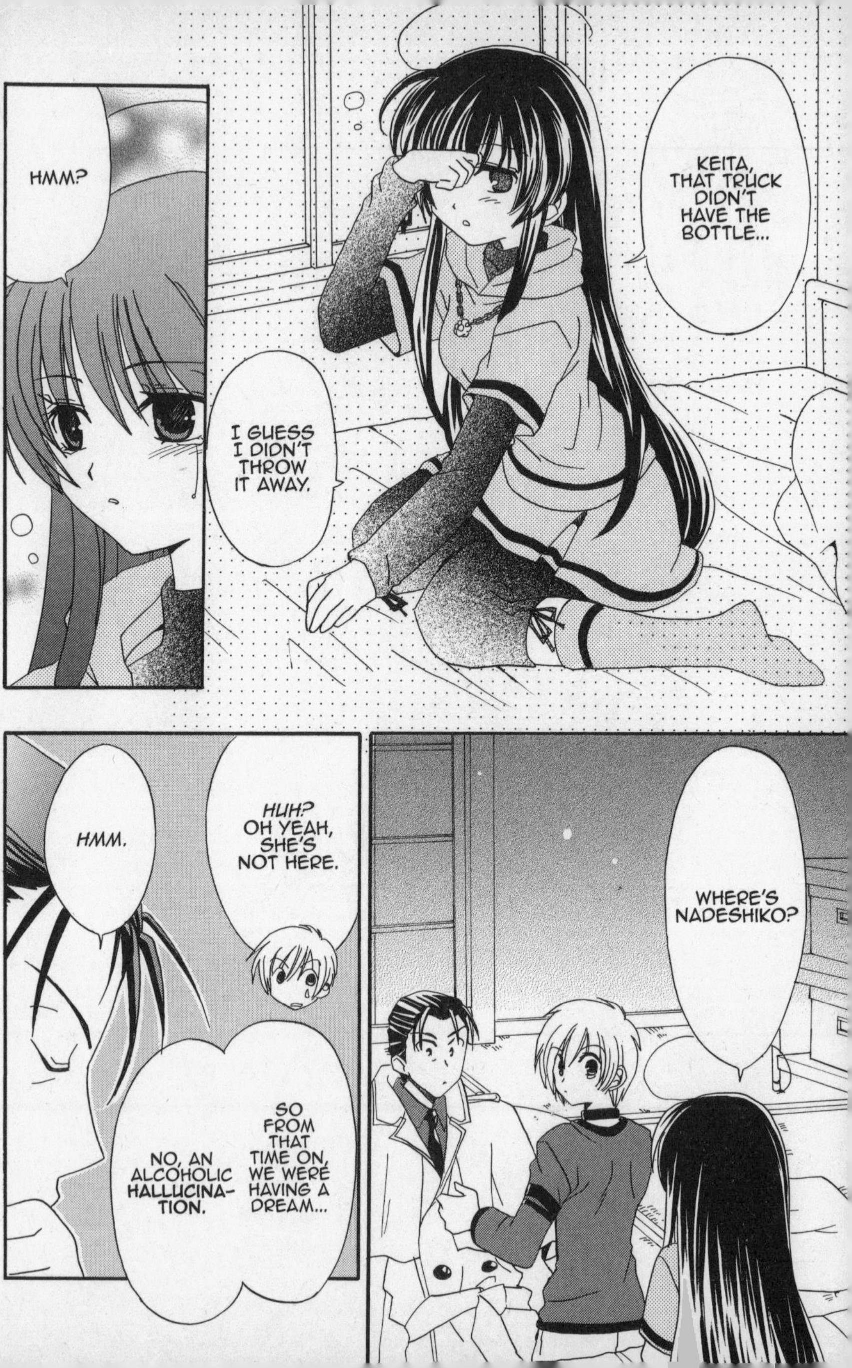
KEITA, THAT TRUCK DIDN'T HAVE THE BOTTLE...
I GUESS I DIDN'T THROW IT AWAY.
HMM?
WHERE'S NADESHIKO?
HUH? OH YEAH, SHE'S NOT HERE.
HMM.
SO FROM THAT TIME ON, WE WERE HAVING A DREAM...
NO, AN ALCOHOLIC HALLUCINATION.

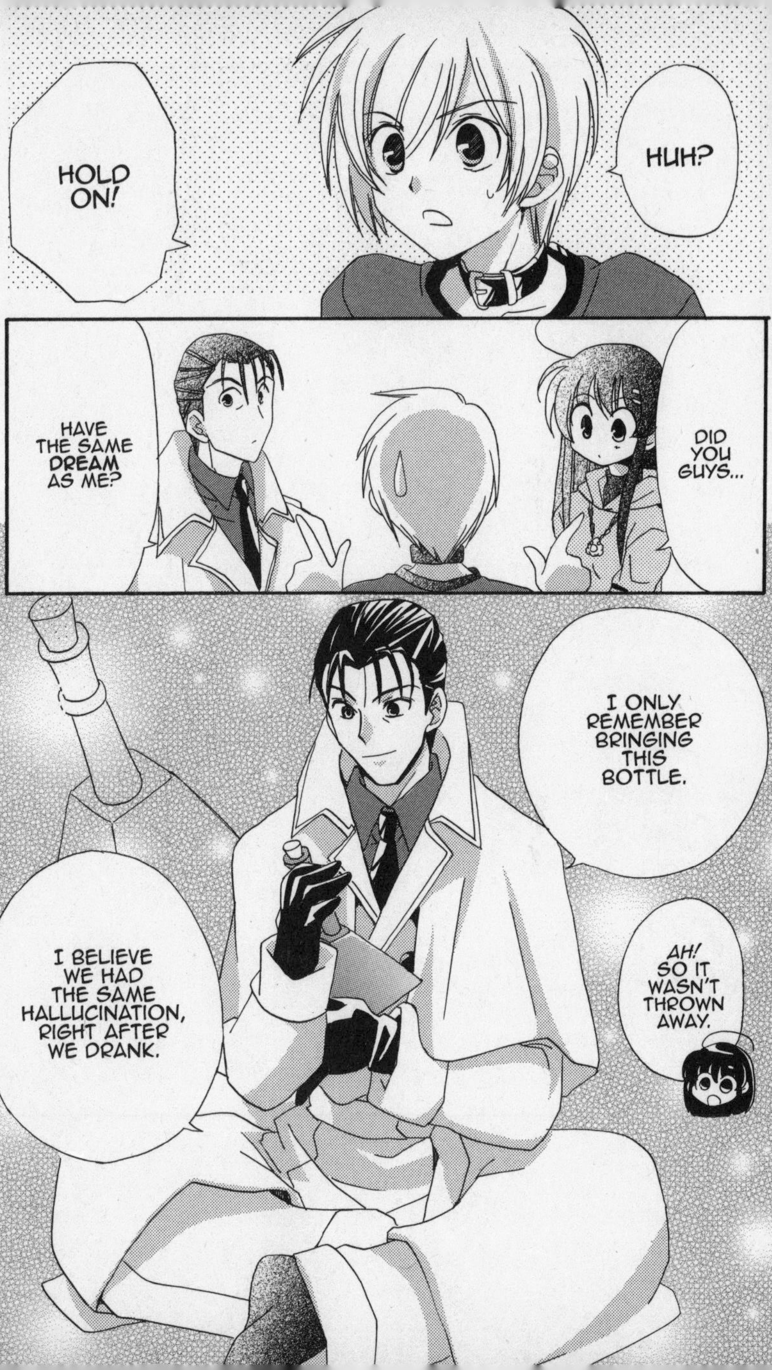
HUH?
HOLD ON!
DID YOU GUYS...
HAVE THE SAME DREAM AS ME?
I ONLY REMEMBER BRINGING THIS BOTTLE.
I BELIEVE WE HAD THE SAME HALLUCINATION, RIGHT AFTER WE DRANK.
AH! SO IT WASN'T THROWN AWAY.

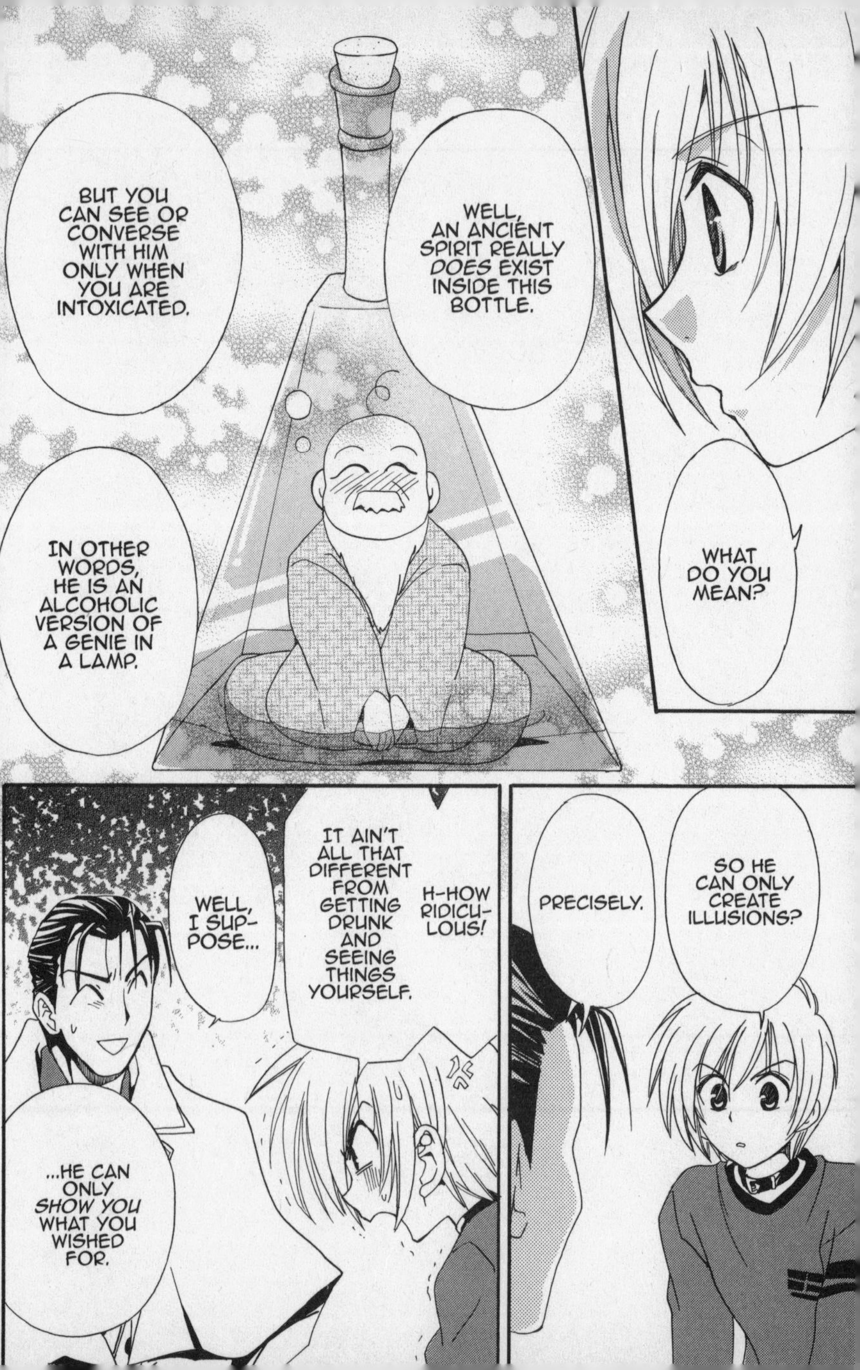
WHAT DO YOU MEAN?
WELL, AN ANCIENT SPIRIT REALLY *DOES* EXIST INSIDE THIS BOTTLE.
BUT YOU CAN SEE OR CONVERSE WITH HIM ONLY WHEN YOU ARE INTOXICATED.
IN OTHER WORDS, HE IS AN ALCOHOLIC VERSION OF A GENIE IN A LAMP.
SO HE CAN ONLY CREATE ILLUSIONS?
PRECISELY.
IT AIN'T ALL THAT DIFFERENT FROM GETTING DRUNK AND SEEING THINGS YOURSELF.
H-HOW RIDICU-LOUS!
WELL, I SUP-POSE...
...HE CAN ONLY *SHOW YOU* WHAT YOU WISHED FOR.

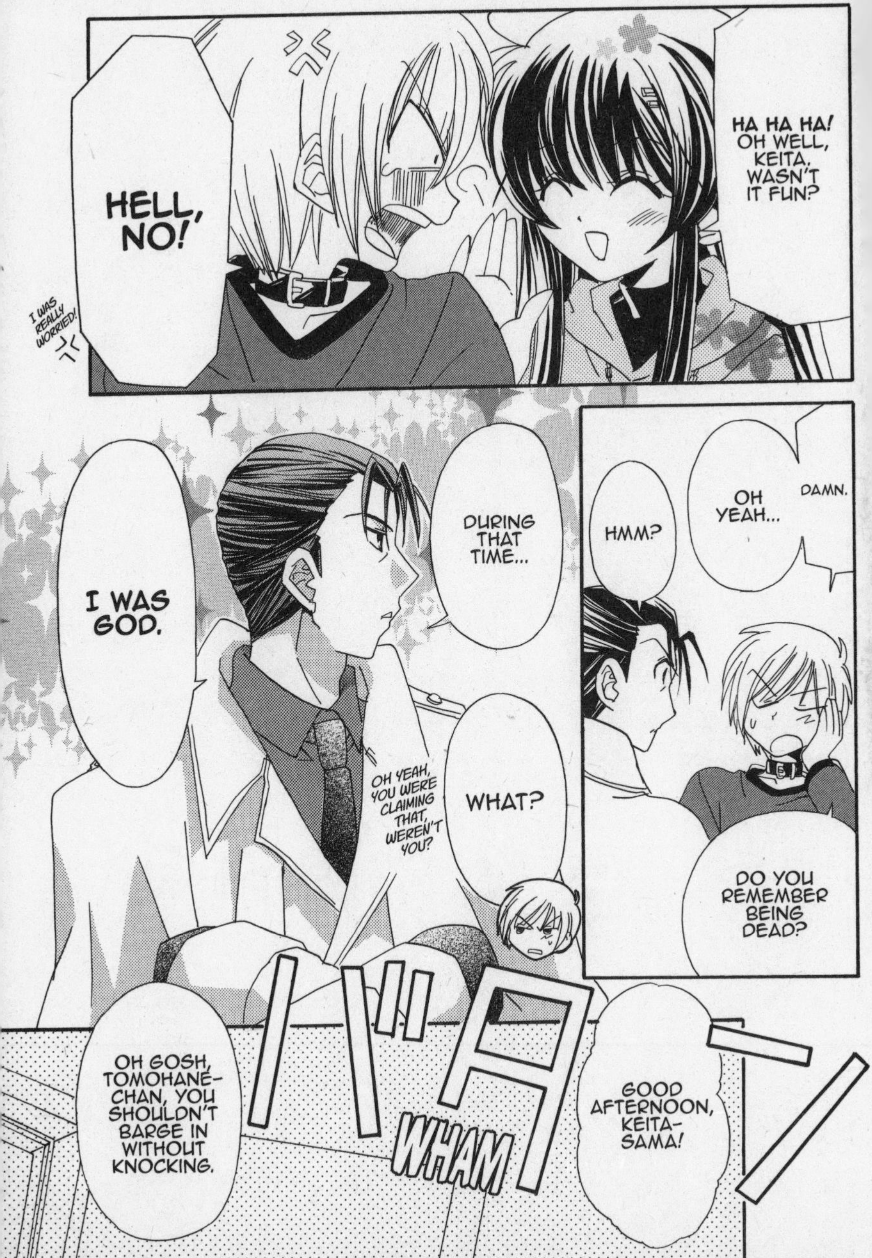
HA HA HA! OH WELL, KEITA, WASN'T IT FUN?
HELL, NO!
I WAS REALLY WORRIED!
DAMN.
OH YEAH...
HMM?
DO YOU REMEMBER BEING DEAD?
DURING THAT TIME...
I WAS GOD.
WHAT?
OH YEAH, YOU WERE CLAIMING THAT, WEREN'T YOU?
GOOD AFTERNOON, KEITA-SAMA!
WHAM
OH GOSH, TOMOHANÉ-CHAN, YOU SHOULDN'T BARGE IN WITHOUT KNOCKING.

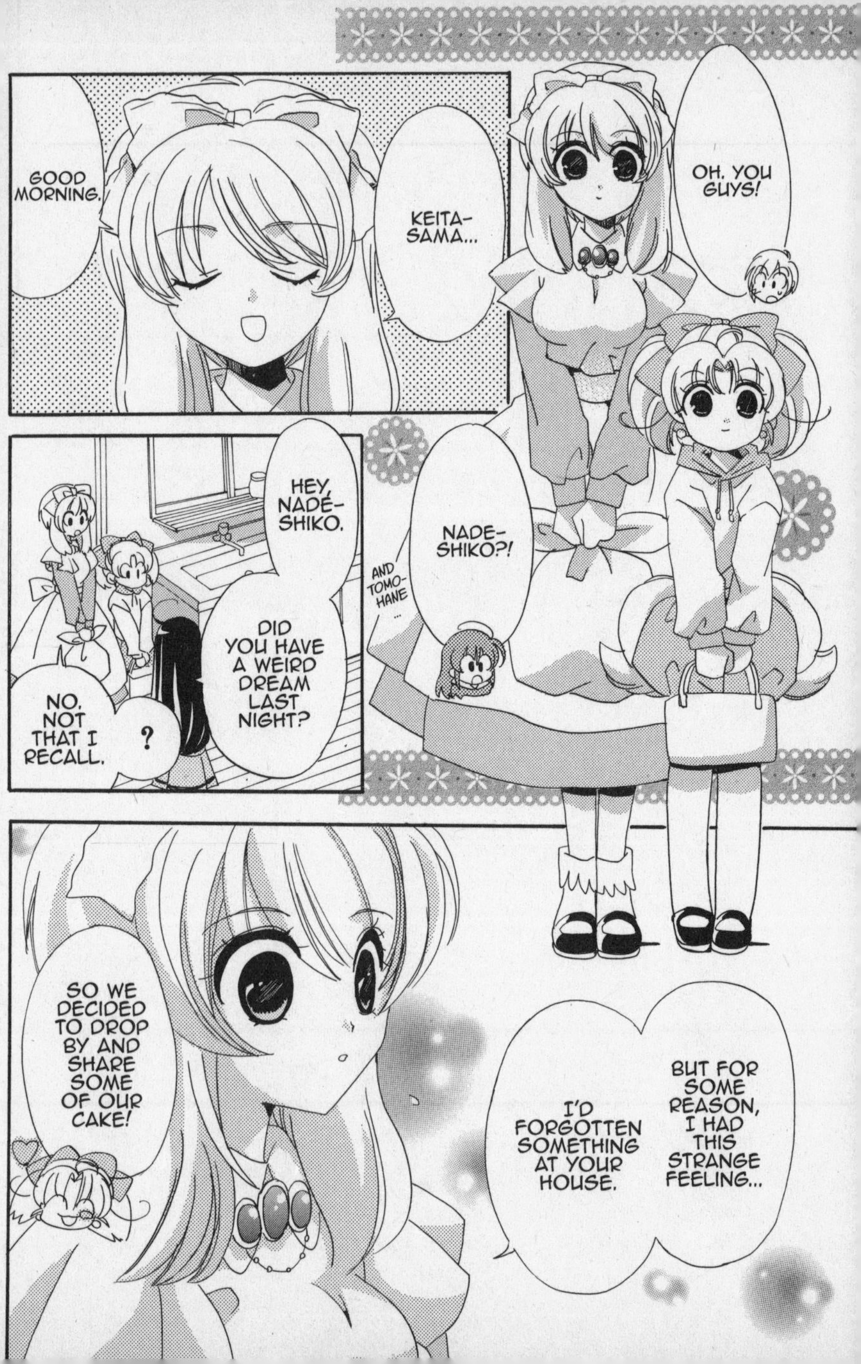
OH, YOU GUYS!
NADE-SHIKO?!
AND TOMO-HANE...
KEITA-SAMA...
GOOD MORNING.
HEY, NADE-SHIKO.
DID YOU HAVE A WEIRD DREAM LAST NIGHT?
?
NO. NOT THAT I RECALL.
BUT FOR SOME REASON, I HAD THIS STRANGE FEELING...
I'D FORGOTTEN SOMETHING AT YOUR HOUSE.
SO WE DECIDED TO DROP BY AND SHARE SOME OF OUR CAKE!

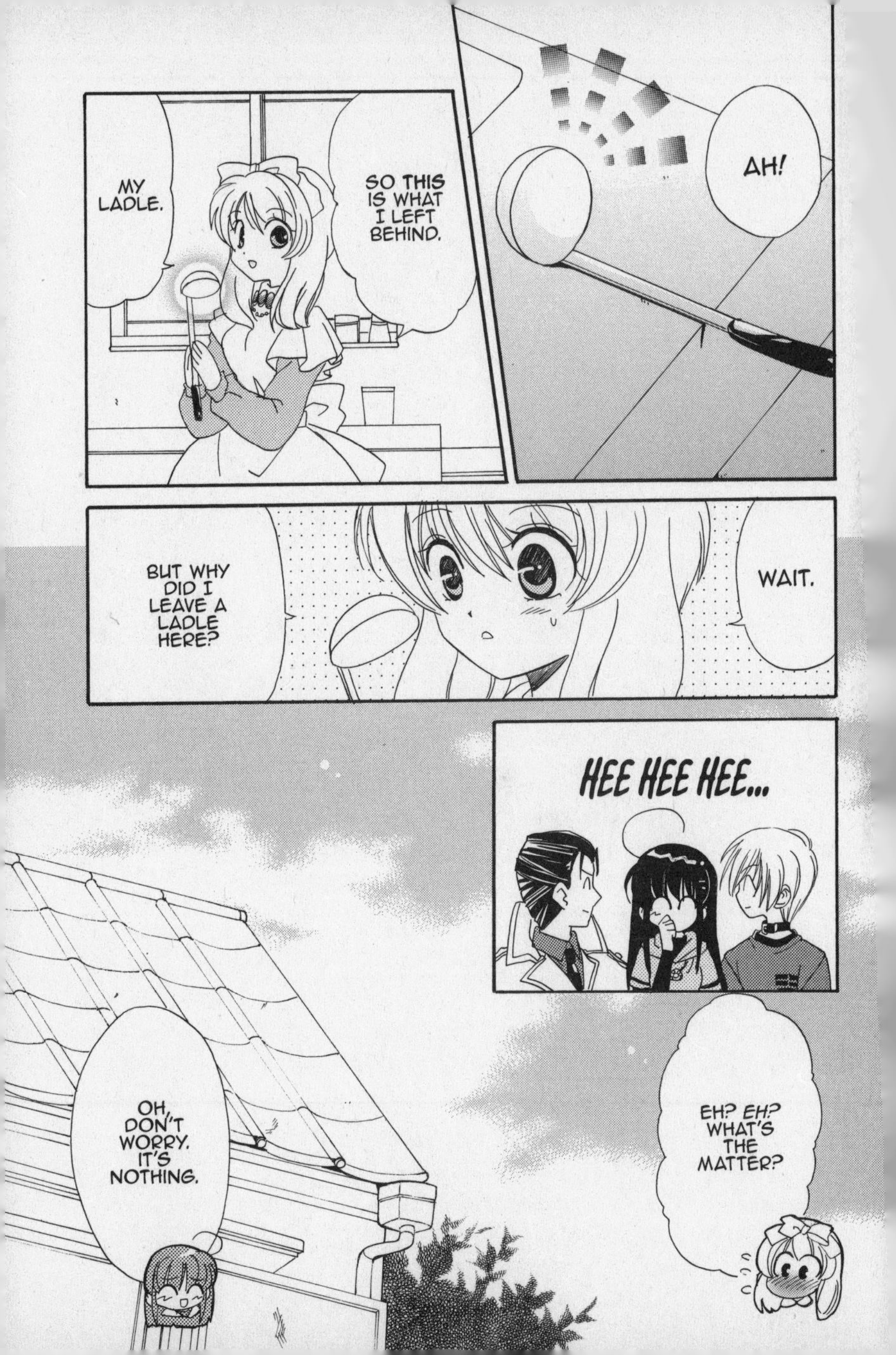
AH!
SO THIS IS WHAT I LEFT BEHIND.
MY LADLE.
WAIT.
BUT WHY DID I LEAVE A LADLE HERE?
HEE HEE HEE...
EH? EH? WHAT'S THE MATTER?
OH, DON'T WORRY. IT'S NOTHING.

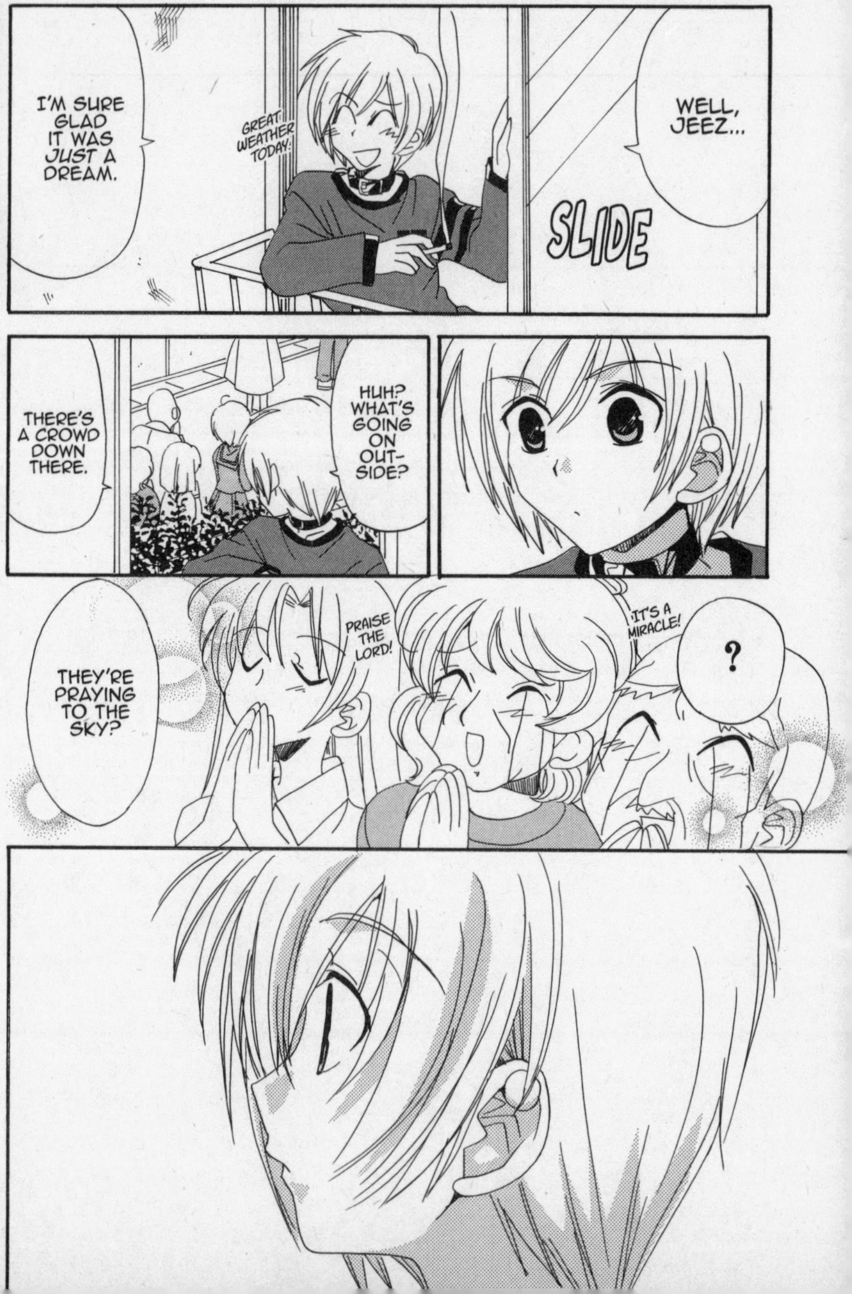
WELL, JEEZ...
SLIDE
GREAT WEATHER TODAY!
I'M SURE GLAD IT WAS JUST A DREAM.
HUH? WHAT'S GOING ON OUT-SIDE?
THERE'S A CROWD DOWN THERE.
?
IT'S A MIRACLE!
PRAISE THE LORD!
THEY'RE PRAYING TO THE SKY?

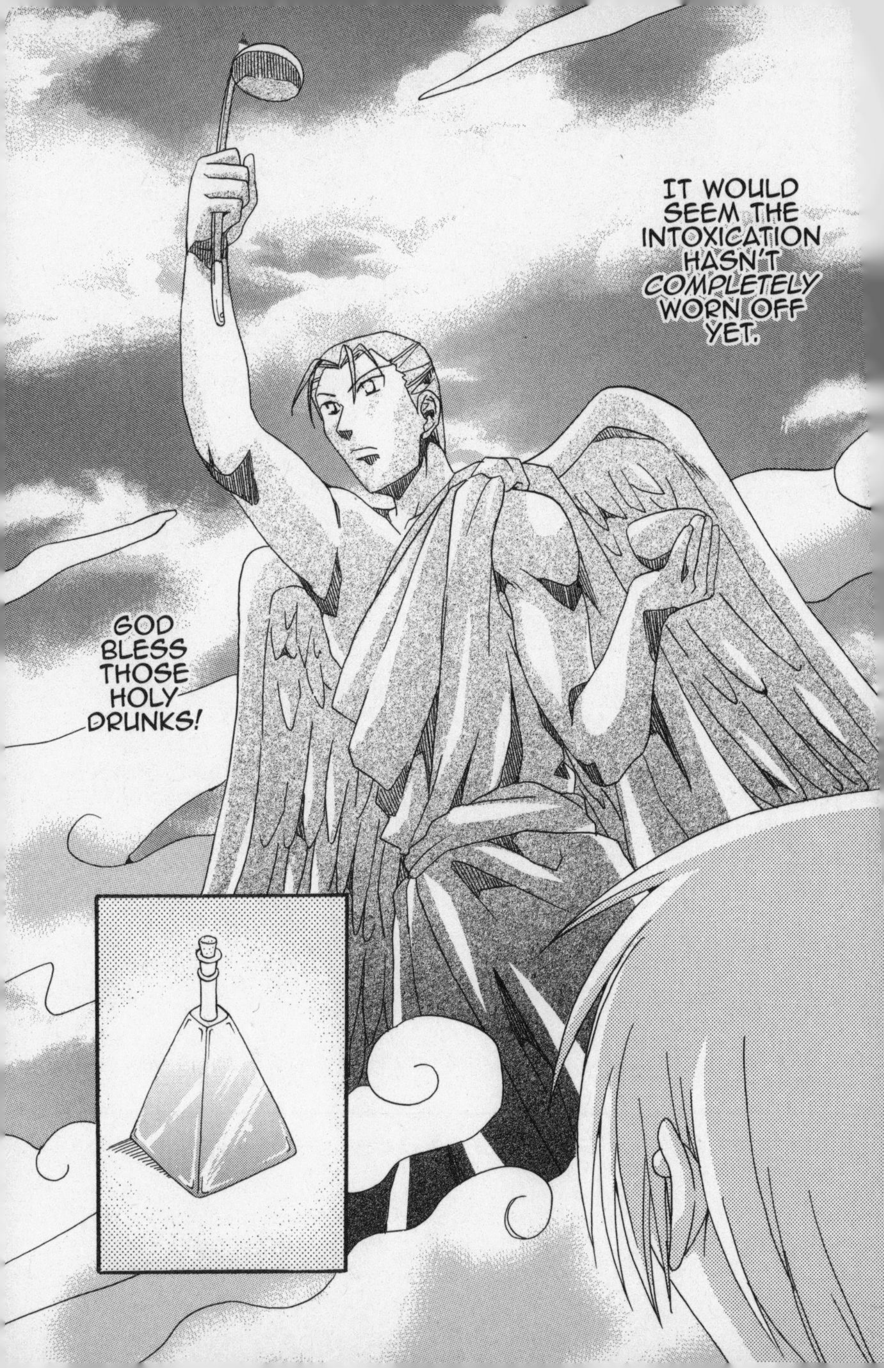
IT WOULD SEEM THE INTOXICATION HASN'T COMPLETELY WORN OFF YET.
GOD BLESS THOSE HOLY DRUNKS!

FROM THE CREATOR

MAMIZU ARISAWA

HELLO, THIS IS ARISAWA.

THE MANGA IS ALREADY UP TO VOLUME 3, AND KAORU HAS FINALLY APPEARED!

MATSUZAWA-SAN DRAWS THIS MANGA WITH FUNNY OR IMPORTANT DETAILS EVEN IN LITTLE CORNERS. PERSONALLY, I REALLY ENJOY THOSE LITTLE DETAILS. I GET A BIG SMILE ON MY FACE WHENEVER I SEE THEM.

AS I READ THIS MANGA, I THOUGHT, "OHH, I WAS THINKING LIKE THIS IN THE EARLIER VOLUMES OF MY LIGHT NOVEL." IT MADE ME REMEMBER EARLIER DAYS AND I WANTED TO RE-READ MY OLDER VOLUMES.

BUT.

THIS MANGA HAS BECOME BETTER THAN THE ORIGINAL.

THERE WILL BE MORE MANGA TO COME, SO PLEASE READ THIS SERIES!

FROM THE AUTHOR, WHO HAS DEVELOPED BUDDING FEELINGS FOR ORANGUTANS.

I AM SERIOUSLY CONSIDERING A TRIP TO SINGAPORE TO PLAY WITH ORANGUTANS. (LOL!)

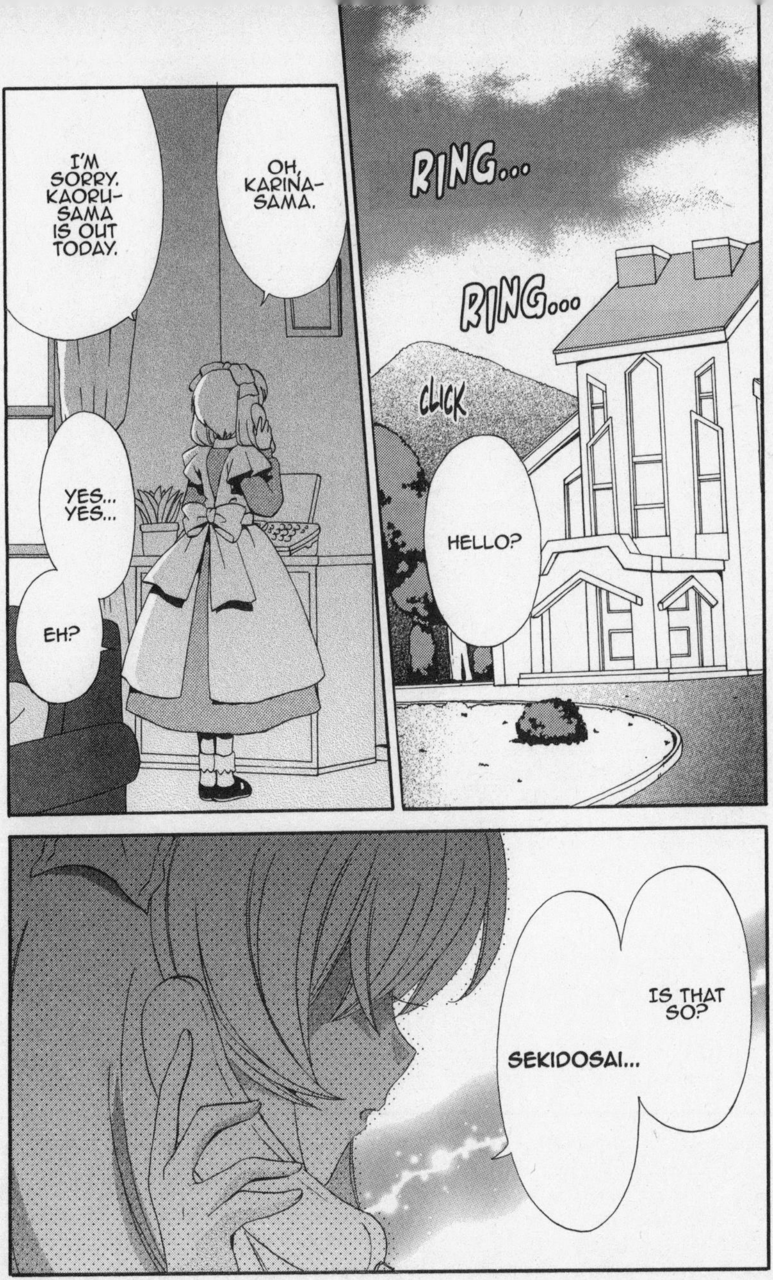
RING...
RING...
CLICK
HELLO?
OH, KARINA-SAMA.
I'M SORRY. KAORU-SAMA IS OUT TODAY.
YES... YES...
EH?
IS THAT SO?
SEKIDOSAI...

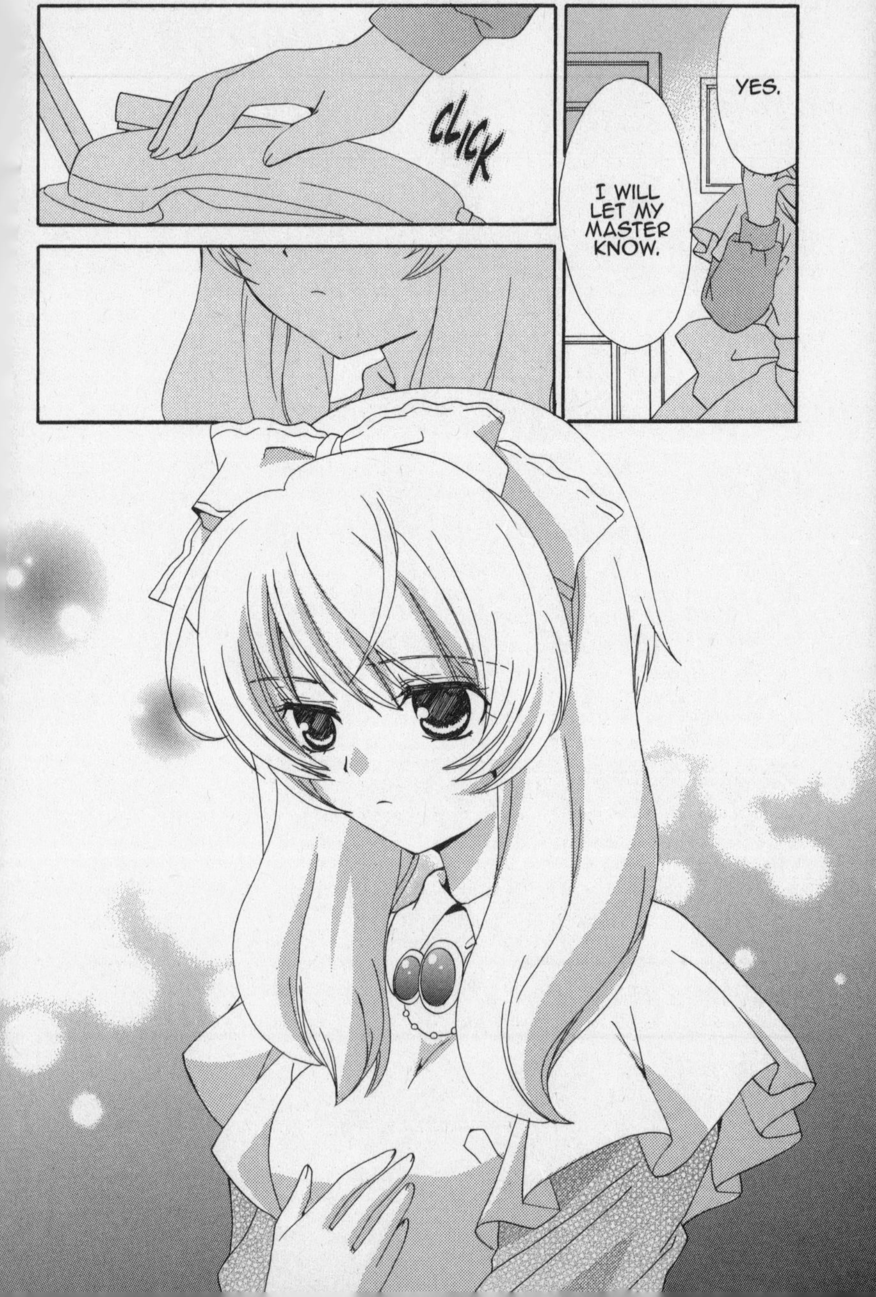
YES.
I WILL LET MY MASTER KNOW.
CLICK

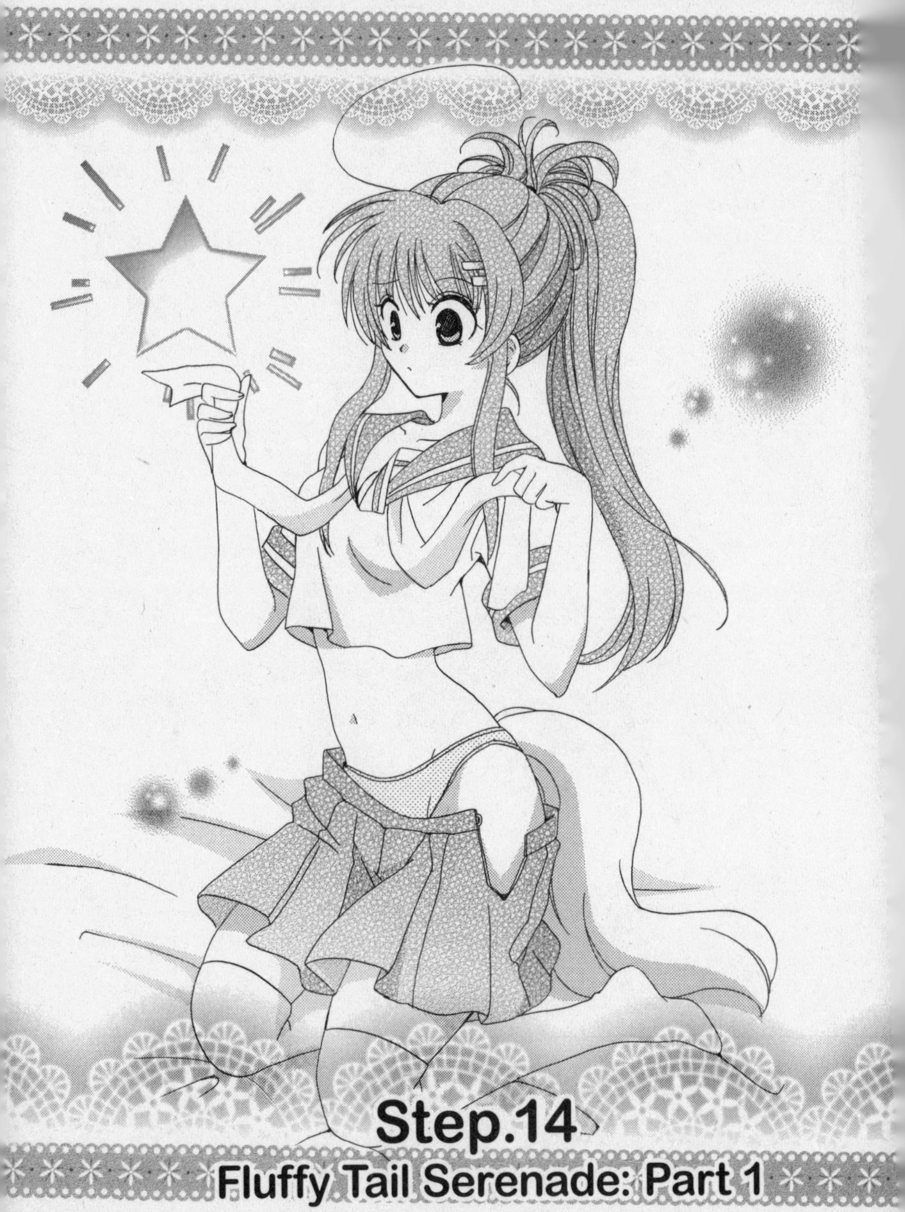

Step.14
Fluffy Tail Serenade: Part 1

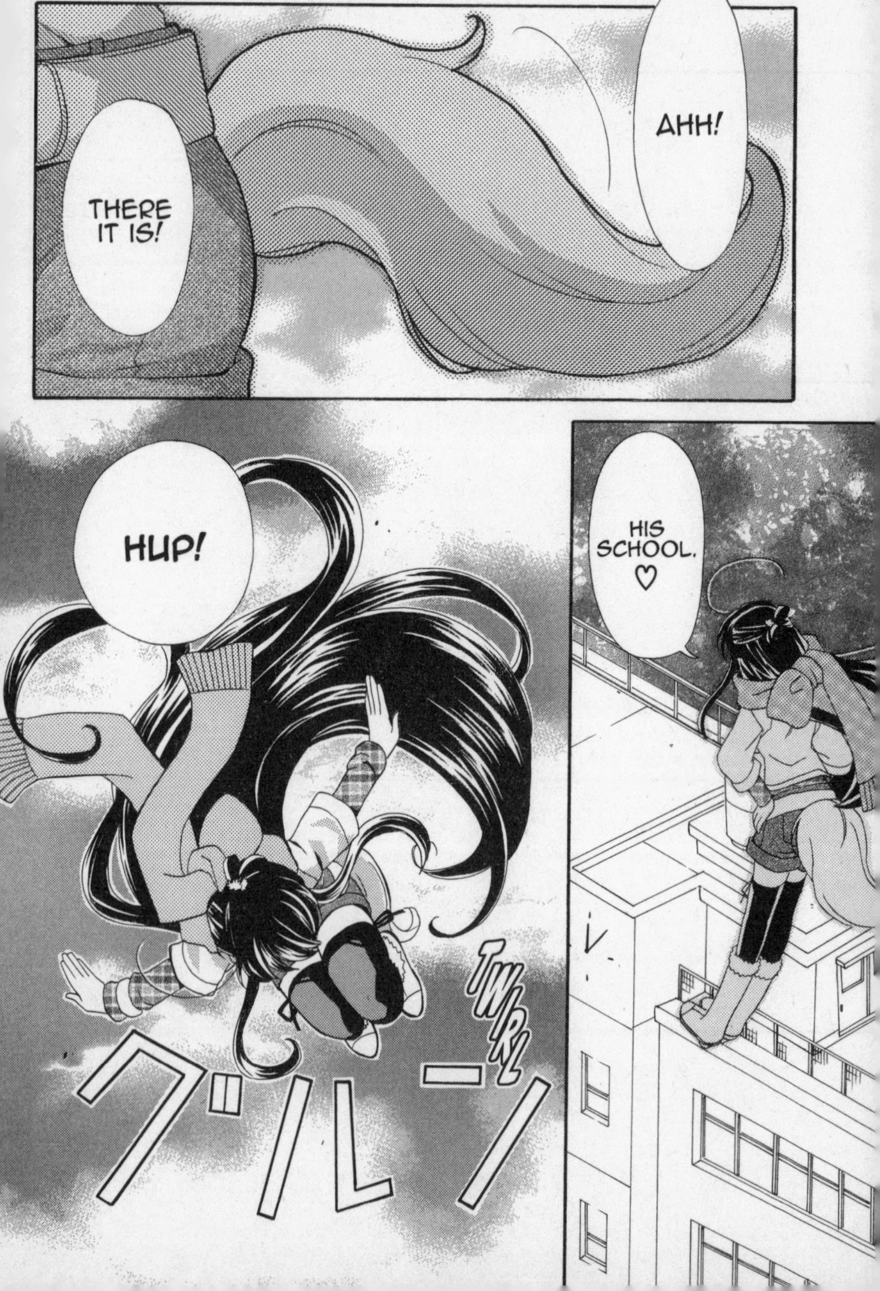
AHH!
THERE IT IS!
HIS SCHOOL. ♡
HUP!
TWIRL
グルーン

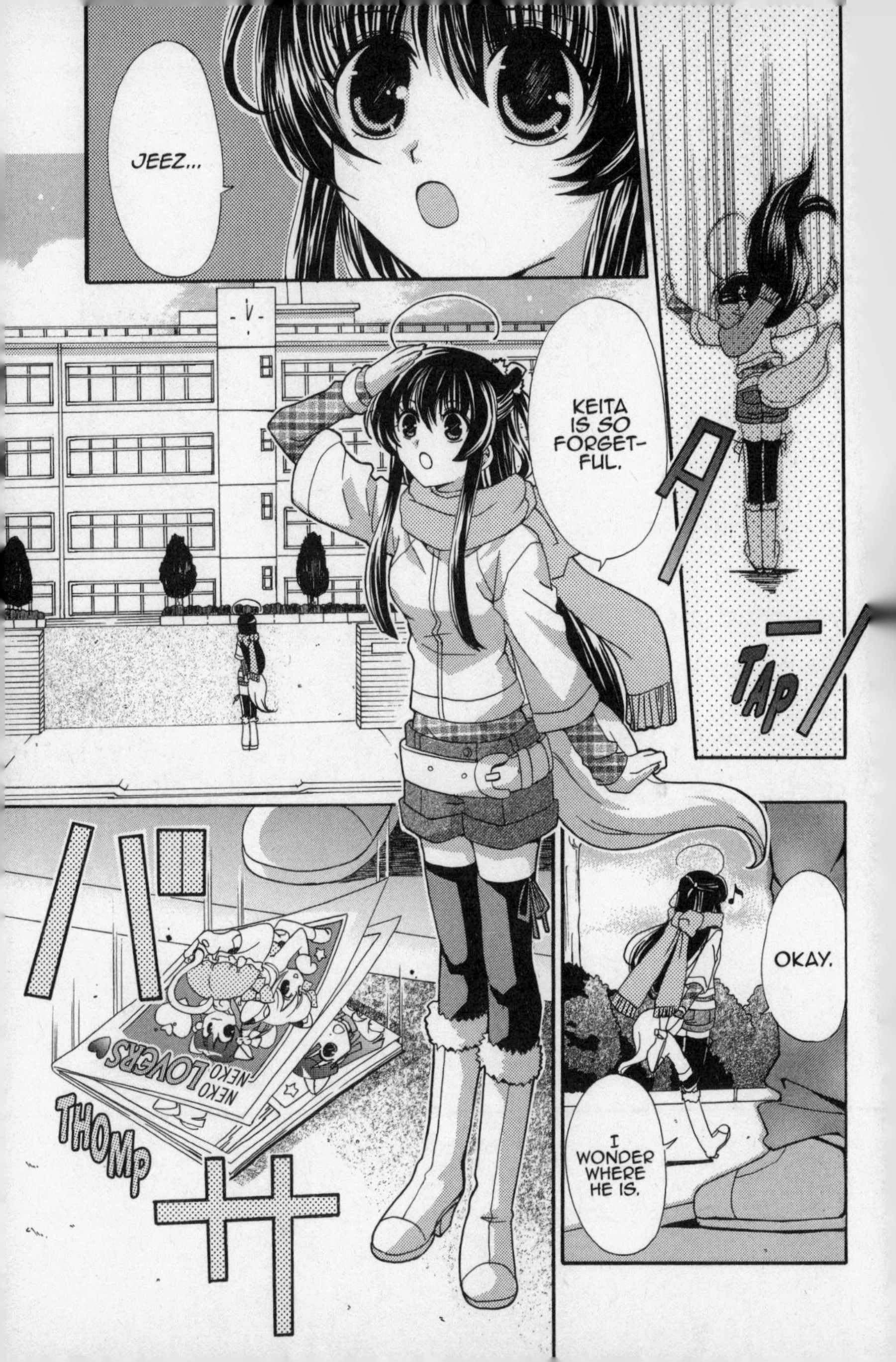
A
TAP
JEEZ...
KEITA IS SO FORGETFUL.
OKAY.
I WONDER WHERE HE IS.
NEKO NEKO LOVERS
THOMP

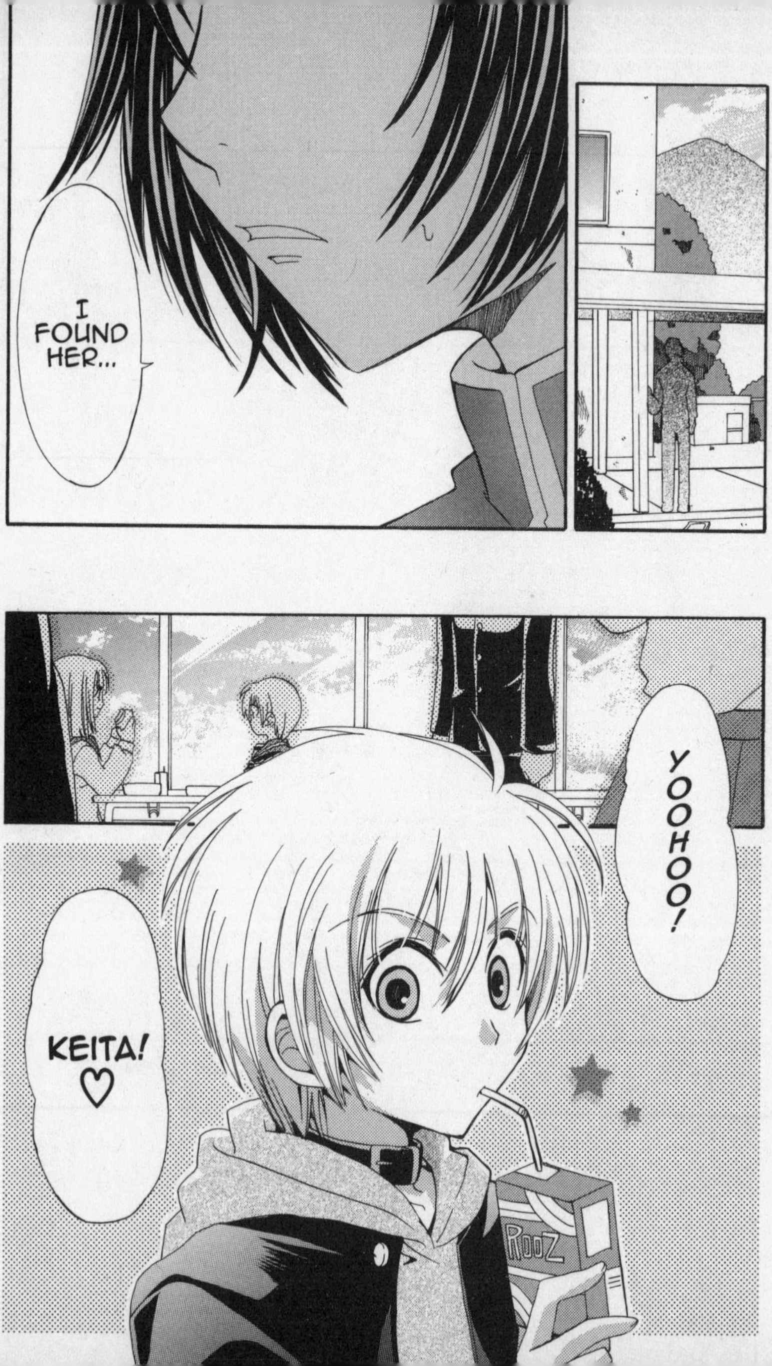
I FOUND HER...
YOOHOO!
KEITA! ♡

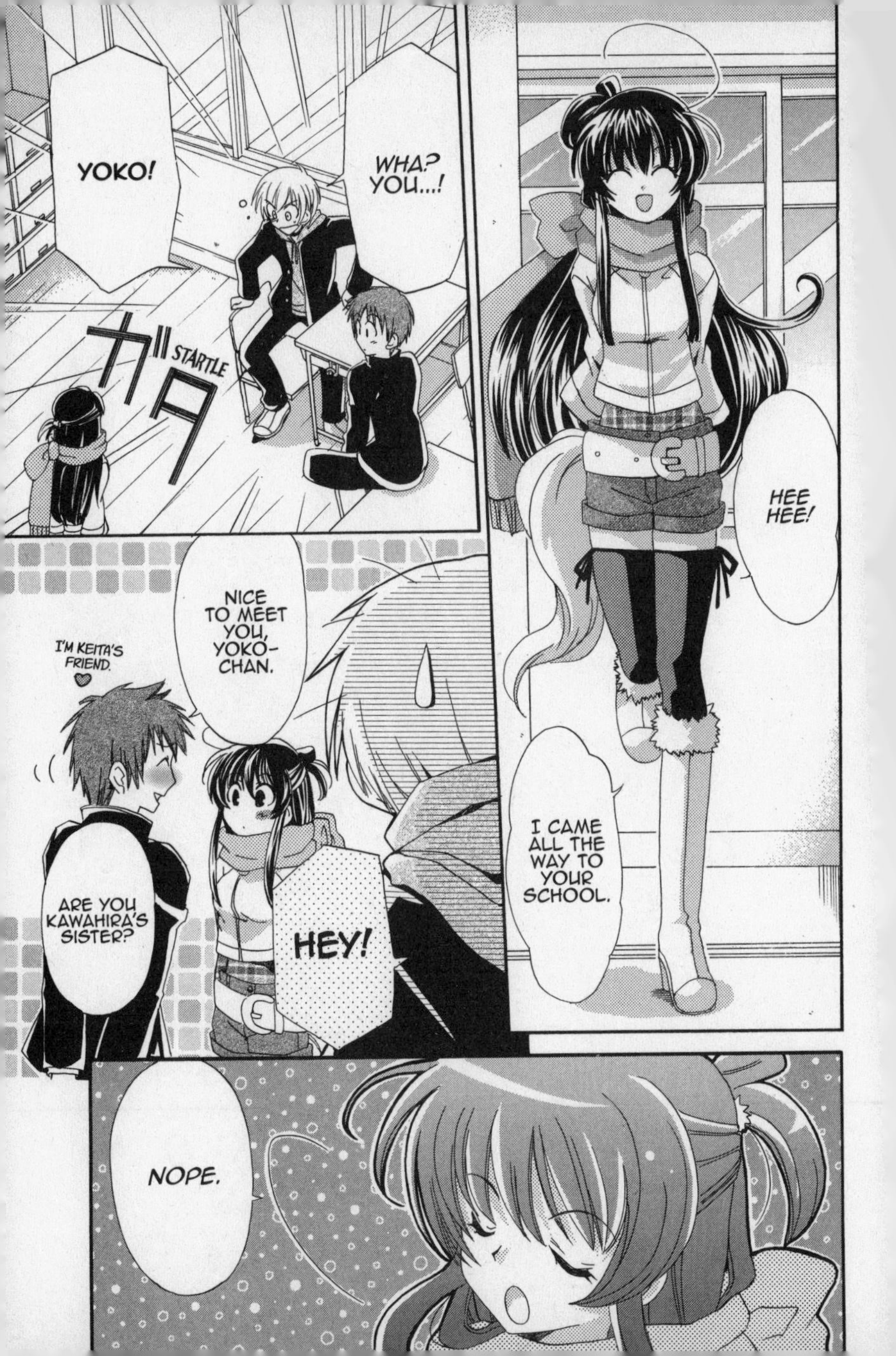
HEE HEE!
I CAME ALL THE WAY TO YOUR SCHOOL.
WHA? YOU...!
YOKO!
カタ STARTLE
NICE TO MEET YOU, YOKO-CHAN.
I'M KEITA'S FRIEND.
HEY!
ARE YOU KAWAHIRA'S SISTER?
NOPE.

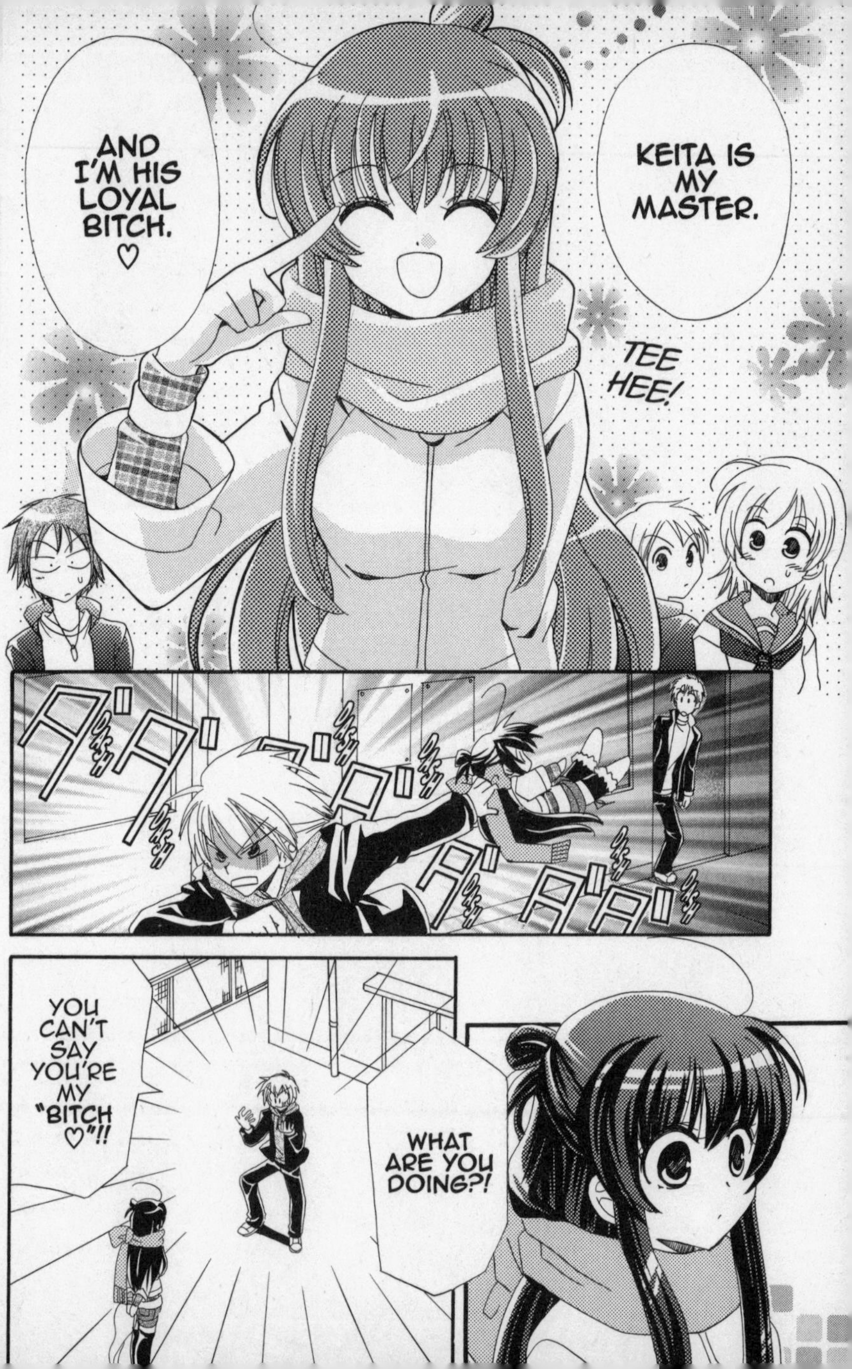
KEITA IS MY MASTER.
TEE HEE!
AND I'M HIS LOYAL BITCH. ♡
WHAT ARE YOU DOING?!
YOU CAN'T SAY YOU'RE MY "BITCH ♡"!!

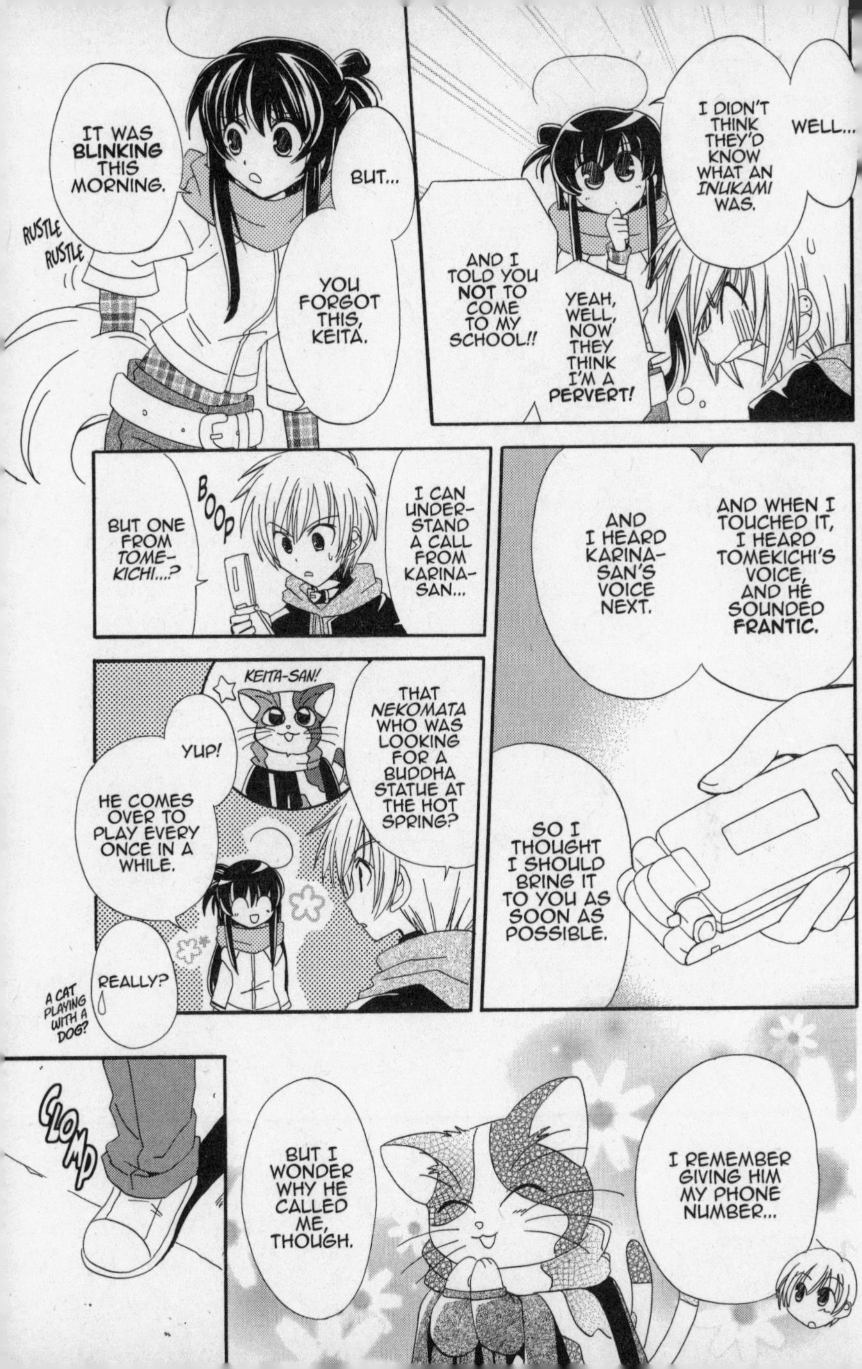

WELL...
I DIDN'T THINK THEY'D KNOW WHAT AN *INUKAMI* WAS.
YEAH, WELL, NOW THEY THINK I'M A PERVERT!
AND I TOLD YOU **NOT** TO COME TO MY SCHOOL!!
BUT...
IT WAS **BLINKING** THIS MORNING.
RUSTLE RUSTLE
YOU FORGOT THIS, KEITA.
AND WHEN I TOUCHED IT, I HEARD TOMEKICHI'S VOICE, AND HE SOUNDED **FRANTIC.**
AND I HEARD KARINA-SAN'S VOICE NEXT.
SO I THOUGHT I SHOULD BRING IT TO YOU AS SOON AS POSSIBLE.
I CAN UNDER-STAND A CALL FROM KARINA-SAN...
BOOP
BUT ONE FROM *TOME-KICHI*...?
THAT *NEKOMATA* WHO WAS LOOKING FOR A BUDDHA STATUE AT THE HOT SPRING?
KEITA-SAN!
YUP!
HE COMES OVER TO PLAY EVERY ONCE IN A WHILE.
REALLY?
A CAT PLAYING WITH A DOG?
I REMEMBER GIVING HIM MY PHONE NUMBER...
BUT I WONDER WHY HE CALLED ME, THOUGH.
CLOMP

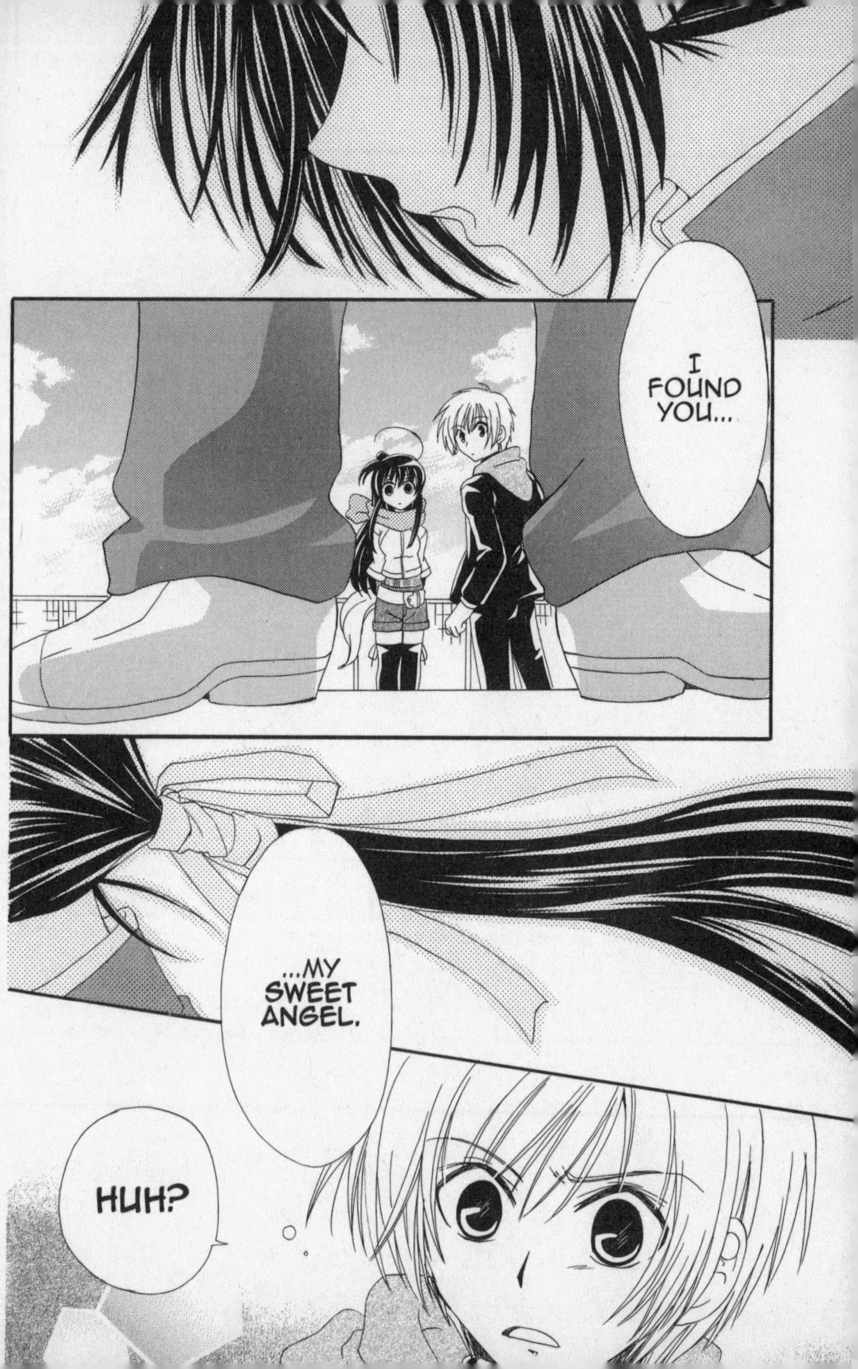

I FOUND YOU...
...MY SWEET ANGEL.
HUH?

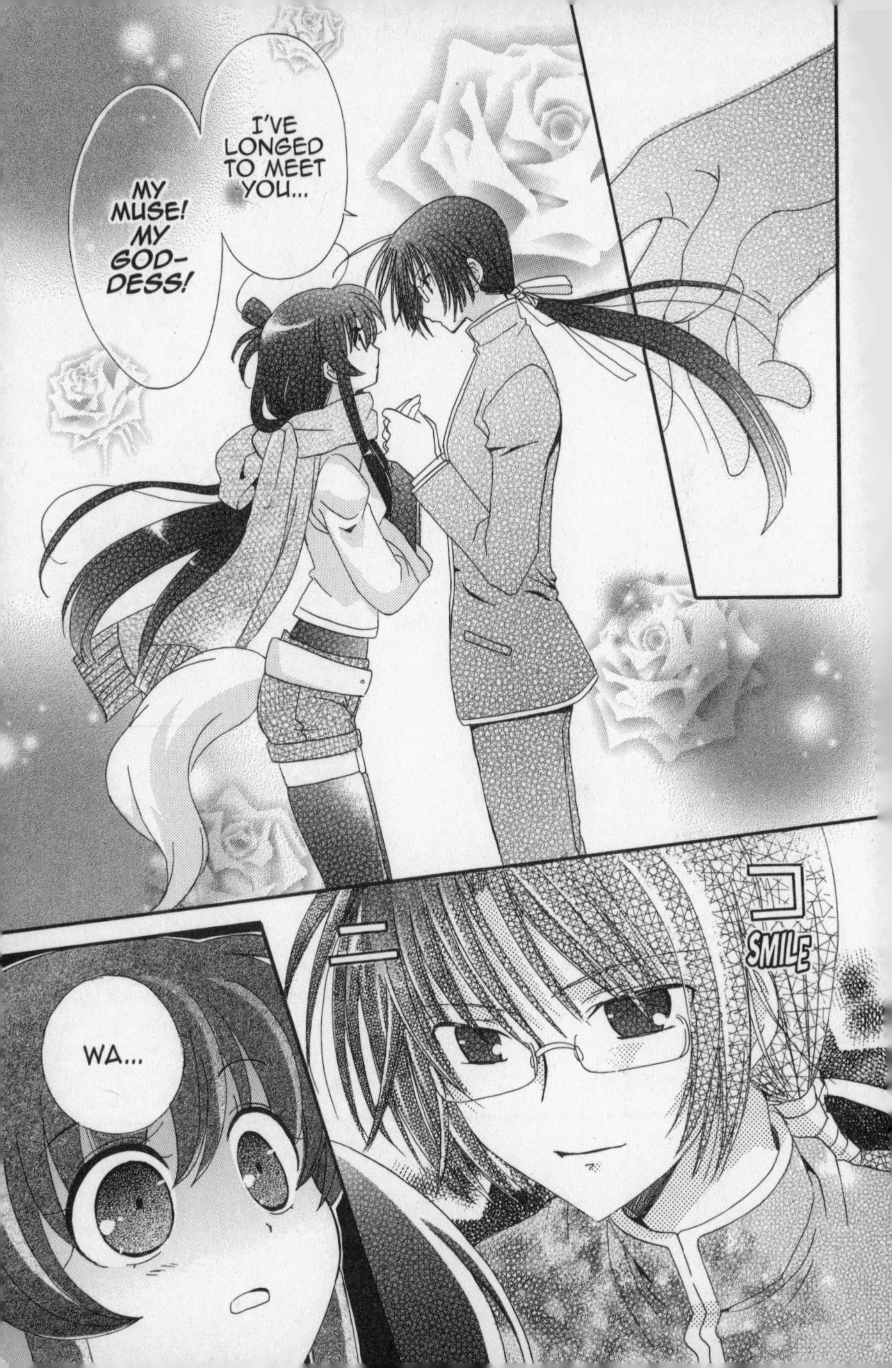
I'VE LONGED TO MEET YOU...
MY MUSE! MY GODDESS!
SMILE
WA...

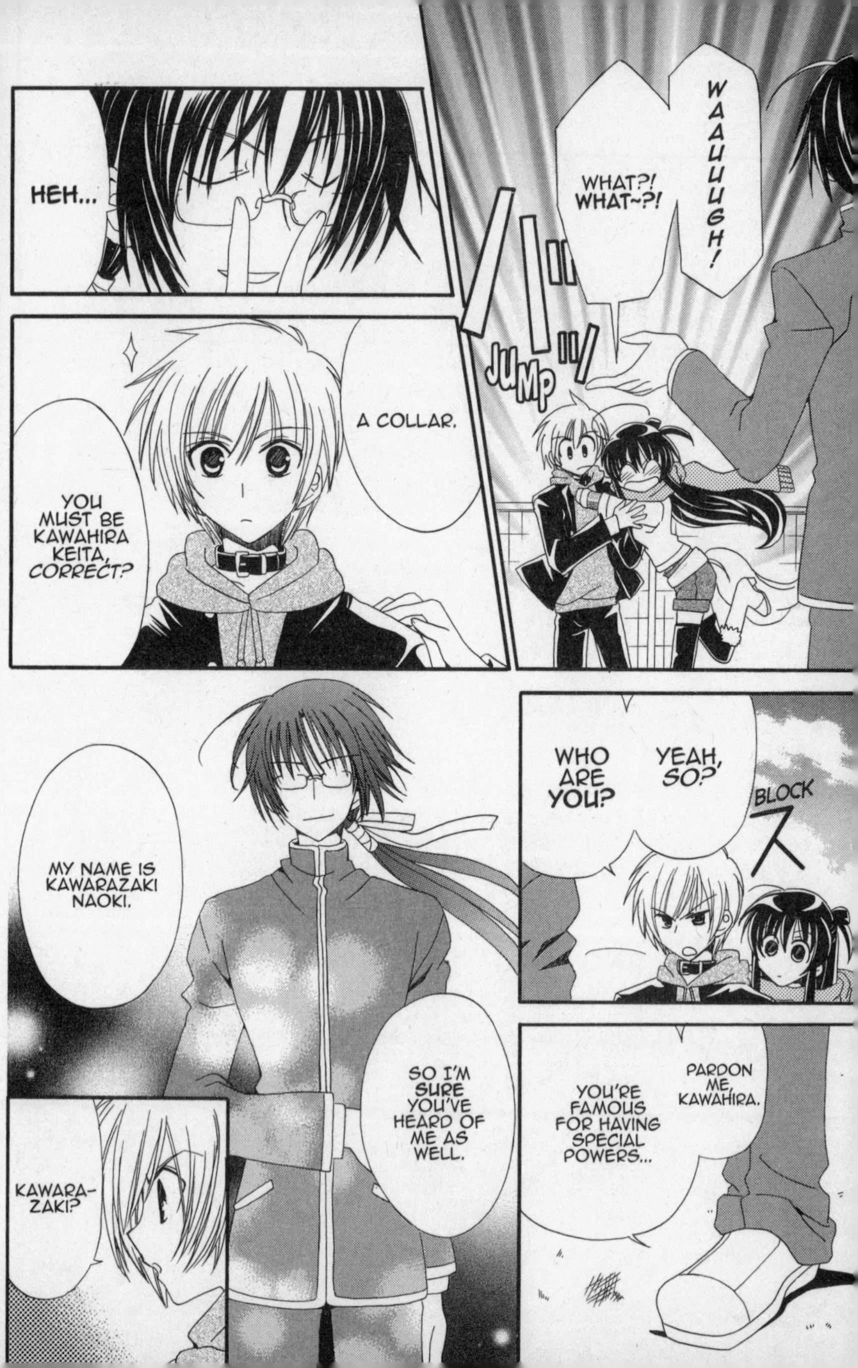
WAAUUUGH!
WHAT?! WHAT~?!
JUMP
HEH...
A COLLAR.
YOU MUST BE KAWAHIRA KEITA, CORRECT?
BLOCK
YEAH, SO?
WHO ARE YOU?
PARDON ME, KAWAHIRA.
YOU'RE FAMOUS FOR HAVING SPECIAL POWERS...
MY NAME IS KAWARAZAKI NAOKI.
SO I'M SURE YOU'VE HEARD OF ME AS WELL.
KAWARA-ZAKI?

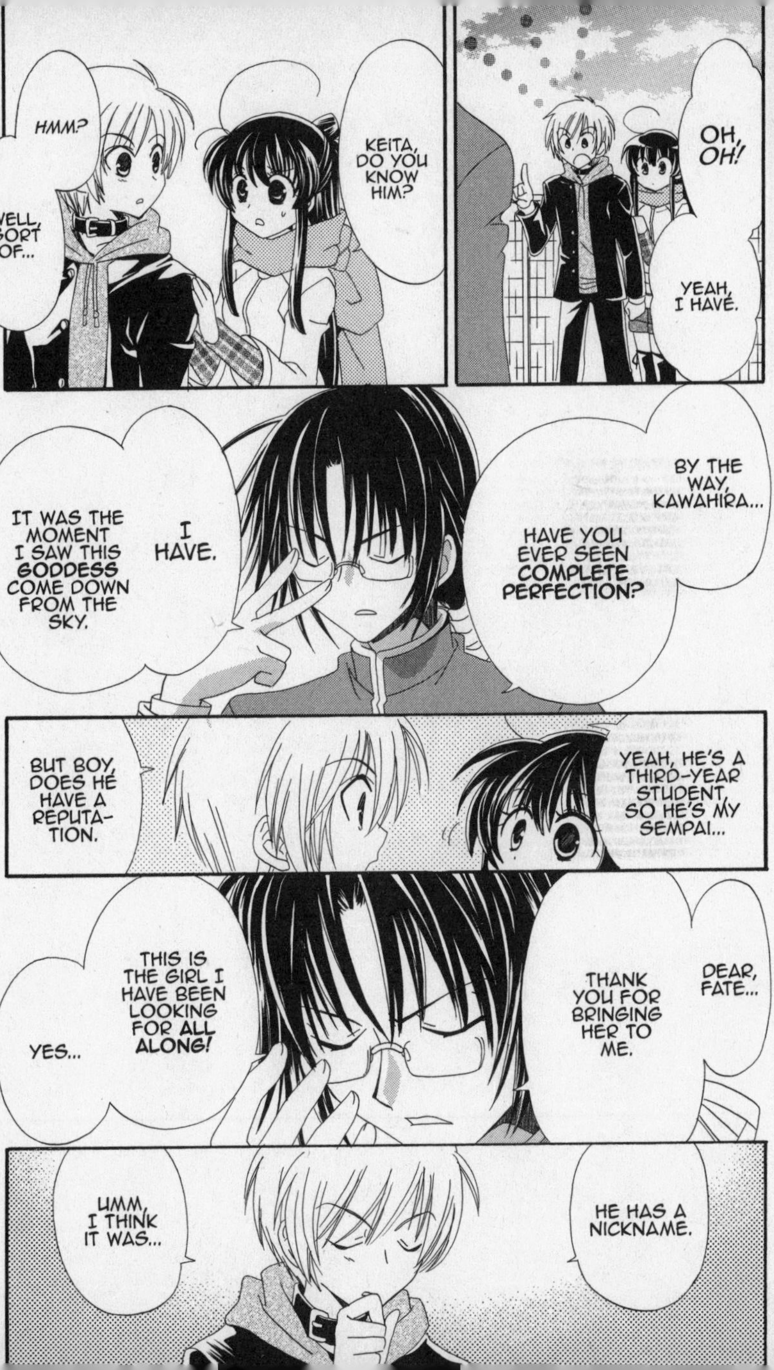
OH, OH!
YEAH, I HAVE.
KEITA, DO YOU KNOW HIM?
HMM?
WELL, SORT OF...
BY THE WAY, KAWAHIRA...
HAVE YOU EVER SEEN COMPLETE PERFECTION?
I HAVE.
IT WAS THE MOMENT I SAW THIS GODDESS COME DOWN FROM THE SKY.
YEAH, HE'S A THIRD-YEAR STUDENT, SO HE'S MY SEMPAI...
BUT BOY, DOES HE HAVE A REPUTATION.
DEAR, FATE...
THANK YOU FOR BRINGING HER TO ME.
THIS IS THE GIRL I HAVE BEEN LOOKING FOR ALL ALONG!
YES...
HE HAS A NICKNAME.
UMM, I THINK IT WAS...

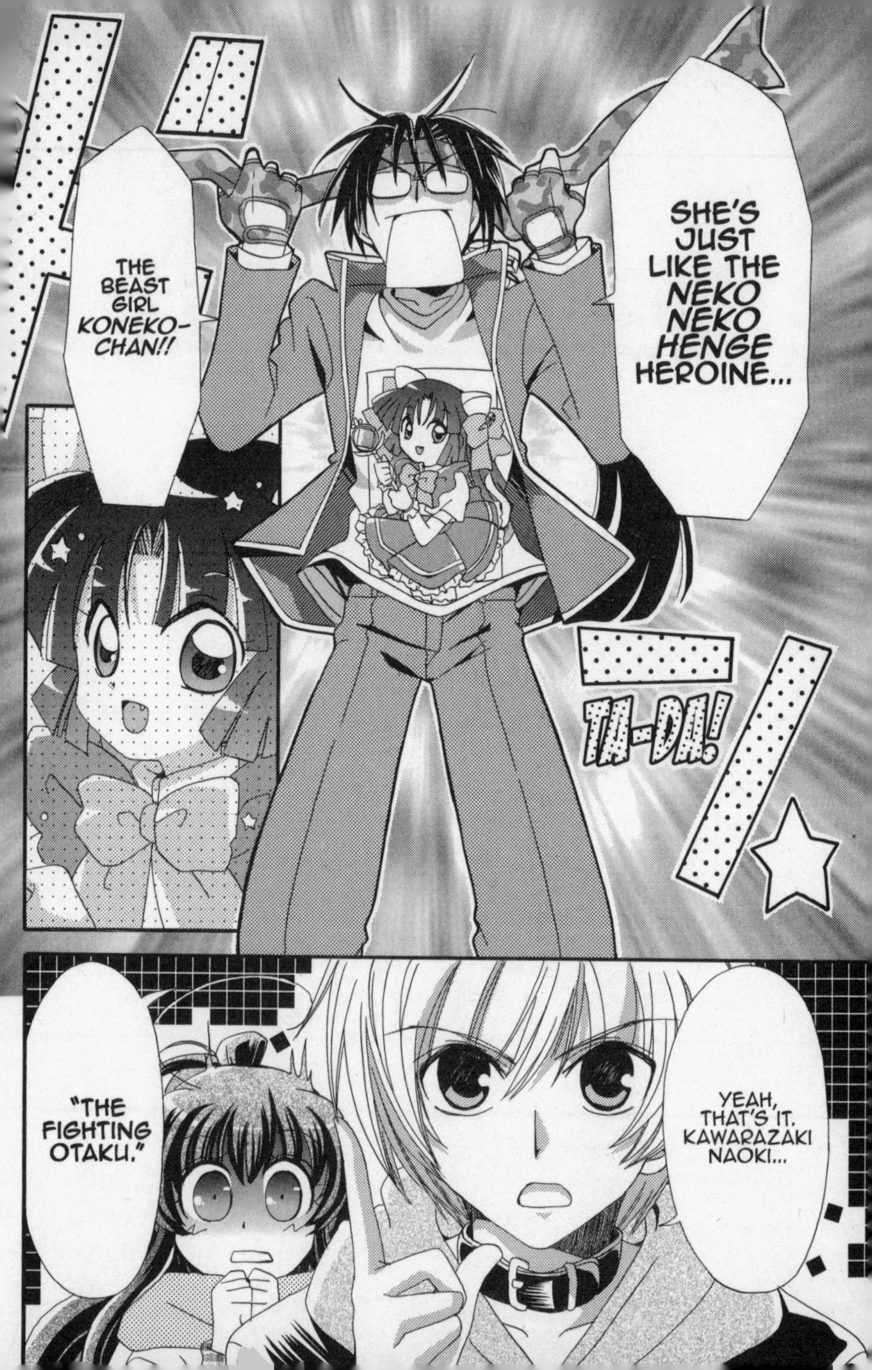
SHE'S JUST LIKE THE NEKO NEKO HENGE HEROINE...
THE BEAST GIRL KONEKO-CHAN!!
TA-DA!
YEAH, THAT'S IT. KAWARAZAKI NAOKI...
"THE FIGHTING OTAKU."

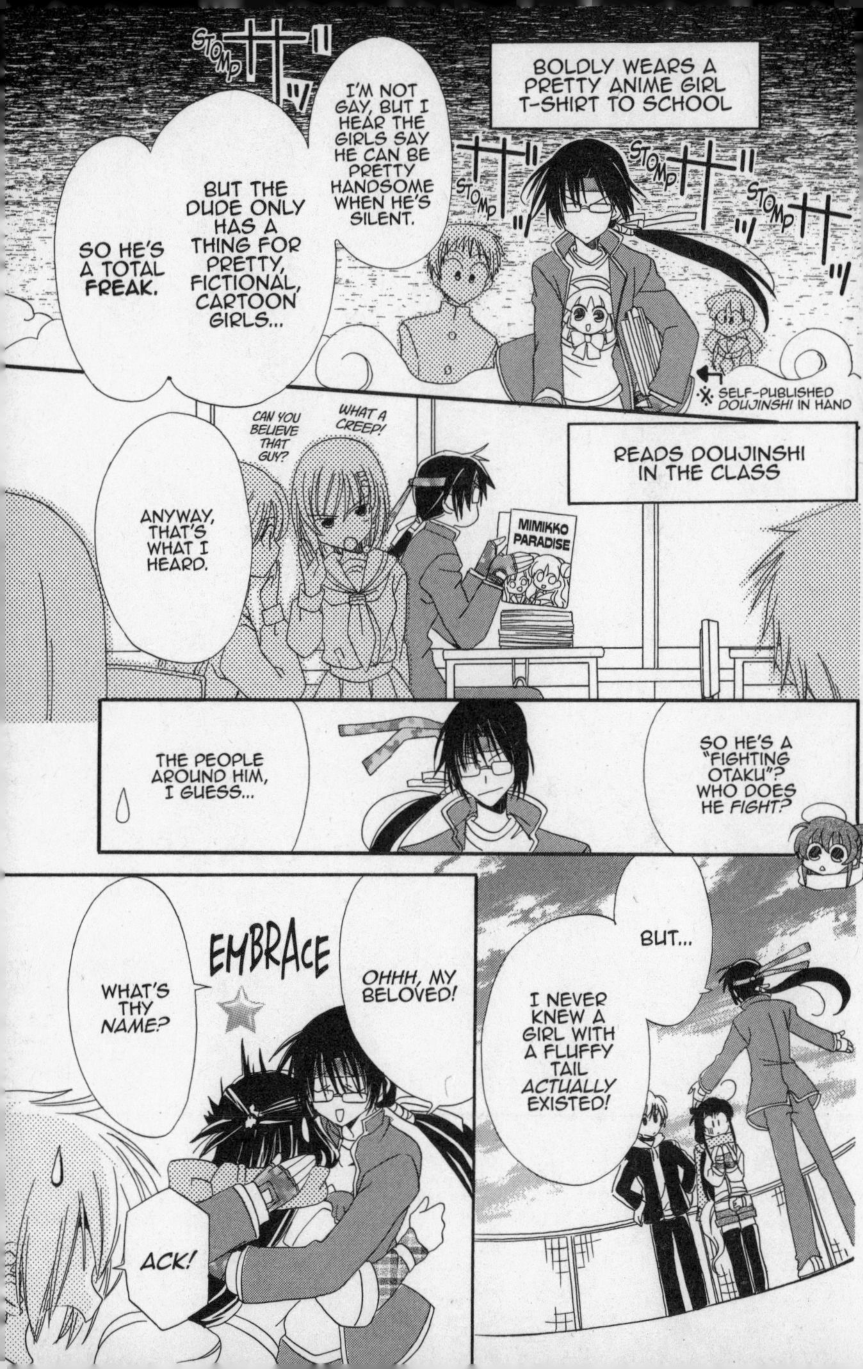
BOLDLY WEARS A PRETTY ANIME GIRL T-SHIRT TO SCHOOL
STOMP
STOMP
STOMP
STOMP
I'M NOT GAY, BUT I HEAR THE GIRLS SAY HE CAN BE PRETTY HANDSOME WHEN HE'S SILENT.
BUT THE DUDE ONLY HAS A THING FOR PRETTY, FICTIONAL, CARTOON GIRLS...
SO HE'S A TOTAL FREAK.
※ SELF-PUBLISHED DOUJINSHI IN HAND
READS DOUJINSHI IN THE CLASS
MIMIKKO PARADISE
WHAT A CREEP!
CAN YOU BELIEVE THAT GUY?
ANYWAY, THAT'S WHAT I HEARD.
SO HE'S A "FIGHTING OTAKU"? WHO DOES HE FIGHT?
THE PEOPLE AROUND HIM, I GUESS...
BUT...
I NEVER KNEW A GIRL WITH A FLUFFY TAIL ACTUALLY EXISTED!
OHHH, MY BELOVED!
EMBRACE
WHAT'S THY NAME?
ACK!

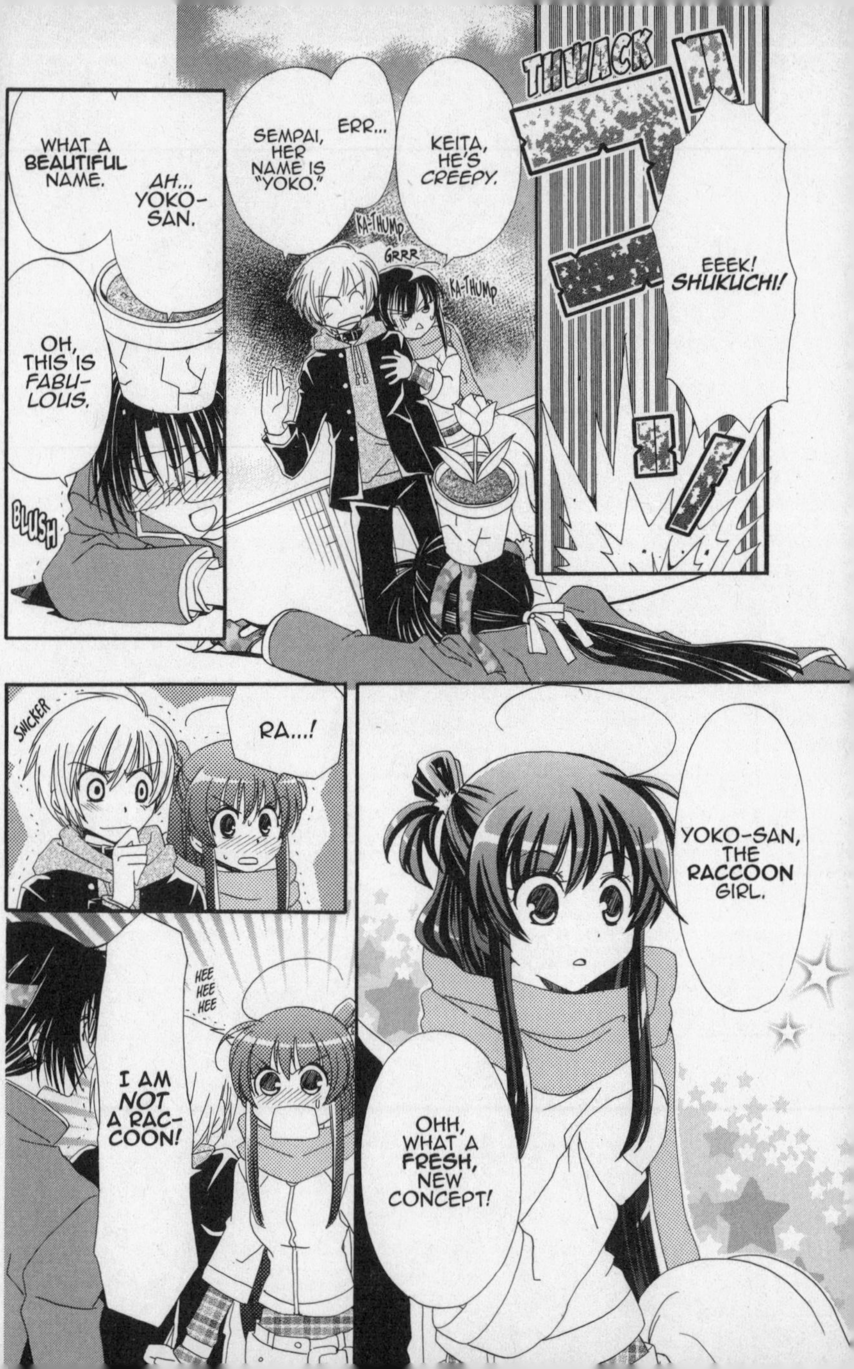
THWACK
EEEK! SHUKUCHI!
KEITA, HE'S CREEPY.
ERR...
SEMPAI, HER NAME IS "YOKO."
KA-THUMP
GRRR
KA-THUMP
AH... YOKO-SAN.
WHAT A BEAUTIFUL NAME.
OH, THIS IS FABULOUS.
BLUSH
YOKO-SAN, THE RACCOON GIRL.
OHH, WHAT A FRESH, NEW CONCEPT!
RA...!
SNICKER
I AM NOT A RACCOON!
HEE HEE HEE

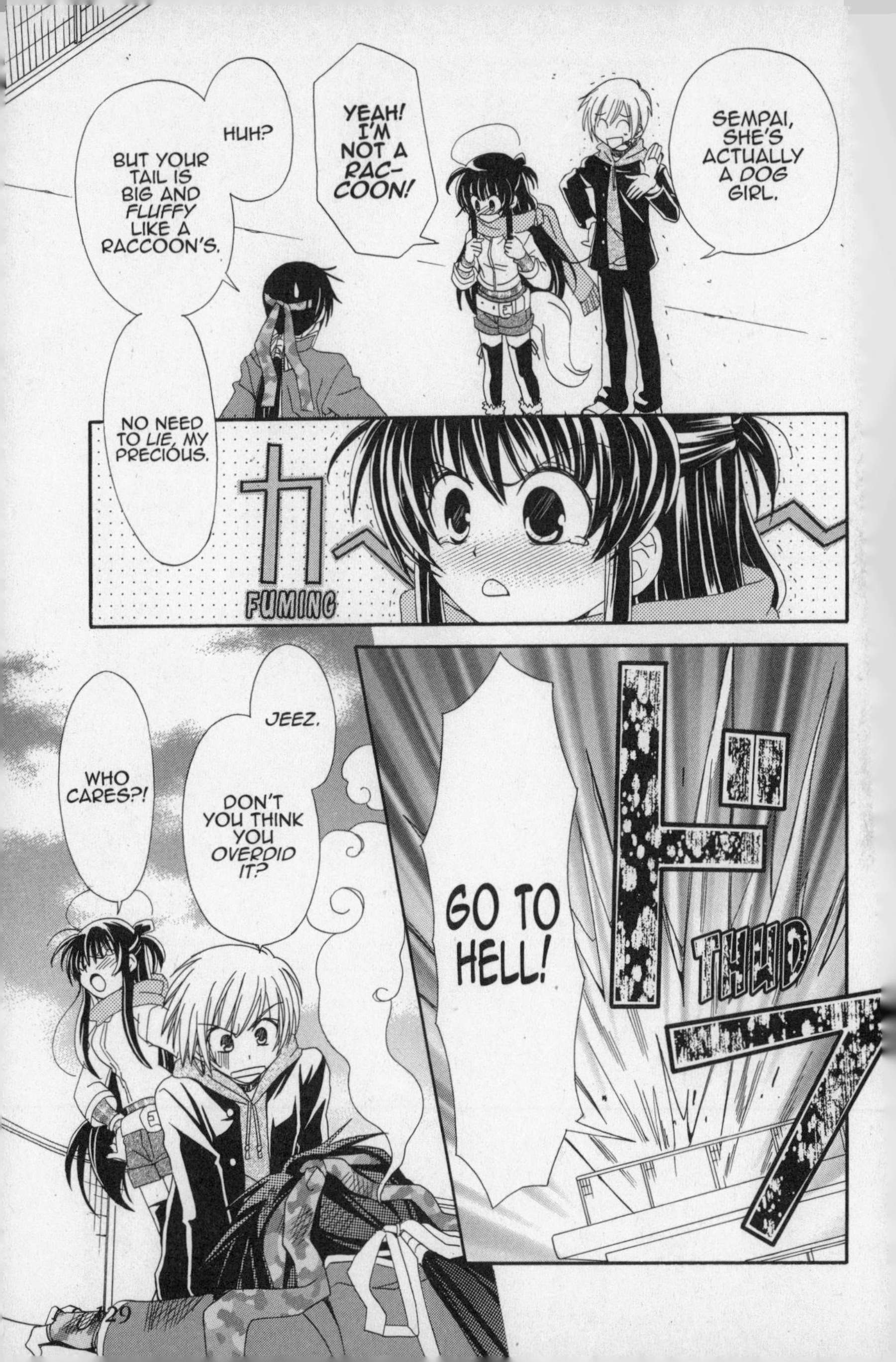
SEMPAI, SHE'S ACTUALLY A DOG GIRL.
YEAH! I'M NOT A RAC-COON!
HUH?
BUT YOUR TAIL IS BIG AND FLUFFY LIKE A RACCOON'S.
NO NEED TO LIE, MY PRECIOUS.
FUMING
GO TO HELL!
THUD
JEEZ.
DON'T YOU THINK YOU OVERDID IT?
WHO CARES?!

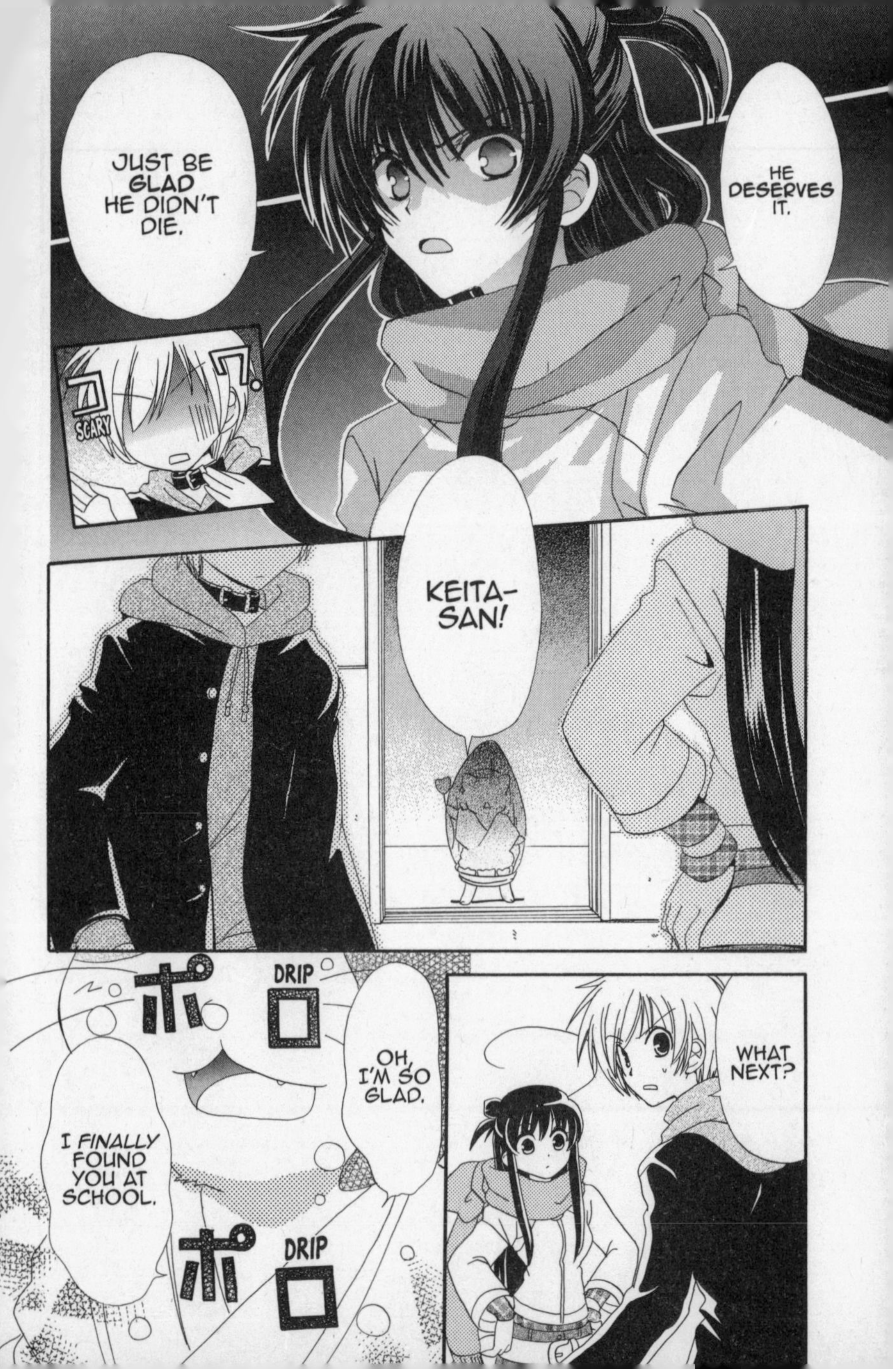
HE DESERVES IT.
JUST BE GLAD HE DIDN'T DIE.
コワ
SCARY
KEITA-SAN!
WHAT NEXT?
ポロ
DRIP
OH, I'M SO GLAD.
I FINALLY FOUND YOU AT SCHOOL.
ポロ
DRIP

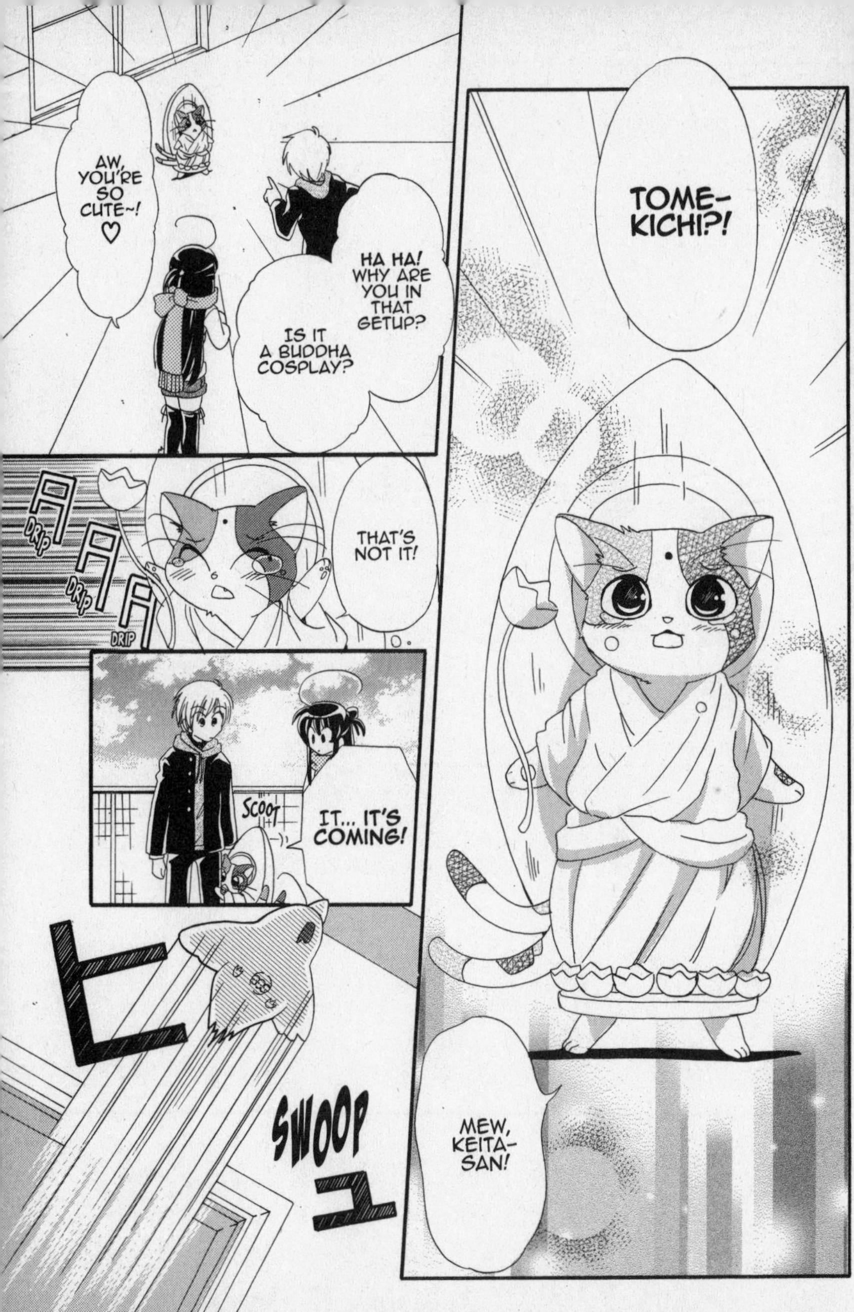
HA HA! WHY ARE YOU IN THAT GETUP?
IS IT A BUDDHA COSPLAY?
AW, YOU'RE SO CUTE~! ♡
THAT'S NOT IT!
DRIP DRIP DRIP
IT... IT'S COMING!
SCOOT
SWOOP
TOME-KICHI?!
MEW, KEITA-SAN!

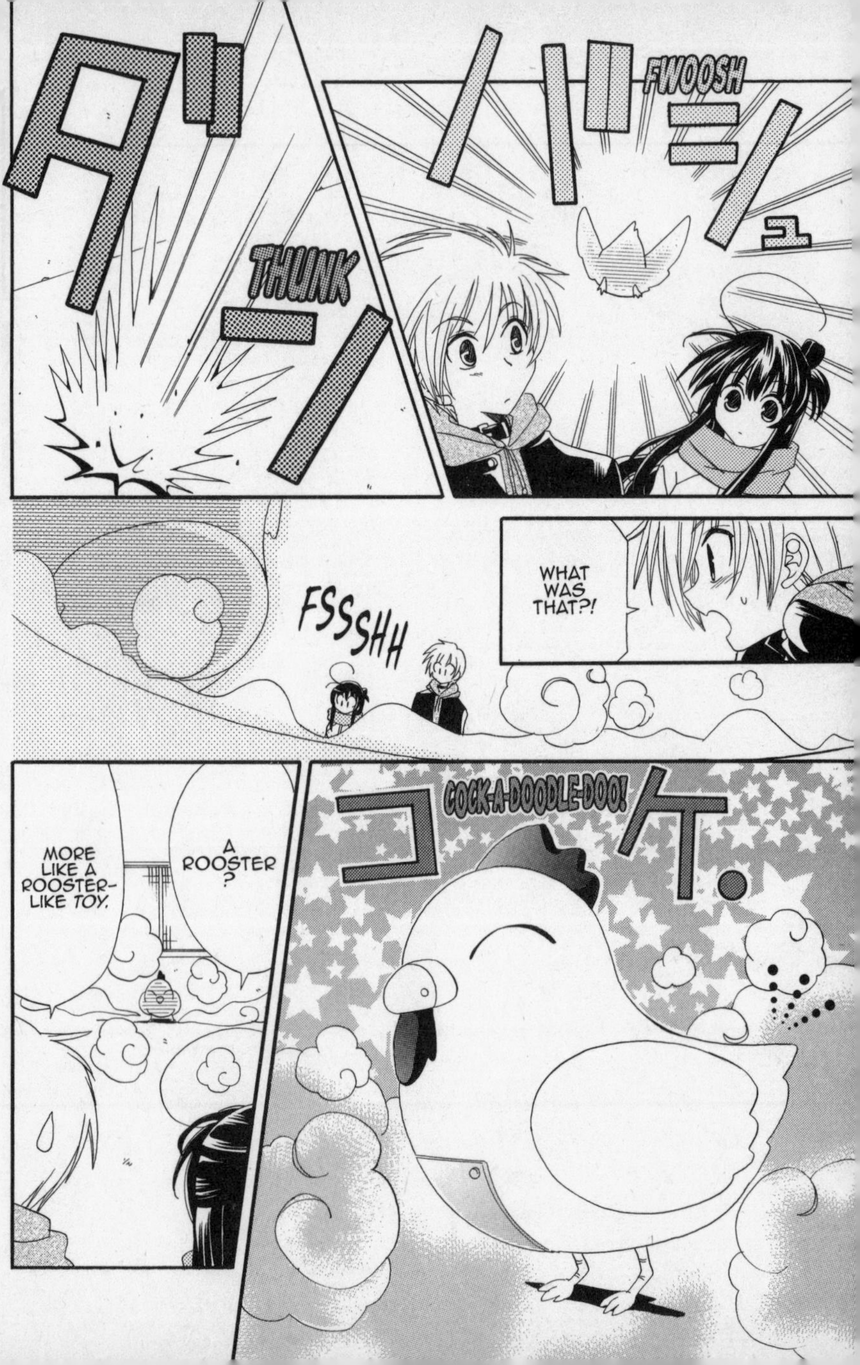

FWOOSH
THUNK
WHAT WAS THAT?!
FSSSHH
COCK-A-DOODLE-DOO!
A ROOSTER?
MORE LIKE A ROOSTER-LIKE TOY.

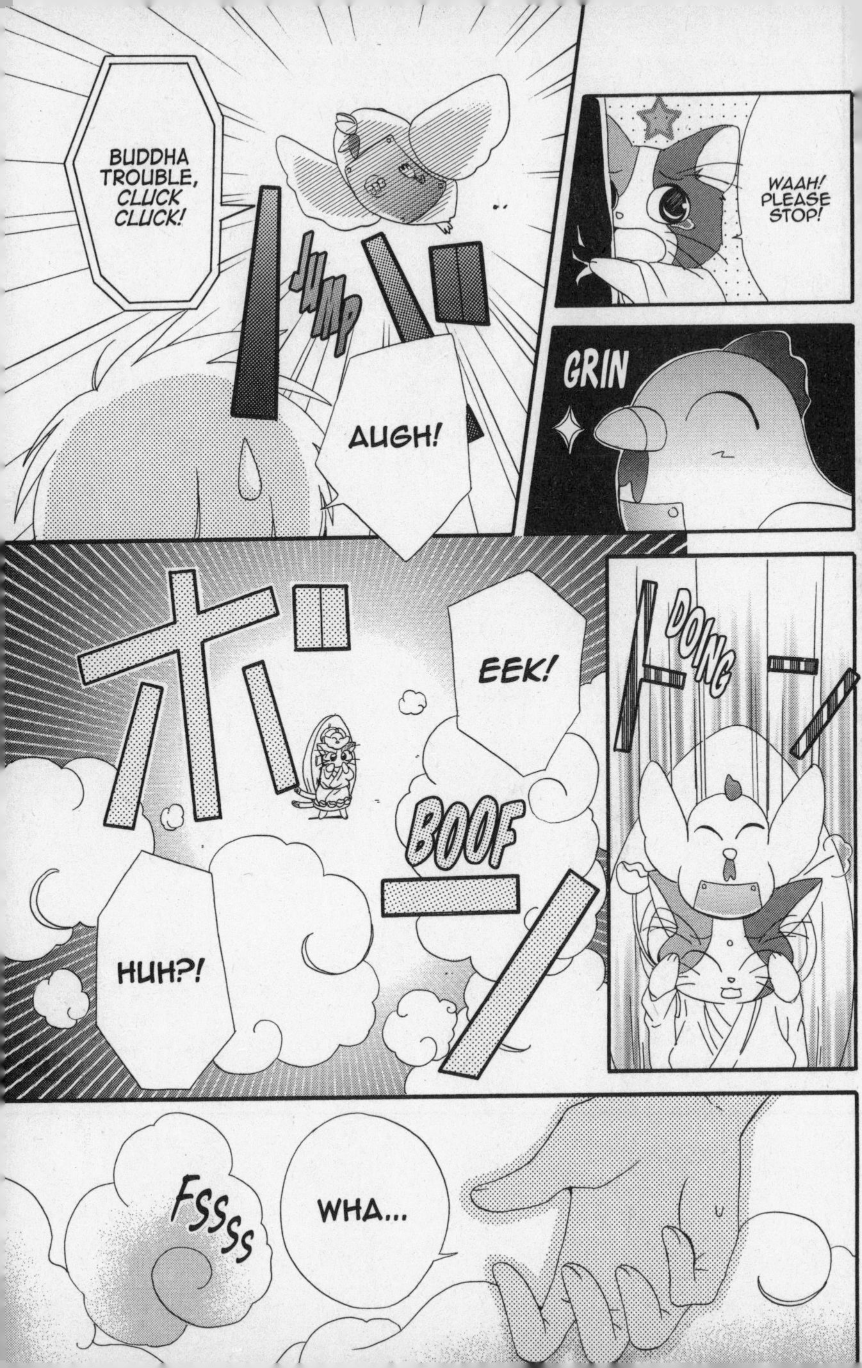
WAAH! PLEASE STOP!
GRIN
BUDDHA TROUBLE, CLUCK CLUCK!
JUMP
AUGH!
DOING
EEK!
BOOF
HUH?!
WHA...
FSSSS

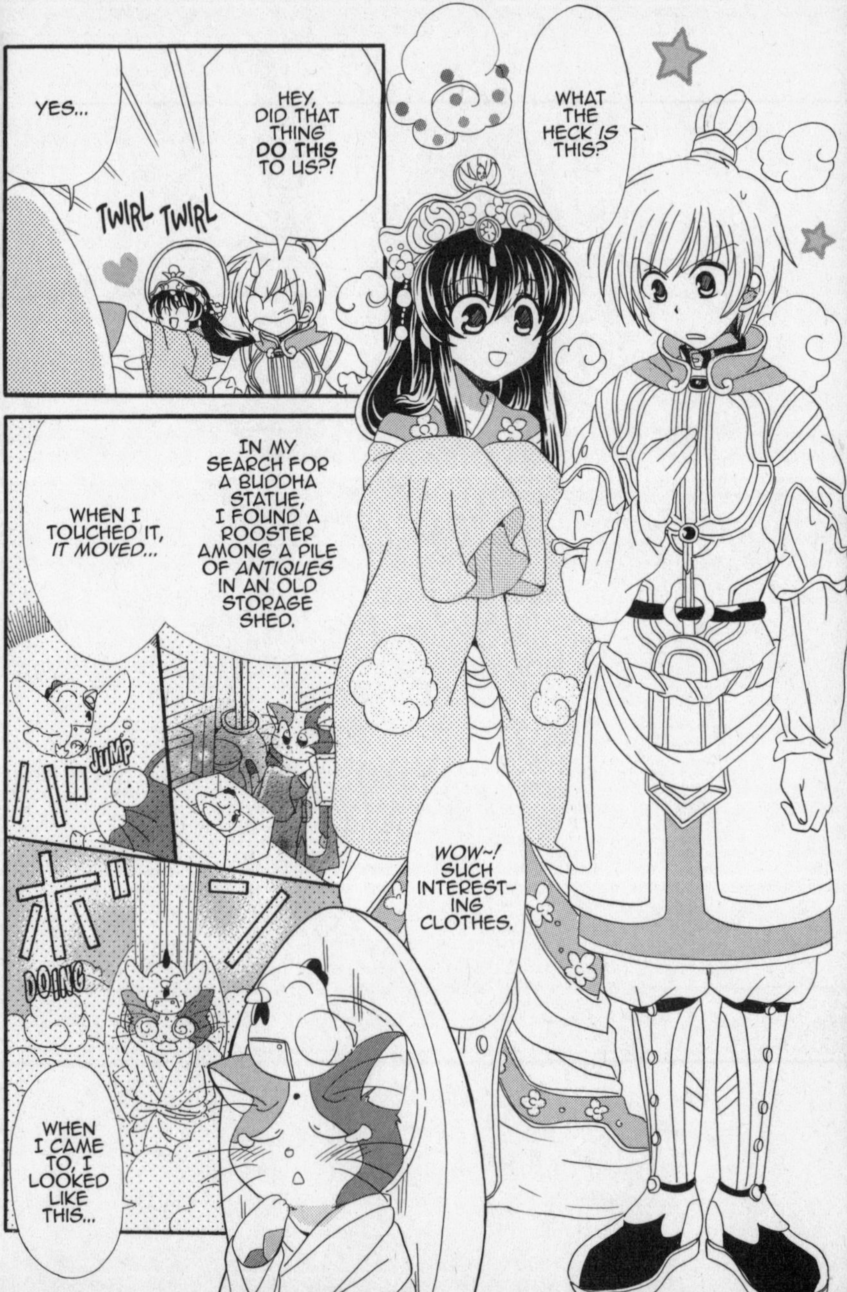
WHAT THE HECK *IS* THIS?
WOW~! SUCH INTERESTING CLOTHES.
HEY, DID THAT THING DO THIS TO US?!
YES...
TWIRL TWIRL
IN MY SEARCH FOR A BUDDHA STATUE, I FOUND A ROOSTER AMONG A PILE OF *ANTIQUES* IN AN OLD STORAGE SHED.
WHEN I TOUCHED IT, *IT MOVED...*
JUMP
DOING
WHEN I CAME TO, I LOOKED LIKE THIS...

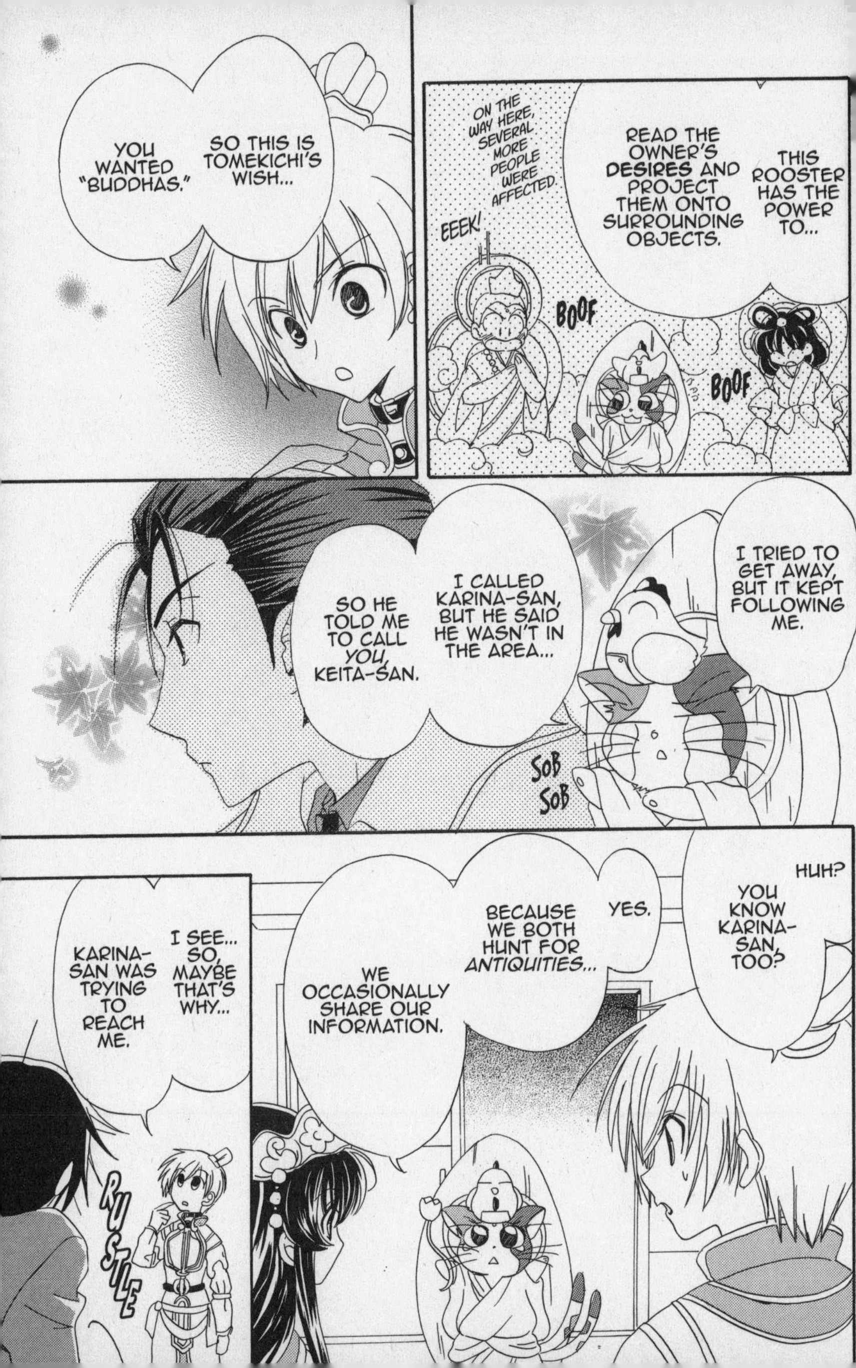
THIS ROOSTER HAS THE POWER TO...
READ THE OWNER'S **DESIRES** AND PROJECT THEM ONTO SURROUNDING OBJECTS.
ON THE WAY HERE, SEVERAL MORE PEOPLE WERE AFFECTED.
EEEK!
BOOF
BOOF
SO THIS IS TOMEKICHI'S WISH...
YOU WANTED "BUDDHAS."
I TRIED TO GET AWAY, BUT IT KEPT FOLLOWING ME.
SOB SOB
I CALLED KARINA-SAN, BUT HE SAID HE WASN'T IN THE AREA...
SO HE TOLD ME TO CALL *YOU*, KEITA-SAN.
HUH?
YOU KNOW KARINA-SAN, TOO?
YES.
BECAUSE WE BOTH HUNT FOR *ANTIQUITIES*...
WE OCCASIONALLY SHARE OUR INFORMATION.
I SEE... SO, MAYBE THAT'S WHY...
KARINA-SAN WAS TRYING TO REACH ME.
RUSTLE

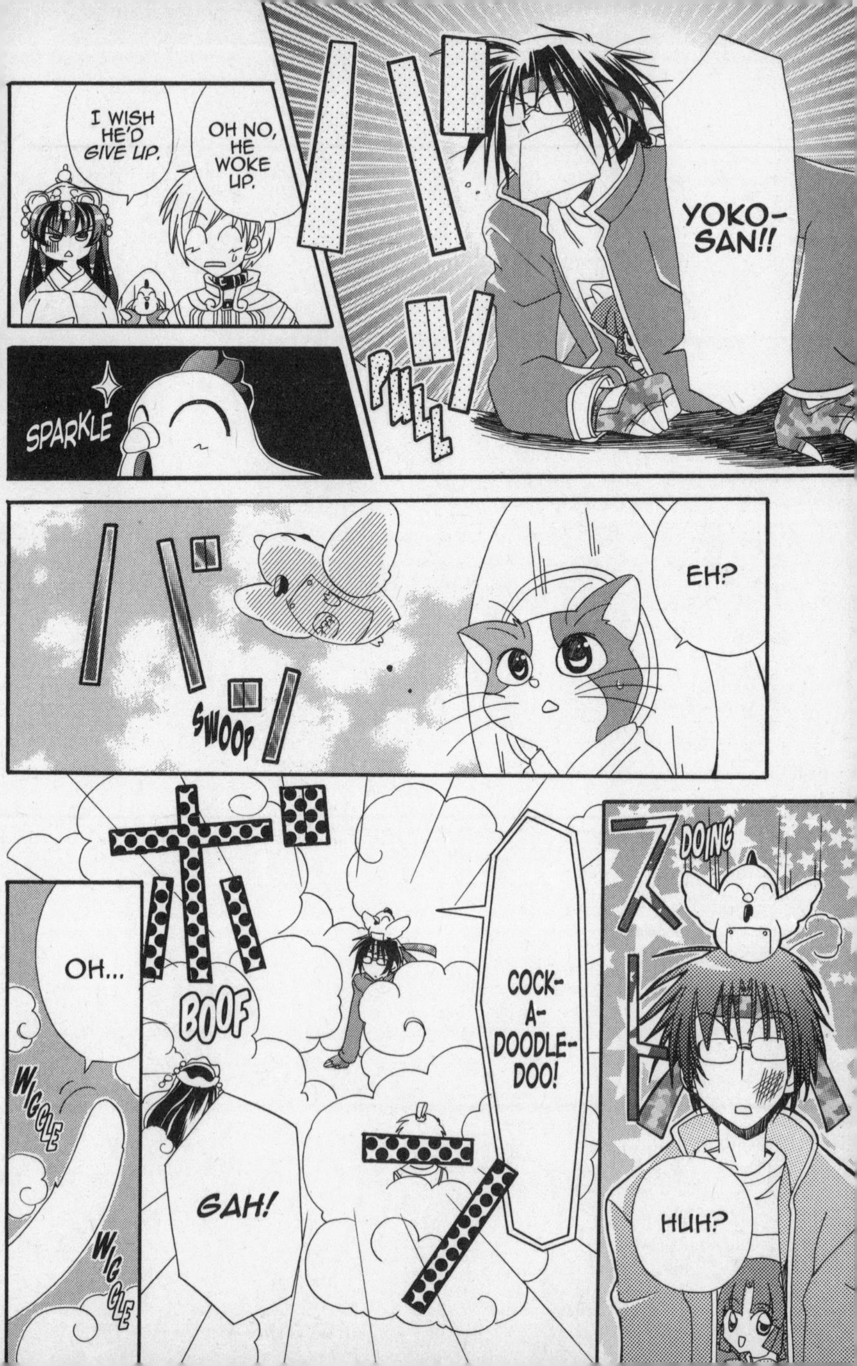
YOKO-SAN!!
PULL
OH NO, HE WOKE UP.
I WISH HE'D GIVE UP.
SPARKLE
EH?
SWOOP
DOING
HUH?
COCK-A-DOODLE-DOO!
BOOF
GAH!
OH...
WIGGLE
WIGGLE

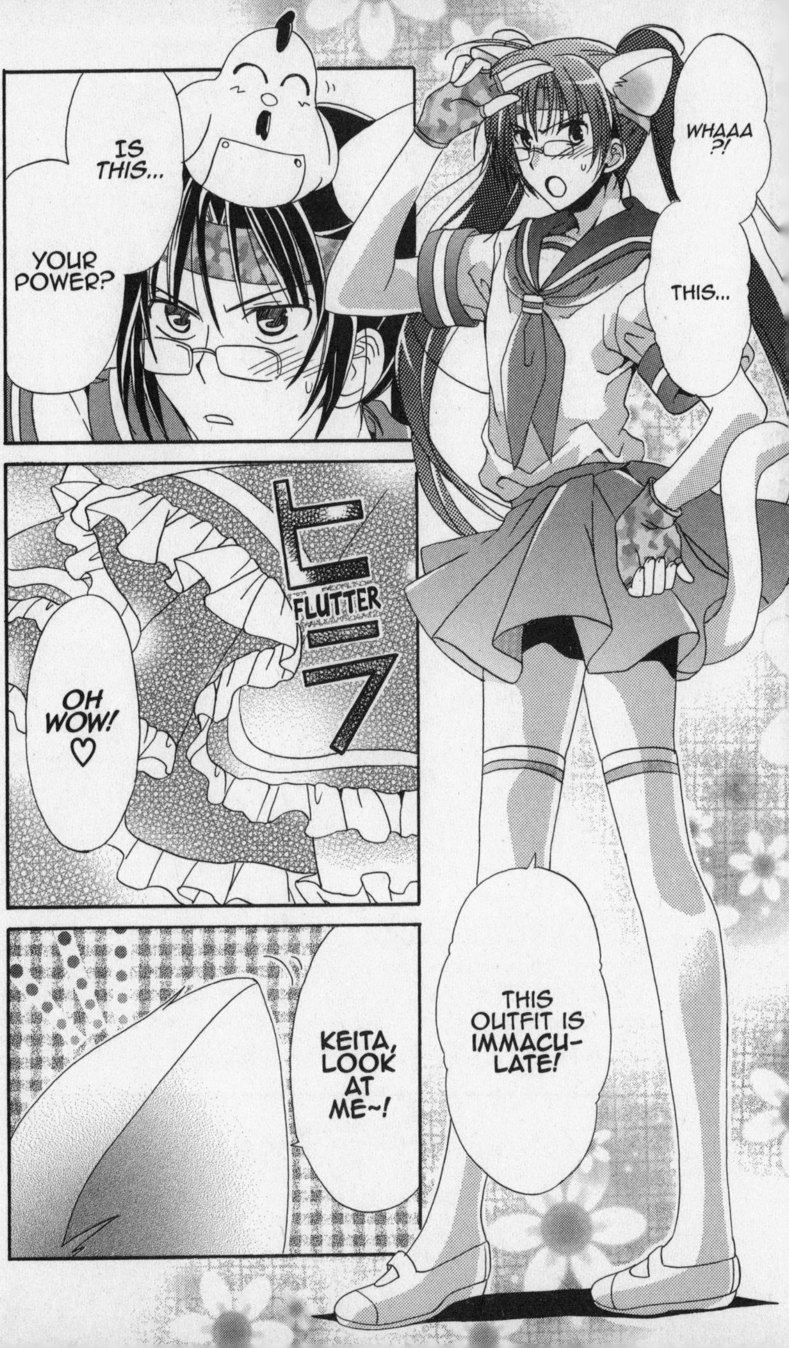
WHAAA ?!
THIS...
THIS OUTFIT IS IMMACU-LATE!
IS THIS...
YOUR POWER?
FLUTTER
OH WOW! ♡
KEITA, LOOK AT ME~!

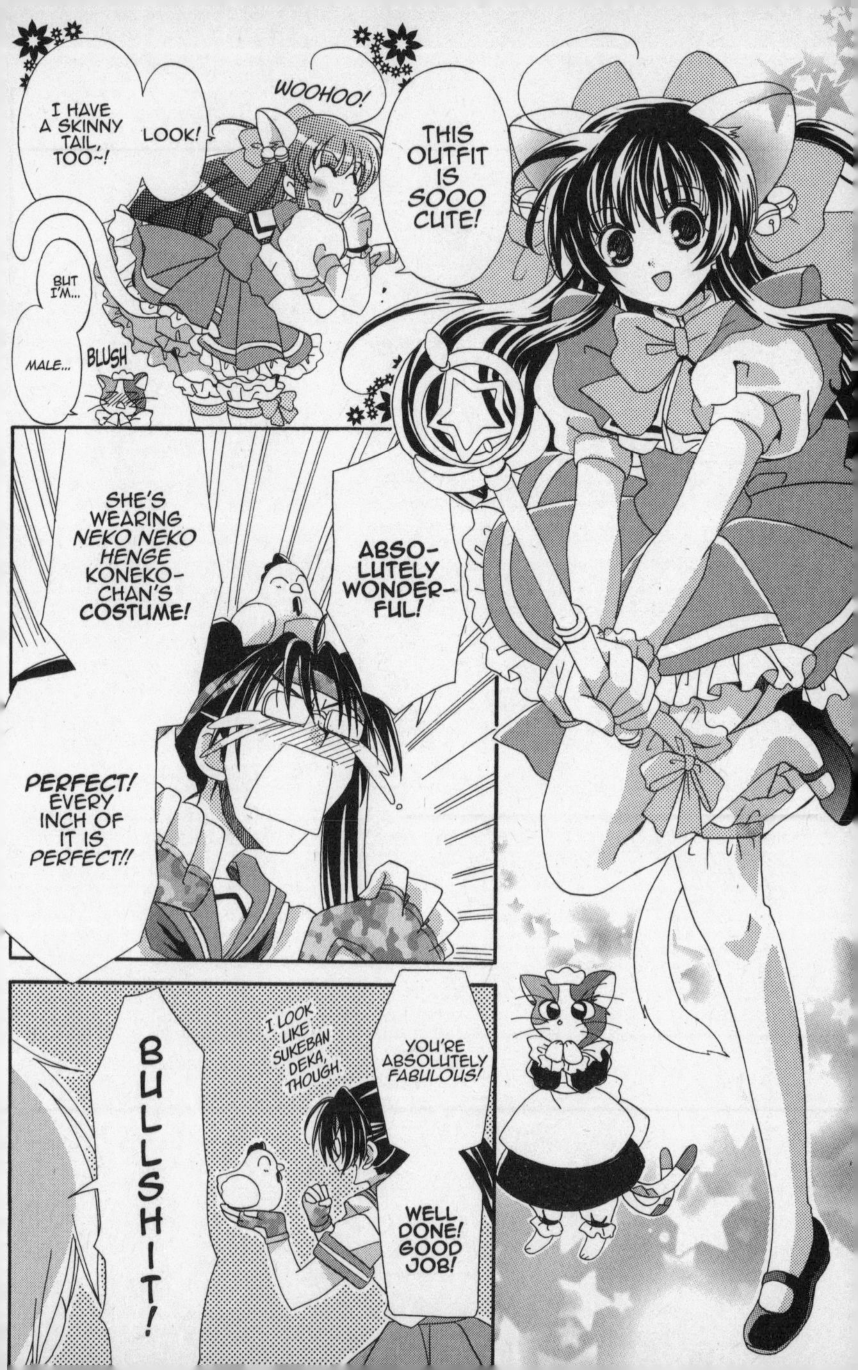
WOOHOO!
THIS OUTFIT IS SOOO CUTE!
LOOK!
I HAVE A SKINNY TAIL, TOO~!
BUT I'M... MALE...
BLUSH
ABSO-LUTELY WONDER-FUL!
SHE'S WEARING NEKO NEKO HENGE KONEKO-CHAN'S COSTUME!
PERFECT! EVERY INCH OF IT IS PERFECT!!
YOU'RE ABSOLUTELY FABULOUS!
WELL DONE! GOOD JOB!
I LOOK LIKE SUKEBAN DEKA, THOUGH.
BULLSHIT!

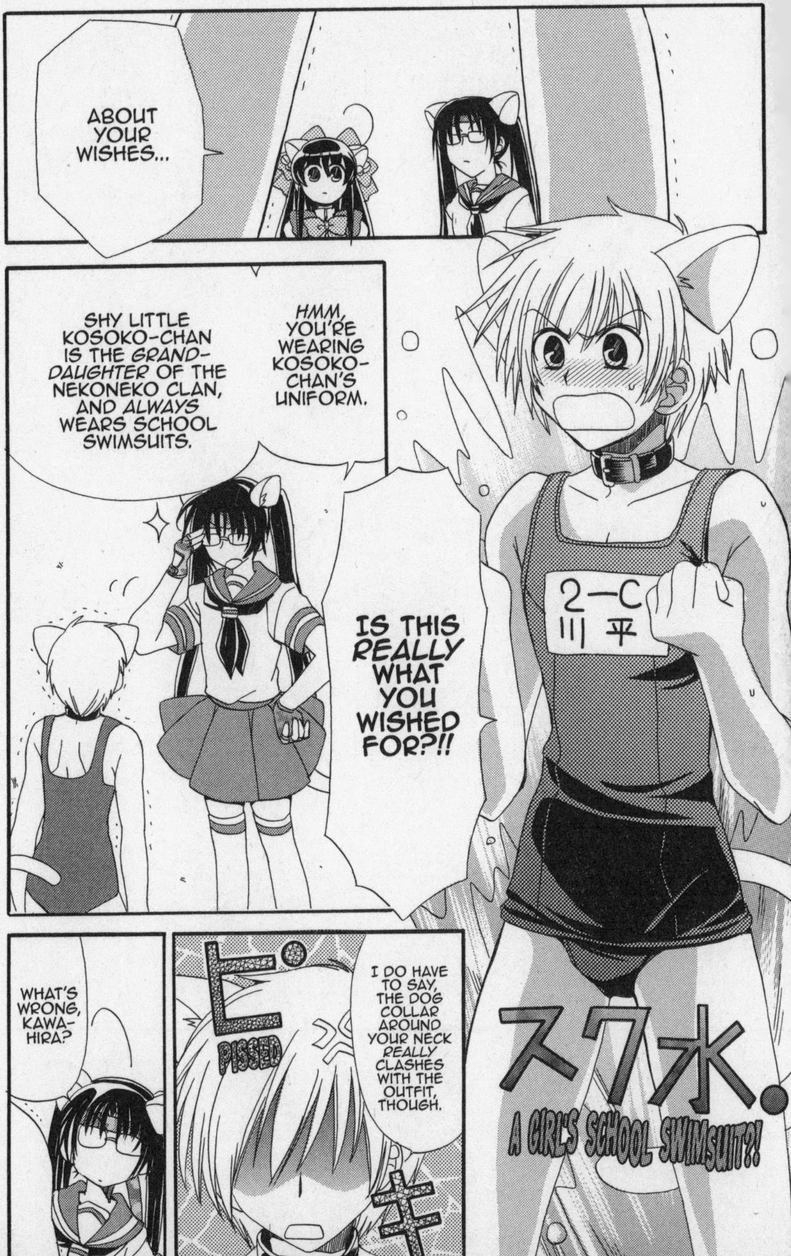
ABOUT YOUR WISHES...
2—C 川平
IS THIS REALLY WHAT YOU WISHED FOR?!!
スク水。
A GIRL'S SCHOOL SWIMSUIT?!
HMM, YOU'RE WEARING KOSOKO-CHAN'S UNIFORM.
SHY LITTLE KOSOKO-CHAN IS THE GRAND-DAUGHTER OF THE NEKONEKO CLAN, AND ALWAYS WEARS SCHOOL SWIMSUITS.
I DO HAVE TO SAY, THE DOG COLLAR AROUND YOUR NECK REALLY CLASHES WITH THE OUTFIT, THOUGH.
ピキ
PISSED
WHAT'S WRONG, KAWA-HIRA?

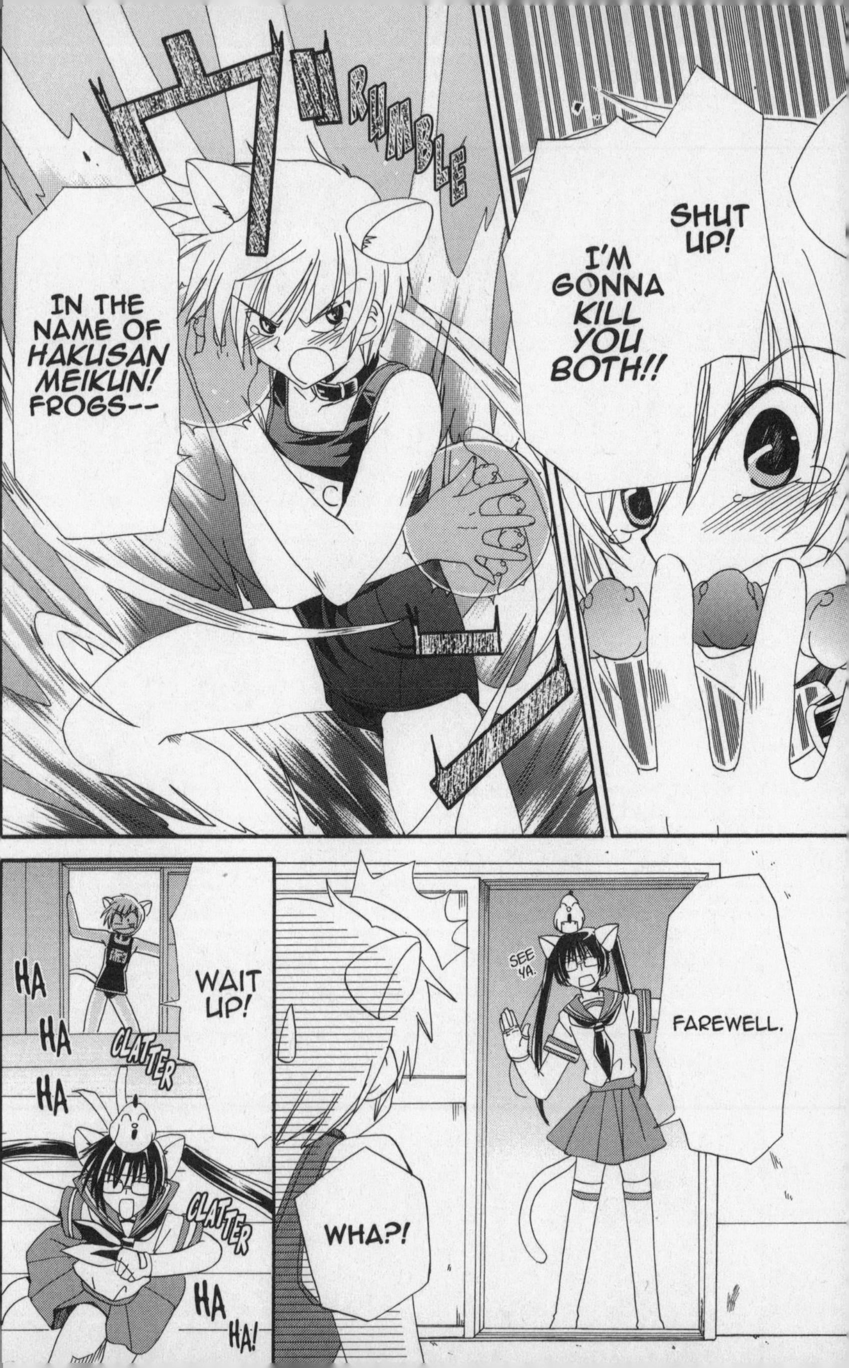
SHUT UP!
I'M GONNA KILL YOU BOTH!!
RUMBLE
IN THE NAME OF HAKUSAN MEIKUN! FROGS--
FAREWELL.
SEE YA.
WHA?!
WAIT UP!
HA
HA
CLATTER
HA
CLATTER
HA
HA!

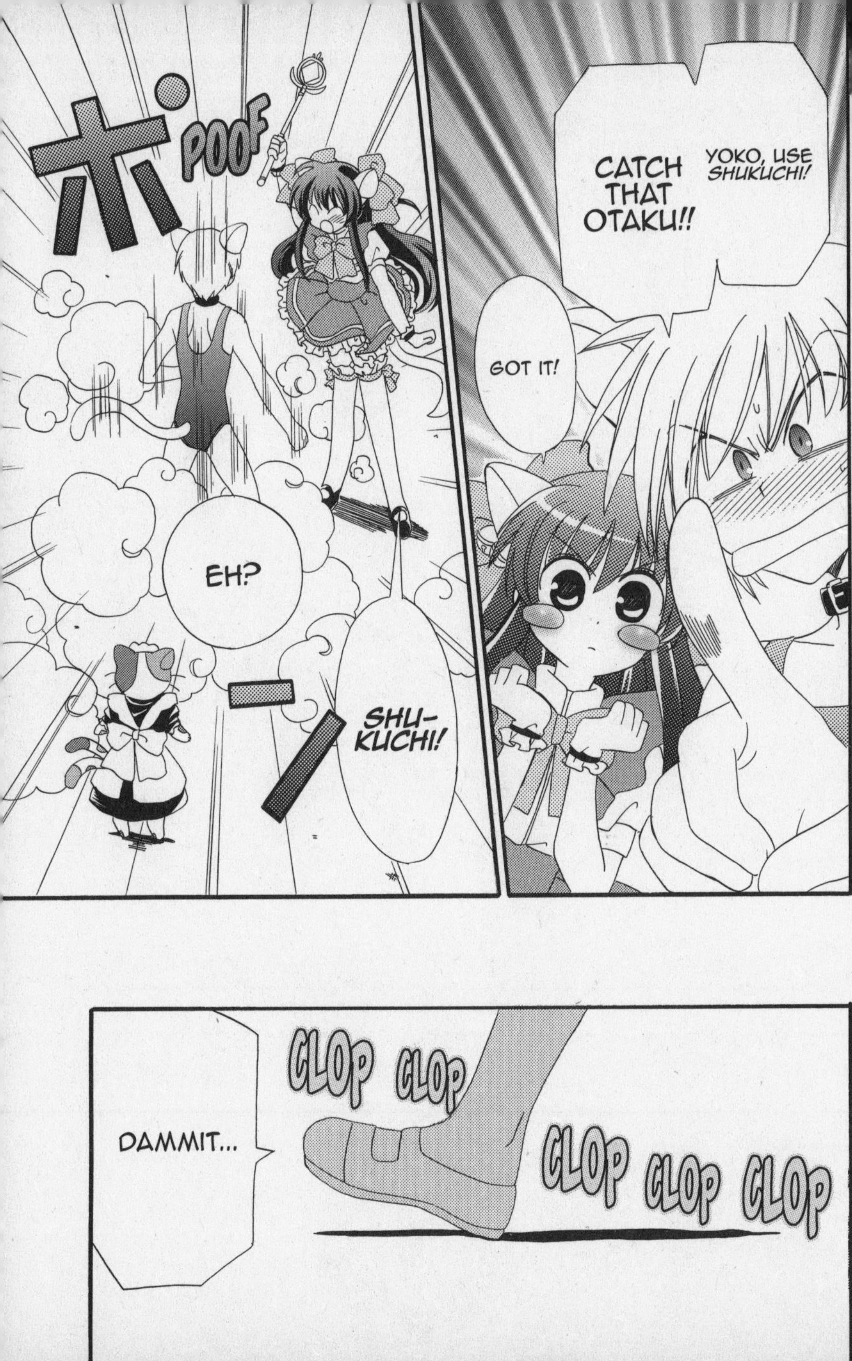
YOKO, USE SHUKUCHI!
CATCH THAT OTAKU!!
GOT IT!
ホ POOF
EH?
SHU-KUCHI!
CLOP CLOP
CLOP CLOP CLOP
DAMMIT...

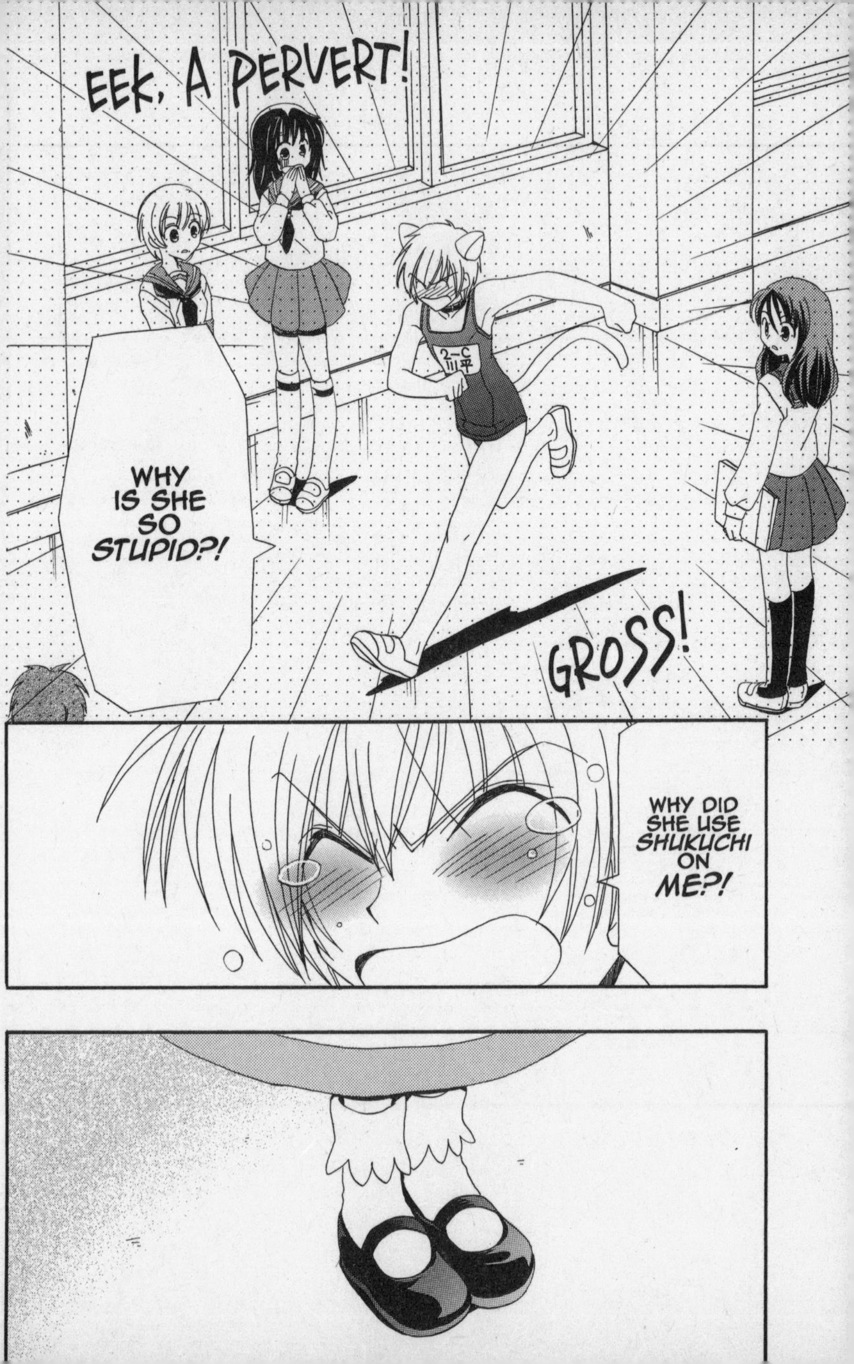
EEK, A PERVERT!
2-C
川平
GROSS!
WHY IS SHE SO STUPID?!
WHY DID SHE USE SHUKUCHI ON ME?!

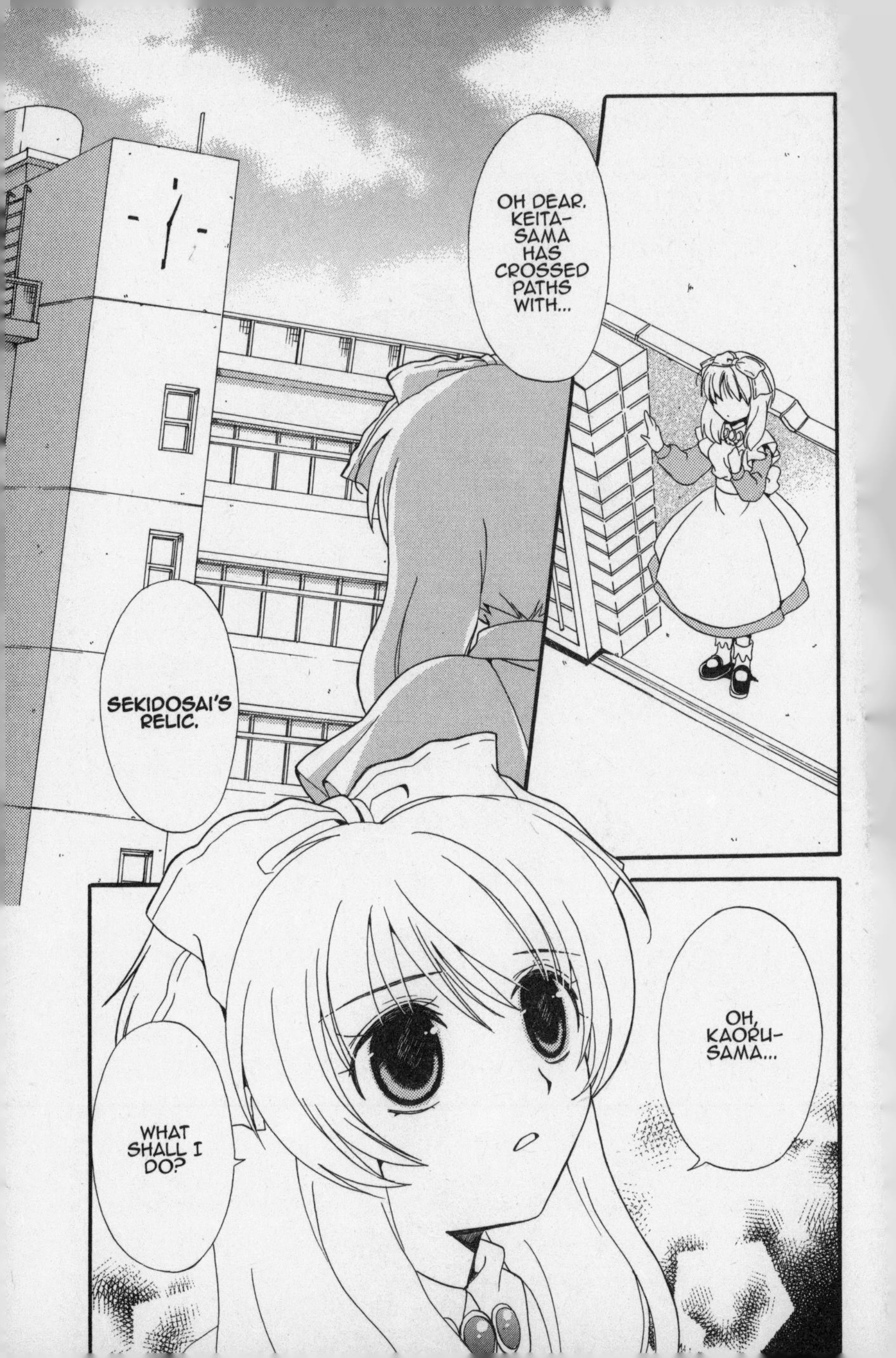
OH DEAR. KEITA-SAMA HAS CROSSED PATHS WITH...
SEKIDOSAI'S RELIC.
OH, KAORU-SAMA...
WHAT SHALL I DO?

From the Character Designer

CONGRATULATIONS ON VOLUME 3! ♡
WELL ACTUALLY, IT'S MORE LIKE I'M SURPRISED THAT IT'S ALREADY VOLUME 3...
TIME FLIES SO QUICKLY.
TO MATSUZAWA-SAN, WHO DRAWS THIS WONDERFUL MANGA...
AS ONE OF THE ORIGINAL CREATORS, I'M DELIGHTED.
TO EXPRESS MY GRATITUDE FOR ALL THE HARD WORK YOU HAVE DONE,
I DREW A "PRECOCIOUS LITTLE TOMOHANE," AS YOU REQUESTED.

'07. JANUARY
KANNA WAKATSUKI

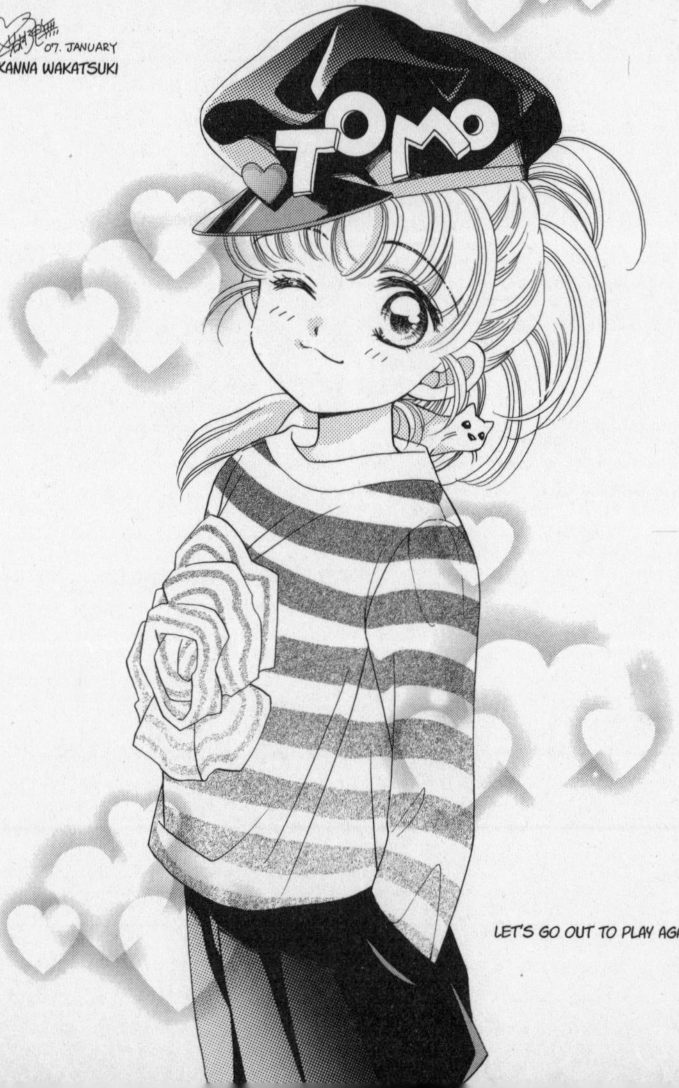
TOMO

LET'S GO OUT TO PLAY AGAIN! ♪

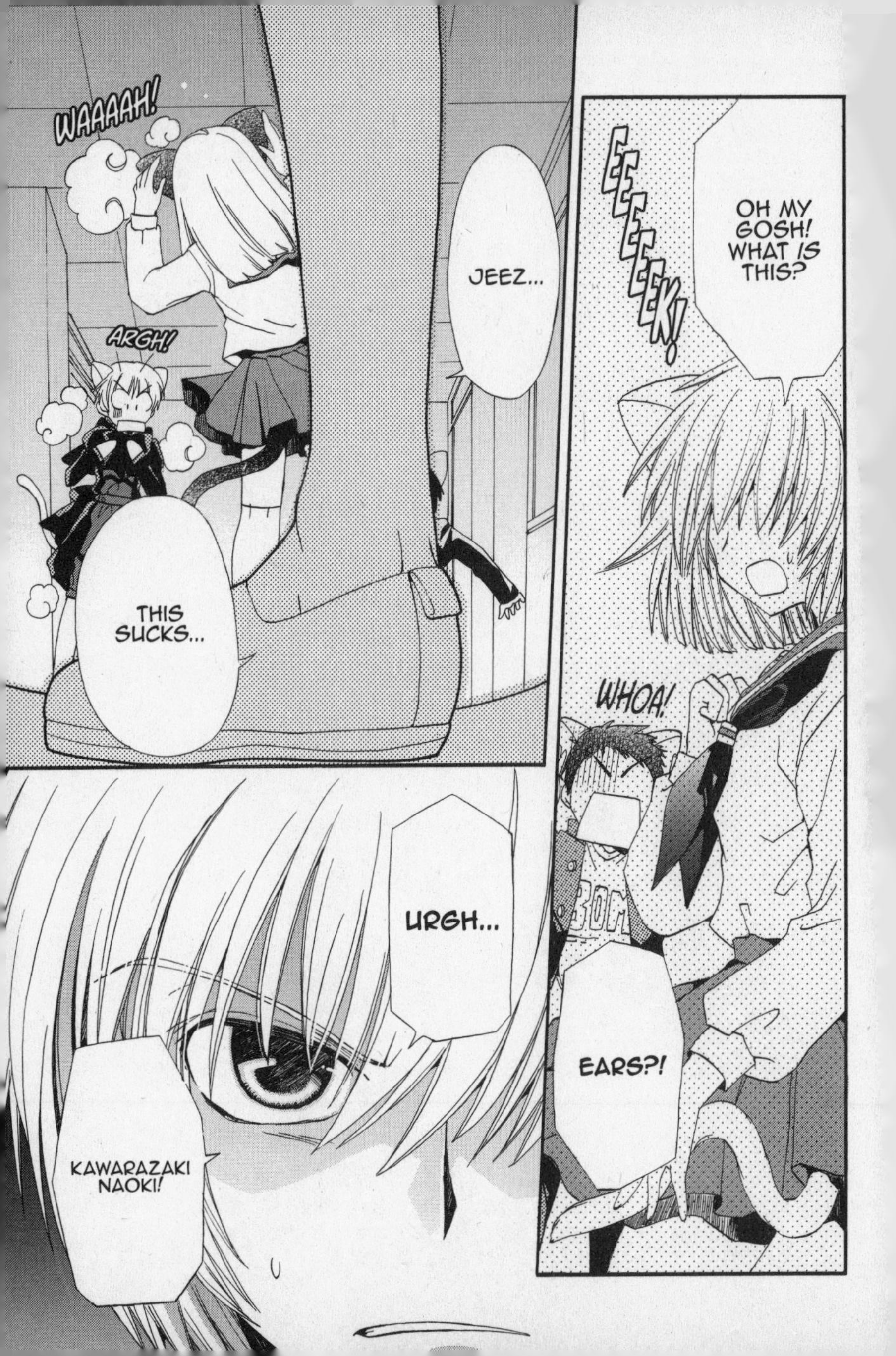
EEEEEK!
OH MY GOSH! WHAT IS THIS?
WHOA!
EARS?!
JEEZ...
WAAAAH!
ARGH!
THIS SUCKS...
URGH...
KAWARAZAKI NAOKI!

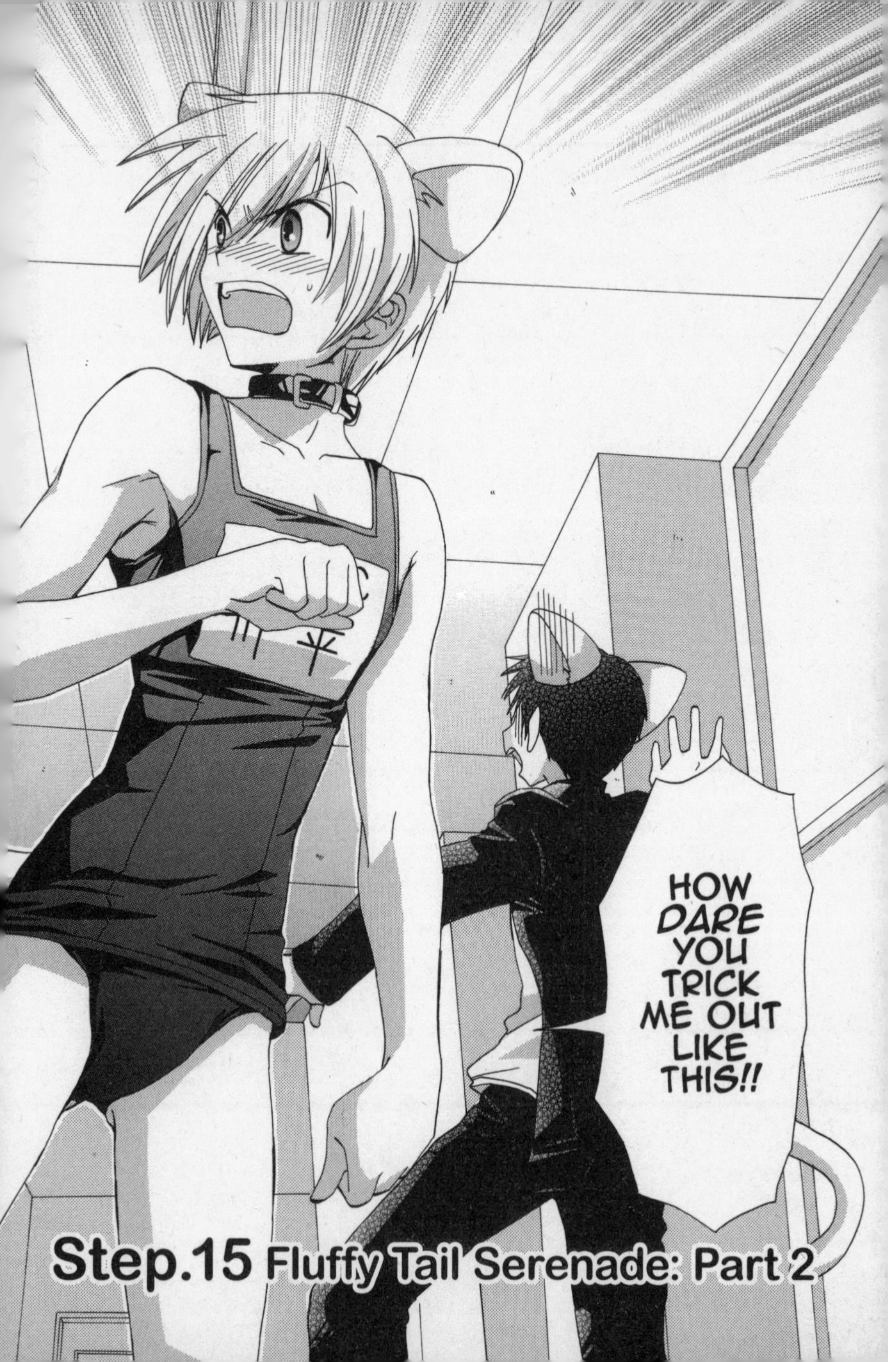
HOW DARE YOU TRICK ME OUT LIKE THIS!!
Step.15 Fluffy Tail Serenade: Part 2

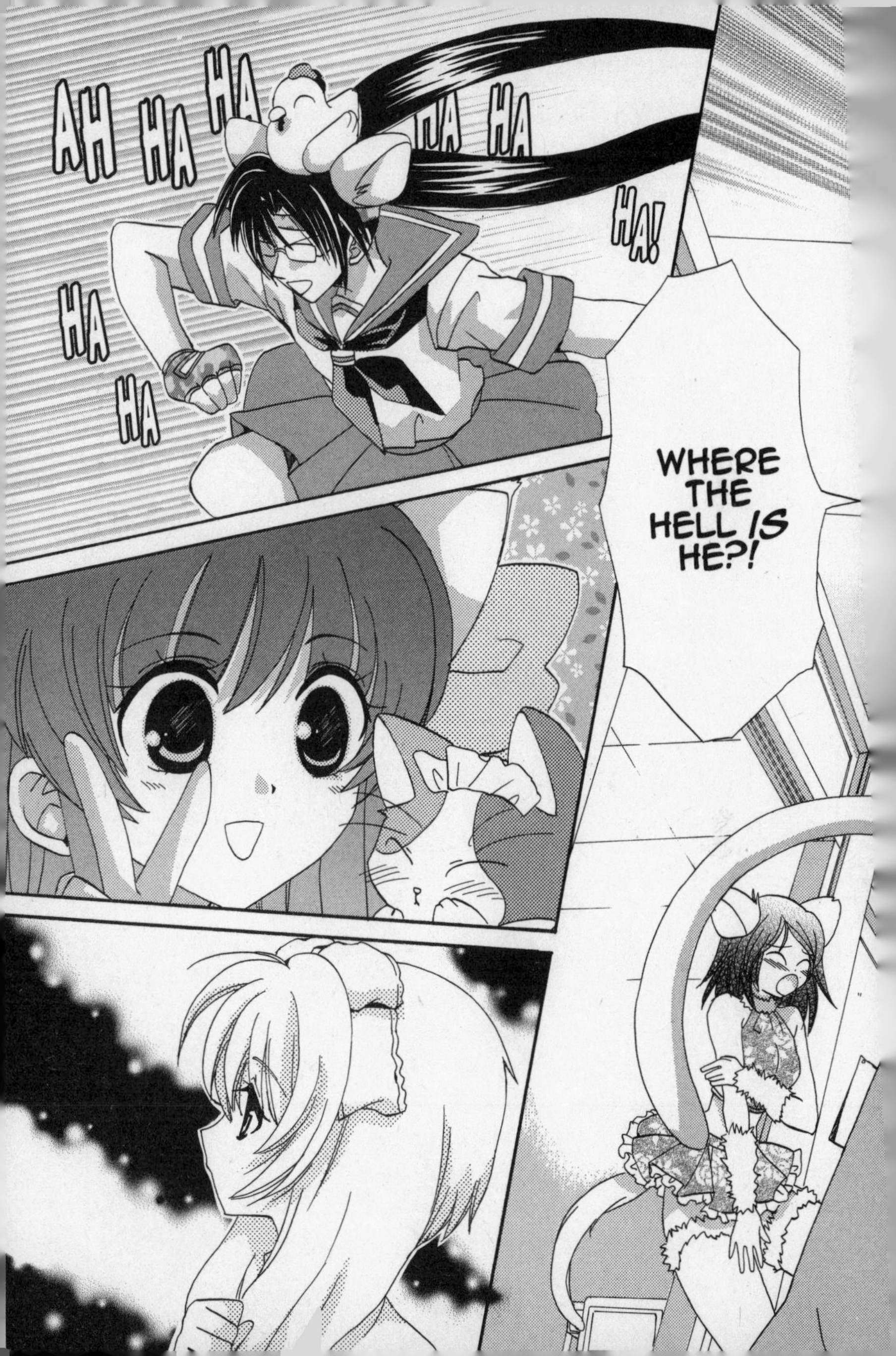
WHERE THE HELL IS HE?!
AH HA HA HA HA HA!
HA HA HA

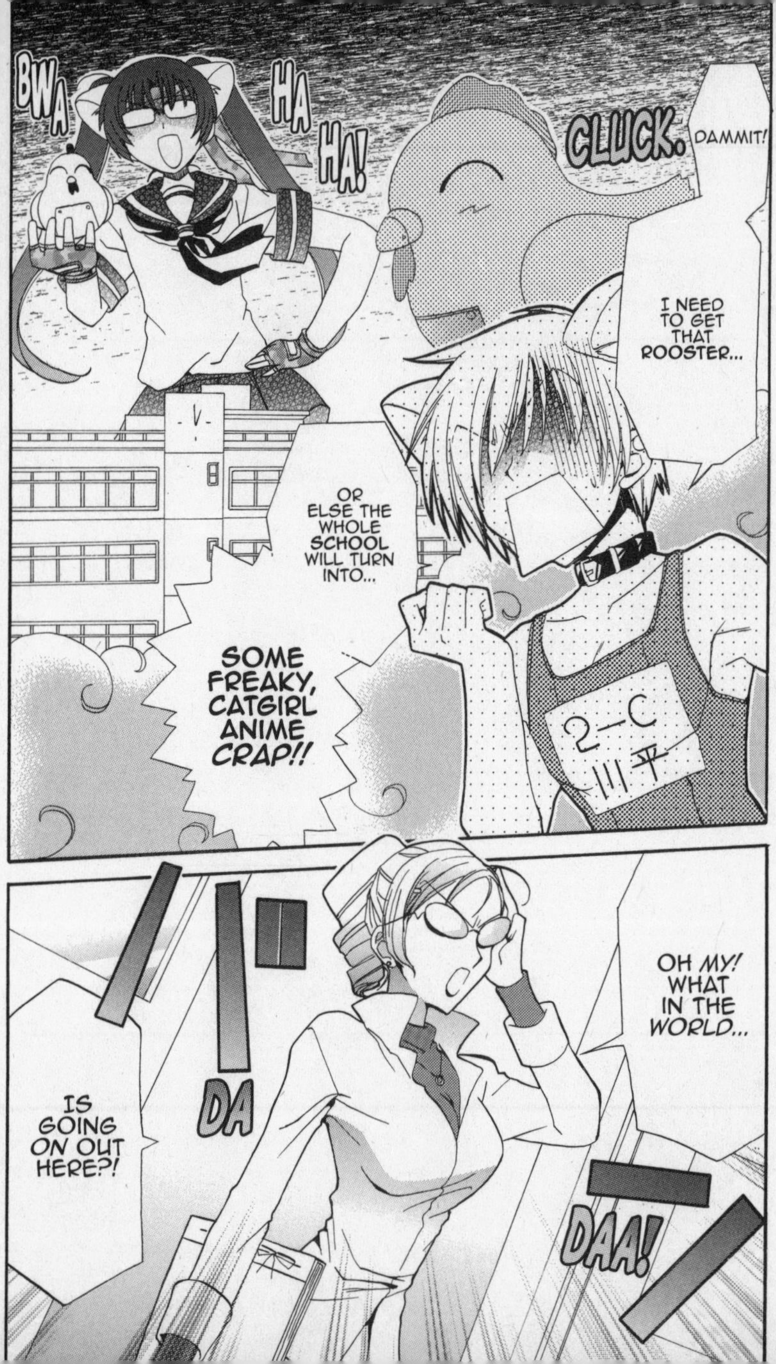
DAMMIT!
CLUCK.
BWA HA HA!
I NEED TO GET THAT ROOSTER...
OR ELSE THE WHOLE SCHOOL WILL TURN INTO...
SOME FREAKY, CATGIRL ANIME CRAP!!
2-C
川平
OH MY! WHAT IN THE WORLD...
DA
DAA!
IS GOING ON OUT HERE?!

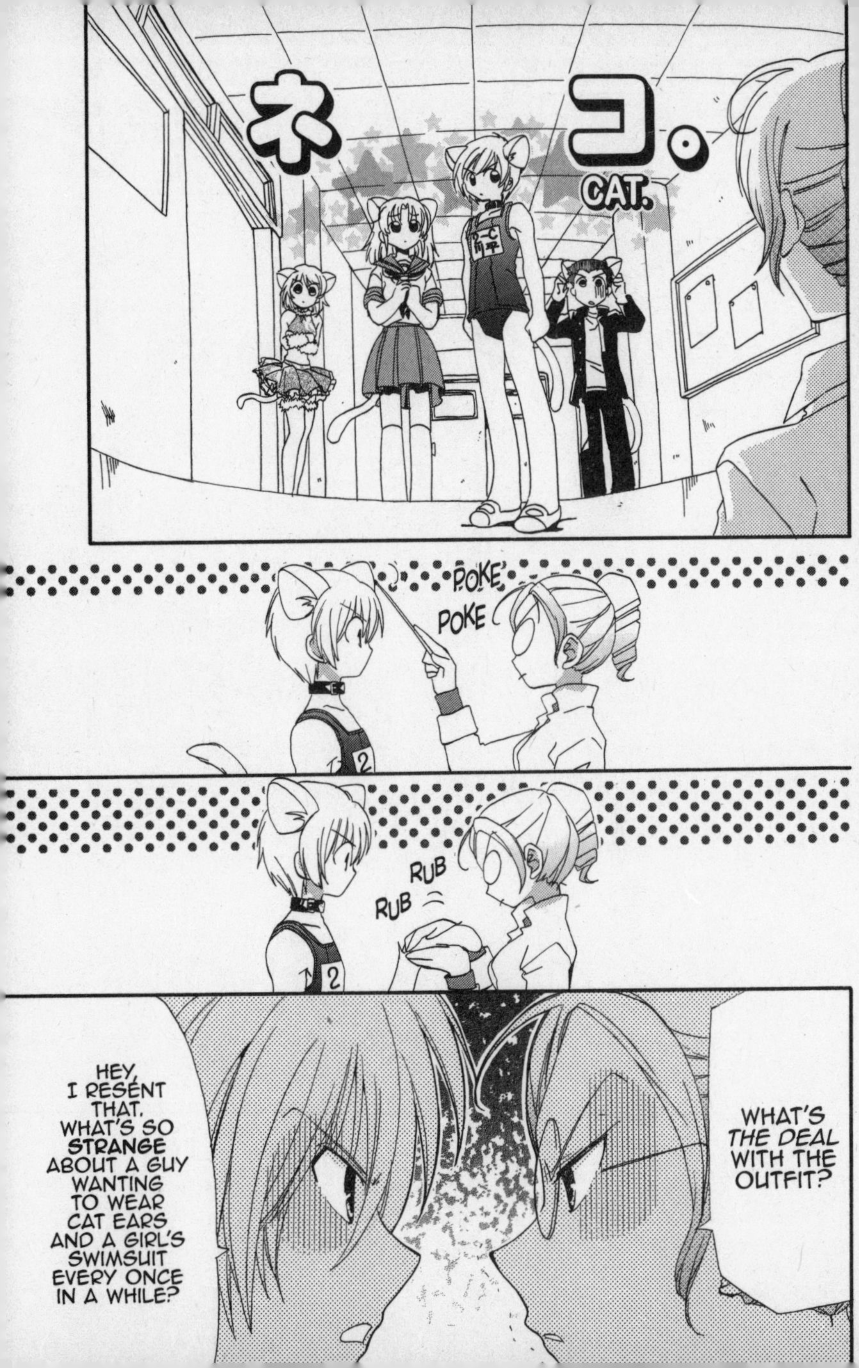
ネコ。
CAT.
POKE
POKE
RUB
RUB
WHAT'S THE DEAL WITH THE OUTFIT?
HEY, I RESENT THAT. WHAT'S SO STRANGE ABOUT A GUY WANTING TO WEAR CAT EARS AND A GIRL'S SWIMSUIT EVERY ONCE IN A WHILE?

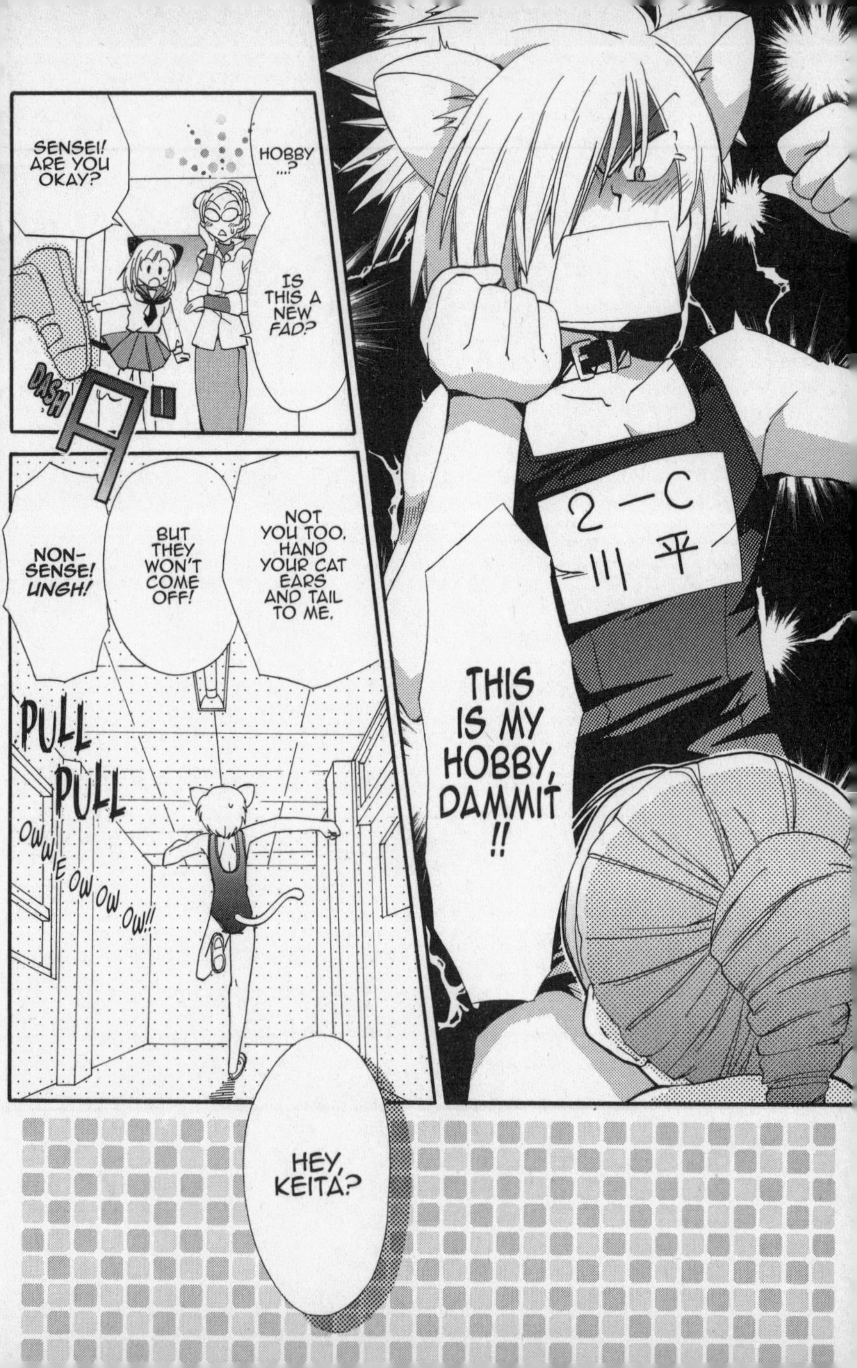
THIS IS MY HOBBY, DAMMIT !!
2—C
川平
HOBBY ...?
SENSEI! ARE YOU OKAY?
IS THIS A NEW FAD?
DASH
NOT YOU TOO. HAND YOUR CAT EARS AND TAIL TO ME.
BUT THEY WON'T COME OFF!
NON-SENSE! UNGH!
PULL
PULL
OWWIE OW OW OW!!
HEY, KEITA?

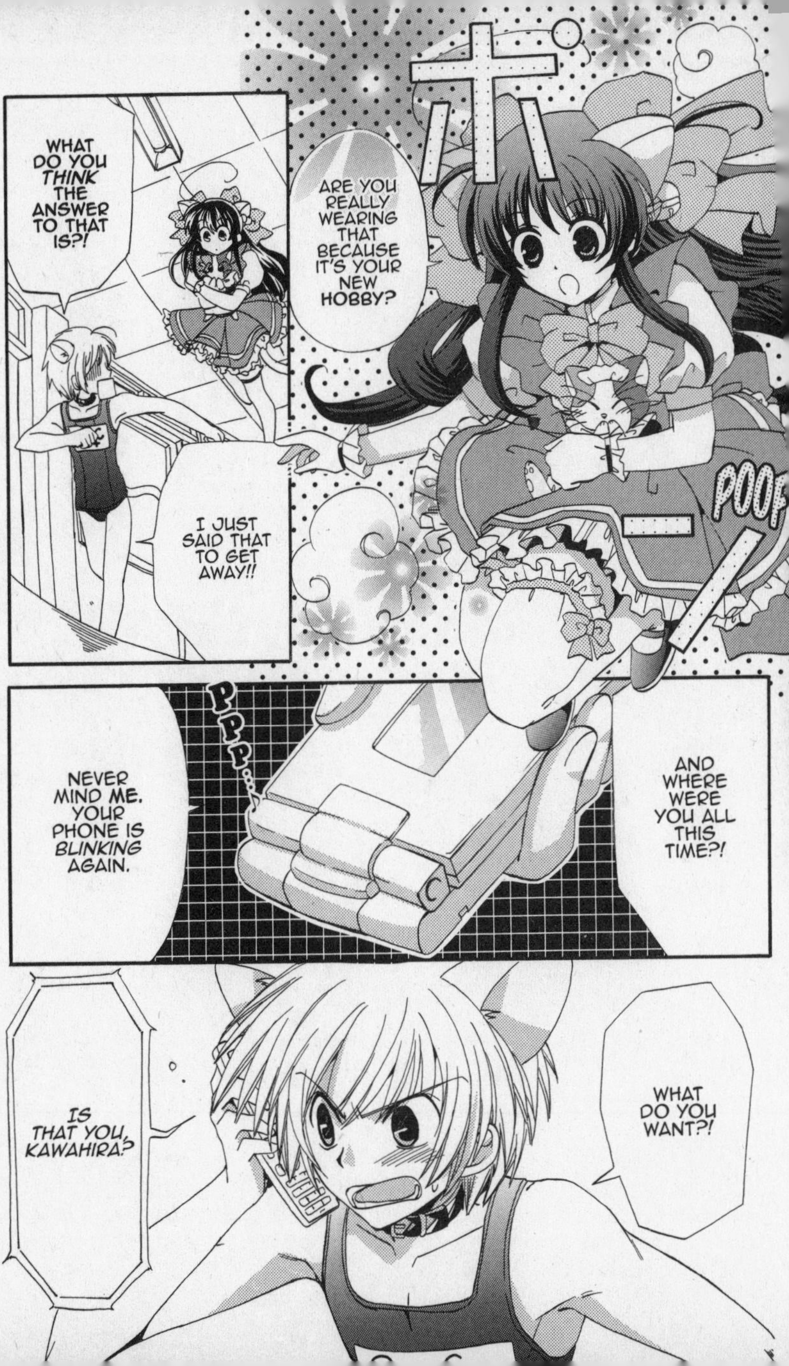
ARE YOU REALLY WEARING THAT BECAUSE IT'S YOUR NEW HOBBY?
POOF
WHAT DO YOU *THINK* THE ANSWER TO THAT IS?!
I JUST SAID THAT TO GET AWAY!!
AND WHERE WERE YOU ALL THIS TIME?!
PPP...
NEVER MIND ME. YOUR PHONE IS *BLINKING* AGAIN.
WHAT DO YOU WANT?!
IS THAT YOU, KAWAHIRA?

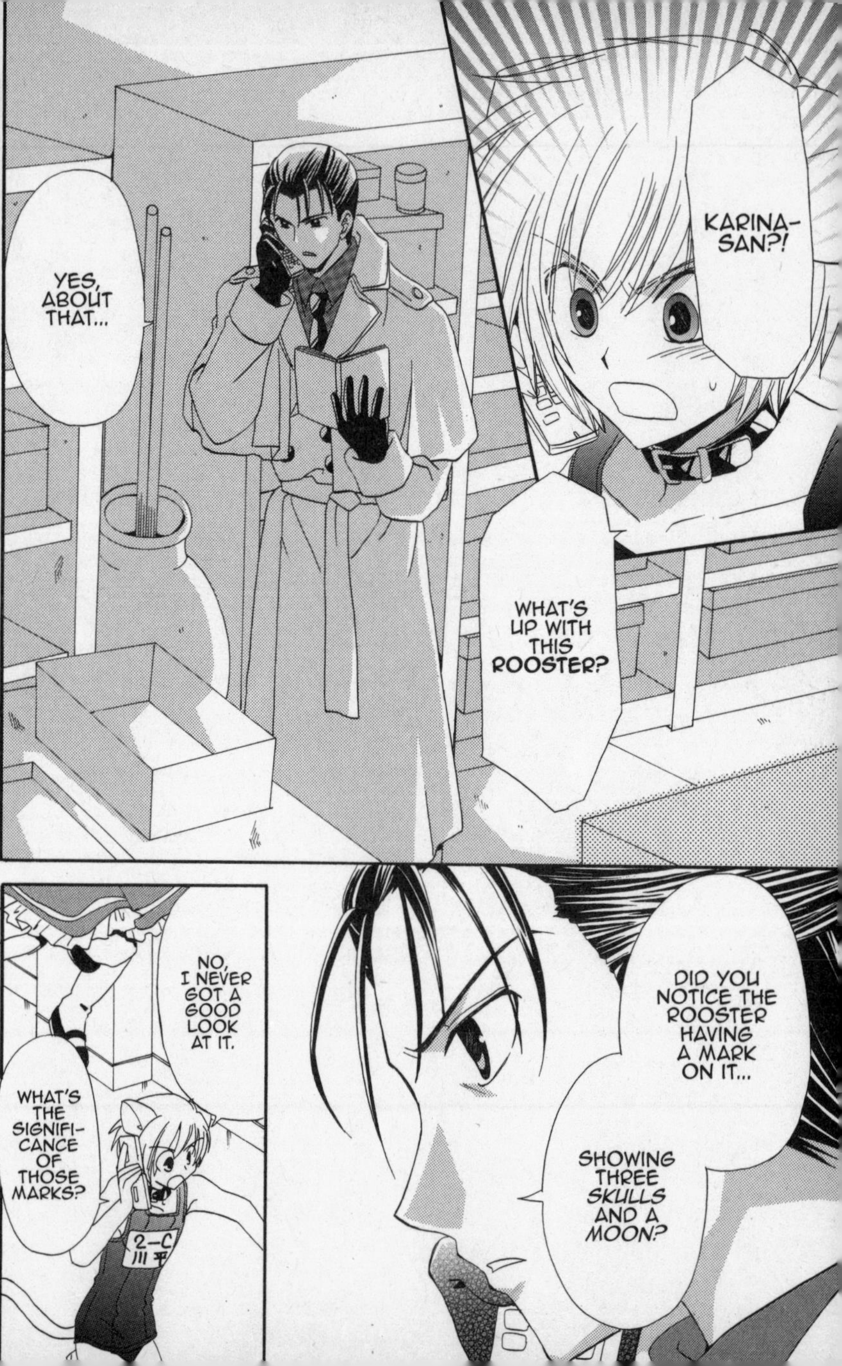
KARINA-SAN?!
WHAT'S UP WITH THIS ROOSTER?
YES, ABOUT THAT...
DID YOU NOTICE THE ROOSTER HAVING A MARK ON IT...
SHOWING THREE SKULLS AND A MOON?
NO, I NEVER GOT A GOOD LOOK AT IT.
WHAT'S THE SIGNIFICANCE OF THOSE MARKS?
2—C
川平

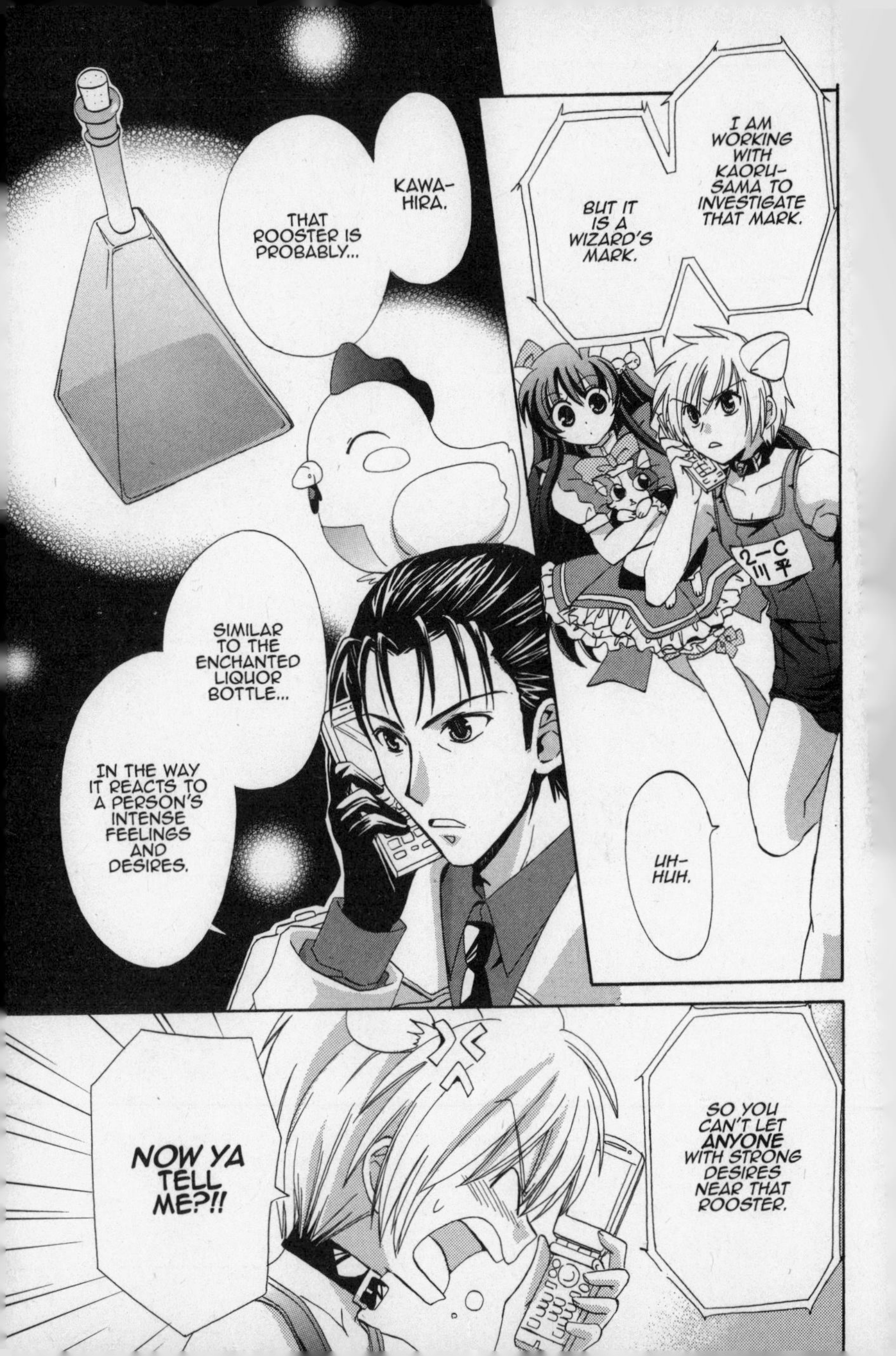
I AM WORKING WITH KAORU-SAMA TO INVESTIGATE THAT MARK.
BUT IT IS A WIZARD'S MARK.
2—C 川平
UH-HUH.
KAWA-HIRA.
THAT ROOSTER IS PROBABLY...
SIMILAR TO THE ENCHANTED LIQUOR BOTTLE...
IN THE WAY IT REACTS TO A PERSON'S INTENSE FEELINGS AND DESIRES.
SO YOU CAN'T LET **ANYONE** WITH STRONG DESIRES NEAR THAT ROOSTER.
NOW YA TELL ME?!!

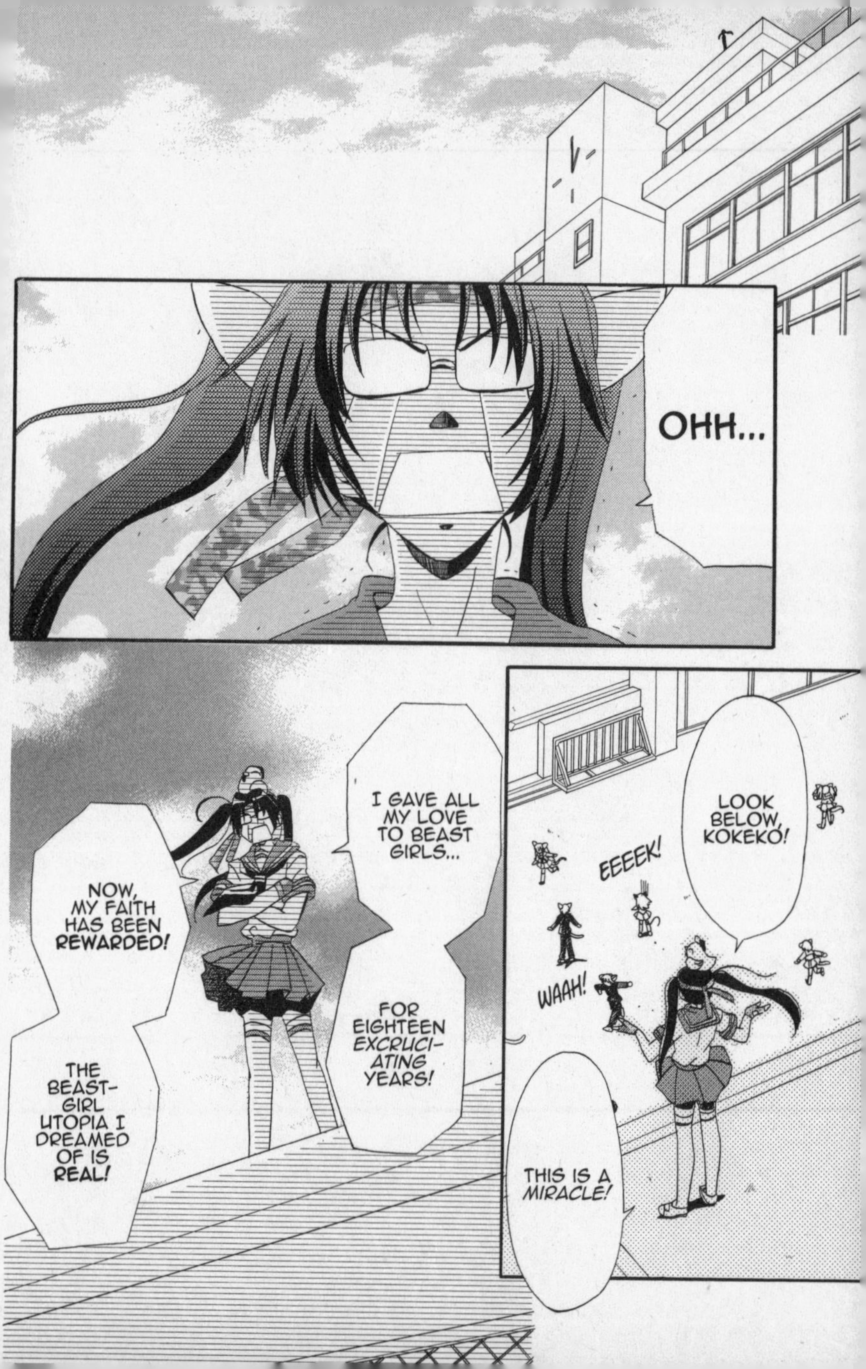
OHH...
LOOK BELOW, KOKEKO!
EEEEK!
WAAH!
THIS IS A MIRACLE!
I GAVE ALL MY LOVE TO BEAST GIRLS...
FOR EIGHTEEN EXCRUCIATING YEARS!
NOW, MY FAITH HAS BEEN REWARDED!
THE BEAST-GIRL UTOPIA I DREAMED OF IS REAL!

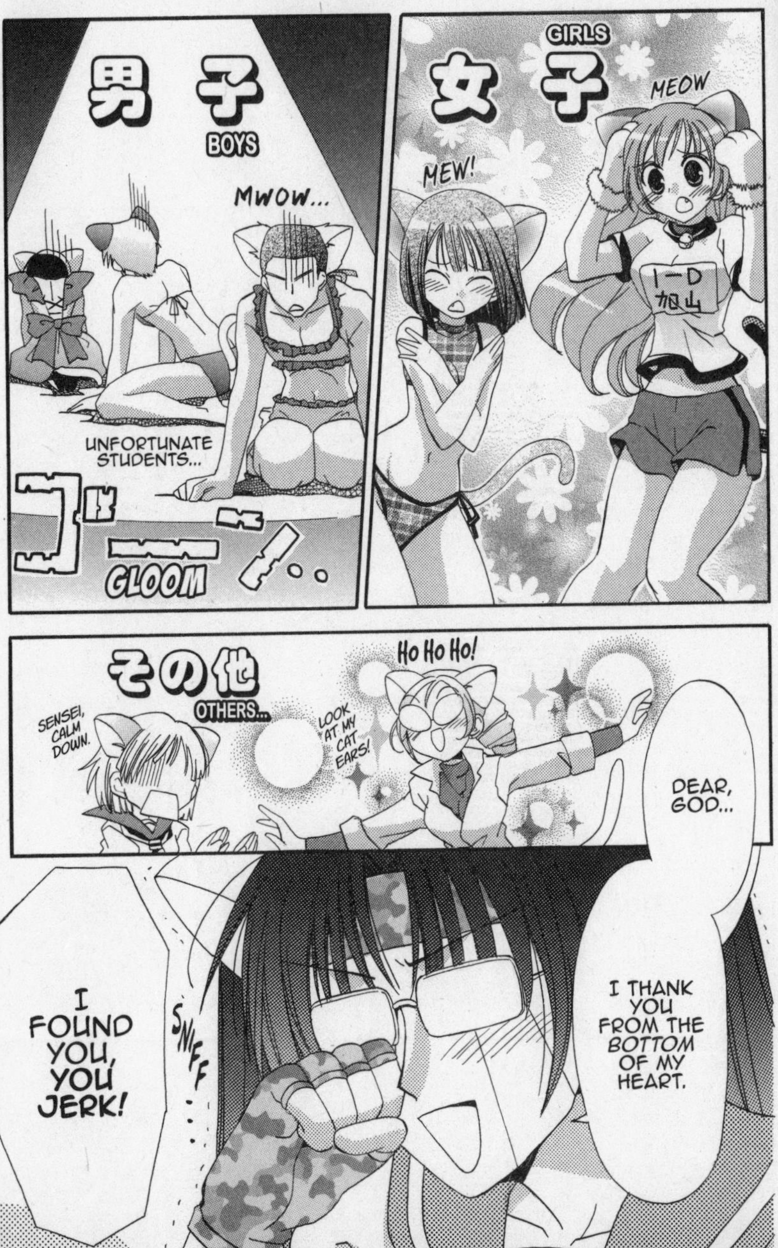
女子
GIRLS
MEOW
MEW!
1-D 加山
男子
BOYS
MWOW...
UNFORTUNATE STUDENTS...
GLOOM
その他
OTHERS...
HO HO HO!
LOOK AT MY CAT EARS!
SENSEI, CALM DOWN.
DEAR, GOD...
I THANK YOU FROM THE BOTTOM OF MY HEART.
SNIFF
I FOUND YOU, YOU JERK!

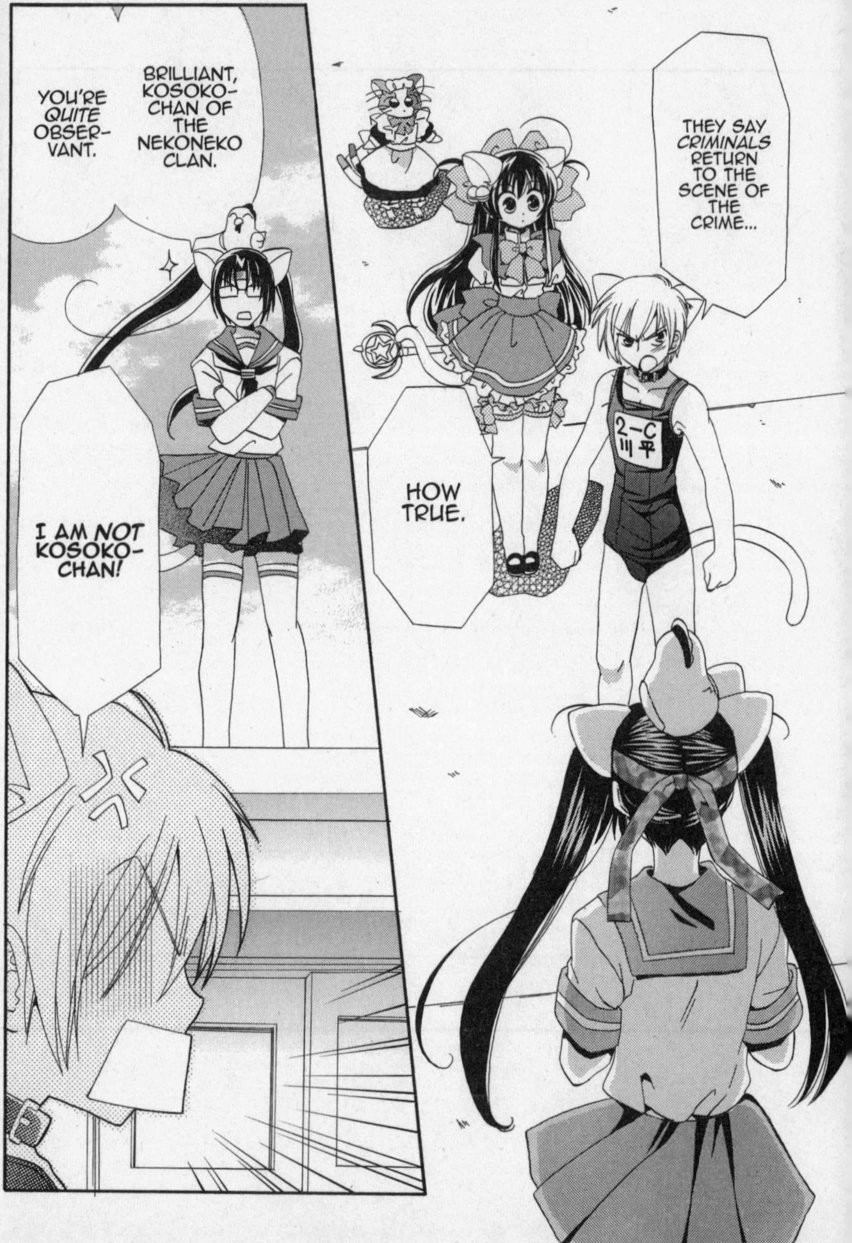
THEY SAY CRIMINALS RETURN TO THE SCENE OF THE CRIME...
HOW TRUE.
2-C 川平
BRILLIANT, KOSOKO-CHAN OF THE NEKONEKO CLAN.
YOU'RE QUITE OBSERVANT.
I AM NOT KOSOKO-CHAN!

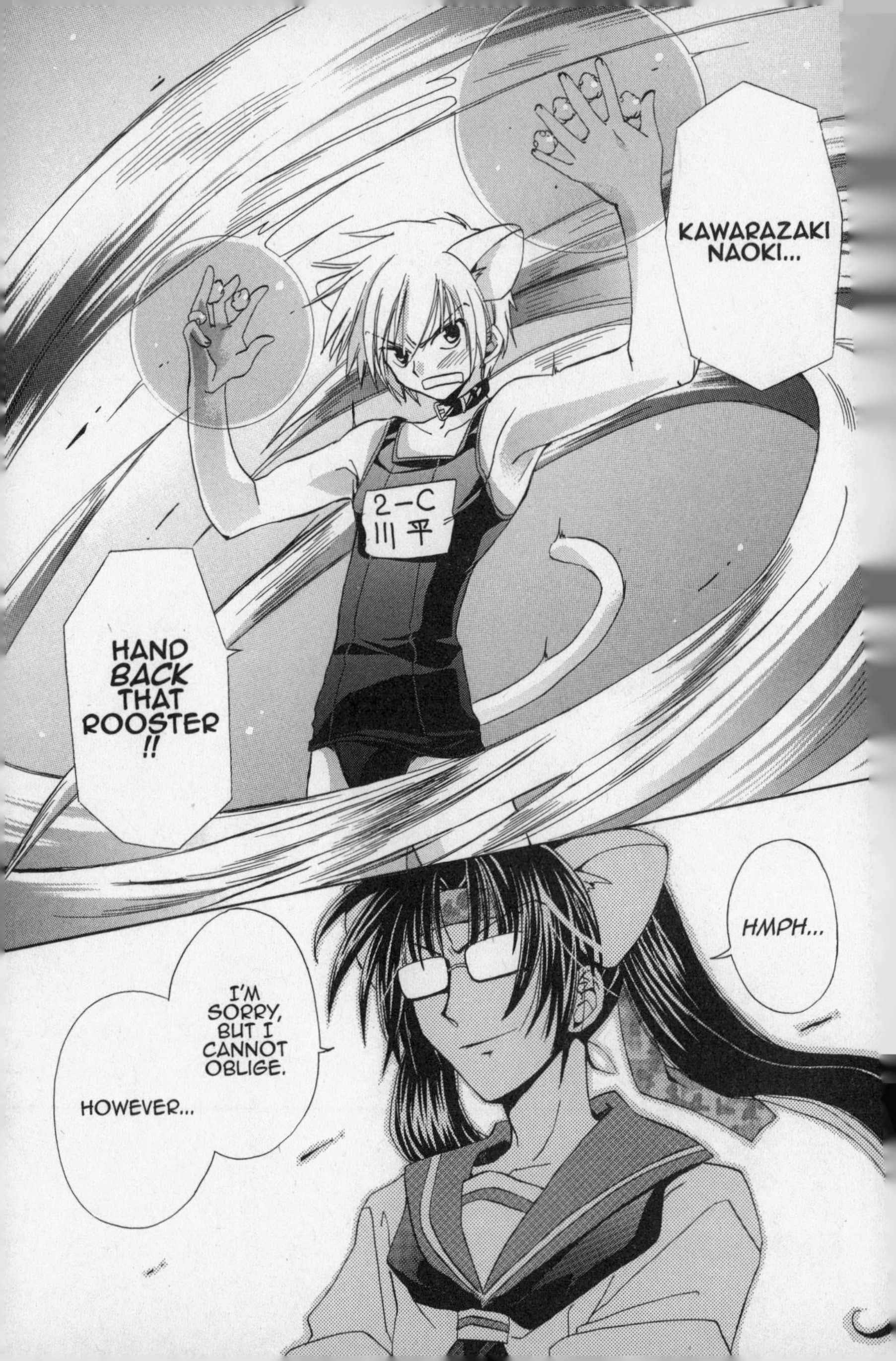
KAWARAZAKI NAOKI...
2-C
川平
HAND BACK THAT ROOSTER !!
HMPH...
I'M SORRY, BUT I CANNOT OBLIGE.
HOWEVER...

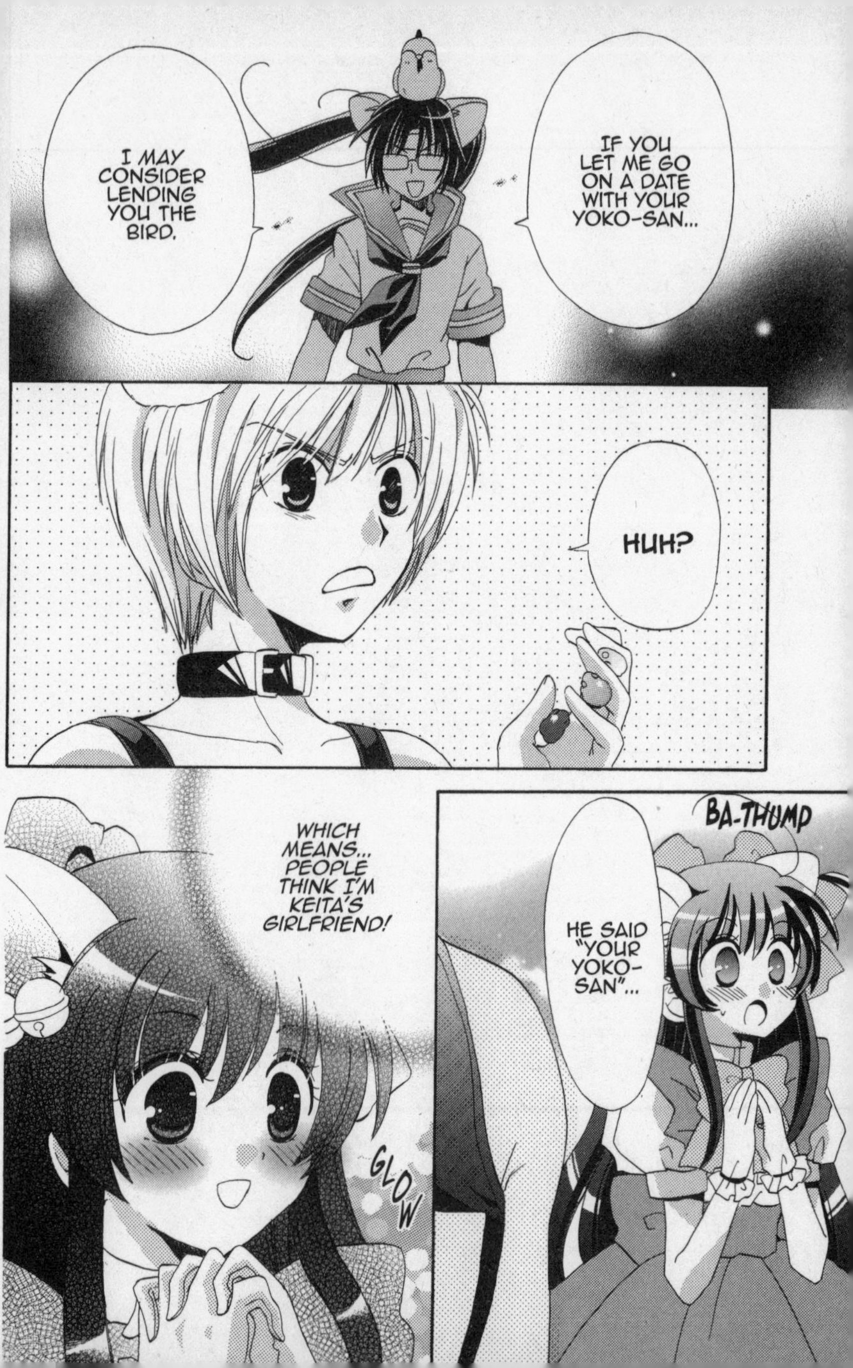
IF YOU LET ME GO ON A DATE WITH YOUR YOKO-SAN...
I MAY CONSIDER LENDING YOU THE BIRD.
HUH?
BA-THUMP
HE SAID "YOUR YOKO-SAN"...
WHICH MEANS... PEOPLE THINK I'M KEITA'S GIRLFRIEND!
GLOW

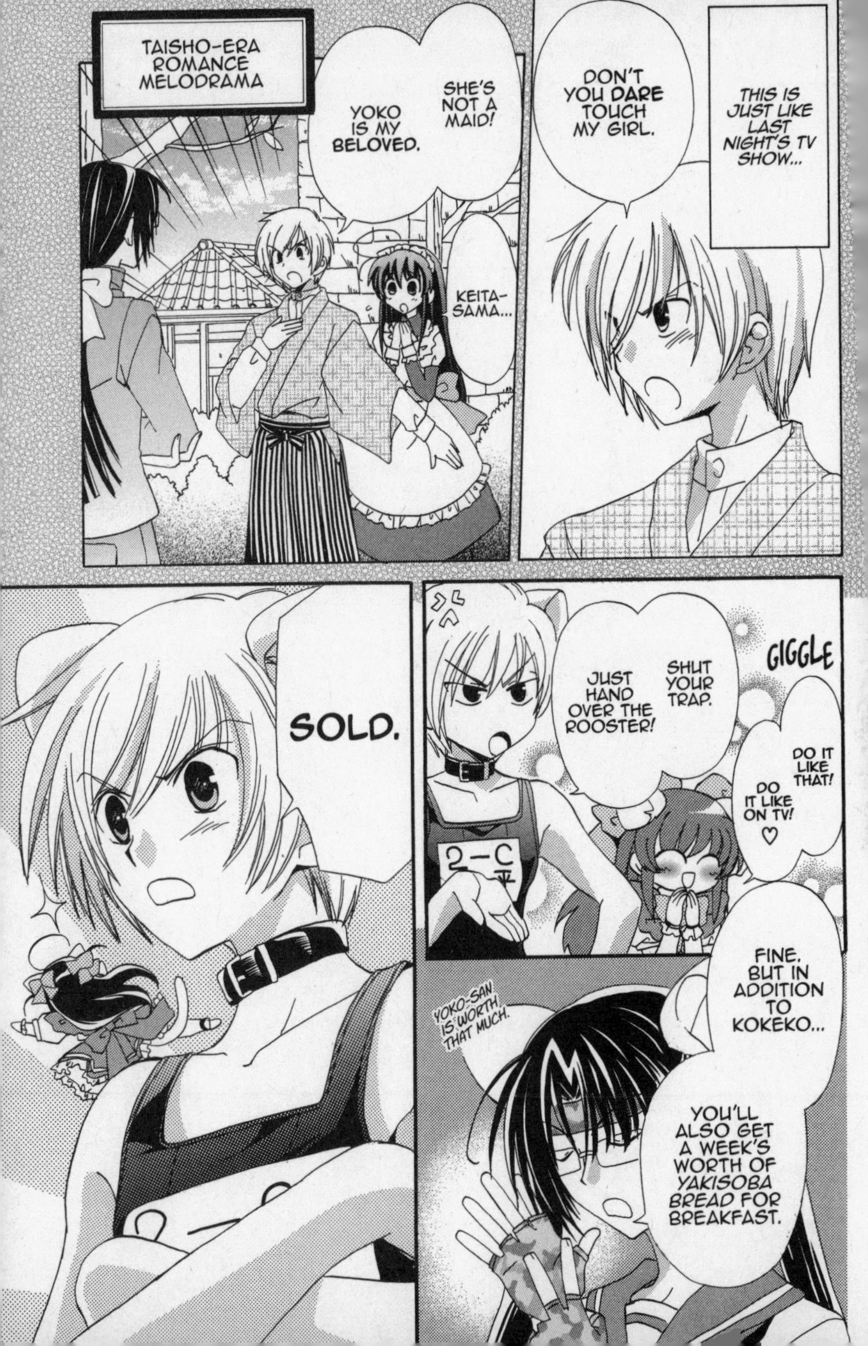
THIS IS JUST LIKE LAST NIGHT'S TV SHOW...
DON'T YOU DARE TOUCH MY GIRL.
SHE'S NOT A MAID!
YOKO IS MY BELOVED.
TAISHO-ERA ROMANCE MELODRAMA
KEITA-SAMA...
GIGGLE
DO IT LIKE THAT!
DO IT LIKE ON TV! ♡
SHUT YOUR TRAP.
JUST HAND OVER THE ROOSTER!
2-C
FINE. BUT IN ADDITION TO KOKEKO...
YOU'LL ALSO GET A WEEK'S WORTH OF YAKISOBA BREAD FOR BREAKFAST.
YOKO-SAN IS WORTH THAT MUCH.
SOLD.

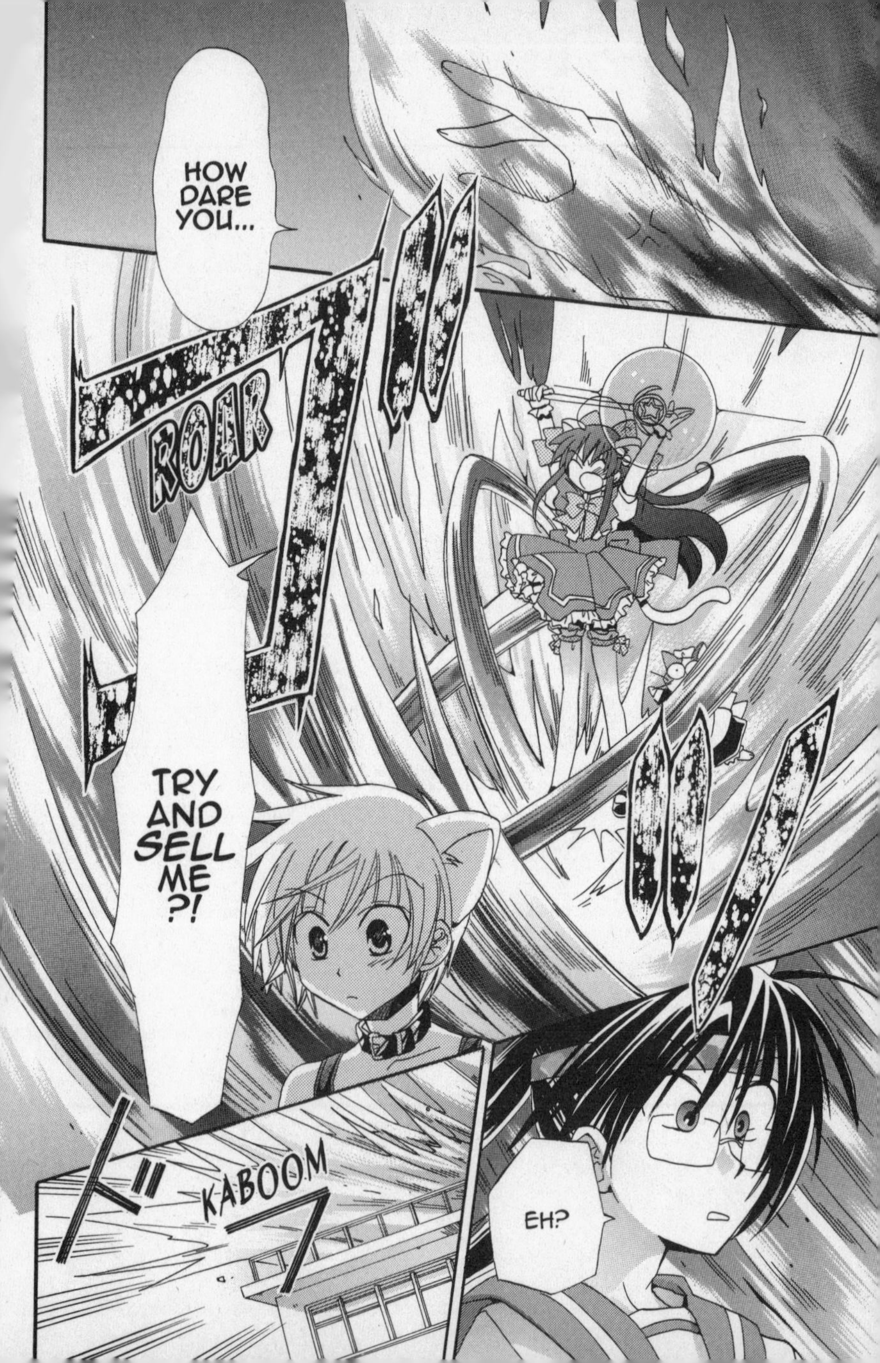
HOW DARE YOU...
ROAR
TRY AND SELL ME?!
EH?
KABOOM

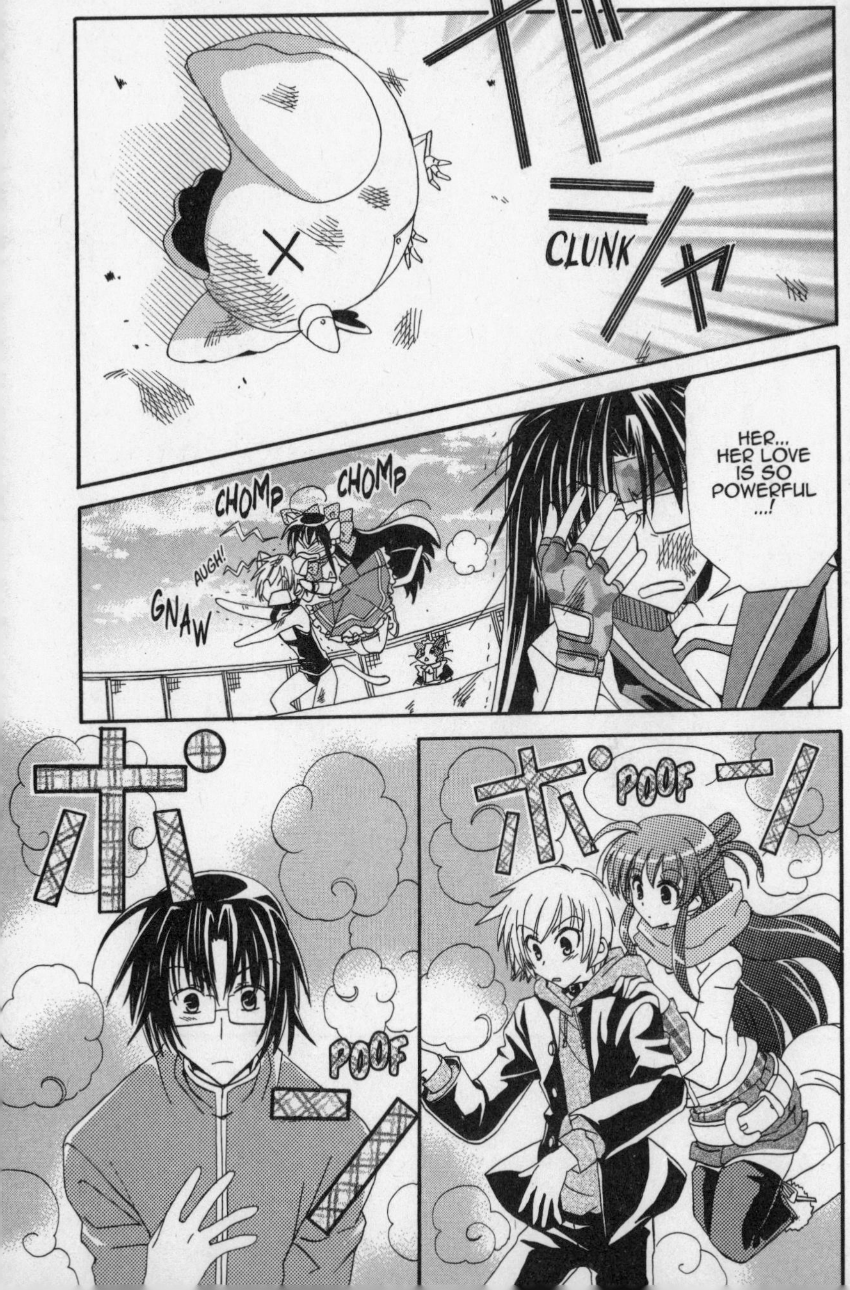
CLUNK
HER... HER LOVE IS SO POWERFUL ...!
CHOMP
CHOMP
AUGH!
GNAW
POOF
POOF

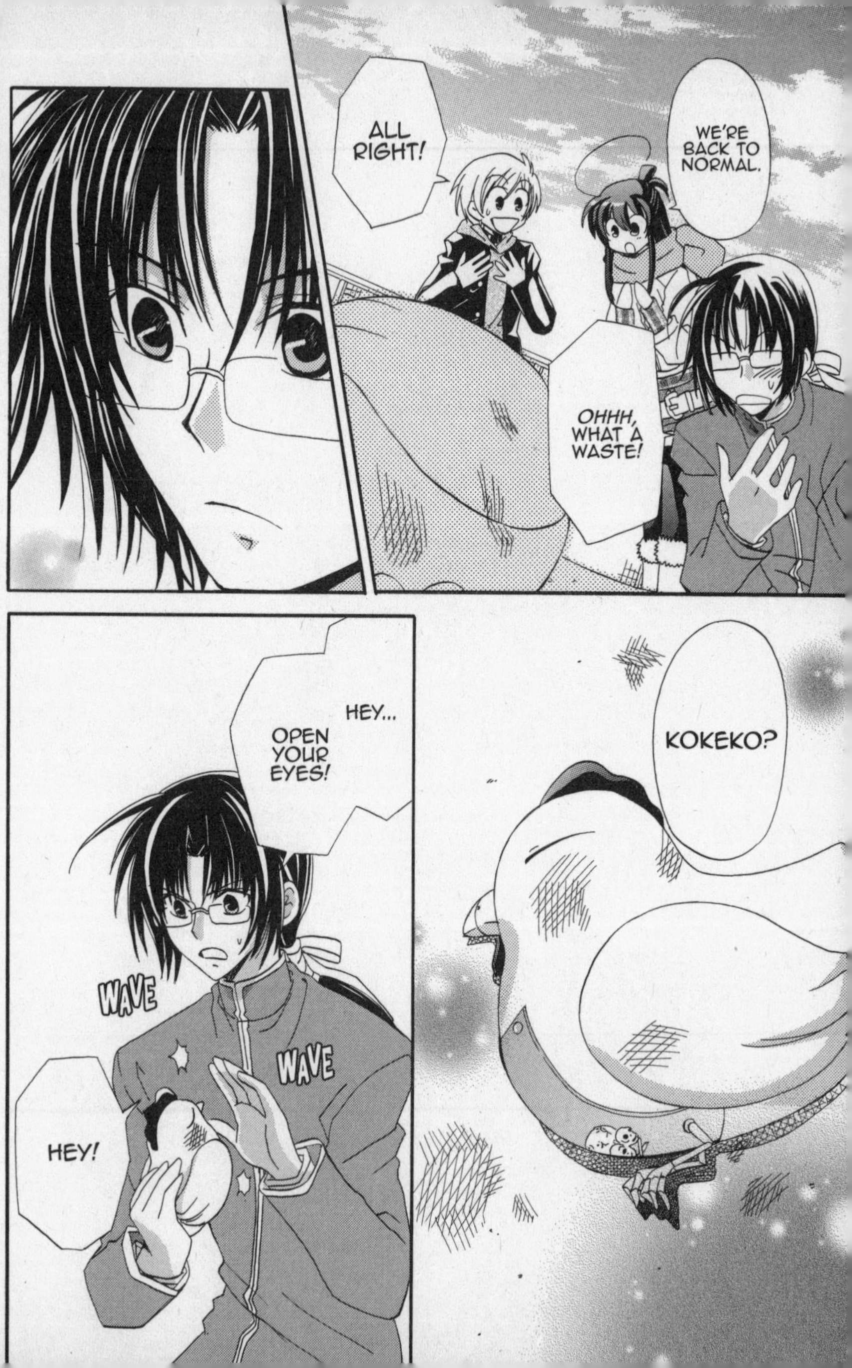
WE'RE BACK TO NORMAL.
ALL RIGHT!
OHHH, WHAT A WASTE!
KOKEKO?
HEY... OPEN YOUR EYES!
WAVE
WAVE
HEY!

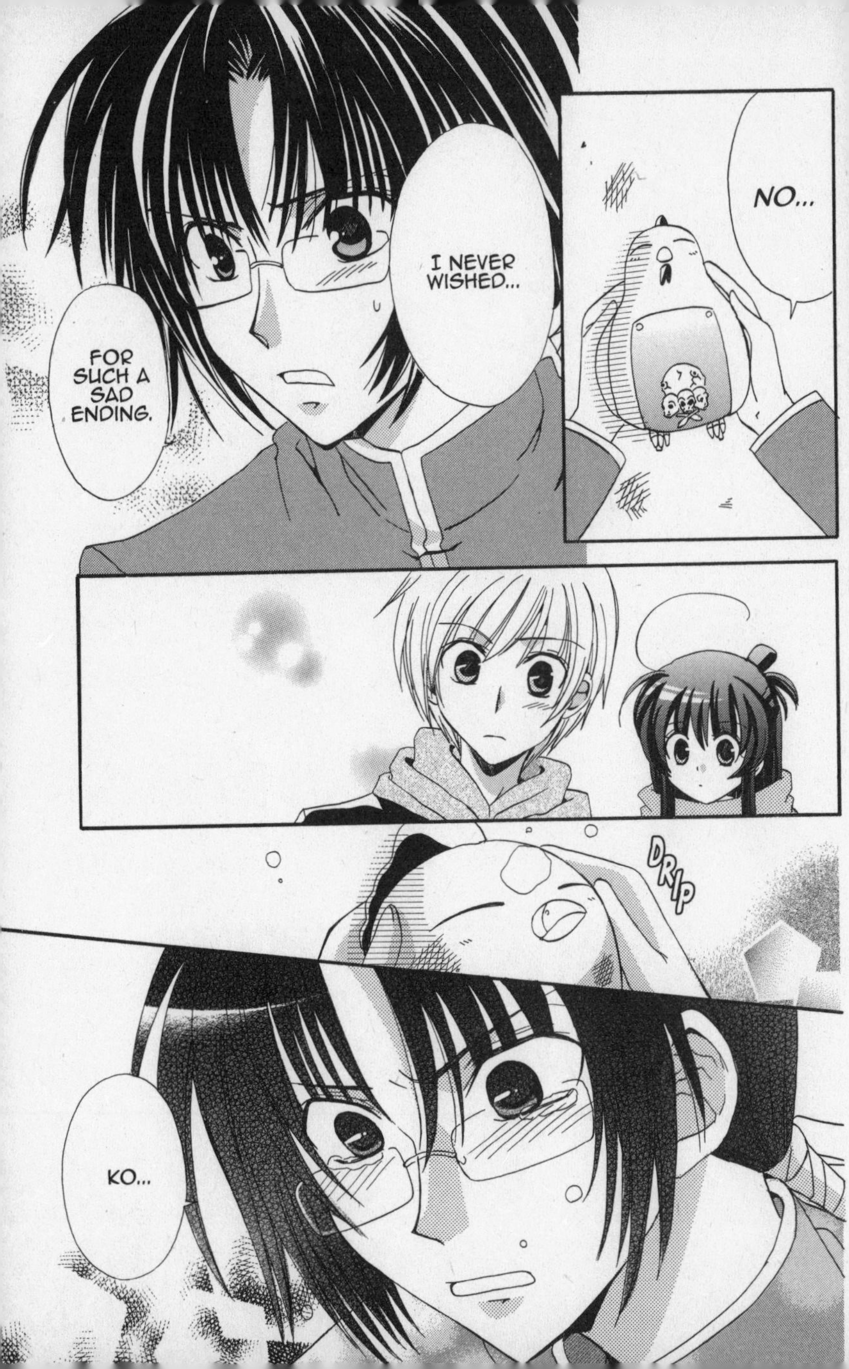
NO...
I NEVER WISHED...
FOR SUCH A SAD ENDING.
DRIP
KO...

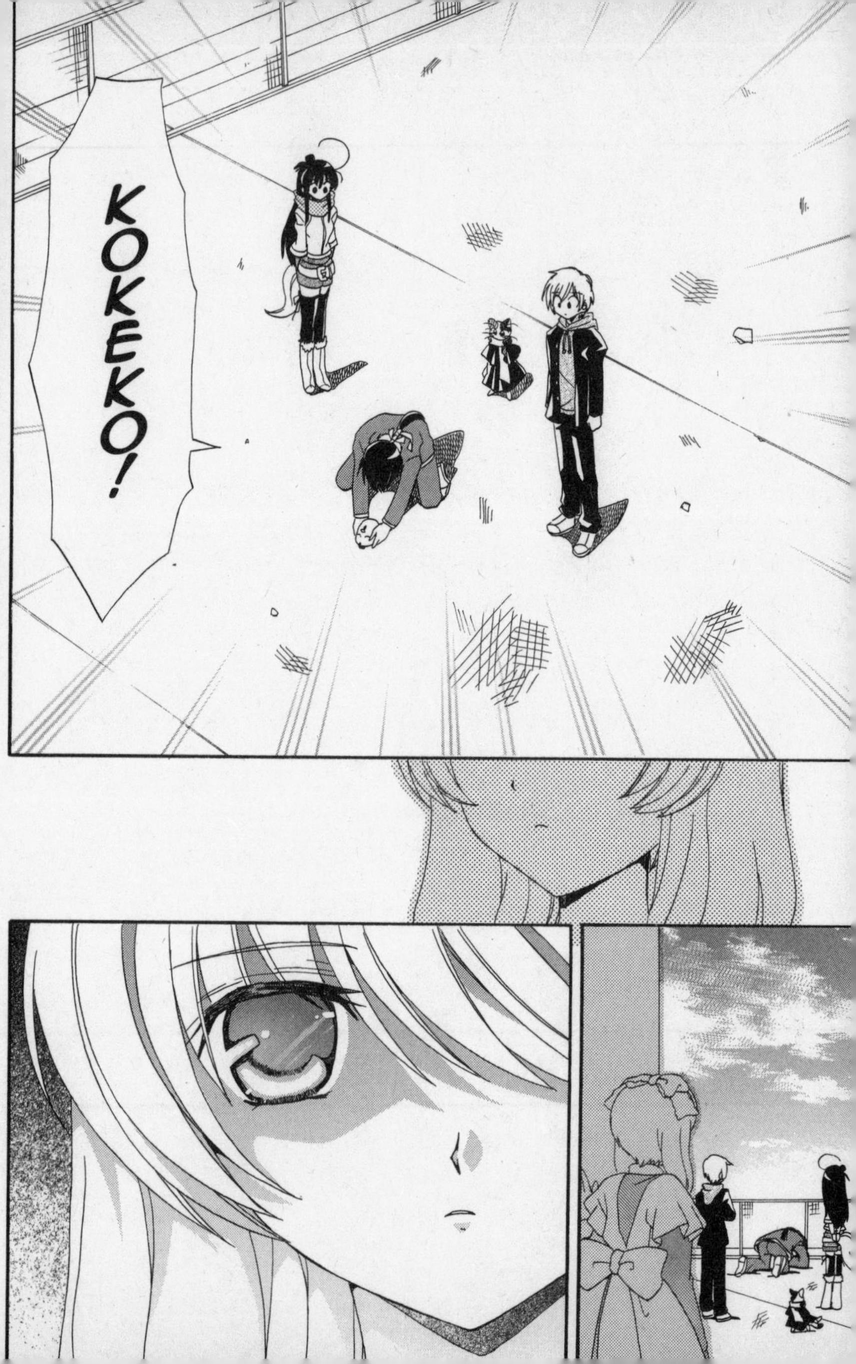
KOKEKO!

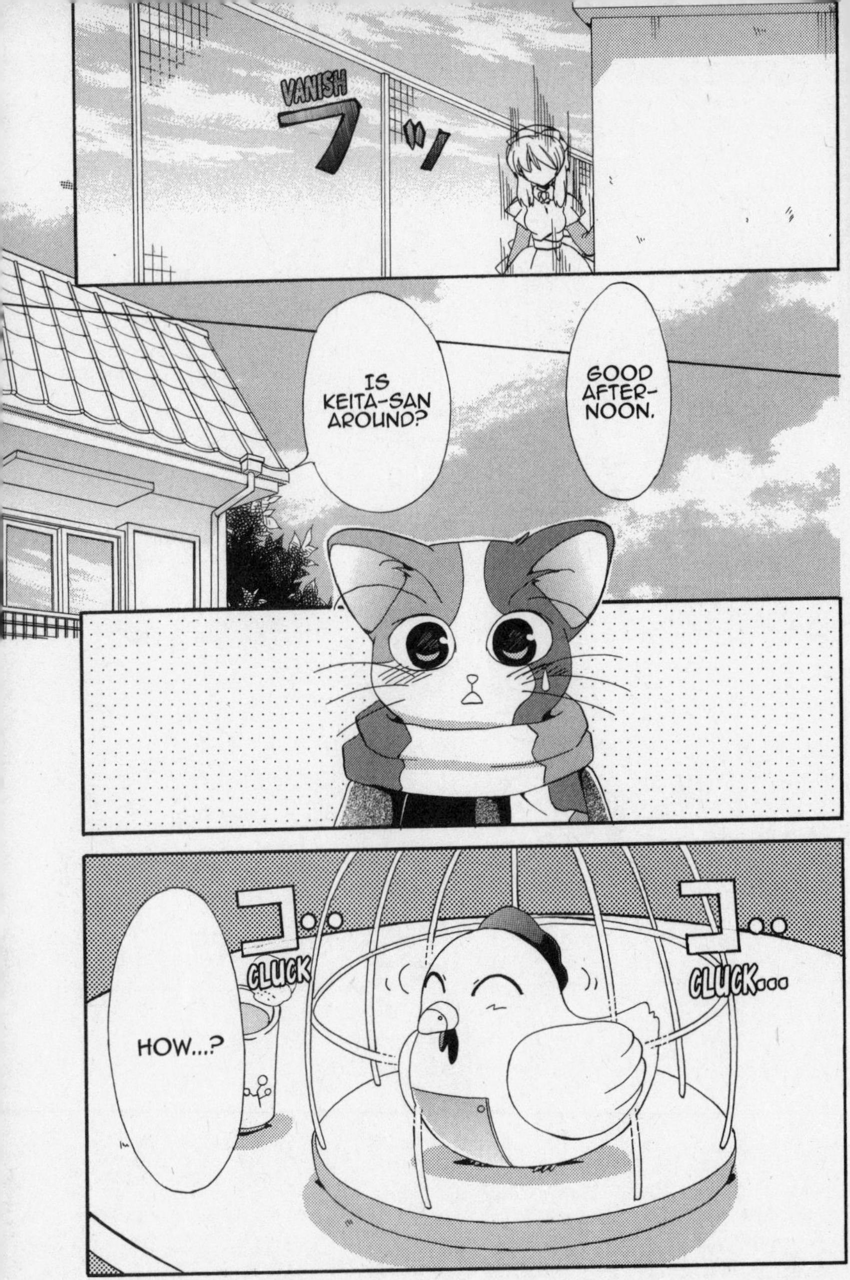
VANISH
GOOD AFTER-NOON.
IS KEITA-SAN AROUND?
CLUCK...
CLUCK
HOW...?

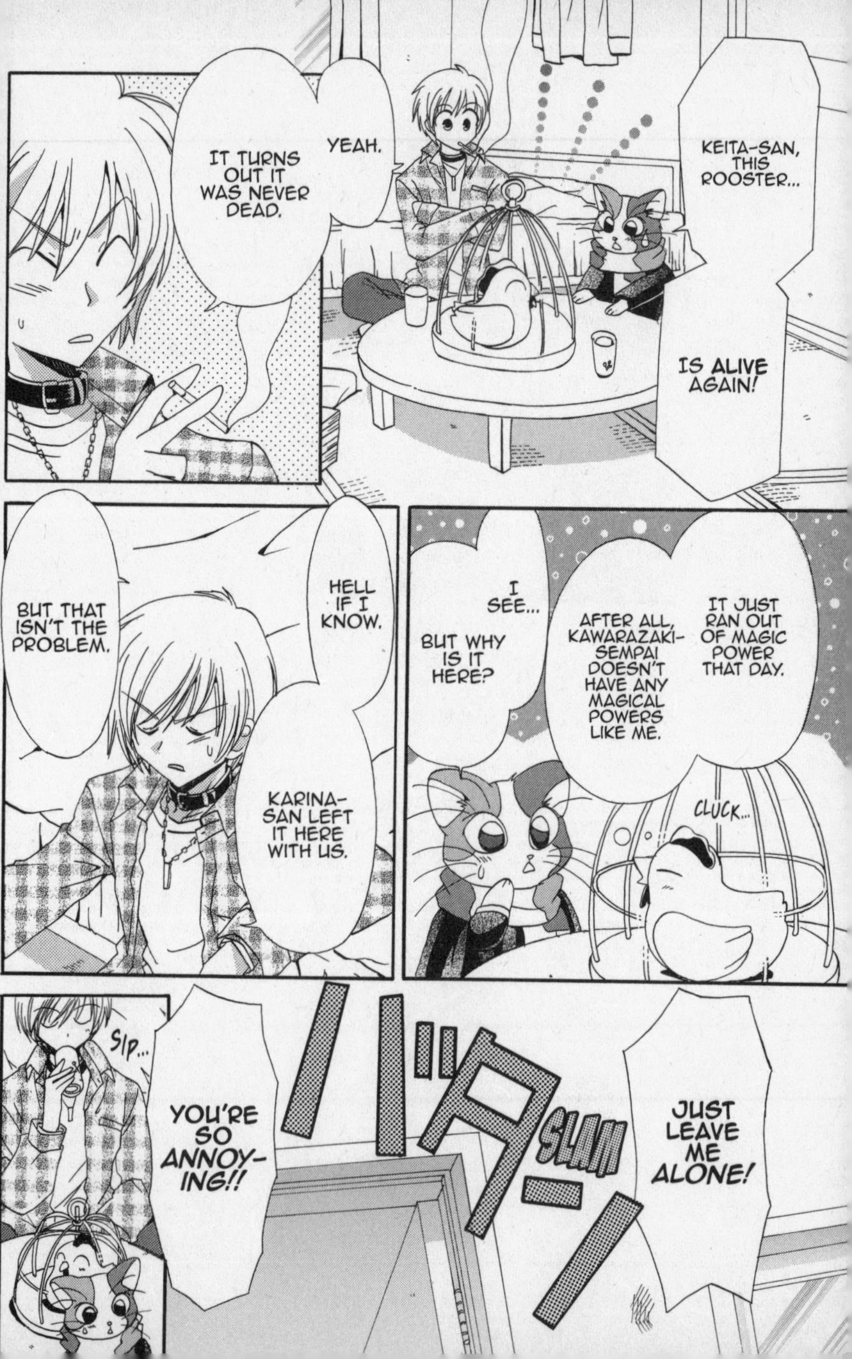
KEITA-SAN, THIS ROOSTER...
IS ALIVE AGAIN!
YEAH.
IT TURNS OUT IT WAS NEVER DEAD.
IT JUST RAN OUT OF MAGIC POWER THAT DAY.
AFTER ALL, KAWARAZAKI-SEMPAI DOESN'T HAVE ANY MAGICAL POWERS LIKE ME.
I SEE...
BUT WHY IS IT HERE?
CLUCK...
HELL IF I KNOW.
BUT THAT ISN'T THE PROBLEM.
KARINA-SAN LEFT IT HERE WITH US.
JUST LEAVE ME ALONE!
SLAM
YOU'RE SO ANNOY-ING!!
Sip...

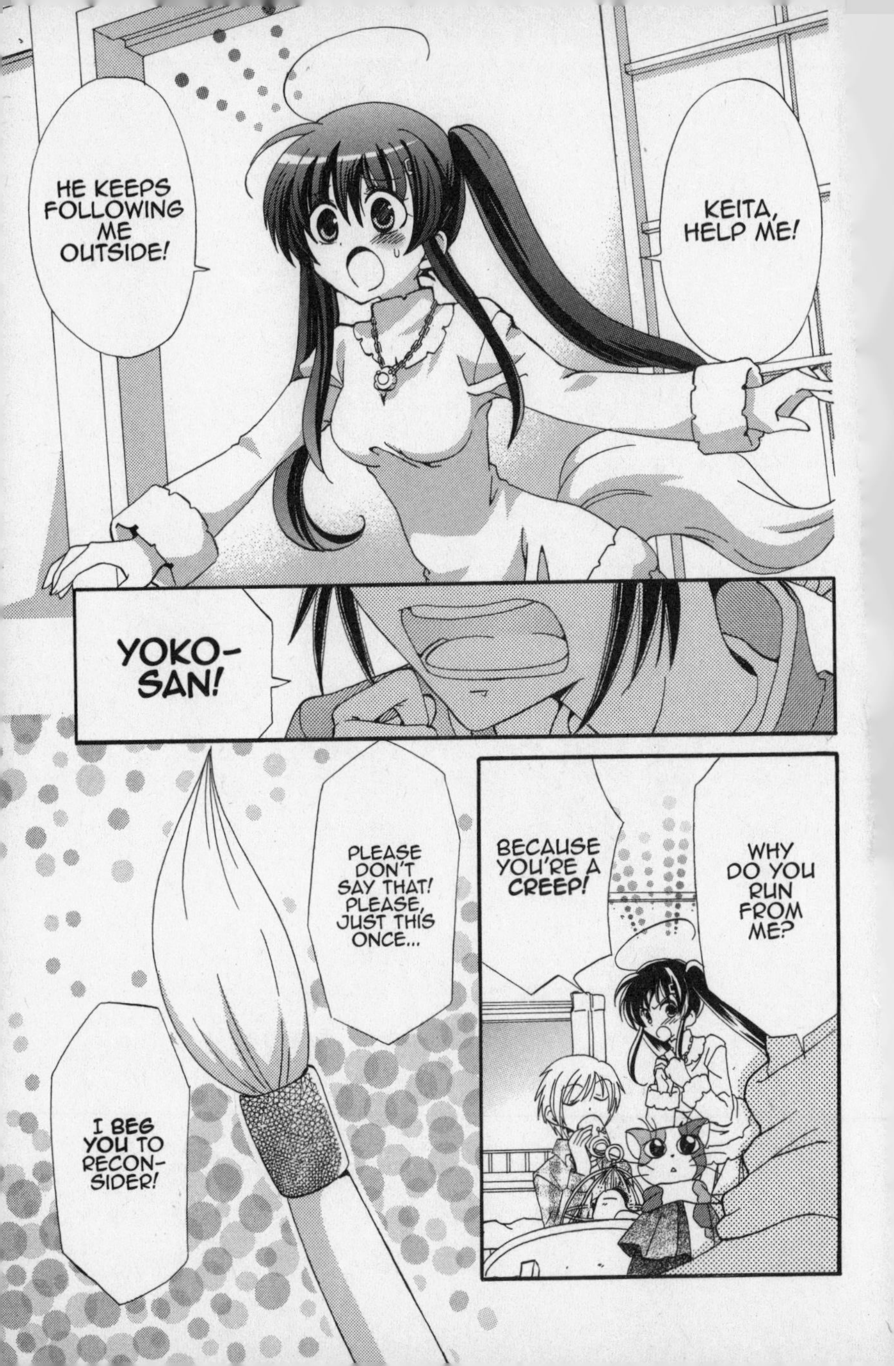
KEITA, HELP ME!
HE KEEPS FOLLOWING ME OUTSIDE!
YOKO-SAN!
WHY DO YOU RUN FROM ME?
BECAUSE YOU'RE A CREEP!
PLEASE DON'T SAY THAT! PLEASE, JUST THIS ONCE...
I BEG YOU TO RECONSIDER!

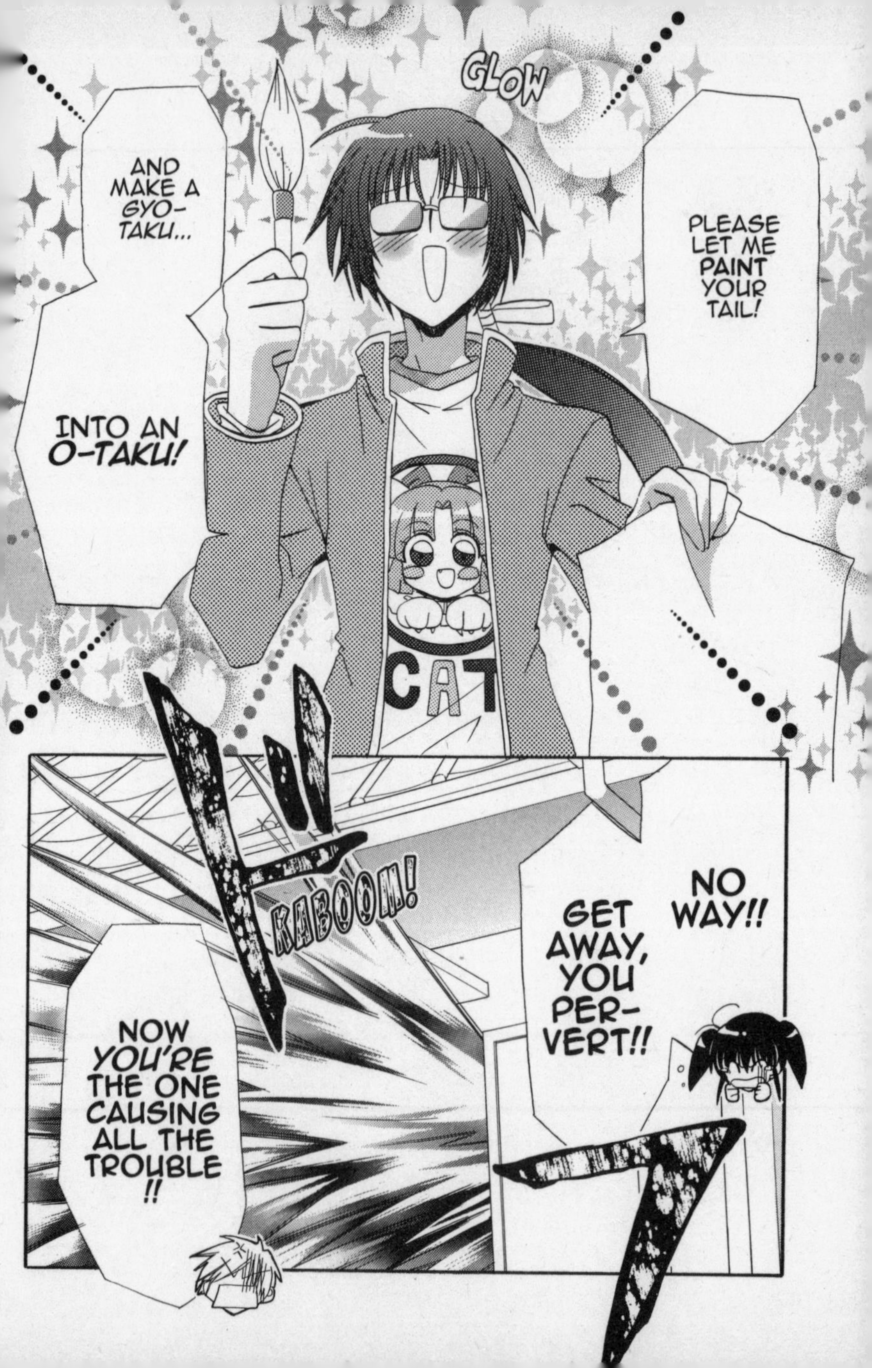
GLOW
PLEASE LET ME PAINT YOUR TAIL!
AND MAKE A GYO-TAKU...
INTO AN O-TAKU!
NO WAY!!
GET AWAY, YOU PER-VERT!!
KABOOM!
NOW YOU'RE THE ONE CAUSING ALL THE TROUBLE!!

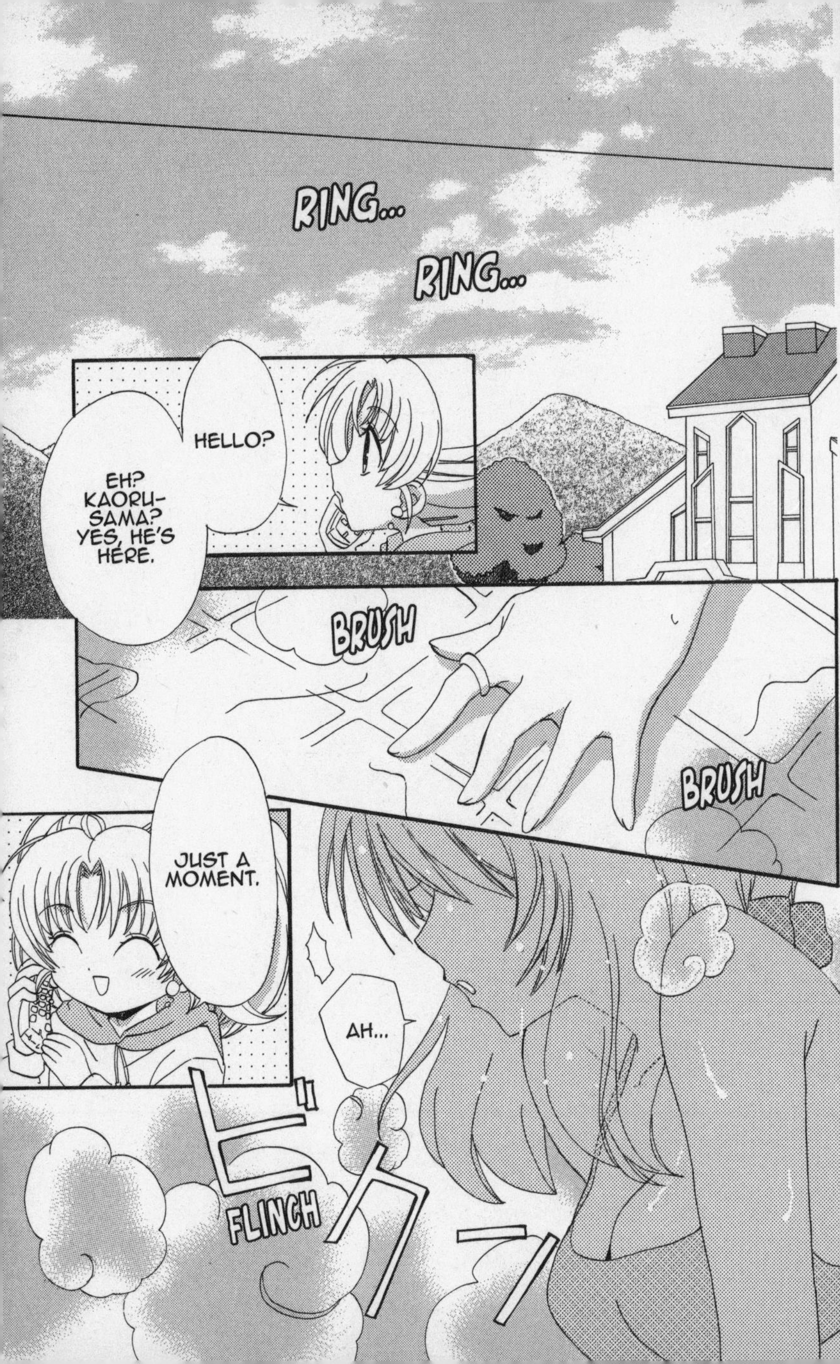
RING...
RING...
HELLO?
EH? KAORU-SAMA? YES, HE'S HERE.
BRUSH
BRUSH
AH...
FLINCH
JUST A MOMENT.

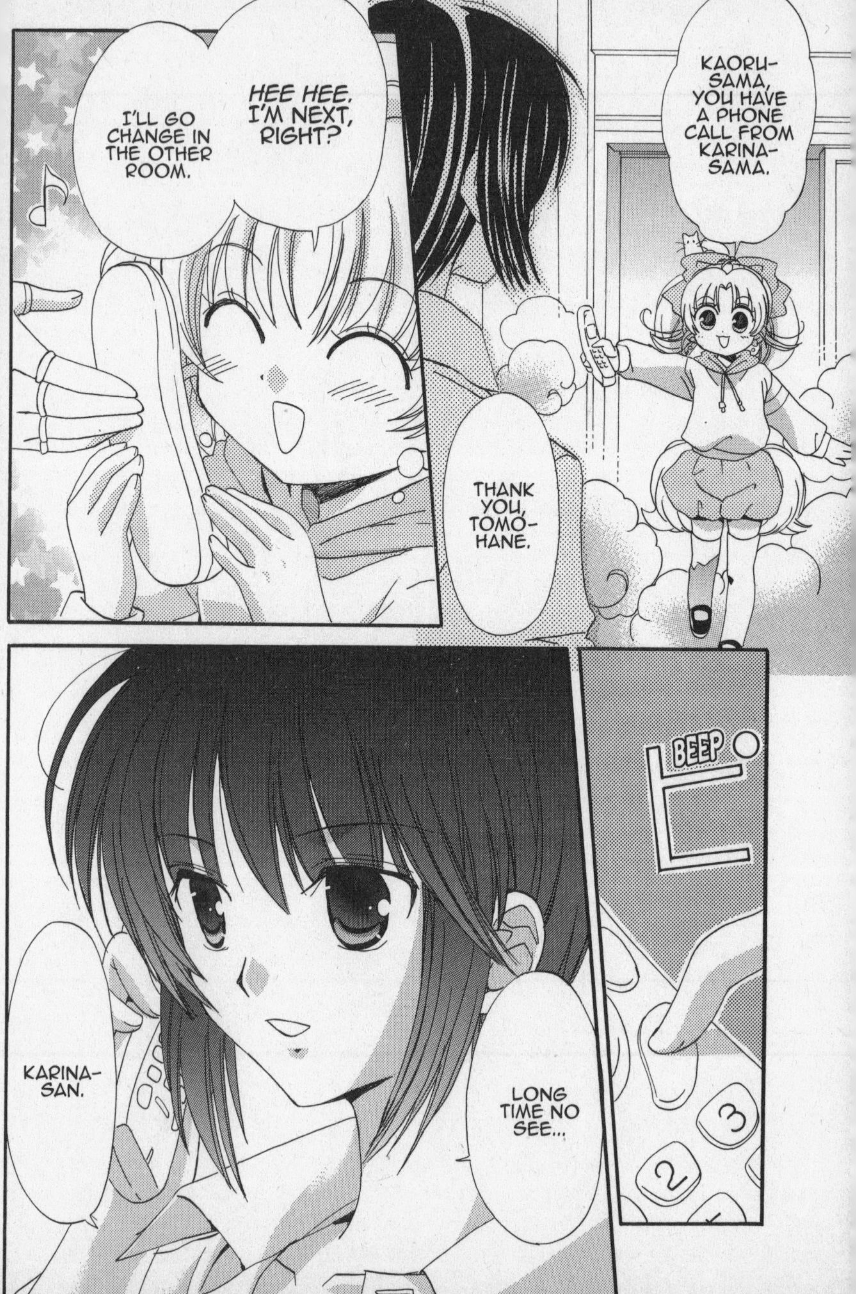
KAORU-SAMA, YOU HAVE A PHONE CALL FROM KARINA-SAMA.
THANK YOU, TOMO-HANE.
HEE HEE. I'M NEXT, RIGHT?
I'LL GO CHANGE IN THE OTHER ROOM.
BEEP
KARINA-SAN.
LONG TIME NO SEE...

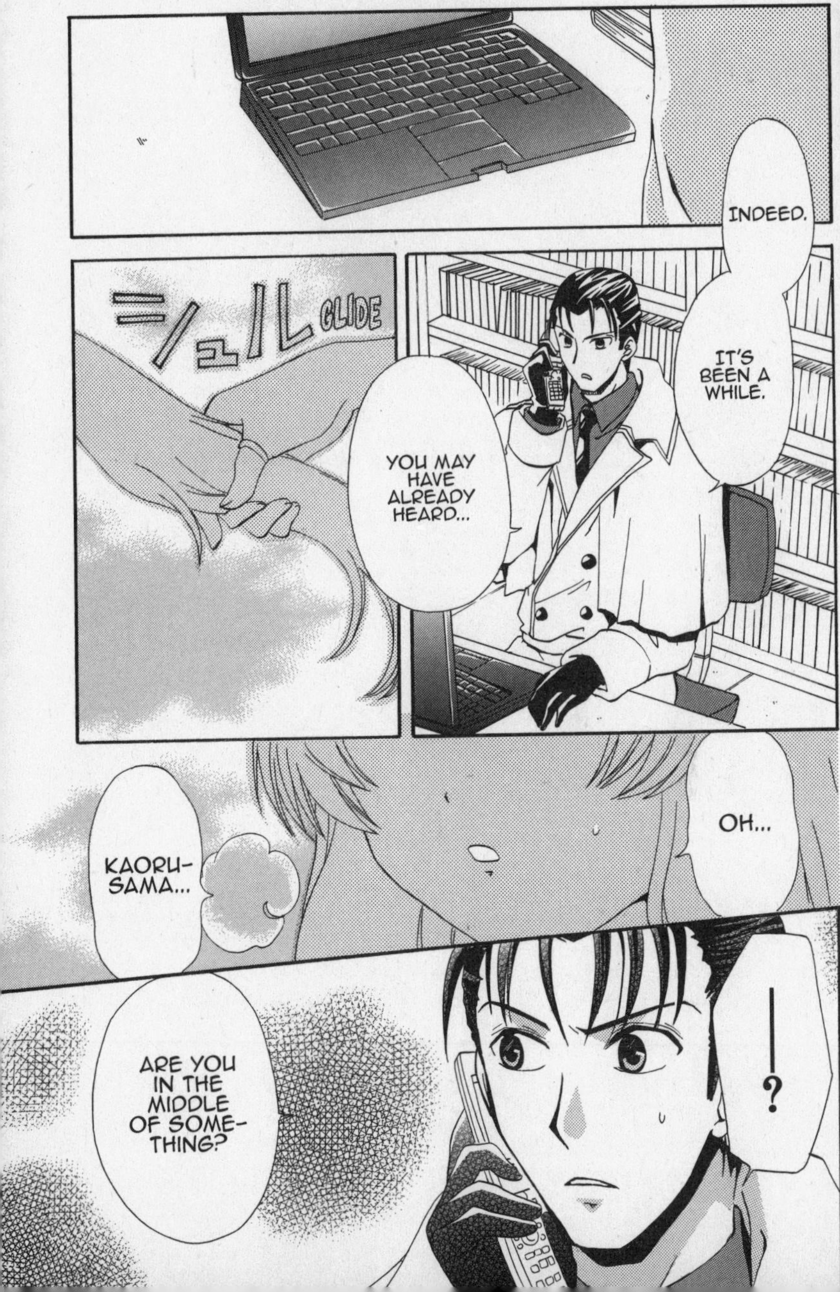

INDEED.
IT'S BEEN A WHILE.
YOU MAY HAVE ALREADY HEARD...
シュル GLIDE
OH...
KAORU-SAMA...
—?
ARE YOU IN THE MIDDLE OF SOME-THING?

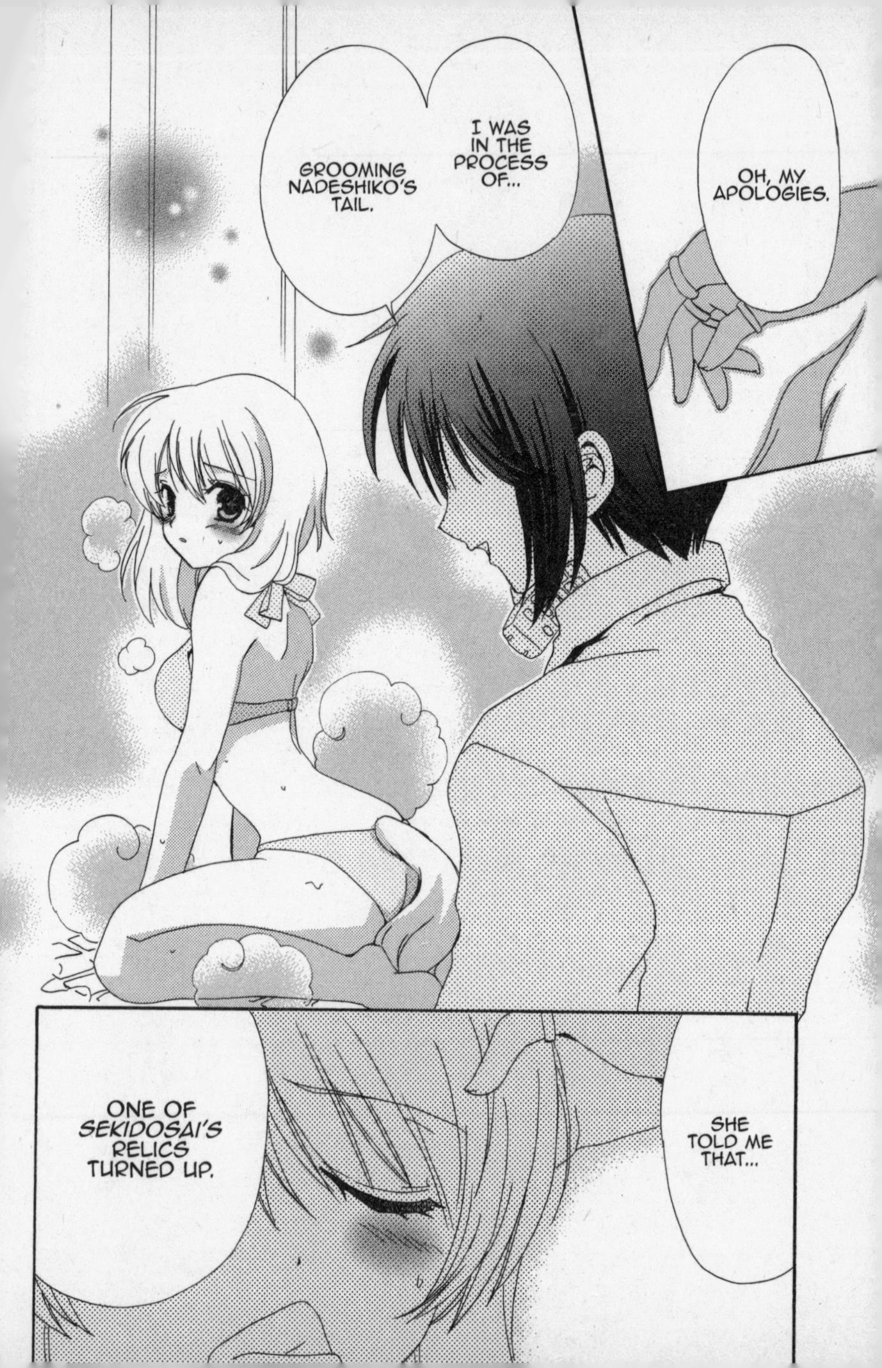
OH, MY APOLOGIES.
I WAS IN THE PROCESS OF...
GROOMING NADESHIKO'S TAIL.
SHE TOLD ME THAT...
ONE OF SEKIDOSAI'S RELICS TURNED UP.

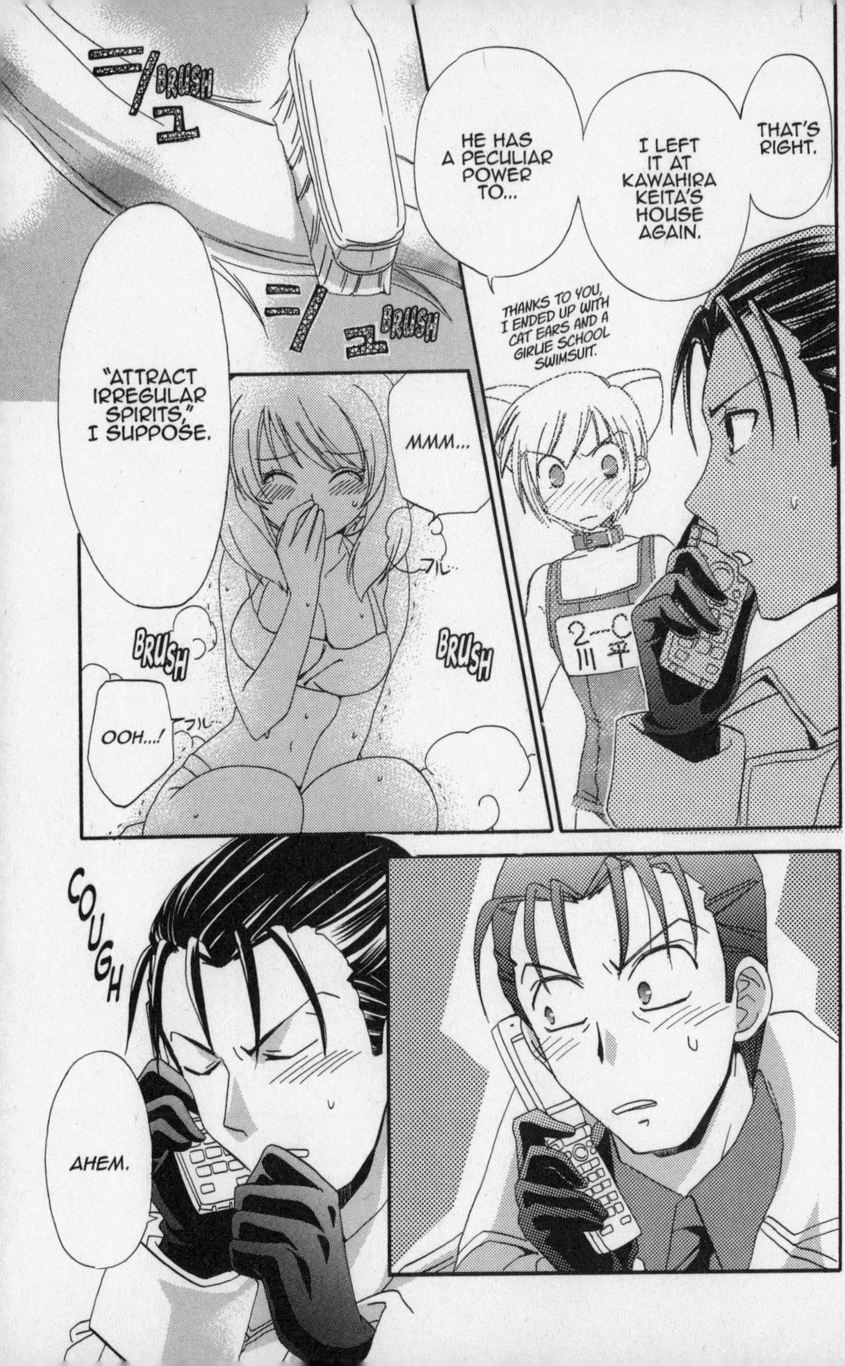
THAT'S RIGHT.
I LEFT IT AT KAWAHIRA KEITA'S HOUSE AGAIN.
HE HAS A PECULIAR POWER TO...
THANKS TO YOU, I ENDED UP WITH CAT EARS AND A GIRLIE SCHOOL SWIMSUIT.
BRUSH
BRUSH
"ATTRACT IRREGULAR SPIRITS," I SUPPOSE.
MMM...
フル...
BRUSH
BRUSH
フル...
OOH...!
COUGH
AHEM.

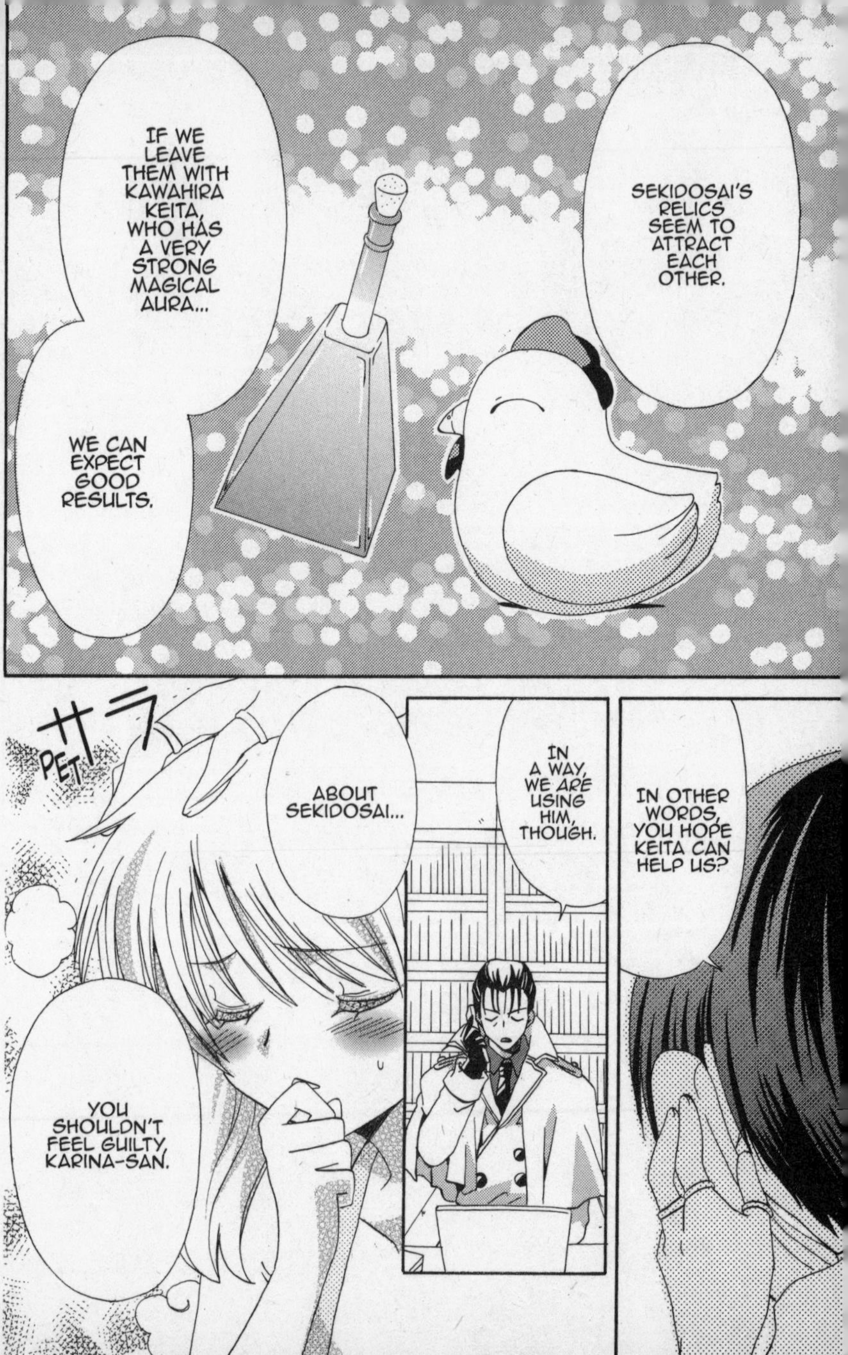
SEKIDOSAI'S RELICS SEEM TO ATTRACT EACH OTHER.
IF WE LEAVE THEM WITH KAWAHIRA KEITA, WHO HAS A VERY STRONG MAGICAL AURA...
WE CAN EXPECT GOOD RESULTS.
IN OTHER WORDS, YOU HOPE KEITA CAN HELP US?
IN A WAY, WE ARE USING HIM, THOUGH.
ABOUT SEKIDOSAI...
サラ
PET
YOU SHOULDN'T FEEL GUILTY, KARINA-SAN.

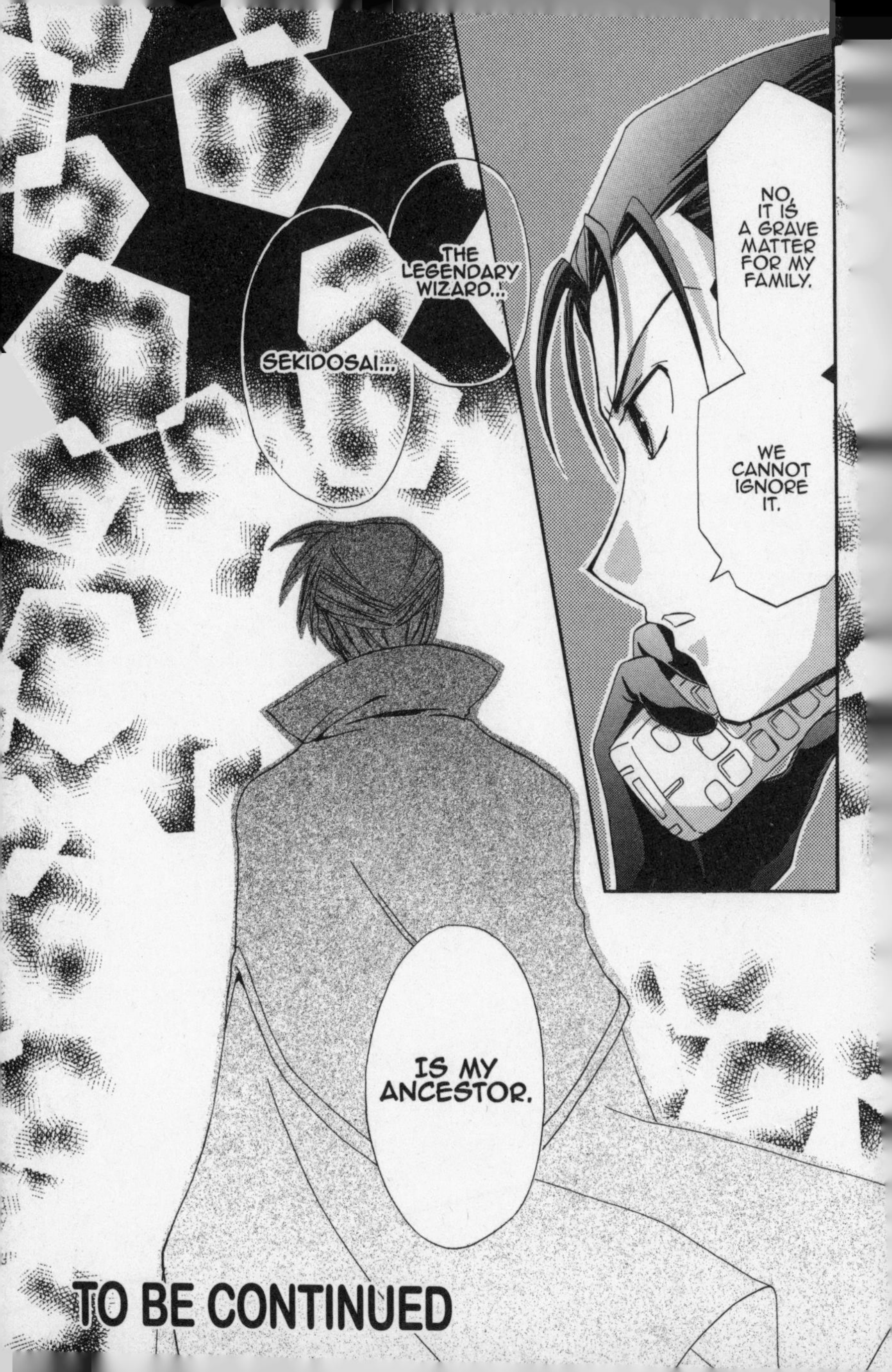
NO, IT IS A GRAVE MATTER FOR MY FAMILY.
WE CANNOT IGNORE IT.
THE LEGENDARY WIZARD...!
SEKIDOSAI...
IS MY ANCESTOR.
TO BE CONTINUED

Afterword!

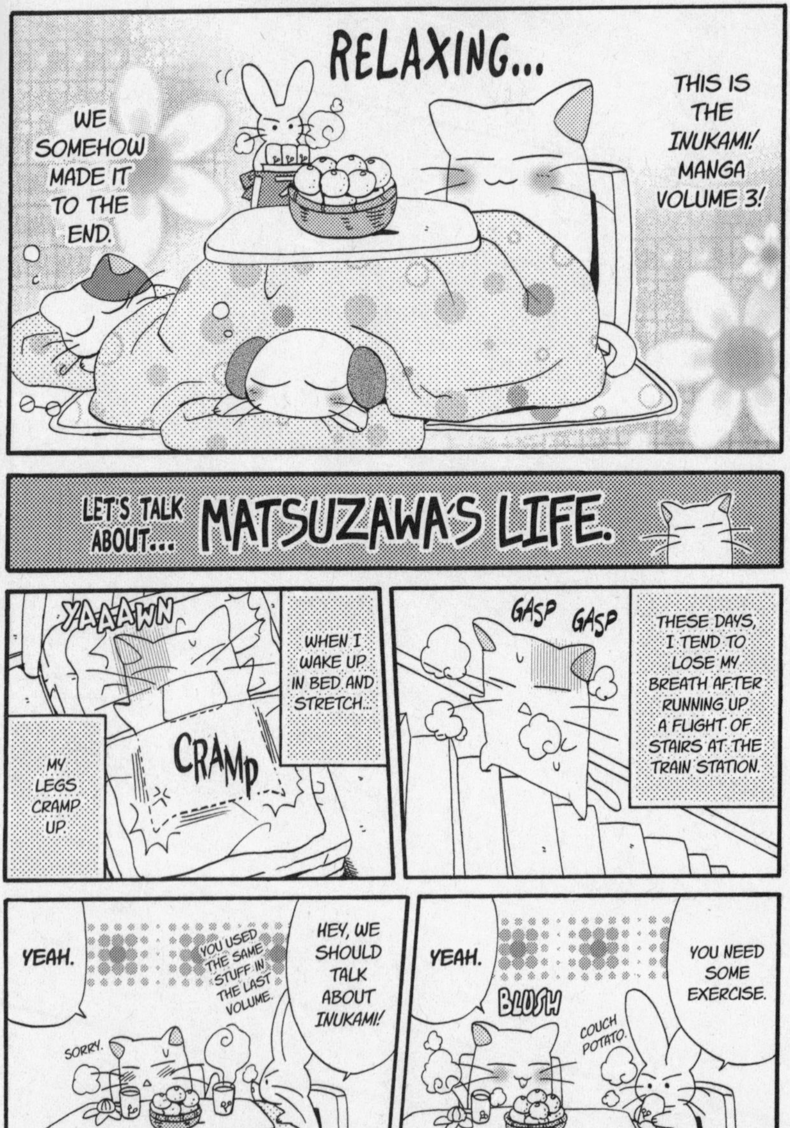
THIS IS THE INUKAMI! MANGA VOLUME 3!
RELAXING...
WE SOMEHOW MADE IT TO THE END.
LET'S TALK ABOUT... MATSUZAWA'S LIFE.
THESE DAYS, I TEND TO LOSE MY BREATH AFTER RUNNING UP A FLIGHT OF STAIRS AT THE TRAIN STATION.
GASP
GASP
WHEN I WAKE UP IN BED AND STRETCH...
YAAAWN
MY LEGS CRAMP UP.
CRAMP
YOU NEED SOME EXERCISE.
COUCH POTATO.
BLUSH
YEAH.
HEY, WE SHOULD TALK ABOUT INUKAMI!
YOU USED THE SAME STUFF IN THE LAST VOLUME.
SORRY.
YEAH.

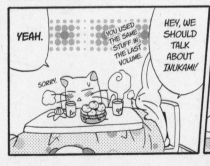

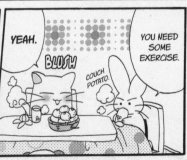

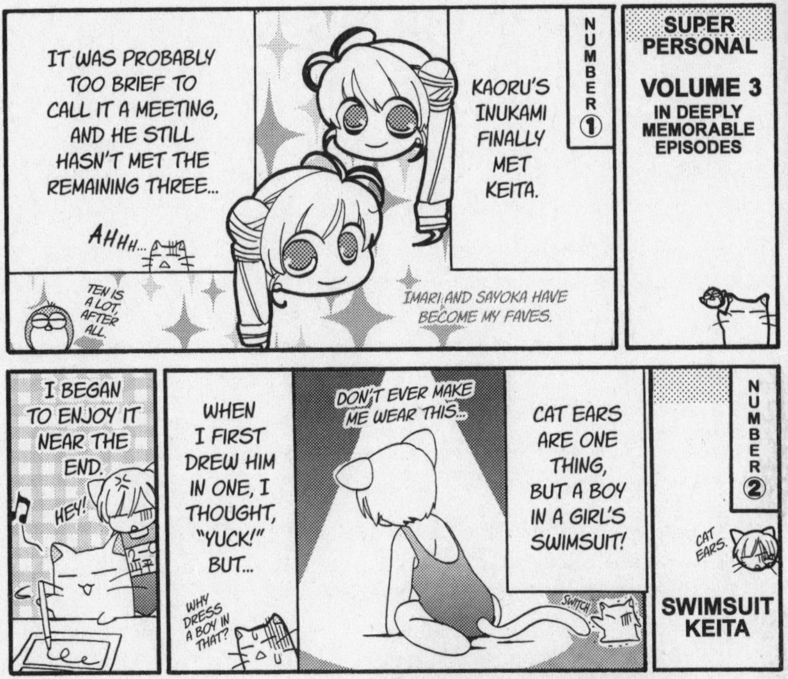
SUPER PERSONAL
VOLUME 3
IN DEEPLY MEMORABLE EPISODES
NUMBER 1
KAORU'S INUKAMI FINALLY MET KEITA.
IMARI AND SAYOKA HAVE BECOME MY FAVES.
IT WAS PROBABLY TOO BRIEF TO CALL IT A MEETING, AND HE STILL HASN'T MET THE REMAINING THREE...
AHHH...
TEN IS A LOT, AFTER ALL.
NUMBER 2
SWIMSUIT KEITA
CAT EARS.
CAT EARS ARE ONE THING, BUT A BOY IN A GIRL'S SWIMSUIT!
DON'T EVER MAKE ME WEAR THIS...
SWITCH
WHEN I FIRST DREW HIM IN ONE, I THOUGHT, "YUCK!" BUT...
WHY DRESS A BOY IN THAT?
I BEGAN TO ENJOY IT NEAR THE END.
HEY!

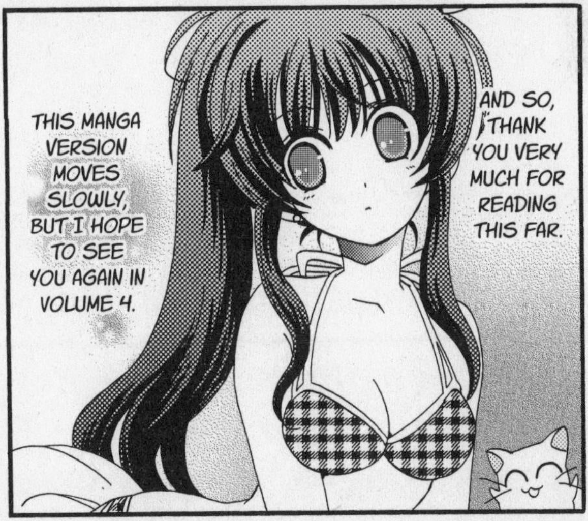
AND SO, THANK YOU VERY MUCH FOR READING THIS FAR.
THIS MANGA VERSION MOVES SLOWLY, BUT I HOPE TO SEE YOU AGAIN IN VOLUME 4.

Special Thanks

- MAMIZU ARISAWA-SAN
- KANNO WAKATSUKI-SAN
- KISHO FUJIYOSHI-SAN
- UTA ICHIKAWA-SAN
- AKIMASA NANJO-SAN
- ALL THE EDITORS
- MY FAMILY
- AND EVERYONE ELSE I COULDN'T MENTION SPECIFICALLY.

HONORIFICS

To ensure that all character relationships appear as they were originally intended, all character names have been kept in their original Japanese name order with family name first and given name second. For copyright reasons, creator names appear in standard English name order.

In addition to preserving the original Japanese name order, Seven Seas is committed to ensuring that honorifics—polite speech that indicates a person's status or relationship towards another individual—are retained within this book. Politeness is an integral facet of Japanese culture and we believe that maintaining honorifics in our translations helps bring out the same character nuances as seen in the original work.

The following are some of the more common honorifics you may come across while reading this and other books:

-san – The most common of all honorifics, it is an all-purpose suffix that can be used in any situation where politeness is expected. Generally seen as the equivalent to Mr., Miss, Ms., Mrs., etc.

-sama – This suffix is one level higher than "-san" and is used to confer great respect upon an individual.

-kun – This suffix is commonly used at the end of boys' names to express either familiarity or endearment. It can also be used when addressing someone younger than oneself or of a lower status.

-chan – Another common honorific. This suffix is mainly used to express endearment towards girls, but can also be used when referring to little boys or even pets. Couples are also known to use the term amongst each other to convey a sense of cuteness and intimacy.

Sempai – This title is used towards one's senior or "superior" in a particular group or organization. "Sempai" is most often used in a school setting, where underclassmen refer to upperclassmen as "sempai," though it is also commonly said by employees when addressing fellow employees who hold seniority in the workplace.

Sensei – Literally meaning "one who has come before," this title is used for teachers, doctors, or masters of any profession or art.

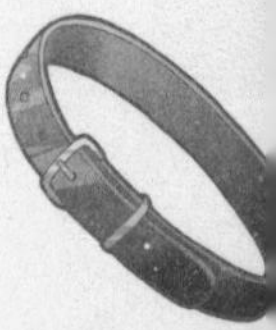

Oniisan – This title literally means "big brother." First and foremost, it is used by younger siblings towards older male siblings. It can be used by itself or attached to a person's name as a suffix (niisan). It is often used by a younger person toward an older person unrelated by blood, but as a sign of respect. Other forms include the informal "oniichan" and the more respectful "oniisama."

Oneesan – This title is the opposite of "oniisan" and means "big sister." Other forms include the informal "oneechan" and the more respectful "oneesama."

TRANSLATION NOTES

Step.11
Doujinshi are fan-made, self-published manga, often with strong sexual themes.

Bozu – Keita misheard "Boys Love" as "bozu," a word that means "young boy" or "Buddhist monk" and can also be slang for someone who shaves his head. Obviously, Boys Love stories usually feature handsome guys with full heads of hair.

Step.12
Sukeban Deka is a well-known anime, manga, and live-action series that starred a punk girl who infiltrated schools on behalf of the police.

Step.13
In Japanese families where Buddhist traditions are observed, it is customary to bury loved ones in a white kimono.

Ojiisan – The Japanese honorific for "Grandfather."

Japanese puns are notoriously hard to translate into a way that makes sense and retains the original comedic tone of the story. In this particular scene, Keita originally says the word *"shitai,"* which Keita uses to mean, "I want to do it," but it also has a double meaning, which is that of "dead body."

Step.14

Sekidosai is the name of a legendary master wizard in the Inukami world. When an object, like the bottle in the last chapter, has his imprint, it has special powers. Karina-san has a very personal reason to be interested in him...

In Japanese folklore, a *nekomata* is a demon cat with a forked tail.

Step.15

Kokeko is Kawarazaki's new nickname for the rooster. It comes from the Japanese version of a rooster's call: *"kokekokko!"*

The Taisho period was 1912 to 1926. It's associated with the beginnings of Japanese democracy.

Yakisoba bread is a bun split down the middle and filled with fried noodles and pork.

A *gyotaku* is a print made by using a painted fish as a stamp. *O-taku* literally means tail print, but an actual otaku print might require Yoko to let him press his painted body against her...

CHARACTER NAME

The name "Nadeshiko" comes from the famous Japanese phrase *"yamato nadeshiko,"* which refers to the "perfect Japanese woman." The American equivalent would be the phrase "all-American girl." Both phrases refer to a woman with qualities that are viewed as traditionally desirable by society.

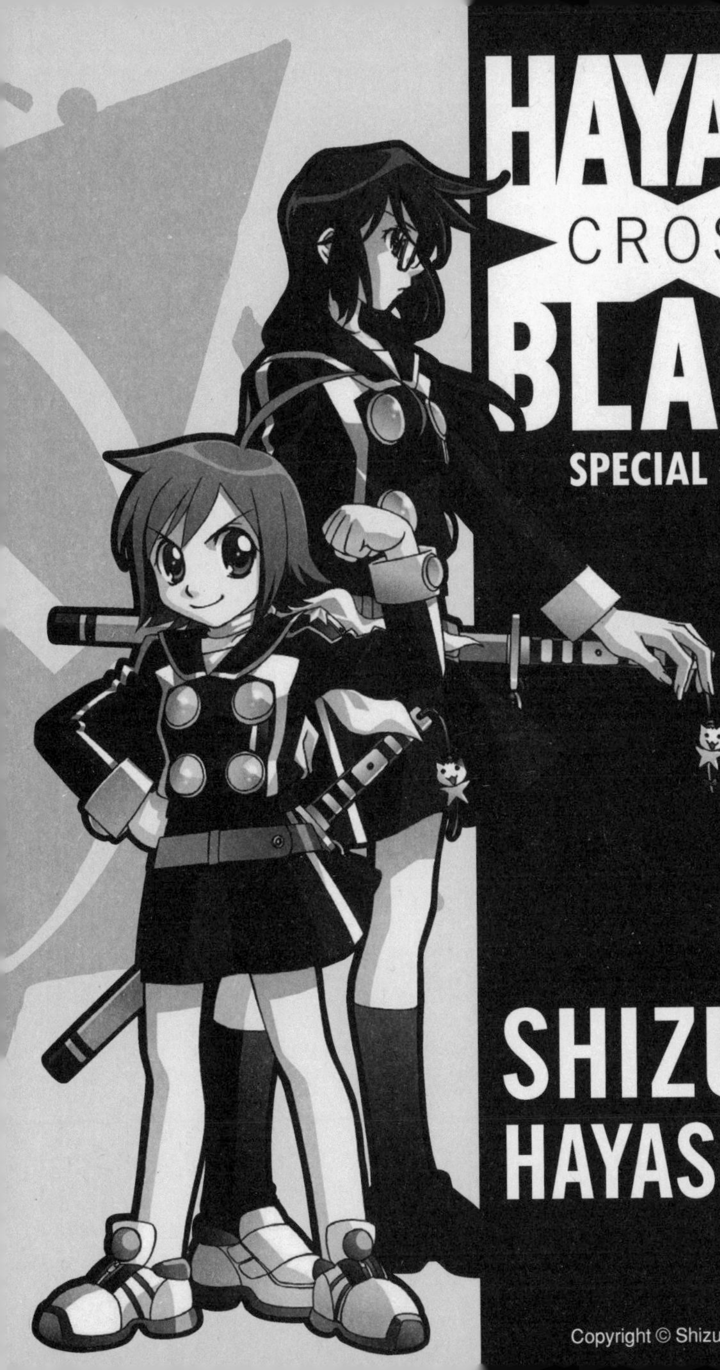

HAYATE CROSS BLADE

SPECIAL PREVIEW

SHIZURU HAYASHIYA

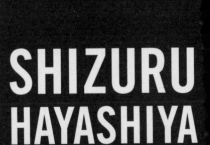

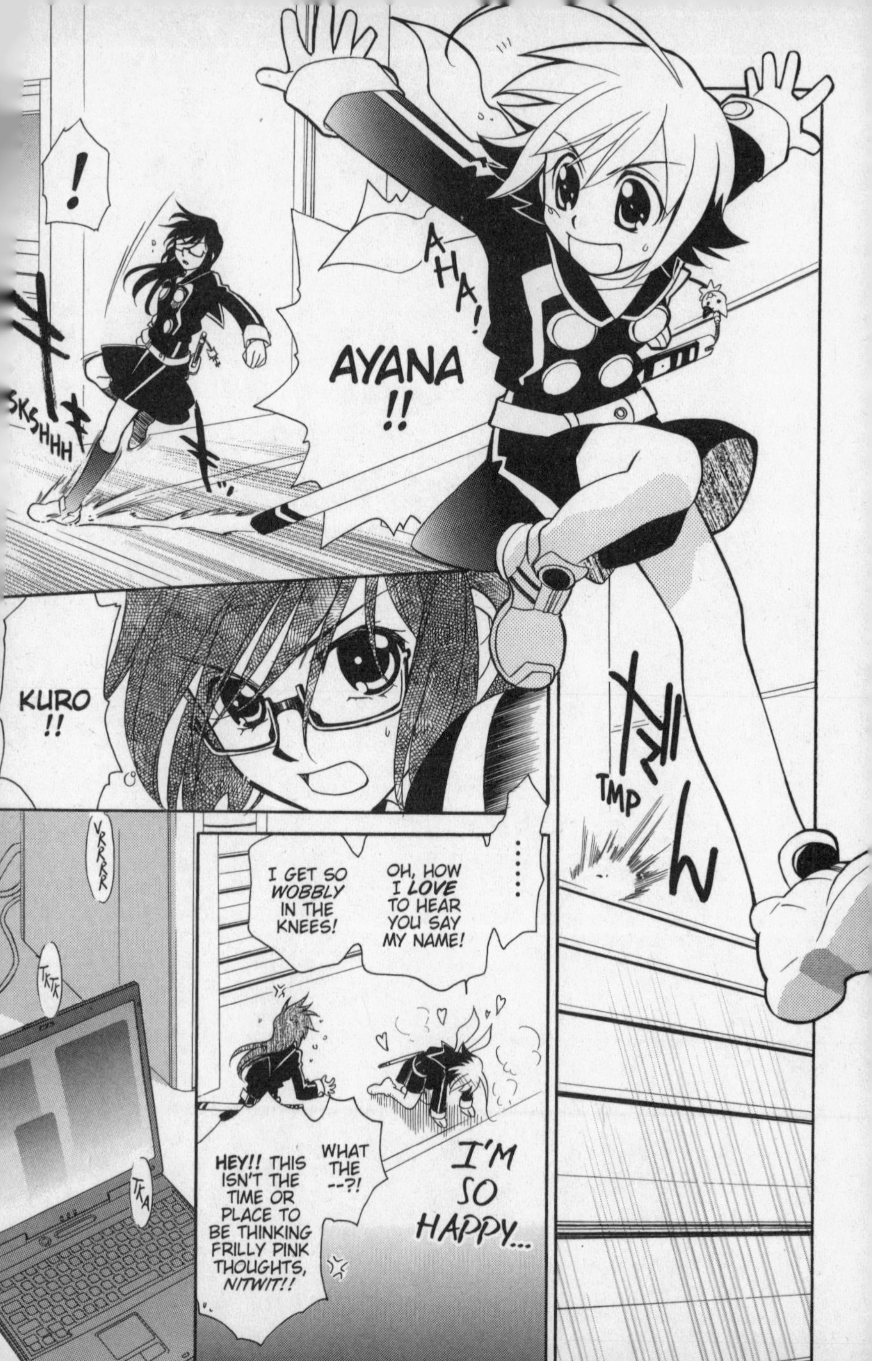

AHA!
AYANA!!
!
SKSHHH
TMP
KURO!!
......
OH, HOW I LOVE TO HEAR YOU SAY MY NAME!
I GET SO WOBBLY IN THE KNEES!
I'M SO HAPPY...
WHAT THE --?!
HEY!! THIS ISN'T THE TIME OR PLACE TO BE THINKING FRILLY PINK THOUGHTS, NITWIT!!
VRRRRR
TKTK
TKA

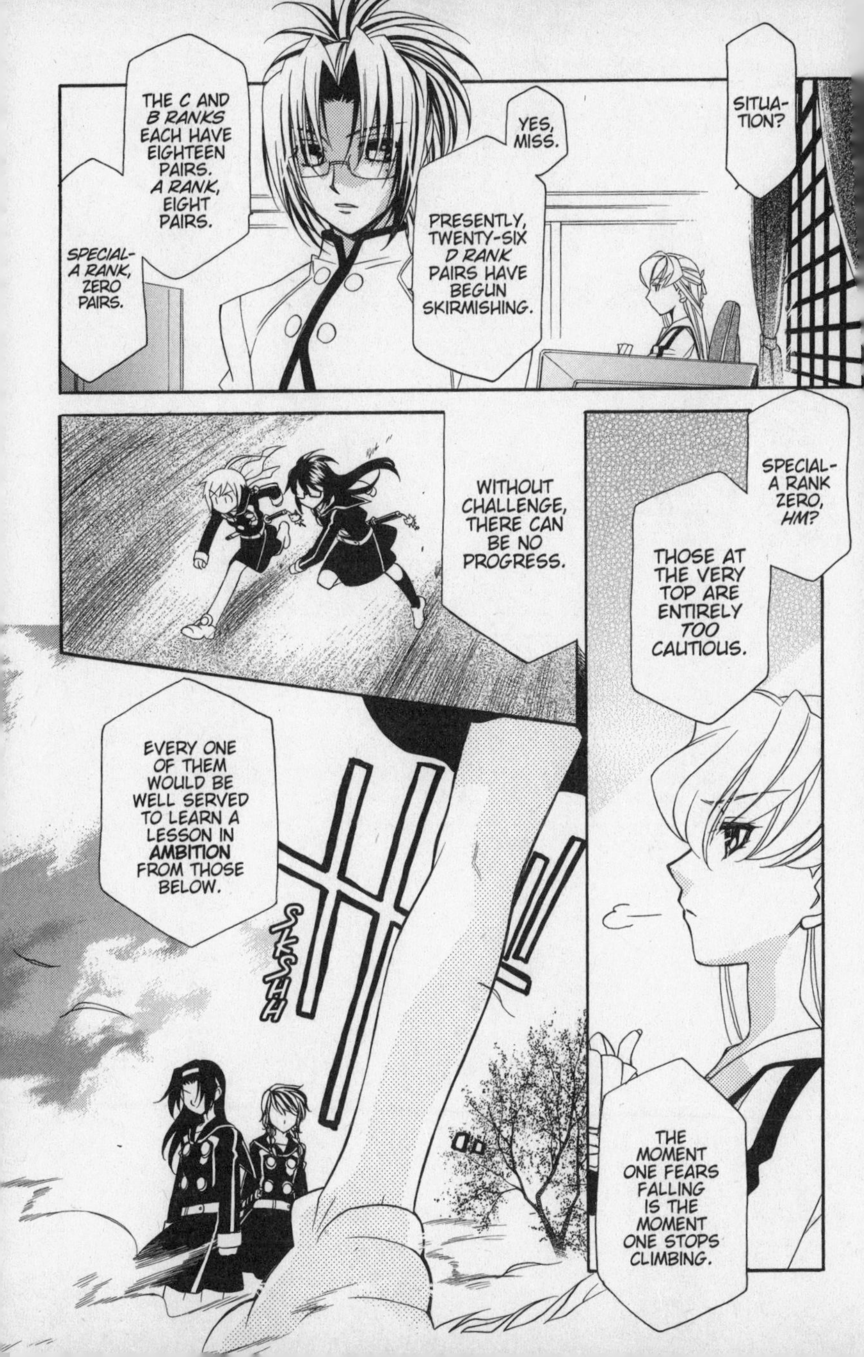
SITUA-TION?
YES, MISS.
PRESENTLY, TWENTY-SIX D RANK PAIRS HAVE BEGUN SKIRMISHING.
THE C AND B RANKS EACH HAVE EIGHTEEN PAIRS. A RANK, EIGHT PAIRS.
SPECIAL-A RANK, ZERO PAIRS.
SPECIAL-A RANK ZERO, HM?
THOSE AT THE VERY TOP ARE ENTIRELY TOO CAUTIOUS.
THE MOMENT ONE FEARS FALLING IS THE MOMENT ONE STOPS CLIMBING.
WITHOUT CHALLENGE, THERE CAN BE NO PROGRESS.
EVERY ONE OF THEM WOULD BE WELL SERVED TO LEARN A LESSON IN AMBITION FROM THOSE BELOW.
SKSHH

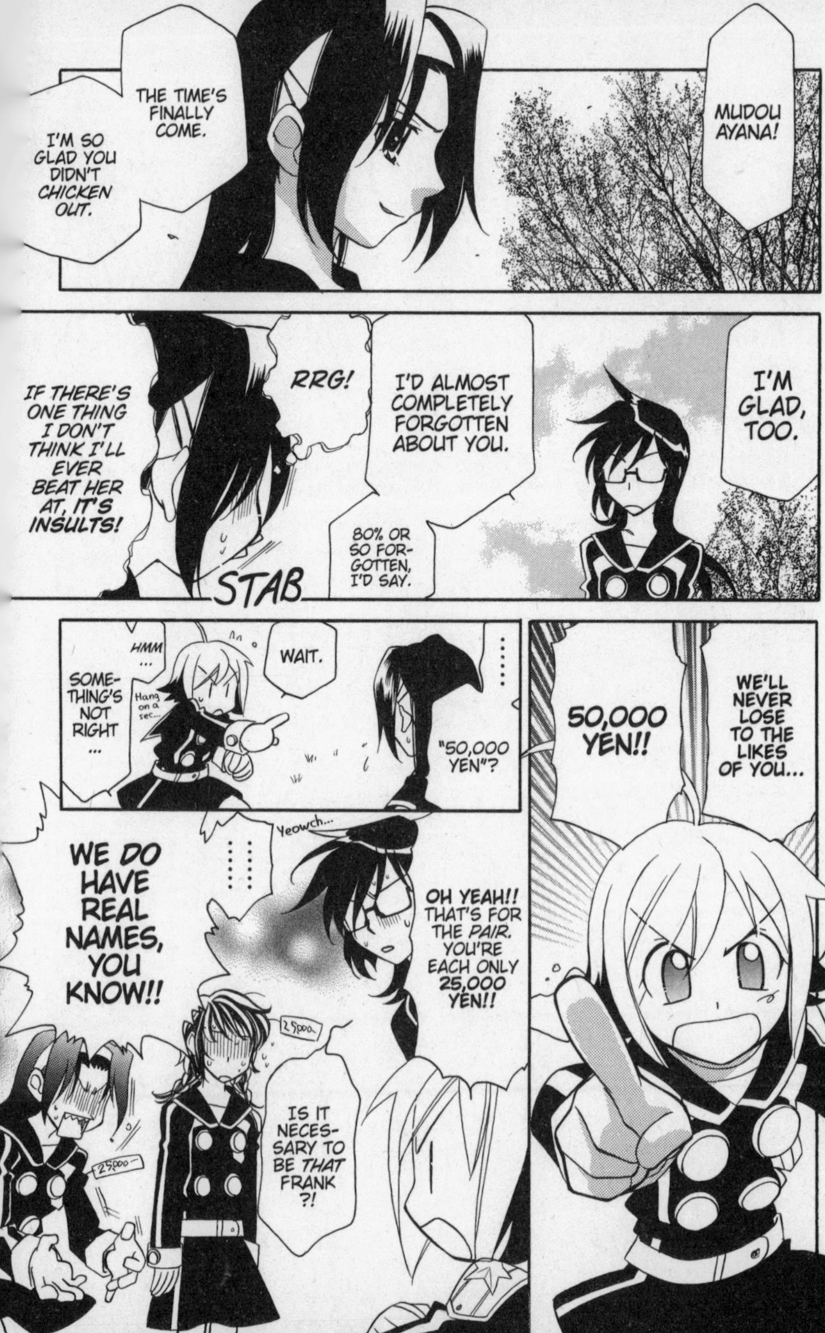
MUDOU AYANA!
THE TIME'S FINALLY COME.
I'M SO GLAD YOU DIDN'T CHICKEN OUT.
I'M GLAD, TOO.
I'D ALMOST COMPLETELY FORGOTTEN ABOUT YOU.
80% OR SO FOR-GOTTEN, I'D SAY.
RRG!
STAB
IF THERE'S ONE THING I DON'T THINK I'LL EVER BEAT HER AT, IT'S INSULTS!
WE'LL NEVER LOSE TO THE LIKES OF YOU...
50,000 YEN!!
......
"50,000 YEN"?
WAIT.
HMM...
SOME-THING'S NOT RIGHT...
Hang on a sec...
Yeowch...
OH YEAH!! THAT'S FOR THE PAIR. YOU'RE EACH ONLY 25,000 YEN!!
......
WE DO HAVE REAL NAMES, YOU KNOW!!
25,000~
IS IT NECES-SARY TO BE THAT FRANK?!
25,000~

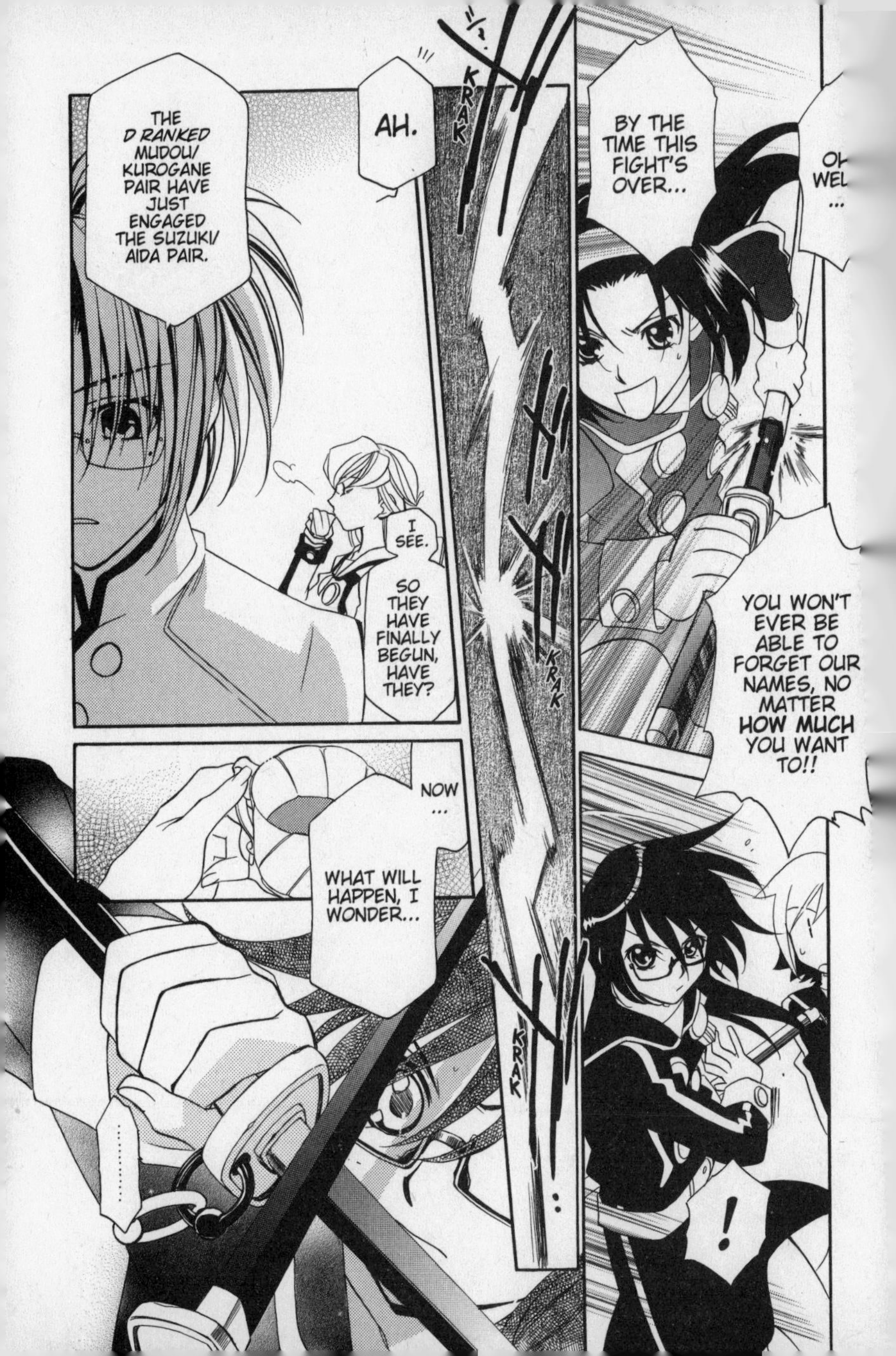
BY THE TIME THIS FIGHT'S OVER...
OH WEL ...
KRAK
YOU WON'T EVER BE ABLE TO FORGET OUR NAMES, NO MATTER HOW MUCH YOU WANT TO!!
KRAK
!
KRAK
AH.
THE D RANKED MUDOU/ KUROGANE PAIR HAVE JUST ENGAGED THE SUZUKI/ AIDA PAIR.
I SEE.
SO THEY HAVE FINALLY BEGUN, HAVE THEY?
NOW ...
WHAT WILL HAPPEN, I WONDER...
......

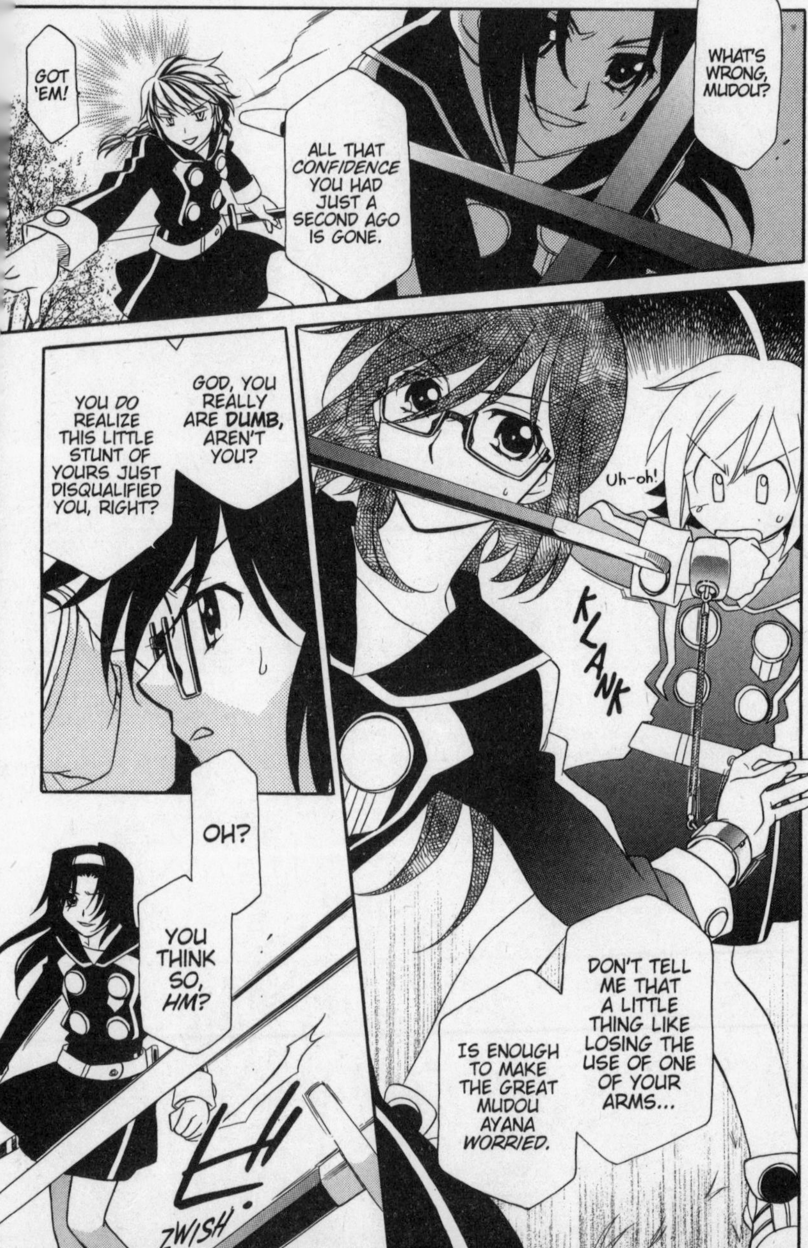
WHAT'S WRONG, MUDOU?
ALL THAT CONFIDENCE YOU HAD JUST A SECOND AGO IS GONE.
GOT 'EM!
Uh-oh!
KLANK
GOD, YOU REALLY ARE **DUMB**, AREN'T YOU?
YOU *DO* REALIZE THIS LITTLE STUNT OF YOURS JUST DISQUALIFIED YOU, RIGHT?
OH?
YOU THINK SO, *HM?*
DON'T TELL ME THAT A LITTLE THING LIKE LOSING THE USE OF ONE OF YOUR ARMS...
IS ENOUGH TO MAKE THE GREAT MUDOU AYANA *WORRIED.*
ZWISH

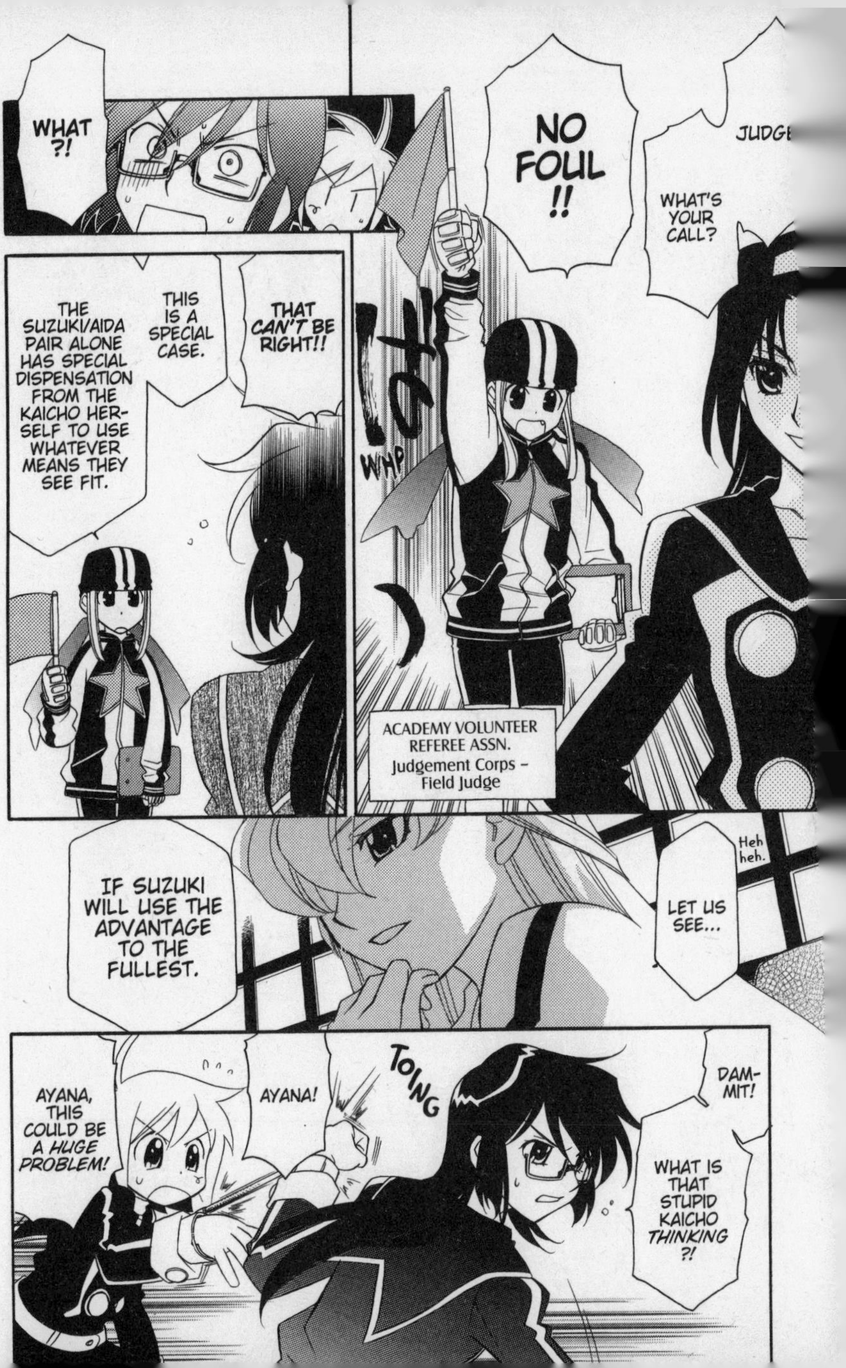
JUDGE
WHAT'S YOUR CALL?
NO FOUL!!
WHP
ACADEMY VOLUNTEER REFEREE ASSN. Judgement Corps – Field Judge
WHAT?!
THAT *CAN'T* BE RIGHT!!
THIS IS A SPECIAL CASE.
THE SUZUKI/AIDA PAIR ALONE HAS SPECIAL DISPENSATION FROM THE KAICHO HERSELF TO USE WHATEVER MEANS THEY SEE FIT.
Heh heh.
LET US SEE...
IF SUZUKI WILL USE THE ADVANTAGE TO THE FULLEST.
DAMMIT!
WHAT IS THAT STUPID KAICHO *THINKING*?!
TOING
AYANA!
AYANA, THIS COULD BE A *HUGE PROBLEM!*

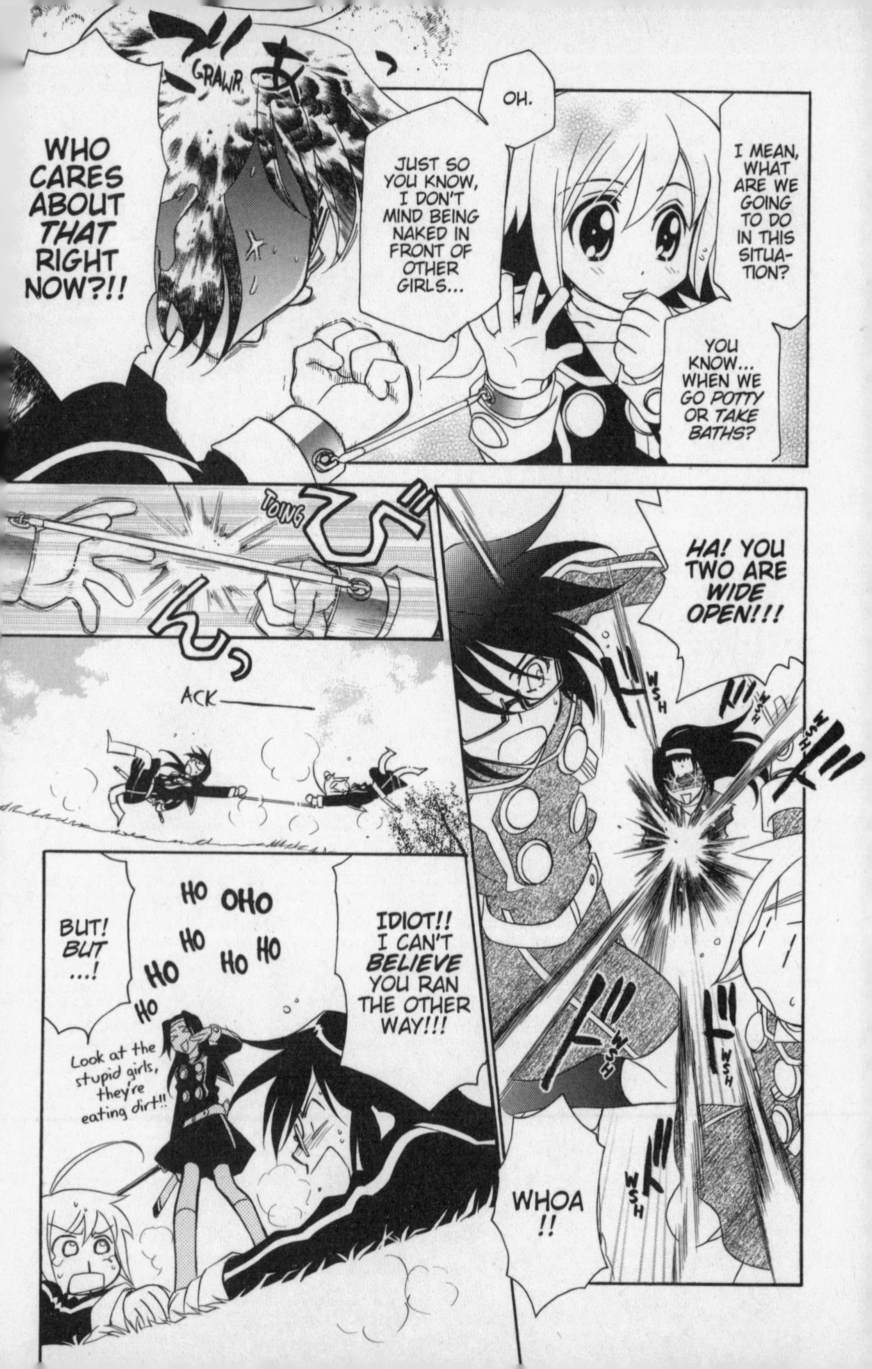
I MEAN, WHAT ARE WE GOING TO DO IN THIS SITUATION?
YOU KNOW... WHEN WE GO *POTTY* OR *TAKE BATHS*?
OH.
JUST SO YOU KNOW, I DON'T MIND BEING NAKED IN FRONT OF OTHER GIRLS...
GRAWR
WHO CARES ABOUT *THAT* RIGHT NOW?!!
HA! YOU TWO ARE *WIDE OPEN!!!*
WSH
WSH
WSH
WSH
WSH
WHOA !!
TOING
ACK
IDIOT!! I CAN'T *BELIEVE* YOU RAN THE OTHER WAY!!!
HO OHO HO HO HO HO HO
BUT! *BUT* ...!
Look at the stupid girls, they're eating dirt!!

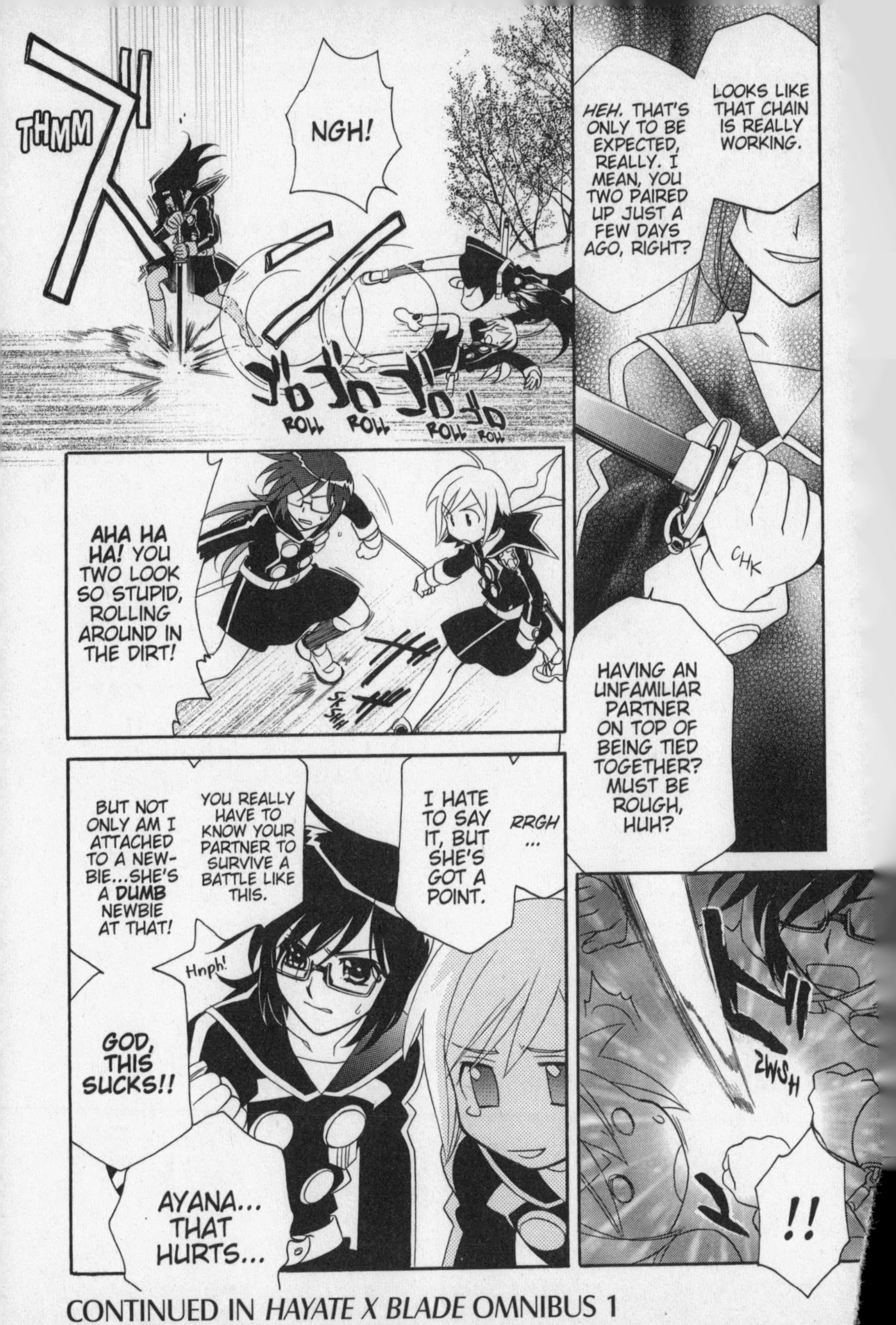
LOOKS LIKE THAT CHAIN IS REALLY WORKING.
HEH. THAT'S ONLY TO BE EXPECTED, REALLY. I MEAN, YOU TWO PAIRED UP JUST A FEW DAYS AGO, RIGHT?
CHK
HAVING AN UNFAMILIAR PARTNER ON TOP OF BEING TIED TOGETHER? MUST BE ROUGH, HUH?
THMM
NGH!
ROLL
ROLL
ROLL
ROLL
AHA HA HA! YOU TWO LOOK SO STUPID, ROLLING AROUND IN THE DIRT!
SKSHH
ZWSH
!!
I HATE TO SAY IT, BUT SHE'S GOT A POINT.
RRGH ...
YOU REALLY HAVE TO KNOW YOUR PARTNER TO SURVIVE A BATTLE LIKE THIS.
BUT NOT ONLY AM I ATTACHED TO A NEW-BIE...SHE'S A DUMB NEWBIE AT THAT!
Hnph!
GOD, THIS SUCKS!!
AYANA... THAT HURTS...

CONTINUED IN *HAYATE X BLADE* OMNIBUS 1

THE END

YOU'RE READING THE WRONG WAY

This is the last page of
Inukami!
Omnibus Collection 1

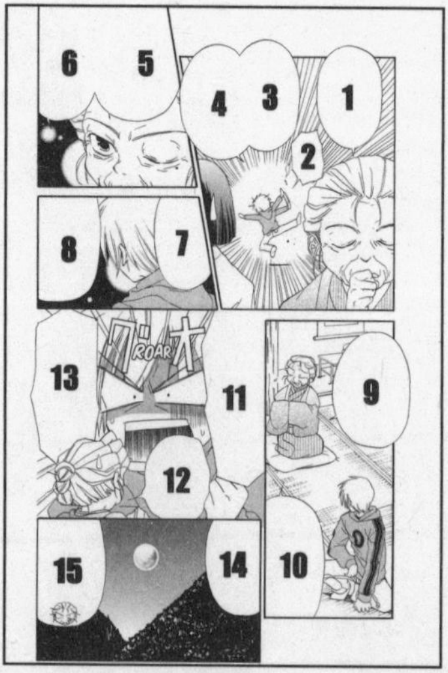
1
2
3
4
5
6
7
8
9
10
11
ROAR
12
13
14
15

This book reads from right to left, Japanese style. To read from the beginning, flip the book over to the other side, start with the top right panel, and take it from there.

If this is your first time reading manga, just follow the diagram. It may seem backwards at first, but you'll get used to it! Have fun!